A TREATISE OF The Pleas of the Crown:

OR,

A SYSTEM of the Principal Matters relating to that SUBJECT, digested under their PROPER HEADS.

BOOK I and II

By *WILLIAM HAWKINS*, Serjeant at Law

The Third Edition, with large ADDITIONS and many hundred new REFERENCES to the Modern Books of Authority published since the Author compiled this TREATISE.

THE LAWBOOK EXCHANGE, LTD.
Clark, New Jersey

ISBN 9781584779360

Lawbook Exchange edition 2011

The quality of this reprint is equivalent to the quality of the original work.

THE LAWBOOK EXCHANGE, LTD.
33 Terminal Avenue
Clark, New Jersey 07066-1321

Please see our website for a selection of our other publications and fine facsimile reprints of classic works of legal history:
www.lawbookexchange.com

Library of Congress Cataloging-in-Publication Data

Hawkins, William, 1673-1746.
A treatise of the pleas of the crown or, a system of the principal matters relating to that subject, digested under their proper heads / by William Hawkins. -- 3rd ed., with large additions and many hundred new references to the modern books of authority published since the author compiled this treatise.
p. cm.
Originally published: London : Printed by E. and R. Nutt, and R. Gosling, 1739.
ISBN-13: 978-1-58477-936-0 (cloth : alk. paper)
ISBN-10: 1-58477-936-5 (cloth : alk. paper)
1. Criminal law--England. 2. Criminal law--England--Digests. 3. Pleas of the crown. I. Title.
KD7950.H39 2009
345.42--dc22

2008040199

Printed in the United States of America on acid-free paper

A

TREATISE

OF

The Pleas of the Crown:

OR,

A SYSTEM of the Principal Matters relating to that SUBJECT, digested under their PROPER HEADS.

BOOK I and II

By *WILLIAM HAWKINS*,
Serjeant at Law

The Third Edition, with large ADDITIONS and many hundred new REFERENCES to the Modern Books of Authority published since the Author compiled this TREATISE.

In the SAVOY:

Printed by E. and R. NUTT, and R. GOSLING, (Assigns of *E. Sayer*, Esq;) for B. Nutt, and sold by S. Birt in *Ave-Mary-Lane*, D. Browne without *Temple-Bar*, J. Shuckburgh in *Fleet-Street*, and J. Stagg in *Westminster-Hall*. MDCCXXXIX.

To the Right Honourable

THOMAS Lord *PARKER*,

Baron of *MACCLESFIELD*,

Lord Chief Juſtice of *ENGLAND*.

MY LORD,

THE following *Treatiſe* containing that Part of the Law, which is peculiarly under the Adminiſtration of the Chief Juſtice of *England*, I preſum'd in regard to the Subject of it, to think of preſenting it to your Lordſhip, which your Goodneſs having been pleaſed to permit, it is with the leſs Uneaſineſs that I venture to make it Publick; for I could not hope to introduce it into the Word with greater Advantage than under your Protection.

This was the real Ground of my Ambition, to dedicate it to your Lordſhip, and not to give my ſelf an Opportunity of publiſhing how much I honour thoſe wonderful Talents, that have raiſed You to ſo high a Station: A private Character indeed may be ſet forth to Advantage, and many Virtues in it be made known by an Addreſs of this Nature, which might otherwiſe have lain for ever concealed: But your Lordſhip's is Publick and Conſpicuous, and can appear no where with ſo much Luſtre as when you ſit in Judgment, where that vaſt Genius you are bleſs'd with, ſhines forth to all the World, adorn'd with all the Improvements that Humane Art can furniſh, and ſupported with the greateſt Courage and Integrity.

And nothing leſs, My Lord, could give You that Command of all the Variety of Buſineſs which comes before You, and that Facility with which You diſpatch it: The moſt intricate Points of Law, that have for Ages lain in Confuſion and Obſcurity, when they fall under your Lordſhip's Conſideration, receive ſuch Light, are ſtated and explain'd with ſuch exact Method, and ſuch Propriety and Beauty of Expreſſion, that the moſt Polite Compoſitions ap-

pear

pear not more Elegant, nor the moſt Demonſtrative more Convincing: This, My Lord, is the agreeable Part of the Exerciſe of your Authority, being no Violence to that general Humanity which you delight to ſhew to all Mankind: But the Duties of your Office require You ſometimes to put on another Character and to ſhew the awful Face of Juſtice, to curb the Rage of an unruly People, and to fright them into their Duty by the Terrors of the Law; and 'tis with Pleaſure all good Men ſee your Lordſhip purſue the prevailing Vices of the Age with ſuch Zeal and Indignation, that Crimes no longer appear leſs odious for being faſhionable, nor are the more ſecure from Puniſhment for being popular.

Theſe, My Lord, are Bleſſings which the whole Nation ſhares in, and have an Influence upon all Parts of the civil Adminiſtration: But we, who have the Honour to attend your Lordſhip at the Bar, are in a more particular Manner to acknowledge our Obligations, for that Candor and Condeſcenſion with which You treat us: The Encouragement You give to our weak Endeavours, no leſs engages our Affections, than your comprehenſive Knowledge and clear and accurate Judgment command our Reverence and Eſteem.

Such Goodneſs charms all that approach and feel it; and it was with univerſal Joy we ſaw your Lordſhip's Firmneſs to the preſent Eſtabliſhment, and great Services to your County, diſtinguiſhed lately by an Acceſſion of Honour from his Majeſty, whoſe Wiſdom in conferring his Favours has eminently appeared, by the many ſignal Benefits the Nation has received from thoſe who have the Honour to ſerve Him. I am with the greateſt Reſpect,

My LORD,

Your Lordſhip's

Moſt obliged,

And moſt Humble Servant,

William Hawkins.

THE

PREFACE.

NOTHING is more common than to hear thoſe who have taken only a ſuperficial View of the Crown-Law, charge it with numberleſs Hardſhips and undiſtinguiſhing Rigour; whereas thoſe, who have more fully examin'd it, agree, that it wants nothing to make it admir'd, for Clemency and Equity, as well as Juſtice, but to be underſtood: It is ſo agreeable to Reaſon, that even thoſe who ſuffer by it, cannot charge it with Injuſtice; ſo adapted to the Common Good, as to ſuffer no Folly to go unpuniſhed, which that requires to be reſtrained; and yet ſo tender of the Infirmities of Human Nature, as never to refuſe an Indulgence, where the Safety of the Publick will bear it; It gives the Prince no Power, but of doing Good; and reſtrains the People from no Liberty, but of doing Evil.

It would be needleſs therefore to ſay any Thing of the Uſefulneſs of this Treatiſe, could I be ſo happy as any Way to come up to the Deſign of it, which was, to vindicate the Juſtice and Reaſonableneſs of the Laws concerning criminal Matters, and to reduce them into as clear a Method, and explain them in as familiar a Manner, as the Nature of the Thing will bear.

Had any of thoſe great Men, who formerly have written on this Subject, gone through the whole Law relating to it, all farther Attempts of this Kind had been unneceſſary. The Treatiſe, publiſhed under the Name of Sir Matthew Hale, *is indeed very uſeful, and written in a clear Method, and with great Learning and Judgment; but is certainly very imperfect in the Whole, and ſeems to be only a Model or*

Plan

Plan of a Work of this Kind, which is ſaid to have been intended by him.

Sir Edward Coke's *third Inſtitute is alſo a Treatiſe of great Learning, and not unworthy of the Hand that produc'd it; but yet it ſeems by no Means a compleat Work, many conſiderable Heads being either wholly omitted in it, or barely touched upon.*

The Treatiſe of Sir Will. Staundforde *ſeems to be writ with great Judgment, but he takes in a very ſmall Compaſs, ſcarce mentioning any Offences under Felonies.*

As for the Treatiſes of Lambard, Crompton, Pulton, *and* Dalton, *they having an Eye chiefly to the Direction of Juſtices of Peace; and, treating of the Crown-Law no farther than as it concerns them, are far from being compleat Syſtems of it.*

Upon the whole, I apprehend that none of the Authors before mentioned were ſo perfect, but that, by reducing all the Laws relating to this Subject, under one general Scheme, they might generally be underſtood with much leſs Difficulty than they have hitherto been. This 'twas induc'd me to write on this Subject, and I hope to finiſh the Whole in two Books, propoſing in this Firſt to ſhew the Nature of criminal Offences; and in the Second, the Manner of bringing Offenders to Puniſhment.

The Editor's Preface.

I*N this Edition Abſtracts of the Statutes made ſince the Author wrote, relating to the Subject of this Treatiſe, have been added. Care has alſo been taken to make additional References to the Reports publiſhed ſince our Author finiſhed this Work, and to Sir* Matthew Hale's Hiſtoria Placitorum Coronæ. *Such References as only tend to confirm what is advanced in the Text are thrown into the Margin; but where new Points or Differences ſeemed to occur, it was thought proper to place them, together with the Abſtracts of the Statutes, by Way of Addition at the End of each Book; by which Means the learned Serjeant's Work is kept unmixed with any Thing of the Editor's, and the Pages of this Edition are made to correſpond with thoſe of the Former, ſo that References to our Author from the Modern Books may be turned to with equal Eaſe as before.*

G. L. Scott.

AN

ANALYSIS

OF

The First BOOK

OF

The Pleas of the Crown.

ALL Persons whatsoever are liable to be punish'd as Criminal Offenders, unless they can excuse themselves, either,

1. In Respect of their Want of Reason: Or,
2. In Respect of their Subjection to the Power of others, ch. 1.

Offences, considered in relation to the Persons against whom they are committed, are either,

1. Such as are more immediately against God: Or,
2. Such as are more immediately against Man.

Offences more immediately against God are either by Common Law or by Statute.

Those at Common Law are either capital or not capital.

The capital are of three Kinds.

1. Heresy, ch. 2.
2. Witchcraft, ch. 3.
3. Sodomy, ch. 4.

Those not capital are either by Common Law or Statute.

Those by Common Law are of five Kinds,

1. Blasphemies against God, ch. 5. sect. 1.
2. Scoffing at the Scriptures, ch. 5. sect. 2.
3. Impostures in Religion, ch. 5. sect. 3.
4. Open Lewdness grosly scandalous, ch. 5. sect. 4.
5. Seditious Words against the established Religion, ch. 5. sect. 6.

Those by Statute are two-fold.

1. Such as are against Religion in general.
2. such as are against the established Church.

Those against Religion in general are of four Kinds.

1. Profanations of the Lord's Day, ch. 6. sect. 1, 2, 3.
2. Profane swearing and Cursing, ch. 6. sect. 4.
3. Drunkenness, ch. 6. sect. 5.
4. Reviling the Lord's Supper, ch. 6. sect. 6.

Those against the established Church are three-fold.

1. Such as concern all Persons in general.
2. Such as more immediately relate to those of the Popish Religion.
3. Such as more immediately regard Protestant Dissenters, ch. 16.

Those which concern all Persons in general, are either,

1. Against the Common Prayer, ch. 7. Or,
2. In accepting or holding an Office without due Conformity to the Church, ch. 8. Or,
3. In Teaching School without conforming to the Church, ch. 9. Or,
4. In not coming to Church, ch. 10, 11.

Those relating more immediately to Persons of the Popish Religion, are of four Kinds,

1. Popish Recusancy, ch. 12.
2. The Offence of saying or hearing of Mass, or other Popish Service, ch. 13.
3. The Offence of not making a Declaration against Popery, ch. 14.
4. The Offence of promoting or encouraging the Popish Religion; either,
   1. In giving or receiving Popish Education, ch. 15. sect. 1, 2, 3. Or,
   2. In professing the Popish Religion, ch. 15. from sect. 4. to sect. 15. Or,
   3. In buying or selling Popish Books, ch. 15. sect. 15.

Offences more immediately against Man are either more immediately against the King, or more immediately against the Subject.

Those more immediately against the King are either capital or not capital.

The capital are either,

1. High Treason: Or,
2. Felonies.

High Treason is either,

1. Such as is within 25 *E.* 3. and other Statutes grounded upon it, and explaining it: Or,
2. Such as depends upon subsequent Statutes.

Of Treason within 25 *Ed.* 3. there are four Species.

1. That which immediately concerns the King, his Wife or Children, ch. 17. sect. 3, 4, &c.
2. That which concerns his Office in the Administration of Justice, ch. 17. sect. 46.
3. That which concerns his Seal, ch. 17. sect. 48.
4. That which concerns his Coin, ch. 17. sect. 54.

Of High Treason depending on subsequent Statutes, there are three Species.

1. Offences in upholding or favouring the Power of the Pope.
2. Offences against the Protestant Succession, ch. 17. sect. 85.
3. Offences in lifting Men without the King's Licence, ch. 17. sect. 86.

Of Offences in upholding or favouring the Power of the Pope, there are five Species.

1. Extolling the Pope's Power, ch. 17. sect. 72.
2. Putting in Ure Popish Bulls, ch. 17. sect. 75.
3. Perverting others, or being perverted to Popery, ch. 17. sect. 76.
4. Receiving Popish Orders or Education in Popish Seminaries, and not submitting, &c. ch. 17. sect. 79.
5. Refusing a second Tender of the Oaths, ch. 17. sect. 84.

Felonies more immediately against the King are of five Kinds.

1. Offences relating to the Coin or Bullion.
2. Offences against the King's Council, ch. 18. sect. 8.
3. The Offence of passing beyond Sea, to serve a Foreign Prince, ch. 18. sect. 10.
4. The Offence of imbezilling the King's Armour, ch. 18. sect. 12.
5. The Offence of relieving a Popish Priest, ch. 18. sect. 14.

Of Felony relating to the Coin or Bullion, there are three Species.

1. The Offence of debasing it, ch. 18. sect. 1.
2. The Offence of unlawfully diminishing it, ch. 18. sect. 2.
3. The Offence of endeavouring by extraordinary Means to increase it, ch. 18. sect. 7.

Of Offences more immediately against the King, not capital, there are two Kinds.

1. *Præmunire.*
2. Misprision.

Offences coming under the Notion of *Præmunire*, are either,

1. Against the Prerogative of the Crown: Or,
2. Against the Authority of the King and Parliament, ch. 19. sect. 44.

Of Offences of this Kind against the Prerogative of the Crown, there are nine Species.

1. Making

1. Making uſe of Papal Bulls, ch. 19. ſect. 12.
2. Derogating from the King's Common Law Courts, ch. 19. ſect. 14.
3. Appealing to *Rome* from any of the King's Courts, ch. 19. ſect. 20.
4. Exerciſing the Juriſdiction of a Suffragan, without the Appointment of the Biſhop of the Dioceſe, ch. 19. ſect. 21.
5. Refuſing to elect or conſecrate the Perſon nominated by the King to a Biſhoprick, ch. 19. ſect. 22.
6. Maintaining the Pope's Power, ch. 19. ſect. 23.
7. Bringing in *Agnus Dei*, ch. 19. ſect. 24.
8. Contributing to the Maintenance of a Popiſh Seminary, ch. 19. ſect. 26.
9. Refuſing the Oaths, ch. 19. ſect. 27.

Miſpriſions more immediately againſt the King are either Negative or Poſitive.

The Negative is commonly called Miſpriſion of Treaſon, ch. 20.

Poſitive Miſpriſions of this kind either amount to Miſpriſion of Treaſon, or do not.

Of ſuch Miſpriſions, amounting to Miſpriſions of Treaſon, there is only one Species; forging foreign Coin not current here, ch. 20. ſect. 7.

Of ſuch Miſpriſions not amounting to Miſpriſion of Treaſon, there are four Kinds,

1. Contempts againſt the King's Palace or Courts of Juſtice, ch. 21.
2. Contempts againſt his Prerogative, ch. 22.
3. Contempts againſt his Perſon or Government, ch. 23.
4. Contempts againſt his Title, ch. 24.

Of Contempts againſt the King's Prerogative, there are three Species.

1. Refuſing to aſſiſt him for the Good of the Publick, ch. 22. ſect. 2.
2. Preferring the Intereſts of a Foreign Prince to that of our own, ch. 22. ſect. 3.
3. Diſobeying the King's lawful Commands or Prohibition, ch. 22. ſect. 4.

Of Contempts againſt the King's Perſon or Government, there are ſix Kinds.

1. Charging the Government with Oppreſſion or weak Adminiſtration, ch. 23. ſect. 2.
2. Doing an Act which impliedly encourages Rebellion, ch. 23. ſect. 4.
3. Endeavouring to frighten the King into a Change of his Meaſures, ch. 23. ſect. 4.
4. Spreading falſe Rumours concerning the King's Intentions, ch. 23. ſect. 5.
5. Charging him with a Breach of his Coronation-Oath, ch. 23. ſect. 6.
6. Speaking contemptuouſly of him, ch. 23. ſect. 7.

Of Contempts againſt the King's Title, there are two Kinds.

1. Denying his Title, ch. 24. ſect. 1.
2. Refuſing to take the Oaths required by Law for the Support of his Government.

Of Offences in refuſing to take ſuch Oaths, there are two Kinds.

1. The Offence of refuſing the Oath required by Common Law, ch. 24. ſect. 3.
2. The Offence of refuſing the Oaths required by Statute.

Of Offences in Refuſing the Oaths required by Statute, there are two Kinds.

1. The Offence of refuſing the Oaths of Allegiance and Supremacy, ch. 24. ſect. 4.
2. The Offence of refuſing the Oath of Abjuration, ch. 24. ſect. 6.

Offences more immediately againſt the Subject are either capital or not capital.

The Capital are either by the Common Law or by Statute.

Thoſe by the Common Law are committed either,

1. Againſt the Life of a Man; or,
2. Againſt his Goods; or,
3. Againſt his Habitation; or,
4. Againſt publick Juſtice.

Thoſe againſt the Life of a Man are either,

1. Caſual, not being occaſioned by the Default or Procurement of any Man, ch. 26. Or,
2. Such as come under the Notion of Homicide, being occaſioned by a Man, ch. 26. ſect. 2.

Of Homicides there are two Kinds.

1. Such as is committed againſt a Man's own Life, ch. 27.
2. Such as is committed againſt the Life of another.

Of Homicide againſt the Life of another, there be two Kinds.

1. Such as amounts not to Felony.
2. Such as amounts to Felony.

Of ſuch Homicide not amounting to Felony there are two Kinds.

1. Juſtifiable

1. Justifiable.
2. Excusable.

Justifiable Homicide is either of a publick or a private Nature.

That of a publick Nature is of two Kinds.

1. Such as happens in the due Execution, ch. 28. sect. 4. and
2. Such as happens in the due Advancement of publick Justice.

Of the latter there are two Kinds.

1. Such as happens in Criminal, ch. 28. sect. 11. And
2. Such as happens in Civil Causes, ch. 28. sect. 17.

Of justifiable Homicide of a private Nature there are two Kinds.

1. Such as happens in killing a Wrong-Doer, ch. 28. sect. 21.
2. Such as happens in killing an innocent Person, ch. 28. sect. 26.

Of excusable Homicide there are two Kinds.

1. Homicide *per infortunium*, ch. 29. sect. 1.
2. Homicide *Se defendendo*, ch. 29. sect. 12.

Homicide against the Life of another, amounting to Felony, is either with or without Malice.

That which is without Malice is called Manslaughter or Chancemedley, ch. 20.

Of such Homicide with Malice there are two Kinds.

1. Murder, ch. 31.
2. Petit Treason, ch. 32.

Of Murder there are two Kinds.

1. Such as is done with express Malice.
2. Such as is done with implied Malice.

Of Murder done with express Malice, there are three Kinds.

1. Such as happens in Duelling, ch. 31. sect. 21.
2. Such as happens in killing another without any Provocation; or but upon a slight one, ch. 31. sect. 32.
3. Such as happens in killing one whom the Person killing intended to hurt in a less Degree, ch. 31. sect. 38.

Murder done with implied Malice, generally happens in the following Instances.

1. Where the principal Intention is to commit another Felony, ch. 31. sect. 41.
2. Where the principal Design is to commit a bare Breach of the Peace, not intended against the Person of him who happens to be slain, ch. 31. sect. 46.
3. Where the chief Motive is to assist a third Person, ch. 31. sect. 49.
4. Where the direct Design is to escape from an Arrest, ch. 31. sect. 55.
5. Where the principal Purpose is to usurp an illegal Authority, ch. 31. sect. 59.
6. Where no Mischief is intended at all, ch. 31. sect. 61.

Of Petit Treason there are three Kinds, ch. 32.

1. Where a Servant kills his Master.
2. Where a Wife kills her Husband.
3. Where an Ecclesiastical Person kills his Prelate.

Of capital Offences at Common Law against the Goods of another, there are two Kinds.

1. Simple Larceny.
2. Mix'd Larceny.

Of simple Larceny there are also two Kinds.

1. Grand Larceny, ch. 32. sect. 1.
2. Petit Larceny, ch. 32. sect. 31.

Mix'd Larceny is either from the Person of a Man, or from his House, ch. 36.

Of mix'd Larceny from the Person there are two Kinds.

1. Robbery, ch. 34.
2. Larceny from the Person, ch. 35.

Also there is another Offence of this Nature call'd Piracy, ch. 37.

Capital Offences at Common Law against the Habitation of a Man are of two Kinds.

1. Burglary, ch. 38.
2. Arson, ch. 39.

Offences more immediately against the Subject, made capital by Statute, are such as are committed.

1. Against Women, (and of these there are two Kinds.
    1. Rape.
    2. Forcible Marriage.)
2. Against the Rights of Marriage, ch. 43.

3. Against

3. Againſt the Members of a Man's Body, ch. 44.
4. Againſt Records, ch. 45.
5. Againſt Cattle, ch. 46.
6. By Purveyors, ch. 47.
7. By Soldiers and Mariners, ch. 48.
8. By Hunters, ch. 49.
9. By Forgers of falſe Deeds, ch. 50.
10. By Gaolers, ch. 51.
11. By Tranſporters of Sheep or Wool, ch. 52.
12. By Servants, ch. 53.
13. By *Egyptians*, ch. 54.
14. By Cutters of Pow-dike, ch. 55.
15. By Treſpaſſers on the Borders, and Rioters, ch. 56.
16. By Bankrupts, ch. 57.
17. By Counterfeiters of Bank-Notes, Exchequer-Bills, Stamps, South-Sea Bonds, Lottery-Orders, &c. ch. 58.

Offences more immediately againſt the Subject not capital, are of two Kinds.

1. Miſpriſion of Felony, ch. 59.
2. Other inferior Offences.

Such inferior Offences are of two Kinds.

1. Such as amount to an actual Diſturbance of the Peace.
2. Such as do not amount to ſuch a Diſturbance.

For the Prevention of the former of theſe Kinds of Offences, the Law has provided two Remedies.

1. By Surety for keeping the Peace, ch. 60.
2. By Surety for the good Behaviour, ch. 61.

Of the abovementioned Offences amounting to the actual Diſturbance of the Peace, there are two Kinds.

1. Such as may be committed by one or two Perſons.
2. Such as require a greater Number.

Of thoſe which may be committed by one or two Perſons there are four Kinds.

1. Aſſaults, ch. 62. ſect. 1.
2. Batteries, ch. 62. ſect. 2.
3. Affrays, ch. 63.
4. Forcible Entries and Detainers, ch. 64.

Of thoſe, which require a greater Number of Perſons, there are three Kinds.

1. Riots, ch. 65. ſect. 1.
2. Routs, ch. 65. ſect. 8.
3. Unlawful Aſſemblies, ch. 65. ſect. 9.

Of ſuch inferior Offences not amounting to an actual Diſturbance of the Peace, there are two Kinds.

1. Such as are committed by Officers.
2. Such as are committed by common Perſons without any Relation to an Office.

Of Offences of this Nature committed by Officers, there are three Species.

1. Neglect or Breach of Duty, ch. 66.
2. Bribery, ch. 67.
3. Extortion, ch. 68.

Of Offences of this Nature, committed by private Perſons, without any relation to any Office, there are two Kinds.

1. Such as are infamous and groſly ſcandalous, proceeding from Principles of down-right Diſhoneſty, Malice or Faction.
2. Such as are of an inferior Nature, and neither infamous nor groſly ſcandalous.

Of Offences of the firſt Sort, there are ſix Species.

1. Perjury, ch. 69.
2. Forgery, ch. 70.
3. Cheats, ch. 71.
4. Conſpiracy, ch. 72.
5. Libels, ch. 73.
6. Keeping of a Bawdy-houſe, ch. 74.

Of Offences of the latter Sort there are two Kinds.

1. Such as more immediately affect the Publick.
2. Such as more immediately affect the Intereſts of particular Perſons.

Of thoſe which more immediately affect the Publick, there are four Kinds.

1. Common Nuſances, ch. 75.
2. Monopolies, ch. 79.
3. Foreſtalling, Ingroſſing, and Regrating, ch. 80.
4. Barratry, ch. 81.

The moſt remarkable Kinds of common Nuſances are,

1. Such as relate to Highways.
2. Such as relate to Publick Houſes, ch. 78.

Thoſe which relate to Highways come under a two-fold Conſideration.

1. As they relate to Highways in general, ch. 76.
2. As they relate to Bridges in particular, ch. 77.

Of the Offences above-mentioned more immediately affecting the Intereſts of particular Perſons there are three Kinds.

1. Uſury, ch. 82.
2. Maintenance.
3. Buying or ſelling a pretended Title, ch. 86.

Maintenance is two-fold.

1. *Ruralis*, ch. 63. ſect. 2.
2. *Curialis*, ch. 83. ſect. 3.

Of Maintenance *Curialis* there are three Species.

1. General Maintenance, ch. 83. ſect. 4.
2. Champerty, ch. 84.
3. Embracery, ch. 85.

An

An Account of the Authors referred to in this Book.

A.

ALeyn	*ALeyn's Reports.*
And. 1, 2.	*Anderson's Reports, first and second Part.*
Aff. 1, 2, 3, 4, &c.	*The Book of Affizes in the Reign of King Edward the third, for the first, second, third, fourth Years, &c.*

B.

Barrow	*Barrow's Supremacy.*
Benloe	*Benloe's Reports.*
Brac. Bracton	*Bracton, De legibus & confuetudinibus Angliæ.*
Bridg.	*Bridgman's Reports.*
Bro.	*Brook's Abridgment.*
Bul. 1, 2, 3.	*Bulftrode's Reports, the first, second and third Part.*

C.

Carth.	*Carthew's Reports.*
Cafes in Parliament	*Sir Bartholomew Shower's Cafes in Parliament.*
Caw. Cawley	*Cawley's Law againft Recufants.*
Co. 1, 2, &c.	*Sir Edward Coke's Reports, the firft and fecond Part, &c.*
Co. Litt.	*Sir Edward Coke's Commentary upon Littleton.*
Comb.	*Comberbach's Reports.*
Cro. E.	*Croke's Reports for the Reign of Queen Elizabeth.*
Cro. Ja.	*Croke's Reports for the Reign of King James the firft.*
Cro. Ca.	*Croke's Reports for the Reign of King Charles the firft.*
Crom.	*Crompton's Office of a Juftice of Peace, printed in the Year 1606.*

D.

Dalif.	*Dalifon's Reports.*
Dalt.	*Dalton's Country Juftice, printed in the Year 1655.*
Danv. Abr. 1, 2, 3.	*D'Anver's Abridgment, firft, fecond and third Part.*
Dav. Davis	*Davis's Reports.*
Dy. Dyer	*Dyer's Reports.*

F.

F. N. B.	*Fitzherbert's Natura Brevium.*
Fitz.	*Fitzherbert's Abridgment.*
Far.	*Farrefley's Reports.*

G.

Gibf. Gibfon	*Gibfon's Codex Juris Ecclefiaftici Anglicani.*
Godb.	*Godbolt's Reports.*

H.

1, 2 H. H. P. C.	*Hale's Hiftoria Placitorum Coronæ, firft and fecond Vol.*
H. P. C.	*Hale's Pleas of the Crown.*
Hard.	*Hardrefs's Reports.*
Hetl.	*Hetley's Reports.*
Hob.	*Hobart's Reports.*
Hutt.	*Hutton's Reports.*

J.

1 Jon. Sir Wm. Jon.	*Sir William Jones's Reports.*
2 Jon.	*Sir Thomas Jones's Reports.*
1 Inft.	*Coke upon Littleton.*
2 Inft.	*The fecond Part of Coke's Inftitutes.*
3 Inft.	*The third Part of Coke's Inftitutes.*
4 Inft.	*The fourth Part of Coke's Inftitutes.*

Keb.

K.	
Keb. 1, 2, 3.	*Keble's Reports, the first, second, and third Part.*
Kell.	*Kellewey's Reports.*
Kelyng, Keyl.	*Kelyng's Reports.*
Kitch.	*Kitchin, of Courts-Leet and Courts-Baron.*
L.	
Lam. Lamb.	*Lambard's Office of Justices of Peace, printed in the Year* 1614.
Lane	*Lane's Reports.*
Latch	*Latch's Reports.*
Leon. 1, 2, 3, 4.	*Leonard's Reports, the first, second, &c. Part.*
Lev. 1, 2,	*Levinz's Reports, the first and second Part.*
Litt.	*Littleton's Reports.*
M.	
Mar.	*March's Reports.*
Mod. 1, 2, 3, &c.	*Modern Reports, first, second, and third Part, &c.*
Mo.	*Moore's Reports.*
N.	
New Abr.	*New Abridgment of the Law.*
Noy	*Noy's Reports.*
O.	
Ow. Owen.	*Owen's Reports.*
P.	
Pal. Palm.	*Palmer's Reports.*
Parsons	*Parsons against Sir Edward Coke's fifth Report.*
Pl. Com.	*Plowden's Commentaries.*
Po. Poph.	*Popham's Reports.*
Pult.	*Pulton, De Pace Regis & Regni.*
R.	
Ray. Raym.	*Raymond's Reports.*
Reg.	*Register.*
R. A. Rol. Ab. 1, 2.	*Rolle's Abridgment, the first and second Part.*
R. R. Rol. Re. 1, 2.	*Rolle's Reports, the first and second Part.*
Rushw. Coll.	*Rushworth's Collections.*
S.	
Salk.	*Salkeld's Reports.*
Saun. 1, 2.	*Saunder's Reports, the first and second Part.*
Sav.	*Savil's Reports.*
Selden's Janus Anglorum	*Jani Anglorum facies altera by Mr. Selden, translated into English by Redman Westcot, and printed in the Year* 1682.
Selden's Epinomis	*England's Epinomis by Mr. Selden, printed in the Year* 1683.
Shower	*Shower's Reports.*
Sid. Syd. 1, 2.	*Siderfin's Reports, the first and second.*
Skin.	*Skinner's Reports.*
St. Tr. Vol. 1, 2, &c.	*State Trials, Vol.* 1, 2, *&c. first Edition.*
S. P. C.	*Staundeford's Pleas of the Crown.*
T.	
Thelo.	*Theloal's Digest of Writs.*
Trem.	*Tremaine's Pleas of the Crown.*
V.	
Vaugh.	*Vaughan's Reports.*
Vent. 1, 2.	*Ventris's Reports, the first and second Part.*
W.	
Wats. Watson	*Watson's Clergy-man's Law, Folio Edition.*
Win. Winch	*Winch's Reports.*
Wood's Inst.	*Wood's new Institute of the Imperial or Civil Law.*
Y.	
Year Books.	
Yel.	*Yelverton's Reports.*

A TREATISE

A TREATISE OF The Pleas of the Crown.

BOOK I.

CHAP. I.

Of the Persons who may be guilty of criminal Offences.

THE Guilt of offending againſt any Law whatſoever, neceſſarily ſuppoſing a wilful Diſobedience, can never juſtly be imputed to thoſe, who are either uncapable of underſtanding it, or of conforming themſelves to it: Therefore, before I come to the ſeveral Kinds of Offences, I ſhall ſhew what Degrees of Diſcretion and Freedom are required in the Commiſſion of them; for the better Underſtanding whereof, I ſhall conſider what Offenders are excuſable,

1. In reſpect of their Want of Reaſon;
2. In reſpect of their Subjection to the Power of others.

Sect.

Sect. 1. As to the first Point it is to be observed, [a] That those who are under a natural Disability of distinguishing between Good and Evil, as Infants under the Age of Discretion, Ideots and Lunaticks, are not punishable by any criminal Prosecution whatsoever. [1]

Sect. 2. Indeed it was [b] anciently holden, in Respect of that high * Regard which the Law has for the Safety of the King's Person, That a Madman might be punish'd as a Traitor, for killing or offering to kill the King; but this is [c] contradicted by the later Opinions.

Sect. 3. And it seems agreed at this [d] Day, That if one, who has committed a capital Offence, become *Non Compos* before Conviction, he shall not be arraigned; and if after Conviction, that he shall not be executed.

Sect. 4. But by 12 *Annæ*, 23. which seems to be agreeable to the [e] ancient Common Law, a dangerous Madman may be kept in Prison till he recover his Senses; and by the Common Law, if it be doubtful whether a Criminal, who at his Trial is in [f] appearance a Lunatick, be such in Truth or not, it shall be tried by an Inquest of Office, to be returned by the Sheriff of the County wherein the Court sits; and if it be found by them that the Party only feigns himself mad, [g] and he still refuse to answer, he shall be dealt with as one that stands mute.

Sect. 5. And if one who wants Discretion commit a [h] Trespass against the Person or Possession of another, he shall be compelled in a civil Action to give Satisfaction for the Damage.

Sect. 6. And he who is guilty of any Crime whatever, thro' his [i] voluntary Drunkenness, shall be punished for it as much as if he had been sober.

Sect. 7. Also he, who incites a Madman to do a Murder or other Crime, is a [k] principal Offender, and as much punishable as if he had done it himself.

Sect. 8. And if it appear by the Circumstances, that an Infant under the Age of Discretion could [l] distinguish between Good and Evil, as if one of the Age of nine or ten Years kill another, and hide the Body, or make Excuses, or hide himself, he may be convicted and condemned, and forfeit, *&c.* as much as if he were of full Age. But in such a Case the Judges will in Prudence respite the Execution in order to get a Pardon: And it is said, That if an Infant apparently wanting Discretion be indicted and found guilty of Felony, the Justices themselves may dismiss him without a Pardon, *&c.*

As to the second Point, *viz.* How far those are to be excused who are under the Power of others:

Sect. 9. 1. A Feme Covert is so much favoured in Respect of that Power and Authority which her Husband has over her, that she shall not suffer any Punishment for committing a bare [m] Theft in Company with, or by Coercion of, her Husband.

Sect. 10. Neither shall she be deemed accessary [n] to a Felony for receiving her Husband who has been guilty of it, as her Husband shall be for receiving her.

Sect. 11. But if she commit a Theft of her own voluntary [o] Act, or by the bare Command of her Husband; or be guilty of Treason, Murder or Robbery, in Company with, or by Coercion of, her Husband, she is punishable as much as if she were Sole.

Sect. 12. Also a Wife may be indicted together with her Husband, and condemned to the Pillory with him for keeping a Bawdy-house; for this is an Offence as to the Government of the House, in which the

I Wife

[a] H. P. C. 10, 43, 65. Pult. 122. b. Dalt. cap. 95. Bro. Coron. 6, 61, 136, 170, 217. 3 H. 7. 1. b. See 1 Hale's History P. C. 16, 17, &c.

[b] 4 Co. 124. b. 2 Rol. Rep. 324.

* Lunatick pardoned Regist. 309. Fitz. Cor. 351.

[c] 3 Inst. 46. H. P. C. 10, 43. Co. Lit. 247. 1 H. H. P. C. 36, 37.

[d] H. P. C. 10. 3 Inst. 4, 6. 1 And. 107, 109. 26 Ass. Pl. 27. Sav. 50, 57. 1 H. H. P. C. 34, 35.

[e] 26 Ass. Pl. 27. Bro. Coron. 101. 1 H. H. P. C. 35.

[f] 1 And. 107. Sav. 50. 1 H. H. P. C. 35.

[g] H. P. C. 226. Sav. 56.

[h] 2 R. A. 547. Pl. 4. Hob. 134. 35 H. 6. 11. b. Co. Lit. 247. b. Bro. Coron. 6. Dalt. ca. 95. 1 H. H. P. C. 15, 16.

[i] Co. Lit. 247. 1 H. H. P. C. 32. Plowd. 19. a.

[k] H. P. C. 43, 44. Keyl. 53. Dalt. ca. 95. 1 H. H. P. C. 617.

[l] H. P. C. 43. 12 Ass. Pl. 30. 3 H. 7. 1. b. 12. b. Bro. Coron. 74, 133. 3 H. 7. 1. b. 12. b. S. P. C. 16. F. H. P. C. 35. 35 H. 6. 11. b. Bro. Coron. 6, 61. 1 H. H. P. C. 26, 27, 434, 569, 570. Infant under seven pardoned, Regist. 309. b.

[m] Keyl. 31. S. P. C. 26. c. 142. c. 27 Ass. 40. H. P. C. 65. 1 H. H. P. C. 45.

[n] 3 Inst. 108. H. P. C. 65. 1 H. H. P. C. 44, 45.

[o] H. P. C. 65. Dalt. ca. 104. 27 Ass. Pl. 40. Fitz. Coro. 199. B. 2 Ch. 29. S. 34. Queen and Williams, Mich. 10 Annæ. 1 Salk. 384.

Wife has a principal Share; and also such an Offence as may generally be presumed to be managed by the Intrigues of her Sex.

Sect. 13. And generally [a] a Feme Covert shall answer as much as if she were Sole, for any Offence, not capital, against the Common Law, or Statute; and (if it be of such a Nature that it may be committed by her alone, without the Concurrence of the Husband) she may be punished for it without the Husband, by Way of Indictment, which being a Proceeding grounded merely on the Breach of the Law, the Husband shall not be included in it for an Offence to which he is no way privy. And [b] if a Woman bring a malicious Appeal for the Death of her Husband, known by her to be alive, she may be imprisoned for her false Appeal, till she make [c] Fine to the King, and the Husband shall go at large. But if a Wife incur the Forfeiture of a penal Statute, * the Husband may be made a Party to an Action or Information for the same, (as he may be generally to any Suit for a Cause of Action given by his Wife,) and shall be liable to answer what shall be recovered thereon.

Sect. 14. 2. Neither [d] a Son, nor a Servant, are excused the Commission of any Crime, whether capital or not capital, by the Command or Coercion ☞ of the Father or Master. [2]

[a] 9 Co. 71. Con. Mo. 813. 1 Sid. 410. 2 Keb. 634. Vide Hob. 93. Noy 103. Savil 25. 1 Rol. Rep. 93, 94, 233, 234. Cro. Ja. 482. 11 Co. 61. b. 62.
[b] 8 H. 4. 17. Pl. 2 Fitz. Coro. 73. Bro. Imprisonm. 100.
[c] See the Citations to Letter a.
* Infra Ch. 10. Sect. 31, 39.
[d] 3 Keb. 34. H. P. C. 66. Moor 813. 1 H. H. P. C. 44.

CHAP. II.

Of Heresy.

OFFENCES considered in Relation to the Persons against whom they are committed, are either,

1. Such as are more immediately against God; or,
2. Such as are more immediately against Man.

Offences more immediately against God are either by Common Law, or by Statute.

Those at Common Law are either capital, or not capital. The capital Offences of this Nature are of three Kinds:

1. Heresy.
2. Witchcraft.
3. Sodomy.

Concerning Heresy I shall consider, See 1 H. H. P. C. 383 to 410.

1. What it is;
2. By whom it is cognizable;
3. How it is punishable.

Sect. 1. As to the first Point it seems, That among Protestants Heresy is taken to be a false Opinion repugnant to some Point of Doctrine clearly revealed in Scripture, and either absolutely essential to the Christian Faith, or at least of most high Importance.

Sect. 2. But it is impossible to set down all the particular Errors which may properly be called Heretical, concerning which there are,

and

and always have been, so many intricate Disputes; However the 1 *El.* 1. which erected the High-Commission-Court, having restrained the same from adjudging any Points to be Heretical, which have not been determined to be such either by Scripture, or by some one of the four first General Councils, or by some other Council, by express Words of Scripture, or by the Parliament with the Assent of the Convocation, it has been since generally holden, that these Rules will be good Directions to Ecclesiastical Courts in Relation to Heresy.

3 Inst. 40. H. P. C. 3.

See Bro. Heresy. 2 Roll. Ab. 226.

Sect. 3. As to the second Point, *viz.* By whom Heresy is cognizable, it is certain, That the Convocation may declare what Opinions are Heretical: But it hath been questioned of late, Whether they have Power at this Day to convene and convict the Heretick?

F. N. B. 269. 12 Co. 56, 57. 3 Inst. 40. H. P. C. 5. Gibson 401, 410. 12 Co. 56, 57, 93. 3 Inst. 40.

Sect. 4. However it is agreed, That every Bishop may convict Persons of Heresy, within his own Diocese, and proceed by Church-Censures against those who shall be convicted; but it is said, That no Spiritual Judge, who is not a Bishop, hath this Power; and it has been questioned, Whether a Conviction before the Ordinary were a sufficient Foundation whereon to ground the Writ *de Hæretico comburendo*, as it is agreed that a Conviction before the Convocation was?

Sect. 5. By 24 *H.* 8. 9. the Archbishop of either Province may cite any Person before him for Heresy, if the immediate Ordinary either consent thereto, or do not his Duty in punishing the same.

27 H. 8. 14. b. 5 Co. 58. a. H. P. C. 4. Hob. 236.

Sect. 6. But it is certain, that a Man cannot be proceeded against at the Common Law in a Temporal Court merely for Heresy; yet if in Maintenance of his Errors he set up Conventicles and raise Factions, which may tend to the Disturbance of the publick Peace, it seemeth that he may in this Respect be fined and imprisoned upon an Indictment, *&c.* at the Common Law.

H. P. C. 4. 1 H. H. P. C. 399, 400.

Sect. 7. Also a Temporal Judge may incidently take Knowledge whether a Tenet be Heretical or not; as where one was committed by Force of 2 *H.* 4. 5. for saying, that he was not bound by the Law of God to pay Tithes to the Curate: And another for saying, That though he was excommunicate before Men, yet he was not so before God. The Temporal Courts, on an *Habeas Corpus* in the first Case, and an Action of false Imprisonment in the other, adjudged neither of the Points to be Heresy within that Statute; for the King's Courts will examine all Things which are ordained by Statute.

3 Inst. 42. 1 Ro. Re. 110. 2 Bulst. 300.

5 Co. 58. 1 And. 191. 2 Leon. 199. 3 Lev. 314. 1 H. H. P. C. 407, 408.

Sect. 8. Also in a *Quare impedit*, if the Bishop plead that he refused the Clerk for Heresy, it seems that he must set forth the particular Point, that it may appear to be Heretical to the Court wherein the Action is brought, which having Conusance of the original Cause must by Consequence have a Power as to all incidental Matters necessary for the Determination of it; and, without knowing the very Point alledged against the Clerk, will not be able to give Directions concerning it to the Jury, who (if the Party be dead) are to try the Truth of the Allegation.

Sect. 9. But if a Man be proceeded against as an Heretick in the Spiritual Court *pro salute animæ*, and think himself aggrieved, his proper Remedy seems to be to bring his Appeal to a higher Ecclesiastical Court, and not to move for a Prohibition from a Temporal one, which, as it seems to be agreed, cannot regularly determine or discuss, what shall be called Heresy.

5 Co. 58. a. 27 H. 8. 14. b.

F. N. B. 269. 3 Inst. 43. H. P. C. 5.

Sect. 10. As to the third Point, *viz.* How Heresy is punishable; there is no Doubt but that at Common Law one convicted thereof, and refusing to abjure it, or falling into it again after he had abjured it, might be burnt by Force of the Writ *de Hæretico comburendo*, which was grantable out of Chancery upon a Certificate of ſuch Conviction; but it is ſaid, That he forfeited neither Lands nor Goods, becauſe the proceedings againſt him were only *pro ſalute animæ*. Doctor and Student, lib. 3. ca. 29. H. P. C. 5.

Sect. 11. But at this Day the ſaid Writ *de Hæretico comburendo* is aboliſhed by 29 *Car.* 2. 9. And all the old Statutes which give a Power to arreſt or impriſon Perſons for Hereſy, or introduced any Forfeiture on that Account, are repealed; yet by the Common Law an obſtinate Heretick being excommunicate, is ſtill liable to be impriſoned by Force of the Writ *de Excommunicato capiendo*, till he make Satisfaction to the Church. And by 9 & 10 *Will.* 3. 32. *If any Perſon having been educated in, or having made Profeſſion of the Chriſtian Religion within this Realm, ſhall be convicted in any of the Courts of* Weſtminſter, *or at the Aſſizes, of denying any one of the Perſons in the Holy Trinity to be God, or of maintaining that there are more Gods than one, or of denying the Truth of the Chriſtian Religion, or the Divine Authority of the Holy Scriptures, he ſhall for the firſt Offence be adjudged uncapable of any Office; and for the ſecond, ſhall be diſabled to ſue any Action, or to be a Guardian, Executor or Adminiſtrator, or to take by any Legacy or Deed of Gift, or to bear any Office Civil or Military, or Benefice Eccleſiaſtical, for ever, and ſhall alſo ſuffer Impriſonment for three Years, without Bail or Mainprize, from the Time of ſuch Conviction.* H. P. C. 4, 5. 12 Co. 44.

CHAP. III.

Of Witchcraft.

Sect. 1. OF Offenders of this Nature there are ſaid to be three Kinds, 3 Inſt. 44. Dalt. ca. 107.

1. Conjurers, who by Force of certain Magick Words endeavour to raiſe the Devil, and compel him to execute their Commands.

2. Witches, who by Way of friendly Conference are ſaid to bargain with an evil Spirit to do what they deſire of him.

3. Sorcerers or Charmers, who by the Uſe of certain ſuperſtitious Forms of Words, or by Means of Images, or other odd Repreſentations of Perſons or Things, &c. are ſaid to produce ſtrange Effects above the ordinary Courſe of Nature.

Sect. 2. All theſe were anciently puniſhed in the ſame Manner as Hereticks, by the Writ *de Hæretico comburendo* after a Sentence in the Eccleſiaſtical Court, and a Relapſe. And it is ſaid alſo, That they might be condemned to the Pillory, &c. upon an Indictment at Common Law. 3 Inſt. 44. F.N.B.269.b. H. P. C. 6. S. P. C. 38. g. Cro. Eliz. 571

Sect. 3. In the Time of King *Edward* the third, one taken with the Head and Face of a dead Man, and a Book of Sorcery, was brought into the King's Bench: But there being no Indictment againſt him, he was ſworn that from thenceforth he would not be a Sorcerer, and then delivered from Priſon, and the Head was burnt at his Charge: But this Method ſeems to be obſolete at this Day. 1 H. H. P. C. 383. 45 Ed. 3. 17. b. Bro. Cor. 15. 2 Keb. 719.

Sect. 4. By 1 *Jac.* 1. *cap.* 12. the only Law now in Force againſt theſe Offenders, they are divided into two Degrees; and thoſe in the firſt Degree, and their Acceſſaries before, ſhall ſuffer as Felons without Clergy; and of theſe there are the four following Species.

H. P. C. 6. 3 Inst. 45. con. 1. *Such as shall use any Invocation or Conjuration of any evil Spirit:* And such seem clearly to be within the Law, tho' no Spirit do actually appear.

H. P. C. 6. 3 Inst. 45. 2. *Such as consult, covenant with, entertain, employ, feed, or reward any evil Spirit to any Intent:* And these are agreed to be within the Statute, though nothing farther be done upon such Consultation, *&c.*

H. P. C. 6. 3 Inst. 45. 3. *Such as take up any dead Person's Body, or any Part thereof, to be used in any Manner of Witchcraft:* And these are also clearly within the Statute, though they do not actually so use it.

H. P. C. 7. 3 Inst. 45. 1 Jon. 143. 4. *Such as exercise any Witchcraft, Inchantment, Charm or Sorcery, whereby any Person shall be killed, destroyed, consumed, or lamed in his or her Body, or any Part thereof:* But none are within this Branch who do not actually effect such Mischief.

Sect. 5. Those in the second Degree shall for the first Offence suffer a Year's Imprisonment, and the Pillory; and for the second, as Felons without Clergy, and these by the manifest Purport of the Words of the Act, which is very obscurely penned, seem to be divided into the two following Species.

1. *Such as take upon them by Withcraft, Inchantment, Charm or Sorcery, to tell where Treasure is to be found, or where Things lost or stolen may be found, or to do any Thing to the Intent to provoke any Person to unlawful Love, or to hurt or destroy any Person in his or her Body, though the same be not effected.*

H. P. C. 8. 3 Inst. 46. 2. *Such as shall use any Witchcraft,* &c. *whereby any Cattle or Goods of any Person shall be destroyed, wasted or impaired:* But those, who take upon them to do this, are not within the Act unless they actually do it. [3] ☞

CHAP. IV.

Of Sodomy.

12 Co. 36, 37. 3 Inst. 58. *Sect.* 1. ALL unnatural Carnal Copulations, whether with Man or Beast, seem to come under the Notion of Sodomy, which was Felony by the ancient Common Law, and punish'd, according to some Authors, with Burning; according to others, with Burying alive: But at this Day by Force of 25 *H.* 8. 6. & 5 *El.* 17. is punished in the same Manner as other Felonies, which are excluded from Clergy.

12 Co. 36, 37. 3 Inst. 58. But Quære, and See 1 H. H. P. C. 628. and Ld. Audley's Case in State Trials. *Sect.* 2. In every Indictment for this Offence, there must be the Words *Rem habuit veneream & carnaliter cognovit*; and consequently some Kind of Penetration, and also of Emission, must be proved; but any the least Degree is sufficient, and Emission is *prima facie* an Evidence of Penetration.

CHAP. V.

Of Offences against God not Capital at Common Law.

OFFENCES more immediately against God not Capital, are either by the Common Law or Statute.

Those by the Common Law are,

1 Ven. 293. 3 Keb. 607, 621. *Sect.* 1. I. All Blasphemies against God, as denying his Being or Providence, and all contumelious Reproaches of Jesus Christ.

Sect. 2. II. All profane Scoffing at the Holy Scripture, or expoſing any Part thereof to Contempt or Ridicule.

Sect. 3. III. Impoſtures in Religion, as falſly pretending to extraordinary Commiſſions from God, and terrifying or abuſing the People with falſe Denunciations of Judgments, *&c.* See the Caſe of James Nailor, and of the French Prophets, &c.

Sect. 4. IV. All open Lewdneſs groſly ſcandalous, ſuch as was that of thoſe Perſons, who expoſed themſelves naked to the People in a Balcony in *Covent-Garden* with moſt abominable Circumſtances. 1 Sid. 168. 1 Keb. 620.

Sect. 5. Offences of this Nature, becauſe they tend to ſubvert all Religion or Morality, which are the Foundation of Government, are puniſhable by the Temporal Judges with Fine and Impriſonment, and alſo ſuch corporal infamous Puniſhment as to the Court in Diſcretion ſhall ſeem meet, according to the Heinouſneſs of the Crime. 1 Ven. 293. 3 Keb. 607, 621.

Sect. 6. V. Seditious Words in Derogation of the Eſtabliſhed Religion are indictable, as tending to a Breach of the Peace; as theſe, Your Religion is a new Religion, and Preaching is but Prattling, and Prayer once a Day is more edifying. 2 R. A. 187. Pl. 1. Cro. Ja. 421.

CHAP. VI.

Of Offences by Statute againſt Religion in general.

OFFENCES by Statute not Capital more immediately againſt God, are either,

1. Such as are againſt Religion in general; or,
2. Such as are againſt the Eſtabliſhed Church.

Thoſe againſt Religion in general are of ſeveral Kinds; as

Sect. 1. I. All Profanation of the Lord's Day; for by 1 *Car.* 1. 1. *There ſhall be no Aſſembly of People, out of their own Pariſhes, on this Day, for any Sport whatſoever; nor any Bull-baiting or Bear-baiting, Interludes, common Plays, or other unlawful Exerciſes and Paſtimes, uſed by any Perſons in their own Pariſhes, on Pain that every Offender ſhall forfeit* 3 s. *and* 4 d. *to the Uſe of the Poor*, &c.

Sect. 2. By 29 *Car.* 2. 7. *No Perſons whatſoever, above fourteen Years old, ſhall exerciſe any worldly Labour, Buſineſs, or Work of their ordinary Calling on the Lord's Day, (except Works of Neceſſity and Charity, and the Dreſſing and Selling of Meat in an Inn and Victualling Houſe, for thoſe who cannot otherwiſe be provided,) on Pain of forfeiting* 5 s. *And no Perſon ſhall publickly cry, or expoſe to Sale, any Goods whatſoever on this Day, (except Milk, which may be ſold before Nine in the Morning, and after Four in the Afternoon,) on Pain of forfeiting the ſame.* Par. 5.

Sect. 3. *Alſo no Drover, Horſe-courſer, Waggoner, Butcher or Higler, ſhall travel, or come to their Inn on this Day, on Pain of twenty Shillings. And no Perſon ſhall Uſe, employ, or travel with any Boat or Barge, without the Allowance of ſome Juſtice of Peace*, &c. *on Pain of five Shillings.* But by 11 and 12 Gul. 21. *Forty Watermen may be appointed by the Company*

pany of Watermen to ply on the Thames, *&c.* And by 9 *Ann.* 23. *Hackney Coach-Men are permitted to work within the Bills of Mortality on Sunday.*

Sect. 4. II. All profane Swearing and Curſing; for by 21 *Jac.* 1. 20. and 6 & 7 Gul. 11. *Every Servant, Day-Labourer, Seaman or Soldier, convicted of profane Curſing or Swearing, forfeits one Shilling, and every other Perſon two Shillings, and ſhall be regiſtred at Seſſions*; and by 13 Car. 2. cap. 9. Artic. 2. *All Perſons in the King's Pay at Sea, for profane Oaths,* &c. *ſhall be puniſhed by Fine and Impriſonment, as the Court Martial ſhall think fit.*

Sect. 5. III. Drunkenneſs, for which by 1 *Jac.* 1. 5. all Perſons whatſoever forfeit five Shillings to the Poor; and for which Seamen may by 13 *Car.* 2. 9. be puniſhed by Fine, *&c.* as the Court Martial ſhall think fit.

Sect. 6. IV. Reviling the Sacrament of the Lord's Supper with contemptuous Words, *&c.* for which (by 1 *Ed.* 6. 1. which was repealed by 1 *Mar.* 2. and revived by 1 *El.* 1.) the Offender ſhall be impriſoned, fined, and ranſomed.

Sect. 7. I ſhall not mention the Offences againſt 2 *&* 3 *Ed.* 6. 19. and 5 *El.* 5. relating to Faſts and Fiſh-days, becauſe it is expreſly declared, That thoſe Statutes are enacted merely on a political Account, and it is made penal to affirm that any eating of Fiſh, or forbearing of Fleſh mentioned therein, is neceſſary to Salvation, or that it is the Service of God.

CHAP. VII.

Of Offences againſt the Common Prayer.

OFFENCES againſt the Eſtabliſhed Church are,

1. Such as concern all Perſons in general;
2. Such as more immediately relate to thoſe of the Popiſh Religion;
3. Such as more immediately regard Proteſtant Diſſenters.

Thoſe which concern all Perſons in general are,

1. Againſt the Common Prayer.
2. In accepting or holding an Office without due Conformity to the Church.
3. In teaching School without conforming to the Church.
4. In not coming to Church.

Sect. 1. And firſt of Offences againſt the Common Prayer, as to which it is to be obſerved, That by 2 *&* 3 *Ed.* 6. 1. and 6 *Ed.* 6. 1. (which were repealed by 1 *Mar.* 2. and revived by 1 *El.* 2.) the Common Prayer Book was firſt eſtabliſhed under ſevere Penalties, but the ſame Penalties being repeated and enlarged by 1 *El.* 2. and 13 *&* 14 *Car.* 2. 4. which enacts the Uſe of the ſame Common Prayer with ſome Alterations; thoſe Statutes of *Ed.* 6. ſeem at this Day to be of little Uſe.

Sect. 2. By 1 *El.* 2. Par. 4, 5 & 6. *If any Parſon, Vicar, or other whatſoever Miniſter, that ought to ſay the ſaid Com. Prayer,* &c. *ſhall refuſe to uſe it in ſuch Church,* &c. *or other Place where he ſhould uſe to miniſter the ſame, or wilfully or ob-*

obstinately standing in the same, use any other Form, or speak any Thing in Derogation of the said Book, or any Thing therein contain'd, he forfeits for the first Offence one Year's Profit of all his Spiritual Promotions, and shall suffer six Months Imprisonment; and for the second Offence shall be deprived, &c. See for the Form of the Indictment, 3 Mod. 78, 79.

In the Construction of this Act it has been resolved,

Sect. 3. I. That under the Words, *Parson, Vicar, or other whatsoever Minister, that ought or should say the said Common Prayer,* &c. those Clergymen who have no Cure are included, as much as those who have one, and that they are punishable for using any other Form, *&c.* inasmuch as by their Ordination they are oblig'd to officiate in the Offices of the Church, *&c.* and it is said, that they are sufficiently shewn to be in Holy Orders by the Word *Clericus* in an Indictment. [4] Dyer 203. pl. 73, 74.

Sect. 4. II. That this Statute being not only in the Affirmative, but also expresly saving the Jurisdiction of Ecclesiastical Courts, does not restrain them from proceeding against these Offenders in their own Methods, as Disturbers of the Unity and Peace of the Church; and consequently that such Persons may be deprived by the said Court according to the Course of the Spiritual Law, for the first Offence. 5 Co. Cawdry's Case, 5. b. 6. a. Poph. 59. 2 Rol. Abr. 222. 5.

Sect. 5. Also it is farther enacted, by 1 *El.* 2. Par. 9. *That if any Person shall in Plays, Songs, or other open Words, speak any Thing in Derogation, Depraving or Despising of the said Book,* &c. *Or by open Fact compel, or otherwise procure or maintain any Minister to say any Common Prayer openly,* &c. *in other Form: Or shall by any of the said Means let any Minister to say the said Common Prayer,* &c. *he shall forfeit one hundred Marks for the first Offence, and four hundred for the second,* &c. (*which if he pay not within six Weeks after Conviction, he shall suffer six Months Imprisonment for the first Offence, and twelve for the second,*) *and for the third Offence shall forfeit all his Goods and Chattels, and shall suffer Imprisonment for Life.*

Sect. 6. It has been made a Question in the Construction of this Clause, Whether if the Party die within six Weeks, the said Forfeiture be not discharged, since by the Act of God the Election of paying it, or suffering Imprisonment in lieu of it, is taken away? Dyer 203. 74. 231. 4.

CHAP. VIII.

Of Offences in accepting or holding an Office without due Conformity to the Church.

OFfences in accepting or holding an Office, without due Conformity to the Church, are of two Kinds,

1. In not receiving the Sacrament both before and after the Acceptance of an Office.

2. In going to any other Place for Religious Worship, than the Church, during the Continuance in an Office.

Sect. 1. As to the first of these Offences, it is enacted by 13 *Car.* 2. Stat. 2. *Cap.* 1. Par. 10, 12. *That no Person shall be placed, elected or chosen, to any Office or Place of Mayor, Alderman, Recorder, Bailiff, Town-Clerk, Common-Council-Man, or other Office of Magistracy, Place or Trust, or other Imploy-*

ment relating to the Government of any City, Corporation, Borough, Cinque-Port, or other Port-Town, who shall not have received the Sacrament, according [5 Mod. 431.] *to the Rites of the Church of* England, *within one Year next before such Election; and that every Person so placed or elected shall take the Oaths of Allegiance and Supremacy at the same Time when the Oath for the due Execution of the said Office,* &c. *shall be administred; and that the said Oaths shall be administred and tendered by those who administer the Oath of Office, and in Default of such, by two Justices of Peace of the Corporation,* &c. (which makes [a] it necessary in a Return to a *Mandamus*, setting forth that the Party did not take the Oaths before the Mayor, *&c.* to add, that he did not take them before two Justices of Peace, *&c.* and it is further enacted, *That on Default hereof every such Election, Placing and Choice shall be void.* And [b] it hath been adjudged to be no Excuse, that the Oaths were not tendered.

[a] 5 Mod. 317, 318. Salk. 428, 429.

[b] 5 Mod. 316, 317, 318. 2 Jon. 121. Salk. 428, 429.

Sect. 2. Also it is enacted by 25 *Car.* 2. *That all Officers Civil and Military, (Except those of Inheritance, appointing sufficient Deputies) and all, who have any Fee,* &c. *by Patent from the King, (Except such as shall be granted for valuable Consideration for Life or Years, and not relate to any Office or Place of Trust; and also all who have any Place of Trust, or any Employment in the King's Houshold, shall take the Oaths of Allegiance and Supremacy, and Test, the next Term, (in the King's Bench or Chancery, or Quarter-Sessions;) and receive the Sacrament within three Months, and give in a Certificate thereof, proved by two Witnesses, to the Court wherein they take the said Oaths. And in Case of Neglect shall be disabled to hold the said Offices,* &c. *and forfeit five hundred Pounds, except Femes Covert,* &c. But [c] it hath been adjudged, that the Persons so disabled lose only their Right to the Profits of their Offices from the Time of such Disability; but that they lose nothing vested in them before. Also [d] it hath been adjudged to be no Excuse, for a Person bound by Law to accept a Corporation Office, that he is disabled to receive the Sacrament, by having been excommunicated; and [e] *Quære*, if it be any Excuse, that his Conscience will not suffer him to take it, being a Protestant Dissenter, *&c.*

[c] Lutw. 910.

[d] 2 Mod. 299.

[e] 2 Vent. 248. King and Larwood. Sal. 167, 168. 2 Vent. 248. Skin. 574. to 577. Carth. 306, 307.

Sect. 3. Notwithstanding the Words of the first of these Acts are so very strong as to make such Election, *&c.* void, and those of the second to make such Persons disabled in Law to all Intents and Purposes whatsoever, to have, occupy or enjoy the said Offices; [f] yet it hath been strongly holden, that the Acts of one under such a Disability being instated in such an Office, and executing the same without any Objection to his Authority, may be valid as to Strangers; for otherwise not only those who no Way infringe this Law, but even those whose Benefit is intended to be advanced by it, might be Sufferers for another's Fault to which they are no Way privy; and one Chasm in a Corporation happening thro' the Default of one Head Officer would perpetually vacate the Acts of all others, whose Authority, in respect of their Admission into their Offices, or otherwise, may depend on his.

[f] Vide 3 Keb. 606, 665, 682, 721. 2 Jon. 81, 137. 2 Lev. 184, 242. 2 Mod. 193, 194.

Sect. 4. By 25 *Car.* 2. Parag. 17. it is expresly provided, *That the said Act shall not extend to Constables, or Church-wardens, or such like inferior Civil Officers, or to a Bailiff of a Manor or Lands, or such like private Officers.* But it hath been questioned, whether it extends to the Censor of the College of Physicians?

5 Mod. 431, 432.

Sect. 5. As to the second Offence of this Kind, *viz.* that of going to any other Place for Religious Worship than the Church, during the Continuance of an Office, it was enacted by 10 *Ann.* 2. *That if any Person having any Office, Civil or Military, or receiving any Pay, Salary, Fee or Wages, by reason of any Grant from the Crown, or having any Command or Place of*

Truſt from the Crown, or admitted into any Service or Employment in the King's Houſhold or Family, or bearing any Office of Magiſtracy, or Place of Truſt, or other Employment relating to the Government of any City, Corporation, Borough, or Cinque-Port, and obliged by 13 *Car.* 2. Stat. 2. Cap. 1. *or* 25 *Car.* 2. 21. *to receive the Sacrament, according to the Uſage of the Church of* England, *ſhould at any Time after Admiſſion into any ſuch Office,* &c. *and during the Continuance in the ſame, knowingly or willingly be preſent at any Aſſembly in* England, Wales, *or* Berwick *on* Tweed, *for the Exerciſe of Religion in other Manner than according to the Church of* England, *at which Aſſembly there ſhall be ten Perſons beſides thoſe of the Family, or at any ſuch Meeting where ſuch Liturgy is uſed, and the King, and ſuch others as ſhall be lawfully appointed to be prayed for, ſhould not be prayed for in expreſs Words,* &c. *he ſhould forfeit forty Pounds; and be diſabled to hold any Office or Employment whatſoever in* England, &c. But this Statute, ſo far as it relates to ☞ this Matter, is repealed by 5 *Geo.* 1. *c.* 4. [5.]

CHAP. IX.

Of Offences in teaching School without conforming to the Church.

Sect. 1. AS to the Offence of teaching School without conforming to the Church, ſo far as it concerns all Perſons in general, it is enacted by 23 *El.* 1. Par. 6 & 7. *That if any Perſon or Perſons, Body Politick or Corporate, ſhall keep or maintain any School-maſter, who ſhall not repair to Church according to the Form of the ſaid Statute, or be allowed by the Biſhop or Ordinary of the Dioceſe, (who ſhall not take any Thing for the ſaid Allowance) they ſhall forfeit for every Month ten Pounds; and ſuch School-maſter preſuming to teach contrary to the ſaid Act, and being thereof convict, ſhall be diſabled to be a Teacher of Youth, and ſhall ſuffer Impriſonment without Bail or Mainpriſe for one Year.*

Sect. 2. And it is farther enacted by 1 *Jac.* 1. 4. Par. 9. *That no Perſon* Carth. 464, 465. *ſhall keep any School, or be a School-maſter, out of the Univerſities or Colleges of this Realm, except it be in ſome publick or free Grammar-School, or in ſome ſuch Nobleman's or Noblewoman's, or Gentleman's or Gentlewoman's Houſe, as are not Recuſants, or where the ſame School-maſter ſhall be ſpecially licenced thereunto by the Archbiſhop, Biſhop, or Guardian of the Spiritualties of that Dioceſe, upon Pain, that as well the School-maſter, as alſo the Party that ſhall retain or maintain any ſuch School-maſter, contrary to the Meaning of the ſaid Statute, ſhall forfeit each of them for every Day, ſo wittingly offending, forty Shillings.*

Sect. 3. But it having been doubted whether ſuch Perſons as are within the Benefit of 1 *Gul. & Mar.* 18. commonly called *The Toleration Act*, are not exempted from the Penalties of the above mentioned Statutes, it was farther enacted by 12 *Ann.* 7. *That whoever ſhall keep any publick or private School or Seminary, or teach any Youth as Tutor or School-maſter, (unleſs he inſtruct them only in Reading, or Writing, Arithmetick, or ſuch mathematical Learning as relates to navigation, or ſome mechanical Art, and that in the* Engliſh *Tongue; or unleſs he ſhall be a Foreigner of a Foreign reformed Church, and teach the Children of ſuch Foreigners only) without having firſt ſubſcribed that Part of the Declaration in* 13 & 14 Car. 2. *which relates to Conformity to the Liturgy of the Church of* England, *and alſo having obtained a Licence from the Biſhop,* &c. *and ſhall be thereof convicted in any of the Courts at* Weſtminſter, *or or at the Assizes, or before Justices of Oyer and Terminer, shall be committed to the common Gaol for three Months*, &c. But this Statute, so far as it relates to this Matter, is repealed by 5 *Geo.* 1. *c.* 4.

As to Popish School-masters in particular, see *Chap.* 15. *Sect.* 3.

CHAP. X.

Of Offences in not coming to Church.

FOR the better Understanding of the Offences of not coming to Church, so far as the same relate to all Persons in general, except such as are within the Indulgence of 1 *Will. & Mar.* 18. which is commonly called *The Toleration Act*, I shall consider:

1. How far Persons are punishable for their own Absence from the Church.

2. How far they are punishable for suffering such Absence in others.

And first, In Order to shew how far Persons are punishable for their own Absence, I shall consider the following Particulars:

1. What Forfeitures of Money, Lands or Goods, such Offenders incur.
2. In what Manner they are to be proceeded against for those Forfeitures.
3. What other Inconveniencies they are subject unto.
4. By what Means they may be discharged.

As to the first Point, I shall consider,

1. What Forfeitures of Money; and,

2. What Forfeitures of Lands and Goods such Offenders are liable unto.

And first, The Forfeitures of Money, to which they are liable, are threefold;

1. That of twelve Pence for the Absence of one Sunday, or other Holy Day.
2. That of twenty Pounds for the Absence of every Month contained in a Conviction.
3. That of twenty Pounds for the Absence of every Month after a Conviction.

Sect. 1. And first, the Forfeiture of twelve Pence for the Absence of one *Sunday*, or other Holy Day, depends upon 1 *El.* 2. by which it is enacted, *That all Persons inhabiting within this Realm, or any other the King's Dominions, shall diligently and faithfully, having no lawful or reasonable Excuse to be absent, endeavour to resort to their Parish Church or Cha-*

2 *pel*

pel accuſtomed, or upon reaſonable Let thereof, to ſome uſual Place, where Common Prayer and ſuch Service of God ſhall be uſed, in ſuch Time of Let, upon every Sunday, and other Days ordained and uſed to be kept as Holy Days, and then and there to abide orderly and ſoberly, during the Time of the Common Prayer, Preaching, or other Service of God there to be uſed and miniſtered, upon Pain of Puniſhment by the Cenſures of the Church, and alſo upon Pain that every Perſon ſo offending ſhall forfeit for every ſuch Offence twelve Pence.

In the Expoſition of this Statute, the following Opinions have been holden.

Sect. 2. I. That the Indictment needs not ſhew that the Party had no reaſonable Excuſe for his Abſence, or that he is an Inhabitant within this Realm, *&c.* But that the Defendant, if he have any Matter of this Kind in his Favour, ought to ſhew it.

2 Leon. 5. Godbolt 148. See 29 El. 6. Par. 5.

Sect. 3. II. That if the Spiritual Court, proceeding upon this Statute, refuſe to allow a reaſonable Excuſe, they may be prohibited; but that if they proceed wholly on their own Canons, they ſhall not be at all comptrolled by the Common Law, (unleſs they act in Derogation from it, as by queſtioning a Matter not triable by them, as the Bounds of a Pariſh, *&c.* for they ſhall be preſumed to be the beſt Judges of their own Laws.

2 Rol. Rep. 438, 455. 1 Bulſt. 159. See Gibſ. 358.

Sect. 4. III. That he who miſbehaves himſelf in the Church, or miſſes either Morning or Evening Prayer, or goes away before the whole Service is over, is as much within the Statute as he who is wholly abſent; and that he who is abſent from his own Pariſh Church, ſhall be put to prove where he went to Church.

1 Rol. Rep. 93. Godbolt 148. Dal. ca. 45. fol. 106. 1 Syd. 230.

Sect. 5. IV. That the Offence in not coming to Church conſiſting wholly in a Non-feaſance, and not ſuppoſing any Fact done, but barely the Omiſſion of what ought to be done, needs not be alledged in any certain Place; for properly ſpeaking, it is not committed any where.

1 And. 139. Hob. 251. See 2 Leon. 167.

Sect. 6. Secondly, The Forfeiture of twenty Pounds for the Abſence of a whole Month contained in a Conviction, depends upon 23 *El.* 1. Par. 5. by which it is enacted, *That every Perſon above the Age of ſixteen Years, who ſhall not repair to ſome Church, Chapel or uſual Place of Common Prayer, but forbear the ſame, contrary to the Tenor of the ſaid Statute of* 1 El. 2. *and being thereof lawfully convicted, ſhall forfeit to the King, for every Month which he or ſhe ſhall ſo forbear, twenty Pounds.*

Precedent of Declaration, Lutw. 201, 208.

In the Expoſition hereof it hath been reſolved,

Sect. 7. I. That this Statute, by inflicting twenty Pounds for a Month's Abſence, diſpenſes not with the Forfeiture of twelve Pence, given by 1 *El.* 2. for the Abſence of one *Sunday*, for both may well ſtand together, and the twelve Pence is immediately forfeited upon the Abſence of each particular Day.

11 Co. 63. b. 1 Rol. Rep. 94.

Sect. 8. II. That theſe Words, *being thereof lawfully convicted*, are no more than the Law would have implied, if they had not been expreſſed, and therefore operate nothing; from whence it follows, That they neither cauſe the Party to forfeit any Thing by a Conviction, unleſs Judgment be given thereon, nor reſtrain the Forfeiture to ſuch Offences only, as are committed after a previous Conviction, inaſmuch as they mean no more than what the Law provides of common Right in every Caſe, *viz.* That the Party ſhall forfeit nothing till he be convicted.

Lutw. 162, 163. 11 Co. 57. b. 59. b. 1 Rol. Rep. 89, 90, 233, 234. Dy. 160. pl. 40. 3 Bulſt. 87.

11 Co. 58.a.b. 60. a. 1 Rol. Rep. 89, 90.

Sect. 9. III. That he who is condemned on Demurrer, or *Nihil dicit*, is ſufficiently convicted within the Act; for whoever is adjudged, is convict, though it follow not that every one, who is convict, is adjudged, *&c.*

Cro. Jac. 529.

Sect. 10. IV. That one, who was ſick for Part of the Time contained in an Information upon this Statute, ſhall not be at all excuſed by Reaſon of ſuch Sickneſs, if it be proved that he was a Recuſant both before and after; for it ſhall be intended that he obſtinately forbore during that Time.

Yel. 100. Cro. El. 835. 2 Rol. Abr. 521. c. Cawley 61.

Sect. 11. V. That the Time of a Month, intended by the Statute, ſhall be computed not by the Kalendar, but by the Number of Days, allowing 28 Days to each, according to the common Rule of expounding Statutes, which ſpeak generally of a Month.

[a] 3 Lev. 333. Lut. 203, 1117. 2 Mod. 240, 241. 1 And. 294, 295.

Sect. 12. Thirdly, The Forfeiture of twenty Pounds for the Abſence of every Month after a Conviction, depends upon 28 (commonly called [a] 29) *El.* 6. Par. 2, 3, 4. and 3 *Jac.* 1. 4. Par. 8, 3. by which it is enacted, *That every Offender being convicted of not coming to Church, contrary to the Purport of the Statutes above mentioned, ſhall pay twenty Pounds for every Month after ſuch Conviction, until he ſhall conform himſelf, and come to Church.*

See 29 El. 6. Par. 1, 8.

Sect. 13. As to the ſecond Branch of this Head, *viz.* What Forfeiture of Lands and Goods ſuch Offenders are liable to, the ſame depends alſo upon 29 *El.* 6. Par. 4. and 3 *Jac.* 1. 4. Par. 8, 9. by which it is enacted, *That if the Offender ſhall make Default of Payment of the twenty Pounds, both for every Month contained in the Conviction, and alſo for every Month ſubſequent, during which he ſhall not conform himſelf to the Church, the King ſhall take, ſeize and enjoy all his Goods, and two Parts of his Hereditaments, Leaſes and Farms, leaving the third Part only of the ſame Hereditaments, Leaſes and Farms, to and for the Maintenance and Relief of the ſame Offender, his Wife, Children and Family, notwithſtanding any prior Conveyance thereof made by ſuch Offender, with Power of Revocation, or to the Uſe of himſelf or his Family. Alſo by the ſaid Statute of* 3 Jac. 1. 4. Par. 11. *the King may refuſe the Penalty of twenty Pounds a Month, tho' it be tendered according to Law, and thereupon ſeiſe two Parts of all the Hereditaments, Leaſes and Farms, which at the Time of ſuch Seizure ſhall be, or afterwards ſhall come to any ſuch Offender, or to any other to his Uſe, or in Truſt for him, or at his Diſpoſition, or whereby or in Conſideration whereof he or his Family ſhall be relieved, maintained or kept, leaving unto him his chief Manſion-Houſe, as Part of his third Part.*

In the Conſtruction of theſe Statutes the following Points have been reſolved.

1 Jones 24, 25. Cawley 171, 172.

Sect. 14. I. That the King by making his Election given him by 3 *Jac.* 1. to ſeize the Offender's Hereditaments, *&c.* waves the Benefit of the twenty Pounds a Month, and the Power of ſeizing the Offender's Goods.

12 Co. 1, 2. 1 Leon. 98. 1 Rol. Rep. 7.

Sect. 15. II. That a Recognizance or Bond taken by ſuch Offenders, either in their own Names or in the Names of others to their Uſe, are within the Statute 29 *El.* for the Words thereof to this Purpoſe are, *That the King ſhall take, ſeize, and enjoy all the Goods, &c.* which in an Act of Parliament will include the whole perſonal Eſtate; and though a Choſe in Action cannot properly be ſaid to be taken or ſeiſed, yet may it properly enough be ſaid to be enjoyed.

Owen 37. 1 Leon. 97. Cawley 107.a.

Sect. 16. III. That no Copyhold Lands are within 29 *El.* (and by the ſame Reaſon it ſeemeth that they are not within 3 *Jac.* 1.) in Reſpect of the Prejudice, which would accrue to the Lord by the Loſs of his Services, *&c.*

Sect. 17. IV. That the Profits of the Lands ſeized by the King by Force of 29 *El.* for the Non-payment of the twenty Pounds a Month, ought not to be applied to the Satisfaction thereof, but that the Lands ought to remain in the King's Hands by Way of Pledge, till the whole Forfeiture be paid ſome other Way; but this Conſtruction of the Statute ſeeming over ſevere, it was provided by 3 *Jac.* 1. 4. Par. 5. *That the Profits of the ſaid Lands ſhould go towards the Satisfaction of the twenty Pounds.* Cro. El. 845. 2 Rol. Rep. 25. Palm. 41. Sir W. Jones 24.

Sect. 18. It hath been queſtioned, Whether an Eſtate conveyed by another in Truſt for a Recuſant, be liable to be ſeized by Force of the ſaid Statute of 29 *El.* becauſe it expreſly avoids ſuch Conveyances only as are made by the Recuſant himſelf *to his own Uſe*, &c. And perhaps if it ſhall plainly appear, That an Eſtate is ſettled *bona fide* in Truſt for a Recuſant, by ſome Friend of his, upon ſome other View, and not meerly with an Intent to evade the Statute, it may be reaſonable to exempt ſuch a Conveyance out of the Meaning of it; however it is clear from the expreſs Words of 3 *Jac.* 1. 4. Par. 11. *That the King, upon his waving the Forfeiture of the twenty Pounds a Month, may ſeize two Parts of all the Hereditaments,* &c. *which ſhall come to any ſuch Offenders, or to others to their Uſe, or in Truſt for them:* Alſo it is ſaid, That the King may ſeize an Eſtate, which is granted to a Recuſant in Truſt for another; and it is certain that the Statute has made no expreſs Proviſion for the *Ceſtui que Truſt.* Lane 105, 106. Cawley 169. See 12 Co. 1, 2. Lane 39.

As to the ſecond general Head of this Chapter, *viz.* In what Manner Offenders of this Nature are to be proceeded againſt for the Forfeitures above mentioned, I ſhall conſider,

1. How they are to be proceeded againſt for the ſaid Forfeitures of Money, and

2. In what Manner for the ſaid Forfeitures of Lands and Goods.

As to the Proſecution for the ſaid Forfeitures of Money, I ſhall ſhew,

1. How they are to be proceeded againſt for the ſaid Forfeiture of twelve Pence for the Abſence of every *Sunday, &c.* and

2. In what Manner for the ſaid Forfeiture of twenty Pounds for the Abſence of every Month contained in a Conviction, and

3. In what Manner for the ſaid Forfeiture of twenty Pounds for the Abſence of every Month after a Conviction.

Sect. 19. And firſt, As to the Recovery of the ſaid Forfeiture of twelve Pence for the Abſence of every *Sunday*, it was enacted by 1 *El.* 2. *That the ſame ſhould be levied by the Church-wardens of the Pariſh where ſuch Offence ſhould be done, to the Uſe of the Poor of the ſame Pariſh, of the Goods, Lands, and Tenements of ſuch Offenders, by Way of Diſtreſs:* But this being defective in not ſhewing by whom, or in what Manner ſuch Offenders ſhould be convicted, or by whom the Warrant for levying the ſaid Forfeiture ſhould be granted; it was farther enacted by 3 *Jac.* 1. 4. Par. 27. *That it ſhall be lawful for any one Juſtice of the Peace of the Limit, Diviſion, or Liberty, wherein the ſaid Party ſhall dwell, upon the Confeſſion of the Party, or the Oath of one Witneſs, to call the ſaid Party before him, and if he ſhall not make a ſufficient Excuſe, and due Proof thereof, to the Satisfaction of the ſaid Juſtice of Peace, that it ſhall be lawful for the ſaid Juſtice of Peace to make a Warrant to the Church-warden of the ſaid Pariſh, where the ſaid Party ſhall dwell, to levy 12 Pence for every ſuch Default, by Diſtreſs and Sale of the Offender's Goods, rendering the Overplus to the ſaid Offender; and that in Default of ſuch Diſtreſs, it ſhall be lawful for the ſaid Juſtice of Peace to commit every ſuch Offender to Priſon, until the ſaid Forfeiture ſhall be paid, which ſhall be employed to the Use of the Poor of the Parish, wherein the Offender shall be resident or abiding at the Time of the Offence.*

Sect. 20. As to the second Point, *viz.* In what Manner the said Offenders are to be proceeded against for the said Forfeiture of twenty Pounds for the Absence of every Month contained in a Conviction, I shall consider,

1. In what Manner the same may be recovered at the Suit of the King, and

2. In what Manner at the Suit of an Informer.

And first, as to the Recovery hereof at the King's Suit, I shall consider,

1. In what Manner it may be recovered at the King's Suit by Way of Indictment.

2. In what Manner by Way of Action or Information.

See 1 Rol. Rep. 94. 11 Co. 63. Cawley 66, 67, 82, 83.

Sect. 21. And first, as to the Recovery hereof at the Suit of the King by Way of Indictment, it was enacted by 23 *El.* 1. Par. 9. *That the Justices of Oyer, Assize, Gaol-Delivery, and Quarter-Sessions of the Peace, might enquire of and determine these Offences, within one Year and a Day:* But by 29 *El.* 6. Par. 2. *It was ordained that all such Convictions should be in the King's Bench, or at the Assizes, or General Gaol-Delivery, and not elsewhere:* However by 3 *Jac.* 1. 4. Par. 7. the Jurisdiction of the Sessions is revived.

Precedent Lut. 203, 1101.

Sect. 22. Also it is farther enacted by 29 *El.* 6. Par. 5. and 3 *Jac.* 1. 4. Par. 7. *That upon an Indictment at the Assizes, Gaol-Delivery, or General Sessions of the Peace, Proclamation shall be made that the Offender render himself to the Sheriff before the next Assizes, Gaol-Delivery or Sessions; and that if he shall not then appear of Record, upon such Default recorded, the same shall be a Conviction in Law, as if a Trial by Verdict on the Indictment had been recorded.* And by Par. 9. *Every such Conviction shall be certified into the Exchequer,* &c. (Sal. 145.)

1 Vent. 355. Raym. 434.

Sect. 23. In the Construction hereof it hath been resolved, I. That such a Conviction shall not be look'd on as a Judgment; for the Words are, *It shall be a Conviction in Law, as if a Trial,* &c. *had been recorded:* And consequently that it cannot be reversed by Writ of Error, which cannot be brought on any Record, which is not a Judgment, and therefore that the Party has no other Remedy against an insufficient Conviction, but to remove it into the Exchequer, and quash it there. Also upon the same Ground it has been holden, That a Forfeiture due to the King, by Force of such a Conviction, shall not be taken to be within the Exception of a general Pardon, which excepts all Forfeitures, *&c.* converted to a Debt by Judgment. (Vide Sal. 145. pl. 5. 11 Co. 65. a. Vide infra Sect. 42.)

Palm. 40, 41. Bridg. 123. 3 Lev. 333. Lut. 1117.

Sect. 24. II. That if the Proclamation do not pursue the Statute, as if it appoint that the Body shall be rendered at next Sessions, *&c.* whereas by the Statute it ought to order a Render to the Sheriff, and that before the next Sessions, the Conviction is insufficient.

Cawley 164. Poph. 29. Keilw. 180. a.

Sect. 25. III. That an actual personal Appearance of the Defendant at the next Sessions, *&c.* will no Way avail him, unless the same be entered of Record.

Hob. 205.

Sect. 26. It hath been holden, That a Man cannot be convicted by Force of this Statute upon a Default on a Proclamation, *&c.* in the King's Bench, because this Court is not mentioned in the Statute: But perhaps this Opinion may justly be questioned, because the Court of King's Bench being the supreme Court of Assise, and Gaol-Delivery, *&c.* in the County where it sits, it seems that a Statute by giving any Power to the Courts of Assize, or Gaol-Delivery, does impliedly give the same to the Court of King's Bench, unless it have some restrictive Words to the contrary. (H. P. C. 156. Cro. Ca. 465. 2 Lev. 179. 2 Mod. 128, 129.)

Sect. 27. If the Defendant do appear, there is no Doubt but that the Proceedings ought to be according to the common Courſe of Law upon other Indictments in all Reſpects, except thoſe which are within the Reſtraint of 3 *Jac.* 1. 4. Par. 16, 17. by which it is enacted, *That no ſuch Indictment, nor any Proclamation, Outlawry or other Proceeding thereupon, ſhall at any Time hereafter be avoided, diſcharged or reverſed, by reaſon of any Default in Form or lack of Form, or other Defect whatſoever, (other than by direct Traverſe to the Point of not coming to Church,* &c.) *but the ſame Indictment ſhall ſtand in Force and be proceeded upon; any ſuch Default of Form, or other Defect whatſoever notwithſtanding, unleſs the Party ſo indicted ſhall conform,* &c. Cro. Ca. 504. Raym. 434.

Sect. 28. However it hath been reſolved,

I. That the Party is only reſtrained from taking Advantage of Defects in the Record it ſelf, and that he may plead any collateral Matter, as a Pardon, or *Autrefoits convict,* &c. 11 Co. 59. b. 65. a. b. 1 Rol. Rep. 95. Cro. Jac. 480, 482.

Sect. 29. II. That he may even reverſe a Judgment after Verdict for any ſuch Defect in the Record it ſelf, as tends to the King's Prejudice, as the Omiſſion of a *Capiatur, &c.* And that he may reverſe an Outlawry for any common Defect, upon putting in Bail, and traverſing the Indictment as to the Point of not coming to Church, which is very agreeable to the Purport of the whole Clauſe, the latter Part whereof ſeems manifeſtly to qualify the Generality of the former. Cro. Ca. 504, 505. Show. 309. 5 Mod. 141. 3 Keb. 591.

Sect. 30. Secondly, As to the Recovery of the ſaid Forfeiture by way of Action or Information at the King's Suit, it was enacted by 35 *El.* 1. Par. 10. *That all and every the ſaid Pains, Duties, Forfeitures and Payments, ſhall and may be recovered and levied to her Majeſty's Uſe, by Action of Debt, Bill, Plaint, Information or otherwiſe, in any of the Courts commonly called the King's Bench, Common Pleas, or Exchequer, in ſuch Sort and in all Reſpects, as by the ordinary Courſe of the Common Laws of this Realm, any other Debt due by any ſuch Perſon in any other Caſe ſhould or may be recovered or levied, wherein no Eſſoin, Protection or Wager of Law ſhall be admitted or allowed.*

Sect. 31. It is ſaid, That the principal End of making this Clauſe, was to enable the Queen to proceed againſt the Husband for the Recuſancy of his Wife, which ſhe could not do by Virtue of any of the former Statutes, by which ſhe had no other Way of proceeding but by Indictment, and conſequently could not charge the Husband for the Forfeiture of the Wife, becauſe ſhe could not make him a Party to the Suit, as ſhe may by Force of this Statute; However it is ſaid, That on a Conviction of the Wife upon an Indictment, the Lands and Leaſes, which the Huſband has in her Right, may be ſeiſed by the Exchequer-Proceſs. 11 Co. 61. b. 62. a. Vide ſupra ca. 1. Sect. 13. Cro. Jac. 482. Bridgm. 122. ſeems cont.

Sect. 32. As to the ſecond Particular, *viz.* In what Manner an Informer may proceed for the Forfeitures aforeſaid, it is enacted by 23 *El.* 1. Par. 11. *That all Forfeitures of any Sums of Money limited by that Act, ſhall be divided into three equal Parts, whereof one Third ſhall be to the Queen, to her own Uſe, one other Third to the Queen, for the Relief of the Poor in the Pariſh where the Offence ſhall be committed, to be delivered by the Warrant of the principal Officers in the Receipt of the Exchequer, without further Warrant from her Majeſty; and the other Third to ſuch Perſon, as will ſue for the ſame in any Court of Record, by Action of Debt, Bill, Plaint, or Information, in which Suit no Eſſoin,* &c. *ſhall be allowed: And that every Perſon which ſhall forfeit any Sums of Money by Virtue of that Act, and ſhall not be able, or ſhall fail to pay the ſame within three Months after Judgment thereof given, ſhall be* 2 Leon. 167. & 29 Eliz. 6. Par. 7.

committed to prison, there to remain until he have paid the same Sums, or conform himself to go to Church, and there do as is aforesaid.

Sect. 33. It has been objected, that this Clause shall not extend to the said Forfeiture of twenty Pounds a Month for not coming to Church, because the same is by the former Part of this Statute given expresly to the Queen, whereas the Forfeitures for saying or hearing Mass, and keeping an unlicenced School-master, are inflicted by the same Statute indefinitely, and not expresly given to any one; from which it is argued, That this latter Clause of Distribution ought only to be applied to the said indefinite Clauses, and not to take from the Queen any Part of that, which was expresly given her before; yet it has been answered and resolved, That it shall equally extend to all; for the Limitation of the Forfeiture to the Queen is mere Surplus, and no more than the Law would have implied, & *expressio eorum, quæ tacite insunt, nihil operatur.*

11 Co. 58. a. See 3 & 6 Par. 1 Rol. Rep. 89.
11 Co. 58. a.

Sect. 34. Also it has been resolved, That an Informer may sue, not only for the third Part which belongs to him, but for the whole Penalty in the Behalf of himself and the King, and that the Judgment shall be that they shall recover, &c.

1 And. 139, 140. B. 2. Ch. 26. Sect. 76.

Sect. 35. Also it has been adjudged, that neither the above mentioned Clause of 29 *El.* 6. which orders, That all Convictions upon 23 *El.* shall be certified into the Exchequer, and also that the Offender shall pay to the Queen twenty Pounds for every Month contained in the Indictment, &c. nor the said Clause in the 35 *El.* 1. by which it is enacted, That all the said Pains, &c. shall be recovered to the Queen's Use, do take away the Suit of the Informer, against one not proceeded against by the King, or the third Part of the Penalty given him by 23 *Eliz.* For the plain Purport of both these Acts is to further the Punishment of Recusants, and therefore inasmuch as they are in the Affirmative, and consistent with 23 *El.* they shall not be construed to abrogate any Part of it.

Supra Sect. 13.
Supra Sect. 33.
11 Co. 61, 62. 1 Rol. Rep. 92, 93.

Sect. 36. Moreover it is manifest, that 29 *El.* 6. extends only to the King's Suit by Indictment, for the Word Indictment is mentioned almost in every Clause.

Sect. 37. And it also follows from hence, That the second Paragraph of the said Statute of 29 *El.* which enacts, That Convictions for this Offence shall be only at Assizes, Gaol-Delivery, or the King's Bench, restrains only Convictions upon Indictments, and consequently does not any Way impeach the Jurisdiction of the Common Pleas or Exchequer, as to Informations, &c.

Hob. 205. Con. 11 Co. 61. a.

Sect. 38. It seems the better Opinion (upon comparing all the Books together, which differ much from one another both in stating the Cases, and giving the Reasons of the Judgments relating to this Matter,) that a Conviction at the King's Suit, whether strictly regular or erroneous, may be pleaded to a Suit by an Informer, because while it stands in Force, it makes the Party liable to the Forfeiture of twenty Pounds a Month, and no one ought to be punished twice for the same Offence: But it hath been resolved, that an erroneous, and strongly holden that a regular, Conviction by Proclamation cannot be pleaded to a new Suit by the King, because such a Conviction is of no greater Effect than a Conviction by Verdict, and consequently the King may wave it and begin anew.

11 Co. 59. b. 65. a. See B. 2. Ch. 26. Sect. 63. Lutw. 208. 1 Rol. Rep. 93. Cro. Jac. 481, 482. Noy 117. Lane 60. Palm. 39, 40, 41. 2 Rol. Re. 108. Bridg. 122, 123.

Sect. 39. But it seems very doubtful, whether the Conviction of a Feme Covert upon an Indictment can be pleaded to an Information against her and her Husband, because the Husband is not liable to pay the Forfeiture recovered upon an Indictment.

Cro. Jac. 481, 482. Bridg. 120, 121, 122. 2 Rol. Re. 108. Vide supra, cap. 1. Sect. 13.

Sect. 40. It ſeems that the ordinary Method of recovering the ſaid Forfeiture of twenty Pounds for every Month contained in a Conviction, either at the Suit of the King, or of an Informer, may ſufficiently appear from what has been already ſaid; but there is an extraordinary Remedy provided by the ſaid Statute of 29 *El.* 6. to enforce the Party to take Care of the Payment of the Forfeiture of the twenty Pounds for every Month contained in an Indictment, whereon he ſhall be convicted, by making his Lands and Goods liable to be ſeized by the King for the Non-payment thereof into the Exchequer, upon ſuch of the Terms of *Eaſter* or *Michaelmas*, as ſhall be next after his Conviction; but this extends not to a Conviction by Way of Action, or Information, as more fully appears from the two next Sections.

Sect. 41. As to the third Point, *viz.* In what Manner the Forfeiture of twenty Pounds for the Abſence of every Month after a Conviction is to be recovered, it ſeems needleſs to enquire how far it may be recovered by an Action or Information for it at the King's Suit, inaſmuch as the ſaid Statutes of 29 *El.* 6. *&* 3 *Jac.* 1. have made a moſt effectual Proviſion for the Payment of it, by expreſly enacting, *That every ſuch Offender being once convicted, ſhall for every Month after ſuch Conviction, without any other Indictment or Conviction, pay into the Exchequer twice in the Year,* viz. *in every* Eaſter *and* Michaelmas *Term, as much as ſhall then remain unpaid, after the Rate of twenty Pounds for every Month after a Conviction, and that for a Default herein the King may ſeize all the Goods, and two Parts of the Hereditaments of ſuch an Offender*, &c.

Sect. 42. But it ſeemeth that theſe Clauſes extend not to any Conviction upon an Information, or Action, *&c.* but only to a Conviction upon an Indictment, for there is no other Suit referred to beſides that of Indictment; alſo it is ſaid, that the ſaid Clauſes extend to no Convictions by Verdict or otherwiſe, unleſs Judgment be given thereon; becauſe, till then nothing is forfeited. And from the ſame Ground it ſeems to follow, That they would not have extended to a Conviction by Default upon Proclamation, if there had been no other Words in the Statute to this Purpoſe, than thoſe by which it is enacted, *That ſuch a Default recorded ſhall be as ſufficient a Conviction in Law of the ſaid Offence, whereof the Party ſtandeth indicted, as if upon the ſame Indictment a Trial by Verdict thereupon had proceeded and been recorded*, which Words of themſelves can by no Means make ſuch a Conviction amount to a Judgment after Verdict, without which their can be no Forfeiture upon any other Conviction; and therefore it ſeemeth that the Forfeiture cauſed by ſuch a Conviction muſt depend upon the other Clauſes of the ſaid Statutes, and the conſtant Tenor of our Law Books, which ſeem to ſuppoſe that a Perſon ſo convicted ſhall be liable to the ſaid Forfeitures, as much as one, againſt whom a Judgment is expreſly given.

Cawley 102, 103. Vide ſupra, Sect. 8. Vide infra, Sect. 56. See 29 El. 6. Par. 6. 3 Jac. 1. 4. Par. 7, 8, 9. Cawley 103, 104.

Sect. 43. As to the ſecond general Branch of this Head, *viz.* In what Manner Offenders of this Nature are to be proſecuted for the Forfeiture of Lands or Goods, it appeareth from the 13th, 14th, 15th, 17th, 18th, 40th and 41ſt Sections of this Chapter, that the King hath his Election either to ſeize all the Goods and two Parts of the Hereditaments and Leaſes of the Offender, upon his making Default in the Payment of twenty Pounds, both for every Month contained in an Indictment, whereon he ſhall be convicted, and alſo for every Month ſubſequent, or elſe to refuſe the ſaid Penalty of twenty Pounds a Month, and thereupon to ſeize two Parts of the Hereditaments and Leaſes of the Offender.

Sect. 44. It alſo appeareth from what hath been ſaid in the forty ſecond Section of this Chapter, that the King hath this Advantage of ſeizing the Lands and Goods of the Offender upon no other Conviction, but ſuch as followeth an Indictment, nor even upon ſuch a Conviction without a Judgment, unleſs it be cauſed by a Default upon a Proclamation; therefore I ſhall add no more to this Head, except theſe two following Obſervations:

2 Inſt. 573. 8 Co. 169. Plowd. 486. *Sect.* 45. I. That the King cannot ſeize the Lands, till it appears by the Return of an Inquiſition to that Purpoſe to be awarded, of what Lands, *&c.* the Offender was ſeized, becauſe the King's Title to Lands ought always to appear of Record.

Bro. Coro. 2, 14, 25, 45, 47, 55, 60. 1 Rol. Rep. 7. 2 Rol. Ab. 184. pl. 3. *Sect.* 46. II. That the King, according to the better Opinion, may ſeize the Goods, but not grant them over, without ſuch an Inquiſition.

Sect. 47. As to the third general Head of this Chapter, *viz.* What Diſabilities, and other Inconveniencies, Offenders of this Kind are liable unto, it is enacted by 3 *Jac.* 1. 5. Par. 8. *That no Recuſant convict ſhall practice either the Common or Civil Law, or Phyſick, or uſe the Trade of an Apothecary, or be Judge or Miniſter of any Court, or bear any Office in Camp, Troop, or Company of Soldiers, or in any Ship, or Fortreſs, but ſhall be utterly diſabled for the ſame, and forfeit for every ſuch Offence, one hundred Pounds.*

Sect. 48. Alſo it is farther enacted by the ſaid Statute of 3 *Jac.* 1. 5. Par. 22. *That ſuch Recuſants, as ſhall be convicted at the Time of the Death of any Teſtator, or at the Time of the Granting of any Adminiſtration, ſhall be diſabled to be Executors or Adminiſtrators; and that no ſuch Perſons ſhall be Guardians to any Child,* &c.

Sect. 49. And it is enacted by 23 *El.* 1. *That every Perſon forbearing the Church twelve Months, ſhall on Certificate thereof into the King's Bench by the Ordinary, a Juſtice of Aſſize and Gaol-Delivery, or a Juſtice of Peace of the County where ſuch Offender ſhall dwell or be, be bound with two ſufficient Sureties in the Sum of two hundred Pounds at the leaſt to the Good Behaviour, and ſo continue bound until ſuch Offender ſhall conform himſelf,* &c.

Sect. 50. As to the fourth general Head of this Chapter, *viz.* By what Means Offenders of this Nature may be diſcharged from the ſaid Forfeitures, *&c.* it is enacted by 23 *El.* 1. Par. 10. *That every Perſon guilty of the above-mentioned Offences, who ſhall before he be thereof indicted, or at his Arraignment or Trial before Judgment, ſubmit and conform himſelf before the Biſhop of the Dioceſe where he ſhall be reſident, or before the Juſtices where he ſhall be indicted, arraigned, or tried, (having not before made like Submiſſion at any his Trial, being indicted for his firſt like Offence,) ſhall upon his Recognition of ſuch Submiſſion in open Aſſizes, or Seſſions of the County where ſuch Perſon ſhall be reſident, be diſcharged of all and every the ſaid Offences againſt the ſaid Statute,* &c.

Sect. 51. Alſo it is enacted by 29 *El.* 6. Par. 6. *That whenſoever any ſuch Offender ſhall make Submiſſion, and become conformable, according to the Form limited by the above mentioned Statute of* 23 El. 1. *or ſhall fortune to die, that then no Forfeiture of twenty Pounds for any Month, or Seizure of the Lands of the ſame Offender, from and after ſuch Submiſſion and Conformity, or Death, and full Satiſfaction of all the Arrearages of twenty Pounds Monthly, before ſuch Seizure due or payable, ſhall enſue, or be continued againſt ſuch Offender, ſo long as the ſame Perſon ſhall continue in coming to Divine Service, according to the Intent of the ſaid Statute.*

Sect. 52. But this Statute being thought not to give ſufficient Encouragement to ſuch Perſons to conform to the Church, becauſe, by the moſt favourable Conſtruction that could be made, it ſtill obliged them to pay ſuch Debts as were due to the King by Force of a Judgment, it was enacted by 1 *Jac.* 1. 4. Par. 2. *That a Recuſant conforming himſelf according to the Meaning of the above mentioned Statutes, &c. ſhall, during ſuch Conformity, be diſcharged of all Penalties, which he might otherwiſe ſuſtain by Reaſon of his Recuſancy.* 1 Rol. Rep. 94.

Sect. 53. And it hath been reſolved, that ſuch Conformity may by Force of this Statute be pleaded as well to the Suit of an Informer as to that of the King; and that after Judgment it will be a good Ground for an *Audita Querela* againſt an Informer; and alſo may be pleaded againſt the King before Execution awarded. Raym. 391, 465. 2 Jon. 187. 1 Mod. 213. 1 Rol. Rep. 95. 2 Bulst. 324, 325.

Sect. 54. However, there ſeems to be no Remedy for ſuch a Perſon to get a Reſtitution of ſuch of the Profits of his Lands, as have been actually taken by the King. Savil 130.

Sect. 55. It ſeemed very doubtful before 1 *Jac.* 1. 4. how far the Lands of an Heir were chargeable with the Forfeitures incurred by his Anceſtor in Reſpect of his Recuſancy; but this ſeems to be for the moſt part cleared by the 3d, 4th and 5th Paragraphs of that Statute, by which it is enacted, *That the Heir, if he be no Recuſant, or were ſuch, and conform, ſhall be freed from all Penalties happening upon him by reaſon of his Anceſtor's Recuſancy, unleſs the two Parts of the Lands were ſeiſed by the King in the Anceſtor's Life, in which Caſe they ſhall continue in the King's Hands till the whole Debt ſhall be levied. But it is farther enacted, that the King ſhall not extend the other third Part of the Lands for the ſaid Penalty.* Lane 92, 93, 106. Cawley 109, 110.

Sect. 56. It ſeems by the manifeſt Purport of this Statute, that the Heir of a Recuſant, being alſo a Recuſant himſelf, has no Remedy, but by conforming, to free his Fee-Simple Lands from any of the Forfeitures incurred by the Conviction of his Anceſtor, whether the Lands were ſeized in the Anceſtor's Life or not: However, it is ſaid, that the Land in Fee-Tail, which he claims from ſuch Anceſtor, is no Way chargeable after the Death of the Anceſtor, with any Forfeitures upon a Conviction by Proclamation, (which has no greater Effect than a Verdict recorded) but only with ſuch, as are due upon a Judgment; which, as it is agreed, charge an Heir in Tail by Force of 33 *H.* 8. 39. Par. 29. which makes an Heir chargeable with the Debts of his Anceſtor by Judgment, Recognizance, Obligation, or other Specialty; but perhaps the Authority of theſe Opinions may juſtly be queſtioned: For tho' a Conviction by Proclamation amount not to a Judgment, yet ſurely it cannot be inferior to an Obligation: And therefore perhaps the Books cited in the Margin are miſreported in this Particular, and the more proper Diſtinction may be this: That an Heir in Tail is chargeable only with the Forfeitures for thoſe Months, which are contained in the Indictment it ſelf, on which a Judgment is afterwards given, or a Conviction by Proclamation recorded, and not for the Months ſubſequent to ſuch Conviction, or Proclamation, inaſmuch as the firſt ſeem to be Debts appearing of Record, the latter not; and the ſame Diſtinction ſeems applicable to ſuch Lands in Tail of an Heir who conforms, as were ſeized in the Anceſtor's Life; but it is clear, that ſuch only of his Lands as were ſo ſeized are in any Caſe liable, whether he claim them in Fee-Simple or Tail. Moore 523. 1 Rol. Rep. 94. Cro. El. 846. Cawley 109, 110, 150, 151, 152. Vide ſupra Sect. 42

CHAP. XI.

Of the Offence of suffering others to be absent from Church.

HAving shewn how far all Persons in general are punishable for their own Absence from the Church, I am now to shew how far they may be punished for the Absence of others; as to which it is enacted by 3 *Jac.* 1. 4. Par. 32, 33, 34. *That whosoever shall retain or keep in his Service, Fee or Livery, or shall willingly maintain, retain, relieve, keep, or harbour, in his House, any Servant, Sojourner, or Stranger, (except a Father or Mother wanting, without Fraud or Covin, other Habitation, or sufficient Maintenance, and also except a Ward, or Person committed to the Custody of another by Authority,) who shall not go to some Church or Chapel, or usual Place of Common Prayer, to hear Divine Service, but shall forbear the same for the Space of one Month,* &c. *shall for every Month, that he shall keep such Servant,* &c. *forfeit ten Pounds.*

CHAP. XII.

Of Popish Recusancy.

AND now we are come to Offences against the Established Church, more immediately relating to those of the Popish Religion, for the better understanding whereof I shall consider:

1. The above mentioned Offence of not coming to Church, so far as it particularly concerns those of this Persuasion.
2. The Offence of saying or hearing Mass, or other Popish Service.
3. The Offence of not making a Declaration against Popery.
4. The Offence of promoting or encouraging the Popish Religion.

And first as to the said Offence of not coming to Church, so far as it particularly concerns those of the Popish Religion, who in respect hereof are commonly called Popish Recusants, I shall consider;

1. How far such Recusants are punishable in their own Persons.
2. How far they make others liable to be punished.

As to the first of these Points, *viz.* How far such Recusants are punishable in their own Persons, it is to be observed, that they are not only liable to all the Forfeitures and Disabilities, and other Inconveniences mentioned in Chap. 10. but also to many particular Disabilities, Restraints and Forfeitures, and other Inconveniences to which no others are liable.

And first they are put under the following Disabilities,

1. That of bringing an Action.

2. That of presenting to a Church.

3. That of bearing any publick Office, or Charge.

4. That of claiming any Part of a Husband's personal Estate.

5. That of claiming an Estate by Curtesy, or by Way of Dower, after a Marriage against Law.

Secondly, They are put under the following Restraints,

1. From going above five Miles from Home.

2. From coming to Court.

3. From keeping Arms.

4. From coming within ten Miles of *London.*

Thirdly, They are liable to the following Forfeitures,

1. That of two Parts of a Jointure or Dower.

2. That of twenty Pounds for not receiving the Sacrament yearly after Conformity.

3. That of one hundred Pounds for an unlawful Marriage.

4. That of one hundred Pounds for an Omission of lawful Baptism.

5. That of twenty Pounds for an unlawful Burial.

Lastly, They are subject to the following Inconveniences,

1. That their Houses may be searched for Reliques, whether they be Men or Women.

2. If they be Women and married, that they may be committed, *&c.*

Sect. 1. As to the first of the said Disabilities, *viz.* That of bringing an Action, it is enacted by 3 *Jac.* 1. 5. Par. 11, 12. *That every Popish Recusant convict shall stand to all Intents and Purposes disabled, as a Person lawfully excommunicated, and as if such Person had been so denounced and excommunicated according the Laws of this Realm, until he or she shall conform,* &c. *And that every Person, sued by such Person so disabled, may plead the same in disabling of such Plaintiff, as if he or she were excommunicated by Sentence in the Ecclesiastical Court. Except the Action of such Recusant do concern some Hereditament or Lease, which is not to be seised into the King's Hands, by Force of some Law concerning Recusancy.*

In the Exposition hereof it hath been resolved,

Sect. 2. I. That the Plea of such a Conviction, like all other Pleas in Disability, ought to be pleaded before Imparlance, and also to conclude with a Demand if the Plaintiff shall be answered. Noy 89. Latch 176, 177. Hetl. 18.

Sect. 3. II. That such Plea ought also to shew before what Justices the Conviction was, that the Court may know where to send for a Certificate thereof, if it be denied; and also that the Record it self, or at least a Certificate thereof, ought to be immediately produced, according to the general Rule of the Law, as to all dilatory Pleas grounded upon Records. Noy 89. Latch 176. 3 Lev. 333, 334.

Sect. 4. III. That if after such a Plea it be certified that the Plaintiff hath conformed, and thereupon the Defendant be ordered to plead in chief, and then the Plaintiff relapse and be convict again, the Defendant cannot plead the same in Disability a second Time. Hetl. 176.

Sect. 5. IV. That it must appear either from the Conviction it self, or by proper Averments, that the Plaintiff is convicted of Popish Recusancy, because no Recusants, except Popish ones, are within the said Clause; however that this is sufficiently set forth, by alledging that the Plaintiff being *Papalis Recusans,* was indicted and convicted *secundum formam Statuti, &c.* 3 Lev. 333, 334, 11, 12.

Sect. 6. And some have gone so far as to hold, That all Popish Recusants convict may be taken up by the Writ * *De Excommunicato capiendo,* and that they are not to be admitted as competent Witnesses in any Cause;

* 2 Bul. 155, 156. The same Point seems admitted, State Trials Vol. 1 fol. 268. Vol. 3 f 423.

Cause; but this seems to be a Construction over severe: For inasmuch as this, like all other Penal Statutes, ought to be construed strictly, and the Words thereof are no more than, That such Persons shall stand disabled, *&c.* as Persons lawfully excommunicate, *&c.* and the Purport thereof may be fully satisfied by the Disability to bring any Action, it seems to be too rigorous to carry them farther.

Cawley 216.

Sect. 7. As to the second of the said Disabilities, *viz.* That of presenting to a Church, the same being at this Day extended by 12 *Ann.* 2. to all Persons making Profession of the Popish Religion, I shall refer the Reader, for the Matters relating to this Head, to Chap. 15, wherein is shewn how penal it is, barely to profess the said Religion; and I shall only take Notice in this Place, that by 1 *Gul. & Mar.* 26. Par. 4. *If the Trustee, Mortgagee, or Grantee of any Avoidance, whereof the Trust shall be for any Popish Recusant convict, shall present without giving Notice in Writing of the Avoidance, to the University,* &c. *within three Months after the Avoidance, he forfeits five hundred Pounds.*

Sect. 8. As to the third of the said Disabilities, *viz.* That of bearing any publick Office or Charge, it is enacted by 3 *Jac.* 1. 5. Par. 9. *That no Popish Recusant convict shall exercise any publick Office, or Charge, in the Commonwealth, but shall be utterly disabled to exercise the same, by himself or his Deputy.*

Sect. 9. It is observable, that this Clause is more strongly penned than that, which immediately precedes it, relating to all Recusants in general, as to the following Particulars:

1. That this extends to all publick Offices and Charges in general, whereas the former extends only to those, which are particularly enumerated.

2. That this expresly disables a Popish Recusant to exercise such an Office by himself or his Deputy, but the other says nothing at all of the Exercise of an Office by a Deputy.

Sect. 10. As to the Fourth of the said Disabilities, *viz.* That of claiming any Part of a Husband's personal Estate, it is enacted by 3 *Jac.* 1. 5. Par. 10. *That every Woman being a Popish Recusant convict, (her Husband not standing convicted of Popish Recusancy) which shall not conform her self and remain conform'd, but shall forbear to repair to some Church or usual Place of Common Prayer, and there hear Divine Service and Sermon, if any then be, and receive the Sacrament of the Lord's Supper, according to the Laws of this Realm, by the Space of one whole Year next before the Death of her said Husband, shall not only be disabled to be Executrix or Administratrix of her said Husband, but also to have or demand any Part of her said Husband's Goods or Chattels, by any Law, Custom or Usage whatsoever*; and by 3 Jac. 1. 5. Par. 13. *Every Woman is put under the like Disability, being a Popish Recusant, who shall be married otherwise than according to the Church of* England.

Sect. 11. As to the Fifth of the said Disabilities, *viz.* That of claiming an Estate by the Curtesy, or by Way of Dower, *&c.* it is enacted by 3 *Jac.* 1. 5. Par. 13. *That every Man, who being a Popish Recusant convict, shall be married otherwise than in some open Church or Chapel, and otherwise than according to the Orders of the Church of* England *by a Minister lawfully authorized, shall be disabled to have any Estate, as Tenant by the Curtesy; and that every Woman being a Popish Recusant convict, who shall be married in other Form than as aforesaid, shall be disabled to claim her Dower or Jointure, or Widow's Estate,* &c.

Sect. 12. As to the first of the above mentioned Restraints, *viz.* That from going above five Miles from Home, *&c.* it is enacted by 35 *El.* 2. and 3 *Jac.* 1. 5. Par. 6, 7. *That every Popish Recusant convict shall repair to* *his Place of Dwelling*, &c. *and not remove above five Miles from thence, unless he be urged by Process*, &c. *or have a Licence from the Privy Council*, &c. *or under the Hands and Seals of four Justices of Peace, with the Assent in Writing of the Lieutenant of the County, or of the Bishop*, &c. (*Every Licence of which Kind by Justices of Peace must express both the particular Cause and the Time for which it is given, and ought not to be granted without a previous Oath of some reasonable Cause,*) *under Pain of forfeiting all his Goods and Hereditaments,* (*whether Freehold or Copyhold,*) *for his Life, or of abjuring the Realm, if he be not worth twenty Marks a Year, or forty Pounds in Goods, unless he recant before Conviction, and also continue conformable.* See Cawley 128, 129, &c. 207, 208.

Sect. 13. Note, That the Privy Council may grant such Licence without any Special Cause or Oath, *&c.* but that the Justices of Peace cannot: And it hath been resolved, That in Pleading a Licence of Justices of Peace, you must expresly shew, that it was made under their Hands and Seals, and also set forth the Cause in particular for which it was granted, and the Time for which it was limited, and that the Party was sworn to the Truth of such Cause, *&c.* Cro. Jac. 352. 1 Rol. Re. 108. Moor 836.

Sect. 14. It is said, That if the same Person be both a Justice of Peace and a Lieutenant, he cannot both join in a Licence as Justice of Peace, and also give his Assent as Lieutenant, but can only act in one Capacity. Cro. Ja. 352. 1 Rol. Re. 108. Moor 836.

Sect. 15. It seems that the Miles shall be computed according to the *English* Manner, allowing 5280 Foot, or 1760 Yards to each Mile, and that the same shall be reckoned not by strait Lines, as a Bird or Arrow may fly, but according to the nearest and most usual Way. Cawley 130, 131. Cro. El. 212.

Sect. 16. As to the Second of the above mentioned Restraints, *viz.* That which relates to the coming to Court, it is enacted by 3 *Jac.* 1. 5. Par. 2. *That no Popish Recusant convict shall come into the Court or House, where the King or his Heir apparent shall be, unless he be commanded so to do by the King, upon Pain of one hundred Pounds*, &c. And it is farther enacted by 30 *Car.* 2. St. 2. Par. 5, 6. *That every Popish Recusant convict, who shall come advisedly into, or remain in the Presence of the King or Queen, or shall come into the Court or House, where they or any of them reside, shall be disabled to hold or execute any Office or Place of Trust Civil or Military, or to sue in Law or Equity, or to be an Executor*, &c. *or capable of any Legacy or Deed of Gift, and shall forfeit for every wilful Offence five hundred Pounds, unless such Person do within the Term next after such his coming or remaining, take the Oaths of Allegiance and Supremacy, and make the Declaration against Transubstantiation and the Invocation of Saints*, &c. *in the Court of Chancery.*

Sect. 17. As to the Third of the above mentioned Restraints, *viz.* That which relates to the keeping of Arms, it is enacted by 3 *Jac.* 1. 5. Par. 27, 28, 29. *That all such Armour, Gun-powder, and Munition of whatsoever Kinds, as any Popish Recusant convict shall have in his own House or elsewhere, or in the Possession of any other at his Disposition, shall be taken from him by Warrant of four Justices of Peace at their General or Quarter-Sessions,* (*except such necessary Weapons, as shall be allowed him by the said four Justices, for the Defence of his Person or House*) *and that the said Armour*, &c. *so taken, shall be kept at the Costs of such Recusant, in such Place as the said four Justices at their said Sessions shall appoint: And that if any such Recusant having such Armour*, &c. *or if any other Person who shall have any such Armour*, &c. *to the Use of such Recusant, shall refuse to discover to the said Justices, or any of them, what Armour he hath, or shall let or hinder the Delivery thereof to any of the said Justices, or to any other Person authorized by their Warrant to take the same, that then every Person so offending shall forfeit his said Armour*, &c. *and alſo be impriſoned for three Months without Bail, by Warrant from any Juſtices of Peace of ſuch County.* And it is farther enacted, *That notwithſtanding the taking away ſuch Armour,* &c. *yet ſuch Recuſant ſhall be charged with the maintaining of the ſame, and with the providing of a Horſe,* &c. *in ſuch Sort as others of his Majeſty's Subjects.* Alſo it is farther enacted by 1 *Will. & Mar.* 15. *That no reputed Papiſt refuſing to make the ſaid Declaration againſt Popery, mentioned in* 30 Car. *ſhall keep Arms*; as is ſet forth more at large *Chap.* 14. *Sect.* 4.

Sect. 18. As to the fourth of the above mentioned Reſtraints, *viz.* That which relates to the coming within ten Miles of *London*, it is enacted by 3 *Jac.* 1. 5. Par. 4, 5. *That no Popiſh Recuſant, &c. ſhall remain within the Compaſs of ten Miles of* London *under Pain of one hundred Pounds, except ſuch Perſons as at the Time of the ſaid Act did uſe ſome Trade, Myſtery, or manual Occupation in* London, *&c. and ſuch as ſhall have their only Dwelling in* London, *&c.* Alſo reputed Papiſts, refuſing to make the Declaration mentioned in the precedent Sections, are to be removed from *London*, &c. by Force of 1 *Will. & Mar.* 9. which is ſet forth more at large in *Cha.* 14. *Sect.* 3.

Sect. 19. As to the firſt of the above mentioned Forfeitures, *viz.* That of two Parts of a Jointure or Dower, it is enacted by 3 *Jac.* 1. 5. Par. 10. *That every married Woman being a Popiſh Recuſant convict, (her Husband not ſtanding convicted of Popiſh Recuſancy) who ſhall not conform her ſelf and remain conformed, but ſhall forbear to repair to ſome Church or uſual Place of Common Prayer, and there to hear Divine Service and Sermon, if any then be, and receive the Sacrament of the Lord's Supper, according to the Laws of this Realm, within one Year next before the Death of her ſaid Husband, ſhall forfeit to the King the Profits of two Parts of her Jointure and Dower of any Hereditaments of her ſaid Husband,* &c.

Sect. 20. As to the ſecond of the above mentioned Forfeitures, *viz.* That of twenty Pounds, *&c.* for not receiving the Sacrament yearly after Conformity, it is enacted by 3 *Jac.* 1. 4. Par. 2, 3. *That if any Popiſh Recuſant convict, who hath conformed himſelf to the Church,* &c. *ſhall not receive the Sacrament in his own Pariſh-Church,* &c. *within one Year after his Conformity, he ſhall forfeit twenty Pounds, and for the ſecond Year forty Pounds, and for every Year after ſixty Pounds,* &c.

Sect. 21. As to the third of the above mentioned Forfeitures, *viz.* That of one hundred Pounds for an unlawful Marriage, it is enacted by 3 *Jac.* 1. 5. Par. 13. *That every Popiſh Recuſant convict, who ſhall be married to a Woman who is no Inheritrix, otherwiſe than according to the Church of* England, *ſhall forfeit one hundred Pounds.*

Sect. 22. As to the fourth of the above mentioned Forfeitures, *viz.* That of one hundred Pounds for the Omiſſion of a lawful Baptiſm, it is enacted by 3 *Jac.* 1. 5. Par. 14. *That every Popiſh Recuſant, who ſhall not cauſe his or her Child to be baptized, within one Month after its Birth, by a lawful Miniſter,* &c. *ſhall forfeit one hundred Pounds,* &c.

Sect. 23. As to the fifth of the above mentioned Forfeitures, *viz.* That of twenty Pounds for an unlawful Burial, it is enacted by 3 *Jac.* 1. 5. Par. 15. *That if any Popiſh Recuſant not being excommunicate, ſhall be buried in any other Place than in the Church or Church-yard, or not according to the Eccleſiaſtical Laws of this Realm, the Executors,* &c. *of ſuch Recuſant, knowing the ſame, or the Party that cauſeth him to be ſo buried, ſhall forfeit twenty Pounds,* &c.

Sect. 24. As to the Inconvenience to which all ſuch Offenders are liable, *viz.* That of having their Houſes ſearched for Reliques, *&c.*

 it

it is enacted by 3 *Jac.* 1. 5. Par. 26. *That any two Juſtices of Peace, and all Mayors, Bailiffs, and chief Officers of Cities, and Towns Corporate, in their reſpective Juriſdictions, may ſearch the Houſe and Lodgings of every Popiſh Recuſant convict for Popiſh Books and Reliques; and that if any Altar, Pix, Beads, Pictures, or ſuch like Popiſh Relique, or any Popiſh Book, be found in the Cuſtody of ſuch Perſon, as in the Opinion of the ſaid Juſtices,* &c. *ſhall be unmeet for him or her to have or uſe, it ſhall be defaced and burnt, if it be meet to be burnt; and if it be a Crucifix or other Relique of any Price, the ſame ſhall be defaced at the General Quarter-Seſſions in the County where it ſhall be found, and then reſtored to the Owner.*

Sect. 25. As to the Inconvenience to which ſuch Offenders being Femes-Covert are liable, *viz.* that of being committed, it is enacted by 7 *Jac.* 1. 6. Par. 28. *That if any married Woman, being a Popiſh Recuſant convict, ſhall not within three Months after her Conviction conform her ſelf and repair to Church and receive the Sacrament,* &c. *ſhe may be committed to Priſon by one of the Privy Council, or by the Biſhop, if ſhe be a Baroneſs; or if under that Degree by two Juſtices of Peace whereof one to be of the* Quorum, *there to remain till ſhe perform,* &c. *unleſs the Husband will pay to the King ten Pounds a Month for her Offence, or elſe the third Part of all his Lands,* &c. *at the Choice of the Husband,* &c.

Sect. 26. And now I am to conſider in the ſecond Place, how far ſuch Recuſants make others liable to be puniſhed; as to which it is to be obſerved, That the Husband of a Popiſh Recuſant convict is not only liable to the Forfeiture of ten Pounds a Month for the Abſence of any of his Servants from Church, by Force of 1 *Jac.* 1. which is ſet forth more at large in the foregoing Chapter, *But is alſo utterly diſabled by the ninth Paragraph of the ſaid Statute, to exerciſe any Publick Office or Charge in the Common-wealth by himſelf or by his Deputy; (except ſuch Husband himſelf, and his Children, which ſhall be above the Age of nine Years abiding with him, and his Servants in Houſhold, ſhall once every Month at leaſt, not having any reaſonable Excuſe to the Contrary, repair to ſome Church or Chapel uſual for Divine Service, and there hear Divine Service; and the ſaid Husband, and ſuch his Children and Servants, as are of meet Age, receive the Sacrament of the Lord's Supper, at ſuch Times as are limited by the Laws of this Realm, and do bring up his ſaid Children in the true Religion.)*

Sect. 27. Alſo it is farther enacted by the ſaid Statute of 3 *Jac.* 1. 5. Par. 26. *That the Houſe of one whoſe Wife is a Popiſh Recuſant convict, may be ſearched by any two Juſtices of Peace,* &c. *for Popiſh Books,* &c.

CHAP. XIII.

Of Offences in ſaying or hearing Maſs or other Popiſh Service.

Sect. 1. AS to the Offence in ſaying or hearing Maſs, it is enacted by 23 *El.* 1. Par. 4. *That every Perſon who ſhall ſay or ſing Maſs, being thereof lawfully convict, ſhall forfeit two hundred Marks, and be committed to Priſon in the next Gaol, there to remain by the Space of one Year, and from thenceforth till he have paid the ſaid Sum of two hundred Marks;*

and

and that every Perſon, who ſhall willingly hear Maſs, ſhall forfeit the Sum of one hundred Marks, and ſuffer a Year's Impriſonment.

Sect. 2. And it is enacted by 11 & 12 *Will.* 3. 4. Par. 2, 3, 4, 5. *That every Perſon, who ſhall apprehend any Popiſh Biſhop, Prieſt or Jeſuit, and proſecute him to Conviction for ſaying Maſs, or exerciſing any other Part of the Function of a Popiſh Biſhop or Prieſt, ſhall receive one hundred Pounds of the Sheriff, and that every ſuch Popiſh Biſhop,* &c. (*except, being a Foreigner, he be entered in the Secretary's Office, and officiate only in the Houſe of a Foreign Miniſter,*) *ſhall be adjudged to perpetual Impriſonment.*

CHAP. XIV.

Of the Offence of not making a Declaration againſt Popery.

THE Offence of refuſing to make a Declaration againſt ſome of the Principal Doctrines of the Popiſh Religion puts all Perſons under the following Reſtraints:

1. From ſitting in Parliament.
2. From holding a Place at Court.
3. From living within ten Miles of *London.*
4. From keeping Arms.

Alſo it puts them under a Diſability of preſenting to a Church.

Sect. 1. As to the firſt of the above mentioned Reſtraints, *viz.* That which relates to the ſitting in Parliament, it is enacted by 30 *Car.* 2. Stat. 2. Chap. 1. *That no Peer ſhall vote or make his Proxy in the Houſe of Peers, or ſit there during any Debate; and that no Member of the Houſe of Commons ſhall vote or ſit there during any Debate after the Speaker is choſen, until ſuch Peer or Member ſhall take the Oaths of Allegiance and Supremacy, and make a Declaration of his Belief that there is no Tranſubſtantiation in the Sacrament of the Lord's Supper; and that the Invocation or Adoration of the Virgin* Mary, *or any other Saint, and the Sacrifice of the Maſs, as they are now uſed in the Church of* Rome, *are Superſtitious and Idolatrous,* &c. *on Pain that every ſuch offender ſhall be adjudged a Popiſh Recuſant convict, and diſabled to hold or execute any Office,* &c. *or from thenceforth to ſit or vote in either Houſe of Parliament, to ſue in Law or Equity, or to be Guardian, Executor or Adminiſtrator, or capable of any Legacy or Deed of Gift, and ſhall forfeit for every wilful Offence five hundred Pounds.*

Sect. 2. As to the ſecond of the above mentioned Reſtraints, *viz.* That which relates to the holding a Place at Court, it is enacted by the ſaid Statute of 30 *Car.* 2. Stat. 2. Par. 9, 12, 13. *That every Perſon who ſhall be a ſworn Servant to the King, ſhall take the ſaid Oaths, and make and ſubſcribe the ſaid Declaration in Chancery, the next Term after he ſhall be ſo ſworn a Servant,* &c. *And that if any ſuch Perſon, neglecting ſo to do, ſhall adviſedly come into or remain in the Preſence of the King or Queen, or ſhall come into the Court or Houſe where they are or any of them reſide, he ſhall ſuffer all the Penalties expreſſed in the foregoing Section, unleſs ſuch Perſon ſo coming into the*

the King's Preſence, &c. *ſhall firſt have Licence ſo to do, by Warrant under the Hands and Seals of ſix Privy Counſellors, by Order of the Privy Council, upon ſome urgent Occaſion therein to be expreſſed, which Licence ſhall not exceed ten Days, and ſhall be firſt filed,* &c. *in the Petty-Bag Office, for any Body to view without Fee,* &c. *and no Perſon be licenced for above thirty Days in one Year.*

Sect. 3. As to the third of the above mentioned Reſtraints, *viz.* That which relates to the living within ten Miles of *London,* it is enacted by 1 *Will. & Mar.* 9. *That every Juſtice of Peace in* London *and* Weſtminſter, *and within ten Miles thereof, ſhall cauſe to be arreſted and brought before him all reputed Papiſts, (except Foreigners, being Merchants, or menial Servants to ſome Ambaſſadour or publick Agent, and except all ſuch as uſed ſome Trade, Myſtery, or ſome manual Occupation at the Time of the ſaid Act, in* London, &c. *and alſo except all ſuch Perſons as had their Dwelling in* London, &c. *within ſix Months before the thirteenth of* February 1688. *and no Dwelling elſewhere, and certified their Names to the Seſſions before the firſt of* Auguſt 1689) *and that every ſuch Juſtice ſhall tender the ſaid Declaration to every ſuch Perſon, and that every ſuch Perſon refuſing the ſame, and afterwards remaining in* London, &c. *or within ten Miles thereof, or being certified to the King's Bench or Quarter-Seſſions, at the next Term or Seſſions, as having refuſed to make the ſaid Declaration, and neglecting to make the ſame in ſuch Court, ſhall ſuffer as a Popiſh Recuſant convict,* &c. See Ch. 12. S. 18.

Sect. 4. As to the fourth of the above mentioned Reſtraints, *viz.* That which relates to the keeping Arms, it is enacted by 1 *Will. & Mar.* 15. *That any two Juſtices of Peace may and ought to tender the ſaid Declaration to any Perſon whom they ſhall know or ſuſpect, or have Information of, as being a Papiſt, or ſuſpected to be ſuch; and that no ſuch Perſon ſo required, and not making and ſubſcribing the ſaid Declaration, or not appearing before the ſaid Juſtices upon Notice to him given, or left at his uſual Abode, by one authorized by Warrant under the Hands and Seals of the ſaid Juſtices, ſhall keep any Arms or Ammunition, or Horſe above the Value of five Pounds, in his own Poſſeſſion, or in the Poſſeſſion of any other Perſon to his Uſe, (other than ſuch neceſſary Weapons, as ſhall be allowed him by the Quarter-Seſſions for the Defence of his Houſe or Perſon) and that any two Juſtices of Peace, by Warrant under their Hands and Seals, may authorize any Perſon in the Day-time, with the Aſſiſtance of the Conſtable or his Deputy or the Tithing-man, to ſearch for all ſuch Arms,* &c. *and Horſes, and ſeize them to the King's Uſe, and that the ſaid Juſtices ſhall deliver the ſaid Arms and Ammunition at the next Quarter-Seſſions in open Court, and that whoever ſhall conceal,* &c. *or ſhall be aiding to the concealing any ſuch Arms or Horſes, ſhall be committed to the common Gaol by Warrant under the Hands and Seals of any two Juſtices of Peace, and alſo forfeit treble the Value; and that thoſe who diſcover any ſuch Arms or Ammunition, ſo as the ſame may be ſeized, ſhall have the full Value thereof, to be awarded to them by the Seſſions,* &c. *and that ſuch Refuſers of the ſaid Declaration,* &c. *ſhall be diſcharged whenever they ſhall make the ſame.* See Ch 12. S. 17.

Sect. 5. As to the above mentioned Diſability of preſenting to a Church, it is enacted by 1 *Will. & Mar.* 26. That whoever ſhall refuſe to make the ſaid Declaration upon ſuch a Tender thereof as is preſcribed by the ſaid Act, ſhall be diſabled to preſent to any Benefice, *&c.* But it ſeems needleſs to ſet forth the Clauſe of the ſaid Statute relating to this Matter at large in this Place, inaſmuch, as by 12 *Annæ* 14. All Perſons whatſoever making Profeſſion of the Popiſh Religion are under the like Diſability, as will appear from *Ch.* 15. *Sect.* 6, 7, *&c.*

CHAP. XV.

Of Offences in promoting or encouraging the Popiſh Religion.

OFFENCES in promoting or encouraging the Popiſh Religion ſeem to be reducible to the following Heads;

1. Giving or Receiving Popiſh Education.
2. Profeſſing the Popiſh Religion.
3. Buying or Selling Popiſh Books.

Sect. 1. The firſt Offence of this Kind, *viz.* That of giving or receiving Popiſh Education depends upon ſeveral Statutes; and firſt it is enacted by 1 *Jac.* 1. 4. Par. 6, 7. *That if any Perſon or Perſons under the King's Obedience ſhall go, or ſend or cauſe to be ſent, any Child or any other Perſon under their or any of their Government, beyond the Seas, out of the King's Obedience, to the Intent to enter into, or reſide in, or repair to any College,* &c. *of any Popiſh Order, Profeſſion or Calling, to be inſtructed, perſwaded, or ſtrengthned in the Popiſh Religion, or in any ſort to profeſs the ſame, every ſuch Perſon ſo ſending ſuch Child,* &c. *ſhall forfeit* 100 *l. And every ſuch Perſon ſo paſſing or being ſent,* &c. *ſhall in reſpect of him or herſelf only, and not in reſpect of any of his Heirs or Poſterity, be diſabled to inherit, purchaſe, take, have or enjoy, any Profits, Hereditaments, Chattels, Debts, Legacies or Sums of Money,* &c. *whatſoever: And that all Eſtates, Terms, and other Intereſts whatſoever to be made, ſuffered or done, to the Uſe or Behoof of any ſuch Perſon, or upon any Truſt or Confidence, mediately or immediately to or for the Benefit or Relief of any ſuch Perſon, ſhall be utterly void.*

Sect. 2. And it is farther enacted by 3 *Jac.* 1. 5. Par. 16. *That if the Children of any Subject within the Realm (the ſaid Children not being Soldiers, Mariners, Merchants, or their Apprentices or Factors) ſhall be ſent or go beyond Sea, to prevent their good Education in* England, *or for any other Cauſe, without the Licence of the King or ſix of his Privy Council (whereof the Principal Secretary to be one) under their Hands and Seals, that then every ſuch Child ſhall take no Benefit by any Gift, Conveyance, Deſcent, Deviſe or otherwiſe of or to any Hereditament or Chattel, till ſuch Child being of the Age of eighteen Years or above, take the Oath of Obedience before ſome Juſtice of Peace of the County, Liberty or Limit, where the Parent of ſuch Child did and ſhall inhabit: And that in the mean Time the next of Kin to ſuch Child, who ſhall be no Popiſh Recuſant, ſhall have the ſaid Hereditaments,* &c. *ſo given,* &c. *until ſuch Child ſhall conform,* &c. *and take the ſaid Oath and receive the Sacrament; and that after ſuch Conformity,* &c. *he who hath received the Profits of the ſaid Hereditaments,* &c. *ſhall accompt for the ſame, and in reaſonable Time make Payment thereof, and reſtore the Value of the ſaid Goods,* &c. *And that whoever ſhall ſend ſuch Child over Seas, ſhall forfeit one hundred Pounds,* which by 11 & 12 *Will.* 3. 4. Par. 6. *ſhall be to the ſole Uſe and Benefit of the Perſon who ſhall diſcover the Offence.*

Sect. 3. Alſo it is enacted by 3 *Car.* 1. 2. *That if any Perſon under the Obedience of the King ſhall go, or ſhall convey or ſend, or cauſe to be ſent or con-*

veyed, any Person out of the King's Dominions, into any Parts beyond the Seas, out of the King's Obedience, to the Intent to enter into, or be resident or trained up, in any Priory, Abbey, Nunnery, Popish University, College or School, or House of Jesuits, Priests, or in a private Popish Family, and shall be there by any Popish Person instructed, perswaded or strengthened in the Popish Religion in any Sort to profess the same, or shall convey or send, or cause to be conveyed or sent, any Thing towards the Maintenance of any Person so going or sent, and trained and instructed, as is aforesaid, or under the Colour of any Charity towards the Relief of any Priory, &c. *or religious House whatsoever; every Person so sending,* &c. *any such Person or Thing, and every Person passing or sent, being thereof convicted,* &c. *shall be disabled to prosecute any Suit in Law or Equity, or to be Executor or Administrator to any Person, or capable of any Legacy or Deed of Gift, or to bear any Office within the Realm. And shall forfeit all his Goods and Chattels, and shall forfeit all his Hereditaments, Offices and Estates of Freehold, during his Life.*

The second Offence of this Kind, *viz.* That of professing the Popish Religion is punished with the following Disabilities,

1. Of taking an Estate in Lands.
2. Of presenting to a Church.

Also it is punished with the following Restraints,

1. From keeping School.
2. From with-holding a competent Maintenance from a Protestant Child.

Sect. 4. As to the first of the above mentioned Disabilities, *viz.* That of taking an Estate in Lands, it is enacted by 11 & 12 *W.* 3. c. 4. *That every Person educated in or professing the Popish Religion, who shall not within six Months after the Age of eighteen Years, take the Oaths of Allegiance and Supremacy, and subscribe the Declaration against Popery mentioned in* 30 Car. 2. *Stat.* 2. *Chap.* 1. *in the Chancery, or King's Bench, or Quarter-Sessions of the County where such Person shall reside, shall in Respect of himself or herself only, and not in Respect of any of his or her Heirs or Posterity, be disabled to inherit or take by Discent, Devise or Limitation, in Possession, Reversion or Remainder, any Lands, Tenements or Hereditaments, in* England *or* Wales, &c. *And during the Life of such Person, and until he take the said Oaths,* &c. *his next of Kin being a Protestant, shall enjoy the same, without being accomptable for the Profits, but shall not do wilful Waste under Pain of forfeiting treble Damages to the Party so disabled: And all Papists, or Persons making Profession of the Popish Religion, are disabled to purchase in their own Names, or the Names of others, to their Use or in Trust for them: And all Estates, Terms and other Interest and Profits whatsoever, out of Lands made to their Use, or on any Trust,* ☞ *mediately or immediately, for their Benefit, are void.* [6]

Sect. 5. In the Construction hereof it was resolved by the House of Lords in *Roper*'s Case, That the Devise of the Residue of Money arising from the Sale of an Estate appointed to be sold for Payment of Debts, *&c.* is within the Statute.

Sect. 6. As to the second of the above mentioned Disabilities, *viz.* That of presenting to a Church, which by 3 *Jac.* 1. 5. Par. 18, 19, 20, 21. and 1 *Will.* & *Mar.* 26. did extend only to Popish Recusants convict, and Persons refusing to make the Declaration against Popery, mentioned in 30 *Car.* 2. Stat. 2. it is enacted by 12 *Ann.* St. 2. c. 14. *That every Papist, or Person making Profession of the Popish Religion,* &c. *and every Mortgagee, Trustee, or Person any ways intrusted by or for such Papist,* &c. *with or without Writing, shall be disabled to present to any Benefice, School, or Hospital,* &c. *or*

Precedent of a Title made under these Statutes. Lut. 1101.

See 11 Geo. 2. c. 17. *or to grant any Avoidance of any Benefice, Prebend or Ecclesiastical Living; and that in all Cases the Universities shall present.*

Sect. 7. Also by Force of the said Statute, *The Ordinary may tender the Declaration against Transubstantiation to any reputed Papist making a Presentation, and upon a Refusal to take the same, the Presentation shall be void: Also the Ordinary may examine every Presentee upon Oath, Whether the Person who presented him, be the true Patron, or only a Trustee? And the Court wherein a* Quare Impedit *shall be brought, may in like Manner examine the Parties, and a Bill may be brought in any Court of Equity to discover such secret Trusts,* &c. *and the Answer of such Persons upon any such Examination or Bill shall be good Evidence against such Patron, in Respect of such a Presentation, but not as to any other Purpose.*

Sect. 8. I do not know that any Resolution hath been given on either of the above mentioned Statutes of 1 *Will. & Mar.* or 12 *Ann.* However the Expositions which were made on 3 *Jac.* 1. seeming to be for the most part applicable to these latter Statutes also, I shall take Notice of the principal of them; as,

Sect. 9. I. That where a Presentment is *pro hac vice* vested in the University by reason of the Patron's being a Popish Recusant at the Time when
7 Co. 57 b. the Church became void, it shall not be devested again by his conforming himself to the Church.

Sect. 10. II. That such a Patron is only disabled to present, and that he
Cawley 230. continues Patron as to all other Purposes, and therefore that he shall confirm the Leases of the Incumbent, *&c.*

Sect. 11. III. That such a Person by being disabled to grant an Avoidance, is no way hindred from granting the Advowson itself in Fee, or for
1 Jon. 19, 20. Life or Years, *bona Fide*, and for good Consideration.

1 Jon. 20, 21, &c. Hob. 126, 127. Mo. 872. *Sect.* 12. IV. That if an Advowson or Avoidance belonging to such a Person come into the King's Hands, by reason of an Outlawry, or Conviction of Recusancy, *&c.* the King, and not the University, shall present.

Sect. 13. As to the first of the above mentioned Restraints, *viz.* that which relates to the keeping School, it is enacted by the said Statute of 11 & 12 *Will.* 3. 4. Par. 3. *That if any Papist, or Person making Profession of the Popish Religion, shall be convict of keeping School, or taking upon themselves the Education or Government, or Boarding of Youth in any Place within this Realm, or the Dominions thereunto belonging, they shall be adjudged to perpetual Imprisonment.*

Sect. 14. As to the second of the above mentioned Restraints, *viz.* that which relates to the Power of a Popish Parent over his Protestant Child, it is enacted by the said Statute of 11 & 12 *Will.* 3. 4. *That if any Popish Parent, in order to compel a Protestant Child to a Change of Religion, shall refuse to allow such Child a sufficient Maintenance, suitable to the Degree and Ability of such Parent, and to the Age and Education of such Child, the Lord Chancellor upon Complaint may make such Order therein, as shall be agreeable to the Intent of the said Act.*

Sect. 15. The third Offence of this Kind, *viz.* that of selling or buying Popish Books depends upon 3 *Jac.* 1. 5. Par. 25. by which it is enacted, *That no Person shall bring from beyond the Seas, nor shall print, buy or sell any Popish Primers, Ladies Psalters, Manuals, Rosaries, Popish Catechisms, Missals, Breviaries, Portals, Legends and Lives of Saints, containing superstitious Matter, printed or written in any Language whatsoever, nor any other superstitious Books, printed or written in the* English *Tongue; on pain of forfeiting forty Shillings for every Book,* &c. *and the Books to be burnt.*

5 CHAP.

CHAP. XVI.

Of Offences against the Established Church by Protestant Dissenters.

Sect. 1. BY 31 *El.* 1. *Obstinate Nonconformists were compellable to abjure the Realm, and were also subject to all the Penalties mentioned in the tenth and eleventh Chapters of this Book; and Dissenters were farther restrained by* 17 Car. 2. 2. & 22 Car. 2. 1. but at this Day by 1 *Will. & Mar.* 18. Par. 2. *All Persons dissenting from the Church, (except Papists, and those who shall in Preaching or Writing deny the Doctrine of the Trinity,) are exempted from all Penal Laws relating to Religion, except* 25 Car. 2. *Chap.* 2. *(by which all Officers of Trust are bound to receive the Sacrament according to the Usage of the Church of* England, *and also to take the Oaths of Allegiance and Supremacy, and the Test;) and also except* 30 Car. 2. *Stat.* 2. *Chap.* 1. *(by which the Members of both Houses of Parliament, and all the King's Sworn Servants are bound to make a Declaration against Transubstantiation and the Invocation of Saints, and the Sacrifice of the Mass,) provided such Dissenters take the Oaths of Allegiance and Supremacy, and make the said Declaration against Transubstantiation,* &c. *and come to some Congregation for religious Worship in some Place registred either in the Bishop's Court, or at Sessions, the Doors whereof shall neither be locked, barred, nor bolted.* Vide 2 Jones 225, 226, 233, 234. Par. 17. Vide supra, Ch. 8. Salk. 572. Par 16, 17, 19.

Sect. 2. Also by Par. 8, 9, 10, 11, 12. *Dissenting Teachers are tolerated, if they take the said Oaths,* &c. *at the General or Quarter-Sessions to be held for the Place where such Persons live, and subscribe the thirty nine Articles of the Church of* England, *except those few scrupled ones concerning Church-Government and Infant-Baptism:* And by 10 *Ann.* 2. Par. 7, 8, 9. *They may qualify themselves as well during a Prosecution upon any Penal Statute, as before, and being qualified in one County may officiate in another, upon producing a Certificate and taking the said Oaths,* &c. *if required.* Vide Salk. 572.

Sect. 3. Also by the said Statute of 1 *Will. & Mar.* Par. 13, 14, 15. *Those who scruple the taking of any Oath, are within the like Indulgence, provided they subscribe the aforesaid Declaration, and also a Declaration of Fidelity to the King, and against the deposing Doctrine and Papal Supremacy; and also profess their Faith in God the Father, and Jesus Christ his eternal Son, the true God, and the Holy Spirit, one God for evermore; and acknowledge the Holy Scriptures of the Old and New Testament to be given by Divine Inspiration.*

Sect. 4. Since this Statute a Prohibition lies to the Spiritual Court proceeding against Persons for Incontinency, who have been married in a licensed Conventicle. 3 Levinz 376.

CHAP. XVII.

Of High Treason.

OF Offences more immediately against Man, some are more immediately against the King, others more immediately against the Subject.

Offences more immediately against the King are either Capital or not Capital.

The Capital Offences of this Nature are either High Treason or Felonies.

Sect. 1. And first of High Treason, concerning which, before 25 *Ed.* 3. 2. there was great Diversity of Opinions, and many Offences were taken to be included in it, besides those expressed in the said Statute; as the killing of the King's [a] Father or Brother, or even of his [b] Messenger; producing the [c] Pope's Bull of Excommunication, and pleading it in Disability; refusing to accuse a Man in the King's Courts, and [d] summoning him to appear, and defend himself before a foreign Prince, and other such like Acts tending to diminish the Royal Dignity of the Crown.

[a] 3 Inst. 7. [b] 22 Ass. 49. [c] 30 Ass. 19. Bro. Trea. 14. [d] 3 Inst. 7. S. P. C. 1. b. See 1 H. H. P. C. 76 to 87.

Sect. 2. But all Treasons were settled by the said Statute of 25 *Ed.* 3. 1. which by 1 *Mar.* Sess. 1 Chap. 1. was re-inforced, and again made the only Standard of Treason; and all Statutes between the said Statutes of 35 *Ed.* 3. and 1 *Mar.* which made any Offences High or Petit Treason, or Misprision of Treason, are abrogated, so that no Offence is at this Day to be esteemed High Treason, unless it be either declared to be such by the said Statute of 25 *Ed.* 3. or made such by some Statute since 1 *Mar.* and therefore I shall consider,

1. Such Offences as are High Treason within the said Statute of 25 *Ed.* 3. or other Statutes grounded thereon, and explaining the same.

See 1 H. H. P. C. 87, 88, &c.

2. Such as are made High Treason by subsequent Statutes.

And first, by the said Statute of 25 *Ed.* 3. there are four Kinds of High Treason.

1. That which immediately concerns the King, his Wife, or Children.

2. That which concerns his Office in the Administration of Justice.

3. That which concerns his Seal.

H. P. C. 7.

4. That which concerns his Coin: And these three last are called Interpretative Treasons.

Sect. 3. That of the first Kind is thus declared by the following Words of the said Statute of 25 *Ed.* 3. *Whereas divers Opinions have been before this Time, in what Case Treason shall be said, and in what not, the King at the Request of the Lords and of the Commons, hath made a Declaration in the Manner as hereafter followeth; that is to say: When a Man doth compass or imagine the Death of our Lord the King, or of my Lady his Queen, or of their eldest Son and Heir: Or if a Man do violate the King's Companion, or the King's eldest Daughter unmarried, or the Wife of the King's eldest Son and Heir: Or if a Man do levy War against our Lord the King in his Realm, or be adherent to the King's Enemies in his Realm, giving them Aid and Comfort in the Realm or elsewhere, and thereof be provably attainted of open Deed by the People of their Condition.*

For the Explication of which I shall consider,

1. The Branch relating to the King and his Relations.

2. That concerning the levying of War, and adhering to the King's Enemies, *&c.*

3. That concerning an Overt Act.

As to the Branch relating to the King and his Relations, I shall consider the following Particulars:

1. Who may be guilty.

2. What is the Import of the Words, *Compass or imagine the King's Death.*

3. Who is a King within the Act.

4. What is the Extent of the Clause concerning the King's Relations.

Sect. 4. As to the first Point, *viz.* who may be guilty,

1. I shall take it for granted at this Day, That all Subjects of the Age of Discretion, and of [a] Sane Memory, whether they be [b] Ecclesiastical or Temporal, Men or Women, are included within those general Words *When a Man doth compass*, &c.

Sect. 5. II. Also it seems clear, That the Subjects of a foreign Prince coming into *England* and living under the Protection of our King, may, in respect of that local Ligeance which they owe to him, be guilty of High Treason, and indicted that they *contra Dominum Regem*, (the Words *naturalem Dominum suum* being omitted) did compass, *&c. contra Ligeantiæ suæ Debitum*. And it is said, That even an Ambassadour committing a Treason against the King's Life, may be condemned and executed here, and that for other Treasons he shall be sent home. And it hath been holden, That there is no Need of the Words *contra ligeantiæ suæ debitum* in an Indictment for a Treason, which is made such by Statute, and is not a Treason in its own Nature. And that there is no Necessity for the Words *contra ligeum supremum Dominum suum* in any Indictment of Treason.

Sect. 6. [c] But it seemeth that Aliens who in an hostile Manner invade the Kingdom, whether their King were at War or Peace with ours, and whether they come by themselves or in Company with *English* Traitors cannot be punished as Traitors, but shall be dealt with by Martial Law. [7]

Sect. 7. [d] It hath been resolved, That one born a natural Subject is bound to such an inseparable Allegiance to our King, that howsoever he may endeavour to renounce it, and transfer his Subjection from his natural to a foreign Prince, yet if he practise what in any other Subject would amount to High Treason he shall suffer as a Traitor.

Sect. 8. As to the second Point, *viz.* the Import of the Words *Compass or imagine the King's Death*, since the said Statute these Words have been so strictly followed, that where a King has been actually murdered, yet not the Killing him, but the Compassing his Death has in the Indictment been laid as the Treason, and the Killing as an Overt Act thereof.

Sect. 9. And such Compassing the King's Death may be manifested not only by Overt Acts of a direct Conspiracy to take away his Life, but also by such as shew such a Design, as cannot be executed without the apparent Peril thereof; as by [e] writing Letters to a foreign Prince, inciting him to invade the Realm; or assembling Men together in order to [f] imprison or [g] depose the King, or to [h] compel him by Force to yield to certain Demands, or to levy War *against* [i] *his Person*.

Sect. 10. But it is possible that it may not be proved by an [k] Act, which directly causes the King's Death; as the Glancing of an Arrow did that of *William Rufus*, proving fatal merely through an unfortunate Accident, and being accompanied with no unlawful Circumstance.

Sect. 11. As to the third Point, *viz.* Who is a King within this Act, It seems agreed, That [l] every King for the Time being, in actual Possession of the Crown, is a King within the Meaning of this Statute: For there is a Necessity that the Realm should have a King, by whom and in whose Name the Laws shall be administred; and the King in Possession being the only Person, who either doth or can administer those Laws, must be the only Person, who has a Right to that Obedience, which is due to him who administers those Laws; and since by Vertue thereof he secures to Us the Safety of our Lives, Liberties and Properties, and all other Advantages of Government, he may justly claim Returns of Duty, Allegiance and Subjection.

[a] See Chap 1.
[b] See Keliw. 181, 182, &c.
3 Inst. 4.
Calvin's Case 6.
Dy. 145. Pl. 62.
Bro. Trea. 31.
3 Inst. 4, 5, 10.
H.P.C. 10, 15.
1 H. H. P. C. 96 to 100, 117.
Hob. 271.
Sal. 630, 631, 633.
1 Ro. Re. 185.
Carthew 319.
Sal. 630, 631.
Skin. 338, 360, 425, 442.
[c] Bro. Treas. 1, 32.
H.P.C. 10, 15.
Calvin's Case 6. b.
3 Inst. 11.
Con. Dalis. 32.
[d] Dy. 300. Pl. 38.
Co. Lit. 129. a.
1 H. H. P. C. 96.
Kelynge 8.
In the Case of the Regicides.
See 1 H. H. P. C. 107, 108.
See 1 H. H. P. C. 108 to 111; 119 to 123.
[e] Dy. 238. Pl. 29.
H. P. C. 11,
3 Inst. 14.
1 H. H. P. C. 120, 122.
[f] 3 Inst. 6, 12. 38.
H. P. C. 11.
[g] Kely. 20, 12.
H. P. C. 11.
Yet this was made a Query in Bro. Treas. 24.
[h] Kelynge 21.
Moor 621.
[i] Kelynge 14, 15, 17, 20, 21.
[k] 3 Inst. 6.
1 H. H. P. C. 107.
[l] H. P. C. 12.
3 Inst. 7.
9 Ed. 4. 1. b.
1 H. H. P. C. 101, 102, &c.

Sect. 12. And this plainly appears even by the prevailing Opinions in the Time of King *Edward* the Fourth, in whose Reign the Distinction between a King *de Jure* and *de Facto* seems first to have begun; and yet it was then laid down as a Principle, and taken for granted in the Arguments of *Bagot*'s Case, That a Treason against *Henry* the Sixth, while he was King, in compassing his Death, was punishable after *Edward* the Fourth came to the Crown, from which it follows, that Allegiance was allowed to have been due to *Henry* the Sixth while he was King, because every Indictment of Treason must lay the Offence, *contra Ligeantiæ Debitum*.

1 H. H. P. C. 60, 61, 102, 103. 9 Ed. 4. 1. b. Bro. Treas. 10, 32. 3 Inst. 7. H. P. C. 12. Dal. ca. 89. f. 223.

Sect. 13. It was also settled, That all judicial Acts done by *Henry* the Sixth while he was King, and also all Pardons of Felony and Charters of Denization granted by him, were valid; but that a Pardon made by *Edward* the Fourth, before he was actually King, was void, even after he came to the Crown.

9 Ed. 4. 1. b. 2. a. Bro. Judg. 42. Charter of Pardon 22. Patents 21. Denizen 3. Exempt. 4. Judgment 42. Fitz-H. Assize 29. Denizen 1. 9 Ed. 4. 1, 2, 11.

Sect. 14. And by the 11 *H.* 7. Chap. 1. it is declared, *That all Subjects are bound by their Allegiance to serve their Prince and Sovereign Lord for the Time being, in his Wars, for the Defence of him and his Land, against every Rebellion Power and Might reared against him*, &c. *and that it is against all Laws, Reason and good Conscience, that they should lose or forfeit any Thing for so doing:* And it is enacted, *That from thenceforth no Persons that attend on the King for the Time being, and do him true and faithful Allegiance in his Wars within the Realm or without, shall for the said Deed and true Duty of Allegiance be convict of any Offence.*

9 Ed. 4. 2. a.

Sect. 15. From hence it clearly follows:

I. That every King for the Time being has a Right to the People's Allegiance, because they are bound thereby to defend him in his Wars against every Power whatsoever.

Sect. 16. II. That one out of Possession is so far from having any Right to our Allegiance by Vertue of any other Title, which he may set up against the King in Being, that we are bound by the Duty of our Allegiance to resist him.

Kel. 14.

Sect. 17. It is true indeed, that after the Restoration of King *Charles* the Second, it was resolved, That all those who acted against, and kept him out of Possession, in Obedience to the Powers then in Being, were Traitors.

Kel. 14, 15. 1 Keb. 315. 1 Keb. 454.

Sect. 18. But it ought to be considered, that it was first resolved by the same Judges, That King *Charles* the Second was King *de Facto* as well as *de Jure*, from his Father's Death; and it is apparent, that no other Person was in Possession of any Sovereign Power known to our Laws.

3 Inst. 7. H. P. C. 12. 1 H. H. P. C. 102.

Sect. 19. However, it is a general uncontested Rule, That upon the Death of a King in actual Possession of the Crown, his Heir is a King within the Act before his Coronation; for without a King to execute the Laws, Justice must fail; and therefore it is a Maxim, That the King never dies.

1 H. H. P. C. 102, 106. 1 Ma. Sess. 3. Ch. 1. H. P. C. 12. 3 Inst. 8.

Sect. 20. A titular King, as the Husband of a Queen Regnant, seems to be within the Words, yet it is clearly not within the Meaning of this Law; and *è converso*, a Queen Regnant is not within the strict Words, and yet she is undoubtedly within the Meaning; for by the Words, *Our Lord the King*, is meant any Person invested with the Regal Power.

Sect. 21. By 1 *Will. & Mar.* Sess. 2. Chap. 2. Par. 9. *Every Person that shall be reconciled to, or hold Communion with, the Church of* Rome, *or profess the Popish Religion, or marry a Papist, shall be excluded, and be for ever uncapable to inherit, possess, or enjoy the Crown of this Realm,* &c. *And in every such Case the People of this Realm are absolved from their Allegiance,* &c.

Sect. 22. As to the fourth Point, *viz.* The Extent of the Clause concerning the King's Relations, it is to be observed,

1. That no Queen or Princess Dowager is any Way within the Purview of it. [8]

2. That if the Companion, (by which Word is meant the Wife) of the King or Prince, consent to an Adulterer; she is no less guilty of High Treason than he.

3. That under the Words, *Their eldest Son and Heir*, the Son of a Queen Regnant is included, and also the second Son after the Death of the first, and perhaps also a collateral Heir apparent, especially if he be declared such by Parliament. [9]

1 H. H. P. C. 124. 3 Inst. 8, 9. H. P. C. 12. 1 H. H. P. C. 128. 3 Inst. 8, 9. H. P. C. 12. 3 Inst. 8, 9. H. P. C. 12. 1 H. H. P. C. 125.

And now we are come to the second general Branch of this Kind of High Treason, *viz.* That concerning the levying of War, *&c.* and adhering to the King's Enemies, *&c.* in treating whereof I shall consider.

1. What Acts shall be said to amount to a levying of War against the King.

2. What shall be said to be an Adherence to the King's Enemies.

See 1 H. H. P. C. 130, 131, &c.

Sect. 23. As to the first Point, it is to be observed, That not only those who directly rebel against the King, and take up Arms in order to dethrone him, but also in many other Cases, those who in a violent and forcible Manner withstand his lawful Authority, or endeavour to reform his Government, are said to levy War against him; and therefore,

Sect. 24. Those that hold a Fort or Castle against the King's Forces, or keep together armed Numbers of Men against the King's express Command have been adjudged to levy War against him. But those who join themselves to Rebels, *&c.* for fear of Death, and retire as soon as they dare, seem to be no way guilty of this Offence.

3 Inst. 10. H. P. C. 14. Bro. Treas. 24. Dal. ch. 89. fo. 224. 1 H. H. P. C. 139.

Sect. 25. II. Those also who make an Insurrection in order to redress a publick Grievance, whether it be a real or pretended one, and of their own Authority attempt with Force to redress it, are said to levy War against the King, altho' they have no direct Design against his Person, inasmuch as they insolently invade his Prerogative, by attempting to do that by private Authority, which he by publick Justice ought to do, which manifestly tends to a downright Rebellion; as where great Numbers by Force attempt to remove certain Persons from the King; or to lay violent Hands on a Privy Counsellor; or to revenge themselves against a Magistrate for executing his Office; or to bring down the Price of Victuals; or to reform the Law or Religion; or to pull down all Bawdy-houses; or to remove all Inclosures in general, *&c.* But where a Number of Men rise to remove a Grievance to their private Interest, as to pull down a Particular Inclosure intrenching upon their Common, *&c.* they are only Rioters. [10]

Moor 621. H. P. C. 14. 3 Inst. 9, 10. 2 And. 5. Kelynge 75, &c. 1 H. H. P. C. 131, 135, 152, 153. Moor 621. Cro. Car. 583. Poph. 122, 123. 2 And. 4, 5. 3 Inst. 9. 1 Ven. 250, 251. H. P. C. 14. Kelynge 76. 1 H. H. P. C. 136.

Sect. 26. In a special Verdict, not only those who are expresly found to have been aiding and assisting a rebellious Insurrection, but perhaps also those who are only found to have acted in the Execution of the intended Violence, or to have attended the principal Offender from the Beginning, though they be not found to have known the Design of the Rising, shall be adjudged guilty of High Treason; but those who are found only to have suddenly joined with them in the Streets, and to have flung up their Hats and hallowed with them, are guilty of no greater Offence than a Riot at most.

1 Sid. 358. 3 And. 66. Pop. 121. 3 Inst. 9. H. P. C. 14. Kelynge 75. 1 H. H. P. C. 138. Moor 621, 622.

Sect. 27. However it is certain, That a bare Conſpiracy to levy ſuch a War cannot amount to Treaſon, unleſs it be actually levied; yet it hath been reſolved, that a Conſpiracy to levy War againſt the King's Perſon may be alledged as an Overt Act of compaſſing his Death, and that in all Caſes, if the Treaſon be actually compleated, the Conſpirators, *&c.* are Traitors as much as the Actors: And [a] that there may be a Levying of War, where there is no actual Fighting. [11] [12]

Sect. 28. As to the ſecond Point, (*viz.*) What ſhall be ſaid to be an Adherence to the King's Enemies, *&c.* this is explained by the Words ſubſequent, *Giving Aid and Comfort to them*; from which it appears, that any Aſſiſtance given to Aliens in open Hoſtility againſt the King, as by ſurrendring a Caſtle of the King's to them for Reward, or ſelling them Arms, *&c.* or aſſiſting [b] the King's Enemies againſt his Allies; or cruiſing in a Ship with Enemies, to the Intent to deſtroy the King's Subjects, is clearly within this Branch; but there is no Neceſſity, expreſly to alledge, that ſuch Adherence [c] was againſt the King, for it is apparent; yet the ſpecial Manner of Adherence muſt be ſet forth: And it is ſaid, that the Succouring a Rebel fled into another Realm is not within the Statute, becauſe a Rebel is not properly an Enemy, and the Statute is taken ſtrictly.

Sect. 29. As to the Branch relating to an Overt Act, I ſhall take it for granted, that ſome Overt Act muſt be alledged in every Indictment of High Treaſon, in compaſſing the Death of the King, *&c.* or levying War, or adhering to the King's Enemies; but there hath been ſome Queſtion concerning what ſhall be ſaid to be ſuch an Overt Act, as to which I ſhall conſider,

1. What Facts amount to ſuch and Overt Act.
2. Whether any Words be ſufficient.

Sect. 30. As to the firſt Point it ſeems clearly agreed by all, That conſpiring the King's Death, and providing Weapons to effect it, or ſending Letters to incite others to procure it, or actually aſſembling People in order to take the King into their Power, and all other ſuch like notorious Facts, done in Purſuance of a treaſonable Purpoſe againſt the King's Perſon, may be alledged as Overt Acts to prove the Compaſſing his Death.

Sect. 31. It has alſo been adjudged, That the [d] levying War againſt the King's Perſon; or the bare [e] conſulting to levy ſuch War; or meeting together and [f] conſulting the Means to deſtroy the King and his Government; or [g] aſſembling with others, and procuring them to attempt the King's Death; or liſting [h] Men in Order to depoſe the King; or [i] printing treaſonable Poſitions, as that the King is accountable to the People, and that they ought to take the Government into their own Hands, *&c.* or publiſhing a Book to prove that [k] the King's Government is Antichriſtian and Heretical, *&c.* may be alledged as Overt Acts to prove the Compaſſing the King's Death.

Sect. 32. As to the ſecond Point, *viz.* Whether any Words are ſufficient Overt Acts? it has been holden, That [l] written Words in a Sermon or other Writing may amount to Overt Acts of compaſſing the King's Death, tho' the ſame neither actually were, nor ever were intended to be, preached or publiſhed; but this Opinion ſeems [m] to be over ſevere, for though it be true, that *ſcribere eſt agere*, yet ſurely it cannot with any Propriety be ſaid, that to write in ſuch a private Manner *eſt apertè agere*, and it ſeems rigorous to make that amount to a malicious Deſign againſt the King, which perhaps was only done by Way of Amuſement or Diverſion.

1 H. H. P. C. 131, 151. Daliſ. 14, 15. St. Tr. Vol. 4. f. 63, 97. H. P. C. 13, 14. Dy. 98. Pl. 56. Kelynge 19, 20. Infra Sect. 31. Hetl. 65. 3 Inſt. 9. [a] Sal. 635. 3 Inſt. 11. 1 H. H. P. C. 165 to 169. 3 Inſt. 10. H. P. C. 14. Daliſ. 89, 224. H. P. C. 115. Vide 2 Ven. 315, 316. [b] Salk. 634, 635. See Vaughan's Trial in the St. Tr. Vol. 4. f. 347, 348, &c. [c] St. Tr. V. 4. f. 347, 348. 3 Inſt. 12, 13. Sal. 635. 1 H. H. P. C. 108. H. P. C. 13. 3 Inſt. 13, 14. Bro. Treaſon 24. 1 H. H. P. C. 108, 109, 110. [d] Kelynge 14, 17. [e] Kelynge 20, 21. St. Tr. Vol. 3. f. 149 to 158, 228. Vol. 4. f. 63, 79, 207, 277, 278, 282. Vol. 3. f. 179. Ruſhw. Strafford's Trial 684. [f] Kelynge 15. St. Tr. Vol. 3. fol. 126. [g] 1 And. 106. [h] 2 Vent. 316. [i] Kelynge 22. St. Tr. Vol. 1. fol. 977. Vol. 3. f. 228. Supra Sect. 24. [k] 2 Rol. Rep. 89, 90. [l] 2 Ro. Re. 89. [m] Cro. Ca. 125. 2 Ro. Re. 89. See the Reverſal of the Attainder of Algernoon Sidney, 1 W. & M. St. c. 7. private Acts.

Sect. 33. But the great Queſtion is, Whether Words only ſpoken can amount to an Overt Act of compaſſing the King's Death? Which having been queſtioned by ſome great Men, and denied by others, I dare not be peremptory concerning it.

S. P. C. 2. Kelynge 13. 3 Inſt. 14, 140. H. P. C. 13.

Sect. 34. However it ſeems agreed, That Words ſpoken only in Contempt and Diſgrace of the King, and not directly ſhewing any Purpoſe to rebel, or any Way to hurt his Perſon, or diſturb his Government, as thoſe which charge him with a perſonal Vice, as Drunkenneſs, *&c.* or a perſonal Defect, as Want of Wiſdom, or Steddineſs, *&c.* ſhall not be ſo far ſtrained, as to be made Overt Acts of compaſſing his Death, *&c.*

Cro. Ca. 125. Cro. Ca. 117, 125.

Sect. 35. Indeed it has been holden, That to affirm that another has a better Title than the King, is High Treaſon, becauſe it tends to draw People from their Allegiance, and to create a Mutiny, *&c.* but perhaps this may be queſtioned, becauſe it cannot certainly appear from ſuch Words, whether the Speaker had a Deſign againſt the King's Perſon or no? However there can be no Doubt, but that ſuch Diſcourſes are highly puniſhable, as great Miſdemeanors, and tending to raiſe Doubts, and diſturb the Government.

Yelv. 107. 2 Ro. Re. 90. Palm. 426.

Sect. 36. Alſo the following Words have been adjudged High Treaſon, If King *Henry* the Eighth will not take back his Wife, he ſhall not be King, but ſhall die;——If the King will arreſt me for High Treaſon I will ſtab him;—— If I knew that *Perkin Warbeck* was the Son of *Edward* the Fourth, I would take his Part againſt *Henry* the Seventh.

1 Ro. Re. 185. 14 H. 8. 12. a. [a] Salk. 631. 2 Ven. 315. St. Tr. Vol. 4. fol. 30, 31, 95, 172. 1 H. H. P. C. 115, 116.

Sect. 37. But however the Laws may ſtand in Relation to ſuch conditional Words, or to looſe [a] Words ſpoken without Relation to any Act, yet it ſeems clear that Words joined to an Act may explain it, and that Words of Perſuaſion to kill the King, or manifeſting an Agreement, or Conſultation, or Directions to that Purpoſe, are ſufficient Overt Acts of Compaſſing his Death; and it hath been ſtrongly holden, that any [b] deliberate Words, which ſhew a direct Purpoſe againſt the King's Life, as theſe, If I meet the King I will kill him, being ſpoken maturely and adviſedly, are ſufficient Overt Acts of compaſſing or imagining his Death.

[b] 1 Ro. Re. 185. Cro. Ca. 117, 118, 125, 332, 333. 1 Lev. 57. Kelynge 13. St. Tr. Vol. 2. f. 133, 135. Vol. 3. fol. 293, 1001.

Sect. 38. [c] And ſince the Compaſſing or Imagining of the King's Death is the Treaſon, and Words be the moſt natural Means of expreſſing the Imagination of the Heart, why ſhould they not be good Evidences of it? Beſides it has been often adjudged, That falſely to charge a Man with ſpeaking Treaſon is actionable, which could not be, if no Words could amount to Treaſon, as in the Arguments of thoſe Caſes it is clearly holden that they may, and not ſo much as made a Queſtion.

1 Keb. 14. 34, 179, 231. Dalt. Ch. 89. fo. 223, 224. 3 Mod. 53. See the Precedent cited Cro. Ca. 118.

Sect. 39. Beſides it is certain, That before the 25 *Ed.* 3. Words might amount to Treaſon; and it is a general Rule, That in doubtful Caſes the Reaſon of the Common Law ought to govern the Conſtruction of a Statute. Alſo [d] there can be no Doubt but that he, who by Command or Perſuaſion induces another to commit Treaſon, is himſelf a Traitor; (for without Queſtion by ſuch Means he would be acceſſary to a Felony; and it is an uncontroverted Rule, That [e] whatever will make a Man an Acceſſary in Felony, will make him a Principal in Treaſon) and yet he does no Act but by Words.

[c] Yelv. 107, 197. Cro. Ja. 276. 406, 413. Hutt. 75. Winch 124. 1 Bulſt. 148. 3 Bulſ. 225. 1 Ro. Re. 444. [d] S. P. C. 2. b.

Sect. 40. As to Sir *Edward Coke*'s Argument from 3 *H.* 7. 14. which makes the [f] Compaſſing the King's Death, or that of any of his Council, *&c.* by the King's Servants, Felony; from whence he infers, that in the Judgment of this Parliament, the Compaſſing the King's Death by bare Words could not be Treaſon before; it may be anſwered, That this Argument extends as well to the King's Servants Compaſſing his Death by any other

[e] H. P. C. 215. [f] 3 Inſt. 38.

Act

Act whatever, as to their doing it by bare Words; for all are equally within the 3 *H.* 7. and yet none will contend, but that the former hath always been Treason.

H. P. C. 13. 1 H. H. P. C. 111, 112. *Sect.* 41. As to the Argument, that Compassing the King's Death by bare Words cannot amount to Treason, within 25 *Ed.* 3. because many late temporary Acts of Parliament have made it Treason, which would be needless if it were so before; it may be answered, That the principal End of those Statutes was to make it Treason to charge the King with Heresy or Schism, or Usurpation, or to affirm that it was lawful to take up Arms against him, which the *Romanists* were apt to be guilty of at the Beginning of the Reformation, and it may be questioned whether these be Overt Acts of High Treason within 25 *E.* 3. Vide 2 Ro. Rep. 89, 90.

Sect. 42. Indeed it is recited in the Preamble of 1 *Mar.* Seff. i. Chap. 1. *That the State of every King consists more assuredly in the Love of the Subject towards their Prince, than in the Dread of Laws made with rigorous Pains; and that Laws made for the Preservation of the Commonwealth without great Penalties are more often obeyed and kept, than Laws made with extream Punishments. And in special such Laws so made, whereby not the Ignorant but also the Learned, minding Honesty, are often trapped, yea many Times for Words only, without other Fact or Deed done or perpetrated; and thereupon the Queen calls to remembrance, that many, as well honourable Persons, as others of good Reputation, had then of late, (for Words only, without other Opinion, Fact, or Deed,) suffered shameful Death, and expresses her Pleasure, that the Severity of such like extream dangerous and painful Laws shall be abolished.* And then follows the enacting Clause, *That from thenceforth none Act or Offence, being by Act of Parliament or Statute made Treason, Petit Treason, or Misprision of Treason, by Words, Writing, Cyphering, Deeds, or otherwise whatsoever, shall be taken, had, deemed, or adjudged to be High Treason, Petit Treason, or Misprision of Treason, but only such as be declared and expressed to be Treason, Petit Treason, or Misprision of Treason, by* 25 Ed. 3. *Nor that any Pains of Death, Penalty or Forfeiture, in any Ways ensue to any Offender for the doing any Treason,* &c. *other than such as by the said Statute of* 25 Ed. 3. *be ordained; any Statute since the said twenty-fifth Year of* Ed. 3. *or other Declaration to the contrary in any wise notwithstanding.*

Sect. 43. And it must be confessed, That this Statute *primâ Facie* seems very much to favour the Opinion, That no Words whatsoever can of themselves amount to Overt Acts of High Treason, inasmuch as one of the principal Mischiefs intended to be redressed by it seems to be, that Men had often suffered as Traitors for Words only; yet the Force of this Objection will be very much lessened, if we consider, that the principal Purport of the said Statute of 1 *Mar.* seems to be, to make the 25 *Ed.* 3. according to the Intention of the Makers of it, the only Standard of Treason, and to abolish all subsequent Statutes, which had made any Offences Treason, which were not contained in the said Statute of 25 *Ed.* 3. but no Way to extenuate the Crimes mentioned in 25 *Ed.* 3. or to take away the Force of any natural Exposition thereof; for the first Part of the Preamble complains of such Laws as not only inflicted Punishments over severe for the Crimes intended to be restrained by them, but were also penned in such a Manner, as to be often apt to entrap the wisest by bare Words; but surely this can no Way be applicable to 25 *Ed.* 3. inasmuch as no Punishments can be thought extream for the Crimes therein restrained, and there can be no Danger from that Statute of any Man's being punished for unwary or innocent Words, inasmuch as there is no Colour to say, that any Words, as such, are punished within that Statute, but only the most wicked Imagination of the Heart, which may be sometimes proved by the Evidence of Words: And it farther appears from the next Part of the Preamble of the said Statute of 1 *Mar.* that it has an Eye only to such Statutes as are above mentioned, inasmuch as it complains of Persons having suffered shameful Deaths for Words only, without other Opinion, Fact, or Deed, which is very applicable to those many Statutes in the Time of *H.* 8. as 26 *H.* 8. 13. and 35 *H.* 8. 3. and some others, which made bare Words High Treason, many of which were so far from purporting a Design against the King's Life, that they were scarce otherwise Criminal, than as they were prohibited by those Statutes; but surely this can have no Relation to 25 *Ed.* 3. either in punishing a Man for such Imaginations of the Heart as are most perversly wicked, or in suffering those Imaginations to be proved upon him from his own Mouth. Also it is farther remarkable, That the enacting Clause restrains only such Offences, as are made High Treason by Statutes subsequent to 25 *Ed.* 3. from being adjudged High Treason by Words, Writing, Cyphering, *&c.* and seems to leave the Offences contained in the said Statute to the same Construction which they had before.

Sect. 44. As to the Authority of Sir *Edw. Coke* in his third Institute it is of the less Weight, because he is said to have been some Time of the contrary Opinion.

3 Inst. 14, 140. 1 Rol. Re. 186.

Sect. 45. Neither does it appear to me, That my Lord Chief Justice *Hale* was at all of this Opinion; for though in the latter Edition of his *Treatise of the Pleas of the Crown*, it be said, That compassing by bare Words is not an Overt-Act, *&c.* yet in the first Edition published in the Year 1678. it is twice said, That it hath been adjudged that Words are ☞ an Overt Act. [13.]

Old Edition 13, 16.

Sect. 46. The second Kind of High Treason concerning the King's Office in the Administration of Justice is expressed in the Words following: *If a Man slay the Chancellor, Treasurer, or the King's Justices of the one Bench or the other, Justices in Eyre, or Justices of Assize, and all other Justices assigned to hear and determine, being in their Places during their Offices.*

1 H. H. P. C. 111 to 120, 312, 322, 323.

Sect. 47. It hath been holden, That this Part of the Statute shall not be extended by Equity, to any other high Officers of State besides these expresly named, nor even to these when they are not in actual Execution of their Offices, nor to any Attempt to kill them, nor even to the actual wounding of them, unless Death ensue. *See the next Chapter.*

H. P. C. 17. 3 Inst. 18, 38. 1 H. H. P. C. 230 to 232.

Sect. 48. The third Kind of High Treason, relating to the King's Seal, is said to have been High Treason at the Common Law, and is expressed in the following Words, *And if a Man counterfeit the King's Great or Privy Seal.*

3 Inst. 15. S. P. C. 2, 3. 1 H. H. P. C. 181 to 184.

Sect. 49. It hath been holden, That these Words extend to the Aiders and Consenters to such Counterfeiting, as well as to the Actors.

H. P. C. 18. S. P. C. 3. a.

Sect. 50. But not to an Intent or Compassing to do it, if it be not actually done.

3 Inst. 15. H. P. C. 18. 1 H. H. P. C. 181.

Sect. 51. [a] Nor to the fixing of the Great Seal to a Patent without a Warrant for so doing.

Sect. 52. [b] Nor to the razing of the Name of one Manor out of a Patent, and putting in that of another, nor to any artificial removing of the true Writing, and adding Matter altogether new: Nor, by the better Opinion, to the taking off the Wax impressed with the Great Seal from a true Patent, and fixing it to a Writing purporting a Grant from the King.

[a] 3 Inst. 15. H. P. C. 18. Con. Dal. c. 89. f. 225. See 1 H. H. P. C. 181, 182. [b] Kelynge 80. 3 Inst. 15.

Sect. 53. [c] Nor to the Counterfeiting of the Sign Manual, or Privy Signet, but this is made High Treason by 1 *Mar.* 6.

12 Co. 15, 16, 17. 3 Inst. 15, 16.

Sect. 54. The fourth Kind of High Treason concerning the Coin is expressed in these Words, *If a Man counterfeits the King's Money, and if a*

2 Keb. 74. Bro. Treas. 3, 17, 48. 40 Ass. 32. 2 H. 4. 25.

H. P. C. 8. Con. S. P. C. 3. Letter B. [c] 1 Rol. Rep. 50, 51.

Man bring falſe Money into this Realm, counterfeit to the Money of England, *as the Money called* Luſhburgh, *or other like to the ſaid Money of* England, *knowing the Money to be falſe, to merchandize or make Payment, in Deceit of our ſaid Lord the King and his People.*

In treating hereof I ſhall conſider,

1. The Branch relating to the counterfeiting of the King's Money.
2. That concerning the bringing of falſe Money into the Realm, *&c.*

In treating of the firſt Branch I ſhall ſhew,

1. What Degree of counterfeiting Money will amount to High Treaſon.
2. What ſhall be ſaid to be the King's Money within this Act.

1 H. H. P. C. 213, 214, 229. Bro. Treaſ. 27. H. P. C. 20. 3 Inſt. 16. Contra 6 H. 7. 13. 3 H. 7. 10. 2 Inſt. 375. 3 Inſt. 17. H. P. C. 127. Kelynge 33. Contra Dyer 296. and 1 H. H. P. C. 233. H. P. C. 19. [a] 3 H. 7. 10. b. H. P. C. 128. Bro. Treaſ. 19. 1 H. H. P. C. 214, 373, 375. [b] 3 Inſt. 577. 3 Inſt. 17. 2 Keb. 36. Dalt. ca. 89. 1 H. H. P. C. 210 to 213.

Sect. 55. As to the Point of counterfeiting, it is ſaid, That thoſe, who coin Money without the King's Authority, are guilty of High Treaſon within this Act, whether they utter it or not; and that thoſe, who have the King's Authority to coin Money, are guilty of High Treaſon, if they make it of baſer Alloy than they ought; and that thoſe alſo are guilty of the ſame Crime, who receive and comfort one who is known by them to be guilty thereof; but that Clippers, *&c.* are not within this Statute.

Sect. 56. [a] But it ſeems, That thoſe, who barely utter falſe Money made within the Realm, knowing it to be falſe, are neither guilty of High Treaſon, nor of a Miſpriſion thereof, but only of a high Miſpriſion: Yet by 8 *&* 9 *Will.* 3. 26. they are in ſome Caſes made guilty of Felony, for which ſee the next Chapter.

Sect. 57. [b] As to the ſecond Point, *viz.* What ſhall be ſaid to be the King's Money? It ſeems, That ſuch only as is coined by the King's Authority either in Gold or Silver within the Realm, and conſequently not braſs Farthings, *&c.* ſhall come under this Denomination. [14.]

Sect. 58. But the Miſchiefs intended to be remedied by this Statute, having been found by Experience not to have been ſufficiently redreſſed by it, as thus reſtrained, the ſame have been farther provided for by ſubſequent Statutes.

Sect. 59. For by 1 *M.* Seſſ. 2. *Ca.* 6. *Thoſe who forge any Foreign Coin of Gold or Silver, which ſhall be current by Conſent of the King, ſhall be guilty of High Treaſon.*

Sect. 60. And by 14 *El.* 3. *Thoſe who forge Money not current,* &c. *their Aiders and Abetters are guilty of Miſpriſion of Treaſon.*

1 H. H. P. C. 327, 328.

Sect. 61. By 5 *El.* 11. *Whoever ſhall waſh, clip, round or file,* And by 18 *El.* 1. *Whoever ſhall impair, diminiſh, falſify, ſcale or lighten, for Lucre or Gain, the proper Money of this Realm, or that of other Realms made current by Proclamation, ſhall be deemed as an Offender in Treaſon, and forfeit all his Chattels abſolutely, and his Hereditaments for Life, but without Corruption of Blood or Loſs of Dower.*

Sect. 62. By 8 *&* 9 *W.* 3. 25. made perpetual by 7 *Annæ* 25. *Whoever ſhall knowingly make or mend, or begin to make or mend, buy, ſell, or have in his Poſſeſſion any Mould or Preſs for coining; or convey ſuch Inſtruments out of the King's Mint, or mark on the Edges any Coin current, or counterfeit or colour or gild any Coin reſembling the current Coin of this Kingdom, or any round Blanks of baſe Metal,* &c. *ſhall be guilty of High Treaſon, but without Corruption of Blood or Loſs of Dower;* And by 7 *Annæ* 25. *The Proſecution for ſuch making,* &c. *may be at any Time within ſix Months.*

Sect. 63. And by Par. 5. *Such Inſtruments may be ſeiſed by any Perſon, and brought before a Juſtice of Peace, in order to be produced in Evidence at the Trial of ſuch Offenders; and after they ſhall be ſo produced, they ſhall be defaced and deſtroyed; and all falſe Money, which ſhall be ſo produced, ſhall be cut in Pieces.*

4 *Sect.*

Sect. 64. By 6 & 7 *Will.* 3. 17. *Whoever ſhall apprehend a Coiner or Clipper,* &c. *and proſecute him to Conviction, ſhall receive of the Sheriff* 40 l. &c. *And, he who being guilty himſelf ſhall diſcover two or three more, ſhall have a Pardon.* B. 2. Ch. 12. Sect. 25.

As to the ſecond Branch concerning the bringing falſe Money into the Realm the following Particulars are obſervable; See 1 H. H. P. C. 225.

Sect. 65. I. That the Money ſo brought muſt be counterfeited according to the Similitude of *Engliſh* Money: But by 1 & 2 *Phil. & Mar.* 11. *It is made High Treaſon to bring into the Realm Money counterfeited according to the Similitude of foreign Coin current here, to the Intent to merchandize therewith.* 1 H. H. P. C. 225, 228, 229, 317. H. P. C. 21. S. P. C. 3.

Sect. 66. II. That it muſt be brought by one, who knows it to be falſe.

Sect. 67. III. That it muſt be brought from a foreign Nation, and not from *Ireland*, or other Place ſubject to the Crown of *England*; for tho' to ſome Purpoſes they be diſtinct from the Realm of *England*, and conſequently Money brought from thence may within the Letter of the Statute be ſaid to be brought into the Realm; yet inaſmuch as the counterfeiting is puniſhable there by the Laws of our King as much as in *England*, the bringing Money from ſuch Places has been conſtrued to be no more within the Act than if they were actually in *England.* 1 H. H. P. C. 225, 226, 317. 3 H. 7. 10. S. P. C. 3. 3 Inſt. 18. H. P. C. 12. Bro. Treaſ. 19. Dal. 89. f. 225.

Sect. 68. IV. That the bare uttering of ſuch Money here by one who brought it not over, is not within this Branch; but by Force of an antient Statute, if falſe Money be found in the Hands of a ſuſpicious Perſon, he may be arreſted till he have found his Warrant. 3 Inſt. 18. H. P. C. 21.

Sect. 69. V. That it is not neceſſary that ſuch falſe Money be actually paid away or merchandized withal, for the Words are to merchandize or make Payment, *&c.* which only import an Intention to do ſo, and are fully ſatisfied whether the Act intended be performed or not: But *Quære*, becauſe both *Coke* and *Hale* ſeem to hold otherwiſe; however it is clear, that bringing over Money counterfeited according to the Similitude of foreign ☞ Coin is Treaſon within 1 & 2 *Phil. & Mar.* 11. [15.] 3 Inſt. 18. H. P. C. 21.

Sect. 70. Alſo in the ſaid Statute of 25 *Ed.* 3. there is this Clauſe, *And becauſe that many other like Caſes of Treaſon may happen in Time to come, which a Man cannot think nor declare at this preſent Time, it is accorded, That if any other Caſe, ſuppoſed Treaſon, which is not above ſpecified, doth happen before any Juſtices, the Juſtices ſhall tarry without any going to Judgment of the Treaſon, till the Cauſe be ſhewed and declared before the King and his Parliament, whether it ought to be judged Treaſon or other Felony.*

Sect. 71. By Virtue of this Clauſe, many Offences which are not High Treaſon within this Statute, as the Murder of an Ambaſſador, *&c.* were declared by the Parliament to be High Treaſon, but theſe and all other ſuch like Declarations are made void by 1 *Mar.* 1. And it ſeems that the Parliament have no ſuch Power at this Day by Virtue of the ſaid Clauſe, inaſmuch as the ſaid Statute of 1 *Mar.* expreſly enacts, *That no Offence ſhall be deemed High Treaſon, but only ſuch as is declared and expreſſed to be ſo by* 25 *Ed.* 3. and takes no Notice of the ſaid Clauſe relating to the Parliament. 1 H. H. P. C. 308. 3 Inſt. 8. 12 Co. 16.

And now we are come to Offences, which have been made High Treaſon ſince the ſaid Statute of 1 *Mar.* and in treating of theſe, we ſhall conſider,

1. Offences in upholding or favouring the Power of the Pope.
2. Offences againſt the Proteſtant Succeſſion.
3. Offence of liſting Men without the King's Licence.

And firſt, Offences in upholding, or favouring the Power of the Pope, ſeem reducible to the following Heads:

1. Extolling the Pope's Power.
2. Putting in Ure Popiſh Bulls.
3. Perverting others, or being perverted to Popery.

4. Re-

4. Receiving Popiſh Orders or Education in Popiſh Seminaries, and not ſubmitting, *&c.*

5. Refuſing a ſecond Tender of the Oaths.

Sect. 72. And firſt, The Offence of extolling the Pope's Power is made High Treaſon by 5 *El.* 1. Par. 2. & 10. by which it is enacted, *That if any Perſon within the Queen's Dominions ſhall by Writing, Cyphering, Preaching or Teaching, Deed or Act, adviſedly and wittingly hold or ſtand with, extol or ſet forth, maintain or defend, the Juriſdiction of the Biſhop of* Rome, *heretofore claimed in this Realm, or by any Speech, open Deed or Act, willingly or adviſedly attribute any ſuch Authority to the See of* Rome; *he ſhall be guilty of a* Præmunire *by the firſt Offence, of High Treaſon by the ſecond, but without Corruption of Blood or Loſs of Dower.* (See 1 H. H. P.C. 331, 332.)

(Dyer 282.) *Sect.* 73. It has been holden, That he, who knowing the Effect of a Book written beyond Sea, brings it over and ſecretly ſells it; and alſo, That he who by Report hearing the Contents thereof commends it; and alſo, That he, who knowing its Contents ſecretly conveys it to a Friend with an Intent to pervert him, is in Danger of the Statute; and it has been reſolved, That he, who having read the Book does afterwards in diſcourſing of it, allow it to be good; and alſo, That whoever writes or prints ſuch a Book, and after publiſhes it, is clearly guilty: But it is ſaid, That he, who having heard of the Contents barely buys and reads the Book, is not within the Statute.

(Sav. 46. Pl. 99.) *Sect.* 74. It has alſo been holden, That if one who is convicted and condemned for an Offence of this Nature, being afterwards demanded by the Judges, Whether he be ſtill of the ſame Opinion? anſwer, That he is, he is guilty of High Treaſon, as having adviſedly maintained the Pope's Power a ſecond Time.

Sect. 75. The ſecond Offence of this Kind, *viz.* That of putting in Ure a Popiſh Bull, is made High Treaſon by 13 *El.* 2. Par. 2 & 3. By which it is enacted, *That if any within the Queen's Dominions ſhall put in Ure, any Bull or Inſtrument of Abſolution or Reconciliation obtained from the See of* Rome; *or ſhall take upon him by Colour thereof to abſolve or reconcile any Perſon; or to grant or promiſe any Abſolution or Reconciliation, or ſhall willingly receive any ſuch Abſolution or Reconciliation, or ſhall obtain from the See of* Rome *any Bull or Writing whatſoever, or publiſh, or any Ways put the ſame in Ure, he is guilty of High Treaſon.* And by Par. 4. *Acceſſaries after the Offence incur a* Præmunire. And by Par. 5, 6. *Thoſe who within ſix Weeks diſcloſe not an Offer of ſuch Bulls,* &c. *to ſome Privy Counſellor,* &c. *are guilty of a Miſpriſion of Treaſon.*

(1 H. H. P. C. 337, 338.) *Sect.* 76. The third Offence of this Kind, *viz.* That of perverting others, or being perverted to Popery, is made High Treaſon by 23 *El.* 1. Par. 2. & 3 *Jac.* 1. 4. Par. 22, 23. by which it is enacted, *That if any one ſhall pretend to have Power, or ſhall put in Practice to withdraw a Subject from his natural Obedience to the King, or to withdraw them for that Intent to the* Romiſh *Religion, or to move to promiſe any Obedience to any foreign Power, or to do any Overt Act to that Intent, or to reconcile one to the See of* Rome; *and if any Perſon ſhall by any Means be willingly withdrawn, or promiſe Obedience, as aforeſaid, he is guilty of High Treaſon.*

(See Cawley 187.) *Sect.* 77. But by 3 *Jac.* 1. 4. *If any Perſon, who is reconciled to the See of* Rome *beyond the Seas, return into the Realm and ſubmit himſelf,* &c. *and take the Oaths within ſix Days after his Return, he is excuſed.*

Sect. 78. It ſeemeth that the bare pretending to ſuch a Power, without any farther Act in endeavouring to perſwade Perſons from their Allegiance, or the bare endeavouring ſo to perſwade them, without any Pretence of ſuch a Power, is High Treaſon within theſe Acts. (Savil 3. Pl. 9.)

Sect. 79.

Sect. 79. The fourth Offence of this Kind, *viz.* That of receiving Popish Orders or Education, *&c.* is made High Treason by 27 *El.* 2. Par. 3. by which it is enacted, *That if any Ecclesiastick born in the Queen's Dominions, and ordained or professed by Popish Authority, shall remain in the Queen's Dominions, or come from beyond Sea, and not submit to some Bishop or Justice of Peace within three Days, and take the Oaths,* &c. *he shall be guilty of High Treason.* 1 H. H. P. C. 336, 337.

Sect. 80. And by Par. 5. *If any Subject, not being an Ecclesiastick, shall not return from a Popish Seminary within six Months after a Proclamation to that Purpose in* London, *and submit,* &c. *within two Days, he shall be guilty of High Treason, whenever he shall otherwise return.*

Sect. 81. And by Par. 13. *If any Subject shall know that any such Priest is within the Realm, and not discover him to some Justice of Peace,* &c. *within twelve Days, he shall be fined and imprisoned at the Queen's Will; and if any Justice of Peace,* &c. *to whom such Matter shall be discovered, shall not give Information to some of the Privy Council,* &c. *within twenty-eight Days, he shall forfeit two hundred Marks.*

In the Construction of this Statute it hath been resolved,

Sect. 82. I. That in an Indictment grounded on this Statute against a Priest remaining here beyond the Time limited by the Statute, it must be alledged, That he was born in the Realm, *&c.* and also that he was ordained, *&c.* by Authority challenged or pretended from the See of *Rome*; but that there is no need to shew in what Place in particular he was born, or whether he were ordained within the Realm, or beyond Sea. Poph. 94.

Sect. 83. II. That one in Popish Orders, being in a Ship in Order to go to *Ireland*, and driven by a Storm into *England*, and immediately apprehended, is not guilty of High Treason within this Act; for his Design of going to *Ireland* was prevented, *& nil efficit conatus, nisi sequatur effectus,* and he was forced into *England* by the Act of God, and against his Will; neither can he be said to remain here within the Intent of the Statute, because he was compelled to it by Reason of the Prosecution. Raym. 377.

Sect. 84. The fifth Offence of this Nature, *viz.* That of refusing a second Tender of the Oaths, is made High Treason by 5 *El.* 1. Par. 11, 12 & 20. by which it is enacted, *That if any Person who shall have a Charge, Cure, or Office in the Church, or an Office or Ministry in an Ecclesiastical Court, or if any Person who shall willfully refuse to observe the Rites of the Church of* England, *after having been admonished by the Ordinary,* &c. *or that shall say or hear private Mass,* &c. *shall refuse a second Tender of the Oaths, he shall be guilty of High Treason, but without Corruption of Blood.* Vide infra Ch. 19.

Sect. 85. Secondly Offences against the Protestant Succession made High Treason are twofold:

1. Denying the Power of the Parliament to limit the Succession of the Crown, which is made High Treason, by 4 *Annæ* 8. Par. 1, 2. and 6 *Annæ* 7. Par. 1, 2. whereby it is enacted, *That whoever shall maliciously, advisedly and directly by Writing or Printing declare, maintain and affirm, That the pretended Prince of* Wales, *or any other hath any Right or Title to the Crown, otherwise than according to* 1 W. & M. ch. 2. or 12 W. 3. ch. 2. *or that the Kings of this Realm, by Authority of Parliament, are not able to make Laws to limit and bind the Crown and the Descent and Government thereof, shall be guilty of High Treason, and that those that maliciously and directly affirm the same by Preaching, Teaching or advised speaking, shall be guilty of a* Præmunire.

2. Endeavouring maliciously, advisedly and directly to hinder any Person, who shall be next in Succession, according to 1 *W.* & *M.* and 12 *W.* 3. which is made High Treason by 1 *Annæ* 17.

Sect. 86. 3. The Offence of listing Men without the King's Licence is made High Treason by 12 *Annæ* 11. by which it is enacted, *That every Subject shall be guilty of High Treason, who shall in the Kingdom of* Great Britain *or* Ireland *list or enter himself in the Service of any foreign Prince or Person as a Soldier, or procure another to be so listed; or to go beyond Sea with such Intent, without the King's Licence, or in the* French *King's Service even with our King's Licence, until the said* French *King shall have disbanded all his* English *Regiments*, &c. But this Act is to continue but for three Years. [16.] ☞

CHAP. XVIII.

Of Felonies more immediately against the King.

FElonies more immediately against the King are of five Kinds:

1. Offences relating to the Coin or Bullion.
2. Offences against the King's Council.
3. The Offence of passing beyond Sea to serve a foreign Prince.
4. Imbezilling the King's Armour.
5. The Offence of relieving a Popish Priest.

Felonies relating to the Coin or Bullion are of three kinds:

1. The Offence of debasing it.
2. The Offence of unlawfully diminishing it.
3. The Offence of endeavouring by extraordinary Means to increase it.

Sect. 1. And first, The Offence of debasing the Coin or Bullion was provided against by many ancient Statutes, which seem to be obsolete at this Day; for the Importation of ill Money was made Felony by 17 *Ed.* 3.
3 Inst. 92, 93. N. 15. (which was never printed,) and so was the Payments of Blanks, (which were made of a base Alloy,) by 2 *H.* 6. 9. and the coining or bringing in Galley Half-pence, Seskins or Doydekins, by 3 *H.* 5. 1. However it is made High Treason to bring in false Money, *&c.* by 25 *Ed.* 3.
Supra Ch. 17. and 1 & 2 *Ph.* & *Mar.* 11. And by 8 & 9 *Will.* 3. 25. Par. 6. *It is made Felony to Blanch Copper for Sale, or to mix blanched Copper with Silver, or knowingly to buy or sell, or offer to Sale blanched Copper alone, or mixt with Silver, or knowingly and fraudulently to buy*, &c. *any Mixture which shall be heavier than Silver, and look, and touch, and wear like Standard Gold, but be manifestly worse, or to receive or pay any Counterfeit milled Money*, &c. *at a lower Rate than the same by its Denomination doth import, or was coined or counterfeited for.* [17.] ☞

Sect. 2. Secondly, The Offence of diminiſhing the Coin or Bullion of the Kingdom has been always thought to be of very ill Conſequence, as tending to impoveriſh the Nation, and to embarraſs Trade, and with an Eye to thoſe Inconveniencies it was made Felony by 17 *Ed.* 3. N. 15. (which was never printed) to tranſport Silver, except Plate carried over by Great Men to ſerve their Houſes; alſo the Tranſportation thereof was prohibited by many other Statutes, as 27 *Ed.* 3. 14. 5 *Rich.* 2. 2. 2 *H.* 4. 16. 2 *H.* 6. 6. and 3 *H.* 8. 1. But this general Reſtraint being found by Experience to be inconvenient to Trade; which by exporting Money to one Market may bring back ſuch Goods, as will more than make up the Loſs, from another, it was enacted by 15 *Car.* 2. 7. Par. 12. *That any Perſon might export any foreign Coin or Bullion without Duty, firſt making an Entry thereof in the Cuſtom-Houſe.* Poph. 149. Hob. 270. 3 Inſt. 92, 93.

Sect. 3. But this Licence having been often abuſed by the Tranſportation of ſuch Silver, which having been coined into *Engliſh* Money or wrought into Plate, was afterwards melted down into the Form of foreign Coin or Bullion, it was, in Order to prevent this Miſchief, enacted by 6 & 7 *Will.* 3. 17. Par. 3. *That none ſhall caſt or make Ingots or Bars of Silver in Imitation of* Spaniſh, *under Pain of five hundred Pounds.* And it is farther enacted by the ſaid Statute, Par. 5. *That no Perſon ſhall tranſport, or cauſe to be tranſported, any molten Silver, but only ſuch as ſhall be marked or ſtamped at Goldſmith's Hall,* &c. *nor even that without a Certificate under the Hands of one of the Wardens of the Goldſmiths Company, that Oath hath been made by the Owner or Owners thereof, and likewiſe by one credible Witneſs, that the ſame is lawful Silver, and that no Part thereof was (before the ſame was molten) the current Coin of this Realm, nor Clippings thereof, nor Plate wrought within this Kingdom,* &c.

Sect. 4. Alſo it is farther enacted, Par. 6. *That any Officer of the Cuſtom-Houſe may ſeize any molten Silver, which ſhall be put on Board any Veſſel, without having ſuch Mark or Stamp, and alſo ſuch Certificate, as is above mentioned.*

Sect. 5. And it is farther enacted, Par. 7. *That if any Broker, not being a trading Goldſmith, or Refiner of Silver, ſhall buy or ſell any Bullion or molten Silver, he ſhall ſuffer Impriſonment for ſix Months without Bail.*

Sect. 6. Alſo it is farther enacted, Par. 13, 14. *That if a Doubt ſhall ariſe upon Bullion ſhipped to be exported, whether the ſame be* Engliſh *or Foreign, the Proof ſhall lie upon the Owner,* &c. *And that if any Perſon ſhall enter or ſhip any Bullion, by the ſaid Act allowed to be exported, other than in the Name of the true Owner, Proprietor or Importer, the Exporter ſhall forfeit the ſame, or the full Value thereof.*

Sect. 7. Thirdly, The Endeavours of ſome Perſons in making Uſe of extraordinary Methods for the producing of Gold and Silver, were found by Experience to be ſo prejudicial to the Publick, both from the laviſh Waſte of many valuable Materials, and alſo from the Ruin of many Families, which had been occaſioned by ſuch uſeleſs Expences, that it was thought neceſſary to put a Check to ſuch Practices by ſome ſevere Law, and for that Purpoſe it was made Felony, by 5 *H.* 4. 4. *to multiply Gold or Silver, or to uſe the Art or Craft of Multiplication.* And it was holden, That the practiſing to find out the Philoſophers Stone, by which it is imagined that all Metals may be made Gold, was Felony within this Statute: But this Reſtraint having been found to have no other Effect, upon the unaccountable Vanity of thoſe, who fancied ſuch Attempts to be practicable, but only to ſend them beyond Sea, to try their Experiments with Impunity in other Countries, the Statute of 5 *H.* 4. was at laſt wholly repealed by 1 *Will.* & *Mar.* 30. Dyer. 88. Pl. 105.

Sect. 8.

Sect. 8. As to the second Kind of Felonies more immediately against the King, *viz.* those which are against his Council, it is enacted by 3 *H.* 7. 14. *That if any sworn Servant in the Chequer-Roll of the King's Houshold, under the State of a Lord, make any Confederacy, Compassing, Conspiracy or Imagination with any Person to destroy or murder the King, or any Lord of this Realm, or any other Person sworn to the King's Council, he shall be guilty of Felony.*

Supra Ch. 17. Sect. 40.

Sect. 9. And it is farther enacted by 9 *Annæ, Chap.* 16. *That if any Person shall attempt to kill, assault, strike or wound any Privy Counsellor in Execution of his Office, he shall suffer as a Felon without Clergy.*

Sect. 10. As to the third Offence of this Kind (*viz.*) That of passing beyond Sea to serve a foreign Prince, it is enacted by 3 *Jac.* 1. 4. Par. 18, 19, 20, 21. *That every Subject, who shall go out of the Realm to serve any foreign Prince or State, or shall pass over the Seas, and there voluntarily serve any such foreign Prince or State, not having before his going taken the Oath of Obedience, shall suffer as a Felon; and that if any Gentleman, or Person of higher Degree, or any Person who hath born any Office or Charge in Camp or Army, shall go out of the Realm to serve such foreign Prince,* &c. *without being bound with two Sureties in a Bond, conditioned that he shall not be reconciled to the See of* Rome, *nor enter into any Conspiracy against the King, he shall be a Felon.*

3 Inst. 80. Dalt. ch. 107. Cawley 182.

Sect. 11. Note, That by 1 *Will. & Mar.* Sess. 1. Chap. 8. this Oath of Obedience is taken away, and the new Oaths of Allegiance and Supremacy enjoined in the Room thereof.

See the next Chapter.

Sect. 12. As to the fourth Offence of this Kind, *viz.* That of imbezilling the King's Armour, it is enacted by 31 *El.* 4. *That if any Person, having the Charge or Custody of the King's Armour, Ordnance, or Munition,* &c. *or of any Victuals provided for the victualling of any Soldiers or Mariners,* &c. *shall for Lucre and Gain, or wittingly, advisedly, and of Purpose to hinder or impeach the King's Service, imbezil, purloin, or convey away any of the same Armour,* &c. *to the Value of twenty Shillings, he shall be judged guilty of Felony.*

Sect. 13. *But such Offender must be prosecuted within the Year next after the Offence done; neither shall he forfeit his Hereditaments any longer than during his Life; nor shall his Blood be corrupted, or his Wife lose her Dower.*

3 Inst. 78, 79. Cawley 90, 91.

Sect. 14. As to the fifth Offence of this Kind, *viz.* That of relieving a Popish Priest, it is enacted by 27 *El.* 2. Par. 4. *That whoever shall wittingly, and willingly receive, relieve, comfort, aid or maintain any Jesuit, Seminary or other Popish Priest,* &c. *being at Liberty or out of Hold, knowing him to be such a Jesuit,* &c. *shall for such Offence be adjudged a Felon without Benefit of Clergy.*

CHAP. XIX.

Of Præmunire.

OFfences more immediately against the King, not capital, come generally under the Titles of *Præmunire,* Misprision, and Contempts. In treating of *Præmunire* I shall consider,

1. What Offences come under this Notion.
2. How they are punished.

And firſt, Offences coming under the Notion of *Præmunire*, ſeem to be reducible to the following general Heads;

1. Offences againſt the Prerogative of the Crown.
2. Offences againſt the Authority of the King and Parliament.

Thoſe of the firſt Kind ſeem to come under the following Particulars;

1. Making Uſe of Papal Bulls.
2. Derogating from the King's Common Law Courts.
3. Appealing to *Rome* from any of the King's Courts.
4. Exerciſing the Juriſdiction of a Suffragan without the Appointment of the Biſhop of the Dioceſe.
5. Refuſing to elect or conſecrate the Perſon nominated by the King to a Biſhoprick.
6. Maintaining the Pope's Power.
7. Bringing in *Agnus Dei*.
8. Contributing to the Maintenance of a Popiſh Seminary.
9. Refuſing the Oaths.

Sect. 1. But inaſmuch as theſe Offences depend chiefly upon Statutes made for the Preſervation of the Sovereignty of the Crown from the Incroachments of the See of *Rome*, I ſhall, in order to ſhew the Reaſonableneſs of theſe Laws, take a ſhort View of thoſe Uſurpations, which made them neceſſary.

Sect. 2. It is the general Opinion, That Chriſtianity was firſt planted in this Iſland by ſome of the Eaſtern Church, which is very probable, from the ancient *Britons* obſerving *Eaſter* always on the fourteenth Day of the Month, according to the Cuſtom of the Eaſt.

Davis 88. con. Selden's Janus Anglorum 27.

Sect. 3. But the *Saxons* being converted about the Year 600. by Perſons ſent from *Rome*, and wholly devoted to the Intereſt thereof, it cannot be expected that ſuch an Opportunity of enlarging the Juriſdiction of that See ſhould wholly be neglected.

Sect. 4. [a] And yet *Parſons*, in his Attempt to anſwer Sir *Edward Coke*'s fifth Report concerning the King's Eccleſiaſtical Authority, is ſcarce able to produce any Inſtances of the Papal Power in this Kingdom before the *Norman* Conqueſt. Indeed he tells us, That four or five Perſons were made Biſhops by the Pope at the firſt Converſion, but offers not any Example thereof between the Year 669 and the Conqueſt; and it is certain, That all Biſhopricks were then conferred by the King's Delivery of a Ring and a Paſtoral Staff.

[a] Parſon's ch. 6. Par. 12, 20, 21, 22, 24, 25, 57, 59. See Barrow from Page 258 to 262. 1 Ro. Ab. 882. 1 Inſt. 134. a. 344. a. Selden's Janus Anglorum 42, 65.

Sect. 5. [b] Neither is he able to produce any Inſtance, that looks like an Appeal to *Rome* before the Conqueſt, except in the Caſe of two Biſhops, and he is forced to own, That even one of the Biſhops was depoſed by two Kings, and could get no Relief againſt either of them, notwithſtanding the Pope's utmoſt Application in his Favour.

[b] Parſons ch. 6. Par. 29, 30, 31, 32, 50, 51, 52, 53, 54, 55, 56. See Barrow from Page 242 to 258. Selden's Janus Anglorum 59, 67, 68.

Sect. 6. Nor can he ſhew more than four or five Inſtances of Exemptions from ordinary Juriſdiction, granted or confirmed by Popes to Religious Houſes in thoſe Days, which plainly ſhews that this Concurrence was not thought neceſſary; and it appears, That our ancient Kings, of their own Authority, exempted ſome Abbeys from Epiſcopal Juriſdiction; and it hath always been a received Rule, even in the Times of Popery, That the Chancellor ſhall viſit a Church of the King's Foundation, notwithſtanding it be not ſpecially exempted.

Parſons ch. 6. from Par. 37 to 48. 1 H. 7. 25. 21 Ed. 3. 60. a. b. 1 Inſt. 144. a. F. N. B. 42. a. 27 Ed. 3. 85. a. 6 H. 7. 14. a. 2 Rol. Abr. 230, 231.

Davis 89. *Sect.* 7. But the Pope, having favoured and supported *William* the first in his Invasion of the Kingdom, took that Opportunity of enlarging his Incroachments, and in this King's Reign began to send his Legates hither; Davis 90, 93. 2 Ro. Re. 103. Palm. 25, 26. Selden's Janus Anglorum 67. and prevailed at first with *Henry* the first, and afterwards with King *John*, to give up the Donation of Bishopricks; and in the Time of King *Stephen* gained the Prerogative of Appeals; and, in the Time of *Henry* the second, exempted all Clerks from the Secular Power.

Selden's Epinomis, cap. 8. Dav. Rep. 91. *Sect.* 8. Indeed this King did at first strenuously withstand these Innovations, and abolished most of them by the Constitutions of *Clarendon:* But upon the Death of *Becket*, who, for having violently opposed the King, was slain by some of his Servants, the Pope got such an Advantage over the King, that he was never after able effectually to execute those Laws.

Sect. 9. And not long after this, by a general Excommunication of the King and People, for several Years, because they would not suffer an Archbishop to be imposed upon them, King *John* was reduced to such Straits, that he was obliged to surrender his Kingdoms to the Pope, and to receive them again, to hold of him for the Rent of a Thousand Marks.

2 Inst. 584. Dav. 95. *Sect.* 10. And in the following Reign of *Henry* the third, partly from the Profits of our best Church Benefices, which were generally given to *Italians*, and others residing at the Court of *Rome*, and partly from the Taxes imposed by the Pope, there went yearly out of the Kingdom Seventy thousand Pounds Sterling.

2 Inst. 580. *Sect.* 11. The Nation being under this Necessity was obliged to provide for the Prerogative of the Prince and the Liberties of the People, by many strict Laws. And in the Reign of *Edward* the first, Religious Houses were prohibited, under high Penalties, to send any Thing to their Superiors beyond Seas; and it was declared by Parliament, That the Pope's taking upon him to dispose of *English* Benefices to Aliens was an Incroachment not to be endured; and soon after, these Grievances produced those more severe Laws against the abovementioned Offences of this Nature, the Particulars whereof are before set forth.

See Register 64. a. 3 Inst. 127. *Sect.* 12. And first the Offence of making Use of Papal Bulls is made a *Præmunire* by many ancient as well as later Statutes; for it is enacted by 25 *Ed.* 3. called the Statute of Provisors, *That whoever shall by a Papal Provision disturb any Patron to present to a Benefice*, &c. *shall be fined and imprisoned till he make full Renunciation*, &c. And it is farther enacted by 25 *Ed.* 3. Stat. 5. Chap. 22. *That if any one purchase a Provision of an Abbey or Priory, he shall be out of the King's Protection.* And by 38 *Ed.* 3. & 12 *R.* 2. 15. & 13 *R.* 2. Stat. 2. Chap. 2. *That whoever shall accept a Benefice contrary to* 25 Ed. 3. *shall be banished.* And by 13 *R.* 2. Stat. 2. Chap. 3. *That whoever shall bring a Sentence of Excommunication against any Person for executing the said Statute of* 25 Ed. 3. *shall suffer Pain of Life and Member.* And by 16 *R.* 2. 5. *That whoever shall purchase or pursue, or cause to be purchased or pursued, in the Court of* Rome *or elsewhere, any Translations, Processes, Sentences of Excommunication, Bulls, Instruments or other Things contrary to the Tenor of that Statute, which touch the King, against him, his Crown, his Regality or his Realm, or bring them within this Realm, or receive them*, &c. *shall be out of the King's Protection, and their Lands and Tenements, Goods and Chattels forfeited to the King; and they shall be attached by their Bodies*, &c. And by 2 *H.* 4. 3. *That whoever shall purchase from* Rome *a Provision of Exemption from ordinary Obedience*; and by 2 *H.* 4. 4. *That whoever shall put in Execution Bulls purchased by those of the Order of* Cisteaux *to be discharged of Tithes, shall incur the like Penalty.* Also Offenders of this Nature are farther restrained by 6 *H.* 4. 1. 7 *H.* 4. 8. 9 *H.* 4. 8. & 3 *H.* 5. 4. *By which the Statutes above mentioned are enforced and explained.* And it is farther enacted by 23 *H.* 8. 21. Sect. 22. *That whoever shall sue for, or execute any Licence, Dispensation, or Faculty from the See of* Rome; and by 28 *H.* 8. 16. (by which all Bulls, Briefs, *&c.* heretofore obtained from *Rome*, are made void) *That whoever shall use, alledge, or plead the same in any Court, unless they were confirmed by that Statute, or afterwards by the King, shall incur the like Penalty.* Yet it hath been holden, That the alledging of an ancient Bull in order to induce another principal Matter, whereon to ground a Title without claiming any Thing from the Bull it self, is not within this Statute. 2 Lev. 251.

Sect. 13. By 13 *El.* 2. those who purchase any Bull, *&c.* from *Rome*, are guilty of High Treason. But those ancient Statutes still continue in force; and it is in the Election of the Crown to proceed either upon them, or 13 *El.* Also by the said Statute of 13 *El.* *The Aiders, Comforters, and Maintainers of such Offenders after the Offence, to the Intent to uphold the said usurped Power, incur a* Præmunire. 1 H. H. P. C. 643. Vide supra Chap. 17. Davis 84.

Sect. 14. The second Offence of this Nature, *viz.* That of derogating from the King's Common Law Courts, is said to have been a High Offence at Common Law, and is made a *Præmunire* by many ancient Statutes; for by 27 *Ed.* 3. 1. & 38 *Ed.* 3. of Provisors, *If any Subject draw any out of the Realm in Plea, whereof the Cognizance pertains to the King's Court, or of Things whereof Judgments be given in the King's Court, or sue in any other Court to defeat or impeach the Judgments given in the King's Court, he shall be warned to appear,* &c. *in proper Person, at a Day containing the space of two Months; at which if he appear not, he and his Proctors,* &c. *shall be put out of the King's Protection, his Lands and Chattels forfeited, his Body imprisoned and ransomed at the King's Will,* &c. 2 Rol. Abr. 176. O. 3. 177. P. 1. 3. Rastal's Entr. 466. b. 467. b. B. 2. C. 48. S. 9. 3 Inst. 125. Bro. Præmunire 3.

Sect. 15. And by 16 *Rich.* 2. 5. *Both those who shall pursue or cause to be pursued in the Court of* Rome *or elsewhere, any Processes or Instruments, or other Things whatsoever which touch the King, against him, his Crown, and Regality or his Realm, and also those who shall bring, receive, notify or execute them, and their Abbettors,* &c. *shall be put out of the King's Protection,* &c.

Sect. 16. In the Construction of these Statutes it was holden, That certain Commissioners of Sewers for summoning one before them who had got a Judgment at Law, and imprisoning him till he would release it, were guilty of a *Præmunire.* 2 Bulst. 299. 3 Inst. 125. Cro. Ja. 336.

Sect. 17. Also there have been formerly many strong Opinions, That [a] Suits in Equity to relieve against a Judgment at Law are within these Statutes; especially if the End thereof be to controvert the very Point determined at Law, or to seek Relief after Judgment in a Case wherein the Law may relieve, as against Excessiveness of Damages, *&c.* But it seems to be generally agreed at this Day, That no such Suit is within the Intention of the said Statutes. [a] 3 Inst. 123, 124. See 4 H. 4. Ch. 23. 2 Chan. Cases 97. Dy. 201. Pl. 64. 301. a. 1 Lev. 241, 242.

Sect. 18. It hath been said, That [b] Suits in the Admiralty or Ecclesiastical Courts within the Realm are within 16 *R.* 2. 5. (by Force of those Words, *or elsewhere*) if they concern Matters, the Cognizance whereof belongs to the Common Law; as where a Bishop deprives an Incumbent of a Donative, or excommunicates a Man for hunting in his Parks, *&c.* or where [c] Commissioners of Sewers imprison a Man for not releasing a Judgment at Law. Hard. 125. 1 Danv. Abr. 764. Pl. 2. 1 Sid. 463. 1 Mod. 59. 3 Keb. 221. [b] 2 Bulst. 299. 1 Ro. Re. 190.

Sect. 19. But it seemeth, That a Suit in those Courts for a Matter which appears not by the Libel it self, but only by the Defendant's Plea, or [c] 3 Inst. 120, 121, 122. Bro. Præmun. 5, 12, 16, 31. 15 H. 7. 9. a.

12 Co. 37. 2 Rol. A. 177. Pl. 2. Moor 838. 12 Co. 37. Cro. Jac. 134.

or other Matter ſubſequent, to be of temporal Cognizance, (as where a Plaintiff libels for Tithes, and the Defendant pleads that they were ſevered from the nine Parts, by which they became a Lay Fee) is not within the Statute, becauſe it appears not that the either Plaintiff or the Judge knew that they were ſevered.

Sect. 20. The third Offence of this Nature, (*viz.*) That of appealing to *Rome* from any of the King's Courts, is made a *Præmunire* by 24 *H.* 8. 12. and 25 *H.* 8. 19. by which it is enacted, *That all ſuch Appeals, as formerly were made to* Rome, *ſhall from henceforth be made to the High Court of Chancery.*

Sect. 21. The fourth Offence of this Nature, (*viz.*) That of exerciſing the Juriſdiction of a Suffragan, without the Appointment of the Biſhop of the Dioceſe, is made a *Præmunire* by 26 *H.* 8. 14. which ſets forth at large for what Towns ſuch Suffragans may be nominated by the King, and alſo how they may be nominated, conſecrated and commiſſioned.

Sect. 22. The fifth Offence of this Nature, (*viz.*) That of refuſing to elect or conſecrate the Perſon nominated by the King to a Biſhoprick, is made a *Præmunire* by 25 *H.* 8. 20. *Par.* 7. by which it is enacted, *That if any Dean and Chapter refuſe to elect the Perſon named in the King's Letter for a Biſhoprick, and to ſignify ſuch Election to the King within twenty Days after the Licence ſhall come to their Hands, or if any Archbiſhop or Biſhop after ſuch Election (or Nomination by the King in Default thereof ſignified unto them by the King) ſhall refuſe within twenty Days to confirm and conſecrate the Perſon ſo ſignified to them, they incur a* Præmunire.

See Chap. 17. *Sect.* 23. The ſixth Offence of this Nature, (*viz.*) That of maintaining the Pope's Power, is made a *Præmunire* upon the firſt Conviction, and High Treaſon upon the ſecond.

Sect. 24. The ſeventh Offence of this Nature, (*viz.*) That of bringing in *Agnus Dei*, is made a *Præmunire* by 13 *El.* 2. Par. 7, 8. by which it is enacted, *That if any one ſhall bring into the Realm,* &c. *any* Agnus Dei, *Croſſes,*
Cawley 52, 53. *Pictures, Beads, or ſuch like ſuperſtitious Things pretended to be hallowed by the Biſhop of* Rome, &c. *and ſhall deliver or offer the ſame to any Subject to be worn or uſed in any wiſe; or if any one ſhall receive the ſame to ſuch Intent, and not*
Cawley 54. *clear himſelf by diſcovering the Offender,* &c. *he ſhall incur a* Præmunire.

Sect. 25. *And ſo ſhall a Juſtice of Peace in the ſame County, who having any Offence in that Act declared unto him, ſhall not declare it to a Privy Counſellor, within ſixteen Days.*

Sect. 26. The eighth Offence of this Nature, (*viz.*) That of contributing to the Maintenance of a Popiſh Seminary, is made a *Præmunire* by 27 *El.* 2. Par. 6.

Sect. 27. The ninth Offence of this Nature, (*viz.*) That of refuſing the Oaths, is made a *Præmunire* by ſeveral Statutes, for by 1 *El.* 1. Par. 19. it is enacted, *That all Eccleſiaſtical Perſons, and all Eccleſiaſtical and Temporal Officers, and all Perſons having the King's Fees or Wages*; and by Par. 26. *That all Perſons taking Orders, or any Degree in any Univerſity within the Realm, ſhall take the Oath of Supremacy under Pain of loſing their Benefices and Offices.* And it is farther enacted by 5 *El.* 1. Par. 5. *That all the Perſons above mentioned, who are required by the ſaid Statute of* 1 El. 1. *to take the ſaid Oath, and all School-maſters, publick and private, Barriſters, Benchers, Readers, Ancients in any Houſe of Court,* &c. *Attornies, Sheriffs, and Officers belonging to the Common or any other Law, or to the Crown, or to any Court whatſoever, ſhall take the ſaid Oath in open Court, before they ſhall be admitted to any ſuch Vocation or Office,* &c. *And if they belong not to any Court, That then they ſhall take the ſame before ſuch Perſon as ſhall admit them to ſuch Vocation,* &c. *or before Commiſſioners appointed under the Great Seal,* &c. And it is farther enacted Par. 6. *That any Bishop may tender the said Oath to any spiritual Person within his Diocese, as well in Places exempt as others*; and by Par. 7. *That Commissioners may be appointed by the Lord Chancellor to tender the same to such Persons as by their Commission they shall be authorized to tender it unto*; and by Par. 8. *That if any Person, compellable by either of the said Acts, or appointed by such Commissioners to take the said Oath, shall refuse to take it on a Tender thereof, he shall incur a* Præmunire. And by Par. 9. *That such Refusal shall be certified within forty Days before the King in his Court of King's Bench, by those who have Authority to tender the said Oath, under the Penalty of one hundred Pounds; and that the Sheriff of the County, wherein the said Court shall sit, may impanel a Jury who shall inquire of such Rufusal in such Manner, as if it had happened in the same County.*

In the Construction of these Statutes it hath been resolved:

Sect. 28. I. That the Obligation to take the said Oath continued after the Death of Queen *Elizabeth*, tho' the Statutes say nothing of her Successors; and the like Resolution also has been made in Relation to the Oaths appointed by subsequent Statutes. Raym. 212. 1 Vent. 171. 2 Keb. 825.

Sect. 29. II. That in a Commission authorizing Persons to tender the said Oath, a general Description of the Persons to whom it shall be tendred is sufficient, without naming them particularly by their Names. Raym. 445.

Sect. 30. III. That if the Person who tendered the Oath as Bishop, was not a Bishop at that Time, the Defendant may give it in Evidence upon the general Issue. Dy. 234. Pl. 15.

Sect. 31. IV. That the said Oath must in Substance be taken in the very Words expressed in the Acts, and cannot be qualified with any Reserve whatever: Yet it hath been resolved, That to use the Words [In Conscience] instead of [in my Conscience] or [Sea of *Rome*] instead of [See of *Rome*] makes no material Variance. 1 Bulst. 197, 198. 1 Vent. 172, 173.

Sect. 32. V. That a Certificate of a Refusal of the said Oath made to the Judges of the said Court of the King's Bench by Name, and not to the King in his said Court, is sufficient within the Meaning of the Statute. Raym. 445.

Sect. 33. VI. That an Ecclesiastical Person is well described in such a Certificate by the Addition of *Legum Doctor, & Sacris Ordinibus constitutus*, without adding *Clericus, &c.* Dy. 234. Pl. 15.

Sect. 34. VII. That such a Certificate being entered of Record, as brought into Court such a Day and Year *per* A. B. *Cancellar.* of such a Bishop is good, without entering that it was so brought *per Mandatum Episcopi.* Dy. 234. Pl. 15.

Sect. 35. VIII. That the Trial must be by a Jury of the County, wherein the Oaths were refused; for the Statute only authorizes an Indictment by a Jury of the County, wherein the Court sits. Dy. 234. Pl. 15.

Sect. 36. IX. That any Misrecital of the very Words of the Oath, in an Indictment for not taking it, is erroneous. See the Books above cited.

Sect. 37. By 3 *Jac.* 1. 4. Par. 13, 14. *Any Bishop, or two Justices of Peace, whereof one is to be of the* Quorum, *might tender the Oath of Obedience therein prescribed, to any Person above the Age of eighteen Years, being under the Degree of Nobility, and convicted or indicted of Recusancy, or not having received the Sacrament twice in the Year past, and also to any suspected Stranger who shall not purge himself upon Oath; and shall certify the Names of such as take the said Oath to the next Quarter-Sessions, and commit those who refuse it till the next Assizes or Sessions, where the same shall be again tendered; and if the said Persons, or any other Persons whatsoever of the Age of eighteen Years, other than Noblemen or Noblewomen, shall there refuse to take it, they incur a* Præmunire, *unless they be Femes Covert, who shall be committed till they take it.* Skin. 11.

Sect. 38. By Par. 41. *The Lords of the Council in like manner may tender the said Oath to any Nobleman or Woman, of the Age of eighteen Years, who refusing the same incur a* Præmunire, *Femes Covert excepted.*

Sect. 39. By 7 *Jac.* 1. 6. Par. 2, 26, 27. *All Persons whatsoever, as well Ecclesiastical as Temporal, of what Estate, Dignity, Pre-eminence, Sex, Quality or Degree soever he or she shall be, above the Age of eighteen Years, being in that Act mentioned and intended, shall take the said Oath; and any Privy Counsellor or Bishop, within his Diocese, may require any Baron or Baroness, of the Age of eighteen Years, and any two Justices of the Peace, whereof one to* See Cawley 246, &c. *be of the* Quorum, *may require any other Person of that Age to take it. And if any Person of or above the said Age and Degree shall be presented,* &c. *for not coming to Church,* &c. *then three of the Privy Council, whereof the Lord Chancellor,* &c. *to be one, shall require such Person to take the said Oath. And if any Person whatsoever, of the said Age and under the said Degree, shall be presented,* &c. *for not coming to Church,* &c. *or if the Minister,* &c. *shall complain to any Justice of Peace,* &c. *and the Justice shall find Cause of Suspicion, then any one Justice of Peace shall require such Person to take the said Oath,* &c. *And all such Persons refusing a Tender of the said Oath, shall be bound over to the Assizes or Sessions, where if they refuse again, they incur a* Præmunire: And Par. 27. *All such Refusers are disabled to execute any publick Place of Judicature, or bear any other Office, (being no Office of Inheritance or ministerial Function) or to practise the Common or Civil Law, Physick or Surgery, or the Art of an Apothecary.*

12 Co. 130, 131. *Sect.* 40. In the Construction of these Statutes it hath been resolved, That the Justices of Peace, *&c.* may send their Warrant to bring such Persons before them, but that they cannot authorize the Constable to break open the Doors to take them.

Sect. 41. But by 1 *Will. & Mar. the Oaths of Supremacy and Obedience prescribed by these Acts were abrogated, and the following Oath and Declaration substituted in their Room.*

I A. B. *do sincerely promise and swear, That I will be faithful and bear true Allegiance to his Majesty King* George.

I A. B. *do swear, That I do from my Heart abhor, detest and abjure, as impious and heretical, that damnable Doctrine and Position, that Princes excommunicated or deprived by the Pope, or any Authority of the See of* Rome, *may be deposed or murdered by their Subjects, or any other whatsoever:*

And I do declare, That no foreign Prince, Person, Prelate, State, or Potentate, hath or ought to have any Jurisdiction, Power, Superiority, Preeminence or Authority Ecclesiastical or Spiritual, within this Realm.

Sect. 42. And by Par. 3, 4, 5. *All Persons who are required to take, or authorized to tender the said abrogated Oaths, or either of them, are in like manner required and authorized to take and tender the said Oath and Declaration, under the same Penalties,* &c. See Chap. 24.

Sect. 43. By 7 *Will.* 3. 24. *Serjeants at Law, Counsellors, Attornies, Solicitors, Proctors, Clerks or Notaries, practising as such in any Court whatsoever, without taking the said Oaths and subscribing the said Declaration, incur a* Præmunire.

Sect. 44. And now I am in the second Place to consider those Offences against the Authority of King and Parliament, which come under the Notion of *Præmunire*, as to which it is enacted by 6 *Ann.* 7. *That if any Person shall maliciously and directly, by Preaching, Teaching, or advised Speaking, declare, maintain and affirm, that the pretended Prince of* Wales, *hath any Right or Title to the Crown of these Realms, or that any other Person or Persons hath or have any Right or Title to the same, otherwise than according to* 1 Will. & Mar. 2. *and* 12 Will. 2. *and the Acts then lately made in* England *and* Scotland, *mutually for the Union of the two Kingdoms; or that the Kings or Queens of this Realm, with the Authority of Parliament, are not able to make Laws to limit the Crown and the Descent,* &c. *thereof, shall incur a* Præmunire.

Sect. 45. As to the second general Point of this Chapter, *viz.* In what manner Offences of this Nature are punished, it is to be observed, That most of the Statutes of *Præmunire* refer the Punishment to 16 *Rich.* 2. 5. which enacts, That those who offend against the Purport thereof *shall be put out of the King's Protection, and their Lands and Tenements, Goods and Chattels forfeited to our Lord the King: And that they be attached by their Bodies if they may be found, and brought before the King and his Council, there to answer to the Cases aforesaid, or that Process be made against them by* Præmunire facias, *in Manner as is ordained in other Statutes of Provisors.*

Sect. 46. Inasmuch as this Statute expresly saith, that such Offenders shall be put out of the King's Protection, and also the Statute of 25 *Ed.* 3. Stat. 5. Chap. 22. had farther added, *That any one might do with a Purchaser of the Provisions, therein prohibited as with the King's Enemy, and that he who should offend against such an one in Body, Lands, or Goods, should be excused,* it was formerly holden, That a Person attainted in a *Præmunire* might 1 Inst. 130.
lawfully be slain by any one, as being the King's Enemy and out of the 12 Co. 68. 3 Inst. 128.
Protection of the Laws, but the latter Opinions seem to have disapproved Bro. Cor. 197.
of this Severity; however it is expresly enacted by 5 *El.* 1. Par. 21, 22. *That it shall not be lawful to kill any Person attainted in* Præmunire, *saving such Pains of Death or other Hurt or Punishment, as heretofore might, without Danger of Law, be done upon any Person that shall send or bring into the Realm, or within the same shall execute, any Process,* &c. *from the See of* Rome.

Sect. 47. But howsoever the Law may stand in Relation to such Persons 1 Inst. 130.
as are within the Exception of this Act, it is certain that no Person whatso- See 1 El. 1. Par. 39.
ever attainted of any *Præmunire* can bring an Action for any Injury whatsoever; and that no one knowing him to be guilty can with Safety give him Aid, Comfort, or Relief.

Sect. 48. But it hath been resolved, That those general Words in the 1 Inst. 130.
Statute 16 *Rich.* 2. 5. That all the Lands and Tenements shall be forfeited, 3 Inst. 126. 2 Lev. 169.
extend not to Land entailed, after the Death of the Offender. B. 2. ch. 49. Sect. 28.

Sect. 49. Also it hath been resolved, That a Statute, by appointing that an Offender shall incur the Penalty and Danger mentioned in the 16 *Rich.* 1 Vent. 173.
2. 5. does not confine the Prosecution for the Offence to the particular Process thereby given. For the Judgment in Præmunire see B. 2. ch. 48. Sect. 9.

CHAP. XX.

Of Misprision of Treason.

Sect. 1. THE Word Misprision has not any certain Signification, but 2 R. 3. 10. b.
is generally applied to all such high Offences as are under the S. P. C. 37. b. Bro. Cor. 174.
Degree of Capital, and nearly bordering thereupon; and it is said that a Treas. 25, 31.
Misprision is contained in every Treason or Felony whatsoever, and that

one

1 H. H. P. C. 374, 652, 708.

one who is guilty of Felony or Treason may be proceeded against for a Misprision only, if the King please.

Offences of this Kind are generally said to be twofold:

1. Negative, which consist in the Omission of something which ought to be done.
2. Positive, which consist in some Misdemeanour actually committed.

1 H. H. P. C. 371, 372. H. P. C. 127. Bract. 118. b. S. P. C. 37. b. 3 Inst. 36.

Sect. 2. The negative Misprision more immediately against the King is commonly called Misprision of Treason, which is an Offence consisting in the bare Knowledge and Concealment of High Treason, (whether it be such by 25 *Ed.* 3. or subsequent Statutes) without any Degree of Assent thereto; and this is declared to be a Misprision only by 2 & 3 *Mar.* 10. But at Law any Delay in discovering High Treason, whatever Excuses the Party might have for it, was deemed an Assent to it, and consequently High Treason. [18.] ☞

H. P. C. 127. Kely. 17, 21.

Sect. 3. And at this Day if the Concealment of High Treason be accompanied with any Circumstances, which shew an Approbation thereof, it amounts to High Treason; as if one, having Notice before-hand that Persons designed to meet in order to conspire against the Government, go into their Company and hear their treasonable Consultation and conceal it; or if one, who has been once accidentally in such Company, and heard such Discourse, meet the same Company a second Time, and hear such like Discourse, and conceal it.

3 H. 7. 10. H. P. C. 127. 3 Inst. 138. 12 Co. 81, 82. Con. Dy. 296. Pl. 21. Infra B. 2. ch. 29. [a] Quære and see 1 H. H. P. C. 233, 234, 237, 613. [b] Kely. 22. H. P. C. 127. S. P. C. 37. b. [c] Kely. 22.

Sect. 4. Also whoever receives and comforts a Traitor, knowing him to be such, whether by counterfeiting of Coin [a], or otherwise, is himself a principal Traitor; for such a Receipt of a Felon makes the Receiver an Accessary to the Felony, and whatever makes an Accessary in Felony, makes a Principal in Treason.

Sect. 5. [b] Neither can a Person, who has Knowledge of a Treason, secure himself by discovering that there will be a Rising in general, without disclosing the very Persons intending to rise; nor even by discovering of these to a private Person, who is no Magistrate.

Sect. 6. [c] But it seems that one who is only told in general that there will be a Rising, without knowing any of the Persons, or Particulars of the Design, is not bound to make any Discovery at all.

1 H. H. P. C. 376, 377.

Sect. 7. There is one positive Misprision which is made Misprision of Treason by 14 *El.* 3. by which it is enacted, That those who forge foreign Coin, not current here, are guilty of Misprision of Treason, &c.

CHAP. XXI.

Of Contempts against the King's Courts.

OTHER positive Misprisions more immediately against the King seem reducible to the following Heads:

1. Contempts against his Palace or Courts of Justice.
2. Contempts against his Prerogative.

3. Contempts against his Person or Government.
4. Contempts against his Title.

Sect. 1. And first, Contempts against the King's Palace, *&c.* have always been looked upon as very high Misprisions, and by the ancient Law before the Conquest, Fighting in the King's Palace was a capital Offence; and by 33 *H.* 8. 12. Par. 7. Malicious Striking in the King's Palace, whereby any Blood shall be shed, is punishable with the Loss of Hand, perpetual Imprisonment, and Fine at the King's Pleasure.

3 Inst. 140. Poph. 206.

Sect. 2. It seems questionable from the Construction of this whole Act, and the general Tenor of the Law-Books, whether Striking in a Palace, wherein the King is not at the Time actually resident, be within the Statute; and it is said that the Instance which is given in the third Institute, of a Person's Hand being cut off for Striking in the Tower, is not warranted by the Record.

See the first Paragraph of the Act. S. P. C. 38. a. Bro. Pain. 16. Dal. cap. 90. 6 Mod. 75, 76. 3 Inst. 140.

Sect. 3. However it is certain, That by the Common Law which continues to this Day, Striking in *Westminster-Hall*, where the King is only present, as represented by his Judges, and by their Administration distributing Justice to his People, is more penal than any Striking in another Place in his actual Presence; for the latter is not punished with the Loss of Hand, unless some Blood be drawn, nor even then with the Loss of Lands or Goods: But if a Person draw his Sword on any Judge, in the Presence of the Court of King's Bench, Chancery, Common Pleas, or Exchequer, or before the Justices of Assize, or Oyer and Terminer, whether he strike or not, or strike a Juror, or any other Person, with or without a Weapon, he shall lose his Hand and his Goods, and the Profits of his Lands during Life, and suffer perpetual Imprisonment, [a] if the Indictment lay the Offence as done *coram Domino Rege*.

2 Inst. 549. 3 Inst. 140. S. P. C. 38. a. Dal. ch. 90. Cro. El. 405. 41 Aff. 25. 22 E. 3. 18. a. Dy. 188. Pl. 10. See B. 2. Ch. 48. Sect. 11. Dalis. 23. 2 Rol. Ab. 76. Pl. 2. 3. H. P. C. 131, 132.

Sect. 4. [b] Neither can one who is guilty of such Offence excuse the same, by shewing that the Person so struck by him gave the first Assault.

1 Keb. 751. 12 Co. 71.

Sect. 5. [c] Also he who rescues a Prisoner from any of the Courts abovementioned, without striking a Blow, shall forfeit his Goods and the Profits of his Lands, and suffer Imprisonment during Life, but not lose his Hand, because he did not strike.

[a] Owen 120. Cro. Eliz. 405. [b] 1 Lev. 106. 6 Mod. 172. Noy 104. Cro. Ja. 367.

Sect. 6. [d] And he who makes an Affray in the Palace-Yard near the said Courts, but out of their View, shall be imprisoned during the King's Pleasure, and severely fined, but not lose his Hand.

[c] 22 E. 3. 13. a. 3 Inst. 141. con. H. P. C. 131.

Sect. 7. And not only those who are guilty of such an actual Violence, but also those who disturb such Courts by threatening or reproachful Words to any Judge sitting in them, are guilty of a High Misprision; and in the Time of *Edward* the First, one *William de Bruce*, who, upon hearing Judgment given against him in the Exchequer, said to the Chief Baron, *Roger, Roger, Thou hast had thy Will of me, which of a long Time thou hast sought, and I will remember it*, was for these Words imprisoned during the King's Pleasure, and ordered to walk from the King's Bench to the Exchequer, bareheaded and ungirt, and to ask Forgiveness, *&c.* And in the Time of *Charles* the First, one *Harrison*, for rushing into the Court of Common Pleas, and saying to Justice *Hutton* sitting there, *I do accuse Mr. Justice* Hutton *of High Treason*, was fined five thousand Pounds, and imprisoned during the King's Pleasure, and ordered to go to all the Courts of *Westminster-Hall* with a Paper on his Head, shewing his Offence, and to make his Submission, *&c.* And these Cases are the more remarkable, because in the first, the Offender was of a very honourable Family; and in

[d] Cro. El. 405. Cro. Ca. 373. Sir W. Jon. 345. Owen 120. 3 Inst. 142. Moor 819.

Cro. Ca. 503, 504. Hutt. 131. Poph. 135.

the ſecond, a Bachelor of Divinity, and yet condemned to ſuch corporal Puniſhment, the loweſt of which is in Judgment of Law higher than the greateſt Fine whatever.

Hob. 220. Moore 563. Poph. 135.

Sect. 8. Alſo all who reflect on the Juſtice or Honour of thoſe High Courts ſeem to be indictable and highly finable; as if one charge an Exemplification under the Great Seal to be contrary to the Original.

1 Lev. 107. 1 Keb. 558.

Sect. 9. Alſo he who gives another the Lie in *Weſtminſter-Hall*, ſitting the Courts, ſhall be bound to his Good Behaviour.

3 Inſt. 141. 12 Co. 71.

Sect. 10. And he, who makes an Affray in the Preſence of any of the King's inferior Courts of Juſtice, is highly finable, but not puniſhable with Loſs of Hand, &c.

[a] Cro. E. 78. 2 R. A. 78. Pl. 4. 6. [b] 1 Sid. 144. con. 2 Rol. Ab. 78. Pl. 4. [c] Owen 113. Moore 470. Cro. El. 581. [d] Raym. 68.

Sect. 11. And he who ſpeaks contemptuous and reproachful Words to the Judge of ſuch a Court in Execution of his Office is [a] immediately finable by ſuch Judge, or, as ſome ſay, may be [b] indicted, &c. as [c] if one give the Lie to a Judge of a Court-Leet in the Face of the Court, or being [d] admoniſhed by him to pull of his Hat, ſay, *I do not Value what you can do*, or tell him in the Face of the Court that he is [e] forſworn, or call [f] him Fool, &c. or [g] ſay, *If I can not have Juſtice here, I will have it elſewhere.*

1 Keb. 451, 465. [e] 2 Rol. Ab. 78. Pl. 4. [f] Cro. El. 78. Moore 247. [g] 1 Sid. 144. 1 Keb. 508. [h] 2 Rol. Ab. 78. Pl. 3. 1 Rol. Re. 245.

Sect. 12. And it was formerly [h] holden that a Man might be indicted for a Slander of the Juſtice of the Nation, by reflecting on a Sentence given in any Court Eccleſiaſtical or Temporal, whether directly, as where one ſaid that ſuch a Sentence given by the High Commiſſion Court, was againſt Law; or obliquely, as where one ſaid that ſuch a Sentence was juſt, but that the Teſtimonies on which it was founded were falſe, or the *Affidavits* equivocating.

Hob. 202. Moore 819.

Sect. 13. But it ſeems the better Opinion at this Day, That a Man cannot be indicted for any ſcandalous or contemptuous Words ſpoken of or to ſuch Officers, not being in the actual Execution of their Office; for ſuch an Offence ſeems rather to proceed from ill Breeding than a Contempt of the Government; and tho' it may be a Cauſe to bind a Man to his Good

1 Ven. 10.

Behaviour, yet it does not ſeem to be of ſuch Conſequence as to be a ſufficient Ground for a publick Proſecution, as for an Offence againſt the common Peace, &c. And agreeably hereto it hath been reſolved, That a

[i] 1 Mod. 35. 2 Keb. 594. [k] 5 Mod. 203. [l] 2 Keb. 494. 5 Mod. 204. 2 Ven. 16. [m] Queen and Wrightſon. Sal. 696. [n] Queen and Soley. Sal. 697. [o] Queen and Legaſley. [p] Queen and Broxham. [q] 6 Mod. 124. Salk. 697. [r] 1 Ven. 10.

Man ſhall not be indicted for ſaying, [i] *That whenever a Burgeſs of ſuch a Town puts on his Gown, Satan enters into him*; or, [k] *That the Mayor and Aldermen of ſuch a Town are as great Villains as any that rob on the Highway*; or, [l] *That the Juſtices of Peace underſtand no more of the Statutes of Exciſe than this Jug, nor one of twenty of the Parliament-Men who made them*; or [m] *That ſuch a Juſtice of Peace is a Fool, and Aſs, and a Coxcomb, for making ſuch a Warrant, and underſtands no more Law than a Slickbill*; or, [n] *That he is not fit to be a Juſtice of Peace; for that he will do right or wrong, according as his Affections lead him*; or, [o] *That ſuch an Order is a Numſcul Order, and that the Juſtice deſerves to be hanged who made it*; or, [p] *That ſuch a Juſtice of Peace is a forſworn Wretch, and that he will fling his Purſe at him*; or for [q] ſaying to a Mayor of a Town, *You, Mr. Mayor, I do not care a Fart for you; You, Mr. Mayor, are a Rogue and a Raſcal*; or, for [r] ſaying, *That the Juſtices of Peace have nothing to do with the Exciſe.*

Sect. 14. And not only thoſe who diſturb the Adminiſtration of Juſtice by direct Contempts offered to the King's Courts, but alſo all ſuch as are guilty of any injurious Treatment of thoſe Perſons who are under the more immediate Protection of thoſe Courts, are highly puniſhable by

3 Inſt. 142. H. P. C. 131. Latch 220.

Fine and Impriſonment; as if a Man aſſault or threaten his Adverſary for ſuing him, or a Counſellor or Attorney for being imployed againſt him, or or a Juror for giving a Verdict against him, or a Gaoler for keeping a Prisoner in safe Custody.

2 Rol. Ab. 76. D. 2.

Sect. 15. Also all who endeavour to stifle the Truth, and prevent the due Execution of Justice, are highly punishable, as those who being examined before the Privy Council concerning their Knowledge of a Crime, whereof a third Person is accused, disclose what passed in such Examination, in order to suppress a farther Discovery; and also all those who dissuade, or but endeavour to dissuade a Witness from giving Evidence against a Person indicted, &c. or who advise a Prisoner to stand Mute on his Arraignment, &c. And it was anciently holden, that if one of the Grand Inquest discover to any Persons indicted the Evidence against them, he is an Accessary to the Offence, whether Treason or Felony; and at this Day it is agreed, that he is guilty of a high Misprision, punishable by Fine and Imprisonment.

Hob. 271. Raym. 376. Trial per Pais 164. H. P. C. 131. 2 Rol. Ab. 77. F. 2. S. P. C. 11. A. 36. B. 27 Ass. 63. Bro. Cor. 113. H. P. C. 131. 3 Inst. 22, 106. See 3 Leon. 207.

CHAP. XXII.

Of Contempts against the King's Prerogative.

Sect. 1. Contempts against the King's Prerogative are of so various a Nature, that they cannot well be reduced to any certain Heads; however, the Principal of them seem to come under the following Particulars:

1. Refusing to assist the King for the Good of the Publick.
2. Preferring the Interests of a foreign Prince to that of our own.
3. Disobeying the King's lawful Commands or Prohibitions.

Sect. 2. First therefore, It is a high Offence for any Subject to deny the King that Assistance for the Good of the Publick, either in his Councils or Wars, which by the Law he is bound to give him; as for a Peer not to [a] come to the Parliament at the Day of Summons, or to [b] depart from thence without the King's Licence; or for a [c] Privy Counsellor to refuse to give his Advice on an Affair of State; or for any [d] private Subject to refuse to serve the King in Person, if he be able, or to find another, if he not able, in the Defence of the Realm, against Rebels and foreign Invaders; or, as some say, to refuse to serve the King for Pay in his Wars abroad.

[a] Moore 778. Pl. 1080. Noy 102. [b] S. P. C. 38. A. Fitz. Coro. 161. [c] 2 Rol. Ab. 211. A. 1. [d] 2 Rol. A. 165. X. 166. Bro. Tenure 44, 73. See 1 Ed. 3. ch. 5. 18 Ed. 3. ch. 7. 25 Ed. 3. ch. 8. 4 H. 4. ch. 13. 11 H. 7. ch. 1 & 18.

Sect. 3. Secondly, It is so high an Offence to prefer the Interests of a foreign Prince to that of our own, that it is criminal to do any Thing which may but incline a Man so to do; as to receive a Pension from a foreign Prince without the Leave of our King.

Cro. Ca. 11. Cromp. Jurisd. 83. b. 84. 3 Inst. 144.

Sect. 4. Thirdly, It is also a high Crime to disobey the King's lawful Commands or Prohibitions; as by obstinately refusing Obedience to his Writs; or contemning a Summons from his Council to appear before them; or not answering such Questions in relation to a Matter wherein the Interest of the State is concerned, as shall be proposed by the Privy Council; or refusing to give Evidence to a Grand Jury concerning a Crime (for which [e] the Court may impose an immediate Fine); or not returning from beyond Sea upon the King's Letters to that Purpose; for which the Offender's Lands shall be seized till he return, and when he does

Cro. Ca. 153. Cro. Ca. 257. Hob. 235. 12 Co. 94. [e] Sal. 278. Pl. 2. Dy. 176. Pl. 30, 31, 128. Pl. 61, 75. b. Moore 109, 779. Lane 43. 3 Inst. 179. Savil 7, 8.

2 Rol. Ab. 208. O. does return he shall be fined) or assembling at a Turnament against the King's express Prohibition; or going beyond Sea against the King's Will F. N. B. 85. 1 Chan. Cases 116. expresly signified, either by the Writ, *Ne exeas Regnum*, (which may be directed as well to a Layman as to a Clergyman, and on the Suggestion of 3 Inst. 178. a private as well as of a publick Matter) or under the Great or Privy Seal or Signet, or by Proclamation.

Cro. Eliz. 655. Book 2. C. 26. Sect. 2. *Sect.* 5. Also every Contempt of a Statute is indictable, if no other Punishment be limited.

CHAP. XXIII.

Of Contempts against the King's Person or Government.

Sect. 1. ALL Contempts against the King's Person or Government are very highly criminal, and punishable with Fine and Imprisonment, and sometimes with the Pillory, by the Discretion of the Judges, upon Consideration of all the Circumstances of the Case; but inasmuch as it is generally obvious to common Sense, in what Cases and to what Degree a Man is guilty of this Offence, and it would be endless to enumerate all the Particulars, I shall content my self with glancing at some of the most general Heads; as,

Cro. Ca. 168. 2 Keb. 336. *Sect.* 2. I. The charging the Government with Oppression or weak Administration; as by saying, *That Merchants are screwed up here in* England *more than in* Turkey; or, *That it is a good World when beggarly Priests are made Lords*, &c.

5 Mod. 363. *Sect.* 3. II. The doing an Act which impliedly encourages Rebellion; as by absolving Persons at the Gallows, who being condemned for High Treason, shew no Sign of Repentance, but persist in justifying the Fact; 3 Mod. 52. or by drinking to the pious Memory of a Person executed for High Treason.

Cro. Ja. 37. Moore 756. Noy 101. *Sect.* 4. III. Endeavouring to frighten the King into a Change of his Measures with Threats of the Uneasiness of his Subjects; as by subscribing a Petition to him, in which it is intimated, that if it be denied, many Thousands will be discontented, *&c.*

Cro. Ja. 38. *Sect.* 5. IV. Spreading false Rumours concerning the King's Intentions; as that he designs to grant a Toleration to Papists, *&c.*

Noy 105. *Sect.* 6. V. Charging him with a Breach of his Coronation Oath.

See Cro. Ca. 117, &c. *Sect.* 7. VI. Speaking contemptuously of him; as by cursing him, *&c.* or giving out that he wants Wisdom, Valour or Steadiness; or in general, doing any Thing which may lessen him in the Esteem of his Subjects, and weaken his Government, or raise Jealousies between him and his People.

1 Syd. 143 Pl 23. *Sect.* 8. Also it is said to be an Offence, for which a Man may be indicted, to refuse in a foreign Port to pay the usual Customs, because it may cause a Breach between our King and the King of the Country. [19.] ☞

CHAP. XXIV.

Of Contempts against the King's Title.

CONTEMPTS against the King's Title are of two Kinds,

1. Denying his Title.
2. Refusing to take the Oaths required by Law for the Support of his Government.

Sect. 1. The first Offence of this Kind, *viz.* That of denying the King's Title, hath by some been carried so high as to be adjudged an Overt-Act of Compassing his Death; however, it is certainly most highly criminal, and punishable with Fine and Imprisonment, and also such infamous corporal Punishment, as to the Discretion of the Court shall seem proper, according to the Heinousness of the Crime and the Circumstances of the Parties; as if a Man in Writing or Discourse shall maintain that the King is an Usurper, or that another hath a better Title to the Crown, &c. for such like Insinuations manifestly tend to raise Tumults and Disorders in the State, and to alienate the Affections of the People from the Prince, and incline them to favour the Pretensions of another; and it is highly presumptuous for private Persons to intermeddle with Matters of so high a Nature; and it will be impossible to preserve the Peace of a Government, unless Subjects will quietly submit themselves to those whom Providence has placed over them, and prefer the publick Good to their own private Inclinations and Opinions: For otherwise, whenever the Title to the Crown shall happen to be contested, it will be impossible to end the Difference without perpetual Civil Broils and Dissensions, and the Prince who prevails will be tempted to esteem those of the contrary Party rather as Enemies than subjects, If he finds them ready and desirous to lay hold of all Opportunities to disturb his Government, and shake off their forced Obedience. And since there is no Tribunal but that of Heaven, to which Princes can appeal for the Decision of their Titles, when that seems so far to have declared in Favour of one as to give him quiet Possession of the Throne, the publick Peace, which is the End of all Government, requires a dutiful Submission to him; and it is the highest Madness to give up that Ease and Security which we may enjoy from a peaceful Obedience, in Exchange for that Disorder, Uncertainty, and Bloodshed, which cannot but be expected from an Attempt to wrest the Sceptre out of the Hands of our Prince; and it is the highest Ingratitude to make no other Return but Disloyalty and Rebellion, for all the Happiness we can enjoy under a just Administration; and it is the greatest of Absurdities to think that the Good of the Community, for the sake of which all Government was instituted, ought not to be preferred before the disputed Title of a particular Person or Family: All we can desire from Government, is the secure Enjoyment of what we may call our own, and whether this, or that Competitor to the Crown be the Instrument of this Happiness to us, seems little to concern us. Let the Title of one out of Possession of the Throne be never so plausible, it must have

Yelv. 107. 2 Rol. Re. 90. Palm. 424.

its original Foundation from ſome poſitive Law; which, when it cannot take Effect without involving a Nation in Diſcord and Confuſion, the avoiding whereof is the very End of all Laws, it muſt give way to the publick Neceſſity of the State; for there can be no human Inſtitution whatſoever, but muſt be limited by this implicit Reſerve from the firſt Principles of Reaſon, that where-ever the Execution of it ſhall be abſolutely inconſiſtent with the Happineſs of the People for whoſe ſake it was ordained, it ought ſo far to be ſuſpended.

Sect. 2. For this and many other ſuch like Reaſons, the Law has always had a moſt tender Regard for the Security of the Prince in Poſſeſſion of the Crown, and as it has made it High Treaſon to compaſs his Death, *&c.* as appears from Chap. 17. Sect. 11, *&c.* ſo hath it alſo made it highly Penal in any inferiour Degree to diſturb or diſquiet his Government.

As to the ſecond Kind of Offences of this Nature, *viz.* That of refuſing to take the Oaths required by Law for the Support of the King's Government; I ſhall conſider,

1. The Offence of refuſing the Oaths required for this Purpoſe by the Common Law.

2. The Offence of refuſing the Oaths required by Statute.

Finch of Law 241, 242. *Sect.* 3. As to the firſt Particular, it ſeems to be a high Contempt at the Common Law to refuſe to take the Oath of Allegiance to the King, which all Laymen above the Age of twelve Years are bound to take at the Torn or Court-Leet, *&c.* and ſurely nothing can be more unreaſonable than to deny the King, whoſe Government we are happy under, all proper Aſſurances of our Fidelity to him; for how can we expect to enjoy the Privileges of Subjects from one to whom we refuſe to acknowledge our ſelves Subjects, or hope for Protection from one, whom we provoke to eſteem us as his Enemies, or blame that Government for treating us as Malecontents, to which we give ſo juſt a Cauſe to ſuſpect our Fidelity? If we conſult the Law of God, that will tell us, *That the Powers that be are ordained of God*; If we will hear the Voice of Reaſon, that will convince us, that not only the Peace and Safety of the Community, but alſo our own Preſervation requires us to pay a dutiful Obedience to thoſe who govern us; and can we think it unlawful to engage our ſelves to do what it is our Duty to do? If we will conſult the Practice of all Nations, that will ſhew us, that even Conqueſt, which is the weakeſt of all Titles, has always been eſteemed to give the Conqueror ſuch a Right to the Obedience of the Conquered, that upon his taking them into his Protection, they have in all Ages been ready to promiſe a reciprocal Obedience; and if we will conſult our own Laws, we ſhall find them to direct us to pay our Allegiance to the King who governs us, as has been fully proved in the Chapter of High Treaſon.

As to the ſecond Kind of Offences of this Nature, *viz.* That of refuſing the Oaths required by Statute for the Support of the Government, I ſhall conſider,

1. The Offence of refuſing the Oaths of Allegiance and Supremacy.

2. The Offence of refuſing the Oath of Abjuration.

Sect. 4. As to the firſt of theſe Offences, *viz.* That of refuſing the Oaths of Allegiance and Supremacy, which ſince the Reformation of Religion have been thought neceſſary to be required from all Perſons, eſpecially from thoſe who are intruſted with an Office, in order to ſecure our Princes from the Intrigues of Popes, who have often taken upon them to diſpence with Oaths of Allegiance made to ſuch Princes whom they are pleaſed to call Hereticks, and to perſwade the People that they may lawfully depoſe thoſe who have ſo far incurred the Diſpleaſure of the Biſhop of *Rome*, as to be excommunicated by him, it having been ſhewn already in Chap. 8. under what Penalties Officers are bound to take the ſaid Oaths and in Chap. 19. Sect. 27, *&c.* how far all Perſons whatſoever are compellable to take them under Pain of incurring a *Præmunire*, I ſhall only take Notice in this Place, of the Method of Proceeding on 1 *Will. & Mar.* 8. by which it is enacted, *That Perſons refuſing the ſaid Oaths being tendered to them by Perſons lawfully authorized to tender the ſame, ſhall be committed by the Perſons making ſuch a Tender for three Months, unleſs they ſhall pay ſuch Sum not exceeding* 40 *s. as the Perſons who ſhall make ſuch Tender ſhall require of them, and if they refuſe again at the End of the three Months, that they ſhall be impriſoned ſix Months, or pay a Sum not above ten nor under five Pounds, and alſo find Sureties for their good Behaviour and Appearance at the next Aſſizes, where if they refuſe the ſaid Oaths, they ſhall be incapable of any Office, and continue bound to their good Behaviour, and if they refuſe the Declaration mentioned in* 30 Car. 2. *they ſhall ſuffer as Popiſh Recuſants convict.*

Sect. 5. It ſeems to be the Intention of this Statute, to give the Government an Election to proceed either on the mild Method therein preſcribed, or the more ſevere one appointed by the former Laws, according to the Circumſtances of the Caſe, and Quality of the Offender, *&c.*

Sect. 6. As to the ſecond Offence of this Kind, *viz.* That of refuſing the Oath of Abjuration, the ſame depends on thoſe Laws, which the Nation has been of late under a Neceſſity of eſtabliſhing, by adding a new Limitation to the Law relating to the Succeſſion of the Crown, excluding all Papiſts from a Poſſibility of inheriting it; who, if they be true to their Engagements to their own Religion, cannot but be falſe to thoſe they may make to ours, and can never be expected to execute thoſe Laws, which they cannot but think void, as being repugnant to the Laws of God; or to defend that Faith which they think damnable; or to obſerve thoſe Oaths, which ſeem to them to have been ordained for the Support of Irreligion. And from theſe Conſiderations they have been diſabled from inheriting the Crown, it ſeeming of abſolute Neceſſity in our preſent Circumſtances for the good of the Community, to make ſuch an Alteration in Law, which like all other human Laws depending meerly on the Policy of Men, ſeems to have nothing in it ſo ſacred as to oblige the People unalterably to abide by it to the Hazard of their common Safety, Peace and Happineſs, for the ſake whereof it was at firſt ordained: For ſurely, there cannot be ſo much Danger to the common Good from ſuch an Alteration, as muſt needs follow from the Government of a Prince, whoſe Conſcience is under the Influence of thoſe, who are implacable Enemies to the Religion of his Country, and who thinks himſelf bound by his Duty to God and his Church to promote that Intereſt, which his People think themſelves under the like Obligations to oppoſe: From which unhappy Circumſtances nothing can be expected but endleſs Factions and Diſcords, and irreconcileable Jealouſies and Diſtruſts between Prince and People, which, if they break not into an open Rupture, will at leaſt be attended with ſuch Convulſions and uneaſineſſes, as render a State of Government ſcarce one Degree more ſecure than a State of Anarchy and Confuſion.

Sect. 7. For the remedying of ſuch like Inconveniences, it having been thought proper to exclude all Papiſts from the Crown, it was likewiſe thought expedient to ſecure the preſent Settlement, by obliging all Officers, *&c.* to take the Oath of Abjuration, as to which it is enacted

by

by 13 *Will.* 3. c. 6. and 1 *Geor.* 1. St. 2. c. 13. *That all Persons who shall be admitted,* &c. *into any Office Civil or Military, (not being an Office of Inheritance, executed by a lawful Deputy) or shall receive any Pay, Salary, Fee or Wages, by Reason of any Patent or Grant from the King, or that have a Command or Place of Trust under the King,* &c. *or shall be admitted into any Service or Imployment in the King's Houshold or Family, or of his Royal Highness* George *Prince of* Wales, *or her Royal Highness the Princess of* Wales, *or their Issue, and all Ecclesiastical Persons, Heads or Governors, of what Denomination soever, and all other Members of Colleges and Halls in any University, that shall be of the Foundation, or enjoy any Exhibition, being of, or as soon as they shall attain the Age of eighteen Years, and all Persons teaching or reading to Pupils in any University or elsewhere, and all School-masters and Ushers, and all Preachers and Teachers of separate Congregations, High or Chief Constables, and every Person who shall act as Serjeant at Law, Counsellor at Law, Barrafter, Advocate, Attorney, Solicitor, Proctor, Clerk, or Notary, by practising in any Manner as such, in any Court or Courts whatsoever within that Part of* Great Britain *called* England, *shall within three Months after they shall be admitted into, or enter upon any such Preferment, Benefice, Office, or Place, or come into such Capacity, or take upon them such Practice, Imployment or Business, take and subscribe the Oaths of Allegiance, Supremacy and Abjuration, at one of the Courts at* Westminster, *or at the General Quarter-Sessions of the Peace where they shall reside, or otherwise they shall be* ipso facto *adjudged incapable, and disabled in Law, to have, occupy, or enjoy the said Offices,* &c. *and if they shall by themselves, or Deputy or Trustee, execute any the said Offices,* &c. *and shall be thereof convict,* &c. *they shall be disabled to prosecute any Suit at Law or Equity, or to be Guardians, Executors, or Administrators, or capable of any Legacy or Deed of Gift, or to be in any Office within this Realm, or to vote at any Election for Members of Parliament, and shall forfeit five hundred Pounds,* &c.

Sect. 8. And it is farther enacted by the said Statute, *That any two Justices of the Peace, or any other Person or Persons who shall be by the King for that Purpose specially appointed by Order in the Privy Council or by Commission under the Great Seal, may administer and tender the said Oaths to any Person whatsoever, whom they shall suspect to be dangerous or disaffected; and that if any Person, to whom the said Oaths shall be so tendered, shall neglect or refuse to take the same; or if any Person being summoned by the said Justices,* &c. *in order to take the said Oaths either in proper Person, or by Notice left at his Place of Abode with one of the Family, shall neglect or refuse to appear,* &c. *such Refusal shall be certified at Sessions,* &c. *and from thence to the King's Bench or Chancery,* &c. *and every such Person so neglecting to take the said Oaths, shall be adjudged a Popish Recusant convict,* &c.

Sect. 9. And it is farther enacted by the said Statute, *That if any Member of either University shall neglect to take and subscribe the said Oaths according to the Intent of the said Act, or to produce a Certificate thereof, under the Hand of some proper Officer of the respective Court, and cause the same to be entered in the Register of the proper College or Hall, within one Month after his having taken and subscribed the said Oaths; and if the Persons in whom the Right of Election of such Member shall be, do neglect to elect some fitting Person in his stead within twelve Months,* &c. *that then the King may, under the Great Seal or Sign Manual, nominate some fitting Person qualified according to the local Statutes of such College,* &c. *and if the Head of any College,* &c. *shall neglect to admit such Nominee, by the Space of ten Days after such Admission shall be demanded of him, that then the local Visitor shall admit the said Nominee; and if such Visitor shall neglect or refuse to admit such Person within the Space of one Month after the same shall be demanded, that then the Court of King's-*

Bench may issue a Writ of Mandamus *to such Visitor to admit such Nominee*, &c.

Sect. 10. And it is farther enacted by the said Statute, *That no Peer shall vote or make his Proxy, or sit in the House of Peers during any Debate, and that no Member of the House of Commons shall vote or sit during any Debate in the said House, after the Speaker is chosen, until he shall have taken the said Oaths*, &c. *under Pain of the Disabilities and Forfeitures above mentioned*, &c.

CHAP. XXV.

Of Felony.

OFfences more immediately against the Subject are either Capital or not Capital.

The Capital are either by the Common Law or by Statute.

Sect. 1. Those by the Common Law come generally under the Title of Felony, which, *ex vi Termini*, signifies *quodlibet crimen felleo animo perpetratum*, and can be expressed by no Periphrasis, or Word equivalent, without the Word *Felonicè*. Vide Spelm. Gloss. verb. Felonia. 1 Inst. 391.

Sect. 2. Felony is said to be included in High Treason, and consequently a Pardon of Felony discharges an Indictment of High Treason, if it want the Word *Proditorie*. H. P. C. 11. 3 H. 7. 10. a. 3 Inst. 15.

Sect. 3. It is always accompanied with an evil Intention, and therefore shall not be imputed to a meer Mistake or Mis-animadversion, as where Persons break open a Door, in order to execute a Warrant, which will not justify such a Proceeding; *Affectio enim tua nomen imponit operi tuo; item crimen non contrahitur nisi nocendi voluntas intercedat.* But the bare Intention to commit a Felony is so very criminal, That at the Common Law it was punishable as Felony, where it missed its Effect thro' some Accident no Way lessening the Guilt of the Offender; but it seems agreed at this Day, That Felony shall not be imputed to a bare Intention to commit it, yet it is certain that the Party may be very severely fined for such an Intention. Brac. lib. 1. ca. 4. S. P. C. 17. a. 27. b. 1 Lev. 146. 1 Sid. 230, 231. 5 Mod. 206.

CHAP. XXVI.

Of casual Death and of Deodands.

OF Capital Offences at Common Law more immediately against the Subject, there are three principal Kinds:

1. Such as are committed against his Life.
2. Such as are against his Goods.
3. Such as are against his Habitation.

Sect. 1. There is another mix'd Kind of Capital Offences, which conſiſts in the Hindrance of the due Proceſs of publick Juſtice, which I ſhall conſider in the ſecond Book, wherein I ſhall treat of the Means of bringing Offenders to their due Puniſhment.

Bract. lib. 3. cap. 4.

Sect. 2. Offences againſt the Life of a Man come under the general Name of Homicide, which in our Law ſignifies the killing of a Man by a Man.

1 H. H. P. C. 471, 472. Crom. 31. a. 1 H. H. P. C. 419.

Sect. 3. But before I treat hereof, it may not be improper to conſider the killing of a Man merely *per infortunium*, occaſioned by ſome ~~Animal or~~ Thing without Life, without the Default or Procurement of another Man, as where one is killed by a Fall from a Horſe or Cart, *&c.* which, though it be not properly Homicide, nor puniſhable as a Crime, yet is taken Notice of by the Law, as far as the Nature of the Thing will bear, in order to raiſe the greater Abhorrence of Murder, and the unhappy Inſtrument or Occaſion of ſuch Death is called a Deodand, and forfeited to the King, in order to be diſpoſed of in pious Uſes by the King's Almoner; as alſo are all ſuch Weapons whereby one Man kills another.

S. P. C. 21. a. 3 Inſt. 58. H. P. C. 34. Pult. 125. a. Dal. cap. 97. 1 H. H. P. C. 422. 2 Keb. 719, 806.

Sect. 4. It ſeems clearly ſettled, That a Horſe, *&c.* killing an Infant within the Age of Diſcretion, are as much forfeited as if he were of Age: But formerly it was holden, That a Horſe or Cart, by a Fall from which an Infant was ſlain, were not forfeited, perhaps for this Reaſon, becauſe the Misfortune might rather ſeem owing to the Indiſcretion of the Infant than any Default in the Horſe, *&c.* But this Diſtinction has not been allowed of late; for the Law does not ground the Forfeiture on any Default in the Things forfeited, ſince it extends it to Things without Life, to which 'tis plain, that no Manner of Fault can be imputed.

S. P. C. 20. b. Pult. 124. b. 1 Sid. 206, 207. 1 Lev. 136. Raym. 97.

Sect. 5. Alſo by the Opinion of our ancient Authors, Things fixed to a Freehold, as the Wheel of a Mill, a Bell hanging in a Steeple, *&c.* may be Deodands, but by the latter Reſolutions they cannot, unleſs they were ſevered before the Accident happened.

6 Mod. 187. 1 Keb. 723, 745. S. P. C. 21. Pult. 125. a. 3 Inſt. 58. H. P. C. 33. 1 H. H. P. C. 422. Cro. Jac. 483. 2 Rol. Re. 23. Popham 136. Salk. 220. S. P. C. 20. b. 21. 3 Inſt. 58. Pult. 125. See S. P. C. 20. b. & Quære. Pult. 124. b. Salk. 220.

Sect. 6. However, as it is agreed by all, a Ship in ſalt Water, whether in the open Sea or within the Body of a County, from which a Man falls and is drowned, is not forfeited, becauſe Perſons at Sea are continually expoſed to ſo many Perils, that the Law imputes ſuch Misfortunes happeing there, rather to them than to the Ship. Alſo it ſeems clear, That when a Man riding on a Horſe over a River is drowned through the Violence of the Stream, the Horſe is not forfeited, becauſe not that, but the Waters cauſed his Death: But it is ſaid, That a Ship by a Fall from which a Man is drowned in the freſh Water ſhall be forfeited, but not the Merchandize therein, becauſe they no way contribute to his Death. And by the ſame Reaſon it ſeems, That if a Man riding on the Shafts of a Waggon fall to the Ground and break his Neck, the Horſes and Waggon only are forfeited, and not the Loading, becauſe it no way contributed to his Death; for which Cauſe, where a Thing not in Motion cauſes a Man's Death, that Part thereof only which is the immediate Cauſe is forfeited. As where one climbing upon the Wheel of a Cart while it ſtands ſtill, falls from it and dies of the Fall, the Wheel only is forfeited: But if he had been killed by a Bruiſe from one of the Wheels being in Motion, the Loading alſo would have been forfeited, becauſe the Weight thereof made the Hurt the greater; and it is a general Rule, That where-ever the Thing which is the Occaſion of a Man's Death is in Motion at the Time, not only that Part thereof, which immediately wounds him, but all Things which move together with it, and help to make the Wound more dangerous are forfeited alſo; for the ☞ Rule is, *Omnia quæque movent ad Mortem, ſunt Deodanda.* [20.]

Sect. 7. In all theſe Caſes, if the Party wounded die not of his Wound within a Year and a Day after he received it, there ſhall be nothing forfeited, for the Law does not look on ſuch a Wound as the Cauſe of a Man's Death, after which he lives ſo long: But if the Party die within that Time, the Forfeiture ſhall have Relation to the Wound given, and cannot be ſaved by any Alienation or other Act whatſoever in the mean Time. H. P. C. 55. S. P. C. 21 b. Dalt. ca. 97. Pl. Com. 260. Kellw. 68. b.

Sect. 8. However, nothing can be forfeited as a Deodand, nor ſeized as ſuch, till it be found by the Coroner's Inqueſt to have cauſed a Man's Death; but after ſuch Inquiſition, the Sheriff is anſwerable for the Value of it, and may levy the ſame on the Town where it fell, and therefore the ☞ Inqueſt ought to find the Value of it. [21.] 5 Co. 110. b. Co.Li. 115.a. Dal. cap. 97. S. P. C. 21.a. Pult. 125. a. See 4 Ed. 1. de Officio Coronatoris. 1 H.H. P. C. 418, 419.

CHAP. XXVII.

Of Felo de ſe.

HOmicide properly ſo called, is either againſt a Man's own Life, or that of another.

In treating of Homicide againſt a Man's own Life, I ſhall conſider:

1. In what Caſes a Man ſhall be ſaid to be a *Felo de ſe.*
2. What he ſhall forfeit for this Offence.

Sect. 1. As to the firſt Point, I ſhall take it for granted, That in this as well as in all other Felonies, the Offender ought to be of the Age of Diſcretion, and *Compos Mentis*, and therefore that an Infant killing himſelf under the Age of Diſcretion, or a Lunatick during his Lunacy, cannot be a *Felo de ſe.* 1 H. H. P.C. 411, 412. Crom.30.a.b. 31. a. H. P. C. 28. Dal. cap. 92. 3 Inſt. 54.

Sect. 2. But here I cannot but take Notice of a ſtrange Notion, which has unaccountably prevailed of late, That every one who kills himſelf, muſt be *Non Compos* of Courſe; for it is ſaid to be impoſſible, That a Man in his Senſes ſhould do a Thing ſo contrary to Nature and all Senſe and Reaſon. 3 Mod. 100.

Sect. 3. If this Argument be good, Self-Murder can be no Crime, for a Madman can be guilty of none: But it is wonderful that the Repugnancy to Nature and Reaſon, which is the higheſt Aggravation of this Offence, ſhould be thought to make it impoſſible to be any Crime at all, which cannot but be the neceſſary Conſequence of this Poſition, That none but a Madman can be guilty of it. May it not with as much Reaſon be argued, That the Murder of a Child or of a Parent is againſt Nature and Reaſon, and conſequently that no Man in his Senſes can commit it? But has a Man therefore no Uſe of his Reaſon, becauſe he acts againſt right Reaſon? Why may not the Paſſions of Grief and Diſcontent tempt a Man knowingly to act againſt the Principles of Nature and Reaſon in this Caſe, as thoſe of Love, Hatred and Revenge, and ſuch like, are too well known to do in others?

Sect. 4. However our Laws have always had ſuch an Abhorrence of this Crime, that not only he who kills himſelf with a deliberate and direct Purpoſe of ſo doing, but alſo in ſome Caſes he who maliciouſly attempts to kill another, and in Purſuance of ſuch Attempt unwillingly kills himſelf, ſhall be adjudged in the Eye of the Law a *Felo de ſe*; for where-ever Death is cauſed by an Act done with a murdrous Intent, it makes the Offender a Murderer; and therefore if *A.* diſcharge a Gun at *B.* with an Intent to kill him, and the Gun breaks and kills *A.* or if *A.* ſtrike *B.* to the Ground, and then haſtily falling upon him wound himſelf with a Knife which *B.* happens to have in his Hand and die, in both theſe Caſes *A.* is *Felo de ſe*, for he is the only Agent. [22.] ☞

Dal. cap. 92. 44 E. 3. 44. 44 Aſſ. 55. Bro. Cor. 12, 14. Dalt. chap. 92.

Sect. 5. But if *B.* being ſo aſſaulted had been driven to the Wall, and holden up a Pitch-fork or Knife, ſtanding in his Defence, and *A.* had haſtily run upon the ſame and been ſlain, *B.* ſhould be adjudged to kill him in his own Defence. And for the ſame Reaſon perhaps in the Caſe above, if *B.* after he had fallen to the Ground, had holden up a Knife or Sword in his Defence, and *A.* had fallen thereon and been ſlain, *B.* ſhould be adjudged to kill him *ſe defendendo*; for here *B.* exerts his Strength in his own Defence, and by ſo doing occaſions the mortal Wound received by *A.*

S. P. C. 16. a. 20. H.P.C.28, 29. Pult. 119. b. Crom. 28. 1 H. H. P. C. 493. Con. 3 Inſt. 54. But the Caſe there is not rightly ſtated, as it is in the Books.

Sect. 6. He, who kills another upon his Deſire or Command, is in the Judgment of the Law as much a Murderer, as if he had done it merely of his own Head, and the Perſon killed is not looked upon as a *Felo de ſe*, inaſmuch as his Aſſent was merely void, as being againſt the Laws of God and Man: But where two Perſons agree to die together, and one of them at the Perſwaſion of the other buys Ratſbane, and mixes it in a Potion, and both drink of it, and he who bought and made the Potion, ſurvives by uſing proper Remedies, and the other dies, perhaps it is the better Opinion, That he who dies ſhall be adjudged a *Felo de ſe*, becauſe all that happened was originally owing to his own wicked Purpoſe, and the other only put it in his Power to execute it in that particular Manner.

Kellw. 136. a. Moore 754. Pl. 1041.

Sect. 7. [a] As to the ſecond Point, *viz.* What ſuch an Offender ſhall forfeit, it ſeems clear that he ſhall forfeit all Chattels Real or Perſonal, which he hath in his own Right, and alſo all ſuch Chattels Real whereof he is poſſeſſed either jointly with his Wife, or in her Right; and alſo all Bonds and other Perſonal Things in Action belonging ſolely to himſelf; and alſo all Perſonal Things in Action, and, as ſome ſay, entire Chattels in Poſſeſſion, to which he was intitled jointly with another, on any Account except that of Merchandize: But it is ſaid, That he ſhall forfeit a Moiety only of ſuch joint Chattels as may be ſevered, and nothing at all of what he was poſſeſſed of as Executor or Adminiſtrator.

[a] S. P. C. 189. F. G. 262, 263. 1 H. H. P. C. 413. H. P. C. 29. Plow. Com. 262, 263. S. P. C. 188. a. Crom. 31. a. 3 Inſt. 55. 19 H. 6. 47. a. 8 E. 4. 24. b. Raym. 7. Plow. Com. 243, 259, 323. b.

Sect. 8. [b] However the Blood of a *Felo de ſe* is not corrupted, nor his Lands of Inheritance forfeited, nor his Wife barred of her Dower.

[b] 1 H.H.P.C. 413. Plow. Com. 261. b. 262. a.

Sect. 9. [c] Alſo no Part of the Perſonal Eſtate is veſted in the King, before the Self-Murder is found by ſome Inquiſition; and conſequently the Forfeiture thereof is ſaved by a Pardon of the Offence before ſuch Finding.

Sect. 10. [d] But if there be no ſuch Pardon, the whole is forfeited immediately after ſuch Inquiſition, from the Time ſuch mortal Wound was given, and all intermediate Alienations are avoided.

Sect. 11. [e] And ſuch Inquiſitions ought to be by the Coroner *ſuper viſum Corporis*, if the Body can be found; and an Inquiſition ſo taken, as ſome ſay, cannot be traverſed. [23.] ☞

[c] 5 Co. 110. b. 3 Inſt. 54. 1 Saund. 362. 1 H. H. P. C. 414. 1 Sid. 150, 162. 2 Mod. 53. 3 Mod. 100, 241, 242. Con. 1 Lev. 8. 1 Keb. 67, 68. [d] Plow. Com. 260. H. P. C. 29. 5 Co. 110. [e] H. P. C. 29. 3 Inſt. 55. See B. 2. Ch. 9. Sect. 52. 1 H. H. P. C. 414 to 417. Far. 16. Salk. 377. Carth. 72. Skin 45.

Sect. 12. But if the Body cannot be found, so that the Coroner, who has Authority only *super visum Corporis*, cannot proceed, the Inquiry may be by Justices of Peace, (who by their Commission have a general Power to inquire of all Felonies) or in the King's Bench, if the Felony were committed in the County where the said Court sits; and such Inquisitions are traversable by the Executor, *&c.* 3 Inst. 55. H. P. C. 29. 2 Lev. 141. 1 H. H. P. C. 414.

Sect. 13. Also all Inquisitions of this Offence being in the Nature of Indictments, ought particularly and certainly to set forth the Circumstances of the Fact, as the particular Manner of the Wound, and that it was mortal, *&c.* and in the Conclusion add, That the Party in such manner murdered himself. Sal. 377.

Sect. 14. Therefore if either the Premisses be insufficient, as if it be found that the Party flung himself into the Water, *& sic seipsum emergit*, which is Nonsense, (because *emergo* signifies only to rise out of the Water) or if there be wanting the proper Conclusion, *& sic seipsum murdravit*, the Inquisition is not good. 3 Lev. 140. 3 Mod. 100 2 Lev. 152. contra Salk. 377.

Sect. 15. Yet if it be full in Substance, the Coroner may be served with a Rule to amend a Defect in Form. 1 Sid. 225, 259. 3 Mod. 101. 1 Keb. 907. See 1 Saund. 273. for Process from the Crown-Office on such an Inquisition against a Debtor of a Felo de se.

CHAP. XXVIII.

Of Justifiable Homicide.

HOMICIDE against the Life of another either amounts to Felony, or does not.

That which amounts not to Felony, is either justifiable and causes no Forfeiture at all, or excusable and causes the Forfeiture of the Party's Goods.

And first of Justifiable Homicide, concerning which I shall premise these general Rules:

Sect. 1. I. It must be owing to some unavoidable Necessity, to which the Person who kills another must be reduced without any manner of Fault in himself. Vid. Sect. 22.

Sect. 2. II. There must be no Malice coloured under Pretence of Necessity; for where-ever a Person who kills another, acts in Truth upon Malice, and takes Occasion from the Appearance of Necessity to execute his own private Revenge, he is guilty of Murder. 2 Rol. Rep. 120, 121. Kelynge 28. H. P. C. 38. Bract. lib. 3. cap. 4. 21 Ed. 1. de Malefactor' in Parcis.

Sect. 3. III. According to the Opinion of the old [a] Books, (which in this respect seem to be contradicted by [b] others more modern) it seems, That one may set forth a Fact, amounting to justifiable Homicide, in a Special Plea to an Indictment or Appeal of Murder; and that the same being found true, he shall be dismissed, without being arraigned or enforced to plead Not guilty. And indeed it seems extreamly hard, That a Sheriff or Judge who condemn or execute a Criminal, *&c.* should be forced on a frivolous Prosecution, to hold up their Hands at the Bar for it, *&c.* But it is agreed, That no one can plead a Fact amounting to Homicide *se defendendo*, or by Misadventure, but that in such a Case the Defendant must plead Not guilty, and give the Special Matter in Evidence:

[a] 22 Ass. 55. 27 Ass. 41. 37 H. 6. 20. 21. a. Bro. Appeal, 5, 129. Bro. Coro. 57, 87, 89. b.
[b] 35 H. 6. 11. b. 58. Bro. Appeal. 122.

2 Inst. 316. 1 Inst. 283. H. P. C. 38. Bro. Coro. 1.

H. P. C. 38.

dence: And it is alſo agreed, That where a Special Fact, amounting to juſtifiable Homicide, is found by the Jury, the Party is to be diſmiſſed, without being obliged to purchaſe any Pardon, *&c.*

Juſtifiable Homicide is either of a publick or private Nature.

That of a publick Nature, is ſuch as is occaſioned by the due Execution or Advancement of publick Juſtice.

That of a private Nature, is ſuch as happens in the juſt Defence of a Man's Perſon, Houſe, or Goods.

And firſt, I ſhall conſider juſtifiable Homicide in the due Execution of publick Juſtice, as to which the following Rules muſt be obſerved:

Dalt. cap. 98. 1 H. H. P. C. 497. 10 Co. 76.

Sect. 4. I. The Judgment, by Virtue whereof any Perſon is put to Death, muſt be given by one who has Juriſdiction in the Cauſe; for otherwiſe both Judge and Officer may be guilty of Felony.

22 E. 4. 33. a. H. P. C. 35.

Sect. 5. And therefore if the Court of Common Pleas give Judgment on an Appeal of Death, or Juſtices of Peace on an Indictment of Treaſon and award Execution, which is executed, both the Judges who give, and the Officers who execute the Sentence, are guilty of Felony, becauſe theſe Courts having no more Juriſdiction over theſe Crimes than mere private Perſons, their Proceedings thereon are merely void, and without any Foundation. [24]

H. P. C. 35. Dalt. cap. 98.

Sect. 6. But if the Juſtices of Peace, on an Indictment of Treſpaſs, arraign a Man of Felony, and condemn him, and he be executed, the Juſtices only are guilty of Felony, and not the Officers who execute their Sentence; for the Juſtices had a Juriſdiction over the Offence, and their Proceedings were irregular and erroneous only, but not void.

[a] 1 Inſt. 128. b. 2 Aſſ. pl. 3. S. P. C. 13. a. 196. 11 H. 4. 12. a. Plow. Com. 306. b. 3 Inſt. 131.

Sect. 7. II. The Judgment muſt be executed by the lawful Officer.

Sect. 8. [a] Indeed it was formerly holden, That any one might as lawfully kill a Perſon attainted of Treaſon or Felony, as a Wolf or other wild Beaſt; and anciently a Perſon condemned in an Appeal of Death, was delivered to the Relations of the Deceaſed, in order to be executed by them.

[b] 27 Aſſ. 41. 1 H. H. P. C. 501. Bro. Appeal. 69. Coro. 67, 197.

Sect. 9. [b] But at this Day, as it ſeems agreed, if the Judge, who gives the Sentence of Death, and, *a fortiori*, if any private Perſon execute the ſame, or if the proper Officer himſelf do it without a lawful Command, they are guilty of Felony.

1 Inſt. 128. b. Dalt. ca. 98. H. P. C. 35. [c] 35 H. 6. 58. b. 1 H. H. P. C. 454, 501.

Sect. 10. [c] III. The Execution muſt be purſuant of, and warranted by the Judgment, otherwiſe it is without Authority; and conſequently if a Sheriff behead a Man where it is no Part of the Sentence to cut off the Head, he is guilty of Felony.

Bro. Appeal. 5. S. P. C. 13. H. P. C. 36, 272. See B. 2. ch. 51.

And now we are come to Juſtifiable Homicide in the due Advancement of publick Juſtice, which I ſhall conſider:

1. In Relation to criminal,
2. In Relation to civil Cauſes.

22 Aſſ. 55. Bro. Cor. 87, 89.

And firſt, Homicide in the Advancement of publick Juſtice in criminal Cauſes may be juſtified in ſeveral Caſes; as,

S. P. C. 13. 3 Inſt. 221. Dalt. cap. 98. H. P. C. 36. Crom. 30. Fitz. Coro. 192, 258, 261. 1 H. H. P. C. 489.

Sect. 11. I. If a Perſon, having actually committed a Felony, will not ſuffer himſelf to be arreſted, but ſtand on his own Defence, or fly, ſo that he cannot poſſibly be apprehended alive by thoſe who purſue him, whether private Perſons or publick Officers, with or without a Warrant from a Magiſtrate, he may be lawfully ſlain by them.

Sect. 12. II. If an innocent Person be indicted of a Felony, where, in Truth, no Felony was committed, and will not suffer himself to be arrested by the Officer who has a Warrant to that Purpose, he may lawfully be killed by him, if he cannot otherwise be taken; for there is a Charge against him, upon Record to which at his Peril he is bound to answer. [25] See the Authorities above cited. Fitz. Coro. 179, 261.

Sect. 13. III. If a Criminal, endeavouring to break the Gaol, assault his Gaoler, he may be lawfully killed by him in the Affray. 1 H. H. P. C. 481, 496.

Sect. 14. IV. If those who are engaged in a Riot, or a Forcible Entry, or Detainer, stand in their Defence, and continue the Force in Opposition to the Command of a Justice of Peace, &c. or resist such Justice endeavouring to arrest them, the Killing of them may be justified; and so perhaps may the killing of dangerous Rioters by any private Persons, who cannot otherwise suppress them, or defend themselves from them, inasmuch as every private Person seems to be authorized by the Law to arm himself for the Purposes aforesaid. Crom. 30. b. 158. b. 1 H. H. P. C. 494, 495. H. P. C. 37. See 1 Geo. 1. 5. par. 3. infra Ch. 65. Sect. 56. Poph. 121.

Sect. 15. V. If Trespassers in a Forest, Chace, Park, or Warren, or any inclosed Ground wherein Deer are kept, will not render themselves to the Keepers, upon an Hue and Cry made to stand to the King's Peace, but fly from, or defend themselves against them, they may be slain by Force of the Statute *de Malefactoribus in Parcis*, and 3 and 4 *Will. & Mar.* 10. S. P. C. 13. b. Crom. 30. b. Dyer 326. Pl. 3. 1 H. H. P. C. 491.

Sect. 16. VI. If either of the Parties fighting in a Combat allowed by Law, for the Trial of some Special Cases, be slain, he who kills him is justified, and the Death of the other is imputed to the just Judgment of God, who is presumed to give the Victory to him who fights in Maintenance of the Truth. Dalt. cap. 98. Plow. Com. 9. b. 3 Inst. 221. 37 H. 6. 21. a.

Secondly, Homicide in the Advancement of Justice in civil Causes, may also be justified in some Cases.

Sect. 17. [a] As where a Sheriff, &c. attempting to make a lawful Arrest in a civil Action, or to retake one who has been arrested and made his Escape, is resisted by the Party, and unavoidably kills him in the Affray. [a] 1 Rol. Re. 189. H. P. C. 37. 3 Inst. 56. Crom. 24. a. Dalt. cap. 98.

Sect. 18. [b] And in such Case the Officer is not bound to give back, but may stand his Ground and attack the Party. [b] H. P. C. 37.

Sect. 19. But no private Person of his own Authority can arrest a Man for a civil Matter, as he may for Felony, &c. Crom. 30. b.

Sect. 20. Neither can the Sheriff himself lawfully kill those who barely fly from the Execution of any civil Process. H. P. C. 37. 1 H. H. P. C. 481.

And now I am to consider justifiable Homicide of a private Nature, in the just Defence of a Man's Person, House or Goods, in treating whereof I shall shew,

1. In what Cases the killing of a Wrong-doer may be justified by Reason of such Defence.
2. Where the killing of an innocent Person may be so justified.

Sect. 21. And first the killing of a Wrong-doer, in the making of such Defence, may be justified in many Cases; as where a Man kills one who assaults him in the Highway to rob or murder him; or the Owner of a House, or any of his Servants, or Lodgers, &c. kill one who attempts to burn it, or to commit in it Murder, Robbery, or other Felony; or a Woman kills one who attempts to ravish her; or a Servant coming suddenly and finding his Master robbed and slain, falls upon the Murderer immediately and kills him; for he does it in the Height of his Sur- 24 H. 8. c. 5. Dalt. cap. 98. 1 H. H. P. C. 486, 487, 493, 494. H. P. C. 32. S. P. C. 14. Bro. Coro. 100, 102. Fitz. Coro. 179, 192, 194, 261, 305. Cro. Ca. 544. 26 Ass. 23. Bro. Cor. 100. Crom. 26. b.

Surprize, and under just Apprehensions of the like Attempt upon himself: But in other Circumstances he could not have justified the killing of such an one, but ought to have apprehended him, *&c.* [26]

Sect. 22. Neither shall a Man in any Case justify the killing another Crom. 27. b. H. P. C. 56. by a Pretence of Necessity, unless he were himself wholly without Fault in bringing that Necessity upon himself; for if a Man, in Defence of an Injury done by himself, kill any Person whatsoever, he is guilty of Manslaughter at least; as where divers Rioters wrongfully detain a House by Force, and kill those who attack it from without, and endeavour to burn it.

Sect. 23. Neither can a Man justify the killing another in Defence of H.P.C.40,57. Cro.Car.538. Dalt. cap. 98. 1 H.H.P.C. 485, 486, 488. his House or Goods, or even of his Person, from a bare private Trespass; and therefore he that kills another, who claiming a Title to his House, attempts to enter it by Force, and shoots at it, or that breaks open his Windows in order to arrest him, or that persists in breaking his Hedges after he is forbidden, is guilty of Manslaughter; and he who in his own Defence kills another that assaults him in his House in the Day-Time, and plainly appears to intend to beat him only, is guilty of Homicide *se defendendo*, for which he forfeits his Goods, but is pardoned of Course; yet it Pult. 119. a. H. P. C. 40. Crom. 28. a. 3 Inst. 138. Poph. 121. seems that a private Person, and *à fortiori*, an Officer of Justice, who happens unavoidably to kill another in endeavouring to defend himself from, or suppress dangerous Rioters, may justify the Fact, inasmuch as he only does his Duty in Aid of the publick Justice.

Sect. 24. And I can see no Reason why a Person, who without Provocation is assaulted by another in any Place whatsoever, in such a Man- N. Bendlo. 47. 1 And. 41. ner as plainly shews an Intent to murder him, as by discharging a Pistol, or pushing at him with a drawn Sword, *&c.* may not justify killing such an Assailant, as much as if he had attempted to rob him: For is not he, who attempts to murder me, more injurious than he who barely attempts to rob me? And can it be more justifiable to fight for my Goods, than for my Life? And it is not only highly agreeable to Reason, that a Man in such Circumstances may lawfully kill another, but it seems also to be Crom. 27. b. 28. b. Dalt. cap. 98. S. P. C. 15. a. 3 Inst. 57. Vide Fitz. Coro. 284. 286, 287. Bacon 33. confirmed by the general Tenor of our Law-Books, which speaking of Homicide *se defendendo*, suppose it done in some Quarrel or Affray; from whence it seems reasonable to conclude, That where the Law judges a Man guilty of Homicide *se defendendo*, there must be some precedent Quarrel in which both Parties always are, or at least may justly be supposed to have been, in some Fault, so that the Necessity, to which a Man is at length reduced to kill another, is in some Measure presumed to have been owing to himself: For it cannot be imagined, That the Law, which is founded on the highest Reason, will adjudge a Man to forfeit all his Goods, and put him to the Necessity of purchasing his Pardon, without some Appearance of a Fault. And though it may be said, That there is none in Chance-medley, and yet that the Party's Goods are also forfeited by that. I answer, That Chance-medley may be intended to proceed from some Negligence, or at least want of sufficient Caution in the Party, who is so unfortunate as to commit it, so that S. P. C. 15. Dalt. cap. 98. he doth not seem to be altogether faultless. Besides, one of the Reasons given in our Law-Books for which Homicide *se defendendo* forfeits Goods, is because thereby a true Man is killed; but it seems absurd, That he who apparently attempts to murder another, which is the most heinous of all Felonies, should be esteemed such, when those who attempt other Felonies, which seem to be much less criminal, are allowed to be killed as downright Villains, not deserving the Protection or Regard of the Law.

Sect. 25. However, perhaps in all these Cases, there ought to be a Distinction between an Assault in the Highway and an Assault in a Town; for in the first Case it is said, That the Person assaulted may justify killing the other without giving back at all: But that in the second Case, he ought to retreat as far as he can without apparently hazarding his Life, in respect of the Probability of getting Assistance. N. Bendl. 47. Crom. 27. b. 28. a. Dal. cap. 98. H. P. C. 42.

II. Also the killing of an innocent Person, in the Defence of a Man's self, is said to be justifiable in some special Cases, as,

Sect. 26. I. If two be shipwreck'd together, and one of them get upon a Plank to save himself, and the other also, having no other Means to save his Life, get upon the same Plank, and finding it not able to support them both, thrust the other from it, whereby he is drowned, it seems that he, who thus preserves his own Life at the Expence of that of another, may justify the Fact by the inevitable Necessity of the Case. Dal. cap. 98.

Sect. 27. If a Man be awakened in the Night with an Alarm that Thieves are in his House, and searching for them in the Dark with his Sword drawn, happen to kill a Person lying hid in a Part of the House, who in Truth had no ill Design, and was brought thither by a Servant in order to assist in cleaning the House, it seemeth that he may justify the Fact, inasmuch as it hath not the Appearance of a Fault. Cro.Car. 538. March 5. 1 H. H. P. C. 42, 43.

CHAP. XXIX.

Of Excusable Homicide.

EXcusable Homicide is either *per infortunium*, or *se defendendo*. See 1 H. H. P. C. 38 to 41, 492, 493.

In treating of which I shall first shew the Nature of each of them distinctly, and then consider those Properties wherein they both agree.

Sect. 1. And first of Homicide *per infortunium*, or by Misadventure, which is where a Man in doing a lawful Act, without any Intent of Hurt, unfortunately chances to kill another; as, 3 Inst. 56. H. P. C. 31. 1 H. H. P. C. 472.

Sect. 2. I. Where a Labourer being at Work with a Hatchet, the Head thereof flies off, and kills one who stands by. 6 Ed. 4. 7. b. Bro. Coro. 59, 148.

Sect. 3. II. Where a third Person whips a Horse on which a Man is riding, whereupon he springs out, and runs over a Child and kills him, in which Case the Rider is guilty of Homicide *per infortunium*; and he who gave the Blow, of Manslaughter. H.P.C.58,59. 1 H. H. P. C. 476.

Sect. 4. III. Where a Workman having first given loud Warning to all Persons to stand clear, flings down a Piece of Timber from a private House standing out of the Road, and thereby kills one who happens to be underneath: (But if any Person fling down such a Piece of Timber idly in Play, or even a Workman fling it down in the Streets of a Town, where the Danger is apparent in respect of the Number of People continually passing by, he is guilty of Manslaughter.) 1 H. H. P. C. 472, 475. Kelynge 40. Bract. lib. 3. cap. 4. Dalt. ca. 96. H. P. C. 31. Bro. Coro. 229.

Sect. 5. IV. Where a Schoolmaster in correcting his Scholar, or a Father his Son, or a Master his Servant, or an Officer in whipping a Criminal condemned to such Punishment, happens to occasion his Death; (yet if such Persons in their Correction be so barbarous, as to exceed all Bounds of Moderation, and thereby cause the Party's Death, they are guilty of Manslaughter at the least; and if they make use of 1 H. H. P. C. 454, 473, 474. Bract. lib. 1. ca. 4. H. P. C. 31. Crom. 28. b. Dalt. cap. 96. Kellw. 136.

Skin. 668. Kelynge 65. Vide 5 Mod. 287, 288, &c.

an Inſtrument improper for Correction, and apparently indangering the Party's Life, as an iron Bar, or Sword, *&c.* or kick him to the Ground, and then ſtamp on his Belly and kill him, they are guilty of Murder.)

Kellw. 108. Bro. Cor. 148. Vide Kelynge 41.

Sect. 6. V. Where one lawfully uſing an innocent Diverſion, as ſhooting at Butts, or at a Bird, *&c.* by the glancing of an Arrow, or ſuch like Accident, kills another.

Kellw. 108, 136. Crom. 29. a. 11 H. 7. 23. a.

Sect. 7. VI. Where a Perſon happens to kill another in playing a Match of Foot-ball, Wreſtling, or ſuch like Sports which are attended with no apparent Danger of Life, and intended only for the Trial, Exerciſe and Improvement, of the Strength, Courage, and Activity of the Parties.

[a] 11 H. 7. 23. a. 3 Inſt. 160. See 1 H. H. P. C. 473. Kellw. 108, 136.

Sect. 8. [a] VII. Where one kills another in fighting at Barriers or Tilting by the King's Command, which by the better Opinion, ſecures him from being guilty of Felony, by Reaſon of any ſuch unfortunate Accident.

H. P. C. 31. Dalt. cap. 96. Hob. 134. Cromp. 29. a. Con. Bro. Cor. 22. [b] H. P. C. 31, 32. [c] H. P. C. 58. Con. Hob. 134. Dalt. cap. 98. H. P. C. 57. Aleyn 12. 1 H. H. P. C. 472, 473.

Sect. 9. [b] But if a Perſon kill another by ſhooting at a Deer, *&c.* in a third Perſon's Park, in the doing whereof he is a Treſpaſſer; or by ſhooting off a Gun, or throwing Stones in a City or Highway, or other Place where Men uſually reſort; or [c] by throwing Stones at another wantonly in Play, which is a dangerous Sport, and has not the leaſt Appearance of any good Intent; or by doing any other ſuch idle Action as cannot but indanger the bodily Hurt of ſome one or other; or by tilting or playing at Handſword without the King's Command; or by parrying with naked Swords covered with Buttons at the Points, or with Swords in the Scabbards, or ſuch like raſh Sports, which cannot be uſed without the manifeſt Hazard of Life, he is guilty of Manſlaughter.

H. P. C. 52, 57. Kelynge 117. 1 H. H. P. C. 39.

Sect. 10. And if a Man happen to kill another in the Execution of a malicious and deliberate Purpoſe to do him a perſonal Hurt, by wounding or beating him; or in the wilful Commiſſion of any unlawful Act, which neceſſarily tends to raiſe Tumults and Quarrels, and conſequently cannot but be attended with the Danger of perſonal Hurt to ſome one or other; as by committing a Riot, robbing a Park, *&c.* he ſhall be adjudged guilty of Murder. [27.]

3 Inſt. 56. Kelynge 117. Supra Ch. 27. Sect. 4. H. P. C. 52. 1 H. H. P. C. 475.

Sect. 11. And *a fortiori* he ſhall come under the ſame Conſtruction, who in the Purſuance of a deliberate Intention to commit a Felony, chances to kill a Man, as by ſhooting at tame Fowl, with an Intent to ſteal them, *&c.* for ſuch Perſons are by no Means favoured, and they muſt at their Peril take Care of the Conſequence of their Actions; and it is a general Rule, That where-ever a Man intending to commit one Felony, happens to commit another, he is as much guilty as if he had intended the Felony which he actually commits.

1 H. H. P. C. 476. H. P. C. 32, 44. 3 Inſt. 57. Dal. cap. 93. 11 H. 7. 23. a. Bro. Coro. 229. Dalt. cap. 97.

Sect. 12. Neither ſhall he be adjudged guilty of a leſs Crime, who kills another, in doing ſuch a wilful Act, as ſhews him to be as dangerous as a wild Beaſt, and an Enemy to Mankind in general; as by going deliberately with a Horſe uſed to ſtrike, or diſcharging a Gun, among a Multitude of People, or throwing a great Stone or Piece of Timber from a Houſe into a Street, through which he knows that many are paſſing; and it is no Excuſe that he intended no Harm to any one in particular, or that he meant to do it only for Sport, or to frighten the People, *&c.*

Vide ſupra Ch. 28. Sect. 23, 24. H. P. C. 40, 41. S. P. C. 15.

Sect. 13. And now I am to conſider Homicide *ſe defendendo*, which ſeems to be where one, who has no other poſſible Means of preſerving his Life from one who combats with him on a ſudden Quarrel, or of defending his Perſon from one who attempts to beat him, (eſpecially if ſuch

Attempt be made upon him in his own House,) kills the Person by whom he is reduced to such an inevitable Necessity.

Sect. 14. And not only he who on an Assault retreats to a Wall, or some such Streight, beyond which he can go no farther, before he kills the other, is judged by the Law to act upon unavoidable Necessity: But also he who being assaulted in such a Manner, and in such a Place, that he cannot go back without manifestly indangering his Life, kills the other without retreating at all. Bro. Coro. 125. 43 Ass. 31. 3 Inst. 56. H. P. C. 41.

Sect. 15. And notwithstanding a Person who retreats from an Assault to the Wall, give the other Wounds in his Retreat, yet if he give him no mortal one till he get thither, and then kill him, he is guilty of Homicide *se defendendo* only. H. P. C. 41. Crom. 28. S. P. C. 15. a.

Sect. 16. And an Officer who kills one that resists him in the Execution of his Office, and even a private Person, that kills one who feloniously assaults him in the Highway, may justify the Fact without ever giving back at all. H. P. C. 41. 3 Inst. 56. Crom. 28. a. Vide supra Ch. 28. Sect. 18.

Sect. 17. According to some good Opinions, even he who gives another the first Blow on a sudden Quarrel, if he afterwards do what he can to avoid killing him, is not guilty of Felony; yet such a Person seems to be too much favoured by this Opinion, inasmuch as the Necessity to which he is at last reduced, was at the first so much owing to his own Fault. And it is now agreed, That if a Man strike another upon Malice Prepense, and then fly to the Wall, and there kill him in his own Defence, he is guilty of Murder. S. P. C. 15. a. Crom. 28. a. See 1 H. H. P.C. 479, 480. Dalt. cap. 98. Kelynge 58. H. P. C. 42. Dalt. cap. 98.

Sect. 18. Thus far of each kind of excusable Homicide distinctly considered, and now I am to consider those Properties wherein they both agree.

Sect. 19. And first it seems clear, That neither of these Homicides are Felonies, because they are not accompanied with a felonious Intent, which is necessary in every Felony. 3 Inst. 56. 2 Inst. 149. Fitz. Coro. 116.

Sect. 20. And from hence it seems plainly to follow, That they were never punishable with Loss of Life: And the same also farther appears from the Writ *de Odio & Atia*, by Vertue whereof, if any Person committed for killing another, were found guilty of either of these Homicides, and no other Crime, he might be bailed; and indeed it seems to be against natural Justice, to condemn a Man to Death, for what is owing rather to his Misfortune than his Fault. 11 H. 4. 93. Pl. 54. Bro. Coro. 80. 15 Ass. Pl. 7. Vide infra Sect. 24.

Sect. 21. It is true indeed, That some of our best Authors have argued from the Statute of *Marlebridge*, ch. 26. which enacts, That *Murdrum de cætero non adjudicetur, ubi Infortunium tantummodo adjudicatum est*, &c. that before this Statute Homicides by Misadventure, or *se defendendo*, were adjudged Murder, and consequently punished by Death. 2 Inst. 56. S. P. C. 16. C.

Sect. 22. But to this it may be answered, That Murder in those Days, signified only the private killing of a Man by one, who was neither seen nor heard by any Witness, for which the Offender, if found, was to be tried by Ordeal, and if he could not be found, the Town in which the Fact was done, was to be amerced sixty-six Marks, unless it could be proved that the Person killed was an *Englishman*, for otherwise it was presumed that he was a *Dane* or *Norman*, who in those Days were often privately made away with by the *English*. And it being a Doubt whether Homicide by Misadventure, &c. were to be esteemed Murder in this Sense, it seems to have been the chief Intent of the Makers of this Statute to settle this Question. Bract. 134. b. Kelynge 121. See 1 H. H. P. C. 425, 448. Bract. 135. a.

H.P.C.98,99. 2 Inst. 315. Dalt. cap. 98. 1 H. H. P.C. 477. *Sect.* 23. II. However it is certain, That notwithstanding neither of these Offences be Felonies, yet a Person guilty of them is not bailable by Justices of Peace, but must be committed till the next coming of the Justices of Eyre or Gaol-Delivery.

Regist. 133.b. 2Inst.42,315. 9 Co. 56. 4 Inst. 182. Bract. 123. Fleta B. 1. Ch. 25. S.P.C. 77.G. 2Inst.43,315. 9 Co. 56. Co. Bail and Mainprize, c. 10. *Sect.* 24. Indeed anciently a Person, committed for the Death of a Man might sue out the Writ *de Odio & Atia*, which by *Magna Charta* 26. is grantable without Fee; and if thereon, by an Inquest taken by the Sheriff, he were found to have done the Fact by Misadventure, or *se defendendo*, he might be mainprized by twelve Men, upon the Writ *de ponendo in Ballium*. But such Writs and Enquiries were taken away by the Statute of *Gloucester*, 9 and 28 *Ed.* 3. 9. And though perhaps they were again revived by 42 *Ed.* 3. 1. which makes all Statutes, contrary to *Magna Charta*, void; yet at this Day they seem to be obsolete, and indeed useless, inasmuch as the Party may probably be sooner delivered in the usual Course, by the coming of the Justices of Gaol-Delivery.

Vide supra Ch.28.Sect.3. 1 H. H. P. C. 478. 4 H. 7. 2. a. Kellw. 53. a. 108. b. 2 Inst. 316. S. P. C. 15. b. 16. b. Fitz. Coro. 297,354,361. Dalt. cap. 96, 98. F. N. B. 246. C. H. *Sect.* 25. III. It is also agreed, That no one can excuse the killing another, by setting forth in a special Plea, that he did it by Misadventure, or *se defendendo*; but that he must plead Not guilty, and give the special Matter in Evidence. And that where-ever a Person is found guilty of such Homicide either upon a special Indictment for the same, or by a Verdict setting forth the Circumstances of the Case on a general Indictment of Murder or Homicide, he shall be discharged out of Prison upon Bail and forfeit his Goods: But that upon removing the Record by *Certiorari* into Chancery, he shall have his Pardon of Course, without staying for any Warrant from the King to that Purpose, as shall be more fully shewn. *B.* 2. *Ch.* 37. *Sect.* 1.

CHAP. XXX.

Of Manslaughter.

HOmicide against the Life of another, amounting to Felony, is either with or without Malice.

3 Inst. 55,57. Dalt. cap. 94. H.P.C.56,57. 1 H. H. P. C. 466. *Sect.* 1. That which is without Malice is called Manslaughter, or sometimes Chance-medly, by which we understand such killing as happens either on a sudden Quarrel, or in the Commission of an unlawful Act, without any deliberate Intention of doing any Mischief at all.

H. P. C. 217. B. 2. Ch. 29. Sect. 24. *Sect.* 2. And from hence it follows, That there can be no Accessaries to this Offence before the Fact, because it must be done without Premeditation.

Sect. 3. But the Learning relating to this Head, being for the most part co-incident with that of others, it will be superfluous to inlarge on it here; and therefore I shall refer the Reader to other Chapters for the particular Case, as to the following Chapter of Murder, from Section 21 to 32. for those concerning Duelling; and to the said Chapter, Sections 47, 48, 49. and to Chapter 28. Sections 14, 15. for such as happen in a Riot, *&c.* and to Chapter 29 from Section 6 to Section 13. for such as fall out in the Execution of a rash, unlawful Action.

Sect. 4. But there is a particular kind of Manſlaughter proper to be conſidered here, from which the Benefit of the Clergy is taken away by 1 *Jac.* See Skin. 666, 667, 668. 1. 8. *Where any Perſon ſhall ſtab or thruſt any Perſon or Perſons that hath not then any Weapon drawn, or that hath not then firſt ſtricken, the Party which ſhall ſo ſtab or thruſt, ſo as the Perſon or Perſons ſo ſtabbed or thruſt, ſhall thereof die within the Space of ſix Months then next following, although it cannot be proved that the ſame was done of Malice fore-thought.*

Sect. 5. It is generally holden, That this Statute is but declarative of 1 Bulſt. 87. the Common Law, and in the Conſtruction thereof, the following Points Kelynge 55. have been reſolved.

Sect. 6. I. That where-ever a Perſon who happens to kill another, was 1 Jon. 240. ſtruck by him in the Quarrel before he gave the mortal Wound, he is out Vide 3 Lev. 266. of the Statute, though he himſelf gave the firſt Blow.

Sect. 7. II. That he only who actually gives the Stroke, and not any H. P. C. 58. of thoſe who may be ſaid to do it by Conſtruction of Law, as being pre- See B. 2. Ch. 33. S. 98. ſent, and aiding and abetting the Fact, are within the Statute; from whence Salk. 542, it follows, That if it cannot be proved by whom the Stroke was given, 543. none can be found guilty within the Statute. Aleyn. 44.

Sect. 8. III. That the Killing of a Man with a Hammer, or ſuch like 1 Jones 432. Inſtrument, which cannot come properly under the Words Thruſt, or Stab, is not a Killing within the Statute; but it ſeems that the diſcharging a Piſtol, or throwing a Pot, or other dangerous Weapon at the Party, is 3 Lev. 266. within the Equity of the Words, *having a Weapon drawn*; for Penal Statutes are conſtrued ſtrictly againſt the Subject, and favourably and equitably for him.

Sect. 9. IV. That there is no need to lay the Concluſion of the In- H. P. C. 58. dictment *contra forma Statuti*, becauſe the Statute makes no new Offence, but only takes away the Privilege of the Clergy from an old one, and leaves it to the Judgment of the Common Law; from whence it follows, That See B. 2. Ch. 25. S. 117. a Perſon indicted on the Statute, may be found guilty of Manſlaughter generally. Alſo from the ſame Ground it hath been reſolved, That if both H. P. C. 58, 266. an Indictment lay, and a Verdict alſo find, a Fact to be *contra formam Sta-* Aleyn 47. *tuti*, which cannot poſſibly be ſo, as that *A.* and *B.* aided and abetted *C. contra formam Statuti*, yet neither ſuch Indictment nor Verdict are void, but *A.* and *B.* ſhall be dealt with in the ſame Manner as they ſhould have been, if thoſe Words *contra formam Statuti* had been wholly omitted, becauſe the Subſtance of the Indictment being found, they may be rejected as Surplus and Senſeleſs: And, *a fortiori*, therefore it is certain, that they ſhall do no Hurt to an Indictment or Verdict containing a Fact which may Cro. Jac. 282. be within the Statute. See 1 H. H. P. C. 467 to 470.

Sect. 10. V. How far the Words *contra formam Statuti*, ſupply a Defect in an Indictment, which does not ſpecially purſue the Statute, See *B.* 2. *Ch.* 25. *Sect.* 116.

CHAP. XXXI.

Of Murder.

HOMICIDE against the Life of another, amounting to Felony with Malice, is either Murder or Petit Treason.

Bract. 134. b. 135. a. Kelynge 121, &c. 1 H. H. P. C. 447, 448. Bract. 121. a.

Sect. 1. And first of Murder, which antiently signified only the private Killing of a Man, for which by Force of a Law introduced by King *Canutus* for the Preservation of his *Danes*, the Town or Hundred where the Fact was done, was to be amerced to the King, unless they could prove that the Person slain were an *Englishman*, (which Proof was called *Engleschire*) or could produce the Offender, *&c.* And in those Days, the open wilful Killing of a Man through Anger or Malice, *&c.* was not called Murder, but voluntary Homicide.

S. P. C. 18. b. 19. a. 1 H. H. P. C. 448.

Sect. 2. But the said Law concerning *Engleschire* having been abolished by 14 *Ed.* 3. 4. the Killing of any *Englishman* or Foreigner through Malice prepense, whether committed openly or secretly, was by Degrees called Murder; and 13 *Rich.* 2. 1. which restrains the King's Pardon in certain Cases, does in the Preamble, under the general Name of Murder, include all such Homicide as shall not be pardoned without special Words; and in the Body of the Act expresses the same by Murder, or Killing by Await, Assault, or Malice prepensed. And doubtless the Makers of 23 *H.* 8. *c.* 1. which excluded all wilful Murder of Malice prepense from the Benefit of the Clergy, intended to include open, as well as private, Homicide within the Word Murder.

1 H. H. P. C. 450.

Sect. 3. By Murder therefore at this Day we understand the wilfull Killing of any Subject whatsoever, through Malice fore-thought, whether the Person slain be an *Englishman* or Foreigner.

And for the better understanding hereof, I shall examine the following Particulars:

1. In what Cases a Man may be said to kill another.
2. In what Places such Killing is within the Cognizance of the Law.
3. Who are such Persons by killing of whom a Man may commit Murder.
4. What Killing shall be adjudged to be Malice prepense, or Murder.

3 Inst. 48. H. P. C. 53. Palm. 548.

Sect. 4. As to the first Point, *viz.* In what Cases a Man may be said to kill another; not only he who by a Wound or Blow, or by Poisoning, Strangling, or Famishing, *&c.* directly causes another's Death, but also in many Cases, he who by wilfully and deliberately doing a Thing which apparently endangers another's Life, thereby occasions his Death, shall be adjudged to kill him.

Crom. 24. b. Pult. 122. a. b. Dalt. cap. 93. 1 H. H. P. C. 431, 432.

Sect. 5. And such was the Case of him who carried his sick Father, against his Will, in a cold frosty Season, from one Town to another, by Reason whereof he died. [28] ☞

Sect. 6. Such alſo was the Caſe of the Harlot, who being delivered of a Child, left it in an Orchard covered only with Leaves, in which Condition it was ſtruck by a Kite, and died thereof.

Crom. 24. b. Dal. cap. 93.

Sect. 7. And in ſome Caſes a Man ſhall be ſaid, in the Judgment of the Law, to kill one who is in Truth actually killed by another, or by himſelf; as where one by Dureſs [a] of Impriſonment compels a Man to accuſe an innocent Perſon, who on his Evidence is condemned and executed; or where one incites a [b] Madman to kill himſelf or another; or where one lays [c] Poiſon with an Intent to kill one Man, which is afterwards accidentally taken by another, who dies thereof.

[a] S.P.C.36. c. 3 Inſt. 91. [b] Dal. cap 93. Supra Ch. 1. S. 7. 1 H. H. P. C. 431, 436, 442, 467. [c] Plow. Com. 474.

Sect. 8. Alſo he who wilfully neglects to prevent a Miſchief, which he may, and ought to provide againſt, is, as ſome have ſaid, in Judgment of the Law, the actual Cauſe of the Damage which enſues; and therefore if a Man have an Ox or Horſe, which he knows to be miſchievous, by being uſed to gore or ſtrike at thoſe who come near them, and do not tie them up, but leave them to their Liberty, and they afterwards kill a Man, according to ſome Opinions, the Owner may be indicted, as having himſelf feloniouſly killed him; and this is agreeable to the *Moſaical* Law. However, as it is agreed by all, ſuch a Perſon is certainly guilty of a very groſs Miſdemeanour. [29]

9 Co. 81. 1 H.H. P. C. 430, 431. Fitz. Corone 311. S. P. C. 17. a. Crom. 24. b. Dalt. cap. 93. Pult. 122. b. H. P. C. 53. Exodus c. 21. v. 29.

Sect. 9. Alſo it is agreed, That no Perſon ſhall be adjudged by any Act whatever to kill another, who doth not die thereof within a Year and a Day after; in the Computation whereof, the whole Day on which the Hurt was done ſhall be reckoned the firſt.

H. P. C. 55. Pult. 123. a. Dalt. cap. 93. S. P. C. 21. d.

Sect. 10. But if a Perſon hurt by another, die thereof within a Year and a Day, it is no Excuſe for the other that he might have recovered, if he had not neglected to take Care of himſelf.

3 Inſt. 53. Kelynge 26. 1 Keb. 17.

Sect. 11. As to the ſecond Point, *viz.* In what Places ſuch killing is within the Conuſance of the Law, it ſeems, That the Killing of one who is both wounded and dies out of the Realm, or wounded out of the Realm and dies here, cannot be determined at Common Law, becauſe it cannot be tried by a Jury of the Neighbourhood where the Fact was done. But it is agreed, That the Death of one who is both wounded and dies beyond Sea; and it is ſaid by ſome, That the Death of him who dies here of a Wound given there, may be heard and determined before the Conſtable and Marſhal, according to the Civil Law, if the King pleaſe to appoint a Conſtable. And it ſeemeth alſo to be clear, That ſuch a Fact being examined by the Privy Council, may by Force of 33 *H.* 8. 23. be tried (in Relation to the principal Offenders, but not as to the Acceſſaries) before Commiſſioners appointed by the King in any County in *England*.

3 Inſt. 48. 1 H. H. P. C. 426. 2 Inſt. 51. Co. Lit. 75. S. P. C. 65. a. Bro. Appeal. 153. Cro. Car. 247. B. 2. Ch. 23 S. 12. 3 Keb. 785. Pl. 34. Con. 3 Keb. 715. Pl. 34. 1 And. 195.

Sect. 12. A Murder at Sea was anciently cognizable only by the Civil Law, but now by Force of 27 *H.* 8. 4. and 28 *H.* 8. 15. it may be tried and determined before the King's Commiſſioners in any County of *England* according to the Courſe of the Common Law; yet the Killing of one who dies at Land of a Wound received at Sea, is neither determinable at Common Law, nor by Force of either of theſe Statutes; but it ſeems, that it may be tried by the Conſtable and Marſhal, or before Commiſſioners appointed, in Purſuance of the aforeſaid Statute of 33 *H.* 8. 23. [30]

3 Inſt. 48, 49. 1 Leon. 270. H. P. C. 54. 3 Inſt. 48.

Sect. 13. It is ſaid by ſome, That the Death of one who died in one County, of the Wound given in another, was not indictable at all at Common Law, becauſe the Offence was not compleat in either County, and the Jury could enquire only of what happened in their own County. But it hath been holden by others, That if the Corps were carried into the

3 Inſt. 48, 49. 1 H. H. P. C. 426, 427. Bro. Coro. 140, 141, 143. Indictm. 13, 45. S. P. C. 90. c. 6 H. 7. 10 a.

Finch Law, 411. S. P. C. 182. c. 45 Aſſ. Pl. 9. Bro. Appeal, 3, 80, 83, 85, 149.

the County where the Stroke was given, the whole might be enquired of by a Jury of the ſame County: And it is agreed, That an Appeal might be brought in either County, and the Fact tried by a Jury returned jointly from each: And at this Day by Force of 2 and 3 *Ed.* 6. 24. the whole is triable by a Jury of the County wherein the Death ſhall happen, on an Indictment found, or Appeal brought, in the ſame County.

B. 2. Ch. 25. S. 39, 40. Cro. Car. 247. 1 Jon. 255.

Sect. 14. Alſo by Force of 26 *H.* 8. 6. a Murder in *Wales* may be enquired of in an adjoining *Engliſh* County, but Appeals muſt ſtill be brought in the proper County.

1 Lev. 118. Latch. 12, 118. 3 Inſt. 50.

Sect. 15. As to the third Point, *viz.* Who are ſuch Perſons by killing of whom a Man may commit Murder; it is agreed, That the malicious Killing of any Perſon, whatſoever Nation or Religion he be of, or of whatſoever Crime attainted, is Murder.

Bract. 121. S. P. C. 21. Bro. Coro. 91. H. P. C. 53. Fitz. Coro. 146, 183, 263. 23 Aſſ. Pl. 94. B. 2. Ch. 29. S. 18. 3 Inſt. 50. 3 Aſſ. 2. Bro. Cor. 68. Dalt. cap. 93. Exodus c. 21. v. 22, 23.

Sect. 16. And it was anciently holden, That the cauſing of an Abortion by giving a Potion to, or ſtriking, a Woman big with Child, was Murder: But at this Day, it is ſaid to be a great Miſpriſion only, and not Murder, unleſs the Child be born alive, and die thereof, in which Caſe it ſeems clearly to be Murder, notwithſtanding ſome Opinions to the contrary. And in this Reſpect alſo, the Common Law ſeems to be agreeable to the *Moſaical*, which as to the Purpoſe is thus expreſſed, *If Men ſtrive and hurt a Woman with Child, ſo that her Fruit depart from her, and yet no Miſchief follow, he ſhall be ſurely puniſhed, according as the Woman's Husband will lay upon him, and he ſhall pay as the Judges determine; And if any Miſchief follow, then thou ſhalt give Life for Life.* [31]

Dyer 186. 1 H. H. P. C. 433.

Sect. 17. It ſeems alſo agreed, That where one counſels a Woman to kill her Child when it ſhall be born, who afterwards does kill it in Purſuance of ſuch Advice, he is an Acceſſary to the Murder.

3 Inſt. 51. Kelynge 127.

Sect. 18. As to the fourth Point, *viz.* What Killing ſhall be adjudged of Malice prepenſe or Murder; it is to be obſerved, That any formed Deſign of doing Miſchief may be called Malice; and therefore that not ſuch Killing only as proceeds from premeditated Hatred or Revenge againſt the Perſon killed, but alſo in many other Caſes, ſuch as is accompanied with thoſe Circumſtances that ſhew the Heart to be perverſly wicked, is adjudged to be of Malice prepenſe, and conſequently Murder.

Kelynge 130. 1 H. H. P. C. 451 to 454.

Sect. 19. And according to this Notion, I ſhall conſider,

1. Such Murder as is occaſioned through an expreſs Purpoſe to do ſome perſonal Injury to him, who is ſlain in particular, which ſeems to be moſt properly called expreſs Malice.

Kelynge 129, 130. 1 H. H. P. C. 455, &c.

2. Such as happens in the Execution of an unlawful Action, principally intended for ſome other Purpoſe, and not to do a perſonal Injury to him in particular who is ſlain, in which Caſe the Malice ſeems to be moſt properly ſaid to be implied.

Sect. 20. As to Murder in the firſt Senſe, ſuch Acts as ſhew a direct and deliberate Intent to kill another, as Poiſoning, Stabbing, and ſuch like, are ſo clearly Murder, that I know not any Queſtions relating thereto worth explaining: But the Caſes, which have born Diſpute, have generally happened in the following Inſtances;

1. In Duelling.
2. In killing another without any Provocation, or but upon a ſlight one.
3. In killing one whom the Perſon killing intended to hurt in a leſs Degree.

Bulſt. 86, 87.

Sect. 21. As to the firſt Inſtance of this Kind, it ſeems agreed, That where-ever two Perſons in cool Blood meet and fight on a precedent Quarrel, and one of them is killed, the other is guilty of Murder, and cannot help himſelf by alledging that he was [a] firſt ſtruck by the Deceaſed; or that he had often [b] declined to meet him, and was prevailed upon to do it by his Importunity; or that it was his only Intent to vindicate his Reputation; or that he meant not to kill, but only to diſarm, his Adverſary: For ſince he deliberately ingaged in an Act highly unlawful, in Defiance of the Laws, he muſt at his Peril abide the Conſequences thereof.

[a] 2 Bulſt. 147. Crom. 22. b. [b] 1 Rol. Rep. 360. 3 Bulſt. 171. H. P. C. 48. 1 H. H. P. C. 452, 453.

Sect. 22. And from hence it clearly follows, That if two Perſons quarrel over Night, and appoint to fight the next Day; or quarrel in the Morning, and agree to fight in the Afternoon; or ſuch a conſiderable Time after, by which, in common Intendment, it muſt be preſumed that the Blood was cooled, and then they meet and fight, and one kill the other, he is guilty of Murder.

3 Inſt. 51. H. P. C. 48. Kelynge 56. 1 Lev. 80.

Sect. 23. And where-ever it appears from the whole Circumſtances of the Caſe, That he who kills another on a ſudden Quarrel, was Maſter of his Temper at the Time, he is guilty of Murder; as if after the Quarrel he fall into other Diſcourſe and talk calmly thereon; or perhaps if he have ſo much Conſideration, as to ſay, That the Place wherein the Quarrel happens is not convenient for Fighting; or that if he ſhould fight at preſent, he ſhould have the Diſadvantage by reaſon of the Height of his Shoes, *&c.*

Kelynge 56. 1 Sid. 177. 1 Lev. 180.

Sect. 24. And if *A.* on a Quarrel with *B.* tell him that he will not ſtrike him, but that he will give *B.* a Pot of Ale to ſtrike him, and thereupon *B.* ſtrike, and *A.* kill him, he is guilty of Murder; for he ſhall not elude the Juſtice of the Law by ſuch a Pretence to cover his Malice.

H. P. C. 48.

Sect. 25. In like Manner if *B.* challenge *A.* and *A.* refuſe to meet him, but in order to evade the Law, tell *B.* that he ſhall go the next Day to ſuch a Town about his Buſineſs, and accordingly *B.* meet him the next Day in the Road to the ſame Town, and aſſault him, whereupon they fight, and *A.* kills *B.* he ſeems guilty of Murder, unleſs it appear by the whole Circumſtances that he gave *B.* ſuch Information accidentally, and not with a Deſign to give him an Opportunity of Fighting.

1 H. H. P. C. 453. Con. Crom. 22. b. and H. P. C. 48.

Sect. 26. And at this Day it ſeems to be ſettled, That if a Man aſſault another with Malice prepenſe, and after be driven by him to the Wall, and kill him there in his own Defence, he is guilty of Murder, in reſpect of his firſt Intent.

Crom. 22. b. Dalt. cap. 93. H. P. C. 47. Kelynge 58, 129.

Sect. 27. And it hath been adjudged, That even upon a ſudden Quarrel, if a Man be ſo far provoked by any bare Words or Geſtures of another, as to make a Puſh at him with a Sword, or to ſtrike at him with any other ſuch Weapon as manifeſtly endangers his Life, before the other's Sword is drawn, and thereupon a Fight enſue, and he who made ſuch Aſſault kill the other, he is guilty of Murder; becauſe that by aſſaulting the other in ſuch an outrageous Manner, without giving him an Opportunity to defend himſelf, he ſhewed that he intended not to fight with him, but to kill him, which violent Revenge is no more excuſed by ſuch a ſlight Provocation, than if there had been none at all.

Crom. 23. a. b. Dalt. cap. 93. Kelyn. 61. and Mawgridge's Caſe.

Sect. 28. But it is ſaid, That if he who draws upon another in a ſudden Quarrel, make no Paſs at him till his Sword is drawn, and then fight with him, and kill him, he is guilty of Manſlaughter only, becauſe that by neglecting the Opportunity of killing the other before he was on

Kelynge 55, 61, 131.

his Guard, and in a Condition to defend himſelf, with like Hazard to
both, he ſhew'd that his Intent was not ſo much to kill, as to combat
with the other, in Compliance with thoſe common Notions of Honour,
which prevailing over Reaſon, during the Time that a Man is under, the
2 Rol. Re. 461. Tranſports of a ſudden Paſſion, ſo far mitigate his Offence in Fighting,
That it ſhall not be adjudged to be of Malice prepenſe.

H. P. C. 48. 3 Inſt. 51. *Sect.* 29. And if two happen to fall out upon a ſudden, and preſently
1 H. H. P. C. agree to fight, and each of them fetch a Weapon, and go into the Field,
453. and there one kill the other, he is guilty of Manſlaughter only, becauſe
he did it in the Heat of Blood.

1 H. H. P. C. *Sect.* 30. And ſuch an Indulgence is ſhewn to the Frailties of humane
452. Crom. 23. a. Nature, That where two Perſons who have formerly fought on Malice, are
Dalt. cap. 93. afterwards to all Appearance reconciled, and fight again on a freſh Quarrel,
H. P. C. 49. 1 Rol. Rep. it ſhall not be preſumed that they were moved by the old Grudge, unleſs it
360. appear by the whole Circumſtances of the Fact.

3 Bulſt. 171. *Sect.* 31. But the Law ſo far abhors all Duelling in cold Blood, That
H. P. C. 51. not only the Principal who actually kills the other, but alſo his Seconds
Dalt. cap. 93. are guilty of Murder, whether they fought or not; and ſome have
gone ſo far as to hold, That the Seconds of the Perſon killed are alſo
equally guilty, in Reſpect of that Countenance which they give to their
Principals in the Execution of their Purpoſe, by accompanying them
1 H. H. P. C. therein, and being ready to bear a Part with them: But ſome have
443. H. P. C. 51. thought this rather too ſevere a Conſtruction to make a Man by ſuch
Reaſoning the Murderer of his Friend, to whom he was ſo far from in-
tending any Miſchief, that he was ready to hazard his own Life in his
Quarrel.

Sect. 32. And now I am to conſider the ſecond Inſtance of this kind,
viz. Such Murder as happens in killing another without any Provocation,
or but upon a ſlight one; as to which it is to be obſerved, That where-
Kelynge 27. ever it appears that a Man killed another, it ſhall be intended, *prima facie*,
that he did it maliciouſly, unleſs de can make out the contrary, by ſhew-
ing that he did it on a ſudden Provocation, &c.

[a] Kelynge *Sect.* 33. Alſo it ſeems to be agreed, That no [a] Breach of a Man's
135. 1 H. H. P. C. Word or Promiſe, no Treſpaſs either to [b] Lands or Goods, no Affront
455, 456. by bare [c] Words or Geſtures, however falſe or malicious it may be, and
2 Rol. Rep. aggravated with the moſt provoking Circumſtances, will excuſe him from
460, 461. being guilty of Murder, who is ſo far tranſported thereby, as immediately
[b] Kelynge 131, &c. to attack the Perſon who offends him, in ſuch a Manner as manifeſtly en-
Dalt. cap. 93. [c] Cro. El. 779. dangers his Life, without giving him Time to put himſelf upon his Guard,
Noy 171. if he kills him in Purſuance of ſuch Aſſault, whether the Perſon ſlain did
1 Sid. 277. 1 Lev. 180. at all fight in his Defence or not; for ſo baſe and cruel a Revenge cannot
Hob. 121. have too ſevere a Conſtruction.

Con. 1 Jon. 432. a. *Sect.* 34. But if a Perſon ſo provoked, had beaten the other only in
Kelynge 131. ſuch a Manner, that it might plainly appear that he meant not to kill, but
only chaſtiſe him; or if he had reſtrained himſelf till the other had put
Kelynge 55, 61, 131. himſelf on his Guard, and then in fighting with him had killed him, he
* Kely. 61, had been guilty of Manſlaughter only.

136. Cro. Jac. 296. *Sect.* 35. * And of the like Offence ſhall he be adjudged guilty, who
12 Co. 87. ſeeing two Perſons fighting together on a private Quarrel, whether ſudden
[d] Kely. 137. or malicious, takes Part with one of them, and kills the other.

1 Vent. 158, 159. *Sect.* 36. Neither can he be thought guilty of a greater Crime, who
Raym. 212. [d] finding a Man in Bed with his Wife, or being actually [e] ſtruck by him,
2 Keb. 829. [e] Kely. 135. or pulled by the Noſe, or fillipped upon the Forehead, immediately kills
3 Mod. 68. 2 him

him; or [a] who happens to kill another in a Contention for the Wall; or [b] in the Defence of his Person from an unlawful Arrest; or [c] in the Defence of his House from those who claiming a Title to it attempt forcibly to enter it, and to that Purpose shoot at it, *&c.* or in [d] the Defence of his Possession of a Room in a Publick House, from those who attempt to turn him out of it, and thereupon draw their Swords upon him; in which Case the killing the Assailant hath been holden by some to be justifiable: But it is certain, That it can amount to no more than Manslaughter.

[a] H. P. C. 57. 3 Inst. 55. [b] Kelynge 137. 1 H. H. P. C 457. [c] H. P. C. 57. Crom. 27. a. 1 H. H. P. C. 445. [d] Kelynge 51.

Sect. 37. Nor was he judged criminal in a higher Degree, who seeing his Son's Nose bloody, and being told by him, That he had been beaten by such a Boy, ran three Quarters of a Mile, and having found the Boy, beat him with a small Cudgel, whereof he afterwards died.

H. P. C. 48. Cro. Jac. 296. 12 Co. 87. 1 Vent. 159. 1 H. H. P. C. 453.

Sect. 38. And now we are come to the third Instance of this kind, *viz.* Such Murder as happens in killing one whom the Person killing intended to hurt in a less Degree; as to which it is to be observed, That where-ever a Person in cool Blood by way of Revenge, unlawfully and deliberately beats another in such a Manner, that he afterwards dies thereof, he is guilty of Murder, however unwilling he might have been to have gone so far.

Kelyn. Mawgridge's Case, 131. H. P. C. 49, 50, 51, 52.

Sect. 39. Also it seems, That he, who upon a sudden Provocation executeth his Revenge in such a cruel Manner, as shews a cruel and deliberate Intent to do Mischief, is guilty of Murder, if Death ensue; as where the Keeper of a Park, finding a Boy stealing Wood, tied him to a Horse's Tail and beat him, whereupon the Horse ran away and killed him.

Cro. Car. 131. 1 Jon. 198. Palm. 545. H. P. C. 49. 1 H. H. P. C. 454.

Sect. 40. And now I am to consider the second general Branch of this Head, *viz.* In what Cases such killing shall be adjudged Murder which happens in the Execution of an unlawful Action, principally intended for some other Purpose, and not to do a personal Injury to him in particular who happens to be slain; and this I shall consider in the following Instances:

1. Where the principal Intention is to commit another Felony.
2. Where the principal Design is to commit a bare Breach of the Peace, not intended against the Person of him who happens to be slain.
3. Where the chief Motive is to assist a third Person.
4. Where the direct Design is to escape from an Arrest.
5. Where the principal Purpose is to usurp an illegal Authority.
6. Where no Mischief is intended at all.

Sect. 41. As to the first Particular, *viz.* Such killing as happens in the Execution of an unlawful Action, whereof the principal Intention was to commit another Felony; it seems agreed, That where-ever a Man happens to kill another in the Execution of a deliberate Purpose to commit any Felony, he is guilty of Murder; as where a Person shooting at tame Fowl, with an Intent to steal them, accidentally kills a Man; or where one sets upon a Man to rob him, and kills him in making Resistance; or where a Person shooting at, or fighting with one Man, with a Design to murder him, misses him and kills another.

1 H. H. P. C. 465, 474. H. P. C. 50. Kelynge 117. H. P. C. 46, 50. Dalt. cap. 93. Moore 87. Pl. Com. 101.

Sect. 42.

Sect. 42. And not only in ſuch Caſes where the very act of a Perſon, having ſuch a felonious Intent, is the immediate Cauſe of a third Perſon's Death, but alſo where it any Way occaſionally cauſes ſuch a Misfortune, it makes him guilty of Murder; and ſuch was the Caſe of the Husband, who gave a poiſoned Apple to his Wife, who eat not enough of it to kill her, but innocently, and againſt the Husband's Will and Perſwaſion, gave Part of it to a Child who died thereof; ſuch alſo was the Caſe of the Wife, who mixed Ratsbane in a Potion ſent by an Apothecary to her Huſband, which did not kill him, but afterwards killed the Apothecary, who to vindicate his Reputation taſted it himſelf, having firſt ſtirred it about. Neither is it material in this Caſe, That the ſtirring of the Potion might make the Operation of the Poiſon more forcible than otherwiſe it would have been; for inaſmuch as ſuch a murderous Intention, which of it ſelf perhaps in ſtrictneſs might juſtly be made puniſhable with Death, proves now in the Event the Cauſe of the King's loſing a Subject, it ſhall be as ſeverely puniſhed as if it had had the intended Effect, the miſſing whereof is not owing to any Want of Malice, but of Power.

(Pl. Com. 474. 3 Inſt. 51. 1 H. H. P. C. 436, 441, 442, 467. 9 Co. 81.)

Sect. 43. But if one happen to be poiſoned by Ratsbane laid in order to deſtroy Vermine, the Perſon by whom he is ſo killed is guilty of Homicide *per infortunium* only, becauſe his Intentions were wholly innocent.

(Pl. Com. 474. 9 Co. 81. b. 1 H. H. P. C. 431.)

Sect. 44. Alſo if a third Perſon accidentally happen to be kill'd by one engaged in a Combat with another upon a ſudden Quarrel, it ſeems that he who kills him is guilty of Manſlaughter only; but it hath been adjudged, That if a Juſtice of Peace, Conſtable or Watchman, or even a private Perſon, be killed in endeavouring to part thoſe whom he ſees fighting, the Perſon by whom he is killed, is guilty of Murder; and that he cannot excuſe himſelf by alledging that what he did was in a ſudden Affray in the Heat of Blood, and through the Violence of Paſſion; for he who carries his Reſentments ſo high, as not only to execute his Revenge againſt thoſe who have affronted him, but even againſt ſuch as have no otherwiſe offended him but by doing their Duty, and endeavouring to reſtrain him from breaking through his, ſhews ſuch an obſtinate Contempt of the Laws, that he is no more to be favoured, than if he had acted in cool Blood.

(H. P. C. 50. 1 H. H. P. C. 441, 446. H. P. C. 45. 3 Inſt. 52. Dalt. cap. 93. Fitz. Coro. 180. Savil 67. Kelynge 66. 22 Aſſ. 71. H. P. C. 50. 4 Co. 40. b. 9 Co. 68. Crom. 25. a. b.)

Sect. 45. Yet it hath been reſolved, That if the third Perſon ſlain in ſuch a ſudden Affray do not give Notice for what Purpoſe he comes, by commanding the Parties in the King's Name to keep the Peace, or otherwiſe manifeſtly ſhewing his Intention to be not to take Part in the Quarrel, but to appeaſe it, he who kills him is guilty of Manſlaughter only, for he might ſuſpect that he came to ſide with his Adverſary.

(Kelynge 66. 1 H. H. P. C. 442.)

Sect. 46. As to the ſecond Inſtance of this kind, *viz.* Such killing as happens in the Execution of an unlawful Action, where the principal Deſign is to commit a bare Breach of the Peace, not intended againſt the Perſon of him who happens to be ſlain; it ſeems clear, That regularly where divers Perſons reſolve generally to reſiſt all Oppoſers in the Commiſſion of any Breach of the Peace, and to execute it in ſuch a Manner as naturally tends to raiſe Tumults and Affrays, as by committing a violent Diſſeiſin with great Numbers of People, hunting in a Park, *&c.* and in ſo doing happen to kill a Man, they are all guilty of Murder; for they muſt at their Peril abide the Event of their Actions, who wilfully engage in ſuch bold Diſturbances of the Publick Peace, in open Oppoſition to, and Defiance of, the Juſtice of the Nation.

(1 H. H. P. C. 442, 443, 463. Savil 67. Moore 86. Palm. 35. Crom. 24. b. 25. a. H. P. C. 47. 5 Mod. 289. Dyer 128. Pl. 60. S. P. C. 17. b.)

Sect. 47. Yet where divers Rioters having forcible Possession of a House, afterwards killed a Person whom they had ejected, as he was endeavouring in the Night forcibly to regain the Possession, and to fire the House, they were adjudged guilty of Manslaughter only, notwithstanding they did the Fact in Maintenance of a deliberate Injury, perhaps for this Reason, because the Person slain was so much in Fault himself. Crom. 28. b. H. P. C. 56. 1 H. H. P. C. 440, 441.

Sect. 48. But if in such, or any other Quarrel, whether it were sudden or premeditated, a Justice of Peace, Constable, or Watchman, or even a private Person, be slain in endeavouring to keep the Peace and suppress the Affray, he who kills him is guilty of Murder; for notwithstanding it was not his primary Intention to commit a Felony, yet inasmuch as he persists in a less Offence with so much Obstinacy, as to go on in it to the Hazard of the Lives of those who no otherwise offend him, but by doing their Duty in Maintenance of the Law, which therefore affords them its more immediate Protection, he seems to be in this Respect equally criminal, as if his Intention had been to commit a Felony. H. P. C. 45. Dalt. cap. 93. 3 Inst. 52. Kelynge 66. 22 Ass. 71. 4 Co. 40. b. 9 Co. 68. Crom. 25.

Sect. 49. As to the third Instance of this kind, *viz.* such killing, as happens in the Execution of an unlawful Action, the principal Motive whereof was to assist a third Person, it seems clear, That if a Master maliciously intending to kill another take his Servants with him, without acquainting them with his Purpose, and meet his Adversary and fight with him, and the Servants seeing their Master engaged take part with him, and kill the other, they are guilty of Manslaughter only, but the Master of Murder. 1 H. H. P. C. 437, 446. Pl. Com. 100, 101. a. Crom. 23. Dalt. cap. 93. H. P. C. 51, 52.

Sect. 50. And therefore it follows, *a fortiori*, That if a Man's Servant, or Friend, or even a Stranger, coming suddenly, see him fighting with another and side with him, and kill the other; or seeing his Sword broken send him another, wherewith he kills the other, he is guilty of Manslaughter only. Crom. 26. b. H. P. C. 57. Dalt. cap. 94. 1 Rol. Rep. 407, 408. 3 Bulst. 206. H. P. C. 52.

Sect. 51. Yet in this very Case if the Person killed were a Bailiff, or other Officer of Justice, resisted by the Master, *&c.* in the due Execution of his Duty, such Friend or Servant, *&c.* are guilty of Murder, whether they knew that the Person slain were an Officer or not. Kelynge 67, 86, 87.

Sect. 52. But perhaps it may be objected, That in this last Case there seems to be no more Malice than in the former; and such third Person being wholly ignorant that the Party killed was an Officer, seems to be no more in Fault than if he had been a Private Person.

Sect. 53. To this it may be answered, That all Fighting is highly unlawful, and that he, who on a sudden seeing Persons engaged in it, is so far from endeavouring to part them, as every good Subject ought, that he takes part with one Side, and fights in the Quarrel, without knowing the Cause of it, shews a high Contempt of the Laws, and a Readiness to break through them on a small Occasion, and must at his Peril take heed what he does, and consequently might perhaps in strict Justice be adjudged in the foregoing Cases to act with Malice, which doth not always signify a particular ill Will against the Person killed, as appears by many of the above mentioned Cases; and though such Person be favoured in respect of the Suddenness of the Occasion, where both the Quarrel and the Persons are private, yet he must not expect such Indulgence where the Fight, in which he so rashly ingages, was begun in open Opposition to the Justice of the Nation, and a Person happens to be killed thereby who engaged in Maintenance thereof, and on that Account is under its more particular Care; and may justly challenge, that his 1 Sid. 160. Noy 50. Plow. Com. 100.

Oppoſers be made Examples to deter others from joining in ſuch unwarrantable Quarrels.

Kelynge 60, 137. Crom. 27. a. Dent's Caſe lately adjudged.

Sect. 54. But if a Man ſeeing another arreſted and reſtrained from his Liberty, under Colour of a Preſs-Warrant or Civil Proceſs, *&c.* by thoſe who in Truth have no ſuch Authority, happen to kill ſuch Treſpaſſers in reſcuing the Perſon oppreſſed, he ſhall be adjudged guilty of Manſlaughter only, notwithſtanding the injured Perſon ſubmitted to them, and endeavoured not to reſcue himſelf, and the Perſon who reſcued him, did not know that he was illegally arreſted; for ſince in the Event it appears, that the Perſons ſlain were Treſpaſſers, covering their Violence with a Shew of Juſtice, he who kills them is indulged by the Law, which in theſe Caſes judges by the Event, which thoſe who engage in ſuch unlawful Actions muſt abide at their Peril.

2 H. H. P. C. 83. Dalt. cap. 93. H. P. C. 45. Crom. 24. a.

Sect. 55. As to the fourth Inſtance of this kind, *viz.* Such Killing as happens in the Execution of an unlawful Action, whereof the direct Deſign was to eſcape from an Arreſt, it ſeems to be agreed, That whoever kills a Sheriff, or any of his Officers, in the lawful Execution of a Civil Proceſs, as on arreſting a Perſon upon a *Capias, &c.* is guilty of Murder.

9 Co. 68. Cro. Jac. 280. 1 H. H. P. C. 457, 458, 462. 9 Co. 66. Cro. Jac. 280. B. 2. Ch. 13. S. 28. 2 H. H. P. C. 85. 6 Co. 68. b. 69. a. Cro. Jac. 486 9 Co. 69. [a]Cro. Car. 372. 1 H. H. P. C. 457. 1 Jon. 346. 1 Lev. 91. 12 Co. 49. [b]H. P. C. 46.

Sect. 56. Neither is it any Excuſe to ſuch a Perſon that the Proceſs was erroneous, (for it is not void by being ſo,) or that the Arreſt was in the Night, or that the Officer did not tell him for what cauſe he arreſted him, and out of what Court, (which is not neceſſary when prevented by the Party's Reſiſtance;) or that the Officer did not ſhew his Warrant, which he is not bound to do at all, if he be a Bailiff commonly known, nor without a Demand, if he be a ſpecial one.

Yet the Killing of an Officer in ſome Caſes will be Manſlaughter only, as,

Sect. 57. I. [a] Where the Warrant by which he acts gives him no Authority to arreſt the Party; as where a Bailiff arreſts *J. S.* a Baronet, who never was knighted, by Force of a Warrant to arreſt *J. S.* Knight.

Sect. 58. II. [b] Where a good Warrant is executed in an unlawful Manner; as if a Bailiff be killed in breaking open a Door or Window to arreſt a Man; or perhaps if he arreſt one on a *Sunday* ſince 29 *Ca.* 2. 7. by which all ſuch Arreſts are made unlawful. [32]

Sect. 59. As to the fifth Inſtance of this kind, *viz.* Such Killing as happens in the Execution of an unlawful Action, whereof the principal Purpoſe was to uſurp an illegal Authority, it ſeems clear, That if Perſons take upon them to put others to Death, either by Virtue of a new Commiſſion wholly unknown to our Laws, or by Virtue of any known Juriſdiction, which clearly extends not to Caſes of this Nature; as if the Court of Common Pleas cauſe a Man to be executed for Treaſon or Felony; or the Court Martial, in Time of Peace, put a Man to Death by the Martial Law, both the Judges and Officers are guilty of Murder.

Supra Ch. 28. S. 5. H. P. C. 46.

Sect. 60. But where Perſons act by Virtue of a Commiſſion, which if it were ſtrictly regular would undoubtedly give them full Authority, but happens to be defective only in ſome Point of Form, it ſeems that they are no way criminal.

Sect. 61. As to the ſixth Inſtance of this kind, *viz.* Such Killing as happens in the Execution of an unlawful Action, where no Miſchief was intended at all, it is ſaid, That if a Perſon happen to occaſion the Death of another, in adviſedly doing any idle wanton Action, which cannot but be attended with the manifeſt Danger of ſome other; as by riding with a

Vide ſupra Ch. 29. S. 12.

Horſe known to be uſed to kick among a Multitude of People, by which he means no more than to divert himſelf by putting them into a Fright, he is guilty of Murder.

Sect. 62. Alſo it hath been anciently holden, That if a Perſon not duly authorized to be a Phyſician or Surgeon, undertake a Cure and the Patient die under his Hand, he is guilty of Felony; but inaſmuch as the Books wherein this Opinion is holden, were written before the Statute of 23 *H.* 8. which firſt excluded ſuch felonious killing, as may be called wilful Murder of Malice prepenſe, from the Benefit of Clergy, it may be well queſtioned, whether ſuch Killing ſhall be ſaid to be of Malice prepenſe, within the Intent of that Statute; however it is certainly highly raſh and preſumptuous for unſkilful Perſons to undertake Matters of this Nature; and indeed the Law cannot be well too ſevere in this Caſe, in order to deter ignorant People from endeavouring to get a Livelihood by ſuch Practiſe, which cannot be followed without the manifeſt Hazard of the Lives of thoſe who have to do with them: But ſurely the charitable Endeavours of thoſe Gentlemen who ſtudy to qualify themſelves to give Advice of this Kind, in order to aſſiſt their poor Neighbours, can by no Means deſerve ſo ſevere a Conſtruction from their happening to fall into ſome Miſtakes in their Preſcriptions, from which the moſt learned and experienced cannot always be ſecure.

S. P. C. 16. b.
Pult. 22. b.
Crom. 27.
43 Ed. 3. 33. b.
Fitz. Coron. 163.
1 H. H. P. C. 429, 430.
See Dal. ch. 9[illegible].

For other Particulars relating to this Head, ſee the Chapter of Principals and Acceſſaries, *in the Second Book.*

CHAP. XXXII.

Of Petit Treaſon.

Sect. 1. AT Common Law not only the Offences ſpecified in 25 *Ed.* 3. but many others alſo were eſteemed Petit Treaſons, which are not ſo at this Day; as [a] Piracy by a Subject; [b] Diſcovery of the King's Counſel by one of the Grand Jury; [c] an Attempt by a Wife to kill her Huſband, &c. But by 25 *Ed.* 3. no Offence ſhall be adjudged Petit Treaſon, except in the following Inſtances:

1. Where a Servant kills his Maſter.
2. Where a Wife kills her Huſband.
3. Where an Eccleſiaſtical Man, ſecular, or religious, kills his Prelate to whom he owes Obedience.

3 Inſt. 20, 28.
[a] 40 Aſſ. Pl. 35.
Infra Ch. 37. S. 2.
[b] 27 Aſſ. 63.
3 Inſt. 22.
Dalt. ca. 91.
[c] S. P. C. 10. b.
See 1 H. H. P. C. 377 to 382.

Sect. 2. And this Statute has been ſo ſtrictly conſtrued, that no other Caſe whatſoever, which cannot be brought within the Meaning of theſe Words, however it may be in its own Nature more heinous, ſhall, by Parity of Reaſon, be expounded to be within the Equity of them; and therefore the Murder of a Father by a Son ſhall not be puniſhed as Petit Treaſon, unleſs the Son may by a reaſonable Conſtruction come under the word Servant, ſerving the Father for Meat, Drink, Clothes, or Wages, in which Caſe he ſhall be indicted by the Name of a Servant.

Dalíſ. 14.
3 Inſt. 20.
H. P. C. 24.
Dalt. ca. 91.
Crom. 91. b.

Sect. 3.

Bro. Treaf. 8, 12. *Sect.* 3. Yet the Murder of a Miftrefs, or of a Mafter's Wife, has been adjudged Petit Treafon within this Statute, for notwithftanding the Plow. Com. 86. Perfons flain can in neither of thefe Cafes in good Grammar, come under 19 H. 6. 47. b. the Word Mafter, yet they are clearly within the Meaning thereof, being 3 Inft. 20. ufed here to fignify any Perfon to whom another ftands related as a Ser- 4 Co. 46. b. vant.

33 Aff. 7. Bro. Coro. 116. *Sect.* 4. Alfo the Murder of a Perfon by one who was his Servant, upon Malice conceived during the Service, though it be not within the ex- S. P. C. 10. prefs Words, is within the Meaning of them, inafmuch as it is but the Plow. Com. 260. a. Execution of the treafonable Intention of the Party, while he was a Ser- 1 Co. 99. b. vant.

Sect. 5. Alfo the Procuring, Aiding, or Abetting, of any of thefe Of- H. P. C. 24. fences, is clearly punifhable within the Meaning of this Act, in the fame S. P. C. 10. N. 3 Inft. 20. manner as it was before; for the plain Intent of the Statutes is only to reftrain the Judges from proceeding againft other Crimes, as Petit Treafons, but no way to alter the Law as to thefe.

H. P. C. 24. *Sect.* 6. And therefore it feems agreed, That Perfons accufed of Petit Treafon fhall be conftrued to be either not guilty at all, or Principal or Acceffary, according to the known Rules of Law in other Cafes; and from hence it follows, That if the Fact appear to have been done upon a fud- H. P. C. 24. den Falling out, or in the Party's neceffary Self-defence, *&c.* it cannot Dalif. 16. be Petit Treafon: For inafmuch as all Petit Treafon implies Murder, and Dalt. ca. 91. is the higheft Degree thereof, where-ever the Circumftances do not make Crom. 19, 20. the Offence Murder, they cannot make it Petit Treafon; and *vice verfa*, Dy. 254. Pl. 103. generally where-ever the Circumftances are fuch as will make the Killing of a Stranger by a Stranger Murder, they make the Killing of a Husband, or Bro. Coro. 119. Mafter, *&c.* Petit Treafon: Yet it hath been adjudged, That if a Wife 40 Aff. 25. or Servant procure a Stranger to kill the Husband, or Mafter, in the Ab- H. P. C. 215. fence of fuch Wife, or Servant, neither the Procurer nor Actor are guilty of 3 Inft. 20, 21, 139. Petit Treafon, but of Murder only; becaufe it is an allowed Maxim, That Crom. 19. b. the Offence of an Acceffary can never be of a higher Kind than that of Dy. 128. Pl. 37. the Principal; but it feems clear, That if the Wife or Servant be either ac- Moor 91. Pl. 227. tually prefent, when the Crime is done, or prefent only in Judgment of Dalif. 16. Law, as being in the fame Houfe, but not in the fame Room, (in which Cafe the Hopes of their immediate Affiftance encourages and imboldens the Murderer to commit the Fact, which otherwife perhaps he would not have dared to do, and makes them guilty in the fame Degree, as if they had B. 2. Ch. 29. actually ftood by with their Swords drawn, ready to fecond the Villany,) S. 89. fuch Wife, or Servant, being Principals as much as the Stranger, are guilty of Petit Treafon, and the Stranger of Murder; but it is faid, That if Dy. 332. Pl. 25. a Wife procure a Servant to kill the Husband, both are guilty of Petit Treafon: And even if a Stranger procure a Wife, or Servant, to kill the Crompt. 41. Pl. 6. Husband, or Mafter, it feems that he may be indicted as Acceffary to Petit Dalif. 16. Treafon.

CHAP.

CHAP. XXXIII.

Of Simple Larceny.

AND now we are come to Offences against the Goods of another, which are generally called Larcenies, from the *Latin* Word *Latrocinium*, of which there are two Kinds:

1. Simple Larceny.
2. Mix'd Larceny.

Simple Larceny is also of two Kinds,
1. Grand Larceny.
2. Petit Larceny.

Sect. 1. Simple Grand Larceny is a felonious and fraudulent taking and H. P. C. 60.
carrying away, by any Person, of the mere Personal Goods of another, Dalt. c. 101. 1 H. H. P. C.
not from the Person, nor out of his House, above the Value of twelve 503, 504.
Pence.

For the better Explication of which Definition, I shall in order consider the several Parts of it; as,
1. What shall be said to be a felonious and fraudulent taking.
2. What shall be said to be a carrying away.
3. By whom the Offence may be committed.
4. What are such Goods the Taking whereof may be felonious.
5. How far such Goods ought to belong to another.
6. Of what Value they must be.

Sect. 2. As to the first Particular, *viz.* What shall be said to be a fe- Kelynge 24.
lonious and fraudulent Taking, it is to be observed, That all Felony in- Bro.Coro. 45,
cludes Trespass, and that every Indictment of Larceny must have the 48, 58, 137, 160.
Words *Felonicè cepit*, as well as *asportavit*; from whence it follows, That H. P. C. 61.
if the Party be guilty of no Trespass in taking the Goods, he cannot be
guilty of Felony in carrying them away.

Sect. 3. And from this Ground it hath been holden, That one who finds 3 Inst. 103.
such Goods as I have lost, and converts them to his own Use *Animo fu-* H. P. C. 61.
randi, is no Felon; and, *a fortiori*, therefore it must follow, That one 1 H. H. P. C.
who has the actual Possession of my Goods by my Delivery, for a special 504, 505, 506.
Purpose, as a Carrier who receives them, in order to carry them to a cer- 13 Ed. 4. 9, 10.
tain Place; or a Taylor who has them in order to make me a Suit of S. P. C. 25. a.
Clothes; or a Friend who is intrusted with them to keep for my Use, can- 3 Inst. 108.
not be said to steal them, by imbeziling of them afterwards.

Sect. 4. And herein our Law differs from the Civil, which, agreeably S. P. C. 25.
to the *Mosaical* Law, having no capital Punishment for bare Thefts, deals See Exod. 22.
with Offences of this Kind as such, as in strict Justice most certainly it may; but our Law, which punishes all Theft with Death, if the Thing stoln be above the Value of twelve Pence, and with corporal Punishment if under, rather chuses to deal with them as civil than criminal Offences, perhaps for this Reason in the above mentioned Case, concerning Goods lost, because the Party is not much aggrieved where nothing is taken but what he had lost before; and for this Cause in the other Cases,

concerning the imbezilling of Goods delivered to another by the Owner, becauſe the Party being intruſted with the whole Poſſeſſion, it may be preſumed that both the Offender and his Offence are known, and conſequently the Perſon injured is ſuppoſed to have a Remedy by Action againſt him, from which Conſideration ſome have made it Part of the Definition of Larceny, that it be committed without the Knowledge of the Owner; and it ſeems rigorous to have Recourſe to ſevere Laws, where probably more gentle ones will be effectual.

Dalt. ch. 101.

Sect. 5. And agreeably hereto it has been reſolved, That even thoſe who have the Poſſeſſion of Goods by the Delivery of the Party, may be guilty of Felony by taking away Part thereof, with an Intent to ſteal it; as if a Carrier open a Pack and take out Part of the Goods; or a Weaver who has received Silk to work; or a Miller who has Corn to grind; take out Part with an Intent to ſteal it; in which Caſes it may not only be ſaid that ſuch Poſſeſſion of a Part diſtinct from the Whole, was gained by Wrong, and not delivered by the Owner, but alſo that it was obtained baſely, fraudulently, and clandeſtinely, in Hopes to prevent its being diſcovered at all, or fixed upon any one when diſcovered.

1 H. H. P. C. 505. 13 Ed. 4. 9, 10. S. P. C. 25. a. Dalt. ca. 102. Kelynge 35. 1 Rol. Ab. 73. Pl. 16.

Sect. 6. Alſo it ſeems generally agreed, That one who has the bare Charge, or the ſpecial Uſe of Goods, but not the Poſſeſſion of them; as a Shepherd who looks after my Sheep; or a Butler who takes care of my Plate, or a Servant who keeps a Key to my Chamber, or a Gueſt who has a Piece of Plate ſet before him in an Inn, may be guilty of Felony, in fraudulently taking away the ſame; for in all theſe Caſes the Offence may as properly come under the Word *Cepit*; the Injury to the Owner is as great, and the Fraud as ſecret, and the Villany more baſe, than if it had been done by a Stranger.

3 H. 7. 12. b. 21 H. 7. 14. b. Bro. Coro. 58, 137. S. P. C. 25. A. Dalt. ca. 102. Moore 246. Poph. 84. 1 H. H. P. C. 505, 506, 667, 668.

Sect. 7. Alſo it ſeems clear, That if a Carrier, after he has brought the Goods to the Place appointed, take them away again ſecretly *animo furandi*, he is guilty of Felony, becauſe the Poſſeſſion which he received from the Owner being determined, his ſecond Taking is in all Reſpects the ſame as if he were a mere Stranger.

H. P. C. 62. 3 Inſt. 107. Bro. Coro. 160. S. P. C. 25. 1 H. H. P. C. 505.

Sect. 8. And not only he who firſt lays his Hands on my Goods himſelf, but in many Caſes he who receives them from another, may be guilty of feloniouſly taking them; as if a Perſon intending to ſteal my Horſe, take out a Replevin, and thereby have the Horſe delivered to him by the Sheriff; or if one intending to rifle my Goods, get Poſſeſſion from the Sheriff, by Virtue of a Judgment obtained, without any the leaſt Colour of Title, upon falſe Affidavits, &c. in which Caſes the making Uſe of legal Proceſs is ſo far from extenuating, that it highly aggravates the Offence, by the Abuſe put on the Law, in making it ſerve the Purpoſes of Oppreſſion and Injuſtice.

1 H. H. P. C. 507. 3 Inſt. 108. H. P. C. 63. Kelynge 43. 1 Sid. 254. Raym. 276.

Sect. 9. Alſo he who ſteals my Goods from *J. S.* who had ſtoln them before, may be indicted, or appealed, as having ſtoln them from me, becauſe in Judgment of Law, the Poſſeſſion as well as Property always continued in me. And for this Cauſe, he who ſteals my Goods in the County of *B.* and carries them to the County of *C.* may be indicted or appealed in the County of *C.* as well as that of *B.* becauſe the Poſſeſſion ſtill continuing in me, every Moment's Continuance of the Treſpaſs is as much a Wrong to it, and may come under the Word *Cepit*, as much as the firſt Taking. Yet a Pirate carrying the Goods whereof he robbed me at Sea, into any County, cannot be indicted for Felony there, becauſe the original Taking was not ſuch a Felony whereof the Common Law takes Conuſance.

13 E. 4. 3. b. H. P. C. 64, 69, 184. S. P. C. 61, 182. Bro. Appeal 84, 100. Coro. 171. 4 H. 7. 5, 6. a. 1 H. H. P. C. 507.

3 Inſt. 113.

Sect. 10. It ſeems not to have been clearly ſettled before 3 & 4 *Will. & Mar.* 9. whether a Lodger, who ſtole the Furniture of his Lodgings, were indictable as a Felon, inaſmuch as he had a kind of ſpecial Property in the Goods, and was to pay the greater Rent in Conſideration of them; but if it had appeared clearly, from the whole Circumſtances of the Caſe, that the firſt Intention of the Party in coming to the Houſe, was not to have the Conveniency of lodging in it, but only, under the Colour thereof, to have the better Opportunity of rifling it, and to elude the Juſtice of the Law, by endeavouring to keep out of the Letter of it, by gaining a Poſſeſſion of the Goods with the Conſent of the Owner, I cannot ſee any good Reaſon why ſuch a Perſon ſhould not be eſteemed as much a Felon as a mere Stranger, inaſmuch as his whole Deſign was to defraud the Law, and the Conſent of the Owner was grounded on a Suppoſition of his coming as a Lodger, and could never have been gain'd if the Truth had appeared, which the Party ſhall get no Advantage by falſifying: And it brings a Contempt upon the Juſtice of the Nation to ſuffer its Laws to be evaded by ſuch little Contrivances: However this Queſtion is now ſettled by the ſaid Statute, which hath enacted and declared, *That if any Perſon or Perſons ſhall take away with an Intent to ſteal, imbezil or purloin any Chattel, Bedding or Furniture, which by Contract or Agreement he or they are to uſe, or ſhall be let to him or them to uſe, in or with ſuch Lodging, ſuch Taking, Imbezilling, or Purloining, ſhall be to all Intents and Purpoſes taken, reputed, and adjudged to be Larceny and Felony, and the Offender ſhall ſuffer as in Caſe of Felony.* Kelynge 24, 81. Shower 50, 57.

Sect. 11. It is recited by 21 *H.* 8. 7. *That before the Time of the ſaid Statute, divers, as well Noblemen, as other the King's Subjects, had, upon Confidence and Truſt, delivered unto their Servants their Caſkets, and other Jewels, Money, Goods and Chattels, ſafely to keep, to the Uſe of their ſaid Maſters or Miſtreſſes, and after ſuch Delivery the ſaid Servants had withdrawn themſelves, and gone away from their ſaid Maſters or Miſtreſſes, with the ſaid Caſkets, Jewels, Money, Goods and Chattels, or Part thereof, to the Intent to ſteal the ſame, and defraud their ſaid Maſters or Miſtreſſes thereof, and ſometime being with their ſaid Maſters or Miſtreſſes, had converted the ſaid Jewels, Money, and other Chattels, or Part thereof, to their own Uſe, which Miſbehaviour ſo done, was doubtful in the Common Law, whether it were Felony or not; and by reaſon thereof the aforeſaid Servants had been in great Boldneſs to commit ſuch or the like Offences.* And thereupon it is enacted, *That all and ſingular ſuch Servants, (being of the Age of eighteen Years, and not Apprentices) to whom any ſuch Caſkets, Jewels, Money, Goods or Chattels by his or their ſaid Maſters or Miſtreſſes ſhall from thenceforth ſo be delivered to keep, That if any ſuch Servant or Servants withdraw him or them from their ſaid Maſters or Miſtreſſes, and go away with the ſaid Caſkets, Jewels, Money, Goods or Chattels or any Part thereof, to the Intent to ſteal the ſame, and defraud his or their ſaid Maſters or Miſtreſſes thereof, contrary to the Truſt and Confidence to him or them put, by his or their ſaid Maſters and Miſtreſſes, or elſe being in the Service of his ſaid Maſter or Miſtreſs, without Aſſent or Commandment of his Maſter or Miſtreſs he imbezil the ſame Caſkets, Jewels, Money, Goods or Chattels, or any Part thereof, or otherwiſe convert the ſame to his own Uſe, with like Purpoſe to ſteal it, That if the ſaid Caſkets, Jewels, Money, Goods, or Chattels, that any ſuch Servant ſhall ſo go away with, or which he ſhall imbezil with Purpoſe to ſteal it, as is aforeſaid, be of the Value of* 40 s. *or above, That then the ſame falſe, fraudulent and untrue Act and Demeanour, from thenceforth, ſhall be deemed and adjudged Felony,* &c.

In the Conſtruction of this Statute the following Opinions have been holden. See 1 H.H.P. C. 667, 668.

Sect. 12.

Dal. ca. 102. H. P. C. 63. *Sect.* 12. I. That it extends only to ſuch as were Servants to the Owner of the Goods, both at the Time when they were delivered, and alſo at the Time when they were ſtoln.

Dy. 5. Pl. 2, 3. H. P. C. 62, 63. 3 Inſt. 105. Dal. ca. 102. *Sect.* 13. II. That it is ſtrictly confined to ſuch Goods as are delivered to keep, and therefore that a Receiver, who having received his Maſter's Rents, runs away with them; or a Servant who being intruſted to ſell Goods, or to receive Money due on a Bond, ſells the Goods, *&c.* and departs with the Money, is not within the Statute; but that a Servant, Dy. 5. Pl. 3. who receives his Maſter's Goods from another Servant to keep for the Maſter, is as much Guilty as if he had received them from the Maſter's own Hands, becauſe ſuch a Delivery is looked upon as a Delivery by the Maſter.

H. P. C. 63. Dal. ca. 102. Dy. 5. *Sect.* 14. III. That it includes not the waſting or conſuming of Goods, howſoever wilful it may be; nor the taking away of an Obligation, or any other bare *Choſe* in Action.

Sect. 15. IV. That it extends not to the Taking of ſuch Things whereof the actual Property is not in the Maſter at the Time; and therefore, That if a Servant having Money, or Corn, *&c.* delivered to him, melt down the Money of his own Head, without the Command of his Maſter, 5 H. 7. 16. a. Crom. 50. Dal. ca. 102. into a Piece of Plate; or turn the Corn into Malt, and then run away with them, that he is not within the Statute, becauſe the Property of theſe Things is ſo far changed, by altering them in ſuch a Manner, that they cannot be known again, and the Maſter cannot afterwards take them without a Treſpaſs; but it is agreed, That if a Servant make a Suit of Clothes of Cloth, or a Pair of Shoes of Leather, delivered to him by the Maſter, and then run away with them, that he is within the Statute, becauſe the Property is no way altered; and even in the firſt Caſe, whether the very Taking of the Plate or Malt, be within the Statute or not; yet I can ſee no Reaſon, why the whole Act of the Servant taken together, ſhould not be looked upon as a Converſion of the Maſter's Goods to his own Uſe, with an Intent to ſteal them, which brings it within the expreſs Letter of the Statute: And it has been reſolved, That a Servant who changes his Maſter's Money from Silver to Gold, and then runs away with it, *&c.* is within the See Crom. 50. Dal. ca. 102. Statute; and I can ſee no good Diſtinction between that and the preſent Caſe.

Sect. 16. The Benefit of the Clergy was taken away from all Felonies within this Statute, by 27 *H.* 8. 17. and reſtored by 1 *Ed.* 6. 12. but taken B. 2. ch. 33. Sect. 66, 67. away again by 12 *Ann.* 7. from all ſuch as ſhall be committed in a Dwelling-houſe or Out-houſe.

Sect. 17. By 7 *Jac.* 1. 7. *If any Sorter, Kember, Carder or Spinſter of Wool, or Weaver of Yarn made of ſuch Wool, ſhall imbezil any Wool or Yarn delivered to him to be wrought, and ſhall be thereof convict before two Juſtices of Peace, according to the Method preſcribed by that Statute, he ſhall be whipped,* &c.

Sect. 18. As to the ſecond Particular, *viz.* What ſhall be ſaid to be ſuch a Carrying away of the Thing ſtoln, as will bring the Caſe within the 3 Inſt. 108. 2 Vent. 215. Word *Aſportavit*, which is neceſſary in every Indictment of Larceny, it ſeems that any the leaſt removing of the Thing taken from the Place 27 Aſſ. 39. S. P. C. 26. a. Bro. Coro. 107. where it was before, is ſufficient for this Purpoſe, tho' it be not quite carried off; and upon this Ground the Gueſt, who, having taken off the Sheets from his Bed, with an Intent to ſteal them, carried them into the 3 Inſt. 109. Dal. ca. 102. Hall, and was apprehended before he could get out of the Houſe, was adjudged guilty of Larceny; ſo alſo was he who having taken a Horſe in a Cloſe with an Intent to ſteal him, was apprehended before he could get him out of the Cloſe; neither is he leſs guilty who pulls off the Wool from another's Sheep, or ſtrips their Skins, with an Intent to ſteal them; or he who intending to ſteal Plate takes it out of a Trunk wherein it was, and lays it on the Floor; and is ſurprized before he can carry it off. 1 H. H. P. C. 508. Dalif. 21. Crom. 36. a. Kelynge 31.

Sect. 19. As to the third Particular, *viz.* By whom Larceny may be committed, It is certain that a Feme Covert may be guilty thereof by ſtealing the Goods of a Stranger, but not by ſtealing her Husband's, becauſe a Husband and Wife are conſidered but as one Perſon in Law; and the Husband, by endowing his Wife at the Marriage with all his worldly Goods, gives her a kind of Intereſt in them; for which Cauſe, even a Stranger cannot commit Larceny in taking the Goods of the Husband by the Delivery of his Wife; as he may by taking away the Wife by Force and againſt her Will, together with the Goods of the Husband. Sup. Ch. 1. S. 9, 10, 11. 1 H. H. P. C. 514, 515, 516, 637, 638. Pult. 127. H. P. C. 65. Bro. Co. 142. Dal ca. 104. 13 Aſſ. 5. 18 Ed. 3. 32. a. Bro. Coro. 77.

Sect. 20. [a] It is ſaid to be no Felony for one reduced to extream Neceſſity, to take ſo much of another's Victuals as will ſave him from ſtarving; but if ſuch his Neceſſity be owing to his Unthriftineſs, ſurely it is far from ☞ being any Excuſe. [33] S. P. C. 94. B. Dal. ca. 104. Crom. 35. [a] Dal. ca. 99. Crom. 33. a. See Proverbs, ch. 6. v. 30.

[b] As to the fourth Point, *viz.* What are ſuch Goods, the ſtealing whereof may amount to Felony, the following Particulars are to be obſerved. [b] 1 H. H. P. C. 509 to 512.

Sect. 21. I. They ought to be no way annexed to the Freehold, and therefore it is no Larceny, but a bare Treſpaſs, to ſteal Corn or Graſs, growing, or Apples on a Tree, or Lead on a Church or Houſe, but it is Larceny to take them being ſevered from the Freehold, whether by the owner, or even by the Thief himſelf, if he ſever them at one Time and then come again at another Time and take them: And the general Reaſon of this Diſtinction between Chattels fix'd to a Freehold and thoſe lying looſe, perhaps may be this; becauſe the former, not being to be removed without Trouble and Difficulty, are not ſo liable to be ſtoln, and therefore need not to be ſecured by ſo ſevere Laws as the others re- ☞ quire. [34] 12 Aſſ. 32. Bro. Coro. 77. 1 Mod. 89. H. P. C. 66. Allen 83. 2 Keb. 875. Pl. 37. 1 Vent. 187. Crom. 37. a. 18 H. 8. 2. S. P. C. 25. b.

Sect. 22. II. They ought to have ſome Worth in themſelves, and not to derive their whole Value from the Relation they bear to ſome other Thing, which cannot be ſtoln, as Paper or Parchment on which are written Aſſurances concerning Lands, or Obligations, or Covenants, or other Securities for a Debt, or other *Choſe* in Action. And the Reaſon wherefore there can be no Felony in taking away any ſuch Thing ſeems to be, becauſe, generally ſpeaking, they being of no Manner of Uſe to any but the Owner, are not ſuppoſed to be ſo much in danger of being ſtoln, and therefore need not to be provided for in ſo ſtrict a manner as thoſe Things which are of a known Price, and every Body's Mcney; and for the like Reaſon it is no Felony to take away a Villein, or an Infant in ☞ Ward, &c. [35] H. P. C. 66, 67. 3 Inſt. 109. Bro. Coro. 155. S. P. C. 25. b. Crom. 27. b. H. P. C. 66. S. P. C. 25. Bro. Coro. 155.

Sect. 23. III. They ought not to be Things of a baſe Nature, as Dogs, Cats, Bears, Foxes, Monkeys, Ferrets, and the like, which, howſoever they may be valued by the owner, ſhall never be ſo highly regarded by the Law, that for their ſakes a Man ſhall die; as he may for ſtealing a Hawk, known by him to be reclaimed, not only by Force of the Statute of 37 *Ed.* 3. 19. but alſo at Common Law, in reſpect of that very high Value which was formerly ſet upon that Bird. H. P. C. 66. 3 Inſt. 109. 7 Co. 18. a. 3 H. 8. 3. b. Crom. 36. a. b. Dalt. ca. 103.

Sect. 24. As to the fifth Point, *viz.* How for the Goods taken away ought to belong to another; it ſeems agreed, That the taking of Goods where- See 1 H. H. P. C. 512 to 515. Bro. Cor. 190.

H. P. C. 67. 22 Aſſ. Pl. 99. 3 Inſt. 108. S. P. C. 25. b. Dalt. ca. 103. Fitz. Cor. 265.

whereof no one had a Property at the Time, cannot be Felony; and therefore, That he who takes away Treaſure-trove, or a Wreck, Waif, or Stray, before they have been ſeized by the Perſons who have a Right thereto, is not guilty of Felony, and ſhall be only puniſhed by Fine, &c.

3 Inſt. 109. H. P. C. 67. Owen 20.

Sect. 25. Neither ſhall he who takes a Fiſh in a River or other great Water, wherein they are at their natural Liberty, be guilty of Felony, as he may be who takes them out of a Trunk or Pond, &c.

7 Co. 18. 22 Aſſ. 95. 22 H. 6. 59. b. 18 Ed. 4. 8. a. Bro. Coro. 92, 155, 164. S. P. C. 25. b. 3 Inſt. 109, 110. 18 H. 8. 2. a. b. Dalt. ca. 92.

Sect. 26. Upon the like Ground it ſeems clear, That a Man cannot commit Felony by taking Deer, Hares, or Conies, in a Foreſt, Chaſe, or Warren, or old Pigeons being out of the Houſe, &c. But it is agreed, That one may commit Larceny in taking ſuch or any other Creatures *feræ naturæ*, if they be fit for Food, and reduced to Tameneſs, and known by him to be ſo; and it ſeems the moſt plauſible Opinion, That it is Felony to ſteal wild Pigeons in a Dove-houſe ſhut up, or Hares or Deer in a Houſe, or even in a Park, incloſed in ſuch a manner that the Owner may take them whenever he pleaſes, without the leaſt Danger of their eſcaping, in which Caſe they are as much in his Power as Fiſh in a Pond, or young Pigeons, or Hawks in a Neſt, &c. in taking of which, for the like Reaſon, it ſeems to be agreed, that Felony may be committed.

H. P. C. 68. 1 H. H. P. C. 511. 7 Co. 17, 18. Dalt. ca. 103. H. P. C. 68. 3 Inſt. 109. ſeem contrary.

Sect. 27. Alſo it ſeems clear, That one may commit Felony by taking away Swans marked or pinioned, or thoſe which are unmarked, if they be kept in a Pond or private River; neither do I ſee why it is not as much Felony to ſteal the Eggs of ſuch Swans or Hawks, as it is to ſteal their young Ones, unleſs it be becauſe 11 *H.* 7. 17. has appointed a leſs Puniſhment for this Offence. [36]

H. P. C. 68. 3 Inſt. 109.

Sect. 28. However, there is no Doubt but that the Taking of Domeſtick Beaſts, as Horſes, Mares, Colts, &c. or of any Creatures whatſoever, which are *domitæ Naturæ*, and fit for Food, as Ducks, Hens, Geeſe, Turkeys, Peacocks, or their Eggs, or young Ones, may be Felony.

S. P. C. 25, 96. A. Dy. 99. Pl. 61. Dal. ca. 103. H. P. C. 67. B. 2. Ch. 23, S. 78. 7 Ed. 4. 14. b. 15. a. S. P. C. 95. H. Dal. ca. 103. 3 Inſt. 110. Bro. Indictm. 33. 1 H. H. P. C. 515. [a] 3 Inſt. 110. 12 Co. 113. H. P. C. 67. Con. Dal. ca. 103.

Sect. 29. Alſo it is ſaid, That there may be Felony in taking Goods the Owner whereof is unknown, in which Caſe the King ſhall have the Goods, and the Offender ſhall be indicted from taking *Bona cujuſdam Hominis ignoti*; and it ſeems, That in ſome Caſes the Law will rather feign a Property, where in Strickneſs there is none, than ſuffer an Offender to eſcape; and therefore it is ſaid, That he who takes away the Goods of a Chapel, or Abbey, in Time of Vacation, may be indicted in the firſt Caſe, for ſtealing *Bona Capellæ*, being in the Cuſtody of ſuch and ſuch, and in the ſecond, for ſtealing *Bona Domus & Eccleſiæ*, &c. and *a fortiori* therefore it follows, That he who ſteals Goods belonging to a Pariſh-Church, may be indicted for ſtealing *Bona Parochianorum*; and it hath been adjudged, That he who takes off a [a] Shrowd from a dead Corps, may be indicted as having ſtoln it from him who was the Owner thereof when it was put on, for a dead Man can have no Property.

[b] 7 H. 6. 43. a. 5 H. 7. 18. b. Bro. Coro. 45, 160. Cro. Eliz. 536. S. P. C. 26. A. 3 Inſt. 110. Mo. Pl. 981. Dalt. ca. 103. [c] H. P. C. 67. Kellew. 70. b.

Sect. 30. And there is a ſpecial Caſe wherein it is ſaid, That a Man may commit Larceny by taking of Things, whereof the abſolute Property is in himſelf; as if *A.* [b] deliver Goods to *B.* being a Tailor, or Carrier, &c. and afterwards, with an Intent to make him anſwer for them fraudulently and ſecretly take them away; for *B.* had a ſpecial Kind of Property in the Goods ſo delivered to him, in reſpect whereof, if a [c] Stranger had ſtoln them, he might have been indicted generally as having ſtoln *B.*'s Goods, and the Injury is altogether as great, and the Fraud as baſe, where they are taken away by the very Owner.

Sect. 31. As to the fixth [a] Point, *viz.* of what Value the Goods ftoln must be, if they be but of the Value of 12 *d.* or under, the Offence can be but Petit Larceny.

[a] 22 Aff. 39. 1 H. H. P. C. 530. Bro. Coro. 84, 85.

S. P. C. 24. H. K. 2 Rol. Re. 78. Dal. ca. 101. 2 Inft. 189. Kelynge 68. H. P. C. 69, 70.

Sect. 32. Yet [b] if two Perfons, or more, together, fteal Goods above the Value of twelve Pence, every one of them is guilty of Grand Larceny, for each Perfon is as much an Offender as if he had been alone.

[b] S. P. C. 24. K. Dal. ca. 101. H. P. C. 70. Crom. 36. a.

Sect. 33. Alfo it [c] feems the current Opinion of all the old Books, That if one at feveral Times fteal feveral Parcels of Goods, each under the Value of twelve Pence, but amounting in the whole to more, from the fame Perfon, and be found guilty thereof on the fame Indictment, he fhall have Judgment of Death as for Grand Larceny; but this Severity is feldom practifed.

[c] S. P. C. 24. I. K. 1 H. H. P. C. 531. Crom. 36. a. Dal. ca. 101. H. P. C. 70. 2 Keb. 719.

In what Cafes fimple Larceny is excluded from the Benefit of the Clergy will be fhewn hereafter in the fecond Book, in the Chapter concerning Clergy.

Sect. 34. And now we are come to Petit Larceny, which feems to agree with Grand Larceny in all the Particulars above-mentioned, except only the Value of the Goods; fo that where-ever an Offence would amount to Grand Larceny, if the Thing ftoln were above the Value of twelve Pence, it is Petit Larceny, if it be but of that Value or under.

H. P. C. 69. 1 H. H. P. C. 503.

Sect. 35. And if one be indicted for ftealing Goods to the Value of ten Shillings, and the Jury find fpecially that he is guilty, but that the Goods are worth but ten Pence, he fhall not have Judgment of Death, but only as for Petit Larceny.

Bro. Coro. 84, 184. S. P. C. 24. L. Dal. ca. 101. Crom. 36. a. Hetl. 66.

Sect. 36. It feems that all Petit Larceny is Felony, and confequently requires the word *Felonicè*, in an Indictment for it; yet it is certain, That it is not punifhed with the Lofs of Life, or Lands, but only with the Forfeiture of Goods and Chattels, and whipping, or other corporal Punifhment.

7 H. 8. 23. Bro. Coro. 2. 219. 1 H. H. P. C. 530. Appeal 72. 143. H. P. C. 70. Con. S. P. C. 24. b. Dalt ca. 101.

CHAP. XXXIV.

Of Robbery.

Sect. 1. MIXT or complicated Larceny is fuch as hath a farther Degree of Guilt in it, as being a Taking from the Perfon of a Man, or from his Houfe.

Sect. 2. Larceny from the Perfon of a Man either puts him in Fear, and then it is called Robbery; or does not put him in Fear, and then it is called barely, Larceny from the Perfon.

Sect. 3. Robbery is a felonious and violent Taking away from the Perfon of another, Goods or Money to any Value, putting him in Fear.

H. P. C. 71. 2 Inft. 68. 1 H. H. P. C. 532.

In

In the Explication whereof, I ſhall conſider the following Particulars:

1. What Taking away will ſatisfy the Word *Cepit* in an Indictment for this Offence.
2. What ſhall be ſaid to be a Taking away from the Perſon.
3. What kind of Taking ſhall be ſaid to be violent.
4. In what Reſpects Robbery differs from other Larcenies.

H. P. C. 72. 44 E. 3. 14. b. 4 H. 4. 3. a. Dalt. cap. 100. S. P. C. 27. f. Crom. 34. a. 3 Inſt. 68. Fitz. Cor. 464.

Sect. 4. As to the firſt Point, *viz.* What Taking away will ſatisfy the Word *Cepit* in an Indictment for Robbery; it ſeems clear, That he who receives my Money by my Delivery, either whilſt I am under the Terror of his Aſſault, or afterwards while I think my ſelf bound in Conſcience to give it him by an Oath to that Purpoſe, which in my Fear I was compelled by him to take, may in the Eye of the Law, as properly be ſaid to take it from me, as he who actually takes it out of my Pocket with his own Hands.

3 Inſt. 69. H. P. C. 72.

Sect. 5. Neither can he who has once actually compleated the Offence, by taking my Goods in ſuch a Manner into his Poſſeſſion, afterwards purge it by any Re-delivery, &c.

S. P. C. 27. g. Crom. 34. 3 Inſt. 69. Dalt. cap. 100. H. P. C. 71, 72. 1 H. H. P. C. 532.

Sect. 6. But he who only attacks me in order to rob me, but does not take my Goods into his Poſſeſſion, though he go ſo far as to cut off the Girdle of my Purſe, by Reaſon whereof it falls to the Ground, is not guilty of Robbery; but highly puniſhable by Fine and Impriſonment, &c. for ſo enormous a Breach of the Peace. [37]

1 H. H. P. C. 533, 534, 537. Crom. 34. a. b.

Sect. 7. Yet in ſome Caſes a Man may be ſaid to rob me, where in Truth he never actually had any of my Goods in his Poſſeſſion; as where I am robbed by ſeveral in one Gang, and one of them only takes my Money, in which Caſe, in Judgment of Law, every one of the Company ſhall be ſaid to take it, in reſpect of that Encouragement which they give to one another, through the Hopes of mutual Aſſiſtance in their Enterprize:

1 And. 116. Pudſey's Caſe. Crom. 34. Dalt. cap. 100. H. P. C. 72. B. 2. Ch. 29. § 8.

Nay, though they miſs of the firſt intended Prize, and one of them afterwards ride from the reſt, and rob a third Perſon in the ſame High-way without their Knowledge out of their View, and then return to them, all are guilty of Robbery, for they came together with an Intent to rob, and to aſſiſt one another in ſo doing.

S. P. C. 27. d. Crom. 34, 35. Dalt. cap. 100. 3 Inſt. 69. H. P. C. 73. 1 H. H. P. C. 533. Sty. Rep. 156. Salk. 613. Carth. 145.

Sect. 8. As to the ſecond Point, *viz.* What ſhall be ſaid to be a Taking away from the Perſon; not only the taking away a Horſe from a Man whereon he is actually riding, or Money out of his Pocket, but alſo the Taking of any Thing from him openly and before his Face, which is under his immediate and perſonal Care and Protection, may properly enough be ſaid to be a Taking from the Perſon: And therefore he who having firſt aſſaulted me takes away my Horſe ſtanding by me, or having put me in Fear, drives my Cattle in my Preſence out of my Paſture, or takes up my Purſe which in my Fright I caſt into a Buſh, or my Hat which fell from my Head, or robs my Servant of my Money before my Face, may be indicted as having taken ſuch Things from my Perſon. [38]

1 H. H. P. C. 533, 534. H. P. C. 71, 72. Crom. 34. b. Dal. cap. 100.

Sect. 9. As to the third Point, *viz.* What kind of Taking ſhall be ſaid to be violent; where-ever a Perſon aſſaults another with ſuch Circumſtances of Terror as put him into Fear, and cauſes him by Reaſon of ſuch Fear to part with his Money, the Taking thereof is adjudged Robbery, whether there were any Weapon drawn or not, or whether the Perſon aſſaulted delivered his Money upon the other's Command, or afterwards gave it him upon his ceaſing to uſe Force, and begging an Alms; for he was put into Fear by his Assault, and gives him his Money to get rid of him. [39]

Sect. 10. And some have gone so far as to hold, That if a Man, meeting another going with his Goods to Market in order to sell them, compel him to sell them to him against his Will, he is guilty of Robbery, though he give for them more than they are worth: But perhaps this Opinion is too severe, because the Grievance to the Party seems rather to proceed from the Perverseness of his Humour, than from any real Injury done to him; and there seems to be no such Enormity in the Intention of the Wrong-doer, as is implied in the Notion of Felony. Crom. 34. b. 35. Dalt.cap.100.

Sect. 11. However it is certain, That the Claim of Property, in the Thing taken away, without any Colour, is no manner of Excuse. 1 H. H. P. C. 509. H. P. C. first Edition 62.

As to the fourth Point, *viz.* In what Respects Robbery differs from other Larcenies.

Sect. 12. I. No other Larceny shall have Judgment of Death, unless the Thing stoln be above the Value of twelve Pence; but Robbery shall have such Judgment, how small soever the Value may be of the Thing taken away. S. P. C. 27. a. Crom. 33. b. Dal. cap.100. H. P.C. 74.

Sect. 13. II. Other Larcenies whether from the Person or not, shall not be supposed to be done with Violence or Terror, but Robbery is always laid as done on an Assault with Violence, and putting the Party in Fear, which is properly thus expressed in an Indictment, ——— *à Persona* J. S. *violenter & felonicè cepit & asportavit in magnum prædicti* J. S. *Terrorem.* H. P. C. 74. 3 Inst. 68. Kelynge 70.

Sect. 14. III. But they all agree in this, That the Offenders had the Benefit of the Clergy at the Common Law, but many of them are at this Day excluded in many Cases by Statute; for which see the Chapter in the second Book concerning Clergy.

CHAP. XXXV.

Of Larceny from the Person.

Sect. 1. Larceny from the Person of a Man without putting him in Fear, is either done privily without his Knowledge, (in which Case it is excluded from the Benefit of the Clergy by 8 *El.* 4.) or openly and avowedly before his Face; as if one take off my Hat from my Head, and run away with it, or come into my Shop and cheapen Goods, and run away with them without paying for them, which is agreed not to be Robbery, and as it seems is more properly indictable as a Trespass than Felony, unless the Offender were either unknown, or immediately fled the Country if he were known; otherwise I have a Remedy against him in the ordinary Course of civil Justice; and it seems rigorous to make such Offences capital, which probably may sufficiently be provided against by more gentle Methods. Dy. 224. Pl. 30. 2Rol.Re.154. H. P. C. 73, 74. 75. Crom. 34. b. Dalt.cap.100. Raym. 275, 276.

Sect. 2. However it is certain, That all open Larcenies from the Person are within the Benefit of the Clergy, except such as are committed in a Dwelling-House, *&c.* to the Value of forty Shillings, from which it is taken away by 12 *Ann.* 7.

1 H. H. P.C. 529. *Sect.* 3. Alſo a private Larceny from the Perſon ſhall have the Benefit
H. P. C. 75. of the Clergy, unleſs it be laid in the Indictment as done *clam* and *ſecretè*, *&c.* in exact Purſuance of the Words of 8 *El.* 4.

H. P. C. 75. *Sect.* 4. And no ſuch Larceny ſhall have Judgment of Death but only
Dalt.cap.100. as of Petit Larceny, if the Jury find the Offender guilty under the Value of twelve Pence; for the Statute does not alter the Nature of the Offence, or make that Capital which was not ſo before, but only leaves the Offender to the Judgment of the Common Law.

CHAP. XXXVI.

Of Larceny from the Houſe.

H. P. C. 76. *Sect.* 1. THE other Branch of complicated Larceny, is that which is from the Habitation of a Man, which though it ſeem to have a higher Degree of Guilt than ſimple Larceny, yet I do not find it diſtinguiſhed from it by the Common Law, either as to the Circumſtances above mentioned, which are requiſite to conſtitute the Offence, or as to the Puniſhment.

Sect. 2. However it is at this Day excluded from the Benefit of the Clergy in many Caſes by ſeveral Acts of Parliament, which I ſhall particularly conſider in the ſecond Book in the Chapter concerning Clergy.

CHAP. XXXVII.

Of Piracy.

Sect. 1. TO what has been ſaid concerning ſuch Larcenies as are Felonies by the Common Law, it may not be improper to add ſomewhat concerning Piracy and Depredation at Sea, which is a capital Offence by the Civil Law. [40]

40 Aſſ. 25. *Sect.* 2. It is ſaid, That before 25 *Ed.* 3. this Offence was puniſhed at
3 Inſt. 115. S. P. C. 10. b. Common Law as Petit Treaſon, if committed by a Subject, and as Felony,
H. P. C. 77. if committed by a Foreigner: However it ſeems agreed, that after that Sta-
28 H. 8. c. 15. tute by which all Treaſon is confined to the Particulars therein ſet down, it
3 Inſt. 112. was cognizable only by the Civil Law.

H. P. C. 77. *Sect.* 3. But this proving very inconvenient, becauſe by that Law no
3 Inſt. 112. Offender ſhall have Judgment of Death, without his own Confeſſion, or direct Proof by Eye-Witneſſes, it was enacted by 28 *H.* 8. 15. *That all Felonies and Robberies,* &c. *upon the Sea, or in any Haven, River, Creek, or Place, where the Admiral or Admirals have or pretend to have Power, Authority or Juriſdiction, ſhall be inquired, tried, heard, determined and judged in ſuch Shires and Places in the Realm, as ſhall be limited by the King's Commiſſion or Commiſſions to be directed for the ſame, in like Form and Condition, as if any ſuch Offence or Offences had been committed or done in or upon the Land, and ſuch Commiſſions ſhall be had under the King's Great Seal, directed to the Admiral or Admi-*

rals, or to his or their Lieutenant, Deputy and Deputies, and to three or four ſuch other ſubſtantial Perſons, as ſhall be named or appointed by the Lord Chancellor of England *for the Time being, from Time to Time, and as oft as Need ſhall require, to hear and determine ſuch Offences, after the common Courſe of the Laws of this Land uſed for Felonies and Robberies,* &c. *done and committed upon the Land within this Realm.*

Sect. 4. And it is farther enacted by the ſaid Statute, *That if any Perſon or Perſons happen to be indicted for any ſuch Offence done, or hereafter to be done, upon the Seas, or in any other Place above limited, that then ſuch Order, Proceſs, Judgment and Execution, ſhall be uſed, had, done and made, to and againſt every ſuch Perſon and Perſons ſo being indicted, as againſt Felons,* &c. *for any Felony,* &c. *upon the Land, by the Laws of the Land is accuſtomed.*

Sect. 5. And it is farther enacted by the ſaid Statute, *That ſuch as ſhall be convict of any ſuch Offence by Verdict, Confeſſion, or Proceſs by Authority of any ſuch Commiſſion, ſhall have and ſuffer ſuch Pains of Death, Loſſes of Lands, Goods and Chattels, as if they had been attainted and convicted of ſuch Offence done upon the Land, and alſo that they ſhall be excluded from the* See the Ch. of
Benefit of the Clergy. Clergy.

In the Expoſition of this Act it has been holden,

Sect. 6. I. That it does not alter the Nature of the Offence, ſo as to make that which was before a Felony only by the Civil Law, now become a Felony by the Common Law; for the Offence muſt ſtill be alledged as done upon the Sea, and is no Way cognizable by the Common Law, but only by Virtue of this Statute, which by ordaining that in ſome Reſpects it ſhall have the like Trial and Puniſhment, as are uſed for Felony at Common Law, ſhall not be carried ſo far as to make it alſo agree with it in other Particulars which are not mentioned: And from hence it follows, That this Offence remains as before of a ſpecial Nature, and that it ſhall not be included in a general Pardon of all Felonies, which, as it was before this Statute, to be expounded of no Felonies which are ſuch only by the Civil Law, ſhall continue ſtill to have the ſame Conſtruction. 3 Inſt. 112, 113. H. P. C. 77. Moore 756. 3 Inſt. 112. Co. Lit. 391. H. P. C. 77.

Sect. 7. From the ſame Ground alſo it follows, That no Perſons ſhall, in Reſpect of this Statute, be conſtrued to be, or puniſhed as, Acceſſaries to Piracy before or after, as they might have been if it had been made a Felony by the Statute, whereby all thoſe would incidentally have been made Acceſſaries in the like Caſes, in which they would have been Acceſſaries to a Felony at Common Law: And from hence it follows, That Acceſſaries to Piracy being neither expreſly named in the Statute, nor by Conſtruction included in it, remain as they were before, and were triable by the Civil Law, if their Offence were committed on the Sea, but if on the Land, by no Law until 11 and 12 *Will.* 3. 7. for 2 and 3 *Ed.* 6. 24. which provides againſt Acceſſaries in one County to a Felony in another, extends not to Acceſſaries to an Offence committed in no County, but on the Sea; but by the ſaid Statute of 11 and 12 *Will.* they are triable in like Manner as the Principals are by the Statute of 28 *H.* 8. 3 Inſt. 112. H. P. C. 77, 215.

Sect. 8. From the ſame Ground alſo it follows, That an Attainder for this Offence corrupts not the Blood, inaſmuch as the Statute only ſays that the Offender ſhall ſuffer ſuch Pains of Death, *&c.* as if he were attainted of a Felony at Common Law; but ſays not that the Blood ſhall be corrupted, *&c.* 3 Inſt. 112. H. P. C. 77. B. 2. Ch. 23. Sect. 12.

Sect. 9. Yet it has been reſolved, That an Offender ſtanding mute on an Arraignment by Force of this Statute, ſhall have Judgment of Pain *Fort & dure*; for the Words of the Statute are, *That a Commiſſion ſhall be directed* 3 Inſt. 114. Dyer 241. Pl. 49, 308. Pl. 73. H. P. C. 78.

directed, &c. *to hear and determine ſuch Offences after the common Courſe of the Laws of the Land*, &c.

Sect. 10. II. It has been holden, That the Indictment for this Offence
3 Inſt. 112. S.P.C. 114. a. muſt alledge the Fact to be done upon the Sea, and muſt have both the Words *Felonicè* and *Piraticè*: And that no Offence is puniſhable by Vir-
1 Rol. Re. 175. tue of this Act as Piracy, which would not have been Felony if done on the Land, and conſequently that the Taking of an Enemy's Ship by an Enemy, is not within the Statute.

Moore 756. 1 Rol. Re. 175. H. P. C. 77. 3 Inſt. 113. *Sect.* 11. III. It is agreed, That this Statute extends not to Offences done in Creeks or Ports within the Body of a County, becauſe they are, and always were, cognizable by the Common Law.

Sect. 12. It is enacted by 11 and 12 *Wil.* 3. 7. which was continued by 1 *Georg.* 25. for five Years, and from thence to the End of the next Seſſions of Parliament, *That all Piracies, Felonies and Robberies committed in or upon the Sea, or in any Place where the Admiral has Juriſdiction, may be tried and determined at Sea or upon the Land, in any of his Majeſty's Iſlands, or Plantations*, &c. *to be appointed by the King's Commiſſion under the Great Seal, or the Seal of the Admiralty, directed to any of the Admirals*, &c. *and ſuch Perſons and Officers by Name, or for the Time being, as his Majeſty ſhall think fit, who ſhall have Power jointly or ſeverally, by Warrant under Hand and Seal of any of them, to commit any Perſon againſt whom Information of any ſuch Offences ſhall be given upon Oath, and to call a Court of Admiralty, which ſhall conſiſt of ſeven Perſons at the leaſt, and ſhall proceed in the Trial of the ſaid Offenders, according to ſuch Directions as are ſet forth at large in the ſaid Statute.*

Sect. 13. And it is farther enacted by the ſaid Statute, Par. 8. *That if any of his Majeſty's natural born Subjects or Denizens of this Kingdom, ſhall commit any Piracy or Robbery, or any Act of Hoſtility, againſt other his Majeſty's Subjects upon the Sea, under Colour of any Commiſſion from any foreign Prince or State, or Pretence of Authority from any Perſon whatſoever, ſuch Offender and Offenders, and every of them, ſhall be deemed, adjudged, and taken to be Pirates, Felons and Robbers; and they and every of them being duly convicted thereof, according to this Act, or the aforeſaid Statute of King* Henry *the Eighth, ſhall have and ſuffer ſuch Pains of Death, Loſs of Lands, Goods and Chattels, as Pirates, Felons and Robbers upon the Seas ought to have and ſuffer.*

Sect. 14. And it is farther enacted by the ſaid Statute, *That if any Commander or Maſter of any Ship, or any Seaman or Mariner, ſhall in any Place where the Admiral hath Juriſdiction, betray his Truſt and turn Pirate, Enemy or Rebel, and piratically and felonioully run away with his or their Ship or Ships, or any Barge, Boat, Ordnance, Ammunition, Goods or Merchandizes, or yield them up voluntarily to any Pirate, or bring any ſeducing Meſſage from any Pirate, Enemy or Rebel, or conſult, combine, or confederate with, or attempt or endeavour to corrupt, any Commander, Maſter, Officer or Mariner to yield up or run away with any Ship, Goods or Merchandize, or turn Pirate, or go over to Pirates, or if any Perſon ſhall lay violent Hands on his Commander, whereby to hinder him from fighting in Defence of his Ship and Goods committed to his Truſt, or that ſhall confine his Maſter, or make or endeavour to make a Revolt in his Ship, ſhall be adjudged to be a Pirate, Felon and Robber; and being convicted thereof, according to the Direction of this Act, ſhall have and ſuffer Pains of Death, Loſs of Lands, Goods and Chattels, as Pirates, Felons and Robbers upon the Seas ought to have and ſuffer.*

Sect. 15. And it is farther enacted by the ſaid Statute, *That all and every Perſon and Perſons whatſoever, who ſhall either on the Land or upon the Seas, wittingly or knowingly ſet forth any Pirate, or aid and aſſiſt, or maintain, procure, command, counſel, or adviſe any Perſon or Perſons whatſoever, to do or commit any Piracies or Robberies upon the Seas; and ſuch Perſon or Perſons ſhall thereupon do or commit any ſuch Piracy or Robbery, then all and every ſuch Perſon or Perſons whatſoever, ſo as aforeſaid, ſetting forth any Pirate, or aiding or aſſiſting, maintaining procuring, commanding, counſelling or adviſing the ſame, either on the Land or upon the Sea, ſhall be adjudged to be Acceſſary to ſuch Piracy and Robbery done and committed:* And further, *That after any Piracy or Robbery is or ſhall be committed by any Pirate or Robber whatever, every Perſon or Perſons, who, knowing that ſuch Pirate or Robber has done or committed ſuch Piracy and Robbery, ſhall on the Land or upon the Sea receive, entertain, or conceal any ſuch Pirate or Robber, or receive or take into his Cuſtody, any Ship, Veſſel, Goods or Chattels, which have been by any ſuch Pirate or Robber piratically and feloniouſly taken, ſhall be, by this Statute likewiſe adjudged to be Acceſſary to ſuch Piracy and Robbery: And that all ſuch Acceſſaries to ſuch Piracies and Robberies, ſhall be enquired of, tried, heard, determined and adjudged according to the common Courſe of the Law, according to the ſaid Statute of* 28 H. 8. *as the Principals of ſuch Piracies and Robberies may be, and no otherwiſe; and being thereupon attainted ſhall ſuffer ſuch Pains of Death, Loſs of Lands, Goods and Chattels, and in like Manner as the Principals of ſuch Piracies, Robberies and Felonies, ought to ſuffer according to the ſaid Statute of* H. 8. *which is declared to be in full* ☞ *Force, any thing in this laſt Act to the contrary notwithſtanding.* [41]

Sect. 16. And by 4 Georg. 1. c. 11. Par. 7. *All Perſons who ſhall commit any Offence for which they ought to be adjudged Pirates, Felons or Robbers, by* 11 & 12 Guli. 3. *may be tried and judged for every ſuch Offence, according to the Form of* 28 H. 8. *and ſhall be excluded from their Clergy.*

CHAP. XXXVIII.

Of Burglary.

AND now we are come to Offences againſt the Habitation of a Man, which are of two kinds: H. P. C. 79. 22 Aſſ. 95. Bro. Cor. 93. 3 Inſt. 63. S. P. C. 30. a. Dalt. cap. 99. Crom. 31. a.

1. Burglary.
2. Arſon.

Sect. 1. Burglary is a Felony at the Common Law, in breaking and entering the Manſion-Houſe of another, or (as ſome ſay,) the Walls or Gates of a walled Town in the Night, to the Intent to commit ſome Felony within the ſame, whether the felonious Intent be executed or not. 1 H. H. P. C. 549. 2 H. H. P. C. 360.

For the better Underſtanding whereof, I ſhall conſider the following Particulars:

1. What ſhall be accounted Night-time for this Purpoſe.
2. Whether there muſt be both an actual Entry and Breaking.
3. What Breaking is ſufficient.
4. What Entry.
5. In what Place this Offence may be committed.
6. What Degree of Guilt is required in the principal Intention.

Sect. 2. [a] As to the firſt Point, *viz.* What ſhall be accounted Night-Time for this Purpoſe; there are ſome Opinions, That Burglary may be committed at any Time after Sun-ſet, and before Sun-riſing; but it ſeems the much better Opinion, That the Word *Noctanter*, which is preciſely neceſſary [a] Dalt. cap. 99. S. P. C. 30. a. Crom 33. a. H. P. C. 79. 3 Inſt. 63. Savil. 47. Crom. 32. a. 7 Co. 6. 1 H. H. P. C. 550, 551.

neceſſary in every Indictment for this Offence, cannot be ſatisfied in a legal Senſe, if it appear upon the Evidence, that there was ſo much Day-light at the Time, that a Man's Countenance might be diſcerned thereby. [42]

Dalt. cap. 99. *Sect.* 3. As to the ſecond Point, *viz.* Whether there muſt be both
Crom. 32. a. an Entry and Breaking; notwithſtanding ſome looſe Opinions to the con-
Dyer 99. a. trary, there ſeems to be no good Cauſe to doubt but that both are re-
S. P. C. 30. a. 3 Inſt. 64. quired to compleat this Offence, for the Words, *fregit* and *intravit*, being
H. P. C. 80. both of them preciſely neceſſary in the Indictment, both muſt be ſatisfied:
1 H. H. P. C. And *à fortiori* therefore there can be no Burglary, where there is neither
551, 555, 559. Con. Dalt. of them; as if on a bare Aſſault upon a Houſe the Owner fling out his
cap. 99. Money.

Crom. 31. b. *Sect.* 4. As to the third Point, *viz.* What Breaking is ſufficient; it
3 Inſt. 64. ſeems agreed, That ſuch a Breaking as is implied by Law in every unlaw-
H. P. C. 80. 1 H. H. P. C. ful Entry on the Poſſeſſion of another, whether it lie open or be incloſed,
551, 552. and will maintain a common Indictment, or Action of Treſpaſs *Quare clauſum fregit*, will not ſatisfy the Words *Felonicè & Burglariter fregit*, except in ſome ſpecial Caſes, in which it is accompanied with ſuch Circum-
H. P. C. 80, ſtances as make it as heinous as an actual Breaking: And from hence it
82. follows, That if one enter into a Houſe by a Door which he finds open,
Con. Dal. 99. or through a Hole which was made there before, and ſteal Goods, &c. or draw any thing out of a Houſe through a Door or Window which
Crom. 34. a. were open before, or enter into a Houſe by the Doors open in the Day-
H. P. C. 81. Dalt. cap. 99. time, and lie there till Night, and then rob and go away, without break-
1 And. 115. ing any Part of the Houſe, he is not guilty of Burglary. But it is certain,
H. P. C. 80. That he would have been guilty thereof if he had opened the Window, or
Dalt. cap. 99. Savil 47. unlocked the Door, or broke a Hole in the Wall, and then had entered, &c. or if having entered by a Door which he found open, or having lain
Dal. cap. 99. Kelynge 67. in the Houſe by the Owner's Conſent, he had but unlatched a Chamber
H. P. C. 81, Door; or if he had come down by the Chimney: (in which Caſe though
82. it might be ſaid, That the Houſe was open there, and ſo not actually bro-
Hutt. 20. ken; yet it was as much incloſed as the Nature of the Thing would bear.) And according to ſome Opinions, he would have been in like Manner guilty, if upon an Aſſault made by him upon the Houſe, with an Intent to rob it, the Owner had opened the Door in order to drive him off, and thereupon he had entered: (in which Caſe, as ſome ſay, the opening of the
Crom. 32. a. Door by the Owner, being occaſioned by the felonious Attempt of the
Con. 1 And. other, is as much imputable to him as if it had been actually done by his
115. own Hands.) [43]

Sect. 5. And it has alſo been reſolved, That where divers Perſons
Kelynge 42. came to a Houſe with an Intent to rob it, and knocked at the Door, pretending to have Buſineſs with the Owner, and being by that Means let in, rifled the Houſe, they were guilty of Burglary: Alſo it hath been adjudged,
Kelynge 63. That thoſe were no leſs guilty, who, having a Deſign to rob a Houſe, took Lodgings in it, and then fell on the Landlord and robbed him; for the Law will not endure to have its Juſtice defrauded by ſuch Evaſions.
Crom. 32. b. And for the like Reaſon, *à fortiori*, it has been reſolved, That where
Dalt. cap. 99. H. P. C. 81. Perſons, intending to rob a Houſe, raiſed a Hue and Cry, and prevailed
1 H. H. P. C. with a Conſtable to make a Search in the Houſe, and having got in by
552. that Means, with the Owner's Conſent, bound the Conſtable, and robbed the Inhabitants, they were guilty of Burglary; for there cannot be a greater Affront to publick Juſtice, than to make Uſe of legal Proceſs as a Stale for ſuch villanous Purpoſes; and therefore the whole Act is eſteemed tortious *ab initio.*

Sect. 6. It is recited by 12 *Annæ*, 7. *That there had been ſome Doubt, Whether the entring into a Manſion-Houſe, without breaking the ſame, with an Intent to commit ſome Felony, and breaking the ſaid Houſe in the Night-time to get out, were Burglary:* And thereupon it is declared and enacted, *That if any Perſon ſhall enter into the Manſion or Dwelling-Houſe of another by Day or by Night, without breaking the ſame, with an Intent to commit Felony, or being in ſuch a Houſe, ſhall commit any Felony, and ſhall in the Night-time break the ſaid Houſe to get out of the ſame, ſuch Perſon is, and ſhall be taken to be, guilty of Burglary, and ouſted of the Benefit of Clergy, in the ſame Manner as if ſuch Perſon had broken and entred the ſaid Houſe in the Night-time, with an Intent to commit Felony there.*

Sect. 7. As to the fourth Point, *viz.* What Entry is ſufficient to this Purpoſe; it ſeems agreed, That any the leaſt Entry, either with the whole, or but with Part of the Body, or with any Inſtrument, or Weapon, will ſatisfy the Word *Intravit* in an Indictment of Burglary; as if one do but put his Foot over a Threſhold, or his Hand, or a Hook, or Piſtol, within a Window, or turn the Key of a Door which is locked on the Inſide, or ☞ diſcharge a loaded Gun into a Houſe, *&c.* [44]

Dalt. cap. 99. H. P. C. 81. 1 And. 115. 1 H. H. P. C. 553, 555. Crom. 31, 32. Crom. 32. a. Con. 1 And. 115.

Sect. 8. Nay, it is certain, That in ſome Caſes one may be guilty of Burglary, who never made any actual Entry at all; as where divers come to commit a Burglary together, and ſome ſtand to watch in adjacent Places, and the others enter, and rob, *&c.* for in all ſuch Caſes, the Act of one is in Judgment of Law the Act of all.

1 H. H. P. C. 439, 555. Crom. 32. a. H.P.C. 80, 81.

Sect. 9. And upon the like Ground, it ſeems difficult to find a Reaſon, why a Servant, who, confederating with a Rogue, lets him in to rob a Houſe, *&c.* ſhould not be guilty of Burglary as much as he; for it is clear, That if the Servant were out of the Houſe, the Entry of the other would be adjudged to be his alſo; and what Difference is there, when he ☞ is in the Houſe? [45]

Con. H. P. C. 81. Dalt. cap. 99.

Sect. 10. As to fifth Point, *viz.* In what Place this Offence may be committed, it ſeems to be the current Opinion at this Day, That it can be only in a Dwelling-Houſe, and that the Indictment for it muſt neceſſarily alledge the Fact *in Domo manſionali.* And Sir *Edward Coke* ſeems to ſay, That the Breaking a Church, *&c.* is therefore Burglary, becauſe the Church is the Manſion-Houſe of God: But I can find nothing in the more ancient Authors to countenance this Nicety; for the general Tenor of the old Books ſeems to be, That Burglary may be committed in breaking Houſes, or Churches, or the Walls, or Gates of a Town. And *Staunforde* and *Anderſon* mention Precedents of Indictments of Burglary *in Domo,* without adding *Manſionali:* However the conſtant Courſe of late Precedents and Opinions makes it certainly a very dangerous if not an Incurable, Fault, to omit the Word *Manſionalis* in an Indictment of Burglary in a Houſe; and therefore without Queſtion, it ought always to be inſerted where the Truth of the Caſe will bear it. But ſure it cannot be neceſſary or proper to have any ſuch Word in an Indictment of Burglary in a Church, which, by all the Books above cited, ſeems to be taken as a diſtinct Burglary from that in a Houſe.

1 H. H. P. C. 550. 4 Co. 40. a. 3 Inſt. 64, 67. H. P. C. 82, 86. 3 Inſt. 64. H. P. C. 82. Bract. 144. b. Bro. Coro. 93. 22 Aſſ. 39, 95. Dalt. cap. 99. 27 Aſſ. 38. 1 And. 302. S. P. C. 30. Poph. 42. 1 H. H. P. C. 549 from Spelman's Gloſſ. Verb. Burglaria. Dalt. cap. 99. [a] 1 H. H. P. C. 556. Crom. 33. b. Dalt. cap. 99.

Sect. 11. [a] However it is agreed by all, That a Houſe wherein a Man dwells but for Part of the Year, or a Houſe which one has hired to live in, and brought Part of his Goods into, but has not yet lodged in; or a Chamber in one of the Inns of Court wherein a Perſon uſually lodges, or a Houſe which a Man's Wife hires without his Privity, and lives in by herſelf without him, may be called his Dwelling-Houſe; and will ſufficiently ſatisfy the Words *Domus manſionalis* in the Indictment, whether any Perſon were actually therein, or not, at the Time of the Offence.

H. P. C. 82. Moor 660. Pl. 903. 4 Co. 40. a. Cro. Car. 474. 1 Jon. 394. H. P. C. 82. Kelynge 54. Poph. 42, 52. 3 Inſt. 64. Skin. 68[illegible]

Sect. 12.

3 Inst. 64. Dalt. cap. 99. Bro. Cor. 180. Crom. 32. b. 1 H. H. P. C. 558, 559. H. P. C. 82.

Sect. 12. Alſo all Out-Buildings, as Barns, Stables, Dairy-Houſes, &c. adjoining to a Houſe, are looked upon as Part thereof, and conſequently Burglary may be committed in them; but if they be removed at any Diſtance from the Houſe, it ſeems that it has not been uſual of late to proceed againſt Offences therein as Burglaries.

Kelynge 27, 52, 83.

Sect. 13. If ſeveral Perſons dwell in one Houſe, as Servants, Gueſts, or Tenants at Will, or otherwiſe having no fix'd and certain Intereſt in any Part thereof, and a Burglary be committed in any of their Apartments; it ſeems clear, that the Indictment ſhall lay the Offence in the Manſion-Houſe of the Proprietor, &c. But if one hire a diſtinct Apartment in a Houſe for his Lodging for a certain Time, and a Burglary be committed therein, I can ſee no good Reaſon why the Indictment may not lay the Offence *in Domo manſionali* of ſuch Lodger; for it ſeems to be agreed, That an Indictment for a Burglary committed in a Chamber in one of the Inns of Court, may lay the Offence *in Domo manſionali* of the Owner of the Chamber; and why may not ſuch an Apartment, with as much Propriety be called the Manſion-Houſe of him that takes it, during the Time that he has a certain Intereſt in it? For ſo long as it is ſevered by the Leaſe, it ſeems in the Eye of the Law to be as diſtinct from the other Parts of the Houſe, as if the Perſon who rents it, had a Freehold or Inheritance in it. And as to the Objection, That he goes into the Houſe by the ſame Door with the other Inhabitants, and therefore is but an Inmate, and the whole ought to be conſidered but as one Houſe; I anſwer, That he muſt have ſome Way to his Apartment as incident to his Intereſt in it, and that ſuch Way lying through a Door which is common to him with others, doth not make the Apartment itſelf in any Reſpect leſs his own, than a Way through a Door belonging to himſelf only would have done.

1 H. H. P. C. 556. Con. Kelynge 83. Vide ſupra. Sect. 11. Crom. 33. a. Dal. cap. 99. Co. Lit. 48. b. H. P. C. 83.

Sect. 14. And if the Law be ſo in this Caſe it ſeems to me very reaſonable alſo, That if ſuch a Lodger take alſo a Cellar in the ſaid Houſe, a Burglary committed in ſuch Cellar, may be alledged *in Domo manſionali* of the Lodger, whether the Cellar had any Communication with the Houſe or not; for ſince it ſeems to be agreed, That a Barn or Stable, or other Out-Building near to a Houſe, ſhall be looked on as Part thereof, why ſhould not ſuch a Cellar have the like Eſtimation? *Sed Quære*, for *Kelynge* ſeems to incline to a different Opinion.

Kelynge 83.

Sect. 15. However it is agreed by all, That if one hire a Part of a Houſe to lodge in, which is actually divided from the reſt, and have a Door of its own to the Street, a Burglary therein may be alledged *in Domo manſionali* of ſuch Perſon.

Sect. 16. But if he had taken it as a Shop or Work-houſe for his Uſe in the Day-time only, it ſeems that a Felony therein cannot be alledged in a Manſion-Houſe; not of him that lets it, becauſe it is ſevered by the Leaſe from that Part of the Houſe which belongs to him, nor of him to whom it is let, becauſe he takes it not to lodge in. [46]

H. P. C. 83. 1 H. H. P. C. 557, 558.

Sect. 17. From what has been ſaid it clearly appears, That no Burglary can be committed by breaking into any Ground incloſed, or Booth, or Tent, &c. for there ſeems to be no Colour from any Authority ancient or modern, to make any Offence Burglary that is not done either againſt ſome Houſe, or Church, or the Walls, or Gates of ſome Town.

H. P. C. 82, 83. 22 Aſſ. 95. Bro. Coro. 93. S. P. C. 30. Dalt. cap. 99. Crom. 31.

Sect. 18. As to the ſixth Point, *viz.* What Degree of Guilt is required in the principal Intention of the Offender, it ſeems clear, That there can be no Burglary but where the Indictment both expreſly alledges, and the Verdict alſo finds, an Intention to commit ſome Felony; for if it appear

Dy. 99. Pl. 58. Dalſ. 22. 3 Inſt. 65.

that the Offender meant only to commit a Trespass, as to beat the Party, &c. he is not guilty of Burglary. However, it seems much the better Opinion, That an Intention to commit a Rape, or such other Crime which is made Felony by Statute, and was a Trespass only at Common Law, will make a Man guilty of Burglary, as much as if such Offence were a Felony at Common Law, because where-ever a Statute makes any Offence Felony, it incidentally gives it all the Properties of a Felony at Common Law. Kelynge 30. H.P.C.83,84. Crom.32. a.b. Con. Dalt. cap. 99. H. P. C. 215. Infra Ch. 40. Sect. 3. 1 H. H. P. C. 562.

CHAP. XXXIX.

Of Arson.

ARSON is a Felony at Common Law, in maliciously and voluntarily burning the House of another by Night or by Day. 1 H. H. P. C. 566. Bro. Coro. 135, 155. S. P. C. 36. 3 Inst. 66. Dal. cap.105. 2 Inst. 188. 11 Co. 29.

For the better Explication whereof I shall consider:

1. What is such a House in which Arson may be committed.
2. Whether this Offence may be committed in the Offender's own House.
3. How much of the House ought to be burnt.
4. With what Degrees of Malice.

Sect. 1. As to the first Point, *viz.* What is such a House in which Arson may be committed; it seems agreed, That not only a Mansion-House, and the principal Parts thereof, but also any other House, and the Outbuildings, as Barns, and Stables, adjoining thereto; and also Barns full of Corn, whether they be adjoining to any House or not, are so far secured by Law, that the malicious burning of them is Arson; and it is said, That in an Indictment they are well expressed by the Word *Domus*, without adding *Mansionalis*. 3 Inst. 67. 4 Co. 20. Dal. ca. 105. 11 H. 7. 1. Bro. Coro. 226. S. P. C. 36. H. P. C. 86. 1 H. H. P. C. 567, 570.

Sect. 2. But it seems that at this Day the Burning of the Frame of a House, or of a Stack of Corn, &c. is not accounted Arson, because it cannot come under the Word *Domus*, which seems at present to be thought necessary in every Indictment of Arson; yet it is said, That anciently the Burning of a Stack of Corn was accounted Arson. And at this Day by 43 *El.* 13. *it is Felony without the Benefit of Clergy, wilfully and of Malice to burn or cause to be burned, or aid, procure, or consent to the Burning of any Barn, Stack of Corn, or Grain, in the Counties of* Northumberland, Cumberland, Westmoreland *and* Durham. And by 22 and 23 *Ca.* 2. 7. *it is Felony, in the Night-time, maliciously, unlawfully, and willingly to burn or cause to be burned any Stacks or Ricks of Corn, Hay, or Grain, Barns, or other Houses, or Buildings, or Kilns, in any Place whatsoever: But the Offender may avoid Judgment of Death by chusing Transportation, and may be proceeded against by any three Justices of Peace, according to the Method prescribed by the Statute*, which is set forth more at large in Chap. 46. 1 H. H. P. C. 568. H. P. C. 86. 3 Inst. 67. 3 Inst. 67. Britt. fo. 16. S. P. C. 36. Dal. cap. 105.

Sect. 3. As to the second Point, *viz.* Whether Arson may be committed in the Offender's own House, it seems clearly agreed, That one seized in Fee, or but possessed for Years, of a House standing by it self at 1 Jon. 351. Cro. Ca. 377.

a Diſtance from all others, cannot commit Felony in burning the ſame: Alſo it ſeems the much ſtronger Opinion, That a Man ſo ſeized or poſſeſſed of a Houſe in a Town, who burns his own with an Intent to burn his Neighbour's, but in the Event burns his own only, is not guilty of Arſon; for by the general Tenor of the Books ſpeaking of this Offence, it ſeems to be ſuppoſed to be done in the Houſe of another, and not of the Offender: Neither ſhall any Act, which is only a Crime in Reſpect of the Injury which it does, or may do, to another, be made a Felony by Reaſon of an Intention thereby to commit a Felony, if ſuch Intention be not executed: However this is certainly an Offence highly puniſhable, in Regard of the Malice thereof, and the great Danger to the Publick which attends it, and the Offender may be ſeverely fined and impriſoned during the King's Pleaſure, and ſet on the Pillory, and bound to his good Behaviour during Life.

1 H. H. P. C. 568, 569. 3 Inſt. 67. Dalt. cap. 105. Cro. Ca. 338. 1 Inſt. 351. H. P. C. 85. Kelynge 29.

Sect. 4. As to the third Point, *viz.* How much of ſuch Houſe ought to be burnt, it ſeems to be clearly agreed, That neither a bare Intention to burn a Houſe, nor even an actual Attempt to do it by putting Fire to Part of a Houſe, will amount to Felony, if no Part of it be burnt; for the Indictment muſt have the Words *Incendit & combuſſit:* But it is certain, That if any Part of the Houſe be burnt, the Offender is guilty of Felony, notwithſtanding the Fire afterwards be put out, or go out of it ſelf.

1 H. H. P. C. 570. H. P. C. 85. Dal. cap. 105. 3 Inſt. 66.

Sect. 5. As to the fourth Point, *viz.* With what Degrees of Malice ſuch Houſe ought to be burnt; it ſeems clear, That if the Fire happened through Negligence or Miſchance, it cannot make him, who is the unfortunate Cauſe of it, guilty of Arſon; for the Indictment muſt alledge the Offence to have been done *Voluntariè ex malitiâ ſuâ præcogitatâ & felonicè.* Yet if one maliciouſly intending only to burn the Houſe of *A.* happen thereby to burn the Houſe of *B.* it is certain that he may be indicted as having maliciouſly burned the Houſe of *B.* for where a felonious Deſign againſt one Man miſſes its Aim, and takes Effect upon another, it ſhall have the like Conſtruction as if it had been levelled againſt him who ſuffers by it.

1 H. H. P. C. 569. 3 Inſt. 67. H. P. C. 85. Plow. Com. 475.

CHAP. XL.

Of Felonies by Statute.

OFFENCES more immediately againſt the Subject, made capital by Statute, and not reduced to any of the foregoing Heads, are ſuch as are committed;

1. Againſt Women.
2. Againſt the Rights of Marriage.
3. Againſt the Members of a Man's Body.
4. Againſt Records.
5. Againſt Cattle.
6. By Purveyors.
7. By Soldiers and Mariners.
8. By Hunters.

9. By Forgers of falſe Deeds.
10. By Gaolers.
11. By Tranſporters of Sheep or Wool.
12. By Servants.
13. By Egyptians.
14. By Cutters of Pow-dike.
15. By Treſpaſſers on the Borders, and Rioters.
16. By Bankrupts.
17. By Counterfeiters of Bank-Notes, Exchequer-Bills, Stamps, South-Sea Bonds, Lottery-Orders, *&c.*

In treating hereof, I ſhall firſt conſider ſuch Points as relate to them all in general, and then deſcend to each Crime in particular, in the Order before ſet down.

As to what relates to them all in general, I will ſhew,

1. Where an Offence ſhall be ſaid to be made Felony by Statute.
2. What is incidentally implied in every ſuch Statute.

Sect. 1. As to the firſt Point it ſeems clear, That not only thoſe Crimes which are made Felonies in expreſs Words, but alſo all thoſe which are decreed to have or undergo Judgment of Life and Member by any Statute, become Felonies thereby, whether the Word Felony were omitted or mentioned. 1 H. H. P. C. 627, 641, 703. Bro. Coro. 204. 3 Inſt. 91. 2 Inſt. 434. Co. Lit. 391.

Sect. 2. But an Offence ſhall never be made Felony by the Conſtruction of any doubtful and ambiguous Words of a Statute, and therefore, if it be only prohibited under Pain of forfeiting all that a Man has, or of forfeiting Body and Goods, or of being at the King's Will for Body, Land, and Goods, it ſhall amount to no more than a high Miſdemeanor, puniſhable by Impriſonment, *&c.* Hob. 293. Co. Lit. 391. Hob. 270, 293. 3 Inſt. 146.

Sect. 3. Alſo where a Statute makes a ſecond Offence Felony, or ſubject to a heavier Puniſhment than the firſt; it is always implied, That ſuch ſecond Offence ought to be committed after a Conviction for the firſt; from whence it follows, That if it be not ſo laid in the Indictment, it ſhall be puniſhed but as the firſt Offence; for the gentler Method ſhall firſt be tried, which perhaps may prove effectual. 1 H. H. P. C. 324, 685, 705. H. P. C. 8. 2 Bulſt. 349. Dy. 323. Pl. 31. 1 Leon. 295.

Sect. 4. As to the ſecond Point, *viz.* What is incidentally implied in every Statute, making an Offence Felony; it ſeems clear, That every ſuch Statute does by neceſſary Conſequence ſubject the Offender to the like Attainder and Forfeiture, *&c.* and alſo does require the like Conſtruction, as to thoſe who ſhall be accounted Acceſſaries before or after, and to all other Intents and Purpoſes, as is incident to a Felony at Common Law. 3 Inſt. 47, 59, 90. 1 H. H. P. C. 704. Crompt. 42. Pl. 13. H. P. C. 215. Dalif. 11, 22. B. 2. Ch. 29. Sect. 13, 14. Sal. 542, 543.

Sect. 5. Yet where ſuch a Statute ſaves the Corruption of Blood, it impliedly ſaves the Deſcent of the Land of the Offender to his Heir: Alſo where it ſaves the Land to the Heir, it prevents the Corruption of Blood ſo far; And it is ſaid, That in both Caſes it ſaves the Wife's Dower, becauſe whereever an Heir takes as Heir, he ſhall not avoid a Title of Dower in Reſpect of the ſame Inheritance. But notwithſtanding ſuch a Saving the Land ſhall be forfeited for the Life of the Offender. 3 Inſt. 47. H. P. C. 8. 3 Inſt. 47. 1 H. H. P. C. 703, 704.

Sect. 6. If one commit an Offence which is made Felony by Statute, and then the Statute be repealed, he cannot be puniſhed as a Felon in Reſpect of that Statute. Bro. Coro. 203.

CHAP.

CHAP. XLI.

Of Rape.

OFFENCES againſt Women made Felonies by Statute are of two Kinds.

See 1 H. H. P. C. 626 to 636.

1. Rape.
2. Forcible Marriage.

In treating of Rape, I ſhall conſider,

1. What ſhall be called a Rape.
2. How it is puniſhed.

Co. Lit. 190. 3 Inſt. 60. 2 Inſt. 180. 12 Co. 37. 3 Inſt. 59,60. See 1 H. H. P. C. 628. and Lord Audley's Caſe in the State Trials. H. P. C. 117.

Sect. 1. As to the firſt Point, It ſeems that Rape is an Offence in having unlawful and carnal Knowledge of a Woman, by Force and againſt her Will: But it is ſaid, That no Aſſault upon a Woman in order to raviſh her, howſoever ſhameleſs and outrageous it may be, if it proceed not to ſome Degree of Penetration, and alſo of Emiſſion, can amount to a Rape; however it is ſaid, That Emiſſion is, *primâ facie*, an Evidence of Penetration.

Ruſhworth's Coll. Part 2. Vol. 1. 94. 3 Inſt. 59.

Dalt. ca. 105. Bro. Parliament 55. 5 Ed. 4. 6. a. Ruſhworth's Coll. Part 2. Vol. I. 100. Bract. 147. S. P. C. 24. Bract. 148. Finch 204. Dal. cap. 107.

Sect. 2. Offences of this Nature are not any way mitigated, by ſhewing that the Woman at laſt yielded to the Violence, if ſuch her Conſent was forced by Fear of Death, or of Dureſs: Nor is it any Excuſe, that ſhe conſented after the Fact, or that ſhe was a common Strumpet; for ſhe is ſtill under the Protection of the Law, and may not be forced. But it was anciently ſaid, to be no Rape to force a Man's own Concubine. Alſo it hath been ſaid by ſome to be no Rape to force a Woman who conceives at the Time; for it is ſaid, That if ſhe had not conſented, ſhe could not have conceived: But this Opinion ſeems very queſtionable, not only becauſe the previous Violence is no way extenuated by ſuch a ſubſequent Conſent, but alſo becauſe if it were neceſſary to ſhew that the Woman did not conceive, the Offender could not be tried till ſuch Time as it might appear whether ſhe did or not, and likewiſe becauſe the Philoſophy of this Notion may very well be doubted of. [47] ☜

1 H. H. P. C. 633. Ruſhworth's Coll. Part 2. Vol. I. 100. Bract. 147. a. Dalt. ca. 107. Crom. 100. a. Dy. 304. Pl. 51. Cro. Ca. 332.

Sect. 3. It is a ſtrong, but not a concluſive Preſumption againſt a Woman, That ſhe made no Complaint in a reaſonable Time after the Fact.

Sect. 4. It was a Queſtion before 18 *El.* 7. Whether a Rape could be committed on a Child of the Age of ſix or ſeven Years; but by that Statute, *whoſoever ſhall unlawfully and carnally know and abuſe any Woman-Child under the Age of ten Years, ſhall ſuffer as a Felon without Clergy.*

Sect. 5. Upon an Indictment for this Offence, it is no way material whether ſuch Child conſented, or were forced; yet it muſt be proved, That the Offender entered into her Body, &c.

B. 2. Ch. 29. Sect. 7, 89. Dalt. ca. 107.

Sect. 6. All who are preſent and actually aſſiſt a Man to commit a Rape, may be indicted as principal Offenders, whether they be Men or Women.

2 *Sect.* 7.

Sect. 7. As to the second Point, *viz.* How Rape is punished, it is said, that of old Time it was Felony, and consequently punishable with Death, especially if the Party ravished were a Virgin, unless such Virgin would accept of the Offender for her Husband, in which Case she might save his Life by marrying him. But afterwards it was looked upon as a great Misdemeanour only, but not Felony; and the Offender was punished with the Loss of his Eyes and Testicles: And by the Statute of *Westm.* 1. 13. It was reduced to a Trespass, subjecting the Offender to two Years Imprisonment, and a Fine at the King's Will. But the Smallness of the Punishment proving a great Encouragement to the Offence, it was made Felony again, by the Statute of *Westminster* 2. 34. and by 18 *El.* 7. it is excluded from the Benefit of Clergy.

1 H. H. P. C. 627. Bract. 147, 148. S. P. C. 21. b. 22, 23. 2 Inst. 181. Dalt. cap. 99. Crom. 32. con. Co. Li. 123. b. Fleta lib. 1. cap. 40. 3 Inst. 180. Quære Fitz. Utlagary 49. Bro. Coro. 169.

CHAP. XLII.

Of Forcible Marriage.

Sect. 1. THE marrying a Woman of Substance by Force, and other Offences of the like Nature, were made Felonies by 3 *H.* 7. 2. which was enacted in the following Words:

Sect. 2. *Where Women as well Maidens as Widows and Wives, having Substances, some in Goods moveable, and some in Lands and Tenements, and some being Heirs Apparent unto their Ancestors, for the Lucre of such Substances, be oftentimes taken by Mis-doers, contrary to their Will, and after married to such Mis-doers, or to other by their Assent, or defiled, to the great Displeasure of God, and contrary to the King's Laws, and Disparagement of the said Women, and utter Heaviness and Discomfort of their Friends, and to the evil Ensample of all other: It is therefore ordained, established and enacted by our Sovereign Lord the King, by the Advice of the Lords Spiritual and Temporal, and the Commons in the said Parliament assembled, and by the Authority of the same, That what Person or Persons from henceforth, that taketh any Woman (so) against her Will unlawfully, that is to say, Maid, Widow, or Wife, that such Taking, Procuring, and Abetting to the same, and also receiving wittingly the same Woman so taken against her Will, and knowing the same, be Felony: And that such Mis-doers, Takers, and Procurators to the same, and Receitors, knowing the said Offence in Form aforesaid, be henceforth reputed and judged as principal Felons: Provided alway, that this Act extend not to any Person taking any Woman, only claiming her as his Ward or Bond-Woman.*

Sect. 3. And by 39 *El.* 9. *All Persons who shall be Principals, or Procurers or Accessaries before such Offence committed, are excluded from the Benefit of the Clergy.*

In the Construction of the said Statute or 3 *H.* 7. 2. the following Points have been resolved.

See 1 H. H. P. C. 660, 661. and Swendsen's Case, St. Tr. Vol. 5. p. 468.

Sect. 4. I. That the Indictment must expresly set forth, both that the Woman taken away had Land or Goods, or was Heir apparent, and also that she was married or defiled, because no other Case is within the Preamble of the Statute, to which the enacting Clause clearly refers; for it does not say, That what Person, &c. that taketh any Woman against her Will, but what Person that taketh any Woman *so* against her Will.

Far. 101, 102. Hob. 182. Cro. Ca. 485. Dalis. 22. 1 And. 115. 3 Inst. 61. H. P. C. 118. Savil 59. 12 Co. 20, 110.

Sect. 5. II. That the Indictment ought allso to alledge, That the taking was for Lucre, becaufe the Words of the Preamble are fo, but that it needs not fet forth, That it was with an Intention to marry or defile the Party, becaufe the Words of the Statute neither require fuch an Intention, nor does the Want thereof any way leffen the Injury.

Hob. 182. Cro. Ca. 485, 489.

Hob. 182. Cro. Ca. 485.

Sect. 6. III. That it is no manner of Excufe, That the Woman at firft was taken away with her own Confent, becaufe if fhe afterwards refufe to continue with the Offender, and be forced againft her Will, fhe may from that Time as properly be faid to be taken againft her Will, as if fhe had never given any Confent at all; for till the Force was put upon her, fhe was in her own Power.

Cro. Ca. 493. 3 Keb. 193. 2 Vent. 243, 244.

Sect. 7. IV. That it is not material whether a Woman fo taken away, be at laft married, or defiled, with her own Confent or not, if fhe were under the Force at the Time, becaufe the Offender is in both Cafes equally within the Words of the Statute, and fhall not be conftrued to be out of the Meaning of it, for having prevailed over the Weaknefs of a Woman, whom by fo bafe Means he got into his Power.

3 Inft. 61. Dalif. 22. S. P. C. 44. Far. 132.

Sect. 8. V. That thofe who after the Fact receive the Offender, but not the Woman, are not Principals within this Statute, becaufe the Words are, *receiving wittingly the fame Woman fo taken*, &c. but it feems clearly, That they are Acceffaries after the Offence, according to the known Rules of Common Law.

Cro. Ca. 482. H. P. C. 119.

Sect. 9. VI. That thofe who are only privy to the Marriage, but no way Parties to the Forcible taking away, or confenting thereto, are not within the Statute.

Cro. Ca. 488. Hob. 183. H. P. C. 119.

Sect. 10. VII. That where a Woman is taken by Force in the County of *A.* and married in the County of *B.* the Offender may be indicted and found guilty in the County of *B.* becaufe the continuing of the Force there amounts to a Forcible Taking within the Statute.

CHAP. XLIII.

Of Offences against the Rights of Marriage.

Cro. El. 94.

Sect. 1. OFFENCES againft the Rights of Marriage, at Common Law, are looked upon as Spiritual Offences, and punifhable only by the Ecclefiaftical Law, but one of them is made Felony, but not excluded from the Benefit of the Clergy, by 1 *Jac.* 1. 11. by which it is enacted, *That if any Perfon or Perfons, within his Majefty's Dominions of* England *and* Wales, *being married, do marry any Perfon or Perfons, the former Husband or Wife being alive, that then every fuch Offence fhall be Felony, and the Perfon and Perfons fo offending, fhall fuffer Death as in Cafes of Felony. And the Party and Parties fo offending, fhall receive fuch and the like Proceeding, Trial, and Execution, in fuch County, where fuch Perfon or Perfons fhall be apprehended, as if the Offence had been committed in fuch County, where fuch Perfon or Perfons fhall be taken or apprehended.*

Sect. 2. But it is provided by the faid Statute, *That nothing therein contained, fhall extend to any Perfon or Perfons whofe Husband or Wife fhall be continually remaining beyond the Seas by the Space of feven Years together, or whofe*

Husband or Wife ſhall abſent him or her ſelf, the one from the other, by the Space of ſeven Years together in any Parts within his Majeſty's Dominions, the one of them not knowing the other to be living within that Time.

Sect. 3. And it is farther provided, *That the ſaid Statute ſhall not extend to any Perſon or Perſons who ſhall be at the Time of ſuch Marriage divorced by Sentence in the Eccleſiaſtical Court, or to any Perſon or Perſons where the former Marriage ſhall be by Sentence in the Eccleſiaſtical Court declared to be void and of no effect: Nor to any Perſon or Perſons, for, or by Reaſon of, any former Marriage had or made within Age of Conſent.*

Sect. 4. Alſo it is farther provided, *That no Attainder for this Offence ſhall make or work any Corruption of Blood, Loſs of Dower, or Diſinheriſon of Heir or Heirs.*

In the Conſtruction of this Statute it has been holden, See 1 H. H. P. C. 692 to 694.

Sect. 5. I. That not only thoſe who are divorced *à vinculo Matrimonii*, but alſo thoſe who are divorced only *à Menſa & Thoro Cauſa Adulterii* or *Sævitiæ*, are within the Exception in this Statute; notwithſtanding there be not the Word *Divortiamus*, but only the Word *Separamus*, in the Sentence; becauſe the Statute, being penal, ſhall be conſtrued favourably, and ſuch Separations are taken for Divorces in common Underſtanding. [58] 3 Inſt. 89. H. P. C. 122. Kelynge 27. Cro. Ca. 461, 462. This is made a Quære.

Sect. 6. II. Where either of the Parties were within the Age of Conſent at the Time of the firſt Marriage, that not only ſuch Perſon as was within ſuch Age, but alſo the other who was above it, is within the Exception of the Statute, becauſe the Power of diſagreeing to ſuch Marriage is equal on both Sides. 3 Inſt. 89. H. P. C. 121. 1 Rol. Ab. 340. Pl. 13, 141. Pl. 14, 15, 16, 17. Co. Lit. 79.

Sect. 7. III. That if the firſt Marriage were beyond Sea, and the latter in *England*, the Party may be indicted for it here, becauſe it is the latter Marriage that makes the Offence; but if the firſt Marriage were in *England*, and the latter beyond Sea, it is ſaid that the Offender cannot be indicted here; *ſed Quære*, why not? for the Words of the Statute are, *That the Parties ſo offending ſhall receive ſuch and the like Proceeding, Trial, and Execution, in ſuch County where ſuch Perſon or Perſons ſhall be apprehended, as if the Offence had been committed in ſuch County, where ſuch Perſon or Perſons ſhall be taken or apprehended.* 1 H. H. P. C. 692. 1 Sid. 171. Kelynge 80.

CHAP. XLIV.

Of Offences againſt the Members of a Man's Body.

IN treating of Offences againſt the Members of a Man's Body, I ſhall conſider,

1. What Offences of this Nature are eſteemed Maims.
2. How they are puniſhed by the Common Law.
3. How they are puniſhed by Statute.

Fleta. lib. c. 40. Brit. 48. Bract. 144. b, 145. S. P. C. 38. b. Co. Lit. 126, 128.

Sect. 1. As to the firſt Point, it ſeems that ſuch a Hurt of any Part of a Man's Body, whereby he is rendered leſs able in Fighting, either to defend himſelf or annoy his Adverſary, is properly Maim. 3 Inſt. 62, 118. Fitz. Coro. 142, 458.

Sect. 2. And therefore the cutting off, or diſabling, or weakening a Man's Hand or Finger, or ſtriking out his Eye or Foretooth, or caſtrating him, are ſaid to be Maims, but the cutting off his Ear, or Noſe, 25 Ed. 3. 94. See the Authors above cited.

Nose, &c. are not esteemed Maims, because they do not weaken, but only disfigure him.

Bract. 144. b. Fleta lib. 1. cap. 40. S. P. C. 37. a. 3 Inst. 62, 118. H. P. C. 133.

Sect. 3. As to the second Point, *viz.* How such Offences are to be punished, it is to be observed, that all Maim is Felony; and it is said, That anciently Castration was punished with Death, and other Maims with the Loss of Member for Member; but afterwards no Maim was punished in any Case with the Loss of Life or Member, but only with Fine and Imprisonment.

See 5 H. 4. c. 5.

Sect. 4. As to the third Point, *viz.* How such Offences are punished by Statute, it is enacted by 22 and 23 *Ca.* 2. cap. 1. *That if any Person shall on Purpose and of Malice fore-thought, and by lying in wait, unlawfully cut out, or disable, the Tongue, put out an Eye, slit the Nose, cut off a Nose, or Lip, or cut off or disable any Limb, or Member of any subject of his Majesty, with Intention in so doing to maim or disfigure, in any the Manners before mentioned, such his Majesty's Subject, That then and in every such Case the Person or Persons so offending, their Counsellors, Aiders and Abettors, knowing of, and privy to the Offence, as aforesaid, shall be and are by the said Statute declared to be Felons, and shall suffer Death as in Cases of Felony without Benefit of Clergy.*

Sect. 5. But it is provided by the said Statute, *That no Attainder of such Felony shall extend to corrupt the Blood, or forfeit the Dower of the Wife, or the Lands, Good or Chattels of the Offender.*

Woodburn and Coke's Case at the Suffolk Assizes, 8 Geo. 1. see the St. Tr. Vol. 6. p. 212.

Sect. 6. If a Man attack another of Malice fore-thought, in order to murder him with a Bill, or any other such like Instrument, which cannot but endanger the Maiming him, and in such Attack happen not to kill, but only to maim him, he may be indicted on this Statute, together with all those who were his Abettors, &c. and it shall be left to the Jury on the Evidence, whether there were a Design to murder by maiming, and consequently a malicious Intent to maim as well as to kill, in which Case the Offence is within the Statute, tho' the primary Intention was Murder.

CHAP. XLV.

Of Offences against Records.

3 Inst. 71, 72. 1 H. H. P. C. 646 to 648.

Sect. 1. AT Common Law the imbezilling, defacing, or altering any Record, without due Authority, was an Offence highly punishable by Fine and Imprisonment, &c. and in many Cases it was made Felony by the following Clause of 8 *H.* 6. 12.

Sect. 2. *It is ordained, That if any Record or Parcel of the same, Writ, Return, Panel, Process, or Warrant of Attorney, in the King's Courts of Chancery, Exchequer, the one Bench or the other, or in his Treasury, be willingly stoln, taken away, withdrawn, or avoided, by any Clerk, or by other Person, because whereof any Judgment shall be reversed: That such Stealer, Taker-away, Withdrawer, or Avoider, their Procurators, Counsellors, and Abettors, thereof indicted, and by Process thereupon made, thereof duly convict by their own Confession, or by Inquest to be taken of lawful Man, (whereof the one half shall be of the Men of any Court of the same Courts, and the other half of other) shall be judged for Felons, and shall incur the Pain of Felony: And that the Judges of the said Courts, of the one Bench or of the other, have Power to hear and determine such Defaults before them, and thereof to make due Punishment, as afore is said.*

In the Construction of this Clause, it hath been holden: 3 Inst. 71.

Sect. 3. I. That it extends only to the Courts which are expresly named; and to the Court of Chancery, so far only as it proceeds according to the Course of the Common Law. 1 H. H. P. C. 649 to 652.

Sect. 4. II. That it extends not to such Offence by the Judges of any Court; for whereas it begins with expresly naming Clerks which are inferior to them, it shall not be intended to include them under the general Words following; however by 8 *R.* 2. 4. *Judges as well as Clerks are to pay a Fine to the King, and make Satisfaction to the Party for falsly entring Pleas, or rasing Rolls, or changing Verdicts to the Disherison of any one*; And they are highly punishable at Common Law for other Offences of like Nature, as for inserting a Bill of Indictment not found by the Jury among those which were found, and such like. And Justice *Ingham* in the Reign of *Edward* the first was fined eight hundred Marks for rasing a Fine of thirteen Shillings and four Pence, set on a poor Man, and making it six Shillings and eight Pence. 3 Inst. 72. 2 R. 3. 10. 3 Mod. 66. Bro. Cor. 174. Tresf. 31. Con. Bro. Presentment 23. Indictment 14, 50. 3 Inst. 72.

Sect. 5. III. That not only such an Alteration whereby a Judgment is actually reversed, but also such whereby it is reversible, whether it were made before or after the Judgment was given, or whether it be or be not afterwards amended by the Court, is within this Act; for those Words in the Statute *whereby any Judgment shall be reversed*, are taken to have the same Purport, as if it were said, whereby any Judgment shall be annulled, or lose its Force or Effect; for it is plain, That the Statute cannot intend that the Judgment must be actually reversed by Writ of Error, because it speaks of stealing or carrying away, or avoiding of Records, which makes it impossible that the Judgment should be reversed at all, because no Writ of Error can remove a Judgment which appears not. And it has been holden, That if *A. B.* be outlawed by the Name of *A. C.* and afterwards the Record be rased, and *A. B.* inserted, the Offence is within the Statute, because the Record against *A. C.* is annulled, and the Judgment prevented, which might have been given on a Writ of Error for this Defect. 2 Rol. Re. 81. 2 R. 3. 10. S. P. C. 36. b. 3 Inst. 72. 11 Rep. 34. b.

Sect. 6. IV. If the Offence were committed partly in one County, and partly in another, but not so as to amount to a compleat Offence within the Statute in either, That the Party cannot be indicted for a Felony, because the Counties cannot join in an Indictment, and that which is done in one cannot be found in another, but that he may be indicted for a Misprision in either County. 2 R. 3. 10. b. 11. S. P. C. 36. 3 Inst. 73.

Sect. 7. V. That the Act, by making those who are Accessary before the Fact principal Felons, does not mean any way to favour those who are Accessary after, but to leave them to the general Construction of the Law. 3 Inst. 72. Con S. P. C. 44. d.

Sect. 8. VI. That by the last Clause of the Act, the Justices of either Bench have a concurrent Authority, and that they which shall first enquire shall proceed; and that if the Offence were committed in the County where the Benches sit, they need no other Commission; but if it were done in another County, that they must have a special Commission: And if in *London*, that they shall have a Commission in which the Mayor shall be omitted, for the Charters of the City, which require that he shall be a Principal in every Commission, extend not to such Causes which are specially limited to particular Judges. 3 Inst 73. 3 Inst. 72. 2 R. 3. 11. a.

Sect. 9. By 21 *Jac.* 1. 26. *It is made Felony without the Benefit of Clergy, but not so as to corrupt the Blood, to acknowledge or procure to be acknowledged, any Fine, Recovery, Deed enrolled, Statute, Recognizance, Bail, or Judgment in the Name of any other Person or Persons not privy or consenting to the same.*

2 Jon. 64. Contra in the Report of the same Case. *Sect.* 10. In the Construction hereof it has been holden, That if a Man personate another in the County of *A.* in putting in Bail before a Judge, and the Bail be filed in the County of *B.* the Trial shall be in the County
1 Ven. 301, 302. of *A.* Also it seems the bare personating of Bail before a Judge is no Fe-
1 Ven. 302. lony, unless the Bail be filed. [49]

Sect. 11. Also it is enacted by 4 & 5 *Will. & Mar.* 4. *That any Person or Persons who shall before any Commissioner authorized to take Bail, by Virtue of the said Statute, in Actions depending in the Courts of King's Bench, Common Pleas, or Exchequer, represent, or personate any other Person or Persons, whereby the Person or Persons so represented and personated, may be liable to the Payment of any Sum or Sums of Money, or Debt, or Damages, to be recovered in the same Suit or Action, wherein such Person or Persons are represented and personated, as if they had really acknowledged and entered into the same, being lawfully convicted thereof, shall be adjudged Felons.*

CHAP. XLVI.

Of Offences relating to Cattle.

BY 22 & 23 *Car.* 2. 7. it is made Felony, *Maliciously, unlawfully, and willingly, to kill or destroy any Horses, Sheep, or other Cattle of any Person or Persons whatsoever in the Night-time, but Liberty is given to the Offender to avoid Judgment of Death, by chusing Judgment of Transportation for seven Years; and any three Justices of Peace for the County, Division, City, Town-corporate, or Place, whereof one to be of the* Quorum, *are authorised to enquire as well by the Oaths of twelve lawful Men, of the same County, as by Examination of Witnesses upon Oath, or by any lawful Ways or Means, which to them shall seem meet, of the said Offences, and in order thereunto to issue out Warrants, as well for the Summoning of Jurors, as for the apprehending of all Persons, who shall or may be suspected thereof, and to take their Examination touching the same, as also to cause all such other Persons as to them shall seem likely to make Discovery thereof, to appear before them, and to give Information upon Oath concerning their Knowledge of the Premisses, so as no Person so to be examined shall in any wise be proceeded against for any Offence concerning which he shall be so examined as a Witness, and shall upon such his Examination make a true Discovery of: And if any Person who shall be thought likely to make such Discovery, being summoned by the said Justices, refuse to appear, or to be examined as a Witness, he may be committed by the said Justices to the County-Gaol, till he shall submit to be examined. Provided, That no Person shall be questioned for any Offence against the Statute, unless he be proceeded against within six Months after the Offence committed.*

CHAP. XLVII.

Of Offences by Purveyors.

2 Inst. 543. *Sect.* 1. ANciently the King's Court was supplied with Necessaries from the ancient Demesnes of the Crown, which were manured for that Purpose, and in respect thereof the Tenants of those Lands had many Privileges, which they still enjoy; but this Method being found to

be troublesome and inconvenient, was by Degrees disused, and afterwards
the King used to appoint certain Officers to buy in Provisions for his
Houshold, who were called Purveyors, and claimed many Privileges by the
Prerogative of the Crown, and seem to have had the Pre-emption of all Noy 101.
such Victuals as were bought by any one to sell again.

Sect. 2. By *Magna Charta*, chap. 21. *The King shall not take the Timber* 28 E. 1. ch 2.
of any Person against his Will, and by many subsequent Statutes, several Offences 36 E. 3. ch. 2, 3, 4, 5, 6.
of Purveyors were made Felonies, as if they took Things above the Value of twelve 5 E. 3. ch 2.
Pence against the Will of the Owner, without Warrant, or without such Ap- 2 Inst. 82. Dalt. ca. 107.
praisement as was directed by those Statutes, or without paying for them, &c. Crom. 48.

Sect. 3. But these Laws having been found by Experience not to have 1 Bulst. 96, 97.
sufficiently provided against the Oppressions of *Persons imployed for making* See Mo. 762,
Provisions for the King's Houshold, Carriages, and other Purveyance for his 770, 778. Noy 101.
Majesty, and several Counties having found themselves obliged to submit to
sundry Rates and Taxes, and Compositions to redeem themselves from such
Vexations and Oppressions, as it is recited by 12 *Car.* 2. 24. Par. 12. it was 1 H. H. P. C. 644.
enacted by the said Statute, *That from thenceforth no Sum or Sums of Mo-
ney, or other Thing shall be taken, raised, taxed, rated, imposed, paid, or le-
vied, for or in regard of any Provision, Carriages, or Purveyance for his
Majesty, his Heirs or Successors.*

Sect. 4. And it is farther enacted by the said Statute, Par. 13. *That no Person or Persons by any Warrant, Commission, or Authority under the Great Seal, or otherwise by Colour of buying or making Provision or Purveyance for his Majesty, or any Queen of* England *for the Time being, or of any the Children of any King or Queen of* England *for the Time being, or that shall be, or for his, their, or any of their Houshold, shall take any Timber, Fuel, Cattle, Corn, Grain, Malt, Hay, Straw, Victual, Cart, Carriage, or other Thing whatsoever, of any the Subjects of his Majesty, his Heirs, or Successors, without the free and full Consent of the Owner or Owners thereof, had and obtained without Menace or Enforcement; nor shall summon, warn, take, use, or require any the said Subjects to furnish or find any Horses, Oxen, or Cattle, Carts, Ploughs, Wains, or other Carriages, for the Use of his Majesty, his Heirs or Successors, or of any Queen of* England, *or of any Child, or Children of any of the Kings or Queens of* England *for the Time being, for the carrying the Goods of his Majesty, his Heirs or Successors, or the said Queens, or Children, or any of them, without such full and free Consent as aforesaid, any Law, Statute, Custom, or Usage to the contrary notwithstanding.*

Sect. 5. And it is farther enacted Par. 14. *That no Pre-emption shall be allowed or claimed in the Behalf of his Majesty, or of any of his Heirs or Successors, or of any of the Queens of* England, *or of any of the Children of the Royal Family, for the Time being, in Market or out of Market, but that it be free to all and every the Subjects of his Majesty, to sell, dispose, or employ his said Goods to any other Person or Persons, as him listeth, any Pretence of making Provision or Purveyance of Victual, Carriages or other Thing for his Majesty, his Heirs or Successors, or of the said Queens, or Children, or any Pretence of Pre-emption in their, or any of their Behalfs notwithstanding. And if any Person or Persons shall make Provision or Purveyance for his Majesty, his Heirs or Successors, or any the Queens, or Children aforesaid, or impress, or take any such Carriages, or other Things aforesaid, on any Pretence or Colour of any Warrant aforesaid, under the Great Seal, or otherwise, contrary to the Intent hereof, it shall be lawful for the Justices of Peace, or such two, or one of them as dwell near, and to the Constables of such Parish or Village where such Occasion shall happen, at the Request of the Party grieved, to commit or cause to be committed, the Party or Parties so doing and offending, to Gaol, till the next Sessions, there to be indicted and proceeded against for the same*, &c.

Sect. 6.

Sect. 6. But this abſolute and univerſal Reſtraint of all Kinds of Purveyance having been found by Experience inconvenient, it was enacted by 13 & 14 *Car.* 2. 20. which has been often continued by ſubſequent Statutes, That the Officers of the Navy may preſs Carriages for the Uſe of his Majeſty's Navy and Ordnance, according to the Regulations preſcribed by that Statute, and the like was enacted by 1 *Jac.* 2. 10. in relation to the King's Royal Progreſſes, &c.

CHAP. XLVIII.

Of Offences by Soldiers and Mariners.

OFFENCES by Soldiers or Mariners, made Felony by Statute, are of three Kinds.

1. Wandering without a Teſtimonial.
2. Departing from the King's Service without Licence.
3. Deſtroying a Ship.

Sect. 1. The firſt of theſe Offences depends upon 39 *El.* 17. by which it is recited, *That divers licentious Perſons contemning both Laws, Magiſtrates, and Religion, had uſed to wander up and down in all Parts of the Realm, under the Name of Soldiers and Mariners, abuſing the Title of that honourable Profeſſion, to countenance their wicked Behaviours, and that ſuch Perſons had uſed to aſſemble themſelves weaponed in the Highways, and elſewhere in Troops, to the great Terror and Aſtoniſhment of her Majeſty's true Subjects, the Impeachment of her Laws, and the Diſturbance of the Peace and Tranquility of this Realm: And that many hainous Outrages, Robberies, and horrible Murders had been daily committed by ſuch diſſolute Perſons*; And thereupon it is enacted, *That all idle and wandering Soldiers or Mariners, or idle Perſons which ſhall be wandering as Soldiers or Mariners, ſhall ſettle themſelves in ſome Service, Labour, or other lawful Courſe of Life, without wandering, or otherwiſe repair to the Places where they were born, or to their Dwelling-Places, if they have any, and there remain, betaking themſelves to ſome lawful Trade or Courſe of Life, as aforeſaid*; *upon Pain, That all Perſons offending contrary to this Act, ſhall ſuffer as in caſe of Felony, without Clergy.*

Sect. 2. And it is farther enacted, *That every idle and wandering Soldier or Mariner, which, coming from his Captain from the Seas, or from beyond the Seas, ſhall not have a Teſtimonial under the Hand of ſome one Juſtice of the Peace, of, or near, the Place where he landed, ſetting down therein the Place and Time, where and when he landed, and the Place of his Dwelling or Birth, unto which he is to paſs as aforeſaid, and a convenient Time therein limited for his Paſſage, or having ſuch Teſtimonial, ſhall wilfully exceed the Time therein limited, above fourteen Days: And alſo, as well every ſuch idle and wandering Soldier or Mariner, as every other idle Perſon wandering, as Soldier or Mariner, which ſhall at any Time hereafter forge or counterfeit any ſuch Teſtimonial, or have with him or them any ſuch Teſtimonial forged, or counterfeited as aforeſaid, knowing the ſame to be counterfeited or forged, in all theſe Caſes, every ſuch Act or Acts to be Felony, and the Offenders to ſuffer, as aforeſaid, without any Benefit of Clergy.*

Sect. 3. And it is farther enacted, *That it ſhall be lawful for the Juſtices of Aſſizes, Juſtices of Gaol-Delivery, and the Juſtices of Peace of every County, and all Juſtices of Peace in Towns corporate, having Authority to hear and determine Felonies, to hear and determine all ſuch Offences in their general Seſſions, and to execute the Offenders, which ſhall be convicted before them, as in Caſes of Felony is accuſtomed, except ſome honeſt Freeholder,* &c. *will take ſuch Offender into his Service for one whole Year, and alſo be bound by Recognizance of ten Pounds, to keep the ſaid Perſon for one whole Year, and bring him to the next Seſſions for the Peace and Gaol-Delivery next enſuing after the ſaid Year; and if any ſuch Perſon ſo retained, depart within the Year, without the Licence of him that ſo retained him, then, to be indicted, tried, and judged as a Felon, and not to have the Benefit of the Clergy.*

Sect. 4. But it is provided by the ſaid Statute, *That if any ſuch idle and wandring Perſon, as aforeſaid, ſhall happen to fall ſick by the Way, ſo that by reaſon of his Weakneſs he cannot travel to his Journey's End within the Time limited within his Teſtimonial, no ſuch Perſon to be within the Danger of this Statute, ſo as he ſettle himſelf in ſome lawful Courſe of Life, as aforeſaid, or repair, as aforeſaid, to the Place where he was born, or was laſt abiding, within convenient Time after the Recovery of his Sickneſs, and there remain as aforeſaid.*

Sect. 5. And it is farther provided by the ſaid Statute, *That if ſuch Soldier or Mariner repairing to his Place of Birth,* &c. *cannot get work, he ſhall be ſet to work by two Juſtices of Peace,* &c.

Sect. 6. And it is farther provided, *That if ſuch Soldier or Mariner reſort to ſome Juſtice of the Peace next adjoining to his Place of Landing, or to ſuch his direct Way home, and make known unto the ſaid Juſtice his Poverty; that the ſaid Juſtice, upon perfect Notice thereof had, may licence the ſame Soldier or Mariner to paſs the next and direct Way to the Place where he is to repair, and to limit him ſo much Time only, as ſhall be neceſſary for his Travel thither; and that in ſuch caſe his Licence being ſo made, and he purſuing the Form of ſuch his Licenſe, ſhall and may, for his neceſſary Relief in his Travel, ask and take the Relief that any Perſon ſhall willingly give him.*

Sect. 7. The ſecond Offence of this Kind, *viz.* That of departing from the King's Service without Licence, depends upon ſeveral Statutes; for it was enacted by 18 *H.* 6. 19. *that Soldiers retained in the manner preſcribed by that Act, departing from their Captains without Licence, ſhall be guilty of Felony*; but this Statute is now of little uſe, becauſe the Method of ☞ retaining Soldiers therein referred to, is diſuſed. [50] 3 Inſt. 86. 6 Co. 27. Co. Lit. 71. Dalt. ca. 107. Cro. Ca. 71. Hutt. 134.

Sect. 8. However by 7 *H.* 7. 1. and 3 *H.* 8. 5. ſtill in Force, *If any Soldier, being no Captain, immediately retained with the King, who ſhall be in Wages and retained, or take any Preſt. to ſerve the King upon the Sea, or upon the Land beyond the Sea, depart out of the King's Service, without Licence of his Captain, he ſhall ſuffer as a Felon, without the Benefit of the Clergy. And all Juſtices of Peace in every ſhire in* England, *where any ſuch Offenders be taken, have Power to enquire of the ſaid Offences, and the ſame to hear and determine, as they may do of Felony, Treſpaſſes, and of other Offences expreſſed in the King's Commiſſion to them made, as though the ſaid Offences were done in the ſame Shire.* 3 Inſt. 86. Dalt. ca. 107. 2 And. 151. 3 Mod. 124. See alſo the other Books above cited, and 1 H. H. P. C. 672 to 680.

Sect. 9. And by 2 *Ed.* 6. 2. *If any Soldier, ſerving the King in his Wars, in any his Dominions, or on the Seas, or beyond the Seas, or in* Scotland, *depart without Licence of the Lieutenant, or Admiral, or Captain,* &c. *with Booty, or otherwiſe, being in the Enemy's Country, or elſewhere in the King's Service, or out of any Garriſon where he ſhall be appointed to ſerve, he ſhall be adjudged a Felon, and excluded from his Clergy; and the Juſtices of eve-* 3 Inſt. 86. 6 Co. 67.

ry Shire where such Offender shall be taken, may enquire of and determine the Offence, &c.

Sect. 10. The third Offence of this Kind, *viz.* That of destroying a Ship, depends upon 22 & 23 Car. 2. 11. and 1 *Annæ*, St. 2. c. 9. by which it is enacted, *That if any Captain, Master, Mariner or other Officer, belonging to any Ship, shall wilfully cast away, burn, or otherwise destroy the Ship to which he belongeth, or procure the same to be done, to the Prejudice of the Owner or Owners thereof, or of any Merchant or Merchants that shall load Goods thereon, he shall suffer as a Felon, without the Benefit of Clergy, and if the Offence were committed in the Admiral's Jurisdiction, shall be tried in the Manner prescribed by* 28 H. 8. 15. [51] [52]

CHAP. XLIX.

Of Offences by Hunters.

3 Inst. 76, 77. Dal. ca. 29. 1 H. H. P. C. 656 to 659.

IT is recited by 1 *H.* 7. 7. *That many great Outrages, Murders, Insurrections and Rebellions had often been occasion'd by Persons in great Numbers, with painted Faces, Visors, and otherwise disguised, and riotously, and in manner of War arrayed, hunting as well by Night as by Day*; and thereupon it is enacted, *That as often as Information shall be made of any such unlawful Huntings by Night, or with painted Faces, to any of the King's Council, or to any Justice of Peace of the County, of any Person suspected thereof, any of the same Council, or Justices, to whom such Information shall be made, may make a Warrant to arrest such Person, and may also examine him of the said Hunting, and of the said Doers in that Behalf; and if the same Person wilfully conceal the said Huntings, or any Person with him defective therein, that then the same Concealment be Felony; and if he then confess the Truth, and all that he shall be examined of, and knoweth in that behalf, that then the said Offences of Huntings be against the King but Trespass finable, by Reason of the same Confession, at the next general Sessions of the Peace to be holden in the same County, by the King's Justices of the same Sessions, there to be sessed. And if any Rescous or Disobedience be made to any Person, having Authority to do Execution or Justice, by any such Warrant, by any Person, the which so should be arrested, so that the Execution of the same Warrant thereby be not had, that then the same Rescous and Disobedience, be Felony; and if any Person or Persons shall be convict of any such Huntings, with painted Faces, Visors, or otherwise disguised, to the Intent they should not be known, or of unlawful Hunting in Time of Night, that then the same Person or Persons so convict, to have like Punition, as he or they should have, if he or they were convict of Felony.*

CHAP. L.

Of Offences by Forgers of False Deeds.

BY 5 *El.* chap. 14. *If a Man be convict or condemned of forging or publishing a forged Deed, and after such Conviction or Condemnation, do commit the like Offence, he is made guilty of Felony, and excluded from the Benefit of Clergy*; as shall more fully be shewn in the Chapter of *Forgery*. 1 H. H. P. C. 682 to 686.

CHAP. LI.

Of Offences by Gaolers.

BY 14 *E.* 3. 10. *If any Keeper of a Prison, or Under-keeper, by too great Duress of Imprisonment, and by Pain, make any Prisoner that he hath in his Ward, to become an Appellor against his Will, he is guilty of Felony:* 1 H. H. P. C. 640, 641. And it is said to be no Way material, whether the Approvement be true S. P. C. 36. C. or false, or whether the Appellee be acquitted or condemned; but at Law 3 Inst. 91. this Offence was esteemed a Misprision only, unless the Appellee were hanged, by reason of the Appeal.

CHAP. LII.

Of Offences by Transporters of Sheep or Wool.

Sect. 1. BY some old Statutes, and 13 & 14 *Car.* 2. 18. the Exportation 3 Inst. 95, 96. of Wool was made Felony; but by 7 & 8 *W.* 3. 28. it is re- 1 W. & M. Seff. 1. cap. 32. duced to a Misdemeanour only, and it is subjected to severe Penalties by 7 & 8 W. 3. many late Statutes. [53] cap. 28.

☞ *Sect.* 2. It is enacted by 8 *El.* 3. *That no Person or Persons shall bring,* 9 & 10 W. 3. cap. 40. *deliver, send, receive, or take, or procure to be brought, delivered, sent, or* 11 & 12 W. 3. *received into any Ship or Bottom, any Rams, Sheep or Lambs, or any manner* cap. 10. *of other Kind of Sheep, being alive, to be carried and conveyed out of this Realm of* England, Wales, *or* Ireland, *or out of any of the King's Dominions, on Pain that every such Person or Persons, their Aiders, Abbettors, Procurers and Comforters, shall for the first Offence forfeit all his Goods for ever, whereof the one Moiety shall be to the King, the other Moiety to him that will sue for the same:* And further, *That every such Offender shall suffer Imprisonment by the Space of one whole Year, without Bail or Mainprize, and at the Year's End, shall in some open Market-Town, in the Fulness of the Market, on the Market-Day, have his left Hand cut off, and that to be nailed*

up,

up, in the openest Place of ſuch Market; and that every Perſon or Perſons eftſoons offending againſt this Statute, ſhall be adjudged a Felon, &c.

CHAP. LIII.

Of Offences by Servants

IT is recited by 33 *H.* 6. 1. *That divers Houſhold-Servants, as well of Lords, as of other Perſons of good Degree, had then of late, ſhortly after the Death of their ſaid Lords and Maſters, violently, and riotouſly, taken and ſpoiled the Goods which were of their ſaid Lords and Maſters at the Time of their Death, and the ſame diſtributed among themſelves*; and thereupon it is enacted, *That after Information made to the Chancellor by the Executors of any ſuch Perſon, or two of them, of ſuch Riot, Taking, and Spoil; the Chancellor, by the Advice of the two Chief Juſtices, and Chief Baron, or two of them, may make out Writs to ſuch Sheriffs as ſhall be thought neceſſary, commanding them to make ſuch Proclamation, as by the ſaid Statute is directed, for the Offenders to appear in the King's Bench at ſuch a Day, whereupon, if they make Default, they ſhall be attainted of Felony; but if they appear, they ſhall be committed or bailed, till they have anſwered the ſaid Executors in ſuch Actions, which the ſaid Executors will declare againſt them, or any of them, for the Riot, Taking, and Spoiling aforeſaid.*

CHAP. LIV.

Of Offences by Egyptians.

BY 1 & 2 *Ph.* & *Mar.* 4. *All outlandiſh Perſons, called* Egyptians, *being of the Age of thirteen Years, who ſhall be tranſported into this Realm of* England *or* Wales, *and continue within the ſame by the Space of one Month*; and by 5 *El.* 20. *All Perſons being of the Age of fourteen Years, who ſhall be ſeen or found within this Realm of* England *or* Wales, *in any Company or Fellowſhip of Vagabonds, commonly called, or calling themſelves,* Egyptians, *or counterfeiting, transforming, or diſguiſing themſelves by their Apparel, Speech, or other Behaviour, like unto ſuch Vagabonds, commonly called or calling themſelves* Egyptians, *and ſhall continue and remain in the ſame, either at one Time, or at ſeveral Times, by the Space of one Month, ſhall ſuffer as Felons, without Benefit of Clergy.*

CHAP. LV.

Of Offences by Cutters of Pow-dike.

IT is recited by 22 *H.* 8. 11. which was repealed by 1 *Ed.* 6. and revived by 2 & 3 *Ph.* & *Mar.* 19. *That divers Perſons had maliciouſly at ſundry Times cut down and broken up, divers Parts of the Dike called the new* Pow-dike *in* Marſhland, *in the County of* Norfolk, *and the broken Dike, otherwiſe called* Oldfelde-Dike *by* Marſhland, *in the Iſle of* Ely, *in the County of* Cambridge: *By Reaſon whereof the Ground within the Country of* Marſhland *in the Counties aforeſaid, had been many Times drowned; and the Inhabitants had not only been put to great Charges and Expences, but alſo had loſt much Cattle, and alſo many People had been drowned in their Beds:* And thereupon it is enacted, *That every ſuch perverſe and malicious cutting down, and breaking up of, any Part or Parts of the ſaid Dikes, or of any other Bank, being Parcel of the Rind and uttermoſt Part of the ſaid Country of* Marſhland, *by any Perſon or Perſons, otherwiſe than in working upon the ſaid Bank or Dikes, for the repairing, fortifying, and amending of the ſame, ſhall be adjudged Felony, and that the Juſtices of Peace of the ſaid Counties of* Norfolk *and* Cambridge, *within the ſaid Iſle, ſhall have full Power at their Seſſions to cauſe Enquiry to be made of every ſuch Offence, to award like Proceſs, Judgment, and Execution, as they have uſed to do upon other Felonies, being Felony at Common Law.*

CHAP. LVI.

Of Offences by Treſpaſſers on the Borders, and Rioters.

IT is recited by 43 *El.* 13. *That then of late Years many of the Queen's Subjects dwelling in the Counties of* Cumberland, Weſtmorland, *and the Biſhoprick of* Durham, *had been taken, ſome from their own Houſes, and other in travelling on the Highway, or otherwiſe, and been carried away as Priſoners, and kept barbarouſly, and cruelly until they had been redeemed by great Ranſoms; and alſo, that then of late Time there had been many Incurſions, Robberies and burning and ſpoiling of Towns, Villages, and Houſes, within the ſaid Counties, ſo that divers of the Queen's Subjects, in the ſaid Counties, had been enforced to pay a certain Rate of Money, Corn, Cattle, or other Conſideration, commonly called Black-mail, to divers inhabiting upon or near the Borders, being Men of Name, and friended and allied with divers in thoſe Parts, who were commonly known to be great Robbers, and Spoil-Takers, within the ſaid Counties, to the End thereby to be by them protected from the Danger of ſuch as uſed to rob and ſteal in thoſe Parts;* and thereupon it is enacted, *That whoſoever ſhall at any Time hereafter without good and lawful Warrant or Authority, take any of her Majeſty's Subjects againſt his or their Will or Wills, and carry them out of the ſame Counties, or detain, force, or impriſon him or them, as Priſoners, or againſt his or their Wills, to ranſom them, or to make Prey or*

Spoil of his or their Perſon, or Goods, upon deadly Feud or otherwiſe: Or whoſoever ſhall be privy, conſenting, aiding, or aſſiſting unto any ſuch Taking, Detaining, or Carrying away, or procure the Taking, Detaining or Carrying away, of any ſuch Perſon or Perſons, Priſoners as aforeſaid: Or whoſoever ſhall take, receive, or carry, to the Uſe of himſelf, or wittingly to the Uſe of any other, any Money, Corn, Cattle, or other Conſideration, commonly called Black-mail, for the protecting, or defending of him or them, or his or their Lands, Tenements, Goods, or Chattels, from ſuch Thefts, Spoils, and Robberies, as is aforeſaid: Or whoſoever ſhall give any ſuch Money, Corn, Cattle, or other Conſideration, called Black-mail, for ſuch Protection as is aforeſaid, and ſhall be of the ſaid ſeveral Offences, or of any of them, indicted and lawfully convicted, or ſhall ſtand mute, or ſhall challenge peremptorily above the Number of twenty before the Juſtices of Aſſizes, Juſtices of Gaol-Delivery, Juſtices of Oyer and Terminer, or Juſtices of Peace, within any of the ſaid Counties, at ſome of their General Seſſions within ſome of the ſaid Counties to be holden, ſhall be reputed, adjudged, and taken to be as Felons, and ſhall ſuffer Pains of Death, without any Benefit of Clergy, &c.

Infra Ch. 65. Sect. 56, &c. Notorious Rioters in ſome Caſes, are made guilty of Felony by 1 *Geo.* 1. *c.* 5. as is ſhewn at large in the Chapter of Riots.

For the Suppreſſion of Thieves and Robbers called Moſs-Troopers, ſee 13 and 14 *Ca.* 2. 22. which is continued by 12 *Annæ*, *Stat.* 1. *c.* 10. for eleven Years, and from thence to the End of the firſt Seſſions of the next Parliament. [54] ☞

CHAP. LVII.

Of Offences by Bankrupts.

Sect. 1. IT is enacted by 4 *Annæ*, 17. which was continued by 7 *Annæ* for ſeven Years, and from thence to the End of the next Seſſion, *That if any Perſon or Perſons who after the 24th of* June 1706. *ſhall become Bankrupt, and againſt whom a Commiſſion of Bankrupt ſhall be awarded, ſhall not within thirty Days next after Notice thereof in Writing, left at the uſual Place of Abode of ſuch Perſon or Perſons, and Notice given in the Gazette, that ſuch Commiſſion is iſſued, and of the Time and Place of Meeting of the Commiſſioners, ſurrender him, her, or themſelves to the ſaid Commiſſioners or ſome of them, and ſubmit to be examined, from Time to Time, upon Oath, by and before the ſaid Commiſſioners, or the major Part of them, and in all Things conform to the ſeveral Statutes which had then been made concerning Bankrupts, and alſo upon ſuch Examination fully and truly diſcloſe and diſcover, how, and in what manner, and to whom, and upon what Conſideration, he, ſhe, or they, hath or have diſpoſed, aſſigned or transferred, any of his, her, or their Goods, Wares, Merchandizes, Money, or other Effects, or Eſtate, and all Books, Papers and Writings, relating thereunto, of which he, ſhe, or they were poſſeſſed, or in or to which he, ſhe, or they were any Way intereſted, or intitled, or which any Perſon or Perſons, had, hath, or have had, in Truſt for him, her or them, or for his, her, or their Uſe, at any Time before or after the iſſuing out of the ſaid Commiſſion, and alſo deliver up unto the ſaid Commiſſioners, or the major Part of the Commiſſioners by the ſaid Commiſſion authorized, all ſuch Part of his, her, or their, the ſaid Bankrupts Goods, Wares, Merchandizes, Effects and Eſtate, and all Books, Papers and Writings relating thereunto, as at the Time of ſuch Examination ſhall be in his, her, or their Poſſeſſion, Cuſtody or*

Power, (his, her, or their Wives and Childrens necessary wearing Apparel only excepted,) then he, she, or they, the said Bankrupt, in Case of any Default or wilful Omission therein, or in any the Premisses, and being thereof lawfully convicted by Indictment or Information, shall suffer as a Felon, without the Benefit of Clergy.

Sect. 2. But it is provided by the said Statute, *That the Lord Chancellor may enlarge the Time for such Persons surrendering themselves, and discovering their Estates, for any Time as he shall think fit, not exceeding sixty Days, so as such Order for so enlarging the Time, be made five Days before the Time on which such Persons were so to surrender themselves*, &c.

Sect. 3. And it is farther enacted by 5 *Annæ*, 22. *That if any Person or Persons who shall become Bankrupt, or any other Person or Persons, by or with his, her, or their Order, Consent, or Privity, shall after the 25th of* April 1707. *remove, carry away, conceal, destroy, or imbezil any of the Goods, Wares, Merchandizes, Moneys, or Effects, whereof he, she, or they, or any Person or Persons in Trust for him, her, or them, is, or are possessed, or intitled unto, to the Value of twenty Pounds or upwards, or any Books of Accompts, Bonds, Bills, Notes, Papers or Writings relating thereunto, with Intent to defraud his, her, or their Creditors, every such Person so becoming Bankrupt, and being thereof lawfully convicted shall suffer as a Felon without Benefit of Clergy.* [55]

CHAP. LVIII.

Of Offences by Counterfeiters of Bank-Notes, Exchequer-Bills, Stamps, South-Sea Bonds, Lottery-Orders, &c.

Sect. 1. AND first as to Counterfeiters of Bank-Notes it is enacted by 8 & 9 *Will.* 3. 19. Par. 36. *That the forging or counterfeiting the Common Seal of the Governor and Company of the Bank of* England, *or of any sealed Bank-Bill, made or given out in the Name of the said Governor and Company, for the Payment of any Sum of Money, or of any Bank-Note of any Sort whatsoever, signed for the said Governor and Company of the Bank of* England, *or the altering or rasing any Endorsement on any Bank-Bill, or Note of any Sort, shall be adjudged to be Felony without Benefit of Clergy.* 11 Geo. 1. Ch. 9. Par. 6.

Sect. 2. Secondly, As to Counterfeiters of Exchequer-Bills, it is enacted, by 7 and 8 *Will.* 3. 31. Par. 78. *That if any Person or Persons shall forge or counterfeit any such Bill of Credit, as by the said Statute the Commissioners of the Treasury were authorized to issue out, or tender in Payment any forged or counterfeited Bill of Credit, or demand Money thereupon at the Exchequer, (knowing the Bill so tendered, or whereupon the Money shall be so demanded, to be actually forged or counterfeited) and with Intention to defraud his Majesty, or any other Person or Persons, every such Person or Persons so offending shall be adjudged a Felon.*

Sect. 3. And the like was enacted by 8 & 9 *Will.* 3. 23. in relation to the Exchequer-Bills issued out by Authority of that Statute, and the Offenders are excluded from the Benefit of the Clergy, as appears from *Washington*; Washington's Abr. 513. but this Part of the Statute is omitted out of the last Volume of the Statutes at large.

Sect. 4. And it is farther enacted by 5 *Annæ*, 13. Par. 22. *That if any Person or Persons shall forge or counterfeit any Exchequer-Bill to be issued by*

Virtue of that Statute, or any Endorsement thereon, or tender in Payment any such forged or counterfeit Exchequer-Bill, or with such counterfeit Endorsement, or demand to have the same exchanged for ready Money by the Governor and Company of the Bank of England *or their Successors, (knowing the Bill so tendered or demanded to be exchanged, or the Endorsement thereon to be forged or counterfeit) and with Intention to defraud her Majesty, her Heirs or Successors, or the said Governor and Company, or their Successors, or any Person or Persons, Body Politick or Corporate, then every such Person or Persons so offending, (being thereof lawfully convicted) shall be adjudged a Felon, and suffer as in Cases of Felony, without Benefit of Clergy.*

Sect. 5. And the like is enacted by 7 *Annæ*, 7. and also by 9 *Annæ*, 7. and by 1 *Georg.* 1. *c.* 12. in relation to Exchequer-Bills made forth in Pursuance of those Acts.

Sect. 6. As to Counterfeiters of Stamps, it is enacted by 9 and 10 *Will.* 3. 25. Par. 59. *That if any Person or Persons whatsoever shall counterfeit or forge any Stamp or Mark to resemble any Stamp or Mark which shall be provided, made or used in pursuance of that Act, or shall counterfeit or resemble the Impression of the same, upon any Vellum, Parchment or Paper, thereby to defraud his Majesty, his Heirs or Successors, of any of the said Duties upon Vellum, Parchment or Paper, or shall utter, vend, or sell Vellum, Parchment or Paper, with such counterfeit Mark or Marks thereupon, knowing such Mark or Marks to be counterfeit, that the Person so offending being thereof convicted in due Form of Law, shall be judged a Felon, and shall suffer Death, as in Cases of Felony, without the Benefit of Clergy.*

Sect. 7. And the like is enacted by 10 *Annæ*, 19. in relation to the Stamps to be provided in Pursuance of that Act, with this Addition, *That those who shall privately and fraudulently use any Stamps or Marks thereby to defraud her Majesty of any Duty upon Vellum, Parchment or Paper by the said Act granted, shall be adjudged in like manner guilty.*

And the like is enacted 10 *Annæ*, 26. and by 12 *Annæ*, 9. and also by 12 *Annæ*, 19. In relation to the Stamps or Marks to be provided in Pursuance of those Statutes.

Sect. 8. As to Counterfeiters of South-Sea Bonds, it is enacted by 9 *Annæ*, 21. *That if any Person or Persons shall forge or counterfeit the common Seal of the South-Sea Company, or shall forge, counterfeit or alter any Bond or Obligation under the common Seal of the said Company, or shall offer to dispose of, or pay away any such forged, counterfeited, or altered Bond, (knowing the same to be such) or shall demand the Money therein contained, or pretended to be due thereon, or any Part thereof, of the said Company, or any of their Officers, knowing the same to be forged, counterfeited, or altered, with Intent to defraud the said Company, or any other Person or Persons, every such Offender shall suffer as a Felon without the Benefit of Clergy.*

Sect. 9. As to Counterfeiters of Lottery-Orders, it is enacted by 12 *Annæ*, 2. *That if any Person or Persons shall forge or counterfeit any Lottery-Order, made in Pursuance of* 9 Annæ, 6 *or* 23. *or* 10 Annæ, 19 *or* 26. *or alter the Number or principal Sum of any such Order, or counterfeit the Hand of any Person to such Order, thereby to procure a fraudulent Assignment, or sell any such Order, knowing the same to be forged or counterfeit, or knowing that the Name of the Owner is forged, in order to procure such fraudulent Assignment; then all and every such Person or Persons being therefore convict, shall suffer as in Cases of Felony, without Benefit of Clergy.*

For other Forgeries relating to Publick Securities, see the Additions from Number [55] to [61] And for other Felonies by later Statutes, see the Additions from [60] to [81] See also the Chapters of *Perjury* and *Forgery*, infra.

CHAP. LIX.

Of Misprision of Felony.

OFFENCES more immediately against the Subject, not capital, are either Misprision of Felony, or other inferior Offences. 1 H. H. P. C.

Sect. 1. It is said, That every Felony includes Misprision of Felony, and may be proceeded against as a Misprision only if the King please, as hath been shewn already in Chapter 20. 652, 708. Bro. Treas. 25. 2 Ric. 3. 10.] S. P. C. 32. d.

Sect. 2. But generally Misprision of Felony is taken for a Concealment of Felony, or a procuring of the Concealment thereof, whether it be Felony by the Common Law, or by Statute. [81] H. P. C. 129. S. P. C. 37. c. 3 Inst. 139.

Sect. 3. For this Offence every common Person is punishable by Fine and Imprisonment at Common Law. And by the Statute of *Westm.* 1. 9. *If the Sheriff, Coroner, or any other Bailiff within a Franchise or without, for Reward or for Prayer, or for Fear, or for any manner of Affinity, conceal, consent, or procure to conceal the Felonies done in their Liberties; or otherwise will not attach nor arrest such Felons (there as they may) or otherwise will not do their Office, for Favour borne to such Mis-doers, and be attainted thereof, they shall have one Year's Imprisonment, and after make a grievous Fine at the King's Pleasure, if they have wherewith; and if they have not whereof, they shall have Imprisonment of three Years.* Bro. Treas. 25. 3 Inst. 173.

Sect. 4. By 3 *H.* 7. 1. *The Justices of the Peace of every Shire of this Realm, for the Time being, may take by their Discretion an Inquest, whereof every Man shall have Lands and Tenements to the yearly Value of forty Shillings at the least, to enquire of the Concealments of other Inquests taken before them, and afore other, of such Matters and Offences as are to be enquired and presented afore Justices of Peace, whereof Complaint shall be made by Bill or by Bills, as well within Franchise as without. And if any such Concealment be found of any Inquest, as is afore rehearsed, had or made within the Year after the same Concealment, every Person of the same Inquest to be amerced for the Concealment, by Discretion of the same Justices of the Peace, the said Amerciaments to be sessed in plain Sessions.*

Sect. 5. To this Title of Misprision of Felony, That of Theftbote seems not improperly reducible, which is where one not only knows of a Felony, but takes his Goods again, or other amends, not to prosecute. 1 H. H. P. C. 619. S. P. C. 40. b. Ch. 43. 3 Inst. 134.

Sect. 6. This Offence is very nearly allied to Felony, and is said to have been anciently punished as such: But at this Day it is punishable only with Ransom and Imprisonment, unless it were accompanied with some Degree of Maintenance given to the Felon, which makes the Party an Accessary after the Fact. H. P. C. 130. S. P. C. 40. b. Fitz. Coro. 353. 2 H. H. P. C. 400. 3 Inst. 134.

2 And 47, 48. Cro. Eliz. 536. B. 2. Ch. 29. Sect. 26, &c.

Sect. 7. But the bare Taking of one's own Goods again, which have been stoln, is no Offence at all, unless some Favour be shewn to the Thief. Bro. Cor. 122. 42 Ass. Pl. 5.

H. P. C. 130. Cro. El. 486. Pl. 3. 1 Rol. Ab. 67. Pl. 27. Fitz. Assise 346.

CHAP. LX.

Of Surety of the Peace.

INferior Offences more immediately againſt the Subject, not capital, either amount to an actual Diſturbance of the Peace, or do not.

And firſt I ſhall conſider ſuch Offences of this Kind, as amount to an actual Diſturbance of the Peace: But before I deſcend to the ſeveral Kinds thereof, it may not be improper firſt to ſhew what Security may be had againſt the Breach of the Peace before it happens; and in order hereto, I ſhall examine how the Breach may be ſecured.

1. By Surety for keeping the Peace.
2. By Surety for the good Behaviour.

As to Surety for keeping the Peace, I ſhall conſider the following Particulars:

1. In what Caſes it ought to be taken *ex Officio.*
2. At whoſe Requeſt it ought to be granted.
3. Againſt whom it ought to be granted.
4. For what Cauſe it is grantable.
5. In what manner it is grantable by the Courts of Chancery and King's Bench.
6. In what manner it is grantable by a Juſtice of Peace.
7. In what manner the Proceſs for it ought to be executed.
8. How ſuch Proceſs may be ſuperſeded.
9. What ought to be the Form of a Recognizance for this Purpoſe.
10. How ſuch a Recognizance may be diſcharged.
11. How ſuch a Recognizance ought to be certified and proceeded upon.
12. How it may be forfeited.

Dalt. cap. 67. fol. 158, 159. Lamb. 77, 78. 9 Ed. 4. 3. a. Bro. Peace 7, 8. Crom. 135, 142. Dalt. cap. 67. 21 E. 4. 40. Crom. 142. b. Dalt. cap. 67.

Sect. 1. As to the firſt Point, *viz.* In what Caſes Surety of the Peace ought to be taken *ex Officio*, it ſeems, That any Juſtice of Peace may, according to his Diſcretion, bind all thoſe to the Peace, who in his Preſence ſhall make any Affray, or ſhall threaten to kill or beat any Perſon, or ſhall contend together with hot Words, or ſhall go about with unuſual Weapons or Attendants, to the Terror of the People; and alſo all ſuch Perſons as ſhall be known by him to be common Barrators; and alſo all thoſe who ſhall be brought before him by a Conſtable for a Breach of the Peace in the Preſence of ſuch Conſtable; and all ſuch Perſons who, having been before bound to keep the Peace, ſhall be convicted of having forfeited their Recognizance.

Dalt. cap. 68. Lamb. 78, 79. Crom. 133. b. 134.

Sect. 2. As to the ſecond Point, *viz.* At whoſe Requeſt the Surety of the Peace ought to be granted; it ſeems agreed at this Day, That all Perſons whatſoever, under the King's Protection, being of ſane Memory, whether they be natural and good Subjects, or Aliens, or attainted of Treaſon, *&c.* have a Right to demand Surety of the Peace.

Dalt. cap. 68. Lamb. 80.

Sect. 3. But it has been queſtioned, whether Jews or Pagans, or Perſons attainted of *Præmunire*, have a Right to it or not.

Sect. 4. However it is certain, That a Wife may demand it againſt her Huſband threatening to beat her outrageouſly, and that a Huſband alſo may have it againſt his Wife.

Dalt. cap. 68. Lamb. 78. Crom. 133.b. 3 Lev. 128.

Sect. 5. As to the third Point, *viz.* Againſt whom the Surety of the Peace ought to be granted; there ſeems to be no Doubt but that it ought upon a Juſt Cauſe of Complaint to be granted by any Juſtice of Peace, againſt any Perſon whatſoever, under the Degree of Nobility, being of ſane Memory, whether he be a Magiſtrate or private Perſon, and whether he be of full Age or under Age, *&c.* But Infants and Femes Covert ought to find Security by their Friends, and not to be bound themſelves; and the ſafeſt Way of proceeding againſt a Peer is by Complaint to the Court of Chancery or King's Bench.

F. N. B. 80.f. Dalt. cap. 68. Lamb. 81,82. Cromp. 134, 135.

See the Books above cited, and Fitz. Subpœna 20.

Sect. 6. As to the fourth Point, *viz.* For what Cauſe the Surety of the Peace is grantable; it ſeems clear, That where-ever a Perſon has juſt Cauſe to fear that another will burn his Houſe, or do him a corporal Hurt, as by killing or beating him, or that he will procure others to do him ſuch Miſchief, he may demand the Surety of the Peace againſt ſuch Perſon; and that every Juſtice of Peace is bound to grant it, upon the Party's giving him Satisfaction upon Oath, that he is actually under ſuch Fear; and that he has juſt Cauſe to be ſo, by Reaſon of the other's having threatened to beat him, or lain in wait for that Purpoſe; and that he does not require it out of Malice, or for Vexation.

Dalt. cap. 67. Lamb. 82. Crom. 135.

Sect. 7. It ſeems alſo the better Opinion, That he who is threatened to be impriſoned by another, has a Right to demand the Surety of the Peace; for every unlawful Impriſonment is an Aſſault and Wrong to the Perſon of a Man: And the Objection, That one wrongfully impriſoned may recover Damages in an Action, *&c.* and therefore needs not the Surety of the Peace, is as ſtrong in the Caſe of Battery as Impriſonment, and yet there is no doubt, but that one threatened to be beaten may demand the Surety of the Peace.

Dalt. cap. 67. Lamb. 82,83. Con. 17 Ed. 4. 4. Bro. Peace 22. Crom. 135 a.

Sect. 8. As to the fifth Point, *viz.* In what manner ſuch Surety is grantable by the Courts of Chancery and King's Bench, it is enacted by 21 Jac. 1. 8. *That all Proceſs for the Peace or good Behaviour to be granted or awarded out of the ſame Courts, or either of them, againſt any Perſon or Perſons whatſoever, at the Suit of, or by the Proſecution of any Perſon or Perſons whatſoever, ſhall be void and of none Effect, unleſs ſuch Proceſs ſhall be ſo granted or awarded, upon Motion firſt made before the Judge or Judges of the ſame Courts reſpectively, (ſitting in open Court, and upon Declaration in Writing upon their corporal Oaths, to be then exhibited unto them by the Parties which ſhall deſire ſuch Proceſs) of the Cauſes for which ſuch Proceſs ſhall be granted or awarded, by or out of the ſaid Courts reſpectively, and unleſs that ſuch Motion and Declaration be mentioned to be made upon the back of a Writ, the ſaid Writings there to be entered and remain of Record: And that if it ſhall afterwards appear unto the ſaid Courts, or either of them reſpectively, that the Cauſes expreſs'd in ſuch Writings, or any of them be untrue, That then the Judge or Judges of the ſaid Courts, or either of them reſpectively, ſhall and may award ſuch Coſts and Damages unto the Parties grieved, for their, or any of their wrongful Vexations in that Behalf, as they ſhall think fit: And that the Party or Parties ſo offending, ſhall and may be committed to Priſon by ſuch Judge or Judges, until he or they pay the ſaid Coſts and Damages.*

See 1 Lev. 53. 1 Syd. 67.

Sect. 9. As to the ſixth Point, *viz.* In what manner ſuch Surety is grantable by a Juſtice of Peace, it ſeemeth certain, That if the Perſon to be bound be in the Preſence of the Juſtice, he may be immediately com-

14 H 7. 8, 9, 10. 9 Ed. 4. 3. 2. Bro. Mainpr. 39.

committed, unleſs he offer Sureties; and from hence it follows, *a fortiori*, That he may be commanded by Word of Mouth to find Sureties, and committed for his Diſobedience; but it is ſaid, That if he be abſent, he Lamb. 85, &c. Dalt. ca. 69. cannot be committed without a Warrant from ſome Juſtice of Peace, in order to find Sureties, and that ſuch Warrant ought to be under Seal, and to ſhew the Cauſe for which it is granted, and at whoſe Suit, and that it may be directed to any indifferent Perſon.

Sect. 10. As to the ſeventh Point, *viz.* In what Manner the Proceſs for the Peace ought to be executed, it ſeems needleſs to give a particular Account of the Execution of the Writ of *Supplicavit*, becauſe I do not find that it is much in Uſe at this Day, and therefore I ſhall refer the Reader for this purpoſe to *Fitzherbert's Natura Brevium*, fol. 80, *&c.* But as to the Execution of a Warrant of a Juſtice, the following Rules are to be obſerved.

Lamb. 89. *Sect.* 11. I. It can be executed only by the Perſons to whom it is directed, or ſome of them, unleſs it be directed to the Sheriff, who may either by Parol, or by Precept in writing, authorize an Officer ſworn and known, to ſerve it, but cannot impower any other Perſon without a Precept in writing.

Sect. 12. II. If the Warrant be made in the common Form, directing the Officer to cauſe the Party complained of to come before ſome Juſtice of Long Quinto, 5 Ed. 4. 12. b. 13. a. Bro. Falſe Impriſ. 18. Dalt. ca. 69. Lamb. 90, 91. Crom. 235. 5 Co. 59. b. Peace, to find ſufficient Surety, *&c.* and if he ſhall refuſe ſo to do, to convey him immediately to Priſon, without expecting any further Warrant, until he ſhall willingly do the ſame, *&c.* the Officer who ſerves it, before he makes any Arreſt, ought firſt to require the Party to go with him, and find Sureties according to the Purport of the Warrant, but upon his Refuſal to do either, he may carry him to the Gaol by Force of the ſame Warrant, without more.

5 Co. 59. Dal. ca. 69. Bro. Falſe Impriſon. 11. 21 H. 7. 21. a. Lamb. 94, 95. *Sect.* 13. III. If the Warrant ſpecially direct, that the Party ſhall be brought before the Juſtice who made it, the Officer ought not to carry him before any other: But if the Warrant be general, to bring him before any Juſtice of Peace, *&c.* the Officer has the Election to bring him before what Juſtice he pleaſes, and may carry him to Priſon for refuſing to find Surety before ſuch Juſtice.

Sect. 14. As to the eighth Point, *viz.* How ſuch Proceſs may be ſuperſeded, it is ſaid, That if one who fears that the Surety of the Peace Dalt. c. 69. will be demanded againſt him, find Sureties before any Juſtice of the Peace of the ſame County, either before or after a Warrant is iſſued againſt him, he may have a *Superſedeas* from ſuch Juſtice, which ſhall diſcharge him from Arreſt from any other Juſtice, at the Suit of the ſame Lamb. 112, 113. See 2 Roll. A. 492. F. Party, for whoſe Security he has given ſuch Surety: Alſo it is ſaid, That an Appearance upon a Recognizance for the Peace may be ſuperſeded, by finding Sureties in the Chancery or King's Bench, and purchaſing a Writ teſtifying the ſame. But this Practice having often been abuſed by turbulent Perſons, who deſervedly fearing to be bound to the Peace or Good Behaviour, by Juſtices of Peace, would procure themſelves to be bound thereto in the ſaid Courts, upon inſufficient Sureties, or upon the colourable Proſecution of ſome Perſon who would be ready at all Times to releaſe them at their Pleaſure; whereupon Writs of *Superſedeas* had been often directed to Juſtices of Peace, commanding them to forbear to arreſt the Parties for ſuch Cauſes; by reaſon whereof ſuch turbulent Perſons uſed to miſdemean themſelves among their Neighbours with Impunity, as it is recited by 21 *Jac.* 1. 8. it is thereupon enacted by the ſaid Statute, *That all Writs of* Superſedeas, *to be granted out of either of the ſaid Courts, ſhall be void, unleſs ſuch Proceſs be granted upon Motion in open Court firſt made,* &c. *upon ſuch ſufficient Sureties, as ſhall appear unto the Judge or Judges of the ſame Court reſpectively, upon Oath, to be aſſeſſed at five Pounds Lands, or ten Pounds in Goods, in the Subſidy Book, at the leaſt; which Oaths, and the Names of ſuch Sureties, with the Places of their Abode, and where they ſtand ſo aſſeſſed in the Subſidy Books, ſhall be entred, and remain of Record in the ſame Courts: And unleſs it ſhall alſo firſt appear unto the ſaid Judge or Judges, from whom ſuch* Superſedeas *is deſired, That the Proceſs of the Peace, or good Behaviour, is proſecuted againſt him or them, deſiring ſuch* Superſedeas, bona fide, *by ſome Party grieved, in that Court, out of which ſuch* Superſedeas *is deſired to be ſo awarded and directed.*

2 Chancery Reports, 68.

Sect. 15. As to the ninth Point, *viz.* What ought to be the Form of ſuch a Recognizance: If it be taken in Purſuance of a Writ of *Supplicavit*, it muſt be wholly governed by the Directions of ſuch Writ; but if it be taken before a Juſtice of Peace, upon a Complaint below, it ſeems that it may be regulated by the Diſcretion of ſuch Juſtice, both as to the Number and Sufficiency of the Sureties, and the Largeneſs of the Sum, and the Continuance of the Time, for which the Party ſhall be bound; and it hath been ſaid, That a Recognizance to keep the Peace as to *A. B.* for a Year, or for Life, or without expreſſing any certain Time, (in which Caſe it ſhall be intended to be for Life) or without fixing any Time or Place for the Party's Appearance, or without binding him to keep the Peace againſt all the King's People in general, is good.

Lamb. 100, 101. Dal. ca. 70.

Sect. 16. However, it ſeems to be the ſafeſt Way to bind the Party to appear at the next Seſſions of the Peace, and in the mean Time to keep the Peace as to the King, and all his Liege People, eſpecially as to the Party, according to the common Form of Precedents.

Lamb. 105. Dal. ca. 124.

Sect. 17. As to the tenth Point, *viz.* How ſuch a Recognizance may be diſcharged, it ſeems agreed, That it may be diſcharged by the Demiſe of the [a] King in whoſe Reign it was taken, or of the [b] principal Party who was bound thereby, if it were not forfeited before; alſo it hath been holden, That it may be diſcharged by the Releaſe of the Party at whoſe Complaint it was taken, being certified together with it, but this may juſtly be queſtioned, becauſe the Recognizance is not to the Subject, but to the King, and conſequently cannot be diſcharged by the Subject, who is not a Party to it; however, ſuch a Releaſe will be a good Inducement to the Court, to which ſuch a Recognizance ſhall be certified, to diſcharge it; and ſo alſo will the Non-Appearance of the Party at whoſe complaint it was taken, in order to pray the Continuance of it; and yet it is ſaid, That the Seſſions in that Caſe may, in their Diſcretion, refuſe to diſcharge it; however, it is certain that ſuch a Recognizance cannot be pardoned, or releaſed by the King, before it is broken, becauſe the Subject has a Kind of Intereſt in it; and it is ſaid, That [d] the Sureties are not diſcharged by their Death, but that their Executors, *&c.* continue bound as their Teſtators, *&c.* were.

[a] Bro. Peace 15. 1 H. 7. 2. [b] 15 H. 7. 2. b. 13. A. 21 Ed. 4. 70. b. Dalt. ch. 71. 1 Lev. 235. [c] Lamb. 110, &c. Crom. 139. b. 169. a. Bro. Peace 17. Crom. 144. b. 1 H. 7. 10 b. 11 H. 7. 12. a. 11 H. 4. 43. a. B. 2. Ch. 26. S. 64. Ch. 37. S. 34. [d] Bro. Peace 17.

Sect. 18. As to the eleventh Point, *viz.* How ſuch a Recognizance ought to be certified, and proceeded upon: If it be taken by Force of a Writ of *Supplicavit*, it needs not be certified till the Juſtice receive a Writ of *Certiorari* to that Purpoſe; but if it be taken upon a Complaint below, it muſt be certified, ſent, or brought to the next Seſſions of the Peace by Force of 3 *H.* 7. 1. that the Party ſo bound may be called; and by the ſame Statute, *If the Party then make Default, the ſame Default ſhall be then recorded, and the ſame Recognizance with the Record of the Default, ſhall*

Lamb. 111. 112, &c. Dalt. ca. 70.

Hill. 1 Geor. 1. between the King and Combs agreed.

be certified into the Chancery, King's Bench or Exchequer: However, if the Party have any Excuse for his not appearing, it seems that the Sessions is not bound peremptorily to record his Default, but may equitably consider of the Reasonableness of such Excuse; and it is said, That the Sessions cannot in any Case proceed against the Party for a Forfeiture of his Recognizance, either in respect of his not appearing, or breaking the Peace, but that the Recognizance in such Case ought to be removed into some of the King's Courts of *Westminster Hall*, who shall proceed by *Scire Facias* upon such Recognizance, and not by Indictment, *&c.*

Dal. ch. 71. Raym. 169. Cro. Ja. 598. 1 Roll. A. 900. Pl. 4.

3 Bulst. 120.

Sect. 19. It seemeth, that in a *Scire Facias* upon such a Recognizance, it is sufficient to lay the Fact alledged for a Breach thereof, as having been done *contra pacem*, without using the Words *Vi & Armis.*

Whether such Scire Facias must shew the Day on which the Sessions was holden, till which the Party was bound to keep the Peace. Cro. Ca. 138.

Bro. Peace 20. Dalt. ch. 72. Lamb. 127, 128.

Sect. 20. As to the twelfth Point, *viz.* How such Recognizance may be forfeited, there is no Doubt but that it may be forfeited by any actual Violence to the Person of another, whether it be done by the Party himself, or by others thro' his Procurement, as Manslaughter, Rape, Robbery, unlawful Imprisonment, *&c.*

Lamb. 115, &c. Dalt. ch. 72. 2 H. 7. 2. b. seems otherwise. 18 Ed. 4. 28. a. 22 Ed. 4. 35. b.

Sect. 21. Also it has been holden, That it may be forfeited by any Treason against the Person of the King, and also by any unlawful Assembly *in Terrorem populi*, and even by Words directly tending to a Breach of the Peace, as by challenging one to fight, or, in his Presence, threatning to beat him, *&c.*

Cro. Ca. 498, 499. See the Books cited in the following Section, and 2 R. A. 545. Pl. 2, 3, 4, 5, 6, 7, 8. 547. E. 3.

Cro. El. 86. Mo. 249. 2 Rol. Re. 199, 227. Palm. 126. Infra Ch. 61. S. 3.

Sect. 22. However, it seems that it shall not be forfeited by bare Words of Heat and Choler, as the calling a Man Knave, Teller of Lies, Rascal, or Drunkard; for though such Words may provoke a cholerick Man to break the Peace, yet they do not directly challenge him to it, nor does it appear that the Speaker designed to carry his Resentment any farther: And it hath been said, That even a Recognizance for the good Behaviour, shall not be forfeited for such Words; from whence it follows, *à fortiori*, That a Recognizance for the Peace shall not.

[a] 2 Ed. 4. 6. 21 H. 7. 39. [b] Dalt. ca. 72. Crom. 136. b. [c] 38 H. 6. 25. 1 Sid. 176, 177. [d] H. P. C. 31. 1 Sid. 177. 21 Ed. 4. 6. [e] Dal. ca. 72. [f] Crom. 28. b. 136. b. F. N. B. 80. F. Hetley 149. Contra 1 Syd. 113, 116. [g] 22 Ass. 56. 2 R. A. 546. C. 22 Ed. 4. 5. a. b. [h] Cro. Ja. 134. 2 R. A. 546. Pl. 35, 59. E.

Sect. 23. Also there are some actual Assaults on the Person of another, which do not amount to a Forfeiture of such a Recognizance; as if an [a] Officer, having a Warrant against one who will not suffer himself to be arrested, beat or wound him in the Attempt to take him; or if a [b] Parent in a reasonable Manner chastise his Child, or a Master his Servant, [c] being actually in his Service at the Time; or a [d] Schoolmaster his Scholar, or a [e] Gaoler his Prisoner, or even a [f] Husband his Wife, as some say; or if [g] one confine a Friend who is mad, and bind, and beat him, *&c.* in such a Manner as is proper in such Circumstances; or if a Man [h] force a Sword from one who offers to kill another therewith; or if a Man gently lay his Hands upon another, and thereby stay him from inciting a Dog against a third Person; or if [i] I beat one (without [k] wounding him, or throwing at him a dangerous Weapon) who wrongfully endeavours with Violence to dispossess me of my Land, or Goods; or the Goods of another delivered to me to be kept for him, and will not desist upon my laying my Hands gently on him, and disturbing him; or if a Man beat, [l] or, as some say, wound, or maim one who makes an

[i] 3 H. 4. 6. b. 9. a. Lutw. 1483. Cro. Ja. 236. Cro. Ca. 138. 19 H. 6. 31. b. 10 E. 4. 6. b. 11 Ed. 4. 28. b. Kellew. 92. a. Yelv. 172. 2 R. A. 547. E. 1, 2. 548. Pl. 2, 3, 4, 5, 6, 7. 549. P. 9, 10, 11. Pult. 5, 6. Crom. 137. a. Dal. ca. 72. Infra Ch. 64. S. 1. [k] 2 R. A. 548. Pl. 4, 8. [l] 41 Ass. 21. 27 Ed. 3. 94. a. 25 Ed. 3. 42. a. 8 H. 4. 8. a. b. 9 Ed. 4. 48. b. 12 Ed. 4. 6. a. Bro de Tort. Demesne 57. 1 Sid. 246. Kely. 128. 2 R. A. 547. F. Pl. 1, 2, 3, 4. 1 Keb. 884, 921. 2 Inst. 316.

Assault upon his Person, or that of his [a] Wife, Parent, Child, or Master; especially if it appear that he did all he could to avoid fighting before he gave the Wound; or if a Man [b] fight with or beat one who attempts to kill any Stranger; or if a Man even [c] threaten to kill one who puts him in Fear of Death in such a Place where he cannot safely fly from him; or if one [d] imprison those whom he sees fighting, till the Heat is over.

[a] 35 H. 6. 50. b. 51. a. 19 H. 6. 31. a. b. 66. a. 12 Ed. 4. 6. a. Crom. 136. b. Dal. ca. 72. 2 R. A. 546. D. 1, 2, 3. 22 E. 4. 45. b.

[b] 12 H. 8. 2. b. [c] 32 H. 6. 18. b. 10 Ed. 4. 6. b. [d] 2 Rol. Ab. 559 E.

Sect. 24. According to some Opinions, a [e] Master shall not forfeit such a Recognizance for beating another in Defence of his Servant, but it is said, That a [f] Servant is liable to such Forfeiture for beating another in Defence of his Master's Son, tho' he were commanded by the Master so to do, because he is not a Servant to the Son; and for the like Reason it is said, That a [g] Tenant shall incur the like Forfeiture for beating another in Defence of his Landlord, *&c.*

[e] 2 R. A. 546. D. 2. 19 H. 6. 31. b. 66. a. Dalt. ca. 72. Crom. 136. b. Con. 9 Ed. 4. 48. b. Salk. 407. 2.

[f] 9 Ed. 4. 48. b. Bro. Tresp. 189. Lamb. 129.

[g] Dalt. ch. 72.

Sect. 25. But it seems agreed, That no one shall forfeit such a Recognizance by a bare Trespass on another's Lands, or Goods, unless it be accompanied with some Violence to the Person. Crom. 136. b. Dalt. ca. 72. Cro. El. 86. Moor 249.

Sect. 26. And it seems to be the better Opinion, That a Man is in no Danger of such a Forfeiture from any Hurt done to another, by playing at Cudgels, or such like Sport, by Consent, because the Intent of the Parties seems no way unlawful, but rather commendable, and tending mutually to promote Activity and Courage; yet it is said, That he who wounds another in fighting with naked Swords, does in strictness forfeit such a Recognizance, because no Consent can make so dangerous a Diversion lawful. Dalt. ca. 22. Bro. Coron. 229. Fitz. Bar. 244.

Sect. 27. But it seemeth, That a Man shall not forfeit such Recognizance, by a Hurt done to another merely thro' Negligence, or Mischance; as where one Soldier hurts another by discharging a Gun in Exercise, without sufficient Caution; for notwithstanding such Person must, in a Civil Action, give the other Satisfaction for the Damage occasioned by his Want of Care, yet he seems not to have offended against the Purport of such a Recognizance, unless he be guilty of some wilfull Breach of the Peace. Ho. 134. 2 R. A. 548. G.

CHAP. LXI.

Of Surety for the Good Behaviour.

AND now we are come to Surety for the Good Behaviour, which being of great Affinity with Surety of the Peace, both as to the Manner in which it is to be taken, superseded, and discharged, *&c.* seems not to require a particular Consideration, save only as to the following Points,

1. For what Misbehaviours it is to be required.
2. For what it shall be forfeited.

Sect. 1. As to the first Point, it is to be observed, That by 34 *Ed.* 3. 1. *Justices of Peace are impowered to restrain Offenders, Rioters, and all other Barrators, and to pursue, arrest, take, and chastise them, according to their Trespass, or Offence; and to cause them to be imprisoned, and duly punished according* to *to the Laws and Customs of the Realm, and according to that which to them shall seem best to do by their Discretions, and good Advisement, and also to inform them, and to enquire of all those that have been Pillors and Robbers in the Parts beyond the Sea, and be now come again, and go wandring, and will not labour as they were wont in Times past; and to take and arrest all those, that they may find by Indictment or by Suspicion, and to put them in Prison, and to take of all them that be not of good Fame, where they shall be found, sufficient Surety and Mainprize of their good Behaviour towards the King and his People, and the other duly to punish, to the Intent that the People be not by such Rioters troubled nor endamaged, nor the Peace blemished, nor Merchants, nor others passing by the Highways of the Realm disturbed, nor put in the Peril which may happen of such Offenders.*

4 Inst. 181. 2H.7.2.b.3.a. Lamb. 115, 116, 117. Dalt. ca. 75.

Sect. 2. In the Construction hereof there seem to have been some Opinions, that the Statute, speaking of those that be not of good Fame, means only such as are defamed, and justly suspected that they intend to break the Peace, and that it does not any Way extend to those who are guilty of other Misbehaviours not relating to the Peace; but this seems much too narrow a Construction, since the above mentioned Expression of Persons of evil Fame, in common Understanding, as properly includes Persons of scandalous Behaviour in other Respects, as those who by their quarrelsome Behaviour give just Suspicion of their Readiness to break the Peace; and accordingly it seems to have been always the better Opinion, That a Man may be bound to his Good Behaviour for many Causes of Scandal which give him a bad Fame, as being contrary to good Manners only; as for [a] haunting Bawdy-houses with Women of bad Fame; or for [b] keeping bad Women in his own House; or for speaking Words of Contempt of an inferiour [c] Magistrate, as a Justice of Peace, or Mayor of a Town, &c. tho' he be not then in the actual Execution of his Office, or of an inferior Officer of Justice, as a Constable, and such like, being in the actual Execution of his Office.

[a] 13H.7.10.b. [b] Crom.140.a. [c] Cro. El. 78. 1 Levin. 52, 53, 107. 11 Co. 98. 1 Ro. Re.224. Latch 220. Con. Cro. El. 689. Palm. 130. 1 Rol. Rep. 227, 228. 3 Bulst. 139, 140. [d] Cro. Ca. 498, 499. [e] Cro. El. 86. Moor 249. Supra Ch. 60. S. 22.

Sect. 3. However, it seems the better Opinion, That no one ought to be bound [d] to the Good Behaviour for any rash, quarrelsome, or unmannerly Words, unless they either directly tend to a Breach of the Peace, or to scandalize the Government, by abusing those who are intrusted by it with the Administration of Justice, or to deter an Officer from doing his Duty; and therefore it seems, That he [e] who barely calls another Rogue, or Rascal, or Teller of Lies, or Drunkard, &c. ought not for such Cause to be bound to the Good Behaviour.

2 Rol. Re. 199, 227. Palm. 126. Dalt. 75. 1 Rol.Re.150. 2 Ventr. 22, 23, 24.

Sect. 4. However, I cannot find any certain precise Rules for the Direction of the Magistrate in this Respect, and therefore am inclined to think, that he has a discretionary Power to take such Surety of all those whom he shall have just Cause to suspect to be dangerous, quarrelsome, or scandalous, as of those who sleep in the Day, and go abroad in the Night, and of such as keep suspicious Company, and of such as are generally suspected to be Robbers, &c. and of Eves-Droppers, and common Drunkards, and all other Persons, whose Misbehaviour may reasonably be intended to bring them within the Meaning of the Statute, as Persons of evil Fame, who, being described by an Expression of so great Latitude, seem in a great Measure to be left to the Judgment of the Magistrate. But if he commit one for want of Sureties, he must shew the Cause, &c. with convenient Certainty.

Palm. 129, 130.

Sect. 5. As to the second Point, *viz.* For what Misbehaviours such a Recognizance shall be forfeited, it is laid down as a general Rule in the Argument of *Stamp* and *Hide*'s Case, That whatever will be a good

Cause to bind a Man to his Good Behaviour, will forfeit a Recognizance for it, yet this is since denied in *Heyward*'s Case; and indeed does by no Means seem to be maintainable, because the Statute in ordering Persons of evil Fame to be bound in this Manner, seems in many Cases chiefly to regard the Prevention of that Mischief which they may justly be suspected to be likely to do; and in that Respect requires them to secure the Publick from that Danger which may probably be apprehended from their future Behaviour, whether any actual Crime can be proved upon them, or not; and it would be extreamly hard in such Cases to make Persons forfeit their Recognizance, who yet may justly be compellable to give one, as those who keep suspicious Company, or those who spend much Money idly, without having any visible Means of getting it honestly, or those who lie under a general Suspicion of being Rogues, &c. Cro Ca. 499. 13 H. 7. 10. b. Dalt. ca. 75.

Sect. 6. However, it seems that such a Recognizance shall not only be forfeited for such actual Breaches of the Peace, for which a Recognizance for the Peace may be forfeited, but also for some others, for which such a Recognizance cannot be forfeited; as for going armed with great Numbers to the Terror of the People, or speaking Words tending to Sedition, &c. and also for all such actual Misbehaviours which are intended to be prevented by such a Recognizance, but not for barely giving Cause of Suspicion of what perhaps may never actually happen. 2 H. 7. 2. b. Cro. Ca. 499.

CHAP. LXII.

Of Assaults and Batteries.

AND now I am come to consider the several Kinds of actual Disturbances of the Peace, and these are; either,

1. Such as may be committed by one or two Persons.
2. Such as require a greater Number.

Those which may be committed by one or two Persons, are,

1. Assaults and Batteries.
2. Affrays.
3. Forcible Entries and Detainers.

As to Assaults and Batteries, I shall consider the following Particulars:

1. What shall be said to be an Assault.
2. What shall be said to be a Battery.
3. In what Cases they may be justified.
4. In what Manner they are to be punished.

Sect. 1. As to the first Point, it seems that an Assault is an Attempt, or Offer, with Force and Violence, to do a corporal Hurt to another; as by striking at him with, or without, a Weapon; or presenting a Gun at him, at such a Distance to which the Gun will carry, or pointing a Pitch-fork at him, standing within the Reach of it; or by holding up Pulton 4. a. 6 Mod. 173, 174. 2 R. A. 545, 10, 11.

1 Vent. 256. 1 Mod. 3. 1 Keb. 921. 40 Ed.3.40.a. 42 Ed. 3. 7. a. 45 Ed. 3. 24. b. 25. a. 22 Aff. 60. 2 R. A. 545. Pl. 1, 2, 3, 4, 5, 6, 7, 8. one's Fiſt at him, or by any other ſuch like Act done in an angry threatening Manner; and from hence it clearly follows, That one charged with an Aſſault and Battery, may be found guilty of the former, and yet acquitted of the latter. But [a] every Battery includes an Aſſault, therefore on an Indictment of Aſſault and Battery, in which the Aſſault is ill laid, if the Defendant be found guilty of the Battery, it is ſufficient. Notwithſtanding the many ancient Opinions to the contrary, it ſeems agreed at this Day, that no Words whatſoever can amount to an Aſſault.

22 Aff. Pl.11. Pult. 3. Lamb. 126. [a] Salk. 384. 6 Mod. 149, 172. 1 Mod. 3. 3 Lev. 404. Skin. 387. *Sect.* 2. As to the ſecond Point, *viz.* What ſhall be ſaid to be a Battery, it ſeems that any Injury whatſoever, be it never ſo ſmall, being actually done to the Perſon of a Man, in an angry, or revengeful, or rude, or inſolent Manner, as by Spitting in his Face, or any Way touching him in Anger, or violently juſtling him out of the Way, are Batteries in the Eye of the Law: But it is ſaid to be no Battery to lay one's Hand gently on another whom an Officer has a Warrant to arreſt, and to tell the Officer that this is the Man he wants.

2 R. A. 546. Pl. 1, 2. *Sect.* 3. As to the third Point, *viz.* In what Caſes an Aſſault and Battery may be juſtified, this is ſo fully ſet forth already in the Chapter of *Surety of the Peace*, that there ſeems to be no need of any farther Conſideration thereof in this Place; and therefore I ſhall only add, That where a Man in his own Defence beats another who firſt aſſaults him, *&c.* he may take an Advantage thereof upon an Indictment, as well as upon an Action; 6 Mod. 172. but with this Difference, that in the firſt Caſe he may give it in Evidence upon the Plea of Not guilty, and in the latter he muſt plead it ſpecially.

Sect. 4. As to the fourth Point, *viz.* How unlawful Aſſaults and Batteries are puniſhed, there is no doubt but that the Wrong-doer is ſubject, both to an Action at the Suit of the Party, wherein he ſhall render Damages, *&c.* and alſo to an Indictment at the Suit of the King, wherein he ſhall be fined according to the Heinouſneſs of the Offence.

CHAP. LXIII.

Of Affrays.

IN treating of Affrays, I ſhall conſider,

1. What ſhall be ſaid to be an Affray.
2. How far it may be ſuppreſſed by a private Perſon.
3. How far by a Conſtable.
4. How far by a Juſtice of Peace.
5. In what Manner the ſeveral Kinds of Affrays may be puniſhed.

3 Inſt. 158. Dalt. ca. 8. *Sect.* 1. As to the firſt Point, it is ſaid, That the Word Affray is derived from the *French* Word *Effraier*, to terrify, and that in a legal Senſe it is taken for a publick Offence, to the Terror of the People, from whence it ſeems clearly to follow, That there may be an Aſſault which Lamb. 125, 126. will not amount to an Affray; as where it happens in a private Place, out of the hearing or ſeeing of any, except the Parties concerned; in which Caſe it cannot be ſaid to be to the Terror of the People; and for

this Cause such a private Assault seems not to be inquirable in a Court-Leet, as all Affrays certainly are, as being common Nusances. 4 H. 6. 10. a. 8 Ed. 4. 5. b.

Sect. 2. Also it is said, that no quarrelsome or threatening Words whatsoever shall amount to an Affray; and that no one can justify laying his Hands on those who shall barely quarrel with angry Words, without coming to Blows; yet it seemeth, That the Constable may, at the Request of the Party threatened, carry the Person, who threatens to beat him, before a Justice of Peace, in Order to find Sureties. H. P. C. 135. 23 E. 4. 45. b. Dalt. ch. 8. Lamb. Constable, 14.

Sect. 3. Also it is certain, That it is a very high Offence to challenge another, either by Word or Letter, to fight a Duel, or to be the Messenger of such a Challenge, or even barely to endeavour to provoke another to send a Challenge, or to fight; as by dispersing Letters to that Purpose, full of Reflections, and insinuating a Desire to fight, *&c.* Poph. 158. 3 Inst. 158. 1 Sid. 186. 1 Keb. 694. Hob. 120, 215. 2 Rol. Ab. 78.

Sect. 4. But granting that no bare Words, in the Judgment of Law, carry in them so much Terror as to amount to an Affray; yet it seems certain, That in some Cases there may be an Affray where there is no actual Violence; as where a Man arms himself with dangerous and unusual Weapons, in such a Manner as will naturally cause a Terror to the People, which is said to have been always an Offence at Common Law, and is strictly prohibited by many Statutes: For by 2 *Ed.* 3. 3. it is enacted, *That no Man, great nor small, of what Condition soever he be, except the King's Servants, in his Presence, and his Ministers in executing of the King's Precepts, or of their Office, and such as be in their Company assisting them, and also upon a Cry made for Arms to keep the Peace, and the same in such Places where such Acts happen, be so hardy to come before the King's Justices, or other of the King's Ministers doing their Office, with Force and Arms, nor bring no Force in Affray of Peace, nor to go nor ride armed by Night nor by Day, in Fairs, Markets, nor in the Presence of the Justices or other Ministers, nor in no part elsewhere, upon Pain to forfeit their Armour to the King, and their Bodies to Prison, at the King's Pleasure. And that the King's Justices in their Presence, Sheriffs, and other Ministers in their Bailiwicks, Lords of Franchises, and their Bailiffs in the same, and Mayors and Bailiffs of Cities and Boroughs, within the same Cities and Boroughs, and Borough-holders, Constables and Wardens of the Peace within their Wards, shall have Power to execute this Act: And that the Justices assigned, at their coming down into the Country, shall have Power to enquire how such Officers and Lords have exercised their Offices in this Case, and to punish them whom they find, that have not done that which pertained to their Office*; and this Statute is farther enforced by 7 *Rich.* 2. 13. and 20 *Rich.* 2. 1. Lamb. 126. 3 Inst. 160. 76. D. 2 Rol. Ab. 78. Pl. 4. H. P. C. 137.

And in the Exposition of it, the following Points have been holden:

Sect. 5. I. That any Justice of Peace, or other Person, who is impowered to execute this Statute, may proceed thereon, either *ex Officio*, or by Force of a Writ out of Chancery formed upon the Statute, and that if he find any Person in Arms contrary to the Form of the Statute, he may seize the Arms, and commit the Offender to Prison; and that he ought also to make a Record of his whole Proceeding, and certify the same into the Chancery, where he proceeds by Force of the said Writ, or into the Exchequer, where he proceeds *ex Officio*. F. N. B. 249. 3 Inst. 161. Dal. ch. 22. Lamb. 168, &c. Dalis. 23. 2 Bulf. 330.

Sect. 6. II. That where a Justice of Peace, *&c.* proceeds upon the said Writ, he may not only imprison those whom he shall find offending against the Statute in his own View, but also those who shall be found by an Inquest taken before him, to have offended in such Manner in his Absence; and I do not see why he may not do the same where he proceeds *ex Officio*; for seeing the said Writ hath no other Foundation but Cro. El. 294. Con. Lamb. 170.

the ſaid Statute, and is the moſt authentick Explication thereof, it ſeemeth that the Rules therein preſcribed, ſhould be the beſt Direction for all Proceedings upon that Statute.

Cro. El. 294.

Sect. 7. III. That the Under-Sheriff may execute the ſaid Writ, being directed to the Sheriff, if it name him only by the Name of his Office, and not by his proper Name, and do not expreſly command him to act in his proper Perſon.

24 Ed. 3. 33. a. b. 21 H. 7. 39. a. 3 Inſt. 161, 162. Con. 2 Rol. 78. d. 2 H. 7. 39. a. 3 Inſt. 162.

Sect. 8. IV. That a Man cannot excuſe the wearing ſuch Armour in Publick, by alledging that ſuch a one threatened him, and that he wears it for the Safety of his Perſon from his Aſſault; but it hath been reſolved, That no one ſhall incur the Penalty of the ſaid Statute for aſſembling his Neighbours and Friends in his own Houſe, againſt thoſe who threaten to do him any Violence therein, becauſe a Man's Houſe is as his Caſtle.

3 Mod. 117, 118. 2 Bulſt. 330.

Sect. 9. V. That no Wearing of Arms is within the Meaning of this Statute, unleſs it be accompanied with ſuch Circumſtances as are apt to terrify the People; from whence it ſeems clearly to follow, That Perſons of Quality are in no Danger of offending againſt this Statute by wearing common Weapons, or having their uſual Number of Attendants with them, for their Ornament or Defence, in ſuch Places, and upon ſuch Occaſions, in which it is the common Faſhion to make uſe of them, without cauſing the leaſt Suſpicion of an Intention to commit any Act of Violence or Diſturbance of the Peace. And from the ſame Ground it alſo follows, That

Crom. 64. a.

Perſons armed with privy Coats of Mail to the Intent to defend themſelves againſt their Adverſaries, are not within the Meaning of this Statute, becauſe they do nothing *in terrorem populi*.

Poph. 121, 122.

Sect. 10. VI. That no Perſon is within the Intention of the ſaid Statute, who arms himſelf to ſuppreſs dangerous Rioters, Rebels, or Enemies, and endeavours to ſuppreſs or reſiſt ſuch Diſturbers of the Peace or Quiet of the Realm; for Perſons who ſo arm themſelves, ſeem to be exempted out of the general Words of the ſaid Statute, by that Part of the Exception in the Beginning thereof, which ſeems to allow all Perſons to arm themſelves upon a Cry made for Arms to keep the Peace, in ſuch Places where ſuch Acts happen.

Lamb. 131. 3 Inſt. 158. H. P. C. 131. 2 Inſt. 52. 22 E. 4. 44. b. Dalt. ca. 8. Lamb. 131. Infra 17.

Sect. 11. As to the ſecond Point, *viz.* How far an Affray may be ſuppreſſed by a private Perſon, it ſeems agreed, That any one who ſees others fighting, may lawfully part them, and alſo ſtay them till the Heat be over, and then deliver them to the Conſtable, who may carry them before a Juſtice of Peace, in order to their finding Sureties for the Peace: Alſo it is ſaid, That any private Perſon may ſtop thoſe whom he ſhall ſee coming to join either Party; and from hence it ſeems clearly to follow, That if a Man receive a Hurt from either Party in thus endeavouring to preſerve the Peace, he ſhall have his Remedy by an Action againſt him; alſo upon the

3 Inſt. 138. Con. Lamb. 131. Dalt. cap. 8.

ſame Ground it ſeems equally reaſonable, That if he unavoidably happen to hurt either Party, in thus doing what the Law both allows and commends, he may well juſtify it, inaſmuch as he is no way in Fault; and the Damage done to the other, was occaſioned by a laudable Intention to do him a Kindneſs.

Lamb. 131. Dalt. cap. 8. 3 Inſt. 158. Bro. Faux. Impriſonment 35, 44. H. P. C. 135. 10 H. 7. 20. 2 Inſt. 52.

Sect. 12. However it ſeems clear, That if either Party be dangerouſly wounded in ſuch an Affray, and a Stander-by, endeavouring to arreſt the other, be not able to take him without hurting, or even wounding him, yet he is no way liable to be puniſhed for the ſame, inaſmuch as he is bound under Pain of Fine and Impriſonment, to arreſt ſuch an Offender, and either detain him till it appear whether the Party will live or die, or carry him before a Juſtice of Peace, by whom he either is to be bailed or committed, *&c.*

Sect. 13. As to the third Point, *viz.* How far an Affray may be suppressed by a Constable; it seems agreed, That a Constable is not only impower'd, as all private Persons are, to part an Affray which happens in his 3 Inst. 158. Presence, but is also bound at his Peril to use his best Endeavours to this H. P. C. 135. Lamb. 132, Purpose, and not only to do his utmost himself, but also to demand the 133. Assistance of others, which if they refuse to give him, they are punishable Dalt. cap. 8. 3 H. 7. 10. b. with Fine and Imprisonment.

Sect. 14. And it is said, That if a Constable see Persons either actually engaged in an Affray, as by Striking, or offering to strike, or drawing Lamb. 132, 133. their Weapons, &c. or upon the very Point of entering upon an Affray, Dalt. ca. 1, 8. as where one shall threaten to kill, wound, or beat another, he may either carry the Offender before a Justice of Peace, to the End that such Ju- H. P. C. 136. stice may compel him to find Sureties for the Peace, &c. or he may im- Dalt. cap. 1, 8. Bro. Surety, prison him of his own Authority for a reasonable Time, till the Heat shall 23, 36. be over, and also afterwards detain him till he find such Surety by Obliga- Cro. El. 375. 9 Ed. 4. 26. a. tion: But it seems, That he has no Power to imprison such an Offender Moor 284. in any other Manner, or for any other Purpose; for he cannot justify the Pl. 436. committing an Affrayer to Gaol till he shall be punished for his Offence: 3 H. 4. 9. a. 22 Ed. 4. 35. b. And it is said, That he ought not to lay Hands on those, who barely con- 10 Ed. 4. 18. tend with hot Words, without any Threats of personal Hurt, and that all 5 H. 7. 6. a. Savil 97, 98. which he can do in such a Case, is to command them under Pain of Imprisonment to avoid Fighting.

Sect. 15. But he is so far intrusted with a Power over all actual Af- 5 H. 7. 6. a. frays, that though he himself is a Sufferer by them, and therefore liable H. P. C. 136. 1 Rol. Re. 238. to be objected against, as likely to be partial in his own Cause, yet he may 2 Bulst. 329. suppress them; and therefore, if an Assault be made upon him, he may not only defend himself, but also imprison the Offender, in the same Manner as if he were no way a Party.

Sect. 16. And if an Affray be in a House, the Constable may break 13 Ed. 4. 9. a. open the Doors to preserve the Peace; and if Affrayers fly to a House 7 Ed. 3. 12. b. Dalt. cap. 8, and he follow with fresh Suit, he may break open the Doors to take 67. them. Lamb. 133, 134.

Sect. 17. But it is said, That a Constable hath no Power to arrest a H. P. C. 135. Man for an Affray done out of his own View, without a Warrant from Cro. El. 375. a Justice of Peace, unless a Felony were done or likely to be done; for Owen 105. H. P. C. 92, it is the proper Business of a Constable to preserve the Peace, not to pu- 136. nish the Breach of it; nor does it follow from his having Power to compel those to find Sureties who break the Peace in his Presence, that he has the same Power over those who break it in his Absence, inasmuch as in such Case it is most proper to be done by those who may examine the whole Circumstances of the Matter upon Oath, which a Constable cannot do; yet it is said, That he may carry those before a Justice of Peace, who Lamb. 131. were arrested by such as were present at an Affray, and delivered by them Dalt. cap. 8. into his Hands.

Sect. 18. As to the fourth Point, *viz.* In what Manner an Affray may be suppressed by a Justice of Peace; there is no Doubt, but that he may H. P. C. 136. and must do all such Things to that Purpose, which a private Man or Dalt. cap. 8. Constable are either enabled, or required by the Law to do: But it is said, Bro. False Imprisonment, That he cannot without a Warrant authorize the Arrest of any Person for 6, 12, 33. an Affray out of his View; yet it seems clear, that in such Case he may 14 H. 8. 7. make his Warrant to bring the Offender before him, in order to compel him Moor 468 Pl. 551 to find Sureties for the Peace.

See 38 Ed. 3. 6. b. 7. a. 22 Aſſ. 56. 5 Mod. 84. H. P. C. 36. Dalt. cap. 8. Poph. 153.

Sect. 19. Alſo it ſeems, That a Juſtice of Peace has a greater Power over one who hath dangerouſly wounded another in an Affray, than either a private Perſon or a Conſtable; for there does not ſeem to be any good Authority, that theſe have any Power at all to take Sureties of ſuch an Offender; but it ſeems certain, That a Juſtice of the Peace has a diſcretionary Power either to commit him or to bail him, till the Year and Day be paſt; but it is ſaid, that he ought to be very cautious how he takes Bail, if the Wound be dangerous; for that if the Party die, and the Offender appear not, he is in Danger of being ſeverely fined, if he ſhall appear upon the whole Circumſtances of the Caſe to have been too favourable.

Aleyn 79.

Sect. 20. As to the fifth Point, *viz.* In what Manner the ſeveral kinds of Affrays are to be puniſhed, it ſufficiently appears from the foregoing Part of this Chapter, how ſuch Affrays as are accompanied with Force and Arms, are to be dealt with upon the Statute of *Northampton*; and therefore I ſhall only examine in this Place, what Penalties other Affrays are liable unto, as to which it is to be obſerved, That all Affrays in general are puniſhable by Fine and Impriſonment, the Meaſure of which is to be regulated by the Diſcretion of the Judges according to the Circumſtances of the Caſe, which very much vary the Nature of this Crime, and in ſome Caſes make it ſo inconſiderable as ſcarce to deſerve to be taken Notice of; and in others make it an Offence of a very heinous Nature, as in the following Inſtances:

1. In Reſpect of the dangerous Tendency thereof.
2. In Reſpect of the Perſons againſt whom it is committed.
3. In Reſpect of the Place wherein it happens.

Poph. 153. 3 Inſt. 158. 1 Sid. 186. 1 Keb. 694. Moor 563. Pl. 763.

Sect. 21. And firſt, an Affray may receive an Aggravation from the dangerous Tendency thereof, as where Perſons coolly and deliberately engage in a Duel, which cannot but be attended with the apparent Danger of Murder, and is not only an open Defiance of the Law, but carries with it a direct Contempt of the Juſtice of the Nation, as putting Men under a Neceſſity of righting themſelves; upon which Conſiderations, Perſons convicted of barely ſending a Challenge, have been adjudged to pay a Fine of one hundred Pounds, and to be impriſoned for one Month without Bail, and alſo to make a publick Acknowledgment of their Offence, and to be bound to their good Behaviour.

Sect. 22. Secondly, An Affray may receive another Aggravation from the Perſons againſt whom it is committed; as where the Officers of Juſtice are violently diſturbed in the due Execution of their Office, as by the Reſcous of a Perſon legally arreſted, or the bare Attempt to make ſuch a Reſcous; for all the Miniſters of the Law are under its more immediate Protection.

12 Co. 101. 1 Keb. 290, 491. 1 Mod. 186.

Sect. 23. Thirdly, An Affray may receive a farther Aggravation from the Place wherein it is committed, and upon this Reſpect all Affrays in the King's Court are ſo ſeverely puniſhed, as hath been ſhewn already in Chapter 21, and upon the ſame Account alſo, all Affrays in a Church or Church-yard, have been always eſteemed very heinous Offences, as being great Indignities to the Divine Majeſty, to whoſe Worſhip and Service ſuch Places are immediately dedicated. And upon this Conſideration, all irreverent Behaviour in theſe Places hath been eſteemed ſo criminal by the Makers of our Laws, that they have not only ſeverely puniſhed ſuch Diſturbances in them which are puniſhable where-ever they happen, as all actual Affrays, *&c.* but alſo ſuch, which if they happen elſewhere, are

are not puniſhable at all; as bare quarrelſome Words, and even ſuch which would be commendable if done in another Place; as Arreſts by Virtue of legal Proceſs: But for the better Underſtanding hereof, I ſhall conſider the ſeveral Statutes made for this Purpoſe.

Sect. 24. And firſt, it is enacted by 5 and 6 *Ed.* 6. 4. *That if any Perſon whatſoever, ſhall by Words only quarrel, chide, or brawl, in any Church or Church-yard, that then it ſhall be lawful unto the Ordinary of the Place where the ſame Offence ſhall be done, and proved by two lawful Witneſſes, to ſuſpend every Perſon ſo offending; that is to ſay, if he be a Layman,* ab ingreſſu Eccleſiæ, *and if he be a Clerk from the Miniſtration of his Office, for ſo long Time as the ſame Ordinary ſhall by his Diſcretion think meet and convenient, according to the Fault.*

Sect. 25. And it is further enacted by the ſaid Statute, *That if any Perſon ſhall ſmite or lay any violent Hands upon any other, either in any Church or Church-yard; that then,* ipſo Facto, *every Perſon ſo offending ſhall be deemed excommunicate, and be excluded from the Fellowſhip and Company of Chriſt's Congregation.*

Sect. 26. And it is alſo further enacted by the ſaid Statute, *That if any Perſon ſhall maliciouſly ſtrike any Perſon with any Weapon in any Church or Church-yard, or ſhall draw any Weapon in any Church or Church-yard, to the Intent to ſtrike another with the ſame Weapon; that then every Perſon ſo offending, and thereof being convicted by Verdict of twelve Men, or by his own Confeſſion, or by two lawful Witneſſes, before the Juſtices of Aſſize, Juſtices of Oyer and Terminer, or Juſtices of Peace in their Seſſions, by Force of this Act, ſhall be adjudged by the ſame Juſtices before whom ſuch Perſon ſhall be convicted, to have one of his Ears cut off,* &c. *and beſides that every ſuch Perſon to be, and ſtand* ipſo Facto *excommunicated, as aforeſaid.*

And in the Expoſition hereof it hath been holden:

Sect. 27. I. That notwithſtanding the Words of the Statute be expreſſed, That he who ſmites another in the Church, *&c.* ſhall, *ipſo Facto*, be deemed excommunicate; yet there ought either to be a precedent Conviction at Law, which muſt be tranſmitted to the Ordinary, or elſe the Excommunication muſt be declared in the Spiritual Court upon a proper Proof of the Offence there; for it is implied in every Penal Law, that no one ſhall incur the Penalty thereof, till he be found guilty upon a lawful Trial; alſo it muſt be intended in the Conſtruction of this Statute, that the Excommunication ought to appear Judicially, for otherwiſe there could be no Abſolution. Dyer 275. Pl. 48. Cro. Ja. 462. 1 Vent. 146. Lit. 149. Hett. 86. Cro. El. 919.

Sect. 28. II. That he who ſtrikes another in a Church, *&c.* can no way excuſe himſelf, by ſhewing that the other aſſaulted him. Cro. Ja. 367.

Sect. 29. III. That Church-wardens, or perhaps private Perſons, who whip Boys for playing in the Church, or pull off the Hats of thoſe who obſtinately refuſe to take them off themſelves, or gently lay their Hands on thoſe who diſturb the Performance of any Part of divine Service, and turn them out of the Church, are not within the Meaning of the Statute. 1 Saund. 13, 14. 1 Sid. 301. 3 Keb. 124. 1 Mod. 168.

Sect. 30. Alſo it is enacted by 1 *Ma.* Seſſ. 2. cap. 3. *That if any Perſon or Perſons, of their own Power and Authority, ſhall willingly and of Purpoſe by open and overt Word, Fact, Act, or Deed, maliciouſly or contemptuouſly moleſt, let, diſturb, vex or trouble, or by any other unlawful Ways and Means, diſquiet, or miſuſe, any Preacher who ſhall be licenced, allowed, or authorized to preach by the Queen's Highneſs, or by any Archbiſhop, or Biſhop of this Realm, or by any other lawful Ordinary, or by any of the Univerſities of* Oxford *and* Cambridge, *or otherwiſe lawfully authorized or charged, by Reaſon of his or their*

Cure, Benefice, or other Spiritual Promotion or Charge, in any of his, or their open Sermon, &c. *or if any Person or Persons shall maliciously, willingly, or of purpose, molest, let, disturb, vex, disquiet, or otherwise trouble any Parson, Vicar, Parish-Priest, or Curate, or any lawful Priest, preparing, saying, doing, singing, ministring or celebrating the Mass, or other such divine Service, Sacraments, or Sacramentals, as was most commonly frequented and used in the last Year of the Reign of the late Sovereign Lord King* Henry *the Eighth, or that at any Time hereafter should be allowed, set forth, or authorized by the Queen's Majesty; or if any Person or Persons shall unlawfully, contemptuously, or maliciously, of their own Power or Authority, pull down, deface, spoil, or otherwise break any Altar or Altars, or any Crucifix, or Cross, in any Church, Chapel, or Church-yard; every such Offender and Offenders, his or their Aiders, Procurers or Abettors, may be apprehended by any Constable, or Church-warden of the Place where such Offence shall be committed, or by any other Officer or Person then being present at the Time of the said Offence; and being so apprehended shall be brought before some Justice of Peace by whom they shall be committed forthwith and within six Days the Matter shall be examined by the same, together with some other Justices; and on Proof by two Witnesses or Confession, the Offender shall be committed for three Months, and also till the next Quarter-Sessions, where, if they repent, they shall be discharged upon giving Sureties for their good Behaviour for a Year, and if they do not repent they shall be committed till they do.*

2 Jon. 159. Con. Aleyn 50. 2 Bulst. 51. *Sect.* 31. It hath been resolved, That the Disturbance of a Minister in saying the present Common Prayer is within this Statute; for the express Mention of such Divine Service, as should afterwards be authorized by Queen *Mary*, doth implicitly include such also as should be authorized by her Successors; for since the King never dies, a Prerogative given generally to one, goes of Course to others.

Sect. 32. Also it is enacted by 1 *Will.* and *Mar.* 18. Par. 19. *That if any Person shall willingly and of Purpose, maliciously or contemptuously come into any Cathedral or Parish Church, Chapel, or other Congregation permitted by the said Act, and disquiet or disturb the same, or misuse any Preacher or Teacher, such Persons, upon Proof before any Justice of Peace, by two or more sufficient Witnesses, shall find two Sureties to be bound by Recognizance in the penal Sum of fifty Pounds, and on Default of such Sureties shall be committed to Prison, there to remain till the next General or Quarter-Sessions, and upon Conviction of the said Offence at the said General or Quarter-Sessions, shall suffer the Pain and Penalty of twenty Pounds.*

CHAP. LXIV.

Of Forcible Entries and Detainers.

Lamb. 135. Dalt. cap. 76. Crom. 70. a. b. *Sect.* 1. IT seems that at the Common Law a Man disseised of any Lands, or Tenements, (if he could not prevail by fair Means,) might lawfully regain the Possession thereof by Force, unless he were put to a Necessity of bringing his Action, by having neglected to re-enter in due Time: And it seems certain, That even at this Day, he who is wrongfully dispossessed of his Goods, may justify the re-taking of them by Force from the Wrong-doer, if he refuse to re-deliver them; for the Violence which happens through the Resistance of the wrongful Possessor, being

Kellw. 92. Yelv. 172. Cro. Ja. 236. Supra Ch. 60. S. 23.

being originally owing to his own Fault, gives him no juſt Cauſe of Complaint, inaſmuch as he might have prevented it by doing as he ought.

Sect. 2. But this Indulgence of the Common Law, in ſuffering Perſons to regain the Lands, they were unlawfully deprived of, having been found by Experience to be very prejudicial to the publick Peace, by giving an Opportunity to powerful Men, under the Pretence of feigned Titles, forcibly to eject their weaker Neighbours, and alſo by Force to retain their wrongful Poſſeſſions, it was thought neceſſary by many ſevere Laws to reſtrain all Perſons from the Uſe of ſuch violent Methods of doing themſelves Juſtice.

Sect. 3. However, even at this Day, in an Action of Forcible Entry grounded on thoſe Laws, if the Defendant make himſelf a Title which is found for him, he ſhall be diſmiſſed without any Inquiry concerning the Force; for howſoever he may be puniſhable at the King's Suit, for doing what is prohibited by Statute, as a Contemner of the Laws, and Diſturber of the Peace, yet he ſhall not be liable to pay any Damages for it to the Plaintiff, whoſe Injuſtice gave him the Provocation in that Manner to right himſelf. 17 H. 7. 17. a. b. 21 H. 6. 39. b. F. N. B. 249. d. Bro. Force, 5, 11, 29.

Sect. 4. Since therefore Offences of this Nature are made ſuch, not by the Common Law, but by Statute; I ſhall for the better Underſtanding thereof, conſider the ſeveral Statutes relating to this Subject.

Sect. 5. And firſt, I find it agreed, That by 2 *Ed.* 3. which is commonly called the Statute of *Northampton*; if there be any Uſe made of Arms to ſtrike a Terror into the Perſons upon whom a Forcible Entry is made, any Juſtice of Peace or other Officer, who is within the Purview of that Statute, may both ſeize the Arms for the King's Uſe, and alſo impriſon the Offenders, but not reſtore the Party injured to his Poſſeſſion; but the ſaid Statute having been fully ſet forth in the foregoing Chapter, I ſhall proceed to thoſe Statutes which more directly relate to this Matter. 3 Inſt. 161. Crom. 162. a. Dalt. cap. 80.

Sect. 6. And firſt it is enacted by 5 *Rich.* 2. 7. in the following Words, *And alſo the King defendeth, That none from henceforth make any Entry into any Lands and Tenements, but in Caſe where Entry is given by the Law; and in ſuch Caſe not with ſtrong Hand, nor with Multitude of People, but only in peaceable and eaſy Manner. And if any Man from henceforth do to the contrary, and thereof be duly convict, he ſhall be puniſhed by Impriſonment of his Body, and thereof ranſomed at the King's Will.*

Sect. 7. But this Statute being found by Experience not ſufficiently to have provided againſt the Miſchief intended to be redreſſed by it, inaſmuch as it gave no ſpeedy Remedy to the Party injured, againſt the Wrong-doer, but left him to the common Courſe of proceeding by way of Indictment or Action, and made no Proviſion at all againſt Forcible Detainers, it was thought neceſſary to ſupply theſe Defects by other additional Laws; and to this Purpoſe it was farther enacted by 15 *Rich.* 2. ch. 2. *That the ſaid Statute and all others made againſt Forcible Entries,* &c. *ſhall be fully executed; and farther, That at all Times that ſuch Forcible Entries ſhall be made, and Complaint thereof cometh to the Juſtices of Peace, or to any of them, that the ſame Juſtices or Juſtice take ſufficient Power of the County, and go to the Place where the Force is made; and if they find any that hold ſuch Place forcibly, after ſuch Entry made, they ſhall be taken and put in the next Gaol, there to abide convict by the Record of the ſame Juſtices or Juſtice, until they have made Fine and Ranſom to the King. And that all the People of the County, as well the Sheriff as others, ſhall be attendant upon the ſame Juſtices, to go and assist the same Justices to arrest such Offenders, upon Pain of Imprisonment, and to make Fine to the King: And in the same Manner it shall be done of them that make such Forcible Entries in Benefices or Offices of Holy Church.*

8 Co. 121. a. Dalt. cap. 22. *Sect.* 8. In the Exposition of this Statute it hath been holden, That one Justice of Peace may make a Record of such a forcible Holding, and that such Record is not traversable, because the Justice of Peace in making thereof, acts not as a Minister, but as a Judge: Also it hath [a] lately been solemnly resolved in Colonel *Leighton*'s Case, That the same Justice may assess the Fine for this Offence, either before the Time of Conviction, or after; but it is said, That such Justice of Peace hath no Power to commit the Offender to Gaol, unless he do it immediately upon the Fact, or unless the Offender shall afterwards refuse to find Sureties for his good Behaviour. Also it was holden by the Court in *Leighton*'s Case above mentioned, That if a Person against whom a Complaint shall be made as having been guilty of a Forcible Entry, shall either traverse the Entry or the Force, or plead that he has been three Years in Possession, the Justice may summon a Jury for the Trial of such Traverse, for it is impossible to determine it upon View; and if the Justice have no Power to try it, it would be easy for any one to elude the Statute by the Tender of such a Traverse, and therefore by a necessary Construction, the Justice must needs have this Power as incidental to what is expresly given him.

Lamb. 151. Dalt. cap. 22. [a] B. R. Hill. 1708. Salk. 353. Kellw. 41. 8. Crom. 195. b. 196. Dalt. cap. 22. Moore 848. Salk. 353.

Sect. 9. But this Statute being likewise very defective in many Respects, as in not giving any Remedy against those who were guilty of a Forcible Detainer after a peaceful Entry; nor even against those who were guilty of both a Forcible Entry and Forcible Detainer, if they were removed before the coming of a Justice of Peace; and in not giving the Justices of the Peace any Power to restore the Party injured by such Force to his Possession; and also in not fixing any Pain on the Sheriff for not obeying the Precepts of the Justices in the Execution of the said Statutes; it was farther enacted by 8 *H.* 6. 9. *That from henceforth where any doth make any Forcible Entry in Lands and Tenements, or other Possessions, or them hold forcibly, after Complaint thereof made within the same County where such Entry is made, to the Justices of the Peace, or to one of them, by the Party grieved, that the Justices or Justice so warned, within a convenient Time, shall cause, or one of them shall cause, the said Statute to be duly executed, and that at the Costs of the Party so grieved.*

Sect. 10. And it is farther enacted by the said Statute, *That though such Persons making such Entries be present, or else departed before the coming of the said Justices or Justice, notwithstanding the same Justices or Justice in some good Town next to the Tenements so entered, or in some other convenient Place according to their Discretion, shall have, and either of them shall have, Authority and Power to enquire by the People of the same County, as well of them that make such Forcible Entries in Lands and Tenements, as of them which the same hold with Force. And if it be found before any of them, that any doth contrary to this Statute, then the said Justices or Justice shall cause to reseize the Lands and Tenements so entered or holden as afore, and shall put the Party so put out, in full Possession of the same Lands and Tenements, so entered or holden as before.*

Sect. 11. And it is farther enacted by the said Statute, *That when the said Justices or Justice make such Inquiries as before, they shall make, or one of them shall make, their Warrants and Precepts to be directed to the Sheriff of the same County, commanding him of the King's Behalf, to cause to come before them, and every of them, sufficient and indifferent Persons, dwelling next about the Lands so entered as before, to enquire of such Entries, whereof every Man which ſhall be impanelled to enquire in this Behalf, ſhall have Land or Tenement of the yearly Value of forty Shillings by the Year at the leaſt, above Reprizes, and that the Sheriff return Iſſues upon every of them at the Day of the firſt Precept returnable, twenty Shillings, and at the ſecond Day forty Shillings, and at the third Time an hundred Shillings, and at every Day after the double. And if any Sheriff or Bailiff within a Franchiſe having Return of the King's Writ, be ſlack, and make not Execution duly of the ſaid Precepts to him directed to make ſuch Enquiries, that he ſhall forfeit to the King twenty Pounds for every Default, and moreover ſhall make Fine and Ranſome to the King. And that as well the Juſtices or Juſtice aforeſaid, as the Juſtices of Aſſizes ſhall have Power to hear and determine ſuch Defaults of the ſaid Sheriffs and Bailiffs, at the Suit of the King, or of the Party grieved,* &c.

Sect. 12. And it is farther enacted by the ſaid Statute, *That Mayors, Juſtices or Juſtice of Peace, Sheriffs and Bailiffs of Cities, Towns and Boroughs having Franchiſe, have in the ſaid Cities, Towns, and Boroughs, like Power to remove ſuch Entries, and in other Articles aforeſaid, riſing within the ſame, as the Juſtices of Peace, and Sheriffs in Counties and Countries aforeſaid have.*

Sect. 13. But it is provided by the ſaid Statute, *That they who keep their Poſſeſſions with Force in any Lands and Tenements, whereof they or their Anceſtors, or they whoſe Eſtate they have in ſuch Lands and Tenements, have continued their Poſſeſſions in the ſame by three Years or more, be not endamaged by Force of this Statute.*

Sect. 14. And the ſaid Proviſo was farther enforced and explained by 31 *El.* 11. by which it is declared and enacted, *That no Reſtitution upon any Indictment of Forcibly Entry, or holding with Force, be made to any Perſon, if the Perſon ſo indicted, hath had the Occupation, or been in quiet Poſſeſſion, for the Space of three whole Years together, next before the Day of ſuch Indictment ſo found, and his Eſtate therein not ended; which the Party indicted may alledge for Stay of Reſtitution, and Reſtitution to ſtay till that be tried, if the other will deny or traverſe the ſame: And if the ſame Allegation be tried againſt the ſame Perſon ſo indicted, he is to pay ſuch Coſts and Damages to the other Party, as ſhall be aſſeſſed by the Judges or Juſtices before whom the ſame ſhall be tried; the ſame Coſts and Damages to be recovered and levied, as is uſual for Coſts and Damages contained in Judgments upon other Actions.*

Sect. 15. In the Conſtruction of theſe Statutes it was holden, That if a Leſſee for Years or Copyholder were ouſted, and the Leſſor or Lord diſſeized, and ſuch Ouſter as well as Diſſeiſin were found in an Indictment of Forcible Entry, the Court might in their Diſcretion award a Reſtitution of Poſſeſſion to ſuch Leſſee or Copyholder, which was by neceſſary Conſequence a Reſeiſin of the Freehold alſo, whether the Leſſor or Lord had deſired or oppoſed it: But it was a great Queſtion, Whether a Leſſee for Years or a Copyholder, being ouſted by the Leſſor or Lord, could have a Reſtitution of their Poſſeſſion within the Equity of 8 *H.* 6. the Words whereof as to this Purpoſe are, that the Juſtice ſhall re-ſeize the Lands, *&c.* by which it ſeems to be implied, That the Party muſt be ouſted of ſuch an Eſtate therein, whereof he may be ſaid to be ſeiſed, which muſt be a Freehold at leaſt.

Crom. 161. b. 166. b.

Yelv. 81. Con. 1 Leon. 327.

Lamb. 155. Crom. 71. Dalt. cap. 77. Savil 68. Pl. 141. Far. 123.

Sect. 16. But to remove this Doubt, it is enacted by 21 *Jac.* 1. 15. *That ſuch Judges, Juſtices, or Juſtice of the Peace, as by reaſon of any Act or Acts of Parliament then in force, were authorized and enabled upon Enquiry, to give Reſtitution of Poſſeſſion unto Tenants, of any Eſtate of Freehold, of their Lands or Tenements, which ſhall be entered upon with Force, or from them withholden by Force, ſhall by Reaſon of that Act have the like, and the ſame Authority and Ability from thenceforth (upon Indictment of ſuch Forcible Entries, or forcible with-holding before them duly found) to give like Reſtitution of Poſ-*

ſeſſion

ſeſſion unto Tenants for Term of Years, Tenants by Copy of Court-Roll, Guardians by Knights-Service, Tenants by Elegit, *Statute-Merchant, and Staple of Lands or Tenements, by them ſo holden, which ſhall be entered upon by Force, or holden from them by Force.*

Latch 182. See Co. Litt. 61. *Sect.* 17. But it hath been holden, that a Tenant by the Verge is not within this Statute, becauſe he is not within the expreſs Words; *ſed Quære*, for ſince ſuch Perſon hath no other Evidence of his Title, but by the Copy of Court-Roll, he ſeems at leaſt to be within the Meaning, if not within the Words, of the Statute; however it ſeems clear, That if a Leſſor eject his Leſſee for Years, and afterwards be forcibly put out of Poſſeſſion again Vide Sal. 587. by ſuch Leſſee, he hath no Remedy for a Reſtitution by Force of any of the Crom. 71. a. 166. b. Dal. ch. 77. above mentioned Statutes, for he cannot have it by 8 *H.* 6. becauſe he always continued ſeized of the Freehold, and clearly he is not within 21 *Jac.* 1. 15.

Lamb. 155. Crom. 71. a. Dal. ch. 77. 2 Keb. 495. *Sect.* 18. However there ſeems to be no Doubt, but that a Juſtice of Peace, *&c.* may in either of the ſaid Caſes, remove the Force and commit the Offender, *&c.*

Sect. 19. Having thus ſet forth the ſeveral Statutes relating to this Subject, together with the Miſchiefs which occaſioned them, and the ſeveral Defects of each of them, I ſhall, for the better Underſtanding of them all in general, proceed to examine the following Particulars:

1. What ſhall be eſteemed an Entry within theſe Statutes.
2. What Entry is to be adjudged forcible.
3. What Detainer.
4. In reſpect of what Kind of Poſſeſſions one may be guilty of ſuch forcible Entry or Detainer.
5. What Perſons may be guilty thereof.
6. What ought to be the Form of a Record grounded upon theſe Statutes.
7. Of what Kind of Poſſeſſions a Reſtitution is to be awarded.
8. To whom ſuch Reſtitution ought to be made.
9. By whom, and in what Manner, it is to be awarded and given.
10. In what Caſes it may be barred by the Continuance of a Poſſeſſion for three Years.
11. For what other Cauſes it may be ſtayed.
12. How it may be ſuperſeded before it is executed.
13. How it may be ſet aſide after it is executed.

Sect. 20. As to the firſt Point, *viz.* What ſhall be eſteemed an Entry within theſe Statutes, it ſeems certain, That if one who pretends a Title to Lands, barely go over them, either with, or without a great Number of Crom. 70. b. Dal. ch. 77. Attendants, armed or unarmed, in his Way to the Church, or Market, or for ſuch like Purpoſe, without doing any Act, which either expreſly or impliedly amounts to a Claim of ſuch Lands, he cannot be ſaid to make an Entry thereinto within the Meaning of theſe Statutes.

Crom. 69. Dal. ch. 77. Con. Cro. Ca. 486. *Sect.* 21. Yet in ſuch Caſe, if he make an actual Claim with any Circumſtances of Force or Terror, he ſeems to be guilty of a forcible Entry within 1 & 15 *Ric.* 2. whether his Adverſary actually quit his Poſſeſſion or not.

Crom. 69. a. Dal. ch. 77. B. 2. ch. 29. Sect. 4. *Sect.* 22. Alſo all thoſe who accompany a Man when he makes a forcible Entry, ſhall be adjudged to enter with him, within the Intent of theſe Laws, whether they actually came upon the Lands, or not.

Sect. 23. So alſo ſhall thoſe who having an Eſtate in Land by a defeaſible Title, continue with Force in the Poſſeſſion thereof, after a Claim made by one who had a Right of Entry thereto.

Crom. 69. b. Dal. ch. 77. Co. Lit. 256, 257.

Sect. 24. But he who barely agrees to a forcible Entry made to his Uſe, without his Knowledge or Privity, ſhall not be adjudged to make an Entry within theſe Statutes, becauſe he no way concurred in, or promoted the Force.

Crom. 69. a. Dal. ch. 77. 2 H. 7. 16. b.

Sect. 25. As to the ſecond Point, *viz.* What Entry is to be adjudged forcible, it ſeems clear, that it ought to be accompanied with ſome Circumſtances of actual Violence or Terror; and therefore, That an Entry which hath no other Force than ſuch as is implied by the Law, in every Treſpaſs whatſoever, is not within theſe Statutes.

Lamb. 140, &c. Dalt. ch. 77. Co. Lit. 257. b.

And therefore, for the better Underſtanding hereof, I ſhall conſider;

1. In Reſpect of what Acts of Violence an Entry may be adjudged forcible.
2. In Reſpect of what Circumſtances of Terror.

Sect. 26. As to the firſt of theſe Particulars, it ſeems to be agreed, That an Entry may be ſaid to be forcible, not only in Reſpect of a Violence actually done to the Perſon of a Man, as by beating him if he refuſe to relinquiſh his Poſſeſſion, but alſo in Reſpect of any other Kind of Violence in the Manner of the Entry, as by breaking open the Doors of a Houſe, whether any Perſon be in it at the ſame Time or not, eſpecially if it be a Dwelling-houſe, and perhaps alſo by any Act of Outrage after the Entry, as by carrying away the Party's Goods, *&c.* which being found in an Aſſiſe of Novel Diſſeiſin, will make the Defendant a Diſſeiſor with Force, and ſubject him to Fine and Impriſonment: And according to ſome Opinions, an Entry may be ſaid to be forcible from the bare drawing up of a Latch, or pulling back the Bolt of a Door; but ſurely ſuch inconſiderable Circumſtances as theſe, which commonly paſs between Neighbour and Neighbour, without any Offence at all, can never bring a Man within the Meaning of theſe Statutes, which ſpeak of Entries with ſtrong Hand, or Multitude of People; and it hath been holden, That an Entry into a Houſe through a Window, or by opening a Door with a Key, is not forcible: And it is ſaid, That if one find a Man out of his Houſe, and forcibly with-hold him from returning to it, and ſend Perſons to take peaceable Poſſeſſion thereof, in the Party's Abſence, yet he is not guilty of a forcible Entry, inaſmuch as he did no Violence to the Houſe, but only to the Perſon of the other: But perhaps this Opinion may juſtly be queſtioned, becauſe though the Force be not actually done upon the Land, nor in the very Act of the Entry, yet ſince it is uſed with an immediate Intent to make ſuch Entry, and is the only Cauſe that it met with no Oppoſition, ſurely it cannot be ſaid, that the Entry is without Force, which whether it be upon, or off the Land, ſeems equally within the Statute.

H. P. C. 116. 2 Rol. Re. 2. Noy 136. 30 Aſſ. 50. 11 H. 4. 16. b. 17. a. 2 Inſt. 235, 236. Dal. ch. 77. Crom. 70. a. b. Moore 656. Pl. 899. Noy 137. Dalt. ch. 77. H. P. C. 138. Lamb. 143. 2 Rol. Re. 2. Lamb. 143. Dal. ch. 77.

Sect. 27. As to the ſecond Particular, *viz.* In reſpect of what Circumſtances of Terror an Entry may be adjudged forcible; it is to be obſerved, That where-ever a Man, either by his Behaviour or Speech, at the Time of his Entry, gives thoſe who are in Poſſeſſion of the Tenements which he claims, juſt Cauſe to fear, that he will do them ſome bodily Hurt, if they will not give way to him, his Entry is eſteemed forcible, whether he cauſe ſuch a Terror, by carrying with him ſuch an unuſual

H. P. C. 128. Lamb. 142, &c. Dal. ca. 77.

10 H. 7. 12. a. Crom. 69. Pl. 14, 24. Number of Servants, or by arming himſelf in ſuch a Manner, as plainly intimates a Deſign to back his Pretenſions by Force, or by actually threatening to kill, maim, or beat thoſe who ſhall continue in Poſſeſſion, or by See the Books above cited. giving out ſuch Speeches as plainly imply a Purpoſe of uſing Force againſt thoſe who ſhall make any Reſiſtance, as if one ſay that he will keep his Poſſeſſion in Spite of all Men, *&c.*

Bro. Dureſs, 12, 16. 1 Inſt. 253. b. Dal. ca. 77. *Sect.* 28. But it ſeemeth that no Entry ſhall be judged forcible from any threatening to ſpoil another's Goods, or to deſtroy his Cattle, or to do him any other ſuch like Damage which is not perſonal.

Lamb. 143. *Sect.* 29. However it is clear, That it may be committed by a ſingle Perſon, as well as by twenty.

H. P. C. 138. *Sect.* 30. As to the third Point, *viz.* What Detainer is to be adjudged forcible, it ſeemeth certain, That the ſame Circumſtances of Violence or Terror, which will make an Entry forcible, will make a Detainer forcible alſo; Lamb. 145. Crom. 70. H. P. C. 139. Dal. ca. 77. Cro. Ja. 199. from whence it ſeems to follow, That whoever keeps in his Houſe an unuſual Number of People, or unuſual Weapons, or threatens to do ſome bodily Hurt to the former Poſſeſſor, if he dare return, ſhall be adjudged guilty of a forcible Detainer, tho' no Attempt be made to re-enter; and it hath been ſaid, That he alſo ſhall come under the like Con- Crom. 70. b. Lamb. 145. ſtruction, who places Men at a Diſtance from the Houſe, in order to aſſault any one who ſhall attempt to make an Entry into it; and that he alſo is Crom. 70. b. Lamb. 145. in like Manner guilty who ſhuts his Doors againſt a Juſtice of Peace coming to view the Force, and obſtinately refuſes to let him come in: Crom. 73. Dal. ca. 77. But it is ſaid, That a Man ought not to be adjudged guilty of this Offence, for barely refuſing to go out of a Houſe, and continuing therein in deſpight of another.

Sect. 31. As to the fourth Point, *viz.* In reſpect of what Kind of Poſſeſſions one may be guilty of a forcible Entry or Detainer within thoſe Statutes it ſeems clear, That one may come within the Danger thereof by [a] 1 Sid. 101. 1 Lev. 90. 1 Keb. 438. [b] Cro. Ja. 41. [c] Cro. Ca. 201. [d] 20 H. 6. 11. a. 22 H. 6. 33. a. Bro. Force, 7. Cro. Ca. 201. [e] Cro. Ca. 201. [f] See Cro. Ca. 486. See Dal. ca. 77. [g] Cro. Ja. 18. [h] Crom. 69, 70. Lamb. 144. Dal. ca. 77. a Force done to Eccleſiaſtical Poſſeſſions, as [a] Churches, [b] Vicaridge-Houſes, *&c.* as much as if the ſame were done to any temporal Inheritance; alſo it hath been holden for a general Rule, That one may be indicted for a forcible Entry into any ſuch incorporeal Hereditament, for which a [c] Writ of Entry will lie, either by the Common Law, as for [d] Rent, or by Statute, as for [e] Tithes, *&c.* but I do not find any good Authority, That ſuch an Indictment will lie for a [f] Common or [g] Office; but it ſeems agreed, That an Indictment of forcible Detainer lies againſt any one, whether he be the Tertenant or a Stranger, who ſhall forcibly diſturb the lawful [h] Proprietor in the Enjoyment of any of the above-mentioned Poſſeſſions; as by violently reſiſting a Lord in his Diſtreſs for a Rent, or by menacing a Commoner with bodily Hurt, if he dare put in his Beaſts into the Common, *&c.* yet it ſeems clear, That no one can come within the Danger of theſe Statutes by a Violence offered to another in reſpect 1 Mod. 73. 2 Keb. 709. of a Way, or ſuch like Eaſement, which is no Poſſeſſion. Alſo it ſeemeth, That a Man cannot be convicted upon View, by Force of 15 *Ric.* 2. 2. of a forcible Detainer of any ſuch Tenement, wherein he cannot be ſaid to have made a precedent forcible Entry, becauſe that Statute gives Vide infra Sect. 40. the Juſtices a Juriſdiction of no other forcible Detainer, but what follows a forcible Entry.

Sect. 32. As to the fifth Point, *viz.* Who may be guilty of a forcible Entry or Detainer within theſe Statutes; it ſeems clear, That no one can come within the Intention thereof by any Force whatſoever done by him in entering into a Tenement, whereof he himſelf had the ſole and lawful Poſſeſſion, both at and before the Time of ſuch Entry; as by breaking open the Doors of his own Dwelling-houſe, or, of a Caſtle, which is his own Inheritance, but forcibly detained from him by one who claims the bare Cuſtody of it; or by forcibly entring into the Land in the Poſſeſſion of his own Leſſee at Will. *Sed Quære.*

Moore 786. Cro. Ja. 18. 2 Keb. 495.

Sect. 33. But it ſeems clear, That a Jointenant, or Tenant in Common, may offend againſt the Purport of theſe Statutes, either by forcibly ejecting, or forcibly holding out his Companion, for tho' the Entry of ſuch a Tenant be lawful *per my & per tout*, ſo that he cannot in any Caſe be puniſhed in an Action of Treſpaſs at the Common Law, yet the Lawfulneſs of his Entry no Way excuſes the Violence, or leſſens the Injury done to his Companion, and conſequently an Indictment of forcible Entry into a Moiety of a Manor, *&c.* is good.

8 Ed. 4. 9. a. 19. a. 10 H. 7. 27. a. Latch 224. Palm. 419.

Sect. 34. Alſo if a Man have been in Poſſeſſion of Land for never ſo long a Time, by a defeaſible Title, and another who hath a Right of Entry thereunto, make a Claim, and yet ſuch wrongful Poſſeſſor ſtill continue his Occupation with Force and Arms, he is puniſhable for a forcible Entry and Detainer againſt the Purport of theſe Statutes, becauſe all the Eſtate whereof he was ſeiſed before ſuch Claim, was wholly defeated by it, and his Continuance in Poſſeſſion afterwards amounted in the Judgment of Law to a new Entry.

Co. Lit. 256, 257. Crom. 69. b. Lamb. 160, 161. Dal. ch. 77.

Sect. 35. It is ſaid, That an Infant or Feme Covert may be guilty within the Intention of theſe Statutes, in reſpect of ſuch actual Violence as ſhall be done by them in Perſon, but not in reſpect of what ſhall be done by others at their Command, becauſe all ſuch Commands of theirs are void: Alſo it is ſaid, That a Feme Covert may be impriſoned for ſuch Offence, but that an Infant ought not, becauſe he ſhall not be ſubject to corporal Puniſhment, by Force of the general Words of any Statute, wherein he is not expreſly named.

Dal. ch. 77. Crom. 69. Co. Lit. 357. b. 1 H. H. P. C. 21. Bro. Impriſon. 43, 45, 75, 101.

As to the ſixth Point, *viz.* What ought to be the Form of a Record grounded upon theſe Statutes, it hath been reſolved,

Sect. 36. Firſt, That it is ſufficient in the Caption of ſuch an Indictment, to ſay, That it was taken before *A. B. & C. D. Juſticiariis ad pacem Domini Regis conſervandam aſſignatis*, without ſhewing that they had Authority to hear and determine Felonies and Treſpaſſes, for the Statute enables all Juſtices of Peace, as ſuch, to take ſuch Indictments.

Palm. 277. Cro. 633.

Sect. 37. Secondly, It hath alſo been reſolved, That the Tenement in which the Force was committed, muſt be deſcribed with convenient Certainty, for otherwiſe the Defendant will neither know the ſpecial Charge to which he is to make his Defence, neither will the Juſtices or Sheriff know how to reſtore the injured Party to his Poſſeſſion; and from hence it follows, That an Indictment of a forcible Entry into a [a] Tenement (which may ſignify any Thing whatſoever, [b] wherein a Man may have an Eſtate of Freehold,) or into a Houſe [c] or Tenement, or into two Cloſes of Meadow [d] or Paſture, or into a Rood [e] or Half a Rood of Land, or into [f] certain Lands belonging to ſuch a Houſe, or into ſuch a Houſe, without ſhewing in what [g] Town it lies, or into a [h] Tenement with the Appurtenances called *Trupenny* in *D.* is not good. But it hath been reſolved, That an Indictment for a forcible Entry *in* [i] *Domum Manſionalem ſive Meſſuagium, &c.* is good, for theſe are Words equipollent: Alſo that ſuch an Indictment for an Entry into a [k] Cloſe, called Serjeant *Hern*'s Cloſe, *&c.* without adding the Number of Acres, is good, for here is as much Certainty as is required in an Ejectment;

Dal. ch. 81.

[a] Dal. 15. 2 Rol. Re. 46. 2 Rol. Ab. 80. Pl. 6. 3 Leon. 102. [b] Co. Lit. 6. a. [c] 2 Rol. Ab. 40. Pl. 4, 5. 1 Rol. Re. 334. Cro. Ja. 633. Palm. 277. [d] 2 Rol. Ab. 81. Pl. 4. [e] 1 Bulſt. 201. [f] 2 Leon. 186. 3 Leon. 102. Bro. forcib. Ent. 23. [g] 2 Leon. 186. [h] 2 Rol. Ab. 80. Pl. 7. [i] Cro. Ja. 633. Palm. 277. [k] Cro. El. 458. 2 Rol. Ab. 80. Pl. 8.

and

and it hath been adjudged, That such Indictment may be void as to such Part thereof only which is uncertain, and good for so much as is certain,
2 Leon. 186. and therefore, that an Indictment for a forcible Entry into a House, and
3 Leon. 102. certain Acres of Land thereto belonging, may be quashed as to the Land, and stand good as to the House.

Sect. 38. Thirdly, It hath been also resolved, That an Indictment,
2 Keb. 495. on 5 or 15 *Rich.* 2. needs not shew who had the Freehold at the Time of
3 Bulst. 71. the Force, because those Statutes seem equally to punish all Force of this
1 Ven. 23, 25. Kind, without any Way regarding what Estate the Party had on whom it was made; yet it seems, That such an Indictment ought to shew that such Entry was made on the Possession of some Person, who had some
2 Keb. 495. Estate in the Tenements, either as a Freeholder or Lessee for Years, *&c.*
Salk. 260-2. for otherwise it doth not appear, that such Entry was made injurious to any one; but it is said, That an Indictment on 8 *H.* 6. must shew, that
Hetley 73. the Place wherein the Force was committed was the Freehold of the Party
Latch 109. 2 Keb. 477, grieved at the Time of such Force; and therefore, That it is not suffi-
499. cient to say that the Defendant with strong Hand, *&c.* entered into such
1 Keb. 191. Cro. El. 754. a House, *existens liberum Tenementum J. S. &c.* without saying, *adtunc ex-*
Noy 131. *istens liberum Tenementum J. S.* for otherwise it may be intended, that it
2 Rol. Re. 65. was his Freehold at the Time of the Indictment only, and not at the
Palm. 426. 1 Sid. 102. Time of the Force; and according to the general Opinion, an Indictment
Con. Yelv. 28. on that Statute cannot warrant an Award of Restitution, unless it find,
1 Bulst. 177. that the Party was seized at the Time; yet it is said, That the Want of such an express finding may be supplied by such Words as necessarily imply, that the Party was seised at the Time of the Force; as where it
Contra 1 Ventr. 306. is expresly laid that the Defendant disseised *J. S. &c.* which is impossible,
3 Leon. 102. unless he had been seised of the Freehold at the same Time; and it hath
Allen 49. been said, That it is sufficient in such an Indictment to say that the Par-
Palm. 277. Con. 2 Rol. ty was *Possessionatus pro termino Vitæ*, without using the Word *Seisitus*,
A. 80. Pl. 9. *&c.* for the same Propriety of Expression is not required in Indictments as
2 Keb. 477. Pleadings; *sed Quære.* Also it is said, That if it do appear either in such
Palm. 277. Cro. Ja. 633, an express or implicit Manner, that the Party injured had the Freehold of
634. the Land at the Time of the Force, it is not necessary to shew farther what Estate in particular he had therein, or by what Title he claims the same; for it is not the Title, but the Possession, which is in Question.
2 Rol. A. 80. And upon the like Ground it hath been adjudged, That an Indictment on
Pl. 3. the said Statute for entering on my Farmer, and forcibly expelling him, and disseising me, is good, without shewing what Estate such Farmer had; for it is sufficient to shew that he had the Possession, and the Injury complained of is the forcible Disseisin done to me, which, being the main Point of the Indictment, if it be sufficiently set forth in Substance, the Indictment is good; yet in this very Case the Want of shewing that such
Yelv. 165. Farmer was ousted, would have been an incurable Fault; because his Possession being my Possession, unless he were ousted, I could not be dis-
Far. 123. seised. Also it hath been holden, That as an Indictment on 8 *H.* 6. must shew that the Party who is put out of Possession was seised of a Freehold, in order to bring him within the Purview of that Statute, so also an Indictment on 21 *Jac.* 1. 15. must shew, That the Party injured was possessed of such an Estate as will bring him within the Provision of
1 Ventr. 306. that Act; and upon this Ground it hath been resolved, That such an In-
1 Sid. 102. 1 Mod. 73. dictment, setting forth in general, that the Party was possessed, or that
2 Keb. 709. he was possessed for a certain Term, without adding, that it was for
Salk. 260. Years, is not good; for in the first Case it may be intended, That he
Far. 123. was possessed only by Virtue of a Lease at Will; and in the second,

That he was poſſeſſed of a Term for Life, in neither of which Caſes he
is within the Benefit of 21 *Jac.* 1. 15. Yet it hath been ſaid, That the
Poſſeſſion of ſuch an Eſtate, as is within that Statute, is ſufficiently ſet
forth in the reciting Part of an Indictment, as thus, *Quod cum J. S.* was 1 Mod. 7[illegible]
poſſeſſed for a certain Term of Years, and being ſo poſſeſſed, was by ſtrong
Hand, *&c.* put out of Poſſeſſion, *&c.* without any direct Allegation of
ſuch a Poſſeſſion.

Sect. 39. Fourthly, it hath been reſolved, That a Repugnancy in ſet-
ting forth the Offence in an Indictment upon any of theſe Statutes, is an
incurable Fault; and upon this Foundation it hath been adjudged, That
an Indictment on 8 *H.* 6. ſetting forth, that the Defandants *Pacificè in-* Aleyn 50.
traverunt, &c. & eum adtunc & ibidem vi & armis diſſeiſiverunt, or that Show. 272. 1 Vent. 108.
J. S. was ſeized and poſſeſſed, is void; and it hath alſo been adjudged, Poph. 205.
That an Indictment on 21 *Jac.* 1. ſetting forth, That the Party injured Raymond 67. 1 Keb. 423,
was poſſeſſed of a Term for Years, or of a Copyhold Eſtate, and that the 428, 435, 472.
Defendants with ſtrong Hand, ouſted, and diſſeiſed him, is void, becauſe
it is abſurd and contradictory to ſet forth a Diſſeiſin of ſuch an Eſtate
whereof it is impoſſible that any Man can be diſſeiſed; alſo it hath been
holden, That an Indictment on 8 *H.* 6. ſetting forth a Diſſeiſin of Land,
adtunc & adhuc exiſtens liberum Tenementum J. S. is void for its Repugnan- 2 Ro. Re. 311. Show. 272.
cy, inaſmuch as it implies, That *J. S.* always continued in Poſſeſſion, 2 Bulſ. 121.
which, if it be true, makes it impoſſible that he could be diſſeiſed at all; 1 Sid. 102.
but ſome have ſaid that this ſeeming Repugnancy may be reconciled, by in-
tending that the Diſſeiſee might re-enter after the Time of the Diſſeiſin, and
before the finding of the Indictment; however it ſeems clear, That if the
Words *Adhuc extratenet* be added, ſuch a Repugnancy cannot be helped
by any Intendment; and that no Reſtitution can be awarded on ſuch an In-
dictment, whether thoſe Words *Adhuc extratenet* be in it or not, becauſe
the Party grieved appears by the Indictment it ſelf to have had the Freehold
at the Time of the finding thereof.

Sect. 40. Fifthly, It hath been reſolved, That an Indictment of a 2 Rol. A. 80. Pl. 10.
forcible Detainer, without ſhewing that the Defendant made an Entry in-
to the ſame Lands, is not good, becauſe the Statute doth not prohibit
one who hath always been in Poſſeſſion, to maintain the ſame with Force:
And it ſeems clear, That a Conviction of a forcible Detainer upon View Palm. 195,
by Force of 15 *Rich.* 2. 2. cannot be good, unleſs it ſhew that the Defen- 196, 197.
dant was alſo guilty of a forcible Entry, for the Words of that Statute Cro. Ja. 19, 20, 32.
are, *That at all Times that ſuch forcible Entries are made, and Complaint there-* Cro. El. 915.
of cometh to the Juſtices, &c. *that the ſame Juſtices,* &c. *ſhall go,* &c. *and
if they find any that hold ſuch Place forcibly, after ſuch Entry made,* &c. by
which it is plain, That the Juſtices have no Juriſdiction by Force of this
Statute, but where the Entry, as well as Detainer, was forcible: Yet in B. R. Hill.
Leighton's Caſe it was reſolved, That ſuch a forcible Entry is ſufficiently ſet 1708.
forth in the Complaint recited in ſuch a Conviction; and it is plain, That
the Statute could not intend that the forcible Entry ſhould be viewed, be-
cauſe it is to precede the Proceedings of the Juſtices; but perhaps it is the
better Opinion, That an Indictment upon 8 *H.* 6. ſetting forth an Entry and
forcible Detainer, without ſhewing whether the Entry were forcible or
peaceable, is good; for there is no *Medium* between a forcible and peace-
able Entry, and an Entry not alledged to have been forcible, ſhall be in-
tended to have been peaceable, or if not ſo, yet it ſeems to be no Way
material, whether it ſhall be taken to have been forcible or peaceable,
becauſe in either Caſe it is equally within the Statute, the Words where-
of as to this Purpoſe are, *Where any doth make forcible Entry in Lands and*

2 Rol. Ab. 80. Pl. 11.
Yelv. 99. Cro. Ja. 151. 1 Sid. 97, 99, 414. 2 Keb. 505. Vide infra, Sect. 59. B. 2. Ch. 25. S. 2.

Tenements, or other Poſſeſſions, or them hold forcibly; by which it appears, That a forcible Detainer is a diſtinct Offence from that of a forcible Entry, and no Way depending on it; and my Lord Chief Juſtice *Holt* ſeemed to be of this Opinion in *Leighton*'s Caſe above mentioned. However it ſeems to be certain, That if a Bill both for a forcible Entry and forcible Detainer be preferred to a Grand Jury, and found *Ignoramus* as to the Entry with Force, and *Billa vera* as to the Detainer, it will not warrant an Award of Reſtitution, but is void, becauſe a Grand Jury cannot find a Bill true for Part, and falſe for Part, as a Petit Jury may.

Salk. 260. 2. Bro. Force. 13. Lamb. 153. Dal. ch. 81.

Sect. 41. Sixthly, It hath been reſolved, That no Indictment can warrant an Award of Reſtitution, unleſs it find that the Wrong-doer both ouſted the Party grieved, and alſo continueth his Poſſeſſion at the Time of the finding of the Indictment; for it is a Repugnancy to award Reſtitution of Poſſeſſion to one who never was in Poſſeſſion, and it is vain to award it to one who doth not appear to have loſt it.

Cro. Ja. 41.
B. 2. ch. 23. S. 88.
Dy. 68. Pl. 28.

Sect. 42. Seventhly, It hath been reſolved, That the Time and Place of the Diſſeiſin are ſufficiently ſet forth in an Indictment, alledging, That the Defendant *Tali die intravit, &c. & ipſum A. B. manu forti diſſeiſivit*, without adding the Words *Adtunc & Ibidem*; for inaſmuch as the Entry and Diſſeiſin are both of them of the ſame Nature, and the one of them naturally tends to cauſe the other, it is implied, that they both happened at the ſame Time; and the forcible Entry being the principal Offence within the Purview of theſe Statutes, and the Diſſeiſin being only added to ſhew that the Party grieved hath a Right to a Reſtitution, as to which the Day of the Diſſeiſin is no Way material, it ſeemeth to be over nice to require a preciſe Exactneſs in ſetting it forth; neither can it be to any Purpoſe to alledge that the Diſſeiſin was at the ſame Place with the Entry, ſince it appears from the Nature of the Thing, that it could not but be ſo; yet in an Indictment of Murder, it is perhaps a fatal Miſtake, not expreſly to ſhew the Day and Place of the Stroke, as well as of the Aſſault, becauſe theſe Offences are of different Kinds, the one being only a Treſpaſs, and the other a Felony, and may well be intended to have happened at different Times and Places, and the giving of the Stroke being the principal Offence, ought to be ſet forth with the moſt exact Certainty.

[a] Noy 125. [b] Cro. Ja. 32. [c] Cro. El. 186. Con. Noy 120.

Sect. 43. Eighthly, It hath been reſolved, That a Diſſeiſin is ſufficiently ſet forth, by alledging, That the Defendant entered, &c. into ſuch a Tenement and diſſeiſed the Party, without adding, either the Words [a] *Illicitè*, or [b] *Expulit*, or [c] *Inde*, for the Word *Diſſeiſivit* implies as much.

Cro. El. 461. Latch 224. 2 Bulſ. 258. B. 2. Ch. 25. S. 92. Con. 1. Keb. 572. 2 Keb. 133, 135. 1 Vent. 265.
7 Ed. 4. 18. a. Dal. 25.

Sect. 44. Ninthly, It hath been reſolved, That an Indictment which purſues the Words of the Statute in alledging an Entry, &c. to have been made *Manu forti*, needs not expreſly alſo to ſay, That it was made *Vi & armis*, becauſe that is implied; alſo it is ſaid, That as the Want of thoſe Words will not vitiate an Indictment which purſues the Statute, ſo neither will the uſing of them make good an Indictment which does not purſue it; yet it hath been reſolved, That ſuch an Indictment may be good without mentioning any Complaint, tho' the Statute ſeems to require it; for it is ſaid, That thoſe Words in the Statute are put in *cauſâ abundanti*; and that if a Juſtice of Peace have by any Means whatſoever Notice of a forcible Entry or Detainer, he may and ought to proceed againſt the ſame according to the ſaid Statute, as being a Diſturbance of the publick Peace, the Preſervation whereof was the chief End of theſe Statutes.

Sect. 45.

Sect. 45. As to the ſeventh Point, *viz.* Of what Kind of Poſſeſſions a Reſtitution is to be awarded; it ſeems that it ought only to be awarded for the Poſſeſſion of ſuch Tenements as are viſible and corporeal, for no one who hath a Right to ſuch as are inviſible and incorporeal, as Rents, Commons, *&c.* can be put out of Poſſeſſion thereof, but only at his own Election, by a Fiction of Law, in order to enable him to recover Damages againſt the Perſon who hath wrongfully diſturbed him in the Enjoyment of them; for ſuch Things being mere Creatures of the Law, and depending entirely upon the Conſtruction thereof, are always in the Poſſeſſion of thoſe whom the Law adjudges to have a Right to ſuch Poſſeſſion, and conſequently all the Remedy that can be deſired againſt a Force offered to a Man in reſpect of ſuch like Poſſeſſions, is to have the actual Force removed, and the Offenders puniſhed for the ſame, which may be done by Force of 15 *Rich.* 2. *&c.*

Dal. ch. 81. Lamb. 153.

Co. Lit. 323.

Sect. 46. As to the eighth Point, *viz.* To whom ſuch Reſtitution ought to be made; it hath been holden, That it ſhall only be given to him who is found by the Indictment to have been put out of an actual Poſſeſſion, and conſequently that it ſhall not be awarded to one who was only ſeized in Law, as to an Heir upon whom a Stranger abateth upon the Death of the Anceſtor, before any actual Entry made by ſuch Heir; and from the ſame Ground it followeth, That it ſhall not be granted to an Heir upon an Indictment, finding a forcible Entry made upon his Anceſtor.

Dalt. ch. 83. Lamb. 153.

Lamb. 154. Dal. ch. 83. Vide Cro. Ja. 199.

Sect. 47. It hath been holden by ſome, That if a Diſſeiſee re-enter peaceably upon the Diſſeiſor, and continue for ſome Time peaceably upon the Tenements in Diſpute, and afterwards detain them with Force, the Diſſeiſor ſhall not be reſtored upon an Indictment finding the ſaid Force, becauſe his Poſſeſſion was at firſt peaceably defeated, and at the Time of the Force, he had, in the Judgment of Law, no Poſſeſſion at all; but I cannot be perſuaded that this Opinion is agreeable to the Intention of the ſaid Statutes, the principal End whereof ſeems to be to oblige all Perſons to refer themſelves to the Courts of Juſtice, for the Deciſion of their Claims to the Poſſeſſion of Land, and to reſtrain them from diſturbing the publick Peace, by ſuch Endeavours to right themſelves; but if ſuch a Practice as this ſhould be allowed, it would be eaſy to evade the Effect thereof by refraining from Violence at firſt, and then forcing the Party to leave the Poſſeſſion of the Premiſſes after a ſhort Continuance thereon in Peace; neither do I ſee any Difference between ſuch a Continuance for the Space of three Days, and a Continuance for three Hours or Minutes, inaſmuch as the ſubſequent Force is in each Caſe equally within the Miſchief intended to be provided againſt by the Statutes; and ſeeing the Statutes of 8 *H.* 6. and 31 *El.* 11. have expreſly provided, That thoſe who have been in Poſſeſſion for three Years, ſhall not be put out of Poſſeſſion by an Indictment of forcible Entry or Detainer; it ſeems plainly to be implied, That no one ſhall have the like Advantage, in reſpect of a Poſſeſſion for a ſhorter Time.

Crom. 162. b. 163. a. b.

Sect. 48. It will be needleſs in this Place to ſhew of what Kind of Hereditaments, or of what Kind of Eſtate therein, the Party who is to be reſtored muſt be found to have been ſeized or poſſeſſed, becauſe this may ſufficiently appear by what hath been ſaid in the foregoing Part of this Chapter.

Sect. 49. As to the ninth Point, *viz.* By whom and in what Manner ſuch Reſtitution may be awarded and given, there is no doubt, but that the ſame Juſtice, before whom an Indictment of forcible Entry or De-

Dal. ca. 82. Dy. 187. tainer ſhall be found, may grant an Award of Reſtitution to the Party; and it is ſaid, That he may execute the ſame either in his own proper Perſon, or make his Precept to the Sheriff to do it.

1 Sid. 156. 1 Keb. 88. 1 Vent. 308. *Sect.* 50. But it ſeems clear, That neither Juſtices of Peace, nor any other Court whatſoever, have Authority to grant a Reſtitution upon a Conviction of any Force taken by them upon View, unleſs the ſame be found by an Indictment, according to the Direction of 8 *H.* 6. c. 9. or 21 Dy. 187. Pl. 6. *Ja.* 1. c. 15. Alſo it ſeems to be agreed, That no other Juſtices of Peace, except thoſe before whom ſuch an Indictment ſhall be found, have any Power, either at Seſſions, or out of it, to make any Award of Reſtitution; Dal. ca. 82. Lamb. 184. and that no other Court whatſoever can perſonally reſtore the Party without a Precept to the Sheriff.

Sect. 51. Alſo it hath been reſolved, That Juſtices of Oyer and Terminer have no Power, either to inquire of a forcible Entry or Detainer, Kellew. 159. Daliſ. 25. 9 Co. 118. b. 11 Co. 65. a. or to award Reſtitution on any ſuch Indictment; becauſe, when a new Power is created by Statute, and certain Juſtices are aſſigned to execute it, it cannot regularly be executed by any other; and inaſmuch as Juſtices of Oyer and Terminer have a Commiſſion entirely diſtinct from that of Juſtices of Peace, they ſhall not, from the general Words of their Commiſſion, *Ad inquirend' de omnibus tranſgr' & de omnibus aliis Articulis & Cauſis cont' formam quorumcunque Statutorum fact' ſive perpetrat'*, be conſtrued to have any ſuch Powers as are ſpecially limited to Juſtices of Peace; yet it hath been reſolved, That the Juſtices of the King's Bench may award Reſtitution upon an Indictment of forcible Entry or Detainer removed be- Far. 138. 7 Ed. 4. 18. a. 4 H. 7. 18. b. Daliſ. 25. 9 Co. 118. b. 11 Co. 65. a. Dal. ch. 82. fore them, becauſe the ſaid Juſtices having a ſupream and ſovereign Juriſdiction over all Matters of a criminal and publick Nature, have always been eſteemed to have Power in all Cauſes of this Nature, being brought Judicially before them, to give the Parties ſuch Remedies in Relation thereto, as they ſhall appear to have a Right to demand, either by Common Law or by Statute.

Lamb. 157. Dal. ch. 82. *Sect.* 52. The Sheriff if need be, may raiſe the Power of the County to aſſiſt him in the Execution of a Precept of Reſtitution, and therefore, if he make a Return thereto, that he could not make a Reſtitution by Reaſon of Reſiſtance, he ſhall be amerced.

Salk. 260. Pl. 1. Carth. 496. *Sect.* 53. As to the tenth Point, *viz.* How ſuch Reſtitution may be barred by the Continuance of a Poſſeſſion for three Years, it appears from the abovementioned Proviſo of 8 *H.* 6. and alſo by 31 *El.* 11. That any one indicted upon theſe Statutes, may alledge ſuch Poſſeſſion to ſtay the A- Far. 138. Dalt. ca. 79. Crom. 71. H. P. C. 139. Dyer 141. Pl. 48. 22 H. 6. 18. b. Bro. Force, 22, 29. Crom. 71. ward of Reſtitution; in the Conſtruction whereof it hath been holden, That ſuch Poſſeſſion muſt have continued without Interruption during three whole Years next before the Indictment; and therefore, That he who having been in Poſſeſſion of Land for three Years, or more, is forcibly ouſted, and then reſtored by Force of the Statute of 8 *H.* 6. cannot juſtify a forcible Detainer, till he have been in Poſſeſſion again for three Years after ſuch Reſtitution; and alſo for the ſame Reaſon it hath been ſaid, That he, who under a defeaſible Title hath been never ſo long in Poſſeſ- Dal. ca. 79. 1 Inſt. 256. H. P. C. 139. Bro. Force, 22. ſion of Land to which another hath a Right of Entry, cannot juſtify ſuch a Detainer at any Time within three Years after a Claim made by him who hath ſuch a Right, becauſe all defeaſible Eſtates in the Land are wholly defeated by ſuch a Claim, and the ſubſequent Continuance in Poſſeſſion amounted to a new Entry.

Dal. ca. 79. 22 H. 6. 18. b. Crom. 71. *Sect.* 54. There have been ſome Opinions, That the three Years Poſſeſſion muſt be of a lawful Eſtate, and conſequently that a Diſſeiſor's Continuance in quiet Poſſeſſion for never ſo many Years, ſhall not juſtify a forcible Detainer; but it ſeems neceſſary to make a Diſtinction between a Detainer againſt him who has a Right of Entry, and a Detainer againſt a Stranger, or one who by his Laches has loſt his Right of Entry; for I do not ſee why three Years Continuance of a defeaſible Poſſeſſion ſhould not juſtify a Detainer by Force againſt a Stranger, inaſmuch as he cannot take Advantage of another's Right, and bare Poſſeſſion is a good Title againſt all Perſons, except him who hath the Right, and cannot be lawfully defeated by any other. Alſo if one who has the mere Right to Lands, have ſo long neglected to recover the Poſſeſſion thereof, till in Judgment of Law he hath no more Right to ſuch Poſſeſſion, till he have recovered it by Action, than a mere Stranger, there doth not ſeem to be any Reaſon that he ſhould have more Advantage againſt a forcible Detainer, than if he were a meer Stranger.

Sect. 55. Alſo it hath been holden, That a peaceable Continuance in Poſſeſſion for three Years after a forcible Entry, under any Title whatſoever, will not juſtify a forcible Detainer, inaſmuch as the Poſſeſſion was at firſt gained by Force; but I cannot think this a reaſonable Conſtruction of the ſaid Statutes, for the Force in the Detainer being after three Years quiet Poſſeſſion, ſeems juſtifiable by the expreſs Words of the Statute; and where the Force uſed in gaining a Poſſeſſion is afterwards wholly laid aſide, there ſeems to be no Colour to ſay, That it makes the ſubſequent Poſſeſſion leſs quiet or peaceable than it would have been, if there had been no Force at all uſed at the firſt.

Sect. 56. It ſeems clear from the expreſs Purview of the ſaid Statute of 31 *El.* 11. that where-ever the Defendant pleadeth ſuch a Poſſeſſion in Bar of Reſtitution upon ſuch an Indictment, either before the Juſtices of Peace, or in the King's Bench, no Reſtitution ought to be awarded till the Truth of the Plea be tried; and it hath been holden, That the Plea of ſuch a Poſſeſſion is good, without ſhewing under what Title, or of what Eſtate ſuch Poſſeſſion was, becauſe it is not the Title, but the Poſſeſſion only, which is material in this Caſe. 1 Keb. 538. The King and Burges. Sal. 261. Pl. 1. 1 Sid. 149. 1 Keb. 538. Raymond 84. 1 Vent. 265.

Sect. 57. It ſeems that from the Wording of 31 *El.* 11. if one who has been in Poſſeſſion for three Years, be ouſted, and the ſame Day re-enter with Force, and alſo be indicted for ſuch Re-entry on the very ſame Day, it may be queſtioned whether the Proſecutor ought to have Reſtitution, inaſmuch as the Words of the Statute are, *That there ſhall be no Reſtitution,* &c. *if the Perſon indicted have been in quiet Poſſeſſion for three Years next before the Day of the Indictment found*; and here the Defendant hath been in Poſſeſſion three Years before the Day of the Indictment, though not three Years before the Indictment, inaſmuch as he was ouſted the ſame Day; but if it be conſidered, That the Circumſtance of finding the Indictment on that Day no way affects the Merits of the Cauſe, or leſſens the Offence any more than if it were found in any other Day; and that Reſtitution muſt have been awarded if it had been found on another Day; and that the Miſchief complained of in the Peamble is, that Perſons were by Colour of ſuch Indictments often turned out of their Poſſeſſions which they had quietly enjoyed for three Years next before ſuch Indictments found, which does not extend to the Defendant in the preſent Caſe, I rather incline to think, that Reſtitution might be awarded to the Proſecutor in this Caſe, inaſmuch as it clearly appears, That the Defendant's Poſſeſſion hath not had three Years uninterrupted Continuance within the Intent of the Statute.

1 Keb. 343. 2 Keb. 49, 571. 1 Sid. 284. Salk. 587, 588.

Sect. 58. As to the eleventh Point, *viz.* For what other Cauſes ſuch Reſtitution may be ſtay'd, it ſeemeth to be ſettled at this Day, That if the Defendant tender a Traverſe of the Force, which muſt be done in Writing, and not by a bare Denial of the Force by Parol, the Juſtice ought not to make any Reſtitution, till the Traverſe be tried; in order whereunto he muſt award a *Venire facias*, whereon a Jury muſt be returned, on whoſe Verdict the Award of Reſtitution ought to depend.

1 Sid. 97, 99. 1 Keb. 427.

Sect. 59. It hath been reſolved, That if ſuch a Jury find Part of the Indictment to be true, and Part of it to be falſe; yet if they find ſo much thereof to be true as will warrant a Reſtitution, the Juſtice ought to reſtore the Party; as where on an Indictment of Forcible Entry and Forcible Detainer, the Jury find that the Entry was peaceful, and the Detainer was only forcible.

Savil 68. Pl. 141. Aleyn 78, 79.

Sect. 60. As the Juſtice is bound to ſtay the Award of Reſtitution, upon the Defendant's tendering a Traverſe of the Force, ſo it hath alſo been ſaid, That he ought not to make ſuch an Award in any Caſe in the Defendant's Abſence, without calling him to anſwer for himſelf; for it is implied by natural Juſtice, in the Conſtruction of all Laws, That no one ought to ſuffer any Prejudice thereby, without having firſt an Opportunity of defending himſelf.

Dyer 187. Pl. 6. H. P. C. 140. Crom. 165. Dalt. cap. 81, 84. Cro. El. 915. Yelv. 32.

Sect. 61. As to the twelfth Point, *viz.* How ſuch a Reſtitution may be ſuperſeded before it is executed, there is no Doubt but that the ſame Juſtices by whom a Reſtitution is awarded upon an Indictment of Forcible Entry or Detainer found before them, may alſo afterwards upon an Inſufficiency of the Indictment appearing unto them, ſuperſede the ſame before it is executed: And it hath alſo been ſaid, That if ſuch an Indictment be taken, and Reſtitution awarded by four or five Juſtices, that two or even one of the ſame Juſtices may ſuperſede the Execution thereof, as well as more or all of them. But it ſeems to be agreed, That no other Juſtices, or other Court whatſoever, have ſuch Power, except the King's Bench.

Cro. El. 915. Yelv. 32. Moore 677. Pl. 921. 1 Keb. 93.

Sect. 62. However it is certain, that a *Certiorari* from the King's Bench is a *Superſedeas* to ſuch Reſtitution; for every ſuch *Certiorari* has theſe Words, *coram nobis terminari volumus & non alibi*, and conſequently it wholly cloſes the Hands of the Juſtices of the Peace, and avoids any Reſtitution which is executed after the *Teſte*, but does not bring the Juſtices of Peace, *&c.* into a Contempt, unleſs they proceed after the Delivering thereof.

Savil 68. Pl. 141. H. P. C. 140. 141. Cro. El. 31. Supra Sect. 58.

Sect. 63. As to the thirteenth Point, *viz.* How ſuch Reſtitution may be ſet aſide after it is executed; it is certain, That the Juſtices of the King's Bench, having a general ſuperintendent Power over all the Proceedings whatſoever of Juſtices of Peace, may ſet aſide any ſuch Reſtitution, if it ſhall appear to them to have been either awarded or executed againſt Law; as where the Indictment whereon it was grounded, being removed before them, appears to be Inſufficient, and thereupon is quaſhed; or the Defendant traverſes the Force and gets a Verdict in the King's Bench, or whereever it ſufficiently appears that the Juſtices of Peace have been irregular in their Proceedings, as by refuſing to try a Traverſe of Force tendered by the Defendant, *&c.*

Noy 119. Yelv. 99. Cro. Ja. 148, 149.

Sect. 64. Yet if an Indictment on theſe Statutes be removed into the King's Bench, and the Defendant having been turned out of Poſſeſſion by the Grant of Reſtitution to the Proſecutor by the Juſtices of Peace, traverſe the Force in the King's Bench, and then the Offence be pardoned by a general Pardon, the Court cannot proceed on the Trial, notwithſtanding the Defendant would wave the Benefit of the Pardon, becauſe it appears judicially, That the King can have no Benefit of a Fine from the Defendant if the Verdict paſs againſt him; and the Court will never falſify an Indictment, which is found by the Oaths of twelve Men, by bare Affidavits; and conſequently in this Caſe the Defendant can have no Remedy to ſet aſide the Reſtitution by controverting the Truth of the Indictment. B. 2. Ch. 37. Sect. 61.

Sect. 65. Neither can a Defendant in any Caſe whatſoever, *ex Rigore Juris*, demand a Reſtitution, either upon the quaſhing of the Indictment, or a Verdict for him on a Traverſe thereof, *&c.* for the Power of granting a Re-reſtitution is veſted in the King's Bench, only by an equitable Conſtruction of the general Words of the Statutes, and is not expreſly given by thoſe Statutes; and is never made uſe of by that Court, but when upon Conſideration of the whole Circumſtances of the Caſe, the Defendant ſhall appear to have ſome Right to the Tenements, the Poſſeſſion whereof he loſt by the Reſtitution granted to the Proſecutor. Raym. 85. 1 Keb. 343, 808. 2 Keb. 505. H. P. C. 141. Cro. El. 916. Salk. 587. Dyer 123. Pl. 34. 2 Keb. 571. Savil 68. Pl. 141.

Sect. 66. The Court of King's Bench hath been ſo favourable to one, who, upon his Traverſe of an Indictment upon theſe Statutes being found for him, hath appeared to have been unjuſtly put out of his Poſſeſſion, that they have awarded him a Re-reſtitution, notwithſtanding it hath been ſhewn to the Court, that ſince the Reſtitution granted upon the Indictment, a Stranger hath recovered the Poſſeſſion of the ſame Land in the Lord's Court. Cro. El. 41.

CHAP. LXV.

Of Riots, Routs, and unlawful Aſſemblies.

IN treating of Riots, Routs, and unlawful Aſſemblies, I ſhall conſider,

1. What ſhall be called a Riot, Rout, or unlawful Aſſembly.
2. How they may be ſuppreſſed and puniſhed by the Common Law.
3. How by Statute.

Sect. 1. And firſt a Riot ſeems to be a tumultuous Diſturbance of the Peace, by three Perſons, [a] or more, aſſembling together of their own Authority, with an Intent mutually to aſſiſt one another, againſt any who ſhall oppoſe them, in the Execution of ſome Enterprize of a private Nature, and afterwards actually executing the ſame in a violent and turbulent Manner, to the Terror of the People, whether the Act intended were of it ſelf lawful or unlawful. [b]

[a] Vide 1 Vent. 251. Salk. 594, 595. Dalt. cap. 85, 86, 87. Cromp. 61, &c. Pult. 25, &c. 3 Inſt. 176. H. P. C. 137. 3 Mod. 141.

For the better Underſtanding whereof, I ſhall conſider the following Particulars:

[b] But ſee Salk. 594. Pl. 4.

1. How far ſuch an Aſſembly may become riotous through the Want of legal Authority expreſſed or implied, or be excuſable by Reaſon of ſuch Authority.

2. How

2. How far the Intention with which the Parties assemble together must be unlawful.

3. With what kind of Violence or Terror the intended Enterprize must be executed.

4. How far the Grievance intended to be redressed must be of a private Nature.

5. Whether the unlawful Execution of an Act in its own Nature lawful may not make an Assembly riotous.

Sect. 2. As to the first Point it seems, That where-ever more than three Persons use Force and Violence, in the Execution of any Design whatever wherein the Law does not allow the Use of such Force, all who are concerned therein are Rioters: But in some Cases wherein the Law authorizes Force, it is not only lawful, but also commendable to make use of it; as for a [a] Sheriff or [b] Constable, or perhaps even for a private [c] Person, to assemble a competent Number of People in Order with Force to suppress Rebels, or Enemies, or Rioters, and afterwards with such Force actually to suppress them; or for a Justice of Peace, who has a just Cause to fear a violent Resistance to raise the *Posse*, in order to remove a Force in making an Entry into, or detaining of Lands. Also it seems to be the Duty of a [d] Sheriff, or other Minister of Justice, having the Execution of the King's Writs, and being resisted in endeavouring to execute the same, to raise such a Power as may effectually enable them to over-power any such Resistance; yet it is said not [e] to be lawful for them to raise a Force for the Execution of a civil Process, unless they find a Resistance; and it is certain, That they are highly punishable for using any needless Outrage, or Violence therein.

[a] 2 And. 67. Poph. 121.
[b] 3 H. 7. 10. b.
[c] Poph. 121. Moore 656.
[d] 2 Inst. 193.
[e] 3 Inst. 161. 2 Inst. 193.
Hob. 62, 264.

Sect. 3. As to the second Point, *viz.* How far the Intention with which such Persons assemble together must be unlawful; it seems agreed, That if a Number of Persons being met together at a Fair, or Market, or Church-ale, or any other lawful and innocent Occasion happen on a sudden Quarrel to fall together by the Ears, they are not guilty of a Riot, but of a sudden Affray only, of which none are guilty but those who actually engage in it, because the Design of their Meeting was innocent and lawful, and the subsequent Breach of the Peace, happened unexpectedly without any previous Intention concerning it; yet it is said, That if Persons, innocently assembled together, do afterwards upon a Dispute happening to arise among them, form themselves into Parties, with Promises of mutual Assistance, and then make an Affray, they are guilty of a Riot, because upon their confederating together with an Intention to break the Peace, they may as properly be said to be assembled together for that Purpose from the Time of such Confederacy, as if their first coming together had been on such a Design: However it seems clear, That if in an Assembly of Persons met together on any lawful Occasion whatsoever, a sudden Proposal should be started of going together in a Body to pull down a House or Inclosure, or to do any other Act of Violence to the Disturbance of the Publick Peace, and such Motion be agreed to, and executed accordingly, the Persons concerned cannot but be Rioters, because their Associating themselves together for such a new Purpose, is no way extenuated by their having met at first upon another; also it seems to be certain, That if a Person seeing others actually engaged in a Riot, do join himself unto them and assist them therein, he is as much a Rioter as if he had at first assembled with them for the same Purpose, inasmuch as he has no Pretence that he came innocently into the Company, but appears to have joined himself unto them, with an Intention

Lamb. 179, &c. Dalt. cap. 86. Crom. 61, 62. 6 Mod. 43. Skin. 118.
Salk. 595.

to second them in the Execution of their unlawful Enterprize; and it would be endless, as well as superfluous, to examine whether every particular Person engaged in a Riot, were in Truth one of the first Assembly, or actually had a previous Knowledge of the Design thereof.

6 Mod. 43.

Sect. 4. As to the third Point, *viz.* With what kind of Violence or Terror, the intended Enterprize must be executed, it hath been holden, That it ought to be accompanied with some Offer of Violence, either to the Person of a Man, or to his Possessions, as by beating him, or forcing him to quit the Possession of his Lands or Goods, *&c.* And from hence it seems to follow, That Persons riding together on the Road with unusual Weapons, or otherwise assembling together in such a Manner as is apt to raise a Terror in the People, without any Offer of Violence to any one in Respect either of his Person or Possessions, are not properly guilty of a Riot, but only of an unlawful Assembly.

Dalt. cap. 85. Lamb. 175. 3 Inst. 176.

Sect. 5. However it seems to be clearly agreed, That in every Riot there must be some such Circumstances, either of actual Force or Violence, or at least of an apparent Tendency thereto, as are naturally apt to strike a Terror into the People; as the Shew [a] of Armour, threatening Speeches, or turbulent Gestures; for every such Offence must be laid to be done *in Terrorem Populi:* And from hence it clearly follows, That Assemblies at Wakes or other Festival Times, or Meetings for exercise of common Sports or Diversions, as Bull-baiting, Wrestling, and such like, are not riotous. And from the same Ground also it seems to follow, That it is possible for more than three Persons to assemble together with an Intention to execute a wrongful Act, and also actually to perform their intended Enterprize, without being Rioters; as if a competent Number of People assembled together, in order to carry off a Piece of Timber to which one of the Company hath a pretended Right, and afterwards do carry it away without any threatning Words, or other Circumstances of Terror. And from the same Ground it seems also to follow, That Persons assembled together in a peaceful Manner to do a Thing prohibited by Statute, as to celebrate Mass, *&c.* and afterwards peacefully performing the Thing intended, cannot be said to be Rioters; for there seems to be no Reason why an Assembly should become riotous barely for doing a Thing contrary to Statute, any more than for doing a Thing contrary to Common Law.

[a] Lamb. 178. Dalt. cap. 87. 3 H. 7. 1. a. 6 Mod. 141. 2 Keb. 558. Con. 1 Rol. Rep. 109.
[b] Lamb. 179. Pulton 25. 3 Keb. 578.
Lamb. 178. Crom. 62. a. Quære.
6 Mod. 141. 2 Keb. 558. Con. 1 Mod. 13. 1 Vent. 369, 380.

Sect. 6. As to the fourth Point, *viz.* How far the Grievance intended, to be redressed must be of a private Nature; it seems agreed, That the Injury or Grievance complained of, and intended to be revenged or remedied by such an Assembly, must relate to some private Quarrel only; as the Inclosing of Lands in which the Inhabitants of a Town claim a Right of Common, or gaining the Possession of Tenements, the Title whereof is in dispute, or such like Matters relating to the Interest or Disputes of particular Persons, and no way concerning the Publick; for where-ever the Intention of such an Assembly is to redress publick Grievances, as to pull down all Inclosures in general, or to reform Religion, or to remove evil Counsellors from the King, *&c.* if they attempt with Force to execute such their Intentions, they are in the Eye of the Law guilty of levying War against the King, and consequently of High Treason, as appears from *Chap.* 17. *Sect.* 25.

Sect. 7. As to the fifth Point, *viz.* Whether the Execution of an Act in its own Nature lawful, may make an Assembly riotous, it hath been generally holden, That it is no way material whether the Act intended to be done by such an Assembly, be of it self lawful or unlawful; from

Quære and Vide Salk. 594, 4. Crom. 64. b. 65 a. Dalt. cap. 87.

whence it follows, That if more than three Perſons aſſiſt a Man to make a Forcible Entry into Lands, to which one of them has a good Right of Entry, or if the like Number in a violent and tumultuous Manner join together in removing a Nuſance, or other Thing which may lawfully be done in a peaceful Manner, they are as properly Rioters, as if the Act intended to be done by them were never ſo unlawful; for the Law will not ſuffer Perſons to ſeek the Redreſs of their private Grievances, by ſuch dangerous Diſturbances of the Publick Peace: However the Juſtice of the Quarrel in which ſuch an Aſſembly doth engage, is certainly a great Mitigation of the Offence.

Lamb. 175, 176. Cromp. 61. Dalt. cap. 85. Bro. Riots, 4, 5. Pulton 25.

Sect. 8. A Rout ſeems to be, according to the general Opinion, a Diſturbance of the Peace by Perſons aſſembling together with an Intention to do a Thing, which if it be executed will make them Rioters, and actually making a Motion towards the Execution thereof: But by ſome Books, the Notion of a Rout is confined to ſuch Aſſemblies only, as are occaſioned by ſome Grievance common to all the Company; as the Incloſure of Land in which they all claim a Right of Common, *&c.* However inaſmuch as it generally agrees with a Riot as to all the reſt of the above mentioned Particulars, requiſite to conſtitute a Riot, which have been already fully explained, except only in this, That it may be a compleat Offence without the Execution of the intended Enterprize, it ſeems not to require any farther Explication.

Crom. 61. a. Bro. Riots, 4. Pulton 25. a. Dalt. cap. 95.

Sect. 9. An unlawful Aſſembly, according to the common Opinion, is a Diſturbance of the Peace by Perſons barely aſſembling together, with an Intention to do a Thing, which if it were executed would make them Rioters, but neither actually executing it, nor making a Motion toward the Execution of it; but this ſeems to be much too narrow a Definition: for any Meeting whatſoever of great Numbers of People with ſuch Circumſtances of Terror, as cannot but endanger the Publick Peace, and raiſe Fears and Jealouſies among the King's Subjects, ſeems properly to be called an unlawful Aſſembly; as where great Numbers, complaining of a common Grievance, meet together, armed in a warlike Manner in order to conſult together concerning the moſt proper Means for the Recovery of their Intereſts; for no one can foreſee what may be the Event of ſuch an Aſſembly.

Hob. 92. Salk. 594, 595. 1 Vent. 369, 380.

21 H. 7. 39. Lamb. 179, 180. H. P. C. 137. Cromp. 64. a. Bro. Riots, 1. 5 Co. 91. b.

Sect. 10. Alſo an Aſſembly of a Man's Friends for the Defence of his Perſon, againſt thoſe who threaten to beat him if he go to ſuch a Market, *&c.* is unlawful; for he who is in fear of ſuch Inſults, muſt provide for his Safety, by demanding the Surety of the Peace againſt the Perſons by whom he is threatened, and not make uſe of ſuch violent Methods, which cannot but be attended with the Danger of raiſing Tumults and Diſorders to the Diſturbance of the Publick Peace: Yet an Aſſembly of a Man's Friends in his own Houſe, for the Defence of the Poſſeſſion thereof, againſt thoſe who threaten to make an unlawful Entry thereinto, or for the Defence of his Perſon againſt thoſe who threaten to beat him therein, is indulged by Law; for a Man's Houſe is look'd upon as his Caſtle.

Poph. 121. 3 H. 7. 1. a. 10 b. Vide ſupra.

Sect. 11. As to the ſecond Point, *viz.* How far Offences of this Nature may be ſuppreſſed and puniſhed by the Common Law; it ſeems clear, That every Sheriff and Under-Sheriff, and alſo every other Peace Officer, as Conſtables, *&c.* may and ought to do all that in them lies towards the ſuppreſſing of a Riot, and may command all other Perſons whatſoever to aſſiſt them therein; alſo it is certain, That any private Perſon may lawfully endeavour to appeaſe all ſuch Diſturbances, by ſtaying thoſe whom he ſhall ſee engaged therein from executing their Purpoſe, and alſo

by ſtopping others whom he ſhall ſee coming to join them; for if private Perſons may do thus much, as it is moſt certain that they may, towards the ſuppreſſing of a common Affray, ſurely *à fortiori* they may do it towards the ſuppreſſing of a Riot: Alſo it hath been holden, That Poph. 121.
private Perſons may arm themſelves in order to ſuppreſs a Riot; from Kelynge 76.
whence it ſeems clearly to follow, that they may alſo make uſe of Arms in the ſuppreſſing of it, if there be a Neceſſity for their ſo doing. However it ſeems to be extremely hazardous for private Perſons to proceed to theſe Extremities; and it ſeems no way ſafe for them to go ſo far in common Caſes, leaſt under the Pretence of keeping the Peace, they cauſe a more enormous Breach of it, and therefore ſuch violent Methods ſeem only proper againſt ſuch Riots as favour of Rebellion, for the ſuppreſſing whereof no Remedies can be too ſharp or ſevere. However it is enacted by 1 *Geor.* 1. c. 5. *That if more Perſons than twelve being unlawfully, riotouſly and tumultuouſly aſſembled, twelve or more of them, ſhall continue together, and not diſperſe themſelves within one Hour after Proclamation made in Purſuance of that Statute, that then every Peace Officer of the Place where ſuch Aſſembly ſhall be, and all Perſons who ſhall be commanded to be aſſiſting to ſuch Officer, may and ought to apprehended all ſuch Rioters, and carry them before ſome Juſtice of Peace; and that if any ſuch Rioter ſhall happen to be killed, maimed, or hurt by Reaſon of their reſiſting ſuch Officer,* &c. *the Officer ſhall be diſcharged,* &c. But the Statute being wholly in the Affirmative, cannot be thought to take away any Part of the Authority in the ſuppreſſing of a Riot, which was before that Time given either to Officers or private Perſons by the Common Law or by Statute.

Sect. 12. Generally Offences of this Nature are puniſhed at the Com- Crom. 61.
mon Law, as Treſpaſſes, by Fine and Impriſonment only; yet ſometimes, Dalt. cap. 46.
where they have been very enormous, they have been puniſhed with the Cro. ca. 507.
Pillory; and anciently, if they were undertaken in Contempt of the King's expreſs Prohibition of their Meeting, under Pain of Forfeiture of Lands, 2 Rol. Ab. 208.
&c. they ſeem to have been puniſhable with ſuch Forfeiture.

Sect. 13. It hath been holden, That the Perſons of whom a Corpo- 21 Ed. 4. 13. b. 14. a.
ration conſiſts being guilty of a Riot, are puniſhable in their Natural, Dalt. cap. 88.
but not in their Politick Capacity; for the Corporation it ſelf cannot be in Fault, becauſe it is inviſible, and exiſts only in Suppoſition of Law; yet there are ſome Precedents by which it appears, that Corporations have been amerced, and their Liberties ſeized into the King's Hands, for ſuffering Cro. Ca. 252.
a dangerous Riot to happen within their Juriſdiction without uſing their 2 H. H. P. C. 155.
Endeavours to ſuppreſs it.

Sect. 14. Women are puniſhable as Rioters, but Infants under the Age of Diſcretion are not.

As to the third Point, *viz.* How far Offences of this Nature may be ſuppreſſed and puniſhed by Statute; I ſhall conſider,

1. How far they may be ſuppreſſed and puniſhed by one Juſtice of Peace.
2. How far by two or more.

Sect. 15. As to the firſt of theſe Points, it is enacted by 34 *Ed.* 3. 1 *That Juſtices of Peace ſhall have Power to reſtrain Offenders, Rioters, and all Barrators; and to purſue, arreſt, take and chaſtiſe them according to their Treſpaſs and Offence; and to cauſe them to be impriſoned, and duly puniſhed,* &c.

Sect. 16.

14 H. 7. 9. b. Crom. 62. a. 63. b. 65. a. Lamb. 181, &c. *Sect.* 16. And this Statute has been liberally construed for the Advancement of Justice; for it has been resolved, That if a Justice of Peace find Persons riotously assembled, he alone without staying for his Companions hath not only Power to arrest the Offenders, and bind them to their good Behaviour, or imprison them if they do not offer good Bail, but that he may also authorize others to arrest them by a bare Parol Command without other Warrant, and that by Force thereof the Persons so commanded, may pursue and arrest the Offenders in his Absence as well as Presence. It is also said, That if a Justice of Peace be sick, and hear that Persons are riotously assembled, he may send his Servants to arrest them, and bring them before him; and that if he hear that Persons are riotously together in a certain Place, and go thither and find none there, he may leave his Servants behind him with a Command to arrest them, when they shall come. Also it is said, That after a Riot is over, any one Justice of Peace may send his Warrant to arrest any Person who was concerned in it, and also that he may send him to Gaol, till he shall find Sureties for his good Behaviour.

Dalt. cap. 46. Bro. Peace 7. Dalt. ca. 46. Pult. 28. Dalt. cap. 46. 14 H. 7. 9. b. Lamb. 181, &c. Cromp. 64. a. Kellw. 41. Cromp. 195. b. Dalt. ca. 46.

[a] Bro. Peace, 7. Kellw. 41. a. Lamb. 181, &c. Pult. 26. a. H. P. C. 137. Cromp. 61. b. 63. a. 65. Dalt. cap. 46. Con. Bro. Judges 10. [b] 8 Co. 121. a. Dalt. cap. 22. *Sect.* 17. But it seems to be agreed, That no one [a] Justice of Peace hath any Power by Force of this Statute, either to record a Riot upon his own View, or to take an Inquisition thereof after it is over: Also if one Justice of Peace proceeding upon this Statute, shall arrest an innocent Person as a Rioter, it seemeth that he is liable to an Action of Trespass, and that the Party arrested may justify the rescuing of himself, because no single Justice of Peace is by this Statute made a Judge of the said Offence. [b] But if a Riot shall be committed by Persons armed in an unusual Manner, contrary to the Statute of *Northampton*, and any one Justice of Peace acting *ex Officio*, in Pursuance of the said Statute, seize the Armour and imprison the Offender, and make a Record of the whole Matter, such a Record cannot be traversed, because it is made by one acting in a judicial Capacity, as appears more at large in the Chapter of Affrays; and for the same Reason, if a Justice of Peace proceeding on the Statute of 15 *Rich.* 2. against Forcible Entries and Detainers, shall upon his own View record a Riot, which shall be committed in the Making of any such Forcible Entry or Detainer, a Riot so recorded cannot be traversed, as hath been shewn in the foregoing Chapter. Also if a Justice of Peace acting as a Judge, by Virtue of any Statute whatsoever, impowering him so to do, make a Record upon his View of a Riot committed in his Presence, such Record shall not be traversed; for the Law gives such an uncontroulable Credit to all Matters of Record, made by any Judge of Record as such, that it will never admit of an Averment against the Truth thereof.

8 Co. 121. a. Dalt. cap. 22. Crom. 65. a. Dalt. cap. 46. Lamb. 317. Vide infra Sect. 25.

Pult. 25. a. 26. a. Lamb. 314. Crom. 62. a. *Sect.* 18. It hath been questioned, Whether a Justice of Peace be authorized by Virtue of the above mentioned Statute of 34 *Ed.* 3. 1. to raise the Power of the County to suppress a Riot; but it seemeth, That by being made a Conservator of the Peace, he hath by Implication of Law all such Powers in Relation thereto, as are incident to the Office of a Conservator of the Peace by the Common Law; and consequently, That he hath a Right of demanding the Assistance of others to enable him to preserve the Peace in the same manner, as every Sheriff and Constable are impowered to demand such Assistance by the Common Law: However there seems to be no Reason to doubt, but that every Justice of Peace is authorized by 17 *Rich.* 2. 8. to raise the Power of the County to repress a Riot; for by the said Statute it is enacted, *That as soon as the Sheriffs, and other the King's Ministers,* (under which Words all Justices of Peace seem clearly to be included,) *shall hear of a Riot, Rout, or other Assembly against*

3 H. 7. 10. b. 3 Inst. 158. Vide supra. Pult. 25, 26. Lamb. 314.

the Peace, they with the Power of the County where ſuch Caſe ſhall happen, ſhall diſturb ſuch Malice with all their Power, and ſhall apprehend all ſuch Offenders, and put them in Priſon, until due Execution of the Law be made of them; and that the Lords and other liege People of the Realm ſhall attend with their whole Strength and Power, the Sheriffs and Miniſters aforeſaid.

Sect. 19. As to the ſecond Point, *viz.* How far Offences of this Nature may be ſuppreſſed and puniſhed by two or more Juſtices of Peace, it is enacted by 13 *H.* 4. 7. *That if any Riot, Aſſembly, or Rout of People againſt the Law, be made in Parties of the Realm, that the Juſtices of Peace, three or two of them at the leaſt, and the Sheriff or Under-Sheriff of the County where ſuch Riot, Aſſembly or Rout ſhall be made hereafter, ſhall come with the Power of the County (if need be) to arreſt them, and ſhall arreſt them; and the ſame Juſtices and Sheriff, or Under-Sheriff, ſhall have Power to record that which they ſhall find ſo done in their Preſence againſt the Law. And that by the Record of the ſame Juſtices and Sheriff, or Under-Sheriff, ſuch Treſpaſſers and Offenders ſhall be convict in the Manner and Form as is contained in the Statute of Forcible Entries.*

Sect. 20. In the Conſtruction of this Statute, compared with the above
mentioned Statute of 17 *Rich.* 2. 8. and alſo with the Statute of 2 *H.* 5. 8.
it hath been holden, That all Perſons whatſoever, and even Noblemen,
and all others of what Condition or Degree ſoever they may be, except Pult. 29. a.
Women, Clergymen, Perſons decrepit, and Infants under the Age of fifteen Lamb. 315. Dalt. cap. 46.
Years, are bound under Pain of Fine and Impriſonment upon reaſonable Cromp. 63. a.
Warning to attend the Juſtices and Sheriffs in the Execution of the ſaid Sta- Lamb. 116.
tute, and not only to arreſt the Rioters, but alſo to conduct them to Priſon.

Sect. 21. Alſo it hath been holden, That thoſe who attend the Juſtices Poph. 120,
in order to ſuppreſs a Riot, may take with them ſuch Weapons as ſhall 121. Crom. 62.
be neceſſary to enable them effectually to do it, and that they may juſtify Dalt. cap. 46.
the Beating, Wounding, and even the Killing of ſuch Rioters as ſhall Lamb. 316.
reſiſt or refuſe to ſurrender themſelves.

Sect. 22. It is ſaid, That the Juſtices of Peace are not only impowered Lamb. 318, 319.
by the ſaid Statute, to raiſe the Power of the County to aſſiſt them, in Dalt. cap. 46.
ſuppreſſing a Riot which ſhall happen within their own View or Hearing, Pult. 29.
but alſo, that they may ſafely do it upon a credible Information given them
of a notorious Riot happening at a Diſtance, whether there were any ſuch
Riot in Truth or not; for it may be dangerous for them to ſtay till they
can get certain Information of the Fact: But they ſeem to be puniſhable Pult. 29. a.
for alarming the Country in this Manner, without ſome ſuch probable Lamb. 315. 316.
Ground of their Proceeding, as would induce a reaſonable Man to think Crom. 64. b.
it neceſſary and convenient. Dalt. cap. 46.

Sect. 23. It ſeems clear from the ſaid Statute, That if the Juſtices, &c.
in going towards the Place where they have heard that there is a Riot, ſhall
meet Perſons coming from thence riotouſly arrayed, they may arreſt them Dalt. cap. 46.
for being aſſembled together in ſuch an unlawful Manner, and alſo make Lamb. 316.
a Record thereof, &c. for the Statute extends to all other unlawful Aſſem- Cromp. 63. a.
blies whatſoever as well as to Riots.

Sect. 24. Alſo it ſeems clear, That after the Juſtices have had a
View of a Riot, they may make a Record thereof, whether the Offen-
ders be in Cuſtody at the ſame Time, or have eſcaped: And it is ſaid,
That the Juſtices may lawfully, upon a freſh Purſuit, arreſt ſuch of the Lamb. 318.
Offenders as ſhall have eſcaped, but that they cannot at another Time Dalt. cap. 46.
award any Proceſs on ſuch a Record, and therefore that they ought to Pult. 29. a. b. 8 Co. 121
ſend it into the King's Bench, if any of the Offenders eſcape from a freſh

Vide infra Sect. 29. Vide ſupra Sect. 15, 16. Purſuit, and that Proceſs ſhall iſſue againſt them from thence: However there ſeems to be no Doubt, but that any of the ſame Juſtices who have recorded a Riot, or any other Juſtice of Peace, may at any Time by Virtue of the above mentioned Statute of 34 *Ed.* 3. 1. arreſt thoſe who have been notoriouſly guilty of a Riot, in order to compel them to find Sureties for their Good Behaviour.

Raym. 386. Cromp. 65. a. 63. a. Dalt. ca. 46. *Sect.* 25. It ſeemeth to be certain, That the Record of a Riot expreſly mentioned to have happened within the View of the Juſtices by whom it is recorded, is a Conviction of ſo great Authority, that it can no way be traverſed, however little Ground in Truth there might be to affirm that any Riot at all was committed, or however innocent the Parties may be of the Fact recorded againſt them. Pult. 29. a. b. Lamb. 316, 317. And it is ſaid, That if one be bound by Recognizance to keep the Peace, and on a *Scire Facias* thereon ſuch a Record of a Riot be produced againſt him, he ſhall not only be concluded thereby from pleading the general Iſſue, but alſo from pleading any Matter of Juſtification whatſoever.

Lamb. 317. Dal. ca. 130. *Sect.* 26. However it ſeemeth clear, That if in ſuch a Record of a Riot it be contained, that the Party was guilty therein of a Felony, or Maim, or Reſcous, the Party ſhall be concluded thereby as to the Riot only, and not as to any of the other Matters, becauſe the Juſtices of Peace have by this Statute a judicial Authority over no other Offences except Riots, Routs, and unlawful Aſſemblies.

Sect. 27. And inaſmuch as ſuch a Record is a final Conviction of the Parties as to all ſuch Matters as are properly contained in it, it ought to be certain both as to the Time and Place of the Offence, and the Number of Perſons concerned therein, and the ſeveral Kinds of Weapons made uſe of by them, and all other Circumſtances of the Fact; for ſince the Parties are concluded from denying the Truth of ſuch a Record, and have no other Remedy to defend themſelves againſt it, but only by taking Advantage of the Inſufficiency of what is contained in it, they may juſtly demand the Benefit of excepting to it, if it do not expreſly ſhew, both that they are guilty within the Meaning of the Statute, and alſo how far they are guilty, and that the Juſtices have purſued the Power given them, by the ſaid Statute; and from the ſame Ground it ſeems alſo to follow, That ſuch a Record may be excepted againſt, if it do not appear to have been made by the Sheriff or Under-Sheriff in Concurrence with the Juſtices.

Lamb. 316. Dalt. ca. 46. Lamb. 319. Raym. 386. Con. Dal. ca. 46.

Sect. 28. It is ſaid that the Offenders being under the Arreſt of the ſaid Juſtices, and alſo convicted by a Record of their Offence, ought immediately to be committed to Gaol by the ſame Juſtices, till they ſhall make Fine and Ranſom to the King, which can be aſſeſſed by no other Juſtices of Peace, except thoſe by whom the Record of the Offence was made; and by 2 *H.* 5. 8. ſuch Fine ought to be larger than it was wont to be before that Statute, for the Support of the Charges of the ſaid Juſtices, &c. whereof Payment ought to be made by the Sheriff, by Indenture thereof between him and them.

Lamb. 317. Dalt. ca. 46.

Sect. 29. It is farther enacted by the ſaid Statute of 13 *H.* 4. 7. that if it ſhall happen, *That ſuch Treſpaſſers and Offenders be departed before the coming of the ſaid Juſtices and Sheriff, and Under-Sheriff, that the ſame Juſtices, three, or two of them ſhall diligently inquire within a Month after ſuch Riot, Aſſembly, or Rout of People ſo made, and thereof ſhall hear and determine according to the Law of the Land.*

Sect. 30. Alſo it is farther enacted by 19 *H.* 7. 13. *That the Sheriff having a Precept directed to him to return a Jury in purſuance of* 13 H. 4. 7. *ſhall return twenty-four Perſons dwelling within the Shire where ſuch Riot, Rout, or unlawful Aſſembly ſhall be ſo committed and done, whereof every of them ſhall have Lands and Tenements within the ſame Shire, to the yearly Value of twenty Shillings of Charter-Land or Freehold, or twenty-ſix Shillings and eight Pence of Copyhold, or of both, over and above all Charges, for to enquire of the ſaid Riot, Rout or unlawful Aſſembly. And that he ſhall return upon every Perſon ſo by him impanelled, in Iſſues at the firſt Day twenty Shillings, and at the ſecond Day forty Shillings, if they appear not, and be ſworn to inquire of the Premiſſes at the firſt Day. And that the Sheriff for every Default,* &c. *ſhall forfeit twenty Pounds,* &c.

Sect. 31. It is not clearly ſettled, whether the Month, within which the Juſtices of Peace are confined to take their Inquiry by Force of theſe Statutes, muſt be reckoned according to the Computation of a Lunar, or of a Solar Month; however it ſeems to be agreed, That if the Juſtices give their Charge to the Jury, and it is ſaid, that if they do but award a Precept for the returning of the Jury, within a Lunar Month, they may take the Verdict afterwards, for the Cauſe being regularly attached in them within the Time preſcribed by the Statute, ſhall be proſecuted as all other Cauſes ought, with ſuch convenient Diſpatch as to the Judges thereof ſhall ſeem proper; and the Statute, by obliging the Juſtices to make ſo ſpeedy an Inquiry, meant not to hurry them in the Execution of it. 1 Sid. 186. 1 Keb. 695. Vide ſupra. Lamb. 322. Dalt. ca. 46. Pult. 29. 6 Mod. 141. Salk. 593.

Sect. 32. It is generally ſaid, That any Juſtices of the County may take ſuch an Inquiry, whether they dwell near the Place where the Riot happened, or at a Diſtance, or whether they went to view the Riot or not; for the Statute ought to be conſtrued as largely as the Words will bear, in Favour of the Juſtices Power in the ſuppreſſing of ſuch Riots; and therefore thoſe Words in the Statute, that the *ſame Juſtices,* &c. *ſhall inquire,* ought to be thus expounded, That the ſame Juſtices who were before impower'd to raiſe the *Poſſe, &c.* ſhall inquire; and it is clear, That any Juſtices in the County are within that Part of the Statute which gives that Power; neither is it any way reaſonable to conſtrue the laſt Clauſe of the ſaid Statute, whereby the Juſtices who dwell nigheſt, are bound to execute the Statute under Pain of one hundred Pounds, in ſuch a Manner as to reſtrain the Juriſdiction of thoſe who by the foregoing Part of the ſaid Statute are authoriſed to execute it; for if ſuch an Expoſition ſhould prevail, the Negligence of the Juſtices who happen to dwell nigheſt would make the Statute wholly ineffectual. Lamb. 322, 327. Dal. ca. 46. Pult. 29. b. Cro. 62. b. 63. a. ſeems contrary. See Sect. 44.

Sect. 33. It ſeems clear from the Wording of the above mentioned Clauſe, that the Sheriff ought not to join with the Juſtices in taking of ſuch an Inquiry, as he ought to do in making a Record of a Riot upon View. Lamb. 321 Raym. 386. Vide Salk. 593. Carth. 383, 384.

Sect. 34. Alſo it ſeems clear from theſe Words in the Statute of 13 *H.* 4. 7. *That the ſame Juſtices ſhall hear and determine,* &c. that they may award Proceſs under their own *Teſte,* againſt thoſe who ſhall be indicted before them of any of the Offences above mentioned, according to the Form of the ſaid Statute; and alſo that they may award the like Proceſs for the Trial of a Traverſe of ſuch an Inquiſition, and do all other Things in relation thereunto, which are of Courſe incident to all Courts of Record. Lamb. 323, 328. Dalt. cap. 46, & cap. 132. Pult. 26. b. Crom. 67.

Sect. 35. But it hath been queſtioned, whether the Juſtices can ſafely diſmiſs the Offenders upon their paying ſuch a Fine as ſhall be impoſed upon Dalt. ca. 45. Crom. 61 b.

upon them without ſome Judgment, for their Impriſonment as well as Fine, inaſmuch as the Statute of 2 *H.* 5. 8. is expreſs, That all Rioters attainted of great and heinous Riots ſhall have one whole Year's Impriſonment at the leaſt, without Bail, *&c.* and that Rioters attainted of Petit Riots, ſhall have Impriſonment, as beſt ſhall ſeem to the King or to his Council.

Crom. 63. a. Pult. 24. b. Dalt. ca. 46. See 1 Leon. 282.

Sect. 36. Formerly, if the Fine impoſed upon Rioters by Juſtices of Peace had been too favourable, it was a common Practice for the Court of Star-Chamber afterwards to impoſe ſuch other Fine as might, together with that which was aſſeſſed by the Juſtices of Peace, be proportionable to the Heinouſneſs of the Offence; and this was ſaid not to be a double Puniſhment for the ſame Offence, but only an Award of due Penalty at ſeveral Times.

Sect. 37. It is farther enacted by the ſaid Statute of 13 *H.* 4. 7. *That if the Truth cannot be found in the Manner as is aforeſaid, then within a Month then next following, the Juſtices, three, or two of them, and the Sheriff, or Under-Sheriff, ſhall certify before the King and his Council all the Deed and the Circumſtances thereof: Which Certificate ſhall be of like Force as the Preſentment of twelve Men; upon which Certificate the ſaid Treſpaſſers and Offenders ſhall be put to anſwer, and they which ſhall be found guilty, ſhall be puniſhed according to the Diſcretion of the King and his Council. And if ſuch Treſpaſſers and Offenders do traverſe the Matter ſo certified, the ſame Certificate and Traverſe ſhall be ſent into the King's Bench, there to be tried and determined, as the Law requireth; and if they appear not before the King and his Council, or in the King's Bench, upon ſuch Proceſs and Proclamation for their Appearance as are required by the ſaid Statute, they ſhall be attainted of the Riot,* &c.

Sect. 38. And it is farther Enacted by 19 *H.* 7. 13. *That if a Riot,* &c. *be not found by the Jury by reaſon of any Maintenance or Embracery of the Jurors, then the ſame Juſtices,* &c. *over and above ſuch Certificate which they muſt and are bound to make by the ſaid Statute of* 13 *H.* 4. 7. *ſhall in the ſame Certificate certify the Names and Miſdemeanours of ſuch Maintainers,* &c. *on Pain that every of the ſaid Juſtices,* &c. *ſhall forfeit twenty Pounds, if they have no reaſonable Excuſe for not certifying the ſame; which Certificate ſo made, ſhall be of like Force as if the Matter were found by Verdict of twelve Men; and every Perſon duly proved to be ſuch a Maintainer,* &c. *ſhall forfeit twenty Pounds,* &c.

Lamb. 323, 326. Pult. 29. b. Dalt. ca. 46.

Sect. 39. In the Conſtruction of theſe Statutes it hath been holden, That the Certificate required by the above mentioned Statutes may be made, either by the Juſtices, *&c.* who went to ſee the Riot, or by thoſe who took the Inquiry; but it ſeems to be moſt proper, That where-ever ſuch an Inquiſition is taken, ſuch Certificate ſhould be made by ſuch Juſtices who made the Inquiry, becauſe they having had the Examination of the Fact, muſt needs be beſt able to judge of the Circumſtances thereof, and in that Reſpect are the moſt proper Perſons to ſupply the Defects of the Inquiry: However the ſaid Statute of 19 *H.* 7. 13. which is grafted on 13 *H.* 4. 7. ſeems clearly to imply, That ſome Juſtices are bound in a more eſpecial Manner to make ſuch Certificate than any others, by impoſing the Penalty of twenty Pounds on thoſe who neglect to make it as they are bound by 13 *H.* 4. 7. which Part of the Statute ſeems to be moſt reaſonably applied to thoſe Juſtices who took the Inquiry, or in Caſe that no Inquiry was taken, to thoſe Juſtices who endeavoured to take one, but by the Fault of others were hindered from taking it; for there was no Need of ſuch an additional Penalty on the neighbouring Juſtices who were bound before to do their Duty in executing 13 *H.* 4. 7.

under Pain of forfeiting one hundred Pounds, as will be ſhewn Section 44, *&c.*

Sect. 40. Alſo it is generally ſaid, That ſuch a Certificate muſt be made within a Month after the Inquiry; and this ſeems to be a very reaſonable Conſtruction where an Inquiry has actually been made; but it may happen that no Inquiry at all may be taken, either through the Default of the Sheriff in not returning a Jury, or the Obſtinacy of the Jurors in refuſing to appear, or the rebellious Humour of the People in not ſuffering the Juſtices to do their Duty; in all which Caſes a Certificate ſeems to be required, both by the Intent and Letter of the Statute, the Words whereof as to this Purpoſe are, *If the Truth cannot be found in the Manner as is aforeſaid, then within a Month then next following, the Juſtices,* &c. *ſhall certify,* &c. And therefore in theſe Caſes it ſeems proper to make a Certificate of the Obſtructions, which prevented the Taking of ſuch an Inquiry, within a Month after they happen. Pult. 29 b. Lamb. 324. Dalt. cap. 46.

Sect. 41. It ſeemeth clear from the plain Words of the Statute, That the Certificate ought to be made to the Privy Council-board, which is clearly diſtinguiſhed, both from the Chancery, and alſo from the King's Bench, which, in ſome Statutes relating to judicial Proceedings, are taken for the King's Council. Lamb. 324. Con. Crompt. 63. b. Dalt ca. 46, & 130. Bro. Præm. 1.

Sect. 42. It is ſaid, That if there be a Variance between the Inquiſition and Certificate, that ſhall be taken which is moſt for the King's Advantage; and therefore if the Inquiſition be of a Riot by ten Perſons, and the Certificate of a Riot by twenty, or by ten in Harneſs; or of a Battery join'd with the Riot, that the Certificate ſhall be preferred, becauſe the Fine to the King ſhall be the greater; but if they differ only as to the Time, it is ſaid that the Inquiſition ſhall be preferred. Pul. 29. b. Cro. 63. b. Lamb. 325. Dal. ca. 46. Lamb. 326. Pul. 29. b.

Sect. 43. Alſo it ſeemeth certain, That ſuch a Certificate, being in Nature of an Indictment at Common Law, ought to comprehend the Certainty of Time, Place, and Perſons, and other material Circumſtances, both of the Riots and Maintenance, *&c.* but perhaps it needs not expreſs the Additions of the Offenders. Dal. ca. 46, & ca. 130. Lam. 321, 322.

Sect. 44. It is farther enacted by the ſaid Statute of 13 *H.* 4. 7. *That the Juſtices of Peace dwelling nigheſt in every County where ſuch Riot, Aſſembly, or Rout of People ſhall be made hereafter, together with the Sheriff or Under-Sheriff of the ſame County, and alſo the Juſtices of Aſſizes, for the Time that they ſhall be there in their Seſſion, in caſe that any ſuch Riot, Aſſembly, or Rout be made in their Preſence, ſhall do Execution of this Statute, every one upon Pain of one hundred Pounds, to be paid to the King as often as they ſhall be found in default of the Execution of the ſame Statute.*

In the Conſtruction of this Clauſe the following Opinions have been holden,

Sect. 45. I. That no Juſtice of Peace is in danger of incurring the Penalty thereof, unleſs he dwell in the County wherein a Riot happens. Lamb. 236. Crom. 63. b. Dal. ca. 46.

Sect. 46. II. That if any Juſtices of Peace, who do not dwell neareſt to the Place, do actually execute the Statute, they excuſe all the reſt. Dal. ca. 46. Lamb. 326. Crom. 63. b. Pult. 30. a.

Sect. 47. III. That if the Juſtices whoſe Dwelling was neareſt at the Time of the Riot, or one of them, happen to die within the Month, thoſe whoſe Dwelling is thereby become the neareſt are bound to execute the Statute in the ſame Manner as the others were. Crom. 62. b.

Lamb. 327. Dal. ca. 46. Pult. 30. a. *Sect.* 48. IV. That notwithstanding those Justices only, who dwell nearest, are liable to the Penalty of the Statute, yet if any others on Notice neglect to supply their Default, they are fineable at Discretion.

Crom. 63. b. Lamb. 327. Dal. ca. 46. Pult. 30. a. *Sect.* 49. V. That if the two Justices, or one of them, do their Duty in executing, or endeavouring to execute the Statute, they shall not incur any Penalty thro' a Default of the Sheriff, *&c.* either in refusing to appear, or to return a Jury, *&c.*

Sect. 50. VI. That the said Justices, *&c.* shall not avoid the Penalty Crom. 61. b. by executing the Statute in Part only, as by recording a Riot without committing the Parties.

Sect. 51. VII. That no Justice, *&c.* is subject to the Penalty of the Dal. ca. 46. said Statute on account of a Petit Riot, but only of such as are notorious, and in nature of Insurrections and Rebellions.

Dy. 210. Pl. 25. Lamb. 328. Pult. 28. b. Crom. 62 b. Dal. ca. 46. *Sect.* 52. VIII. That if a Justice of Peace, *&c.* had no express Notice given him of the Riot, he shall be excused, unless it were so very flagrant, that by common Intendment, every one dwelling near it could not but have Notice thereof.

Crom. 62. b. Lamb. 322. Pult. 28. Dalt. ca. 46. Crom. 64. a. *Sect.* 53. IX. That the Acquiescence or Agreement of the Parties aggrieved is no Excuse to the Justices, because they ought, *ex Officio*, to make the Inquiry, and make Proclamation whether any will give Evidence for the King, *&c.* and may bind such of the Parties grieved as shall refuse to prosecute their Complaint to their Good Behaviour.

Sect. 54. Also it is farther enacted by 2 *H.* 5. 8. *That upon any Default of the said Justices,* &c. *touching the Execution of* 13 H. 4. *a Commission shall be awarded at the Instance of the Party grieved, to enquire as well of the Truth of the Case, as of the Default of the said Justices,* &c. *and that the said Commissioners shall presently return into Chancery the Inquests before them taken; and that the Jurors, who shall make Inquiry, shall be worth* 10 l. per Annum, *and shall be returned by the Coroners, if the Sheriff, supposed to be in Default, continue in his Office,* &c. *See the Statute.*

Sect. 55. Also it is farther enacted by 2 *H.* 5. 9. and 8 *H.* 6. 14. *That the Lord Chancellor, upon Complaint made to him, that a dangerous Rioter is fled into Places unknown, and also upon a Suggestion under the Seals of two Justices of Peace and the Sheriff, that the common Fame and Voice runneth in the County of the Riot, may award a* Capias *against the Party returnable in Chancery upon a certain Day,* &c. *and afterwards a Writ of Proclamation returnable in the King's Bench,* &c.

Sect. 56. But all the Penalties of the above mentioned Statutes having been found by Experience not to be sufficient to restrain the Rage of the Populace from breaking out into dangerous Tumults, whenever they happen to be perswaded that they lie under any real or pretended Grievance, it was thought necessary to make a farther Provision against such insolent Disturbances of the Peace, by more severe Laws; and to this End it was enacted by 1 *Geor.* 1. *c.* 5. *That if any Persons to the Number of twelve, or more, being unlawfully, riotously, and tumultuously assembled together, to the Disturbance of the publick Peace, and being required or commanded by any Justice of Peace, Sheriff of the County, or Under-Sheriff, or by the Mayor, Bailiff or Bailiffs, or other Head-Officer or Justice of the Peace of any City, or Town corporate, where such Assembly shall be, by Proclamation to be made in the King's Name, immediately to disperse themselves, and peaceably to depart to their Habitations, or to their lawful Business, under the Pains of the said Statute, shall afterwards unlawfully, riotously, and tumultuously continue together by the Space of one Hour after such Proclamation made, or after a wilful Let or Hindrance of a Justice*

ſtice of Peace, &c. *from making the ſaid Proclamation, ſhall be adjudged Felons without Benefit of Clergy.*

Sect. 57. And it is farther enacted by the ſaid Statute, *That if any Perſon or Perſons ſhall with Force and Arms wilfully and knowingly oppoſe, obſtruct, or in any Manner wilfully and knowingly, let, hinder, or hurt any Perſon,* &c. *who ſhall begin to proclaim, or go to proclaim, according to the Proclamation appointed by the ſaid Statute, whereby ſuch Proclamation ſhall not be made, they ſhall be adjudged Felons without Benefit of Clergy.*

Sect. 58. And it is farther enacted by the ſaid Statute, *That if any Perſons unlawfully, riotouſly, and tumultuouſly aſſembled together, to the Diſturbance of the Publick Peace, ſhall unlawfully and with Force demoliſh or pull down, or begin to demoliſh or pull down, any Church or Chapel, or any Building for religious Worſhip, certified and regiſtered according to* 1 Will. & Mar. 18. *which is commonly called* The Toleration Act, *or any Dwelling-houſe, Barn, Stable, or other Out-houſe, they ſhall be adjudged Felons without Benefit of Clergy.*

Sect. 59. And it is farther enacted by the ſaid Statute, *That when-ever any ſuch Church,* &c. *ſhall be demoliſhed,* &c. *by any ſuch Rioters,* &c. *the Inhabitants of the Town or Hundred wherein the Riot happened, ſhall be bound to make good the Damage,* &c.

CHAP. LXVI.

Of Offences by Officers in general.

OFFENCES under the Degree of capital, more immediately againſt the Subject, not amounting to an actual Diſturbance of the Peace, are either;

1. Such as are committed by Officers; or,
2. Such as are committed by common Perſons without any Relation to an Office.

Offences by Officers ſeem reducible to the following Heads:

1. Neglect, or Breach of Duty.
2. Bribery.
3. Extortion.

Sect. 1. As to the firſt of theſe Offences, I take it to be agreed, That in the Grant of every Office whatſoever, there is this Condition implied by common Reaſon, that the Grantee ought to execute it diligently and faithfully: For ſince every Office is inſtituted, not for the ſake of the Officer, but for the good of ſome other, nothing can be more juſt, than that he, who either neglects or refuſes to anſwer the End for which his Office was ordained, ſhould give way to others who are both able and willing to take Care of it. And therefore it is certain, That an Officer is liable to a Forfeiture of his Office, not only for doing a Thing directly contrary to the Deſign of it, but alſo for neglecting to attend his Duty Co Lit. 233. 234.

Duty at all uſual, proper, and convenient Times and Places, whereby any Damage ſhall accrue to thoſe, by or for whom he was made an Of-
9 Co. 50. Co. Lit. 233. ficer. And ſome have gone ſo far as to hold, That an Office concerning the Adminiſtration of Juſtice, or the Common Wealth, ſhall be forfeited for a bare Non-Uſer, whether any ſpecial Damage be occaſioned thereby or not: But this Opinion doth not appear to be warranted by any Reſo-
[a] 39 H. 6. 32. 20 Ed. 4. 5. b. 22 Aſſ. 34. 2 H. 7. 11. b. Plow. Com. 379. Long Quinto Ed. 4. 27. 11 Ed. 4. 1. lution in Point, and the [a] Authorities which are cited to maintain it, do not ſeem to come up to it: However it cannot but be very reaſonable, That he who ſo far neglects a publick Office, as plainly to appear to take no manner of Care of it, ſhould rather be immediately diſplaced, than the publick be in danger of ſuffering that Damage, which cannot but be expected ſome Time or other from his Negligence.

Sect. 2. But it would be endleſs to enumerate all the particular Inſtances, wherein an Officer may be diſcharged or fined; and it alſo ſeems needleſs to endeavour it, becauſe they are generally ſo obvious to common Senſe, as to need no Explication; for what can be more plain, than
[b] 9 Co. 50. a. [c] Raym. 216. [d] Cro. Ja. 42. b. that a Gaoler deſerves to be diſcharged and fined, for voluntarily [b] ſuffering his Priſoners to eſcape, or for [c] barbarouſly miſuſing them? What can be more evident, than that a [d] Sheriff is juſtly puniſhable for perſwading a Jury to underprize Goods in the Execution of a *Fieri Facias, &c.* And therefore I ſhall leave the particular Caſes of this Nature to every Man's own Judgment, which, from the Conſideration of the general Rules above mentioned, and the various Circumſtances of every Caſe, will eaſily diſcern how far each Offence of this Kind deſerves to be puniſhed.

CHAP. LXVII.

Of Bribery.

IN treating of Bribery, I ſhall conſider,

1. What it is.
2. How it is puniſhable.

3 Inſt. 145. *Sect.* 1. And firſt, Bribery in a ſtrict Senſe is taken for a great Miſpriſion of one in a judicial Place, taking any valuable Thing whatſoever, except Meat and Drink of ſmall Value, of any one who has to do before him any way, for doing his Office, or by Colour of his Office, but of the King only.

3 Inſt. 149. Hob. 9. Cro. Ja. 65. *Sect.* 2. But Bribery in a large Senſe is ſometimes taken for the receiving or offering of any undue Reward, by or to any Perſon whatſoever, whoſe ordinary Profeſſion or Buſineſs relates to the Adminiſtration of publick Juſtice, in order to incline him to do a Thing againſt the known Rules of Honeſty and Integrity; for the Law abhors any the leaſt Tendency to Corruption in thoſe who are any way concerned in its Adminiſtration, and will not endure their taking a Reward for the doing a Thing which deſerves the ſevereſt of Puniſhments.

3 Inſt. 148. *Sect.* 3. Alſo Bribery ſometimes ſignifies the taking or giving of a Reward for Offices of a publick Nature; and ſurely nothing can be more

palpably prejudicial to the Good of the Publick, than to have Places of the highest Concernment, on the due Execution whereof the Happiness of both King and People doth depend, disposed of not to those who are most able to execute them, but to those who are most able to pay for them; nor can any thing be a greater Discouragement to Industry and Virtue, than to see those Places of Trust and Honour, which ought to be the Rewards of those who by their Industry and Diligence have qualified themselves for them, conferred
on such who have no other Recommendation but that of being the highest Bid- Vide Noy
ders; neither can any thing be a greater Temptation to Officers to abuse their 102. Moore 781.
Power by Bribery and Extortion, and other Acts of Injustice, than the Consideration of the great Expence they were at in gaining their Places, and the Necessity of sometimes straining a Point to make their Bargain answer their Expectation; for which Reasons, among many others, it is expresly enacted by 12 *Rich.* 2. 2. *That the Chancellor, Treasurer, Keeper of the Privy Seal, Steward of the King's House, the King's Chamberlain, Clerk of the Rolls, the Justices of the one Bench and of the other, Barons of the Exchequer, and all other, that shall be called to ordain, name, or make Justices of the Peace, Sheriffs, Escheators, Customers, Comptrollers, or any other Officer or Minister of the King, shall be firmly sworn that they shall not ordain, name, or make, any of the above mentioned Officers, for any Gift or Brocage, Favour or Affection, nor that none which sueth by himself, or by others, privily, or openly, to be in any Manner of Office, shall be put in the same Office, or in any other, but that they make all such Officers and Ministers of the best and most lawful Men, and sufficient to their Estimation and Knowledge.* Also it is farther enacted by 4 *H.* 4.
5. *That no Sheriff shall let his Bailiwick to Farm to any Man, for the Time* Vide Noy
that he occupieth such Office, &c. Also it is enacted by 5 & 6 *Ed.* 6. 16. *That if* 102. Moore 781.
any Person shall bargain or sell, or take any Reward, or Promise of any Reward for any Office, or the Deputation of any Office, any way concerning the King's Revenue, or the Keeping of his Castles, or the Administration or Execution of Justice, (unless it be such an Office as had been usually granted before the making of the said Act by the Justices of the King's Bench, or common Pleas, or by Justices of Assize) that then every such Person so bargaining or selling, or taking such Reward, or Promise, &c. *shall not only forfeit his Right to such Office, or to the Nomination thereof, but also every Person who shall give any such Reward or Promise,* &c. *shall be adjudged a disabled Person in Law, to have or enjoy such Office,* &c.

In the Construction of this Statute of 5 & 6 *Ed.* 6. the following Points have been resolved;

Sect. 4. I. That the Offices of Chancellor, Register, and Commissary in Cro. Ja. 269.
Ecclesiastical Courts, are within the Meaning of the Statute, inasmuch as 3 Inst. 148. Salk. 468.
those Courts do not only determine Matters which are brought before them, 2 Lev. 289.
merely *pro salute Animæ*, but also have the Decision of Disputes concerning 4 Vent. 187, 467.
the Lawfulness of Matrimony and Ligitimation of Children, which touch the Inheritance of the Subjects, and also hold Plea of Legacies and Tithes,
&c. in which respects they are Courts of Justice; but it hath been adjudged, 2 Lev. 151.
that no Office in Fee is within the Statue.

Sect. 5. II. That one, who makes a Contract for an Office contrary to Hob. 75. Co. Litt. 234.
the Purport of the said Statute, is so far disabled to hold the same, that he Cro. Ca. 361.
cannot at any Time during his Life be restored to a Capacity of holding it by Cro. Ja. 386.
any Grant or Dispensation whatsoever. Sal. 466, 468.

III. That a Bond by a Deputy of an Office to pay a certain Sum, at all 6 Mod. 234. 3 Co. 32. b.
Events is within the Statute, and consequently totally void, tho' it also con- Cro. Eliz.
tain other Conditions which, if they stood by themselves would be good; but 529, 530. 1 And. 107,
not a Bond to pay Half the Profits, or a certain Sum out of the Profits of 150.
the Office for a Deputation.

IV. That the Statute extends not to Offices in the Plantations. Salk. 411. Quære 2 Mo. 45.

3 Inst. 145. *Sect.* 6. As to the second Point, *viz.* How Bribery is punishable; it is said, That at Common Law, Bribery in a Judge, in relation to a Cause de- 1 H. H. P. C. 262. pending before him, was looked upon as an Offence of so heinous a Nature, that it was sometimes punished as High Treason before the 25 *Ed.* 3. And at 1 Leon. 295. Cro. Ja. 65. Rushw. Collections, part 1. fol. 31. this Day it is certainly a very high Offence, and punishable, not only with the Forfeiture of the Offender's Office of Justice, but also with Fine and Imprisonment, &c.

Sect. 7. Also all the other above mentioned Kinds of Bribery, taken in a large Sense, seem to be punishable with Fine and Imprisonment, &c. and in the Time of King *James* the First, the Earl of *M.* Lord High Treasurer 3 Inst. 148. of *England*, being impeached by the Commons for refusing to hear Petitions referred to him by the King, till he had received great Bribes, and for other such like Misdemeanors, was, by Sentence of the Lords, deprived of all his Offices, and disabled to have any for the Future, or to sit in the Parliament, and was fined fifty thousand Pounds, and imprisoned during the King's Pleasure. [82] ☞

CHAP. LXVIII.

Of Extortion.

IN treating of Extortion, I shall consider,

1. What shall be called Extortion;
2. How it shall be punished.

Co. Lit. 368. 10 Co. 102. a. *Sect.* 1. As to the first Point it is said, that Extortion in a large Sense signifies any Oppression under Colour of Right; but that in a strict Sense it signifies the Taking of Money by any Officer, by Colour of his Office, either where none at all is due, or not so much is due, or where it is not yet due.

2 Inst. 209. Co. Lit. 368. *Sect.* 2. It is said, That at the Common Law, which was affirmed by the Statute of *Westminster* 1. 26. it was Extortion for any Sheriff or other Minister of the King, whose Office did any way concern the Administration or Execution of Justice, or the common Good of the Subject, to take any Reward whatsoever for doing his Office, except what he received from the King: And surely this was a most excellent Institution, highly tending to promote the Honour of the King, and the Ease of the 42 Ed. 3. 4. b. 5. a. 2 Rol. Ab. 266. H. 1. People, and hath been always thought to conduce so much to the publick Good, that all Prescriptions whatsoever which have been contrary to it have been holden to be void; and upon this Ground it hath been resolved, 4 Inst. 274. Moore 523. 2 Inst. 209. That the Prescription, by virtue whereof the Clerk of the Market claimed certain Fees for the View and Examination of all Weights and Measures, &c. was merely void.

21 H. 7. 17. 2 Inst. 210. 2 Inst. 176. S. P. C. 49. A. *Sect.* 3. But it hath been holden, That the Fee of twenty Pence, commonly called the Bar-Fee, which hath been taken, Time out of Mind, by the Sheriff, of every Prisoner who is acquitted, and also the Fee of one Penny, which was claimed by the Coroner of every Visne, when he came before the Justices in Eyre, are not within the Meaning of the said Statute, because they are not demanded by the Sheriff or Coroner for doing any Thing relating to their Offices, but claimed as Perquisites of Right belonging to them, whether they do any thing or

not. But there seemeth to be no Necessity for this Distinction, for it cannot be intended to be the Meaning of the Statute to restrain the Courts of Justice, in whose Integrity the Law always reposes the highest Confidence, from allowing reasonable Fees for the Labour and Attendance of their Officers: For the chief Danger of Oppression is from Officers being left at their Liberty to set their own Rates on their Labour, and make their own Demands; but there cannot be so much Fear of these Abuses, while they are restrained to known and stated Fees, settled by the Discretion of the Courts, which will not suffer them to be exceeded, without the highest Resentment. 21 H. 7. 17. Co. Lit. 368.

Sect. 4. Also it having been found by Experience, That generally it is vain to expect that any Officers who depend upon a known fixed Salary, without having any immediate Benefit from any particular Instances of their Duty, should be so ready in undertaking, or diligent in executing them, as they would be, if they were to have a present Advantage from them; it hath been thought expedient to permit them to take certain Fees in many Cases, but it is certain that they are guilty of Extortion, if they take any Thing more: Also it hath been resolved, That a Promise to pay them Money for the doing of a Thing, which the Law will not suffer them to take any thing for, is merely void, however freely and voluntarily it may appear to have been made; for if once it should be allowed, That such Promises could maintain an Action, the People would quickly be given to understand how kindly they would be taken, and happy would that Man be who could have his Business well done without them. 3 Inst. 149. 2 Inst. 210. Co. Lit. 368. 1 Rol. A. 16. Pl. 2, 3, 5. 26, 41. 1 Rol. R. 313. Noy 76. 1 Jones 65. Cro. El. 654. Moore 468. Cro. Ja. 103.

Sect. 5. As to the second Point, *viz.* How Extortion shall be punished, there is no doubt, but that at Common Law it is severely punishable, at the King's Suit, by Fine and Imprisonment; and also by a Removal from the Office, in the Execution whereof it was committed. Also Extortion in Sheriffs, Escheators, Bailiffs, Gaolers, the King's Clerk of the Market, and other inferiour Ministers and Officers of the King, whose Offices do any way concern the Administration or Execution of Justice, or the common Good of the Subject, or for the King's Service, have a farther additional Punishment by the above mentioned Statute of *Westminster* 1. 26. by which it is enacted, *That no Sheriff, nor other King's Officer, shall take any Reward to do his Office, but shall be paid of that which they take of the King, and that he who so doth, shall yield twice as much, and shall be punished at the King's Pleasure.* 2 Rol. A. 32, 33, 75. Pl. 1, 2. Raymond 315. 2 Inst. 209.

CHAP. LXIX.

Of Perjury.

OFFENCES under the Degree of capital, more immediately against the Subject, not amounting to an actual Disturbance of the Peace, which may be committed by private Persons, without any Relation to an Office; are either,

1. Such as are infamous, and grosly scandalous, proceeding from Principles of downright Dishonesty, Malice, or Faction.
2. Such as are of an inferiour Nature, and neither infamous, nor grosly scandalous.

Those

Thoſe of the firſt Kind ſeem to be reducible to the following Heads;

1. Perjury, and Subornation of Perjury.
2. Forgery.
3. Cheats.
4. Conſpiracy.
5. Keeping of a Bawdy-houſe.
6. Libels

And firſt of Perjury, and Subornation of Perjury, of both which there are two Kinds:

1. By the Common Law.
2. By Statute.

Sect. 1. Perjury, by the Common Law, ſeemeth to be a wilful falſe Oath, by one who being lawfully required to depoſe the Truth in any Proceeding in a Courſe of Juſtice, ſwears abſolutely, in a Matter of ſome Conſequence to the Point in queſtion, whether he be believed, or not?

For the better Underſtanding whereof, I ſhall conſider the following Particulars:

1. How far this Offence muſt be wilful.
2. In what Kind of Proceedings it may be committed.
3. In what Caſes an Oath may be ſaid to be ſo far lawfully adminiſtred, that he who takes it may become guilty of Perjury.
4. In what Kind of Oaths Perjury may be committed.
5. Whether the Matter of the Oath muſt be falſe.
6. How far the Oath muſt be abſolute.
7. How far the Things ſworn ought to be material to the Point in Queſtion.
8. How far the falſe Oath muſt be credited.

5 Mod. 350. *Sect.* 2. As to the firſt Particular, *viz.* How far this Offence muſt be wilful, it ſeemeth that no one ought to be found guilty thereof without clear Proof, That the falſe Oath alledged againſt him was taken with ſome Degree of Deliberation; for if upon the whole Circumſtances of the Caſe it ſhall appear probable, That it was owing rather to the Weakneſs than Perverſeneſs of the Party, as where it was occaſioned by Surprize, or Inadvertency, or a Miſtake of the true State of the Queſtion, it cannot but be hard to make it amount to voluntary and corrupt Perjury, which is of all Crimes whatſoever the moſt Infamous and Deteſtable.

Sect. 3. As to the ſecond Particular, *viz.* In what Kind of Proceed-
Cro. El. 168, 169. Noy 128. 2 Rol. Ab. 257. Hob. 62.
ings this Offence may be committed, it ſeems to be clearly agreed, That all ſuch falſe Oaths as are taken before thoſe who are any ways intruſted with the Adminiſtration of publick Juſtice, in relation to any Matter before them in Debate, are properly Perjuries; and it ſeems to have been holden by ſome, That all ſuch falſe Oaths, as are taken before Perſons authorized by the King to examine Witneſſes in relation to any Matter whatſoever, wherein his Honour or Intereſt are concerned, are alſo puniſhable as Perjuries. And ſurely there can be no Offence of this Nature which will not juſtly deſerve a publick Proſecution, in as much as if it ſhould once prevail, it would make it impoſſible to have any Law whatſoever

5 ſoever

ſoever duly executed, and expoſe the Lives, Liberties, and Properties, of the moſt Innocent, to the Mercy of the greateſt Villains: And therefore it hath been holden, That not only ſuch Perſons are indictable for Perjury, who take a falſe Oath in a Court of Record, upon an Iſſue therein joined, but alſo all thoſe who forſwear themſelves in a Matter judicially depending before any Court of [a] Equity, or Spiritual [b] Court, or any other [c] lawful Court, whether the Proceedings therein be of Record or not [d] or whether they concern the Intereſt of the King or Subject: And it is ſaid to be no way material, whether ſuch falſe Oath be taken in the Face of a Court, or before Perſons authorized by it to examine a Matter, the Knowledge whereof is neceſſary for the right Determination of a Cauſe; and [e] therefore, That a falſe Oath before a Sheriff, upon a Writ of Inquiry of Damages, is as much puniſhable as if it were taken before the Court on a Trial of the Cauſe. Alſo it ſeemeth, That any falſe Oath is puniſhable, as Perjury, which tends to miſlead the Court in any of their Proceedings relating to a Matter judicially before them, though it no way affect the principal Judgment which is to be given in the Cauſe; as where a [f] Perſon who offers himſelf to be Bail for another, knowingly, and wilfully ſwears that his Subſtance is greater than it is. Alſo it hath been reſolved, That not only ſuch Oaths as are taken upon judicial Proceedings, but alſo all ſuch as any way tend to abuſe the Adminiſtration of Juſtice, are properly Perjuries; as where one [g] takes a falſe Oath before a Juſtice of Peace, in order to induce him to compel another to find Sureties for the Peace, *&c.* or where a Perſon forſwears himſelf [h] before Commiſſioners appointed by the King to inquire of the Forfeitures of his Tenants Eſtates, *&c.* whereby he makes them liable to be ſeized by Exchequer-Proceſs: Alſo it hath been ſaid, That a falſe Oath is puniſhable as Perjury, in ſome Caſes, wherein the King's Honour or Intereſt is concerned, though it do not concern the Adminiſtration of Juſtice; as where one ſwears a falſe Oath concerning the Poſſeſſion of Lands, before Commiſſioners appointed by the King to inquire of ſuch Perſons whoſe Titles to the Lands in their Poſſeſſion are defective, and want the Supply of the King's Patents: And this is certainly an Offence of a very heinous Nature, [i] tending not only to fruſtrate the King's gracious Purpoſe, but to abuſe his Goodneſs by inducing him to grant his Patents to thoſe who are out of Poſſeſſion, and no way within the Intent of the Commiſſion, which, inſtead of quieting the Poſſeſſions of the Subjects, cannot but end in the greateſt Diſturbance of them. However it ſeemeth certain, That no Oath whatſoever in a mere private Matter, howſoever wilful or malicious it may be, is puniſhable as Perjury in a criminal Proſecution; for private Injuries are left to be redreſſed by private Actions; and upon this Ground it hath been holden, That a falſe Oath taken by one upon the making of a Bargain, that the Thing ſold is his own, is not puniſhable as Perjury. Alſo from what hath been ſaid it appears, That the Notion of Perjury is confined to ſuch publick Oaths only as affirm or deny ſome Matter of Fact, contrary to the knowledge of the Party; and therefore, That it doth not extend to any promiſſory Oaths whatſoever; from which it clearly follows, That no Officer, publick or private, who neglects to execute his Office in Purſuance of his Oath, or acts contrary to the Purport of it, is indictable for Perjury, in reſpect of ſuch Oath; yet it is certain, That his Offence is highly aggravated by being contrary to his Oath, and therefore, that he is liable to the ſeverer Fine on that Account.

[a] Cro. El. 907. Skin. 327. 1 Sid. 418. 1 Rol. A. 40. Pl. 16, 17, 18, 20, 21. 5 Mod. 348.
[b] Cro. El. 185, 609. 2 Rol. Re. 410. 1 Rol. A. 40. Pl. 12. 1 Leon. 131. Con. Dy. 243. Pl. 53.
[c] 2 Rol. Ab. 257. Pl. 2. 1 Rol. Ab. 41. Pl. 19. 42, 30. Winch 3. 5 Mod. 348. Hutton 34. 1 Mod. 55. Yelv. 27. Cro. El. 297, 342, 348, 905.
[d] 12 Co. 101. Cro. Ja. 212. Con. Cro. Ja. 120. Vide Sect. 18.
[e] 1 Rol. Ab. 39. Pl. 3. 42, 27.
[f] Cro. Ca. 146.
[g] 2 Rol. Re. 410. 2 Rol. Ab. 77. Pl. 5.
[h] Noy 100. Moor 627
[i] Hob. 62.
Cont. 1 Vent. 369, 370.
3 Rol. Ab. 257. Pl. 4
2 Rol. Ab. 257. Pl. 5. 3 Inſt. 166.

Sect. 4. As to the third Particular, *viz.* In what Caſes an Oath may be ſaid to be ſo far lawfully adminiſtred, that he who takes it may become guilty of Perjury by ſwearing falſly; it ſeemeth clear, That no Oath whatſoever taken before [a] Perſons acting merely in a private [b] Capacity, or [c] before thoſe who take upon them to adminiſter Oaths of a publick Nature, without legal Authority for their ſo doing, or [d] before thoſe who are legally authorized to adminiſter ſome kinds of Oaths, but not thoſe which happen to be taken before them, or even [e] before thoſe who take upon them to adminiſter Juſtice by Virtue of an Authority ſeemingly colourable, but in Truth unwarranted and meerly void, can ever amount to Perjuries in the Eye of the Law, becauſe they are of no Manner of Force, but are altogether idle: And from the ſame Ground it ſeemeth alſo clearly to follow, That no falſe Oath in an Affidavit, made before Perſons falſly pretending to be authorized by a Court of Juſtice to take Affidavits in relation to Matters depending before ſuch Court, can properly be called Perjury, becauſe no Affidavit, is any way regarded, unleſs it be made before Perſons legally intruſted with a Power to take it, as being both of ſufficient Ability to aſk all proper Queſtions of the Party who ſhall make ſuch Affidavit, and alſo of ſuch Integrity as not to ſuffer any Thing to be inſerted therein, to the Truth whereof the Party hath not ſworn. And though it may be ſaid, That an Affidavit taken before Perſons falſly pretending to be commiſſioned for ſuch Purpoſe by the Courts of Juſtice, doth directly tend to impoſe upon ſuch Courts, and may poſſibly happen through Surprize to be read, and may alſo in its own Nature be altogether as heinous, as if it had been made before Perſons regularly impowered to take it; yet inaſmuch as it is of it ſelf of no manner of Validity, and is no otherwiſe regarded, than as it hath the Appearance of being ſworn before Perſons legally commiſſioned, without which it would have no manner of Credit, it ſeemeth that Offences of this Nature are moſt properly puniſhed, by ſeverely chaſtiſing thoſe who uſurp ſuch an Authority of adminiſtring of Oaths, without any legal Warrant. However it hath been adjudged, That a falſe Oath, taken before Perſons who having been commiſſioned to examine Witneſſes, happen to proceed after the Demiſe of the King who gave them their Commiſſion, and before Notice thereof, may be puniſhed as Perjury; for it would be of the utmoſt ill Conſequence to make ſuch Proceedings void; and therefore though all ſuch Commiſſions be in Strictneſs legally determined by the Demiſe of the King, who gave them, without any Notice; yet for the Neceſſity of the Caſe, whatever is done under them before ſuch Notice, muſt be ſuffered to ſtand good; for otherwiſe the moſt innocent and moſt deſerving Subjects would be unavoidably expoſed to numberleſs Proſecutions for doing their Duties, without any Colour of a Fault. And *Quære*, Whether a Perjury in a Court whoſe Proceedings are afterwards reverſed by Error, may not ſtill be puniſhed as Purjury, notwithſtanding ſuch Reverſal.

Sect. 5. As to the fourth Particular, *viz.* In what kind of Oaths Perjury may be committed, it ſeemeth clear, That a Man may be in Danger of being guilty thereof, not only in reſpect of a falſe Oath, taken by him as a Witneſs for another, but alſo in reſpect of a falſe Oath taken by him in his own Cauſe, either in an Anſwer to Queſtions put to him in a Court of [f] Law or [g] Equity, having Power to purge him upon Oath concerning his Knowledge of the Matters in Diſpute, or in his [h] Affidavit concerning ſome collateral Matter, wherein the Parties own Oaths are allowed to be taken. But it ſeems, That a Juror who gives a Verdict contrary to manifeſt Evidence, is not properly guilty of Perjury within the above mentioned Deſcription, becauſe he is not ſworn to depoſe the Truth, but

[a] 2 Rol. Ab. 257. 3 Inſt. 165. Yelv. 72.
[b] Cro. El. 169. 3 Inſt. 165.
[c] 1 Sid. 274. 2 Rol. Ab. 257. Pl. 6. Latch 38, 132.
[d] Yelv. 111. 3 Inſt. 166. See 4 Inſt. 97, 98. 29 Ca. 2. 25. 2 Rol. Re. 427. 4 Inſt. 278.
3 Inſt. 165.
Cro. Ca. 97, 98, 99.
1 Ventr. 181. 1 Syd. 148.
[f] 1 Rol. Ab. 40. Pl. 15, 83. Pl. 9. Cro. El. 609.
[g] 1 Leon. 127. Cro. El. 135, 905. 1 Rol. Ab. 40. Pl. 16, 17, 18. 69. Pl. 42. 1 Sid. 244.
[h] 1 Rol. Re. 79. Noy 128. 5 Mod. 348. Moor 656. Pl. 900. 2 Keb. 452. 2 Rol. Ab. 77. Pl. 4, 5.

only to give a true Judgment upon the Depoſition of others, and in many Caſes is not puniſhable at all *in foro humano*, as ſhall be ſet forth more at large in the Chapter of Conſpiracy.

Sect. 6. As to the fifth Particular, *viz.* How far the Matter of the
Oath which may amount to Perjury, muſt be falſe, it [d] is ſaid not to be [d] Palm. 294.
material whether the Fact which is ſworn, be in itſelf true or falſe; for Hetley 97. 2 Rol. Ab.
howſoever the Thing ſworn may happen to prove agreeable to the Truth, 77. Pl. 5.
yet if it were not known to be ſo by him who ſwears to it, his Offence 3 Inſt. 166. Con. 3 Mod.
is altogether as great as if it had been falſe inaſmuch as he wilfully ſwears, 122.
That he knows a Thing to be true, which at the ſame Time he knows nothing of, and impudently endeavours to induce thoſe before whom he ſwears to proceed upon the Credit of a Depoſition, which any Stranger might make as well as he.

Sect. 7. As to the ſixth Particular, *viz.* How far the Oath muſt be ab-
ſolute, it is ſaid, That no Oath ſhall amount to Perjury unleſs it be ſworn 3 Inſt. 166.
abſolutely and directly; and therefore, That he who ſwears a Thing according as he thinks, remembers or believes, cannot in reſpect of ſuch an Oath be found guilty of Perjury.

Sect. 8. As to the ſeventh Particular, *viz.* How far the Thing ſworn
ought to be material to the Point in Queſtion, it ſeemeth clear, That if the Vide infra Sect. 22.
Oath for which a Man is indicted of Perjury, be wholly foreign from that Aleyn 79.
Purpoſe, or altogether immaterial, and neither any way pertinent to the 1 Rol. Ab. 41.
Matter in Queſtion, not tending to aggravate or extenuate the Damages, Pl. 25. 78. Pl. 3.
nor likely to induce the Jury to give a readier Credit to the ſubſtantial Cro. El. 500.
Part of the Evidence, it cannot amount to Perjury, becauſe it is meerly Salk. 514.
idle and inſignificant; as if upon a Trial, in which the Queſtion is, whe- Noy 36. 2 Rol. Re.
ther ſuch a one was *Compos* or not, a Witneſs introduces his Evidence by 145.
giving a Hiſtory of a Journey which he took to ſee the Party, and hap- Cro. Ca. 321. Hob. 53.
pens to ſwear falſly in Relation to ſome of the Circumſtances of the Jour- Carth. 422.
ney. Alſo it hath been adjudged, That where a Witneſs being asked by a 5 Mod. 345,
Judge, whether *A.* brought a certain Number of Sheep from one Town 348.
to another all together? anſwered, That he did ſo; where in Truth *A.* did
not bring them all together, but Part at one Time and Part at another, 2 Rol. Re. 41.
yet ſuch Witneſs was not guilty of Perjury, becauſe the Subſtance of the Queſtion was, Whether *A.* did bring them at all or not, and that manner of bringing them was only a Circumſtance. And upon the ſame Ground
it is ſaid to have been adjudged, That where a Witneſs being asked, whe- 2 Rol. Re. 42.
ther ſuch a Sum of Money were paid for two Things in Controverſy between the Parties? anſwered, That it was, where in Truth it was paid only for one of them by Agreement, ſuch Witneſs ought not to be puniſhed for Perjury; becauſe as the Caſe was it was no way material whether it were paid for one or both. Alſo it is ſaid to have been reſolved, That a
Witneſs who ſwore that one drew his Dagger and beat and wounded Hetley 97.
J. S. where in Truth he beat him with a Staff, was not guilty of Perjury, becauſe the beating only was material. But perhaps in all theſe Caſes it ought to be intended, That the Queſtion was put in ſuch a Manner, that the Witneſs might reaſonably apprehended that the ſole Deſign of putting it, was to be informed of the ſubſtantial Part of it, which might induce him through Inadvertency to take no Notice of the circumſtantial Part, and give a general Anſwer to the ſubſtantial; for otherwiſe, if it appear plainly, That the Scope of the Queſtion was to ſift him as to his Knowledge of the Subſtance, by examining him ſtrictly concerning the Circumſtances, and he give a particular and diſtinct Account of the Circumſtances, which afterwards appears to be falſe; ſurely he cannot but be

guilty of Perjury, inasmuch as nothing can be more apt to incline a Jury to give Credit to the substantial Part of a Man's Evidence, than his appearing to have an exact and particular Knowledge of all the Circumstances relating to it. And upon these Grounds, I cannot but think the Opinion of those Judges very reasonable, who held, That a Witness was
2 Rol. Re. 368. Palm. 382. guilty of Perjury, who in an Action of Trespass for breaking the Plaintiff's Close, and spoiling it with Sheep, deposed that he saw thirty or forty Sheep in the said Close, and that he knew them to be the Defendant's, because they were marked with such a Mark, which he knew to be the Defendant's Mark, where in Truth the Defendant never used such a Mark; for the giving such a special Reason for his Remembrance could not but make his Testimony more credible than it would have been without it; and though it signified nothing to the Merits of the Cause, whether the Sheep had any Mark at all or not, yet inasmuch as the assigning such a Circumstance in a Thing immaterial had such a direct Tendency to corroborate the Evidence concerning what was most material, and consequently was equally prejudicial to the Party, and equally criminal in its own Nature, and equally tending to abuse the Administration of Justice, as if the Matter sworn had been the very Point in Issue, there doth not seem to be any Reason why it should not be equally punishable. But I cannot find this Matter any where thoroughly settled or debated, and therefore shall leave it to every Man's own Judgment, which from the Consideration of the Circumstances of each particular Case, may generally without any great Difficulty discern whether the Matter in which Perjury is assigned, were wholly impertinent, idle, and insignificant, or not, which seems to be the best Rule for determining whe-
1 Sid. 274. ther it be punishable as Perjury or not. But it is said in *Siderfin*, speaking as I suppose of an Answer in Chancery, that a Man may be guilty of Perjury at the Common Law by swearing a Thing not material; but surely this ought not to be understood in so great a Latitude, as if it were meant that every Falsity in such an answer must needs be Perjury, howsoever foreign, circumstantial and trivial the Point wherein it is assigned may be, which is directly contrary to what seems to be clearly taken for granted in other Books. And therefore perhaps where it is said that a Man may be guilty of Perjury in a Thing not material, no more may be meant, but that he may be as well guilty thereof, by answering to a Matter not charged in the Bill, as by answering to the Matters therein contained, which may alone be said to be material, because the Defendant is not obliged in his Answer to take Notice of any thing else; or else perhaps the Meaning may be, That in a Prosecution for Perjury at Common Law, setting forth a false Oath in such an Answer, relating to the Thing said to be in Variance, the Falsity shall be intended
1 Keb. 935, 941. *primâ facie* to have been some way material in the Cause, unless the contrary be proved by the other Side: Whereas in all Prosecutions upon the Statute, it is necessary expresly to shew in what manner the false Oath is
Vide infra Sect. 23. material to the Cause in Question, because that Statute, extending only to such Perjuries whereby some Person is grieved, cannot maintain a Prosecution which does not bring the Case within the Purview of it, by shewing that some one was grieved by the Injury complained of, which he could not
Cro. Ja. 212. 12 Co. 101. 2 Leon. 198. be, unless the Thing sworn were some way material. However it seemeth to be clear, That a Man may as well be guilty of Perjury by a false Oath tending to extenuate or aggravate the Damages, as by an Oath which is direct to the Fact in Issue.

Sect. 9. As to the eighth Particular, *viz.* how far the false Oath must be credited, it hath been holden not to be material upon an Indictment of Perjury at Common Law, whether the false Oath were at all credited or whether the Party in whose Prejudice it was intended, were in the Event any way aggrieved by it or not, inasmuch as this is not a Prosecution grounded on the Damage to the Party, but on the Abuse of publick Justice. 3 Leon. 230. 2 Leon. 211.

Sect. 10. Subornation of Perjury by the Common Law, seems to be an Offence in procuring a Man to take a false Oath amounting to Perjury, who actually takes such Oath; but it seemeth clear, That if the Person incited to take such an Oath do not actually take it, the Person by whom he was so incited is not guilty of Subornation of Perjury; yet it is certain, That he is liable to be punished not only by Fine, but also by infamous corporal Punishment. 1 Rol. Ab. 41. Pl. 21, 57. Pl. 5, 79. Pl. 2. Yelv. 72. Cro. Ja. 158. Cro. Ca. 337. 2 Keb. 399. 3 Mod. 122. Far. 101.

Sect. 11. Thus far of Perjury and Subornation of Perjury by the Common Law, and now I shall proceed to examine in what Manner these Offences are restrained by Statute; as to which it is to be observed, that it is enacted by 5 *El.* 9. *That whoever shall unlawfully and corruptly procure any Witness, or Witnesses by Letters, Rewards, Promises, or by any other sinister and unlawful Labour or Means whatsoever, to commit any wilful and corrupt Perjury, in any Matter or Cause whatsoever, depending in Suit and Variance, by any Writ, Action, Bill, Complaint or Information, in any wise concerning any Lands, Tenements or Hereditaments, or Goods, Chattels, Debts or Damages, in any of the King's Courts of Chancery,* White-hall, *or elsewhere, within any of the King's Dominions of* England *or* Wales, *or the Marches of the same, where any Person or Persons shall have Authority by Virtue of the King's Commission, Patent or Writ, to hold Plea of Land, or to examine, hear, or determine, any Title of Lands, or any Matter or Witnesses concerning the Title, Right, or Interests of any Lands or Tenements, or Hereditaments, or in any of the King's Courts of Record, or in any Leet, View or Frank-Pledge or Law-Day, Ancient Demesne-Court, Hundred-Court, Court-Baron, or in the Court or Courts of the Stannary in the Counties of* Devon *or* Cornwal, *or shall unlawfully and corruptly procure or suborn any Witness or Witnesses, who shall be sworn to testify* in perpetuam rei Memoriam, *shall for such Offence being thereof lawfully convicted or attainted, forfeit the Sum of forty Pounds. And if any such Offender so being convicted or attainted, shall not have any Goods or Chattels, Lands, or Tenements, to the Value of forty Pounds, that then every such Person shall suffer Imprisonment by the Space of one half Year without Bail or Mainprize, and stand upon the Pillory the Space of one whole Hour, in some Market-Town, next adjoining to the Place where the Offence was committed, in open Market there, or in the Market-Town it self where the Offence was committed.*

Sect. 12. Also it is farther enacted by the said Statute, Par. 5. *That no Person being so convicted or attainted, shall from thenceforth be received as a Witness in any Court of Record, in any of the King's Dominions of* England, Wales, *or the Marches of the same, till such Judgment against him shall be reversed by Attaint, or otherwise; and that upon every such Reversal, the Party grieved shall recover Damages against the Party who did procure the said Judgment so reversed to be first given,* &c. See 1 Sid. 216.

Sect. 13. And it is farther enacted Par. 6. *That if any Person or Persons shall either by the Subornation, unlawful Procurement, sinister Perswasion, or Means of any other, or by their own Act, Consent or Agreement, wilfully, and corruptly commit any Manner of wilful Perjury, by his or their Deposition, in any of the Courts before mentioned, or being examined* ad perpetuam rei Memoriam, *That then every such Offender being duly convicted or attainted shall forfeit twenty*

Pounds, and have Imprisonment by the Space of six Months without Bail or Mainprize; and the Oath of such Offender shall not from thenceforth be received in any Court of Record in England *or* Wales, *until such Judgment shall be reversed*, &c. *on which Reversal the Party grieved shall recover Damages in the Manner before mentioned.* And it is farther enacted Par. 7. *That if such Offender shall not have Goods or Chattels to the Value of twenty Pounds, That then such Person shall be set on the Pillory in some Market-Place within the Shire, City, or Borough, where the Offence shall be committed, by the Sheriff or his Ministers, if it shall fortune to be without any City or Town-Corporate; and if it happen to be within any such City or Town-Corporate, then by the head Officer of such City*, &c. *where he shall have both Ears nailed*, &c.

Sect. 14. And it was farther enacted Par. 8. 9. *That one Moiety of the said Forfeiture shall be to the King, and the other Moiety to such Person as shall be grieved, hindred, or molested, by Reason of any of the Offences before mentioned, that will sue for the same*, &c. *and that as well the Judge and Judges of every such of the said Courts where any such Suits shall be, and whereupon any such Perjury shall be committed, as also the Justices of Assize and Gaol-Delivery, and Justices of Peace at their Quarter-Sessions, both within the Liberties and without, may enquire of, hear, and determine all Offences against the said Act.*

Sect. 15. But it is provided Par. 11. *That the said Act shall no way extend to any Spiritual or Ecclesiastical Court, but that every such Offender as shall offend in Form, as aforesaid, shall be punished by such usual and ordinary Laws as are used in the said Courts.*

Sect. 16. Also it is provided Par. 13. *That the said Statute shall not restrain the Authority of any Judge, having absolute Power to punish Perjury before the Making thereof, but that every such Judge may proceed in the Punishment of all Offences, punishable before the making of the said Statute, in such wise as they might have done, and used to do, to all Purposes, so that they set not upon the Offender less Punishment than is contained in the said Act.* From whence it seemeth undoubtedly to follow, That the Court of King's Bench, *&c.* proceeding upon an Indictment, or Information of Perjury or Subornation of Perjury at Common Law, may not only set a discretionary Fine on the Offender, but also condemn him to the Pillory, without making any Inquiry concerning the Value of his Lands or Goods.

But for the better Understanding of the other Parts of this Statute I shall consider the following Particulars:

1. How far the very Words of the Statute must be pursued in a Prosecution grounded thereon.
2. In what kind of Oaths one may incur the Danger thereof.
3. How far the false Oath must appear to have been prejudicial to some Person.

[a] 2 Leon. 211. 3 Leon. 230. Shower 190. [b] Hetl. 12. Cro. El. 147. [c] Savil 43. [d] 2 Leon. 214. 3 Leon. 230. Het. 12. Savil 43. Cro. El. 147. [e] Cro. El. 105.

Sect. 17. As to the first of these Particulars it hath been holden, That in every Prosecution on this Statute the Words thereof must be exactly pursued, and therefore that an Indictment or Action on the said Statute, alledging that the Defendant deposed such a Matter [a] *falso & deceptivè*, or [b] *falso & corruptè*, or [c] *falso & voluntarie*, without expresly saying, that he did it *voluntarie & corrupte*, is not good; and that such a Defect cannot be [d] supplied by adding the Words *contra formam Statuti*, or concluding *& sic voluntarium & corruptum commisit Perjurium:* Also it hath been [e] holden, That it is necessary expresly to alledge that the Defendant was sworn, and therefore that it is not sufficient to say, that *tacto per se sacro Evangelio falso deposuit.*

Sect. 18. However it hath been resolved, That it is not necessary to shew whether the Party, who is accused of Perjury, did take the false Oath through the Subornation of another, or without any such Subornation, notwithstanding the Words of the Statute are, *if any Person either by the Subornation, unlawful Procurement, sinister Perswasion, or Means of any other, or by their own Act, Consent or Agreement commit wilful Perjury*, &c. for inasmuch as there is no Medium between the two Branches of this Distinction, so that all Perjury whatsoever must needs come within one of them; and it is no way material under which of them it doth come, it is a reasonable Exposition to look on the said Words as put into the Statute *ex abundanti*, seeing they express no more than the Law must needs have implied without them; from whence it follows, That they operate no more than if they had not been expressed, and consequently shall not oblige the Prosecutor necessarily to pursue them, which would put him under the Difficulty not only of proving the Perjury, which alone is material, but also of shewing it to be within one of the Branches of the said Distinction, which is nothing to the Purpose. 3 Bulst. 147. Vide supra Ch. 10. Sect. 8.

Sect. 19. As to the second of the above mentioned Particulars, *viz.* In what kind of Oaths one may incur the Danger of this Statute, it hath been resolved, That no one can be guilty of Perjury within the Meaning thereof, in any Case wherein a Man may not possibly be guilty also of Subornation of Perjury within the same Statute; for it is very reasonable to give the whole Statute the same Construction; nor can it well be intended, that the Makers thereof, who expresly inflict a greater Penalty on Subornation of Perjury, than on the Perjury it self, should mean to extend the Purview of the Law in relation to what they esteemed the lesser Crime, farther than in relation to that which they esteemed the greater; from whence it hath been argued and determined, That because that Part of the Statute, which concerns Subornation of Perjury, extends only to Subornation of Perjury in *Matters depending in Suit by Writ, Action, Bill, Plaint, or Information, in any wise concerning Lands, Tenements, or Hereditaments, or Goods, Chattels, Debts, or Damages*, &c. therefore the following Clause concerning Perjury it self, tho' it be penned in more general Words, shall come under the same Restriction. 5 Co. 99. a. And from hence it clearly follows, That no Perjury upon an Indictment, or criminal Information, can bring a Man within the Danger of this Statute, because they are omitted in the above mentioned Clause. Also upon this Ground it seems easy to account for the Judgment in *Price*'s Case, Cro. Ja. 120. who being indicted for a Perjury supposed to be committed by him in an Information for the King, which as I suppose must be intended to have been a criminal one, was discharged upon an Exception taken to the Indictment; but if the Information whereon the said Perjury was supposed to have been committed, had been of a civil Nature, 3 Inst. 164. I do not see any Reason why it should not be as well within the Meaning, as it seems to be expresly within the Words of the Statute; for surely the Opinion, That the King cannot by Indictment, which is his own proper Suit, punish his own Witness, who swears for him, cannot be agreeable to Law, because however the Perjury of such a Witness may seem to tend to promote the King's Interest in relation to the Cause which happens to be in Dispute; yet certainly it is as heinous a Crime in its own Nature, and as much an Abuse to Justice, and of the same ill Consequence to the Publick, and consequently as worthy of the King's Resentment, as if it had been taken against him.

Sect. 20. Also it hath been resolved, that this Statute extends to no other Perjury except that of a Witness, not only because the Clause con-

concerning Subornation, to which the ſubſequent Clauſe concerning Perjury hath a Reference, relates to Perjury by Witneſſes only, but alſo becauſe the Clauſe concerning Perjury mentions only Perjury committed by Perſons in their Examinations, *ad perpetuam rei memoriam*, or elſe in their Depoſitions in ſome of the Courts above mentioned, which in common Speech are taken for ſuch Oaths only as are taken by a Witneſs; and from hence it follows, That no one can come within the Statute by Reaſon of any falſe Oath in an [a] Anſwer to a Bill in Chancery, or in [b] ſwearing the Peace againſt another, or in a [c] Preſentment made by him as Homager of a Court-Baron, or by Reaſon of a falſe [d] Wager of Law, or for taking a falſe Oath before [e] Commiſſioners appointed by the King to make an Inquiry concerning his Title to certain Lands.

[a] Cro. El. 148. 2 Leon. 201. Daliſ. 84. Yelv. 120.
[b] 2 Rol. Ab. 77. Pl. 5.
[c] 2 Leon. 201.
[d] 1 Noy 7, 108. Finch 450.
[e] Moore 627.

2 Rol. Ab. 77. Pl. 4. 1 Rol. Re. 79. 3 Keble 345.

Sect. 21. Alſo it hath been ſaid, That he who makes a falſe Affidavit againſt a Man in a Court of Juſtice, is not within this Statute; but perhaps the Books wherein this Opinion is holden, ought to be intended only of ſuch Affidavits which no way relate to a Cauſe depending in Suit before ſuch Court; for if they be of ſuch a Nature, That either of the Parties in Variance be grieved, hindered, or moleſted in Reſpect of their Cauſe in ſuch Court by Reaſon of the Perjury; as where a Trial is put off, or a Judgment or Execution ſet aſide upon a falſe Affidavit, the Offence ſeems to be not only within the Meaning of the Statute, but alſo within the very Letter of it, unleſs the Words, Witneſſes and Depoſitions, are confined to ſo ſtrict a Signification, as to bear no kind of Application to any other Perſons or Oaths, except thoſe which are made uſe of upon the Trial of the Iſſue in Queſtion, for which I cannot find any good Authority. However partly perhaps from this Notion, and partly becauſe the Statute ſpeaks expreſly only of Depoſitions in the Courts above mentioned, it hath been queſtioned, Whether a falſe Oath before a Sheriff upon a Writ of Inquiry of Damages, be within the Statute or not? But if it be conſidered, That the Party to whoſe Prejudice ſuch a falſe Oath is taken, is as much grieved by it as if it had been taken in the very Court, and the principal Judgment of the Cauſe depends upon ſuch an Inquiry; and the Depoſitions made before the Sheriff, may as properly be ſaid to be Depoſitions in the Court, by which the Sheriff is commiſſioned to take the Inquiry, as Depoſitions taken before Juſtices of *Niſi Prius*, upon a Trial of an Iſſue joined in a ſuperior Court, which are undoubtedly within the Meaning of the Statute; and alſo inaſmuch as thoſe who give Evidence before a Sheriff upon ſuch an Inquiry may in the common Uſe of the Word, be as properly called Witneſſes, as thoſe who give Evidence before the Court in which an Iſſue is joined, it ſeemeth to be the more plauſible Opinion, that ſuch a Perjury is within the Statute: But ſince it is diſputable, whether it be ſo or no, and it is certain that it is Perjury at Common Law, and that in all Caſes whatſoever where a Man takes a falſe Oath, which is not Perjury within the Statute, but is looked on as Perjury at Common Law, he is ſtill puniſhable for it by Indictment or Information at the Common Law, it is certainly moſt adviſeable to proſecute ſuch an Offender at the Common Law, and not upon the Statute.

Vide 2 Leon. 40.

1 Rol. Ab. 30. Pl. 3. 42. Pl. 27.

See the Authorities above cited.

Cro. Jac. 8.

Sect. 22. As to the third Particular, *viz.* How far the falſe Oath muſt appear to have been prejudicial to ſome Perſon, it hath been collected from the abovementioned Clauſe which giveth an Action to the Party grieved by the Offences mentioned in the Statute, That no falſe Oath is within the Meaning thereof, which does not give ſome Perſon a juſt Cauſe of Complaint; and upon this Ground it hath been ſaid, That he who ſwears a Thing which is true, but not known by him to be ſo, is not within the Statute, becauſe howſoever heinous his Offence may be in its own Nature; yet, when it proves in the Event to be in Maintenance of the Truth, it cannot be ſaid to give him a juſt Cauſe of Complaint, who would take Advantage againſt another from his Want of legal Evidence to make out the Juſtice of his Cauſe. 3 Inſt. 166. Vide ſupra Sect. 6. Con. Hetley 97.

Sect. 23. Alſo from the ſame Ground it ſeemeth clearly to follow, That no falſe Oath can be within the Statute, unleſs the Party againſt whom it was ſworn ſuffered ſome kind of Diſadvantage by it, for otherwiſe it cannot be ſaid that any one was grieved, hindred, or moleſted by it; and therefore it is certain, That in every Proſecution upon the Statute, it is neceſſary to ſet forth the Record of the Cauſe wherein the Perjury complained of is ſuppoſed to have been committed; and alſo to prove at the Trial of the Cauſe, that there is actually ſuch a Record, by producing the Record it ſelf, or a true Copy thereof, which muſt agree with that which is ſet forth in the Pleadings, without any material Variance; for otherwiſe it cannot legally appear, That there ever was ſuch a Suit depending, wherein the Party might be prejudiced in the Manner ſuppoſed: Alſo it ſeems to be agreed, That it is neceſſary not only to ſet forth the Point wherein the falſe Oath was aſſigned, but alſo to ſhew in what Manner it conduced to the Proof or Diſproof of the Matter in Debate between the Parties; and it hath been adjudged, That an Indictment ſetting forth a Suit concerning the Manor of *Dale*, and aſſigning a falſe Oath concerning the Manor (*Manerium prædictum innuendo*) is not good, becauſe it no otherwiſe appears, That the falſe Oath did concern the Manor of *Dale*, but by the *Innuendo*, which is not a ſufficient Averment. Alſo upon the ſame Ground it ſeems to be ſafeſt in a Proſecution upon the Statute for a falſe Oath in Chancery, to ſet forth the Bill and Anſwer, That the Plaintiff may appear to have been aggrieved by it; and for the ſame Reaſon it ſeemeth alſo, That you ought, in ſuch a Proſecution of a Witneſs in Chancery, to ſet forth the Interrogatory in particular, and to ſhew how it was material: Alſo it hath been reſolved, That as in an Action on the Statute brought by one Perſon, it muſt appear, That the falſe Oath was prejudicial to the Plaintiff; ſo in an Action by more than one, it muſt appear to have been prejudicial to every one of the Plaintiffs: And it hath been ſaid, That it is not ſufficient to ſhew that the falſe Oath cauſed the Court to make an Award againſt the Plaintiff, unleſs it alſo appear that ſuch an Award was prejudicial to him, and therefore where the Plaintiff at a Trial in Ejectment challenged a Juror, and proved his Challenge by a falſe Oath, by reaſon whereof the Inqueſt was not taken, and conſequently the Poſſeſſion of the Defendant, who had a defeaſible Title, continued longer than it otherwiſe would have done; it hath been adjudged, That ſuch a Defendant cannot have an Action on the Statute againſt ſuch Witneſs, becauſe in Truth he gained an Advantage by the Perjury. Alſo it hath been holden, That it is not ſufficient to ſhew that the Perjury, for which an Action is brought upon the Statute, was actually prejudicial to the Plaintiff, unleſs it be alſo ſhewn to have been made in ſome Cauſe which may properly be ſaid to have been depending in Suit between him and the Perſon for whom the Witneſs was examined; and therefore it hath been holden, That where *A.* brought a Bill in Chancery againſt *B.* and the Lord Keeper, by an Order made *C.* to be as a Party to the Bill againſt *B.* and afterwards a Commiſſion went forth to examine Witneſſes between *B.* and *C.* upon which *D.* being produced as a Witneſs on the Part of *C.* ſwore directly

Vide ſupra, Sect. 8. & 3 Inſt. 167. Coke Ent. 164. 6 Mod. 168. 2 Rol. Re. 76. 1 Keb. 452, 935, 941. Raym. 202. 2 Leon. 12. 2 Rol. Re. 427. Cro. Ca. 351, 352, 353. 1 Keb. 452. Cro. El. 428. 1 Keb. 935, 941. 1 Sid. 106. 2 Leon. 12. 3 Leon. 68. 2 Leon. 4[illegible]

Yelv. [illegible]. for him against *B.* whereupon a Decree was made against *B.* yet *B.* cannot have an Action on the Statute, because *C.* was not a Party to the Suit, but came in *à Latere*, by an Order; and it is said, That the Words of the Statute are, *where one is grieved by a Deposition in a Suit between Party and Party*; but perhaps the Authority of this Opinion may justly be questioned, not only because the Words of the Statute whereon it is grounded are mistaken, but also because the Offence seems in Truth to be both within the Meaning and Letter of the Law, since thereby a Person is grieved in respect of a Cause depending in Suit in a Court mentioned in the Statute: However
2 Leon. 198. there seems to be no Doubt, but that a Perjury which only tends to increase or
1 Keb. 9. lessen the Damages to be given to a Plaintiff, is as much within the Statute,
Raymond 74. as any Perjury which goes directly to the the Point of the Issue: Also it
1 Sid. 148. 2 Keb. 718, 854. seemeth to be settled, That Perjury in a Cause wherein an erroneous Judgment is given, is a good Foundation of a Prosecution upon the Statute,
1 Keb. 531. while such Judgment stands unreversed.

For late Statutes concerning Perjury, see the Additions [83] [84] ☞

CHAP. LXX.

Of Forgery.

OF Forgery there are two Kinds:

1. By the Common Law.
2. By the Statute.

Sect. 1. Forgery by the Common Law seemeth to be an Offence in falsly and fraudulently making or altering any Matter of Record, or any other authentick Matter of a publick Nature; as a Parish Register, or any Deed or Will.

For the better Understanding whereof, I shall endeavour to shew:

1. In what Cases the Making or Altering of a Writing, shall be said to be so far false and fraudulent, as to amount to Forgery.
2. That a Man may be guilty of Forgery in respect of all the above mentioned Writings, and of no other.

Sect. 2. As to the first Particular, it is said to be possible for a Man knowingly to make a Deed in his own Name, and also to sign and seal it himself, which yet in Judgment of Law may be no better than a downright Forgery; as if a Man make a Feoffment of certain Lands to *J. S.*
3 Inst. 169. Pult. 46. b. 27 H. 6. 3. and afterwards make a Deed of Feoffment of the same Lands to *J. D.* of a Date prior to that of the Feoffment to *J. S.* in which Case he is said to be guilty of Forgery, because he knowingly falsifies the Date, in order to defraud his own Feoffee, by making a second Conveyance which at the Time he had no Power to make: Also it is said, That his
Moore 655. Crime would have been no less, if by his Conveyance he had passed only an equitable Interest for good Consideration, and had afterwards by
Noy 101. Moore 759, 760. such a subsequent antedated Conveyance endeavoured to avoid it. Also in many other Cases a Writing may be said to be forged where neither
3 Inst. 170. Con. Dy. 288. b. the Hand nor Seal of any one are forged; as where one being directed to draw up a Will for a sick Person, doth insert some Legacies therein of

2 his

his own Head; or where one finding another's Name at the Bottom of a Letter at a considerable Distance from the other Writing, causes the Letter to be cut off, and a general Release to be written above the Name, and then takes off the Seal, and fixes it under the Release; or where one inserts into an Indictment the Names of those against whom in Truth it was not found; or where one makes any fraudulent Alteration of the Form of a true Deed in a material Part of it; as by making a Lease of the Manor of *Dale* appear to be a Lease of the Manor of *Sale*, by changing the Letter *D*. into an *S*. or by making a Bond for five hundred Pounds, expressed in Figures, seem to have been made for five Thousand, by adding a new Cypher. But Sir *Edward Coke* seems to say, That a Deed so altered may more properly be called a false than a forged Writing, because it is not forged in the Name of another, nor his Seal nor Hand counterfeited. But I see no good Reason why such an Alteration of a Deed should not as properly be called Forgery, as the entire Making of a new Deed in another's Name; for in both Cases not only the Fraud and Villany are the very same, but also a Man's Hand and Seal are falsly made use of to testify his Assent to an Instrument, which after such an Alteration is no more his Deed than a Stranger's. Also the Notion of Forgery doth not seem so much to consist in the counterfeiting a Man's Hand and Seal, which may often be done innocently, but in the endeavouring to give an Appearance of Truth to a mere Deceit and Falsity, and either to impose that upon the World as the solemn Act of another, which he is no way privy to, or at least to make a Man's own Act appear to have been done at a Time when it was not done, and by Force of such a Falsity to give it an Operation, which in Truth and Justice it ought not to have, as appears by the foregoing Cases in this Section, to most of which Sir *Edward Coke* himself seems to agree.

3 Inst. 171. 3 Mod. 66. 3 Inst. 169. Moore 619. 3 Inst. 169. Vide Moore 619. 3 Mod. 66. Vide 2 Rol. Ab. 28, 29. 11 Co. 27.

Sect. 3. But it seemeth to be clear, That he who writes a Deed in another's Name, and seals it in his Presence, and by his Command, is not guilty of Forgery, because the Law looks on this as the other's own Sealing.

Pult. 46. 21 H. 6. 4. b. Moore 619. Noy 99. Salk. 375.

Sect. 4. Also it hath been adjudged, That he shall not be punished for Forgery who razeth out the Word *Libris* out of a Bond made to himself, and putteth in *Marcis*, because here is no Appearance of a fraudulent Design to cheat another, and the Alteration is prejudicial to none but to him who makes it, whose Security for his Money is wholly avoided by it; yet it is said, That it would be Forgery, if by the Circumstances of the Case it should any way appear to have been done with an Eye of gaining an Advantage to the Party himself, or of prejudicing a third Person: Also it is holden, That such an Alteration, even without these Circumstances is a Misdemeanour, though it be no Forgery.

Sect. 5. It hath been resolved, That a Man shall not be adjudged guilty of Forgery for writing a Will for another without any Directions from him, who becomes *Non Compos* before it is brought to him; for it is not the bare writing an Instrument in another's Name without his Privity, but the giving it a false Appearance of having been executed by him, which makes a Man guilty of Forgery.

Moore 760.

Sect. 6. It is said, That regularly a Man cannot commit an Act of Forgery by a bare Nonfeasance, as by omitting a Legacy out of a Will, which he is directed to draw for another; yet it hath been holden by some, even in this very Case, That if the Omission of a Bequest to one cause a material Alteration in the Limitation of a Bequest to another, as where the Omission of a Devise of an Estate for Life to one Man causeth a Devise

Moore 760. Noy 101.

Devise of the same Lands to another to pass a present Estate, which otherwise would have passed a Remainder only, he who makes such an Omission is guilty of Forgery.

1 Sid. 142.

Sect. 7. It seemeth to be no way material, whether a forged Instrument be made in such a Manner, That if it were in Truth such as it is counterfeited for, it would be of Validity, or not; and upon this Ground it hath been adjudged, That the Forgery of a Protection in the Name of *A. B.* as being a Member of Parliament, who in Truth at the Time was not a Member, is as much a Crime as if he were.

And now I am to shew in the second Place, That a Man may be guilty of Forgery at Common Law, in respect of any of the above mentioned Writings, and of no other.

1 Rol. Ab. 65. Pl. 1, 2. 76 Pl. 3. Yelv. 146. Cro. El. 178. 3 Mod. 66.

Sect. 8. And first it is clear, That one may be guilty thereof by the Common Law, by counterfeiting a Matter of Record; for, since the Law gives the highest Credit to all Records, it cannot but be of the utmost ill Consequence to the Publick, to have them either forged or falsified.

Sect. 9. Secondly, Also there seemeth to be no Doubt, but that one may be guilty of this Crime by the Common Law, by forging any other authentick Matter of a publick Nature, as a [a] Privy Seal, or a [b] Licence from the Barons of the Exchequer to compound a Debt, or a [c] Certificate of Holy Orders, or a [d] Protection from a Parliament Man.

Sect. 10. Thirdly, It is also unquestionable, That a Man may be in like Manner guilty of Forgery at Common Law, by forging a [e] Deed, and surely there cannot be any Reason to doubt, but that one may be equally guilty by forging a [f] Will, which cannot be thought to be of less Consequence than a Deed, but I do not find this Point any where directly holden.

Sect. 11. As to other Writings of an inferiour Nature, it seems to have been generally laid down as a [g] Rule, That the Counterfeiting of them is not properly Forgery; [h] and some have gone so far as to hold, That the Forging another's Hand, and thereby receiving Rent due to him from his Tenants, is not punishable at all; and therefore it cannot but be more safe to proceed against Offences of this Nature, as Cheats than as Forgeries; but surely it cannot be proved by any good Authority, That such base Crimes are wholly disregarded by the Common Law, as not deserving a publick Prosecution; for the Opinion in the Books above cited, That they are punishable by no Law, seems by no Means to be maintainable, since many of them are most certainly punishable by Force of 33 *H.* 8. 1. which is set forth at large in the following Chapter; neither can it be a convincing Argument, That they are not punishable at Common Law, [i] because they are of a private Nature; since Deeds concerning private Matters are also of a private Nature, as much as other Writings concerning such Matters; yet no one will say, That the Making a false Deed concerning a private Matter is not punishable at Common Law; but perhaps it may be reasonable to make this Distinction between the Counterfeiting of such Writings, the Forgery whereof hath been already shewn to be properly punishable as Forgery, and the Counterfeiting of other Writings of an inferiour Nature, that the former is in it self criminal, whether any third Person be actually injured thereby, or not, but that the latter is no Crime, unless some one receive a Prejudice from it.

[a] 1 Rol. Ab. 68. Pl. 33. Cro. Ca. 326. 1 Jon. 325.
[b] 1 Rol. Ab. 65. Pl. 5. 2 Bulf. 137.
[c] 1 Lev. 138.
[d] 1 Sid. 142.
[e] 1 Rol. Ab. 66. Pl. 10. Raymond 81. Owen 47. 1 Sid. 278. 3 Leon. 170.
[f] Moore 760. Noy 101. Dy. 302. b.
[g] 1 Rol. Re. 431. 1 Sid. 16, 155, 451. 1 Rol. Ab. 66. Pl. 8, 9. Winch 40, 90. 3 Leon. 231. 1 Leon. 101. Cro. El. 296. 853. 3 Bulf. 265.
[h] Cro. El. 166. Yelv. 146. 3 Bulf. 265.
[i] Yelv. 146.

Sect. 12. Thus far of Forgery by the Common Law, and now I am to consider Forgery by the Statute, which depends upon 5 *El.* 14. by which it is enacted, *That if any Person or Persons upon his or their own Head and Imagination, or by falſe Conſpiracy and Fraud with others, ſhall wittingly, ſubtilly, and falſly forge or make, or ſubtilly cauſe, or wittingly aſſent to be forged or made, any falſe Deed, Charter, or Writing ſealed, Court-Roll, or the Will of any Perſon or Perſons in Writing, to the Intent that the State of Freehold or Inheritance of any Perſon or Perſons, of, in, or to any Lands, Tenements, or Hereditaments, Freehold or Copyhold, or the Right, Title, or Intereſt, of any Perſon or Perſons, of, in, or to the ſame, or any of them, ſhall, or may be moleſted, troubled, defeated, recovered or charged; or ſhall pronounce, publiſh, or ſhew forth in Evidence, any ſuch falſe and forged Deed, Charter, Writing, Court-Roll, or Will, as true, knowing the ſame to be falſe and forged, as is aforeſaid, to the Intent above remembred,* (*except being an Attorney, Lawyer, or Counſellor, he ſhall for his Client, plead, ſhew forth, or give in Evidence ſuch falſe and forged Deed,* &c. *to the forging whereof he was not Party nor Privy*) *and ſhall be thereof convicted, either upon Action or Actions of Forgery of falſe Deeds, to be founded upon the ſaid Statute, at the Suit of the Party grieved, or otherwiſe, according to the Order and due Courſe of the Laws of this Realm,* &c. *ſhall pay unto the Party grieved his double Coſts and Damages, to be found or aſſeſſed in that Court where ſuch Conviction ſhall be, and alſo ſhall be ſet upon the Pillory in ſome open Market-Town, or other open Place, and there have both his Ears cut off, and alſo his Noſtrils ſlit and cut, and ſeared with a hot Iron,* &c. *and ſhall forfeit to the King the whole Iſſues and Profits of his Lands and Tenements, and ſuffer perpetual Impriſonment,* &c. See Pult. 45, 46. Par. 15.

Sect. 13. And it is farther enacted by the ſaid Statute, Par. 3. *That if any Perſon or Perſons, upon his or their own Head or Imagination, or by falſe Conſpiration or Fraud had with any other, ſhall wittingly, ſubtilly, and falſly forge or make, or wittingly, ſubtilly and falſly cauſe or aſſent to be made and forged, any falſe Charter, Deed or Writing, to the Intent that any Perſon or Perſons ſhall or may have or claim any Eſtate or Intereſt for Term of Years, of, in, or to any Manors, Lands, Tenements, or Hereditaments, not being Copyhold, or any Annuity in Fee-ſimple, Fee-tail, or for Term of Life, Lives or Years, or ſhall, as is aforeſaid, forge, make, or cauſe, or aſſent to be made or forged, any Obligation, or Bill obligatory, or any Acquittance, Releaſe, or other Diſcharge of any Debt, Accompt, Action, Suit, Demand, or other Thing perſonal; or ſhall pronounce, publiſh, or give in Evidence,* (*except as before excepted*) *any ſuch falſe or forged Charter, Deed, Writing, Obligation, Bill obligatory, Acquittance, Releaſe, or Diſcharge, as true, knowing the ſame to be falſe and forged, and ſhall be thereof convicted by any of the Ways and Means aforeſaid, he ſhall pay unto the Party grieved his double Coſts and Damages, to be found and aſſeſſed in ſuch Court where the ſaid Conviction ſhall be had, and ſhall be alſo ſet upon the Pillory in ſome open Market-Town, or other open Place, and there have one of his Ears cut off, and alſo ſhall ſuffer Impriſonment for one Year,* &c. Latw. 190.

Sect. 14. And it is farther enacted by the ſame Statute, Par. 7 & 8. *That if any Perſon or Perſons being convicted or condemned of any of the Offences aforeſaid by any the Ways or Means above limited, ſhall after any ſuch his or their Conviction or Condemnation, eftſoons commit or perpetrate any of the ſaid Offences in Form aforeſaid, that then every ſuch ſecond Offence ſhall be adjudged Felony without Benefit of Clergy, ſaving to all Perſons other than the ſaid Offenders, and ſuch as Claim to their Uſes, all ſuch Rights,* &c. *which they ſhall have to any the Hereditaments of any ſuch Perſon, ſo as is aforeſaid convicted or attainted, at any Time before,* &c. *ſaving alſo the Dower of ſuch Offender's Wife, and the Right of his Heir.*

Sect. 15. And it is farther enacted by the ſaid Statute, Par. 10. *That all Juſtices of Oyer and Terminer, and Juſtices of Aſſize, ſhall have Power to inquire of, hear and determine the Offences aforeſaid.*

Sect. 16. But it is provided, Par. 9, 12 & 16. *That this Act or any Thing therein contained, ſhall not extend to any Ordinary, or his Commiſſary,* &c. *for putting their Seal of Office to any Will to be exhibited unto them, not knowing the ſame to be falſe or forged, or for Writing of the ſaid Will, or Probate of the ſame, nor to any Proctor,* &c. *of any Eccleſiaſtical Court, for the Writing, ſetting forth, or Pleading of any Proxy made according to the Eccleſiaſtical Law,* &c. *for the Appearance of any Perſon being cited to appear in ſuch Court; nor to any Archdeacon, or Official, for putting their authentick Seal to the ſaid Proxy or Proxies, nor to any Eccleſiaſtical Judge for admitting the ſame; nor to any Perſon who ſhall plead or ſhew forth any Deed or Writing exemplified under the great Seal of* England, *or under the Seal of any other authentick Court of this Realm; nor to any Perſon who ſhall cauſe any Seal of any Court to be ſet to any ſuch Deed, Charter, or Writing enrolled, not knowing the ſame to be falſe or forged.*

1 H. H. P. C. 682 to 687. In the Conſtruction of this Statute, the following Points have been holden,

Sect. 17. I. That a falſe Cuſtomary of a Copyhold Manor, made in Parchment under the Seals of ſeveral Tenants of the Manor, and containing in it divers falſe Cuſtoms, apparently tending to the Diſheriſon of the Lord, and falſly pretending by its Title to be ſet forth by the Conſent of all the Tenants, and Allowance of the Lord, is within the firſt Branch of Forgery mentioned in the Statute, as being a ſealed Writing made to the Intent to moleſt the Inheritance of the Lord. (Dy. 322. Pl. 26. 3 Leon. 108.)

Sect. 18. II. That the Forgery of a Leaſe for Years, or of a Grant of a Rent-Charge for Years, in the Name of one who is ſeized of a Freehold or Inheritance, is alſo within the ſaid firſt Branch of the Statute, becauſe the ſaid Branch is penned in general Words extending to any Moleſtation whatſoever of ſuch Eſtate, without mentioning any Eſtate or Intereſt, in the Claim whereof ſuch Moleſtation ſhall conſiſt; and from this Ground it follows, That thoſe Words in the ſecond Branch of Forgery mentioned in the Statute, *to the Intent that any Perſon ſhall claim any Eſtate or Intereſt for Term of Years,* &c. are meant only of ſuch Forgeries which relate to ſuch an Eſtate or Intereſt *in eſſe* before. (3 Inſt. 170. Noy 42. 3 Inſt. 170. Noy 42.)

Sect. 19. III. That the Forgery of a Will in Writing of one poſſeſſed of ſuch an Eſtate, mentioning a Bequeſt thereof, is within the ſaid ſecond Branch of the Statute, as being a falſe Writing, made to the Intent that ſome Perſon may claim an Eſtate for Years; notwithſtanding the ſaid Branch makes no expreſs Mention of a Will, as the firſt doth. (Dy. 302. Pl. 45.)

3 Leon. 170. *Sect.* 20. IV. That the Forgery of a Leaſe of Lands in *Ireland* is not within either of the Branches of the Statute.

Sect. 21. V. That the Forgery of a Deed containing a Gift of mere perſonal Chattels, is alſo no way within the Statute, the Words whereof to this Purpoſe are, *If any Perſon ſhall forge any Obligation or Bill Obligatory, or any Acquittance, Releaſe, or other Diſcharge of any Debt, Account, Action, Suit, Demand, or other Thing perſonal.* (3 Leon. 170.)

Sect. 22. VI. That the Forgery of a Statute-Merchant, or of a Recognizance in the Nature of a Statute-Staple, by acknowledging them in the Name of another are within the Statute, as being Obligations, becauſe they muſt have the Seal of the Party, by the expreſs Words of the Statutes, which appoint in what Manner ſuch Statute or Recognizance ſhall be taken: But that the Forgery of the Statute-Staple is no way within the Statute, becauſe it needeth not the Seal of the Party, but only the Seal of the Staple provided for it. (See Ch. 42. & 62. 15 H. 7. 15. a. 2 Rol. A. 466. Pl. 2, 3, 4, 5. Con. 3 Inſt. 171.)

Sect. 23. VII. That he who is truly informed by another, that a Deed is forged, is in danger of the Statute if he afterwards publiſh the ſame to be true; notwithſtanding the Words of the Statute be, *If any one ſhall publiſh*, &c. *ſuch falſe and forged Deed*, &c. *knowing the ſame to be falſe or forged.* 3 Inſt. 171.

Sect. 24. VIII. That the double Damages to be awarded to the Party grieved by a forged Releaſe of an Obligation, *&c.* ſhall be governed by the Penalty, and not by the true Debt appearing in the Condition. 3 Inſt. 172.

Sect. 25. IX. That one who hath been convicted of publiſhing a forged Deed, may become guilty of Felony by forging another Deed afterwards, as well as by publiſhing any ſuch Deed, notwithſtanding the ſecond Offence be not of the very ſame Nature with the firſt; for the Words of the Statute are, *If any Perſon being convicted or condemned of any of the Offences aforeſaid*, &c. *ſhall, after any ſuch Conviction or Condemnation, eftſoons commit any of the ſaid Offences.* 3 Inſt. 172.

Sect. 26. X. That notwithſtanding it be neceſſary in every Proſecution upon the Statute ſtrictly to purſue the very Words of it, (for which Cauſe it hath been reſolved, That an Indictment, ſetting forth the Forgery of a Writing indented, without adding, that it was ſealed, is inſufficient;) yet there is no Neceſſity that the Tranſlation of ſuch Words be made in proper claſſical *Latin*, ſo that it be intelligible; and upon this Ground it hath been adjudged, That an Indictment, ſetting forth that the Defendant *ſuper Caput ſuum proprium* did forge, *&c.* meaning thereby to expreſs that he did it of his own Head, is ſufficient. 3 Keb. 356, 367. 3 Inſt. 169. See 1 Keb. 849. 2 Keb. 129. 2 Levin. 221. Other Caſes of this Kind, 2 Keb. 129, 245, 501, 532. Far. 150.

Sect. 27. XI. That upon an Indictment of Treſpaſs, Forgery and Publication of a Deed, a Verdict finding the Defendant guilty *de Tranſgreſſione & Forgeria prædictis prout ſuperius in Indictamento ſupponitur*, is ſufficient, becauſe thoſe Words *de Tranſgreſſione prædict'* include the whole: Alſo perhaps ſuch a Verdict may be ſufficient for another Reaſon, becauſe the Offence is equally within the Statute, and the Puniſhment the very ſame, whether the Party be guilty both of the Forgery and Publication, or of one of them only. 1 Vent. 23, 24. Salk. 342, 375. Pl. 18. 2 Levin. 111, 221. 3 Keb. 353.

☞ *See the* Additions [85] [86] *for the late Acts againſt Forgery*, & ſupra Ch. 58.

CHAP. LXXI.

Of Cheats.

Of Cheats puniſhable by publick Proſecution, there are two Kinds,

1. By the Common Law.
2. By Statute.

Sect. 1. And firſt it ſeemeth, That thoſe which are puniſhable at Common Law, may in general be deſcribed to be deceitful Practices, in defrauding or endeavouring to defraud another of his known Right by Means of ſome artful Device, contrary to the plain Rules of common Honeſty; as by [a] Playing with falſe Dice; or by [b] cauſing an illiterate Perſon to execute a Deed to his Prejudice, by reading it over to him in Words

[a] 2 Rol. Rep. 107. Cro. Ja. 497, 498. 2 Rol. Ab. 78. H. 1, 2. 1 Keb. 849. Par. Caſe 6. Mod. 42. Far. 40.
[b] 1 Sid. 312.

[a] 1 Sid. 431. [b] Noy 103. [c] Noy 99. Moor 630. Cro. El. 531. 1 Mod. 46. 2 Jon. 64. [d] Noy 99. [e] See the Books above cited, but 2 Rol. A. 863. C. & 12 Co. 123, are contrary.

Words different from thoſe in which it was written; or by [a] perſwading a Woman to execute Writings to another, as her Truſtee upon an intended Marriage, which in Truth contained no ſuch Thing, but only a Warrant of Attorney to confeſs a Judgment, *&c.* or by [b] ſuppreſſing a Will, or by [c] levying a Fine in another's Name, or [d] ſuing out an Execution upon a Judgment for him, or acknowledging an Action in his Name without his Privity, and againſt his Will; in which Caſes, by ſome good [e] Opinions, the Record may be vacated.

[f] 6 Mod. 105. Salk. 379. 5 Mod. 18.

Sect. 2. It [f] ſeemeth to be the better Opinion, That the deceitful receiving of Money from one Man to another's Uſe, upon a falſe Pretence of having a Meſſage and Order to that Purpoſe, is not puniſhable by a criminal Proſecution, becauſe it is accompanied with no manner of artful Contrivance, but wholly depends on a bare naked Lie; and it is ſaid to be needleſs to provide ſevere Laws for ſuch Miſchiefs, againſt which common Prudence and Caution may be a ſufficient Security.

See the Authorities cited in Sect. 1.

Sect. 3. Some of the above mentioned Offences are puniſhable, not only with Fine and Impriſonment, but alſo with farther infamous Puniſhment, (as cheating with falſe Dice, eſpecially if the Offender be a common Gameſter) others are puniſhable with Fine and Impriſonment only, by the Diſcretion of the Judges, which is regulated by the Circumſtances of each particular Caſe; and ſome of them are made Felonies by 21 *Jac.* 1. 26. as appeareth from Chapter 45.

1 H. H. P. C. 506.

Sect. 4. Offences of this Kind by Statute depend upon 33 *H.* 8. 1. by which it is enacted, *That if any Perſon or Perſons ſhall falſly and deceitfully obtain or get into his or their Hands or Poſſeſſion, any Money, Goods, Chatels, Jewels, or other Things of any other Perſon or Perſons, by Colour and Means of any privy falſe Token, or counterfeit Letter made in another Man's Name, to a ſpecial Friend or Acquaintance, for the obtaining of Money,* &c. *from ſuch Perſon, and ſhall be thereof convicted, by Witneſs taken before the Lord Chancellor, or before the Juſtices of Aſſize, or before the Juſtices of Peace of any County, City, Borough, Town, or Franchiſe in their general Seſſions, or by Action in any of the King's Courts of Record, every ſuch Offender ſhall ſuffer ſuch Puniſhment by Impriſonment, ſetting upon the Pillory, or otherwiſe by any corporal Pain, except Pains of Death, as ſhall be appointed by thoſe before whom he ſhall be ſo convict.*

Sect. 5. And it is farther enacted by the ſaid Statute, *That as well the Juſtices of Aſſize for the Time being, as alſo two Juſtices of Peace in the ſame County, whereof the one to be of the* Quorum, *may call and convene by Proceſs, or otherwiſe, to the ſaid Aſſizes, or general Seſſions, any Perſon being ſuſpected of any of the Offences aforeſaid, and to commit or bail him till the next Aſſizes or general Seſſions,* &c.

3 Inſt. 123.

Sect. 6. Sir *Edward Coke* is of Opinion, That the Offender cannot be fined in a Proſecution upon this Statute, becauſe it is expreſly ordained, That ſome corporal Puniſhment ſhall be inflicted, and no other is mentioned; however, there is a Precedent in *Croke*'s Reports, by which it appears, That one convicted on ſuch a Proſecution hath been adjudged not only to ſtand on the Pillory, but alſo to pay a Fine of five hundred Pounds, and to be bound with good Sureties to his good Behaviour.

Cro. Ca. 564.

CHAP. LXXII.

Of Conſpiracy.

FOR the better Underſtanding of the Nature of Conſpiracy, I ſhall conſider the following Particulars:

1. Who may be ſaid to be guilty of it.
2. In what Manner ſuch Offenders are to be puniſhed.

Sect. 1. As to the firſt Point, there can be no better Rule than the Statute of 33, or rather 21 *Ed.* 1. the Intent whereof was to make a final Definition of Conſpirators, to which Purpoſe it declareth, *That Conſpirators be they that do confeder or bind themſelves by Oath, Covenant or other Alliance, that every of them ſhall aid and bear the other falſly and maliciouſly to indict, or cauſe to indict, or falſly to move and maintain Pleas, and alſo ſuch as cauſe Children within Age to appeal Men of Felony, whereby they are impriſoned and ſore grieved; and ſuch as retain Men in the Country with Liveries or Fees for to maintain their malicious Enterprizes; and this extendeth as well to the Takers as to the Givers. And Stewards and Bailiffs of great Lords, who by their Seigniory, Office, or Power, undertake to bear or maintain Quarrels, Pleas, or Debates that concern other Parties than ſuch as touch the Eſtate of their Lords or themſelves.* 2 Inſt. 562.

Sect. 2. From this Definition of Conſpirators it ſeems clearly to follow, That not only thoſe who actually cauſe an Innocent Man to be indicted, and alſo to be tried upon the Indictment, whereupon he is lawfully acquitted, are properly Conſpirators, but that thoſe alſo are guilty of this Offence, who barely conſpire to indict a Man falſly and maliciouſly, whether they do any Act in Proſecution of ſuch Conſpiracy or not; for the Words of the Statute ſeem expreſly to include all ſuch Confederacies under the Notion of Conſpiracy, whether there be any Proſecution thereof or not; and if ſuch a Confederacy be within the Letter of the Statute, there ſeems to be no Manner of Reaſon to ſay, That they are not alſo within the Meaning of it, ſince it is a high Contempt of the Law, barely to engage in ſuch an Aſſociation to abuſe it, to ſerve the Purpoſes of Oppreſſion and Injuſtice; neither can it be a ſevere Conſtruction which will bring a Crime ſo evidently contrary to the firſt Principles of common Honeſty, within the Meaning of a Law, the Words whereof do plainly ſeem to extend to it. And therefore I cannot but queſtion the Accuracy of that Deſcription of Conſpiracy which is given in the third *Inſtitute,* whereby the lawful Acquittal of the Party grieved is required to make the Offenders guilty of this Crime. It is true indeed, That a bare Conſpiracy to indict a Man will not maintain a Writ of Conſpiracy at the Suit of the Party grieved, becauſe it doth not do him any actual Damage; alſo it muſt be confeſſed, That it is often laid down as a general Rule, and taken for granted, That no ſuch Conſpiracy is a good Foundation for ſuch a Writ, unleſs the Plaintiff be lawfully acquitted; and it is certain, That there is no formed Writ of Conſpiracy in the Regiſter for a malicious Indictment or Appeal; but what ſuppoſes ſuch Indict- 3 Inſt. 143. F. N. B. 114. D. 1 Danv Abr. 211. 2. 213. 1, 2. S.P.C.173.A. 174. B. D. 175. A. Bro Coro. 80, or 89.

Indictment or Appeal to have been actually brought, and the Party to have been legally discharged; from whence it follows, That no one can have the Benefit of any such Writ in the Register, who upon a false Accusation, is put to the Trouble and Vexation of being apprehended, examined, or committed, &c. without being ever indicted or appealed. However it is certain, That an Acquittal by Verdict is not always necessary to maintain such a Writ, for it appears by the Register it self, That where one brought such a Writ in the usual Form, having it in the Words *quousque acquietatus fuisset*, &c. against one who had been nonsuited in a malicious Appeal of Felony brought against him, his Writ was abated, because such a Nonsuit would not make good the Words *quousque acquietatus fuisset*, and yet he afterwards brought a new Writ, wherein he used the Words *quietus recessit*, instead of *acquietatus fuisset*, and recovered. And why may not a new Writ as well be formed in any other Case, which is as much within the Mischief of the Statute as this? Or what Colour can there be to say, That the malicious putting of a Man to the unreasonable Charge, Scandal, and Trouble, of a criminal Prosecution, which is so palpably groundless, as not to have Probability enough to induce a Grand Jury to find an Indictment, should not be as good a Foundation of Complaint, and a Grievance as much within the Meaning of the Statute, as the putting one to the Charge and Vexation of a groundless Action, either in a Temporal or Spiritual Court, for which it appears by the [a] Register, That a Writ of Conspiracy doth lie without making use either of the Words *acquietatus fuisset*, or *quietus recessit?* Neither can it be said, That the Opinion I contend for is wholly unsupported by Authority, as appears from the *Poulterer*'s Case in [b] *Coke*'s ninth Report. However since it is certain, That an [c] Action on the Case in the Nature of such Writ doth lie for a false and malicious Prosecution, for any Crime, whether capital, or not capital, tho' it doth not proceed to an actual Indictment, or Appeal, and that the same Damages may be recovered in such Action, as in a Writ of Conspiracy, it hath been thought needless to inquire, whether such Writ may be maintained for such a Prosecution, or not. But howsoever the Law may stand in Relation to Writs of Conspiracy, there seems to be no manner of Reason that the stated Form of such Writs should any Way restrain a Proceeding by way of Indictment or Information against Persons which are apparently within both the Letter and Meaning of the Statute. Also it seems certain, That a Man may not only be condemned to the Pillory, but also to be branded for a false and malicious Accusation, but since it doth not appear to have been solemnly resolved, that such an Offender is indictable upon the Statute, it seems to be more safe and advisable to ground an Indictment of this Kind upon the Common Law, than upon the Statute, since there can be no Doubt, but that all Confederacies whatsoever, wrongfully to prejudice a third Person, are highly criminal at Common Law, as where divers Persons confederate [d] together by indirect Means to impoverish a third Person, or [e] falsly and maliciously to charge a Man with being the reputed Father of [f] a Bastard-Child, or to maintain one another in any Matter, whether it be true or false.

Appeal 68. 1 Rol. Ab. 110. Pl. 2. 111. Pl. 5. 114. Pl. 3. 9 Co. 56, 57. Regist. 134. 1 Jon. 93, 94.

Bro. Coro. 6, or 8. 33 H. 6. 1. Regist. 134. b. See S. P. C. 174. D. Vide 2 Inst. 407, 562.

[a] Regist. 134. F.N.B. 116. B. Finch 306. 2 Inst. 562. 1 Keb. 254.

[b] 9 Co. 56. b.

[c] 1 Jon. 93, 94. 1 Leon. 107. Cro. El. 70, 134. Palm. 315. Cro. Ja. 130, 357. Latch 79. Cro. Ca. 15. 2 Rol. Re. 236, 237. 2 Bulst. 270, 271. 1 Rol. Re. 109. 1 Rol. A. 112. Pl. 11, 12, 13. 113. Pl. 14. 213. Pl. 3. Ray. 135, 180. Con. 1 Bulst. 185. Yelv. 116. Hutt. 49. Cro. El. 563. 9 Co. 57. a.

[d] 1 Levin. 62, 126. 1 Sid. 174. 1 Keb. 350.

[e] 1 Levin. 62. 1 Mod. 185, 186. 1 Sid. 68. 1 Keb. 254.

[f] 27 Ass. 44. 9 Co. 56. b. 2 Rol. Ab. 77. Pl. 2, 3. See Moore 788. Salk. 174. 1 Vent. 303, 304. 6 Mod. 185.

Sect. 3. Neither doth it seem to be any Justification of a Confederacy to carry on a false and malicious Prosecution, That the Indictment or Appeal, which was preferred, or intended to be preferred, in Pursuance of it, was [a] Insufficient, or that the Court wherein the Prosecution was carried on, or designed to be carried on, had no Jurisdiction of the Cause, or that the Matter of the Indictment did import no Manner of [b] Scandal, so that the Party grieved was in Truth in no Danger of losing either his Life, Liberty, or Reputation; for notwithstanding the Injury intended to the Party against whom such a Confederacy is formed, may perhaps be inconsiderable; yet the Association to pervert the Law in order to procure it, seems to be a Crime of a very high Nature, and justly to deserve the Resentment of the Law.

[a] Palm. 45. 3 Keb. 141. Stile 157. 1 Rol. Ab. 110. Pl. 2. 1 Rol. Ab. 111. Pl. 7. 9 Co. 26. b. Yelv. 46, 117. Cro. El. 563. 2 Bulst. 270, 271. Cro. Ja. 357.

1 Rol. Rep. 109. [b] Regist. 134. F. N. B. 116. F. 3 Ass. Pl. 13. 11 H. 7. 25. b. 26. a. 1 Rol. Ab. 112. Pl. 10. 2 Mod. 52, 306. Con. 2 Keb. 881.

Sect. 4. Neither [c] is it any Plea for one who is prosecuted for such an unlawful Confederacy, That nothing more was intended by him, but only to give his Testimony in a legal Course of Justice against the Party to whose Prejudice such Confederacy is supposed to have been formed; for notwithstanding it may be said, That it would be a great Discouragement to legal Proceedings to make Persons liable to a criminal Prosecution, for barely intending to give their Evidence, and it would be a Pre-judging of a Cause to try the Truth of the Testimony intended to be given in it before the Cause it self is determined; yet the Law will rather venture this Mischief, than suffer so flagrant a Villany to go unpunished. However if there be any Probability, That the principal Cause will ever be tried, it seems proper to apply to the Court to stay the Trial of the Confederacy till the Merits of the principal Cause be determined.

[c] 9 Co. 55. b. 56, 57. 12 Co. 23, 90, 91, 92. Cro. El. 70, 71, 134. 1 Leon. 107. 1 Rol. Ab. 113. Pl. 5. 114. Pl. 4, 5. 115. Pl. 7. Winch 28, 54. Latch 79, 80. Con. 1 Rol. Ab. 110. Pl. 1. F. N. B. 115. E. 27 H. 8. 2. a. b.

Sect. 5. Yet it [d] seems to be certain, That no one is liable to any Prosecution whatsoever, in respect of any Verdict given by him in a criminal Matter, either upon a Grand or Petit Jury; for since the Safety of the Innocent, and Punishment of the Guilty, doth so much depend upon the fair and upright Proceeding of Jurors, it is of the utmost Consequence, that they should be as little as possible under the Influence of any Passion whatsoever. And therefore, lest they should be biassed with the Fear of being harrassed by a vexatious Suit, for acting according to their Consciences, (the Danger of which might easily be insinuated, where powerful Men are warmly engaged in a Cause and throughly prepossessed of the Justice of the Side which they espouse) the Law will not leave any Possibility for a Prosecution of this Kind. It is true indeed, the Jurors were formerly sometimes questioned in the Star-Chamber, for their Partiality in finding a manifest Offender not guilty; but this was always thought a very great Grievance; and surely as the Law is now settled by *Bushel*'s Case, there is no Kind of Proceeding against Jurors in respect of their Verdicts in criminal Matters allowed of at this Day. As to the Objection, That an Attaint lies against a Jury for a false Verdict in a civil Cause, and that there is as much Reason to allow of it in a criminal one; it may be answered, That in an Attaint, a Man's Property only is brought into Question a second Time, and not his Liberty or Life; and also it may be generally presumed, That a Jury is likely to be equally influenced with the Fear of an Attaint from either of the contending Parties, whereas if any such Examinations of their Proceedings were allowed in criminal Causes, they might be often in great Danger of one Side, by incurring the Resentment of a powerful Prosecutor, and provoking him to call their Conduct into Question for their supposed Partiality; but they could have little to fear from an injured Criminal, who would seldom be in Circumstances to make his Prosecution formidable.

[d] 22 Ass. 77. 27 Ass. 12. 9 H. 6. 44. b. Bridgm. 130, 131. 21 E. 3. 17. a. 47 E. 3. 17. a. 12 Co. 23, 24. Regist. 134. F. N. B. 115. C. D. 27 H. 8. 2. S. P. C. 172, 173.

12 Co. 23. 24. Vaugh. 135.

F. N. B. 105, 106.

12 Co. 24. See Vaughan 138, 139. 12 Ed. 4. 18. 21 Ed. 4. 67. a. S. P. C. 173.

Sect. 6. And as the Law has exempted Jurors from the Danger of incurring any Puniſhment in reſpect of their Verdicts in criminal Cauſes, it hath alſo freed the Judges of all Courts of Record from all Proſecutions whatſoever, except in the Parliament, for any Thing done by them openly in ſuch Courts as Judges. For the Authority of a Government cannot be maintained, unleſs the greateſt Credit be given to thoſe who are ſo highly intruſted with the Adminiſtration of Publick Juſtice; and it would be impoſſible for them to keep up in the People that Veneration of their Perſons, and Submiſſion to their Judgments, without which it is impoſſible to execute the Laws with Vigour and Succeſs, if they ſhould be continually expoſed to the Proſecutions of thoſe whoſe Partiality to their own Cauſes would induce them to think themſelves injured.

12 Co. 24.

Yet if a Judge will ſo far forget the Dignity and Honour of his Poſt, as to turn Solicitor in a Cauſe which he is to judge, and privately and extrajudicially tamper with Witneſſes, or labour Jurors, he hath no Reaſon to complain, if he be dealt with according to the ſame Capacity, to which he ſo baſely degrades himſelf.

Sect. 7. It appears not only from the Words of the Statute, but alſo from the plain Reaſon of the Thing, That no Confederacy whatſoever to maintain a Suit can come within the Danger of the Statute, unleſs it be both falſe and malicious;

1 Rol. Ab. 111. Pl. 6. 112. Pl. 8. 115. Pl. 7.

for it would be a moſt dangerous Diſcouragement of all legal Proſecutions, if thoſe who engage in them upon a probable Ground, ſhould be in Danger of being found guilty of ſo heinous a Crime upon their not being able to bring their Suits to their intended Effect;

Bro. Coro. 89. S. P. C. 173. 22 Aſſ. 77.

and from hence it clearly follows, that if the Defendants to an Indictment or Appeal in Murder be fgund guilty of Homicide *ſe defendendo*, or by Miſadventure, or get off by pleading the King's Pardon, their Proſecutors are in no Danger of being puniſhed as Conſpirators: And from the ſame Ground it alſo follows, That if the Defendants in a Writ of Conſpiracy can ſhew a probable Cauſe of Suſpicion, they ſhall be diſcharged; as where being accuſed of a Conſpiracy for indicting a Perſon of Larceny,

1 Leon. 107. Cro. El. 134.

they can ſhew that a Larceny was committed at ſuch a Time and Place, and that the Party charged by them for ſuch Larceny was found by them at the ſame Time and Place, with ſuſpicious Circumſtances;

Kelw. 81. b. 83. b. 20 H. 7. 11.

or where Perſons being charged with a Conſpiracy for indicting another for feloniouſly carrying away a Woman, with great Violence and Numbers, are able to prove that they ſaw the Perſons whom they ſo accuſed riding armed in a warlike Manner, and following after thoſe who in Truth actually did the Felony, and that it was the common Report of the Country that they were all of the Company.

20 H. 7. 11. Kellw. 81. b. Cro. El. 134. 1 Leon. 107.

But ſome have ſaid, That there is a Neceſſity to plead ſuch Matter ſpecially, and that it cannot be given in Evidence on the General Iſſue.

Sect. 8. It plainly appears from the Words of the Statute, That one Perſon alone cannot be guilty of Conſpiracy within the Purport of it; from whence it follows, That if all the Defendants who are proſecuted for ſuch a Conſpiracy be acquitted but one, the [a] Acquittal of the reſt is the Acquittal of that one alſo; alſo upon the ſame Ground it hath been holden, That no ſuch Proſecution is maintainable againſt a [b] Huſband and Wife only, becauſe they are eſteemed but as one Perſon in Law, and are preſumed to have but one Will. But it is certain, That an Action on the [c] Caſe in the Nature of a Conſpiracy may be brought againſt one only: Alſo [d] it hath been reſolved, That if ſuch an Action be brought

[a] 8 H. 4. 6. b. 28 Aſſ. Pl. 12. S. P. C. 173. C. D. E. 174. A. Cro. El. 701. 5 Mod. 222, 223. 1 Rol. A. 111. Pl. 5. 112.

Pl. 9. [b] 38 Ed. 3. 3. a. b. S. P. C. 174. a. [c] 1 Rol Ab. 111. Pl. 5. 112. Pl. 9. F. N. B. 116. Cro. Ja. 194. Cro. Ca. 239. 3 Mod. 220. [d] 1 Rol. Ab. 111. Pl. 5. 112. Pl. 9. Cro. El. 701. 6 Mod. 170. 1 Saund. 228. Raymond 180. 2 Keb. 497.

gainst several Persons, and all but one be acquitted, yet Judgment may be given against that one only.

Sect. 9. As to the second Point, *viz.* In what manner Offenders of this Nature are to be punished, it is clear, That those who are convicted of Conspiracy at the Suit of the [a] Party shall only have Judgment of Fine and Imprisonment, and to render to the Plaintiff his Damages. Also it is certain, That he who is convicted at the Suit of the [b] King, of a Conspiracy to accuse another of a Matter which may touch his Life, shall have Judgment that he shall lose the Freedom and Franchise of the Law, (whereby he is disabled to be put upon any Jury, or to be sworn as a Witness, or even to appear in Person in any of the King's Courts;) and also that his Houses, Lands, and Goods, shall be seised into the King's Hands, and his Houses and Lands estreped and wasted, his Trees rooted up and arrased, and his Body imprisoned. And this is commonly called a villainous Judgment, and is given by the Common Law, and not by any Statute, and is said generally in some [c] Books, to be the proper Judgment upon every Conviction of Conspiracy, at the Suit of the King, without any Restriction to such as endangered the Life of the Party; but I do not find this Point any where settled.

[a] 24 Ed. 3. 34. b. 3 Inst. 143. 2 Inst. 383; 562. S. P. C. 175.

[b] 24 Ed. 3. 34. b. 3 Inst. 143. 2 Inst. 562. S. P. C. 175. 27 Ass. Pl. 59.

[c] See the Books above cited. 27 Ass. Pl. 59. S. P. C. 175.

CHAP. LXXIII.

Of Libels.

IN treating of Libels, I shall consider,

1. What shall be said to be a Libel.
2. Who are liable to be punished for it.
3. In what Manner they are to be punished.

Sect. 1. As to the first Point it seemeth, That a Libel in a strict Sense is taken for a malicious Defamation, expressed either in Printing or Writing, and tending either to blacken the Memory of one who is dead, or the Reputation of one who is alive, and to expose him to publick Hatred, Contempt or Ridicule. 5 Co. 121. 5 Mod. 165, 166.

Sect. 2. But it is said, That in a larger Sense the Notion of a Libel may be applied to any Defamation whatsoever, expressed either by Signs or Pictures, as by fixing up a Gallows against a Man's Door, or by painting him in a shameful and ignominious Manner. 5 Co. 121 b. Skin. 123, 124.

Sect. 3. And since the chief Cause for which the Law so severely punishes all Offences of this Nature, is the direct Tendency of them to a Breach of Publick Peace, by provoking the Parties injured, and their Friends and Families to Acts of Revenge, which it would be impossible to restrain by the severest Laws, were there no Redress from Publick Justice for Injuries of this kind, which of all others are most sensibly felt; and since the plain Meaning of such Scandal as is expressed by Signs or Pictures, is as obvious to common Sense, and as easily understood by every common Capacity, and altogether as provoking, as that which is expressed by Writing or Printing, why should it not be equally criminal? 5 Co. 121.

Sect. 4. And from the same Ground it seemeth clearly to follow, That such Scandal as is expressed in a scoffing and ironical Manner, Hob. 215. Poph. 139.

 makes

makes a Writing as properly a Libel, as that which is expressed in direct Terms; as where a Writing in a taunting Manner reckoning up several Acts of Publick Charity done by one, says, *You will not play the Jew, nor the Hypocrite*, and so goes on in a Strain of Ridicule to insinuate, that what he did was owing to his Vain-Glory; or where a Writing, pretending to recommend to one the Charracters of several great Men for his Imitation, instead of taking Notice of what they are generally esteemed famous for, pitched on such Qualities only which their Enemies charge them with the Want of; as by proposing such a one to be imitated for his Cou-
Brown's Case. rage who is known to be a great Statesman, but no Soldier, and another to be imitated for his Learning, who is known to be a great General, but no Scholar, &c. which Kind of Writing is as well understood to mean only to upbraid the Parties with the Want of these Qualities, as if it had directly and expresly done so.

Sect. 5. And from the same Foundation it hath also been resolved, That a Defamatory Writing expressing only one or two Letters of a Name, in such a Manner, that from what goes before and follows after, it must needs be understood to signify such a particular Person, in the plain, obvious,
Hurt's Case, Trin. 12 Annæ. and natural Construction of the whole, and would be perfect Nonsense if strained to any other Meaning, is as properly a Libel, as if it had expressed the whole Name at large; for it brings the utmost Contempt upon the Law, to suffer its Justice to be eluded by such trifling Evasions: And it is a ridiculous Absurdity to say, That a Writing which is understood by every the meanest Capacity, cannot possibly be understood by a Judge and Jury.

5 Co. 125. b. Hob. 253. Moore 627. *Sect.* 6. And from the same Ground it farther doth appear, That it is far from being a Justification of a Libel, that the Contents thereof are true, or that the Person upon whom it is made, had a bad Reputation, since the greater Appearance there is of Truth in any malicious Invective, so much the more provoking it is.

5 Co. 125. *Sect.* 7. Nor can there be any Doubt, but that a Writing which defames private Persons only, is as much a Libel as that which defames Persons intrusted with a Publick Capacity, inasmuch as it manifestly tends to create ill Blood, and to cause a Disturbance of the Publick Peace: However it
2 Rol. Re. 86. is certain, That it is a very high Aggravation of a Libel that it tends to scandalize the Government, by reflecting on those who are intrusted with the Administration of Publick Affairs, which doth not only endanger the Publick Peace, as all other Libels do, by stirring up the Parties immediately concerned in it to acts of Revenge, but also has a direct Tendency to breed in the People a Dislike of their Governors, and incline them to Faction and Sedition.

Sect. 8. But it hath been resolved, That no false or scandalous Mat-
[a] 1 Lev. 240. 1 Sid. 414, 415. 1 Saund. 131. 2 Keb. 832. [b] 4 Co. 14. b. [c] Dyer 285. Pl. 37. ter contained in a [a] Petition to a Committee of Parliament, or in [b] Articles of the Peace exhibited to Justices of Peace, or in any other [c] Proceeding in a regular Course of Justice, will make the Complaint amount to a Libel; for it would be a great Discouragement to Suitors to subject them to Publick Prosecutions, in respect of their Applications to a Court of Justice. And the chief Intention of the Law in prohibiting Persons to revenge themselves by Libels, or any other private Manner, is to restrain them from endeavouring to make themselves their own Judges, and to oblige them to refer the Decision of their Grievances, to those
[d] 2 Keb. 832. Con. 4 Co. 14. b. whom the Law has appointed to determine them. Also [d] it seemeth to have been holden by some, That no Want of Jurisdiction in the Court, to which such a Complaint shall be exhibited, will make it a Libel, be-

cause the Mistake of the proper Court is not imputable to the Party, but to his Counsel. Yet if it shall manifestly appear from the whole Circumstances of the Case, That a Prosecution is intirely false, malicious, and groundless, and commenced, not with a Design to go through with it, but only to expose the Defendant's Character under the Shew of a legal Proceeding; I cannot see any Reason why such a Mockery of Publick Justice should not rather aggravate the Offence, than make it cease to be one, and make such Scandal a good Ground of an Indictment at the Suit of the King; as it makes the Malice of their Proceeding a good Foundation of an Action on the Case at the Suit of the Party, whether the Court had a Jurisdiction of the Cause or not. But it is said, that no Presentment of a Grand Jury can be a Libel, not only because Persons who are supposed to be returned without their own seeking, and are sworn to act impartially, shall be presumed to have proper Evidence for what they do, but also because it would be of the utmost ill Consequence any way to discourage them from making their Inquiries with that Freedom and Readiness which the Publick Good requires. For which Considerations, it seems reasonable to exempt them from the Fear of any Kind of Prosecution in respect of their Inquiries, as hath been shewn more at large in the Chapter of Conspiracy.

See 1 Danv. Abr. 208, 209, 210, 211. and the foregoing Chapter of Conspiracy.

Moore 627.

Sect. 9. However it seems clear, That no Writing whatsoever is to be esteemed a Libel, unless it reflect upon some particular Person; and it seems, That a Writing full of obscene Ribaldry, without any Kind of Reflection upon any one, is not punishable at all by any Prosecution at Common Law, as I have heard it agreed in the Court of King's Bench; yet it seems, That the Author may be bound to his good Behaviour, as a scandalous Person of evil Fame.

See the Chapter concerning Surety for the good Behaviour.

Sect. 10. As to the second Point, *viz.* Who are liable to be punished for a Libel, it is certain that not only he who composes, or procures another to compose it, but also that he who publishes, or procures another to publish it, are in Danger of being punished for it; and it is said, not to be material whether he who disperses a Libel knew any Thing of the Contents or Effect of it or not; for nothing could be more easy than to publish the most virulent Papers with the greatest Security, if the Concealing the Purport of them from an illiterate Publisher would make him safe in dispersing them. Also it hath been said, That if he who hath either read a Libel himself, or hath heard it read by another, do afterwards maliciously read or repeat any Part of it, in the Presence of others, or lend or shew it to another, he is guilty of an unlawful Publication of it. Also it hath been holden, That the Copying of a Libel shall be a conclusive Evidence of the Publication of it, unless the Party can prove that he delivered it to a Magistrate to examine it, in which Case the Act subsequent is said to explain the Intention precedent. But it seems to be the better Opinion, That he who first writes a Libel dictated by another, is thereby guilty of making it, and consequently punishable for the bare Writing; for it was no Libel till it was reduced to Writing.

9 Co. 59. b. Moore 627, 813.

Moore 627. Con. 9 Co. b. 59. b.

Moore 627, 813. 9 Co. 59. b.

9 Co. 59. b. Moore 813.

5 Mod. 167.

Vide Salk. 417, 418, 419. Carth. 407 to 410.

Sect. 11. Also it hath been resolved, [a] That the sending of a Letter full of provoking Language to another, without publishing it, is highly punishable; and if the bare making of a Libel be an Offence, whether it be published or not, as it seemeth to be holden in some [b] Books, surely the Sending of it to the Party reflected upon, must be a much greater Crime, inasmuch as it so manifestly tends to a Disturbance of the Peace.

[a] 1 Keb. 931. 1 Levinz 139. 12 Co. 34. Poph. 139. Ray. 201. 1 Sid. 270. 1 Mod. 58. Hob. 62, 215. 3 Inst. 174. 4 Inst. 180, 181.

Sect. 12. Also it seems to be agreed, That he who delivers a Paper full of Reflections on any Person, in Nature of a Petition to a Committee of

[b] 5 Mod. 167. 9 Co. 59. b. 1 Keb. 832.

1 Saund. 133. 1 Levinz 240. 1 Sid. 414, 415. of Parliament, to any other Perſons except the Members of Parliament, may be puniſhed as the Publiſher of a Libel, in reſpect of ſuch a Diſperſing thereof among thoſe who have nothing to do with it.

[a] 9 Co. 59. b. Moore 813. [b] 9 Co. 59. b. Moore 813. [c] Moore 627. 1 Vent. 31. 2 Keb. 502. Salk. 418. Carth. 409. *Sect.* 13. But it hath been reſolved, That he who barely reads a Libel in the Preſence [a] of another, without knowing it before to be a Libel, or who hearing a Libel read by another, [b] laughs at it, or who [c] barely ſays, That ſuch a Libel is made upon ſuch a Perſon, whether he ſpeak it with or without Malice, or who is only proved to have had a Libel in his Cuſtody, ſhall not in reſpect of any ſuch Act be adjudged the Publiſher of it. But the having in one's Cuſtody a written Copy of a Libel publickly known, is an Evidence of the Publication of it.

Moore 627. *Sect.* 14. Alſo it hath been holden, That he who repeats Part of a Libel in Merriment without Malice, and with no Purpoſe of Defamation, is no way puniſhable; but it ſeemeth, That the Reaſonableneſs of this Opinion may juſtly be queſtioned; for Jeſts of this Kind are not to be endured, and the Injury to the Reputation of the Party grieved is no way leſſened by the Merriment of him who makes ſo light of it.

1 Keb. 832. 1 Saund. 133. 1 Levinz 240. 1 Sid. 414, 415. Skin. 124. *Sect.* 15. But it ſeemeth to be ſettled, That the bare Printing of a Petition to a Committee of Parliament (which would be a Libel againſt the Party complained of, if it were made for any other Purpoſe, than as a Complaint in a Courſe of Juſtice) and delivering Copies thereof to the Members of the Committee, ſhall not be look'd upon as the Publication of a Libel, inaſmuch as it is juſtified by the Order and Courſe of Proceedings in Parliament, whereof the King's Courts will take judicial Notice.

Cro. Ca. 175, &c. *Sect.* 16. As to the third Point, *viz.* In what manner Offenders of this Kind are to be puniſhed, there ſeemeth to be no Doubt, but that they may be condemned to pay ſuch Fine, and alſo to ſuffer ſuch corporal Puniſhment, as to the Court in Diſcretion ſhall ſeem proper, according to the Heinouſneſs of the Crime, and the Circumſtances of the Offender.

CHAP. LXXIV.

Of the Offence of keeping a Bawdy-Houſe.

THE Offence of keeping a Bawdy-Houſe being of ſo groſs a Nature, and there being alſo ſo few Queſtions relating to it worth conſidering, I ſhall paſs it over with theſe following Obſervations:

1. That it comes under the Cognizance of the Temporal Law, as a Com-
Kitchen 11. a. 3 Inſt. 205. mon Nuſance, not only in reſpect of its endangering the Publick Peace, by drawing together diſſolute and debauched Perſons, but alſo in reſpect of its apparent Tendency to corrupt the Manners of both Sexes, by ſuch an open Profeſſion of Lewdneſs.

2. That a Feme-Covert is puniſhable for this Offence as much as if ſhe were ſole, as more fully hath been ſhewn, Chap, 1. Sect. 12.

3. That a Lodger who keeps only a ſingle Room for the Uſe of Bawdry,
Salk. 382. is indictable for keeping a Bawdy-Houſe; but that the bare Solicitation of Chaſtity is not indictable.

4. That Offenders of this Kind are puniſhable not only with Fine and Impriſonment, but alſo with ſuch infamous Puniſhment as to the Court in Diſcretion ſhall ſeem proper.

CHAP. LXXV.

Of Common Nuſances.

OFFENCES under the Degree of capital, more immediately againſt the Subject, not amounting to an actual Diſturbance of the Peace, which may be committed by private Perſons without any Relation to an Office, and which are of an inferiour Nature to the ſix Kinds of Offences laſt treated of, being neither infamous nor groſly ſcandalous, ſeem to be reducible to the following Heads:

1. Such as more immediately affect the Publick.
2. Such as more immediately affect the Intereſts of particular Perſons.

Offences of this Kind, more immediately affecting the Publick, are four-fold;

1. Common Nuſances.
2. Monopolies.
3. Foreſtalling, Ingroſſing, and Regrating.
4. Barratry.

And firſt of Common Nuſances; for the better underſtanding whereof I ſhall firſt conſider them in general, and then deſcend to thoſe relating to Highways, and Publick Houſes, which ſeem to be the moſt remarkable general Heads of this Offence.

As to Common Nuſances in general I ſhall conſider,

1. What ſhall be ſaid to be a Common Nuſance.
2. How it may be removed,
3. How it may be puniſhed.

Sect. 1. As to the firſt Point it ſeems, That a Common Nuſance may be defined to be an Offence againſt the Publick, either by doing a Thing which tends to the Annoyance of all the King's Subjects, or by neglecting to do a Thing which the Common Good requires.

2 Rol. Ab. 83.

Sect. 2. But Annoyances to the Intereſt of particular Perſons are not puniſhable by a publick Proſecution as Common Nuſances, but are left to be redreſſed by the private Actions of the Parties aggrieved by them.

2 Rol. Ab. 83.

Sect. 3. And from hence it clearly follows, That no Indictment for a Nuſance can be good, which lays it to the Damage of private Perſons only; as where it accuſes a Man of [a] Surcharging ſuch a Common; or of [b] incloſing ſuch a Piece of Ground, wherein the Inhabitants of ſuch a Town have a Right of Common, to the Nuſance of all the Inhabitants of ſuch a Town; or of diſturbing a [c] Water-courſe running to the Mill of *J. S. ad grave Damnum J. S. & Tenentium ſuorum*, without ſaying *omnium Ligeorum Domini Regis*; or of doing a Nuſance to a Thing no way appearing to be of a Publick Nature, *ad grave* [d] *Damnum*, or [e] *Detrimentum*, or [f] *commune No-*

1 Sid. 209.
[a] 2 Rol. Ab. 83. Pl. 7.
[b] 27 Aſſ. Pl. 6. 2 Rol. Ab. 83. Pl. 7, 12, 13. Cro. El. 90.
[c] 2 Rol. Ab. 83. Pl. 10. Vid. 1 Ventr. 26.

[d] 2 Rol. Ab. 83. Pl. 11. [e] 1 Mod. 107. [f] 1 Rol. Re. 406. 3 Keb. 284. Cro. El. 414. Cro. Jac. 382. 1 Saund. 135. Cro. El. 148. 2 Keb. 461.

2 Leon. 183, 184. 9 Co. 113. 1 Vent. 208. 3 Keb. 28. *cumentum omnium Ligeorum Domini Regis prope Inhabitantium*; yet it hath been resolved, That an Indictment for not repairing a Bridge by Reason whereof it was ruinous, *ita quod Ligei Domini Regis per eam transire non possunt*, and concluding, *ad Nocumentum eorundem*, is good without using the Words *ad Nocumentum omnium Ligeorum, &c.* for by the King's liege People shall be understood, all his liege People.

Sect. 4. Also it is said, That the Law hath so tender a Regard for the Interest of the King and of Religion, That an Indictment for doing a Thing which plainly appears immediately to tend to the Prejudice of either of them, is good, though it do not expresly complain of it as a common Grievance; and upon this Ground it hath been resolved, That an Indictment for converting the King's Money to one's own Use is good, without more. And upon the same Foundation also it hath been holden, That an Indictment for breaking and digging up the Wall of the Church of such a Town, *ad Nocumentum Burgi Ligeorum Domini Regis*, is good. (27 Ass. Pl. 19, 20. 2 Rol. Ab. 83. Pl. 1, 2, 3. 2 Rol. Ab. 84. Pl. 14.)

Sect. 5. Also it hath been said, That an Indictment of a common Scold, by the Words *communis Rixatrix*, which seem to be precisely necessary in every Indictment of this Kind, is good, though it conclude *ad commune Nocumentum diversorum* instead of *omnium, &c.* perhaps for this Reason, because a common Scold cannot but be a common Nusance. And upon the like Ground it seems that it may probably be argued, That an Indictment for laying Logs in the Stream of a navigable publick River, *ad Nocumentum J. S.* may be maintained, because it cannot but be a common Nusance. And if the Law be so in this Case, why should not also an Indictment setting forth a Nusance to a Way, and expresly and unexceptionably shewing it to be a Highway, be good, notwithstanding it conclude *in Nocumentum diversorum Ligeorum, &c.* without saying *omnium*; for why should such a Conclusion be more necessary in an Indictment for one Kind of Nusance than for any other? And perhaps the [a] Authorities which seem to contradict this Opinion, might go upon this Reason, That in the Body of the Indictment, it did not appear with sufficient Certainty, whether the Way, wherein the Nusance was alledged, were a Highway, or only a private Way; and therefore that it shall be intended from the Conclusion of the Indictment, That it was a private Way. (6 Mod 11. 178, 213, 239, 311. Moor 847. 2 Keb. 410. 1 Keb. 161. 1 Rol. Re. 201. [a] Cro. El. 148. 2 Keb. 461. Vid. 2 Rol. Ab. 83. Pl. 11.)

Sect. 6. There is no Doubt but that common Bawdy-Houses are indictable as common Nusances, as hath been more fully shewn in the foregoing Chapter; also it hath been said, That all common Stages for Rope-Dancers, and also all common Gaming-houses, are Nusances in the Eye of the Law, not only because they are great Temptations to Idleness, but also because they are apt to draw together great Numbers of disorderly Persons, which cannot but be very inconvenient to the Neighbourhood. (1 Mod. 76. 2 Keb. 846. 3 Keb. 464. 5 Mod. 142. 1 Vent. 169.)

Sect. 7. Also it hath been holden, That a common Play-house may be a Nusance, if it draw together such Numbers of Coaches or People, *&c.* as prove generally inconvenient to the Places adjacent; and it seems to be a proper Distinction between Play-houses and the Nusances mentioned in the foregoing Section, That Play-houses having been originally instituted with a laudable Design of recommending Virtue to the Imitation of the People, and exposing Vice and Folly, are not Nusances in their own Nature, but may only become such by Accident, whereas the others cannot but be Nusances. (1 Rol. Re. 109. 5 Mod. 142. See Rushworth's Coll. Part 2. Vol. 1. fol. 220, 247. Skin. 625 to 630.)

Sect. 8. It hath been resolved, That neither an old nor a new [b] Dovecote, whether it were erected by the Lord of a Manor, or one of his Tenants, ([b] 2 Rol. Ab. 138. f. 139. f. 1, 2, 3. 265. E. 1.)

Tenants, is a common Nusance; for if a Dove-cote were a common Nusance, it could never become lawful by any Licence or Prescription whatsoever, because every Nusance is a *Malum in se*; but it is certain, that a Dove-house may be justified by a Prescription, and that it is so far countenanced by the Law, as to be [a] demandable in a *Præcipe* before any Land whatsoever which is not built upon, and that the Owner may justify the Taking another's [b] Hawk, which he shall find at his Dove-house, flying at his Pigeons; and from hence it seems clearly to follow, That though a Tenant, who builds a Dove-house without the Licence of the Lord of the Manor, may perhaps be liable to an Action on the Case at the Suit of such Lord, whose Prerogative is said to be incroached upon by the erecting such a House without his Licence, yet he cannot be punished for it by a publick Prosecution.

[2 Rol. Re. 4, 30. Cro. Ja. 382, 491. Moor 238. 1 Rol. Re. 136, 201. Popham 143. Con. 5 Co. 104. b. a F. N. B. 2. c. b 16 E. 4. 7. b. Quære Moor Pl. 580 & 621. Cro. El. 548.]

Sect. 9. But perhaps it may be argued, That if this Reasoning be good, it will follow from the same Ground, That a Gate erected in a Highway will be also no Nusance; because, if it were, it could not be justified by any Prescription, as it is agreed that it may be; but to this it may be answered, That the Erecting of such a Gate is therefore a Nusance; because it interrupts the People in that free and open Passage which they before enjoyed, and were lawfully intitled to; but where such a Gate has continued Time out of Mind, it shall be intended, That it was set up at first by Consent, on a Composition with the Owner of the Land on the laying out the Road, in which Case the People had never any Right to a freer Passage than what they still enjoy.

[1 Jones 221. Cro. Ca. 184. 1 Bulf. 203. 2 Rol. Ab. 137. C.]

Sect. 10. It hath been holden, That it is no common Nusance to make Candles in a Town, because the Needfulness of them shall dispense with the Noisomness of the Smell; but the Reasonableness of this Opinion seems justly to be questionable, because whatever Necessity there may be that Candles be made, it cannot be pretended to be necessary to make them in a Town; and surely the Trade of a Brewer is as necessary as that of a Chandler; and yet it seems to be agreed, That a Brew-house, erected in such an inconvenient Place, wherein the Business cannot be carried on without greatly incommoding the Neighbourhood, may be indicted as a common Nusance: And so in the like Case may a Glass-House or Swine-yard.

[2 Rol. Ab. 139. Pl. 2. Cont. 3 Mod. 138. 2 Keb. 500. Vide 1 Danv. A. 173, 174. Salk. 458, 460.]

Sect. 11. It seemeth certain, That it is a common Nusance to divert Part of a publick navigable River, whereby the Current of it is weakened, and made unable to carry Vessels of the same Burden, as it could before. Also it hath been holden to be a common Nusance to divide a House in a Town for poor People to inhabit in, by reason whereof it will be more dangerous in the Time of Infection of the Plague.

[Noy 103. 2 Rol. Ab. 139. Pl. 3.]

Sect. 12. As to the second Point, *viz.* How a Nusance may be removed; it seemeth to be certain, That any one may pull down or otherwise destroy a common Nusance, as a new Gate, or even a new House erected in a Highway, *&c.* for if one whose Estate is, or may be, prejudiced by a private Nusance actually erected, as a House hanging over his Ground, or stopping his Lights, *&c.* may justify the entring into another's Ground, and pulling down and destroying such a Nusance, whether it were erected before or since he came to the Estate, surely it cannot but follow *à fortiori*, That any one may lawfully destroy a common Nusance: And as the Law is now holden, it seems, that in a Plea, justifying the Removal of the Nusance, you need not shew that you did as little Damage as might be.

[2 Rol. Ab. 144. S. Cro. Ca. 184. 1 Jon. 221. 2 Rol. A. 145. U. W. Salk. 459. Yelv. 142. 5 Co. 101. b. 9 Co. 54. b. 1 Rol. Rep. 9 E. 4. 35. Bro. Nusance 14. 1 Jon. 221. Salk. 458.]

Sect. 13. It hath been adjudged, That if a River be ſtopped, to the
37 Aſſ. 10. 2 Rol. Ab. 137. A. Nuſance of the Country, and none appear bound by Preſcription to clear it, thoſe who have the Piſcary, and the neighbouring Towns, who have a common Paſſage and Eaſement therein, may be compelled to do it.

Sect. 14. As to the third Point, *viz.* In what Manner common Nu-
6 Mod. 11, 178, 213. ſances may be puniſhed; it is ſaid, That a common Scold is puniſhable by being put into the Ducking-Stool, and there is no Doubt, but that whoever is convicted of another Nuſance, may be fined and impriſoned;
2 Rol. Ab. 84. Pl. 15. and it is ſaid, That one convicted of a Nuſance, done to the King's Highway may be commanded by the Judgment to remove the Nuſance at his own Coſts; and it ſeemeth to be reaſonable, That thoſe who are convicted of any other common Nuſance ſhould alſo have the like Judgment.

CHAP. LXXVI.

Of Nuſances relating to Highways.

AND now I am particularly to conſider ſuch Nuſances as relate to Highways, and publick Houſes;

And firſt for the better Underſtanding of thoſe which concern Highways, I ſhall conſider:

1. Such as relate to Highways in general.
2. Such as relate to Bridges in particular.

For the better Underſtanding of Nuſances relating to highways in general, I ſhall examine the following Particulars:

1. What ſhall be ſaid to be a Highway.
2. At whoſe Charge and by whom it ought to be repaired.
3. In what Manner it is to be inlarged.
4. How the Surveyors thereof ſhall be appointed.
5. How ſuch Surveyors ought to execute their Office.
6. What ſhall be ſaid to be a Nuſance to the Highway.
7. How ſuch Nuſances are to be removed and puniſhed.
8. In what Manner thoſe who are charged with any Offence relating to the Highway, are to be proceeded againſt.
9. How Perſons ſo proceeded againſt may defend themſelves.

As to the firſt Point, *viz.* What ſhall be ſaid to be a Highway, it is ſaid that there are three Kinds of Ways:

1. A Footway, which is called in *Latin*, *Iter*.
2. Co. Lit. 56. a. A Pack and Prime-way, which is both a Horſe and Foot-way, and called in *Latin*, *Actus*.
3. A Cart-way, which contains the other two; and alſo a Cart-way, and is called in *Latin*, *Via* or *Aditus*, and this is either com-

mon to all Men, and then it is called, *Via Regia*, or belongs to some City or Town, or private Person, and then it is called *Communis Strata*.

Sect. 1. It seemeth that any one of the said Ways, which is common to all the King's People, whether it lead directly to a Market-Town, or only from Town to Town, may properly be called a Highway, and that any such Cartway may be called the King's Highway, and that a Nusance in any of the said Ways is punishable by Indictment in the Court-Leet; for Indictments for [a] stopping Horseways, and [b] Footways, have often been allowed, and where others have been quashed, no other Reason has been given for it, but that the Way was not called a common Way or Highway; and in [c] Books of the best Authority, a River common to all Men, is called a Highway; and it is laid [d] down as a general Rule, That Nusances to any Way common to all Men, are inquirable in the Leet, and Horse-Causeys are taken Notice of by [e] Parliament; and therefore there seems to be no Reason why any Way leading from Village to Village, which does not terminate there, but is also a Thoroughfare to other Towns, may not properly be called a common or Highway, or why a Nusance therein should not be indictable, whether it directly lead to a Market-Town or not; for since such a Way lies open to all the King's Subjects, a Nusance therein [f] cannot but be a common Nusance, and if it be not punishable by Indictment it would not be punishable at all, inasmuch as it [g] seems to be certain, That it is not punishable by Action, because if one Man might bring his Action in Respect of the Possibility of the Damage which he might receive from it, all other Men may do the like, which would introduce a Multiplicity of Actions; and therefore the Distinction which is taken in some [h] Books concerning this Matter seems to be very reasonable, That every Way from Town to Town may be called a Highway, because it is common to all the King's Subjects, but that a Way to a Parish-Church, or to the common Fields of a Town, or to a private House, or perhaps to a Village which terminates there, and is for the Benefit of the particular Inhabitants of such Parish, House, or Village only, may be called a private Way, but not a Highway, because it belongeth not to all the King's Subjects, but only to some particular Persons, each of which, as it seems, may have an Action on the Case for a Nusance therein.

Palm. 389. 6 Mod. 255. [a] Cro. El. 63. [b] 1 Vent. 208. 2 Keb. 178. 3 Keb. 26. 6 Mod. 255. [c] 27 Ass. 23. [d] Co. Lit. 56. a. 5 Ed. 4. 2. b. [e] 3 & 4 W. & M. 12. [f] Kitchin 35. a. Palm. 389. 2 Rol. Re. 412 [g] Moore 180. Pl. 321. Cro. E. 664. Co. Lit. 56. a. 27 H. 8. 27. a. [h] 1 Vent. 189. Kitch. 35. a. 1 Vent. 208. 3 Keb. 28. Co. Lit. 56.

Sect. 2. It hath been holden, that if there be a Highway in an open Field, and the People have used, Time out of Mind, when the Ways are bad, to go by Outlets on the Land adjoining, such Outlets are Parcel of the Way; for the King's Subjects ought to have a good Passage, and the good Passage is the Way, and not only the beaten Track; from whence it follows, That if such Outlets be sown with Corn, and the beaten Track be founderous, the King's Subjects may justify going upon the Corn.

1 Rol. A. 390. Pl. 1.

Sect. 3. It seemeth to be agreed, That an ancient Highway cannot be changed without the King's Licence first obtained upon a Writ of *Ad quod dammum*, and an Inquisition thereon found, That such a Change will not be prejudicial to the Publick; and it is said, That if one change a Highway without such Authority, he may stop the new Way whenever he pleases; and it seemeth, That the King's Subjects have not such an Interest in such new Way as will make good a general Justification of their going in it as in a common Highway, but that in an Action of Trespass brought by the Owner of the Land against those who shall go over it, they ought to shew specially, by Way of Excuse, how the old Way was obstructed, and the new one set out; also it is said, That the Inha-

Cro. Ca. 266, 267. Vaugh. 341. Cro. Ca. 267. Yelv. 141, 142.

Inhabitants are not bound to keep Watch in ſuch a new Way, or to make Amends for a Robbery therein committed, or to repair it.

Cro. Ca. 267. *Sect.* 4. However it is certain, That a Highway may be changed by the Act of God; and therefore it hath been holden, That if a Water which has been an ancient Highway, by Degrees changes its Courſe, and goes over different Ground from that whereon it uſed to run, yet the Highway continues in the new Chanel, in the ſame Manner as in the old. 22 Aſſ. 93. 1 Rol. A. 390.

As to the ſecond Point, *viz.* At whoſe Charge, and by whom the Highway ought to be repaired, I ſhall conſider:

1. What Proviſion is made by the Common Law concerning this Matter.
2. What by Statute.

[a] 1 Rol. Ab. 890. [b] March 26. 1 Vent. 90, 183, 189. H. P. C. 144. 8 H. 7. 5. *Sect.* 5. As to the firſt of theſe Particulars, it ſeems to be agreed, That of common Right, the general Charge of Repairing all Highways lies on the Occupiers of the Lands in the Pariſh wherein they are; but it is ſaid, That the Tenants of the Lands adjoining are bound to ſcowr their Ditches, and there is no Doubt but particular Perſons may be burthened with the general Charge of Repairing a Highway, in two Caſes:

1. In Reſpect of an Incloſure of the Land wherein it lies.
2. In Reſpect of a Preſcription.

1 Rol. Ab. 390. B. Cro. Ca. 366. 1 Sid. 464. *Sect.* 6. And firſt a particular Perſon may be bound to repair a Highway in Reſpect of an Incloſure, as where the Owner of Lands not incloſed, next adjoining to the Highway, incloſes his Lands on both Sides thereof, in which Caſe he is bound to make a perfect good Way, and ſhall not be excuſed for making it as good as it was at the Time of the Incloſure, if it were then any way defective, becauſe, before the Incloſure, the People uſed, when the Way was bad, to go for their better Paſſage, over the Fields adjoining, out of the common Track, which Liberty is taken away by the Incloſure.

1 Sid. 464. *Sect.* 7. Alſo it hath been holden, That if one incloſe Land on one Side, which hath been anciently incloſed of the other Side, he ought to repair all the Way, but that if there be not ſuch an ancient Incloſure of the other Side, he ought to repair but Half that Way: And it is ſaid, That where-ever one is bound to repair a Highway in reſpect of an Incloſure, and lays it open again as it was before, he ſhall be freed from the Charge of repairing it.

2 Saund. 160. 27 Aſſ. 8. 21 Ed. 4. 38. b. Brook Preſcription 49, 78. Far. 54, 55. *Sect.* 8. Secondly, A particular Perſon may be bound to repair a Highway in reſpect of a Preſcription; and it is ſaid, That a Corporation aggregate may be compelled to do it by Force of a general Preſcription, That it ought and hath uſed to do it, without ſhewing, that it uſed to do ſo in Reſpect of the Tenure of certain Lands, or for any other Conſideration, becauſe ſuch a Corporation in Judgment of Law never dies, and therefore, if it were ever bound to ſuch a Duty, it muſt needs continue to be always ſo; neither is it any Plea, That ſuch Corporation have always done it out of Charity; for what it hath always done, it ſhall be preſumed to have been always bound to do; but it is ſaid,
21 Ed. 4. 31. b. That a Perſon cannot be charged with ſuch a Duty by a general Preſcription from what his Anceſtors have done, becauſe no one is bound to do what his Anceſtors have done, unleſs it be for ſome ſpecial Reaſon, as the

5

the having Land deſcended from ſuch Anceſtors, which are holden by ſuch like Service, *&c.* yet it ſeems, That an Indictment charging a Tenant in Fee-ſimple with having uſed of Right to repair ſuch a Way *ratione Tenuræ Terræ ſuæ*, is certain enough, without adding, That his Anceſtors, or thoſe whoſe Eſtate he hath, have always ſo done, for that is implied in ſaying, That he has always uſed to do it *ratione Tenuræ ſuæ*. Alſo an Occupier, as ſuch, though at Will only, is indictable for ſuffering a Houſe ſtanding upon the Highway to be ruinous, *&c.* and the Words *ratione Tenuræ*, *&c.* if added, are Surplus. Kellew. 52. a. Latch 206. Salk. 357, 2.

Sect. 9. However it ſeemeth certain, That whether a particular Perſon be bound to repair a Highway by Incloſure, or Preſcription, *&c.* yet the Pariſh cannot take Advantage of it upon the Plea of Not guilty to an Indictment againſt them for not repairing it, but ought to ſet forth their Diſcharge in a ſpecial Plea. 1 Mod. 112. 3 Keb. 301. 1 Ven. 256.

And now I am to conſider in the ſecond Place, at whoſe Charge, and by whom the Highway ought to be repaired by Force of the Statute; for the better Underſtanding whereof, I ſhall examine:

1. Who are by Statute compellable to work in the Repairs thereof in their own Perſons, or by others.
2. Who may be aſſeſſed to a Rate made for the Defraying of the extraordinary Charges of ſuch Repairs.
3. What other Proviſions have been made to this Purpoſe.
4. In what manner the Profits of Lands ſettled in Truſt for the Repairs of the Highways ſhall be imployed.

Sect. 10. As to the firſt Point, it is enacted by 2 & 3 *Ph. & Mar.* 8. Par. 2. and 22 *Car.* 2. 12. *That the Pariſhioners of every Pariſh ſhall endeavour themſelves to the Amending of the Highways therein, and ſhall be chargeable thereunto as followeth*; that is to ſay, *Every Perſon for every Plough-land in Tillage or Paſture, That he or ſhe ſhall occupy in the ſame Pariſh, and every other Perſon keeping there a Draught or Plough, ſhall find and ſend at every Day and Place to be appointed for the amending of the Ways in the Pariſh, one Wain or Cart, furniſhed after the Cuſtom of the Country, with Oxen, Horſes, or other Cattle, and all other Neceſſaries meet to carry Things convenient for that Purpoſe, and alſo two able Men with the ſame, upon Pain of every Draught making Default, ten Shillings; and every Houſholder, and alſo every Cottager and Labourer of that Pariſh, able to labour, and being no hired Servant by the Year, ſhall by themſelves, or one ſufficient Labourer for every of them, upon every of the ſaid Days, work and travel in the Amendment of the ſaid Highways, upon Pain of every Perſon making Default, to loſe for every Day, one Shilling and Six-pence: And if the ſaid Carriages of the Pariſh, or any of them ſhall not be thought needful by the Surveyors, to be occupied upon any of the ſaid Days, that then every ſuch Perſon that ſhould have ſent any ſuch Carriage, ſhall ſend to the ſaid Work, for every Carriage ſo ſpared, two able Men, there to labour for the Day, upon Pain to loſe for every Man not ſo ſent to the ſaid Work, Twelve-pence; and every Perſon and Carriage abovesaid ſhall have and bring with them ſuch Shovels, Spades, Picks, Mattocks, and other Tools and Inſtruments as they do make their own Ditches and Fences withal, and ſuch as be neceſſary for their ſaid Work: And all the ſaid Perſons and Carriages ſhall do and keep their Work, as they ſhall be appointed by the ſaid Superviſors, or one of them, eight Hours of every the ſaid Days, unleſs they ſhall be otherwiſe licenced by the ſaid Superviſors, or one of them.* 22 Car. 2. 12. Par. 9.

Sect. 11.

Sect. 11. And it is farther enacted by 18 *El.* 10. Par. 2. *That every Person or Persons (except such as dwell in the City of* London) *that shall be assessed to the Payment of any Subsidy to Her Majesty, to five Pounds in Goods, or forty Shillings in Lands, or above, during all such Time as he shall stand so assessed and not altered, and being none of the Parties chargeable for the Amendment of Highways by any former Law, but as a Cottager, shall find two able Men yearly to labour in the Highways, at the Times appointed.*

Sect. 12. And it is farther enacted by the said Statute, Par. 3. *That every other that shall occupy a Plough-land in Tillage or Pasture, lying in several Parishes, shall be chargeable to the making of the Ways within the Parish where he dwelleth, as far forth, and in such Manner and Form as any Person having a Plough-land in any one Parish, is or ought to be chargeable.*

Dal. ca. 26. 3 Keb. 568. 2 Keb. 617.

Sect. 13. It was made a great Doubt in the Construction of these Statutes, what should be accounted a Plough-land within the Purview of them, for the settling whereof it was enacted by 7 & 8 *W.* 3. 29. *That any Person that shall have in his or her Occupation, Wood-land, or other Land, to the Value of fifty Pounds* per Annum, *shall be adjudged and deemed to have a Plough-land, as to all, or any of the Purposes within any of the Statutes before that Time made, of or concerning the Highways, any Thing in Them, or any Usage, or Custom to the contrary, in any wise notwithstanding.*

Sect. 14. Also it is farther enacted by the above mentioned Statute of 22 *Car.* 2. 12. Par. 8. *That in such Places where there is no Use of Carts, and Teams for the Amendment of the Highways, but the Usage and Practice is to carry Stones, Gravel, Earth, or other Materials for such Amendment, upon the Backs of Horses, or by any other Kinds of Carriages; that in all such Places the Inhabitants using any such Horses or other Carriages, shall send in such their Horses as are accustomed to that Kind of Labour, and such their other Carriages, with able Persons to work with the same, in like Manner, and under the like Directions, Forfeitures and Penalties, as by any former Statute for repairing of Highways, is appointed for Carts and Teams.*

In the Exposition of these Statutes the following Opinions have been holden,

[a] 3 Keb. 255, 476. 1 Ven. 273. Watf. ca. 40. 2 Inst. 704.

Sect. 15. I. That [a] Persons in Holy Orders are within the Purview of them, in respect of their Spiritual Possessions, as much as any other Persons whatsoever, in respect of any other Possessions, for the Words are general, and there is no Kind of Intimation that any particular Persons shall be exempted more than others.

[b] Raym. 186. 3 Keb. 567, 468. Vide Dalt. ca. 26. 2 Keb. 617.

Sect. 16. II. [b] That he who keeps several Draughts in a Parish is bound to send a Team for each Draught, whether he occupy any Land in the Parish, or not; and in like Manner, That he who occupies several Plough-lands, ought to send a Team for each Plough-land, whether he keep any Draught, or not.

[c] Palm. 389. 2 Rol. Re. 412.

Sect. 17. III. That [c] notwithstanding the Words of the Statute extend only to the Occupiers of Land, yet if the Owner neither occupy them, nor let them, but suffer them to lie fresh, he shall be charged as much as if he had occupied them, for there is no Reason that the Publick shall suffer for his Negligence.

Dalt. ca 26.

Sect. 18. IV. That it is no Excuse for the Inhabitants of a Parish, being indicted at Common Law for not repairing the Highways, That they have done the full Work required of them by Statute, for since these Statutes are wholly in the Affirmative, and made in Aid of the Common Law, and to supply the Defects thereof, they shall not be construed to abrogate any Provision thereby made for these Purposes.

Sect. 19.

Sect. 19. *Dalton* is of Opinion, That he who keeps a Draught and but two Horses, ought to attend therewith at the Times appointed, and that if he carry with them such Loads as they are able to draw, he shall be excused. Dalt. ca. 26.

Sect. 20. As to the second Point, *viz.* Who may be assessed to a Rate made for the defraying of the extraordinary Charges of such Repairs, it is enacted by the above mentioned Statute of 22 *Car.* 2. 12 Par. 10, 11. and 3 & 4 *W.* & *M.* 12. *That where the Justices of the Peace of any County, City, or other Place, or the major Part of them, at their General or Quarter-Sessions, shall be fully satisfied that the common Highways, Causeys, Bridges, Streets or Pavements, within any Parish, Township, or Hamlet,* &c. *within their respective Jurisdiction, cannot be sufficiently amended, repaired, and supported, by Means of the Laws then in Force, without the Help of the said Acts*; *in all such Cases one or more Assessment, or Assessments, upon all and every the Inhabitants, Owners, and Occupiers of Lands, Houses, Tenements, and Hereditaments, or any personal Estate, usually rateable to the Poor, within any such Parish, Township, or Hamlet,* &c. *shall be made, levied, collected, and allowed, by such Person and Persons, and in such Manner as the said Justices by their Order at such Sessions shall direct and appoint in that Behalf: And the Money thereby raised shall be imployed and accounted for, according to the Order and Directions of the said Justices, for and towards the Amending, Repairing, Paving, Cleansing and Supporting such Highways, Causeys, and Bridges, from Time to Time, as Need shall require, and the said Assessments shall be levied by Distress and Sale of Goods on Non-Payment upon Demand,* &c. *Provided that no such Assessment or Assessments to be made in any one Year, shall exceed the Rate of Six-pence in the Pound of the yearly Value of any Lands, Houses, Tenements and Hereditaments, so assessed, nor the Rate of Six-pence for twenty Pounds in personal Estate.*

Sect. 21. An it is farther enacted by the above mentioned Statute of 7 & 8 *W.* 3. 29. *Par.* 4. *That if any Inship, Liberty, Precinct, or Vill, that uses to repair their own Highways, shall have levied the Rate of Six-pence in the Pound, and imployed the same towards the Repair of the Highways, and yet the said Highways are not sufficiently repaired, in such Cases it shall be lawful for the Justices of the Peace at their special Sessions to be held every four Months, for the Consideration of the Highways, to order the whole Parish to contribute to the Repairing thereof.*

Sect. 22. It is recited by 3 & 4 *W.* & *M.* 12. *That divers Parishes and Townships, having not any Gravel-stones, Quarries, nor any other Materials fitting or convenient for the Amending or Repairing of the Highways within the said Parishes and Townships, the Surveyors of the Highways of such Parishes and Townships, had been forced to lay out their own Money for the Buying of such Materials as were necessary for that Purpose, and yet had no Remedy by any Law then in Force for a Reimbursement of such Expences*; and thereupon it is enacted, *That upon Notice given by the Surveyor or Surveyors of the Highways to the Justices of the Peace at their special Sessions, and Oath made of what Sum or Sums of Money, he or they have or hath so laid out and expended, upon Amending and Repairing of the said Highways, the Justices of Peace, or any two of them, at their special Sessions, may by Warrant under their Hands and Seals, cause an equal Rate to be made for the Re-imbursing the said Surveyor or Surveyors, the Monies by him or them laid out as aforesaid, upon all the Inhabitants of such Parish or Township where such Monies are expended, according to the Rules and Methods prescribed by* 43 El. 2. *which Rate being confirmed and allowed by the said Justices in their special Sessions, shall be collected and gathered by the said Surveyor or Surveyors of the Highways*; *and if any Person or Persons refuse to pay the Monies so assessed on him or them, that then the same shall be levied by the said Surveyors by Distress and Sale of the Goods and Chattels of the Persons so refusing, rendring to the Party the Overplus, reasonable Charges for making the said Distress first to be deducted. If the Justices refuse to make such a Rate, they are compellable by* Mandamus *from the King's Bench, on* Affidavit *of the Monies having been laid out; and the* Mandamus *shall be directed to the Justices of the County, and served on those of the privy Sessions.*

The King against the Inhabitants of Newton in Cheshire.

Sect. 23. As to the third Point, *viz.* What other Provisions have been made to this Purpose, it is enacted by the said Statute of 3 & 4 *W. & M.* 12. *That no Fine, Issue, Penalty, or Forfeiture, for not repairing any Highway, shall be returned into the Court of Exchequer, or other Court, but shall be levied and paid into the Hands of the Surveyors of the Parish or Place, to be applied towards the Repair and Amendment of such Highway; and that if any Fine, Penalty, or Forfeiture, imposed on any Parish or Place, for not repairing the Highways, shall hereafter be levied on any one, or more, of the Inhabitants of such Parish or Place, that then such Inhabitant or Inhabitants shall make his or their Complaint to the Justices of the Peace at their special Sessions, and the said Justices, or any two of them, are by the said Statute impowered and authorized by Warrant under their Hands and Seals, to cause a Rate to be made, according to the Form and Manner* [a] *aforesaid, for the Re-imbursing such Inhabitant or Inhabitants the Money so levied on him or them, as aforesaid, which Rate so made, and confirmed by two Justices, as aforesaid, shall be collected, and levied by the Surveyor or Surveyors of the Highways of such Parish or Place so presented or indicted, as aforesaid, and the said Surveyor or Surveyors shall within one Month next after the Making and Confirming the Rute aforesaid, pay unto the Inhabitant or Inhabitants, such Money so levied on him or them, as aforesaid.*

[a] See the precedent Section.

Sect. 24. Also the later Statutes which have imposed any Penalties on Surveyors of the Highways, or others, for any Offences relating to the Highways, have generally ordained that the Whole, or Part thereof, shall be applied to the Repairs of the Highways of the Place wherein the Offence shall be committed, as will more fully appear in the subsequent Part of this Chapter.

Sect. 25. As to the fourth Point, *viz.* In what Manner the Profits of Lands settled in Trust for the Repairs of the Highways shall be employed, it is enacted by the above mentioned Statute of 22 *Car.* 2. 12. *Par.* 2. *That where any Lands have been, or shall be given for the Maintenance of Causeys, Pavements, Highways and Bridges, all such Persons that are, or shall be, enfeoffed, or trusted with any such Lands, shall let them to farm at the most improved yearly Value without Fine; and that the Justices of Peace in their open Sessions shall enquire by such Ways and Means as they think fitting, into the Value of all such Lands so given, or to be given, and order the Improvement and Imployment of the Rents and Profits thereof, according to the Will and Direction of the Donor of such Lands, if they find that the Persons so intrusted, have been negligent or faulty in the Performance of their Trust, (except such Lands have been given to the Uses aforesaid, to any College or Hall in either of the Universities of this Kingdom, which have Visitors of their own) any Law, Statute, Usage, or Custom, to the contrary notwithstanding.*

Sect. 26. As to the third general Head of this Chapter, *viz.* In what Manner the Highway is to be enlarged, it is enacted by 13 *Ed.* 1. *Stat.* 2. commonly called the Statute of *Winchester*, Chap. 5. *That Highways leading from one Market-Town to another shall be enlarged, so that there be neither Dyke, Tree, nor Bush, whereby a Man may lurk to do Hurt, within two hundred Foot of the one Side, and two hundred Foot of the other Side of the Way: So that the Statute shall not extend to Ashes, nor unto great Trees,* &c. *and if by Default of the Lord that will not avoid the Dyke, Underwood, or Bushes, in the Manner aforesaid, any Robberies be done therein, the Lord shall be answerable for the Felony, and if Murder be done, the Lord shall make a Fine at the King's Pleasure: And if the Lord be not able to fell the Underwoods, the Country shall aid him threin. And the King willeth, that in his Demean Lands and Woods within his Forest, and without, the Ways shall be enlarged, as before is said. And if per-case a Park be taken from the Highway, it is requisite that the Lord shall set his Park the Space of two hundred Foot from the Highways, as before is said; or that he make such a Wall, Dyke, or Hedge, that Offenders may not pass nor return to do Evil.*

Sect. 27. Also it is enacted by the above mentioned Statute of 3 & 4 *W.* & *M.* 12. *That the Surveyors of the Highways shall make every Cartway leading to any Market-Town, eight Foot wide at the least, and as near as may be, even and level.*

Sect. 28. And it is farther enacted and declared by the same Statute, *That no Horse-Causey, or Causey for Horses, travelling upon, or in any publick Highway, be less or under three Foot in Breadth.*

Sect. 29. Also it is enacted by 8 & 9 *W.* 3. 15. *That the Justices of the Peace of any County, City, Riding, Division, Liberty, or Place, or the major Part of them, being five at the least, at their Quarter-Sessions, shall have Power to enlarge or widen any Highways in their respective Countries, Ridings, Divisions, Liberties, or Places, so that the Ground to be taken into the said Highways do not exceed eight Yards in Breadth, and that the said Power do not extend to pull down any House, or to take away the Ground of any Garden, Orchard, Court, or Yard: And for the Satisfaction of the Persons who are Owners of, or may be interested in, the said Ground that shall be laid into the said Highways, the said Justices are by the said Statute impowered to impanel a Jury before them, and to administer an Oath to the said Jury, That they will assess such Damages to be given, and Recompence to be made to the Owners and others interested in the said Ground, for their respective Interests, as they shall think reasonable, not exceeding five and twenty Years Purchase for Lands so laid out, and likewise such Recompence as they shall think reasonable for the Making of a new Ditch and Fence to that Side of the Highway that shall be so enlarged, and also Satisfaction to any Person that may be otherwise injured by the enlarging of the said Highways: And upon Payment of the said Money so awarded, or leaving it in the Hands of the Clerk of the Peace of the respective County, for the Use of the Owner, or of others interested in the said Ground, the Interest of the said Persons shall be for ever divested out of them, and the Ground that shall be laid into any Highway by Virtue of the said Act, shall be esteemed a publick Highway to all Intents and Purposes whatsoever; and the said Justices shall have Power to order one or more Assessment or Assessments to be made, levied, or collected, upon all and every the Inhabitants, Owners, or Occupiers of Lands, Houses, Tenements or Hereditaments, in their respective Parishes or Places that ought to repair the same, to such Person or Persons, and in such Manner as the said Justices at such Sessions shall direct and appoint; and the Money thereby raised shall be employed and accounted for, according to the Order and Direction of the said Justices, for and towards the Purchasing of the Land to enlarge the said Highways, and for the Making the said Ditches and Fences: And the said Assessments shall, by Order of the said Justices, be levied by the Overseers of the Highways, by Distress and Sale of the Goods of Persons so assessed, not paying the same within ten days after Demand, rendring the Overplus of the Value of the Goods so distrained to the Owner and Owners thereof (the necessary Charges being first deducted).*

Sect. 30. But it is provided by the said Statute, *That no such Assessment or Assessments made in any one Year, for enlarging of Highways, shall exceed the Rate of Six-pence in the Pound of the yearly Income of any Lands, Houses,*

Tene-

Tenements, and Hereditaments, nor the Rate of Six-pence in the Pound for personal Estates.

Sect. 31. Also it is farther enacted by the said Statute, *That the Justices of Peace at their Quarter-Sessions, at the Request of any Person, for the putting in Execution the Powers contained in the said Act for the Enlarging of Highways, shall issue out their Precepts to the Owner or Owners of Ground, or others interested in the same, that are to be laid into the said Highways, to appear at the next Quarter-Sessions, or shew Cause why the said Highways should not be enlarged.*

Sect. 32. And it is farther enacted, *That if any Order or Decree shall be made by the said Justices for the laying out of Ground for the Enlarging of Highways, the Owners or Proprietors of the said Ground shall have free Liberty, within eight Months after such Order, to cut down any Wood or Timber growing upon the said Ground, or upon the Neglect thereof, that the same shall be sold by Order of the said Justices, and the Owners of such Wood or Timber shall receive the full of what shall be made thereof, the Charges being first deducted.*

Sect. 33. And it is farther enacted, *That any Person grieved by the Order or Decree of the said Justices may appeal to the Judges of Assize at the next Assize only to be held for the County where such Decree or Order shall be made, and any of the said Judges are by the said Statute impowered to examine, affirm, or reverse the said former Order and Decree, as in Judgment they shall think fit, and if affirmed, to award Costs against such Appellants for their Vexation and Delay, and to cause the same to be levied by Distress and Sale of the Appellant's Goods, rendring the Overplus to the said Appellants.*

Sect. 34. And it is farther enacted by the said Statute, *That where any common Highway shall be inclosed after a Writ of* Ad quod damnum *issued, and Inquisition thereupon taken, any Person grieved by such Inclosure, may make his Appeal to the Quarter-Sessions of the County to be held next after such Inquisition taken, which shall finally hear and determine such Appeal; and if no such Appeal be made, then the said Inquisition and Return entred and recorded by the Clerk of the Peace of such County at the Quarter-Sessions, shall be for ever afterwards binding to all Persons whatsoever.*

Sect. 35. As to the fourth general Head of this Chapter, *viz.* In what Manner the Surveyors of the Highways shall be appointed, it is enacted by 3 & 4 *Will. & Mar.* 12. *That upon the six and twentieth Day of* December *in every Year, unless that Day be Sunday, and then on the seven and twentieth, the Constables, Headboroughs, Tithing-men, Church-wardens, Surveyor or Surveyors of the Highways, and Inhabitants in every Parish, shall assemble together, and the major Part of them as are so assembled, shall make a list of the Names of a competent Number of the Inhabitants in their Parish, who have an Estate in Lands, Tenements, or Hereditaments, in their own Right, or their Wives, of the Value of ten Pounds by the Year, or a personal Estate of the Value of one hundred Pounds, or are Occupiers or Tenants of Houses, Lands, Tenements, or Hereditaments, of the yearly Value of thirty Pounds, if any such there be; or if there be no such Persons in the Parish, then the said List to be of the most sufficient Inhabitants of such Parish, and shall return such List unto two or more of the Justices of the Peace in or near the Division of the County in which their Parish lies, at a special Sessions to be held for that Purpose within the said Division, on the third Day of* January *next following, unless it shall happen on a Sunday, and then to be the fourth of the same Month, or within fifteen Days after; for which Purpose the said Justices are required to hold a special Sessions at some Place within that Division where the Parish lies, and to give Notice of the Time and Place where they intend to hold the same, to the Constables, Headboroughs, Tithingmen, Church-wardens, and Surveyors of the Highways of every*

Parish within the said Division, at least ten Days before the Holding of the said Sessions; and the said Justices shall then and there, out of the said Lists, according to their Discretion, and the Largeness of the Parish by Warrant under their Hands and Seals, nominate and appoint one, two, or more, as they shall think fit, and approve of, being of like Sufficiency as aforesaid, to be Surveyor or Surveyors of the Highways of every Parish within the Division, or for any Hamlet, Precinct, Liberty, Tithing or Town, of and in the same Division, for the Year ensuing; which Nomination and Appointment shall by the Constables, Headboroughs, Tithingmen, or Surveyors of the Highways for the Time being, or some of them, be notified to the Person or Persons so nominated, chosen, and appointed, by the said Justices within six Days after such Nomination, by serving him or them with the said Warrant or Warrants, or by leaving the same, or a true Copy thereof, at his or their Houses or usual Places of abode; and from thenceforth the Person or Persons so nominated and appointed, shall be Surveyor or Surveyors of the Highways, for the Parish, Town, Village, Hamlet, Precinct, or Tithing, for which he shall have been so nominated, chosen, and appointed for the Year ensuing, and shall take upon him and them respectively and duly execute the said Office according to the former Laws made concerning the Highways, and the said Act; and if the said Persons so nominated and served with the said Warrant shall refuse, or neglect so to do, he or they so refusing and neglecting, shall forfeit the Sum of five Pounds, to be levied on his or their Goods and Chattels, by Distress and Sale of the same, by Warrant under the Hand and Seal of two or more Justices of the Peace of the same Division, or in Default thereof any neighbouring Justices of the Peace for the said County, which Warrant the said Justices are required to make upon Information of any one credible Witness upon Oath; the one Moiety of which Forfeiture shall go to him that shall inform, and the other Moiety for and towards the Repair of the Highways of the same Parish, rendring the Overplus to the Party whose Goods shall be distrained, the Charges of the Distress and Sale being first deducted; and in Case of such Neglect or Refusal, the said Justices are impowered to nominate and appoint some other fit Person or Persons to perform the said Office, who upon like Notice of such Nomination and Appointment, shall take upon him or them, and duly execute the said Office, and if he or they neglect or refuse so to do, shall forfeit the like Sum of five Pounds, to be levied and disposed of as aforesaid; and if the Constables, Headboroughs, Tithingmen, Church-wardens, and Surveyor or Surveyors of the Highways of any Parish, Town, Liberty or Precinct, or some of them, shall not return the said List of Names in such Manner, as in this Act is directed, every of them so neglecting, shall forfeit the Sum of twenty Shillings, to be levied in the Manner, and imployed to the Uses aforesaid.

Sect. 36. And it is farther enacted by the said Statute of 3 & 4 *W.* & *M.* 12. *That if any Justice of the Peace shall neglect or refuse to do what is required of him by the said Act, he shall forfeit five Pounds, one Moiety whereof shall go to the Person that shall sue for the same, the other Moiety to be employed in the Repairs of the Highways of the Parish where the Person who shall sue for the same inhabits, to be recovered in any of the King's Courts of Record, by Action of Debt,* &c.

Sect. 37. As to the fifth general Head of this Chapter, *viz.* In what Manner the Surveyors of the Highways ought to execute their Office, it is enacted by the said Statute of 3 & 4 *W.* & *M.* 12. *That every Surveyor of the Highways, appointed as by the said Act is directed, shall within fourteen Days next after the first Acceptance of the said Office, and so from Time to Time every four Months, during his being Surveyor, take a View of all the Roads, common Highways, Water-Courses, Bridges, Causeys, and Pavements within the Parish, Town, Village, Hamlet, Precinct, or Tithing, for which he is appointed*

Surveyor, that are to be repaired by the ſaid Pariſh, &c. *and ſhall make a Preſentment upon Oath, in what State and Condition he finds the ſame, to ſome Juſtices of the Peace of the ſame Diviſion, if then reſident there, otherwiſe to ſome neighbouring Juſtice of the Peace for the ſaid County, and in Default thereof ſhall incur the Penalty aforeſaid, as if he or they had refuſed or neglected to accept and execute the ſaid Office, unleſs he ſhall have ſome reaſonable Excuſe for omitting the ſame, to be allowed of by two Juſtices of the Peace of the ſame Diviſion,* &c. *And what Defaults and Annoyances they ſhall find in any of the ſaid Highways,* &c. *they ſhall from Time to Time the next Sunday immediately after Sermon, give publick Notice of the ſame in the Pariſh Church, and if the ſame ſhall not be removed, repaired, and amended within thirty Days after ſuch Notice given, that then the ſaid Surveyor or Surveyors ſhall within thirty Days remove, repair, and amend the ſame, and diſpoſe of the ſame Annoyances, to and for the Repair of the ſaid Highways; and the ſaid Surveyor or Surveyors ſhall be re-imburſed what Charges and Expences they ſhall be at in ſo doing, by the Parties who ſhould have done the ſame; and in Caſe the ſaid Parties ſhall upon Demand refuſe or neglect to pay the ſaid Surveyors their ſaid Charges, then the ſaid Surveyors ſhall apply themſelves to any Juſtice of the Peace within the Diviſion of the County wherein ſuch Highway is, and in Default thereof to any neighbouring Juſtice for the ſaid County, and upon his or their making Oath before ſuch Juſtice of the Notice to the Defaulter in manner aforeſaid, the ſaid Surveyors ſhall be repaid all ſuch their Charges as ſhall be allowed to be reaſonable by the ſaid Juſtice, to be levied in Manner aforeſaid.*

Sect. 38. Alſo it is enacted by the above mentioned Statute of 22 *Car.* 2. 12. Par. 12. *That the Surveyors ſhall appoint ſix Days for the providing Stones Gravel, and other Materials, for the Amendment of, and for working in the Highways, having reſpect to the Seaſon of the Year, and the Weather, and giving Notice publickly ſome convenient Time before the ſeveral Days; at which Days all Perſons liable to the ſaid Work, ſhall attend and work accordingly: And the ſaid Surveyors,* &c. *ſhall make Return of the Defaulters, within one Month after every Default made, to ſome neighbouring Juſtice of the Peace of the ſame County; and the ſaid Juſtice ſhall preſent the ſame at the Quarter-Seſſions of the Peace held next after ſuch Return made unto him; and the Offenders ſhall reſpectively incur the ſame Forfeiture, Pains and Penalties, inflicted and appointed by the Laws then in Force for the Amending of the Highways.*
Salk. 357. And it has been adjudged, That the Juſtices ought to fix the Particular Days, and not generally to appoint ſix Days between ſuch and ſuch a Day.

Sect. 39. It is enacted by 5 *El.* 13. *That it ſhall be lawful for the Surveyors of the Highways, for the better Reparation of the Ways, within their ſeveral Limits (if it ſhall be ſo to them thought neceſſary) to take or carry away of the Rubbiſh or ſmalleſt broken Stones of any Quarry or Quarries lying and being within the Pariſh where they ſhall be Surveyors, without Licence, Controlment, or Impeachment of the Owner, ſo much as by their Diſcretions ſhall be deemed neceſſary for the Amendment of the ſaid Ways: And that for the Fault of any Quarry not being within their ſaid Pariſh or Limits, or in Default of Rubbiſh not to be found in any ſuch Quarry, it ſhall be lawful for every ſuch Surveyor, for the Uſe aforeſaid, in the ſeveral Grounds of any Perſon or Perſons being within the Pariſh and Limits where they ſhall be Surveyors, and nigh adjoining to the Way wherein ſuch Reparations ſhall be thought neceſſary to be made, and wherein Gravel, Sand, or Cinders is likely to be found, to dig or cauſe to be digged for Gravel, Sand, or Cinders, and likewiſe to gather Stones lying upon any Lands or Grounds within the Pariſh, and meet to be uſed to ſuch Purpoſe, and thereof to take and carry away ſo much as ſhall be by them thought neceſſary to be employed in the Amendment of the ſaid Highways.*

Sect. 40. But it is provided by the said Statute, Par. 4. *That it shall not be lawful to any such Supervisor by Virtue of the said Act to cause any Rubbish to be digged out of any Quarry or Quarries, but only shall extend to such Rubbish as shall be found there ready digged by the Owner or Owners of the said Quarry or Quarries, or otherwise by his or their Licence and Commandment; nor shall not extend to give Authority to any Supervisor to dig or cause to be digged any Gravel, Sand, or Cinders in the House, Garden, Orchard, or Meadow of any Person, nor that it shall be lawful to any such Supervisor to cause any more Pits to be digged for Gravel in any several and inclosed Ground than one only; and that the same Pit or Hole so digged for Gravel, as is aforesaid, shall not by any Way be in Breadth or Length, above ten Yards over at the most: And that every such Supervisor as shall cause any such Pit to be made and digged for Gravel, Sand, or Cinders, as is abovesaid, shall within one Month next after such Digging or Pit made, cause the same to be filled and stopped up with Earth, at the Costs and Charges of the Parishioners, upon Pain to forfeit to the Owner or Owners of the Soil wherein any such Pit shall be made and digged, for every Default five Marks to be recovered by Action of Debt,* &c.

Sect. 41. And it is farther enacted by the same Statute, Par. 6. *That every Supervisor shall within the Limits where he shall be Supervisor, have Authority to turn a Water-Course, or Spring of Water, being in any Highway, into any Ditch of the several Ground of any Person whatsoever next adjoining to the said Ways, in such Manner as by the said Supervisors shall be thought meetest.*

Sect. 42. Also it is enacted by the above mentioned Statute of 18 *El.* 10. Par. 7. *That where any Soil hath been cast into the common Highway, or common faring Way, that there is a Bank between the said Way and the Ditch, it shall be lawful for the said Surveyors,* &c. *to make Sluices or other Devices by their Discretions, to convey the Water out of the said Way into the Ditch; any Law, Right, Interest, or Usage, to the contrary notwithstanding.*

Sect. 43. And it is farther enacted by the said Statute of 3 & 4 *W.* & *M.* 12. *That it shall be lawful for the said Surveyors, where the Ditches and Drains already made are not sufficient to carry of the Water that lies upon the Highways, to make new Ditches and Drains in and through the Lands next adjoining to the said Highways, and keep them scoured, cleansed, and open, and come upon any of the Lands with their Workmen for so doing.*

Sect. 44. Also it is enacted by the above mentioned Statute of 5 *El.* 13. Par. 8. *That every Surveyor for the Time being, shall within one Month next after Default or Offence made by any Person, contrary to the Provision and true Meaning of either of the said Statutes of* 2 & 3 Ph. & Mar. 8. *or* 5 *El.* 13. *present every such Default or Offence, to the next Justice of Peace for the Time being, under pain of forty Shillings.*

Sect. 45. And it is enacted by the said Statute of 22 *Car.* 2. 12. Par. 1. *That all Constables and Surveyors of the Highways, from Time to Time during their Continuance in their Offices, shall cause the several Acts of Parliament then in Force, touching the Repairing the Highways, to be put in Execution, and the Penalties thereby imposed to be levied and disposed of, as by the said several Act is directed: And every Constable or Surveyor of the Highways refusing or neglecting to put the said Acts in Execution, or wilfully suffering any Waggons or Carts to pass thro' their respective Limits with more Cattle, or in other Manner than by Law is allowed, shall incur the like Penalty of forty Shillings,* &c.

Sect. 46. And it is farther enacted by the said Statute of 3 & 4 *W.* & *M.* 12. *That the Justices of the Peace of every County shall in their respective Divisions once in four Months, hold a special Sessions, and shall thereunto summon*

summon all the Surveyors of the Highways within that Division to come before them, and shall give them a Charge to do their Duty, and declare to them what they are obliged to do by Virtue of that, or any former Act; after which the said Surveyors shall make a Presentment unto them upon Oath, of the State and Condition of the Highways within their respective Parishes, Towns, Hamlets, &c. *and what Offences and Neglects any are guilty of, contrary to the Meaning of any Statute made concerning the Highways, or any Thing relating thereunto: And before any such Surveyor shall go out of, or be discharged from his Office, he shall at some such special Sessions, give an Account upon Oath of all Money that hath come to his Hands, which ought to be employed in amending of the Highways, and how he hath disposed of the same; and in case any Moneys shall remain in his Hands, he shall deliver the same to the Surveyors of the Highways, that shall serve for the same Parish, Town, or Hamlet,* &c. *for the Year ensuing, and in case of Failure, to forfeit the double Value of what shall be adjudged to be in his Hands, by the said Justices,* &c.

Sect. 47. And it is enacted by 6 *Annæ*, 29. *That if any Surveyor shall neglect to put either that or any former Law for repairing Highways in Execution, he shall forfeit five Pounds, to be levied by Distress,* &c. *by Warrant of one Justice of the Peace.*

As to the sixth general Head of this Chapter, *viz.* What shall be said to be a Nusance to the Highway, I shall consider:

1. What shall be said to be such a Nusance at Common Law.
2. What by Statute.

Kitch. 34, 35. *Sect.* 48. As to the first Point, there is no Doubt but that all Injuries whatsoever to any Highway, as by digging a Ditch, or making a Hedge overthwart it, or laying Logs of Timber in it, or by doing any other Act, which will render it less commodious to the King's People, are publick Nusances at Common Law.

2 Rol. Ab. 137. B. 265. c. 2. *Sect.* 49. Also it seemeth to be clear, That it is no Excuse for one who layeth such Logs in the Highway that he laid them only here and there, so that the People might have a Passage by Windings and Turnings through the Logs: Yet it is said to be no Nusance for the Inhabitants of a Town to unlade Billets, *&c.* in the Street before their Houses, by reason of the Necessity of the Case, unless they suffer them to continue there an unreasonable Time, after they are unloaded. (2 Rol. Ab. 137. B. 2, 3.)

Sect. 50. There is no Doubt but that it is a Nusance at Common Law to erect a new Gate in a Highway, as hath been more fully shewn in the precedent Chapter; also it seemeth clear, That it is a like Nusance to suffer the Ditches adjoining to a Highway, to be foul, by reason whereof it is impaired, or to suffer the Boughs of Trees growing near the Highway, to hang over the Road in such a Manner as thereby to incommode the Passage. (8 H. 7. 5. a. Kitch. 34, 35. 8 H. 7. 5. b.)

Sect. 51. As to the second Point, *viz.* What shall be said to be a Nusance to the Highway by Statute; not only all the above mentioned Nusances, which are such at Common Law, are esteemed also Nusances by Statute, but there is also one particular Nusance which is made such by Statute, and doth not seem to be taken Notice of by Common Law, and that is the Drawing of a travelling Carriage with more than six Horses in Length, the Permitting whereof hath occasioned the Carrying of such excessive Loads in such Carriage, that the Weight thereof hath in many Places rendred the Roads unpassable. (5 Geo. 1. 12.)

As to the ſeventh general Head of this Chapter, *viz.* How ſuch Nuſances are to be removed and puniſhed, I ſhall conſider the following Particulars:

1. In what Order Hedges and Ditches, adjoining to the Highway, ought to be kept.
2. How far all Trees and Buſhes are to be removed from the Highway.
3. In what Manner all other Annoyances obſtructing the Highway are to be removed.
4. How far all Perſons are puniſhable for taking away Things made uſe of for the Benefit of the Highway.
5. How far they may be puniſhed for drawing a Carriage with more than five Horſes in Length.

Sect. 52. As to the firſt Particular, *viz.* In what Order Hedges and Ditches, adjoining to the Highway, ought to be kept; it is ſaid, That he who hath Lands next adjoining to a Highway, is bound of common Right to ſcowr his Ditches; but it is ſaid, That he who hath Lands next adjoining to ſuch Lands, is not bound by the Common Law ſo to do, without ſome ſpecial Preſcription for that Purpoſe; and perhaps it is the better Opinion, That he who hath Trees next adjoining to the Highway, and hanging over it to the Annoyance of the People, is bound by the Common Law to lop the ſame; and it ſeems clear, That any Perſon may juſtify the Lopping ſuch Trees, ſo far as to avoid the Nuſance. 8 H. 7. 5. a. b. Kitch. 34, 35. Dal. ca. 26. H. P. C. 144. 8 H. 7. 5. a. b.

Sect. 53. However it is enacted by 5 *El.* 13. Par. 7. *That the Hays, Fences, Dykes, or Hedges, next adjoining on either Side, to any High or Common faring Way, ſhall from Time to Time be dyked, ſcowered, repaired, and kept low, by the Owner or Owners of the Ground or Soil, which ſhall be incloſed with the ſaid Hays, Fences, Dykes, or Hedges aforeſaid,* &c.

Sect. 54. And it is farther enacted by 18 *El.* 10. Par. 5. *That whoever ſhall not repair, ditch, or ſcowr, any Hays, Fences, Ditches, or Hedges adjoining to any Highway, or Common faring Way, according to the true Intent of the above mentioned Statute of* 5 El. 13. *ſhall forfeit for every ſuch Offence ten Shillings, to be levied by the Surveyors,* &c.

Sect. 55. And it is farther enacted by 3 *&* 4 *W. & M.* 12. *If any Owner or Occupier of Lands next adjoining to any Highway, not twenty Foot broad, ſhall neglect to cleanſe or ſcowr their Ditches, Gutters and Drains, adjoining to the ſaid Highways, or cauſe the Earth taken out thereof to be carried away, and lay ſufficient Trunks, Tunnels or Bridges, where any Cartways are, into the ſaid Grounds, for the Space of ten Days after Notice thereof given by a Surveyor,* &c. *every ſuch Offender ſhall forfeit five Shillings,* &c.

Sect. 56. And it is farther enacted by the ſaid Statute of 3 *&* 4 *W. & M.* 12. *That the Poſſeſſors of the Land next adjoining to any Highways, where they are not twenty Foot broad, ſhall from Time to Time, and at all Times, keep their Hedges plaſht, cut, or pruned, ſo as no Tree, Buſh, or ſhard, ſhall ſtand or grow in ſuch Highway, nor Bough or Branch be ſuffered to hang over the ſame, or any Part thereof; but the ſaid Hedges ſhall be kept cut and pared right up from the Roots, and not permitted in any ſort to ſpread into or hang over the Highway, or any Part thereof, to the End that there may be a free and clear Paſſage for the Travellers, and all Sorts of Carriages loaden, without being any ways prejudiced or obſtructed by any Hedges, Trees, Boughs, or Branches whatſoever,*

ſoever, and that the Sun may freely ſhine into the ſaid Ways, to dry and amend the ſame.

Sect. 57. Alſo it is farther enacted by the above mentioned Statute of 18 *El.* 10. Par. 6. *That every Occupier of Lands adjoining to the Grounds adjoining to any Highway, or common faring Way, where any Ditching or Scowring ſhould or ought to be, as aforeſaid, ſhall from Time to Time, as Need ſhall require, ditch and ſcowr in his Grounds ſo adjoining, whereby the Water conveyed from the ſaid Highway,* &c. *over the Ground next adjoining, may have Paſſage over ſuch next Ground ſo adjoining, on Pain of Forfeiture for every Time ſo offending for every Rod not ſo ditched and ſcowred, twelve Pence.*

Sect. 58. As to the ſecond Particular, *viz.* How far all Trees and Buſhes are to be removed from the Highway, it appears from the above mentioned Statute of *Wincheſter*, Chapter 5. *That no ſmall Tree or Buſh, whereby a Man may lurk to do hurt, ought to be ſuffered to ſtand within two hundred Foot of either Side of a Highway leading from one Market-Town to another.*

Sect. 59. And it is farther enacted by the ſaid Statute of 5 *El.* 13. Par. 7. *That all Trees and Buſhes growing in the Highways, ſhall be cut down by the Owner or Owners of the Ground or Soil,* &c. And it is alſo enacted by the ſaid Statute of 18 *El.* 10. Par. 7. *That whoever ſhall not cut down, or keep low all Trees and Buſhes, growing in or next adjoining to any the ſaid Ways, according to the Intent of the above mentioned Statute of* 5 El. 13. *ſhall forfeit ten Shillings.*

Sect. 60. Alſo it is enacted by the ſaid Statute of 3 & 4 *W.* & *M.* 12. *That no Tree, Buſh, or Shrub ſhall be permitted to ſtand or grow in any Highway not full twenty Foot broad, but the ſame ſhall be cut down, grubbed up, and carried away by the Owner or Owners of the Land or Soil, where the ſame ſhall ſtand or grow, within ten Days after Notice to him or them given by the ſaid Surveyors, or any of them, on Pain to forfeit for every Neglect, five Shillings,* &c.

Sect. 61. As to the third Particular, *viz.* In what Manner all other Annoyances obſtructing the Highway are to be removed; it ſeems clear,
1 Jon. 222. That, by the Common Law any one may abate a Nuſance to a Highway, and remove the Materials, but not convert them to his own Uſe, as hath
Vide 4 Aſſ. 3. more fully been ſhewn in the precedent Chapter; alſo it ſeemeth, That an
17 Ed. 3. 9. b. 2 Rol. Ab. Heir may be indicted for continuing an Incroachment, or other Nuſance to
137. B. 4. a Highway, begun by his Anceſtor, becauſe ſuch a Continuance thereof a-
142. K, L. mounts in the Judgment of Law to a new Nuſance.

Sect. 62. But the Common Law, not having been thought ſufficiently to have provided againſt Miſchiefs of that Kind, it was enacted by the above mentioned Statute of 18 *El.* 10. Par. 7. *That no Perſon, having any Ground adjoining to any Highway, or Common faring Way, leading to any Market-Town, ſhall caſt or ſcowr any Ditch, and throw or lay the Soil thereof into the Highway, and ſuffer it to lie there by the Space of ſix Months, to the Annoyance of the ſaid Highway, or Common faring Way, upon Pain of Forfeiture for every Load of Soil ſo caſt into the Highway, or Common faring Way, in Ditching or Scowring, twelve Pence: And that the Surveyors may make Sluces thro' Banks occaſioned by the caſting ſuch Soil into any Highway,* &c.

Sect. 63. And it is farther enacted by the above mentioned Statute of 3 & 4 *W.* & *M.* 12. *That no Perſon ſhall lay in any Highway not twenty Foot broad, any Stone, Timber, Straw, Dung, or other Matter, whereby the ſame ſhall be any ways obſtructed or annoyed, on Pain to forfeit for every ſuch Offence, five Shillings,* &c. And it is farther enacted, *That if any Timber, Stone, Hay, Straw, Stubble, or other Matter for the making of Dung, or on any other Pre-*

tence whatsoever, shall be laid in any Highway, as aforesaid, whereby the same shall be any ways obstructed or annoyed, the Owners or Possessors of the Lands next adjoining to the same, shall clear the said Way by removing the said Timber, Stone, Hay, Straw, Dung, or other Matter, and have, take, and dispose of the same to his and their own Use; and if any such Owner or Occupier of Lands next adjoining to the said Highways, shall neglect to clear the said Ways of the said Nusances, he shall forfeit five Shillings, &c.

Sect. 64. As to the fourth Particular, *viz.* How far all Persons are punishable for taking away Things made Use of for the Benefit of Highways, it is enacted by the above mentioned Statute of 7 & 8 *W.* 3. 29. *That every Person who shall pull up, cut down, or remove, any Post, Block, great Stone, Bank of Earth, or other Security, which was set up, placed, and made, for securing any Horse or Foot Causey, in a publick Highway, from Waggons, Wains and Carts, shall upon Complaint to any Justice of the Peace of the Place or Division where such Offence shall be proved by the Oath of one credible Witness,* &c. *forfeit twenty Shillings, one Moiety thereof to the Surveyors,* &c. *and the other Moiety to him that shall discover the same.*

Sect. 65. As to the fifth Particular, *viz.* How far Persons may be punished for drawing a Carriage with more than five Horses in Length, it is enacted by the above mentioned Statutes of 22 *Car.* 2. 12. Par. 6, 7. and 7 & 8 *Will.* 3. 29. and also by 6 *Annæ*, 29. and 9 *Annæ*, 18. and 1 *Geo.* 1. *c.* 11. *That no travelling Waggon, Wain, Cart, or Carriage, wherein any Burdens, Goods and Wares shall be carried and drawn (other than such Carts and Carriages as shall be imployed in or about Husbandry and Manuring of Land, and in carrying of Hay, Straw, Corn* [a] *unthrashed, Chalk, Timber for Shipping, Materials for Building, Stones of all Sorts, or such Ammunition or Artillery as should be for the Service of his Majesty, his Heirs or Successors) shall at any one Time be drawn or go in any common or publick Highway or Road, with above five Horses, Oxen, or Beasts in Length, (except* [b] *only where such five Horses shall not be sufficient to draw such Cart or Waggon up any steep Hill, or out of any foul Place, in which Case it shall be lawful to join any Horses from another Cart or Waggon then travelling that Road, with the Consent of the Owner or Driver of such Cart or Waggon, to help such insufficient Horses up such steep Hill, or out of such foul Place) on Pain of* [c] *forfeiting five Pounds, one Moiety to the Surveyor of the Highways of the Place where such Offence shall be committed, for the Repairs of the said Highways, and the other Moiety to him who shall discover and prosecute for the same, to be levied by Distress of all, or any of the Horses, Oxen, or Beasts af any Person offending against the said Statutes, which* [d] *Distress may be made by any Person whatsoever,* (without any Warrant, as it seemeth from 9 *Annæ*, 18.) *And the Beasts so distrained are to be delivered forthwith to the Surveyor of the Highways, or other Parish Officer, of the Place where the Offence shall be committed; and if the said Penalty be not paid within three Days, the said Surveyor or other Parish Officer, may, by Warrant of one Justice of the Peace, sell the said Distress, and deliver the Money raised thereby to the said Justice, who is to distribute the Penalties in the Manner above directed, rendring the Overplus to the Owner, the Charges being first deducted; or if the Offender shall immediately pay the said Penalty to the Person who shall make such Distress, or to the Surveyor, or other Parish Officer, where the Offence shall be committed; then the Person so receiving the same, shall deliver it to the next Justice of the Peace, to be by him distributed, as aforesaid. Provided that if any Person shall refuse or neglect to carry any of the said Beasts by him so distrained, to the Surveyor, or other Parish Officer, as aforesaid, he shall forfeit twenty Pounds, to be levied of his Goods by Warrant of one Justice of the Peace,* &c. *And if any Surveyor, or other Parish Officer, shall refuse or*

neglect

See the Statute of 5 Geo. 1. c. 12.

[a] 1 Geo. 1. Stat. 2. c. 11.

[b] 6 Annæ, 29. 9 Annæ, 18.

[c] 6 Annæ, 29.

[d] 9 Annæ, 18.

neglect to deliver any Sum of Money, or Penalty by him received, to the ſaid Juſtice, he ſhall forfeit twenty Pounds to be levied, &c. *as aforeſaid.* Additions [87]

Sect. 66. And it is farther enacted by the ſaid Statute of 9 *Annæ*, 18. *That if any Perſon employed by any Carrier, or other Perſon ſubject to the Penalties mentioned in the ſaid Act, ſhall drive, or aſſiſt in the Driving of any travelling Waggon,* &c. *with more than ſix Horſes,* &c. *the Perſon ſo offending ſhall forfeit five Pounds, to be levied and diſpoſed of in like Manner as the Forfeitures before mentioned are directed and appointed.*

Sect. 67. As to the eighth general Head of this Chapter, *viz.* In what Manner thoſe, who are charged with any Offence relating to the Highway, are to be proceeded againſt, it is enacted by the above mentioned Statute of 2 & 3 *Ph. & M.* 8. *That the Steward of every Leet may enquire by the Oaths of the Suitors of all Offences which ſhall be committed within the Leet, againſt every Article of the ſaid Statute, and to aſſeſs ſuch Fines and Amerciaments for the ſame, as ſhall be thought meet by the ſaid Steward: And in Default of ſuch Inquiry or Preſentment, the Quarter-Seſſions of every Place may inquire of the ſame Offences which ſhall be committed within the Limits of their Commiſſion, and to aſſeſs ſuch Fines as they, or two of them, whereof one to be of the* Quorum, *ſhall think meet: And the Steward of the every Leet ſhall make Eſtreats indented of all the Fines, Forfeitures, and Amerciaments, for the Defaults preſented before him, and ſhall deliver the one Part thereof ſealed and ſigned by him to the Bailiff and High Conſtable of every Hundred, Rape, Lathe, or Wapentake, wherein the Default ſhall be preſented, and the other Part to the Conſtable and Church-wardens of the Pariſh wherein the Defaults were made; the ſame to be yearly delivered within ſix Weeks after the Feaſt of* Michaelmas: *And the Clerk of the Peace ſhall make the like Eſtreats indented of the Fines,* &c. *for the Defaults preſented before the Juſtices of the Peace,* &c. *The which Eſtreats ſhall be ſufficient Warrant to the ſaid Bailiff, or chief Conſtable, to levy the ſaid Fines,* &c. *by Way of Diſtreſs: And if no ſufficient Diſtreſs can be found by the ſaid Bailiff or Chief Conſtable; or if the ſaid Offender ſhall obſtinately refuſe to pay the ſaid Fine,* &c. *and do not pay the ſame within twenty Days after a lawful Demand of the ſame by the ſaid Officer, he ſhall forfeit the double Sum that he ſhould before have paid.*

Sect. 68. And it is farther enacted by the ſaid Statute, *That every of the ſaid Bailiffs and Head Conſtables, ſhall at leaſt once every Year, betwixt the firſt Day of* March *and the laſt Day of* April, *make a true Account and Payment of all ſuch Sums of Money, (to the Conſtable and Church-wardens of every Pariſh wherein the Offences were committed, or to two of them) as he ſhall have collected upon any of the ſaid Eſtates, on Pain of, to forfeit for every Time he ſhall not ſo do, forty Shillings.*

Sect. 69. And it is farther enacted by the ſaid Statute, *That all Fines,* &c. *which ſhall be due for any Offence againſt the Purview thereof, ſhall be to the Church-wardens of every Pariſh wherein the Offences ſhall be committed, to be beſtowed on the Highways in the ſaid Pariſhes: And the ſaid Church-wardens ſhall have Authority to call the ſaid Bailiff and Head Conſtable to account, before the Juſtices of Peace, or two of them, whereof one to be of the* Quorum, *by Bill, Information, or otherwiſe: The which Juſtices ſhall have Authority to take the ſaid Account, and to commit the ſaid Bailiff and Head Conſtable to Priſon till he ſhall pay all ſuch Arrearages as ſhall be adjudged by the ſaid Juſtices; and every of the ſaid Bailiffs and Head Conſtables upon their Accounts ſhall have allowed for every Pound he ſhall collect and pay, Eight-pence for his own Pains, and Twelve-pence for the Fees of the Clerk of the Peace, or Steward of the Leet, for the Eſtreats indented of every ſeveral Pariſh that they ſhall deliver as is aforeſaid;*

And the Succeſſors of every Church-warden ſhall have the like Action of Account againſt their Predeceſſors, as is before appointed againſt the Bailiff.

Sect. 70. And it is enacted by the above mentioned Statute of 5 *El.* 13. Par. 8. *That every Surveyor ſhall within one Month after any Default or Offence againſt the ſaid Statute of* 2 & 3 Ph. & Mar. 8. *or the ſaid Statute of* 5 El. 13. *preſent every ſuch Offence to the next Juſtice of Peace, on Pain to forfeit for every ſuch Offence in ſuch Sort, not by him preſented, forty Shillings: And that every ſuch Juſtice of Peace to whom any ſuch Offence ſhall be ſo preſented, ſhall certify the ſame Preſentment at the next general County Seſſions, on Pain to forfeit for not certifying of every ſuch Preſentment of every ſuch Offence, five Pounds; and that the Juſtices of Peace of every County, where the ſaid Offences ſhall be committed, may enquire thereof at their Quarter-Seſſions, and aſſeſs ſuch Fines for the ſame, as they or two of them, whereof one to be of the* Quorum *ſhall think meet.*

Sect. 71. And it is farther enacted by the ſaid Statute, Par. 9. *That every Juſtice of Peace may of his own proper Knowledge, in the open General-Seſſions, make Preſentment of any Highway not well and ſufficiently repaired and amended, or of any other Default or Offence, contrary to either of the ſaid Statutes of* 2 & 3 Ph. & Mar. 8. *or* 5 El. 18. *And that every Preſentment made by any ſuch Juſtice of Peace upon his own Knowledge, as is aforeſaid, ſhall be as good, and of the ſame Force, Strength, and Effect in the Law, as if the ſame had been preſented, found, and adjudged, by the Oath of twelve Men: And that for every ſuch Default ſo preſented, as is aforeſaid, the Juſtices of Peace of the ſaid County ſhall immediately, at the ſaid General-Seſſions, have Authority to aſſeſs ſuch Fines, as to them, or two of them, whereof the one to be of the* Quorum, *ſhall be thought meet: Saving to every Perſon that ſhall be touched by any ſuch Preſentment his lawful Traverſe to the ſame Preſentment, as he might have upon any Indictment of Treſpaſs, or forcible Entry, by the Laws of this Realm, before the making of this Statute.*

Sect. 72. It hath been holden in the Expoſition of this Clauſe, That the Party againſt whom ſuch a Preſentment ſhall be made, cannot take any Traverſe to the Want of Repair of ſuch Highway; but it is agreed, That he may plead that ſome other Perſon ought to repair the ſame, and traverſe his own Obligation to do it. Neither can I ſee upon what Reaſon the former Opinion is grounded, that he cannot traverſe the Want of Repair of ſuch Highway, for ſince the Statute expreſly *ſaves to every Perſon who ſhall be touched by any ſuch Preſentment, his lawful Traverſe to the ſame, as he might have to an Indictment of Treſpaſs or forcible Entry*; and ſince it ſeems clear, That every Defendant to any ſuch Indictment may traverſe the whole Matter alledged againſt him, as hath been ſhewn more at large, Chap. 64. Sect. 58. why may he not as well have the ſame Benefit in the preſent Caſe? And though the Record of a Juſtice of Peace acting by Force of any Statute, as a Judge, be not traverſable; yet it ſeems hard by ſuch a general Rule, to make any Record not traverſable, which by the expreſs Words of the Statute, which authorizes the making of it, is allowed to be traverſable: It is true indeed, That a Preſentment in a Court-Leet is not traverſable, unleſs it touch the Party's Freehold: But I do not ſee why ſuch a Preſentment in Purſuance of this Statute ſhould have the like Privilege ſince the Statute hath no Mention of ſuch Preſentments in Courts-Leet, but gives the like Traverſe as is allowed by Law upon any Indictment of Treſpaſs, &c.

Kellew. 34. Crom. 131. Dalt. ca. 26.

See Carth. 212, 213. Supra, ch. 64. Sect. 18.

5 H. 7. 4. a. Dy. 13. b.

Sect. 73. It is farther enacted by the ſaid Statute of 5 *El.* 13. Par. 10. *That all ſuch Fines,* &c. *to be aſſeſſed by the ſaid General-Seſſions, ſhall be eſtreated*

 ed

ed and levied in ſuch Manner, and imployed to ſuch Uſes and Intents, as in the ſaid Statute of 2 & 3 Phil. & Mar. *are appointed.*

Sect. 74. And it is farther enacted by the above mentioned Statute of 18 *El.* 10. Par. 8. *That all Juſtices of Aſſize, Juſtices of Oyer and Terminer, and Juſtices of the Peace in their Seſſions, and Stewards of Leets in their Leets, ſhall hear and determine every Offence, Matter, and Cauſe, that ſhall grow, come, or riſe, by Reaſon of the ſaid Statute.*

Sect. 75. Alſo it is enacted by the above mentioned Statute of 22 *Car.* 2. 12. Par. 9. *That if any Perſon ſhall fail in his reſpective Days Labour in every Year towards the Repairing of the Highways, or neglect to ſend his reſpective Carriages,* &c. *required by Law; the Surveyors ought to make Complaint thereof to the next Juſtices of the Peace, who ought upon Proof by Oath of one credible Witneſs, to levy by Diſtreſs and Sale of Goods,* &c. *for every Day-Labourer failing, as is aforeſaid, one Shilling and ſix Pence; for every Man and Horſe, that ſhall make Default three Shillings; and for every Cart with two Men, ten Shilling for every reſpective Day wherein they ſhall make Default; which Penalties ſhall be imployed towards the Repairs of the Highways,* &c.

Sect. 76. And it is farther enacted by the ſame Statute, Par. 10. and 3 & 4 *Will. & Mar.* 12. *That the Aſſeſſments to be made, in Purſuance of theſe Statutes, for the Repairs of the Highways, ſhall be levied by Diſtreſs and Sale of the Goods of every Perſon ſo aſſeſſed, not paying the ſame within ten Days after Demand, rendring the Overplus to the Owner the neceſſary Charges being firſt deducted.*

Sect. 77. It will be needleſs to ſhew in this Place in what Manner the ſeveral Penalties for other Offences againſt the above mentioned Statutes concerning the Highways, are to be recovered, becauſe the ſame may appear from the foregoing Part of this Chapter, wherein the ſeveral Clauſes of the ſaid Statutes relating to the ſaid Offences are ſet forth.

Sect. 78. It is enacted by the ſaid Statute of 22 *Car.* 2. 12. Par. 4. *That all Defects of Repairs of Cauſeys, Pavements, Highways or Bridges, ſhall be preſented in the County only where ſuch Cauſeys,* &c. *lie, and not elſewhere; and that no ſuch Preſentment or Indictment ſhall be removed by* Certiorari, *or otherwiſe, out of the ſaid County, till ſuch Indictment or Preſentment be traverſed, and Judgment thereupon given.*

See B.2.Ch.27. S. 37, 46, 47.

Sect. 79. And it is farther enacted by the ſaid Statute of 3 & 4 *W. & M.* 12. *That all Matters concerning Highways, Cauſeys, Pavements, and Bridges, mentioned in the ſaid Act, ſhall be determined in the County where the ſame do lie, and not elſewhere; and that no Preſentment, Indictment, or Order, made by Virtue of the ſaid Act, ſhall be removed by* Certiorari *out of the ſaid County into any other Court.*

Sect. 80. Yet it hath been reſolved, That if the Quarter-Seſſions, under Pretence of the Juriſdiction given them by theſe Statutes, take upon them to do a Thing manifeſtly exceeding their Authority, as to make an Order on Surveyors of the Highways to make up their Accounts before a ſpecial Seſſions, their Proceedings may be removed by *Certiorari* into the King's Bench, and there quaſhed; for the Quarter-Seſſions have no manner of Power given them to intermeddle originally with ſuch Accounts, but only by Way of Appeal.

Queen and Bramby, Mic. 10 Ann.

Sect. 81. It is enacted by the ſaid Statute of 3 & 4 *W. & M.* 12. *That no Perſon ſhall be puniſhed for any Offence againſt the ſaid Act, unleſs ſuch Offender be proſecuted for the ſame within ſix Months after the Offence committed, and that no Perſon who ſhall be puniſhed for any Offence by Virtue of the ſaid Act, ſhall be puniſhed for the ſame Offence by Virtue of any other Act, or Law whatſoever.*

Sect. 82. As to the ninth general Head of this Chapter, *viz.* In what manner Perſons proceeded againſt for any of the abovementioned Offences may defend themſelves; it is enacted by the ſaid Statute of 3 & 4 *W.* & *M.* 10. *That if any Perſon ſhall find himſelf aggrieved with an Aſſeſſment or Rate, or other Act by the ſaid Juſtices of Peace, the general Quarter-Seſſions of the Peace, may take ſuch Order therein, as to them ſhall be thought convenient, and the ſame to conclude and bind all the ſaid Parties.*

Sect. 83. Alſo it ſeems to be implied in the Conſtruction of theſe as well as of all other Penal Statutes, That no one ought to be convicted of any Offence againſt them, without having Notice of the Accuſation made againſt him, and an Opportunity of defending himſelf. And therefore I ſhall take it for granted, that generally no one ought to be puniſhed for any of the above mentioned Offences, without being called upon to anſwer for himſelf, and having Liberty to traverſe the Matters alledged againſt him; it is true indeed, That it is generally holden, That no Traverſe can be taken againſt a Preſentment by a Juſtice of Peace of his own Knowledge, as to the Want of Repair; yet this Opinion ſeems juſtly queſtionable for the Reaſons alledged in the ſeventy-ſecond Section of this Chapter.

Vide ſupra. Ch. 64. Sect. 58, 59, 60.

Sect. 84. However it is certain, That in all other Caſes, whoever is indicted or preſented in any Court, except a Court-Leet, for any Offence relating to the Highways, may traverſe the whole Matter alledged againſt him in ſuch Indictment or Preſentment; but it ſeemeth to be agreed, That he, who is preſented for ſuch an Offence in a Court-Leet, can only traverſe it ſo far as it concerns his Freehold, as by charging him with being bound to ſuch Repairs in reſpect of the Tenure of his Lands, &c. for which Purpoſe it is certain, that he may remove it by a *Certiorari* into the King's Bench, and there traverſe it; alſo there is no Doubt, but that after Conviction, or upon a Demurrer, or Confeſſion, any one may take Exceptions to any ſuch Indictment or Preſentment in any Court for the Want of legal Form; but the Court in Diſcretion will very rarely ſuffer a Man to take ſuch Exceptions, before ſuch Conviction or Confeſſion, without a Certificate and Affidavit, that the Ways are in good Repair.

5 H. 7. 4. a. Dy. 14. Pl. 64. Finch 386.

And. 234; 1 Keb. 256, 291, 829. 2 Keb. 715, 728.

Sect. 85. Therefore for the better Underſtanding in what Caſes it may be ſafe to demur to, or confeſs an Indictment or Preſentment of this Kind, I ſhall lay down the following Rules concerning them.

Sect. 86. I. That it is [a] ſafeſt in every ſuch Indictment to ſhew both the Place from which, and alſo the Place to which the Way ſuppoſed to be out of Repair doth lead, yet Exceptions for Want of ſuch Certainty, have ſometimes been [b] diſallowed; however it ſeems certain, That there is no Neceſſity to ſhew [c] that a Highway leads to a Market-Town, becauſe every Highway leads from Town to Town.

[a] 2 Rol. Ab. 81. Pl. 18. Palm. 420.
[b] 2 Keb. 715, 728. 3 Keb. 89, 644. 1 Brown 6.
[c] Palm. 389. 2 Ro. Re. 412.

Sect. 87. II. That it is neceſſary [d] in every ſuch Indictment expreſly to ſhew in what Place the Nuſance complained of was done, for which [e] Cauſe an Indictment for ſtopping a Way at *D.* leading from *D.* to *C.* is not good, for it is impoſſible that a Way leading from *D.* ſhould be in *D.* and no other Place is alledged.

[d] 3 Keb. 644.
[e] 2 Rol. Ab. 81. Pl. 18.

Sect. 88. III. That every ſuch Indictment ought alſo certainly to ſhew to what Part of the Highway the Nuſance did extend, as by ſhewing how many Foot in Length, and how many Foot in Breadth it contained, or otherwiſe the Defendant will neither know of the Certainty of the Charge, againſt which he is to make his Defence, neither will the Court be able from the Record to judge of the Greatneſs of the Offence, in order to aſſeſs a Fine anſwerable thereunto; and upon this Ground it hath

Cro. Ja. 324.

2 Rol Ab 80. Pl. 14. 81 Pl. 16.

hath been adjudged, That an indictment for ſtopping a certain Part of the King's Way at *K.* is naught, for the Uncertainty thereof: Alſo it hath been reſolved, That the Place wherein ſuch a Nuſance is alledged, is not ſuffi-
2 Rol. Ab. 81. Pl. 7.
ciently aſcertained in ſuch an Indictment, by ſhewing that it contained ſo many Foot in Length, and ſo many in Breadth, by Eſtimation.

Sal. 359. 6 Mod. 255, 256. [a] Cro. El. 63. [b] See 2 R. A. 83. C. 1 Vent. 208. Poph. 206. 2 Keb. 728. [c] 1 Vent. 208. 3 Keb. 28.

Sect. 89. IV. That every ſuch Indictment muſt ſhew, That the Way wherein a Nuſance is alledged, is a Way common to all the King's People, for which cauſe it hath been reſolved, That an Indictment for a Nuſance to a [a] Horſe-way, without adding that it is a Highway, is naught; and upon the ſame Ground it ſeemeth alſo, That an Indictment for a Nuſance to a common Foot-way to the Church of *D.* for [b] all the Pariſhioners of *D.* is not good; yet it [c] ſeems, That if thoſe laſt Words, *viz. For all Pariſhioners of* D. had been omitted, ſuch an Indictment might be maintained.

[d] Noy 93. 3 Keb. 855. But the contrary was adjudged Paſch. 5 Geo. 1. between the King and Corrack, according to Ventr. 331. Vide 2 Keb. 514. Raym. 182. [e] 3 Keb. 58.

Sect. 90. V. That it is not ſafe in an Indictment againſt a common Perſon for not repairing a Highway, which he ought to have done in Reſpect of the Tenure of certain Lands, barely to ſay that he was bound to repair it, *ratione Tenuræ Terræ*, without adding [d] *ſuæ*; alſo it is ſaid, That in an Indictment againſt a [e] Biſhop, *&c.* for not repairing a Highway, in reſpect of certain Lands, it ought to be ſhewn in what Capacity he ought to repair it, becauſe otherwiſe it cannot be known in what Capacity the Proceſs is to be awarded againſt him.

Sect. 91. VI. That in every ſuch Indictment the Fact alledged againſt the Defendant muſt be expreſſed in ſuch proper Terms, that it may clearly appear to the Court to have been a Nuſance; and for this Cauſe it hath been reſolved, That a Preſentment for diverting a Highway is not good, becauſe a Highway cannot be diverted, but muſt always continue in the ſame Place
1 And. 234. Poph. 206.
where it was, howſoever it be obſtructed, and a new Way made in another Place.

Sect. 92. VII. That an Indictment againſt a Man for ſtopping a Highway in his own Land is good, without laying the Offence done *Vi & Armis.* Alſo it is ſaid, That a Preſentment that a Highway in ſuch a Place is
2 R. A. 79. L.
decayed by the Defaults of the Inhabitants of ſuch a Town is good without naming any Perſon in Certainty. But it hath been adjudged, That an Indictment againſt particular Perſons muſt ſpecially charge them every one; for which Cauſe it hath been reſolved, That an Indictment againſt ſeveral for
2 R. A. 81. Pl. 6, 7.
not repairing their Streets, that they & *eorum uterque*, did not repair them, is not good.

1 Syd. 140. Carth. 213.
Sect. 93. VIII. That the Defendants ought not to plead *quod non debent reparare*, without ſhewing who ought.

Salk. 358. 6 Mod. 163.
Sect. 94. That the Defendants ſhall not be diſcharged by ſubmitting to a Fine, but a *Diſtringas* ſhall go *in infinitum* till they repair. [88] ☞

CHAP. LXXVII.

Of Nuſances relating to Bridges.

AND now I am in the ſecond Place to conſider Nuſances relating to Bridges in particular; for the better Underſtanding whereof, I ſhall examine:

1. How publick Bridges are to be repaired by the Common Law.
2. How by the Statute.

As to the firſt Point, I ſhall conſider,

1. In what Manner, and by whom ſuch Bridges are to be repaired by Common Law.
2. In what Manner Perſons bound to ſuch Repairs are to be proceeded againſt.

Sect. 1. As to the firſt of theſe Particulars, it ſeemeth to be clear, That thoſe who are bound to repair ſuch Bridges, muſt make them of ſuch Height and Strength, as ſhall be anſwerable to the Courſe of the Water, whether it continue in the old Chanel, or make a new one; and that they are not puniſhable as Treſpaſſers, for entring on any adjoining Land, for ſuch Purpoſe, or for laying thereon the Materials requiſite for ſuch Repairs. Alſo it ſeemeth to be clearly [a] ſettled, That of common Right the Charge of repairing all common Bridges, lies upon the County wherein they are, unleſs Part thereof be within a Franchiſe; in which Caſe it is ſaid, That ſo much as is within the Franchiſe ſhall be repaired by thoſe of the Franchiſe.

43 Aſſ. Pl. 43. Dalt. ca. 14.

[a] 2 Inſt. 701. H. P. C. 143. Cro. Ca. 365. 6 Mod. 307. Salk. 358, 359.

Sect. 2. Alſo it ſeemeth to be [b] certain, That ſuch Charge may be caſt upon a Corporation aggregate, either in reſpect of a ſpecial Tenure of certain Lands, or in reſpect of a ſpecial Preſcription, and that it may be caſt upon any other Perſons by reaſon of ſuch a ſpecial Tenure, as hath been ſhewn more at large under the ſecond general Head of the precedent Chapter. But it is [c] ſaid, That a Man ſhall not be bound to repair a new Bridge built by himſelf, for the common Good: But that the County ſhall be bound to repair it, if it become of publick Convenience.

[b] 2 Inſt. 700, 701. H. P. C. 143. Dal. ca. 14. Far. 54, 55.

[c] 2 Inſt. 701. 6 Mod. 307. Salk. 359. See Cro. Ca. 365.

Sect. 3. As to the ſecond Particular, *viz.* In what Manner Perſons bound to ſuch Repairs, are to be proceeded againſt; it ſeemeth to be clear, [d] That any particular Inhabitant or Inhabitants of a County, or Tenant or Tenants of Land charged to the Repairs of ſuch a Bridge, may be made Defendants to an Indictment for not repairing it, and be liable to pay the whole Fine aſſeſſed by the Court for the Default of ſuch Repairs, and ſhall be put to their Remedy at Law for a Contribution from thoſe who are bound to bear a proportionable Share in the Charge, for the Neceſſity of the Caſe requires the greateſt Expedition in Caſes of this Nature.

[d] 1 Jon. 273. Poph. 192. 6 Mod. 307. Salk. 358.

Sect. 4. Alſo it hath been [e] reſolved, That it is not ſufficient for the Defendants to an Indictment for not repairing a Bridge, to excuſe themſelves, by ſhewing either that they are not bound to repair the Whole, or any Part of the Bridge, without ſhewing what other Perſon is bound to repair the ſame; and it is ſaid, That in ſuch Caſe the whole Charge ſhall be laid upon ſuch Defendants, by reaſon of their ill Plea.

[e] 2 Levin. 112. Poph. 192. 43 Aſſ. Pl. 37.

43 Aſſ. Pl. 37. Bro. Preſentment, 22, and 29.

Sect. 5. It is ſaid, That where ſuch Defendants plead, that *A. B.* ought to repair the Bridge mentioned in the Indictment, and take a Traverſe to the Charge againſt themſelves, the Attorney General in this ſpecial Caſe may take a Traverſe upon a Traverſe, and inſiſt that the Defendants are bound to the Repairs, and traverſe the Charge alledged againſt *A. B.* and that an Iſſue ought to be taken on ſuch ſecond Traverſe; and that the Attorney General may afterwards ſurmiſe, that the Defendants are bound to repair it, and that the whole Matter ſhall be tried by an indifferent Jury, &c.

See 1 Sid. 140.

2 Levin. 112.

6 Mod. 307. *Sect.* 6. It ſeems that no Inhabitant of a County ought to be a Juror for the Trial of an Iſſue, whether the County be bound to ſuch Repairs or not, but it is ſaid that he may be a good Witneſs.

Sect. 7. As to the ſecond Point, *viz.* In what Manner ſuch Bridges are to be repaired by Statute, it is enacted by 22 *H.* 8. 5. *That the Juſtices of Peace in every Shire of this Realm, Franchiſe, City, or Borough, or four of them at the leaſt, whereof one to be of the* Quorum, *may inquire, hear, and determine, in their General Seſſions, of all manner of Annoyances of Bridges broken in the Highways, to the Damage of the King's liege People, and to make ſuch Proceſs and Pains upon every Preſentment afore them, for the Reformation of the ſame, againſt ſuch as owen to be charged for the Making or Amending of ſuch Bridges, as the King's Juſtices of his Bench uſe commonly to do; or as it ſhall ſeem by their Diſcretions to be neceſſary and convenient for the ſpeedy Amendment of ſuch Bridges.*

Sect. 8. And it is farther enacted, Par. 2 & 3. *That where it cannot be known and proved what Hundred, Riding, Wapentake, City, Borough, Town or Pariſh, nor what Perſon certain, or Body Politick, ought of Right to make ſuch Bridges decayed, by reaſon whereof ſuch decayed Bridges, for Lack of Knowledge of ſuch as owen to make them, for the moſt part lie long without any Amendment, to the great Annoyance of the King's Subjects, in every ſuch Caſe the ſaid Bridges, if they be without City or Town-corporate, ſhall be made by the Inhabitants of the Shire or Riding, within which the ſaid Bridge decayed ſhall happen to be: And if it be within any City or Town-corporate, then by the Inhabitants of every ſuch City or Town-corporate wherein ſuch Bridges ſhall be. And if Part of any ſuch Bridges ſo decayed happen to be in one Shire, Riding, City, or Town-corporate, and the other Part thereof in another Shire, Riding, City, or Town-corporate, or if Part be within the Limits of any City or Town-corporate, and Part without, or Part within one Riding, and Part within another, that then in every ſuch Caſe the Inhabitants of the Shires, Ridings, Cities, or Towns-corporate, ſhall be charged and chargeable to amend, make and repair ſuch Part and Portion of ſuch Bridges ſo decayed, as ſhall lie and be within the Limits of the Shire, Riding, City, or Town-corporate, wherein they be inhabited at the Time of the ſame Decays.*

Sect. 9. And it is farther enacted, Par. 4. *That in every ſuch Caſe where* Vide 1 Keb. 422. *it cannot be known and proved what Perſons, Lands, Tenements, and Bodies politick owen to make and repair ſuch Bridges, that for ſpeedy Reformation and Amending of ſuch Bridges, the Juſtices of Peace within the Shires or Ridings wherein ſuch decayed Bridges being out of Cities and Towns-corporate, and if it be within Cities or Towns-corporate, then the Juſtices of Peace within every ſuch City or Town-corporate, or four of the ſaid Juſtices at the leaſt, whereof one to be of the* Quorum, *within the Limits of their ſeveral Commiſſions and Authorities, may call before them the Conſtables of every Town and Pariſh, being within the Shire, Riding, City or Town-corporate, as well within Liberty as without, wherein ſuch Bridges or any Parcel thereof ſhall happen to be, or elſe two of the moſt honeſt Inhabitants within every ſuch Town or Pariſh in the ſaid Shire, Riding, City or Town-corporate, by the Diſcretion of the ſaid Juſtices of Peace,* &c. *And at and upon the Appearance of ſuch Conſtables or Inhabitants, the ſaid Juſtices of Peace,* &c. *with the Aſſent of the ſaid Conſtables or Inhabitants, may tax, and ſet every Inhabitant in any ſuch City, Town or Pariſh, within the Limits of their Commiſſions and Authorities, to ſuch reaſonable Aid and Sum of Money, as they ſhall think by their Diſcretions convenient and ſufficient for the Repairing, Re-edifying, and Amending of ſuch Bridges, and after ſuch Taxation made the ſaid Juſtices ſhall cauſe the Names and Sums of every particular Perſon ſo by them taxed, to be written in a Roll indented. And ſhall alſo have Power and Authority to make two Collectors of every Hundred, for Collection of all ſuch Sums of Money by them ſet and taxed, which Collectors receiving the one Part of the ſaid Roll indented, under the Seals of the ſaid Juſtices, ſhall have Power and Authority to collect and receive all the particular Sums of Money therein contained, and to diſtrain every ſuch Inhabitant as ſhall be taxed, and refuſe Payment thereof, in his Lands, Goods and Chattels, and to ſell ſuch Diſtreſs, and of the Sale thereof retain and perceive all the Money taxed, and the Reſidue, (if the Diſtreſs be better) to deliver to the Owner thereof: And that the ſame Juſtices, or four of them, within the Limits of their Commiſſions and Authorities, may alſo name and appoint two Surveyors, which ſhall ſee every ſuch decayed Bridge repaired and amended from Time to Time, as often as need ſhall require, to whoſe Hands the ſaid Collectors ſhall pay the ſaid Sums of Money, taxed, and by them received: And that the Collectors and Surveyors, and every of them, and their Executors and Adminiſtrators, and the Executors and Adminiſtrators of them, and every of them, from Time to Time, ſhall make a true Declaration and Accompt to the Juſtices of Peace of the Shire, Riding, City, or Town-corporate, wherein they ſhall be appointed Collectors or Surveyors, or to four of the ſame Juſtices, whereof one to be of the* Quorum, *of the Receipts, Payments, and Expences of the ſaid Sums of Money: And if they or any of them refuſe that to do, that then the ſame Juſtices of Peace, or four of them, from Time to Time by their Diſcretions, ſhall have Power and Authority to make Proceſs againſt the ſaid Collectors and Surveyors, and every of them, their Executors and Adminiſtrators, and the Executors and Adminiſtrators of every of them, by Attachments under their Seals, returnable at the General Seſſions of Peace: And if they appear, then to compel them to accompt, as is aforeſaid; or elſe if they or any of them refuſe that to do, then to commit ſuch of them as ſhall refuſe, to ward, there to remain without Bail or Mainpriſe, till the ſaid Declaration and Accompt be truly made.*

Sect. 10. And it is farther enacted, Par. 5. *That where any Bridge or Bridges lien in one Shire or Riding, and ſuch Perſons Inhabitants, Bodies Politick, Lands or Tenements, which owen to be charged to the Making and Amending of ſuch Bridges, lien and abiden in another Shire or Riding, or where ſuch Bridges been within any City, or Town-corporate, and the Perſons Inhabitants, Bodies Politick, Lands or Tenements, that owen to make or repair any ſuch Bridges lien and been out of the ſaid Cities and Town-corporate, in every ſuch Caſe the Juſtices of Peace of the Shire, City, or Town-corporate, within which ſuch decayed Bridges, or any Part thereof, ſhall happen to be, ſhall have Power to inquire, hear, and determine all ſuch Annoyances, being within the Limits of their Commiſſions and Authorities. And if the Annoyance be preſented, then to make Proceſs into every Shire within this Realm, againſt ſuch as owen to make, or amend any ſuch Bridges ſo preſented before them to be decayed, to the Annoyance, and Let of the Paſſage of the King's Subjects, and to do further in every Behalf in every ſuch Caſe, as they might do by Authority of the ſaid Act, in Caſe that the Perſons,* &c. *which owen to be charged to the Amending or Making of ſuch Bridges,* &c. *were in the ſame Shire,* &c. *where ſuch Annoyance ſhall happen to be. And that all Sheriffs, and Bailiffs of Liberties and Franchiſes, ſhall truly ſerve and execute Proceſs as ſhall come to their Hands from the ſaid Juſtices of Peace, afore whom any Preſentment ſhall be had for any ſuch Annoyance, according to the Tenor and Effect of the ſaid Proceſs to them directed,* &c. *on Pain to make ſuch Fine as ſhall be ſet on them by the Diſcretion of the ſaid Juſtices.*

Sect. 11. But it is provided, Par. 6. *That nothing in the ſaid Act contained ſhall be prejudicial to the Liberties of the five Ports, or Members of the ſame: And for Reformation of Annoyance of Bridges within the ſaid Ports and Mem-*

Members: It is farther enacted, Par. 7. *That the Warden, Mayors, and Bailiffs elected, and Jurates of the same Ports, and every of them, have Power and Authority to inquire, hear, and determine all manner of common Annoyances of Bridges within the same Ports and Members, and to make such Process, Pains, Taxations, and all other Things within the same Ports and Members, as the Justices of Peace may do in other Shires or Places out of the same Ports, by Virtue of the said Act in every Behalf.*

Sect. 12. And it is farther enacted, Par. 8. *That the said Justices,* &c. *may allow such reasonable Costs and Charges to the said Surveyors and Collectors, as by their Discretion shall be thought convenient.*

Sect. 13. And it is farther enacted, Par. 9. *That such Part and Portion of the Highways in every Part of this Realm, as well within Franchise as without, as lie next adjoining to any Ends of any Bridges within this Realm, distant from any of the said Ends by the Space of three hundred Foot, be made, repaired and amended, as often as need shall require; and that the Justices of Peace in every Shire of this Realm, Franchise, City, or Borough, or four of them at the least, whereof one to be of the* Quorum, *within the Limits of their Commissions and Authorities, may inquire, hear, and determine in their General Sessions, all Manner of Annoyances of and in such Highways, so being and lying next adjoining to any Ends of Bridges within this Realm, distant from any one of the Ends of such Bridges three hundred Foot, and to do in every Thing concerning the Making, Repairing, and Amending such Highways,* &c. *in as large and ample Manner as they might and may do, to and for the Making, Repairing, and Amending of Bridges, by Virtue of the said Act.*

In the Construction of this Statute the following Opinions have been holden:

2 Inst. 701. Salk. 359. 6 Mod. 255, 256. *Sect.* 14. I. That no private Bridges are within the Purview thereof, but only such as are common in the Highways, where all the King's liege People have, or may have Passage.

2 Inst. 701, 702. *Sect.* 15. II. That unless the Justices of Peace of a County, or Town, *&c.* be four in Number, and one of them of the *Quorum*, they have no manner of Jurisdiction by Virtue of this Statute; but it is said, That the Justices of Peace of the County, in which such Town, being not a County of it self, and wanting such a Number of Justices, shall lie, may by Virtue of the first Clause of the Statute, determine all Annoyances of Bridges within such Town, *&c.* if it be known what Persons in certain are bound to repair the same: But if it be not known, it seems that such Annoyances are left to the Remedy of the Common Law, because the Clause which in
2 Inst. 704. such Case authorises the Justices of Peace to tax all the Inhabitants, seems expresly to confine the Power of taxing the Inhabitants of such Towns to their own Justices, *&c.*

Sect. 16. III. That all Housholders dwelling in any County, or Town,
2 Inst. 703. *&c.* whether they occupy any Lands or not; and also all Persons who have Lands in their own Possession or Manurance, whether they dwell in the same County, *&c.* or not; and also all Bodies Politick, either residing in, or having Lands in their own Hands in a County, *&c.* are liable to be taxed as Inhabitants, within the Meaning of the Statute.

2 Inst. 704. Vide 1 Keb. 91. *Sect.* 17. IV. That the Taxation to be made in Pursuance of the Statute ought to be assessed distinctly on each Inhabitant, and not on a whole Hundred, Parish, or Town in general.

Sect. 18. V. That all Privileges of Exemptions and Discharges from Contribution to the Repairs of decayed Bridges, whether such Exemptions

tions were originally derived from Charter or Act of Parliament, or any other Foundation whatſoever, are taken away by the expreſs Words of the Statute, *That the Juſtices*, &c. *ſhall tax and ſet every Inhabitant.* 2 Inſt. 704.

Sect. 19. It hath been queſtioned whether a Borough which hath no Bridge within its own Limits, be not liable to contribute to the Repairs of a County-Bridge. 1 Keb. 68.

CHAP. LXXVIII.

Of Nuſances relating to Publick Houſes.

FOR the better Underſtanding of Nuſances relating to publick Houſes, I ſhall conſider:

1. In what Manner they are prevented and reſtrained by the Common Law.
2. In what Manner by Statute.

Sect. 1. As to the firſt Point it ſeems to be agreed, That the Keeper of an Inn may by the Common Law be indicted and fined, as being guilty of a publick Nuſance [a] if he uſually harbour Thieves, or Perſons of ſcandalous Reputation, or [b] ſuffer frequent Diſorders in his Houſe, or take exorbitant Prices, or ſet [c] up a new Inn in a Place, where there is no Manner of Need of one, to the Hindrance of other ancient and well governed Inns, or [d] keep it in a Place in reſpect of its Situation, wholly unfit for ſuch a Purpoſe. [a] Palm. 374. 2 Ro. Re. 345. [b] H.P.C. 146. Cro. Ca. 549. Dalt. ca. 7. [cd] H.P.C. 146. Dalt. ca. 7. Palm. 374. 2 Ro. Re. 345. [e] Palm. 374. 2 Ro. Re. 345.

Sect. 2. And it ſeems alſo to be clear, That if one who keeps a common Inn, refuſe either to receive a Traveller as a Gueſt into his Houſe, or to find him Victuals or [e] Lodging, upon his tendring him a reaſonable [f] Price for the ſame, he is not only liable to render [g] Damages for the Injury in an Action on the Caſe at the Suit of the Party grieved, but may alſo be [h] indicted and fined, at the Suit of the King; alſo it is ſaid, That he may be compelled by the Conſtable [i] of the Town to receive, and entertain ſuch a Perſon as his Gueſt, and that it is no way [k] material whether he have any Sign before his Door or not, if he make it his common Buſineſs to entertain Paſſengers. [f] 10 H. 7. 8. a. 39 H. 6. 18. b. 19. a. 9 Co. 87. b. [g] Dy. 158. Pl. 33. Bro. Ac. ſur caſ. 76, 92. [h] H. P. C. 146. Dalt. ca. 7. [i] 5 E. 4. 2. b. Dalt. ca. 7. [k] Palm. 374. 2 Ro. Re. 345, 346.

Sect. 3. It ſeems to have been always clearly [l] agreed, That he who has an Inn by Preſcription, may lawfully enlarge it upon the ſame Land which has been uſed with it, either by erecting new Buildings thereon, or turning Stables into Chambers of Entertainment, and that he ſhall have the ſame Privilege in ſuch new Parts of his Houſe as in any of the old. [l] 2 Rol. A. 84. Pl. 8. 85. Pl. 9.

Sect. 4. Alſo it ſeems to be [m] ſettled at this Day, That any Perſon may lawfully ſet up a new Inn, unleſs it be inconvenient to the Publick in ſome of the Reſpects taken Notice of in the firſt Section, and that he has no Need of any Licence from the King for this Purpoſe, for the Keeping of an Inn is no Franchiſe, but a lawful Trade, open to every Subject. But if an Inn degenerate into an Ale-houſe, by ſuffering diſorderly Tipling, it ſhall be deemed as ſuch. [m] 2 Rol. A. 84. A. Salk. 45. 2 Rol. Re. 345. Palm. 367, 374. 2 Keb. 506. 1 Bulſ. 109. Salk. 45.

Sect. 5. As to the second Point, *viz.* In what manner Nusances of this Kind are prevented and restrained by Statute, it is enacted by 12 *Ed.* 2. 6. *That no Officer in City or in Borough, that by reason of his Office ought to keep Assizes of Wines and Victual, so long as he is attendant to that Office, shall not merchandize for Wines nor Victuals, neither in Gross nor by Retail; and if any be convict of such Offence, the Merchandize shall be forfeited to the King, and the third Part thereof delivered to the Party that sued for the same*, &c.

Vide F. N. B. 172. Regist. 184.

Sect. 6. And it is farther enacted by 6 *Rich.* 2. 9. *That no Victualler shall have, exercise, or occupy any judicial Office in any Town, but only where no other Person sufficient may be found to have the same Office. In which Case yet the same Judge, for the Time that he shall continue in the said Office, shall utterly omit and abstain himself and his from the Exercise of Victualling, upon Pain of forfeiting his Victuals so sold.*

Sect. 7. And it is farther enacted by 3 *H.* 8. 8. *That as often as any Victualler chosen to bear any Office within any City, Borough, or Town-corporate, which for the Time that he shall stand and be in such Office should have the Assessing and Correction for selling of Victuals, that then two discreet and honest Persons of the same City, Borough, or Town-corporate, not being Victuallers, nor any of them being a Victualler, shall be chosen by the Commonalty of the same City, Borough, or Town-corporate, in like Form as the said Officer shall be chosen: Which two Persons, with the said Officer, shall be sworn truly to sess and set the Prices and Assizes of Victual there, for the Time that any such Victualler shall abide in the same Office: And that then it shall be lawful to all and every of the said Officers, after the same Victuals be set and sessed by the same Officer, and the said two Persons, or one of the same two Persons, the other being absent, to merchant and sell Wines, and all other Victual in Gross, and at Retail, during the Time that he shall be in any such Office, without any Thing therefore to forfeit: The said Statute, Act, and Ordinance of* 12 E. 2. *or any other Act or Acts, Ordinance, or Statute to the contrary made in any wise notwithstanding.*

Vide Cro. Ja. 609, 610. 2 Rol. Re. 225, 226.

Sect. 8. Also it is enacted by 21 *Jac.* 1. 21. *That all Hostlers or Innholders shall sell their Horse bread, and their Hay, Oats, Beans, Pease, Provender, and also all Kind of Victual, both for Man and Beast, for reasonable Gain, having Respect to the Prices for which they shall be sold in the Markets adjoining, without taking any Thing for Litter.* And it is farther enacted by the said Statute, *That every Hostler and Innkeeper dwelling in any Town or Village, being a Thorough-fare, and no City, Town-corporate, or Market-Town, wherein any common Baker, having been an Apprentice to the Trade for seven Years, is dwelling, may make within his House Horse-bread sufficient, lawful, and of due Assize, according to the Price of Grain or Corn, any Thing in the said Statute contained to the contrary notwithstanding.* And it is farther enacted, *That if the Horse-bread, which any of the said Hostlers or Innholders shall make, be not sufficient, lawful, and of due Assize, according to the Price of Grain and Corn, as abovesaid; or that if any of them shall offend in any Thing contrary to this Act, the Justices of Assize, Justices of Oyer and Terminer, Justices of Peace in every Shire, Liberty, or Franchise within this Realm, Sheriffs in their Turns, and Stewards in their Leets, may inquire, hear, and determine, the said Offences of the said Hostlers and Innholders, who shall be fined for the first Offence, according to the Quantity of the Offence, and for the second Offence shall be imprisoned for one Month, and for the third shall stand upon the Pillory*, &c.

Sect. 9. And it is enacted by 5 & 6 *Ed.* 6. 25. *That the Justices of Peace within every Shire, City, Borough, Town-corporate, Franchise, or Liberty within this Realm, or two of them at the least, whereof one to be of the* Quorum, *shall have full Power and Authority within every Shire, City,* &c. *to remove, discharge, and put away common Selling of Ale and Beer in common Ale-houses and Tippling-houses.*

Sect. 10. And it seems to have been the general Opinion in the Construction of this Clause, That an Alehouse-keeper suppressed in Pursuance of it, cannot be afterwards licenced again but in open Sessions. Dal. ca. 7. H. P. C. 147.

Sect. 11. And it is farther enacted by the said Statute of 5 & 6 *Ed.* 6. 25 Par. 1 & 6. *That none shall be admitted or suffered to keep any common Ale-house or Tippling-house, except in Fairs, but such as shall be allowed in the open Sessions, or by two Justices of Peace, whereof one to be of the* Quorum: *And that the said Justices shall take Bonds and Surety from Time to Time, by Recognizance, of such as shall be allowed to keep any common Ale-house or Tippling-house, as well for and against the using of unlawful Games, as also for the Maintenance of good Order within the same, as by their Discretion shall be thought necessary and convenient; for making of every which Recognizance the Parties bound shall pay but twelve Pence.*

Sect. 12. And it is farther enacted, Par. 2. *That the said Justices shall certify the same Recognizance at the next Quarter-Sessions of the same Shire, City, or Borough,* &c. *there to remain of Record before the Justices of Peace of the Shire,* &c. *upon Pain of forfeiting for every such Recognizance taken, and not certified, three Pounds six Shillings eight Pence.*

Sect. 13. And it is farther enacted, Par. 3. *That the Justices of Peace of every Shire, City, Borough,* &c. *may at their Quarter-Sessions by Presentment, Information, or otherwise by their Discretion, inquire of all such Persons as shall be allowed to keep any Ale-house or Tippling-house, and that be bound by Recognizance, as is abovesaid, if any of them have done any Act whereby they have forfeited the same Recognizance: And the said Justices shall upon every such Presentment or Information, award Process against every such Person so presented or complained upon before them, to shew why he should not forfeit his Recognizance, and may also hear and determine the same by all such Ways and Means, as by their Discretion shall be thought good.*

Sect. 14. And it is farther enacted, Par. 4. *That if any Person, other than such as shall be allowed by the said Justices, shall obstinately, and upon his own Authority, take upon him to keep a common Ale-house, or Tippling-house, or shall contrary to the Commandment of the said Justices, or two of them, use commonly Selling of Ale and Beer, except in Fairs; that then the said Justices, or two of them, whereof one to be of the* Quorum, *shall for every such Offence commit every such Person so offending, to the common Gaol within the said Shire, City, Borough,* &c. *there to remain without Bail or Mainprize by the Space of three Days; and before his Deliverance the said Justices shall take his Recognizance with two Sureties, That he shall not keep any common Ale-house, Tippling-house, or use commonly Selling of Ale or Beer, as by the Discretion of the said Justices shall seem convenient.*

Sect. 15. And it is farther enacted, Par. 5. *That the said Justices shall make Certificate of every such Recognizance and Offence, at the next Quarter-Sessions for the same Shire, City, Borough,* &c. *which Certificate shall be a sufficient Conviction of the same Offence; and the said Justices upon the said Certificate made, shall in open Sessions assess the Fine for every such Offence, at twenty Shillings.*

Sect. 16. And it is farther enacted by 3 *Car.* 1. 3. *That if any Person shall upon his own Authority, not being thereunto lawfully licenced, take upon him to keep a common Ale-house or Tippling-house, or use commonly selling of Ale, or Beer, Cyder, or Perry, except in Fairs, every such Person shall for every such Offence, forfeit twenty Shillings to the Use of the Poor of the Parish where such*

Offence

Offence shall be committed, the same Offence being viewed by any Mayor, Bailiff, or Justice of Peace, or other Head-Officer within the several Limits, or confessed by the Party so offending, or proved by the Oath of two Witnesses, to be taken before any Mayor, Bailiff, or other Head-Officer, or any Justice of Peace, being within the Limits of their Commission; the said Penalty to be levied by the Constables or Church-wardens of the Parish, or Parishes, where the said Offence shall be committed, who shall be accountable therefore to the Use of the Poor of the said Parish, by Way of Distress, to be taken and detained by Warrant or Precept from the said Mayor, Bailiff, or Justice, &c. *by whom the said Offence shall be viewed,* &c. *And for Default of Satisfaction within three Days next ensuing, the said Distress to be by the said Constables, or Church-wardens, apprized and sold, and the Overplus to be delivered to the Party offending; and if such Offender shall not have sufficient Goods and Chattels, whereby the said twenty Shillings may be levied by Way of Distress, as aforesaid, or shall not pay the said Sum of twenty Shillings within six Days after such Conviction, as aforesaid, the said Mayor, Bailiff, or Justice,* &c. *before whom the said Offender shall be so convicted, shall commit such Offender to some Constable, or other inferior Officer of the City, Borough, or Parish,* &c. *where the Offence shall be committed, to be openly whipped, as the said Justice shall limit or appoint. And if such Constable,* &c. *shall neglect to execute the said Precept or Warrant, or to execute by himself, or some other, upon the Offender, the Punishment limited by the said Statute, the said Mayor,* &c. *may commit him to the common Gaol of the said County, City, or Town,* &c. *there to remain till the said Offender shall be by him or some other punished and whipped; or until the Person so neglecting shall have paid forty Shillings to the Use of the Poor of the Parish, for his said Contempt. And if any such unlicenced Alehouse-keeper shall offend in any the Premisses the second time, and be thereof convicted in Manner and Form aforesaid, the said Mayor, Bailiff, or Justice,* &c. *shall commit him to the House of Correction, there to remain for one Month, and be dealt withal as an idle, lewd, and disorderly Person: And if such Person shall again offend, and be convict, as aforesaid, he shall be committed to the said House of Correction, as aforesaid, there to remain till by the Order of the General-Sessions for the County, City, or Borough,* &c. *he shall be delivered from thence. Provided that such Offender as shall be punished by Virtue of this Act, shall not be punished again for the same Offence by the above mentioned Statute of* 5 & 6 Ed. 6. *And that such Offender as shall be punished by Virtue of the said Statute of* 5 & 6 Ed. 6. *shall not be punished again by Virtue of this Act.*

Sect. 17. Also it is enacted by 1 Jac. 1. 9. and 4 Jac. 1. 15. and 21 Jac. 1. 7. and 1 Car. 1. 4. *That if any Inn-keeper, Victualler, or Alehouse-keeper, or any Keeper of a Tavern, or one who sells Wine in his House, and also keeps an Inn, or Victualling in his House, do permit or suffer any Person, whether such Person be an Inhabitant of the Place where such Inn,* &c. *shall be, or not to continue Drinking or Tippling in any Inn or Victualling-house,* &c. *other than such as shall be invited by any Traveller, and shall accompany him only during his necessary Abode there; and other than Labouring and Handicraftsmen in Cities, and Towns-corporate, and Market-Towns upon the usual working Days, for one Hour at Dinner-time, to take their Diet in an Alehouse; and other than Labourers and Workmen, who for the following of their Work by the Day, or by the Great, in any City, Town-corporate, Market-Town, or Village, shall for the Time of their said continuing in Work there, sojourn, lodge, or victual in any Inn, Ale-house, or other Victualling-house; or other than for urgent and necessary Occasions, to be allowed by two Justices of Peace, That then every such Inn-keeper,* &c. *shall forfeit ten Shillings to the Use of the Poor of the Parish where such Offence shall be committed; the same Offence being viewed and seen by any*

Mayor, Bailiff, or Justice of Peace within their several Limits, or found by Verdict on a Trial upon an Indictment at Assizes, Sessions, or Court-Leet, or proved by the Oath of [a] *one Witness to be taken before any Mayor or Bailiff,* &c. *or any one Justice of the Peace, or by the voluntary Confession of any Offender, after which Confession the Oath of such Offender shall be taken, and be a sufficient Proof against any other Offending at the same Time.* 4 Jac. 1. 5. [a] 21 Jac. 1. 7.

Sect. 18. And it is farther enacted by the said Statute of 1 *Jac.* 1. 9. Par. 3. *That the said Penalty of ten Shillings shall be levied by the Constables or Church-wardens of the Parishes where the Offence shall be committed, by way of Distress, and for Default of Satisfaction within six Days, the same to be presently appraised and sold, and the Surplusage to be delivered to the Party of whom the Distress was taken, and for Want of sufficient Distress the Party offending to be by the said Mayor,* &c. *committed to the common Gaol, there to remain till the said Penalty be paid. And if the said Constables or Church-wardens do neglect their Duty in levying the said Penalties, or in Default of Distress, do neglect to certify the same within twenty Days to the said Mayor,* &c. *every Person so offending shall forfeit forty Shillings, to the Use of the Poor of the Parish where such Offence shall be committed, to be levied by Distress of Goods, by Warrant from any one Justice of Peace,* &c. *to be taken and detained six Days; within which, if Payment be not made, the same Goods to be appraised and sold,* &c.

Sect. 19. But it is provided by the said Statute of 1 *Jac.* 1. 9. *That the Punishment of such as shall offend against the same, within either of the two Universities, or the Precincts or Liberties of the same, shall be done upon the Offenders, and Justice ministred in this Behalf, according to the Intent of the said Law, by the Governours, Magistrates, Justices of the Peace, or other principal Officers of either of the said Universities, to whom in other Cases the Administration of Justice, and Correction and Punishment of Offenders by the Laws of this Realm and their several Charters doth belong; and that no other within their Liberties for any Matter concerning the said Law contrary to their several Charters, do intermeddle, and that all Penalties to be forfeited by Virtue of the said Act, within either of the Universities or the Liberties or Precincts of the same, shall be levied by the Officers or Ministers of either of the said Universities, to be from Time to Time in that Behalf appointed by the Vice-Chancellors thereof for the Time being respectively, and that all Powers and Authorities given by the said Act, shall by the Governours, Magistrates, and principal Officers abovesaid, of either of the said Universities, be duly executed within either of the said Universities,* &c.

Sect. 20. And it is farther enacted by 4 *Jac.* 1. 5. and 21 *Jac.* 1. 7. *That whoever shall be drunk, and within* [a] *six Months after such Offence, shall be convict thereof either on an Indictment at Assizes or Sessions, or Court-Leet, or before any* [b] *Justice of Peace in any County, or any Justice of Peace, or other Head Officer in any City or Town-corporate, upon View or Confession, or by Oath of one Witness, shall forfeit five Shillings, to be paid within one Week after Conviction, to the Church-wardens of the Parish where the Offence shall be committed,* &c. *And if such Person shall refuse or neglect to pay the said Forfeiture, the same shall be levied of his Goods by Warrant or Precept from the said Court, or Judge before whom the same Conviction shall be: And if the Offender be not able to pay the said Sum of five Shillings, he shall be committed to the Stocks for every Offence, there to remain six Hours; and if he shall be convicted a second Time of the like Offence, he shall be bound to the* [c] *good Behaviour, with two Sureties in a Recognizance of ten Pounds. And if any Constable or other inferiour Officer of the Place where the Offence shall be committed,* &c. *do neglect the due Correction of the said Offender, or the due Levying of the said Penalties, he shall forfeit ten Shillings to the Use of the Poor,* &c. *to be levied by way of Distress, by Warrant from any Mayor,* &c.

[a] 4 Jac. 1. 5. Par. 11.
[b] 21 Jac. 1. 7. 4 Jac. 1. 5.
[c] Par. 6.

Sect. 21. And it is farther enacted by the said Statute of 4 *Jac.* 1. 5. and 21 *Jac.* 1. 7. and 1 *Car.* 1. 4. *That if any Person shall remain or continue drinking or tippling in any Inn, Victualling-house, Ale-house, or* [a] *Tavern,* &c. *whether he be an* [b] *Inhabitant of the Place at the Time of such drinking, or not; and the same be viewed by any Mayor, or other Head-Officer, or Justice of Peace, or confessed by the Offender, or proved by one Witness in the Manner prescribed for the above mentioned Offence of suffering Tippling in publick Houses, unless it be in such Cases as are excepted in the above mentioned Act, relating to the said Offence of suffering tippling,* &c. *Every Person so offending, and being convict* [c] *within six Months, shall forfeit three Shillings and four Pence, to the Use of the Poor of the Parish where the Offence shall be committed, to be levied by way of Distress in such Manner as the above mentioned Forfeitures for Drunkenness are to be levied: And if any such Offender be not able to pay the said Forfeiture, any Mayor, Head Officer, Justice of Peace, or Court where any such Conviction shall be, may set him in the Stocks for four Hours.*

[a] 1 Ca. 1. 4.
[b] 21 Jac. 1. 7.
Supra Sect. 17.
[c] 4 Jac. 1. 5. Par. 11.
Supra Sect. 20.

Sect. 22. And it is farther enacted by the said Statute of 4 *Jac.* 1. 5. Par. 7. *That all Constables, Church-wardens, Headboroughs, Tithingmen, Aleconners and Sidemen shall in their several Oaths incident to their several Offices, be charged in like Sort to present the Offences contrary to the said Statute.*

Sect. 23. But it is provided by the same Statute, Par. 8. *That nothing therein contained shall in any wise abridge the Ecclesiastical Jurisdiction.* And it is farther provided, Par. 9. *That no Offender, who hath once been punished for his Offence against any Article of the said Act, by any the Ways or Means before limited, shall be eftsoons punished for the same Offence by any other Ways or Means.*

Sect. 24. And it is farther provided, Par. 10. *That nothing in the said Act contained shall be prejudicial to either of the Universities, but that the Chancellor, Master, and Scholars,* &c. *may as fully use and enjoy all their Jurisdictions, Rights, Privileges, and Charters, as before the said Statute they had or might have done; any Thing in the said Act to the contrary notwithstanding.*

Sect. 25. And it is enacted by 7 *Jac.* 1. 10. *That if any Person being an Alehouse-keeper, shall be lawfully convicted for any Offence committed against any of the Branches of either of the said Acts of* 1 Jac. 1. 9. *or* 4 Jac. 1. 5. *he shall for the Space of three Years next ensuing the said Conviction, be utterly disabled to keep any such Alehouse.* [89] ☞

CHAP. LXXIX.

Of Monopolies.

FOR the better Understanding the Nature of the Offence of procuring or making Use of a Monopoly, I shall consider:

1. What shall be said to be a Monopoly.
2. In what Manner the procuring, or making Use thereof, are restrained by the Common Law.
3. In what Manner by Statute.

Sect. 1. As to the first Point, it seemeth that a Monopoly is an Allowance by the King, to any Person or Persons, of the sole Buying, Selling, Making, Working, or Using of any Thing, whereby any Person is sought to be restrained from any Freedom which he had before, or hindred from his lawful Trade.

3 Inst. 181. Noy 182.

As to the second Point it seemeth, That the procuring or making use of such Monopolies, is restrained by the Common Law two ways,

1. By declaring all Grants of this Kind to be void.
2. By making those who procure or make use of them, liable to be fined.

Sect. 2. And first it is said, Tat all Grants of this Kind relating to any known Trade, are made void by the Common Law, as being against the Freedom of Trade, and discouraging Labour and Industry, and restraining Persons from getting an honest Livelihood by a lawful Employment, and putting it in the Power of particular Persons to set what Prices they please on a Commodity; all which are manifest Inconveniences to the Publick.

Sect. 3. And upon this Ground it hath been [a] resolved, That the King's Grant to any particular Corporation of the sole Importation of any Merchandize is void, whether such Merchandize be prohibited by Statute or not.

See Skin. 132 to 137. 165 to 173. 197 to 204. 223 to 226. East-India Company and Sandys.

Sect. 4. And for the like Reasons also it hath been resolved, That the Grant of the sole [b] Ingrossing of Wills and Inventories in a spiritual Court, or of the sole [c] Making of Bills, Pleas and Writs in a Court of Law, to any particular Person, is void.

[a] 2 Rol. Ab. 214. 3 Inst. 182. 2 Inst. 61.
[b] 2 Rol. Ab. 214. Pl. 4.
[c] 1 Jones 231. 2 Rol. Ab. 214. Pl. 5. 3 Mod. 75.

Sect. 5. Also it hath been adjudged, That the King's Grant of the sole Making, Importing, and Selling of [d] Playing-Cards, is void, notwithstanding the Pretence, That the Playing with them is a Matter meerly of Pleasure and Recreation, and often much abused, and therefore proper to be restrained; for since the Playing with them is in itself lawful and innocent, and the Making of them an honest and laborious Trade, there is no more Reason why any Subject should be hindred from getting his Livelihood by this than by any other Employment.

[d] 11 Co. 84. 85, &c. Mo. 671. Pl. 919. Noy 173, &c. 2 Inst. 47.

Sect. 6. But it seemeth clear, That the King may for a reasonable Time make a good Grant to any one of the sole Use of any Art invented or first brought into the Realm by the Grantee, as shall be shewn more at large in the 14th, 15th, and 16th Sections of this Chapter. Also it seems to be the better Opinion, That the King may grant to particular Persons the sole Use of some particular Imployments, (as of Printing the Holy Scriptures and Law Books, *&c.*) whereof an unrestrained Liberty might be of dangerous Consequence.

Noy 182, 183. 1 Mod. 256. 3 Keb. 792. 3 Mod. 75.

Sect. 7. Secondly, Also it is holden, That the procuring or making Use of an unlawful Monopoly, is farther restrained by the Common Lay, by subjecting those who are guilty thereof to a Fine and Imprisonment for the Offence, as being *Malum in se*, and contrary to the ancient and fundamental Laws of the Kingdom: And it is said, That there are Precedents of Prosecutions of this Kind in former Days, but I cannot find any modern Instance thereof.

3 Inst. 181. 2 Inst. 47, 61.

Sect. 8. As to the third Point, *viz.* In what Manner the procuring and making Use of a Monopoly are restrained by Statute, it is declared and enacted by 21 *Jac.* 1. 3. *That all Monopolies, and all Commissions, Grants, Licences, Charters and Letters Patents to any Person or Persons, Bodies*

Politick

Politick or Corporate whatſoever, of or for the ſole Buying, Selling, Making, Working, or Uſing of any Thing within this Realm, or Wales, *or of any other Monopolies, and all Proclamations, Inhibitions, Reſtraints, Warrants of Aſſiſtance and all other Matters whatſoever any Way tending to the Inſtituting, Strengthening, Furthering, or Countenancing of the ſame, or any of them, are altogether contrary to the Laws of this Realm, and ſo are and ſhall be utterly void, and of none Effect, and in no wiſe to be put in Ure or Execution.*

Sect. 9. And it is farther enacted, Par. 3. *That all Perſons, Bodies Politick and Corporate whatſoever, ſhall be diſabled and uncapable to have, uſe, exerciſe or put in Ure, any Monopoly, or any ſuch Commiſſion, Grant, or Licence,* &c. *or other Thing tending as aforeſaid, or any Liberty, Power, or Faculty, grounded, or pretended to be grounded, upon them, or any of them.*

Sect. 10. And it is farther declared and enacted, Par. 2. *That all Monopolies, and all ſuch Commiſſions, Grants and Licences,* &c. *and all other Things tending as aforeſaid, and the Force and Validity of them, ought to be, and ſhall be examined, heard, tried, and determined, by and according to the Common Laws of this Lealm, and not otherwiſe.*

3 Inſt. 182, 183. *Sect.* 11. In the Conſtruction of this Clauſe it hath been holden, That all Matters of this Kind ought to be tried in the Courts of Common Law only, and not at the Council-Table, or in the Court of Chancery, or any other Court of like Nature.

Sect. 12. And it is farther enacted, Par. 4. *That if any Perſon ſhall be hindred, grieved, diſturbed, or diſquieted, or his Goods or Chattels any way ſeized, attached, diſtrained, taken, carried away or detained, by Occaſion or Pretext of any Monopoly, or of any ſuch Commiſſion, Grant or Licence,* &c. *or other Matter or Thing tending as aforeſaid, and will ſue to be relieved in any of the Premiſſes, he ſhall have his Remedy for the ſame at the Common Law, by Action grounded on the ſaid Statute, to be heard and determined in the King's Bench, Common Pleas or Exchequer, againſt the Party by whom he ſhall be ſo hindred or grieved,* &c. *or by whom his Goods ſhall be ſo ſeized or attached,* &c. *wherein every ſuch Perſon, which ſhall be ſo hindred or grieved,* &c. *or whoſe Goods ſhall be ſo ſeized or attached,* &c. *ſhall recover three Times ſo much as the Damages which he ſuſtained by Means of ſuch Hindrance,* &c. *and double Coſts; and in ſuch Suits, or for the ſtaying or delaying thereof, no Eſſoin, Protection, Wager of Law, Aid Prayer, Privilege, Injunction, or Order of Reſtraint, ſhall be in any wiſe, prayed, granted, admitted, or allowed, nor any more than one Imparlance: And if any Perſon ſhall after Notice that the Action depending is grounded upon the ſaid Statute, cauſe or procure any Action at the Common Law grounded thereon to be ſtayed or delayed before Judgment, by Colour or Means of any Order, Warrant, Power or Authority, ſave only of the Court wherein ſuch Action ſhall be depending, or after Judgment ſhall cauſe or procure the Execution to be ſtayed or delayed by Colour or Means of any Order, Warrant, Power or Authority, ſave only by Writ of Error or Attaint, that then the ſaid Perſon or Perſons ſo offending, ſhall incur a* Præmunire.

3 Inſt. 183. *Sect.* 13. It is ſaid, That the firſt Branch of this laſt Clauſe relating to the delaying of Cauſes of this Kind before Judgment, not only extendeth to the Privy Council, Chancery, Exchequer-Chamber, and the like, but alſo to thoſe who ſhall procure any Warrant from the King for ſuch Purpoſe; and it is ſaid, That the latter Branch, relating to the delaying of Execution after Judgment, extendeth even to the Judges of the Court where the Cauſe is depending.

Sect. 14. But it is provided, Par. 6. *That no Declaration in the Statute mentioned ſhall extend to any Letters Patents and Grants of Privilege for the Term of fourteen Years or under, of the ſole working or making of any manner of new Manufactures within this Realm*; (under which Words Manufactures newly brought into the Realm from beyond Sea are included, tho' they were not new there) *to the true and first Inventor and Inventors of such Manufactures, which others, at the Time of making such Letters Patents and Grants, shall not use, so as also they be not contrary to the Law, nor mischievous to the State, by raising Prices of Commodities at home, or hurt of Trade, or generally inconvenient: The said fourteen Years to be accompted from the Date of the first Letters Patents, or Grant of such Privilege, but that the same shall be of such Force as they should be, if the said Act had never been made, and of none other.* Salk. 447.

Sect. 15. It hath been resolved, That no new Invention concerning the working of any Manufacture, is within the Meaning of this Exception, unless it be substantially new, and not barely an additional Improvement of an old one. 3 Inst. 184.

Sect. 16. Also it hath been holden, That a new Invention to do as much Work in a Day by an Engine, as formerly used to imploy many Hands, is not within the said Exception, because it is inconvenient in turning so many labouring Men to Idleness. 3 Inst. 184.

Sect. 17. Also it seemeth clear, that no old Manufacture in use before, can be prohibited in any Grant of the sole Use of any such new Invention. 3 Inst. 184.

Sect. 18. And it is farther provided, Par. 7. *That nothing in the said Act contained shall extend to any Grant or Privilege, Power, or Authority whatsoever before the said Act, made, granted, allowed, or confirmed by any Act of Parliament, so long as the same shall continue in Force.*

Sect. 19. And it is farther provided, Par. 9. *That nothing in the said Act contained shall be in any wise prejudicial to any City, Borough, or Town-corporate within this Realm, concerning any Grants, Charters, or Letters Patents to them made, or concerning any Custom used by or within them, or unto any Corporations, Companies, or Fellowships of any Art, Trade, Occupation, or Mystery, or to any Companies or Societies of Merchants within this Realm, erected for the Maintenance, Enlargement, or ordering of any Trade or Merchandize: But that the same Charters, Customs, Corporations,* &c. *and their Liberties and Immunities shall be of such Force and Effect as they were before the making of the said Act, and of none other; any Thing before in the said Act contained to the contrary in any wise notwithstanding.*

Sect. 20. And it is farther provided, Par. 10. *That nothing in the said Act contained shall extend to any Letters Patents, or Grants of Privilege, concerning Printing; nor to any Commission, Grants, or Letters Patents concerning the digging, making, or compounding of Salt-Peter, or Gun-Powder; or the casting or making of Ordnance, or Shot for Ordnance: Nor to any Grant or Letters Patents of any Office erected before the making of the said Statute, and then in Being, and put in Execution, other than such Offices as had been decried by Proclamation: But that all such Grants,* &c. *shall be of the like Force and Effect, and no other, as if the said Act had never been made.*

Sect. 21. But it is enacted by 16 *Car.* 1. 21. *That it shall be lawful for all Persons, as well Strangers, as natural born Subjects, to import any Quantities of Gun-Powder whatsoever, paying such Customs and Duties for the same as by Parliament shall be limited: And that it shall be lawful for all his Majesty's Subjects of this his Realm of* England, *to make and sell any Quantities of Gun-Powder at his Pleasure, and also to bring into this Kingdom any Quantities of Salt-Peter, Brimstone, or any other Materials for the making of Gunpowder: And that if any Person shall put in Execution any Letters Patents, Proclamation, Edict, Act, Order, Warrant, Restraint, or other Inhibition whatsoever, whereby the Importation of Gun-Powder, Salt-Peter, Brimstone, or other the Materials afore mentioned, shall be any ways prohibited or restrained, he shall incur a* Præmunire.

Sect. 22. And it is farther provided by the ſaid Statute of 21 *Jac.* 1. 3. Par. 11. 12. *That nothing in the ſaid Act contained ſhall extend to any Commiſſion or Grant concerning the digging, compounding, or making of Allum, or Allum-Mines,* &c. *nor concerning the Licencing of the Keeping of any Tavern, or ſelling of Wines, to be ſpent in the Manſion-Houſe, or other Place, in the Tenure or Occupation of the Party ſelling the ſame, and a farther Proviſion is made in the latter Part of the Statute, for ſome particular Grants to particular Corporations and Perſons, as* Newcaſtle *upon* Tine, *&c.*

3 Inſt. 185. *Sect.* 23. But it is ſaid, That the ſaid Clauſe relating to Allum was needleſs, becauſe all ſuch Mines belong of Courſe to the Perſons in whoſe Grounds they are, and therefore no Privilege concerning them can be granted, but in the King's own Ground.

CHAP. LXXX.

Of Foreſtalling, Ingroſſing and Regrating, and other Offences of the like Nature.

FOR the better underſtanding the Nature of Foreſtalling, Ingroſſing and Regrating, and other ſuch like Offences, I ſhall conſider,

1. How ſuch Offences are treated by the Common Law.
2. How by Statute.

As to the firſt Point, I ſhall conſider:

1. What is eſteemed an Offence of this Kind by the Common Law.
2. How ſuch Offence is puniſhable by the Common Law.

[a] 43 Aſſ. 38. 3 Inſt. 195, 196. Bro. Indictment, 40. Preſentment, 12. [b] Crom. 80. b. [c] Crom. 80. b.

Sect. 1. As to the firſt of theſe Particulars it is ſaid, That all Endeavours whatſoever to enhanſe the common Price of any Merchandize, and all Kinds of Practices which have an apparent Tendency thereto, whether by ſpreading falſe [a] Rumors, or by [b] buying Things in a Market before the accuſtomed Hour, or by buying and ſelling again the ſame Thing in the ſame [c] Market, or by any other ſuch like Devices, are highly Criminal at Common Law, and that all ſuch Offences antiently came under the general Notion of Foreſtalling, which included all Kinds of Offences of this Nature.

Sect. 2. And ſurely there can be no Attempt of this Kind, but muſt be looked upon as a high Offence againſt the Publick, inaſmuch as it ſo apparently tends to put a Check upon Trade, to the general Inconvenience of the People, by putting it out of their Power to ſupply themſelves with a Commodity, without an unreaſonable Expence, which often proves extremely oppreſſive to the poorer Sort, and cannot but give juſt Cauſe of Complaint to the richeſt.

3 Inſt. 196. H. P. C. 152. *Sect.* 3. But it hath been reſolved, That any Merchant, whether he be a Subject or a Foreigner, bringing Victuals, or any other Merchandize into the Realm, may ſell the ſame in Groſs, but that no Perſon can lawfully buy within the Realm any Merchandize in Groſs, and ſell the ſame

 in

in Grofs again, becaufe by fuch Means the Price will be inhanfed, for the more Hands any Merchandize paffeth through, the dearer it muft grow, becaufe every one will make his Profit of it: And if fuch Practices were allowable, a rich Man might ingrofs into his Hands a whole Commodity, and then fell it at what Price he fhould think fit; which is of fuch dangerous Confequence, that the bare Ingroffing of a whole Commodity with an Intent to fell it at an unreafonable Price, is an Offence indictable at the Common Law, whether any Part thereof be fold by the Ingroffer, or not. Cro. Ca. 231, 232.

Sect. 4. And fo jealous is the Common Law of all Practices of this Kind, that it will not fuffer Corn to be fold in the Sheaf, perhaps for this Reafon, becaufe by fuch Means the Market is in Effect foreftalled. 3 Inft. 197. H. P. C. 152.

Sect. 5. As to the fecond Particular, *viz.* In what manner Offences of this Kind are punifhable by the Common Law; it is faid, That by an antient Statute the Offender was to be grievoufly amerced for the firft Offence; for the fecond, to be condemned to the Pillory; for the third, to be imprifoned; and for the fourth, to be compelled to abjure the Vill: And there feems to be no Doubt, but that at this Day all Offenders of this Kind are liable to a Fine and Imprifonment, anfwerable to the Heinoufnefs of their Offence, upon an Indictment at Common Law. 3 Inft. 195.

As to the fecond Point, *viz.* In what manner thefe Offences are treated by Statute, I fhall confider;

1. What particular Provifions have been made relating to this Matter.
2. What Cafes have been excepted out of thofe Provifions.
3. In what Manner the Offenders are to be proceeded againft.

The particular Provifions of this Nature are five-fold;

1. The obliging all Victuallers to fell at a reafonable Price.
2. The allowing all Foreigners free Liberty of importing and felling Victuals.
3. The giving the great Officers of State a Power to tax the Price of Victuals.
4. The prohibiting Confpiracies to raife the Price of Victuals.
5. The prohibiting all Foreftalling, Ingroffing, and Regrating.

Sect. 6. The firft of the faid Provifions depends upon 23 *Ed.* 3. 6. by which it is enacted, *That Butchers, Fifhmongers, Regrators, Hoftelers, Brewers, Bakers, Poulterers, and other Sellers of all Manner of Victual, fhall be bound to fell the fame for a reafonable Price, having refpect to the Price that fuch Victual fhall be fold at in the Places adjoining; fo that fuch Sellers have moderate Gains, reafonably to be required, according to the Diftance of the Place from whence the faid Victuals be carried, on pain to forfeit double the Value,* &c. *And the chief Officers of Towns are required to fee this Statute executed, on Pain of paying the treble Value of the Thing fold,* &c.

Sect. 7. The fecond of the above mentioned Provifions depends upon 6 *R.* 2. 10. and 11 *Ric.* 2. 7. and 1 *H.* 4. 17. by which it is enacted, *That all manner of Aliens, being of the Amity of the King, coming into any Town of the Realm with Fifh, or other Victual, fhall be under the King's efpecial Protection, and may cut their Fifhes and Victuals in Pieces, and in part, or in all, at Retail, or in Grofs, as to them beft fhall feem, to fell and make their Profit,* &c. And it is farther enacted by 14 *H.* 6. 6. *That if any Man difturb any Alien to fell his Fifh in Grofs, or at Retail, in Part or in Whole, contrary to the above*

above mentioned Ordinances, and thereof be duly attainted at the Suit of the King, or of the Party, he shall forfeit ten Pounds, &c.

Sect. 8. The Third of the above mentioned Provisions depends upon 25 *H.* 8. 2. by which it is enacted, *That to remedy the frequent Rise of the Price of Cheese, Butter, Capons, Hens, Chickens, and other necessary Victuals for Man's Sustenance, by ingrossing and regrating the same; the Lord Chancellor and other high Officers of State,* &c. *may, upon Complaint of any inhansing of the Prices of such Victuals without Ground or reasonable Cause, in any Part of the King's Dominions, set and tax reasonable Prices of such Victuals: And that after Proclamation made of such Prices, all Farmers, Owners, Broggers, and all other Victuallers whatsoever, having or keeping any such Victuals to the Intent to sell, shall sell the same to such of the King's Subjects as will buy them at such Prices as shall be taxed by such Proclamation, under the Pains to be limited in the said Proclamation.*

Vide infra S. 36.

Sect. 9. But it is provided, *That the Officers of Cities, Boroughs, or Towns-corporate, and all other Persons having Authority to set Prices of such Victuals, may set such Prices in such Manner as if the said Act had not been made.*

Sect. 10. The fourth of the above mentioned Provisions depends upon 2 & 3 *E.* 6. 15. by which it is enacted, *That if any Butchers, Brewers, Bakers, Poulterers, Cooks, Coster-mongers or Fruiterers, shall conspire, covenant, promise, or make any Oaths, that they shall not sell their Victuals but at certain Prices; or if any Artificers, Workmen, or Labourers, do conspire, covenant, or promise together, or make any Oaths, that they shall not make or do their Works, but at a certain Price or Rate; or shall not enterprise, or take upon them to finish what another hath begun, or shall do but a certain Work in a Day, or shall not work but at certain Hours and Times, every such Person so conspiring,* &c. *shall forfeit for the first Offence ten Pounds, and if he pay not the same within six Days, shall suffer twenty Days Imprisonment; and for the second Offence shall forfeit twenty Pounds,* &c. *and for the third, forty Pounds,* &c. *And if any such Conspiracy, Covenant, or Promise be made by any Society, Brotherhood, or Company, of any Craft, Mystery or Occupation of the Victuallers above mentioned, with the Presence or Consent of the more Part of them, that then immediately upon such Act of Conspiracy,* &c. *over and besides the particular Punishment before appointed, their Corporation shall be dissolved; and that the said Offences shall be determined at the Assizes, Sessions of the Peace, or Court-Leet. See* 22 & 23 Car. 2. 15.

Sect. 11. The fifth of the above mentioned Provisions depends chiefly upon 3 & 4 *E.* 6. 21. and 5 & 6 *E.* 6. 14. By the first of which Statutes it is enacted, *That no Person, not being an Inn-holder, or Victualler, selling by Retail in his House, shall buy to sell again any Butter or Cheese, unless he sell the same again by Retail, in open Shop, Fair, or Market, not selling more than a Weight of Cheese, or a Barrel of Butter at one Time.*

Vide infra S. 36.

Sect. 12. And it is farther enacted by the said Statute of 5 & 6 *E.* 6. 14. which is the principal Statute relating to this Matter, *That whosoever shall buy, or cause to be bought, any Merchandize, Victual, or any other Thing whatsoever, coming by Land or by Water toward any Market or Fair to be sold in the same, or coming toward any City, Port, Haven, Creek or Road of this Realm, or* Wales, *from any Parts beyond the Sea, to be sold; or make any Bargain, Contract, or Promise for the having or buying of the same, or any Part thereof so coming as is aforesaid, before the same shall be in the Market, Fair, City, or Port,* &c. *ready to be sold; or shall make any Motion by Word, Letter, Message, or otherwise, to any Person or Persons, for the inhansing of the Price, or dearer selling of any Thing above mentioned; or else disswade, move, or stir any one coming to the Market or Fair, to abstain or forbear to bring or convey any of the*

the Things above rehearſed, to any Market, Fair, City, or Port, &c. *to be ſold, ſhall be deemed a Foreſtaller.*

Sect. 13. It hath been reſolved, That an Indictment upon this Clauſe, charging the Defendant with meeting *J. S.* at ſuch a Place near a certain Town, and there buying of him certain Goods, which he was about to ſell in the Market of ſuch Town, is inſufficient, becauſe it is not expreſly ſaid, that the Goods ſo bought were coming to the Market to be ſold. 1 Rol.Re 421.

Sect. 14. And it is farther enacted by the ſaid Statute of 5 & 6 *Ed.* 6. 14. Par. 2. *That whoſoever ſhall by any Means, regrate, obtain, or get into his Hands or Poſſeſſion, in any Fair or Market, any Corn, Wine, Fiſh, Butter, Cheeſe, Candles, Tallow, Sheep, Lambs, Calves, Swine, Pigs, Geeſe, Capons, Hens, Chickens, Pigeons, Conies, or other dead Victual whatſoever, that ſhall be brought to any Fair or Market to be ſold, and do ſell the ſame again in any Fair or Market holden in the ſame Place, or within four Miles thereof, ſhall be taken for a Regrator.*

Sect. 15. And it is farther enacted, Par. 3. *That whoſoever ſhall engroſs or get into his Hands by buying, contracting or promiſe taking, other than by Demiſe, Grant, or Leaſe of Land or Tithe, any Corn growing in the Fields, or any other Corn or Grain, Butter, Cheeſe, Fiſh, or other dead Victuals whatſoever, within the Realm of* England, *to the Intent to ſell the ſame again, ſhall be reputed an unlawful Ingroſſer.*

In the Conſtruction of the laſt mentioned Clauſes the following Opinions have been holden:

Sect. 16. I. That [a] Salt is a Victual within the Meaning of it, not only becauſe it is of Neceſſity of it ſelf for the Food and Health of Man, but alſo becauſe it ſeaſoneth and maketh wholeſome Beef, Pork, and other Victuals, in which Reſpect it ſeemeth it ſelf to come under the Notion of Victual, and ſeemeth to be ſo underſtood by the Makers of 13 *El.* 25. as appears from Par. 21. of that Statute.

Sect. 17. II. That ſuch [b] Victual only as is neceſſary for the Food of Man is within the Purview of it; and therefore that Apples, and Cherries, and ſuch like Fruits, are not within the Intent of it; for the Words are, *Corn, or Grain, Butter, Cheeſe, Fiſh, or other dead Victuals,* which Words are ſaid to import the ſame as if it had been ſaid, or other dead Victuals of like Quality: Alſo it is ſaid, That there is not any Thing prohibited within the Statute, but what hath a Proviſo, how in ſome Kind it might be bought; and therefore, ſince there is not any ſuch Proviſo for Apples, that they never were intended to be reſtrained: And agreeably hereto it hath been holden, That neither [c] Hops nor [d] Malt are within the Meaning of the Statute.

Sect. 18. III. That the Buying of Corn, with an Intent to make [e] Starch of it, and then to ſell it, is not within the ſaid Clauſe, becauſe it is not bought to be ſold again in the ſame Nature in which it was bought, but to be firſt altered by a Trade or Science, and then ſold again. And for the like Reaſon it ſeemeth to be the better [f] Opinion, That the Buying of Corn in order to make Meal of it, and then to ſell it, is no way within the ſaid Clauſe; and that the Buying of [g] Barley with an Intent to make it into Malt, and then to ſell it, had no need of the Exception made for it in the ſaid Statute.

Sect. 19. IV. That there is no Neceſſity in an Information or Indictment grounded on the ſaid Clauſe for ingroſſing any Victual therein mentioned, to ſay, [h] That the Defendant did not come by it by a Demiſe of Land

[a] Inſt. 195. H. P. C. 152. Cro. Ca. 231.

[b] 3 Inſt. 195. H. P. C. 152. Cro. Ca. 231. Owen 135. Cro. Ja. 214.

[c] Cro.Ca.231.

[d] 3 Inſt. 196. H. P. C. 152. Con. Owen 135. 1 Rol.Re. 12.

[e] Bridg. 5, 6. Owen 135.

[f] Moore 595. Pl. 810. Cro. Ca. 231. Con. Owen 135.

[g] Cro.Ca.231. 3 Inſt. 196. See Chap. 33 Sect. 15, 18. Con. Owen 135

[h] 1 Jon. 157.

Land, &c. but that the Defendant, if he have any such Matter to alledge in his Defence, may give it in Evidence.

2 Leon. 39. *Sect.* 20. V. That in every such Information, &c. the Words of the Statute must be precisely pursued, and therefore that it is not sufficient to say, That the Defendant bought so much Corn, &c. because the Words are, *shall ingross, or get into his Hands, by buying,* &c.

Sect. 21. And it is farther enacted by the said Statute of 5 & 6 *E.* 6. 14. Par. 4, 5, 6. *That whoever shall offend in any of the Things before recited, and be thereof duly convicted, shall for the first Offence, suffer Imprisonment for two Months, and forfeit the Value of the Goods so by him bought or had; and for the second Offence, shall suffer Imprisonment for one half Year, and forfeit the double Value of the Goods,* &c. *and for the third Offence, shall be set on the Pillory, and forfeit all his Goods, and be committed to Prison during the King's Pleasure.*

Sect. 22. And from hence it seems clearly to follow, as well as from the general Rules of Law, That no Information for any of the above mentioned Offences against the said Statute, can be good, without shewing in certain the Quantity of the Thing in Relation to which the Defendant is supposed to have incurred the Penalty, not only because otherwise the Judgment to be given on such an Information can never be pleaded in Bar of any other, because it cannot appear that both of them were brought for the same Thing, but also because it cannot appear to the Court what Forfeiture the Defendant ought to incur, unless the Extent of the Offence, which is to be the Measure of it, be specially set forth: And for these Reasons it hath
2 Bulst. 317. Cro. Ca. 381. been adjudged, That an Information for ingrossing Corn, the Quantity whereof is expressed by the Word *Cumulus* only, is not good; yet it is said, That
6 Mod. 32. an Indictment for ingrossing *magnam quantitatem frumenti*, is sufficient.

Sect. 23. And it is farther enacted by the said Statute of 5 & 6 *E.* 6. 14. Par. 8. *That if any Person having sufficient Corn and Grain, for the Provision of his own House, and sowing of his Grounds for one Year, do buy any Corn in any Fair or Market, for the Change of his Seed, and do not bring to the same Fare or Market the same Day, so much Corn as he shall fortune to buy for his Seed, and sell the same if he can, as the Price of Corn then goeth in the said Market or Fair, that then every such Person shall forfeit the double Value of the Corn so bought.*

Sect. 24. And it is farther enacted, Par. 9. *That if any Person shall buy any manner of Oxen, Ronts, Steers, Kine, Heifers, Calves, Sheep, Lambs, Goats or Kids living, and sell the same again alive, unless he keep and feed the same five Weeks, he shall lose the double Value of the Cattle so bought and sold, one Moiety whereof shall be to the King, and the other Moiety to him that will sue for the same.*

The principal Exceptions out of the above mentioned Statutes seem to be reducible to the following Heads:

1. Such as relate to Corn.
2. Such as relate to Butter and Cheese, and dead Cattle.
3. Such as relate to Beer, Cyder, and Mum.
4. Such as relate to Fish.
5. Such as relate to Wine, Oil, Sugar, Salt, &c.
6. Such as relate to Fishmongers, Victuallers, Butchers, Poulterers, &c.
7. Such as relate to Badgers and Drovers.
8. Such as relate to Lessors, &c.
9. Such as relate to Shipping and Castles.
10. Such as relate to Towns-Corporate.

Sect. 25. As to the first of these Exceptions relating to Corn, it is enacted by the said Statute of 5 & 6 *Ed.* 6. 14. Par. 7. *That the buying of any such Barley, Bigge, or Oats, as any Person (not forestalling) shall buy to convert into Malt or Oat-meal in his own House, and so shall be converted indeed, shall not be taken to be within the said Act.*

Sect. 26. It seemeth to be the better Opinion, That if there had been no such Exception, yet the Buying of Corn for such Purpose should not be intended to have been within the Purview of the Statute, as hath been more fully shewn already *Sect.* 18. But upon the Supposition, that such an Exception was necessary, it hath been holden that the Buying of Corn and Turning it into Malt in another's House, because it was of so great a Quantity, that it could not be malted in the Buyer's own House, is not within the Benefit of it. Owen 135.

Sect. 27. And it is farther enacted by 1 *W.* & *M.* Sess. 1. Ch. 12. *That when Malt or Barley,* Winchester *Measure, shall be at twenty-four Shillings a Quarter or under; Rye at thirty-two Shillings a Quarter or under; and Wheat at forty-eight Shillings a Quarter or under, in any Port of* England *or* Wales; *every Person who shall put on Ship-board in* English *Shipping, the Master and two Thirds of his Mariners being their Majesties Subjects, any Sorts of the Corn aforesaid, from any such Ports where the Rates shall not then be higher than as aforesaid, with Intent to export the said Corn to Parts beyond the Seas, shall bring a Certificate in Writing under his Hand, containing the Quantity and Quality of the Corn so shipped, to the Persons appointed to collect the Customs within any such Port; and upon Proof of such Certificate by one or more credible Persons upon Oath, and upon Bond given by every such Exporter of two hundred Pounds for every hundred Tun of Corn so shipped, and so proportionably, that the said Corn, (Dangers of Seas excepted) shall be exported beyond the Seas, and not landed again in* England, Wales, Guernsey, Jersey, *or* Berwick *on* Tweed, *shall receive from the said Persons appointed to receive the Customs, for every Quarter of Barley or Malt ground or unground, two Shillings and Six-pence; for every Quarter of Rye ground or unground, three Shillings and Six-pence; for every Quarter of Wheat ground or unground, five Shillings, without any Custom, Fee, or Reward to be paid for the same. And upon Certificate returned under the common Seal of the chief Magistrate in any Place beyond Sea, or under the Hands and Seals of two known* English *Merchants upon the Place, that such Corn was there landed, or upon Proof by credible Persons that such Corn was taken by Enemies, or perished at Sea, the Examination and Proof thereof being left to the Receivers of the Customs, the Bond shall be delivered up to be cancelled; and the Monies so paid, shall be allowed as paid to their Majesties.*

Vide 5 & 6 Ed. 6. 14. Par. 12, 13. 5 El. 5. Par. 26. 1 Ja. 1. 25. Par. 26. 21 Ja. 1. 28. 3 Ca. 1. 4. 12 Ca. 2. 4.

Sect. 28. As to the Second of the above mentioned Exceptions, relating to Butter and Cheese, and dead Cattle, it is enacted by 21 *Jac.* 1. 22. *That neither of the above mentioned Statutes of* 3 & 4 Ed. 6. 21. *or* 5 & 6 Ed. 6. 14. *or any other Provision whatsoever before that Statute made, concerning the Sale of Butter and Cheese in open Shop, Fair or Market, or the Providing or Buying of any Butter or Cheese, shall in any wise extend to any Cheesemonger, or Tallow-Chandler, free of the City of* London, *and having been brought up as an Apprentice seven Years, trading in Butter and Cheese, for such Butter and Cheese, and either of them, as he shall sell in* London, Westminster, *or* Southwark, *for the Victualling of any Ship of the King or Subject, or to any Butter and Cheese, which he shall sell by any Quantities at one Time, and to one Person, not exceeding four Wey of Cheese, or four Barrels of Butter, without Fraud, so as he sell the same in open Shop, Fair, or Market: Provided that if the Justices of Peace of any County at their Quarter-Sessions, shall declare that such Traders shall forbear to buy any Butter or Cheese, for any Time within such County;*

Vide supra Sect. 11, 14, 15, &c.

County; that then during the Time of such Restraint, the said Traders in Butter and Cheese, that shall buy any such Butter or Cheese, and sell the same again by retail, contrary to any of the said Acts, shall not be freed from the Penalties thereof.

Sect. 29. And it is farther enacted by 3 & 4 *W. & M.* 8. *That it shall be lawful for every Person, native or foreign, at any Time, to ship, lade, carry, and transport, or export, from any Place within* England, Wales, *or* Berwick *on* Tweed, *in any Part of the World in Amity with their Majesties, all Sorts of Beef, Pork, or Hogs-flesh, Butter, Cheese, or Candles, free from any Custom or Imposition whatsoever.*

Sect. 30. As to the Third of the above mentioned Exceptions relating to Beer, Cyder, and Mum, it is enacted by 1 *Will. & Mar.* Seff. 1. Ch. 22. *That any Person may export any strong Ale, strong Beer, Cyder or Mum to be spent beyond the Seas, paying Custom for the same, at the Rate of one Shilling for every Tun, in such manner as is set forth more at large in the said Statute.*

Sect. 31. As to the Fourth of the above mentioned Exceptions relating to Fish, it is enacted by the said Statute of 5 & 6 *Ed.* 6. 14. Par. 7. *That the Buying of any dried or salted Fish, Herring, or Sprats (not forestalled) and sold for reasonable Prices, shall not be deemed any Offence contrary to the said Act.*

Sect. 32. And it is farther enacted by the said Statute, Par. 15. *That it shall be lawful for any Subject, dwelling within one Mile of the main Sea, to buy all manner of Fish fresh or salted, (not forestalling the same) and to sell the same again at reasonable Prices.*

Sect. 33. And it is farther enacted by 5 *El.* 5. Par. 13. *That so much of the said Statute of* 5 & 6 Ed. 6. 14. *and so much of all other Statutes against Regrators, Ingrossers, and Forestallers, as concerneth the Buying of Sea-fish unsalted, or Mud-fish, to be taken and brought in any* English *Subjects Ships, Crayers, or other Vessels, into any Place of this Realm, shall be utterly repealed for so much of the said Fish, as any Buyer upon the Sea by way of Forestalling or Regrating, shall bring and discharge in any Port or Haven within this Realm.*

Sect. 34. As to the Fifth of the above mentioned Exceptions relating to Wine, Oil, Sugar, Salt, *&c.* the same Exception is made in Relation to Wine, Oil, and Salt by the said Statute of 5 *El.* 5. Par. 13. as is set forth in the last Section concerning Fish unsalted, or Mud-Fish.

Sect. 35. And it is farther enacted by 13 *El.* 25. Par. 21. *That the said Statute of* 5 & 6 Ed. 6. 14. *is not meant to extend, nor shall extend to any Wines, Oils, Sugars, Spices, Currans, nor other foreign Victuals, brought into this Realm from beyond the Seas, Fish and Salt only excepted.*

Sect. 36. As to the Sixth of the above mentioned Exceptions relating to Fishmongers, Victuallers, Butchers and Poulterers, *&c.* it is enacted by the said Statute of 5 & 6 Ed. 6. 14. *That the Buying of any Victual by any Fishmonger, Butcher or Poulterer, as concern his own Faculty, Craft, or Mystery, otherwise than by Forestalling, which shall sell the same again upon reasonable Prices by Retail; or the Buying of any Wine or other dead Victual above mentioned, being Meat for Man's Sustenance, by any Innholder, or other Victualler, to sell the same by Retail within his House, or to any of his Neighbours for their Sustenance, for reasonable Prices, shall not be deemed any Offence contrary to the said Act.*

Cro. Ca. 314. 1 Rol. Re. 88, 12. 1 Jon. 320. *Sect.* 37. Notwithstanding this Exception it hath been resolved, That any of the Persons therein mentioned may be indicted for ingrossing Victuals, with an Intent to sell them again, against the Form of the Statute; for it shall be intended that they ingrossed, and did not sell at reasonable Prices.

4 *Sect.* 38.

Sect. 38. As to the ſeventh of the above mentioned Exceptions relating to Badgers and Drovers, it is enacted by the ſaid Statute of 5 & 6 E. 6. 14. Par. 7. *That the Buying of any Corn, Fiſh, Butter, or Cheeſe, by any ſuch Badger, Lader, Kidder, or Carrier, that ſhall be allowed to that Office by three Juſtices of Peace,* &c. *which ſhall ſell or deliver in open Fair or Market, or to any other Victualler, or to any other Perſon for the Proviſion of his Houſe, all ſuch Corn, Grain, Butter and Cheeſe, as any ſuch Perſon ſhall buy, or cauſe to be bought, and that within one Month next after he ſhall ſo buy any ſuch Corn, Grain, Butter or Cheeſe, ſo that the ſame ſhall be bought without Foreſtalling, ſhall not be deemed any Offence contrary to the ſaid Statute.*

Sect. 39. And it is farther enacted by the ſame Statute, Par. 12. *That it ſhall be lawful to every Perſon who ſhall be allowed by three Juſtices of Peace, to buy (otherwiſe than by Foreſtalling) Corn, Grain, or Cattle, to be carried by Water from any Place within this Realm, or* Wales, *unto any other Place within the ſaid Realm, or Dominions, if he ſhall without Fraud embark within forty Days next after he ſhall have bought the ſame, or taken Covenant, or Promiſe for the buying thereof, and with all poſſible Expedition tranſport the ſame to ſuch Place as his Cocket ſhall declare, and there unlade the ſame, and bring a Certificate thereof from a Juſtice of Peace of the County, or Head-Officer of the Town and Cuſtomer of the Port where it ſhall be unladen,* &c. *to be directed to the Cuſtomer and Comptroller of the Port where it ſhall be embarked.*

Sect. 40. And it is farther enacted by the ſame Statute, Par. 16, 17. *That it ſhall be lawful for any Perſon known for a common Drover, being licenced by three Juſtices of Peace,* &c. *to buy Cattle in ſuch Shires where Drovers had been wont in Times paſt, accuſtomably to buy Cattle at their free Liberty and Pleaſure, and to ſell the ſame as is aforeſaid, at reaſonable Prices, in common Fairs or Markets, diſtant from the Place where he ſhall buy the ſame forty Miles, ſo that the ſame Cattle be not bought by way of Foreſtalling.*

Sect. 41. And it is farther enacted by 5 *El.* 12. and 13 *El.* 25. Par. 20. *That no Drover of Cattle, Badger, Lader, Kidder, Carrier, Buyer or Tranſporter of Corn or Grain, Butter and Cheeſe, ſhall be licenſed to any ſuch Office or Doing, in any County except* Weſtmorland, Cumberland, Lancaſter, Cheſter *or* York, *but only in the General open Quarter-Seſſions of the Peace, to be holden in the Shire where ſuch Perſon ſo to be allowed ſhall dwell, and ſhall have dwelled three Years next before the* Teſte *of his Licence: And that no Perſon be admitted to any of the ſaid Offices or Doings, but ſuch only as be or have been married Men, and ſhall be at the Time of ſuch Licence to be granted, Houſholders, and not Houſhold-Servants, nor Retainers to any Perſon, and of the Age of thirty Years: And that ſuch Licences ſhall be good only for one Year next after the Date, and ſhall bear Date of the Day and Place where the ſaid Seſſions ſhall be holden, and ſhall be ſigned and ſealed with the proper Hands and Seals of three Juſtices preſent at the ſame Seſſions, whereof one to be of the* Quorum, *on Pain that every Perſon that ſhall take any Licence contrary to this Ordnance, ſhall forfeit five Pounds, and that all Licences made otherwiſe than is before expreſſed, ſhall be void; and that the Juſtices in the ſaid Seſſions ſhall by their Diſcretion, take Bond and Surety from Time to Time, by Recognizance of ſuch as ſhall be allowed a common Drover of Cattle, Badger, or Lader,* &c. *that they nor any of them ſhall by Colour of ſuch Licence foreſtal, or engroſs, or otherwiſe do any Thing contrary to the Meaning of the ſaid Statute of* 5 & 6 E. 6. 14. *And that every ſuch Licence and Recognizance ſhall be made and written by the Clerk of the Peace of every County, where ſuch Licence ſhall be granted, or by his Deputy, and by no other Perſon; and that every Perſon that ſhall have any ſuch Licence, ſhall pay to the Clerk of the Peace,* &c. *Twelve-pence only; and for every ſuch Recognizance, eight Pence; and for regiſtring the ſame*

Licence and Recognizance, four Pence, and that the ſaid Clerk, &c. *for the ſaid Fee, ſhall keep one Regiſter-Book, and therein ſhall regiſter and write all the Names, Surnames, and Dwelling-Places of ſuch as ſhall be ſo licenced, with a brief Entry of the ſaid Licence, and of the Day, Time, and Place where it ſhall be granted; and that the ſaid Clerk of the Peace ſhall bring the ſaid Book to every Seſſions, that it may appear what Number of Licences have been granted. And that no Perſon ſhall by Authority of any ſuch Licence, buy any Corn or Grain out of open Fair or Market to ſell again, unleſs he ſhall be thereunto licenced by ſpecial and expreſs Words contained in ſuch Licence, on Pain to forfeit five Pounds for every Time that he ſhall do to the contrary, and that one Moiety of the Forfeitures afore rehearſed, ſhall be to the Queen, and the other to him who will ſue for the ſame,* &c.

Sect. 42. As to the Eighth of the above mentioned Exceptions relating to Leſſors, it is enacted by the ſaid Statute of 5 & 6 *E.* 6. 14. Par. 7. *That the Taking of any Cattle, Corn, Grain, Butter, Cheeſe, or any other Thing in the ſaid Statute mentioned, reſerved without Fraud or Covin, upon any Leaſe for Life or Years, ſhall not be deemed any Offence contrary to the ſaid Statute.*

Sect. 43. As to the Ninth of the above mentioned Exceptions relating to Shipping and Caſtles, it is farther enacted by the ſame Paragraph of the ſaid Statute. *That the ſame ſhall not extend to Proviſion made, without Fraud, by any Perſon, of any of the Things in the ſaid Statute mentioned, for the victualling of any Ship, Caſtle, or Fort, within the King's Dominions, without Foreſtalling, which ſhall be employed only to that Uſe and Purpoſe,* &c.

Sect. 44. As to the Tenth of the above mentioned Exceptions relating to Towns-Corporate, it is farther enacted by the ſame Paragraph, *That the ſaid Statute ſhall not extend to any common Proviſion to be made without Fraud by any Perſon, of any of the Things in the ſaid Statute mentioned, for any City, Borough, or Town-corporate.*

Sect. 45. Alſo it is enacted by the ſaid Statute of 5 *El.* 12. Par. 9. concerning the licenſing of Badgers, *&c. That nothing therein contained ſhall in any wiſe extend to the Prejudice of the Liberty of any City or Town-corporate, but that every of them may aſſign and licence Purveyors, for the Proviſion of the ſame, as they might have done before.*

Sect. 46. As to the third Point, *viz.* In what Manner Offenders of this Kind are to be proceeded againſt, it is enacted by the ſaid Statutes of 5 & 6 *E.* 6. 14. Par. 10, 11. and 5 El. 12. Par. 8. *That the Juſtices of Peace of every County at their Quarter-Seſſions may enquire, hear, and determine, all the Offences contrary to either of the ſaid Acts, by Inquiſition, Preſentment, Bill, or Information before them exhibited, and by Examination of two lawful Witneſſes, or by any of the ſame Ways or Means, by their Diſcretion, and make Proceſs thereupon, as though they were indicted before them by Inquiſition, or by Verdict of twelve Men or more; and upon the Conviction of the Offender, by Information or Suit of any other than the King, make Extracts of the Moiety of the Forfeitures to be levied to the King's Uſe,* &c. *and award Execution of the other Moiety for the Complainant,* &c. *by* Fieri facias, *or* Capias *as the King's Juſtices at* Weſtminſter *uſe to do,* &c. *and if ſuch Conviction ſhall be at the King's Suit, the Whole ſhall be levied to his Uſe only.*

Sect. 47. Alſo it is provided by 31 *El.* 5. which ordains that Informations for Offences againſt Penal Statutes, muſt be laid in the proper County, *That nothing in the ſaid Statute contained, ſhall extend to any Information or Declaration, for any Offence compriſed in any Statute made againſt Ingroſſing, Regrating, or Foreſtalling, where the Penalty or Forfeiture ſhall appear to be to the Value of twenty Pounds, or above, but that every ſuch Offence may be laid in any County at the Pleaſure of the Informer.*

See B. 2. Ch. 26. Sect. 26 to 40.

CHAP. LXXXI.

Of Barratry.

IN treating of Barratry, I ſhall conſider:

1. Who ſhall be ſaid to be a Barrator.
2. In what Manner ſuch an Offender is to be proceeded againſt.
3. To what Puniſhment he is liable.

Sect. 1. As to the firſt Point it ſeems, That a Barrator is a common Co. Lit. 368.
Mover, Exciter, or Maintainer of Suits or Quarrels, either in Courts, or 8 Co. 36. b.
in the Country.

Sect. 2. And it is ſaid not to be material, whether the Courts wherein Co. Lit. 368.
ſuch Suits are commenced, be of Record or not, or whether ſuch Quarrels 8 Co. 36. b.
in the Country relate to a diſputed Title of Poſſeſſions or not: But that all Kinds of Diſturbances of the Peace, and the Spreading of falſe Rumors and Calumnies, whereby Diſcord and Diſquiet may grow among Neighbours, are as proper Inſtances of Barratry, as the Taking or Keeping the Poſſeſſion of Lands in Controveſy.

Sect. 3. But it hath been holden, That a Man ſhall not be adjudged a
Barrator in Reſpect of any Number of falſe Actions brought by him in his 1 Rol. Abr.
own Right; however if ſuch Actions be merely groundleſs and vexatious 355. A.
without any Manner of Colour, and brought only with a Deſign to oppreſs 3 Mod. 98.
the Defendants, I do not ſee why a Man may not as properly be called a 8 Co. 36. b.
Barrator for bringing ſuch Actions himſelf, as for ſtirring up others to bring them.

Sect. 4. But it ſeems, That an Attorney is in no Danger of being
judged guilty of an Act of Barratry, in reſpect of his maintaining an- 3 Mod. 97, 98.
other in a groundleſs Action, to the commencing whereof he was no way privy.

Sect. 5. Alſo it ſeems clear, That no one can be a Barrator in reſpect
of one Act only; for every Indictment for ſuch Crime muſt charge the 8 Co. 36. b.
Defendant with being *Communis Barractator.*

Sect. 6. It ſeems to have been holden, That a Feme Covert cannot be
indicted as a common Barrator, but this Opinion ſeems juſtly queſtionable; 2 Rol. Re. 39.
for ſince a Feme Covert is as capable of exciting Quarrels, in the frequent
Repetition whereof the Notion of Barratry ſeems to conſiſt, as if ſhe were See Chap. 1.
ſole, why ſhould ſhe not as properly be indictable for it? Sect. 13.

Sect. 7. As to the ſecond Point, *viz.* In what Manner Offenders of this Kind are to be proceeded againſt, it is enacted by 34 *E.* 3. 1. *That in every County ſhall be aſſigned for the Keeping of the Peace one Lord, and with him three or four of the moſt worthy of the County,* &c. *and that they ſhall have Power to reſtrain Offenders, Rioters, and all other Barrators, and to purſue, arreſt, take, and chaſtiſe them, according to their Treſpaſs or Offence; and ſo cauſe them to be impriſoned and duly puniſhed according to the Law and Cuſtoms of the Realm, and according to that which to them ſhall ſeem beſt to do by their Diſcretions and good Adviſement,* &c.

Sect. 8.

Con. B. 2. Ch. 8. Sect. 38, 39. Yelv. 46. *Sect.* 8. It seemeth from these Words, That Justices of Peace (as such) have Cognizance of Barratry without any other Commission, *sed Quære*;
2 Rol. R. 151. for the contrary Opinion seems to have been holden in *Rolle*'s Reports.

Sect. 9. However it seems clear, That no general Indictment of this
1 Mod. 288. 1 Sid. 282. Cro. Ja. 526. Kind, charging the Defendant with being a common Oppressor, and Disturber of the Peace, and Stirrer up of Strife among Neighbours, is good, without adding the Words *communis Barractator*, which is a Term of Art appropriated by the Law to this Purpose.

[a] 2 Rol. Abr. 79. Pl. 3. 82. Pl. 6. Cro. Ja. 527. Cro. Ca. 340. *Sect.* 10. [a] Also it seemeth to be certain, That an Indictment of Barratry concluding *contra formam Statuti*, is good, tho' no Statute be made directly against it, but only for the Punishment of it, supposing it an Offence at Common Law.

2 Keb. 409, 410. Cro. El. 148. [b] 2 Keb. 410. Cro. El. 195. Con. Latch 194. 2 H. H. P. C. 180. *Sect.* 11. [b] Also it hath been holden, That an Indictment of this Kind may be good, without alledging the Offence at any certain Place; because from the Nature of the Thing, consisting in the Repetition of several Acts, it must be intended to have happened in several Places; for which Cause it is said, That a Trial ought to be by a Jury from the Body of the County.

Palm. 450. 1 Rol. Re. 295. [c] Cro. Ja. 527. *Sect.* 12. [c] But it hath been resolved, That such an Indictment is not good, without concluding *contra Pacem, &c.* for this is an essential Part of it.

[d] 5 Mod. 18. *Sect.* 13. [d] Also it seemeth to be settled Practice, not to suffer the Prosecutor to go on in the Trial of an Indictment of this Kind, without giving the Defendant a Note of the particular Matters, which he intends to prove against him; for otherwise it will be impossible to prepare a Defence against so general and uncertain a Charge, which may be proved by such a Multiplicity of different Instances.

Hutton 104. *Sect.* 14. As to the third Point, *viz.* In what Manner Offenders of this Kind are to be punished; it is said, That if they be common Persons, they are to be fined and imprisoned, and bound to their good Behaviour; and if they be of any Profession relating to the Law, that they ought also to be farther punished, by being disabled to practise for the Future. Vide 1 Dan. Abr. 111. Pl. 6. 113. Pl. 15.

CHAP. LXXXII.

Of Usury.

OFFENCES under the Degree of Capital more immediately against the Subject, not amounting to an actual Disturbance of the Peace, which may be committed by private Persons without any Relation to an Office, and which are neither infamous nor grosly scandalous, and more immediately affect the Interests of particular Persons, seem to be reducible to the following Heads:

1. Usury.
2. Maintenance.
3. The Offence of buying or selling pretended Titles.

In treating of Uſury, I ſhall conſider:

1. What it is.
2. How it is reſtrained by Common Law.
3. How by Statute.

Sect. 1. And firſt it ſeems, that Uſury, in a ſtrict Senſe, is a Contract upon the Loan of Money to give the Lender a certain Profit for the Uſe of it, upon all Events, whether the Borrower make any Advantage of it, or the Lender ſuffer any Prejudice for the Want of it, or whether it be repaid on the Day appointed, or not.

Wood's Inſt. 171. 3 Inſt. 151. See Bro. Uſury 12.

Sect. 2. And in a larger Senſe it ſeemeth, That all undue Advantages taken by a Lender againſt a Borrower come under the Notion of Uſury, whether there were any Contract in relation thereto, or not; as where one in Poſſeſſion of Land, made over to him for the Security of a certain Debt, retains his Poſſeſſion after he hath receiv'd all that is due from the Profits of the Land.

Gibſ. 1070.

Sect. 3. But it hath been reſolved, That an Agreement to pay double the Sum borrowed, or other Penalty on the Non-payment of the principal Debt at a certain Day, is not uſurious, becauſe it is in the Power of the Borrower, wholly to diſcharge himſelf, by repaying the Principal according to the Bargain.

2 Ro. A. 801. Pl. 2, 3. 802. Pl. 4. 26 E. 3. 71. a. 2 Inſt. 89.

Sect. 4. As to the ſecond Point, *viz.* How Uſury is reſtrained by the [a] Common Law; it is ſaid, That anciently it was holden to be abſolutely unlawful for a Chriſtian to take any Kind of Uſury, and that whoſoever was guilty of it, was liable to be puniſhed by the Cenſures of the Church in his Life-time; and that if after Death any one was found to have been an Uſurer while living, all his Chattels were forfeited to the King, and his Lands eſcheated to the Lord of the Fee.

[a] 3 Inſt. 151. 2 Rol. A. 800, 801. 2 Inſt. 506, 507. Palm. 293. 294.

Sect. 5. Alſo it ſeemeth to have been the Opinion of the Makers of ſome late Acts of Parliament, as 5 *Ed.* 6. 20. 13 *El.* 8. Par. 5. and 21 *Jac.* 1. 17. Par. 5. That all Kinds of Uſury are contrary to good Conſcience.

Sect. 6. [b] And agreeably hereto it ſeemeth formerly to have been the general Opinion, That no Action could be maintained on any Promiſe to pay any Kind of Uſe for the Forbearance of Money, becauſe that all ſuch Contracts were thought to be unlawful, and conſequently void.

[b] 2 Ro. A. 801. 26 Ed. 1. 71. a. 1 Rol. Ab. 18. Pl. 14, 15. 2 Rol. Re. 239, 240, 469. Palm. 293.

Sect. 7. But it ſeems to be generally agreed at this Day, [c] That the Taking of reaſonable Intereſt for the Uſe of Money is in it ſelf lawful, and conſequently that a Covenant or Promiſe to pay it, in Conſideration of the Forbearance of a Debt, will maintain an Action: For why ſhould not one who has an Eſtate in Money be as well allowed to make a fair Profit of it, as another who has an Eſtate in Land? And what reaſon can there be, that the Lender of Money ſhould not as well make an Advantage of it as the Borrower? Neither do the Paſſages in the *Moſaical* Law, which are generally urged againſt the Lawfulneſs of all Uſury, if fully conſidered, ſo much prove the Unlawfulneſs, as the Lawfulneſs of it; for if all Uſury were againſt the Moral Law, why ſhould it not be as much ſo in reſpect of Foreigners, of whom the *Jews* were expreſly allowed to take it, as in Reſpect of thoſe of the ſame Nation, of whom alone they were forbidden to receive it? From whence it ſeems clearly to follow, That the Prohibition of it to that People was merely political, and conſequently doth not extend to any other Nation.

[c] 1 Rol. A. 25. Pl. 35. 2 Rol. A. 782, 802. H. 1. Pl. 4. Winch 114, 120. Cro. Ja. 378, 379. 1 Vent. 198. 199. 3 Keb. 15. Cro. Ca. 273. 1 Vent. 198. Exod. 22. ver. 25. Levit. 25. ver. 36, 37. Deuter. 23. ver. 19, 20.

Sect. 8. As to the third Point, *viz.* How Usury is restrained by Statute, it is enacted by 12 *Annæ*, 16. *That no Person whatsoever, shall upon any Contract which shall be made from and after the nine and twentieth Day of* September, 1714. *take, directly or indirectly, for Loan of any Money, Wares, Merchandize, or other Commodities whatsoever, above the Value of five Pounds, for the Forbearance of one hundred Pounds for a Year, and so after that Rate for a greater or lesser Sum, or for a longer or shorter Time; and that all Bonds, Contracts, and Assurances whatsoever, made after the Time aforesaid, for Payment of any Principal, or Money to be lent, or covenanted to be performed upon or for any Usury, whereupon or whereby there shall be reserved or taken above the Rate of five Pounds in the Hundred, as aforesaid, shall be utterly void,* (tho' the Reservation be of so much if requested, and the Request be never made) *and that all and every Person or Persons whatsoever, which shall after the Time aforesaid, upon any Contract to be made after the said nine and twentieth Day of* September, *take, accept, and receive, by Way or Means of any corrupt Bargain, Loan, Exchange, Chevizance, Shift, or Interest of any Wares, Merchandize, or other Thing or Things whatsoever, or by any deceitful Way or Means, or by any Covin, Engine, or deceitful Conveyance, for the forbearing or giving Day of Payment for one whole Year, of and for their Money or other Thing, above the Sum of five Pounds for the forbearing of one hundred Pounds for a Year, and so after that Rate for a greater or lesser Sum, or for a* [a] *longer or shorter Term, shall forfeit and lose for every such Offence the treble Value of the Money, Wares, Merchandize, and other Things so lent, bargained, exchanged, or shifted.* And Note, That the treble Value is not forfeited, unless something be taken above the legal Rate; but the very Contract alone avoids the Security.

3 Keb. 259, 260. 1 Vent. 253.

[a] Vide Cro. Ja. 25. Mo. 644. Pl. 819. Noy 41. Cro. Ca. 283.

Cro. Eliz. 20.

Sect. 9. And it is farther enacted by the said Statute, *That every Scrivener, Broker, Solicitor, and Driver of Bargains for Contracts, who shall, after the said nine and twentieth Day of* September, *take or receive, directly or indirectly, any Sum or Sums of Money, or other Reward or Thing, for Brokage, Soliciting, Driving or Procuring the Loan, or forbearing of any Sum or Sums of Money, over and above the Rate or Value of five Shillings for the Loan, or forbearing of one hundred Pounds, for a Year, and so rateably; or above twelve Pence, over and above the Stamp-Duties, for making or renewing of the Bond or Bill for Loan, or forbearing thereof, or for any Counterbond or Bill concerning the same, shall forfeit for every such Offence twenty Pounds, with Costs of Suit, and suffer Imprisonment for half a Year, the one Moiety of all which Forfeitures shall be to the Queen, the other to him that will sue for the same, in the same County where the several Offences are committed,* &c.

The Expositions which were made of the former Statutes of Usury being equally applicable to this which is penned almost in the very same Words, I shall take Notice of the Principal of them; as,

Dalif. 12. Con. Raym. 147.

Sect. 10. I. That a Contract made before the Statute is no way within the Meaning of it, and therefore that it is still lawful to receive six *per Cent.* in respect of any such Contract.

Sect. 11. II. That a Bond made to secure a just Debt payable with lawful Interest, shall not be avoided by reason of a corrupt Agreement between the Obligors, to which the Obligee was no way Privy: As where *A.* being indebted to *B.* in 100 *l.* agrees to give him 30 *l.* for the Forbearance of that 100 *l.* for a Year, and gives him a Bond of 60 *l.* for Payment of the 30 *l.* and for the Payment of the 100 *l.* enters into a Bond of 200 *l.* together with *B.* for the Payment of a true Debt of 100 *l.* due from *B.* to *C.*

2 And. 121. Moor 752. Pl. 1035. Cro. Ja. 32, 33. Yel. 47.

Sect. 12. III. That the Receipt of higher Interest than is allowed by the Statute, by Virtue of an Agreement subsequent to the first Contract, does not avoid an Assurance fairly made, and agreeable to the Statute, but only subjects the Party to the Forfeiture of treble Value, for the Words are, *That all Assurances for the Payment of any Principal*, &c. *whereupon or whereby there shall be reserved or taken above the Rate of* 5 l. *in the Hundred*, &c. *shall be utterly void.* 1 Mod. 69. 3 Keb. 142. 2 Mod. 307. 1 Saund. 294. Raym. 196. 2 Keb. 525, 690. 1 Bulf. 17.

Sect. 13. IV. That in an Assurance for the Payment of fifty Shillings for the Use of 100 *l.* for six Months, the Computation shall be by Kalendar and not by Lunar Months, because by the latter the Interest would exceed the Rate allowed by the Statute. Noy 37. 1 Leon. 96.

Sect. 14. V. That the Receipt of Interest before the Time when it is in Strictness due, being voluntarily paid by the Debtor for the greater Convenience of the Creditor, or for any other such like Consideration, without any Manner of corrupt Practice, or any previous Agreement of this Kind at the making of the first Contract, does not make the Party liable to the Forfeiture of the treble Value. 1 Bulf. 17, 20. Yel. 30, 31. Noy 171. 2 Keb. 690. Con. 1 Leon. 96.

Sect. 15. VI. That the Grant of an Annuity for Lives not only exceeding the Rate allowed for Interest, but also exceeding the known Proportion for Contracts of this Kind, in Consideration of a certain Sum of Money, is not within the Meaning of the Statute, unless there were some underhand Bargain for the Security of the Repayment of the Principal or Consideration-Money. Cro. Ja. 253. Noy 151. 2 Levinz 7, 8. Vid. 2 Rol. A. 782. H. 1.

Sect. 16. VII. That no Contract is usurious, by which the Lender runs the Hazard of losing all his Money, both Principal and Interest: As where on the Loan of a certain Sum for a Year, for the Victualling of a Ship, it is agreed, That if the Ship return, the Lender shall have so many thousand Fishes at such a Rate, which exceeds the Interest allowed by the Statute, and if the Ship never return, or if it perish by unavoidable Casualties of Sea, Fire, or Enemies, that then he shall have nothing: Or where on the Loan of 30 *l.* a Bond is given for the Payment of 100 *l.* on the Marriage of a Daughter of one of the Parties; provided, That if either of them should die before, that then nothing should be paid: But it is clear, That if the Interest only be hazarded on such a Contract, and the whole Principal secured, the Whole is usurious. Also it hath been resolved, That an Agreement to pay more than the lawful Interest for the Loan of a certain Sum at such a Day, if *A. B.* shall be then alive, and if he shall be dead, then to pay such a Sum which is less than the Principal, is void by the Statute; for if such a Contingency would exempt the Case out of the Statute, by the same Reason twenty Lives might be added, and the Statute wholly evaded. Cro. Ja. 208, 209, 508, 509. 1 Keb. 539, 711. 2 Ro. Re. 48. 1 Lev. 54. 1 Sid 27. 3 Keb. 304. Vide Cro. El. 741. 2 Ro. Re. 48. Cro. Ja. 508. 5 Co. 70. Moor 397. Cro. Eliz. 642, 643, 741. Lutw. 468, 469. Carth. 68.

Sect. 17. VIII. That an Assurance made in Pursuance of a fair Agreement for such Interest as is allowed by the Statute, shall not be avoided by the Fault of the Scrivener, who draws it up in such a Manner as to bring it within the express Letter of the Statute: As where the Parties agree, That 5 *l.* shall be paid for the Loan of 100 *l.* for a Year, and the Scrivener in drawing the Bond for it, doth, without the Knowledge of the Parties, who are illiterate Persons, make the 5 *l.* payable at the End of half a Year: Or where on the fair Loan of 100 *l.* agreed to be paid with common Interest, a Mortgage is made for the 100 *l.* with a Proviso, That it shall be void on Payment of 105 *l.* at the End of one Year, without any Covenant for the Mortgagor to take the Profits till Default be made of Payment, so that in Strictness the Mortgagee is intitled both to the Interest and Profits. Cro. Ja. 677, 678. 2 Ro. Re. 414, 415. Hetley 11. 1 Jon. 396. Cro. Ca. 501. 2 Ventr. 83. 2 Mod. 307. 2 Rol. A. 793, 798, 5.

5 Co. 70. b.

Sect. 18. IX. That the Loan of Money for lawful Intereſt allowed by the Statute, ſhall not be conſtrued to be within the Purview of it, in reſpect of any Expectations which the Lender may have of a voluntary Gratuity to be given him by the Borrower, if there be no Kind of Agreement relating to it.

5 Co. 69. Cro. Ja. 509. 5 Co. 69. b. See Mo. 397. 2 And. 16.

Sect. 19. X. That the Reſervation of a greater Sum than is allowed by the Statute for Intereſt, upon the Non-payment of the Principal at the End of the Year is not uſurious within the Statute, becauſe it is in the Power of the Borrower to avoid the Payment of the Money ſo reſerved, by paying the Principal at the Day appointed; yet it ſeemeth clear, That if it were originally agreed, that the principal Money ſhould not be paid at the Time appointed, and that ſuch Clauſe was inſerted only with an Intent to evade the Statute, the whole Contract is void; for the Conſtruction of Caſes of this Nature muſt be governed by the Circumſtances of the whole Matter, from which the Intention of the Parties will appear in the making of the Bargain, which, if it was in Truth uſurious, is void, however it may be diſguiſed by a ſpecious Aſſurance.

[a] 3 Co. 80. 9 Co. 36. b. 1 Jon. 203. 1 Ro. Re. 41, 42. 2 Ventr. 83, 108. 2 Leon. 166. Con. Cro. El. 25, 588. 1 Sid. 182. b. [b] Salk. 22. Pl. 2. Skin. 411, 412.

Sect. 20. XI. That a [a] Fine levied, or Judgment ſuffered, in Purſuance of an uſurious Contract, may be avoided by an Averment of the corrupt Agreement, as well as any common Specialty, or parol Contract. And in an *Aſſumpſit* [b] if it appear, either upon the Evidence, or from the Plaintiff's own Expreſs Shewing in his Declaration, that the Contract was uſurious, he cannot recover. But a Specialty cannot be avoided by Uſury appearing on Evidence or on the Face of the Condition, but it muſt be pleaded.

[c] Cro. Ja. 252, 508. 2 Rol. Re. 48. 2 Lev. 7, 8.

Sect. 21. XII. That it is not [c] material whether the Payment both of the Principal and alſo of the uſurious Intereſt be ſecured by the ſame [d] or by different Conveyances, but that all Writings whatſoever for the ſtrengthening ſuch a Contract, are void.

[d] Lutw. 273. 466. [e] Cro. Ja. 440.

Sect. 22. XIII. That a Contract reſerving to the Lender a greater Advantage than is allowed by the Statute, is equally within the Meaning of it, [e] whether the whole be reſerved by way of Intereſt, or in Part only under that Name, and in Part by way of Rent for a Houſe, let at a Rate plainly exceeding the known Value.

3 Keb. 142. Con. Noy 2.

Sect. 23. XIV. That a ſecond Bond made after the Forfeiture of a former, and conditioned for the Receipt of Intereſt according to the Penalty of the forfeited Bond, is as much within the Statute as if it had been made before the Forfeiture; for if ſuch a Practice ſhould be allowed, nothing could be more eaſy than to elude the Statute; and though the whole Penalty be due in Strictneſs to the Obligee, yet the true principal Debt is in Conſcience no greater after the Forfeiture of the Bond than it was before.

1 And. 49. 1 Sid. 285. 3 Mod. 35. 1 Keb. 629. Noy 143. Cro. Ja. 440. Vide Cro. Ca. 501. Precedents. 2 Vent. 81. Lutw. 468.

Sect. 24. XV. That in pleading an uſurious Contract by way of Bar to an Action, you muſt ſet forth the whole Matter ſpecially, becauſe it lay within your own Privity; but that in an Information on the Statute for making ſuch a Contract, it is ſufficient to ſet forth the corrupt Bargain generally, becauſe Matters of this Kind are ſuppoſed to be privily tranſacted, and ſuch Information may be brought by a Stranger.

Sect. 25. XVI. [f] That in every ſuch Information it is neceſſary expreſly to ſet forth the Place where the corrupt Bargain was made.

[f] 1 Leon. 96, 97. 1 Leon. 148. 149.

Sect. 26. XVII. That if an uſurious Contract in the County of *D.* be pleaded in Bar to an Action on a Bond ſaid to be made in the County of *E.* the Trial ſhall be in the County of *D.* becauſe the Ground of the Matter is the uſurious Contract, and the Bond is confeſſed by the Plea.

Sect. 27. XVIII. That he who hath agreed to pay Money upon an usurious Contract, shall not be admitted to give Evidence upon an Information against the Usurer, unless he have paid off the whole Debt; for by such Means a Man might avoid his own Act and Deed. Co. Lit. 6. b. 2 Rol. A. 685. 2 Raymond 191. B. 2. Ch. 46. Sect. 24.

Sect. 28. XIX. That an Information for an usurious Contract on a Loan of Money, cannot be supported by Evidence of such a Contract on a Bargain concerning Wares sold. 1 Leon. 95, 96.

CHAP. LXXXIII.

Of Maintenance.

Sect. 1. MAintenance is commonly taken in an ill Sense, and in general seemeth to signify an unlawful Taking in Hand, or Upholding of Quarrels or Sides, to the Disturbance or Hinderance of common Right, and is said to be twofold: Co. Lit. 368. b. 2 Inst. 208, 212.

Sect. 2. I. *Ruralis*, or in the Country; as where one assists another in his Pretensions to certain Lands, by taking or holding the Possession of them for him by Force or Subtilty, or where one stirs up Quarrels, and Suits in the Country, in relation to Matters wherein he is no way concerned: And this Kind of Maintenance is punishable at the King's Suit by Fine and Imprisonment, whether the Matter in Dispute any way depended in Plea or not, but is said not to be actionable. Co. Lit. 368. b. 2 Inst. 213. 1 Ric. 1. ch. 4. 2 Rol. Abr. 115. F.

Sect. 3. II. *Curialis*, or in a Court of Justice, where one officiously intermeddles in a Suit depending in any such Court which no way belongs to him, by assisting either Party with Money or otherwise, in the Prosecution or Defence of any such Suit. Pult. 25. 2 Inst. 212. 2 Rol. A. 115. F.

Of this second Kind of Maintenance there seem to be three Species:

1. Where one maintains another without any Contract to have Part of the Thing in Suit, which generally goes under the common Name of Maintenance.
2. Where one maintains one Side, to have Part of the Thing in Suit, which is called Champerty.
3. Where one laboureth a Jury, which is called Embracery.

For the better Understanding of the first of the above mentioned Species, I shall examine:

1. What shall be said to amount to an Act of Maintenance.
2. In what Respects some such Acts may be justifyed.
3. How far Offences of this Kind are restrained by the Common Law.
4. How far by Statute.

Sect. 4. As to the first Point, it seemeth clear, That whoever assists another with Money to carry on his Cause, as by retaining one to be of Counsel for him, or otherwise bearing him out in the whole or Part of the Expence of the Suit, may properly be said to be guilty of an Act of Maintenance, as it seems to be taken for granted in the [a] Books cited in the Margin.

[a] 28 H. 6. 7. b. 12. a. 34 H. 6. 25, 26. a. b. 9 E. 4. 32. a. 21 H. 7. 40. b. 6 E. 4. 5. b. 19 E. 4. 3. b. 31 H. 6. 9. Bro. Maintenance, 7, 14, 17, 20, 24, 43, 44, 52. 2 Rol. A 118. Pl. 5, 6.

Sect. 5. Also it is said, That not only he who lays out his Money to assist another in his Cause, but also that he who by his Friendship or Interest

tereſt ſaves him that Expence which he might otherwiſe be put to, or but endeavours ſo to do, is alſo guilty of Maintenance; as where [a] one perſwades, or but endeavours to perſwade a Man to be of Counſel for another *gratis.*

[a] 28 H. 6. 7. b. 12. b. 34 H. 6. 25. b. 9 E. 3. 32. a. Bro. Maintenance, 6, 7, 20.

Sect. 6. Alſo it is ſaid, That all ſuch Perſons may properly be called Maintainers, who give or but endeavour to give any other Kind of Aſſiſtance to either of the Parties, in the Management of the Suit depending between them; as by [b] opening the Evidence to the Jury; or by [c] giving Evidence officiouſly without being called upon to do it; or by ſpeaking in the Cauſe as [d] one of Counſel with the Party; or by [e] retaining an Attorney for him; or [f] perhaps for barely going along with him to enquire for a Perſon learned in the Law.

[b] 22 H. 6. 5. b. Bro. Maintenance, 14. Cro. El. 735. [c] 28 H. 6. 6. a. 11 H. 6. 41. b. Bro. Maintenance, 5, 51. Fitz. Maintenance, 10. 2 Rol. Abr. Pl. 118. Pl. 7, 8. [d] Hetley 78, 79. [e] 1 Rol. Ab. 593. Pl. 11. [f] 19 E. 4. 3. b. 12 E. 4. 14. b. Hetl. 79.

Sect. 7. Alſo it hath been ſaid, That thoſe ſhall come under the like Notion, who give any publick Countenance to another in Relation to any ſuch Suit; as where one of great Power and Intereſt ſays [g] publickly, That he will ſpend twenty Pounds on one Side, or that he will give twenty Pounds to labour the Jury, whether in Truth he ſpend one Penny or not; or where ſuch a Perſon [h] comes to the Bar with one of the Parties, and ſtands by him while his Cauſe is tried, whether he ſay any Thing or not; for ſuch Kinds of Practices do not only tend to diſcourage the other Party from going on in his Cauſe, but alſo to intimidate Juries from doing their Duty. But it ſeems, That a bare [i] Promiſe to maintain another, is not in it ſelf Maintenance, unleſs it be either in reſpect of the publick Manner in which, or the Power of the Perſon by whom, it is made.

[g] 22 H. 6. 5. b. Bro. Maintenance, 14. Fitz. Maintenance, 8. [h] 22 H. 6. 6. b. 11 H. 6. 39. b. 19 E. 4. 3. b. Bro. Maintenance, 51. [i] 9 H. 7. 18. b. Bro. Champerty, 9.

Sect. 8. Alſo it is ſaid to be as much Maintenance for a [k] Juror, as for any other Perſon, to ſollicit a Judge to give Judgment according to the Verdict, becauſe after a Juror has given his Verdict, he has nothing more to do: But it is ſaid to be no [k] Maintenance for a Juror to exhort his Companions to join with him in giving ſuch a Verdict as ſeems to him to be right.

[k] Bro. Maintenance 40. 18 E. 4. 1. Pl. 6. 2. Pl. 8. 17 E. 4. 5. b. Bro. Maintenance, 39.

Sect. 9. However it ſeems clear, [l] That a Man is in no Danger of being judged guilty of an Act of Maintenance, for giving another friendly Advice, what Action is proper for him to bring for the Recovery of a certain Debt, or what Method is ſafeſt to take to free him from ſuch an Arreſt, or what Counſellor or Attorney is likely to do his Buſineſs moſt effectually; for it would be extreamly hard to make ſuch neighbourly Acts of Kindneſs, which ſeem rather commendable than blame-worthy, to come under the Notion of Maintenance, which always ſeems to imply a contentious, and over-buſy intermeddling in other Mens Matters, in which reſpect it is ſo highly Criminal. Yet it is ſaid, that a Man of great Power not learned in the Law, may be guilty of Maintenance, by telling another who aſks his Advice, that he has a good Title.

[l] 12 E. 4. 14. b. 19 E. 4. 3. b. 22 H. 6. 35. a. Bro. Maintenance, 17. 3 Rol. Ab. 118. Pl. 2.

Fitz. Maintenance, 21.

Sect. 10. Alſo it hath been ſaid, That no one can be guilty of Maintenance, in reſpect of any Money given by him to another before any Suit is actually commenced; yet if it plainly appear, That it was given merely with a Deſign to aſſiſt him in the Proſecution or Defence of an intended Suit, which afterwards is actually brought; ſurely it cannot but be as great a Miſdemeanor in the Nature of the Thing, and equally criminal at Common Law, as if the Money were given after the Commencement of the Suit, though perhaps it may not in Strictneſs come under the Notion of Maintenance.

3 H. 6. 54. a. Fitz. Maintenance, 18. Bro. Maintenance, 1.

Sect. 11. However it is certain, That one may as properly be ſaid to be guilty of Maintenance, within the Meaning of the Words *adhuc manutenet,*

47 Ed. 3. 10. a. Bro. Champerty, 2.

nutenet, in an Action of Maintenance, for supporting another after Judgment, as for doing it hanging the Plea; because the Party grieved may be discouraged thereby from bringing a Writ of Error or Attaint.

As to the second Point, *viz.* In what Respects some Acts of this Kind may be justified, I shall consider the following Particulars:

1. How far they are justifiable in Respect of an Interest in the Thing in Variance.
2. How far in Respect of Kindred or Affinity.
3. How far in Respect of other Relations.
4. How far in Respect of Charity.
5. How far in Respect of the Profession of the Law.

Sect. 12. As to the first of these Particulars, *viz.* How far some Acts of this Kind are justifiable in Respect of an Interest in the Thing in Variance, it seemeth to be clearly agreed, That if a [a] Tenant in Tail, or for Life, be impleaded, he in Remainder or Reversion may lawfully maintain the Defence of the Suit with his own Money: And upon the like Ground it seems to be clear, That if in an Action of Trespass, &c. brought by or against a [b] Lessee for Years, the Inheritance come into Question, the Lessor may lawfully maintain his Lessee, and give [c] Evidence to prove the Inheritance in himself; for though the Judgment which may be given against the Lessee cannot directly bind his Inheritance, yet the Verdict may be a Prejudice to his Title, being given on a Supposal of his not having a good one: Also it hath been [d] admitted as clear Law, That if one seized in Fee of certain Land, bring an Action of Trespass, *quare Clausum fregit*, and then alien the Land, and afterwards in the Trial of the Cause it be questioned whether the Inheritance at the Time of the supposed Trespass belonged to the Plaintiff or Defendant, the Alienee may lawfully produce Evidence to prove that the Inheritance was in the Plaintiff, because the Plaintiff's Title is now become his own.

[a] 19 E. 4. 3. b. 9 H. 6. 64. Bro. Maintenance, 3, 53. 2 Rol. A. 117. O. 2.
[b] 6 E. 4. 2. b. 2 Rol. Ab. 117. O. 3. Bro. Maintenance, 33.
[c] 39 H. 6. 20. a. Bro. Maintenance, 28.
[d] 14 H. 6. 7. b. Bro. Maintenance, 23. 2 Rol. Ab. 117. O. 4.

Sect. 13. Also it hath been said, that not only those who have a certain Interest, but also that those who have a bare Contingency of such an Interest in the Lands in Question, which possibly may never come *in esse*, may in like manner lawfully maintain another in an Action concerning such Lands; from whence it follows, That if I grant to *B.* that if my Lessee for Life shall die during my Life, that then he shall have the Land for ten Years, and after my Lessee be impleaded, *B.* may maintain him.

9 H. 6. 64. A. B. 2 Rol. Ab. 117. O. 5.

Sect. 14. And it hath been said, That not only those who have a Contingency of such an Interest, which it is in no Man's Power to bar them of, if the Contingency happen, may justify such Maintenance, but that those also shall have the same Privilege, who by the Act of God, have the immediate Possibility of such an Interest, though it be in the Power of another to deprive them of it; and therefore that an Heir Apparent, or the Husband of such an Heir, may lawfully maintain the Ancestor in an Action concerning the Inheritance of the Land whereof he is seised in Fee.

14 H. 7. 2. a. 19 Ed. 4. 3. b. 21 H. 6. 16. b. 2 Inst. 564. 2 Rol. A. 115. H, I.

Sect. 15. But it is said, That the Grantee of a Reversion, before the late Statute for Amendment of the Law which made all Attornment needless, could not maintain the Tenant of the Land without Attornment, because his Possibility was wholly created by the Act of the Party, and could not be executed but by the voluntary Attornment of the Tenant, which there was no Remedy to compel him to make by the Common Law; but perhaps the Authority of this Opinion may be questionable, especially if such Grant were made for good Consideration: For since those who have only an equitable Interest in Lands, may lawfully main-

9 H. 6. 64. a. 2 Rol. Ab. 117. Pl. 7.

tain

tain others in Actions relating to those Lands, as shall more fully be shewn in the seventeenth Section; and since the Grantor in Equity shall stand in-
34 H. 6. 30. b. trusted for the Grantee after the Grant, and the Tenant may be enforced by a Court of Equity to attorn to him, I do not see any good Reason why such Grantee should be esteemed such a Stranger to the Land, that he may not lawfully defend an Action concerning it, in the Event whereof he is so nearly concerned.

11 H. 6. 41. Bro. Maintenance, 51. 2 Rol. Ab. 118. Pl. 8.

Sect. 16. But it seems clear, That he who is bound to warrant Lands, may lawfully maintain the Tenant in the Defence of his Title, because he is bound by the Warranty to render other Lands to the Value of those which shall be evicted.

[a] 34 H. 6. 30. b. 15 H. 7. 2. a. 2 E. 4. 2. a. Bro. Maintenance, 19, 30. [b] Noy 100. Moore 620. Pl. 847. See 39 H. 6. 19. b. 20. a. Fitz. Maintenance, 14. [c] 34 H. 6. 30. b. 15 H. 7. 2. a. Noy 52. Cro. El. 552. 1 Sid. 217. Bro. Maintenance, 19.

Sect. 17. Also it seems to be agreed, That he who hath an equitable Interest in Lands or Goods, or even in a Chose in Action, may lawfully maintain another in an Action relating thereto; and therefore it seemeth to be clear, That a Man may lawfully [a] maintain those who are infeoffed of Lands in Trust for him, in any Action concerning those Lands, and that if he sell them to another, the Vendee shall have the same Privilege; also it hath been [b] resolved, That where *A.* was bound as a Surety for *B.* and *B.* thereupon made a Deed of Gift of certain Sheep to *A.* in order to save him harmless from the said Bond, with an implied Trust that the Sheep should be returned to *B.* if *A.* should not be damnified, and afterwards an Action was brought against *A.* for the Taking of the Sheep, *B.* might justify the Maintaining of him in respect of the said Trust: Also it seemeth to be [c] certain, That the Assignee of a Bond, or other Chose in Action, being made over to him for good Consideration, in Satisfaction of a precedent Debt due *bonâ fide* to him, and not merely in Consideration of the intended Maintenance, may either maintain the Obligee in an Action brought by him for the Debt, or commence an original Action in his Name, for he hath an equitable Interest in the Debt.

[d] 18 Ed. 4. 2. b. Bro. Maintenance, 41. Hob. 92. 2 Rol. Ab. 118. Pl. 8. Noy 99. Moore 562. Pl. 764, 788. Pl. 1088. 1 Rol. Re. 57.

Sect. 18. Also it seemeth to be [d] agreed, That where-ever any Persons claim a common Interest in the same Thing, as in a Way, Church-yard, or Common, *&c.* by the same Title, they may maintain one another in a Suit relating to the same.

[e] 34 H. 6. 26. a. 14 H. 6. 6. b. 18 Ed. 4. 12. b.

Sect. 19. It is said, That he who is [e] Bail for another, may take Care to have his Appearance recorded, but that he ought not to intermeddle any farther.

[f] 20 H. 6. 1. 6 Ed. 4. 5. b. 14 H. 7. 2. a. [g] 6 Ed. 4. 5. b. Fitz. Maintenance, 16. [h] 21 H. 6. 15. b. 11 H. 6. 41. b. 42. a. 12 H. 6. 2. Pl. 7. 19 Ed. 4. 3. b. 9 H. 6. 64. a. 9 Ed. 4. 32. a. [i] 19 Ed. 4. 5. a. 2 Inst. 564. 6 Ed. 4. 5. [k] 21 H. 6. 16. b. 2 Inst. 564.

Sect. 20. As to the second of the said Particulars, *viz.* How far some Acts of this Kind are justifiable in respect of Kindred or Affinity, it seems to be agreed, That whoever is any way of Kin or Affinity to either of the Parties, so long as the same [f] continues, or but related to him by being his [g] Godfather, may lawfully [h] stand by him at the Bar, and counsel and assist him, and also pray another to be of Counsel to him, but that he cannot justify the laying out of any of his own [i] Money in the Cause, unless he be either [k] Father, or Son, or Heir Apparent to the Party, or the Husband of such an Heiress.

Vide supra Sect. 14.

As to the third of the said Particulars, *viz.* How far some Acts of Maintenance are justifiable in respect of other Relations, I shall consider,

1. How far a Lord may maintain his Tenant.
2. How far a Tenant may maintain his Lord.
3. How far a Master may maintain his Servant.
4. How far a Servant may maintain his Master.
5. How far one Neighbour may maintain another.

Sect. 21. As to the first Point it seems certain, That not only the [a] Lord, but also the *Cestui que Use* of a Seigniory, may come with the Tenant to a Trial in an Assize against him, and stand by him and assist him, and also pray the Sheriff to return an indifferent Jury: Also it seemeth, That the [b] Lord of a Town in an Action brought against the Inhabitants, wherein a Right to a common Burying-place, claimed by them, is brought into Question, may maintain them in the Defence of their Right, by shewing authentick Evidence thereof to the Jury: And in some [c] Books it is said generally, That the Lord may maintain his Tenant, without saying, how far he may do it; and I do not find it any where expresly holden, That the Lord may justify laying out his own Money in Defence of his Tenant's Title; but it seemeth the better Opinion, That he may as well justify it as any other of the above mentioned Acts of Maintenance; for the Lord, by accepting a Man for his Tenant, seemeth to take him under his immediate [d] Protection; and inasmuch as the Lands were originally derived from the Lord, and he hath the continual Benefit of the Services due from them, the Law in many Cases of [e] Common Right, obliges him to warrant them unto his Tenant, and where it doth not oblige him, surely it will at least permit him to do it: But it [f] seems clear, That he cannot maintain him in respect of any Lands not holden of him.

Sect. 22. As to the second Point, *viz.* How far a Tenant may maintain his Lord, it is said, That he may justify [g] Coming with his Lord, and Standing with him at a Trial; but I cannot find any Thing more relating to this Matter in any of the Books.

Sect. 23. As to the third Point, *viz.* How far a Master may maintain his Servant, it is said, That the Master may go along with his [h] Servant, or with his [i] Chaplain, being retained to live in his House with him, in order to [k] retain Counsel, and that he may pray one to be of Counsel for him, and also that he may go with him to the [l] Trial and stand with him and aid him while the Cause is tried, but ought not to speak in the Court in favour of his Cause. Also it is said, That if my Servant be arrested in an Action of [m] Debt, I may assist him with Money in order to keep him out of Prison, that I may have the Benefit of his Service: But it is said, That the Master, in real Actions, cannot justify Laying out Money for his Servant, unless he hath some of his Wages in his Hand; which, if the Servant be willing, the Master may safely lay out on his Behalf.

Sect. 24. As to the fourth Point, *viz.* How far a Servant may maintain his Master, it seemeth clear, That a Person generally retained by another as his Servant to do all manner of Services, and not for a [n] particular Occasion only, may justify [o] Riding about to speed his Business, and Going to [p] Counsel in his Behalf, and Shewing his Evidences to the Counsel or to the Jury, and [q] Standing by him at a Trial between him and another; but it is certain, that he cannot lawfully lay out any of his own [r] Money to assist the Master in his Suit.

Sect. 25. As to the fifth Point, *viz.* How far one Neighbour may assist another, it seems clear, That a Man may lawfully go with his [s] Neighbour to inquire for a Person learned in Law, but that he [t] ought not to give him any Money towards carrying on his Suit.

Sect. 26. As to the fourth Instance wherein some Acts of this Kind are justifiable, *viz.* That relating to Charity, it seems to be [u] agreed, That any one may lawfully give Money to a poor Man to enable him to carry on his Suit. Also it hath been adjudged, That any one may safely go

[a] 11 H. 6. 39. b. 40. a. 2 Rol. Ab. 117. N. Bro. Maintenance 50.
[b] 18 Ed. 4. 2. b. Bro. Maintenance 41. 2 Rol. Ab. 116. G.
[c] 9 H. 6. 64. a. Bro. Maintenance 3.
[d] Co. Lit. 65. a.
[e] Co. Lit. 101, 384.
11 H. 6. 42. a. 2 Rol. A. 117.
[f] Fitz. Maintenance 25.
[g] 11 H. 6. 42. a. 2 Rol. Ab. 116. K.
[h] Hetley 79.
[i] 19 H. 6. 30. b.
[k] 28 H. 6. 7. b. 12. b. 13. b. 34 H. 6. 25. b. 26. a. b. Bro. Maintenance 6, 14. Fitz. Maintenance 20. Con. Fitz. Maintenance 13.
[l] 19 H. 6. 30. b. 11 H. 6. 42. a. 2 Rol. Ab. 116. K. Hetley 79.
[m] 21 H. 7. 40. b. Moor 814. Bro. Maintenance 24. 31 H. 6. 9. b. 19 Ed. 4. 3. b. 2 Rol. Ab. 116. K. Hetley 79. Bro. Maintenance 44, 52.
[n] 39 H. 6. 5. b. 6. a. Con. Keil. 50. b.
[o] 19 E. 4. 3. b.
[p] 19 H. 6. 31. b.
[q] 11 H. 6. 42. a.
[r] 3 H. 6. 53. b. 54. a. 11 H. 6. 10. b. 11. a.
[s] 19 E. 4. 3. b. 12 Ed. 4. 14. b.
[t] 19 E. 4. 3. b. 2 Rol. A. 118.
[u] 21 H. 6. 16. b. 9 H. 6. 64. a. 22 H. 6. 35. a. Bro. Maintenance 14

[a] 19 E. 4. 3. b. 34 H. 6. 25. b. 15 H. 7. 2. a. Bro. Maintenance 7.

with a [a] Foreigner who cannot ſpeak *Engliſh*, to a Counſellor, and inform him of his Caſe.

As to the fifth Inſtance wherein ſome Acts of this Kind may be juſtified, *viz.* that relating to the Profeſſion of the Law, I ſhall conſider,

1. How far they are juſtifiable in a Counſellor.
2. How far in an Attorney.

[b] 11 H. 6. 10. b. 11. a. 2 Rol. Ab. 116. M. 2 Inſt. 564. [c] Fitz. Maintenance 8. 22 H. 6. 6.

Sect. 27. As to the firſt Point, there is no Doubt but that a [b] Counſellor, having received his Fee, may lawfully ſet forth his Client's Cauſe to the beſt Advantage; but it is certain, That he can no more juſtify [c] giving him Money to maintain his Suit, or threatening a Juror, than any other Perſon.

[d] 13 H. 4. 16. b. Kellway 50. b. Hob. 117. 2 Inſt. 564. 2 Rol. Abr. 116. M. Fitz. Maintenance 21. [e] 3 Mod. 98. Vid. 2 Danv. 487, 12, 13, 14. Winch 52. 1 Jon. 208. Cro. Ca. 159, 194. Con. Cro. El. 425, 459, 760. Moor 366. Pl. 500. 2 Rol. Ab. 114. Pl. 4. 115. Pl. 6. [f] 2 Rol. Ab. 114. Pl. 5. 2 Rol. Ab. 115. Pl. 6. Winch 53. [h] 2 Inſt. 214.

Sect. 28. As to the ſecond Point, there is no Doubt but that an Attorney may [d] lawfully proſecute or defend an Action in the Court wherein he is an allowed Attorney, in the Behalf of any one by whom he ſhall be ſpecially retained, and that he may aſſiſt his Client, by laying out his own Money for him to be repaid again, and alſo may maintain an Action againſt him for the ſame by Virtue of ſuch a Retainer, without any ſpecial Promiſe; and it is ſaid alſo, That Attornies may juſtify ſuch Maintenance in other Courts, wherein they are not [e] allowed Attornies, but that they cannot have an Action for the Money ſo laid out without a ſpecial Promiſe, and that they are more juſtified by a general [f] Retainer to proſecute for another all his Cauſes, than if they were not retained at all; and it is certain that they ought not to carry on a Cauſe for another at their own Expence, with a Promiſe never to expect a Repayment. And it [g] ſeems juſtly queſtionable, whether Sollicitors who are no Attornies, can in any Caſe juſtify the Laying out their Money in another's Suit.

Sect. 29. However it is certain, That no Counſellor or Attorney can juſtify the Uſing any deceitful Practice, in Maintenance of a Client's Cauſe, and that they are liable to be ſeverely puniſhed for all Miſdemeanours of this Kind, not only by the [h] Common Law, but alſo by Statute; for it is enacted by *Weſtminſter* 1. 29. *That if any Serjeant, Pleader, or other, do any manner of Diſceit or Colluſion in the King's Court, or conſent unto it, in Diſceit of the Court, or to beguile the Court of the Party, and thereof be attainted, he ſhall be impriſoned for a Year and a Day, and from thenceforth ſhall not be heard to plead in that Court for any Man. And if he be no Pleader, he ſhall be impriſoned in like manner by the Space of a Year and a Day at the leaſt. And if the Treſpaſs require greater Puniſhment, it ſhall be at the King's Pleaſure.*

In the Conſtruction of this Statute the following Points have been holden,

11 E. 4. 3. b. Bro. Diſceit, 28. 2 Inſt. 215, 216. Dyer 249. Pl 84. 2 Inſt. 215. F. N. B. 98.

Sect. 30. I. That Counſellors, *&c.* who are not ſworn, are as much within the Meaning of it as Serjeants, *&c.* who are ſworn.

Sect. 31. II. That all Fraud and Falſhood, tending to impoſe upon or abuſe the Juſtice of the King's Courts, are within the Purview of it, as in the following Inſtances:

Sect. 32. Firſt, Where an Attorney ſues out an *Habere facias ſeiſinam*, falſly reciting a Recovery in a real Action, where in Truth there was no Recovery at all, and by Colour thereof puts the suppofed Tenant in the Action out of his Freehold.

Sect. 33. Secondly, Where one brings a *Præcipe* againft a poor Man, knowing that he had nothing in the Land, on Purpofe to get the Poffeffion from the true Tenant. 2 Inft. 215.

Sect. 34. Thirdly, Where one procures an Attorney to appear for a Man, and confefs Judgment without any Warrant. 41 E. 3. 1. b. 2 Inft. 215. Dy. 362. Pl. 13.

Sect. 35. Fourthly, Where one pleads a falfe Plea, known to be utterly groundlefs, and invented merely with a Defign to delay Juftice, and abufe the Court; and therefore it is faid, That if a Client defire his Attorney to plead fuch a Plea, the Attorney ought to enter upon the Roll, *Non fum veraciter informatus, ideo nihil dicit.* 10 E. 4. 9. b.

Sect. 36. As to the third general Point of this Chapter, How far Offences of this Kind are reftrained by the Common Law, it feemeth, That all Maintenance is ftrictly prohibited by the Common Law, as having a manifeft Tendency to Oppreffion, by encouraging and affifting Perfons to perfift in Suits, which perhaps they would not venture to go on in upon their own Bottoms; and therefore it is faid, That all Offenders of this Kind are not only liable to an [a] Action of Maintenance at the Suit of the Party grieved, wherein they fhall render fuch Damages as fhall be anfwerable to the Injury done to the Plaintiff, but alfo that they may be [b] indicted as Offenders againft publick Juftice, and adjudged thereupon to fuch Fine and Imprifonment, as fhall be agreeable to the Circumftances of the Offence. Alfo it feemeth, That a Court of Record may commit a Man for an [c] Act of Maintenance done in the Face of the Court. 2 Inft. 208. 212. [a] 11 H. 6. 11. a. 2 Inft. 208. 2 Rol. Ab. 114. D. 8 H. 5. 8. a. [b] 2 Rol. Ab. 114. D. 2 Inft. 208, 212. [c] Hetley 79.

Sect. 37. As to the Fourth general Point of this Chapter, How far Offences of this Kind are punifhed by the Statute, it is enacted by 1 *Ed.* 3. 14. which was farther enforced by 20 *Ed.* 3. 4. *That none of the King's Minifters, nor no Great Man of the Realm, by himfelf nor by other, by fending of Letters, nor otherwife, nor none other great nor fmall, fhall take upon them to maintain Quarrels nor Parts in the Country, to the Let and Difturbance of the Common Law.*

Sect. 38. And it is farther enacted by 1 *R.* 2. 4. *That none of the King's Counfellors, Officers or Servants, nor any other Perfon within the Realm of* England, *of whatfoever Eftate or Condition they be, fhall take or fuftain any Quarrel by Maintenance, in the Country or elfewhere, upon grievous Pain, that is to fay, the faid Counfellors and the King's Great Officers, upon a Pain which fhall be ordained by the King himfelf, by the Advice of the Lords of his Realm; and other lefs Officers and Servants of the King's, as well in the Exchequer, and all his other Courts and Places, as of his own Meiny, upon Pain to lofe their Offices and Services, and to be imprifoned, and then to be ranfomed at the King's Will, every of them according to their Degree, Eftate, and Defert: And all other Perfons through the Realm, upon Pain of Imprifonment, and to be ranfomed as aforefaid.*

In the Conftruction of thefe Statutes the following Points have been holden:

Sect. 39. I. That Maintenance of a Suit in a Court-Baron is as much within the Purview thereof as Maintenance in a Court of Record. Fitz. Maintenance 24. 3 H. 6. 53. b. 54. a.

Sect. 40. II. That *Nul tiel Record* is a good Plea to an Action of Maintenance brought on thefe Statutes; and therefore, That he who barely affifts another in taking out an Original, which never is returned, is not liable to any fuch Action. Bro. Maintenance 1. Fitz. Maintenance 18.

Sect. 41.

Fitz. Maintenance 17, 26. *Sect.* 41. III. That it is not material, whether the Plaintiff in an Action on the ſaid Statutes were nonſuited, or recovered in the Action wherein the Maintenance is ſuppoſed.

Reg. 182. b. *Sect.* 42. Alſo it is certain, That he who fears that another will maintain his Adverſary, may by way of Prevention have an original Writ grounded on the ſaid Statute prohibiting him ſo to do.

Sect. 43. Alſo all Perſons are prohibited to give or receive any Liveries or Badges for Maintenance, under ſevere Penalties, by 1 *R.* 2. 7. 7 *H.* 4. 14. 13 *H.* 4. 3. 8 *H.* 6. 4. and 8 *E.* 4. 2.

Sect. 44. And it is farther enacted by 32 *H.* 8. 9. *That no Perſon whatſoever ſhall unlawfully maintain, or cauſe or procure any unlawful Maintenance, in any Action, Demand, Suit, or Complaint in any of the King's Courts of the Chancery,* Whitehall, *or elſewhere, where any Perſon ſhall have Authority by Virtue of the King's Commiſſion, Patent or Writ, to hold Plea of Lands, or to examine, hear or determine any Title of Lands, or any Matter of Witneſſes, concerning the Title, Right, or Intereſt of any Lands, Tenements, or Hereditaments; and alſo that no Perſon whatſoever do unlawfully retain, for Maintenance of any Suit or Plea, any Perſon or Perſons, or embrace any Freeholders or Jurors, or ſuborn any Witneſs by Letters, Rewards, Promiſes, or any other ſiniſter Labour or Means, for to maintain any Matter or Cauſe, or to the Diſturbance or Hindrance of Juſtice, or to the Procurement, by Occaſion of any manner of Perjury by falſe Verdict or otherwiſe, in any manner of Courts aforeſaid, upon Pain to forfeit for every ſuch Offence ten Pounds, the one Moiety thereof unto the King, and the other Moiety to him that will ſue for the ſame by Action of Debt,* &c.

Sect. 45. It ſeemeth that in an Information on this Statute it is not
Savil 41, 42. ſufficient to ſay, That the Defendant maintained the Party without adding that he did it unlawfully.

Noy 68. Cro. E. 594. *Sect.* 46. Alſo it is ſaid to have been adjudged, That Maintenance of a Suit in a Spiritual Court, is neither within this nor any of the other above mentioned Statutes concerning Maintenance.

Savil 41, 42. *Sect.* 47. Alſo it hath been holden, That in an Information on this Statute, it is neceſſary to ſhew that a Plea was depending, and therefore that it is not ſufficient to ſay that a Bill ways exhibited.

CHAP. LXXXIV.

Of Champerty.

2 Inſt. 208. Co.Lit.368.b. *Sect.* 1. AND now we are come to the ſecond Species of Maintenance, called Champerty, which is the unlawful Maintenance of a Suit in Conſideration of ſome Bargain to have Part of the Thing in Diſpute, or ſome Profit out of it.

Sect. 2. Having ſhewn in the precedent Chapter what ſhall amount to an Act of Maintenance, and how far all Maintenance in general, and conſequently Champerty, is puniſhable by the Common Law; I ſhall only take Notice in this Place, how far this Offence in particular is reſtrained by Statute, and to that End ſhall ſet down in Order the ſeveral Statutes relating to it, and ſhew in what Manner they have been expounded.

Sect. 3. And first, it is enacted by the Statute of *Westminster* 1. 25. *That no Officers of the King by themselves nor by other, shall maintain Pleas, Suits, or Matters hanging in the King's Courts, for Lands, Tenements, or other Things, for to have Part or Profit thereof by Covenant made between them; and he that doth, shall be punished at the King's Pleasure.*

In the Construction of this Statute the following Opinions have been holden:

Sect. 4. I. That by the King's Courts therein mentioned, are intended only his Courts of Record. 2 Inst. 208.

Sect. 5. II. That under the Word Covenant, which in a strict Sense signifieth only an Agreement by Deed, all Kinds of Promises and Contracts of this Kind are included, whether they be made by Writing or Parol. F.N.B. 172 L. 2 Inst. 209, 563.

Sect. 6. III. That Maintenance in personal Actions to have Part of the Debt or Damages, is as much within this Statute as Maintenance in real Actions for a Part of the Land. 47 Ass. Pl. 5. 47 Ed. 3. 9. b.

Sect. 7. IV. That Maintenance in Consideration of a Rent granted out of Land in Variance, is within this Statute, but that Rent granted out of other Lands is no way within the Purview of it. F. N. B. 172. K, M. 2 Inst. 209. 47 Ed. 3. 9. b. 47 Ass. 5.

Sect. 8. V. That it hath been holden not to be material, whether he who brings a Writ of Champerty, did in Truth suffer any Damage by it, or whether the Plea wherein it is alledged be determined or not. Con. 9 H. 7. 18. b. Fitz. Champerty, 4.

Sect. 9. VI. That the [a] Maintenance of the Tenant or Defendant is as much within the Meaning of the Statute, as the Maintenance of a Demandant or Plaintiff. Bro. Champerty, 2. [a] 21 E. 3. 52. a. 30 Ed. 3. 3. b. 4. a.

Sect. 10. VII. That [b] such Grants only of Part of the Thing in Suit, which are made merely in Consideration of the Maintenance are within the Meaning of the Statute, and not such as are made in Consideration of a precedent honest Debt, which is agreed to be satisfied with the Thing in Demand when recovered. 2 Rol. Ab. 113. Pl. 3. [b] 15 H. 7. 2. a. Bro. Champerty, 6.

Sect. 11. And it is farther enacted by the Statute of *Westminster*, 2. 49. *That the Chancellor, Treasurer, Justices, nor any of the King's Counsel, no Clerk of the Chancery, nor of the Exchequer, nor any Justice or other Officer, nor any of the King's House, Clerk nor Lay, shall not receive any Church, nor Advowson of a Church, Land, nor Tenement in Fee, by Gift, or by Purchase, or to Farm, nor by Champerty, nor otherwise, so long as the Thing is in Plea before the King, or before any of his Officers, nor shall take no Reward thereof. And that he that doth contrary to this Act, either himself or by another, or make any Bargain, shall be punished at the King's Pleasure, as well he that purchaseth as he that doth sell.*

In the Construction of this Statute the following Opinions have been holden:

Sect. 12. I. That it extendeth only to the Officers therein named, and not to any other Persons. 2 Inst. 484, 485.

Sect. 13. II. That it so strictly restrains all such Officers from purchasing any Land hanging a Plea, that they cannot be excused by a Consideration of [c] Kindred or Affinity, and that they are within the Meaning of the Statute by barely making such a Purchase, whether [d] they maintain the Party in his Suit or not, [e] whereas such a Purchase for good Consideration, made by any other Person, of any Ter-tenant, is no Offence, unless it appear that he did it to maintain the Party. [c] 2 Inst. 485. [d] 2 Inst. 484. 50 Ass. Pl. 3. Bro. Champerty, 8. Fitz. Champerty, 6. [e] 22 E. 3. 10. b. 52. a. 2 Inst. 484. F. N. B. 172. D, E.

Sect. 14. And it is farther enacted by 28 *E.* 1. 11. in the following Words, *because the King hath heretofore ordained by Statute, That none of his Ministers shall take no Plea for Maintenance, by which Statute other Officers were not bounden before this Time, the King will that no Officer, nor any other, (for to have Part of the Thing in Plea) shall not take upon him the Business that is in Suit; nor none upon any such Covenant shall give up his Right to another; and if any do and be attainted thereof, the Taker shall forfeit unto the King so much of his Lands and Goods, as doth amount to the Value of the Part that he hath purchased for such Maintenance. And to obtain this, whosoever will, shall be received to sue for the King before the Justices before whom the Plea hangeth, and the Judgment shall be given by them. But it may not be understood hereby, that any Person shall be prohibited to have Counsel of Pleaders, or of learned Men in Law, for his Fee, or of his Parents and next Friends.*

In the Construction of this Statute the following Points have been holden:

Sect. 15. I. That a [a] Conveyance executed, hanging a Plea, in Pursuance of a Bargain made before, is not within the Meaning of it.

Sect. 16. II. That Champerty in any Action at [b] Common Law, whether it be real, personal, or mixt, is within this Statute: Also it seems the better Opinion, That the Purchase of Land while a Suit of [c] Equity concerning it is depending, is within the Purview of it.

Sect. 17. III. That a [d] Lease for Life, or Years, or a voluntary Gift of Land, hanging a Plea, is as much within the Statute as a Purchase for Money.

Sect. 18. IV. That a Surrender made by a [e] Lessee to his Lessor is not within the Meaning of the Statute; for since the Lessor may lawfully maintain his Lessee without such a Surrender, as hath been more fully shewn in the precedent Chapter, surely *à fortiori*, he may do it after the Surrender.

Sect. 19. V. That no [f] Conveyance, or Promise thereof, relating to Lands in Suit, made by a Father to his Son, or by any Ancestor to his Heir Apparent, is within the Statute, since it only gives them the greater Encouragement to do what by Nature they are bound to do.

Sect. 20. VI. That the [g] Giving of Part of the Land in Suit, after the End of it, to a Counsellor for his Wages, is not within the Meaning of it, if it evidently appears that there was no Kind of precedent Bargain relating to such Gift; but it seems [h] dangerous to meddle with any such Gift, since it cannot but carry with it a strong Presumption of Champerty.

[a] 30 Ass. Pl. 15. 8 Ed. 4. 13. 2 Inst. 563. Fitz. Champerty, 13. F. N. B. 172. D.

[b] 47 Ed. 3. 9. b. 47 Ass. 5. 2 Inst. 563.

[c] Moore 655. Pl. 898. Con. 2 Rol. Ab. 113. Pl. 2.

[d] 8 E. 4. 13. b. Bro. Champerty, 10. F. N. B. 172. C.

[e] F. N. B. 172. E. 2 Inst. 564.

[f] 2 Inst. 564. F. N. B. 172. H.

[g] 13 H. 7. 17. a. Bro. Champerty, 3.

[h] 2 Inst. 564.

4

CHAP.

CHAP. LXXXV.

Of Embracery.

FOR the better Underſtanding of the Nature of Embracery, I ſhall conſider,

1. What Kind of Maintenance comes under the Notion of Embracery.
2. What Acts of this Nature are altogether unlawful.
3. In what Circumſtances ſome Kinds of them may be lawful.
4. How far this Offence is reſtrained by the Common Law.
5. How far by Statute.

Sect. 1. As to the firſt Point it ſeems clear, That [a] any Attempt whatſoever to corrupt, or influence, or inſtruct a Jury, or any way to incline them to be more favourable to the one Side than to the other, by Money, Promiſes, Letters, Threats, or Perſwaſions, except only by the Strength of the Evidence and the Arguments of the Counſel in open Court, at the Trial of the Cauſe, is a proper Act of Embracery, [b] whether the Jurors, on whom ſuch Attempt is made give any Verdict or not, or whether the Verdict given be true or falſe.

Sect. 2. [c] And the Law ſo far abhors all Corruption of this Kind that it prohibits every Thing which has the leaſt Tendency to it, what ſpecious Pretence ſoever it may be covered with, and therefore it will not ſuffer a mere Stranger, ſo much as to labour a Juror to appear and act according to his Conſcience.

Sect. 3. Alſo it is ſaid, That generally the giving of Money to a Juror [d] after the Verdict, without any precedent Contract in Relation to it, is an Offence ſavouring of the Nature of Embracery; becauſe if ſuch Practices were allowable, it would be eaſy to evade the Law, by giving Jurors ſecret Intimations of ſuch an intended Reward for their Service, which might be of as bad Conſequence as the giving of Money before-hand. But it ſeems clear, That the giving of Jurors ſuch a reaſonable Recompence, as is uſually allowed them for their Expences in travelling, *&c.* and which may fairly be expected by them from either Side that ſhall prevail, is no way criminal, becauſe if no ſuch Allowance were to be expected, it would be often difficult to prevail with Perſons to ſerve on a Jury at their own Charge; and therefore by Experience it hath been found neceſſary to permit the Parties to give Jurors ſome Amends for their Charges.

Sect. 4. It hath been adjudged, That the bare [e] Giving of Money to another to be diſtributed among Jurors, is an Offence of the Nature of Embracery, whether any of it be afterwards actually ſo diſtributed or not; alſo it is [f] clear, That it is as Criminal in a Juror, as in any other Perſon, to endeavour to prevail with his Companions to give a Verdict for one Side by any Practices whatſoever, except only by Arguments from the Evidence which was produced, and Exhortations from the general Obligations of Conſcience to give a true Verdict. And there can be no Doubt but

[a] F.N.B. 171. B. C. Co.Lit. 369.a. Moore 815. Pl. 1104.

[b] 21 H.6. 20.a. 22 H.6. 5.b. 37 H.6. 31.a. Bro. Decies tantum, 10, 11, 13. Co.Lit. 369.a. Mo. 815. Pl. 1104.

[c] 13 H.4. 16.b. Moore 806. Cro. El. 816. Co.Lit. 159.b. 369. a.

[d] 39 Aſſ. 19. Bro. Decies, 14.

[e] 22 H.6. 5.b. 28 H.6. 7.b. 12.b. 31 H.6. 8.b. 9. Bro. Maintenance, 6, 14.

[f] 17 Ed. 4. 5.b. 18 Ed. 4. 4.b. Bro. Maintenance, 32, 39.

[a] 1 Saund. 301.

but that all fraudulent Contrivances whatsoever to secure a Verdict, are high Offences of this Nature; as where Persons by [a] indirect Means procure themselves or others, to be sworn on a *Tales* in order to serve one Side.

[b] 13 H. 4. 16. b. 17. a. 11 H. 6. 11. a. 2 Rol. A. 116. L. 6. M. 3. [c] 19 H. 6. 31. b. 13 H. 4. 17. a. [d] 2 Bulst. 25. Noy 102.

Sect. 5. As to the second Point, *viz.* what Acts of this Kind are altogether unlawful, it seems clear, That neither the Party himself, nor his Counsel, nor Attorney, nor any Person whatsoever, can justify any indirect Practices of influencing a Jury, either by giving [b] or promising them Money, or [c] menacing them, or [d] instructing them in the Cause beforehand, &c.

Co. Li. 369. a. Moore 815. Pl. 1104. [e] Dyer 48. Pl. 19. Co. Lit. 157. b. 369. a. Moore 813. Pl. 1101. Hob. 294. Noy 102. [f] Hob. 294.

Sect. 6. As to the third Point, *viz.* In what Circumstances some Acts of this Nature may be lawful, it seemeth clear, That any Person who may justify any other Act of Maintenance, may safely labour a Juror to [e] appear and give a Verdict according to his Conscience, but that no other Person can justify intermeddling so far, and that no one whatsoever can justify the labouring a Juror [f] not to appear.

Sect. 7. As to the fourth Point, *viz.* How far Offences of this Kind are restrained by the Common Law, there can be no Doubt but that they subject the Offender either to an Indictment or Action, in the same Manner as all other Kinds of unlawful Maintenance do by the Common Law: Also it seemeth, That if an Act of Embracery were not known before the Trial of a Cause, so that the Party to whose Prejudice it was intended, had no Opportunity to prevent the ill Effects of it, by challenging the Juror who was practised upon, it will be a good Ground to move the Court to set aside the Verdict.

Sect. 8. As to the fifth Point, *viz.* How far Offences of this Kind are restrained by Statute, it is enacted, by 5 *Ed.* 3. 10. *That if any Juror, in Assizes, Juries, or Inquests, take of the one Party or of the other, and be thereof duly attainted, that hereafter he shall not be put in any Assizes, Juries or Inquests, and nevertheless he shall be commanded to Prison, and further ransomed at the King's Will. And the Justices before whom such Assizes, Juries and Inquests shall pass, shall have Power to enquire and determine according to this Statute.*

Sect. 9. And it is farther enacted by 34 *Ed.* 3. 8. *That in every Plea, whereof the Inquest or Assize doth pass, if any of the Parties will sue against any of the Jurors, that they have taken of his Adversary or of him, for to give their Verdict, he shall be heard, and shall have his Plaint by Bill presently before the Justices, before whom they did swear, and that the Juror be put to answer without any Delay; and if they plead to the Country, the Inquest shall be taken* maintenant. *And if any Man other than the Party will sue for the King against the Juror, it shall be heard and determined as afore is said. And if the Juror be attainted at the Suit of other than the Party, and maketh Fine, the Party that sueth shall have Half the Fine; and that the Parties to the Plea shall recover their Damages by the Assessment of the Inquest. And that the Juror so attainted have the Prison of one Year, which Imprisonment the King granteth, that it shall not be pardoned for any Fine; and if the Party will sue by Writ, before other Justices, he shall have the Suit in the Form aforesaid.*

Sect. 10. And it is farther enacted by 38 *Ed.* 3. 12. *That if any Jurors in Assizes sworn, and other Inquests to be taken between the King and Party, or Party and Party, do any Thing take by them, or other of the Party, Plaintiff, or Defendant to give their Verdict, and thereof be attainted by Process contained in the said Statute of* 34 E. 3. *be it at the Suit of the Party that will sue for himself, or for the King, or any other Person, every of the said Jurors shall pay ten Times as much as he hath taken. And that he that will sue, ſhall have the one half, and the King the other half. And that all the Embraceors to bring or procure ſuch Inqueſt in the Country to take Gain or Profit ſhall be puniſhed in the ſame Manner and Form as the Jurors. And if the Juror or Embraceor ſo attainted, have not whereof to make Gree in the Manner aforeſaid, he ſhall have the Impriſonment of one Year: And the Intent of the King, of Great Men, and of the Commons is, That no Juſtice nor other Miniſter ſhall enquire of Office, upon any of the Points of this Article, but only at the Suit of the Party, or of other, as afore is ſaid.*

In the Conſtruction of theſe Statutes the following Points have been holden:

Sect. 11. I. That all Actions of *Decies tantum* being founded on an Offence ſuppoſed to have been committed in ſome former Action appearing upon Record, it will be a good Plea in Bar, either that there is no [a] ſuch Record at all, or that there is not any ſuch [b] Record by which it may appear that the Juror was ſworn, and that it is a good [c] Exception in Abatement of the Writ, that there is a Variance in the firſt Record from that in the Declaration in the preſent Action; yet it is ſaid, That it is not neceſſary to [d] ſhew the whole Record in certain, but only ſo much of it as conveys the Plaintiff to his Action. [a] 5 Ed. 4. 3. a. Bro. Decies tantum, 2, 11. [b] 37 H. 6. 31. a. Bro. Decies tantum, 13. [c] 9 H. 6. 1. Bro. Decies tantum, 1. [d] 34 H. 6. 4. b.

Sect. 12. II. That it is not [e] ſufficient to ſhew that the Defendants took Money in order to embrace a Jury, without ſhewing alſo that they actually diſpoſed of it accordingly. [e] 37 H. 6. 31. a. F. N. B. 171. C.

Sect. 13. III. That the [f] Plaintiff muſt ſhew in certain how much was received, or otherwiſe the Court will not know for what Sum to give Judgment. [f] Pl. Com. 85.

Sect. 14. IV. That the giving of Money to a Juror [g] after the Verdict is not within the Statute, unleſs there were ſome precedent Contract relating to it. [g] 39 Aſſ. 19. Bro. Decies tantum, 14.

Sect. 15. V. That it is not [h] material whether the Jurors gave any Verdict or not, or if they did give one, whether it were true or falſe. [h] 21 H. 6. 31. a. 37 H. 6. 31. a. Bro. Decies tantum, 10, 13. F. N. B. 171. C. B.

Sect. 16. VI. That all the Jurors and Embraceors may be joined in one Action, notwithſtanding they ſeverally received different Sums, becauſe all was received in order to give the ſame Verdict, which could not but be the entire Act of all the Jurors. But it ſeems, That each Defendant ought to plead ſeverally, that he did not take Money in the Manner as the Plaintiff hath declared. Co. Lit. 369. a. Dy. 95. Pl. 39. 40 Ed. 3. 3. b. 36 H. 6. 28. b. Bro. Decies tantum, 3, 4. F. N. B. 171. a. Finch 255. 21 H. 6. 20.

Sect. 17. VII. That the [i] Defendants ought not to plead generally, Not guilty, but that they ought ſpecially to deny the Taking of the Money, *&c.* [i] Bro. Decies tantum, 1. 18 Savil. 42.

Sect. 18. VIII. [k] That the Plaintiff ſhall be paid the Moiety of the Money due to him on a Judgment in *Decies tantum* before the King, becauſe the King's Moiety is not due as a Debt but as a Fine; and wherever the King is intitled to a Fine from the Suit of a Subject, the Plaintiff ſhall firſt be ſatisfied. [k] 41 E. 3. 15. a. 44 E. 3. 36. b. Bro. Decies tantum, 5, 7.

Sect. 19. IX. That the Husband [l] alone may bring a *Decies tantum* for an Embracry in a former Action brought by him and his Wife, becauſe by a *Decies tantum* Money only is to be recovered wherein the Wife can claim no Share. [l] 7 H. 4. 2. b. 3. a. 43 E. 3. 16. a. Bro. Decies tantum, 9. 19.

Sect. 20. X. That he who buys Land to maintain a Suit at a lower Price than it is known to be worth, is as much within the Statute, for ſo much as the [m] Land is worth more than he gave, as if he had received it in Money. [m] 41 Ed. 3. 9. b. Bro. Decies tantum, 4. 1 Rol. Ab. 579. A.

[a] 5 E. 4. 2. b. 3. a. B. 2. Ch. 26 S. 64. Bro. Decies tantum, 15. Cro. El. 138, 583. 11 Co. 65. b. 3 Inst. 194. *Sect.* 21. XI. That this being a popular Action may be barred by the [a] King's Release, being made before any Action brought, but that it cannot be barred by the Release of the Party grieved; and from the same Ground also it follows, that the Party grieved needs not in such Action declare of any Damages done to him by the Embracery; but if he do, it is said, That he [b] ought to lay them severally against each Defendant, or else that his Writ shall abate, unless he will release them: But perhaps there may be good Reason to question this Opinion, for why may not the Damages be as well recovered, as the Action jointly laid against all the Defendants?

[b] 44 E. 3. 36. b. Bro. Decies tantum, 7.

[c] 44 E. 3. 12. a. 47 E. 3. 4. a. Bro. Decies, 6, 8. *Sect.* 22. XII. That no [c] Process of Outlawry lies in this Action, but only a *Capias* or Distress infinite, upon a *Nihil* returned, and that such Distress ought to be of the Lands which the Defendants had at the Time of the Writ of *Decies tantum* purchased, and not of those which they had at the Time of the Inquest; and that no *Capias* [d] into a foreign County lies against the Jurors, because it shall be presumed that they are in the County wherein they were returned on the Jury; but clearly this Reason can no way be extended to the Embraceors: And perhaps it may be over favourable to carry it so far in Relation to the Jurors, especially since the Distress infinite can only affect the Lands which they had at the Time of the *Decies tantum*, before which they may possibly have sold those which they had at the Return of the *Venire*; and why should not the Sheriff's present Return that the Defendants have nothing in the County, over-ballance the Presumption chiefly grounded on the former Return, with which the present is not inconsistent, being made at a subsequent Time.

[d] 47 E. 3. 4. a.

Vide 6 E. 4. 11. a. b. 2 Rol. Ab. 277. B.

CHAP. LXXXVI.

Of the Offence of buying or selling a pretended Title.

FOR the better understanding the Offence of buying or selling a pretended Title, I shall consider:

1. How it is restrained by Common Law.
2. How by Statute.

Moore 751. Pl. 1031. Hob. 115. Pl. Com. 80. a. 88. a. *Sect.* 1. As to the first Point, it seemeth to be a High Offence at Common Law to buy or sell any doubtful Title to Lands known to be disputed, to the Intent that the Buyer may carry on the Suit, which the Seller doth not think it worth his while to do, and on that Consideration sells his Pretensions at an Under-Rate; and it seemeth not to be material, whether the Title so sold be a good or bad one, or whether the Seller were in Possession or not, unless his Possession were lawful and uncontested; for all Practices of this Kind are by all Means to be discountenanced, as manifestly tending to Oppression, by giving Opportunities to Great Men to purchase the disputed Titles of others, to the great Grievance of the adverse Parties, who may often be unable or discouraged to defend their Titles against such powerful Persons, which perhaps they might safely enough maintain against their proper Adversary.

Sect. 2. As to the second Point, *viz.* How far Offences of this Kind are restrained by Statute, it is recited by 1 *R.* 2. 9. *That many Persons having true Title to Lands, and also in Personal Actions were wrongfully delayed of their Rights and Actions, by Means that the Defendants did commonly make Gifts and Feoffments of their Lands in Debate, and of their Goods, to Lords, and other Great Men, against whom the said Pursuants for Menace that was made to them, neither could nor durst make their Pursuits: And also that many Persons often times used to disseise others, and anon after such Disseisin to make divers Feoffments, sometimes to Lords and other Great Men, to have Maintenance, and sometimes to Persons unknown, to the Intent to delay the said Disseisees,* &c. And it is thereupon enacted, *That from thenceforth no Gift, or Feoffment, of Lands, Tenements or Goods, be made, by such Fraud or Maintenance; and that if any be in such wise made, they shall be holden for none and of no Value; and that the said Disseisees shall from thenceforth have their Recovery against the first Disseisor, as well of the Lands and Tenements, as of their double Damages, without having Regard to such Alienations, so that the Disseisees commence their Suits within the Year next after the Disseisin done.*

In the Construction of the Statute it hath been holden:

Sect. 3. That Feoffments of this Kind are only void in Respect of the Disseisees, but that they are effectual between the Feoffor and Feoffee, *&c.* Bro. Feoffments de terres, 1, 19. Co.Lit.369.a.

Sect. 4. And it is farther enacted by 32 *H.* 8. 9. *That no Person or Persons whatsoever shall bargain, buy, or sell, or by any Ways or Means, obtain, get, or have any pretended Rights or Titles, or take, promise, grant, or covenant to have any Right or Title, of any Person or Persons, in, or to any Manors, Lands, Tenements, or Hereditaments, but if such Person or Persons, which shall so bargain, sell, give, grant, covenant, or promise the same, their Ancestors, or they by whom he or they claim the same, have been in Possession of the same, or of the Reversion or Remainder thereof, or taken the Rents or Profits thereof, by the Space of one whole Year next before the said Bargain, Covenant, Grant, or Promise made, upon Pain that he that shall make any such Bargain, Sale, Promise, Covenant, or Grant, to forfeit the whole Value of the Lands, Tenements or Hereditaments so bargained, sold, promised, covenanted, or granted, contrary to the Form of this Act. And the Buyer or Taker thereof, knowing the same, to forfeit also the Value of the said Lands, Tenements, or Hereditaments so by him bought, or taken as is abovesaid. The one Half of the said Forfeitures to be to the King, and the other Half to the Party that will sue for the same in any of the King's Courts of Record, by Action of Debt, Bill, Plaint, or Information. In which Action, Bill, Plaint, or Information, no Essoin, Protection, Wager of Law, nor Injunction shall be allowed.*

Sect. 5. But it is provided by the said Statute, *That it shall be lawful to any Person, being in lawful Possession, by taking of the yearly Farm, Rents, or Profits, of, or for any Manors, Lands, Tenements, or Hereditaments, to buy, obtain, get, or have by any reasonable Way or Means, the pretensed Right or Title of any other Person or Persons, hereafter to be made to, of, or in such Manors, Lands, Tenements, or Hereditaments, whereof he or they shall so be*

in

in lawful Possession, any Thing in the said Act contained to the contrary notwithstanding.

Sect. 6. And it is farther provided, *That the said Statute shall not extend to charge any Person with any of the above mentioned Penalties, except such Person be sued for the Offence within one Year.*

In the Construction of this Statute the following Opinions have been holden :

Pl.Com.83.b.

Sect. 7. I. That it is not material whether any Suit be depending concerning the Lands contracted for, or not, whereas the Statutes set forth in the precedent Chapters extended only to Contracts concerning Lands which were actually in Suit.

Lit. Rep. 369. B. 2. Ch. 25. S. 101. Pl. Com. 84. Cro. Ca. 233. Dy. 74. Pl. 19, 20. Contr. 1 And. 76.

Sect. 8. II. That in an Action on this Statute, the Plaintiff needs not recite it, because the Judges are bound *ex Officio* to take Notice of it, being of a publick Nature ; but that if he do recite it, he must, at his Peril, take Care to recite it certainly, because it is the Ground of his Action ; and the Court will not aid him by intending that there is another Statute to maintain his Action, different from that whereon he himself hath founded it.

1 Leon. 167. Lit. Rep. 369.

Sect. 9. III. That in such an Action against the Buyer of a pretended Title, it ought expresly to appear, That the Defendant did know that the Seller had not been in Possession the Year before ; and *vicê versâ*, that in such an Action by the Buyer the contrary ought to appear, for otherwise it may be intended, that he was *Particeps Criminis*, and therefore ought not to have any Share of the Penalty.

Dy. 74. Pl. 19, 20. Pl. Com. 80, 81, 87, 88. Cro. Ca. 233.

Sect. 10. IV. That it is not sufficient to shew, That the Seller had not been in Possession, *&c.* a Year before, without expresly averring that he had a pretended Right or Title, because that is the Point of the Action.

[a] Cro.Ca. 233. [b] 4 Co. 26. a. Co.Lit.369.b. Moore 655. Pl. 898. [c] Pl. Com. 80, 81, 87. Dy. 74. Pl. 19, 20, 374. Pl. 17. [d] Co. Lit. 369. a. b. Con. Moore 266. Pl. 414. Dy. 374. Pl. 17. [e] Co. Lit. 369. b.

Sect. 11. V. That it is not [a] sufficient to set forth the Value of the Land at the Time of the Conveyance executed, without shewing the Value at the Time of the Bargain, because the Forfeiture is governed by the latter.

Sect. 12. VI. That a Contract for a [b] customary Right to a Copyhold Estate, or for a Lease for [c] Years, is as much within the Statute as a Contract for the Fee-Simple ; for the Words of the Statute are, *any Right or Title*, and such Contracts are as much within the Mischief intended to be redressed by the Statute as any others can be: But it is [d] said, That a Lease for Years made with an Intent to try the Title in Ejectment, is not within the Meaning of the Statute, because it is in a kind of Course of Law, [e] unless it be made to a powerful Man to sway the Cause.

Pl. Com. 81, 85. Dy. 74. Pl. 19, 20.

Sect. 13. VII. That in an Action for the making such a Lease for Years, it is not necessary precisely to set forth the Commencement and End of it, because the Plaintiff is supposed to be a Stranger to it.

1 Leon. 166. 1 And. 76, 77.

Sect. 14. VIII. That a Lease for Years by one out of Possession being made off the Land, is as much within the Statute as if it had been made upon the Land, though it be wholly void in Law ; for it is a Lease in Reputation, and taken for such among the Vulgar, and tends as much to disquiet the Possession as if it had been effectual in Law.

Sect. 15. IX. That no Conveyance made by one, who hath the uncontested Possession, and undisputed absolute Propriety of Lands, is any Way within the Meaning of the Statute, because it no Way favours of Maintenance, and can be prejudicial to no one; from whence it follows, That a Disseisor obtaining the Release of the Disseisee, or a Mortgagor redeeming his Land, are in no Danger of the Statute in Respect of any Contract by them made, concerning such Land after such Release or Redemption. Bro. Maintenance 38. Pl. Com. 88, 89. Co. Lit. 369. a.

Sect. 16. X. That one, who gains the Possession of Lands, by Virtue of a Judgment at Law in Affirmance of an ancient Title, cannot come within the Meaning of this Statute in Respect of any Lease made of such Lands; for it can never be imagined, That it was the Intent of the Statute to oblige all Persons who should recover their Lands, to occupy them themselves, which would be generally inconvenient, and often wholly impracticable; and therefore it must be admitted from the Necessity of the Case, That such Persons may lawfully lease their Lands and Houses to proper Tenants, to be manured and occupied for the usual Rents: But if it shall appear, That the Title to such Lands is still contested notwithstanding such Recovery, and that such Lease was in Truth designed for the Maintenance of the Title, I can see no Reason why it should not be as much within the Statute as any Case whatsoever. However there seems to be no Doubt, but that if a Disseissee enter upon a Disseisor, being in Possession of the Land under a pretended Title, and immediately sell it to a Stranger, he is as much within the Statute as if he had been out of Possession at the Time of such Sale; for notwithstanding his Entry was lawful, and he had both the absolute Property and Possession of the Land, yet inasmuch as the Disseisor claims a Title to it, which is yet in Dispute, such a Sale by the Disseisee seems within the Intent of the Statute, which meant absolutely to restrain all Persons from transferring their disputed Titles to any Stranger whatsoever. But it is said, that such a Sale by a Father to his Son and Heir Apparent, is excepted out of the general Purview of the Statute, by common Reason, which by the Ties of Nature as well as of Interest, obliges such a Son to maintain his Father; yet it hath been holden that such a Sale to a Brother of the half Blood is within the Statute. Pl. Com. 88, 89. Moor 655. Pl. 898. 1 Leon. 166, 167. Co. Lit. 369. a. seems contrary. Savil 95, 96. 1 Leon. 167. Mo. 656. 1 Leon. 167. Savil 95, 96.

Sect. 17. XI. It is said that the above mentioned Proviso, That one, who is in lawful Possession by taking the yearly Rents or Profits of Lands, *&c.* may lawfully buy the pretended Right of any other Person by reasonable Means, is no more than the Law would have implied, if it had not been expressed; for such a Contract cannot possibly be to the Wrong of any one, and tends rather to quiet Suits than to promote them. And from the like Reason also it is said, That a Disseisor may lawfully get the Release of the Disseisee, though his Possession was unlawful; and it seems clear, That such a Release cannot come within the Meaning of the Statute, if the Disseisee had the true Right, and no other had any Pretence of Title to the Land; for in such Case it is clear, That the End of the Release is not for Maintenance, but for the Settlement of all Disputes: But if such a Disseisee had had but a contested Title, and such Release were intended only to enable the Disseisor to defend himself with the dubious Title of his Disseisee, surely it cannot but be as much within the Meaning of the Statute, as any Conveyance to one wholly out of Possession. However it seems clear, That those Co. Lit. 369. b.

Inſtances in the ſaid Proviſo by which it is ſhewn how it ſhall appear, that the Perſons who are permitted to contract for pretended Titles are in Poſſeſſion, as by the receiving of Rent, *&c.* are only put for Examples, and that thoſe, who are any Way whatſoever lawfully ſeized in Poſſeſſion, Reverſion, or Remainder, are within the Benefit of the Proviſo; but it ſeems
Co.Li.369. b. clear, That they can only juſtify the Taking ſuch a Conveyance as will ſtrengthen the Eſtate whereof they are ſeiſed, and that they cannot take a Covenant from a Stranger to convey the Land to them, when he ſhall have recovered it on a pretended Right, becauſe ſuch a Covenant ſeems clearly to ſavour as much of Maintenance, as if they had been Strangers to the Land.

F I N I S.

Notes and Additions to the Firſt Book.

IF a Man be a Lunatick, and this be proved, yet the Law preſumes the acts of ſuch a Perſon to be committed in thoſe Intervals, wherein he has the Uſe of Reaſon, unleſs by Circumſtances it appears they were committed in the time of his Diſtemper; and this holds in Civil Caſes as well as in Criminal. 1 *H. H. P. C.* 34. Page 2. N° [1]

A Man *ſurdus & mutus a Nativitate* is in Preſumption of Law an Ideot, but if it appears that he hath Underſtanding, he may be tried, and ſuffer Judgment and Execution. *Hale, ibid.*

Neither does the King's Command excuſe an unlawful Act. See 1 *H. H. P. C.* 44, and the Authorities in the Notes there, *(b) (d)* Page 3. N° [2]

But by 9 *Geo.* 2. *c.* 5. this Statute of 1 *James* 1. is repealed, and no Proſecution whatſoever is to be carried on againſt any Perſon for Witchcraft, Sorcery, *&c.* but Perſons pretending to Witchcraft, *&c.* or undertaking to tell Fortunes, or pretending from their Skill in any occult or crafty Science, to diſcover ſtolen Goods, ſhall be impriſoned for one Year, and once in every Quarter of the ſaid Year ſtand on the Pillory by the Space of one Hour; and ſhall be obliged to give Sureties for their good Behaviour, in ſuch Sum, and for ſuch Time, as the Court, by which ſuch Judgment ſhall be given, ſhall judge proper. Page 6. N° [3]

Offenders having no Spiritual Promotion, are by 1 *El. c.* 2. *ſect.* 7 and 8. to be impriſoned for one Year for the firſt Offence, and for the ſecond, to be impriſoned for Life. Page 9. N° [4]

But it is provided by the ſaid Act 5 *Geo.* 1. *c.* 4. *ſect.* 2. *That if any Mayor or other Magiſtrate ſhall knowingly and willingly reſort to any publick Meeting for religious Worſhip, other than the Church of* England, *in the peculiar Habit of, or attended with, the Enſigns of his Office, he ſhall be diſabled to hold ſuch Office, and be adjudged incapable of any publick Employment whatſoever, in* England, Wales, Berwick, Jerſey *and* Guernſey. Page 11. N° [5]

By 1 *Geo.* 1. *ſtat.* 2. *c.* 55. Papiſts not taking the Oaths, or not regiſtring their Eſtates, and in the manner mentioned in the Act, ſhall forfeit the Fee ſimple of ſuch Lands, *&c.* two Thirds to the King, and one Third to any Proteſtant ſuing, *&c.* This is enforced by 9 *Geo.* 1. *c.* 24. *ſect.* 5. but by 10 *Geo.* 1. *c.* 4. *ſect.* 1. Women, Reverſioners, Mortgagees, and Truſtees are excepted, and by *ſect.* 10. the Clauſe of the former Acts relating to the Forfeiture of Fee ſimple Lands, *&c.* is repealed, and the Penalty for not taking the Oaths, or not Regiſtring, is reduced to the Forfeiture of the full Value of one Year's Rent of all the Lands, *&c.* not regiſtred, two Thirds to the King, and one Third to the Perſon who ſhall ſue for the ſame. See likewiſe for the Inrollment of Deeds and Wills by Papiſts, 3 *Geo.* 1. *c.* 18. Enlarged by 11 *Geo.* 2. *c.* 11. and amended by 11 *Geo.* 2. *c.* 17. Page 31. N° [6]

But an Alien ſubject to a foreign State at War with ours, living here as an Inhabitant or Trader, whether he ſettled here before the War broke out, or after, if he compaſs the King's Death, may be dealt with as a Traitor; therefore the general Words in *Co. P. C.* 5. where it is ſaid that an *Alien Enemy* cannot be guilty of Treaſon, muſt be taken with the Allay given in *Calvin*'s Caſe, *f.* 6. *b. That he come to invade this Realm, and be taken in War.* The like may be ſaid of ſuch as are ſent over merely as Spies by a foreign Prince in Hoſtility. 1 *H. H. P. C.* 92 to 95. Page 35. N° [7]

The *King's Companion* is his Wife, during the Marriage between them. A Queen divorced from the King *a vinculo Matrimonii*, as for Conſanguinity, *&c.* is not a Queen within this Act, tho' the King be living. This was the Caſe of *Katharine*, *Henry* the Eighth's firſt Queen; as alſo of his ſecond Wife *Anne Bullen*, who was alſo divorced *a vinculo*, and the Divorce was confirmed by 28 *H.* 8. *c.* 7. but tho' the Marriage was declared null *ab initio*, yet there was a Clauſe in the ſaid Act, to pardon all Treaſons committed againſt the Queen or her Daughter *Elizabeth*, the Nullity not being thought a ſufficient Diſcharge. 1 *H. H. P. C.* 124. Page 37. N° [8]

The

Notes and Additions to the Firſt Book.

Page 37. N° [9] *The eldeſt Son and Heir* extends not to a collateral Heir, tho' declared Heir apparent to the Crown, unleſs there be a ſpecial Proviſion for that Purpoſe by Act of Parliament, 1 *H. H. P. C.* 125. where alſo it is made a *Quære*, whether the Compaſſing the Death of Prince *Richard*, after the Death of his Father *Edward* the Black Prince, and during the Life of his Grandfather *Edward* the Third, would have been Treaſon within the Statute 25 *Edw.* 3. for *Richard* was Heir, and the Heirſhip could not be deveſted by any after born Child; and in Page 126, it is ſaid that tho' it may probably be Treaſon within the Intent of this Act, yet it is fitteſt to be firſt decided by Parliament, according to the Caution uſed in the Statute 25 *Edw.* 3.

If the King have two Daughters only, and no Son, the *eldeſt Daughter* is not within the Words, nor Intent, of the King's eldeſt Son, for a Son may be born after; but Statutes have made temporary Proviſions in this Caſe. 1 *H. H. P. C.* 126.

The Clauſe relating to the Violating *the King's eldeſt Daughter unmarried*, extends to a ſecond Daughter, the eldeſt being dead. But at Common Law, this Treaſon extended to any of the Daughters. *Britton*, *c.* 22. § 71. And ſee ſeveral other Caſes and *Quæries* relating to this Clauſe in 1 *H. H. P. C.* 128, 129.

Page 37. N° [10] Riding armed upon a private Quarrel or Deſign againſt a common Perſon, is not Levying War againſt the King, nor would it be high Treaſon, tho' there were really a War levied between two Noblemen, or others, upon a private Quarrel between them, but only a great Riot and Contempt. 1 *H. H. P. C.* 131, 133 to 138, 140, 141, 152, 260.

Page 38. N° [11] In the Clauſe about levying War, the Statute ſays *en ſon Realm*. The Realm of *England* comprehends the narrow Seas; and therefore if a War be levied upon thoſe Seas, as if any Subject invade the King's Ships, this is a Levying War within his Realm, 1 *H. H. P. C.* 154, 325, and is within the 25 *Edw.* 3. but the bare detaining of ſuch Ships, or of the King's Caſtles, ſeems not to be Levying War within this Statute 1 *H. H. P. C.* 146. but was made Treaſon by the 5 and 6 *Edw.* 6. *c.* 11. (ſince repealed.) See 1 *H. H. P. C.* 294, 296.

Page 38. N° [12] *Ireland*, tho' Part of the Dominions of the Crown of *England*, yet is no Part of the Realm of *England*, as was ruled in Time of *Edw.* 1. Yet for Levying War or other Treaſon in *Ireland*, the Offender may be tried in *England*, by 35 *H.* 8. *c.* 2. for Treaſons done out of the Realm. 1 *H. H. P. C.* 155. See *B.* 2. *ch.* 25. *ſect.* 52, 53.

The ſame that is ſaid of *Ireland*, may be ſaid of *Man*, *Jerſey*, *Guernſey*, *Sark* and *Alderney*, which are Parcel of the Dominions of the Crown of *England*, but not within the Realm of *England*; but they have ſpecial Laws of their own, applicable to Criminals, and Juriſdiction for their Trials. 1 *H. H. P. C.* 155, 156, ſee alſo the ſame Author, *p.* 156, 157, 158. concerning *Wales*, which is certainly within the Kingdom of *England*, and therefore not within the Statute 35 *H.* 8. *c.* 2. for Trial of foreign Treaſons.

Page 41. N° [13] According to Sir *Matthew Hale*, in his *Hiſt. Plac. Coron.* Words, unleſs committed to writing, are not regularly an overt Act within the Stat. 25 *Edw.* 3. See *p.* 111, to 118.

Page 42. N° [14] Sir *Matthew Hale's Hiſt. P. C.* 211, 212, makes it a *Quære*, whether the Counterfeiting of Farthings and Half-pence, made current by Proclamation, be not Treaſon within the 25 *Edw.* 3. but he ſeems to incline to the Negative. See alſo 2 *Inſt.* 577.

Page 43. N° [15] But *Hale's Hiſt. P. C.* 229, differs from *Coke*, and ſays, that the Intent only to merchandize or make Payment with ſuch foreign Money ſo imported, is ſufficient to make it Treaſon by this Statute.

Page 46. N° [16] Stat. 9 Geo. 2. c. 30. ſect. 1. *Any Perſon enliſting himſelf, or hiring, or retaining, any Perſon, being a Subject of his Majeſty, with an Intent to cauſe ſuch Perſon to enliſt, or procure any ſuch Perſon to go beyond Sea, in order to ſerve any foreign Prince or State as a Soldier, without Leave firſt obtained under his Majeſty's Sign Manual, ſuch Offender ſhall ſuffer as a Felon, without Benefit of Clergy.*

Sect. 2. *Any Offence againſt this Act committed out of this Realm, may be alledged to be committed, and may be enquired of, and tried in any County in* England.

Page 46. N° [17] *Skin.* 109. cites the Caſe of *Pargiter*, which was tried at the Bar, where an Information was exhibited againſt him, for an Offence at Common Law, for having ſold an Inkhorn mixed with baſe Metal for Sterling. The Court was of Opinion, that the ſelling ſuch Metal, tho' but for a reaſonable Price, was an Offence, and that no ſuch Metal ſhould be made.

In 1 *H. H. P. C.* 48. it is made a *Quære*, whether a Wife can be guilty of Misprision of Treason committed by her Husband. Page 56. N° [18]

See in *Skin.* 637, 638, *The King* and *Cowper*, *&c.* an Information at Common Law preferred against the Defendants, for hiring a Ship to go over to *France*, during the War between *England* and that Kingdom, with an Intent to assist the King's Enemies *in Contempt. Dom. Reg. &c.* The Court held it to be a great Offence at Common Law, bordering upon Treason; and the Defendants were fined accordingly. Page 60. N° [19]

A Man falls from his Horse against a Trunk, whereof he dies, the Horse is forfeit as a Deodand, but not the Trunk, 3 *Edw.* 3. *Fitz. Coron.* 341. but see a strong Authority in 1 *H. H. P. C.* 420, 421, that in this Case, the Horse is not forfeited, unless he throw his Rider. Page 67. N° [20]

The Inquisition may also be before the Commissioners of Gaol-Delivery, *Oyer* and *Terminer*, or of the Peace, if omitted by the Coroner; and hence it is, that neither these Goods, nor the Goods of Felons of themselves, Felons and other outlawed Persons, can be claimed by Prescription, because there must appear a Title to them by Matter of Record, before they are forfeited. 1 *H. H. P. C.* 419. Page 67. N° [21]

Lord *Hale* is of Opinion, that the last Case of this *Sect.* is only Death *per Infortunium*, and that the Opinion of *Dalton*, *c.* 92. is not warranted by the Authorities he cites, 1 *H. H. P. C.* 413, but that if *A.* had struck *B.* with a Knife, intending to kill him, and missing *B.* had struck and killed himself, there he had been *felo de se. Ibid.* Page 68. N° [22]

But Lord *Hale*, *Vol.* 1. *p.* 416, 417, is of Opinion, that an Inquisition taken before the Coroner *super visum corporis*, is traversable. See *B.* 2. *ch.* 9. *sect.* 52. Page 68. N° [23]

1 *H. H. P. C.* 497, 498, seems of the contrary Opinion, and that it is not Felony, but only a great Misprision in the Judges of the Common Pleas, in case of Appeal by Original, or in Justices of the Peace, in case of Indictment of Treason, to give Judgment and award Execution. Page 70. N° [24]

If *A.* not being indicted, but only suspected by *B.* resists or flies upon *B.*'s offering to arrest him, and is killed, if no Felony was committed, or *B.* had no probable Cause of Suspicion, this is at least Manslaughter in *B.* If a Felony had been committed, tho' *A.* be not guilty, yet *B.* having Cause to suspect him, may justify Imprisoning him; but *Quære*, if *B.* should kill *A.* in the Pursuit, whether this will excuse him from Manslaughter. 1 *H. H. P. C.* 490. See also 2 *H. H. P. C.* 83, 119. And in case *B.* be a Constable or Officer, see 2 *H. H. P. C.* 92, 93. If Felony be committed by one, and another arrest him not knowing the Truth, the Law is the same as if he knew it, only he does it at his Peril. 2 *H. H. P. C.* 78. Page 71. N° [25]

A Man killing one who attempts to ravish his Wife or his Daughter, is within the Privilege of *se defendendo*, if it could not otherwise be prevented; but if it might, he is guilty of Manslaughter. 1 *H. H. P. C.* 485, 486. Page 72. N° [26]

If the unlawful Act be only *malum prohibitum*, as by the Stat. 33 *H.* 8. *c.* 6. *No Person, not having Lands*, &c. *of the Yearly Value of one hundred Pounds* per Annum, *may keep a Gun, upon Pain of Forfeiture of ten Pounds*; then supposing a Person not qualified shoots at a Bird, and by Mischance kills the By-stander, by the breaking of the Gun or by some other Accident, this according to Lord *Hale*, amounts only to Chance-medley. 1 *H. H. P. C.* 475, 476. Page 74. N° [27]

Or by imprisoning a Man so strictly that he dies; and therefore where any one dies in Gaol, the Coroner ought to be sent for to inquire after the manner of his Death. 1 *H. H. P. C.* 432. see *B.* 2. *Ch.* 9. *Sect.* 21. Page 78. N° [28]

If he does not know the Beast used to hurt People, he is not to be punished; but if the Beast be *feræ Naturæ*, he is bound at his Peril to keep him up safe. 1 *H. H. P. C.* 430, 431, 617. Page 79. N° [29]

By 2 Geo. 2. c. 21. *If any Person be feloniously Stricken, or Poisoned upon the Sea, or at any Place out of* England, *and dies in* England, *or Stricken or Poisoned in* England, *and dies on the Sea, or out of* England; *in either Case an Indictment found by Jurors of the County in which such Death, Stroke or Poisoning, happened respectively, shall be as effectual at Law, against Principals and Accessaries, and all Courts shall proceed in the same Manner, and Offenders have the same Trial*, &c. (*Challenges for the Hundred excepted*) *as if the Stroke, Poisoning and Death had happened in the County where the Indictment is found.* Page 79. N° [30]

Page 80. N° [31] Lord *Hale, H. P. C.* 433. is of Opinion that the Causing an Abortion by giving a Woman a Potion, or striking her, is not Murder nor Manslaughter, because the Child is not yet *in rerum natura*; nor can it be legally known, whether it were killed or not; and he says it would not be Homicide, tho' such Child were born alive and baptized, and afterwards died of the Stroke given the Mother; for this he cites 1 *Ed.* 3. 23. *b. Fitz. Coron.* 146.

He who gives a Potion to destroy the Child, if it kills the Mother, is guilty of Murder. 1 *H. H. P. C.* 429.

Page 86. N° [32] If a Bailiff enter by the outer Door happening to be open, he may break open the inner Door, and killing him in this Case would be Murder. 1 *H. H. P. C.* 458, 459. See how far Officers are justified in breaking open Doors, and consequently when the Persons killing them are guilty of Murder. *Ibid.* and 2 *H. H. P. C.* 94. and *B.* 2. *Ch.* 14.

Page 93. N° [33] But in 1 *H. H. P. C.* 54. it is said, this Rule by the Law of *England* is false; and therefore if a Person being under Necessity for want of Victuals or Clothes steal another Man's Goods, it is Felony.

Page 93. N° [34] Stat. 4 Geo. 2. c. 32. *Every Person who shall steal, rip, cut or break with Intent to steal, any Lead, Iron Bar, Iron Gate, Iron Palisadoe, or Iron Rail fixed to any Dwelling-House or other Building, or fixed in any Garden, Court-Yard, Fence, or Outlet belonging to any Building, shall be guilty of Felony, and transported for Seven Years, and every Person aiding or abetting in stealing, ripping,* &c. *or buying or receiving such Lead, Iron,* &c. *knowing the same to be stolen, shall be subject to the same Punishment.*

Page 93. N° [35] Stat. 2 Geo. 2. cap. 25. sect. 3. *If any Person steal or take by Robbery any Exchequer Orders or Tallies, intitling any other Person to any Annuity or Share in any Parliamentary Fund, or any Exchequer Bills, Bank Notes,* South-Sea *Bonds,* East-India *Bonds, Dividend Warrants of the Bank,* South-Sea *Company,* East-India *Company, or any other Company, Bills of Exchange, Navy Bills or Debenturs, Goldsmiths Notes for Payment of Money, or other Bonds or Warrants, Bills or Promissory Notes for the Payment of Money, being the Property of any other Person, notwithstanding any of the said Particulars are termed in Law a* Chose in Action, *it shall be deemed Felony of the same Nature, and with or without Benefit of Clergy, as if the Offender had stolen,* &c. *any other Goods of like Value with the Money due on such Orders,* &c.

Sect. 5. *No Attainder for any Offence hereby made Felony shall work Corruption of Blood, Loss of Dower, or Disherison of Heirs.*

Sect. 6. *This Act shall continue for five Years.*

Revived and made perpetual, 9 *Geo.* 2. *cap.* 18. *sect.* 1.

Page 94. N° [36] Takers of *Hawks* Eggs are not guilty of Larceny, but are punishable by Fine and Imprisonment upon the *Stat.* 11 *H.* 7. *c.* 17. and 31 *H.* 8. *c.* 12. 1 *H. H. P. C.* 511.

Page 96. N° [37] Stat. 7 Geo. 2. c. 21. sect. 1. *If any Person shall, with any offensive Weapon assault, or shall by Menaces or in a violent Manner, demand any Money, Goods or Chattels, from any Person, with an Intent to rob such Person, every such Offender shall be guilty of Felony, and transported for Seven Years.*

Sect. 2. *And if such Felon shall break Gaol, or escape, or return from Transportation to* Great Britain *or* Ireland, *before the Expiration of the said Term, he shall suffer as a Felon, without Benefit of Clergy.*

Page 96. N° [38] But *Quære* whether the taking the Purse or Hat, *&c.* in the Presence or before the Face of the Person robbed, be necessary to make the Offence Robbery, as in the Case put by *Hale, H. P. C. p.* 533. from *Dalton*; if *B.* flying from the Thief lets falls his Hat, and the Thief take it and carry it away? If such Presence be necessary, it seems very easy to elude the Law.

Page 97. N° [39] But if Words of Menace be not used till after a clandestine Taking, it is only Larceny, as in the Case of *Harman* and *Halfpenny*, in 1 *H. H. P. C.* 534, 535. where *Halfpenny* going up a Bank to open a Gap, *Harman* slipt his Hand into his Pocket and took his Purse, and upon *Halfpenny*'s seeing it in *Harman*'s Hand and demanding it again, *Harman* threatned him, if he spoke of it, and went off with the Purse. This was ruled only Stealth, and the Offender had his Clergy.

Page 98. N° [40] In 2 *H. H. P. C.* 14, 15, it is said that the Court of *King's Bench* had certainly a concurrent Jurisdiction with the Admiralty, in Cases of Felonies done upon the Narrow Seas or Coasts, tho' it were High Sea, because within the King's Realm of *England*. But that this Jurisdiction of the Common Law Courts, was interrupted

rupted by a ſpecial Order of the King and Council, 35 *Ed.* 3. And that ſince the 38 *Ed.* 3. it does not appear that the Courts of Common Law took Cognizance of Crimes committed upon the High Seas.

Stat. 8 Geo. 1. c. 24. ſect. 1. *If any Commander of a Ship or other Perſon ſhall* Page 101. N° [41]
any wiſe trade with any Pirate, or ſhall furniſh any Pirate with Ammunition or Stores, or fit out any Ship with ſuch Deſign, or confederate or correſpond with any Pirate, knowing him to be ſuch; every ſuch Offender ſhall be adjudged guilty of Piracy, and ſhall be tried according to the Statute of 28 H. 8. c. 15. *and the* 11 *&* 12 W. 3. c. 7. made perpetual by the 6 Geo. 1. c. 19. *and being convicted ſhall ſuffer as a Pirate. And Perſons belonging to any Ship, who ſhall upon meeting any Merchant Ship upon the High Seas, forcibly board ſuch Ship, and tho' they do not carry off ſuch Ship, ſhall throw over board or deſtroy any Part of her Goods, ſhall be puniſhed as Pirates.*

Sect. 2. *Every Ship fitted out with Deſign to trade with or ſupply any Pirate, and all the Goods put on board ſuch Ship, ſhall be* ipſo facto *forfeited, one Moiety to the King, and the other to the Informer, to be recovered in the High Court of Admiralty.*

Sect. 3. *All Perſons declared Acceſſaries by the* 11 *&* 12 W. 3. *are hereby declared principal Offenders.*

Sect. 4. *Offenders convicted on this Act ſhall be excluded from the Benefit of Clergy.*

This Act is made perpetual by 2 *Geo.* 2. *c.* 28. *ſect.* 7.

The Word *Noctanter* is to be applied to all that follows, *viz. fregit & intravit,* ſo Page 102. N° [42]
that if the Breaking were in the Day-time, and the Entry by Night, or *vice verſa,* this will not be Burglary. But if the Breaking be one Night, with an Intent to enter and commit Felony another Night, which is done accordingly, this ſeems to be Burglary according to 1 *H. H. P. C.* 551.

Sir *Matthew Hale, H. P. C.* 552. ſays that in an Arraignment for Burglary be- Page 102. N° [43]
fore him, he was doubtful whether Creeping down a Chimney were Burglary, till it appeared that ſome Bricks had been thereby looſened and thrown down into the Room.

But if he ſhoot without the Houſe and the Bullet comes in, this ſeems to be no Page 103. N° [44]
Entry to make Burglary. *Quære* 1 *H. H. P. C.* 555.

In 1 *H. H. P. C.* 553. it is ſaid to be Burglary in both. Page 103. N° [45]

But if one break open a Study or Counting-Houſe, or Shop within the Houſe, Page 104. N° [46]
this is Burglary, tho' none uſually lodge in the Study; and the ſame Law ſeems to be, if one break open a Cupboard or Counter fixed to the Houſe, *Quære* 1 *H. H. P. C.* 555. but not a Cheſt, becauſe it is no Part of the Houſe, *ibid.* 554. but it is Felony without Benefit of Clergy by Statutes. See *B.* 2. *Ch.* 33. of Clergy, *ſect.* 64.

A Woman being a Man's Concubine is no Exception at this Day. 1 *H. H. P. C.* Page 108. N° [47]
628. And the Opinion of Mr. *Finch*, cited by *Dalton*, and by *Stamford* from *Britton*, that it can be no Rape if the Woman conceive, ſeems to be no Law. 1 *H. H. P. C.* 731.

The Divorce intended is certainly not *a vinculo Matrimonii*, for then without Page 111. N° [48]
the Aid of a *Proviſo* either Party might freely marry; but it muſt be intended of a Divorce *a Menſa & Thoro.* The Doubt in *Cro. Car.* 461. is whether a Divorce *cauſa ſævitiæ* was within this Exception, becauſe it ſeemed rather to be a proviſional Separation for the Wife's Safety and Maintenance, than a Divorce; but it was never reſolved. 1 *H. H. P. C.* 694.

Bail taken before a Judge is not Bail within this Statute till it be filed of Page 114. N° [49]
Record; and if it be not filed, the acknowledging thereof in another's Name, makes not Felony, but a Miſdemeanor only. 1 *H. H. P. C.* 696.

See the Act which has been Annually paſt of late Years, intitled, *An Act for* Page 117. N° [50]
puniſhing Mutining and Deſertion, and for the better Payment of the Army and their Quarters. By which Soldiers for the Offences of Mutiny or Deſertion, *&c.* are ſubjected to Military Law, and the Judgment of a Court Martial. And by which the King is impowered to make Articles of War.

And by 12 *Annæ, ſtat.* 2. *c.* 18. *ſect.* 6. made Perpetual by 4 *Geo.* 1. *c.* 12. it is en- Page 118. N° [51]
acted, *That if any Perſon ſhall make, or be aſſiſting in making any Hole in a Ship, or ſhall ſteal any Pump belonging to any Ship in Diſtreſs, or ſhall be aiding or abetting to ſuch ſtealing, or ſhall wilfully do any Thing tending to the immediate Loſs or Deſtruction of ſuch Ship, ſuch Perſon ſhall be guilty of Felony without Benefit of Clergy.*

Stat. 11 Geo. 1. c. 29. ſect. 6. *If any Owner of, Captain, Maſter, Officer or Mariner,* Page 118. N° [52]
belonging to any Ship, ſhall wilfully caſt away, burn, or otherwiſe Deſtroy the Ship of which

he

he is Owner, or to which he belongs, or procure the same to be done, with Intent to prejudice any Person that hath or shall underwrite any Policy of Insurance thereon, or any Merchant that shall load Goods thereon, or any Owner of such Ship, the Person so offending shall suffer as a Felon without Benefit of Clergy.

Page 119. N° [53] By 4 Geo. 1. c. 11. sect. 6. *Persons imprisoned for exporting Wool,* &c. *refusing to plead, Judgment shall be entered against them by Default; and if they pay not the Sum recovered against them, within three Months after Judgment, they shall be transported as Felons; and if they return to* Great Britain *or* Ireland *before the Expiration of Seven Years, they shall suffer as Felons without Benefit of Clergy.*

Page 122. N° [54] This Act of the 13 & 14 *Car.* 2. *c.* 22. is continued by the 6 *Geo.* 2. *c.* 37. *sect.* 7. to the First of *September* 1744, *&c.* and the Clause in the 18 *Car.* 2. *c.* 3. *sect.* 2. taking away the Benefit of Clergy from great and notorious Thieves and Spoil-Takers in the Counties of *Northumberland* and *Cumberland*; as also the Clauses in the 29 & 30 *Car.* 2. *c.* 2. *sect.* 2 and 3. empowering the Justices of Peace for the said Counties respectively, to take Security from the Persons by them employed, for the Preservation of the said Counties from Theft and Rapine; *&c.* are likewise revived and continued to the said First of *September* 1744.

Page 123. N° [55] By the 5 *Geo.* 2. *c.* 30. *sect.* 1. continued by the 9 *Geo.* 2. *c.* 18. until the 29th of *September* 1743, and from thence to the End of the next Sessions of Parliament the Time limited for Bankrupts to surrender themselves is forty-two Days, which by *sect.* 3. of the said Stat. may be enlarged by the Chancellor, Lord Keeper, *&c.* to any Time not exceeding fifty Days, to be computed from the End of the said forty-two Days; so as such Order for enlarging the Time be made at least six Days before the Time such Bankrupts were to surrender themselves. And the Bankrupt not surrendering himself, and refusing to make Discovery, or imbeziling, *&c.* is to be adjudged a Felon without Benefit of Clergy.

Page 124. N° [56] These Clauses making it Felony without Benefit of Clergy, to forge Exchequer-Bills, Stamps, Lottery Tickets or Orders, as also Annuity Orders, are usually repeated or referred to in all Acts of Parliament directing the Issuing Exchequer-Bills, *&c.* See the 9 *Geo.* 1. *c.* 12. *sect.* 4. relating to Annuity Orders made in pursuance of that Act, and the Acts therein mentioned.

Page 124. N° [57] Stat. 6 Geo. 1. c. 11. sect. 50. *If any Person shall forge, counterfeit or alter any Receipt, (of the* South-Sea *Company) Warrant, or Endorsement or Writing thereupon or therein, or shall tender such forged,* &c. *Receipt,* &c. *knowing the same to be forged, to the said Company, or to any of their Officers, or shall offer to dispose of the same, knowing the same to be forged, and with Intent to defraud the said Company, or any other Person; such Offender shall be adjudged a Felon without Benefit of Clergy.*

Page 124. N° [58] Stat. 6 Geo. 1. c. 18. sect. 13. *If any Person shall forge or counterfeit the Common Seal of either of the Corporations for Assurance, or shall forge, counterfeit or alter any Policy, Bill, Bond or Obligation, under the Common Seal of either the same Corporations, or shall offer to dispose of or pay away any such forged Policy, Bill,* &c. *knowing the same to be such, or shall demand the Money therein contained, or pretended to be due thereon, or any Part thereof, from such Corporation or their Officers, with Intent to defraud,* &c. *every such Offender shall be guilty of Felony, without Benefit of Clergy.*

Page 124. N° [59] Stat. 8 Geo. 1. c. 22. sect. 1. *If any Person shall forge or counterfeit, or procure to be forged, or knowingly and wilfully act or assist in the Forging any Letter of Attorney, or other Authority to transfer, assign,* &c. *any Share, or Part of such Share, of and in the capital Stocks of Bodies corporate established by Act of Parliament, or to receive Annuities or Dividends, or shall forge the Name of any Proprietor, or of any Person intitled to any Annuity or Dividend, or to any such pretended Letter of Attorney, or shall fraudulently demand any Share in Stock transferred, or such Annuity, Dividend or Part thereof, to be received by Virtue of such forged Letter of Attorney, or shall falsely personate any Proprietor of the said Shares, Annuities and Dividends, and thereby transfer, or endeavour to transfer the Stock, or receive the Money of such Proprietor, every such Offender shall be adjudged guilty of Felony, without Benefit of Clergy.*

Page 124. N° [60] Stat. 12 Geo. 1. c. 32. sect. 9. *If any Person shall forge, or procure to be forged, or assist in forging the Name or Hand of the Accountant General of the Court of* Chancery, *the Register, the Clerk of the Report-Office, or any of the Cashiers of the Bank of* England, *to any Certificate, Report,* &c. *in Order to the Receiving any of the Money or Effects of the Suitors of the Court of* Chancery, *or shall forge any Certificate, Report,* &c. *made by such Accountant General, or any Bond under the Seal of the* East-India *Company,*

pany, or any Indorsement or Assignment thereon, or on any Bond under the Seal of the South-Sea *Company, or shall utter or publish any such, knowing the same to be forged, with an Intent to defraud,* &c. *every such Offender shall be guilty of Felony without Benefit of Clergy.*

Stat. 1 Geo. 1. stat. 2. c. 48. *If any Person shall maliciously set on Fire, or burn any Wood, Underwood, or Copice, or any Part thereof, such Person shall suffer as a Felon.* Page 124. N° [61]

Stat. 4 Geo. 1. c. 11. sect. 4. *Where any Person taketh Money or Reward, under pretence of helping any Person to stolen Goods, he shall (unless he apprehends the Felon, and causes him to be brought to Trial, and gives Evidence against him) be guilty of Felony, and suffer the Penalties according to the Nature of the Felony committed in stealing such Goods, as if he had stolen them himself.* Page 124. N° [62]

For other Matters in this Statute, as also in 6 *Geo.* 1. *c.* 23. relating to the Transportation of Felons, see *B.* 2. *Ch.* 33. *sect.* 135, 136, *&c.*

Stat. 6 Geo. 1. c. 21. sect. 34. *If Officers of the Customs be forcibly hindred, beaten or wounded in the due Execution of their Office, by Persons tumultuously assembled, and armed with Clubs or other Weapons, to the Number of Eight or more, all Persons so hindering, beating,* &c. *with their Assistants, being convicted thereof, shall be transported for a Term not exceeding Seven Years, according to the Manner set forth in* 4 Geo. 1. c. 11. *and Offenders returning to* Great Britain *or* Ireland *before the Expiration of their Term, shall suffer as Felons without Benefit of Clergy.* Page 124. N° [63]

Stat. 6 Geo. 1. c. 23. sect. 11. *If any Person shall wilfully and maliciously assault any Person in the publick Streets or Highways, with Intent to tear, spoil, cut, burn or deface, and shall tear, spoil,* &c. *the Cloaths of such Persons, such Offender shall be guilty of Felony; and the Court, before whom he shall be tried, shall have Power to transport him for Seven Years.* Page 124. N° [64]

Stat. 8 Geo. 1. c. 18. sect. 6. *All Persons who shall be found passing (knowingly and willingly) with any foreign Goods landed from any Ship, without due Entry and Payment of Duties, in their Custody, from any of the Coasts of this Kingdom, or within the Space of twenty Miles of any of the said Coasts, and shall be more than five Persons in Company, or shall carry any offensive Arms, or wear any Mask or other Disguise, when passing with such Goods, or shall forcibly hinder or resist any of the Officers of the Customs or Excise, in the Seizing any Sort of run Goods, shall be deemed and taken to be Runners of foreign Goods within the Meaning of this Act; and being convicted shall be adjudged Felons, and transported for Seven Years; and such Offenders, returning to* Great Britain *or* Ireland *before the Expiration of the said Term, shall be guilty of Felony without Benefit of Clergy.* Page 124. N° [65]

This Act by 2 *Geo.* 2. *c.* 28. *sect.* 6. is continued to the 29th of *September* 1744, *&c.*

Stat. 9 Geo. 1. cap. 22. sect. 1. *If any Persons being armed with Swords, Fire Arms or other offensive Weapons, and having their Faces blacked, or being otherwise disguised, shall appear in any Forest, Chase, Paddock or Grounds inclosed, wherein Deer are usually kept, or in any Warren or Place where Hares or Conies are usually kept, or in any Highway, Heath, Common or Down; or shall unlawfully and wilfully hunt, wound, kill or steal, any red or fallow Deer, or rob any Warren or Place where Conies or Hares are usually kept; or steal or take Fish out of any River or Pond; or if any Persons shall unlawfully and wilfully hunt,* &c. *any red or fallow Deer, kept in any of his Majesty's Forests or Chases inclosed with Fences, or in any Park,* &c. *inclosed, where Deer are usually kept, or shall unlawfully and maliciously break down the Head of any Fish-pond, whereby the Fish shall be lost; or shall unlawfully and maliciously kill, maim or wound, any Cattle, or cut down or destroy any Trees planted in any Avenue or growing in any Orchard, Garden or Plantation, for Ornament, Shelter or Profit; or shall set fire to any House, Barn or Out-house, or to any Hovel, Cock, Mow or Stack of Corn, Straw, Hay or Wood; or shall wilfully and maliciously shoot at any Person in any Dwelling-house or other Place; or shall knowingly send any Letter without a Name subscribed thereto, or signed with a fictitious Name, demanding Money, Venison, or other valuable Thing; or shall forcibly rescue any Person, being lawfully in Custody of an Officer or other Person, for any of the said Offences; or if any Person shall by Gift or Promise of Reward, procure any other to join him in any such unlawful Act, every Person so offending, being convicted, shall be guilty of Felony, and shall suffer Death without Benefit of Clergy.* Page 124. N° [66]

Sect. 4. *If any Person shall be charged with any of the said Offences before two Justices of the County where the same were committed, by Information of one credible Person on Oath by him subscribed, such Justices shall certify such Information to one of the Principal Secretaries of State, who is to lay the same before his Majesty in Council, whereupon his Majesty may make his Order in Council, commanding such Offender to surrender himself within forty Days to the Justices of the King's Bench, or to a Justice of Peace, to answer the Offences wherewith he shall stand charged; which Order shall be printed in the next* London Gazette, *and transmitted to the Sheriff of the County where the Offence shall be committed, and shall within six Days after the Receipt thereof be proclaimed by him or his Officers, between Ten in the Morning and Two in the Afternoon, in the Market-Places on the Market-Days of two Market-Towns in the County, near the Place where such Offence was committed; and a Copy of the Order shall be affixed in some publick Place in such Market-Towns; and if such Offender shall not surrender pursuant to such Order, he shall be deemed convicted and attainted of Felony, and shall suffer Death without Benefit of Clergy; and the Court of King's Bench, or the Justices of* Oyer *and* Terminer *or Gaol-Delivery for the County where the Offence is sworn in such Information to have been committed, upon producing such Order in Council under the Seal of the Council, may award Execution against such Offender, as if he had been convicted in the said Court,* &c.

Sect. 5. *Every Person, who, after the Time appointed for the Surrender of any Person so charged, shall conceal, abet or succour him, knowing him to be so charged and required to surrender, being convicted thereof, shall suffer Death as a Felon without Benefit of Clergy. Continued by* 10 Geo. 2. c. 32. *till the first of* September, 1744, *&c.*

Page 124. N° [67] Stat. 9 Geo. 1. c. 28. sect. 1. *If any Person shall, within the Place commonly called the Mint, or the pretended Limits thereof, wilfully obstruct the serving or executing of any Writ, Warrant or legal Process whatsoever, or shall assault or abuse any Person serving such Writ,* &c. *whereby such Person shall receive bodily Hurt;*

Sect. 2. *Or shall oppose any Officer of Justice or any Person aiding such Officer, in the Execution of any Writ,* &c. *or shall make Rescous of any Prisoner taken upon such Writ,* &c. *or shall knowingly conceal any Prisoner so taken, or any Person who rescued such Prisoner, or shall be any ways aiding in resisting such Officer, or in rescuing such Prisoner, or shall exercise any unlawful Jurisdiction, or execute or join in executing any pretended Rule for supporting any pretended Privilege within the said Place or Limits thereof, or for opposing the due Execution of legal Process; such Offender shall be guilty of Felony, and transported as other Felons.*

Sect. 3. *And if any Person wearing any Vizard, Mask, or being otherwise disguised, shall within the said Mint, or pretended Limits thereof, join in, aid or abet any Riot or Tumult there, or shall in any such Disguise oppose the Execution of any legal Process, or assault and abuse any Person serving such Process; such Offender shall be guilty of Felony without Benefit of Clergy. And all Persons aiding, abetting or concealing such disguised Person, shall be guilty of Felony and transported.*

Sect. 14. *If any Person so residing, or pretending to reside in the said Mint, shall perjure himself in any of the Matters in this Act mentioned, he shall be guilty of Felony without Benefit of Clergy.*

Page 124. N° [68] Stat. 12 Geo. 1. c. 34. sect. 6. *If any Person shall assault or abuse any Master Woolcomber or Master Weaver, or other Person concerned in the Woollen Manufacture, whereby such Master,* &c. *shall receive any bodily Hurt, for not complying with the illegal By-Laws, Ordinances,* &c. *in the Statute mentioned; or if any Person shall knowingly send any Writing or Message, threatning Harm to such Master Woolcomber,* &c. *or to destroy,* &c. *any of their Houses, Trees or Cattle, for not complying with the Demands or Pretences of their Workmen, or for not complying with such illegal By-Laws; every such Offender shall be guilty of Felony and transported.*

Sect. 7. *If any Person shall break into any House or Shop, with Intent to cut or destroy any Serge, or other Woollen Goods, in the Loom, or any Tools employed in the Making thereof, or shall wilfully and maliciously destroy any such Serges,* &c. *in the Loom or on the Rack, or destroy any Rack, on which such Serges,* &c. *are dried; or shall destroy any Tools used in the Making such Serges,* &c. *without the Consent of the Owner; every such Offender shall be guilty of Felony without Benefit of Clergy.*

Sect. 8. *The like Penalties to be extended to Combers of Kersey and Wool, to Frame-work-knitters and Weavers, and to Makers of Stockings.*

Stat.

Notes and Additions to the First Book.

Stat. 12 Geo. 1. c. 36. sect. 3. *Persons wilfully and maliciously burning, blowing up,* Page 124. N° [69]
pulling down, or destroying the Bridge from Fulham *to* Putney, *or any Part thereof, or attempting so to do, or without Authority taking away any Works thereto belonging, or procuring the same to be done, whereby the said Works may be damaged; such Offenders shall be adjudged Felons without Benefit of Clergy.*

Stat. 1 Geo. 2. Sess. 2. c. 19. sect. 1. *If any Person shall break down any Turnpike,* Page 124. N° [70]
&c. *he shall be sent to Gaol or to the House of Correction for three Months, and be whipt publickly*

Sect. 2. *And convicted of a second Offence shall be adjudged a Felon and transported for seven Years.*

This Act is continued by 5 *Geo.* 2. *c.* 33. for five Years, which further enacts, *That any Person maliciously destroying any Turnpike,* &c. *shall for the first Offence be guilty of Felony and transported for seven Years, and returning from Transportation before the Expiration of the said Term, shall be guilty of Felony without Benefit of Clergy.* Both these Acts are continued by 8 *Geo.* 2. *c.* 20. for five Years. See the Act in N° [74.]

Stat. 4 Geo. 2. c. 16. sect. 1. *Any Person who shall feloniously take or steal, or shall* Page 124. N° [71]
procure any other Person to steal from any Whitening or Bleaching Croft, Field, &c. *or from any Building made Use of by any Whitster,* &c. *for whitening Linen, Fustian or Cotton Cloth, or any Thread, Yarn,* &c. *to the Value of ten Shillings, or shall buy or receive any such Goods, knowing them to be stolen, shall be guilty of Felony without Benefit of Clergy, unless the Court, before whom the Conviction shall be, shall think it reasonable upon the Circumstances of the Case that the Offender, instead of suffering Death, should be transported; in which Case the Offender shall be transported for seven Years, in the Manner directed by* 4 Geo. 1. c. 11. and 6 Geo. 1. c. 23.

Sect. 2. *Offenders refusing to be transported, or breaking prison, escaping, or returning before the Term expired, shall suffer Death.*

Stat. 4 Geo. 2. c. 18. sect. 1. *If any Person shall within* Great Britain *or* Ireland, *or* Page 124 N° [72]
any other of his Majesty's Dominions, or without, falsely make, forge, or counterfeit, or cause to be falsely made, &c. *or knowingly assist in false making,* &c. *any Pass for any Ship, commonly called a* Mediterranean Pass, *or shall counterfeit the Seal of the Admiralty Office, or the Hand of the Lord High Admiral, or of any Commissioner for executing the Office of Lord High Admiral, to any such Pass; or shall alter or erase any true Pass issued by the Lord Admiral or Commissioners,* &c. *or shall utter and publish as true any such false, forged,* &c. *Pass, knowing the same to be such; every such Offender shall suffer as a Felon without Benefit of Clergy.*

Sect. 2. *Such Offences committed any where out of the Realm may be tried in any County of* Great Britain.

Stat. 6 Geo. 2. c. 37. sect. 5. *If any Person shall maliciously break or cut down* Page 124. N° [73]
the Bank of any River, or any Sea Bank, whereby any Lands shall be overflowed or damaged, every Person so Offending shall be guilty of Felony without Benefit of Clergy.

Sect 6. *If any Person shall maliciously cut any Hop-binds growing on Poles in any Plantation of Hops; every Person so offending shall be guilty of Felony without Benefit of Clergy.*

By 10 *Geo.* 2. *c.* 32. These Clauses are to be in force till the First of *September* 1744, *&c.*

Stat. 8 Geo. 2. c. 20. *Any Person who shall maliciously destroy any Turnpike-Gate,* Page 124. N° [74]
Post, Rail, Wall, Chain or other Fence set up, or to be set up, to prevent Passengers from passing by without paying Toll, directed to be paid by Act of Parliament, or any Lock, Sluice, Floodgate, or other Works erected on any Navigable River by Authority of Parliament; or shall forcibly rescue any Person lawfully in Custody for such Offence; such Offender shall be guilty of Felony without Benefit of Clergy.

Attainder on this Act not to work Corruption of Blood, Loss of Dower or Forfeiture.

This Statute together with the 1 *Geo.* 2. *stat.* 2. *c.* 19. and 5 *Geo.* 2. *c.* 33. are to continue for five Years, from the 15th of *May* 1735, and from thence to the End of the then next Session of Parliament.

Stat. 9 Geo. 2. c. 29. sect. 5. *Any Person wilfully and maliciously destroying the Bridge* Page 124. N° [75]
to be built from Westminster *to the opposite Shore, or any Part thereof, or attempting so to do, or, without Authority from the Commissioners, removing or taking away any Works thereto belonging, whereby the said Bridge may be damaged, or in any wise directing or procuring the same to be done, shall suffer as a Felon without Benefit of Clergy.*

Stat,

Page 124. N° [76] Stat. 9 Geo. 2. c. 35. sect. 1. *All Persons having incurred any Penalty by the Clandestine running of Goods,* &c. *before the 27th of* April 1736, *or for resisting, beating,* &c. *any Officer in the due Execution of his Duty, shall be indemnified,* &c.

Sect. 7. *Provided that if any Person, who hath been guilty of any Offence before mentioned, for which he is liable to be transported as a Felon, shall take the Benefit of this Act, and shall afterwards be guilty of the like Offence, then every such Person being convicted of the said Offence hereafter to be committed, and upon Proof made that such Person had committed any of the same Offences before the making of this Act, and had taken the Benefit thereof for his Discharge, shall be guilty of Felony without Benefit of Clergy.*

Sect. 10. *All Persons (to the Number of Three or more, armed with Fire Arms or other offensive Arms) upon Conviction of their being assembled and armed, in order to be assisting in the Clandestine running of prohibited or uncustomed Goods, shall be adjudged guilty of Felony, and transported for seven Years; and if such Offenders return into* Great Britain *or* Ireland *before the Expiration of the said Term, they shall suffer as Felons without Benefit of Clergy.*

Sect. 13. *All Persons who, to the Number of Two or more in Company, shall be found passing within five Miles from the Sea Coast, or from any Navigable River, with any Horse, Cart, or Carriage, whereon there shall be laden more than six Pounds of Tea, or Brandy or other Spirits exceeding the Quantity of five Gallons, not having paid the Duties by Law charged thereon, and not having a Permit for the same, or any other foreign Goods to the Value of Thirty Pounds Sterling, landed from any Ship, without due Entry and Payment of Duties, and shall carry any offensive Arms, or wear any Mask or Disguise, when passing with such Goods; or shall forcibly assault or resist any of the Officers of the Customs or Excise in the Seising any run Goods, or other Execution of their Office, shall be deemed Runners of foreign Goods within the Intent and Meaning of the* 8 Geo. 1. c. 18. *and every such Offender shall be guilty of Felony, and transported for seven Years; and such Offender returning to* Great Britain *or* Ireland, *before the Expiration of the said Term, shall suffer as a Felon without Benefit of Clergy.*

Sect. 28. *If any Officer of the Customs or Excise being on board any Ship, Boat, or Vessel, within the Limits of any of the Ports of this Kingdom, be forcibly hindred, wounded or beaten, in the due Execution of his Office, by any Person whatsoever, all Persons so forcibly hindering,* &c. *and all such as shall act in their Assistance, shall be transported for a Term not exceeding seven Years; and if such Offenders shall return before the Expiration of their said Term, they shall suffer as Felons without Benefit of Clergy.*

Page 124. N° [77] Stat. 10 Geo. 2. c. 31. sect. 8. *If any greater Number of Persons shall be taken into or carried in any Tilt-Boat, Row-Barge, Ferry-Boat, or other Boat or Wherry, than are respectively allowed to be carried by this Act, and any Passenger shall then be drowned, every Person who shall work or navigate such Tilt-Boat, Row-Barge,* &c. *offending therein, and being thereof convicted, shall be guilty of Felony, and transported as a Felon.*

Page 124. N° [78] Stat. 10 Geo. 2. c. 32. sect. 4. *All the Provisions made in the* 9 Geo. 1. c. 22. *for bringing Offenders against the said Act to Justice, and the Persons who shall conceal, abet or succour such Offenders,* &c. *shall, during the Continuance of the said Act, extend to all Offences by unlawfully or maliciously breaking or cutting down the Bank of any River or Sea-Bank, or by unlawfully and maliciously cutting Hop-Binds, or by wilfully and maliciously setting on fire any Delph of Coal.*

Sect. 6. *If any Person shall maliciously set on fire, or cause to be set on fire, any Mine, Pit, or Delph of Coal or cannel Coal, every Person so offending shall be guilty of Felony without Benefit of Clergy.*

Sect. 7. *If any Person hereafter convicted of coursing, hunting, taking in Toils, killing, wounding or taking away, any red or fallow Deer, in any open or uninclosed Forest or Chase where Deer are usually kept, (for which by the* 3 & 4 W. & M. c. 10. *he is only liable to pecuniary Penalties, and not punishable by* 9 Geo. 1. c. 22.) *shall, during the Continuance of the* 9 Geo. 1. c. 22. *be guilty of a second Offence of the like Nature, such Offender shall be transported for seven Years; and such Offender returning to* Great Britain *or* Ireland *within the said seven Years shall be guilty of Felony without Benefit of Clergy.*

Sect. 9. *If any Persons armed with Fire Arms or other offensive Weapons shall, during the Continuance of the said* 9 Geo. 1. c. 22. *come into any Forest, Chase or Park, wherein Deer are usually kept (be the same inclosed or not inclosed) with an Intent to hunt, take in Toils,* &c. *any Deer, and shall there beat, or wound, any Keeper,* &c. *in the Exe-*

*cution of his Office; every ſuch Offender ſhall be tranſported for ſeven Years, and ſuch Of-
fender returning within the ſaid Term, ſhall ſuffer as a Felon without Benefit of Clergy.*

Stat. 11 Geo. 2. c. 22. ſect. 1. *If any Perſon ſhall wilfully and maliciouſly beat,* Page 124. N° [79]
*wound, or uſe any Violence to any Perſon, with Intent to hinder him from buying of any
Corn or Grain; or ſhall ſtop or ſeiſe any Waggon or other Carriage, or Horſe loaded with
Wheat, Flower, Meal, Malt or other Grain, on the Way from any City, Market-Town or
Sea-Port, and maliciouſly break or deſtroy the ſame or Part thereof, or the Harneſs of the
Horſes drawing the ſame, or ſhall take of, kill or wound any of ſuch Horſes, or beat or
wound the Drivers of ſuch Waggon,* &c. *ſo loaded, in order to ſtop the ſame; or ſhall ſcatter
ſuch Wheat,* &c. *or ſhall take or damage the ſame or any Part thereof; every ſuch Offender
ſhall be ſent to Gaol or the Houſe of Correction for any Time not exceeding three Months,
nor leſs than one Month, and ſhall be once publickly whipt.*

Sect. 2. *And if any Perſon ſo convicted ſhall commit any of the ſaid Offences a ſecond
Time, or if any Perſon ſhall maliciouſly throw down or deſtroy any Storehouſe or Granary,
or other Place, where Corn ſhall be kept in Order to be exported; or ſhall enter any ſuch
Storehouſe,* &c. *and carry away any Corn,* &c. *or ſhall throw abroad or ſpoil the ſame;
or ſhall enter any Ship, or Veſſel, and carry away, throw out or ſpoil any Grain intended
for Exportation; every ſuch Offender ſhall be guilty of Felony and tranſported for ſeven Years,
and ſuch Offender returning before the Expiration of the ſeven Years ſhall ſuffer as a Felon
without Benefit of Clergy.*

Stat. 11 Geo. 2. c. 26. ſect. 2. *If any Perſons to the Number of five or more, ſhall in* Page 124. N° [80]
*a tumultuous and riotous Manner aſſemble themſelves to reſcue any Offender againſt the
9 Geo. 2.* for laying a Duty on Retailers of Spirituous Liquors, *&c. or to aſſault,
beat, or wound any Perſon who ſhall give any Information or Evidence againſt, ſeiſe, or
bring to Juſtice any Perſon offending againſt the ſaid Act; then all Perſons ſo aſſembling them-
ſelves, and their Aiders and Abettors, ſhall be adjudged guilty of Felony, and may be tranſport-
ed by the Courts before whom they ſhall be convicted for ſeven Years, upon the like Terms as
are enacted by* 4 Geo. 1. c. 11 and 6 Geo. 1. c. 23.

Upon the Commiſſion of Felony, looking on without uſing any Means to take the Page 125. N° [81]
Felon, is puniſhable as Miſpriſion of Felony. *1 H. H. P. C.* 431, 448, 449, 533.
2 H. H. P. C. 75, 76. See alſo *B. 2. Ch. 12. ſect. 1.*

By *2 Geo. 2. c. 24.* for preventing Bribery and Corruption in the Election of Mem- Page 170. N° [82]
bers of Parliament, it is enacted, *That every Elector ſhall take an Oath, if demanded, that
he has not received any Reward, Promiſe,* &c. *for his Vote, which Oath the preſiding Officer
ſhall adminiſter under the Penalty of* 50 l. *And the returning Officer admitting an Elec-
tor to poll, before taking the demanded Oath, forfeits* 100 l. Alſo it is enacted, *That the re-
turning Officer ſhall immediately after Reading the Writ take an Oath that he has received no
Reward,* &c. *for making a Return. And the returning Officer or Electors convicted of
Perjury ſhall ſuffer all the legal Penalties of Perjury, and be incapable of voting at any
Election for Members of Parliament; and Perſons having or claiming to have a Vote,
and taking any Reward to vote or to forbear voting, forfeit* 500 l. *and ſhall be diſabled from
voting at any Election of Members of Parliament, and ſhall alſo be diſabled to hold any Of-
fice or Franchiſe, to which they are, or may afterwards be entitled, as if they were naturally
dead. And every Officer, to whom the Execution of any Writ for electing Members of Par-
liament does belong, for every wilful Offence againſt this Act ſhall forfeit* 50 l.

Stat. 9 Geo. 2. c. 35. ſect. 24. *If any Perſon ſhall offer any Bribe to any Officer of the
Cuſtoms or Exciſe, to do any Act whereby his Majeſty might be defrauded in his ſaid Re-
venues, every Perſon ſhall for every ſuch Offence, forfeit* 50 l.

Stat. 2 Geo. 2. c. 25. ſect. 2. *Any Perſon guilty of wilful Perjury or Subornation* Page 182. N° [83]
*of Perjury may (beſides the Puniſhment already inflicted by Law for ſuch Crimes) be ſent to
the Houſe of Correction, or be tranſported for a Term not exceeding ſeven Years; and if
any Perſon ſo committed or tranſported ſhall voluntarily eſcape or break Priſon, or return
from Tranſportation before the Expiration of his Term, ſuch Perſon ſhall ſuffer as a Felon
without Benefit of Clergy.*

Stat. 10 Geo. 2. c. 26. ſect. 18. *If any Priſoner or other Perſon enabled to take the Be-* Page 182. N° [84]
*nefit of this Act (for the Relief of Inſolvent Debtors) ſhall be convicted of wilful Perjury,
in any of the Matters in this Act mentioned; he ſhall ſuffer as a Felon without Benefit of
Clergy.*

Stat. 2 Geo. 2. c. 25. ſect. 1. *If any Perſon ſhall forge or procure to be forged, or aſſiſt* Page 187. N° [85]
in forging any Deed, Will, Teſtament, Bond, Writing obligatory, Bill of Exchange,

 Pro-

Promiſſory Note for Payment of Money, Indorſement or Aſſignment of any Bill of Exchange, or Promiſſory Note for Payment of Money, or any Acquittance, or Receipt for Money or Goods; or ſhall utter or publiſh as true any forged Deed, Will, &c. *knowing the ſame to be forged, with an Intent to defraud any Perſon; every ſuch Offender ſhall be guilty of Felony without Benefit of Clergy.*

Page 187. N° [86] Stat. 7 Geo. 2. c. 22. *If any Perſon ſhall falſely make, alter or forge, or procure to be falſely made, altered,* &c. *or aſſiſt in falſely making,* &c. *any Acceptance of any Bill of Exchange, or the Number or principal Sum of any accountable Receipt for any Note, Bill, or other Security for Payment of Money, or any Warrant or Order for Payment of Money, or Delivery of Goods, or ſhall utter or publiſh any ſuch falſe Acceptance, Bill, Receipt,* &c. *with Intent to defraud any Perſon; every ſuch Offender ſhall ſuffer as a Felon without Benefit of Clergy.*

Page 216. N° [87] Stat. 5 Geo. 1. c. 12. ſect. 1. *No Waggon travelling for Hire ſhall be drawn with more than ſix Horſes, and no ſuch Cart with more than three, on Pain of forfeiting all the Horſes above ſix in a Waggon, and three in a Cart, with all the Accoutrements, to the ſole Uſe of him who ſhall ſeiſe the ſame.*

Sect. 2. *And the Perſon who ſhall make ſuch Seiſure ſhall deliver the Things ſo ſeiſed into the Cuſtody of the Conſtable, or other pariſh Officer of the ſame or adjacent Town or Pariſh, (who are hereby required ſafely to keep the ſame) till the Perſon who made ſuch Diſtreſs ſhall make Proof upon Oath before ſome Juſtice of the Peace of the Offence committed, and the ſaid Juſtice is hereby required to iſſue his Precept to the ſaid Officer to deliver the Things ſo forfeited to the Party who ſeiſed the ſame for his ſole Uſe, paying ſuch reaſonable Charge for the keeping,* &c. *as the ſaid Juſtice ſhall allow.*

Sect. 3. *No ſuch travelling Waggon, having the Wheels bound with Streaks or Tire of a leſs Breadth than two Inches and a half, when worn, or being ſet on with roſe-headed Nails, ſhall be drawn with more than three Horſes, on Pain of forfeiting all above three,* &c.

Sect. 4. *And if any Perſon ſhall hinder or attempt to hinder the Seiſing, or carrying away any Seiſure, for any Forfeiture in this Act, or ſhall reſcue the ſame, or uſe any Violence to the Perſon making ſuch Seiſure, ſuch Perſon ſhall upon Proof, made by Oath before a Juſtice of the Peace for the County wherein ſuch Offence is done, be committed to the Common Gaol for three Months without Bail, and ſhall forfeit ten Pounds to be levied by Diſtreſs,* &c.

Sect. 5. *Provided nothing in this Act ſhall extend to ſuch Waggons, Carts or Carriages as ſhall be employed about Husbandry, or in carrying of Cheeſe, Butter, Hay, Straw, Corn unthraſhed, Coals, Chalk, or any one Tree or Piece of Timber, or any one Stone, or Block of Marble, Carravans, and the covered Carriages of Noblemen and Gentlemen, for their own private Uſe, or ſuch Timber, Ammunition or Artillery as ſhall be for the Service of his Majeſty, his Heirs and Succeſſors.*

Page 220. N° [88] On this Subject of Highways, ſee alſo the *Stat.* 1 *Geo.* 1. *c.* 52. for making the Laws for repairing the Highways more effectual. *Stat.* 6 *Geo.* 1. *c.* 6. for preventing the Carriage of exceſſive Loads of Meal, Malt, Bricks and Coal within ten Miles of *London* and *Weſtminſter*. *Stat.* 7 *Geo.* 2. *c.* 9. to oblige Poſſeſſors of Lands to cut and keep low ſuch Hedges as are adjoining to the Highways. *Stat.* 9 *Geo.* 2. *c.* 18. for explaining and amending the Clauſe in 1 *Geo.* 1. *ſtat.* 2. *c.* 52. relating to Scavengers.

Page 230. N° [89] By 2 *Geo.* 2. *c.* 28. *ſect.* 11. it is enacted, *That no Licence ſhall be granted to any Perſon to keep a common Inn or Alehouſe, or to retail Brandy,* &c. *but at a general Meeting of the Juſtices of Peace, acting in the Diviſion where the ſaid Perſon dwells, to be holden for that Purpoſe.*

An Alphabetical Index of the Principal Matters contained in this Book.

How

Index to the First Book.

Index to the First Book.

Evasion.

The

In-

Index to the First Book.

What

Church,

Penal

In

Whether

How

FINIS.

A TREATISE OF The Pleas of the Crown:

OR,

A SYSTEM of the Principal Matters relating to that SUBJECT, digested under their PROPER HEADS.

BOOK II.

By *WILLIAM HAWKINS*,
Serjeant at Law.

The Third Edition, with large ADDITIONS and many hundred new REFERENCES to the Modern Books of Authority published since the Author compiled this TREATISE.

In the SAVOY:
Printed by E. and R. NUTT, and R. GOSLING, (Assigns of *E. Sayer*, Esq;) for B. Nutt, and sold by S. Birt in *Ave-Mary-Lane*, D. Browne without *Temple-Bar*, J. Shuckburgh in *Fleet-Street*, and J. Stagg in *Westminster-Hall*. MDCCXXXIX.

To the Right Honourable

THOMAS Lord *PARKER*,

Baron of *MACCLESFIELD*,

AND

Lord High Chancellor of *Great Britain*.

MY LORD,

THE Experience I have ſo often had of your Lordſhip's Goodneſs, cannot but encourage me to hope for the Continuance of it: And the Succeſs of my former Endeavours under the Protection of your Lordſhip's Name, is a ſufficient Aſſurance, That if I can be ſo happy as to have your Lordſhip's Approbation and Encouragement, I need not deſire any other.

NOR is my Application to your Lordſhip in Behalf of a Common Law Treatiſe, any way diſcouraged by your Lordſhip's Removal to the Station you at preſent adorn; for tho' the Publick Good, and his Majeſty's Service, have put you under a Neceſſity of leaving the Common Law Courts, yet nothing can ever make you ceaſe from being the moſt aſſured Friend and Patron, as well as the moſt exquiſite Maſter of the Common Law. And the Greateſt Lovers of it have the leſs Regret for the Loſs of your Lordſhip's Preſence among them, from the Honour the Law it ſelf has received by your Lordſhip's Advancement, whereby the World has been effectually convinc'd, That nothing ſo much conduces to make a

Consummate Chancellor, as the most perfect Skill and Experience in the Common Law.

IT is with the utmost Pleasure we observe your Lordship with so much Steadiness adhere to those stated Boundaries of Property, which our Ancestors have always had in such high Veneration, and which your Lordship never departs from, but in such Cases, wherein evident Equity, Common Sense, and Natural Justice, undeniably point out an Exception.

IT is to your Lordship we are obliged for the Removal of that Vulgar Prejudice, That the Rules of Law and Equity could not possibly be reconciled: As your Lordship had formerly convinced us, That there is nothing in the Common Law rightly understood, that is any way repugnant to Equity; you have now given us the like Satisfaction, That there is no Rule of Equity skilfully applied, that in the least contradicts the true Reason of the Common Law.

I am,

My LORD,

With the greatest Respect,

Your Lordship's most dutiful,

and most obliged Servant,

William Hawkins.

AN
ANALYSIS
OF
The Second BOOK
OF
The Pleas of the Crown.

ALL Courts of criminal Jurisdiction are Courts of Record, (ch. 1. sect 14.) and derive their Authority from the Crown, ch. 1. sect. 1, *&c.*

The Principal Courts of this Kind are,

1. The Court of the Lord High Steward, ch. 2.
2. The Court of King's Bench, ch. 3.
3. The Court of the Constable and Marshal, ch. 4.
4. The Court of the Justices of *Oyer* and *Terminer*, ch. 5.
5. The Court of Justices of Gaol-Delivery, ch. 6.
6. The Court of the Justices of Assise and *Nisi prius*, ch. 7.
7. The Court of Sessions of Justices of Peace, ch. 8.
8. The Court of the Coroner, ch. 9.
9. The Sheriff's Torn, ch. 10.
10. The Court Leet, ch. 11.

The first Thing to be done in order to the bringing a Criminal to Justice is to arrest him.

Arrests are either without Process from a Court of Record, or by Virtue of such Process.

And first, Arrests without such Process, are either.

1. By Private Persons, or,
2. By Publick Officers.

Arrests of this Kind by Private Persons are either,

1. Such as are commanded and enjoined by Law, (ch. 12. sect. 1. to 8.) or,
2. Such as are permitted by Law, ch. 12. sect. 8. to 18.) or,
3. Such as are rewarded by Law, (ch. 12. sect. 22, *&c.*

Arrests of this Kind by Publick Officers, are either,

1. By Watchmen, ch. 13. sect. 1 to 7.) or,
2. By Constables, (ch. 13. sect. 7 to 12.) or,
3. By Bailiffs of Towns, (ch. 13. sect. 12.) or,
4. By Justices of Peace, which are either,
    1. By Parol, (ch. 13. sect. 14.) or,
    2. By Warrant, ch. 13. sect. 15. *to the End of the Chapter.*

Persons arrested are either to be bailed, ch. 15.

Or committed, ch. 16.

Per-

Persons may be criminal, in preventing the Bringing of Offenders to Publick Justice, several Ways,

1. Before any Arrest made,
2. After an Arrest.

Persons may be so guilty before any Arrest made,

1. By opposing an Arrest, ch. 17. sect. 1.
2. By suffering a Criminal to escape, ch. 17. sect. 2, 4.
3. By flying from an Arrest, ch. 17. sect. 3. ch. 49. sect. 14, 15, 16.

Persons may be so Guilty after an Arrest, either in Respect of an Arrest of themselves, or of others.

Their Offence in Respect of an Arrest of themselves, if without Force, is called an Escape, ch. 17. sect. 5.

If with Force, is called a Breach of Prison, ch. 18.

Their Offence in Respect of the Arrest of others, is either,

1. Without Force, or,
2. With Force.

Such Offences, without Force, come under the Notion of Escapes, and are either,

1. By Officers, (ch. 19.) or,
2. By Private Persons, ch. 20.

Such Offences with Force come under the Notion of Rescous, ch. 21.

Secondly, Arrests by Process from a Court of Record may be made by Virtue of two Kinds of Process,

1. Upon such as is awarded by the Discretion of the Court, upon a bare Suggestion, or the Knowledge of the Justices.
2. Upon such as is awarded on an Appeal, Indictment, or Information.

Process of the first Kind is generally called an Attachment, (ch. 22.) and lies either against,

1. The Officers of the Court, as,
   1. Sheriffs and Bailiffs, ch. 22. sect. 2 to 6.
   2. Attornies, ch. 22. sect. 6 to 12.
   3. Other Officers of the Court, ch. 22. sect. 12.
   4. Jurors, ch. 22. sect. 14 to 25. or,
2. Against other, as,
   1. Inferior Judges, ch. 22. sect. 25. to 30.
   2. Counsellors, ch. 22. sect. 30.
   3. Gaolers, ch. 22. sect. 31.
   4. Any other Persons whatsoever, ch. 22. sect. 33. *to the End of the Chapter.*

Process on an Appeal, Indictment, or Information, supposes such Appeal, Indictment, or Information to be first exhibited.

An Appeal is either.

1. By an innocent Person, which may either be by Writ, or by Bill, ch. 23.
2. By an Offender confessing himself Guilty, who is commonly called an Approver, ch. 24.

Indictments (ch. 25.) are of two Kinds,

1. Such as are grounded on the Common Law, ch. 25. sect. 55 to 99.
2. Such as are grounded on Statute, ch. 25. sect. 99 to 118.

Informations are of two Kinds,

1. Such as are merely the Suit of the King, ch. 26. sect. 1 to 17.
2. Such as are partly the Suit of the King, and partly the Suit of the Party, ch. 26. sect. 17. *to the End of the Chapter.*

Process on an Appeal, Indictment, or Information, may be either considered,

1. In General, without any Particular Regard to Process of Outlawry, ch. 27. sect. 1 to 113.
2. In Particular, with Regard to such Process only, ch. 27. sect. 113. *to the End of the Chapter.*

A Criminal being brought into Court is to be arraigned, or put upon his Trial, the Manner whereof may be considered,

1. As it relates to all Criminals in general, ch. 28.
2. As it relates to Principals and Accessaries in Particular, ch. 29.

The Party being arraigned, either,

1. Stands Mute, (ch. 30.) or,
2. Confesses, (ch. 31.) or,
3. Pleads.

Pleas are either,

1. Dilatory, or,
2. In Chief.

The Dilatory are either,

1. Declinatory, or,
2. In Abatement, ch. 34.

The Declinatory are either,

1. Of the Privilege of Sanctuary, (ch. 32.) or.
2. Of the Benefit of Clergy, ch. 33.

Pleas in Chief are either,

2. Of

1. In Bar, or,
2. The General Iſſue, ch. 38.

The Principal Pleas in Bar are,

1. That of *Autrefoits acquit*, ch. 35.
2. That of *Autrefoits attaint* or *convict*, ch. 36.
3. That of Pardon, ch. 37.

The Plea of Not Guilty is triable either,

1. By the Country, or,
2. By the Peers, (ch. 44.) or,
3. By Battle, ch. 45.

In order for a Trial by the Country a Jury muſt be returned,

1. From the proper County, ch. 40.
2. By proper Proceſs, ch. 41.
3. Before a proper Court, ch. 42.

The Jurors being returned into Court may in many Caſes be challenged.

Such Challenges may be conſidered either,

1. Without any particular Regard to Aliens, or,
2. As they particularly relate to Aliens, ch. 43. ſect. 34. *to the End of the Chapter*.

Thoſe of the firſt Kind, are either,

1. Such as may be taken on the Part of the King, (ch. 43. ſect. 2, 3.) or,
2. Such as may be taken on the Part of the Priſoner,

A Challenge may be taken on the Part of a Priſoner, either,

1. Peremptorily, (ch. 43. ſect. 5 to 10.) or,
2. For Cauſe, ch. 43. ſect. 10 to 34.

The Jury being ſworn, are to be guided by their Evidence, ch. 46.

Whereupon they muſt give ſome Verdict, either General or Special, ch. 47.

Judgments in Criminal Caſes are of two Kinds,

1. Such as expreſly ſentence the Party to the Puniſhment proper for his Crime.
2. Such as give no ſuch expreſs Sentence.

Of Judgments by ſuch expreſs Sentence there are two Kinds,

1. Such as are fix'd and ſtated, and always the ſame for the ſame Species of Crimes, ch. 48. ſect. 2 to 14.
2. Such as are diſcretionary and variable according to the different Circumſtances of each Caſe, ch. 48. 14 to 21.

Of Judgments which give no ſuch expreſs Sentence, there are alſo two Kinds,

1. Outlawry, ch. 48. ſect. 21, 22, 23.
2. Abjuration, ch. 48. ſect. 24.

The moſt conſiderable Conſequences of an Attainder, *&c.* are,

1. The Forfeiture of Lands and Goods, ch. 49. ſect. 1 to 42.
2. The Loſs of the Wife's Dower, ch. 49. ſect. 42 to 47.
3. The Corruption of Blood, ch. 49. ſect. 47. *to the End of the Chapter*.

Forfeitures of Lands and Goods are either,

1. By the Common Law, (ch. 49. ſect. 1 to 18.) or,
2. By Statute, ch. 49. ſect. 18 to 30.

Judgments may be avoided either,

1. Without Writ of Error, (ch. 50. ſect. 10 to 17.) or,
2. By Writ of Error,

They may be avoided by Writ of Error, either,

1. For Faults apparent in the Record, (ch. 50. ſect. 1.) or,
2. For Matters *dehors* the Record, ch. 50. ſect. 2 to 10.

The Party condemned is either to be,

1. Reprieved, (ch. 51. ſect. 8, 9.) or,
2. Executed, ch. 51. ſect. 1 to 8.

A TREATISE

A

TREATISE

OF

The Pleas of the Crown.

BOOK II.

CHAP. I.

Of Courts of criminal Jurisdiction in general.

HAVING in the first Book endeavoured to shew the Nature of criminal Offences, I am now to shew, in what Manner the Offenders are to be brought to Punishment; and in Order hereto I shall consider,

1. The Nature of the Courts, which have Jurisdiction over such Offences.
2. In what Manner the Offenders are to be proceeded against by such Courts.

And

And firſt, for the better Underſtanding of the Nature of ſuch Courts, I ſhall premiſe ſome Conſiderations concerning them in general, and then conſider the Nature of the Principal of them in particular.

As to the Nature of ſuch Courts in general I ſhall conſider,

1. What is requiſite to the Conſtitution of their Authority.
2. What is incidental to all ſuch Courts in general.

S.P.C. 54, 55.

Sect. 1. As to the firſt Point I ſhall take it for granted, That the King being the ſupreme Magiſtrate of the Kingdom, and intruſted with the whole executive Power of the Law, no Court whatſoever can have any ſuch Juriſdiction, unleſs it ſome Way or other derive it from the Crown.

Dalt. ch. 1. S. P. C. 54. b. 4 Inſt. 71. 2 R. 3. 11. a. Speed 521, 524. 1 Rol. Ab. 535.

Sect. 2. Yet it ſeems, That the King himſelf cannot ſit in Judgment upon any Indictment, becauſe he is one of the Parties to the Suit; and therefore where it is ſaid in ſome of our ancient Hiſtories, that our Kings have ſometimes ſate in Perſon with the Juſtices at the Arraignment of great Offenders, probably it ought not to be intended that they came as Judges, but as Spectators only, for the greater Solemnity of the Proceeding.

[a] 4 Inſt. 70, 71. 4 Inſt. 103. 8 H. 4. 13. b. 14. a. 20. 2 R. 3. 11. [b] Madox's Hiſtory of the Exchequer, from Fol. 5 to 17. and Fol. 56 to 85. Dalton ch. 1. [c] 28 Aſſ. pl. 52. [d] 4 Inſt. 73.

Sect. 3. And it is ſaid by [a] Sir *Edward Coke*, That the King has committed and diſtributed all his Power of Judicature to ſeveral Courts of Juſtice; and though it may be argued with the higheſt Probability both from the Nature of the Thing, and the conſtant Tenor of our [b] ancient Records and Hiſtories ſince the Conqueſt, and alſo from the Form of all Proceſs in the King's Bench and Chancery, which is always made returnable before the [c] King himſelf, That in old Time our Kings in Perſon, often determined Cauſes between Party and Party, proper for thoſe Courts; yet at this Day, by the long, conſtant and uninterrupted Uſage of many Ages, our [d] Kings ſeem to have delegated their whole judicial Power to the Judges of their ſeveral Courts, which by the ſame immemorial Uſage have gained a known and ſtated Juriſdiction, regulated by certain and eſtabliſhed Rules, which our Kings themſelves cannot alter without an Act of Parliament.

6 H. 7. 4. b. 5. a. Bro. Pat. 53. 4 Inſt. 125, 127. 6 Co. 11. b. 12 a. 2 H. H. P. C. 105. Skin. 273.

Sect. 4. For it ſeems to be clearly agreed, That the King cannot give any Addition of Juriſdiction to an ancient Court, but that all ſuch Courts muſt be holden in ſuch Manner, and proceed by ſuch Rules, and in ſuch Caſes only, as their known Uſage has limited and preſcribed; and from hence it followeth, That as the Court of King's Bench cannot be authorized to determine a mere real Action between Subject and Subject, ſo neither can the Court of Common Pleas to inquire of Felony or Treaſon.

4 Inſt. 87. 1 Sid. 338.

Sect. 5. Nay, it is ſaid by ſome, That the King is ſo far reſtrained by the ancient Forms in all Caſes of this Nature, that his Grant of a judicial Office for Life, which has been accuſtomed to be granted only at Will, is void.

42 Aſſ. 12, 13. 4 Inſt. 164. Bro. Commiſſion, 15, 16. F.N.B. 110. b. Bro. Indictment, 22, 38. See 12 Co. 31.

Sect. 6. And the Law is ſo jealous of any Kind of Innovation, in a Matter ſo highly concerning the Safety of the Subject, as not to endure any the leaſt Deviation from the old known ſtated Forms, however immaterial it may ſeem, as will be more fully ſhewn, *Ch.* 5. *Sect.* 1.

Sect. 7.

Sect. 7. And from the like Reaſon it follows, that Commiſſions to [a] ſeize the Goods and impriſon the Bodies of all Perſons, who ſhall be notoriouſly ſuſpected of Felonies or Treſpaſſes, without any Indictment or other legal Proceſs againſt them, are illegal and void.

Sect. 8. And it is ſaid, That the King cannot grant any new Commiſſion whatſoever, that is not warranted by ancient Precedents, however neceſſary it may ſeem, and conducive to the publick Good; and therefore [b] Commiſſions to aſſay Weights and Meaſures, being of a new Invention, were condemned by Parliament; and it is ſaid by [c] Sir *Edward Coke*, That the King could not authorize Perſons to take Care of Rivers and the Fiſhery therein, according to the Method preſcribed by the Statute of *Weſtm.* 2. *Ch.* 47. before the Making of that Statute.

Sect. 9. As all Judges muſt derive their Authority from the Crown, by ſome Commiſſion warranted by Law, they muſt alſo exerciſe it in a legal Manner, and hold their Courts in their proper Perſons; for they cannot act by [d] Deputy, nor any Way transfer their Power to another, as the [e] Judges of Eccleſiaſtical Courts may.

Sect. 10. [f] But it ſeems, That regularly where there are divers Judges of a Court of Record, the Act of any one of them is effectual, eſpecially if their [g] Commiſſion do not expreſly require more.

Sect. 11. It hath been [h] reſolved, That by the Common Law, all Patents of the Juſtices of either Bench, Barons of the Exchequer, Sheriffs, Eſcheators, Commiſſioners of *Oyer* and *Terminer*, Gaol-Delivery, and of the Peace, are determined by the Death of the King who made them. Alſo it ſeems [i] certain, That at the Common Law (before 1 *Ed.* 6. 7. ſet forth more at large, *Ch.* 6.) if one had been convicted of any Offence before any ſuch Commiſſioners, and the King had died before Judgment, no Judgment at all could have been given, becauſe the King was dead for whom the Judgment was to have been given, and becauſe the Authority of the Judges was determined. Alſo it is ſaid, that at [k] Common Law a Perſon attainted in the Time of a former King, could not have been executed without a new Warrant. Yet it hath been adjudged, That the Authority of a [l] Coroner or Verderor ceaſes not by the Demiſe of the King in whoſe Reign they were choſen; and that the Office of a [m] Sheriff, in ſuch Places where he is choſen by a Corporation, having by its Charter the Inheritance of the Office, does not determine by the Demiſe of the King; from whence it ſeems alſo to follow, That no other Corporation-Officer, who by the Charter is inveſted with any judicial Authority, loſes it by ſuch Demiſe.

Sect. 12. And to prevent the Diſorders and other Inconveniences, which may happen upon the Death of a King, from the Want of Perſons armed with competent Authority to execute the Laws, before the Succeſſor can have Time to appoint others, it was enacted by 7 & 8 *Gul.* 3. 27. *Sect.* 21. *That no Commiſſion either Civil or Military, ſhall ceaſe, determine, or be void, by Reaſon of the Death and Demiſe of his ſaid Majeſty, or of any of his Heirs or Succeſſors, Kings or Queens of this Realm; but that every ſuch Commiſſion ſhall be, continue, and remain in full Force and Virtue, for the Space of ſix Months next after any ſuch Death or Demiſe, unleſs in the mean Time ſuperſeded, determined, or made void by the next and immediate Succeſſor, to whom the Imperial Crown of this Realm, according to the Act of Settlement in the ſaid Statute before mentioned, is limited and appointed to go, remain or deſcend.*

Sect. 13. And it is further enacted by 1 *Annæ*, Stat. 1. c. 8. Par. 2. *That no Patent or Grant of any Office or Imployment, either Civil or Military, hereafter to be made, ſhall ceaſe, determine, or be void, by Reaſon of the Death*

or

[a] 42 Aſſ. 5. Bro. Commiſſion, 3, 15, 16. 2 Inſt. 54.

[b] 4 Inſt. 163, 245. 18 E. 3. ch. 14.

[c] 2 Inſt. 478.

[d] 1 Rol. Abr. 382. b. 6 Mod. 87. 9 E. 4. 30. b. 31. a. Bro. Judges, 11.

[e] Latch. 7.

[f] Bro. Coron. 201. 14 H. 4. 34. b. 35. a. 23 Aſſ. pl. 7. 39 H. 6. 41. b. 42. a. S. P. C. 53. Letters B, C. Con. Daliſ. 24, 25. Hob. 70. 2 Rol. A. 673. Crompt. 121.

[g] 27 Aſſ. 23. 2 Rol. Abr. 677. G.

[h] Daliſ. 15. Benloe 79. Dy. 165. pl. 2. 1 And. 44. 4 E. 4. 44. Bro. Judges, 32. 1 E. 5. 1. Crom. Jur. 126. a.

[i] 7 Co. 31.

[k] 1 Aſſ. pl. 8. Bro. Coron. 66.

[l] Daliſ. 15. Dy. 165. pl. 2. 2 Inſt. 175. 1 Levinz 120. Bro. Coron. 201. Commiſſion, 19. Crom. Jur. 126 a. But this is made a Quære 4 E. 4. 44. a. b. and Bro. Officer, 25. and denied in S. P. C. fol. 49. Letters B, C.

[m] 7 Co. 30. b.

or Demise of any King or Queen of this Realm, but that every such Patent or Grant shall be, continue, and remain in full Force for six Months, next after any such Death or Demise, unless in the mean Time superseded, determined, or made void by the next immediate Successor, to whom the Crown is limited and appointed to go, remain or descend.

And it is farther enacted, Par. 5. *That no Commission of Assize,* Oyer *and* Terminer, *general Gaol-Delivery, or of Association, Writ of Admittance, Writ of* Si non omnes, *Writ of Assistance, or Commission of the Peace, shall be determined by the Death of any King or Queen of this Realm; but every such Commission and Writ shall be and continue in full Force for six Months next ensuing, notwithstanding such Demise, unless superseded and determined by the next Successor: And also no original Writ, Writ of* Nisi Prius, *Commission, Process or Proceedings whatsoever, in, or issuing out of, any Court of Equity, nor any Process or Proceedings upon any Office or Inquisition, nor any Writ of* Certiorari, *or* Habeas Corpus, *in any Matter or Cause, either Criminal or Civil, nor any Writ of Attachment, or Process for Contempt,* &c. *shall be determined, abated, or discontinued, by the Demise of any King or Queen of this Realm; but every such Writ,* &c. *shall remain in full Force, to be proceeded upon, as if such King or Queen had lived.*

[a] 2 Inst. 311, 312. Far. 128. Reg. 111. b. F.N.B. 85. f. 16. a. 239. d. 1 Rol. Ab. 543. E, F. pl. 3. Co. Lit. 117. b. 260. a. 2 Lev. 93. 1 Mod. 215. 3 Lev. 205. 8 Co. 38. b.
[b] Salk. 200.
[c] 11 H. 6. 12. b. 1 Rol. Ab. 219. Y. 8 Co. 38. b. 11 Co. 43. b. Cro. El. 581. 1 Sid. 145. Brook Leet, 12, 36.
[d] F. N. B. 82. Dalton ch. 1. Lamb. ch. 3. 10 H. 6. 10. b. Cromp. 7. 11 Co. 43. b. seems contrary.
[e] 1 H. 7. 26. a. 3 Inst. 29.
[f] 27 Ass. pl. 23. 2 Rol. A. 77. G. Bro. Indictment, 17. Crom. 121, 122. Salk. 201. Far. 2

As to the second Point, *viz.* What is incidental to all such Courts in general, I shall only take Notice of the following Particulars;

Sect. 14. First, That all Courts of this Kind must be Courts of [a] Record; for a Court which is not of Record, can neither impose any Fine on an Offender, nor award a *Capias* against him, nor even hold Plea of a common Trespass *Vi & Armis*; and from hence it clearly follows, That no Proceedings of any Court of criminal Jurisdiction, can be removed into a Superior, but by Writ of Error or *Certiorari*; and that no Averment can be taken against the Truth of any Thing recorded in any such Court; [b] and that all Courts of Common Law, that have Power given them to fine and imprison, are thereby made Courts of Record.

Sect. 15. Secondly, That [c] all such Courts may injoin the People to keep Silence under a Pain, and impose reasonable Fines, not only on such as shall be convicted before them of any Crime on a formal Prosecution, but also on all such as shall be guilty of any Contempt in the Face of the Court, as by giving opprobrious Language to the Judge, or obstinately refusing to do their Duty as Officers of the Court; and it is said, That all such Courts, except the Court-Leet, may also imprison all such Offenders: Also it seems, [d] That even a Court-Leet is so far intrusted with the Keeping of the Peace within its own Precinct, that the Steward of it may by Recognizance bind any Person to the Peace, who shall make an Affray in his Presence, sitting the Court, or may commit him to Ward, either for want of Sureties, or by Way of Punishment, without demanding any Sureties of him, in which Case he may afterwards impose a Fine according to his Discretion; from whence it follows *à fortiori*, that other superior Courts of Record have the like Power.

Sect. 16. Thirdly, That no [e] Judge of any such Court is compellable to deliver his Opinion before-hand, in Relation to any Question which may after come judicially before him.

Sect. 17. That no such Judge is any Way punishable for a mere [f] Error of Judgment, as hath been more fully shewn in the first *Book, Chap.* 17. *Sect.* 6.

Sect. 18. It is questioned, whether all Courts of Record may not discharge any Person arrested, during his Journeying to or from such Courts, or necessary Attendance there by Process from any other Court: However it seems to be agreed, That any such Court may discharge a Person who shall be so arrested in the Face of it. Lamb. 403. Quære 1 Keb. 845. 1 Lev. 159. 1 Brown 15. Raym. 100. Bro. Privilege, 35. Crompt. 180.

CHAP. II.

Of the Court of the High Steward of England.

AND now I am to consider the Nature of the principal Courts of criminal Jurisdiction in particular, and

1. Of the Court of the High Steward of *England.*
2. The Court of King's Bench.
3. The Court of the Constable and Marshal.
4. The Court of the Justices of *Oyer* and *Terminer.*
5. The Court of the Justices of Gaol-Delivery.
6. The Court of the Justices of Assize and *Nisi Prius.*
7. The Court of the Sessions of the Justices of the Peace.
8. The Court of the Coroners.
9. The Sheriff's Torn.
10. The Court-Leet.

The Office of High Steward of *England*, which anciently was Hereditary, not having been granted to any one since the Reign of King *Henry* the Fourth, but only *pro hac vice*, either for the Trial of a Peer on an Indictment for a capital Offence, or for the Determination of the Pretensions of those who claim to hold by Grand Serjeanty, to do certain honourable Services to the King at his Coronation: It seems needless to make a particular Inquiry, concerning the Authority of the Court of this High Officer, of which very little Mention is made in our ancient Records, or Law-Books; and therefore I shall content my self with remarking in this Place in general, That anciently the Duty of this Office consisted in supervising and regulating next under the King the Administration of Justice, and all other Affairs of the Realm, whether Civil or Military, and that no one under the Degree of Nobility is capable of so honourable a Post; and for the particular Manner of executing this Office in the Trial of a Peer, I shall refer the Reader to the Chapter concerning the Trial of Peers. 4 Inst. 58, 59. Mad. History of the Exchequer, 33, &c. Crompton of Courts, 84. Fleta, lib. 2. Ca. 2, 3. 2 H.H.P.C. 7. 3 Inst. 28. 13 H. 8. 11. b. 4 Inst. 59. S. P. C. 152. infra Ch. 3. Sect. 1.

CHAP. III.

Of the Court of King's Bench.

Vide fupra, Ch. 1. Sect. 3. and Madox, ch. 19. [a] Madox, fol. 21. and 135. 2 H.H.P.C.6. 1 Rol. Ab. 94. Letter A. and 95. Letter B. 2 Inft. 24, 25, 26. [b] See Madox, Ch. 19. Quære 2 Inft. 21, 22, 23. 1 Inft. 71. [c] Madox 543. [d] Dyer 187. Pl. 6. Madox 543, 544. Crompton of Courts, 78. B.

Sect. 1. THE whole Jurifdiction which is now diftributed among the feveral Courts of *Weftminfter-Hall*, feems in the firft Reigns after the Conqueft, to have been lodged in one Court, commonly called the King's Court, wherein Juftice is faid to have been adminiftred fometimes by the King himfelf in Perfon, and fometimes by the High Jufticier, who was an [a] Officer of very great Authority, and ufed in the King's Abfence beyond-fea to govern the Realm as Vice-Roy.

Sect. 2. Out of this Court the Courts of [b] Common Pleas and Exchequer feem to have been derived, fome Time before the making of the Statute of *Magna Charta*; the former of which Courts properly determines Pleas merely Civil, and the latter thofe relating to the Revenue of the Crown. And after the [c] Erection of thefe Courts, the fupreme Court feems by Degrees to have obtained the Name of the Court of King's Bench, and hath always retained a fupreme Jurifdiction in all criminal Matters, and alfo in certain perfonal Caufes, and is ftill [d] fuppofed to have always the King himfelf in Perfon fitting in it.

For the better Underftanding the Nature of this Court, I fhall confider the following Particulars:

1. In what Manner it corrects all Kinds of Mifdemeanors of all Perfons in general.
2. How far it reforms inferior Courts.
3. How far its Prefence fufpends the Power of all other Courts.
4. What Rules are to be obferved in the Form of its Proceedings.

See 16 Ca. 1. ca. 10. fect. 2. 11 Co. 98. 4 Inft. 71. 2 H. H. P. C. 2, 5, 6.

Sect. 3. As to the firft Point, it is certain, That this Court is intrufted with the higheft Jurifdiction, not only over all capital Offences, but alfo all other Mifdemeanors whatfoever of a publick Nature, tending either to a Breach of the Peace, or to the Oppreffion of the Subject, or to the raifing of Faction, Controverfy, or Debate, or to any Manner of Mifgovernment; fo that whatfoever Crime is manifeftly againft the Publick Good, it comes within the Conufance of this Court, though it do not directly injure any particular Perfon; neither can any private Subject, who has not forfeited his Right to the Protection of the Law, fuffer any Kind of unlawful Violence or grofs Injuftice againft his Perfon, Liberty, or Poffeffions, from any Perfon whatfoever, without a proper Remedy from this Court, not only for Satisfaction of the private Damage, but alfo for the exemplary Punifhment of the Offender.

1 Sid. 168. See the Preamble of 16 Ca. 1.

Sect. 4. Neither is it neceffary in a Profecution of any fuch Offence in this Court, to fhew a Precedent of the like Crime formerly punifhed here, agreeing with the prefent in all its Circumftances; for this Court being the *Cuftos Morum* of all the Subjects of the Realm, where-ever it meets with an Offence contrary to the firft Principles of common Juftice, and of dangerous Conſequence to the Publick, if non reſtrained, will adapt ſuch a Puniſhment to it as is ſuitable to the Heinouſneſs of it.

Sect. 5. And ſo high a Truſt doth the Law repoſe in the Juſtice and Integrity of this Court, as generally to leave it to the Diſcretion of its Judges to inflict ſuch Fine and Impriſonment, and even infamous Puniſhment on Offenders, as the Nature of the Crime, conſidered in all its Circumſtances, ſhall require; neither doth it confine them to make uſe of their own Priſon, but leaves them at Liberty to commit Offenders to any Priſon in the Kingdom, which they ſhall think moſt proper, and doth not ſuffer any other Court to remove or bail any Perſons condemned to Impriſonment by them.

Mo. 666. Pl. 913. 1 Sid. 145.

Sect. 6. Alſo this Court hath ſuch a ſovereign Juriſdiction in criminal Matters, that it may proceed as [a] well on Indictments found before other Courts, and removed into this by *Certiorari*, as on Indictments or Informations originally commenced in it, whether the Courts before whom ſuch Indictments were found be determined or ſuſpended, or ſtill *in eſſe*, and whether the Proceedings be grounded on the Common Law, or on ſome Statute making a new Law concerning an old Offence, and appointing certain Juſtices to execute it, as the Statutes of [b] forcible Entries, and the [c] Statute of *Philip* and *Mary*, againſt Perſons taking away Females under the Age of ſixteen Years from their [d] Guardians, *&c.* Neither doth a Statute which appoints, That all Crimes of a certain Denomination ſhall be tried before certain Judges, exclude the Juriſdiction of this Court without expreſs negative Words; upon which Ground it hath been reſolved, That [e] 33 *H.* 8. 12. which enacts, That all Treaſons, *&c.* within the King's Houſe, ſhall be determined before the Lord Steward of the King's Houſe, *&c.* doth not reſtrain this Court from proceeding againſt ſuch Offences: But where a Statute creates a [f] new Offence, which was not taken Notice of by the Common Law, and erects a new Juriſdiction for the Puniſhment of it, and preſcribes a certain Method of Proceeding, it ſeems queſtionable, how far this Court has an implied Juriſdiction in ſuch a Caſe.

[a] Dalif. 25. 2 H. H. P. C. 3, 105. Carth. 6. 44 E. 3. 31 b. Cromp. Juriſd. 131.
[b] 9 Co. 118. See B. 1. Ch. 64. Sect. 51.
[c] Cro. Ca. 465. 2 Lev. 179. 2 Mod. 128, 129, 130.
[d] 3 Keb. 75. 94, 106, 273.
[e] 2 Inſt. 549. 2 Jones 53. 2 H. H. P. C. 5, 9.
[f] See 1 Sid. 296. the Books above cited and the Chapter concerning Indictments.

Sect. 7. But it is certain, That the Law has ſo high a Regard to this Court, that it will not ſuffer a [g] Record regularly removed into it from an inferior one, to be remanded [h] after the Term in which it came in, (except in ſome few [i] Special Caſes;) [k] yet if the Juſtices perceive, that there is any Practice in endeavouring to remove any ſuch Record, or that the ſole Intention of ſuch Removals is the Delay of Juſtice, they may on their Diſcretion refuſe to receive ſuch Record, and may before it is filed remand it back again, for the Expedition of Juſtice; and upon this [k] Ground, as I ſuppoſe, where one who had pleaded Not guilty to an Appeal below, and at his Trial had challenged ſo many of his Jury, that the Inqueſt could not be taken for want of Jurors, whereupon a new *Diſtringas* was awarded, removed himſelf in the Court of King's Bench, he was ordered to be remanded: Alſo by the Conſtruction of the Statutes, which impower the Common Law Courts of *Weſtminſter*, to grant a [l] *Niſi Prius* for the Trial of Iſſues joined in thoſe Courts, the Juſtices of the King's Bench may grant ſuch Trial, as well in Caſes of Treaſon and Felony as in other common Caſes; becauſe, for ſuch Trial, not the Record it ſelf is ſent down, but only the Tranſcript of it.

[g] 22 E. 3. 6 b. 2 H. H. P. C. 3. 29 Aſſ. 43. 40 Aſſ. 29. 1 Rol. Ab. 534. G. 2. 492. K. 1. 4 Inſt. 73. S. P. C. 158.
[h] 1 Rol. Rep. 85.
[i] Cro. Car. 297. 1 Saunders 97, 99. 1 Lev. 223. 1 Sid. 329.
[k] 4 Inſt. 74, 75. 16 E. 4. 5. a. Bro. Coron. 162.
[l] 4 Inſt. 74. Ray. 364.

Sect. 8. And it is recited by 6 *H.* 8. 6. *That divers Felons and Murderers, upon feigned and untrue Surmiſes, had oftentimes removed as well their Bodies as their Indictments, by Writ and otherwiſe, before the King in his Bench, and could not by the Order of the Law be remitted and ſent down to the Juſtices*

of

of Gaol-Delivery, or of the Peace, nor other Juſtices, nor Commiſſioners, to proceed upon them after the Courſe of the Common Law. And thereupon it is enacted, *That the Juſtices of the King's Bench have full Authority by their Diſcretions, to remand and ſend down, as well the Bodies of all Felons and Murderers, brought or removed before the King in his Bench, as their Indictments, into the Counties where the ſame Murders or Felonies have been committed and done; and to command all Juſtices of Gaol-Delivery, Juſtices of Peace, and all other Juſtices and Commiſſioners, and every of them, to proceed and determine, upon all the aforeſaid Bodies and Indictments ſo removed, after the Courſe of the Common Law, in ſuch Manner as the ſame Juſtices of Gaol-Delivery, Juſtices of Peace, and other Commiſſioners, or any of them, might or ſhould have done, if the ſaid Priſoners or Indictments had never been brought into the ſaid King's Bench.*

Cromp. Jur. 213. 2 H. H. P. C. 3, 4, 41.

Ray. 367.

Sect. 9. In the Conſtruction of this Statute it ſeems to have been holden, That it ſhall not be extended by Equity to High Treaſon.

Sect. 10. As to the ſecond Point, *viz.* How far the Court of King's Bench reforms inferior Courts, there is no Doubt, but that this Court, being the higheſt Court of Common Law, hath not only Power to reverſe erroneous Judgments given by inferior Courts, but alſo to puniſh all inferior Magiſtrates, and all Officers of Juſtice, for all wilful and corrupt Abuſes of their Authority, againſt the known, obvious, and common Principles of natural Juſtice, but not for mere Miſtakes, which an honeſt well meaning Man may innocently fall into.

[a] H.P.C. 156. 2 H.H.P.C. 4. 9 Co. 118. b. 27 Aſſ. pl. 1. 3 Inſt. 27. 4 Inſt. 73. [b] 21 H. 7. 29. b. Bro. Commiſſion, 10. Vide infra Ch. 5. Sect. 3. [c] 4 Inſt. 73. [d] 4 Inſt. 73. Dy. 286. Pl. 45. [e] Keilw. 152. b. [f] Keilw. 153.

Sect. 11. As to the third Point, *viz.* How far the Preſence of this Court ſuſpends the Power of all other Courts, it is certain, That this being the [a] ſupreme Court of *Oyer* and *Terminer*, Gaol-Delivery, and *Eyre*, doth ſo far ſuſpend the Power of all other Juſtices of this Kind, in the County wherein it ſits, during the Time of its ſitting in it, (if ſuch Juſtices have [b] Notice of its ſitting there, and even without ſuch [c] Notice, as ſome ſay,) that all Proceedings commenced before any ſuch Juſtices during ſuch Time are void; yet it [d] ſeems, That ſuch Juſtices may proceed upon Indictments taken in a foreign County and removed before them, becauſe the Court of King's Bench hath nothing to do with ſuch Indictments, unleſs they be removed into it. Alſo there ſeems to be the ſame Reaſon, That ſuch Juſtices may proceed on Indictments taken before them, of Offences in the ſame County before the Term; for it is ſaid in [e] *Keilway*, That if an Appeal be commenced before Juſtices in *Eyre*, and afterwards another Appeal be brought in the King's Bench, it will be a good Plea that another Appeal is depending; which ſhews that the King's Bench ought not without a *Certiorari*, &c. to intermeddle in an Appeal, whereof another Court is legally poſſeſſed before; and the Reaſon ſeems to be the ſame as to Indictments: And it is ſaid in the ſame [f] Book, That if the King's Bench and Juſtices in *Eyre* are in one County, yet this ſhall not change the Power of the Juſtices in *Eyre*, but that if the King will make Proceſs for any Thing not commenced before the Juſtices of *Eyre*, as to ſuch Thing their Power is ceaſed; by which it ſeems to be implied, that as to what was commenced before them, their Power continues: However, it is certainly the [g] ſafeſt way for any of the Juſtices above mentioned proceeding on any ſuch Indictment, to have a Special Commiſſion for that Purpoſe, and it is moſt adviſable, that ſuch Commiſſion bear *Teſte* in the Term.

[g] 3 Inſt. 24. 4 Inſt. 73. H. P. C. 156, 157. [h] Co. Entries, 57. b. 58. b. 60. a. [i] Co. Entries, 354. b. 355. b. 356. b. 358. a.

Sect. 12. As to the fourth Point, What Rules are to be obſerved in the Form of the Proceedings of this Court, it ſeemeth, That all Proceſs upon [h] Writs of Appeal, and alſo all Proceſs upon [i] Indictments removed hither by *Certiorari* from a foreign County, ought to be made returnable

2 *coram*

coram nobis ubicunque fuerimus, but that all Proceſs upon [a] Bills of Appeal [a] Co. Entries
againſt one *in cuſtodia Mareſchalli*, and perhaps alſo upon [b] Indictments 52. a. b.
commenced in the King's Bench, ought to be returnable *coram nobis apud* 58. b. 60.a. [b] Co. Entries
Weſtmonaſterium: Alſo it has been [c] reſolved, That where the Court pro- 352.a. 353.b.
ceeds on an Offence committed in the ſame County wherein it ſits, the 361. a. Con. Co. En-
Proceſs may be made returnable immediately; but that where it proceeds on tries 360. a.
an Offence removed by *Certiorari* from another, there muſt be fifteen Days 363. a. [c] 9 Co. 118. b.
between the *Teſte* and Return of every Proceſs. Co.Lit.134.b.
1 Lev. 61.
1 Sid. 72. 2 Rol. Ab. 626. pl. 4, 5. 2 Inſt. 550, 568.

CHAP. IV.

Of the Court of the Conſtable and Marſhal.

FOR the better Underſtanding the Nature of this Court, it may not be improper to premiſe ſome general Conſiderations concerning the ancient Juriſdiction of thoſe high Officers before whom it is holden.

Sect. 1. As to Office of High Conſtable of *England*, which an- Dy. 285. b.
ciently was Hereditary, the ſame being eſteemed of too high Authority 4 Inſt. 127.
to be ſafely intruſted with any Subject, but only *pro hac vice*, ſince the Far. 125.
Reign of King *Henry* the Eighth, and there being very little to be found Mad. Hiſtory
in our ancient Records and Hiſtories, concerning the particular Power of the Exche-
or Authority of this high Officer, our moſt learned Antiquaries ſeem to quer, folio 27, 28, 29.
be able to give us little more than their own Conjectures concerning this Matter. However there is no Doubt, but that he was an Officer of very great Power both in War and Peace; and indeed his very Name im-
ports no leſs; for the Word Conſtable ſignifying in general a Commander Madox 27.
or Officer, he who was called Conſtable of *England*, or the King's Con-
ſtable, or ſometimes, by way of Eminency, the Conſtable, without any Madox 28.
other Addition, cannot but be thought to have been a Perſon of the higheſt Command and Authority; and the Statute of 13 *R.* 2. (which is at large ſet forth in the following Part of this Chapter,) reſtraining his Juriſdiction to Things touching War, not determinable by the Common Law, in relation to which it requires him to proceed according to ancient Uſage, clearly ſuppoſes him to have an ancient eſtabliſhed Authority concerning theſe Matters: And it ſeems to have been ſomewhat doubtful,
before the making of the ſaid Statute, Whether the Conſtable and Mar- 48 E. 3. 3.
ſhal had not a general Juriſdiction over all Contracts whatſoever made be- 13 H. 4. 4, 5.
yond Sea.

Sect. 2. Neither do there ſeem to be any greater Footſteps in Antiquity, of the original Inſtitution of the Office of the Lord Marſhal, or of his Power, or Authority; for anciently there were ſeveral Officers of the King's Houſhold, who were called Marſhals, as the Marſhals of his
[a] Horſes, of his [a] Birds, and of his [a] Meaſures, who had certain Salaries [a] Madox 30.
allotted them, for the Management or well ordering of the Things committed to their Charge. And in the ancient Records relating to thoſe
Officers, there ſeems no more to be meant by having the Marſhalſy of Madox 30, 31.
a Thing, than to have the Overſight, or Charge, or Ordering of it: Alſo in our old Records, there are ſome Officers taken Notice of by the Name of Marſhals, who are mentioned only in general to have been Ser-
vants of the King's Houſhold, without any farther Account of the Na- Madox 29, 30.

1 Rol. Ab. 527. K. ture of their Office or Duty in particular. However, we find that in the
22d Year of King *Edw.* 3. the Parliament granted Fifteenths on divers Con-
ditions, one of which was, That there ſhall be no Mareſchalſy in *Eng-
land*, except the Mareſchalſy of the King, and of the Guardian of *Eng-
land*, when the King ſhall be out of *England*. And it ſeems clear, That
there was one Marſhal ſuperior to the reſt, who was ſometimes called the
Madox 31, 32, 33. Maſter-Marſhal, at other Times the King's Marſhal, the Marſhal of *Eng-
land*, or the Earl Marſhal, being an Officer of very great Authority both
[a] Fleta Lib. 2. Ca. 4. Co. Lit. 74. in War and Peace, whoſe principal Office in [a] Time of War, was to regu-
late the Incampments of the Army, and to aſſign to the Troops their re-
[b] Madox 33. ſpective Poſts in the Day of Battle; and in [b] Time of Peace, to provide for
the Security of the King's Perſon in his Palace, to diſtribute the Lodgings
there, and to preſerve Peace and Order in the King's Houſhold, and to be
[c] 4 Inſt. 123. Caſes in Parliament 60. aſſiſtant to the Conſtable in Determining Cauſes, and alſo to [c] execute the
Orders both of the Court of the Conſtable, wherein he himſelf ſate as
[d] Fleta Lib. 2. Ca. 3. Judge, and of the [d] Court of the High Steward, to which he ſeems to have
been only an Officer.

Sect. 3. But whatever might be the original Inſtitution of theſe Officers,
or the Nature of their Authority, it is certain their Juriſdiction is at pre-
ſent declared, limited and reſtrained by certain Acts of Parliament, before
Madox 29. the Making whereof, we have ſcarce any Thing memorable on Record con-
cerning this Matter.

Sect. 4. And firſt it is enacted by 8 *R.* 2. 5. as followeth, *Becauſe divers Pleas concerning the Common Law, and which by the Common Law ought to be examined and diſcuſſed, are of late drawn before the Conſtable and Marſhal of* England, *to the great Damage and Diſquietneſs of the People: It is agreed and ordained, That all Pleas and Suits touching the Common Law, and which ought to be examined and diſcuſſed at the Common Law, ſhall not hereafter be drawn or holden by any Means before the aforeſaid Conſtable and Marſhal, but that the Court of the ſame Conſtable and Marſhal ſhall have that which belongeth to the ſame Court, and that the Common Law ſhall be executed and uſed, and have that which to it belongeth, and the ſame ſhall be executed and uſed, as it was accuſtomed to be uſed in the Time of King* Edward.

Sect. 5. And it is farther declared by 13 *R.* 2. 2. in the following Words, *Becauſe that the Commons do make a grievous Complaint, that the Court of the Conſtable and Marſhal hath incroached to him and daily doth incroach Contracts, Covenants, Treſpaſſes, Debts and Detinues, and many other Actions pleadable at the Common Law, in great Prejudice of the King, and of his Courts, and to the great Grievance and Oppreſſion of the People: Our Lord the King, willing to ordain a Remedy againſt the Prejudices and Grievances aforeſaid, hath declared in this Parliament, by the Advice and Aſſent of the Lords Spiritual and Temporal, the Power and Juriſdiction of the ſaid Conſtable, in the Form that followeth: To the Conſtable it pertaineth to have Cognizance of Contracts touching Deeds of Arms and of War out of the Realm, and alſo of Things that touch War within the Realm, which cannot be determined nor diſcuſſed by the Common Law, with other Uſages and Cuſtoms to the ſame Matters pertaining, which other Conſtables heretofore have duly and reaſonably uſed in their Time. Joining to the ſame, That every Plaintiff ſhall declare plainly his Matter in his Petition, before that any Man be ſent for to anſwer thereunto. And if any will complain, That any Plea be commenced before the Conſtable and Marſhal, that might be tried by the Common Law of the Land, the ſame Plaintiff ſhall have a Privy Seal of the King without Difficulty, directed to the ſaid Conſtable and Marſhal, to ſurceaſe in that Plea, until it be diſcuſſed by the King's Council, if that Matter ought of Right to pertain to that Court, or otherwiſe to be tried by the Common Law of the Realm of* England, *and also that they surcease in the mean Time.*

Sect. 6. And it is farther enacted by 1 *H.* 4. 14. as followeth, *For many great Inconveniencies and Mischiefs, that often have happened, by many Appeals made within the Realm of* England *before this Time, it is ordained and established from henceforth, That all the Appeals to be made of Things done within the Realm, shall be tried and determined by the good Laws of the Realm, made and used in the Time of the King's noble Progenitors; and that all the Appeals to be made of Things done out of the Realm, shall be tried and determined before the Constable and Marshal of* England *for the Time being: And moreover, it is accorded and assented, That no Appeal be from henceforth made, or in any wise pursued in Parliament in Time to come.*

For the better Understanding of the Construction of these Statutes, and the Nature of this Court, I shall examine the following Particulars:

1. How far the said Court hath Conusance of Points of Honour in general.
2. Whether it can punish private Persons for marshalling Funerals.
3. Whether it can be holden by a Lord Marshal alone without a Constable.
4. Whether its Power as to Appeals of Treason be superseded by 26 or 35 *H.* 8. or 5 and 6 *Ed.* 6. 11. or 1 and 2 *Ph.* and *Mar.* 10.
5. By what Law, and in what Manner it proceeds.
6. Whether it may be prohibited if it exceeds its Jurisdiction.
7. Whether it can be holden by Commission.

Sect. 7. As to the first Point it is observable, That the above mentioned Statute of 13 *R.* 2. declares the Jurisdiction of this Court, in Relation to Things done within the Realm in these Words, *To the Constable pertaineth Conusance*, &c. *of things that touch War within the Realm, which cannot be determined nor discussed by the Common Law:* From whence it seems to follow, That this Court has nothing to do with a meer Civil Matter, no way relating to War; and therefore the Proceedings of the Court of the Lord Marshal, in the Time of King *Charles* the First, for bare scandalous Words, reflecting on the [a] Honour or Gentility of Families, seem no way to be maintained; yet it seems to be taken for granted in some [b] Books, That Disputes concerning Precedency, and Points of Honour, and Satisfaction therein, are proper for this Court: Neither do I find, That the Proceedings therein against Persons for falsly assuming the Name and Arms of honourable Families, were censured or disallowed by the [c] learned Members of the Committee of the House of Commons in the Year 1639. who were appointed to inquire into the Abuses of this Court. And it seems to be [d] admitted in the Argument of *Oldis*'s Case, That all Matters of this Nature are proper for this Court; yet it seems to be a large Interpretation to make these Things relate to War, so as to come within the Declaration above mentioned; and the Rule laid down in [e] *Rolle*'s *Reports*, that the Marshal has Power given him where the Common Law gives no Remedy, seems no way maintainable from the said Statute; for it doth not say in general, That to the Constable pertaineth Conusance of Things, which cannot be determined by the Common Law, but of Things of War, *&c.* which cannot be thereby determined; [f] neither is it a conclusive Argument, that a Matter which is remediless by the Common Law, must have a Remedy from some other Law; yet inasmuch as by the Preamble of the said Statute,

1 H. H. P. C. 500.

[a] Rushworth's Coll. Part 2. Vol. 2. 1055, 1056.

[b] Hob. 121. 1 Rol. Re. 87. 2 Lev. 134 Show. 353. 1 Sid. 353. 1 Lev. 230.

[c] Rushworth's Coll. Part 2. Vol. 2. 1055, 1056.

[d] Parliament Cases 64, 65.

[e] 1 Rol. Re. 87.

[f] 13 H. 4. 4 b. 5. a.

tute, its chief Intention appears to be to prevent Incroachments on the Common Law; and ſuch Proceedings in Matters whereof the Common Law hath no Conuſance, cannot be ſaid any way to incroach upon it: And inaſmuch as the ſaid Statute is wholly declarative, and hath no negative Words; and the conſtant Practice, which is the beſt Interpreter of Laws, and the general Opinion of Lawyers, ſeem to countenance ſuch Proceedings, I ſhall not take upon me to determine how far they may be warrantable.

1 Lev. 230. 2 Sid. 353. Show. Rep. 353.

Sect. 8. As to the ſecond Point, *viz.* Whether this Court can puniſh private Perſons for Marſhalling Funerals; though it ſhould be granted, That the Marſhalling of publick Funerals belongs to the Heralds, who are Attendants on this Court, and that no other Perſons without their Licence can lawfully intermeddle therein; yet it does by no Means follow, That the Marſhal has Power to puniſh thoſe who ſhall be guilty of any ſuch Incroachment; but the proper Remedy ſeems to be by Action on the Caſe at Common Law, and not by a Suit in this Court, which by the above mentioned Statutes of 8 and 13 *R.* 2. has Cognizance only of ſuch Matters, which cannot be determined nor diſcuſſed by the Common Law: And this ſeems to be the principal Reaſon of Dr. *Oldis*'s Caſe, wherein a Suit in the Marſhal's Court againſt one *Donmille*, for taking upon him without Licenſe to paint Arms and Eſcutcheons, and cauſing them to be fixed to Herſes, and providing and lending Palls for Funerals, and painting Arms for one who had no Right to their Uſe at the Funeral, and marſhalling ſeveral Funerals, &c. was prohibited by the Court of Exchequer, upon great Deliberation, with the Advice of the reſt of the Judges, and the Judgment was afterwards confirmed by the Houſe of Lords.

Caſes in Parliament 58, &c.

[a] Caſes in Parliament 65, 66. Far. 127, 128. [b] Ruſhworth's Coll. Part 2. Vol. 2. 1056. [c] S. P. C. 65. Cromp. Juriſdiction 82. 2 Inſt. 51. 4 Inſt. 123. Co. Lit. 261. a. 391. b. [d] 13 H. 4. 46. 37 H. 3. 5. a. 48 E. 3. 3. b. 37 H. 6. 20. b. 21. a. [e] 30 H. 6. 6. b. 13 H. 4. 5. a. [f] 1 Inſt. 74. b. Ruſhworth's Coll. Part 2. Vol. 1. 107, 112, &c. Caſes in Parliament 61. 1 Lev. 230. Hutton 3. [g] Caſes in Parliament 60, 61. [h] See Ch. 1. S. 10.

Sect. 9. As to the Third Point, *viz.* Whether this Court can be holden by the Lord Marſhal alone without the Conſtable, it was ſtrongly inſiſted in the [a] Arguments made uſe of in Dr. *Oldis*'s Caſe, That the Lord Marſhal cannot hold this Court without the Conſtable; and this was alſo the Opinion of the [b] above mentioned learned Committee of the Houſe of Commons in the Year 1639. And it is certain, That all our ancient [c] Law-Books and [d] Reports which ſpeak of this Court, ſpeak of it either as the Court of the Conſtable and Marſhal, or of the Conſtable [e] only; and it is obſervable, that the above mentioned Statute of 13 *R.* 2. which in the Preamble ſpeaks of this Court, as the Court of the Conſtable and Marſhal, in the Body of the Act mentions the Conſtable only. And it is farther remarkable, That where-ever the Conſtable is mentioned together with the Marſhal, as Judge of this Court, he is always put before him; which ſeems to intimate, that he is look'd upon as the principal Judge of it: And it is agreed by [f] all, That the Marſhal cannot determine an Appeal of Death, or Treaſon, without a Conſtable; but on the other Side it may be argued, That the Reaſon why an Appeal of a capital Matter neceſſarily requires a Conſtable as well as Marſhal, is, becauſe 1 *H.* 4. which orders how ſuch an Appeal ſhall be brought, is expreſs, That it ſhall be tried and determined before the Conſtable and Marſhal of *England* for the Time being; whereas the other Statutes only provide againſt the Incroachments of this Court, and do not mention in what Manner, or before whom it ſhall be holden; but they ſeem to refer ſuch Queſtions to ancient Uſage; ſo that if [g] before theſe Statutes the Court was uſually holden before the Conſtable and Marſhal jointly and ſeverally, [h] according to the common Uſage of other Courts, which generally may be holden before one Judge in the Abſence of the reſt, it ſeems a reaſonable Conſtruction of the ſaid Statutes to allow this Court ſtill to be ſo holden; neither is it probable, That the Lord Marſhal upon the Extinguiſhment of the hereditary Office of the Conſtable, ſhould from Time to Time in the [a] Reigns of King *Henry* the Eighth, Queen *Elizabeth*, and King *James* the Firſt, hold this Court by himſelf without any Conſtable, and alſo often be aſſiſted therein by the Judges of the Common Law, unleſs it were then well known, that ſuch his Proceeding was warranted by the ancient and eſtabliſhed Uſage of his Court; and it is very extraordinary, That our Judges and Lawyers ſhould [b] generally take it as a Thing granted, that the Marſhal is at this Day the proper Judge of Points of Honour, *&c.* if it were imagined that he has no Power to act without the Concurrence of a Conſtable.

[a] Caſes in Parliament 60, 61. Far. 126. 4 Inſt. 126

[b] Hob. 121. 1 Rol. Rep. 87. 2 Lev. 134. Show. 353. 1 Sid. 353. 1 Lev. 250.

Sect. 10. As to the fourth Point, *viz.* Whether the Power of this Court as to Appeals of Treaſon, be ſuperſeded by the Statutes of 26 *H.* 8. 13. or 35 *H.* 8. 2. or 5 and 6 *Ed.* 6. 11. or 1 and 2 *Ph.* and *Mar.* 10. it is obſervable that it is enacted by the ſaid Statutes of *H.* 8. and *Ed.* 6. *That all Manner of Treaſons,* &c. *done out of this Realm ſhall from thenceforth be inquired, heard and determined before the Juſtices of the King's Bench, or before Commiſſioners,* &c. *in like Manner to all Intents and Purpoſes, as if they had been done in the ſame Shire wherein they ſhall be inquired of,* &c. And it is enacted by the ſaid Statute of 1 and 2 *Ph.* and *Mar.* 10. *That from thenceforth all Trials for any Treaſon, ſhall be had and uſed only according to the due Order and Courſe of the Common Law:* Yet it hath been adjudged, That none of theſe Statutes take away the Juriſdiction of this Court in Relation to ſuch Treaſon: For the ſaid Statutes of *H.* 8. and *Ed.* 6. being wholly in the Affirmative, and it being their chief Intention to ſupply a Defect in the Common Law, which had provided no Method for the Trial of ſuch Offences by Jury, they ſhall not without expreſs Words be conſtrued to take away the Authority of an ancient Court, confirmed by Parliament; and therefore the above mentioned Expreſſion, That all ſuch Treaſons ſhall be tried by the King's Bench, *&c.* ſhall be taken to purport no more than that the King's Bench, *&c.* ſhall have Authority to try them; and as to the 1 and 2 *Ph.* and *Mar.* the plain Import thereof ſeems to be, to reſtore the ancient Manner of Trial by the Courſe of the Common Law to all Treaſons within it's Juriſdiction, which had been much altered by ſome Statutes in the former Reigns; and this is fully ſatisfied by aboliſhing all Innovations in the Proceedings at Common Law, and has no Relation to Caſes no Way within its Conuſance.

Caſes in Parliament 62. Ruſhworth's Coll. Part 2. Vol. 1. 107. 4 Inſt. 124.

Ruſhworth's Coll. Part 2. Vol. 1. 107. Dyer 131. pl. 75. 3 Inſt. 24. 4 Inſt. 124.

Sect. 11. As to the fifth Point, *viz.* By what Law and in what Manner this Court proceeds, there is no Doubt but that it ought to follow its own Cuſtoms and Uſages ſo far as they go, and in Caſes omitted the Rules of the [c] Civil Law: And becauſe this is not a Court of Common Law, a [d] Condemnation in it for a Capital Offence cauſes neither Forfeiture of Lands nor Corruption of Blood; neither can an Error in its Proceedings be remedied by Writ of Error, but only by Appeal to the King: And yet the Judges of the Common Law take Notice of the Juriſdiction of this Court, and give Credit to a Certificate of its Judges, for the Trial of an [e] Iſſue concerning its Proceedings; [f] for the Civil Law is as much the Law of the Land, in ſuch Caſes wherein it has been always uſed, as the Common Law is in others.

[c] 4 Inſt. 125. 2 Inſt. 51. 1 Inſt. 261. 37 H. 6. 3. b. 20. b.

[d] 4 Inſt. 125. Ruſhworth's Coll. Part. 2. Vol. 1. 107. 113, &c. Caſes in Parliament 62. 2 Inſt. 51.

[e] 4 Inſt. 125, 341. Caſes in Parliament 62.

[f] 30 H. 6. 6. b. 37 H. 6. 3. b. 20. b. 21. a.

Sect. 12. It is queſtioned, Whether the [g] King hath any Remedy in this Court againſt an Offender, by Way of Indictment or Information by the Attorney General.

[g] Hutt. 5.

Sect. 13. As to the sixth Point, *viz.* Whether this Court may be prohibited, if it exceeds its Jurisdiction, it is expresly resolved in *Oldis*'s Case, That the said Court being holden before the Lord Marshal only, may be prohibited by the Courts of Common Law, if it exceed its Jurisdiction, and it is strongly insisted on in the Argument of that Case, That the Court of the Constable and Marshal, may also be prohibited; but there having been no Court holden before a Constable and Marshal for these many Years, and there seeming to be small Likelihood of its being revived, I shall refer the Reader for the farther Examination of this Matter to the learned Sir *Bartholomew Shower*'s Report of the said Case. [1] ☞

Cases in Parliament 61, 66.

Sect. 14. As to the seventh Point, *viz.* Whether the said Court can be holden by Commission; it seems to be the better Opinion of the Court in *Parker*'s Case, That during the Lunacy of an Earl Marshal, it may well be holden before Commissioners deputed to exercise his Office; and it seems hard to say, That such Commissions, founded on the plain Necessity of the Case, and intended to prevent a Failure of Justice, as to Cases of which no other Court hath Conusance, are against the Purview of the Petition of Right, made in the Third Year of the Reign of King *Charles* the First; which, complaining that Commissions had been granted for the Trial of certain Capital Offences and other Outrages, by the Martial Law, under Pretence whereof divers of the King's Subjects had been put to Death, prays that from thenceforth no Commissions of like Nature might issue forth to be executed as aforesaid.

1 Lev. 230. 1 Sid. 353.

CHAP. V.

Of the Court of the Justices of Oyer *and* Terminer.

FOR better Understanding of the Nature of the Courts of the Justices of *Oyer* and *Terminer* and Gaol-Delivery, I shall premise some Considerations concerning them in general, and then consider the Nature of each of them in particular.

Sect. 1. But in the first place, it may not be improper to remark, That the Prerogative authorizing these or any other Justices, is inseparably united to the Crown, not only by the Common Law, but also by Statute to which Purpose it is enacted by 27 *H.* 8. 24. *That no Person or Persons, of what Estate, Degree or Condition soever they be, shall have any Power or Authority to make any Justices of Eyre, Justices of Assise, Justices of Peace, or Justices of Gaol-Delivery: But that all such Officers and Ministers shall be made by Letters Patent under the King's Great Seal, in the Name and by the Authority of the King's Highness, in all Shires, Counties Palatine,* Wales, &c. *or any other his Dominions,* &c. *any Grants, Usages, Allowance, or Act of Parliament to the contrary notwithstanding.*

Lamb. B. 1. ch. 5. Co. Lit. 114. 1 Lev. 219.

As to what belongs to Justices of *Oyer* and *Terminer*, and Gaol-Delivery in general I shall examine:

1. By what Kind of Instruments they must be constituted.
2. How their Authority may be suspended, revived or determined.

3. How far the precise Letter of their Commissions must be observed by such Justices.
4. What Form is to be observed in the Adjournment of such Commissions.
5. How far the Power given by them, may be extended by other Commissions to other Justices, or committed to fewer than were appointed by the former.
6. Whether such Justices can sit in one County to try Offences in another.
7. Where their Records are to be kept after they are determined.
8. Whether the same Justices at the same Time may execute both Commissions.

Sect. 2. As to the first Point, *viz.* By what Kind of Instrument such Justices must be constituted; it seems to be laid down as a general Rule in some of the old Books, That though a Justice may be discharged by Writ under the Great Seal, yet that he cannot be made a Justice by such Writ, but only by [a] Commission: And it seems to be holden, both by [b] Sir *Edward Coke* and Sir [c] *Matthew Hale*, If any such Justices have their Authority by Writ, though made in the same Form and Words, that a legal Commission ought to have, yet their Proceedings are void; and yet it seems, that nothing more is meant by these Expressions, if strictly examined, than that all such Justices must derive their Authority from such Instruments as are of a known, stated, and allowed Form, warranted by ancient Precedents; and 'tis only a Dispute of Words, whether such Instruments are to be called Writs or Commissions; for if you take the Import of the Word *Writ* from [d] *Finch*'s Definition of it, who says, That it is a *Latin* Letter of the King's, from his higher Courts of Record, in Parchment, sealed with his Seal, and *tested* by him, it seemeth that the most approved Forms of Commissions of *Oyer* and *Terminer*, &c. may well enough come under the general Notion of Writs, which by the last mentioned [e] Author are divided into Writs Original and Commissional: And accordingly we find, That Commissions of *Oyer* and *Terminer*, Association, and *si non omnes*, granted upon special Occasions, are called Writs both by the [f] Register, and also by [g] *Fitzherbert*, who yet seems not to approve of this general Notion of the Word *Writ*, and says, That these Commissions should not properly be called Writs. Also it is said by Sir *Edward Coke* in his Comment upon the Statute of *Westminster* the second, *Ch.* 32. which mentions the Writ of *Oyer* and *Terminer*, that Commissions were anciently granted by Writ, by which he seems to imply, That they are otherwise granted at this Day; but he doth not tell us the Distinction between a Writ and Commission; neither can I find that the modern Precedents differ from the old ones; but on the contrary, that it hath always been agreed, That it is the safest Way to follow the old ones: But I must confess, That I cannot find a certain Instance from any [h] Book of Authority, wherein general Commissions of *Oyer* and *Terminer* are called Writs. However, as to the Resolutions of the Judges in 42 *Ass.* *pl.* 12, 13. which are but briefly and obscurely reported, and yet seem to be the chief Foundation of what is said in the later Books relating to this Matter; the Authority thereof seems to amount to no more than these two following Points: First, That Justices appointed by Commission to hear and determine certain Offences, cannot receive an additional Power by Writ directing them to inquire of other Offences; and this seems to be the Sense of [i] *Staunford* and [k] *Fitzherbert*

[a] Long Quinto Ed.4.13.27 b. 42 Ass. pl. 12, 13. Bro. Ass. 384. Commission, 16, 18. Indictment, 22, 38, 39. Finch 247.

[b] 4 Inst. 164.

[c] H.P.C.161. 1 H. H. P. C. 498. 2 H. H. P. C. 23.

[d] Finch 237. See Theloal's Digest of Originals, 1. b. 2. b.

[e] Finch. 312, 318. See Theloal, 2. b.

[f] Register 123.b. 124.b.

[g] F.N.B. 110, 111. Crom. Jur. 131.

[h] Vide infra, sect. 34.

[i] S.P.C.94. A.

[k] Fitz. Indictment, 7. See Br. Commission, 16, 18. Indictment, 22, 38, 39. 12 Co. 31.

[a] 12 Co. 31. *herbert* in Relation to this Matter. [a] Secondly, That Writ impowering Persons to inquire of Offences, without authorizing them also to determine them, are illegal, except in such Cases wherein they are allowed by [b] Register 121. S. P. C. 84. ancient Usage, as where [b] Writs of this Kind to Sheriffs before the Statute of 28 *E.* 3. 9. And therefore where it is generally said in some [c] 1 And. 106. See Pl. Com. 390. [c] Books, That Commissions have been directed to certain Persons to inquire of certain Offences, in order to have them afterwards tried before other Justices, it seems, that it ought to be understood, That such Commissions were in the common Form of Commissions of *Oyer* and *Terminer*, though they be spoken of only as Commissions of Inquiry. As to the [d] Fol. 111, 112, 29. b. 137, 138. Resolution in the *Long* [d] *Quinto* of *Edward* the Fourth, which is the other principal Authority concerning this Matter, the Import thereof seems to be no more than this, That a Person cannot legally be associated to Justices of Assise by a Writ directed to such Justices, reciting a Commission of Association to such Person, and commanding the Justices to receive him, unless there be also produced a Commission of Association directed to such Person; for that the King cannot make a Justice by such Writ directed to others; by which it seems to be implied, That by a proper Writ he may do it. And it is certain, That the Commission of Association directed to the Party himself, is called a Writ both by the [e] Register 124. b. [e] Register, [f] *Fitzherbert*, and [g] *Finch*, and also by [h] Sir *Edward Coke*, as [f] F.N.B. 111. well as the Writ of Admittance directed to the other Justices. However it seems clearly to be agreed by all these Books, That the best Rule of [g] Finch 318. [h] 4 Inst. 107. judging of the Validity of any such Commissions, is their Conformity to known and ancient Precedents; and this seems to be the best Reason of the Resolution in 1 *And.* 296. wherein it is adjudged, That a Commission to a Corporation, appointing some of its principal Members to be Justices of Gaol-Delivery, together with those whom the King should appoint from Time to Time was void: For such an Authority depending on the precarious Appointment of other Justices, is not agreeable to the known Forms of such Commissions; but the other Reason given in that Book, for such newly appointed Justices not joining with the former, because their Authority commences at several Times, seems not conclusive; for the Authority of Justices, appointed by Writ of Association, is of a subsequent Commencement from that of the Justices in the first Commission; and yet it is certain, That such may act jointly together, as will more fully appear in the following Chapter.

2 H. H. P. C. 24, 25. *Sect.* 3. As to the second Point, *viz.* How the Authority of such Justices may be suspended, revived or determined, there is no Doubt, but that their Power is wholly suspended by the Court of King's Bench sitting in the same County for which they are commissioned, during the Time of such Sitting, especially if they have Notice thereof, as hath been more fully shewn *Chap.* 3. *Sect.* 10. and it seems, That their Jurisdiction is revived of Course, when the said Court no longer sits there, without any Writ of *Procedendo*, &c. Also it is certain, that their [i] Au- [i] Register, 124, 125. 12 Ass. 21. 4 Inst. 163. H. P. C. 162. thority may be suspended by a Writ of *Supersedeas*, which is grantable on Proof that their Commission was unduly granted, in which Case their Power may be restored by a Writ of *Procedendo*, without any new Commission. But a Commission once determined, cannot be revived by any Writ of *Procedendo*, nor the Justices authorized a-new without another Commission.

Sect. 4. Such Commiſſions may be determined expreſly or impliedly; expreſly, by an abſolute Repeal or Countermand from the King; impliedly, ſeveral Ways. 4 Inſt. 163.

Sect. 5. Firſt, By the Demiſe of the King by whom they were granted; but this Miſchief is in a great Meaſure obviated by late Statutes, as hath been more fully ſhewn, *Ch.* 1. *Sect.* 11, 12, 13.

Sect. 6. Secondly, According to ſome Opinions, by the Juſtices Acceptance of any new Name of Dignity, as of that of Duke, Knight, or Serjeant, *&c.* But this is remedied by 1 *Ed.* 6. 7. by which it is enacted, *That if any Perſon being in any of the King's Commiſſions whatſoever, ſhall fortune to be made or created Duke, Archbiſhop, Marqueſs, Earl, Viſcount, Baron, Biſhop, Knight, Juſtice of the one Bench or of the other, or Serjeant at Law, or Sheriff, yet that notwithſtanding he ſhall remain Commiſſioner,* &c. But it hath been queſtioned, whether the Dignity of a Baronet which has been created ſince that Statute, be within the Equity of it? Bro. Commiſſion, 4, 22. Cro. Ca. 104. Lit. Rep. 81.

Sect. 7. Thirdly, By holding a Seſſion without adjourning it, if the Commiſſion have no Time limited for its Continuance; as where it is appointed *pro hac vice* only; but if it be granted for a certain Time, or *quamdiu nobis placuerit*, it does not neceſſarily require any Adjournment; and therefore, if the Court holden by Virtue of ſuch Commiſſion, break up without any Adjournment, or upon a void one, as being made without the Conſent of the Majority of the Commiſſioners, yet it may be holden again on a new Summons. Crom. Jur. 125. b. H. P. C. 161. 4 Inſt. 165. Bro. Commiſſion, 12. Dalſ. 24, 25. Vide Dyer 205. Pl. 5. 4 Inſt. 165. 1 Leon. 270.

Sect. 8. Fourthly, By granting a new Commiſſion to other Perſons of the ſame Nature with the former, though but for Part of the Diſtrict for which the former was granted, as ſome ſay: And whether [a] ſuch new Commiſſion be for a certain Time, or *pro hac vice* only; yet the former Commiſſions ſhall remain [b] in Force, ſo far as they are conſiſtent with the latter; and therefore it ſeems certain, that a Commiſſion of the Peace is not determined, as to its Authority relating to the Peace, by a new Commiſſion to hear and determine Felonies. But it hath been [c] holden, That it is determined as to its Authority relating to Felonies; but this ſeems juſtly queſtionable, not only as being contrary to common Practice, but alſo becauſe Juſtices of Peace, as ſuch, ſeem to have Authority by 34 *E.* 3. to hear and determine Felonies, without any ſpecial Clauſe in their Commiſſion, for that Purpoſe, as will more fully be ſhewn *Ch.* 8. But it ſeems certain, That a Commiſſion of [d] Gaol-Delivery ſhall not be determined by a new Commiſſion of *Oyer* and *Terminer*, becauſe they are of different Natures. [e] Alſo it ſeems to be clear not only from 2 & 3 *Ph. & Mar.* 18. ſet forth more at large, *Sect.* 12. but alſo in Caſes not within the Statute, that a Commiſſion of the Peace for a certain Town determines not the Authority of the Corporation, having a Grant from the King, that the Mayor and his Succeſſors ſhall be Juſtices of the Peace within its Limits, becauſe ſuch a Grant is irrevocable. [f] Alſo it ſeems certain, That no new Commiſſion doth determine an old one, unleſs the former Commiſſioners have Notice of it. 10 Ed. 4. 7.

[a] Bro. Commiſſion, 7.
[b] Bro. Commiſſion, 8, 24.
[c] Bro. Commiſſion, 8.
[d] Bro. Commiſſion, 24.
[e] Bro. Commiſſion, 5.
[f] H.P.C. 162. 1 H. H. P. C. 499. 2 H. H. P. C. 25. 4 Inſt. 165. 34 Aſſ. 8. Bro. Commiſſion, 6. 14.

Sect. 9. Such Notice may be given expreſly or impliedly; expreſly, by [g] ſhewing the new Commiſſion to the former Commiſſioners, which certainly determines the Power of all thoſe, to whom it is ſhewn; impliedly, two manner of Ways.

[g] H.P.C. 162. 4 Inſt. 165. Keilw. 116. Crom. Jur. 125. b.

Sect. 10. I. By [h] holding a Seſſion by Force of the new Commiſſion, which ſeemeth to be agreed to be a Matter ſo notorious, that the firſt Juſtices ſhall be preſumed to have Notice of it.

[h] 34 Aſſ. 8. Bro. Commiſſion, 14. Moore 186. Pl. 333. H. P. C. 162. 2 H. H. P. C. 25. 4 Inſt. 165. Dyer 355. Pl. 36.

H. P. C. 162. 4 Inſt. 165. Bro. Crommiſſion, 6. Keilw. 116.

Sect. 11. II. According to the general Opinion, by proclaming the new Commiſſion in the County.

Sect. 12. As the Authority of the Juſtices appointed by any former Commiſſion, is determined by a Grant of a new one in the Manner abovementioned, ſo likewiſe were all Proceedings before ſuch Juſtices diſcontinued at the Common Law; to remedy which Inconvenience it was enacted by 1 *Ed.* 6. 7. Par. 6. *That no manner of Proceſs, or Suit made, ſued, or had before any Juſtices of Aſſiſe, Gaol-Delivery, Oyer and Terminer, Juſtices of Peace, or other of the King's Commiſſioners, ſhall not in any wiſe be diſcontinued by the making and publiſhing of any new Commiſſion or Aſſociation, or by altering the Names of the Juſtices of Aſſiſe, Gaol-Delivery, Oyer and Terminer, Juſtices of Peace, or other the King's Commiſſioners, but that the new Juſtices of Aſſiſe, Gaol-Delivery, and of the Peace, and other Commiſſioners, may proceed in every Behalf, as if the old Commiſſions, Juſtices and Commiſſioners, had ſtill remained and continued not altered.*

1 Sid. 348. 2 Keb. 292. Bro. Coro. 178.

Sect. 13. And it is farther enacted by 2 & 3 *Ph. & Mar.* 18. *That all and ſingular Commiſſions granted to any City or Town-Corporate, not being a County in it ſelf, for the keeping of their Peace and Delivery of the Priſoners remaining in the Gaols of any ſuch City or Town-Corporate, ſhall ſtand, remain, and be good, and available and effectual in the Law, to all Intents, Conſtructions and Purpoſes, the granting of any like Commiſſion of Peace or Gaol-Delivery, to any Commiſſioner or Commiſſioners for the Conſervation of the Peace, or Delivery of the Priſoners remaining in the Gaol of any Shire, Lathe, Rape, Riding, or Wapentake within the Realm of* England, *bearing Date after the ſaid Commiſſion or Commiſſions granted as is aforeſaid, to any ſuch City or Town-Corporate, not being, as aforeſaid, a County in it ſelf, to the contrary notwithſtanding.*

Daliſ. 25. 12 Aſſ. Pl. 21. Crom. Jur. 126. Long quinto E. 4. 133. a. Daliſ. 25. 3 Inſt. 31. 2 H. H. P. C. 24. H. P. C. 160. Bro. Commiſſion, 18. Kelynge 57.

Sect. 14. As to the third Point, *viz.* How far the preciſe Letter of ſuch Commiſſions muſt be obſerved by the Juſtices, it is ſaid to be agreed, That if a Commiſſion of *Oyer* and *Terminer*, &c. be awarded to certain Perſons to inquire at ſuch a Place, they can neither open their Commiſſion at another, nor adjourn it thither, nor give Judgment there; and that if they do, all their Proceedings ſhall be eſteemed as *coram non judice:* Yet it is agreed, That Juſtices appointed by Commiſſion *pro hac vice*, may adjourn their Commiſſion from one Day to another, though there be no Words in their Commiſſion to ſuch Purpoſe; for nothing can be more reaſonable, than to intend that a general Commiſſion authorizing Perſons to do a Thing, does implicitly allow them convenient Time for the doing of it.

[a] Raym. 115. [b] 1 Sid. 348. 2 Keb. 284, 292.

Sect. 15. As to the fourth Point, *viz.* What Form is to be obſerved in the Adjournment of ſuch Commiſſions, having already in the foregoing Part of this Chapter, in the 6th and 13th Sections, incidentally treated of the principal Queſtions relating to this Matter, I ſhall only take Notice in this Place, That it ſeems moſt proper to [a] enter all ſuch Adjournments in the Preſent Tenſe; yet it is ſaid, That the Entry of them in the Preter Tenſe, is made good by the Multitude of Precedents: [b] However it is ſaid, That the Court will never intend that there was an Adjournment, if no Entry at all were made of it.

2 H. H. P. C. 23.

Sect. 16. As to the fifth Point, *viz.* How far the Power given by ſuch Commiſſions may be extended by new ones to other Juſtices, or committed by fewer than were appointed by the former; it is certain, That new Commiſſioners of this Kind may be added to the former by a Writ or Commiſſion of Aſſociation, which ſetting forth the Purport of the former Commiſſion, declares the King's Pleaſure to aſſociate to the Perſons, appointed by the firſt, thoſe to whom ſuch new Writ or Commiſſion is directed, provided that ſuch new Juſtices attend at the Times and Places appointed by the former; and it is uſual to direct another Writ to the former Juſtices, commanding them to admit ſuch new Juſtices as their Aſſociates with the Proviſo above mentioned; and the Writ to the Perſons ſo aſſociated is always Patent, and that to the other Juſtices to admit them is Cloſe. But it hath been [a] reſolved, That the firſt Juſtices are not bound by ſuch Writ to admit the Perſons named in it as their Aſſociates, unleſs they produce ſuch Patent of Aſſociation as is above mentioned directed to themſelves, as hath been more fully ſhewn in the firſt Section of this Chapter. And it hath been [b] queſtioned, Whether a ſpecial Commiſſion of Aſſociation, relating only to a particular Cauſe, can aſſociate the Perſons named in it to Juſtices appointed by a general Commiſſion? Alſo it hath been holden, That the King can grant but one Patent of Aſſociation to one Commiſſion.

Regiſter 124. F. N. B. 111. B. Finch 318, 319. H. P. C. 159, 162. 4 Inſt. 165. [a] Long quinto E. 4. 137. [b] Long quinto E. 4. 111, 112, 130, 131. Fitz. Aſſize, 17. 32 H. 6. 10.

Sect. 17. If after Juſtices have ſat by Virtue of a Commiſſion, and taken divers Indictments, and awarded Proceſs thereon, they ſhall all, or ſome of them die, the King may grant a new Commiſſion to thoſe who are living only, or to others, commanding them to continue the Proceedings begun, and to proceed upon ſuch Proceſs, and to hear and determine all the Offences in the former Commiſſion: And thereupon the King ſhall ſend a Writ unto the Executors of the Juſtices who are dead, to ſend the Rolls, Records, and Proceſſes touching the Premiſſes, before the new Commiſſioners, &c.

Regiſter 128. F. N. B. 111. D. 113, 114.

Sect. 18. After a Writ of Aſſociation, it is uſual to make out a Writ of *Si non omnes*, directed both to the firſt Juſtices, and alſo to thoſe who are ſo aſſociated to them, which reciting the Purport of the two former Commiſſions, commands the Juſtices, That if all of them cannot conveniently be preſent, ſuch a Number of them may proceed, &c.

Regiſter 124. F. N. B. 111. 2 H. H. P. C. 23.

Sect. 19. As to the ſixth Point, *viz.* Whether ſuch Juſtices may ſit in one County to try Offences in another? It ſeems agreed, That regularly all Offences are to be inquired of, heard, and determined in the County wherein they were committed, and that the King cannot authorize the taking of them in another; yet it was adjudged in the Caſe of the City of *Glouceſter*, That if the King grant to a City the Privilege of being a County of it ſelf, diſtinct from the County within which it lies, with a *Salvo* or Reſervation, That the Juſtices of *Oyer* and *Terminer*, &c. for the County at large, may ſtill ſit in ſuch City, ſuch Reſervation makes the City ſtill remain Part of the County for ſuch Purpoſe, and conſequently, that an Indictment found within ſuch City, of an Offence in the County at large, is good. Alſo it is certain, That by a ſpecial Cuſtom Indictments of Offences within a County, may be taken in a Place out of it; as they are in Fact taken both for *Middleſex* and *London* at the Seſſions-Hall at *Newgate*, which ſtands in *London*; for it ſhall be intended, That at the original Diviſion of *London* from *Middleſex*, there was a ſpecial Proviſion made for this Purpoſe. Alſo it is certain, That the King may grant a ſpecial Commiſſion of *Oyer* and *Terminer*, to ſit in one County for hearing and determining Offences, whereof Indictments have been found in another: But it is agreed, That the Trial muſt be by the Jurors of the proper County.

2 H. H. P. C. 21, 22. 3 Inſt. 27. H. P. C. 162, 163. Dy. 286. Pl. 45. Poph. 16, 17. 1 And. 291, 292. 3 Inſt. 27. H. P. C. 162, 163. Dy. 286. Pl. 45. Raym. 193. Popham 17. 3 Inſt. 27. H. P. C. 162, 163. Dy. 286. Pl. 45. Pl. Com. 390.

Sect. 20. As to the ſeventh Point, *viz.* Where the Records of ſuch Juſtices are to be kept after they are determined, it is enacted by 9 *Ed.* 3. 5. *That Juſtices of Aſſize, Gaol-Delivery, and of Oyer and Terminer, ſhall ſend all their Records and Proceſſes determined and put in Execution, to the Exchequer at* Michaelmas, *every Year once, to be delivered there; and the Trea-*

2 H. H. P. C. 31, 36. 14 H. 7. 15. b.

ſurer and Chamberlains, which for the Time ſhall be, having the Sight of the Commiſſions of ſuch Juſtices, ſhall receive the ſame Records and Proceſſes of the ſaid Juſtices under their Seals, and keep them in the Treaſury, as the Manner is; ſo that the Juſtices always do firſt take out the Eſtreats of the ſaid Records and Proceſſes againſt them, to ſend to the Exchequer as they were wont before.

9 H. 7. 9. a. b. Bro. Commiſſion, 17, 24. Crom. Jur. 126. b. 2 H. H. P. C. 34, 166. H. P. C. 160. Fitz Coro. 47. 9 H. 7. 9.

Sect. 21. As to the eighth Point, *viz.* Whether the ſame Juſtices at the ſame Time may execute both the Commiſſion of *Oyer* and *Terminer*, and alſo that of Gaol-Delivery? It ſeems certain at this Day, That the ſame Perſons being authorized by both theſe Commiſſions, may proceed by Virtue of the one in thoſe Caſes, wherein they have no Juriſdiction by the other, and execute both at the ſame Time, and make up their Records accordingly; but this doth not ſeem to have been clearly agreed in former Times.

And now I am to conſider the Nature of each of the above mentioned Commiſſions in particular; and firſt of that of *Oyer* and *Terminer*, concerning which I ſhall endeavour to ſhew;

1. Its ſeveral Kinds.
2. To what Caſes the Juriſdiction given by it doth extend.
3. To whom, and on what Occaſions it is grantable.

As to the firſt Point, theſe Commiſſions are of two Kinds:

1. General.
2. Special.

4 Inſt. 162, 163. Crom. Jur. 131. Pl. Com. 384. b. 2 Inſt. 419. 2 H. H. P. C. 22, 23.

Sect. 22. At this Day the common Form of ſuch a General Commiſſion, is to authorize the Perſons to whom it is directed, or three or four of them, of which Number either ſuch or ſuch particular Perſons among them are ſpecially appointed to be, to inquire by the Oaths of lawful Men, and by other Means, of all Treaſons, Felonies and Miſdemeanors, being ſpecially mentioned, and of all others, in ſuch and ſuch Counties, and to hear and determine the ſame at certain Days and Places, to be appointed by them, *&c.* For which Purpoſe the King acquaints them, That he hath ſent a Writ to the Sheriffs of ſuch Counties, commanding them to return a
Regiſter 123. Jury before them, at ſuch Days and Places as ſhall be notified by them, in order to make Inquiries of ſuch Offences, *&c.*

34 Aſſ. pl. 8. 42 Aſſ. pl. 5. 2 Inſt. 419.

Sect. 23. It is obſervable, That the above mentioned Commiſſion makes no mention of the Suit of the Party; but it ſeems to have been anciently the moſt common Form of ſuch Commiſſion to direct the Juſtices to hear and determine Offences, as well at the Suit of the Party as of the King.

2 H. H. P. C. 10 to 22.

Of Special Commiſſions of *Oyer* and *Terminer*, there are many Precedents in our ancient Law Books; as firſt,

[a] Regiſt. 123. F. N. B. 110.

Sect. 24. I. [a] For the inquiring and determining of ſome particular enormous Violencedone to the Party, at whoſe Complaint the Commiſſion is ſued.

[b] Regiſter 125, 127. F. N. B. 112, 113.

Sect. 25. II. [b] Or for inquiring and determining of Treſpaſſes done to the Poſſeſſions of a Biſhoprick while the Temporalties were in the King's Hands.

[c] Regiſter 126. F. N. B. 112.

Sect. 26. III. [c] Or for inquiring and determining of Injuries offered to Merchants, *&c.* under Pretence that their Ships were wrecked.

Sect. 27. IV. Or for inquiring and determining of Oppressions of Under-Sheriffs and Bailiffs, and other Officers; after which the King may send a Writ to the High Sheriff, commanding him as far as in him lies, to remove such Persons from their Offices till such Inquiries be made. Register 126. F. N. B. 112. Letters D, E.

Sect. 28. V. Or for inquiring into the Want of Reparations of Sea-Walls, Ditches, Gutters, Sewers, Bridges, &c. Register 127, 128. F. N. B. 113.

Sect. 29. VI. For hearing and determining the Right and Title of certain Persons claiming an Office, &c. Yet we find in *Dyer*, That the Defendant, sued before such Commissioners, demurred to the Jurisdictiou of the Court; and it seems not to be clearly settled there whether such Commission be good. Crom. Jur. 132. Dyer 175. pl. 25, 26.

Sect. 30. It is observable, That some of these special Commissions are mentioned to be granted at the Complaint of the [a] particular Persons supposed to be aggrieved; others at the Complaint of [b] divers Persons in general without naming them, and [c] others without any Complaint at all. 2 Inst. 419. [a] Register 123. a. 125. a. b. 126. a. 127. a. [b] Register 125. b. [c] Register 127. a.

Sect. 31. Also there are Precedents of other Commissions of like Nature, granted on particular Occasions; but such special Commissions having been of late much disused, I shall refer the Reader for a more exact Knowledge of them to the *Register*, and *Fitzherbert's Natura Brevium*.

Sect. 32. As to the second Point, *viz.* To what Cases the Jurisdiction given by the Commission of *Oyer* and *Terminer* doth extend; it is generally said, That the Justices have no Power from it to proceed against any Persons, but those who are indicted before themselves, because the Words of it are, That they shall inquire, hear and determine; by which it seems to be implied, That they must inquire of an Offence before they proceed to hear and determine it: But this Reasoning depending wholly on the Wording of general Commissions, which are made in such Form, doth by no Means prove that a special Commission of *Oyer* and *Terminer*, reciting an Indictment of a particular Person, and authorizing the Justices to send for and proceed upon it to try the Offender, is not good; and accordingly we find, That the Attainder of *Dudley*, afterwards Earl of *Leicester*, by Virtue of such a Commission, was not objected against on this Account, in the Arguments concerning it, reported in *Plowden's Commentaries*. Bro. Commission 24. 4 Inst. 164. H. P. C. 161. 12 Co. 32. 2 H. H. P. C. 21, 27. Skin. 32. Crom. Jur. 131, 132. Plow. Com. 385, 386, &c.

Sect. 33. It seems to be [a] agreed, That where a Statute prohibits a Thing, and doth not appoint in what Court it shall be punished, the Offender may be indicted before Justices of *Oyer* and *Terminer*, because the King hath a Prerogative of suing in what Court he will. But it hath been [b] adjudged, That if such Statute appoint that the Offence shall be determined in any of the King's Courts of Record, it can be proceeded against only in one of the Courts of *Westminster-Hall*; because those being the highest Courts of Record, shall be intended to be only spoken of *secundum excellentiam*; and if the Act should be taken literally to intend any Court of Record whatsoever, the Sheriff's Turn, Court-Leet, and Pie-powders, and all other inferior Courts of Record, would be within the Purview of it: And it is farther reasonable to construe the Statute to extend to the said Courts of *Westminster* only, because the King's Attorney always attends there, whose Office it is, if the Defendant plead a special Plea, to make a Replication; yet both Sir *Edward Coke* and Sir *Matthew Hale* seem to be of Opinion, That on a Statute so worded, the Prosecution may be in any Court of *Oyer* and *Terminer*. And indeed seeing the abovementioned Limitation of such Suits to Courts of Record, is no more than the Law would have implied, if it had not been expres- [a] Dy. 236. pl. 24. Crom. Jur. 132. 4 Inst. 164. [b] Dy. 236. pl. 24. 6 Co. 19. b. 20. a. Cro. Jac. 538. Cro. Eliz. 737. Cro. Ca. 146. Salk. 178. 4 Inst. 164, 165. H. P. C. 161. 2 H. H. P. C. 29, 30. seem. contr.

ſed: And it is agreed, That if it had not been expreſſed, the Suit might be in any Court of *Oyer* and *Terminer*, it may be reaſonably argued, that it may be brought in any ſuch Court notwithſtanding ſuch Limitation, according to the common Maxim, *quod expreſſio eorum quæ tacitè inſunt,* Fitz. Eſſoin, 173. *nihil operatur*; eſpecially conſidering that the Court holden before Juſtices of *Oyer*, &c. is a Court of Record of a very high Nature, and much regarded by the Law. And as to the Objection, that the Conſtruction contended for, would extend ſuch Suits to all inferior Courts of Record, it may be anſwered, that it would only extend them to ſuch Courts of a general Juriſdiction, wherein Suits of like Nature may properly be brought, and not to Courts of a limited Authority, inſtituted for ſpecial Purpoſes, and confined either to Offences at the common Law, as the Court-Leet and Sheriff's Turn are, or to Contracts of a ſpecial Nature, as the Court of Pie-powders is: As to the Objection, That it is moſt reaſonable to conſtrue the Statute, to intend only ſuch Courts wherein the King's Attorney attends, the ſame may be ſaid in Relation to Proſecutions on Statutes, which mention no Court at all wherein they ſhall be brought; and yet Dy. 236. pl. 24. it ſeems to be certain, That ſuch Proſecutions may be brought in any Court of *Oyer* and *Terminer*: Neither do I find any Reaſon aſſigned, why the King's Prerogative, of chooſing in what Court he will commence a Suit, ſhould be reſtrained without expreſs Words in this Caſe, where Courts are mentioned in general, more than in the others where they are not mentioned at all. Beſides, it ought to be conſidered, That if ſuch Proſecutions are to be confined to the Courts of *Weſtminſter*, no Offence againſt any ſuch Statute in any County, but that wherein the King's Bench ſits, could be indicted at all; for it is certain, that no Offence can be inquired of out of the County wherein it was committed: Alſo ſince 21 *Jac.* 1. 4. ſet forth more at large in the Chapter concerning *Informations*, which reſtrains all Proſecutions whatſoever on Penal Statutes to their proper Counties, (as the Conſtruction of the ſaid Statute is now ſettled) if Suits on ſuch Statutes could be brought only in *Weſtminſter-Hall*, no Offences out of *Middleſex* could be proſecuted at all.

Sect. 34. As to the third Point, *viz.* To what Perſons, and on what Occaſions, Commiſſions of *Oyer* and *Terminer* are grantable, it is enacted by the Statute of *Weſtminſter* 2 Cap. 29. *That a Writ of Treſpaſs* (ad audiendum & terminandum,) *from henceforth ſhall not be granted before any Juſtices, except Juſtices of either Bench, and Juſtices in Eyre, unleſs it be for an heinous Treſpaſs, where it is neceſſary to provide ſpeedy Remedy, and our Lord the King of his ſpecial Grace hath thought it good to be granted.*

Sect. 35. And it is farther enacted by 2 *E.* 3. Ch. 2. *That Oyers and Terminers ſhall not be granted but before Juſtices of the one Bench or the other, or the Juſtices Errants, and that for great Hurt or horrible Treſpaſſes, and of the King's ſpecial Grace, after the Form of the Statute abovementioned.*

Sect. 36. Alſo it is enacted by 34 *Ed.* 3. 1. *That Writs of* Oyer *and* Terminer *be granted according to the Statutes thereof made, and that the Juſtices which ſhall be thereto aſſigned, be named by the Court, and not by the Party.*

Sect. 37. It may perhaps be argued from the general Words of theſe Statutes, That no Commiſſion of *Oyer* and *Terminer* ought to be granted to any, but ſuch Juſtices as are therein mentioned, and on ſuch ſpecial Occaſions. And Sir *Edward Coke* in his Comment on the ſaid Statute of 2 Inſt. 418. *Weſtminſter* 2. does not ſhew whether all ſuch Commiſſions in general are meant to be reſtrained by it, or ſuch only as are of a particular Nature; yet if the Intention of the ſaid Statutes be fully examined, it ſeems reaſonable to confine the Purview of them to ſpecial Commiſſions of *Oyer* and *Terminer*, granted at the Complaint of particular Perſons, upon ſome great Injury ſuggeſted to have been done to them; not only for that ſuch ſpecial Commiſſions, for redreſſing of a particular Grievance at the Suit of the Party, ſeem to come more properly and generally under the Notion of Writs, than general Commiſſions iſſued by the King as the common Diſpenſer of Juſtice to his People, without any particular Application from, or Regard to any particular Perſon; but alſo becauſe there may be a Miſchief to the Subject from ſuch ſpecial Commiſſions, which cannot be feared from the general ones; for the Party who ſues out ſuch a ſpecial Commiſſion, may thereupon take out a Writ to the Sheriff, commanding him to arreſt the Goods ſuppoſed to be wrongfully taken away, and to keep them in ſafe Cuſtody till ſome Order be made concerning them, by the Juſtices aſſigned to determine the Matter, which may be very inconvenient to the Perſon complained of: Neither can it be imagined, that the Statute intended to reſtrain general Commiſſions to enormous Treſpaſſes, which could not but hinder the due Execution of Juſtice, which requires the Puniſhment of all Kinds of Miſdemeanours, of which ſuch Commiſſioners are the uſual and proper Judges. But it is reaſonable indeed, that ſuch ſpecial Commiſſions ſhould not be granted but upon urgent Occaſions; and accordingly we find Precedents for the ſuperſeding of them, where the King has been informed, that he was impoſed upon in granting them on a Suggeſtion, that the Injury complained of was of a heinous Nature, where in Truth it was but a ſlight inconſiderable Treſpaſs.

Theloal's Digeſt of Writs 1, 2. & ſupra Sect. 1. 2 Inſt. 419.

Regiſter 126, 127. 2 Inſt. 419. F.N.B. 112. F.

Regiſter 124, 125. 12 Aſſ. pl. 21.

For other Particulars concerning the Proceedings of Juſtices of *Oyer* and *Terminer*, ſee the Chapter concerning *Approver*, and the Chapter concerning *Proceſs againſt the Jury*.

CHAP. VI.

Of the Court of the Juſtices of Gaol-Delivery.

FOR the better Underſtanding of the Nature of the Commiſſion of Gaol-Delivery, I ſhall conſider,

1. What ought to be the Form of it.
2. What Juriſdiction the Juſtices authorized by it have by the Common Law.
3. What by Statute.
4. In what Place they ought to hold their Seſſions.

Sect. 1. As to the firſt Point, having already ſhewn that all judicial Commiſſions muſt be agreeable to ancient Precedents, I ſhall only ſhew in this Place, the Purport of the moſt uſual Commiſſion of Gaol-Delivery, which is a Patent in Nature of a Letter from the King to certain Perſons, appointing them his Juſtices, or two or three of them, of which Number either ſuch or ſuch a particular Perſon among them is eſpecially required to be, and authorizing them to deliver his Gaol, at ſuch a Place, of the Priſoners in it; for which Purpoſe it commands them to meet at ſuch Place, at the Time which they themſelves ſhall appoint, and informs them,

Ch. 1. from Sect. 4. to Sect. 9. and Ch. 5 Sect. 1.

4 Inſt. 168. Crom. Jur. 125. 2 H. H. P.C. 32.

them, that for the fame Purpofe the King hath commanded his Sheriff of the fame County, to bring all the Prifoners of the fame Gaol, and their Attachments before them, at fuch Day to be appointed by them.

H. P. C. 158. 2 H. H. P. C. 32, 33. 4 Inft. 168, 169. Bro. Coron. 179. 12 Co. 32.

Sect. 2. As to the fecond Point, *viz.* What Jurifdiction Juftices of Gaol-Delivery have by the Common Law; it feems to be clear, That they may by Common Law proceed upon any Indictment of Felony or Trefpafs, found before other Juftices, againft any Perfon in the Prifon mentioned in their Commiffion, and not determined; and therefore thefe Words in the Statute of 4 *E.* 3. Ch. 2. *That the Juftices affigned to deliver the Gaols fhall have Power to deliver the fame Gaols of thofe that fhall be indicted before the Juftices of Peace,* feem only to be in Affirmance of the Common Law; and herein the Authority of thefe Juftices differs from that of Juftices of *Oyer* and *Terminer*, who regularly can proceed only againft Perfons indicted before themfelves, as hath been more fully fhewn in the precedent Chapter, *Sect.* 32.

[a] Cro. Eliz. 90, 179. Bro. Commiffion 24. 1 And. 111, Fitz. Coron. 47. [b] 1 And. 111, 112. H.P. C. 158. 2 H. H. P. C. 34. 4 Inft. 168.

Sect. 3. But it is faid in fome [a] Books, That Juftices of Gaol-Delivery, as fuch, have no Power to take any Indictment; but the Common Opinion, that they have fuch Power, feems much more agreeable to Reafon; for [b] furely it cannot but be implied in their Commiffion to deliver Prifons of their Prifoners, that they muft have Authority to make fuch Deliverance by due Courfe of Law, which cannot be without a Proclamation, if there be no Profecution, or a proper Trial, if there be one, in Order to which there muft be an Accufation of Record, without which the Prifoner cannot be arraigned or tried.

[c] S. P. C. 183. Letter A. 2 Rol. Rep. 12. Crom. Jur. 28. Fitz. Coron. 47. 1 And. 111.

Sect. 4. Alfo it hath been [c] holden, That Juftices of Gaol-Delivery, as fuch have no Power to deliver the Gaol of Perfons committed for High Treafon, perhaps for this Reafon, becaufe this being a Crime of fo high a Nature, and againft the King himfelf, fhall not be included in the general Words of a Commiffion, nor tried without the King's fpecial Direction; and this Opinion feems to be much favoured by the Preamble of the Statute of 3 *H.* 5. Ch. 7. wherein it is recited, *That the Punifhment of counterfeiting Money,* (which is a Species of Treafon) *pertaineth not to any Judges of the Realm, but to the King's Juftices before himfelf, or to fpecial Commiffioners thereto affigned*; and thereupon it is enacted, *That Juftices of Affize fhall have Power by the King's Commiffion to hear and determine the Offence abovementioned:* Yet the contrary Opinion is not only warranted by very great [d] Authorities, but alfo it feems more agreeable to Reafon; for fince the Words of the Commiffion are general, and include all Prifoners alike without any Exception, why fhould thofe who are accufed of Treafon, be conftrued to be out of the Meaning of them more than others? efpecially confidering, that the greater the Crime is for which a Man is imprifoned, the greater Hardfhip it is for him to lie under the Terror of a Profecution for it, without being admitted to an Opportunity of clearing his Innocence: And the Statute of 1 *Ed.* 6. 7. which authorizes fubfequent Commiffioners of Gaol-Delivery, to give Judgment of Death againft fuch as were found guilty before other Commiffioners of Gaol-Delivery, of Treafon, *&c.* and reprieved before Judgment, clearly fuppofes fuch Juftices to have Power in Treafon as well as in other Cafes.

[d] 4 Inft. 169. H.P. C. 159. 2 H. H. P. C. 35. 1 And. 112. and the next Ch. Sect. 4.

Fitz. Coron. 77.

Sect. 5. It feems clear from the Words of the Commiffion, that thefe Juftices have nothing to do with any Perfons not in Cuftody of the Prifon mentioned in it, except in fome fpecial Cafes; for if Part only of thofe who were Accomplices to the fame Felony be in fuch Prifon, and other Part of them out of it; fuch Juftices for the Neceffity of the Cafe,

3 may

may [a] receive an Appeal against those who are out of the Prison, as well as those who are in it; which Appeal after the Trial of such Prisoners, shall be removed into the King's Bench, and Process shall issue from thence against the rest: But if those out of Prison should be omitted in such Appeal, they could never be put into any other, because there can be but one Appeal for one Felony. Also it is said both by [b] *Staundford*, and [c] *Hale*, That such Justices may receive an Appeal by Bill against one let to Bail. [2] But I cannot find any Authority in the [d] Books, cited by them for that Purpose, to warrant this Opinion; for though it be true, That the Court of King's Bench may receive an Appeal by Bill, against one for whom Bail is filed, as being *in Custodiâ Mareschalli*; yet this seems to depend on the particular Usage of that Court. And I do not find it said in any Book, That those who are bailed by any other Court, are looked upon as Prisoners in the Prison belonging to such Court, but only in the Custody of their Sureties, who may detain them where-ever they please: However, it seems to be agreed by all the Books above-mentioned, That such Justices have no more to do with one let to Main-prize, than if he were at large, because such Person can in no Sense be said to be a Prisoner, since it is not in the Power of his Sureties to detain him in their Custody, as will be more fully shewn in the Chapter concerning *Bail*.

[a] 9 H. 4. 1. b. 4 Co. 47. b. S. P. C. 64. D.
[b] S. P. C. 64. C, D. 65. A. 159, 160.
[c] H. P. C. 179. Quære 4 Inst. 169.
[d] 32 H. 6. 4. a. 39 H. 6. 27. b. 9 H. 4. 2. a. 13 H. 4. 10. b. 21 H. 7. 33 a. Fitz. Mainprize, 12, 13. Dy. 99. Pl. 62. Bro. Appeal, 11, 19, 51, 123.

Sect. 6. It seems clear, That such Justices have not only Power to discharge such Prisoners, as upon their Trial shall be acquitted; but also all such against whom, upon Proclamation made, no Evidence shall appear to indict them; which neither Justices of Peace, nor Justices of *Oyer* and *Terminer* can do. 4 Inst. 167. Fitz. Coron. 47. H. P. C. 158. 2 H. H. P. C. 34.

Sect. 7. Also there seems to be no Doubt, but that the Justices of Gaol-Delivery may award Execution, against such Prisoners as have been outlawed for Felony before Justices of Peace. 15 H. 7. 5. b. 4 Inst. 169. H. P. C. 158. 2 H. H. P. C. 35.

Sect. 8. Also notwithstanding the Commission of Justices of Gaol-Delivery be in Strictness determined after the End of their Session, yet it seems to be settled at this Day, That they have Power either to order the Execution or Reprieve of the Persons who have been condemned before them. Dyer 205. Pl. 5. H. P. C. 160. 2 H. H. P. C. 35.

Sect. 9. Also it is said by some, That the Justices of Gaol-Delivery may by the Common Law punish those who unduly bail Prisoners, as being guilty of a negligent Escape; but it seems needless strictly to examine this Matter, since they have certainly such Power by Statute, as will be more fully shewn in the following Part of this Chapter. Cont. Cromp. Jur. 126. Quære S. P. C. 132. Letter B. S. P. C. 77. a. 25 E. 3. 39. a.

As to the third Point, *viz.* What Jurisdiction Justices of Gaol-Delivery have by Statute, I shall consider the same,

1. In Relation to Appellees.
2. To irregular Bailment of Prisoners.
3. To Sheriffs, &c. refusing to receive Prisoners.
4. To Persons convicted before former Justices.
5. To Offences created by Statute.

Sect. 10. As to the first Particular, it is enacted by 28 *E.* 1. *That they may award Process into a foreign County against those who shall be appealed before them by an Approver*, as shall be more fully shewed in the Chapter concerning *Approvers*. 2 H. H. P. C. 36.

Sect. 11. As to the second Particular, *viz.* The Power of such Justices in Relation to the Bailment of Prisoners, it is enacted by 27 *Ed.* 1. *cap.* 3. commonly called the Statute *De finibus*, *That Justices of Assise shall deliver the Gaols of Counties where they take Assises*, &c. *and inquire if Sheriffs, or any other, have let out by Replevin Prisoners not repleviable, or have offended in any Thing contrary to the Form of the Statute of* Westinster 1. Cap. 15. *and whom they shall find guilty, they shall chasten and punish in all Things according to the Form of the Statute aforesaid.*

F. N. B. 251. H. H. P. C. 158. 4 Inst. 169. *Sect.* 12. But this Statute mentioning only Justices of Assise, it may perhaps be questioned, whether it is to be extended by Equity, to Justices of Gaol-Delivery by special Commission, not being Justices of Assise.

Sect. 13. However, it is enacted by 4 *Ed.* 3. *cap.* 2. *That Justices assigned to deliver Gaols, shall have Power to enquire of Sheriffs, Gaolers, and others in whose Ward Persons indicted before Wardens of the Peace shall be, if they make Deliverance, or let to Mainprize any so indicted, which be not mainpernable, and to punish the said Sheriffs, Gaolers and others, if they do any Thing against this Act.*

Sect. 14. It is observable, that this Statute saith only in general, That such Justices shall have Power to punish the Offenders therein mentioned, without saying, That they shall punish them according to the S. P. C. 77. a. Form of the Statute of *Westminster* 1. as the above mentioned Statute *de finibus* does; yet it is said, That they may punish them according to the Form of the said Statute of *Westminster*, as much as if it had been expressed.

Sect. 15. Also it is enacted by 1 & 2 *Ph.* & *Mar.* 13. *That if any Justice of the Peace of the* Quorum, *or Coroner, shall offend against the Purview of the said Statute, either as to bailing Prisoners, or taking their Examinations, or the Information of those that bring them before them, or not putting the same in Writ, or not certifying them to the next Gaol-Delivery, or not putting in Writing the Evidence given to a Jury on a Coroner's Inquest, of Murder or Manslaughter, or not binding over material Witnesses against Persons accused of Felony, to give Evidence at the next General Gaol-Delivery, or not certifying such Evidence, and also such Recognizances,* &c. *the Justices of Gaol-Delivery of the Place where such Offence shall be committed upon due Proof thereof by Examination before them, shall for every such Offence set such Fine as they shall think meet,* &c.

Sect. 16. As to the third Particular, *viz.* The Power of such Justices in Relation to Sheriffs, &c. refusing to receive Prisoners, it is enacted by 4 *E.* 3. *cap.* 10. *That Justices of Gaol-Delivery shall punish Sheriffs and Gaolers, refusing to take Felons into their Custody from Constables and Townships, without being paid for such Receipt.*

Sect. 17. As to the fourth Particular, *viz.* The Power of such Justices, in Relation to Persons convicted before former Justices, it is enacted by 1 *E.* 6. *cap.* 7. *That where any Person or Persons shall be found guilty of any Treason or Felony, for the which Judgment of Death should or may ensue, and shall be reprieved to Prison without Judgment at that Time given against him, her, or them so found guilty, those Persons that at any Time hereafter, shall by the King's Letters Patent be assigned Justices to deliver the Gaol, where any such Person or Persons found guilty shall remain, shall have full Power and Authority to give Judgment of Death against such Person so found guilty, and reprieved, as the same Justices (before whom such Person or Persons was or were found guilty) might have done, if their Commission of Gaol-Delivery had remained and continued in full Force and Strength.*

Sect. 18. It hath been holden, That this Statute extends not to Convictions before Justices of *Oyer* and *Terminer*, not only because Convictions before Justices of Gaol-Delivery only are mentioned, but because the Proceedings before Justices of *Oyer* and *Terminer*, after the *Oyer* determined, ought to remain in the King's Bench, and the Records before the Justices of Gaol-Delivery with the *Custos Rotulorum*. 12 Co. 33. Bro. Oyer & Terminer.

Sect. 19. Also it seemeth, That since the Statute speaks only of Persons reprieved before Judgment, it gives subsequent Commissioners no manner of Power over Persons condemned by former Justices; and therefore it hath been holden, That if a Person condemned by former Justices, plead a Pardon before their Successors, they have no Power to allow it, but that the Record ought to be removed by *Certiorari* into the King's Bench, and the Prisoner also by *Habeas Corpus*, and that there the Pardon shall be allowed or disallowed. And from the same Reason it seems to follow, That subsequent Justices have no [a] Power from this Statute to award the Execution of Persons condemned by former Justices, and reprieved by them: But if Judgment had not been given by the former Justices, there is no Doubt but that the subsequent ones might by Force of this Statute have allowed the Pardon, or given Judgment, and awarded Execution, &c. as the first might have done. Also it hath been adjudged, That not only such subsequent Justices as are authorized by the same King, by whom the former were commissioned, but also that the Justices of the next King may have the like Power by Virtue of this Statute. Dalison 20. Quære Dy. 165. Pl. 4. [a] 2 H. H. P. C. 35. contra. 7 Co. 31. b. Dalison 20.

Sect. 20. As to the fifth Particular, *viz.* The Jurisdiction of Justices of Gaol-Delivery in Relation to Offences created by Statute; By 33 *H.* 8. 9. Par. 20. They may punish those who keep unlawful Gaming Houses, or use unlawful Games. By 5 *Eliz.* 9. Par. 9. They have Jurisdiction over Perjury and Subornation of Perjury against the Form of that Statute. By 8 *Eliz.* 3. They may punish those who transport Sheep alive. By 23 *Eliz.* 1. Par. 9. They may enquire of, hear and determine Offences against that Statute in not coming to Church; and generally they have the like Power in other Statutes, creating new Offences, which it would be too tedious particularly to set down in this Place.

Sect. 21. As to the fourth general Point of this Chapter, *viz.* In what Place Justices of Gaol-Delivery ought to hold their Sessions, it is enacted by 6 *Ric.* 2. 5. *That Justices assigned to take Assizes and deliver Gaols, shall hold their Sessions in the principal and chief Towns of every of the Counties where the Shire-Courts of the same Counties were then holden, or hereafter should be holden.* For other Matters relating to these Justices, see Chapter 7. concerning *Justices of Assise and* Nisi Prius, and the Chapter concerning *Process.*

CHAP.

CHAP. VII.

Of the Court of the Justices of Assise *and* Nisi Prius.

Sect. 1. THE Power of Justices of Assise, whether as such, or as Justices of *Nisi Prius*, in Relation to criminal Matters, depending wholly on Statute, I shall only take Notice of the principal Branches of their Jurisdiction of this Kind, given them by several Acts of Parliament; and for more particular Inquiries concerning their Authority in other Cases, and the Nature, Extent and End of their Commission, shall refer the Reader to Sir *Edward Coke*'s 4*th Institute, fol.* 158, *&c.* and to his 12*th Report, fol.* 32. and to Mr. *Crompton*'s *Treatise concerning the Jurisdiction of Courts, fol.* 204, *&c.*

The most considerable Parts of their Jurisdiction in criminal Matters, proper to be considered in this Place, are such as relate,

1. To the Delivery of Gaols.
2. To Counterfeiters of Money.
3. To Appellees.
4. To Conspirators, Maintainers, and other Offenders of the like Nature.
5. To Offences of Sheriffs, Gaolers and other Officers.
6. To capital Offences tried by Writ of *Nisi Prius*.
7. To the Counties for which such Justices of Assise may be commissioned.

Sect. 2. As to the first of these Particulars, it is enacted by 27 *Ed.* 1. commonly called the Statute *de finibus, cap.* 3. *That Justices assigned to take Assizes, in every County where they do take Assizes, as they be appointed incontinent after the Assizes taken in the Shires, shall remain both together if they be lay; And if one of them be a Clerk, then one of the most discreet Knights of the Shire being associate to him that is a Layman by the King's Writ, shall deliver the Gaols of the Shires, as well within Liberties as without, of all Manner of Prisoners, after the Form of the Gaol-Deliveries of those Shires, before Times used. And the same Justices shall inquire then, if Sheriffs or any other have let out by Replevin Persons not repleviable,* &c.

Sect. 3. Also it is recited by 2 *Ed.* 3. 2. *That Offenders had been greatly encouraged, because the Justices of Gaol-Delivery and of* Oyer *and* Terminer *had been procured by great Men against the Form of the said Statute of* 27 *Ed.* 1. and thereupon it is enacted, *That such Justices shall not be made against the Form of the said Statute.*

S. P. C. 57. b. Raym. 375. H. P. C. 164. 12 Co. 32. *Sect.* 4. It seems to have been the most general Opinion in the Construction of the above mentioned Statute of 27 *Ed.* 1. That the Purview of it extends only to Cases of Felony; and this is farther confirmed by the Recital of the Statute of 3 *H.* 5. set forth more at large in the following Part of this Chapter, by which it is declared, That no Judges but those of the King's Bench, or special Commissioners, have Power to
S.P.C. 57, 58. punish Counterfeiters of Money. Also it is argued, That the Purview of

the said Statute of 3 *H.* 5. impowering Justices of Assise, having the King's Commission for such Purpose, to hear and determine the Offences of such Persons, would be vain and to no Purpose, if such Justices, as such, had Power over such Offences before, by Virtue of the said former Statute: And yet perhaps the contrary Opinion is the more plausible; for since the said Statute is intended for the greater Expedition of Justice, and the Words of it expresly extend to all Manner of Prisoners, why should they be restrained by a violent Interpretation, inconsistent with the natural and obvious Sense of them? And since Justices of Gaol-Delivery, armed only with a general Commission to deliver Gaols of the Prisoners in them, are, according to the better Opinion at this Day, authorized to deliver such Gaols of Persons accused of Treason, as well as of others committed for Crimes of an inferior Nature, why should not the said Statute, the Intent whereof is to give Justices of Assise like Power with Justices of Gaol-Delivery, be construed to give them as large a Power? And as to the Arguments drawn from the Opinion of the Makers of the above mentioned Statute of 3 *H.* 5. it may be answered, that perhaps the Purport of the said Recital may amount to no more than this, that no other Judges but those therein mentioned, would venture to take upon them a Power to try such Offences, because it was not clearly settled that they had Authority to do it.

Vide infra Sect. 9.
Vide supra cap. 6. Sect. 4.

Sect. 5. It seems to be the general Opinion, That Justices of Assise, as such, by Force of the said Statute of 27 *E.* 1. may deliver Gaols without any special Commission for that Purpose; and this seems to be most agreeable to the Purview of the said Statute, if such Justices be Laymen; for seeing the Act provides only, That if one of them be a Clerk, then one of the Knights of the County being associate by Writ to him that is a Layman shall deliver the Gaols; and make no Mention of any such Writ where both are Laymen; but only says in general, That in such Case they shall remain both together, it seems to imply that Laymen being Justices of ☞ Assise, shall have such Power of Course. [3]

H. P. C. 164. 2 H. H. P. C. 40, 403. S. P. C. 57. b. Crom. Jur. 126. Dy. 99. pl. 62.

Sect. 6. As to the second Particular, *viz.* The Power of these Justices in Relation to Counterfeiters of Money, it is recited by the Statute of 3 *H.* 5. *cap.* 7. *That Counterfeiting, Clipping, Washing, and other Falsity of Money, had then of late abounded, for that the Punishment of the same pertaineth not to any Judges of the Realm, but to the King's Justices before himself, or special Commissioners thereto assigned,* &c. and thereupon it is enacted, *That the King's Justices assigned to take Assises in all the Counties of* England, *shall have Power by the King's Commissions, to hear and determine in their Sessions, as well of the Counterfeiting and of the bringing such false Money into the Realm, as of Clipping, washing, and every other Falsity of the said Money.*

See the precedent Chap. Sect. 4. and the 15th Sect. of this Chapter.

Sect. 7. It seems clear from the manifest Purport of this Statute, That Justices of Assize can claim no Power from it over any of the Offences therein mentioned, without a special Commission for such Purpose; but this Statute being wholly in the Affirmative, and no way intended to abridge but inlarge the Jurisdiction of such Justices; it seems clear, That if they had Authority as Justices of Gaol-Delivery, by Virtue of the above mentioned Statute *De finibus*, without any special Commission, to deliver Persons in Prison for such Crimes, (which Question is more fully handled in the precedent Part of this Chapter) they may still lawfully proceed upon the said Statute in the same Manner as before.

S. P. C 58. H. P. C. 164.

Supra Sect. 4. Crom. Jur. 126.

Sect. 8. As to the third Particular, viz. The Power of Justices of Assise in relation to Appellees, it is enacted by 28 *Ed.* 1. commonly called the Statute *De Appellatis, That such Justices may award Process into any foreign County against Persons appealed by Approvers, and proceed against them,* &c.

Dyer 99. pl. 62. 12 Co. 32. *Sect.* 9. It is made a Doubt in *Dyer's Reports*, by what Warrant Justices of Assise hold Plea of an Appeal of Robbery; and it is there holden, That they do it by Virtue of the Commission of Gaol-Delivery: But it seems, that it ought not to be intended to be the Meaning of this Report, That Justices of Assise have no Jurisdiction as to an Appeal of Robbery, without an express Commission of Gaol-Delivery; for since Justices of Assise, as such, have Power by the above mentioned Statute *De finibus* to deliver Gaols of all Manner of Prisoners, after the Form of the Gaol-deliveries of the Shires wherein they sit, why should they not by Force of those general Words, deliver such Gaols of Persons proceeded against by Way of Appeal commenced before them, as well as of those proceeded against by Way of Indictment, as it seems to be
22 Ed. 4. 19. a. Bro. Appeal, 113. 4 Inst. 159. taken for granted in other Books that they may? And therefore it seems to be reasonable to take the above mentioned Report of *Dyer* in this Sense, That Justices of Assise may hold Plea of Appeals of Robbery by the Commission of Gaol-Delivery, given them implicitly by the said Statute *De finibus*, in respect whereof they seem to have all the Power of Justices of Gaol-Delivery, whether given them by the Common Law or by Statute, as fully appears from what immediately follows the above mentioned Passage in the said Report, wherein it is said, That the
Dyer 99. pl. 62. Statute of 2 or 3 *H.* 7. gives Justices of Assise the Power by express Words as to Appeals of Death; but it is certain, that the said Statute
3 H. 7. ch. 1. of *H.* 7. does not expresly mention Justices of Assise, but saith only, That the Wife, *&c.* may commence an Appeal before the Sheriff and Coroners, or before the King in his Bench, or Justices of Gaol-Delivery; and yet it is holden in the said Report, That this Statute expresly extends to Justices of Assise; from which it seems manifestly to follow, That such Justices are taken to be included under the general Notion of Justices of Gaol-Delivery.
13 Co. 32. 4. Inst. 159.

Sect. 10. As to the fourth Particular, *viz.* The Power of Justices of Assise in Relation to Conspirators, Maintainers, and other Offenders of the like Nature, it is enacted by 28 *Ed.* 1. commonly called *Articuli super chartas*, ch. 10. *That Justices assigned to take Assises, when they come into the Country to do their Office, shall upon every Plaint made unto them of Conspirators, false Informers, and evil Procurers of Dozens, Assises, Inquests, and Juries, award Inquest thereupon without Writ, and shall do Right to the Plaintiffs without Delay.* And it is farther enacted by 4 *Ed.* 3. 11. *That the Justices of Assise, whensoever they come to hold their Sessions, or to take Inquests upon* Nisi Prius, *shall inquire, hear and determine, as well at the Suit of the King as at the Suit of the Party, of Maintainers, Bearors, Conspirators,* &c. And the like is ordained by 20 *Ed.* 3. 6. by which it is enacted, *That such Justices shall have Commissions to inquire of Maintainers and common Embraceors,* &c.

Register 188. *Sect.* 11. Also it is enacted by 5 *Ed.* 3. 10. *That the Justices before whom any Assise, Inquest or Jury shall pass, may inquire and determine the Offence of any Juror in taking Money of either Party,* &c.

Sect. 12. But it is ordained by 38 *Ed.* 3. 12. *That no Justice,* &c. *inquire of Offices of the said Offence, but only at the Suit of the Party, or of other,* &c.

Sect. 13. And it is farther enacted by 32 *H.* 8. *ch.* 9. *That the Justices of Assise of every Circuit within this Realm, and elsewhere within the King's Dominions, shall in every County within their Circuits, twice in the Year cause open Proclamation to be made, as well of the said Statute as of all others made against unlawful Maintenance, Champerty, Embracery,* &c.

Sect. 14. As to the fifth Particular, *viz.* The Power of Justices of Assise

Aſſiſe in Relation to the Offences of Sheriffs, Gaolers, and other Officers, it is enacted by 20 *Ed.* 3. 6. *That Juſtices of Aſſiſe ſhall have Commiſſions ſufficient to inquire of Sheriffs, Eſcheators, Bailiffs of Franchiſes and their Miniſters, and of the Gifts which they take to execute their Office*, &c.

Sect. 15. Alſo it is enacted by 23 *H.* 6. 10. *That Juſtices of Aſſiſes in their Seſſions, ſhall have Power to inquire, hear and determine of Office without ſpecial Commiſſion, of and upon all Sheriffs, Under-Sheriffs, Clerks, Bailiffs, Gaolers, Coroners, Stewards, Bailiffs of Franchiſes, or any other Officer or Miniſter doing contrary to the ſaid Statute, as by extorting Money for the omitting of an Arreſt, or ſhewing Eaſe or Favour to thoſe who ſhall be arreſted, or by admitting Perſons to Bail, or denying them the Benefit of it, contrary to the Form of the ſaid Statute.*

Sect. 16. Alſo it is enacted by 1 *H.* 8. 7. *That Juſtices of Aſſiſe and of the Peace, ſhall have Authority to inquire of and determine, as well by Examination as by Preſentment, the Default of Coroners in not taking an Inqueſt without Fee or Reward, on the View of the Body of any Perſon ſlain by Miſadventure.*

Sect. 17. As to the ſixth Particular, *viz.* the Power of Juſtices of Aſ- 1 H. H. P. C.
ſiſe, in Relation to capital Offences tried by Writ of *Niſi Prius*, it is enacted 350. 2 H. H. P. C.
by 14 *H.* 6. 1. *That the Juſtices before whom Inquiſitions, Inqueſts and Ju-* 403.
ries, ſhall be taken by the King's Writ of Niſi Prius, *ſhall have Power in all* Raym. 367.
the Caſes of Felony and Treaſon, to give their Judgments, as well where a Man is acquit of Felony or of Treaſon, as where he is thereof attainted, the Day and Place where the ſaid Inquiſitions, Inqueſts, and Juries be ſo taken, and then from thenceforth to award Execution to be made by Force of the ſame Judgments.

Sect. 18. In the Conſtruction of this Statute it hath been holden, That
if the Plaintiff in Appeal be nonſuited before Juſtices of *Niſi Prius*, they 22 Ed. 4. 19. a.
have no Power to arraign the Defendant at the Suit of the King on the De- 2 H. H. P. C.
claration in the Appeal, as Juſtices before whom an Appeal is originally com- 41, 403.
menced may do: And the Reaſon of this Conſtruction ſeems to be this, becauſe the Statute only mentioning that Juſtices of *Niſi Prius* ſhall give Judgment where the Defendant is acquitted or attainted, leaves their Juriſdiction upon a Nonſuit as it was before. But it ſeems certain, That on the Acquittal of an Appellee ſuch Juſtices have Power to inquire of the Abettors, and alſo of the Sufficiency of the Plaintiff to anſwer the Damages;
for ſince the Statute of *Weſtm.* 2. Ch. 12. gives ſuch Power to the Ju- Dyer 120.
ſtices before whom an Appeal ſhall be heard and determined; and now by pl. 12.
Force of 14 *H.* 6. it may be heard and determined before Juſtices of Crom. Jur. 212.
Niſi Prius, it ſeems neceſſarily to follow, That Juſtices of *Niſi Prius* ſhall 4 Inſt. 160.
have ſuch Power ſince the ſame Statute of 14 *H.* 6. And from the ſame rea- 22 Ed. 4. 19. a.
ſoning it ſeems alſo to follow, That ſuch Juſtices may give Judgment for the 10 Ed. 4. 14. b. 2 Inſt. 386.
Damages; but conſtant Experience hath over-ruled it to the contrary. Bro. Niſi Prius, 27.

Sect. 19. As to the ſeventh Particular, *viz.* for what Counties Juſtices 2 H. H. P. C.
of Aſſiſe may be commiſſioned, it is enacted by 8 *Rich.* 2. 2. *That no Man* 32.
of Law ſhall be from thenceforth Juſtice of Aſſiſes, or of the common Deliverance of Gaols, in his own Country.

Sect. 20. Alſo it is enacted by 33 *H.* 8. Ch. 24. *That no Juſtice, nor other Man learned in the Laws of this Realm, ſhall uſe, nor exerciſe the Office of Juſtice of Aſſiſe within any County where the ſaid Juſtice was born, or doth inhabit, on Pain of* 100 l. &c. *Provided that the ſaid Act ſhall not extend to any Perſon who ſhall be Clerk of Aſſiſes, and Aſſociate to any Juſtice of Aſſiſe, nor to any Mayor, Sheriff, Recorder, Steward, Bailiff, Sewter, or other Officer being born or dwelling within any City, Borough or Town within this Realm of* England, &c. *Nor to Juſtices of either Bench for taking, hearing, or determining Aſſiſes in the one Bench or the other, nor to the Juſtices, Juſtice-Clerks, or Clerk of Aſſiſes, in the Dutchy and County Palatine of* Lancaſter.

CHAP.

CHAP. VIII.

Of the Court of Seſſions of Juſtices of Peace.

BEFORE I come to conſider the Nature of the Court of Seſſions of Juſtices of Peace, I ſhall premiſe,

1. In what Manner Conſervators of the Peace were provided by the Common Law.
2. In what Manner Juſtices of Peace have been ordained by the ſeveral Statutes concerning them.
3. How they are to be commiſſioned in Purſuance of thoſe Statutes.
4. What is moſt obſervable from the ſaid Statutes and Commiſſions.

As to the firſt Point it ſeems, that Conſervators of the Peace by the Common Law, were of two Sorts;

1. Thoſe who in Reſpect of their Offices had Power to keep the Peace, but were not ſimply called by the Name of Conſervators of the Peace, but by the Name of ſuch Offices.
2. Thoſe who were conſtituted for this Purpoſe only, and were ſimply called by the Name of Conſervators or Wardens of the Peace.

[a] Lamb. B. 1. Ch. 3. Dalt. Ch. 1.
[b] Bro. Recognizance, 14, 19. Dalt. Ch. 1.
[c] Lamb. B. 1. Ch. 3.

Sect. 1. And firſt of thoſe of the firſt Sort, of which the King's [a] Majeſty is certainly the Principal, from whom all Authority of this Kind was originally derived, and who ſtill continues to have the ſame in his own Perſon; yet it is ſaid, [b] That he cannot take a Recognizance for the Keeping the Peace, becauſe it is a Rule in Law, That no one can take any Recognizance, who is not either a Juſtice of Record, or by Commiſſion; alſo it ſeems certain, That [c] no Duke, Earl or Baron, as ſuch, have any greater Authority to keep the Peace than mere private Perſons.

[d] Dalt. Ch. 1. Lamb. B. 1. Ch. 3. Crompt. 6. b.

Sect. 2. The [d] Lord Chancellor or Lord Keeper of the Great Seal, the Lord High Steward of *England*, the Lord Marſhal, and Lord High Conſtable of *England*, and every Juſtice of the King's Bench, and, as ſome ſay, the Lord Treaſurer have, as incident to their Offices, a general Authority to keep the Peace throughout all the Realm, and to award Proceſs for the Surety of the Peace, and to take Recognizances for it. And the Maſter of the Rolls hath alſo the like Power, either as incident to his Office, or at leaſt by Preſcription.

[e] 10 H. 6. 7. b. Lamb. B. 1. Ch. 3.

Sect. 3. Alſo every [e] Court of Record, as ſuch, hath Power to keep the Peace within its own Precinct, as hath been more fully ſhewn, *Ch.* 1. *Sect.* 15. And the Juſtices of Gaol-Delivery may take Surety of the Peace from a Priſoner before them, who was committed for not finding ſuch Surety.

Sect. 4. Also every Sheriff is a principal [a] Conservator of the Peace within his County, and may without Doubt, *ex Officio*, award Process of the Peace, and take Surety for it; and it seems the better [b] Opinion, That the Security so taken by him is by the Common Law looked on as a Recognizance or Matter of Record, and not as a common Obligation, or Matter *in Pais* only; for that it is taken by him by Virtue of the King's Commission, by which he is intrusted with the Custody of the County, and consequently has by it an implied Power of keeping the Peace within such County; and it is a general [c] Rule, That whatsoever is done by Virtue of the King's Commission ought to be taken as a Matter of Record.

[a] Lamb. B. 1. Ch. 3. 12 H. 7. 17. b. Bro. Peace, 13. Cro. Car. 26. [b] Bro. Recognizance, 5. F.N.B. 81. D. 82. Dalt. ch. 11. Lamb. B. 1. Ch. 13. Quære Bro. Recognizance, 5, 14, 16, 18.

Sect. 5. Also every [d] Coroner is another principal Conservator of the Peace within the County of which he is a Coroner, and may certainly bind any Person to the Peace who makes an Affray in his Presence: But it seems the better Opinion, That he has no Authority to grant Process for the Peace; and it seems clear, That the Security taken by him for the keeping of the Peace, (except only where it is taken by him as Judge of his own Court for an Affray done in such Court,) is not to be looked on as a Recognizance, but as an Obligation; because it is not taken by one who acts as a Judge of Record, or by the King's Commission, as all [e] Recognizances ought to be.

[c] See the Books above cited. 9 E. 4. 30. b. 31. a. [d] Cromp. 6. Lamb. B. 1. Ch. 3. [e] See the Books cited S. 1. Letter b. and S. 4. Letter b.

Sect. 6. Also every High and Petit Constable are by the Common Law Conservators of the Peace within their several Limits, and may take such Order for the keeping of the same, as hath been more fully shewn, *B.* 1. *Ch.* 63. *S.* 13, 14, *&c.*

Crompt. 6. b.

Secondly, Conservators of the Peace by the Common Law, who were constituted for that Purpose only, and were simply called by the Name of Conservators or Keepers of the Peace, were of two Kinds:

1. Ordinary.
2. Extraordinary.

Those of the first Kind were either,

1. By Tenure, or
2. By Election, or
3. By Prescription.

Sect. 7. Conservators of the Peace by Tenure were those who held Lands of the King by this Service, among others, of being Conservators of the Peace, within such a District.

Lamb. B. 1. Ch. 3.

Sect. 8. Conservators of the Peace by Election, were those who were chosen to such Office in Pursuance of the King's Writ to such Purpose, (as all Sheriffs anciently were, and as Coroners still are) by the Freeholders of a County in the County-Court; after which Election it was usual for the King to send another Writ to the Persons so chosen, commanding them diligently to attend their said Office till they should receive a Command from the King to the contrary.

Lamb. B. 1. Ch. 3.

Sect. 9. Conservators of the Peace by Prescription, were those who claimed such Power from an immemorial Usage in themselves and their Predecessors or Ancestors, or those whose Estate they had in certain Lands, to exercise the like Power, which wholly depended upon such Usage both as to its Extent, and the Manner in which it was to be exercised.

Bro. Peace, 18. Prescription, 79. 22 Ed. 4. 35 b. Lamb. B. 1. Ch. 3.

[a] 21 Ed. 4. 67. a. *Sect.* 10. It is [a] questioned indeed by some, whether any such Power can be claimed by Usage? Yet if the Power of holding Pleas and even Courts of Record, which are of so high a Nature, and imply a Power of keeping the Peace within their own Precincts, may be claimed by Usage, as it seems to be [b] certain, that they may; it seems strange that the bare Authority of keeping the Peace in a certain District may not as well be claimed by such Usage.

[b] Co. Lit. 114. b. Doctor and Student B. 1. Ch. 7.

[c] Dalt. B. 1. fol. 3. Crompt. 6. b. *Sect.* 11. It [c] seems, That the Power of such Conservators of the Peace, whether by Tenure, Election, or Prescription, was no greater than that of Constables at this Day, unless it were enlarged by some special Grant or Prescription.

Lamb. B. 1. Ch. 3. *Sect.* 12. The extraordinary Conservators of the Peace were Persons specially commissioned, in Times of imminent Danger either from Rebels or foreign Invaders, to take care of and defend such a particular District committed to their Charge, and to preserve the Peace within the Limits of it; and these had Power to command the Sheriff with his whole *Posse* to aid and assist them.

2 H. H. P. C. 42. *Sect.* 13. And now I am in the second Place to shew, in what Manner Justices of Peace have been ordained by the several Statutes concerning them, the first whereof is 1 *Ed.* 3. *Ch.* 16. which is in the following Words, *For the better keeping and Maintenance of the Peace, the King willeth that in every County, good Men and lawful, which be no Maintainers of Evil, or Barrators in the Country, shall be assigned to keep the Peace.*

Sect. 14. And it is farther enacted by 4 *Ed.* 3. 2. *That there shall be assigned good and lawful Men in every County to keep the Peace; and at the Time of the Assignments Mention shall be made, that such as shall be indicted or taken by the said Keepers of the Peace, shall not be let to Mainprise by the Sheriffs, nor by none other Ministers, if they be not mainpernable by the Law; nor that such as shall be indicted, shall not be delivered but at the Common Law. And the Justices assigned to deliver the Gaols, shall have Power to deliver the same Gaols of those that shall be indicted before the Keepers of the Peace; and that the said Keepers shall send their Indictments before the Justices,* &c.

Sect. 15. And it is farther enacted by 18 *Ed.* 3. 2. *That two or three of the best Reputation in the Counties, shall be assigned Keepers of the Peace by the King's Commission. And at what Time need shall be, the same with other wise and learned in the Law shall be assigned by the King's Commission, to hear and determine Felonies and Trespasses done against the Peace in the same Counties, and to inflict Punishment reasonably according to the Law and Reason, and the Manner of the Deed.*

Sect. 16. And it is farther enacted by 34 *Ed.* 3. 1. *That in every County of* England, *shall be assigned for the keeping of the Peace, one Lord, and with him three or four of the most worthy in the County, with some Learned in the Law, and they shall have Power to restrain the Offenders, Rioters, and all other Barrators, and to pursue, arrest, take and chastise them according to their Trespass or Offence; and to cause them to be imprisoned and duly punished according to the Law and Customs of the Realm, and according to that which to them shall seem best to do by their Discretion and good Advisement; and also to inform them, and to inquire of all those who have been Pillors and Robbers in the Parts beyond the Sea, and be now come again, and go wandering, and will not labour as they were wont in Times past; and to take and arrest all those that they may find by Indictment, or by Suspicion, and to put them in Prison, and to take of all them that be not of good Fame, where they shall be found, sufficient Surety and Mainprise of their good Behaviour towards the King and his People, and the other duly to punish, to the Intent that the People be not by such Rioters or Rebels troubled nor endamaged,*

endamaged, nor the Peace blemished, nor Merchants nor other passing by the Highways of the Realm disturbed, nor put in the Peril which may happen of such Offenders; and also to hear and determine at the King's Suit, all Manner of Felonies and Trespasses done in the same County, according to the Laws and Customs aforesaid.

Sect. 17. And it is enacted by 17 *R.* 2. 10. *That in every Commission of the Peace through the Realm, where need shall be, two Men of Law of the same County where such Commission shall be made, shall be assigned to go and proceed to the Deliverance of Thieves and Felons, as often as they shall think it expedient.*

Sect. 18. And it is farther enacted by 2 *H.* 5. Stat. 1. Ch. 4. *That the Justices of Peace in every Shire named of the* Quorum, (*except Lords and the Justices of either Bench, and the Chief Baron, and Serjeants at Law, and the King's Attorney for the Time that they shall be occupied in the King's Service,*) *shall be resiant in the same Shire, and shall make their Sessions four Times by the Year,* viz. *in the first Week after* Michaelmas, Epiphany, Easter, *and the Translation of St.* Thomas *the Martyr, and oftner if Need be, and that the same Justices hold their Sessions throughout* England *in the same Weeks every Year.* 36 Ed. 3. 12. Lamb. B. 4. Ch. 19. Crompt. 123. 2 H. H. P.C. 49.

Sect. 19. Also it is enacted by 2 *H.* 5. Stat. 2. Ch. 1. *That Justices of Peace shall be made in the Counties of* England, *of most sufficient Persons dwelling in the same Counties, by the Advice of the Chancellor and of the King's Counsel, without taking other Persons dwelling in foreign Counties to execute such Office, except the Lords and the Justices of Assises to be named by the King and his Counsel; and except all the King's Chief Stewards of the Lands and Seigniories of the Dutchy of* Lancaster, *in the North Parts, and in the South, for the Time being.*

Sect. 20. Also it is enacted by 1 *Mar.* Sess. 2. Ch. 8. *That no Person having or using the Office of a Sheriff of any County, shall use or exercise the Office of a Justice of Peace, by Force of any Commission or otherwise, in any County where he shall be Sheriff, during the Time only that he shall exercise the said Office, or Sheriffwick: And that all Acts done by such Sheriff by Authority of any Commission of the Peace, during the Time abovesaid, shall be void.* Crompt. 121.

Sect. 21. Also there are many other Statutes concerning the Power of Justices of Peace, all of which it would be endless to enumerate; therefore I have only taken Notice of those which concern their Authority in general; and for those which concern the particular Branches of it, I shall refer the Reader to the Books which treat principally of this Subject.

Sect. 22. As to the third Point, *viz.* In what Manner Justices of the Peace are to be commissioned in Pursuance of the several Statutes concerning them; it is observable, That the Commission of the Peace hath often been altered in several Reigns, and that the present Form of it was settled by the Judges about the thirty-third Year of Queen *Elizabeth*, and is in Substance as followeth: 2 H. H.P.C. 42, 43. 4 Inst. 171. Lamb. B. 1. Ch. 9.

Sect. 23. Beginning with a Salutation from the King to the several Persons named in it, it afterwards assigns them and every one of them, jointly and severally, the King's Justices, to keep the Peace in such a County; and to cause to be kept all Statutes made for the Good of the Peace and quiet Government of the People, as well within Liberties as without; and to punish all those who shall offend against any of the said Statutes; and to cause all those to come before them, or some of them, who shall threaten any of the People as to their Persons, or the burning of their Houses, in order to compel them to find Surety for the Peace or Good Behaviour; and if they shall refuse to find such Surety, to cause them to be safely kept in Prison till they shall find it.

Sect. 24. Then it goes on and assigns them, and every two or more of them, (of which Number either such or such a particular Person among them is is ſpecially required to be) Juſtices to inquire by the Oath of good and lawful Men of the ſame County, of all Felonies, Witchcrafts, Inchantments, Sorceries, Magick Art, Treſpaſſes, Foreſtallers, Regrators, Ingroſſers, and Extortions whatſoever, and of all other Offences of which Juſtices of the Peace may lawfully inquire; alſo of all thoſe who ſhall go or ride armed, &c. or in Companies, to the Diſturbance of the Peace; and alſo of all Inholders and others who ſhall offend in the Abuſe of Weights or Meaſures, or ſelling of Victuals, &c. and alſo of all Sheriffs, Bailiffs, Stewards, Conſtables, Gaolers, and other Officers, who ſhall be faulty in the Execution of their Offices; and to inſpect all Indictments taken before them, or any of them, or other former Juſtices of the Peace for the ſame County; and to make and continue Proceſs againſt all the Perſons ſo indicted, till they ſhall be taken, or render themſelves, or be outlawed; and to hear and determine all the Felonies, and other Offences aforeſaid: Provided, that if a Caſe of Difficulty ſhall ariſe, they ſhall not proceed to give Judgment, except in the Preſence of ſome Juſtice of one of the Benches or of Aſſiſe.

Sect. 25. And then it commands them to make Inquiries of the Premiſſes, and to hear and determine the ſame at certain Days and Places, which they or any ſuch two or more of them ſhall appoint.

Sect. 26. And then it goes on and commands the Sheriff of the County to return before them at certain Days and Places to be made known to him by them, ſuch and ſo many lawful Men of his Bailiwick, by whom the Truth of the Premiſſes may be beſt known and inquired.

Sect. 27. And then concludes, by aſſigning ſome one of them Keeper of the Rolls of the Peace in the ſame County; and commanding him to cauſe to be brought before himſelf and his Fellows, at the ſaid Days and Places, the Writs, Precepts, Proceſſes and Indictments aforeſaid.

And now I am in the fourth Place to ſhew, What is moſt obſervable from the ſaid Statutes and Commiſſions; in order to which I ſhall endeavour to ſhew,

1. What Statutes concerning the Peace may be executed by ſuch Juſtices.
2. How far the Juſtices of Peace for a County may act out of it, or within a Liberty.
3. What Commiſſions of this Kind require a ſpecial Suit to the King for the granting of them.
4. How far ſuch Juſtices have Power to proceed on Indictments not taken before themſelves.
5. By what name they are to be deſcribed.
6. What Authority they have in Relation to Felonies.
7. What in relation to Treaſon, *Præmunire*, and Miſpriſion of Treaſon.
8. What in relation to inferior Offences.

Lamb. B. 1. Ch. 9. Dalt. Ch. 5. Crompt. 7, 8.

Sect. 28. As to the firſt Point, *viz.* What Statutes concerning the Peace may be executed by ſuch Juſtices, it ſeems certain, That by Virtue of the ſaid Commiſſion they may execute all Statutes whatſoever, made for the better keeping of the Peace, and conſequently thoſe of *Wincheſter* and *Weſtminſter*, and all others concerning the Peace, made before the Reign of *Edward* the Third, in whoſe Time Juſtices of Peace were firſt inſtituted; for all thoſe Statutes were expreſly mentioned in the ancient Commiſſions of the Peace, and have always been undoubtedly taken to be included in the general Words of the preſent Commiſſion; and yet none of the Statutes which ordain the Office of Juſtices of Peace, ſay any Thing concerning the Execution of the said former Statutes, so that the Power of Justices of Peace in Relation to those Statutes, seems intirely to depend on the King's Commission, and yet hath always been unquestionably allowed; from whence it appears, That regularly the King by his Commission, may authorize whom he pleases to execute an Act of Parliament.

As to the second Point, *viz.* How far the Justices of Peace for a County may act out of it or within a Liberty; it is said, That they have no coercive Power when out of the County; and therefore that an Order of Barstardy, or for Payment of Labourers Wages, made by them out of the County, is not binding; yet it is said, That Recognizances and Informations voluntarily taken before them in any Place, are good: And it is to be observed, [4] Cro.Car. 211, 212. 2 H. H. P. C. 51.

Sect. 29. That the Justices of Peace for a County have, by their Commission, an express Authority as well within Liberties as without; from whence it seems clearly to follow, That they may execute their Office within a Town, which has a special Commission of the Peace for its own Limits, unless such Commission have a Clause, that no other Justices, except those named in it, shall any way concern themselves in the keeping of the Peace within the Liberties of such Town; and it may be questioned, whether such a special Clause in such a Commission, do absolutely make void the Act of any County-Justice within such Town? since the Commission for the County seems as fully to give those named in it a Jurisdiction over all such Towns within the Precinct of it, as such Commission for a Town doth exclude them: And the Justices for the County seem to be under no Necessity of informing themselves of the Contents of a Commission, which they have nothing to do with; yet if they have express Notice given them of such a restraining Clause, and proceed to act within such Town in Defiance of it, they may perhaps be punishable for their Contempt of the King's Prohibition; and yet perhaps it may be questioned whether their Acts be void, for the Reasons abovementioned. 2 H. H. P. C. 47, 48. Lamb. B. 1. Ch. 9. Cont. Cromp. 8. 20 H. 7. 6, 7, 8.

Sect. 30. As to the third Point, *viz.* What Commissions of this Kind require a special Suit to the King for granting of them; it seems agreed, That notwithstanding all such Commissions must be in the King's Name, as hath been more fully shewn, *Ch.* 5. *Sect.* 1. yet there is not any need of a special Suit or Application to, or Warrant from the King, for the granting of them; for this is only requisite for such as are of a particular Nature, as constituting the Mayor of such a Town, and his Successors, perpetual Justices of the Peace within their Liberties, *&c.* which Commissions are neither revocable by the King, nor determinable by his Death, as the common Commission for the Peace is, which is made of Course by the Lord Chancellor according to his Discretion. Lamb. B. 1. Ch. 5. Brook, Commission, 5. Dalt. Ch. 3. 1 Lev. 219.

Sect. 31. As to the fourth Point, *viz.* How far Justices of Peace have Power to proceed on Indictments not taken before themselves, it is certain, That subsequent Justices of Peace may proceed upon Indictments taken before their Predecessors; but this seems chiefly to depend upon 11 *H.* 6. 6. which, *reciting the Inconvenience that Pleas and Processes upon Indictments before Justices of Peace had often been discontinued by making of new Commissions of the Peace, to the great Loss of the King,* &c. *ordains that such Pleas, Suits, and Processes before Justices of the Peace, shall not be discontinued by new Commissions of the Peace, but stand in Force: And that the new Justices, after that they have the Records of the same Pleas and Processes before them, may continue, and finally hear and determine the same,* &c. And this is farther confirmed by 1 *Ed.* 6. 7. Par. 6. But it is certain that they cannot Crom. 2, 9. 2 H. H. P. C. 46. Cromp. 9. H. P. C. 166, 167.

proceed on an Indictment taken before a Coroner, or Juſtices of *Oyer* and *Terminer*, or Gaol-Delivery, nor deliver Perſons ſuſpected by Proclamation: But by 1 *Ed.* 4. 2. they are enabled to proceed on Indictments taken before the Sheriff at his Torn.

Sect. 32. As to the fifth Point, By what Name ſuch Juſtices are to be deſcribed, it is obſervable, That they are expreſly commiſſioned by the 2 Rol.Ab.95. Name of Juſtices of Peace; and in no Part of their Commiſſion are called by the Name of Keepers of the Peace; yet, inaſmuch as by 18 *E.* 3. 2. which is one of the firſt Statutes made concerning their Inſtitution, they are expreſly called Keepers of the Peace; and the principal End of their Office is for the keeping of the Peace, and their uſual Deſcription in *Certiorari's* is by the Name of Keepers of the Peace; it hath been adjudged, That the Caption of an Indictment, (whereof Juſtices of Peace have Conuſance,) *coram* A. B. & C. D. *Cuſtodibus Pacis & Juſticiariis Domini Regis*, in ſuch a Place, is good, without expreſly naming them Juſtices of Peace. The King and Hawkins, Mich. 3 Geor. 1. Alſo it hath been reſolved, That the Deſcription of Juſtices of Peace by the Name of *Juſticiarii Domini Regis ad pacem conſervandam, &c.* is good without ſaying, *ad pacem Domini Regis*, for that it is neceſſarily implied.

Sect. 33. As to the ſixth Point, *viz.* What Authority Juſtices of Peace have in relation to Felonies, it is obſervable, That ſuch of the ſaid Juſtices as are of the *Quorum* only, are expreſly authorized to inquire of, and hear and determine Felonies and Treſpaſſes, and that the abovementioned Statute of 18 *E.* 3. after it hath ordained, *That ſome Perſons ſhall be aſſigned Keepers of the Peace by the King's Commiſſion*, ſaith in another diſtinct Clauſe, *That at what Time need ſhall be, the ſame ſhall be aſſigned by the King's Commiſſions to hear and determine Felonies and Treſpaſſes*, &c. From whence it is inferred, That Juſtices of Peace have no Power to hear and [a] determine Felonies, unleſs they be authorized ſo to do by the expreſs Words of their Commiſſion: And this Opinion is farther confirmed by the Authority of the Year-Books of [b] 2 *R.* 3. 9. *a. b.* and 12 *H.* 7. 25. *a.* wherein it is adjudged, That a *Certiorari* to remove certain Indictments taken before Juſtices of Peace was not good, becauſe it named them only Juſtices of Peace, without adding that they were alſo aſſigned to hear and determine Felonies, &c. Yet it ſeems, That it may probably be argued for the contrary Opinion, that the Statute of 34 *E.* 3. 1. is expreſs, that the Perſons aſſigned for the keeping of the Peace, ſhall have Power among other Things to hear and determine Felonies and Treſpaſſes, &c. And this ſeems to be the principal Ground of the Reſolution in the Caſe of Cro. Jac. 32. Yelv. 46. 2 Rol. Rep. 151. Dy. 69. Pl. 29. *Barnes* and *Conſtantine*, wherein it is adjudged, That the ſetting forth of an Indictment in a Declaration as taken before Juſtices of Peace, being alſo aſſigned to hear and determine Felonies, &c. was well juſtified upon *Oyer* of the Record, wherein it was entered as taken before Juſtices of Peace, without adding, That they were aſſigned to hear and determine Felonies, &c. And as to the Authority of *Staundford* and *Hale*, it may be anſwered, That their Opinion is expreſly grounded on the Wording of the Statute of 18 *E.* 3. And it does not appear that they conſidered the Purport of 34 *E.* 3. As to the Authority of 2 *R.* 3. 9. it may be anſwered, That the *Certiorari* therein mentioned, was for the Removal of an Indictment for counterfeiting Coin, and that the Power of Juſtices of Peace to take ſuch an Indictment, depends wholly upon the Statute of 3 *H.* 5. 7. whereby it is enacted, *That the Juſtices of Peace throughout the Realm, ſhall have Power by the King's Commiſſions to inquire of the ſaid Offence.* And as to what is ſaid in 12 *H.* 7. 25. it may be anſwered, that the *Certiorari* therein mentioned was to remove certain Indictments, but it doth not appear from the Book what thoſe Indictments were; ſo that it is poſ-

[a] Crompt. 120. b. S. P. C. 53. a. 58. and 96. Letter E. H. P. C. 165, 207. 2 H. H. P. C. 43, 44.

[b] Brook, Indictment, 32, 50.

ſible they might be of a ſpecial Nature, not within the general Purview of 34 *E.* 3. *ſed Quære.* However it is certain, That ſuch a Clauſe in the Commiſſion of Juſtices to hear and determine Felonies, *&c.* gives them no Juriſdiction over an Offence, which by Statute, is ſpecially appointed to be determined by Juſtices of *Oyer* and *Terminer*, becauſe ſuch Juſtices ſhall be intended to mean ſuch Juſtices of *Oyer* and *Terminer* only, which properly and uſually are ſo called, and not thoſe who are diſtinctly known by another Name. And from hence it follows, That Juſtices of Peace have no Power to take an Indictment upon the Statute of 5 *Eliz.* 14. concerning Forgery, nor on the 2 & 3 *Ed.* 6. 24. againſt Acceſſaries in one County to Felonies in another, nor on any other Statute which ſpecially limits the Juriſdiction of determining any other Felony to other Juſtices of a particular Denomination. Yet inaſmuch as all Felonies include in them a Breach of the Peace, and 2 & 3 *Ph.* & *Mar.* 10. which directs Juſtices of Peace to take the Examinations of all ſuch Perſons as ſhall be committed by them for Felony, ſeems to ſuppoſe them to have a general Power of committing all Perſons accuſed of any Kind of Felony; and the general Practice has always been agreeable hereto; it is ſaid, That Juſtices of Peace may take the Examination of Perſons brought before them for any Kind of Felony, and commit them to Priſon; and alſo take the Information of the Proſecutors upon Oath, and bind them over to proſecute; and to commit thoſe who ſhall refuſe to be ſo bound, if it appear that they can give material Evidence. Alſo inaſmuch as the ſaid Statute of 2 & 3 *Ph.* & *Mar.* 10. and alſo 1 & 2 *Ph.* & *Mar.* 13. direct Juſtices of Peace, in Caſe of Homicide and other Felonies, to take the Examination of the Offenders, and the Information of others, and to certify the ſame to the Juſtices of Gaol-Delivery; it hath been generally thought adviſable for Juſtices of Peace to proceed no farther in Relation to any Felonies, though within their Commiſſion, except only Petit Larcenies.

H. P. C. 165. 2 H. H. P. C. 44. 9 Co. 118. b. Cro. El. 87, 601, 697. 2 Rol. Ab. 96. Pl. 2.

Dalton Ch. 20. H. P. C. 167, 168. 2 H. H. P. C. 44.

H. P. C. 169. 2 H. H. P. C. 46.

Sect. 34. As to the ſeventh Point, *viz.* What Authority Juſtices of Peace have in Relation to Treaſon, *Præmunire*, and Miſpriſion of Treaſon; it ſeems to be agreed, That notwithſtanding none of theſe Offences are within the Letter of their Commiſſion; yet inaſmuch as they are againſt the Peace of the King, and of the Realm, any Juſtice of Peace may either upon his own Knowledge, or the Complaint of others, cauſe any Perſon to be apprehended for any ſuch Offence. And it is the Opinion both of *Dalton* and Sir *Matthew Hale*, That ſuch Juſtice may take the Examination of the Perſon ſo apprehended, and the Information of all thoſe who can give material Evidence againſt him, and put the ſame in Writing; and alſo bind over ſuch who are able to give any ſuch Evidence to the King's Bench, or Gaol-Delivery; and certify his Proceedings to the ſame Court, to which he ſhall bind over ſuch Informers. And this Opinion ſeems to be agreeable to conſtant Practice, eſpecially ſince the Statutes of 1 & 2 *Ph.* & *Mar.* 13. and 2 & 3 *Ph.* & *Mar.* 10. which directing Juſtices of Peace to proceed in this Manner againſt Perſons brought before them for Felony, ſeem to give them a diſcretionary Power of proceeding in like Manner againſt Perſons accuſed of the abovementioned Offences.

Lamb. 226.

Dalt. Ch. 90. H. P. C. 168. 2 H. H. P. C. 44.

Sect. 35. Alſo by 3 *H.* 5. Ch. 7. *Juſtices of Peace ſhall have Power by the King's Commiſſions to inquire of Counterfeiting, Clipping, Waſhing, and other Falſity of Money of the Land, and thereupon to make Proceſs by* Capias *only, againſt thoſe who before them ſhall be thereof indicted.*

Sect. 36. And by 5 *El.* 1. Sect. 3. *Juſtices of Peace may inquire of the Offence of maintaining the Pope's Power, and ſhall certify every Preſentment made*

made before them of any ſuch Offence, into the King's Bench, within forty Days after it ſhall be made, &c.

1 Leon. 239. *Sect.* 37. And by 23 *E.* 1. Sect. 8. *They may inquire of all Offences againſt that Act, or againſt the Acts of the firſt, fifth, or thirteenth Years of the ſaid Queen's Reign, touching acknowledging of the King's ſupreme Government in Cauſes Eccleſiaſtical, or other Matters touching the Service of God, or coming to Church, or Eſtabliſhment of true Religion in this Realm, within one Year and a Day after every ſuch Offence committed.*

Sect. 38. As to the eighth Point, *viz.* What Authority Juſtices of Peace have in Relation to inferior Offences, it would be endleſs to enumerate all the Offences within their Juriſdiction, concerning which there have been ſuch great Numbers of Statutes; and therefore I ſhall content my ſelf in this Place with obſerving, that by the abovementioned Statute of 34 *Ed.* 3. 1. and alſo by the expreſs Words of their Commiſſion, they are impowered to hear and determine all Treſpaſſes, which is a Word of a very general Extent, and in a large Senſe not only comprehends all inferior Offences, which are properly and directly againſt the Peace, as Aſſaults and Batteries, and ſuch like, but alſo all others which are ſo on-[a] 6 Mod. 128. ly by Conſtruction; as all Breaches of the Law in general are [a] ſaid to be: Yet it hath been of late ſettled, that Juſtices of Peace have no Juriſ-[b] Salk. 406. Crompt. 120. b. Lamb. B. 1. Ch. 12. diction over [b] Forgery or Perjury at the Common Law, the principal Reaſon of which Reſolution as I apprehended, was, that inaſmuch as the chief End of the Inſtitution of the Office of theſe Juſtices, was for the Preſervation of the Peace againſt perſonal Wrongs, and open Violence; and the Word Treſpaſs in its moſt proper and natural Senſe, is taken for ſuch kind of Injuries, it ſhall be underſtood in that Senſe only in the ſaid Statute and Commiſſion, or at the moſt to extend to ſuch other Offences only as have a direct and immediate Tendency to cauſe ſuch [c] 1 Lev. 139. 1 Sid. 271. 1 Keb. 559, 772,788,931. 2 Keb. 138. Contra Cro. Jac. 421. Tr. 13 Annæ. Breaches of the Peace, [c] as Libels, and ſuch like, which on this Account have been adjudged indictable before Juſtices of Peace: And for this Reaſon, principally as I apprehended, the Court of King's Bench in the Caſe of one *Pitt*, ſince the abovementioned Reſolution concerning Perjury and Forgery, refuſed to quaſh an Indictment found at a Seſſion of the Peace for a Libel, but ordered the Defendant to demur to it, if he thought fit. [d] Latch 173. Poph. 208. [d] And upon the like Reaſon perhaps the former Opinion, That one may be indicted before Juſtices of Peace for being a common Night-Walker and Haunter of Bawdy-Houſes, may not be thought to contradict the abovementioned Reſolution.

Cro. Jac. 32. Yelv. 46. Con. 2 Rol. Rep. 151. *Sect.* 39. And Juſtices of Peace by Virtue of the abovemention'd Statute of 34 *Ed.* 3. 1. ſeem to have a Juriſdiction over Barrators, and ſuch like Offenders, whether they be mentioned in their Commiſſion or not. And it ſeems clear, That Juſtices of Peace have Juriſdiction of all inferior Crimes within their Commiſſion, whether ſuch Crimes be mentioned in King and Loggain. any Statute concerning them or not; for that all ſuch Crimes are either directly, or at leaſt by Conſequence, and Judgment of Law, againſt the Peace, and upon this Ground principally, as I apprehended, it was lately reſolved, That they may take an Indictment of Extortion.

Sect. 40. And now I am to conſider the Nature of the Court of theſe Juſtices Seſſions, by which we underſtand an Aſſembly of two or more of them, whereof one is of the *Quorum*, at a certain Day and Place before appointed, in order to inquire, hear and determine, in Purſuance of their Commiſſion, of any Cauſes or Matters therein contained. And for the better Underſtanding hereof, I ſhall conſider the following Particulars.

1. By whom, and in what Manner such Court is to be summoned and appointed.
2. What Persons are bound to give their Attendance at it.
3. Whether it have any Power over its own Members.
4. The Difference between General and Special, and Quarter-Sessions.

Sect. 41. As to the first Point, It seems clear from the express Words of the Commission, That any two such Justices, whereof one is of the *Quorum*, may hold such Court at such Days and Places as shall be appointed by them, and that the Sheriff is bound to return proper Juries, and that the *Custos Rotulorum* ought to bring the Rolls of the Peace before them, &c. Lamb. B. 4. ch. 2, & 20.

Sect. 42. And from hence it seems to follow, That any two such Justices may direct their Precept under their *Teste* to the Sheriff, for the Summons of the Sessions of the Peace, thereby commanding him to return a Grand Jury before them, or their Fellow Justices at a certain Day and Place, and to give Notice to all Stewards, Constables and Bailiffs of Liberties, to be present and do their Duties at such Day and Place, and to proclaim in proper Places throughout his Bailiwick, that such Sessions will be holden at such Day and Place, and to attend there himself to his Duty, &c. Lamb. B. 4. ch. 20.

Sect. 43. And it is said, That such a Precept by any two such Justices, cannot be superseded by any of their Fellows, but only by Writ out of Chancery. Lamb. B. 4. ch. 2. Crompt. 122. b.

Sect. 44. It is said, That such Justices may hold such a Session without any such Summons, which seems to be a well grounded Opinion, as to their proceeding on Indictments before taken before themselves or others, or on other particular Occasions, for which there is no need either for the Attendance of the Grand Jurors, or Officers, &c. Lamb. B. 4. ch. 2.

Sect. 45. As to the second Point, *viz.* What Persons are bound to give their Attendance at the Court of Sessions, there is no Doubt but that the Sheriff, (who is bound both to return his Precept, and also to take the Charge of all the Prisoners who shall be committed to him) and also all Constables of Hundreds, who are to make their Presentments required by several Statutes, (as that of Hue and Cry, and those relating to Highways and Ale-Houses, &c.) and also all Bailiffs of Franchises, and all Persons returned on a Jury, and the [a] Keeper of the House of Correction, &c. are bound to attend on every such Summons as is abovementioned, on Pain of being amerced for their Default at the Discretion of the Court, &c. Lamb. B. 4. ch. 3. See the Statute of Winchester, and B. 1. Ch. 78. Sect. 22. and Ch. 76. Sect. 45. [a] Vide 7 Jac. ch. 4.

Sect. 46. As to the third Point, *viz.* Whether the Court of Sessions have any Power over its own Members; it seems certain, That it hath no Authority to amerce any Justice of Peace for his Non-Attendance at any such Court, as the Justices of Assise may for the Absence of any such Justice at the Gaol-Delivery; for it is a general Rule, That *inter pares non est potestas*, it being reasonable rather to refer the Punishment of Persons in a judicial Office, in Relation to their Behaviour in such Office, to other Judges of a superior Station, than to those of the same Rank with themselves; and therefore it seems to have been holden, That if a Justice of Peace at the Sessions, who is not of the *Quorum*, shall use such Expressions towards another who is of the *Quorum*, for which if he were a private Person, he might be committed or bound to his Good Behaviour; yet the Sessions hath no Authority to commit him, or to bind him to his Good Behaviour: And yet it seems to be agreed, that if a Justice of Peace give just Cause to Lamb. B. 4. ch. 3. Crompt. 122. a. Fitz. Justices de Peace, 3. Lamb. B. 4. ch. 3. Crompt. 122.

to any Person to demand the Surety of the Peace against him, he may be compelled by any other Justice to find such Security, as hath been shewn Ch.60.Sect.5. in the first Book; for the publick Peace requires an immediate Remedy in all such Cases.

Sect. 47. As to the fourth Point, *viz.* The Difference between General Lamb. B. 4. ch. 19. and Special and Quarter-Sessions, Mr. *Lambard* seems to make no Distinction between General and Quarter-Sessions, but to take them as synonymous Lamb. B. 4. ch. 20. 2 H.H. P. C. 49, 50. Terms. But it seems the better Opinion, That Quarter-Sessions are a Species only of General Sessions, and that such Sessions only are properly called General Quarter-Sessions, which are holden in the four Quarters of the Year in Pursuance of the abovementioned Statute of 2 *H.* 5. 4. set forth more at large in the fifteenth Section of this Chapter; and Salk. 474. pl. 11. 476. pl. 16. 480. pl. 29. 482. pl. 34. 5 Mod. 329. Comber. 448. Carth. 222. that any other Sessions holden at any other Time for the general Execution of the Authority of Justices of Peace, which by the abovementioned Statute, Justices of the Peace are authorized to hold oftner than at the Times therein specified, if Need be, may be properly called General Sessions; and that those holden on a special Occasion for the Execution of some particular Branch of their Authority, may properly be called Special Sessions.

CHAP. IX.

Of the Court of the Coroner.

a 2 Inst. 31. S. P. C. 48, 49. b 4 Inst. 271. 2 Inst. 31. c Ch.8.Sect.3. d F. N. B. 397. *Sect.* 1. CORONERS are [a] ancient Officers by the Common Law; so [b] called, because they deal principally with the Pleas of the Crown, and [c] were of old Time the principal Conservators of the Peace within their County; and there still ought to be a certain Number of them in every County; in [d] some more, in others less, according as the Usage hath been. [5]

4 Inst. 271. 2 Inst. 175. Before I come to the particular Consideration of their Duty and Authority, it may not be improper to premise the following Particulars:

1. What Persons are qualified to be Coroners.
2. In what Manner they are to be placed in their Office.
3. How they may be discharged.

Sect. 2. As to the first Point, it is enacted by the Statute of *Westm.* 1. Ch. 10. in the following Words, *Forasmuch as mean Persons and indiscreet, now of late are commonly chosen to the Office of Coroners, where it is requisite, that Persons honest, loyal and wise, shall occupy such Offices: It is provided, That through all Shires sufficient Men shall be chosen to be Coroners of the most loyal and most wise Knights, which know, will, and may best attend upon such Offices, and which lawfully shall attach and present Pleas of the Crown.*

Sect. 3. It is observable, That this Statute seems expresly to require that none under the Degree of Knighthood shall be chosen a Coroner, and that the Statute of *Merton*, Chapter the Third, which was made near 23 Ass. pl. 7. 4 Inst. 271. Regist. 177.b. F. N. B. 164. forty Years before, seems to suppose, That all Coroners were Knights: And it is farther remarkable, that in the Writ *de Coronatore exonerando*, it is mentioned as a sufficient Cause for the Discharge of a Coroner, that he is not a Knight; yet in as much as the principal Intent of putting those Words into the Statute, was to prevent the Choosing of Persons of mean Ability, which is sufficiently answered, by choosing Men of good Substance and Credit: And it has been generally found impracticable to find Knights enough in any County willing to undertake this Office, and the constant Usage of many late Ages, which is the best Interpreter of Laws, hath suffered Persons of good Ability, under the Degree of Knights, to be chosen and continue Coroners, without any Objection against them on this Account; it seems certain, That at this Day it is no good Cause to remove a Coroner, that he is not a Knight. For why should not such Usage be as well allowed to make such an Explanation of the Law concerning Coroners, as it unquestionably hath done of that relating to the Representatives of a County in Parliament, who by the Writ for their Election are expresly required to be *duo Milites gladio cincti*, and yet may certainly be well chosen in Pursuance of that Writ, though they be under the Degree of Knights?

S. P. C. 48. e. 2 Leon. 160, 161. F. N. B. 164. 2 Inst. 176. 2 H. H. P. C. 55. Co. Lit. 109. b.

Sect. 4. It is further enacted by 14 *E.* 3. 8. *That no Coroner be chosen, unless he have Land in Fee sufficient in the same County, whereof he may answer to all Manner of People.*

Sect. 5. As to the second Point, *viz.* In what Manner Coroners are to be placed in their Office, it is observable, That they do not receive their Authority from the King's Commission, but from the Election of the County in Pursuance of the King's Writ, issuing out of and afterwards returned into the Chancery: And this is the Reason why their Authority does not determine by the Demise of the King, as that of all Judges, acting by the King's Commission only, regularly does, as hath been more fully shewn, *Ch.* 1. *Sect.* 11.

2 H. H. P. C. 55.

Sect. 6. The abovementioned Writ for the Election of a Coroner is in this Form: First it recites the Death or Discharge of one or more former Coroners, and then commands the Sheriff to cause one other or more, as the Case is, to be chosen, in a full County-Court, by the Assent of the County, according to the Form of the Statute in that Case made and provided; who having taken his Oath in the usual Manner, may do all Things which belong to the Office of a Coroner, *&c.* and then it concludes with commanding the Sheriff to certify to the Court the Name of the Person chosen, *&c.*

See the Form of such Certificate in Rastal's Entries, 133.

Sect. 7. [a] A Coroner, being chosen by Virtue of such Writ, shall be sworn by the Sheriff, that he will lawfully do what belongs to the Office of a Coroner, *&c.*

Sect. 8. [b] And inasmuch as he is chosen by the County, if he be insufficient, and not able to answer such Fines, and other Duties in respect of his Office, as he ought, the County, as his Superior, shall answer for him.

[a] S. P. C. 49. d 2 H. H. P. C. 55. F. N. B. 163. M. 4 Inst. 271. [b] 2 Inst. 174, 175. 2 H. H. P. C 56.

Sect. 9. And it is enacted by 28 *E.* 3. 6. *That all Coroners of the Counties, shall be chosen in the full Counties by the Commons of the same Counties, of the most meet and lawful People, that shall be found in the same Counties, to execute the said Office: Saved always to the King and other Lords, who ought to make such Coroners, their Seigniories and Franchises.*

From this Statute the two following Points are observable.

Sect. 10. First, That all such Elections are appointed by it to be made by the Commons of the Counties, without mentioning Freeholders; and yet inasmuch as the said Statute was made in Affirmance of the Common Law, and [c] none but Freeholders are Suitors to the County-Court,

F. N. B. 164. S. P. C. 49. B. [c] 2 Inst. 99. 2 Rol. Abr. 121. F.

Court, and that Usage hath always been, both before and since the said Statute, for such only to vote, it is certain, that none but Freeholders have a Voice at any such Election.

a H. H. P. C. 53, 54. Co. Lit. 114. a.

Sect. 11. Secondly, That it is clearly supposed by the said Statute, that not only the King, but also other Lords have the Franchise of making Coroners: From whence it seems reasonable to infer, That the King may lawfully claim such Franchise by Prescription, and that other Lords may claim it by Grant from the Crown; but it is a Privilege of so high a Nature, that no Subject can well intitle himself to it by Prescription only.

Register 177. a. b. F. N. B. 163, 164. S. P. C. 48. Letter E. 8 Co. 41. b. 2 Inst. 32.

Sect. 12. As to the third Point, *viz.* In what Manner Coroners may be discharged from their Office; it is certain, That if any of them be so far engaged in any other publick Business in the County, that he cannot have Leisure enough to attend the Office of a Coroner; or if he be chosen Verderor of a Forest, or if he have not sufficient Lands in the same County, whereon to live according to his State and Degree, or if he be disabled either by old Age, or any inveterate Disease, as the Palsy, or the like, to execute his Office, as he ought, and as some say, if he follow any common Trade, he may be discharged by the Writ *De Coronatore exonerando*, which being directed to the Sheriff, after a Recital of the particular Cause of the Discharge of such Coroner, commands him to cause another to be chosen in his Room. [6]

Register 177. b. 178. a. F.N.B.164.d. S. P. C. 49.

Sect. 13. But if any Writ of this Kind be grounded on an untrue Suggestion, the Coroner may procure a Commission from the Chancery to inquire of the Truth of it, and to return the Inquiry before the King into the Chancery; and if upon such Commission the Suggestion be disproved, the King may make a *Supersedeas* to the Sheriff, that he do not remove such Coroner; or if he have removed him, That he suffer him to execute the Office as he did before.

And now I am particularly to consider the Duty and Authority of a Coroner; for the better Understanding whereof, I shall examine the following Points:

1. In what Places he hath a Jurisdiction.
2. How far he is impowered, and in what Manner he ought to take an Inquisition.
3. How far to receive and proceed on a Bill of Appeal.
4. How far to receive and proceed on the Appeal of an Approver.
5. How far to take the Abjuration of a Felon.
6. How far the Act of any one of them shall be as effectual as if it had been done by all.
7. In what Cases he may lawfully take a Fee for the Execution of his Office.
8. In what Cases a Matter recorded by, or found before him, admits of no Traverse.

As to the first Point, *viz.* In what Places a Coroner hath Jurisdiction, I shall consider:

1. How far he hath a Jurisdiction of Offences committed on the Sea.
2. How far a Coroner of the County may intermeddle with Offences done within the Verge of the Court, and *vice versa*.

a Owen 122. Moore 892. pl. 1255. 2 H. H. P. C. 54. H. P. C. 171. S. P. C. 51. Letter K.

Sect. 14. As to the first Particular, it is laid down as a general Rule by [a] some, That he may inquire of a Felony committed on the Arms of the Sea, where a Man may see from the one Side to the other; but by others,

thers, who seem to be more accurate, his [a] Power is confined to such Parts of the Sea, where a Man standing on the one Side, may see what is done on the other: But it seems to be [b] agreed, That he hath no Jurisdiction of Offences committed in the open Sea, between the high and low Water-Mark when the Tide is in; but that he hath an Authority over Offences committed in such Places when the Tide is out.

[a] Fitz. Coron. 399. 4 Inst. 140. 2 Rol. Abr. 169. pl. 7.
[b] 3 Inst. 113. 5 Co. 107.

Sect. 15. As to the second Particular, *&c.* How far a Coroner of the County may intermeddle with Offences done within the Verge of the Court, *& vice versa*, it is said, [c] That at the Common Law, as the Coroner of the King's House had nothing to do with an Offence committed in the County out of the Verge, so neither had the Coroner of the County any Thing to do with an Offence committed within the Verge. And therefore it seems, That before the Statute of *Articuli super Chartas*, if a Person had been killed any where within the Verge of the Court, and the King had removed his Court before the Coroner of the King's House had taken an Indictment, no Coroner at all had any Jurisdiction of the Fact; not the Coroner of the County, because he had nothing to do with what happened within the Verge of the Court; not the Coroner of the King's House, because his Authority ceased when the Place where the Matter happened, ceased to be within the Verge of the Court; and this seems to be confirmed by the Statute of *Articuli super Chartas*, Ch. 3. whereby it is recited, that before the making of that Act, *Many Felonies committed within the Verge had been unpunished, because the Coroners of the County had not been authorized to inquire of Felonies done within the Verge, but the Coroner of the King's House, which never continued in one Place; by Reason whereof there can be no Trial made in due Manner, nor the Felons put in Exigent, nor outlawed, nor any Thing presented in the Circuit, the which had been to the great Damage of the King, and nothing to the Preservation of the Peace:* And thereupon it is ordained, *That from thenceforth in Cases of the Death of Men whereof the Coroners Office is to make View and Inquest, it shall be commanded to the Coroner of the County, that he with the Coroner of the King's House, shall do as belongeth to his Office, and enroll it,* &c. It is said indeed by Sir *Edward Coke*, That if a Murder had been committed within the Verge, and the King had removed before any Indictment taken by the Coroner of the Verge, the Coroner of the County might have inquired of the same at the Common Law, *ne maleficia remanerent impunita:* But since no Authority is cited by him for the Maintenance of this Opinion, and the Argument brought to prove it is founded on a mistaken Supposition, in as much as it doth by no Means follow, That such Offences would be dispunishable if they could not be inquired of by the Coroner of the County, since they might certainly be indicted before Justices of *Oyer* and *Terminer*, or of the Peace, who have a general Jurisdiction throughout the whole County; the contrary Opinion seems rather the more Plausible, as being more agreeable to the Purport of the said Statute, and the general Tenor of our Law Books.

[c] 2 Leon. 160. 4 Co. 46. b. 2 H. H. P. C. 54, 55.

2 Inst. 550.

2 Inst. 549. 4 Co. 46. b. 47. a. 4 Co. 47.

Sect. 16. But it is certain, That an Indictment taken before the Coroner of the County, and the Coroner of the King's House, of an Offence not appearing by the Indictment it self, to have happened within the Verge of the Court, is insufficient; for that every material Part of an Indictment ought to be found by the Oaths of the Indictors, and cannot be supplied with any Averment; and it doth not appear by the Indictment, that the Coroner of the King's House had any Authority to take it, and it shall not be said to be void, and *coram non judice*, as to the Coroner of the King's House, and good as to the Coroner of the County, inasmuch as the Record is entire, and the Indictment was taken entirely

4 Co. 47. 2 Inst. 550.

before both; and peradventure the Jury was directed principally by the Coroner of the Houſe, and the Witneſſes examined and ſworn by him.

2 H. H. P. C. 55. 4 Co. 46. a. 3 Inſt. 134. 2 Leon. 160. the ſame Caſe, but no Reſolution.

Sect. 17. It hath been reſolved, That if the ſame Perſon be Coroner of the County, and alſo of the King's Houſe, an Indictment of Death taken before him as Coroner both of the King's Houſe, and of the County, is good, becauſe the Miſchief expreſſed in the Statute, is remedied as well when both Offices are in the ſame Perſons as when they are in divers.

Sect. 18. Alſo it is enacted by 33 *H.* 8. 12. Par. 1 & 3. *That all Inquiſitions upon the View of Perſons ſlain within any of the King's Palaces or Houſes, or any other Houſe or Houſes, at ſuch Time as his Majeſty ſhall happen to be there demurrant or abiding in his Royal Perſon, ſhall be taken by the Coroner for the Time being of the King's Houſhold, without any adjoining or aſſiſting of another Coroner of any Shire within this Realm, by the Oath of twelve or more of the Yeomen, Officers of the King's Houſhold, returned by the two Clerks Controllers, the Clerks of the Check, and the Clerks Marſhals, or one of them, for the Time being, of the ſaid Houſhold, to whom the ſaid Coroner of the ſame Houſhold ſhall direct his Precept, which Coroner ſhall be from Time to Time appointed by the Lord Great Maſter, or Lord Steward for the Time being; and that the ſaid Coroner ſhall certify under his Seal, and the Seals of ſuch Perſons as ſhall be ſworn before him, all ſuch Inquiſitions before the ſaid Lord Maſter or Lord Steward,* &c. [7]

As to the ſecond general Point, *viz.* How far a Coroner is impowered, and in what Manner he ought to take an Inquiſition, I ſhall conſider his Authority of this Kind,

1. In Relation to Death.
2. In Relation to other Matters.

As to his Authority to take an Inquiſition of Death, I ſhall examine,

1. In what Caſes and in what Manner he ought to take ſuch Inquiſition.
2. What farther Care muſt be taken by him for the Proſecution of the Offender, after taking the Inquiſition.
3. What high Credit the Law gives to it.

Bract. 121. Fleta B. 1. Ch. 25.

Sect. 19. As to the firſt of theſe Particulars, it is enacted by 4 *E.* 1. commonly called the Statute *de officio Coronatoris, That the Coroner upon Information, ſhall go to the Places where any be ſlain, or ſuddenly dead or wounded, and ſhall forthwith command four of the next Towns, or five or ſix, to appear before him in ſuch a Place; and when they are come thither, the Coroner upon the Oath of them ſhall inquire in this Manner; that is to wit, if they know where the Perſon was ſlain, whether it were in any Houſe, Field, Bed, Tavern, or Company, and who were there. Likewiſe it is to be inquired who were culpable, either of the Act, or of the Force, and who were preſent, either Men or Women, and of what Age ſoever they be, (if they can ſpeak or have any Diſcretion.) And how many ſoever be found culpable by Inquiſition in any of the Manners aforeſaid, they ſhall be taken and delivered to the Sheriff, and ſhall be committed to the Gaol: And ſuch as be founden, and be not culpable, ſhall be attached until the Coming of the Juſtices, and their Names ſhall be written in the Coroners Rolls. If it fortune any ſuch Man be ſlain, which is found in the Fields, or in the Woods, firſt it is to be inquired whether he were ſlain in the ſame Place or not, And if he were brought and laid there, they ſhall do as much as they can, to fol-*

low their Steps that brought the Body thither, whether he were brought upon a Horſe, or in a Cart. It ſhall be inquired alſo, if the dead Perſon were known, or elſe a Stranger, and where he lay the Night before; and if any be found culpable of the Murder, the Coroner ſhall immediately go unto his Houſe, and ſhall inquire what Goods he hath, and what Corn he hath in his Grange; and if he be a Freeman, they ſhall inquire how much Land he hath, and what it is worth yearly, and further, what Corn he hath upon the Ground. And when they have thus inquired upon every Thing, they ſhall cauſe all the Land, Corn, and Goods to be valued, in like Manner as if they ſhould be ſold incontinently, and thereupon they ſhall be delivered to the whole Townſhip, which ſhall be anſwerable before the Juſtices for all. And likewiſe of his Freehold, how much it is worth yearly over and above the Service due to the Lords of the Fee, and the Land ſhall remain in the King's Hands, until the Lords of the Fee have made Fine for it. And immediately upon theſe Things being inquired, the Bodies of ſuch Perſons being dead or ſlain ſhall be buried. In like Manner it is to be inquired of them that be drowned, or ſuddenly dead, and after ſuch Bodies are to be ſeen, whether they were ſo drowned or ſlain, or ſtrangled by the Sign of a Cord tied ſtrait about their Necks, or about any of their Members, or upon any other Hurt found upon their Bodies, whereupon they ſhall proceed in the Form aboveſaid; and if they were not ſlain, then ought the Coroner to attach the Finders, and all other in Company.

Sect. 20. *Alſo all Wounds ought to be viewed, the Length, Breadth, and Deepneſs, and with what Weapons, and in what Part of the Body the Wound or Hurt is, and how many be culpable, and how many Wounds there be, and who gave the Wound; all which Things muſt be inrolled in the Roll of the Coroners. Alſo Horſes, Boats, Carts, &c. whereby any are ſlain, that properly are called Deodands, ſhall be valued and delivered unto the Towns as before is ſaid.*

Sect. 21. It is obſervable, That this Statute being wholly Directory and in Affirmance of the Common Law, doth neither reſtrain the Coroner from any Branch of his Power, nor excuſe him from the Execution of any Part of his Duty not mentioned in it, which was incident to his Office before; and from hence it follows, That though the Statute mention only his Taking Inquiries of the Death of Perſons ſlain or drowned or ſuddenly dead, yet he may and ought to inquire of the Death of all Perſons whatſoever who die in Priſon, to the End that the Publick may be ſatisfied, whether ſuch Perſons came to their End by the common Courſe of Nature, or by ſome unlawful Violence, or unreaſonable Hardſhips put on them by thoſe under whoſe Power they were confined.

Fitz. Coron. 421. 3 Inſt. 52, 91. Cro. Coron. 168. S. P. C. 51. 1 H. H. P. C. 432. 2 H. H. P. C. 57.

Sect. 22. And the like Reaſon alſo ſeems to be the beſt Ground of the Reſolution which we find in ſome [a] Books, That there is no Neceſſity that it appear in a Coroner's Inqueſt, that it was taken by the Oaths of Perſons of the next adjacent Towns, but that it is ſufficient to ſay, That it was taken by the Oaths of lawful Perſons of the County, inaſmuch as ſuch Inquiſitions being good before the ſaid Statute, which is wholly Declaratory, muſt needs be ſo ſtill; but it [b] ſeems, That it ought to appear in every ſuch Inquiſition, at what Place, and by what Jurors by Name it was taken, and that ſuch Jurors were ſworn, and that the Reaſon given in ſome Books that ſuch Inqueſts ſhall be intended to have been taken by the Men of the next Towns ſeems very harſh, if it be ſuppoſed neceſſary to be taken by ſuch Perſons; for that ſuch Intendment would be contrary to the general Rule of the Law, which will not ſuffer any material Part of an Indictment to be taken by Intendment.

[a] 1 Sid. 204. 1 H. H. P. C. 416. 1 Keb. 723, 744, 745. Con. Latch 166. Poph. 210. Co. Ent. 354.
[b] Cro. El. 31.

1 Sid. 204. 1 Keb. 745.

Sect. 23.

Sect. 23. Alſo it is farther remarkable, that the Statute doth not expreſly ſay, That the Coroner ſhall take his Inqueſt on the View of the dead Body, and that an Inqueſt otherwiſe taken by him, ſhall be void: And yet it is clearly agreed by all the [a] Books, That a Coroner has no Manner of Power to take an Inquiſition of Death without a View of the Body, and that any ſuch Inqueſt taken by him without ſuch View, is meerly void. And for this Reaſon it hath been [b] adjudged, That if a dead Body, in a Priſon, or other Place, whereupon an Inqueſt ought to be taken, be interred, [8] or ſuffered to lie ſo long, that it putrify before the Coroner hath viewed it, the Gaoler or Townſhip ſhall be amerced. Alſo it hath been [c] reſolved, That a Coroner may lawfully within convenient Time, as the Space of fourteen Days after the Death, take up a dead Body out of the Grave in order to view it, not only for the taking of an Inqueſt where none hath been taken before; but alſo for the taking of a good one, where an inſufficient one hath been taken before. But if the Body cannot be [d] found, or have lain ſo long before the Coroner hath viewed it, that he can be no Way aſſiſted from the View in the taking of his Inqueſt; or if there be Danger of infecting People in digging of it up, the Inqueſt ought not to be taken by the Coroner, (unleſs he have a ſpecial Writ or Commiſſion for that Purpoſe) but by Juſtices of Peace, or other Juſtices authorized to inquire of, hear and determine Felonies, *&c.* who ſhall take the Inqueſt on the Teſtimony of Witneſſes; but none can take an Inqueſt on View in any Caſe, but the Coroner.

Sect. 24. If a [e] Coroner take an Inqueſt after a Body hath been ſo long buried, that it may reaſonably be preſumed, that the View of it could be of no Manner of Uſe for the Information of the Jurors, the Court into which the Inquiſition is returned will in Diſcretion refuſe to receive or file it, upon Affidavit of the whole Circumſtances of the Proceeding.

Sect. 25. [f] Yet it is not neceſſary, That the Inquiſition be taken in the very ſame Place where the Body was viewed; for it hath been reſolved, That an Inquiſition taken at *D.* on the View of a Body lying dead at *L.* may be good.

Sect. 26. As the Coroner hath no Power from the ſaid Statute, nor from 3 *H.* 7. 1. to inquire of any Acceſſaries to a Felony after the Fact; ſo neither hath he any ſuch Power by the [g] Common Law; for he has nothing to do with any but thoſe who ſome Way or other cauſed the Party's Death: And therefore it hath been reſolved, That an Indictment of *J. S.* before a Coroner for having received and comforted one who had been guilty of a Murder, is void.

Sect. 27. But it is certain, That a Coroner may inquire of the Acceſſaries before the Fact, as well as of the Principals; and that he [h] alſo may inquire, whether any in ſuch Manner found to have been guilty, did fly for the Offence; for which Flight they forfeit all their Goods and Chattels.

Sect. 28. Alſo it is [i] certain, That a Coroner may and ought to inquire of all the Circumſtances of the Party's Death, and alſo of all Things which occaſioned it; and [k] therefore it is ſaid, That if it be found by his Inqueſt, that the Perſon deceaſed was killed by a Fall from a Bridge into a River, and that the Bridge was out of Repair by the Default of the Inhabitants of ſuch a Town, and that thoſe Inhabitants are bound to repair it, the Townſhip ſhall be amerced.

[a] Fitz. Coron. 107. 2 H. H. P. C. 58. S. P. C. 51. G. 2 Lev. 141. Latch 166. Noy 87. 2 R. 3. 2. pl. 5. 21 Ed. 4. 70. b. H. P. C. 170. Poph. 209.

[b] Fitz. Coron. 329, 339, 421. H. P. C. 170. S. P. C. 51. 1 Keb. 278. pl. 74.

[c] 21 Ed. 4. 70. b. 2 R. 3. 2. pl. 5. 2 H. H. P. C. 58, 59. S. P. C. 51. H. P. C. 170. Bro. Coron. 167, 173.

[d] S. P. C. 51. H. P. C. 170. 2 Lev. 141. Latch 166. 1 Vent. 352. Poph. 209. Sal. 190, 377. Noy 87. 2 Rol. Abr. 96. pl. 3. 1 Rol. Rep. 217.

[e] The King and Cauſey, Hillary, 3 Georg. 1.

[f] Latch 166. See Poph. 209.

[g] 4 H. 7. 18. b. Fitz. Forfeiture, 10. 1 H. H. P. C. 416. 2 H. H. P. C. 63. S. P. C. 183. Letter D. Keilw. 67. Daliſ. 32. Moor 29. pl. 95.

[h] S. P. C. 183. Letters C. D. 2 Lev. 141, 152. 2 H. H. P. C. 63, 65. Keilw. 68. b. H. P. C. 170. Bro. Coron. 151. 8 Ed. 4. 4. a. vide infra Section 51.

[i] Keilw. 67. 1 H. H. P. C. 422. 2 H. H. P. C. 62.

[k] Aleyn 51.

Sect. 29. Also it is agreed, That if a Coroner be remiss in coming to do his Office when he is sent for, *&c.* he shall be amerced, by Virtue of the abovementioned Statute *De conoratoribus.* Also it is farther enacted by 3 *H.* 7. 1. *That if any Person be slain or murdered in the Day, and the Murderer escape untaken, the Township where the said Deed is so done, shall be amerced for the said Escape, and that the Coroner have Authority to inquire thereof upon the View of the Body dead: And that if any Coroner be remiss and make not Inquisitions upon the View of the Body dead, he shall forfeit for every Default an hundred Shillings.*

S. P. C. 51. H. Salk. 377. Fitz. Coron. 292. H. P. C. 170. 1 H. H. P. C. 424. 2 H. H. P. C. 58.

Sect. 30. As to the second Particular, *viz.* What farther Care must be taken by a Coroner for the Prosecution of the Offender, after taking Inquisition of Death against him, it is farther enacted by the said Statute of 3 *H.* 7. 1. *That after the Felony found, the Coroners deliver their Inquisition afore the Justices of the next general Gaol-Delivery, in the Shire where the Inquisition is taken, the same Justices to proceed against such Murderers if they be in the Gaol, or else the same Justices to put the same Inquisitions afore the King in his Bench. And if any Coroner do not in such Manner certify his Inquisition, he shall forfeit an hundred Shillings.*

Sect. 31. Also it is enacted by 1 & 2 *Ph.* & *Mar.* 13. *That every Coroner, upon any Inquisition before him found, whereby any Person or Persons shall be indicted for Murder or Manslaughter, or as Accessary or Accessaries to the same, before the Murder or Manslaughter committed, shall put in Writing the Effect of the Evidence given to the Jury before him, being material: And shall bind all such by Recognizance or Obligation, as do declare any Thing material to prove the same, to appear at the next general Gaol-Delivery to be holden within the County, City, or Town-Corporate where the Trial thereof shall be, then and there to give Evidence against the Party so indicted at the Time of the Trial, and shall certify as well the same Evidence, as such Bond or Bonds in Writing, as he shall take, together with the Inquisition or Indictment before him taken and found, at or before the Time of his said Trial thereof to be had or made: And in Case any Coroner shall offend in any Thing contrary to the true Intent and Meaning of this Act, the Justices of Gaol-Delivery of the Shire, City, Town, or Place where such Offence shall happen to be committed, upon due Proof thereof, by Examination before them, shall for every such Offence set such Fine on every such Coroner, as they shall think meet, and estreat the same as other Fines and Amerciaments assessed before Justices of Gaol-Delivery ought to be.*

Sect. 32. And it is enacted by 1 *H.* 8. 7. *That if any Coroner shall not endeavour himself to do his Office upon any Person dead by Misadventure, he shall forfeit forty Shillings.*

Sect. 33. As to the third Particular, *viz.* What high Credit the Law gives to an Inquisition of Death found before a Coroner, it seems [a] certain, That anciently the Judges would not receive a Verdict, acquitting a Person of the Death of a Man found against him by a Coroner's Inquest, unless the Jury so acquitting the Defendant, had found at the same Time what other Person did the Fact, or by what other Means the Party came to his Death; because it appeared by the Coroner's View upon Record, that a Person was killed: But it is [b] agreed, That the Judges cannot compel a Jury to make such farther Inquiry on an Acquittal of a Defendant from any other Indictment, because it doth not in such Manner appear of Record by any such Inquisition, that a Person is dead: And it seems hard to reconcile the said Practice of compelling a Jury to find such farther Matter with Reason in any Case, unless it appear in the Course of the Evidence by what other Means, not mentioned in the Indictment, the Party lost his Life; for it seems strange, That a Jury should be

[a] 13 E. 4. 3. pl. 7. 37 Ass pl. 13. 11 H. 4. 93. pl. 51. 14 H. 7. 2. pl. 7. Fitz. Coron. 213. Keilway 686. S. P. C. 181. 2 H. H. P. C. 301. Letters B. C. Finch of Law 415. Brook, Appeal, 42, 122. Bro. Indictment, 10, 35. Bro. Coron. 32, 39, 52, 117.

[b] See the Books above cited.

be in any Case compelled to find a Matter upon their Oaths, which they have no Evidence to support; and therefore if it no Way appear to them, by what other Means the Death in Question was occasioned, it seems difficult to maintain that it shall not be sufficient for them to declare so to the Court.

Sect. 34. How high a Credit is given by the Law to a Coroner's Inquisition of Self-Murder, or of the Flight of a Person indicted for the Death of another, will be more fully shewn in the three last Sections of this Chapter.

[a] 35 H. 6. 27. b. 27 Ass. pl. 55. a. Fitz. Coron. 206. Bro. Appeal, 111. [b] S. P. C. 51. I. K. [c] H. P. C. 171. [d] 4 Inst. 271. 2 Inst. 147. [e] See the Statute at large. [f] Britton 3.

Sect. 35. As to the second general Point, *viz.* What Authority a Coroner hath to take an Indictment of other Matters, it is expresly said in some [a] Books, That a Coroner hath no Power *Ex officio* to inquire of any Felony, but only of the Death of a Man upon View. And both [b] *Staunford* and [c] *Hale* [9] seem to speak doubtfully of this Matter upon the Authority of those Books; and [d] Sir *Edward Coke* seems expresly to declare his Opinion, That a Coroner hath no Power to take an Indictment in any other Case: Yet since it is expresly declared by the abovementioned [e] Statute *De officio Coronatoris*, That a Coroner ought to inquire of the Breakers of Houses; and it is said by [f] *Britton*, That he may inquire of Rape, and of the Breach of a Prison; and such Power hath never been expresly taken from him; it seems hard to say, That he may not still make such Inquiries, if he please; for as to the Authority of 27 *Ass.* 55. & 35 *H.* 6. 27. *b.* which are cited for the Maintenance of the contrary Opinion, it may be answered, That this Point is not resolved in either of those Books, but only spoken of incidentally; for the very Point resolved in 27 of *Assizes*, seems to be no more than this, That a Coroner hath no Power to take an Indictment of an Accessary after the Fact; and that which is said in 35 *H.* 6. concerning this Matter is only brought in by Way of Argument concerning a Point of a quite different Nature.

Bracton, B. 3. Ch. 6.

Sect. 36. However there seems to be no Doubt but that the Coroner may and ought to inquire of Treasure-trove, concerning which it is enacted by the said Statute of 4 *E.* 1. *De officio Coronatoris, That a Coroner being certified by the King's Bailiffs, or other honest Men of the Country, shall go to the Places where Treasure is said to be found.* And it is farther enacted in the following Part of the same Statute in these Words, *A Coroner ought also to inquire of Treasure that is found, who were the Finders, and likewise who is suspected thereof: And that may be well perceived where one liveth riotously, haunting Taverns, and hath done so of long Time; hereupon he may be attached for this Suspicion by four or six, or more Pledges, if he may be found.*

S.P.C. 51. K. Bracton 120. b.

Sect. 37. It is also said, That a Coroner may inquire of Royal Fishes, as Sturgeons, Whales.

2 H. H. P. C. 66.

Sect. 38. As to the third general Point, *viz.* How far a Coroner is impowered to receive and proceed on a Bill of Appeal, I shall endeavour to shew,

1. How far he is authorized to receive such Appeal.
2. How far to proceed upon it.
3. In what Manner it may be removed by *Certiorari.*

[a] See the Statute at large. [b] Bract. 122. a. b. 147. Fleta, lib. 1. cap. 25. Britton, fol. 5. S. P. C. 64. 22 Ass. 97, 98. Finch 321.

Sect. 39. As to the first of these Particulars, it appears clearly from the abovementioned [a] Statute of 4 *E.* 1. *De officio Coronatoris*, and also from our ancient [b] Law-Books, That a Coroner in the County-Court may receive an Appeal of any Felony or Mayhem, upon the Plaintiff's finding ſufficient Pledges to the Sheriff for the Proſecution of the Suit. And it is obſervable, That the ſaid Books generally mention the Coroner as the Perſon before whom ſuch Appeal is to be commenced, without joining any other with him; from whence it ſeems clearly to be intimated, That the Coroner is the [b] only Perſon who hath a Juriſdiction in this Matter; and that at Common Law he might [c] receive ſuch Appeal without the Concurrence of any other, as he certainly may the Appeal of an Approver, *&c.* But it being provided by the Statute of *Weſtminſter* 1. *cap.* 10. That the Sheriff ſhall have Counter-Rolls with the Coroners, it ſeems, That no Appeal ſince that Statute is well commenced before the Coroner, [d] unleſs the Sheriff be alſo preſent, in order to take a Counter-Roll of the Proceeding: But it ſeems, That the Sheriff by Virtue of this Statute, is no more a Judge of the Matter than he was before; and therefore where it is ſaid by the Statute of 3 *H.* 7. 1. That an Appeal of Felony may be commenced before the Sheriff and Coroners of the County where it was done, it ſeems reaſonable to intend the Meaning of the Statute to be, that it may be commenced before them in the ſame Manner as before, and not without expreſs [e] Words to make any Alteration of the Juriſdiction given them by the Common Law.

Sect. 40. But it is [f] certain, That a Coroner hath no Power to receive a Bill of Appeal of any Offence done out of the County whereof he is Coroner, becauſe the Offender cannot be tried by the County: But it is agreed, That he may receive the Appeal of an Approver, or take the Abjuration of one, who acknowledges a Felony done by him in any County, becauſe that after ſuch Confeſſions there is no Need of any Trial.

Sect. 41. As to the ſecond Particular, *viz.* How far a Coroner may proceed upon ſuch Appeal, it ſeems [g] probable, That before the Statute of *Magna Charta, cap.* 17. Coroners might try Offenders as well as receive Accuſations againſt them; but it is [h] agreed, That they cannot proceed ſo far ſince that Statute, by which it is enacted, *That no Sheriff, Conſtable, Coroner, or other Bailiff of the King, ſhall hold Pleas of the Crown.* Alſo it is agreed, [i] That Proceſs may be awarded in the County-Court on ſuch Appeals till the Exigent; but [k] it ſeems queſtionable, whether ſuch Proceſs may properly be ſaid to be awarded by the Sheriff and Coroner jointly, ſince the Coroner being the only Judge, as I have endeavoured to prove, *Sect.* 39, it ſeems to be moſt proper that the Proceſs be awarded by him only: Neither doth it ſeem clear, That the abovementioned Statute of *Magna Charta*, doth reſtrain the Coroner from awarding an Exigent, and thereon outlawing an Appellee; for ſince, as it is agreed by all, an Offender might become attainted by an Abjuration of a Felony made before a Coroner; why not as well by an Outlawry pronounced by him? And accordingly we find it taken for granted in ſome of the [l] old Books of the beſt Authority ſince this Statute, that Appellees may be outlawed for not ☞ appearing on Proceſs before the Coroner. [10]

Sect. 42. As to the third Particular, *viz.* In what Manner an Appeal before the Coroner may be removed by *Certiorari*, there [m] is no Doubt but that it may be removed either into the King's Bench or Chancery, by *Certiorari* directed to the Coroners and Sheriff. But it hath been [n] reſolved, That it cannot be removed by ſuch Writ directed to the Sheriff only, becauſe the Coroner is the Judge, and the Sheriff hath only a Counter-Roll ☞ by Virtue of the abovementioned Statute of *Weſtm.* 1. *cap.* 10. [11]

Sect. 43.

[a] Con. 17 Aſſ. pl. 5. Bro. Appeal, 56. H. P. C. 171. S. P. C. 52. D. 64. Letter B.
[b] 2 Inſt. 176. 4 H. 6. 16. a. Bro. Appeal, 44.
[c] H. P. C. 172. 2 H. H. P. C. 67.
[d] 39 H. 6. 41. a. 4 H. 6. 16. a. Contra, Bro. Appeal, 44.
[e] Quære S. P. C. 64. b.
[f] H. P. C. 171. 172. 2 H. H. P. C. 67. S. P. C. 52. D. 53. Fitz. Coron. 437.
[g] See Dalton's Sheriff, cap. 106. 2 H. H. P. C. 56.
[h] 22 Aſſ. 97, 98. Bract. 147. a. Fleta, lib. 1. cap. 25. 2 Inſt. 30, 31, 32. 2 H. H. P. C. 67. Bro. Appeal, 56, 62. Coron. 82.
[i] S. P. C. 64. H. P. C. 171.
[k] Contra, S. P. C. 64. H. P. C. 171. 27 Aſſ. 47.
[l] 22 Aſſ. 97. Fitz. Coron. 184. Con. Bro. Appeal, 82. Quære Bro. Appeal, 109. S. P. C. 64. H. P. C. 171.
[m] S. P. C. 64 Letter B. 70. Letter C. H. P. C. 171, 172. 2 Inſt. 176.
[n] 14 H. 4. 15 b. 16 a. 2 H. H. P. C. 67. Bro. Appeal, 44. 2 Inſt. 176. S. P. C 64 Letter B. 70. Letter C.

Sect. 43. As to the fourth general Point, *viz.* How far a Coroner is authorized to receive and proceed on the Appeal of an Approver, there is no Doubt but that the Coroner alone may receive such Appeal, [a] whether the Offence were committed in the same or in any other County, and may also award Process to the Sheriff against the Appellee, being in the same County, till it come to the Exigent; and it [b] seems, That it may be probably argued, that he may award Process even to an Outlawry, as hath been more fully shewn in the forty-first Section of this Chapter: But it is certain, That he cannot award any Process against an Appellee in a foreign County, but must leave it to the [c] Justices of Gaol-Delivery, or others, before whom the Appeal is afterwards recorded, who shall award Process against such Appellees in such Manner, as shall be more fully set forth in the Chapter concerning *Approvers*, *Sect.* 22.

Sect. 44. As to the fifth general Point, *viz.* How far a Coroner is authorized to take the Confession and Abjuration of a Felon, there seems to be no Doubt but that he may record the Confession of the Breach of Prison by any Felon, *&c.* and also the [d] Confession of any Felony by an Approver; but the Law relating to these Matters being in great Measure obsolete, it seems needless over nicely to inquire into it; also it is certain that he might take an Abjuration, but this not having been in Use since 21 *Jac.* 1. 28. *Sect.* 6. 7. by which it is enacted, *That no Sanctuary or Privilege of Sanctuary, shall be admitted or allowed in any Case*, I shall only touch upon it, and take Notice, That at the Common Law, if a Person accused of any Felony (except [e] Sacrilege,) [f] whether in the same or any other County, for which he was liable to Judgment of [g] Death, and not charged with [h] High Treason, nor (as [i] some say) with Petit Treason, had fled to any [k] Church or Church-yard, and within [l] forty Days confessed himself guilty before the Coroner, and declared all the particular [m] Circumstances of the Offence, and thereupon taken the Oath in that Case provided, (the [n] Substance whereof was that he abjured the Realm, and would depart as soon as possible, at the Port which should be assigned him, and never return without Leave from the King, *&c.*) he saved his Life, if he observed the Terms of the Oath, by going with all [o] convenient Speed the nearest Way to the Port assigned, *&c.* but he was [p] attainted of the Felony by such Abjuration without more, and consequently forfeited his Lands and Goods, *&c.*

Sect. 45. As to the sixth general Point, *viz.* How far the Act of any one Coroner is as effectual as if it were done by all, it seems clear, That [q] where-ever Coroners are authorized to act as Judges, as in the taking of an [r] Inquisition of Death, or receiving an Appeal of Felony, *&c.* the Act of any one of them, who first proceeds in the Matter, is of the same Force as if all had joined in it; but it is said, That after [s] such Proceeding by one of them, the Act of any other will be void: Also it seems certain, That where Coroners are impowered only to act [t] ministerially, as in the Execution of Process directed to them upon the Default or Incapacity of the Sheriff, all their Acts will be void wherein they do not all join, [12.]

Sect. 46. As to the seventh general Point, *viz.* In what Cases a Coroner may lawfully take a Fee for the Execution of his Office, it is enacted by the Statute of *Westm.* 1. *cap.* 10. which was made in Affirmance of the Common Law, 2 *Inst.* 176. [u] *That no Coroner demand or take any Thing of any Man to do his Office, upon pain of great Forfeiture to the King.*

Sect. 47.

[a] H.P.C. 172. 2 H.H.P.C. 67, 68. S.P.C. 53. a. See Sect. 40.
[b] S.P.C. 73. H.P.C. 172.
[c] S.P.C. 53, 73. H.P.C. 172. Fitz. Co. 462. 29 Ed. 3. 42.
[d] Vid. Sect. 36 & 49.
[e] Fitz. Coron. 420. S.P.C. 117. Letter B. 3 Inst. 115.
[f] Sup. Sect. 40.
[g] Bro. Coron. 183. S.P.C. 123. Letter A. Finch of Law 388, 389.
[h] Bro. Coron. 181. S.P.C. 116. G. Finch of Law 388.
[i] S.P.C. 116. Letter G. 117. Letter A. Bro. Coron. 181. Finch 388.
[k] S.P.C. 116. Letter F. 3 Inst. 115. Finch of Law 388.
[l] S.P.C. 117, 118. 3 Inst. 117.
[m] S.P.C. 117, Letter E. Fitz. Co. 54. 3 H. 7. 12. pl. 6.
[n] S.P.C. 119, 120. Finch of Law 389.
[o] 7 H. 7. 7. pl. 11. Bro. Coron. 145. S.P.C. 121.
[p] Fitz. Coron. 425. S.P.C. 122. c. Finch of Law 389. 3 Inst. 217.
[q] S.P.C. 53. a. 14 H. 4. 34. b.
[r] 2 H.H.P.C. 56, 58. Vid. supra Ch. 1. S. 10.
[s] 2 H.H.P.C. 59. Fitz. Co. 107. S.P.C. 52. A. H.P.C. 172.
[t] S.P.C. 53. 14 H. 4. 34, 35, a. 39 H. 6. 40. b. 41, 42.
[u] See Book 1. Ch. 68

Sect. 47. But it is enacted by 3 *H.* 7. 1. *That a Coroner have for his Fee upon every Inquisition taken upon the View of a Body slain* 13 s. 4 d. *of the Goods and Chattels of the Slayer and Murderer, if he have any Goods; and if he have no Goods, of such Amerciaments as shall fortune any Township to be amerced for the Escape of the Murderer*, &c.

Sect. 48. But the Coroners endeavouring to extend this Statute to Persons slain by Misadventure, it was enacted by 1 *H.* 8. 7. *That upon a Request made to a Coroner to come and inquire upon the View of any Person slain, drowned, or otherwise dead by Misadventure, the said Coroner shall diligently do his Office, without taking any Thing therefore, upon Pain to every Coroner that will not endeavour himself to do his Office, (as afore is said) or that taketh any Thing for doing of his Office upon every Person dead by Misadventure, for every Time forty Shillings.*

As to the eighth general Point, *viz.* In what Cases a Matter recorded by, or found before a Coroner, admits of no Traverse, I shall consider the same in Relation,

1. To Abjurations or Confessions made before him.
2. To Escapes.
3. To Flights.
4. To Self-Murders.

Sect. 49. As to the first Particular it is said, That his Record of an [a] Abjuration, or of the Confession of [b] breaking a Prison, or of the Confession of a Felony by an [c] Approver, is of so great Authority, as not only to estop the Party from taking any Traverse to his having made such Confession, but also from alledging that what was said by him was extorted by Duress, or other unfair Means. Also it seems that if the Party plead, That he is not the same Person who abjured, *&c.* and the [d] Coroner record that he is the same Person, such Record is conclusive, *&c.* But in these [e] Cases it seems, That the Judge for the better Information of his Conscience, may in his Discretion, if he think fit, take an Inquiry from the People living next to the Place, of the whole Circumstances of the Matter, *&c.*

[a] H.P.C. 171. Fitz. Co. 124. S. P. C. 52. Letter B.
[b] S. P. C. 32. Letter H. 52. Letter B. 25 E. 3. 42. pl. 35. Fitz. Coron. 134, 243, 435.
[c] Fitz. Coron. 118, 169. 12 Assises, pl. 29.
[d] Fitz. Coron. 124. S. P. C. 52. Letter B.
[e] Fitz. Coron. 118, 124, 169. 12 Ass. 29. Bro. Coron. 75.

Sect. 50. As to the second Particular, *viz.* That relating to Escapes found before a Coroner, it is [f] said, That if it be found by a Coroner's Inquest, that a Murder was committed in such a Town, and that the Murderer escaped untaken, the Township cannot traverse such Escape, because it makes them only liable to an Amerciament, *& de minimis non curat Lex.*

[f] S. P. C. 34. Letters A. B. 35. Letter F. 183. Letter D. See Fitz. 352.

Sect. 51. As to the third Particular, *viz.* That relating to a Flight found before a Coroner, it seems, That if a Person indicted of a Murder by a Coroner's Inquest, be also found to have fled for it, and afterwards upon his Trial be [g] acquitted of the Murder, and also found not to have ☞ fled for it; yet he shall forfeit his Goods, [13] because such a finding that he did not fly by a Jury, who as some say, had nothing to do with it, and ought not to have been charged with such Inquiry, shall not controul the Coroner's Inquest, which is of such Authority, that immediately upon the Flight, the Party's Goods shall be delivered to the Township, which shall be answerable for them. Also it seems [h] generally to be taken for granted, That the Party has no Remedy whatsoever to traverse such Flight found against him by a Coroner's Inquest; for that such Inquest is of very great Authority, [i] inasmuch as all Persons of the neighbouring

[g] 13 H. 4. 13. pl. 6. Fitz. Forfeiture, 29, 32, 35. 5 Co. 109. b. Dyer 238. pl. 36. H. P. C. 271. 1 H. H. P. C. 363. 2 H. H. P. C. 154.

[h] Bro. Coron. 151. 8 E. 4. 4. a. 2 Lev. 141. Bro. Traverse per sans ceo, 229. 3 Keb. 564, 566. 1 H. H. P. C. 363, 414, 415, 417. 2 H. H. P. C. 63, 64, 301. [i] 2 Inst. 147, 148. 3 Keb. 366.

Towns, above the Age of twelve Years, are bound to attend at the taking of it; and yet I cannot find any direct Resolution settling this Point; but on the contrary it is certain, That Sir *William Staundford* makes a Quære of it, and the Reason abovementioned, which is brought to support the great Credit of such Inquests holds as strongly against the Traversing them as to the Point of the Offence, in which Respect it is at this Day generally holden that they may be traversed, as will be more fully shewn in the next Section. And surely the other Reason which is given for this Opinion, That the Party only forfeits his Chattels by such finding, and therefore shall not traverse it, because the Law reckons Chattels among those *minima de quibus non curat Lex*, is very harsh and unaccountable; and it is very hard to say, That a Man shall be liable to forfeit all his Goods, which may perhaps be all that he is worth, by an [a] Inquest taken in his Absence, without either hearing him, or giving him an Opportunity of defending himself.

1 H. H. P. C. 363.

Sect. 52. As to the fourth Particular, *viz.* That relating to Self-Murder found before a Coroner, it is strongly holden in some [b] Books, that no Inquest of this Kind admits of any Traverse; but the contrary Opinion being also holden by [b] Books of as great Authority, and seeming also to be more agreeable to the general Tenor of the Law in other Cases; it seems to be the better Opinion, That such Inquest being moved into the King's Bench by *Certiorari*, may be there traversed by the Executor or Administrator of the Person deceased, and perhaps also [c] by the King or the Lord of the Manor, *&c.*

[a] 3 Inst. 55. 2 Lev. 141. H. P. C. 29. 1 Vent. 181, 182.

[b] 8 Ed. 4. 4. a. B. 1. Ch. 27. Sect. 11. and the Books there cited. Bro. Coron. 151. 2 Lev. 141, 152. 2 Keb. 859. 2 Jon. 198. 1 Vent. 278. 3 Keb. 564, 566, 604, 800.

[c] See the Books above cited.

Sect. 53. Also if it [d] appear, That a Coroner hath been guilty of any corrupt Practice in the taking of an Inquisition, it seems that a *Melius inquirendum* shall be awarded for the taking a new one by special Commissioners, who shall not proceed on the View of the Body, but on the Testimony of Witnesses; and the Coroner shall have nothing to do in the taking such new Inquest, because it appears from his former Misbehaviour, that he is not fit to be trusted; but [e] where his Inquisition is quashed for a Defect in Point of Form only, he may and ought to take a new one, in like Manner as if he had not taken any before. [14] ☞

[d] Cro. El. 371. 3 Keb. 800, 856. 1 Mod. 82. Salkeld 190. Carth. 72. 2 Keb. 859. 1 Vent. 181, 182, 352. 3 Mod. 80, 100, 238. Con. 2 Jones 198.

[e] 2 Rol. Abr. 32. Pl. 5. 21 Ed. 4. 70. b. Salkeld 190. 2 H. H. P. C. 59.

CHAP. X.

Of the Sheriff's Torn.

Sect. 1. THE Sheriff's Torn is the King's Court of Record, holden before the Sheriff for redressing of common Grievances within the County; for the better Understanding the Nature whereof I shall examine the following Points.

Finch 241. F. N. B. 82. 2 H. H. P. C. 70.

1. The original Institution of this Court.
2. At what Time and in what Place it must be holden.
3. What Persons owe Suit to it.
4. What Authority the Sheriff (or his Steward) hath as Judge of it.
5. What Kind of Offences are inquirable in it.
6. Within what Place such Offences must arise.
7. By what Jurors and in what Manner Indictments in it ought to be found.
8. In what Manner they are to be proceeded upon.
9. In what Manner they are to be traversed and determined.

Sect. 2. As to the first Point it is observable, That by the [a] Common Law, every Sheriff ought to make his Torn or Circuit throughout every Hundred in his County twice in the Year, in order to hold a Court in every such Hundred for the Reformation of common Grievances, and the Preservation of the Peace and good Government of the Kingdom. For which Purpose all the [b] Inhabitants of such Hundreds, being above the Age of twelve Years, and not specially privileged, (in such Manner as shall be more fully set forth under the third Point,) are bound to attend at such Courts, in order to make Inquiries of all such Offences; and also to give Security to the Publick for their good Behaviour, by taking an Oath to be faithful to the King, and to observe his Laws, and also by incorporating themselves into some Free-Pledge or Tithing, which formerly signified a certain Number of Families living together in the same Precinct, the Masters whereof were every one of them mutually bound for each other, and punishable for the Default of any Member of any such Family, in not appearing to answer for himself on any Accusation made against him.

[a] 9. Co. Preface. Dalton's Sheriff 385. Magna Charta 35. 2 Inst. 70, 71, 73, 122. Bro. Leet, 42. Britton 71.
[b] See the Books above cited. Fleta B. 1 Ch. 27. Bract. 124. b. 2 Inst. 121. Lambard of Constables 8. Keilw. 141. a.

Sect. 3. And the better inforcing of this Order seems anciently to have been the principal End of holding this Court, the Style whereof even to this Day, must be *Curia visus franci plegii Domini Regis tenta apud* C. *coram vicecomite in turno suo tali die, &c.* But it hath been resolved, That the Law doth not take Notice of any such Court, under the Style of *Turn' Vicecom' tent' tali die*; for the Word *Torn* properly taken, doth not signify the Sheriff's Court, but his Perambulation.

2 Inst. 71, 72. Dalt. Sheriff 385, 391. Fitz. Leet, 11.

Sect. 4. As to the second Point, *viz.* At what Time, and in what Place, this Court is to be holden, it is said, That at the Common Law, it might be holden at any Place within the Hundred, and as often as the Sheriff thought fit: But this having been found to give the Sheriff too great a Power of oppressing the People, by holding his Court at such Times

6 H. 7. 2. b. Dalt. Sheriff 390. Contra Co. Lit. 115. Kitchen 44. b. Dalt. Sheriff 390.

Times and Places at which they could not conveniently attend in order thereby for his own Advantage, to increaſe the Number of his Amercements, it was enacted by the Statute of *Magna Charta*, 35. *That no Sheriff or his Bailiff, ſhall make his Torn through a Hundred but twice in a Year, and at the Place accuſtomed*, viz. *once after* Eaſter, *and again after the Feaſt of St.* Michael; *and that the View of Frank-pledge ſhall be at the Term of St.* Michael.

Sect. 5. And it is farther enacted by 31 *E.* 3. Ch. 15. *That every Sheriff ſhall make his Torn yearly, one Time within the Month after* Eaſter, *and another Time within the Month after St.* Michael; *and if they hold them in other Manner, that then they ſhall loſe their Torn for the Time.*

Sect. 6. And it ſeems [a] certain, That ſince theſe Statutes, the Sheriff is indictable for holding this Court at another Time, than what is therein limited, or at an unuſual Place.

Sect. 7. Alſo it hath been [b] reſolved, That an Indictment found at a Sheriff's Torn, appearing to have been holden at another Time, is void.

Sect. 8. But it is obſervable, That neither of theſe Statutes do expreſly mention a Court-Leet, and therefore it is ſaid in ſome [c] Books, That they do not extend to it; neither do I find any Reſolution, That an ancient Court-Leet holden at any other Time, or at an unuſual Place, is void: But on the contrary it is [d] ſaid, That a Court-Leet may be holden at any Place within the Precinct which the Lord thinks fitting. And it ſeems to be [e] agreed, That a Preſcription to hold ſuch Court oftner than twice in the Year is good; which ſeems hardly reconcileable with the general Rule of Law, That no Preſcription can ſtand good againſt a Statute which has negative Words, if a Court-Leet be conſtrued to be within the Purview of the abovementioned Statutes. It is true indeed, That both Sir *Edward Coke* and *Kitchen*, endeavour to ſolve this Difficulty, by offering a Diſtinction that the ſaid Rule extends not to Statutes made in Affirmance of the Common Law; but it is queſtionable how far this will amount to a good Anſwer, ſince it ſeems to be holden by [f] others of good Authority, that the ſaid Statutes were not made in Affirmance of the old Law, but are introductory of a new one; yet it is certainly ſafeſt to hold a Court-Leet at the Times accuſtomed, for it is [g] ſaid, That if it be holden at an unuſual Time it is void. And it [h] ſeems, That no Court-Leet granted ſince the Statute, can be holden at any other Time than what is limited by it, becauſe every ſuch Court is derived out of the Torn, to which the Statute certainly did extend.

Sect. 9. It hath been [i] holden, That in every Caption of an Indictment taken in a Sheriff's Torn, or Court-Leet, the Day whereon it was taken ought to be ſet forth, that it may appear not to have been on a Sunday.

Sect. 10. As to the third Point, *viz.* What [k] Perſons owe Suit to the Sheriff's Torn, it is certain, That regularly all Perſons above the Age of twelve Years, are by the Common Law bound to appear at this Court in their proper Perſons, and that no Perſons ſo bound to appear, are within the Benefit of the Statute of [l] *Merton*, Ch. 10. which allows Suit-Service to be performed by Attorney. And that not only Maſters of Families, but alſo all their Servants are bound to pay ſuch Suit, and that every [m] Maſter may be amerced for ſuffering a Servant to continue with him a Year and a Day, without being put into the Decennary, *&c.*

[a] Dy. 151. pl. 4. Keilw. 192. Dalt. Sheriff 390, 391.

[b] 38 H. 6. 7. a. 6 H. 7. 2. b. 3. a. S. P. C. 84. 2 H. H. P. C. 70. See 2 Danv. Ab. 256. pl. 14. 2 Inſt. 71. 2 Saund. 290.

[c] Bro. Leet, 23. 2 Leon. 74. 1 Rol. Rep. 201.

[d] 8 H. 7. 4. b. Kitchen 44. b. Owen 35. Daliſ. 61.

[e] Co. Lit. 115. a. Kitchen 8, 44. Cro. El. 125, 245. 1 Rol. Rep. 201.

[f] Dalt. Sheriff 390. 6 H. 7. 2. b.

[g] 38 H. 6. 7. a. Fitz. Leet, 2. Bro. Leet, 32. 2 Saund. 291.

[h] Cro. El. 245. Con. 2 Inſt. 72. 2 Saund. 291.

[i] 2 Keb. 731. 1 Vent. 107. 2 Saund. 290.

[k] See Sect. 2.

[l] 2 Inſt. 99.

[m] 41 E. 3. 26. b. 45 E. 3. 26. b.

Sect. 11. But [a] Tenants in Ancient Demesne are privileged by the Common Law from coming to this Court, unless they and their Ancestors have Time out of Mind used to come to it: Also [b] Parsons of Churches have the like Privilege by the Common Law; and all [c] Peers of the Realm, and Women have the same Privilege by the Statute of *Marlebridge*, *cap.* 10. (and perhaps by the Common Law) unless their Presence be especially required for some particular Cause.

Sect. 12. Also it seems [d] clear, That by the Common Law, as well as the said Statute of *Marlebridge*, *cap.* 10. no Man can be obliged to do Suit to any such Court, within the Precincts whereof he doth not reside, in Respect of any Lands which he may have within the Jurisdiction of it; for that no Suit of this Kind is due in Respect of the Tenure of any Lands, but only in Respect of the personal Residence of the Party. And [e] if a Man have a House which stands upon the Precincts of two Leets, it is said, That he shall do his Suit to the Court within the Jurisdiction of which his Bed-Chamber lies: And if [f] one have a House and Family in two Leets, it seems that he ought to do his Suit to that, wherein for the most part he personally resides, but no Man can be of two Leets; and therefore one who lives within a [g] private Leet, cannot be obliged to do Suit to the Sheriff's Torn, or to any other grand Leet, unless such private Leet, for some Default of the Lord, be seized into the King's Hands, or [h] unless the Lord of the Leet neglect to hold his Court.

As to the fourth Point, *viz.* What Authority the Sheriff (or his [i] Steward) hath as Judge of this Court, I shall consider the same in Relation,

1. To Indictments.
2. To Fines and Amercements in general.
3. To the Appointment of Constables.

Sect. 13. As to the first of these Points, it seems, That by the Common Law he might proceed to [k] hear and determine any Offence within his Jurisdiction, being indicted before him and requiring a Trial. But it is clear, that he is restrained from this Power by the Statute of *Magna Charta*, *cap.* 17. By which it is enacted, *That no Sheriff, Constable, or other Bailiff of the King, shall hold Pleas of the Crown:* And it seems, That this Statute also extends to the [l] Stewards of Courts-Leet, who cannot deliver any Persons indicted before them of Felony, but must refer them to the Justices of Gaol-Delivery; neither can they try any Person indicted before them of any other Offence, and therefore there is no Remedy to avoid such Presentments before them as are traversable, but [m] by removing them into the King's Bench, *&c.* as will be more fully shewn under the ninth Point.

Sect. 14. But it is certain, That the above mentioned Statute of *Magna Charta* 17. doth neither restrain the Sheriff's Torn, nor the Court-Leet, from taking [n] Indictments or Presentments, or awarding Process thereon in the same Manner as before; but this Power of awarding such Process, having been abused by the Sheriffs in their Torns, [o] was taken from all of them, (except those of *London*,) but not from any Court-Leet, by 1 *Ed.* 4. 2. which is more fully set forth under the eighth general Point of this Chapter.

[a] F.N.B. 161. Letter C. Dalt. Sheriff 387. 2 Inst. 121. Quære Bro. Leet, 38.
[b] F.N.B. 160. Cap. 2 Inst. 121. Regist. 175.
[c] 2 Inst. 120, 121. Regist. 175. F. N. B. 160, 161. Dalt. Sheriff 186. Bract. 124. b.
[d] Regist. 175. F. N. B. 160. Dalt. Sheriff 387.
[e] 2 Inst. 122. Dalt. Sheriff 387.
[f] 2 Inst. 122. Dalt. Sheriff 387.
[g] 2 Inst. 122. See 19 H. 6. 1. 33 H. 6. 9.
[h] Cro. Jac. 584. Finch 246. Dalt. Sheriff 388. See the next Chapter, Sect. 3.
[i] Dalt. Sheriff 388. 2 H. H. P. C. 70.
[k] Dalt. Sheriff 400. 2 H. H. P. C. 69.
[l] 2 Inst. 32. Dalt. Sheriff 400. 2 H. H. P. C. 71.
[m] 8 H. 4. 17. a. Bro. Leet 11. 27 H. 8. 2. Kitch. 22, 23. H. P. C. 175. 1 Ed. 3. ch. 17.
[n] Kitchen 42. b. Finch 386. 1 Ed. 3. ch. 17. 2 H. H. P. C. 69, 71.
[o] Dalt. Sheriff 400, 401. 2 H. H. P. C. 71.

As to the ſecond Point, *viz.* The Sheriff's Authority in his Torn in Relation to Fines and Amercements, I ſhall conſider,

1. In what Caſes he may, and in what Manner he ought to impoſe a Fine.
2. In what Caſes he ought to award an Amercement.
3. In what Manner ſuch Amercement is to be awarded and affeered.
4. In what Manner ſuch Fine or Amercement is to be recovered.
5. What farther Penalty may be added to ſuch Fine or Amercement.

Sect. 15. As to the firſt Particular, it ſeems clear, That the Sheriff's Power in this Court is ſtill the ſame as anciently it was, in all Caſes not within either of the above mentioned Statutes of *Magna Charta* or 1 *E.* 4. from whence it follows, That he ſtill continues a Judge of Record, and may impoſe a Fine on all ſuch as are guilty of [a] any Contempt in the Face of the Court; alſo there ſeems to be no Doubt, but that he may impoſe what reaſonable Fine he ſhall think fitting, upon a [b] Suitor refuſing to be ſworn, or upon a [c] Bailiff refuſing to make a Panel, *&c.* or upon a [d] Tithingman neglecting to make his Preſentment, or upon one of the Jury [e] refuſing to preſent the Articles wherewith they are charged, or upon a Perſon duly choſen [f] Conſtable, refuſing to be ſworn.

Sect. 16. But it hath been [g] reſolved, That all ſuch Fines ought to be ſeverally impoſed on each particular Offender, and not jointly upon all of them, except where a whole Vill is to be fined; in which Caſe, for the Neceſſity of the Thing, a joint Fine upon all is good.

Sect. 17. As to the ſecond Particular, *viz.* In what Caſes the Sheriff in his Torn ought to award an Amercement, it ſeems that he hath a diſcretionary Power [h] either to award a Fine or Amercement for Contempts to the Court, as for a Suitor's refuſing to be ſworn, *&c.* Alſo there ſeems to be no Doubt, but that at the Common Law he might, as the Steward of a Court-Leet ſtill may, award an [i] Amercement of any Perſon indicted for an Offence not Capital within his Juriſdiction, without any farther Proceeding or Trial: And it ſeems to be taken for granted in [k] ſome Books, That he might in ſuch Caſes impoſe a Fine on the Offender, if he thought fit; and the Statute of *Ed.* 4. 2. which reſtrains him from levying any Fines or Amercements on Indictments found before him, clearly ſuppoſes him to have had a Power of impoſing ſuch Fines; from all which it ſeems probable, that in ſuch Caſes he had, and that the Steward of a Court-Leet ſtill hath, a Power, either to amerce or fine the Offender, eſpecially if the [l] Crime were any Way enormous, as an Affray accompanied with wounding, *&c.*

Sect. 18. As to the third Particular, *viz.* In what Manner ſuch Amercement is to be awarded and affeered, it ſeems, That if by an Amercement be meant the Judgment, that the Party ſhall be *in miſericordia Domini Regis*, this being a [m] judicial Act, ought to be the Act of the Court only, and requires not the Concurrence or Aſſent of the Jury or any other, as appears from the conſtant Form of all Entries: Neither do I ſee any Reaſon why ſuch an Award of a *Miſericordia* by a Judge of a Court-Leet, ſhould expreſs any certain Sum for which the Party ſhould be *in Miſericordia*, except in ſuch Caſes only where no other Perſon is afterwards to affeer it; for in other Caſes the Award of a *Miſericordia* is only in order to authorize others to fix the Sum, which the Party

[a] See Book 1. ch. 21. ſect. 11. and the firſt Chapter of this Book, Sect. 15.
[b] Fitz. Leet, 11. Dalt. Sheriff 400. 2 Inſt. 142, 143. 44 E. 3. 19. b.
[c] 7 H. 6. 12. b.
[d] 10 H. 6. 7. b. 8 Co. 38. b.
[e] See 8 Co. 38. b. 39. a. Dalt. Sheriff 401. Dy. 211. b.
[f] 8 Co. 38. Dalt. Sheriff 400.
[g] 1 Rol. Rep. 33, 73. 11 Co. 42. b. 43. b. Dyer 211. b.
[h] Dalt. Sheriff 400. Fitz. Leet, 11. See 8 Co. 39, 40. Kitchen 43. b.
[i] Bro. Leet. Keilw. 66. Skin. 392. Finch 468. Kitchen 51, 52.
[k] Fitz. Torn, 4. 8 E. 4. 5. pl. 15. Dalt. Sheriff 401.
[l] 8 Ed. 4. 5. pl. 15.
[m] 1 Jones 301. Cro. Car. 275. 8 Co. 38. b. 40. b.

Party is to pay to the King for his Default; and in such [a] Cases the Courts of *Westminster-Hall*, never do more than award that the Party be *in Misericordia*, without mentioning any Sum in certain; and there seems no Reason, why the Judge of a Cout-Leet should not follow the same Rule; and accordingly I find the Opinion of the Lord Chief Justice [b] *Hobart*, which is the Chief Ground of a Resolution in [c] *Levinz*'s third Report, That every such Award of an Amercement must express a certain Sum, [d] over-ruled of late by Court of King's Bench.

Sect. 19. But if by an Amercement be meant, the Taxing or Reducing to a Certainty, the Sum to be paid by the Party to the King, upon the Award of his being *in Misericordia*; it [e] seems, That if it be for an Offence indicted, it ought to be done by certain Officers called Affeerors, being specially chosen and sworn for this Purpose. It is true [f] indeed, That the common Entry of an Amercement upon a Presentment in a Court-Leet is, that the Party is amerced, or *in Misericordia* to such a Sum, without distinguishing between the Award of the *Misericordia*, and the Assessment of the Amercement, or shewing by whom they are made; yet in Judgment of Law the Award of the *Misericordia* is the Act of the Court only, and the Assessment of the Sum to be paid, the Act of the Affeerors, and so it ought to be pleaded. But if the [g] Amercement be for a Contempt to the Court, it may be settled by the Judge himself, and needs no other Affeerment; for the [h] Judge of every Court of Record is the most proper Judge of all Contempts offered to such Court; and an Amercement of this Kind is in [i] Nature of a Fine, and called so in some [k] Books; and it seems to be a general [l] Rule, That no Fine for a Contempt is within the Statutes which require that Amercements be affeered.

Sect. 20. As to the fourth Particular, *viz.* In what Manner such [m] Fines and Amercements are to be recovered; it seems, That the King or Lord have an Election of common Right, either to distrain for them, or to bring an Action of Debt; for the better Understanding of the Nature of which Remedies, I shall first lay down some Rules concerning both of them in common, and then descend to each of them in particular.

As to what concerns the said Remedies in common, I shall lay down the following Rules:

Sect. 21. First, That it is safest in every Avowry, or Declaration of this Kind, expresly to [n] shew that the Offence was committed within the Jurisdiction of the Court: For if it were not, all the Proceeding were *coram non Judice*; and a Court shall not be presumed to have a Jurisdiction, where it doth not appear to have one. But perhaps it is not necessary to alledge in the Presentment it self, that [o] the Offence arose within the Jurisdiction of the Court; yet it is certainly adviseable to have such an Allegation, and that [p] perhaps may supply the Want of the Averment of Jurisdiction in the Pleadings.

Sect. 22. Secondly, That it is [q] adviseable expresly to alledge, that the Offence was committed as well as that it was presented, *&c.* yet I cannot find any express Opinion to this Purpose; but on the contrary it is observable, that the [r] Precedents of Pleadings of this Kind in the best Authors, do not expresly aver that the Offence was committed, but only that it was presented, and that it arose in such a Place within the Jurisdiction of the Court, *&c.* It is true indeed, that it hath been generally [s] holden, That in an Avowry or Declaration for an Amercement in

[a] 8 Co. 40. b. See Rastal's Entries 553. a. b. 606. F. N. B. 76. Letter A.
[b] Hobart 129. 1 Rol. Ab. 542. pl. 5.
[c] 3 Lev. 206. 3 Mod. 138.
[d] Salk. 56.
[e] 8 Co. 40. b. 3 Lev. 206. See Rastal's Entries 606. a. b. Kitchen 46. See Keilw. 66. a. 3 Keb. 362.
[f] Kitchen 51, 52, 53.
[g] Rastal's Entries 151. b. 7 H. 6. 12. b. 10 H. 6. 7.
[h] 8 Co. 40, 41. 2 Leon. 242. 3 Mod. 138.
[i] Brook Amercement 50.
[k] Savil 93. Co. Entries 572. 8 Co. 38. b. Rast. Ent. 553. 8 Co. 38, &c. 2 Inst. 196.
[l] Magna Charta 14. W. 1. 18.
[m] Rastal's Ent. 151, 553, 606. 2 H. 4. 24. b. 10 H. 6. 7. Cro. E. 581. Raym. 68. Savil 93, 94.
[n] Hob. 129. See Rastal's Ent. 553. a. b. Co. Ent. 572, 573.
[o] Hob. 129.
[p] See Rastal's Ent. 606.
[q] 2 Rol. Rep. 40. Raym. 337. Salk. 107. 108.
[r] Rastal's Entries 151, 553, 606. Co. Ent. 573.
[s] Moor 75. Cro Jac. 582. Cro. El. 748, 885, 886. 3 Leon. 7, 8. 1 Leon. 242.

in a Court-Baron, it is as neceſſary to alledge that the Offence was committed, as that it was preſented: But to this it may be anſwered, That a Court-Baron is not a Court of Record, and conſequently not of ſo high Authority as the Sheriff's Torn or a Court-Leet; neither are Preſentments in a Court-Baron, nor even in any other Court whatſoever, ſo highly credited by the Law as thoſe made in a Torn or Leet, which admit of no Traverſe to the Truth of them, except in ſome ſpecial Caſes, as will be more fully ſhewn under the ninth general Point of this Chapter.

Sect. 23. Thirdly, That it is ſafeſt in [a] ſetting forth a Preſentment, or an Afeerment of an Amercement, to ſhew the Names of the Preſentors and Affeerors; yet I cannot find this done in any of [b] *Raſtal's* Precedents; and ſome have ſaid, That it is neceſſary to ſet forth the Names of the Preſentors in an Action of Debt, but not in Replevin.

Sect. 24. Fourthly, That it is adviſeable to ſhew, that proper [c] Notice was given of the Holding of this Court, yet this I find omitted in ſome [d] Precedents; and perhaps the contrary Opinion may be the better, for that every Court of Record ſhall be preſumed to obſerve all neceſſary previous Incidents for the Holding of it, and all Perſons within its Juriſdiction ſhall be intended to have Notice of it. And for the like Reaſon perhaps, it is not neceſſary in an Avowry for a [e] Diſtreſs for ſuch Fine or Amercement, to ſhew that the Party had previous Notice what it was.

As to the Recovery of ſuch Fines and Amercements by Way of Diſtreſs, I ſhall obſerve,

Sect. 25. Firſt, That it ſeems to be [f] ſettled at this Day, That a Diſtreſs is incident of common Right to every Fine and Amercement in a Sheriff's Torn or Court-Leet, whether the ſame belong to the King or to a Subject, if the Offence for which they were impoſed be of common Right incident to the Juriſdiction of ſuch Courts; but [g] if ſuch Offence were only the Neglect of a Duty created by Cuſtom, it is queſtionable whether it do not require the like Cuſtom for a Diſtreſs, though the Duty be of a publick Nature; but if it be for the [h] private Benefit of a Subject, it ſeems clear, That no Diſtreſs is incident to it without a ſpecial Cuſtom.

Sect. 26. Secondly, That the Sheriff, or Lord of a Leet, may for ſuch Fines or Amercements diſtrain the Goods of the Offender in [i] any Lands within the County or Precinct of the Leet, of whomſoever they ſhall be holden, except [k] only in ſuch Lands which ſhall be in the King's Hands; for that all ſuch Lands, while they continue in the King's Poſſeſſion, are wholly out of the Juriſdiction of ſuch Courts.

Sect. 27. Thirdly, That ſuch a Diſtreſs may lawfully be taken in the [l] Highway; for that the Statute of *Marlebridge, cap.* 15. which prohibits the Taking of a Diſtreſs there, is to be intended only of Diſtreſſes taken for Services due by Way of Tenure of Lands.

Sect. 28. Fourthly, That ſuch Fines and Amercements being for a perſonal Offence, no [m] Stranger's Beaſts can lawfully be deſtrained for them, though they have been levant and couchant on the Lands of the Offender.

Sect. 29. Fifthly, That it ſeems to be [n] agreed, That where any ſuch Court is in the King's Hands, the Goods diſtrained for ſuch Fines and Amercements may lawfully be ſold, after they have been kept a reaſonable Time, as the Space of ſixteen [o] Days; and it ſeems the better

[a] Keilw. 66. a. 3 Keb. 362. Co. En. 572, 773.
[b] Raſtal 553. 606.
9 E. 4. 40. b.
[c] 10 H. 7. 15. pl. 12. 1 Vent. 105. Raym. 204. Coke's Ent. 572, 573. Raſtal's Ent. 553, 606. 1 Rol. Abr. 365. pl. a. 468. pl. b. 2 Rol. Abr. 136. 1 Rol. Rep. 201.
[d] Co. Ent. 572, 573. Raſtal's Ent. 553, 606.
[e] 45 E. 3. 9. a. b. Raſt. Ent. 553, 606.
[f] 1 Rol. Abr. 665. F. 666. pl. 2, 3. 1 Ro. Re. 201. 11 Co. 45. a. 8 Co. 41. Cro. Jac. 382. 10 H. 7. 15. pl. 12. 10 H. 6. 7. Con. 11 H. 7. 14. a. 21 H. 7. 40. b.
[g] 1 Vent. 105. Raym. 204. 2 Keb. 701, 739, 745.
[h] 1 Ro. R. 76. 11 Co. 44. b.
[i] 2 H. 4. 24. b. 47 E. 3. 13. a. Bro. Leet, 28, 41. Fitz. Avowry 194. 1 Rol. Abr. 670. L. 1, 2, 3, 4. 2 Inſt. 104.
[k] 47 Ed. 3. 12, 13. Fitz. Diſtr. 15. 1 Rol. Abr. 670. pl. 5.
[l] 2 Inſt. 131. 47 E. 3. 13. a. 1 And. 72.
[m] 47 E. 3. 13. a. 41 E. 3. 26. b. Bro. Diſtr. 3. F. N. B. 100. H. Owen 146. Noy 20. Con. 1 Rol. A. 669. pl. 20.
[n] Hetley 62. Finch 476.
[o] Hetley 62.

[a] Opinion, That where any ſuch Court is in the Hands of a common Perſon, if the Goods were diſtrained for an Offence of a publick Nature, they may be ſold of common Right, without any ſpecial Cuſtom for that Purpoſe.

Sect. 30. Sixthly, That no Bailiff can lawfully diſtrain for any ſuch Fine or Amercement, without a ſpecial [b] Warrant for ſo doing, which muſt be ſet forth by him in an Avowry or Juſtification of ſuch a Diſtreſs.

Sect. 31. As to the Recovery of ſuch Fines and Amercements by Action of Debt, being ſcarce able to find any Thing remarkable concerning this Matter, except what hath been already taken Notice of, I ſhall content my ſelf with this one Obſervation, That the Defendant ſhall [c] not be ſuffered to wage his Law in any ſuch Action, becauſe it is grounded on the Act of a Court of Record.

Sect. 32. As to the fifth Particular, *viz.* What farther Penalty may be added to ſuch Fines and Amercements, there ſeems to be no Doubt, but that upon a Preſentment of a common Nuſance in a Torn or Leet, the Sheriff or Steward may either amerce the Perſon preſented, and [d] alſo order him to remove the Nuſance by ſuch a Day, under Pain of forfeiting a certain Sum, or may order him to remove it under ſuch a Pain [e] without amercing him at all. But it ſeems doubtful, Whether ſuch Perſon be bound at his Peril, to take Notice of and obey ſuch Order, being made in his [f] Abſence, unleſs expreſs Notice be given him of it; but if he have ſuch Notice it ſeems clear, That he ſhall forfeit the Pain upon a Preſentment at another Court, that he hath not removed ſuch Nuſance, [g] without any farther Proceeding: Alſo it ſeems, That no ſuch Pain can be affeered to any [h] leſſer Sum than what is at firſt ſet; and it is ſaid, That every ſuch Pain when forfeited, may be recovered [i] either by Diſtreſs or Action of Debt, in the ſame Manner as a Fine or Amercement may be: And this Point ſeeming to be agreed by moſt of the Books cited in the Margent, it ſeems probable, That the Reaſon of the Judgment is miſtaken in *Fletcher* and *Ingram*'s Caſe, as reported by Mr. Serjeant [k] *Salkeld*, wherein the contrary Opinion is ſaid to have been holden.

Before I come to the Third Point, *viz.* The Authority of the Sheriff as Judge of the Torn, in Relation to the Appointment of Conſtables, I ſhall in brief premiſe ſome Conſiderations concerning the Antiquity and Nature of the Office of a Conſtable.

Sect. 33. And firſt, as to the Antiquity of the Office of a Conſtable, it ſeems to be the [l] better Opinion, That both Conſtables of Hundreds, which are commonly called High Conſtables, and alſo Conſtables of Tythings, which are at this Day commonly called Petit Conſtables or Tythingmen, and where anciently called Chief Pledges, were by the Common Law, and not firſt ordained by the Statute of *Wincheſter*, *cap.* 6. as it is holden by [m] ſome that they were; for that Statute doth not ſay, That there ſhall be ſuch Officers conſtituted, but clearly ſeems to ſuppoſe that there were ſuch before the making of it.

Sect. 34. As to the Nature of this Office, there ſeems to be no Doubt but that the [n] original Inſtitution of it was for the better Preſervation of the Peace; for which Purpoſe a Conſtable is ſaid to be authorized by the Common Law to [o] arreſt Felons, and alſo all ſuſpicious [p] Perſons that go abroad in the Night, and ſleep by Day, or reſort to Bawdy-Houſes

[a] 3 H. 7. 4. 6. b. 8 Co. 41. b. 1 Rol. Rep. 76. Noy 17. Quære Het. 62. 1 Bulſt. 53. 11 H. 7. 14. a. 21 H. 7. 40. b.
[b] 3 Mod. 138. Cro. El. 698, 748. Moor 574, pl. 789, 607. pl. 839. 2 Keb. 745. Salk. 108.
[c] 10 H. 6. 7. Co. Lit. 295. Fitz. Ley. 5. 43. 2 Rol. Abr. 106 pl. 1, 2, 8.
[d] See Kitchen 51, 52, 53.
[e] See Kitchen 51, 52, 53. Co. Entr. 573. 1 Rol. Abr. 468. pl. 6. Cro. Jac. 382.
[f] 1 Rol. Abr. 468. pl. 6. 2 Rol. Abr. 136. 1 Rol. Re. 201. Aleyn 78. 5 Mod. 130, 131.
[g] Co. Ent. 573.
[h] 3 Leon. 7, 8. Moor 75. pl. 205. Co. Ent. 573. Bro. Leet 37.
[i] 8 Co. 41. b. Keilw. 66. b. Cro. Jac. 382. 1 Rol. Rep. 201. 1 Rol. Abr. 468. pl. 6. Contra Bro. Leet 37.
[k] Salk. 175. See 5 Mod. 96, 130, 131.
[l] Salk. 175. 381. 12 H. 7. 18 a. Owen 105. Finch 336. Kitch. 47, 48. 4 Inſt. 265. Poph. 13. Contra Cro. El. 375, 376. Lamb Conſtable, 5, 9, 10. 6 Co. 77. b.
[m] Lamb. Conſtable, 5. 4 Inſt. 267.
[n] See the Books cited, Sect. 33.
[o] See Ch. 12.
[p] Kitchen 48. 13 H. 7. 10. b. 2 H. H. P. C. 88.

[a] B. 1 Ch. 63.
[b] Lamb. Conſtable, 5, 6, &c.
45 E. 3. 27.
[c] See Raſt. Entries 151.
Crompt. 212.
Dalt. Sheriff 388.
Kitchen 47.

Houſes, or keep ſuſpicious Company, and to ſuppreſs [a] Affrays : And to the ſame End alſo it [b] ſeems, That he ought by the ancient Common Law, to preſent at the Torn or Leet all thoſe within his Precinct, who have not been admitted into ſome Tything and ſworn to the King's Allegiance; and it ſeems that he ſtill ought by the Law in [c] uſe at this Day, to preſent all Offences inquirable in the Torn or Leet ; yet in the Oath ſet down by *Kitchen*, he only ſwears to preſent all Bloodſheds, Outcries, Affrays, and Reſcouſes done within his Office.

[d] Salk 380, 381.
[e] 5 Mod. 130. Salk. 175.
[f] Salk. 381. 2 Rol. Rep. 78.

Sect. 35. Alſo it is [d] ſaid, That a Conſtable was at the Common Law a ſubordinate Officer to the Conſervators of the Peace ; and conſequently ſince the Office of ſuch Conſervators hath been diſuſed, and Juſtices of Peace conſtituted in their Stead, it hath been always holden, That the Conſtable is the proper Officer to a Juſtice of Peace, and bound to execute his Warrants ; and therefore it hath been [e] reſolved, That where a Statute authorizes a Juſtice of Peace to convict a Man of a Crime, and to levy the Penalty by Warrant of Diſtreſs, without ſaying to whom ſuch Warrant ſhall be directed, or by whom it ſhall be executed, the Conſtable is the proper [f] Officer to ſerve ſuch Warrant, and indictable for diſobeying it.

1 H. H. P.C. 581.
2 H. H. P. C. 88.
[g] 1 Rol. Abr. 591. A.
Moor 845.
Crompt. 222.
3 Bulſt. 77.
Dalt. cap. 1.
1 Rol. Rep. 274.
1 Sid. 355.
1 Lev. 233.
March 30.
Quære 2 Keb. 309.
1 Sid 355.

Sect. 36. Yet in as much as the Office of a Conſtable is wholly miniſterial and no way Judicial, it ſeems, That he may appoint a Deputy to execute a [g] Warrant directed to him, when by Reaſon of Sickneſs, Abſence, or otherwiſe, he cannot do it himſelf. For the Publick Good requires, That their ſhould be always ſome Officer ready at Hand to execute ſuch Warrants, and the too rigorous Reſtraint of the Service of them to the proper Officer, could not but ſometimes Cauſe a Failure of Juſtice ; yet I do not find it ſettled, That a Conſtable can make a Deputy without ſome ſuch ſpecial Cauſe. [15]

For the better Underſtanding of the Authority of the Sheriff, as Judge of the Torn, in Relation to the Appointment of Conſtables, I ſhall conſider the following Particulars :

1. Whether the Sheriff in his Torn hath Power to make or remove a Conſtable.
2. What Perſons are privileged from being Conſtables.
3. In what Manner Perſons duly choſen Conſtables, may be puniſhed for refuſing to be ſworn.
4. What Remedy Perſons having a Right to this Office, or to be diſcharged, may have to be admitted into, or reſtored to it, or diſcharged of it.
5. What Power Juſtices of Peace have in Relation to theſe Matters.

[h] Dalt. Sheriff 400.
1 Rol. Rep. 34.
[i] 2 Jones 212.
Lamb. Conſtable, 8.
Salk. 175.

Sect. 37. As to the firſt Particular, *viz.* Whether the Sheriff in his Torn, hath Power to make or remove a Conſtable, it being ſaid in ſome [h] Books, That both High and Petit Conſtables are to be choſen and appointed by the Sheriff in his Torn ; and by [i] others, that they are to be choſen by the Decennary, it ſeems difficult to determine to whom this Power doth of common Right belong ; yet it ſeems clear, That whether a Conſtable be to be choſen by the Sheriff or Decennary, yet he is to be ſworn and placed in his Office by the Sheriff, as being Judge of the Court. Alſo it ſeems certain, That a Cuſtom for chooſing a Conſtable either Way, is good ; and it ſeems to have been the Opinion of the Makers of 13 & 14 *Car.* 2. 12. That the Lords of the Courts-Leet have this Power of

Common Right; for the said Statute, on the Neglect of such Lords to appoint a Constable, gives to Justices of Peace the sole Power of making one; from whence it seems probable, That the Makers of that Statute thought that the like Power did originally belong of common Right to such Lords, and consequently to the Sheriff in his Torn, where there is no Court-Leet: But [a] it hath been said, That a Custom in a Town that the Inhabitants shall serve the Office of a Constable by Turns, according to the Situation of their several Houses, is not good; for that by such a Course it may come to a Woman's Turn to be Constable, as Inhabitant of one of those Houses; yet we find such Customs allowed to be good in later Books; and it seems, That the Consequence of the Reasoning abovementioned may well be denied, since such Woman in such Case may procure another to serve for her.

[a] Cro Car. 389. 2 Keb. 309, 578. 1 Lev. 266. 1 Sid. 355.

Sect. 38. However it seems clear, That the Sheriff or Steward having Power to place a [b] Constable in his Office, have by Consequence a Power of removing him.

[b] Bulst. 174.

Sect. 39. As to the second Particular, *viz.* What persons are privileged from being Constables, it [c] seems certain, That if a sworn Attorney or other Officer of any of the Courts of *Westminster-hall* be chosen into this Office, he may have a Writ of Privilege for his Discharge; for that all such Officers, being bound to give their personal Attendance to such Courts, shall be privileged from all such inferior Offices, which it is apparent that for the most part they cannot personally execute: And it hath been resolved, That such Officers shall have this Privilege, not only where there is no special Custom concerning the Election of Constables, but [d] also where they are chosen by a particular Custom, in respect of their Estates or otherwise; for that no such Custom shall be intended to be more ancient than the Usages of those Courts, and therefore shall give way to them: And upon the like Reasons I find it [e] taken for granted, That practising Barristers at Law, and the Servants of Members of Parliament, have the same Privilege, but I know not of any Resolution to this Purpose.

[c] Noy 112, 113. March 30. Cro. Ca. 389. 2 Keb. 477.

[d] 2 Keb. 508. pl. 84. Cro. Ca. 389. 1 Lev. 265, 266.

[e] 1 Mod. 22. 2 Keb. 578. 1 Mod. 13.

Sect. 40. Also it hath been resolved, That an [f] Alderman of *London* is not compellable to be a Constable, for that as an Alderman he is bound to be present in the City for the good Government of it.

[f] 1 Jon. 462. Cro. Ca. 585.

Sect. 41. But [g] it hath been holden, That a Captain of the King's Guards, being presented to serve as Constable, in Pursuance of a Custom in respect of his Lands in a Town, cannot claim this Privilege; for that notwithstanding he be bound by his Office to personal Attendance on the King's Person, yet such Office being of late Institution, shall not prevail against an ancient Custom: Also it [h] seems, That a practising Physician being chosen Constable in Pursuance of such Custom, has no Remedy for his Discharge; for that there are no Precedents of this Kind, and his Calling is private; yet if such an Officer, or a [i] Gentleman of Quality who hath no such Office, or a practising Physician, be chosen Constable of a Town, which has sufficient Persons besides to execute this Office, and no special Custom concerning it, perhaps he may be relieved by the King's Bench: But it [k] seems, That even a Custom cannot exempt fitting Persons from serving the Office of Constable, where there are not sufficient besides them to execute it. Yet these Points seem not to be settled, as appears by the various Opinions in the Books concerning this Matter which are very differently reported.

[g] See 3 Keb. 309. 1 Sid. 272, 355. 1 Lev. 233. 1 Keb. 933.

[h] 2 Keb. 578. 1 Mod. 22.

[i] 1 Keb 429. Con. 2 Keb. 578.

[k] Sid. 272. See 1 Keb. 933.

Sect. 42.

Sect. 42. It is alledged in the Petition of the *London* Surgeons, whereon the Statute of 5 *H.* 8. *cap.* 6. is made, *That the Wardens and Fellowship of the Craft and Mystery of Surgeons infranchised in the City of* London, *not passing in Number twelve Persons, for the continual Service and Attendance that they at all Hours and Times give to the King's People, have been exempted and discharged from all Offices and Business, wherein they should use or bear any Manner of Armour or Weapon,* &c. And thereupon it is enacted and established, *That from thenceforth the said Wardens and Fellowship be discharged, and not chargeable of Constableship, Watch, and all manner of Office bearing any Armour,* &c. *and also that the said Act extend to all Barber-Surgeons, admitted and approved to exercise the said Mystery of Surgeons, according to the Form of the Statute made in that Behalf, so that they exceed not, nor be at any Time above the Number of twelve Persons.*

2 Keb. 578. *Sect.* 43. And it seems, That by the Equity of this Statute, and the ancient Custom of the Realm, all Surgeons have been allowed the like Privilege.

Sect. 44. Also it is enacted by 32 *H.* 8. 40. *That the President of the Commonalty and Fellowship of the Science and Faculty of Physick in* London, *and the Commons and Fellows of the same, shall not be chosen Constables in the City of* London *or Suburbs of the same,* &c. Yet it seems to have been
Vide supra Sect. 41. holden, That the Equity of this Act doth not extend to other Physicians not mentioned in it; perhaps for this Reason, because Physicians have no such special Custom for their Discharge as Surgeons are said to have.

Sect. 45. Also it is enacted 6 *W.* 3. 4. which hath been continued by subsequent Statutes, *That all Persons using the Art of an Apothecary, who have been brought up and served as Apprentices in the said Art for seven Years, according to the Statute of* 5 Eliz. *shall be freed and exempted from the Office of Constable, in the Counties and Places where they live, for so long as they use and exercise the said Art.*

Sect. 46. As to the third Particular, *viz.* In what Manner Persons duly chosen Constables may be punished for refusing to be sworn, it seems that no Person can lawfully be committed for such Refusal without more;
Cro. Car. 567. Co. Ent. 572. 5 Mod. 130. Salk. 175. 8 Co. 38. but it is said, That if the Party be present in the Court he may be fined, and that if he be absent, and have a certain Time and Place appointed him for the taking of the Oath before a Justice of Peace, and have also express Notice of such Appointment, and be presented at the next Court, for having refused to take it accordingly, he may be amerced: Also it seems, That in either Case he may be indicted either at the Sessions of the Peace, or before Justices of *Oyer* and *Terminer*: And it is advisable in all Pleadings in any Action concerning such a Fine or Amercement, and in all Indictments for such Refusal, specially and expresly to set forth the Manner of every such Election, Appointment, Notice and Refusal,
[a] 1 Mod. 24. [b] 5 Mod. 96, 129. [c] Aleyn 78. 5 Mod. 96, 129, 130, 131. 1 Keb. 418. Vide supra fol. 66. [d] 1 Keb. 416. 6 Co. 77 b. and [a] before whom the Court was holden: And it hath been adjudged, That it is insufficient to say in general, that the Party was [b] *Debito modo electus*, or *Legitime electus*, or that he had [c] Notice thereof, without setting forth the special Circumstances of such Notice, *&c.* Also it is [d] said to have been adjudged, That an Indictment for not finding a sufficient Person to serve the Office of Constable, without shewing that the Party refused to serve it himself, is insufficient; and it is said not to be sufficient to shew, That a Man was presented and returned to be a chief Pledge, without shewing that there were other inferior Pledges.

Sect. 47. As to the fourth Particular, *viz.* What Remedy Perſons having a Right to be Conſtables or to be diſcharged, may have to be admitted into or reſtored to their Office or diſcharged of it; it ſeems clear at this Day, That the Court of King's Bench having the ſupreme Control of all inferior Juriſdictions, may upon the Complaint of any Perſon apprehending himſelf to be unjuſtly aggrieved in any ſuch Reſpect, award a Writ to the Judge of the Court, thereby commanding him to ſwear, reſtore, or diſcharge the Party as the Caſe ſhall be; whereupon if ſuch Judge do not obey ſuch Writ, nor an *Alias* and *Pluries* to the ſame Purpoſe, nor return a ſufficient Cauſe to the Court to juſtify his not obeying it, the Court will at laſt award a preremptory *Mandamus.* 1 Rol. Abr. 535. Letter F. 541. pl. 5, 6. 2 Rol. Rep. 82. Con. 1 Bulſt. 174.

Sect. 48. Alſo it hath been holden, That a Perſon duly choſen Conſtable at a Court-Leet, and refuſed to be ſworn by the Steward, may be relieved by the Seſſions of the Peace; but this Point ſhall be more fully conſidered in the next Section. 2 Jon. 212.

Sect. 49. As to the fifth Particular, *viz.* What Power Juſtices of Peace have in Relation to theſe Matters, it is obſervable, That the Conſtable being a principal Peace-Officer, and it being neceſſary for the Preſervation of the Peace, that every Vill ſhould be furniſhed with one; the Juſtices of Peace have ever ſince the Inſtitution of their Office, taken upon them as Conſervators of the Peace, not only to ſwear Conſtables which have been choſen at a Torn or Leet, but alſo to nominate and ſwear thoſe who have not been choſen at any ſuch Court, on the Neglect of the Sheriffs or Lords to hold their Courts, or to take Care that ſuch Officers are appointed in them; alſo it ſeems, That ſuch Juſtices have always uſed for good Cauſe to diſplace ſuch Officers which have been ſo choſen and ſworn by them; and this Power of Juſtices of Peace having been confirmed by the uninterrupted Uſage of many Ages ſhall not now be diſputed, but ſhall be preſumed to have been grounded on ſufficient Authority. And ſome have carried this Point ſo far, as to allow the Juſtices at their Seſſions to ſwear one who was choſen at the Leet, and unduly rejected by the Steward, who had ſworn another in his Place. Salk. 175. pl. 1, 2, 176. 1 Mod. 13. 2 Jon. 212. 1 Bulſt. 174. Aleyn 78. Dalt. Ch. 121. fol. 366, 367. 1 Bulſt. 174. Salk. 176. Con. 1 Bulſt. 174.

Sect. 50. However it is certain, That Juſtices of Peace had Power to nominate and ſwear Conſtables on the Default of the Torn or Leet, before the Statute of 13 & 14 *Car.* 2. 12. Par. 15. and therefore, that they have ſuch Authority in ſome Caſes not mentioned in that Statute, which reciting, *That the Laws and Statutes for apprehending Rogues and Vagabonds had not been duly executed, ſometimes for want of Officers, by Reaſon Lords of Manors do not keep Court-Leets every Year for the making of them; doth enact, That in Caſe any Conſtable, Headborough, or Tithingman ſhall die or go out of the Pariſh, any two Juſtices of Peace may make and ſwear a new Conſtable, Headborough, or Tythingman, until the ſaid Lord ſhall hold a Court, or until next Quarter-Seſſions, who ſhall approve of the ſaid Officers ſo made and ſworn as aforeſaid, or appoint others, as they ſhall think fit; and if any Officer ſhall continue above a Year in his or their Office, that then in ſuch Caſe the Juſtices of Peace in their Quarter-Seſſions may diſcharge ſuch Officers, and may put another fit Perſon in his or their Place until the Lord of the ſaid Manor ſhall hold a Court as aforeſaid.* See the Books cited in the precedent Section.

As to the fifth general Point of this Chapter, *viz.* What Kind of Offences are inquirable in the Sheriff's Torn, I ſhall premiſe the following Obſervations,

4 Inſt. 261. Cromp. 213.

1. That it is no certain Rule, That ſuch Offences as are omitted in 18 *E.* 2. concerning the View of Frank-Pledge are not within the Juriſdiction of the Torn or Leet.

Fitz. Torn, 5. infra Sect. 52.

2. That Offences made Treaſon or Felony or in any other Manner, having a Reſtraint by Statute ſuperadded to that of the Common Law, are not inquirable here in reſpect of any ſuch Statute, but only as Offences at the Common Law; for that the Juriſdiction of theſe Courts is wholly confined to Offences at Common Law.

Keilw. 66. b.

3. That no Offence whatſoever is cogniſable in any ſuch Court, unleſs it aroſe ſince the holding of the laſt Court.

Offences inquirable in this Court are either,

1. Capital, or
2. Not Capital.

The Capital are either,

[a] Crompt. 212. b. Dalt. Sheriff 292. 7 H. 6. 12. b. 10 H. 6. 7. a. Quære Bro. Leet, 26. [b] 9 H. 6. 44. b. [c] Inf. Sect. 58. [d] Kitchen 8, 9, 22. H. P. C. 173. 6 H. 7. 4. b. 5. a. See the next Section. [e] 10 H. 6. 7. a. Kitchen 9, 10. Cromp. 212. Dalt. Sheriff 392. [f] 9 H. 6. 44. b. 22 E. 4. 22. b. 7 H. 6. 12. Fitz. Torn, 5. 40 Aſſ. 30. Bro. Leet, 18, 26. Finch 241. Kitchen 22. [g] Kitchen 22. 18 E. 2. View of Frank-pledge. 2 Inſt. 181. 22 E. 4. 22. 6 H. 7. 4. b. 5. a. Fitz. Torn, 5. Leet, 3. 1 H. H. P. C. 632. 2 H. H. P. C. 69, 71.

1. Treaſons, or
2. Felonies.

Sect. 51. And firſt as to Treaſons, it is ſaid in [a] ſome Books, That the Sheriff in his Torn may inquire of them all in general, and in [b] others, that he may inquire of all which are not againſt the King's Perſon; but I can find no Reaſon given for this Diſtinction: And ſince it is a general Rule, That Offences are inquirable in this Court, in Reſpect of their being of a publick Nature, on which Account the loweſt Offences againſt the King, as [c] Mortmains and Purpreſtures, and ſuch like, are inquirable in it; it ſeems ſtrange, That the higheſt ſhould be exempted. However it is [d] clear, That the Sheriff has no Power to inquire of any Offence made Treaſon by Statute, as of a Treaſon, but only as it was an Offence at Common Law.

Sect. 52. Secondly, As to Felonies, it is alſo generally ſaid in [e] ſome Books, That the Sheriff in his Torn may inquire of all Kinds of Felonies, and in [f] others, That he may inquire of all except of the Death of a Man, or Rape, of the firſt of which it is ſaid, That he cannot inquire, becauſe it is not a common Nuſance, but only a Wrong to a ſingle Perſon: But if this Reaſoning be the only Foundation for this Opinion, it ſeems difficult to maintain it; for if an Aſſault and Battery of a ſingle Perſon being accompanied with Bloodſhed or Robbery, be inquirable in this Court, in reſpect of the Enormity of the Offence, and the Danger to the Publick from ſuffering ſuch Offenders to go unreſtrained, it ſeems ſtrange if ſuch an Aſſault proceed to Murder, that it ſhould not be inquirable in it alſo: But it is [g] ſaid, That the Sheriff cannot inquire of Rape as of a Felony, becauſe it is made a Felony by the Statute of *Weſtminſter* 2. 34. by which it is enacted, That he who raviſhes a Woman, ſhall have Judgment of Life and Member: But if this Statute had only repealed the 13th of *Weſtminſter* 1. (by which this Offence, which was a Felony at Common Law, was made a Treſpaſs only,) it ſeems that it would have reſtored the Juriſdiction of the Sheriff's Torn over it as a Felony, becauſe then it would have been a Felony by the Common Law again; but now it being a Felony only by the Statute, it is inquirable as a Treſpaſs only in this Court.

Offences not Capital inquirable in the Sheriff's Torn, are either,

1. Such as amount to an actual Treſpaſs, or
2. Such as do not amount to ſuch a Treſpaſs.

Sect. 53. And firſt, as to ſuch Offences amounting to an actual Treſpaſs it is agreed, [a] That an Aſſault and Battery is inquirable here if there be any Bloodſhed in it, but otherwiſe not; becauſe in ſuch Caſe it is not looked on as a common Grievance, but as an Injury to a particular Perſon.

Sect. 54. Secondly, That all [b] Affrays are alſo inquirable here, for that they are *in terrorem Populi.*

Sect. 55. Thirdly, That the common [c] Breaking of Hedges, Walls, or Dykes, may alſo be inquired of in this Court, but not the Breaking of any particular Hedge, for that it is no common Grievance.

Sect. 56. Fourthly, Alſo it is commonly ſaid, that all [d] Pound Breaches may be inquired of in this Court, as being common Grievances, in direct Contempt of the Authority of the Law, by which Pounds are provided for the legal Detainment of Diſtreſſes till they ſhall be delivered by due Courſe of Law.

Sect. 57. Offences under the Degree of Capital, not amounting to an actual Treſpaſs, and inquirable in this Court, either immediately concern the King's Intereſt, or do not.

Sect. 58. As to thoſe which immediately concern the King's Intereſt, it ſeems to be agreed, That all [e] Purpreſtures or Incroachments upon the King, and [f] Alienations in Mortmain, and [g] Seiſures of Treaſure-trove, or of [h] Waifs or [h] Eſtrays, or Goods [h] wrecked, belonging to the King, may be inquired of in this Court: But it ſeems [i] queſtionable, Whether a Preſcription in a Court-Leet to inquire of the Seiſure of ſuch Things belonging to the Lord of it, being a Subject, be good or not, ſince it is againſt the general [k] Rule of the Law, for the Court-Leet to take Conuſance of Treſpaſſes done to the private Damage of the Lord, becauſe that would make him his own Judge.

Sect. 59. As to Offences of this Kind, which do not immediately concern the King's Intereſt, it ſeems to be a general [l] Rule, That all common Nuſances are indictable in this Court; as all Annoyances to common Bridges or Highways, [m] Bawdy-houſes, &c. and alſo all other ſuch like Offences, as [n] Selling corrupt Victuals or Expoſing them to Sale, [o] Breaking the Aſſiſe of Beer and Ale, Neglecting to hold a [p] Fair or Market in Purſuance of a Grant or Preſcription: Alſo it ſeems, That the Keeping of [q] falſe Weights or Meaſures is indictable in this Court, whether it appear that they were actually made Uſe of or not: Alſo it is ſaid, that all common Diſturbers of the Peace may be here indicted, as [r] Barrators, common [r] Scolds, [r] Eves-droppers, and alſo all common Oppreſſors, as [s] Uſurers, &c. and alſo all [t] dangerous and ſuſpicious Perſons as Vagabonds; or thoſe who go abroad in the Night, and ſleep in the Day, or thoſe who inordinately haunt Taverns, having no viſible Means to live by, &c. And alſo all [u] Suitors to the Court who ſhall make Default, &c. And [x] alſo all thoſe who ſhall levy a Hue and Cry without Cauſe, or ſhall neglect to levy one where they ought, or to purſue one rightly levied.

18 E. 4. 5. b. Dy. 233. pl. 14. 1 R. 3. 1. a. 4 H. 6. 18. 18 E. 2. View of Frank-pledge. Kitch. 37, 38. [b] 4 H. 6. 10. a. 1 R. 3. 1. a. Bro. Leet, 15. Kitchen 11. [c] Kitch. 11. Bro. Leet, 26. 22 E. 4. 23. Finch 241. [d] Dalt. Sheriff 394. Kitch. 11, 37. Contra 4 Leon. 12. [e] Dalt. Sheriff 393. [f] Kitch. 23, 38, 39. [g] Kitch. 40. 18 Ed. 2. View of Frank-pledge. [h] Kitch. 12, 13, 23, 40. Dalt. Sheriff 393. Crompt. 213. [i] 44 E. 3. 19. pl. 14. [k] 1 Saunders 135. Raym. 160. 12 H. 4. 8. b. [l] 1 R. 3. 1. 4 H. 6. 10. 22 E. 4. 22, 23. 1 Rol. Abr. 541, 542, 543. [m] Kitch. 11. [n] 1 R. 3. 1. Bro. Leet, 1. 4 Inſt. 261. Kitch. 11, 23. [o] 2 Inſt. 72. 4 E. 4. 24. 4 Inſt. 262. Rol. Ab. 543. [p] Cromp. 212. [q] 18 E. 2. View of Frank-pledge. Con. Kitch. 11. b. Dalt. Sh. 395. [r] Kitch. 11. Hob. 246. [s] Crompt. 212. Dalt. Sh. 394. [t] 18 E. 2. View of Frank-pledge. Kitch. 11. [u] Kitch. 10. b. [x] Dalt. Sheriff 394. 18 E. 2. View of Frank-pledge.

Sect. 60.

[a] Kitch. 13. See the next Chapter. [b] See Kitch. 12. 2 Danv. Ab. 291. [c] 1 Rol. Abr. 541. 2 Rol. Abr. 83. pl. 7. [d] 1 Rol. Ab. 542. pl. 11, 12. Lane 55, 56.

Sect. 60. Alſo [a] it is ſaid, That every Vill within the Precinct of a Torn, is indictable in it for not having a Pair of Stocks, and ſhall forfeit five Pounds.

Sect. 61. Alſo by [b] Statute, many other Offences are inquirable in this Court, which it would be too long to enumerate in this Place.

Sect. 62. But it hath been [c] reſolved, That a Man cannot be amerced in a Court-Leet for ſurcharging a Common, becauſe this only concerns the private Intereſt of the Inhabitants.

[e] 11 H. 7. 14. 21 H. 7. 40. b. 5 Co. 63. Hob. 212. Kitch. 45. [f] 1 Danv. 735. pl. 10. 737. pl. 1, 2, 3. Kitch. 78. [g] See Ch. 11. Sect. 6.

Sect. 63. Yet it hath been [d] holden, That if there be a By-Law made in a Court-Leet, in Purſuance of a Cuſtom to make By-Laws, That no one ſhall receive a poor Man to be his Tenant, who ſhall be chargeable to the Town, under a certain Penalty; and afterwards an Inhabitant offend againſt ſuch By-Law, he may be preſented at the Court-Leet and compelled to pay ſuch Penalty: But if ſuch By-Laws be valid, it ſeems clear, That they depend entirely on the Cuſtom, and are not binding of common Right; for that the Court-Leet, as ſuch, hath nothing to do with ſuch Matters of a private Nature: And how far any ſuch Court may receive from a ſpecial Cuſtom, a new collateral Power of a different Nature from what naturally belongs to it, may deſerve to be conſidered; but it [e] ſeems, That of common Right any Court-Leet with the Aſſent of the Tenants, may make By-Laws under certain Penalties, in Relation to Matters properly within the Conuſance of ſuch Court, as the Reparation of the Highways, *&c.* Alſo there [f] ſeems to be no Doubt, but that by Cuſtom a Court-Baron may make By-Laws, for the well regulating of Commons and ſuch like private Matters; and therefore where a Court-Leet and Baron are holden together at the ſame Place, as they uſually are, it ſeems, That what is tranſacted therein in Relation to publick Matters, ſhall be applied to the [g] Juriſdiction of the Court-Leet, and what is done in Relation to private Matters, ſhall be intended to be done by the Court-Baron.

[h] Dalton's Sheriff 385. Finch 241, 242. Cro. Jac. 551. ſeems contrary. [i] Crom. 212. Dalt. Sheriff 388. [k] 2 Inſt. 120, 122. [l] 1 Rol. Ab. 543. Letter D. Crompt. 212. a. Co. Lit. 168. b. Bro. Preſentment, 1. Dalt. Sheriff 395, 396. 3 Keb. 230. [m] See the Books above cited, and 10 H. 4. 4. a. 12 H. 7. 18. Mo. 607. Finch 246. Cro. Jac. 584, 551. Cont. 4 Inſt. 261. [n] Cro. Jac. 551.

Sect. 64. As to the ſixth general Point of this Chapter, *viz.* Within what Place Offences indictable in the Sheriff's Torn muſt ariſe, it ſeemeth that it is not material, Whether ſuch [h] Offences did ariſe within the Hundred in which the Torn is holden, or not; for though the Sheriff ought to hold his Torn in every particular Hundred, yet it ſeems, That in each of them he holds it for the whole County; and it is certain, That he hath a general Juriſdiction throughout the whole; yet it ſeems, That the Jurors ſhall not be charged on their [i] Oaths to preſent any Offences, but thoſe ariſing within their particular Hundreds: Alſo it is provided by the Statute of *Marlbridge*, *cap.* 10. That thoſe who have Tenements in different [k] Hundreds, ſhall not be compelled to come to any Torn, but only in the Bailiwick wherein they ſhall be converſant: Alſo it [l] ſeems clear, That no Offence ariſing within the Precincts of a Leet, is inquirable in the Torn, unleſs there hath been a Neglect to preſent it in the Leet: But after ſuch a Neglect it ſeems the better [m] Opinion, That it is inquirable in the Torn, leaſt otherwiſe there ſhould be a Failure of Juſtice: Yet it ſeems certain, That in pleading you [n] cannot juſtify the Proceedings of the Sheriff's Torn againſt any Offence ariſing within a Leet, without expreſly alledging that the Leet had neglected to inquire of it; for that ſuch a Neglect is not to be preſumed, where it doth not appear.

2 Inſt. 387. 2 H. H. P. C. 70, 152. *

Sect. 65. As to the ſeventh general Point of this Chapter, *viz.* By what Jurors, and in what Manner, Indictments in the Sheriff's Torn ought to be found, it is enacted by the Statute of *Weſtminſter*, 2. 13. *That the Sheriff ſhall take no Inqueſt either* ex Officio, *or by Virtue of the King's*

Writ, but by twelve lawful Men at the least, who shall put their Seals to such Inquisitions; and the same is also provided as to Bailiffs of Franchises.

Sect. 66. In the Construction of this Statute it hath been holden, That if there be more than twelve Jurors, and all agree to the Inquisition, all must set their Seals to it; but that it is sufficient, if twelve of them only agree, for those twelve to set their Seals. Dalt. Sheriff 389.

Sect. 67. And it is farther enacted by 1 *R.* 3. *cap.* 4. *That no Officer return or impanel any Person to be taken or put in any Inquiry in any Sheriff's Torn, but such as be of good Name and Fame, and having Freehold to the yearly Value of* 20 s. *or Copyhold to the yearly Value of* 26 s. 8 d. *on Pain of* 40 s. &c. *And that every such Indictment before any Sheriff in his Torn otherwise taken, shall be void.*

Sect. 68. And *Note*, That Courts-Leet seem to be within the Letter of the said Statute of *Westminster* 2. and are said by some to be within the Equity of the said Statute of 1 *R.* 3. but this seems questionable; for it is said, by some Books, That any Person happening to be present at a Court-Leet, or to be riding by the Place where it is holden, may for the want of Jurors be compelled by the Steward to be sworn, whether he be Resident within the Precincts of the Leet or not; by which it seems to be implied, That any Person whatsoever is capable of being put upon the Jury in a Court-Leet. 2 Inst. 388. S. P. C. 85. b. 7 H. 6. 13. a. 12 H. 7. 18. b. Bro. Leet, 14. 3 H. 7. 4. b.

Sect. 69. And to prevent the Altering or Imbezilling of any such Indictment, it is enacted by 1 *E.* 3. Stat. 2. Ch. 17. *That the Sheriffs and Bailiffs of Franchises, and all other that do take Indictments in their Torns or elsewhere, where Indictments ought to be made, shall take such Indictment by Roll indented, whereof the one Part shall remain with the Indictors, and the other Part with him that taketh the Inquest; so that the Indictments shall not be imbezilled as they have been in Times past; and so that one of the Inquests may shew the one Part of the Indenture to the Justices, when they come to make Deliverance.* 2 Inst. 388. S. P. C. 85. a.

Sect. 70. And there is no Doubt, but that this Statute extends as well to Courts-Leet, as to the Sheriff's Torn. 2 H. H. P. C. 71.

Sect. 71. Also there are many particular Customs and Usages in Relation to the Taking of Indictments in these Courts; but it seems to have been antiently the most general Course, to impanel not only a Grand Jury, but also a Jury of twelve Men, which was commonly called the Petit Jury; and that all Offences were first presented by the Headboroughs, and the Presentments affirmed by the Petit Jury, before they were brought to the Grand Jury: However it seems, That no Exception can be taken to any such Indictment, in Respect of the Non-observance of any such Custom or Usage; for that no Averment lies against the Acts of a Court of Record, and every Judge of such Court shall be presumed to act according to the Rules of it. Keilw. 141. a. 148. a. Dalt. Sheriff 388, 389. Crompt. 212. 213. Keilw. 66. b. 9 H. 6. 44. b.

Sect. 72. What is above said concerning Indictments taken before the Sheriff in his Torn, is to be intended of such only as are taken before him *ex Officio*; for that he is restrained to take any such Indictment, by Virtue of any Writ or Commission by 28 *E.* 3. 9. *Which reciting that the People had suffered many Mischiefs, for that Sheriffs of divers Counties, by Virtue of Commissions and general Writs granted to them at their own Suit, for their singular Profit to gain of the People, had made and taken divers Inquests, to cause to indict the People at their Will, and had taken Fine and Ransom of them to their own Use, and had delivered them; whereas such Persons indicted were not brought before the King's Justices to have Deliverance, doth thereupon enact, for to eschew all such Mischief, that all such Commissions and Writs before made, be utterly repealed, and that from thenceforth no such Commmissions nor Writs shall be granted.* 2 H. H. P. C 69.

F.N.B. 92. C. 144. I. 250. A. Cro. E. 371. Salk. 190.

Sect. 73. Yet it seemeth not to be clearly settled, Whether by Virtue of this Statute, all such Writs and Commissions, and the Proceedings thereon, be made wholly void or not.

2 Inst. 388. H. P. C. 103, 104, 173. S P. C. 77. F, G. 84. A. Dalt. Sheriff 388, 389. 3 Mod. 238. Book 1. Ch. 29. Sect. 20, 24.

Sect. 74. As to the eighth general Point of this Chapter, *viz.* In what Manner Indictments in the Sheriff's Torn are to be proceeded upon, it is recited by 1 *E.* 4. 2. *That many of the King's People by inordinate and infinite Indictments and Presentments of Felonies and other Offences, taken before Sheriffs at their Torns or Law-Days, (which were oftentimes affirmed by Jurors having no Conscience, nor any Freehold, and often by the Sheriff's menial Servants) had been arrested and imprisoned, and constrained to make grievous Fines and Ransoms, after which they had been enlarged out of Prison, and the said Indictments and Presentments imbezilled and withdrawn.* And thereupon it is enacted, *That all Indictments and Presentments before any of the King's Sheriffs in his Counties, except in* London, *their Under-Sheriffs, Clerks, Bailiffs or Ministers at their Torns or Law-Days, they nor any of them shall have Power to attach, arrest, or put in Prison, or to levy or take any Fine or Amerciament of any Person so indicted or presented, by Reason of any such Indictment or Presentment, but that the said Sheriffs and Under-Sheriffs, Clerks or Bailiffs, and their Ministers, shall deliver all such Indictments and Presentments to the Justices of Peace at their next County-Sessions, on Pain of* 40 l. *And that the said Justices of Peace shall have Power to award Process upon all such Indictments and Presentments as the Law doth require, and in like Form as if the said Indictments and Presentments were taken before the said Justices of Peace; and also to arraign and deliver all such Persons so indicted and presented before the said Sheriffs,* &c. *And such Persons which shall be indicted or presented of Trespass, shall make such a Fine as shall seem lawful by their Discretions. And the Estreats of the said Fines and Amerciaments shall be inrolled, and by Indenture be delivered to the said Sheriffs, Under-Sheriffs, their Clerks, Bailiffs, or Ministers, or some of them, to the Use and Profit of him that was Sheriff at the Time of such Indictments or Presentments taken. And if any of the said Sheriffs, their Under-Sheriffs, Clerks, Bailiffs, or their Ministers, do arrest, attach or put in Prison, or cause any Fine or Ransom to be taken, or levy any Amerciament, of any Person or Persons so indicted or presented, by Reason or Colour of any such Indictment or Presentment taken before them, at their Torns or Law-Days above rehearsed, before that they have Process from the said Justices of Peace, or Estreats delivered out, of the said Indictments or Presentments so brought, delivered, and presented to them, that then the Sheriffs which so do, shall forfeit an Hundred Pounds.*

2 H. H. P. C. 70, 71, 142. S. P. C. 87. D. 4 E. 4. 31. a. Fitz. Torn, 3.

Sect. 75. It is observable, That by the Words of this Statute, Justices of Peace may award Process on any such Indictments, in like Manner as if they had been taken before themselves; and yet it is clear, That if the Sheriff's Torn had no Authority to take the Indictment removed before such Justices, they have no Power to proceed upon it, as they might have done, if it had been taken before themselves; for the Statute in giving them such Power to proceed upon Indictments in the Sheriff's Torn, must be intended to mean such only as were there lawfully taken, not those which were void *ad initio*, as being taken *coram non Judice*; nor is there the least Intimation in the Statute, of an Intent to inlarge the Sheriff's Power in taking Indictments, but the whole Purport of it is to restrain him from proceeding on them. And to this Purpose it hath been so largely construed, That not only the Judge of the Court is punishable for awarding such Process, but also the Officer for obeying it.

1 Jon. 301. Cro. Ca. 275.

Sect. 76. As to the ninth general Point of this Chapter, *viz.* In what Manner Indictments in the Sheriff's Torn are to be traversed and determined; it seems to be [a] agreed, That a Presentment by [b] twelve or more in a Torn or Leet, of any Offence within the Jurisdiction of the Court, being neither Capital nor concerning any Freehold, subjects the Party to a Fine or Amerciament without any farther Proceeding, and binds him for ever after the Day on which it is found, and admits of no Traverse to the Truth of it; but [c] some say, That the Party may have a Writ of false Presentment against the Jurors, the same Day on which the Indictment is found; yet it seems agreed, That no Instance can be shewn of any such Writ being actually brought: But if the Presentment concern the Party's Life or [d] Freehold, as if it charge him with not repairing such a Highway, which he is charged to be bound to repair by the Tenure of his Land; it seems clear, That he may remove it into the King's Bench and traverse it; but not if it barely charge his Person, as for digging a Ditch in the Highway, or not cutting the Branches of his Trees hanging over it, *&c.* Also it [e] seems, That a Man may in like Manner traverse an Indictment of an Offence wholly out of the Jurisdiction of a Court-Leet; as of an Affray or Nusance done out of the Precinct of it, or of the Non-Appearance of a Person at a Leet, who lives out of the Precinct of it. But if the Affray or Nusance were within the Precinct of the Leet, it seems, That no one can traverse it in Respect of his own not living in it; and that a Person who lives within the Precinct of a Leet, shall have no Traverse to a Presentment for not appearing at it.

[a] Finch 386. Keilw. 52. a. 66. b. 3 Mod. 138. Dyer 13. pl. 45.

[b] Keil. 141. a. 45 E. 3. 26. b. 27. a.

[c] Fitz. Bar. 271. Keilw. 66. b. 41 Ed. 3. 28.

[d] 5 H. 7. 4. a. Br. Trav. 183. Keilw. 52, 66, 67. Dy. 13. pl. 64.

[e] Keilw. 66, 67. 41 E. 3. 27.

Sect. 77. But it seems certain, That at this Day, neither the Torn nor Leet, have any Power to try any Traverse whatsoever, as hath been more fully shewn, *Sect.* 13. But it is certain, that the Justices of Peace may by Force of the abovementioned Statute of 1 *E.* 4. try a Man indicted of Felony before the Sheriff in his Torn: Also it seems, That they may try a Person upon any other Indictment in the Torn, which is traversable at Common Law, but that they have no Power to take any Traverse of any other Indictment in the Torn; for that the Words of the Statute are only *That they may award Process on any such Indictments, as if they had been taken before themselves, and also arraign and deliver the Persons indicted,* which must be intended of those indicted of Felony, who only are said to be arraigned, *And that Persons indicted of Trespass, shall make Fines,* &c. *by their Discretion,* without saying, That they shall be tried; by which it seems to be implied, That Persons so indicted shall be fined, as they usually were before in the Torn, and still are in the Leet, and that in some Cases without any farther Trial, as is more fully shewn in the precedent Section.

CHAP.

CHAP. XI.

Of the Court-Leet.

Finch 246. *Sect.* 1. A Court-Leet is a Court of Record, having the ſame Juriſdiction within ſome particular Precinct, which the Sheriff's Torn hath in the County: And therefore ſince it hath been ſhewn in the pre-
[a] Sect. 45, &c. cedent Chapter, at what [a] Time and in what Place the Sheriff's Torn is to
[b] Sect. 10, &c. be holden, and what Perſons owe Suit to it, and what [b] Authority the
[c] Sect. 13, &c. Judge of it hath in Relation to his Proceeding on [c] Indictments, and alſo
[d] Sect. 17, &c. in Relation to [d] Fines and Amerciaments, and the [e] Appointment of Con-
[e] Sect. 33, &c. [f] Sect. 51, &c. ſtables; and having alſo ſhewn what [f] Kind of Offences are inquirable in
[g] Sect. 64, &c. this Court, and within what [g] Place ſuch Offences muſt ariſe, and by what
[h] Sect. 65, &c. [h] Jurors and in what Manner, Indictments in it are to be found, and in
[i] Sect. 74, &c. what Manner they are to be [i] proceeded upon, traverſed and determined; and ſince the Court-Leet hath regularly the very ſame Juriſdiction with the Sheriff's Torn as to all theſe Points, except in ſome ſpecial Caſes, which have been already taken Notice of in the Chapter concerning the Sheriff's
2 Inſt. 71, 72. Torn; I ſhall refer the Reader to the ſaid Chapter for all theſe Particulars,
22 Ed. 4. 22. and ſhall only conſider in this Place,

1. The End of inſtituting the Court-Leet.
2. How far it exempts thoſe who live within its Precincts from the Torn.
3. How far it is ſubject to the Overſight of the Torn.
4. For what Cauſes it may be forfeited.
5. What ought to be the Form of a Caption of an Indictment in it.

12 H. 7. 18. *Sect.* 2. As to the firſt Point it ſeems, That anciently all People who
2 Inſt. 71, 72. now owe Suit to any Court-Leet were bound to come to the Sheriff's Torn, in order there to take the Oath of Allegiance to the King, and
1 Jon. 283. to be incorporated into ſome Tithing, and for ſuch other Purpoſes as are
6 Co. 77. b. ſet forth more at large in the precedent Chapter, *Sect.* 2. But it being more for the Eaſe of the People, to have Courts of this Kind holden in their own Townſhips or Manors; by Degrees, Grants of ſuch Courts were obtained from the King for moſt Manors and Towns, not only by
Dyer 30. pl. 209. the Lords of Manors, but alſo by other Perſons, who had no Lands in the Places for which they obtained ſuch Grants: And for a Recompence to ſuch Grantees, for the Charge and Trouble they were ſuppoſed to have been at in procuring ſuch Grants, it was uſual for the Inhabitants, who had the Benefit of them, to agree to pay a certain Sum of Money, called
13 H. 4. 9. Capitage, or *certum Letæ*, *&c.* at every ſuch Court-Leet; and for the Non-
11 Co. 42. payment of this Duty or Refuſal to preſent it, ſuch Grantees may preſcribe
1 Rol. Rep. 32, 73. to amerce the Defaulters, and to deſtrain for the Amercement; but no ſuch
1 Rol. Abr. 211. A. C. Preſcription ſhall be allowed for any other Matter whatſoever of a private Nature.

Sect. 3. As to the ſecond Point, *viz.* How far a Court-Leet exempts thoſe who live within the Precincts of it from the Torn, it ſeems to be a general [a] Rule, That no Man can be within two Leets at the ſame Time, and in the ſame Reſpect; from whence it follows, That he who reſides within the Precincts of a Leet, the Lord whereof doth duly hold his Court, cannot be compelled to come to the Torn, or any other ſuperior Leet, for the Taking the Oath of Allegiance, or any other ſuch like Purpoſe, which may be as well anſwered by his Attendance at his own Leet: Yet if ſuch private Leet have not the general Juriſdiction of the Torn, but be [b] ſpecially granted for two or three Articles of it only; it ſeems, That the Inhabitants within its Precinct muſt attend the Sheriff's Torn for all ſuch Matters of which ſuch private Leet hath no Juriſdiction: Alſo it [c] ſeems to be a good Preſcription for a Grand Leet, (to which other inferior Leets may be ſubordinate in the ſame Manner as that is to the Torn,) to oblige the Chief Pledges, and a certain Number of the Inhabitants of every Town within its Precinct, to appear at every ſuch Grand Leet, to inquire of ſuch Offences as have not been inquired of in the inferior Leets.

Sect. 4. As to the third Point, *viz.* How far the Court-Leet is ſubject to the Overſight of the Torn; it is ſaid, That the Sheriff's Torn as an [d] Overſeer of this Court, is to inquire whether the Tithings be whole or no, and to preſent Defaults that are not redreſſed in the Leet; and it ſeems alſo, That it may of common Right inquire of the Concealment of Offences inquirable in Leets, and of the Defaults of the Lords of ſuch Courts: However it [e] ſeems clear, That a Preſcription to this Purpoſe is good. And there is no Doubt, but that if a Leet be [f] ſeiſed into the King's Hands, all thoſe who owed Suit to it ought to come to the Torn.

Sect. 5. As to the fourth Point, *viz.* For what Cauſes a Court-Leet may be forfeited, it ſeems, That this being a Franchiſe not intended to be granted for the private Benefit of the Grantee, but for the Good of the Publick, from the more eaſy and convenient Adminiſtration of Juſtice, ſhall not only be forfeited by Acts of groſs and palpable Oppreſſion and Injuſtice, [g] but alſo by bare Omiſſions, in not making it anſwer the End of its Inſtitution; as in the not [h] puniſhing Offenders in the ſame Manner as the Law requires, or in [i] neglecting to hold a Court when it ought to be holden, (at leaſt if ſuch Neglects be often repeated, and without a reaſonable Excuſe,) or in not [k] providing an able Steward to diſcharge the Office, or in not taking Care to have ſuch other Officers, or other Things as are neceſſary for the Execution of Juſtice, as Conſtables and Ale-Taſters, *&c.* and [l] Pillory and Tumbrel; but it is [m] ſaid, That a Vill may be bound by Preſcription to provide a Pillory and Tumbrel, and [n] that every Vill is bound of common Right to provide a Pair of Stocks. *Quære.*

Sect. 6. As to the fifth Point, *viz.* What ought to be the Form of the Caption of an Indictment in a Court-Leet, it hath been [o] reſolved, 1. That the Caption of an Indictment, *ad Cur, Viſ. Franc. Pleg. cum Cur. Baron. &c.* is good; for that the Words *cum Cur. Baron.* ſhall be rejected; and it cannot but be intended that the Indictment was taken by that Court, which alone hath the Colour of Authority to take it.

Sect. 7. 2. [p] That the not Setting forth in the Caption, whether ſuch Court be holden by Grant or Preſcription, is helped by the Multitude of Precedents.

[a] Dalt. Sheriff 402, 403. 1 Jon. 283. 6 Co. 77. b. 18 H. 6. 13. Fitz. Leet, 1. Cro. Jac. 584. See Ch. 10. Sect. 12. Con. Kitch. 34. 1 Rol. Abr. 542. b.

[b] Keilw. 141. a. 142. a. 2 Rol. Abr. 203. pl. 7.

[c] Cro. Jac. 583. Raym. 204. Cro. Car. 75, 76. See Ch. 10. Sect. 12, 64.

[d] Finch 246. See Ch. 10. Sect. 64. Dalt. Sheriff 387, 391.

[e] Cro. Jac. 584.

[f] 2 Rol. Abr. 203. pl. 7. Finch 246.

[g] Co. Lit. 233. a. Kitch. 33. Cro. Jac. 155. 9 Co. 50. 2 Rol. Abr. 155. O. 11 Ed. 4. 1. 2 H. 7. 11. b.

[h] 1 Jon. 383. Keilw. 148. b. 152. a.

[i] Kitch. 33.

[k] 1 Jon. 283.

[l] Fitz. Leet, 12. Cro. Eliz. 125, 698. Mo. 573, 574, 607. 1 Jon. 283.

[m] Cro. Eliz. 698. Mo. 607.

[n] Kitch. 13 a. Carter 29. Con. Moor 573, 574. 1 Jon. 283.

[o] Vide ſupr. ch. 10. Sect. 9. Salk. 195.

[p] Salk. 200. pl. 2

CHAP. XII.

Of Arreſts by private Perſons.

HAVING thus endeavoured to ſhew the Nature of the Courts which have Juriſdiction over criminal Offences. I am now to ſhew in what Manner Offenders are to be proceeded againſt by ſuch Courts; and in Order hereto I ſhall conſider,

1. How they are to be apprehended.
2. In what Manner and in what Caſes they are to be bailed.
3. In what Caſes and in what Manner they are to be committed to Priſon.
4. How far they and their Aſſiſtants are puniſhable for an Hindrance in bringing them to publick Juſtice.

As to the firſt of theſe Points I ſhall conſider,

1. In what Manner ſuch Offenders are to be apprehended by private Perſons.
2. In what Manner by publick Officers.
3. In what Caſes it is lawful to break open Doors in Order to apprehend them.

As to Arreſts of ſuch Offenders by private Perſons, I ſhall examine,

1. Where Arreſts of this Kind are commanded and injoined by Law.
2. Where they are permitted by Law.
3. Where they are rewarded.

Sect. 1. As to the firſt Point it ſeems clear, That [a] all Perſons whatſoever who are preſent when a Felony is committed, or a dangerous Wound given, are bound to apprehend the Offender, on Pain of being fined and impriſoned for their Neglect, [b] unleſs they were under Age at the Time.

Sect. 2. And for this [c] Cauſe, by the Common Law if any Homicide be committed, or dangerous Wound given, whether with or without Malice, or even by [d] Miſadventure or Self-Defence, in any Town or in the [e] Lanes or Fields thereof, in the Day-time, and the Offender eſcape, the Town ſhall be amerced, and if out of a Town, the [f] Hundred ſhall be amerced.

Sect. 3. And ſince the Statute of *Wincheſter*, *cap.* 5. which ordains that [g] walled Towns ſhall be kept ſhut from Sun-ſetting to Sun-riſing, if the Fact happen in any ſuch Town by Night or by Day, and the Offender eſcape, the Town ſhall be amerced.

[a] 3 Inſt. 53, 139, 152. H. P. C. 89, 90. 1 H. H. P. C. 448, 449. 3 H. 7. cap. 1. 2 Inſt. 52. Fitz. Coron. 293.

[b] Fitz. Coron. 395. 2 H. H. P. C. 75, 76.

[c] H. P. C. 89, 90. 2 H. H. P. C. 73, 75, 76. 3 H. 7. cap. 1. 3 Inſt. 53. 4 Inſt. 183. Cro. Car. 252. 3 Leon. 207. Fitz. Coron. 238, 293, 299, 352, 425. Cont. 1 Leon. 107.

[d] 2 Inſt. 315. Fitz. Coron. 302.

[e] Dyer 210. pl. 25.

[f] S. P. C. 34. E. P.

[g] S.P.C. 34. a. 3 Inſt. 53. 7 Co. 6. b. 7. a.

Sect. 4. And as all [a] private Perſons are bound to apprehend all thoſe, who ſhall be guilty of any of the Crimes above mentioned in their View; ſo alſo are they with the utmoſt Diligence to purſue, and endeavour to take all thoſe who ſhall be guilty thereof out of their View, upon a Hue and Cry levied againſt them.

Sect. 5. [b] Hue and Cry is the Purſuit of an Offender from Town to Town till he be taken, which all who are preſent when a Felony is committed, or a dangerous Wound given, are by the Common Law as well as by Statute, bound to raiſe againſt the Offenders who eſcape, on Pain of Fine and Impriſonment: Alſo it [c] ſeems certain, That a Man may lawfully raiſe it againſt one who ſets upon him in the Highway to rob him: Alſo it is enacted by the Statute of [d] *Wincheſter*, *cap.* 4. That Hue and Cry ſhall be levied upon any Stranger who ſhall not obey the Arreſt of the Watch in the Night-Time; and [e] 21 *E.* 1. which was made againſt Treſpaſſers in Foreſts, Chaſes, Parks and Warrens, ſeems to allow the Levying thereof upon any ſuch Offenders. But if a Man take upon him to [f] levy a Hue and Cry without ſufficient Cauſe, he ſhall be puniſhed as a Diſturber of the Peace.

Sect. 6. In Order rightly to raiſe a Hue and Cry, you ought to go to the Conſtable of the next Town, and declare the Fact, and [g] deſcribe the Offender, and the Way he is gone; whereupon the Conſtable ought immediately, whether it be Night or Day, to raiſe his own Town, and make a Search for the Offender: And upon the not Finding him, to ſend the like Notice, with the utmoſt Expedition, by Horſemen as well as Footmen, to the Conſtables of all the neighbouring Towns who ought in like Manner to ſearch for the Offender, and alſo to give Notice to their Neighbouring Conſtables, and they to the next, till the Offender be found. [16]

Sect. 7. Alſo every [h] private Perſon is bound to aſſiſt an Officer demanding his Help for the Taking of a Felon, or the Suppreſſing an Affray, or Apprehending the Affrayers, *&c.*

[a] H. P. C. 90. 1 H. H. P. C. 448, 449, 484, 593. 2 H. H. P. C. 75, 76. 3 Inſt. 117. 2 Inſt. 172.
[b] 3 Inſt. 116, 117. 1 H. H. P. C. 588. 2 H. H. P. C. 99, 102. Dalt. Juſtice, ch. 28. 109. 2 Inſt. 172. Fitz. Coron. 395. Cro. El. 654. Crompt. 178, 179.
[c] 9 E. 4 26. b.
[d] 13 Ed. 1.
[e] Keble's Statutes, fol. 59.
[f] 29 E. 3. 39. Fitz. Treſp. 252. Crompt. 179. 2 H. H. P. C. 100, 101. 21 H. 7. 28. a.
[g] 3 Inſt. 116. Dalt. Juſtice, cap. 28. 109. H. P. C. 91. Cromp. 178, 179.
[h] B. 1. Ch. 63. Sect. 13.

Arreſts of Offenders by private Perſons permitted by Law, are either,

1. By their own Authority: Or,
2. By a Warrant from a Juſtice of Peace.

Arreſt of this Kind by their own Authority, are either,

1. In Reſpect of Treaſon or Felony: Or,
2. In Reſpect of inferior Offences.

Arreſts of this Kind in Reſpect of Treaſon or Felony, are either,

1. For the Suſpicion of ſuch Crimes already done, or ſuppoſed to have been done: Or,
2. To prevent their being done.

As to ſuch Arreſts for ſuch Suſpicion, I ſhall endeavour to ſhew,

1. What are ſufficient Cauſes of Suſpicion.
2. By whom the Perſon arreſted muſt be ſuſpected.
3. Whether any ſuch Cauſe will juſtify an Arreſt, where no Treaſon or Felony at all hath been committed, *&c.*
4. In what Manner an Arreſt for ſuch Suſpicion is to be juſtified in Pleading.

Sect. 8.

Sect. 8. As to the firſt Particular, *viz.* What are ſufficient Cauſes of Suſpicion, I ſhall take Notice of ſome of the Principal of them, which are generally agreed to juſtify the Arreſt of an innocent Perſon for Felony, as,

Sect. 9. I. The common [a] Fame of the Country, But it [b] ſeems, That it ought to appear upon Evidence, in an Action brought for ſuch an Arreſt, that ſuch Fame had ſome probable Ground.

Sect. 10. II. The [c] living a vagrant, idle and diſorderly Life, without having any viſible Means to ſupport it.

Sect. 11. III. The being in [d] Company with one known to be an Offender, at the Time of the Offence; or [e] generally at other Times keeping Company with Perſons of ſcandalous Reputations.

Sect. 12. IV. The being found in ſuch Circumſtances as induce a ſtrong Preſumption of Guilt; as [f] coming out of a Houſe wherein Murder has been committed, with a bloody Knife in one's Hand; or being found in [g] Poſſeſſion of any Part of Goods ſtolen, without being able to give a probable Account of coming honeſtly by them.

Sect. 13. V. The Behaving one's ſelf in ſuch Manner as betrays a Conſciouſneſs of Guilt; as [h] where a Man being charged with a Treaſon or Felony, ſays nothing to it, but ſeems tacitly by his Silence to own himſelf guilty; or where a Man accuſed of any ſuch Crime, upon hearing that a Warrant is taken out againſt him, doth abſcond.

Sect. 14. VI. The being [i] purſued by an Hue and Cry.

Sect. 15. As to the ſecond Particular, *viz.* By whom the Perſon muſt be ſuſpected, upon ſuch an Arreſt for Suſpicion; it ſeems to be [k] agreed, That the Law hath ſo tender a Regard to the Liberty and Reputation of every Perſon, That no Cauſes of Suſpicion whatſoever, let the Number and Probability of them be ever ſo great, will juſtify the Arreſt of an innocent Man, by one who is not himſelf induced by them to ſuſpect him to be guilty, whether he make ſuch Arreſt of his own Head, or in Obedience to the Commands of a private Perſon, or even of a [l] Conſtable.

Sect. 16. As to the third Particular, *viz.* Whether any ſuch Cauſe of Suſpicion will juſtify an Arreſt where no Treaſon or Felony at all hath been committed, or dangerous Wound given: It is holden in ſome [m] Books, That none of the above mentioned Cauſes will in any Caſe juſtify the Arreſting a Man for the Suſpicion of a Crime, where in Truth no ſuch Crime hath been committed either by him or any other Perſon whatſoever. But howſoever this Rule may in general be true, it ſeems very hardly maintainable in the Caſe of an Arreſt of an innocent Perſon upon a Hue and Cry levied againſt him, in ſuch a Place where his Character is unknown, and with ſuch other Circumſtances, that the People of the County have no Reaſon to preſume it groundleſs; for in ſuch Caſes, it would be a great Inconvenience to diſcourage Perſons from following a Hue and Cry, with that Vigour and Diligence, which the Law expects, and the Publick Good requires, by making them liable to an Action if it ſhould in the Event prove to have been levied without ſufficient Cauſe, which they cannot take Time to examine without delaying their Purſuit: And ſince the Perſon injur'd by ſuch an ill-grounded Hue and Cry, has a good Action againſt him that raiſed it, there ſeems to be no Neceſſity, that he ſhould alſo have a Remedy againſt another. And this Opinion ſeems to be the more plauſible, for that among the [n] Books [o] cited to maintain the contrary, [p] that which alone doth directly affirm it, ſeems to go upon an Argument manifeſtly inconcluſive; for it ſays, That an Hue and Cry is not a ſufficient Authority to arreſt a Man unleſs a Felony be done, becauſe the Words of the

[a] 2 H. 7. 15. b. 16. 1 H. H. P. C. 588. 2 H. H. P. C. 81.
[b] 5 H. 7. 4. b. 5. a. 11 E. 4. 4. b. Dy. 236. p. 26. Bridg. 62.
[c] 7 E. 4. 20. a. H. P. C. 91. Keilw. 81. Pult. 13. a.
[b] 2 Inſt. 52. Crom. 98, 99. S. P. C. 97. Bracton 143.
[c] 7 E. 4. 20. a. 17 E. 4. 5. b. H. P. C. 91. Pult. 13. b.
[d] 7 E. 4. 20. a. Keilw. 71. Pult. 13. a. H. P. C. 91.
[e] 2 Inſt. 52. Crompt. 98.
[f] 11 E. 4. 4. b. 12 Co. 92.
[g] 7 E. 4. 20. a. Cro. E. 901. Cro. Jac. 190, 191. Pult. 136. H. P. C. 91. 12 Co. 92. Moor 600. pl. 828.
[h] Crom. 98, 99. Fitz. Cor. 24.
[i] 29 El. 871. 29 E. 3. 39. Fitz. Treſp. 252. 5 H. 7. 5. a. 21 H. 7. 28. a. H. P. C. 91.
[k] 10 H. 7. 17. b. 2 H. H. P. C. 79. 2 H. 7. 15. b. 16. a. 5 H. 7. 4. b. 5. a. 7 Ed. 4. 20. a. 20 E. 4. 6. b. 11 E. 4. 4. b. Cro. El. 871. H. P. C. 93. 12 Co. 92.
[l] 10 H. 7. 17. b. 2 H. 7. 15. b. 16. a. 17 E. 4. 5. a. b.
[m] 2 Inſt. 173. Cro. Jac. 194. 2 H. H. P. C. 78. H. P. C. 91. 2 H. 7. 3. a. 27 H. 8. 23. a. 8 E. 4. 3. b. 3 Inſt. 118. b. Fitz. Treſp. 252. 29 E. 3. 39. 2 Rol. Abr. 559. D.
[n] 29 E. 3. 39. 11 E. 4. 4. b. 2 H. 7. 15.
[o] 2 Inſt. 173.
[p] 5 H. 7. 5. a.

the Statute of *Weſtminſter* 1. *cap.* 9. are, That all Men ſhall be ready upon Hue and Cry to arreſt Felons; but where no Felony is done, there can be no Felon, *&c.* to which it may be replied, That this Argument, if it prove any Thing, proves that none but Felons can be arreſted on a Hue and Cry, which ſeems to be manifeſtly falſe; for it is agreed by all the Books, That if a Felony be actually committed, an innocent Perſon on whom a Hue and Cry for it is levied, may lawfully be arreſted: Alſo there ſeems to be no Doubt, but that he who barely attempts to rob a Man, or who dangerouſly wounds him, may ſafely be purſued and taken by a Hue and Cry, and yet there is no Pretence to call ſuch a Perſon a Felon. [17]

Vide ſupra Sect. 4, 5.

Sect. 17. And if it be granted lawful to arreſt a Man on an Hue and Cry where no Felony hath been committed; from the like Grounds it ſeems alſo to follow, That it is lawful to arreſt a Man on the Warrant of a Juſtice of Peace, where no Felony hath been committed; but this Point ſhall be more fully conſidered in the next Chapter.

Sect. 18. As to the fourth Particular, *viz.* In what Manner an Arreſt for ſuch Suſpicion is to be juſtified in Pleading; it ſeems to be certain, That whoever would juſtify the Arreſt of an innocent Perſon, by Reaſon of any ſuch Suſpicion, muſt not only ſhew that he ſuſpected the Party [a] himſelf, but muſt alſo ſet forth the [b] Cauſe which induced him to have ſuch a Suſpicion, that it may appear to the Court to have been a ſufficient Ground for his Proceeding; Alſo it ſeems [c] certain, That regularly he ought expreſly to ſhew, that the very ſame Crime for which he made the Arreſt, was actually committed. But [d] if a Man have ſeveral Cauſes of ſuch Suſpicion, he is not bound to inſiſt upon ſome one of them only, but may alledge them all; for that the Replication *De ſon tort Demeſne*, anſwers the whole. As [e] where a Man arreſts another, who is actually guilty of the Crime for which he is arreſted, it ſeems, That he needs not in juſtifying it, ſet forth any ſpecial Cauſe of his Suſpicion, but may ſay in general, that the Party feloniouſly did ſuch a Fact, for which he arreſted him, *&c.*

[a] Vide ſupra Sect. 15.
[b] 2 Inſt. 52. Finch 340. 17 E. 4. 5. a. b. 1 E. 4. 20. a. Bridgm. 62. 2 H. H. P. C. 78. 7 H. 4. 35.
[c] 8 E. 4. 3. b. 27 H. 8. 23. a. Cro. Jac. 194. Finch 340.
[d] 7 E. 4. 20. a. 2 H. H. P. C. 81. 17 E. 4. 5. a. b. Bridgm. 62. Finch 394. 4 H. 7. 1. b. 2. a.
[e] 10 E. 4. 17. b. Fitz. Faux Impriſonm. 5.

Sect. 19. As to the arreſting of Offenders by private Perſons of their own Authority, permitted by Law for the Prevention of Treaſon or Felony only intended to be done; it [f] ſeems, that any one may lawfully lay hold on another, whom he ſhall ſee upon the Point of committing a Treaſon or Felony, or doing any Act which would manifeſtly endanger the Life of another, and may detain him ſo long till it may reaſonably be preſumed, that he hath changed his Purpoſe; and upon this Ground it [g] ſeemeth to be the better Opinion, That not only a Conſtable, but any private Perſon, who ſhall ſee another expoſe an Infant in the Street, and refuſe to take it away, may lawfully apprehend and detain him, till he ſhall conſent to take Care of it.

[f] 9 E. 4. 26. b. See B. 1. Ch. 60. Sect. 23.
[g] Popham 12, 13. Owen 98. Moore 284. 2 H. H. P. C. 88.

Sect. 20. As to the Arreſt of Offenders by private Perſons of their own Authority, permitted by Law, for inferior Offences; it [h] ſeems clear, That regularly no private Perſon can of his own Authority arreſt another for a bare Breach of the Peace after it is over; for if an Officer cannot juſtify ſuch an Arreſt, without a Warrant from a Magiſtrate, ſurely *à fortiori* a private Perſon cannot: Yet it is holden by [i] ſome, that any private Perſon may lawfully arreſt a ſuſpicious Night-walker, [18] and detain him till he make it appear, that he is a Perſon of good Reputation. Alſo it hath been [k] adjudged, That any one may lawfully apprehend a common notorious Cheat, going about the Country with falſe Dice, and being actually caught playing with them, in order to have him before a Juſtice of Peace; for the publick Good requires the utmoſt Diſcouragement

[h] See B. 1. Ch. 63. Sect. 13, 14, 17.
[i] Latch 173. 4 H. 7. 18. b. Poph. 208. Quære 4 H. 7. 1. b. 2. a. 5 H. 7. 5. a. 2 Inſt. 52.
[k] 1 Jon. 249. Cro. Ca. 234. 2 Rol. Abr. 546. C. 2.

of all such Persons, and the Restraining of private Persons from arresting them without a Warrant from a Magistrate, would often give them an Opportunity of escaping: And from the Reason of this Case it seems to follow, That the Arrest of any other Offenders by private Persons, for Offences in like Manner scandalous and prejudicial to the Publick, may be justified.

Cromp. 147. 14 H. 8. 16. a. *Sect.* 21. As to Arrests of such Offenders by private Persons, having a Warrant from a Justice of Peace permitted by Law, there is no Doubt but that where the Law authorizes Justices of Peace to direct their Warrants to such Persons, it doth implicitely authorize the Execution of them by them.

As to the third general Point of this Chapter, *viz.* In what Cases the Arrests of Offenders by private Persons are rewarded by Law, I shall give a short Account of the Statutes concerning this Matter, in Relation,

1. To Robbers in Highways.
2. To Counterfeiters and Clippers of the Coin.
3. To Shoplifters and other Offenders of like Nature.
4. To Burglars and felonious Breakers of Houses.

Sect. 22. And first as to Robbers in Highways it is enacted by 4 & 5 *W. & M.* 8. *That whoever shall apprehend and take one or more Thief or Robber in any Highway or Road in* England *or* Wales, *and prosecute him or them till he or they be convicted of any Robbery, committed in or upon any Highway, Passage, Field or open Place, shall receive from the Sheriff of the County where such Robbery and Conviction shall be, without paying any Fee for the same, for every such Offender so convicted* 40 l. *within one Month after such Conviction and Demand thereof made, by tendring a Certificate to the said Sheriff under the Hand or Hands of the Judge or Justices before whom such Felon or Felons shall be convicted; and in Case any Dispute shall arise, between the Persons so apprehending any the said Thieves and Robbers touching their Right to the said Reward, That then the said Judge or Justices so respectively certifying, shall by their said Certificate direct and appoint the said Reward to be paid in such Shares and Proportions as to them shall seem just and reasonable. And if any such Sheriff shall die or be removed before the Expiration of one Month after such Conviction and Demand made, That then the next Sheriff shall pay the same within one Month after Demand and Certificate brought as aforesaid: And the Sheriff making Default in paying the said Sum, shall forfeit double as much.*

Sect. 23. And it is farther enacted, *That if any Person shall be killed by any such Robber in endeavouring to apprehend, or making Pursuit after him, the Executors or Administrators,* &c. *of such Person, shall receive* 40 l. *from the Sheriff,* &c. *upon Certificate delivered under the Hands and Seals of the Judge or Justices of Assize for the County where the Fact was done, or the two next Justices of the Peace, of such Person being so killed, which Certificate the said Judge or Justices, upon sufficient Proof before them made, are immediately required to give without Fee or Reward.*

Sect. 24. And it is farther enacted, *That every Person who shall so take, apprehend, prosecute, or convict such Robber as aforesaid, shall have as a farther Reward, the Horse, Furniture and Arms, Money and other Goods of such Robber, that shall be taken with him; any their Majesties Right or Title, Bodies Politick or Corporate, or the Right or Title thereunto of the Lord of any Manor or Franchise, or of him or them lending or letting the same to Hire to any such Robber notwithstanding: Provided that this shall not be extended to take away the Right of any Person to such Horses, Furniture and Arms, Money or other Goods, from whom the same were before feloniously taken.*

Sect. 25. Secondly as to Counterfeiters and Clippers of the Coin, it is enacted by 6 & 7 *Gul.* 3. 17. *That whoever shall apprehend any Person who shall counterfeit any of the current Coin of this Realm, or for Lucre clip, wash, file, or otherwise diminish the same, or shall cause to be brought into the Kingdom any clipt, false, or counterfeit Coin, and prosecute such Person to Conviction, shall have from the Sheriff of the County where such Conviction shall be, forty Pounds upon the Judge's Certificate,* &c.

Sect. 26. Thirdly, As to Shoplifters, &c. it is enacted by 10 & 11 *W.* 3. 23. *That whosoever shall take and prosecute to Conviction, any Person who by Night or Day shall in any Shop, Warehouse, Coach-house or Stable, privately and feloniously steal any Goods, Wares, or Merchandizes, of the Value of* 5 *s.* (*though such Shop,* &c. *were not broken, and though no Person were in such Shop,* &c.) *or shall assist, hire, or command any Person to commit such Offence, shall have a Certificate thereof* Gratis *from the Judge or Justices, expressing the Parish or Place where such Felony was committed; and if any Dispute shall happen about the Right to such Certificate, the Judge or Justices shall direct and appoint the said Certificate into so many Shares, to be divided among the Persons therein concerned, as to the said Judge,* &c. *shall seem reasonable, which Certificate (before any Benefit has been made of it) may be once assigned over, and no more, and the original Proprietor or Assignee shall by Virtue thereof, be discharged from all Parish and Ward Offices, within the Parish or Ward wherein the Felony was committed; and the said Certificate shall be enrolled by the Clerk of the Peace of the County, for the Fee of one Shilling: And in Case any Person happen to be slain by any such Felons by endeavouring to apprehend them, his Executors,* &c. *shall have the like Reward,* &c.

Sect. 27. Fourthly, As to Burglars and felonious Breakers of Houses, it is enacted by 5 *Annæ,* 31. *That every Person who shall take any one guilty of Burglary, or the felonious breaking and entring any House in the Day-time, and prosecute them to Conviction, shall receive above the Reward given by the abovementioned Statute of* 10 & 11 W. 3. *the Sum of* 40 l. *within one Month after such Conviction*; concerning which the same Rules in Effect are prescribed, as are provided by the abovementioned Statute of 4 & 5 *W.* & *M.* 8. concerning the Reward of 40 *l.* to be paid to those who shall apprehend a Highwayman. [19] [20]

CHAP. XIII.

Of Arrests by publick Officers.

ARRESTS of Offenders by publick Officers, are either by Virtue of Process from some Court of Record, or without such Process.

Arrests of this Kind by Virtue of such Process, shall be considered hereafter in their proper Place.

Arrests by publick Officers without such Process, are either

1. By Watchmen.
2. By Constables.
3. By Bailiffs of Towns, or
4. By Justices of Peace.

Sect. 1.

Sect. 1. But before I consider the Nature of each of these in particular, I shall take it for granted, That where-ever any such Arrest may be justified by a private Person, in every such Case *a fortiori* it may be justified by any such Officer. As to Arrests by Watchmen, I shall first premise in what Manner Watch is to be kept in every Town, and then shall shew the Power of the Watchmen.

Sect. 2. And first as to the keeping Watch in every Town, it is enacted by the Statute of *Winchester*, Ch. 4. *That from thenceforth all Towns be kept as it had been used in Times passed, That is to wit, from the Day of* Ascension *unto the Day of St.* Michael, *in every City six Men shall keep at every Gate, in every Borough twelve Men, in every Town six or four, according to the Number of Inhabitants of the Town, and shall watch the Town continually all Night, from the Sun-setting to the Sun-rising.*

Sect. 3. And it is farther enacted by 5 *H*. 4. 3. *That the Watch to be made upon the Sea-Coasts through the Realm, shall be made by the Number of the People in the Places, and in Manner and Form, as they were wont to be made in Times past, and that in the same Case the Statute of* Winchester *be observed and kept; and that in the Commissions of the Peace this Article be put in, That the Justices of Peace have Power thereof to make Inquiry in their Sessions from Time to Time, and to punish them which be found in Default after the Tenor of the said Statute.*

Sect. 4. It hath been resolved, That a Stranger who is not an Inhabitant of a Town, [a] cannot be compelled by Virtue of the said Statute of *Winchester* to keep Watch in it; but it seems to be agreed, That every Inhabitant is bound to keep it in his Turn, or to [b] find another sufficient Person to keep it for him; from whence it follows, That he is indictable for a Refusal: But it is [c] not agreed, That he may be committed by the Constable till he consent to do his Duty.

[a] Cro. El. 204.
[b] Vide Co. Lit. 70. a.
[c] Cro. El. 204.

2 H. H. P. C. 96.

Sect. 5. As to the Power of Watchmen, it is farther enacted by the said Statute of *Winchester*, Ch. 4. *That if any Stranger do pass by the Watch, he shall be arrested until Morning. And if no Suspicion be found, he shall go quit; and if they find Cause of Suspicion, they shall forthwith deliver him to the Sheriff, and the Sheriff may receive him without Damage, and shall keep him safely until he be acquitted in due Manner. And if they will not obey the Arrest, they shall levy Hue and Cry upon them, and such as keep the Town shall follow with Hue and Cry with all the Town and the Towns near, and so Hue and Cry shall be made from Town to Town, until that they be taken, and delivered to the Sheriff as before is said: And for the Arrestments of such Strangers none shall be punished.*

Poph. 208. Latch 173.

Sect. 6. It is holden, That this Statute was made in Affirmance of the Common Law, and that every private Person may by the Common Law arrest any suspicious Night-walker, and detain him till he give a good Account of himself, as hath been more fully shewn in the precedent Chapter, Section 20.

Secondly, As to such Arrests by Constables, I shall endeavour to shew,

1. How far they may be justified by their own Authority.
2. How far by Virtue of a Warrant from a Justice of Peace.

Sect. 7. And first, as to the Justifying of such Arrests by the Constable's own Authority; it seems difficult to find any Case, wherein a Constable is impowered to arrest a Man for a Felony committed or attempted, in which a private Person might not as well be justified in doing it: But the chief Difference between the Power and Duty of a Conſtable and a private Perſon, in Reſpect of ſuch Arreſts, ſeems to be this, That the [a] former has the greater Authority to demand the Aſſiſtance of others, and is liable to the ſeverer Fine for any Neglect of this Kind, and has no ſure Way to diſcharge himſelf of the Arreſt of any Perſon apprehended by him for Felony, [b] without bringing him before a Juſtice of Peace in order to be examined, as ſhall be more fully ſhewn in the 16th Chapter; whereas a private Perſon having made ſuch an Arreſt, needs only to deliver his Priſoner into the Hands of the Conſtable.

[a] 3 Inſt. 158. Lamb. Conſtable, 12. 17 E. 4. 5. a. b. 3 H. 7. 1. a. 2 H. 7. 15. b.
[b] H. P. C. 91, 112. 10 E. 4. 17. b. 2 H. H. P. C. 81.

Sect. 8. But it is ſaid, That a Conſtable hath Authority not only to arreſt thoſe whom he ſhall ſee actually engaged in an Affray, but alſo to detain them till they find Sureties of the Peace, as hath been more fully ſhewn in the [c] firſt Book; whereas a private Perſon ſeems to have no other Power in a bare Affray, not attended with the Danger of Life, but only to ſtay the [d] Affrayers till the Heat be over, and then deliver them to the Conſtable, and alſo to ſtop thoſe whom he ſhall ſee coming to join either Party: But it is difficult to find any Inſtance wherein a Conſtable hath any greater Power than a private Perſon over a Breach of the Peace out of his View; and it ſeems clear, That he cannot juſtify an Arreſt for any ſuch Offence, without a Warrant from a Juſtice of Peace, *&c.*

[c] Ch. 63. Sect. 14, 17.
[d] B. 1. ch. 63. ſect. 11, 12.

Sect. 9. As to the Juſtifying ſuch Arreſts by Conſtables, by Virtue of a Warrant from a Juſtice of Peace, it ſeems [e] clear, That ſuch an Arreſt unlawfully made by a Conſtable without a Warrant, cannot be made good by a Warrant taken out afterwards; alſo it hath been [f] holden, That if a Conſtable, after he hath arreſted the Party by Force of any ſuch Warrant, ſuffer him to go at large, upon his Promiſe to come again at ſuch a Time and find Sureties, he cannot afterwards arreſt him by Force of the ſame Warrant: However, if the Party return and put himſelf again under the Cuſtody of the Conſtable, it ſeems, that it may be probably argued, That the Conſtable may lawfully detain him, and bring him before the Juſtice in Purſuance of the Warrant; for if a Perſon taken by Virtue of a civil Proceſs, and voluntarily ſuffered by the Sheriff to eſcape, may afterwards upon his Return to the Priſon be kept by the Sheriff by Virtue of the ſame Proceſs, unleſs the Plaintiff rather chuſe to take Advantage of the Eſcape againſt the Sheriff; ſurely *a fortiori* upon an Arreſt for a Crime, in which Caſe it is to be preſumed, That the Publick Good requires that the Party be brought to Juſtice, it ſhall likewiſe be lawful to detain a Perſon returning to the Officer after ſuch an Eſcape: However as the Law ſeems [g] not to be ſettled in Relation to ſuch an Eſcape after an Arreſt by Virtue of civil Proceſs; ſo neither doth it ſeem to be clear in Relation to an Eſcape after an Arreſt by Force of ſuch a Warrant from a Juſtice of Peace.

[e] Dy. 244. pl. 61. Fitz. Bar. 248. Crompt. 149. a. 2 Keb. 705. Dalt. cap. 117. fol. 338.
[f] Crom. 148. 2 Keb. 206. Dalt. ch. 117. 13 E. 4. 9. a.
[g] See 1 Danv. Abr. 633. pl. 4. 635. pl. 11. Hob. 202. 1 Lev. 21. Cro. Ca. 75. 2 Keb. 206.

Sect. 10. But it ſeems clear, That a Conſtable cannot juſtify any Arreſt by [h] Force of a Warrant from a Juſtice of Peace, which expreſly appears in the Face of it, to be for an Offence whereof a Juſtice of Peace hath no Juriſdiction, or to bring the [i] Party before him at a Place out of the County for which he is a Juſtice. But it ſeems, That he both may and ought to execute a general Warrant to bring a Perſon before a Juſtice of Peace, to anſwer ſuch Matters as ſhall be objected againſt him on the Part of the King; for that the Officer ought to preſume, That the Juſtice hath a Juriſdiction of the Matter, which he takes [k] Conuſance of, unleſs the contrary appear; and it may often endanger the Eſcape of the Party to make

[h] 14 H. 8. 16. Crompt. 147, 148.
[i] Crompt. 149. b.
[k] Dalt. ch. 117. 1 H. H. P. C. 577. 2 H. H. P. C. 111.

Dalt. ch. 117. Crompt. 147, 148. 1 H. H. P. C. 577. 2 H. H. P. C. 114, 150. Cro. Jac. 81. H. P. C. 93. 3 Inſt. 177. Yet ſee a Precedent of this Kind, Dalt. 114.

make known the Crime he is accuſed of. But it ſeems to be very queſtionable, Whether a Conſtable can juſtify the Execution of a general Warrant to ſearch for Felons or ſtolen Goods; becauſe ſuch Warrant ſeems to be illegal in the very Face of it; for that it would be extremely hard to leave it to the Diſcretion of a common Officer to arreſt what Perſons, and ſearch what Houſes he thinks fit: And if a Juſtice cannot legally grant a blank Warrant for the Arreſt of a ſingle Perſon, leaving it to the Party to fill it up, ſurely he cannot grant ſuch a general Warrant, which might have the Effect of an Hundred blank Warrants.

Dalt. ch. 117. Crompt. 147, 148. Dalt. Juſtice, cap. 118. 14 H. 8. 16. See ch. 12. ſect. 15. Cont. 4 Inſt. 177. H. P. C. 93, 94.

Sect. 11. Yet perhaps it is the better Opinion at this Day, That any Conſtable, or even private Perſon, to whom a Warrant ſhall be directed from a Juſtice of Peace to arreſt a particular Perſon for Felony, or any other Miſdemeanor within his Juriſdiction, may lawfully execute it, whether the Perſon mentioned in it be in Truth guilty or innocent, and whether he were before indicted of the ſame Offence or not, and whether any Felony were in Truth committed or not; for however the Juſtice himſelf may be puniſhable for granting ſuch a Warrant without ſufficient Grounds, it is reaſonable that he alone be anſwerable for it, and not the Officer, who is not to examine or diſpute the Reaſonableneſs of his Proceeding; and therefore it ſeems that the old Books, (cited in the foregoing Chapter, Sect. 15, 16.) which ſay generally, That no one can juſtify an Arreſt upon a Suſpicion of Felony, unleſs he himſelf ſuſpect the Party, and unleſs the Felony were in Truth committed, ought to be intended only of Arreſts made by a Perſon of his own Head, or in Obedience to the Command of a Conſtable, or other ſuch like miniſterial Officer, and not of ſuch as are made in Purſuance of the Warrant of a

Dalt. ch. 118, 121. 6 Mod. 179. Cro. E. 130. 1 Leon. 187.

[a] 4 Inſt. 177. 14 H. 8. 16. [b] 6 Mod. 179. [c] 14 H. 8. 16. Bro. Faux Impriſonment, 33. [d] 2 H. 7. 3. pl. 9, 15. pl. 1. 4 H. 7. 2. a. 5 H. 7. 4, 5. 10 H. 7. 17. 20 H. 7. 12. 7 E. 4. 20. 8 E. 4. 3. b. 9 E. 4. 26. b. 10 E. 4. 17. b. 11 E. 4. 4. b. 13 E. 4. 9. a. 17 E. 4. 5. 7 E. 4. 35. Dyer 236. [e] 10 H. 7. 17. [f] 2 H 4 ch. 15.

Juſtice of Peace; for inaſmuch as it ſeems to have been the conſtant and allowed Practice of late, to make out Warrants on the Suſpicion of Felony, before any Indictment hath been found againſt the Perſon ſuſpected; and the ſame ſeems to be countenanced by 1 & 2 *Ph.* & *Mar.* 13. and 2 & 3 *Ph.* & *Mar.* 10. which direct in what Manner Perſons brought before Juſtices of Peace upon Suſpicion, ſhall be examined in Order to their being committed or bailed; and ſince the ancient [a] Opinion, That a Juſtice of Peace cannot make out a Warrant againſt a Man for Felony, who has not been indicted before, hath been [b] contradicted by conſtant Experience; and ſince in the very ſame [c] Report in which this Rule is laid down, That a Juſtice of Peace cannot make a Warrant againſt a Perſon who has not been indicted; it ſeems nevertheleſs to be agreed, That ſuch a Warrant is a good Juſtification for the Officer; and ſince none of the [d] Books cited by Sir *Edward Coke* to maintain the contrary Opinion, mention the Caſe of an Arreſt by Force of a Warrant from a Juſtice of Peace, but generally relate only to Arreſts by private Perſons of their own Authority, or by the Command of a Conſtable; and ſince too, the [e] Caſe, which is fulleſt to the Purpoſe, wherein it is reſolved, That an Arreſt of a Perſon by the Command of a Biſhop for ſaying, That he was not bound to pay Tithes, could not be juſtified by Force of the [f] Statute, which authorized Biſhops to arreſt Perſons for Hereſy, for which this Reaſon is given among others, That the Biſhop himſelf could not juſtify ſuch an Arreſt, and conſequently could not authorize another to make it; it may be anſwered, That the Reſolution in that Caſe doth not wholly depend upon this Reaſon, but rather perhaps upon theſe, that the Biſhop's Command was by Parol only, and not by Writing, and that the Statute gave him no Juriſdiction over Points not Heretical; and that the Power of Impriſoning

4 Perſons

Persons for mere Matters of Opinion ought to be strictly construed: And farther, since the Person injured by an Arrest on a Justice's Warrant, hath a good Action against the Justice who granted it, if he did it maliciously of his own Head, in Order to oppress or defame the Party without any probable Ground of Suspicion, and therefore there is no Necessity of giving a farther Remedy against the Officer who obeys the Warrant: And farther, since it is in general a great Discouragement to Officers, to subject them to Actions for endeavouring to serve the Publick, by paying Obedience to the Precepts of those whose Officers they are; it would certainly be very difficult at this Day to maintain an Action against them for any Arrest of this Kind, unless the Warrant appear to be for a Matter whereof the Justice has no Jurisdiction. It seems indeed to be holden in *Broucher*'s Case in *Croke*'s second Report, That where an Officer arrests a Man by Force of a Warrant from a Magistrate, *pro certis Causis*, without shewing any Cause in particular, he cannot justify himself in an Action brought against him for such Arrest, without setting forth the particular Cause in his Plea; and yet in this very Report it seems to be allowed, That such a general Warrant is good; and if so, it seems strange, That the Officer should not be justified by setting forth the Truth of his Case; since if there were no good Cause to justify the Granting of the Warrant, the Magistrate ought to answer for it, not the Officer. [21]

Cro. El. 130. 1 Leon. 187.

Cro. Jac. 81.

Sect. 12. Thirdly, As to such Arrests by Bailiffs of Towns, it is enacted by the abovementioned Statute of *Winchester*, Ch. 4. *That in great Towns being walled, The Gates shall be closed from the Sun setting until the Sun rising, and that no Man do lodge in the Suburbs, nor in any Place out of the Town, from nine of the Clock until Day, without his Host will answer for him: And the Bailiffs of Towns every Week, or at the least every fifteenth Day, shall make Inquiry of all Persons being lodged in the Suburbs, or in foreign Places of the Towns; and if they do find any that have lodged or received any Strangers or suspicious Persons against the Peace, the Bailiffs shall do Right therein.* And surely it cannot be doubted, but that by Force hereof such Bailiffs may lawfully arrest and detain any such Stranger, being found under probable Circumstances of Suspicion, till he shall give a good Account of himself.

Sect. 13. Fourthly as to such Arrests by Justices of Peace, I shall first take it for granted, That where-ever an Arrest of this Kind by a private Person, or inferior Officer acting of their own Authority, is either permitted or enjoined by the Law, in every such Case, *a fortiori*, such an Arrest by a Justice of Peace in Person, is also permitted or enjoined.

H. P. C. 93.

Arrests by the Command of Justices of Peace, as such, are either,

1. By Parol.
2. By Warrant.

Sect. 14. And first, As to such Arrests by Parol, it seems, That any such Justice may lawfully, by Word of Mouth, authorize any one to arrest another, who shall be guilty of any actual Breach of the Peace in his Presence, or shall be engaged in a Riot in his Absence, as hath been more fully shewn in the first Book, Ch. 65. Sect. 16. [22].

Dalt. c. 117.

As to ſuch Arreſts by the Warrant of a Juſtice of Peace, I ſhall endeavour to ſhew,

1. In what Caſes a Warrant for ſuch an Arreſt may lawfully be made by ſuch a Juſtice.
2. In what Form it ought to be made.
3. How it is to be executed.

As to the firſt Point, I ſhall conſider,

1. For what Offences ſuch a Warrant may be granted.
2. Upon what Evidence.

Sect. 15. And firſt, as to the Offences for which ſuch a Warrant may be granted, there ſeems to be no Doubt, but that it may be lawfully granted by any Juſtice of Peace for Treaſon, Felony or *Præmunire*, or Supra ch. 8. ſect. 33, 34. any other Offence againſt the Peace, as hath been more fully ſhewn in the Chapter concerning *Juſtices of Peace*: Alſo it ſeems clear, That whereever a Statute gives to any one Juſtice of Peace a Juriſdiction over any Dalt. ch. 117. 12 Co. 130, 131. Offence, or a Power to require any Perſon to do a certain Thing ordained by ſuch Statute, it impliedly gives a Power to every ſuch Juſtice to make out a Warrant to bring before him any Perſon accuſed of ſuch Offence, or compellable to do the Thing ordained by ſuch Statute; for it cannot but be intended, that a Statute giving a Perſon Juriſdiction over an Offence, doth mean alſo to give him the Power incident to all Courts, of compelling the Party to come before him. And it would be to little Purpoſe to authorize a Man to require another to do a Thing, if it were to be underſtood that the Perſon authorized had no Power to compel the Party to come before him.

Sect. 16. But it ſeems, That anciently no one Juſtice of Peace could Dalt. ch. 117. Bro. Peace, 6. legally make out a Warrant for an Offence againſt a penal Statute, or other Miſdemeanor, cognizable only by a Seſſions of two or more Juſtices; for that one ſingle Juſtice of Peace hath no Juriſdiction of ſuch Offence, and regularly thoſe only who have Juriſdiction over a Cauſe can award 6 Mod. 179. Proceſs concerning it. Yet the long, conſtant, univerſal and uncontrolled Practice of Juſtices of Peace ſeems to have altered the Law in this Particular, and to have given them an Authority in Relation to ſuch Arreſts, not now to be diſputed.

H. P. C. 93. 4 Inſt. 177.b. *Sect.* 17. But I do not find any good Authority, That a Juſtice can juſtify Sending a general Warrant to ſearch all ſuſpected Houſes in general for ſtollen Goods, as hath been more fully ſhewn, *Sect.* 10. [23] ☜

Sect. 18. Secondly, As to the Evidence on which ſuch a Warrant is to be granted, it ſeems probable, That the Practice of Juſtices of Peace 2 H. H. P. C. 108, 109. 6 Mod. 179. Quære Dalt. 117. Con. 14 H. 8. 16. in Relation to this Matter alſo, is now become a Law, and that any Juſtice of Peace may juſtify the Granting of a Warrant for the Arreſt of any Perſon upon ſtrong Grounds of Suſpicion for a Felony or other Miſdemeanor, before any Indictment hath been found againſt him. Yet inaſmuch as Juſtices of Peace claim this Power rather by Connivance, than any expreſs Warrant of Law, and ſince the undue Execution of it may prove ſo highly prejudicial to the Reputation as well as the Liberty of the Party, a Juſtice of Peace cannot well be too tender in his Proceedings of this Kind, and ſeems to be puniſhable not only at the Suit of the King, but alſo of the Party grieved; if he grant any ſuch Warrant groundlesly and maliciously, without such a probable Cause, as might induce a candid and impartial Man to suspect the Party to be guilty.

Cro. El. 130. 1 Leon. 187.

Sect. 19. And since both *Coke* and *Hale* seem to disapprove of such Warrants granted upon Suspicion, and the old Books seem generally to disallow all Arrests for the Suspicion of Felony made by any other Person whatsoever, except the very Person who hath the Suspicion; it is certainly a safe Way of Proceeding for him, who hath the Suspicion to make the Arrest in his proper Person, and to get a Warrant from a Justice of Peace to the Constable to keep the Peace. [24]

4 Inst. 177. H. P. C. 93. Supr. sect. 10. ch. 12. sect. 15.

Sect. 20. And perhaps there may be this Difference between the Warrant of a Justice of Peace, for such Causes which he has not Authority to hear and determine as Judge without the Concurrence of others, and such Warrant for an Offence which he may so determine, without the Concurrence of any other: That in the former Case, inasmuch as he rather proceeds ministerially than judicially, if he act corruptly, he is liable to an Action at the Suit of the Party, as well as to an Information at the Suit of the King: But in the latter Case he is punishable only at the Suit of the King, for that regularly no Man is liable to an Action for what he doth as Judge.

Cro. El. 130. 1 Leon. 187. 1 Danv. Abr. 179. pl. 1, 2, 6. Carth. 492.

As to the second Point, *viz.* In what Form such a Warrant is to be made; I shall lay down the following Rules:

Sect. 21. I. That [a] it ought to be under the Hand and Seal of the Justice who makes it out.

Sect. 22. II. That it [b] ought to set forth the Year and Day wherein it is made, That in an Action brought upon an Arrest made by Virtue of it, it may appear to have been prior to such Arrest.

Sect. 23. III. That it is [c] safe, but perhaps not necessary, in the Body of the Warrant to shew the Place where it was made; yet it seems necessary to set forth the County in the Margin, at least if it be not set forth in the Body.

Sect. 24. IV. That it may be made either in the Name of the King, or of the Justice himself, as appears from the Precedents above referred to.

Sect. 25. V. [d] That if it be for the Peace or Good Behaviour, it is advisable to set forth the special Cause upon which it is granted; but if it be for Treason or Felony, or other Offence of an enormous Nature, it is said, That it is not necessary to set it forth; and it seems to be rather discretionary, than necessary to set it forth in any Case.

Sect. 26. VI. [e] That such a Warrant may be either general, to bring the Party before any Justice of Peace of the County, or special, to bring him before the Justice only who granted it.

Sect. 27. VII. [f] That it may be directed to the Sheriff, Bailiff, Constable, or to any indifferent Person by Name, who is no Officer; for that the Justice may authorize any one to be his Officer, whom he pleases to make such, yet it is most advisable to direct it to the Constable of the Precinct wherein it is to be executed; [g] for that no other Constable, and *a fortiori* no private Person, is compellable to serve it.

[a] 1 H. H. P. C. 577. 2 H. H. P. C. 111. Dalt. cap. 117. 3 Inst. 76. 14 H. 8. 16.
[b] Dalt. cap. 117. See the Precedents in Dalt. cap. 121.
[c] Dalt. cap. 117, 221. Lamb. 85, 86. Crompt. 147, 232, &c.
[d] Dalt. c. 117. Supra sect. 10. 2 H. H. P. C. 111.
[e] Dalt. cap. 117. 1 Rol. Rep. 375. 5 Co. 59. b. Bro. Peace, 9.
[f] Dalt. cap. 117. Cromp. 147. 14 H. 8. 16. Bro. Peace, 6. Salk. 176.
[g] Salk. 176. 1 H. H. P. C. 582. 2 H. H. P. C. 110.

As to the third Point, *viz.* In what Manner such Warrant is to be executed, I shall lay down the following Rules,

Sect. 28. I. That a Bailiff, or a Constable, if they be sworn and commonly known to be Officers, and act within their own Precincts,

8 E. 4. 14. a. 14 H. 7. 9. b. 6 Co. 54. 9 Co. 69. 1 H. H. P.C. 583. 2 H. H. P. C. 116.

need not ſhew their Warrant to the Party; notwithſtanding he demand the Sight of it; but that theſe and all other Perſons whatſoever making an Arreſt, ought to acquaint the Party with the Subſtance of their Warrants, and that all private Perſons to whom ſuch Warrants ſhall be directed, and even Officers, if they be not ſworn and commonly known, and even theſe, if they act out of their own Precincts muſt ſhew their Warrants, if demanded.

Dalt. cap. 117. 8 E. 4. 14. a.

Sect. 29. II. That the Sheriff having ſuch Warrant directed to him, may authorize others to execute it; but that every other Perſon to whom it is directed, muſt perſonally execute it; yet it ſeems, That any one may lawfully aſſiſt him.

Carth. 508. Salk. 176.

Sect. 30. III. That if a Warrant be generally directed to all Conſtables, no one can execute it out of his own Precinct; but if it be directed to a particular Conſtable by Name, he may execute it any where within the Juriſdiction of the Juſtice.

C H A P. XIV.

Where Doors may be broken open in Order to make an Arreſt.

Sect. 1. AND now I am to conſider in what Caſes it is lawful to break open Doors, in Order to apprehend Offenders; and to this Purpoſe I ſhall premiſe, That the Law doth never allow of ſuch [a] Extremities but in Caſes of Neceſſity; and therefore, That no one can juſtify the Breaking open another's Doors to make an Arreſt, unleſs he firſt ſignify to thoſe in the Houſe the Cauſe of his Coming and requeſt them to give him Admittance.

[a] 27 Aſſ. 35. 4 Inſt. 177. 5 Co. 91, 92. Dalt. cap. 78. 2 H. H. P.C. 103, 116, 117. H. P. C. 90. Fitz. Execution, 25 2.

Sect. 2. But where a Perſon authorized to arreſt another who is ſheltered in a Houſe, is denied quietly to enter into it, in Order to take him; it ſeems generally to be agreed, That he may juſtify Breaking open the Doors in the following Inſtances.

[b] 27 Aſſ. 35. 12 Co. 131. 4 Inſt. 131. [c] Moor 606, 668. [d] Dalt. cap. 78. Crom. 170. b.

Sect. 3. I. Upon a [b] *Capias* grounded on an Indictment for any Crime whatſoever, or upon a [c] *Capias* from the [d] King's Bench or Chancery, to compel a Man to find Sureties for the Peace or Good Behaviour, or even upon a Warrant from a Juſtice of Peace for ſuch Purpoſe.

[e] Moor 606, 668.

Sect. 4. II. Upon a [e] *Capias utlagatum*, or *Capias pro fine*, in any Action whatſoever.

Cro. El. 908. Yelv. 28. Dalt. cap. 78. [f] 2 Jones 233, 234.

Sect. 5. III. Upon the [f] Warrant of a Juſtice of Peace, for the Levying of a Forfeiture in Execution of a Judgment or Conviction for it grounded on any Statute which gives the Whole, or but Part of ſuch Forfeiture to the King, and authorizes the Juſtice of Peace to give ſuch Judgment or Conviction for it.

[g] Dalt. cap. 22 and 78.

Sect. 6. IV. Where a [g] forcible Entry or Detainer is either found by Inquiſition before Juſtices of Peace, or appears upon their View.

[h] H.P.C. 90, 93. [i] H.H. P. C. 588, 589. Dalt. cap. 78. 13 E. 4. 9. a. 13 E. 3. 7. b.

Sect. 7. V. [h] Where one known to have committed a Treaſon or Felony, or to [i] have given another a dangerous Wound, is purſued either with or without a Warrant, by a Conſtable or private Perſon: But where one lies under a probable Suſpicion only, and is not indicted, it ſeems the

4 better

better [a] Opinion at this Day, That no one can justify the Breaking open Doors in Order to apprehend him. [25]

[a H. P. C. 91. 4 Inst. 117. Con. 13 E. 4. 9. a. Bro. Coron. 159. Dalt. cap. 78. Fitz. Bar. 110.]

Sect. 8. VI. Where an [b] Affray is made in an House in the View or Hearing of a Constable; or where those who have made an Affray in his Presence fly to a House, and are immediately pursued by him, and he is not suffered to enter; in Order to suppress the Affray in the first Case, or to apprehend the Affrayers in either Case.

[b H. P. C. 134, 135. 2 H. H. P. C. 95. Crom. 170. b. Dalt. cap. 78. Bro. Faux Imprisonment, 6.]

Sect. 9. VII. Where-ever a [c] Person is lawfully arrested for any Cause and afterwards escapes, and shelters him in a House.

[c 6 Mod. 173, 174, 211. Skin. 8. Salk. 79.]

Sect. 10. Also it is enacted by 3 & 4 *Jac.* 1. Par. 35. *That upon any lawful Writ, Warrant or Process awarded to any Sheriff or other Officer, for the Taking of any Popish Recusant, standing excommunicated for such Recusancy, it shall be lawful, if need be, to break open any House.*

Sect. 11. But it hath been resolved, That where Justices of Peace are, by Virtue of a Statute, authorized to require Persons to come before them, to take certain Oaths prescribed by such Statute, the Officer cannot lawfully break open the Doors of the Persons who shall be named in any Warrant made in Pursuance of such Statute, in Order to be brought before the Justices to take such Oath, because such Warrant is not grounded on a precedent Offence; neither doth it appear, That the Party either is or will be guilty of any: But it seems clear, That if an Officer enter into any House to serve any such Warrant, and the Doors of the House be locked upon him, being in such House, he or his Friends may justify Breaking them open, in Order to regain his Liberty; for that even in the Execution of civil Process, the Law allows of the Breaking open Doors in the like Circumstances.

[Palm. 52, 53. Cro. Jac. 555.]

CHAP. XV.

Of Bail.

Sect. 1. AND now I am to consider in what Manner, and in what Cases Offenders are to be bailed; as to which it is to be observed, That where-ever a Person is brought before a Justice of Peace upon an Accusation of Treason or Felony, he must be either bailed or committed, unless it manifestly appear that no such Crime was committed, or that the Cause for which alone the Party was suspected, was totally groundless; in which Cases only it is lawful to discharge him without Bail.

[H. P. C. 98. Crompt. 154. 2 H. H. P. C. 120, 121.]

For the better Understanding of the Nature of Bail, I shall consider the following Points:

1. The Nature of Bail and Mainprize in general.
2. What shall be said to be sufficient Bail.
3. The Offence of taking insufficient Bail.
4. The Offence of granting it where it ought to be denied.

5. The

5. The Offence of denying, delaying or obſtructing it, where it ought to be granted.
6. In what Caſes it is grantable.
7. In what Form it is to be taken.
8. What ſhall forfeit the Recognizance.

And firſt, as to the Nature of Bail and Mainpriſe in general, I ſhall endeavour to ſhew,

1. In what Reſpects they agree.
2. In what they differ.

Sect. 2. As to the firſt Particular it ſeems, That the Words Bail and Mainpriſe, are often uſed promiſcuouſly in our [a] Law-Books and [b] Acts of Parliament, as ſignifying one and the ſame Thing; and it is [c] certain That Bail and Mainpriſe agree in this Notion, that they ſave a Man from Impriſonment in the common Gaol, by his Friends undertaking for him before certain Perſons for that Purpoſe authorized, that he ſhall appear at a certain Day, and anſwer the Crime with which he is charged, and be juſtified by Law.

Sect. 3. As to the ſecond Particular, The chief, if not the [d] only, Difference between Bail and Mainpriſe ſeems to be this, That a Man's Mainpernors are [e] barely his Sureties, and cannot juſtify the Detaining or Impriſoning of him themſelves, in Order to ſecure his Appearance: But that a Man's Bail are looked upon as his [f] Gaolers of his own chooſing and that the [g] Perſon bailed is in the Eye of the Law for many Purpoſes, eſteemed to be as much in the Priſon of the Court by which he is bailed, as if he were in the actual Cuſtody of the proper Gaoler. But I do not find this Point clearly ſettled in Relation to any other Court beſides the King's Bench, as hath been more fully ſhewn *Ch.* 6. *Sect.* 4. However it ſeems certain in every Bailment, That if the Party bailed be [h] ſuſpected by his Bail as likely to deceive them, he may be detained by them, and enforced to appear according to the Condition of the Recognizance, or may be [i] brought by them before the Juſtice of Peace, by whom he ſhall be committed, unleſs he find new Sureties.

Sect. 4. As to the ſecond Point, *viz.* What ſhall be ſaid to be ſufficient Bail, it ſeems to be [k] agreed, That no Perſon ought in any Caſe to be bailed for Felony by leſs than two; and it is [l] ſaid to be the Practice of the King's Bench, not to admit any Perſon to Bail upon a *Habeas Corpus* on a Commitment for Treaſon or Felony without four Sureties: Alſo [m] it ſeems to have been anciently an eſtabliſhed Rule, That none under the Degree of Subſidy-men, ſhould be admitted to bail any Perſon for a capital Crime: But the Manner of granting Taxes by Way of Subſidy having been of late for many Years diſuſed, this Rule at preſent ſeems to be of little Uſe: But the only ſure Way of proceeding in this Caſe, is to take Care that every one of the Bail be of Ability ſufficient to anſwer the Sum in which they are bound, which [n] ought never to be leſs than forty Pounds for a capital Crime, but may be as much higher as the Juſtices in Diſcretion ſhall think fit to require, upon Conſideration of the Ability and Quality of the Priſoner, and the Nature of the Offence: And if it ſhall ſeem doubtful, whether the Perſons who offer themſelves to be Sureties, be able to anſwer ſuch Sum; it is [o] ſaid, That the Perſon who is to take the Bail, may examine them on their Oaths concerning their Sufficiency: And if a Perſon who has Power to take Bail be ſo far im-

[a] 2 H.H.P.C. 124. Dalt. cap. 114. Lamb. 340. 4 Inſt. 180.
[b] 1 Ric. 3. 3. 3 H. 7. 3. 1 & 2 Ph. & Mar. 13.
[c] H. P. C. 96. Dalt. cap. 114.
[d] 4 Inſt. 179, 180.
[e] Fitz. Mainpriſe, 12, 13. Bro. Mainpriſe, 89. Coke, Bail & Mainpriſe, Ch. 3. and the Books cited under Letters f. g. h. Cont. 4 H. 6. 8 pl. 21. 32 H. 6. 4. pl. 3.
[f] 1 H.H.P.C. 325. 2 H. H. P. C. 85, 124, 125. H. P. C. 98. Fitz. Mainpriſe, 12, 13.
[g] S.P.C. 64. D. 21 H. 7. 33. pl. 26. 22 H. 6. 59. pl. 13. 39 H. 6. 27. pl. 39. 32 H. 6. 4. pl. 3. Supra ch. 6. ſect. 4.
[h] Fitz. Mainpriſe, 12, 13. Dalt. cap. 114. Brook Mainpriſe, 99. 2 H. H. P. C. 127.
[i] H.P.C. 96. Dalt. cap. 114.
[k] 2 H.H.P.C. 125. H. P. C. 97. Dalt. cap. 114. See 10 Co. 101.
[l] Stile's Practical Regiſter 110.
[m] Dalt. cap. 70 & 114. H. P. C. 97.
[n] Dalt. cap. 114. H. P. C. 97.
[o] Dalt. cap. 114. Cromp. 194. 2 H. H. P. C. 125.

posed upon as to suffer a Prisoner to be bailed by insufficient Persons, it is said, That either he, or any other Person who hath Power to bail him, may require the Party to find better Sureties, and to enter into a new Recognizance with them, and may commit him on his Refusal, for that insufficient Sureties are as no Sureties. H. P. C. 96. Dalt. cap. 70, & 114.

Sect. 5. But Justices must take Care, That under Pretence of demanding sufficient Surety, they do not make so excessive a Demand, as in effect amounts to a Denial of Bail; for this is looked on as a great Grievance, and is complained of as such by 1 *W. & M. Seff.* 2. by which it is declared, *That Excessive Bail ought not to be required.*

Sect. 6. As to the third Point, *viz.* the Offence of taking insufficient Bail, it seems clear; That where-ever a Sheriff, in Pursuance of the Statute of *Westminster*, *cap.* 15. Or Justices of Peace in Pursuance of the subsequent Statutes, grounded on the said Statute of *Westminster* 1. and set forth more at large in the following Part of this Chapter, shall admit any Person to bail for Felony, with insufficient Sureties, who shall not afterwards appear according to the Condition of the Recognizance, the Justices of Assise may, by Force of 27 *Ed.* 1. *chap.* 3. commonly called the Statute *de finibus levatis*, impose such Fine on such Sheriff or Justices of Peace, as to such Justices of Assise in their Discretion shall seem proper. But if a Prisoner, who is bailed by insufficient Sureties, do appear according to the Condition of the Recognizance, it seems that those who admitted him to bail are safe, inasmuch as the End of the Law is answered, and the Appearance of the Prisoner as effectually procured by such Sureties, as if they had been never so sufficient. Vide Supra, cap. 6. Sect. 10, 11, &c. Dalt. cap. 114. H. P. C. 97.

Sect. 7. As to the fourth Point, *viz.* The Offence of granting Bail where it ought to be denied: There is no Doubt but that the Bailing of a Person who is not bailable by Law, is punishable either at Common Law, as a negligent Escape, as shall be more fully shewn in the Chapter concerning Escapes, or as an Offence against the several Statutes concerning Bail. S. P. C. 33. F. 77. A. 25 E. 3. 39. Pl. 22. Fitz. Escape, 4. Coron. 246. H. P. C. 97, 113.

Sect. 8. And first it is enacted by the Statute of *Westminster* 1. 15. *That if the Sheriff, or any other, let any go at large by Surety, that is not replevisable, if he be Sheriff, or Constable, or any other Bailiff of Fee, which hath keeping of Prisons, and be thereof attainted, he shall lose his Fee and Office for ever. And if the Under-Sheriff, Constable, or Bailiff of such as have Fee for keeping of Prisons, do it contrary to the Will of his Lord, or any other Bailiff being not of Fee, they shall have three Years Imprisonment, and make Fine at the King's Pleasure.* 1 H. H. P. C. 596, 597.

Sect. 9. Also it is enacted by 27 *Ed.* 1. commonly called the Statute *de finibus levatis, cap.* 3. *That the Justices assigned to take Assises,* &c. *when they deliver the Goods,* &c. *shall inquire if Sheriffs, or any other, have let out by Replevin Prisons not replevisable, or have offended in any Thing contrary to the Form of the said Statute of* Westminster 1. *and whom they shall find Guilty they shall chasten and punish in all Things, according to the Form of the said Statute.* Vide supra, Chap. 6. Sect. 11, 12, &c.

Sect. 10. And it is farther enacted by 4 *Ed.* 3. 2. *That at the Time of the Assignment of Keepers of the Peace, Mention shall be made, That such as shall be indicted, or taken by them, shall not be let to Mainprise by the Sheriffs, nor by none other Ministers, if they be not mainpernable by Law; nor that none who are indicted shall be delivered but by the Common Law. And that the Justices assigned to deliver the Gaols, shall have Power to inquire of Sheriffs, Gaolers, and others, in whose Ward such Persons indicted shall be, if they make Deli-* Vide supra, Cap. 6. Sect. 13, 14.

verance, or let to Mainprise, any so indicted, which be not mainpernable; and to punish the said Sheriffs, Gaolers, and others, if they do any Thing against the said Act.

Sect. 11. And it is enacted by 1 & 2 *Ph. & Mar.* 13. *That no Justice or Justices of Peace, shall let to Bail or Mainprise any Person or Persons, which for any Offence or Offences, by them, or any of them committed, be declared not to be replevised or bailed, or be forbidden to be replevised or bailed, by the abovementioned Statute of* Westminster *the* first, cap. 15. *And that the Justices of Gaol-Delivery of the Place where such Justices of the Peace shall be guilty of such Offence, upon due Proof thereof, by Examination before them, shall for every such Offence set such Fine on every such Justice, as the same Justices of Gaol-Delivery shall think meet,* &c.

Sect. 12. It hath been resolved, That it is no Excuse for Justices of Peace admitting a Person to Bail, who was in Truth committed for a Cause not bailable by Law, that they did not know that he was commit-
Poph. 96. ted for such Cause; and that no other Cause of his Commitment was men-
Dalt.cap.114. tioned in his *Mittimus* but the Suspicion of Felony; for that they ought, at their Peril, to have informed themselves of the Cause for which the Party was committed, that they might be satisfied that he was bailable by Law.

Sect. 13. As to the fifth Point, *viz.* The Offence of denying, delaying, or obstructing Bail, where it ought to be granted; this seems to be a
Vide 14 H. 7. 7. Pl. 19. H. P. C. 97. Dalt.cap.114. Misdemeanor, not only by the Statute, but also by the Common Law, and punishable thereby as an Offence against the Liberty of the Subject, not only by Action at the Suit of the Party wrongfully imprisoned, but also by Indictment at the Suit of the King.

H. P. C. 97. Dalt.cap.114. 14 H. 7. 10.a. Bro. Peace, 7. Mainprise, 39. *Sect.* 14. But it seems clear, That he who has Power to bail another is not bound to demand of him to find Sureties, and to forbear committing him 'till he shall refuse to find them; but may well justify his Commitment, unless the Party himself shall offer his Sureties.

Sect. 15. The principal Statutes relating to this Offence, are the abovementioned Statute of *Westminster*, 1. 15. and the Statute *de finibus*, *cap.* 3. and 31 *Car.* 2. *cap.* 2. commonly called the *Habeas Corpus* Act: By the first whereof it is enacted, *That if any with-hold Prisoners replevisable, after that they have offered sufficient Surety, he shall pay a grievous Amerciament to the King. And if he take any Reward for the Deliverance of such, he shall pay double to the Prisoner, and also shall be in the great Mercy of the King.* And by the latter of the said Statutes it is enacted, *That Justices of Assise shall inquire if Sheriffs, or any other, have offended in any Thing contrary to the said Statute of* Westminster, *and whom they shall find Guilty they shall punish in all Things according to the Form of the said Statute.*

Sect. 16. Also it is recited by the above mentioned Statute of 31 *Car.* 2. *That great Delays had been used by Sheriffs, Gaolers, and other Officers, to whose Custody the King's Subjects had been committed for criminal, or supposed criminal Matters; in making Return of Writs of* Habeas Corpus, *by standing out an* Alias *and* Pluries, *and sometimes more, and by other Shifts to avoid their yielding Obedience to such Writs, contrary to their Duty, and the known Laws of the Land, whereby many Subjects had been long detained in Prison, in such Cases where by Law they were bailable,* &c. And thereupon it is enacted, *That whensoever any Person shall bring any* Habeas Corpus *directed unto any Person whatsoever, for any Person in his Custody, and the said Writ shall be served upon the said Officer, or left at the Gaol or Prison with any of the Under-Officers, Under-Keepers, or Deputy of the said Officers or Keepers, that the said Officer or Officers, his or their Under-Officers, Under-Keepers, or Deputies, shall, within three Days after ſuch Service thereof, (unleſs the Commitment were for Treaſon or Felony plainly and ſpecially expreſſed in the Warrant of Commitment) upon Payment or Tender of the Charges of bringing the ſaid Priſoner, to be aſcertained by the Judge or Court that awarded the ſame, and endorſed on the ſaid Writ, not exceeding* 12 d. *per Mile, and on Security given by his own Bond, to pay the Charges of carrying back the Priſoner, if he ſhould be remanded, and that he will not make any Eſcape by the Way, make Return of ſuch Writ, and bring, or cauſe to be brought, the Body of the Party ſo committed, or reſtrained, unto or before the Lord Chancellor, or Lord Keeper, or the Judges or Barons of the Court from which the ſaid Writ ſhall iſſue, or ſuch other Perſons before whom the ſaid Writ is made returnable, according to the Command thereof; and ſhall then likewiſe certify the true Cauſes of his Detainer or Impriſonment, unleſs the Commitment be in a Place beyond twenty Miles Diſtance,* &c. *and if beyond the Diſtance of twenty, and not above one hundred Miles, then within the Space of ten Days, and if beyond the Diſtance of one hundred Miles, then within the Space of twenty Days.*

Sect. 17. And it is further enacted, Par. 3. *That all ſuch Writs ſhall be marked in this Manner,* Per Statutum triceſimo primo Caroli Secundi Regis; *and ſhall be ſigned by the Perſon that awards the ſame. And if any Perſon ſhall be, or ſtand committed or detained as aforeſaid, for any Crime, unleſs for Treaſon or Felony, plainly expreſſed in the Warrant of Commitment, in the Vacation-time, it ſhall be lawful for ſuch Perſon ſo committed or detained (other than Perſons Convict, or in Execution by legal Proceſs) or any one on his Behalf, to complain to the Lord Chancellor, or Lord Keeper, or any Juſtice of either Bench, or Baron of the Exchequer of the Degree of the Coif; and the ſaid Lord Chancellor,* &c. *Juſtice or Baron, on View of the Copy of the Warrant of the Commitment, or otherwiſe on Oath that it was denied, are authorized and required, on requeſt in Writing by ſuch Perſon, or any in his Behalf, atteſted and ſubſcribed by two Witneſſes, who were preſent at the Delivery of the ſame, to grant an* Habeas Corpus *under the Seal of the Court whereof he ſhall be one of the Judges, to be directed to the Officer in whoſe Cuſtody the Party ſhall be returnable* immediate *before the ſaid Lord Chancellor,* &c. *Juſtice or Baron; and on Service thereof as aforeſaid, the Officer,* &c. *in whoſe Cuſtody the Party is, ſhall within the Times reſpectively before limited, bring him before the ſaid Lord Chancellor, Juſtice or Baron before whom the ſaid Writ is returnable; and in Caſe of his Abſence, before any other of them, with the Return of ſuch Writ, and the true Cauſes of the Commitment and Detainer. And thereupon, within two Days after the Party ſhall be brought before them, the ſaid Lord Chancellor, Juſtice or Baron, before whom the Priſoner ſhall be brought as aforeſaid, ſhall diſcharge the ſaid Priſoner from his Impriſonment, taking his Recognizance, with one or more Sureties, in any Sum according to their Diſcretions, having Regard to the Quality of the Priſoner and Nature of the Offence, for his Appearance in the King's Bench the Term following, or in ſuch other Court wherein the Offence is properly cogniſable, as the Caſe ſhall require; and then ſhall certify the ſaid Writ with the Return thereof, and the Recogniſance, into ſuch Court; unleſs it be made appear to the ſaid Lord Chancellor,* &c. *that the Party ſo committed is detained upon a legal Proceſs, Order or Warrant, out of ſome Court that hath Juriſdiction of criminal Matters; or by ſome Warrant ſigned and ſealed with the Hand and Seal of any of the ſaid Juſtices or Barons, or ſome Juſtice or Juſtices of the Peace, for ſuch Matters or Offences, for the which by Law the Priſoner is not bailable.*

Sect. 18. But it is provided, Par. 4. *That if any Perſon ſhall have wilfully neglected by the Space of two whole Terms after his Impriſonment, to pray a* Habeas Corpus *for his Enlargement, he ſhall not have a* Habeas Corpus *to be granted in Vacation-time, in Purſuance of this Act.*

Sect. 19.

Sect. 19. And it is farther enacted, Par. 5. *That if any Officer*, &c. *shall neglect or refuse to make the Returns aforesaid, or to bring the Body of the Prisoner according to the Command of the said Writ, within the respective Times aforesaid, or shall not within six Hours after Demand deliver a true Copy of the Commitment*, &c. *he shall forfeit for the first Offence* 100 l. *for the second* 200 l. *and be made uncapable to hold his Office*, &c.

Sect. 20. And it is farther enacted, Par. 6. *That no Person who shall be set at large upon any* Habeas Corpus, *shall be again imprisoned for the same Offence by any Person whatsoever, other than by the legal Order and Process of such Court wherein he shall be bound by Recognizance to appear, or other Court having Jurisdiction of the Cause, on Pain of* 500 l.

Sect. 21. And it is farther enacted, Par. 7. *That if any Person who shall be committed for Treason or Felony, plainly and specially expressed in the Warrant of Commitment; upon his Prayer or Petition in open Court the first Week of the Term, or the first Day of the Sessions of Oyer and Terminer, or general Gaol-Delivery, to be brought to his Trial, shall not be indicted some Time in the next Term, Sessions of Oyer and Terminer, or general Gaol-Delivery after such Commitment, the Justices of the said Courts shall, upon Motion in open Court, the last Day of the Term, or Sessions, set at Liberty the Prisoner upon Bail; unless it appear upon Oath, that the Witnesses for the King could not be produced the same Term*, &c. *And if such Prisoner, upon his Prayer*, &c. *shall not be indicted and tried the second Term, or Sessions, he shall be discharged from his Imprisonment.*

Sect. 22. And it is farther enacted, Par. 10. *That it shall be lawful for any Prisoner, as aforesaid, to move and obtain his* Habeas Corpus *as well out of the Chancery or Exchequer, as the King's Bench or Common Pleas: And if the said Lord Chancellor or Lord Keeper, or any Judge or Judges, Baron or Barons for the Time being, of the Degree of the Coif, of any of the Courts aforesaid, in the Vacation-Time, upon View of the Copy of a Warrant of Commitment or Detainer, or on Oath made that such Copy was denied, shall deny any Writ of* Habeas Corpus, *by this Act required to be granted, being moved for as aforesaid, they shall severally forfeit to the Party grieved, the Sum of* 500 l.

Sect. 23. But it is provided, Par. 18. *That after the Assises proclaimed for that County where the Prisoner is detained, no Person shall be removed from the common Gaol upon any* Habeas Corpus *granted in Pursuance of this Act; but upon such* Habeas Corpus *shall be brought before the Judge of Assise in open Court, who thereupon shall do what to Justice shall appertain.* But it is provided nevertheless, Par. 19. *That after the Assises are ended, any Person detained may have his* Habeas Corpus *according to the Direction of this Act.*

Sect. 24. It is observable, that this Statute makes the Judges liable to an Action at the Suit of the Party grieved in one Case only, which is the refusing to award a ***Habeas Corpus*** in Vacation-time; and seems to leave it to their Discretion in all other Cases, to pursue its Directions in the same Manner as they ought to execute all other Laws, without making them subject to the Action of the Party, or to any other express Penalty or Forfeiture: And this is most agreeable to the general Reason of the Law, which regularly will not suffer a Judge to be liable to an Action for what he does as Judge.

B. 1. Ch. 72. Sect. 6. & B. 2. Ch. 1. Sect. 17.

As to the sixth Point, *viz.* In what Cases Bail is grantable, I shall endeavour to shew,

1. Where it is grantable by a Sheriff.
2. Where by a Justice of Peace.
3. Where by Justices of Gaol-Delivery.
4. Where by the Courts of *Westminster* Hall.

As to the firſt Point, I ſhall firſt conſider, where Bail is grantable by a Sheriff *ex Officio*; and ſecondly, where by Virtue of a Writ.

Sect. 25. As to the firſt Particular, it is holden by [a] ſome, That by the Common Law the Sheriff might, by Virtue of his Office, as principal Conſervator of the Peace, bail any Perſon arreſted on Suſpicion of Felony, or for any other Offence which is bailable.

Sect. 26. Alſo it hath been holden, [b] that a Conſtable had the like Power by the Common Law: And it may [c] probably be inferred from the Recitals of the Writs of Mainpriſe in the Regiſter, that by the Common Law the Sheriff had Power to bail Perſons indicted of Larceny in a [d] Court-Leet, and alſo Perſons indicted as [d] Acceſſaries to a Felon, and Perſons appealed by [e] Approvers, after the Death of the Approvers, &c. But it ſeems that the Sheriff [f] had no Power *ex Officio*, to bail any Perſon indicted of any Crime before Juſtices of Peace. And it is certain, [g] that neither the Sheriff, nor Conſtable could, in any of the Caſes above mentioned, take Bail by Recognizance, but only by Obligation. And ſome [h] have holden, That the Statutes which impower Juſtices of Peace to admit Perſons to Bail, on an Accuſation of Felony, and particularly preſcribe in what Manner they ſhall do it, have taken away all Power of this Kind from the Sheriff and Conſtable; yet others ſeem to be of another Opinion, becauſe the ſaid Statutes are wholly in the Affirmative.

Sect. 27. But it ſeems certain, [i] That by the Common Law, the Sheriff might bail any Perſon who was indicted before him at his Torn, for Felony, or any other Crime that is bailable; becauſe he might both award Proceſs, and alſo give Judgment againſt the Perſon ſo indicted: And it is a general [k] Rule, That whoſoever is Judge of the Offence, may bail the Offender. But it is holden, [l] That at this Day the Sheriff has loſt his Power, by Reaſon of 1 *Ed.* 4. *cap.* 2. ſet forth more at large *cap.* 10. *ſect.* 74. by which it is enacted, That the Sheriff ſhall not proceed on any ſuch Indictment, but ſhall remove it to the next Seſſions of Peace.

[a] Daliſon 11. See the Preamble of 13 Ed. 1. cap. 15. Regiſter, 83. b. 169. S. P. C. 74. Letter D. Fitz. Coron. 297. contra 2 Inſt. 190.
[b] Daliſon 11. Contra 2 Inſt. 190.
[c] Regiſter 269. a.
[d] Regiſter 270.
[e] Regiſter 269. b.
[f] Regiſter 133. b. 270. b. 271. a. b.
[g] Supra cap. 8. ſect. 4, 5. Daliſon 11.
[h] Daliſon 11.
[i] H. P. C. 106. 2 H. H. P. C. 148, 149. 2 Inſt. 190. Regiſter 269.
[k] Lamb. 342, 348. S. P. C. 74. Letter E. 2 Inſt. 190.
[l] H. P. C. 106.

As to the ſecond Particular, it ſeems, That Bail is grantable by a Sheriff by Virtue of the following Writs. 2 H. H. P. C. 141 to 149.

1. That of *Odio* & *Atia*.
2. That of Mainpriſe.
3. That of *Homine replegiando*.

Sect. 28. But having already, in *Book* 1. *Cap.* 29. *Sect.* 20 and 24. incidently ſhewn the Nature of the firſt of theſe Writs, which ſeems to be in great Meaſure obſolete at this Day, I ſhall refer the Reader to what is there ſaid concerning it.

Sect. 29. Secondly, Of the Writ of Mainpriſe little Notice is taken in the late Books; yet the Law relating to it ſeems to be ſtill in Force in many Caſes; and conſequently in ſuch Caſes, thoſe who are bailable, and have been refuſed the Benefit of Bail, may ſtill by Virtue thereof be delivered out of Priſon (upon their Finding Sureties [m] to the Sheriff that they will appear and anſwer to the Crimes alledged againſt them, before the Juſtices in the Writ mentioned, &c.) as thoſe [n] who are impriſoned for a ſlight Suſpicion of Felony, or indicted of Larceny [o] before the Steward of a Leet, or of Treſpaſs [p] before Juſtices of Peace, and many other [q] Perſons, all which it will be needleſs to enumerate.

[m] Regiſter 269, 270.
[n] F. N. B. 250. b. Regiſter 269. a.
[o] F. N. B. 250. C. Regiſter 269. a. 2 Inſt. 290.
[p] F. N. B. 250. G. 251. C. Regiſter 133. b. 270. b. 271. b.
[q] F. N. B. 250, 251. Regiſter 269, &c.

[a] H. P. C. 104. [b] 2 Inst. 190. [c] F. N. B. 250. A. 4 Inst. 182. Coke, Bail and Mainprise, cap. 10. Vide supra cap. 10. sect. 72, 74.

Sect. 30. But as to that which is said in general, both by Sir *Matthew Hale* [a] and Sir *Edward Coke*, [b] in Relation to this Matter from which it may seem to have been the Opinion of those Authors, That no Writ of Mainprise is grantable at this Day; it may be answered, That this is to be understood [c] only of the Writ of Mainprise, for Persons indicted before the Sheriff in his Torn, in relation to whom he has no judicial Power at this Day, and consequently no Power to bail them *ex Officio*; from whence it follows, That the Writ of Mainprise for such Persons, being grounded on a Suggestion that the Sheriff had unjustly refused before to admit them to bail, cannot now be proper, because he cannot be said to have unjustly refused to do a Thing which he had no Power to do. But this can be no Manner of Reason why the Writ of Mainprise should not be still grantable in other Cases. [26]

F. N. B. 66, 67, 68. Register 78, 79. Register 79. a. F. N. B. 68. C. 2 H. H. P. C. 141. Vide supra Section 26. [d] 1 Sid. 210. Skin. 61, 76, 227, 337. Carth. 286, 287. Far. 9. 4 Mod. 183.

Sect. 31. Thirdly, As to the Writ of *Homine replegiando*, there seems to be no Doubt but that at the Common Law the Sheriff might deliver any Persons out of Prison by Virtue of this Writ, except in those special Cases mentioned in the Statute of *Westminster* 1. *cap.* 15. which is set forth more at large in the next Section: And if he had returned, that the Plaintiff had been eloigned out of the County by the Defendant, he might afterward, by Virtue of a *Capias in Withernam* against such Defendant, whether he were a Peer or Commoner, have taken and imprisoned him till the Plaintiff should be replevied. But the Writ of *Homine replegiando* has been much disused of late, in such Cases wherein Justices of Peace have been authorized to admit Persons to Bail; yet whether the Statutes which gave such Authority to Justices of Peace, being wholly in the Affirmative, do take away the Sheriff's Power in the Cases mentioned in those Statutes, may deserve to be considered. However there can be no Doubt but that in other Cases the Writ of *Homine replegiando*, [d] and *Capias in Withernam* are very proper and effectual Remedies.

2 H. H. P. C. 127 to 136. [e] See Sect. 41. 2 Inst. 190.

Sect. 32. But for the better Understanding the Sheriff's Power in this Particular, I shall set down, and endeavour to explain so much of the said Statute of *Westminster* 1. *cap.* 15. as relates to it, which is enacted as followeth. *Forasmuch as Sheriffs, and others who have taken and kept in Prison Persons detected of Felony, and incontinent have let out by Replevin such as were not replevisable, and have kept in Prison such as were replevisable, because they would gain of the one Party, and grieve the other: And forasmuch as before this Time it was not determined which Persons were replevisable, and which not; but only those that were taken for the Death of a Man, or by Commandment of the King, or of the Justices, or for the Forest: It is provided, and by the King commanded, that such Prisoners as before were outlawed, and they which have abjured the Realm, Provors, and such as be taken with the Manner,* [e] *and those which have broken the King's Prison, Thieves openly defamed and known, and such as be appealed by Provors, so long as the Provors be living (if they be not of good Name) and such as be taken for House-burning feloniously done, or for false Money, or for counterfeiting the King's Seal, or Persons excommunicate, taken at the Request of the Bishop, or for manifest Offences, or for Treason touching the King himself, shall be in no wise replevisable by the common Writ, nor without Writ: But such as be indicted of Larceny by Enquests taken before Sheriffs, or Bailiffs by their Office, or of light Suspicion, or for Petit Larceny, that amounteth not above the Value of twelve Pence, if they were not accused of some other Larceny aforetime, or accused of Receipt of Thieves or Felons, or of Commandment, or Force, or of Aid in Felony done, or accused of some other Trespass, for which one ought not to lose Life or Member, and a Man ap-*

proved by a Provor, after the Death of the Provor (if he be no common Thief, nor defamed) shall be henceforth let out by sufficient Surety, whereof the Sheriff will be answerable, and that without giving ought of their Goods.

For the better Exposition hereof, I shall distinctly consider,

1. That Part of the Preamble which declares, what Persons had always been agreed not to be replevisable.
2. That Part of the Purview which shews what other Persons shall not be replevisable.
3. That which shews what Persons shall be replevisable.

Of those who by Preamble are declared to have always been agreed to be irreplevisable, there are four Kinds. 2 H. H. P. C. 129 to 132.

1. *Those who are taken for the Death of a Man.*
2. *Those who are taken by the Commandment of the King.*
3. *Those who are taken by the Commandment of the Justices.*
4. *Those who are taken for the Forest.*

Sect. 33. As to the first of these Particulars, it is observable that the Statute declares generally, That those imprisoned for the Death of a Man have always been taken to be irreplevisable, without making any Di- 2 H. H. P. C. stinction between such Homicide as is malicious, and that which happens 129. 2 Inst. 186. by Misadventure, or in Self-Defence. And it is further to be observed, that the Statute of *Glocester*, *cap.* 9. provides, *That where a Man kills another by Misfortune, or in his Defence, or in other Manner without Felony, he* 2 Inst. 315. *shall be put in Prison 'till the next Coming of the Justices in Eyre, or Justices* 2 H. H. P. C. *assigned to the Gaol-Delivery*, &c. 138. And agreeably hereto we find, That all Persons in general, who are taken for the Death of a Man, are excepted out of the Writ [a] *de Homine replegiando:* And that even the superior [b] [a] Register 77. b. Courts, which are not restrained by these Statutes, have yet been always F.N.B. 66.E. cautious of bailing Persons imprisoned for any Homicide, except in such [b] 25 Ed. 3. 42. special Cases as shall be set forth more at large in the following Part of this pl. 27. 41 Aff. pl. 14. Chapter. 37 Aff. pl. 12.

Sect. 34. Also it seems agreed, That Justices of Peace, who have Pow- 29 Aff. 44. er at this Day to bail a Man arrested for a light Suspicion of Homicide, 1 Ro. Re. 268. cannot bail any such Person for Manslaughter, or even excusable Homicide, 44 Ed. 3. 38. if it manifestly appear that he was guilty of the Fact, let it be ever so pl. 34. plain that it cannot amount to Murder, as shall be shewn more at large in 21 Ed. 4. 71. a. the following Part of this Chapter [c]. [c] Sect. 63.

Sect. 35. And it is enacted by 3 *H.* 7. 1. *That if it happen, that any Person named as Principal or Accessary, be acquitted of any Murder at the King's Suit, within the Year and Day, that then the same Justices before whom he is acquitted, shall not suffer him to go at large, but either remit him to Prison, or bail him, after their Discretion, 'till the Year and Day be passed.*

Sect. 36. As to the second Particular, *viz.* That concerning those who 2 Inst. 186, are taken by the Commandment of the King, it seems, That the Words of 187. the Statute concerning them are to be understood of such only as are im- S. P. C. 72. E. 1 Rol. Rep. prisoned either by the King's personal Command, or by the Command of 134. his Privy Council, which is looked upon to be as it were incorporated Dalt. ch. 114. with him and to speak with his Mouth; and accordingly we find the Register 77. b. Exception in the Writ of *Homine replegiando*, relating to Persons imprisoned by the King, thus expressed in the Register, *Nisi capti sunt per speciale præceptum nostrum*; by which it seems to be implied, That this Exception is not

not to be applied generally to every Command whatſoever of the King: To which it may be added, That if it were to be underſtood in ſo large a Senſe, it would extend even to thoſe who are taken by a *Capias* in a per-

S. P. C. 72. E.

ſonal Action, for that every ſuch *Capias* is the Commandment of the King; but it ſeems certain, That a Defendant taken by ſuch a *Capias* is repleviſable by the Common Law. But Perſons impriſoned by the ſpecial Command of the King, or of his Privy Council, are ſo far from being replevi-

[a] 1 And. 298. 1 Rol. Rep. 134, 192. pl. 31, 32. 219. 1 Leon. 70. Bro. Mainpriſe, 37. Contra Moor 839. 1 And. 158.

ſable by the Sheriff, that they have formerly [a] been adjudged not to be bailable even by the Court of King's Bench: However at this Day the Law is otherwiſe declared and ſettled by Parliament, as ſhall be ſhewn more at large in the following Part of this Chapter. [27]

Sect. 37. As to the third Particular, *viz.* That concerning Perſons impriſoned by the Command of the Juſtices, it is obſervable, That the Exception in the Writ of *Homine replegiando*, in the Regiſter, [b] concerning

[b] Regiſter 77. b. [c] F. N. B. 66. E. [d] S. P. C. 73. [e] 2 Inſt. 187. [f] Dalt. cap. 114.

Perſons ſo impriſoned, is reſtrained to thoſe who are taken by the ſpecial Command of the King's Chief Juſtice. But by *Fitzherbert* [c] and *Staunford* [d], *Coke* [e] and *Dalton*, [f] the Words of the Statute relating to Perſons ſo impriſoned, ſeem to be underſtood in a large Senſe of any of the King's Juſtices in general, as of thoſe of Aſſiſe, as well as of thoſe of the Courts of *Weſtminſter-Hall.* But it ſeems that they are not to be underſtood generally of Perſons impriſoned by any Command whatſoever of ſuch Juſtices, for that thoſe who are impriſoned by their ordinary Command, not

S. P. C. 73. Dalt. ch. 114. F. N. B. 251. B.

by Way of Puniſhment, but in Order only to be ſafely kept, are ſaid to be repleviſable by the Sheriff, in Caſes not prohibited by the Statute; and therefore it ſeems, That they muſt be taken in a more reſtrained Senſe, of thoſe only who are impriſoned by the abſolute Command of ſuch Juſtices by

S. P. C. 73. Dalt. ch. 114. 24 Ed. 3. 33. pl. 25.

Way of Puniſhment, as for a Miſdemeanor done in their Preſence, or for other Contempts, or ſuch like Matters, which lie rather in their Diſcretion than in their ordinary Power; and it ſeems that a Commitment by the Chief Juſtice, without ſhewing any Cauſe whatſoever, ſhall be intended

1 Rol. Rep. 131.

to be for ſome ſuch Matter; and there can be no Doubt but that a Perſon under ſuch a Commitment is irrepleviſable by the Sheriff. Alſo it hath been holden, That a Perſon ſo committed is not bailable upon a *Habeas Corpus:* But how far Perſons committed by the abſolute Command of one Court, are bailable by another, ſhall be more fully conſidered in the following Part of this Chapter.

Sect. 38. As to the fourth Particular, *viz.* That concerning thoſe who

[g] Regiſter 77. b. 4 Inſt. 314. [h] Vide 1 Inſt. 2. a. 233. a. [i] Regiſter 80. b. F. N. B. 67. D. Vide Plowd. Com. 124. a. [k] 9 H. 3. 10. & 16. [l] 34 Ed. 1. commonly called, Ordinatio Foreſtæ.

are impriſoned for the Foreſt, who alſo are excepted out of the Writ [g] of *Homine replegiando*; it ſeems that the ſaid Exception is to be underſtood as well of Foreſts in the Hands of Subjects, [h] as of thoſe in the Hands of the King; but it ſeems, that it is to be underſtood ſtrictly of proper Foreſts only, and not to be extended [i] by Equity to Chaſes or Parks. And as to Impriſonments for Offences in Foreſts, the Law has been much mitigated by later Statutes; for it is recited by 1 *Ed.* 3. *cap.* 8. *That divers Perſons had been undone by the Chief Keepers of Foreſts,* &c. *againſt the Form of the Great Charter* [k] *of the Foreſt, and againſt the Declaration* [l] *made by King* Edward 1. *by which he granted, That Treſpaſſes done, in his Foreſt, of Vert and Veniſon, ſhould be preſented at the next Swainmote, before the Foreſters,* &c. *and that ſuch Preſentments made before ſuch Foreſters,* &c. *ſhould by the Oaths of Knights, and other diſcreet and lawful Men,* &c. *by the common Aſſent of all the ſaid Miniſters, be ſolemnly written, and with their Seals enſealed: And that if any Indictment ſhould be in any other Manner made, that the ſame ſhould be void.* And thereupon it is ordained, *That from thenceforth no Man ſhall be taken nor impriſoned for Vert or Veniſon, unleſs he be taken with the Manner, or else indicted after the Form before specified: And then the chief Warden shall let him to mainprise 'till the Eyre of the Forest, without any Thing taken for his Deliverance. And if the said Warden will not so do, he shall have a* [a] *Writ out of the Chancery,* &c. *to be at Mainprise till the Eyre. And if the Warden shall not obey such Writ, the Plaintiff shall have a* [b] *Writ to the Sheriff to attach the said Warden before the King, at a certain Day,* &c. *And the Sheriff (the Verders being called to him) shall deliver him that is so taken, by good Mainprise, in the Presence of the Verders, and shall deliver the Names of the Mainpernors to the same Verders, to answer in the Eyre before the Justices,* &c. And it is farther enacted, by 7 *R.* 2. 4. That *no Man shall be imprisoned by any Officer of the Forest without due Indictment, or being taken with the Manner, or trespassing in the Forest,* &c.

[a] F. N. B. 67. A. Regiſter 80. b.
[b] F. N. B. 67. B. Regiſter 80. b.

Sect. 39. And *Note,* That Persons so indicted, or taken with the Manner, being imprisoned by such Officers, have their Election either to be mainprized by twelve Mainpernors, by Virtue of the Writ of *Homine replegiando,* given by the said Statute of 1 *Ed.* 3. 8. or to be bailed upon a *Habeas Corpus,* by the Judges of *Westminster-Hall,* &c. And if a Person be imprisoned for any Offence relating to the Forest, without having been first indicted for it, or taken with the Manner, there seems to be no Doubt but that he may have an Action of false Imprisonment, and may also be mainprised or bailed in the Manner abovementioned.

4 Inst. 290. Register, 80. b. F. N. B. 67. A. B. C. 45 Ed. 3. 7. pl. 8. 4 Inst. 290. Register 80. a. b.

And now I am to consider that Part of the Purview of the above recited Statute of *Westminster* 1. 15. which shews what other Persons are not replevisable, of which there are two Sorts.

2 H. H. P. C. 132 to 135.

1. Such as are excluded from the Benefit of a Replevin, in respect of the Notoriety of their Offence.
2. Such as are excluded from it in respect of the Heinousness of the Crime alledged against them.

Persons excluded from the Benefit of a Replevin, in respect of the Notoriety of their Offence, are of two Kinds.

1. Those who by an express or implied Judgment, Sentence or Conviction, or their own Confession, appear to be Guilty.
2. Those who are under violent Presumptions of Guilt.

Sect. 40. And first, Of those who by Judgment, Sentence, Conviction or Confession, appear to be Guilty, some are excluded from the Benefit of a Replevin by the express Words of the Statute, as *Those who are outlawed, or have abjured the Realm; Persons excommunicate, taken at the Request of the Bishop, and Provors.* And all other [c] Persons who are condemned, or convicted of Felony, or any other [d] heinous Crime whatsoever, whether by their own Confession, or by Verdict General or Special; [e] and also all those [f] who on their Examination own themselves guilty of a Felony alledged against them, and are charged in their *Mittimus* with the Felony so confessed, seem to be excluded from it by Parity of Reason, and the manifest Intent of the Statute; for [g] Bail is only proper where it stands indifferent whether the Party be Guilty or Innocent of the Accusation against him, as it often does before his Trial; but where that Indifferency is removed, it would, generally speaking, be absurd to bail him: And agreeably hereto the Statute of 2 *H.* 5. *cap.* 2. provides, even as to civil Causes, *That if upon a Writ of* Certiorari, *or* Corpus cum causa, *out of Chancery, it shall be returned that the Prisoner is con-*

[c] S. P. C. 74. H. P. C. 101. Dalt. cap. 114. 1 Rol. Rep. 268. 15 H. 7. 9. Pl. 8. Kelynge 90. 3 Bulst. 113, 114.
[d] Vide infra S. 44.
[e] Dy. 179. pl. 42. 1 Bulst. 87, 88. 15 H. 7. 9. a.
[f] 3 Bulst. 114. 1 Rol. Rep. 268. 4 Inst. 178.
[g] 2 Inst. 188. Dyer 179. pl. 42. H. P. C. 100, 101.

demned by Judgment given against him, he shall be remanded, &c. Also 23 *H.* 6. *cap.* 10. which ordains, That Sheriffs, *&c.* shall let out of Prison Persons in their Custody by Force of any Writ, *&c.* in Personal Actions, or on Indictments of Trespass, by sufficient Sureties, *&c.* expresly excepts *All such as shall be in their Ward by Condemnation, Execution*, &c. And therefore it cannot but be reasonable to intend, That the said Statute of *Westminster* 1. put the Cases of Persons outlawed and excommunicate as Examples only; meaning thereby to intimate, That all other Persons under the like Circumstances should be in like Manner irreplevisable: Yet it is certain, that the Court of King's Bench may, in their Discretion, in some special Cases, bail a Person upon an Outlawry of Felony; as [a] where he pleads that he is not of the same Name, and therefore not the same Person with him that was outlawed; or alledges [b] any other Error in the Proceedings. Also it seems, That the Court of King's Bench, or Justices of Gaol-Delivery, may bail [c] a Person convicted of Manslaughter, or, as some say, of any other Felony, for which he afterwards gets the King's Pardon. And [d] there seems to be no Doubt at this Day, but that they may also bail any Person who is found guilty before them of Homicide in Self-defence, or by Misadventure. Also it is certain, That if a Person appear to be imprisoned for an Excommunication, in a Cause of which the Spiritual Court hath no Conusance, he may be delivered either upon a *Habeas Corpus*, or by quashing or superseding the Writ of *Excommunicato capiendo*.

See the Books above cited. H. P.C. 101. S. P. C. 74. Letter A. 2 Inst. 188. [a] 5 H. 7. 16. pl. 7. [b] 19H. 6. 2. a. [c] Bro. Mainprise, 94. H. P. C. 101. 105. [d] H.P.C. 101. 105. F.N.B. 246. C. Contra Fitz. Coron. 297. 354. Quære S. P. C. 74. D.

Secondly, Of those who are under violent Presumptions of Guilt, and in that respect are excluded by the Statute from the Benefit of a Replevin, there are several Kinds.

H. P.C. 101. Carth. 79. 2 Inst. 188. H. P.C. 102. Vide cap. 18. S. 1. & 4.

Sect. 41. I. *Those who are taken with the Manner* (or rather the *Mainer*, that is, with the thing stolen, as it were, in their Hands) and by Parity of Reason, those who are taken freshly upon a Hue and Cry. [28]

Sect. 42. II. *Those who have broken the King's Prison*, and by the same Reason those who have broken any other Prison, which the Law presumes that no Innocent Person will do.

Sect. 43. III. *Those who are appealed by Provors*, who regularly are not bailable, because the Approver, by confessing his own Guilt, induces a strong Presumption against those whom he accuses of the same Crime of which he owns himself guilty; yet by the express Words of the Statute, *If the Person appealed by an Approver be of good Reputation, he may be bailed, even in the Life of the Approver; and, unless he be a notorious Felon, he may be bailed after his Death.* And by Parity of Reason, he may also be bailed, if the Approver waive [e] his Appeal, or be vanquished, [f] unless there be some other Cause to detain him in Prison, as the Appeal of some other Approver, *&c.* And if a Person disabled by Law to become an Approver, as one attainted, [g] *&c.* appeal another of High Treason, it seems that the Person so appealed ought to be bound [h] to his Good Behaviour towards the King: But [i] if such Person had appealed him of Felony only, it seems that he ought to have been wholly discharged, if there had been no other Accusation against him.

H. P C. 102. 2 Inst. 188. Register 269. b. [e] 25 Ed. 3. 42. pl. 27. H. P. C. 102. Fitz. Mainprise, 1. 2 Inst. 188. [f] 25 Ed. 3. 42. pl. 31. Fitz. Mainprise, 2. [g] H. P. C. 192. [h] Fitz. Coron. 387. [i] Bro. Coron. 81, 211.

Sect. 44. IV. *Thieves openly known and notorious*, who, as it seems, ought not to be bailed for any fresh Felony, whereof there is probable Evidence against them. But how far Persons accused of any Crime shall be so far esteemed likely to have committed it, from their former scandalous Behaviour, as to be presumed guilty upon slight Evidence, seems in great measure to be left to the Discretion [k] of the Person who hath Power to bail them; who, upon Consideration of the Circumstances of the whole Matter,

17 Ass. pl. 4. 11 Ass. pl. 27. [k] H.P.C. 102.

ter, and the Probabilities of both Sides, if he find it reaſonable ſtrongly to preſume them to be guilty, ought not to bail but commit them.

Sect. 45. V. *Perſons taken for open and manifeſt Offences*, which ſeems to be underſtood of inferior Crimes of an enormous Nature, under the degree of Felony, as dangerous Riots, [a] ſavouring of High Treaſon, [b] ſcandalous Extortions, Conſpiracies, [c] by Juſtices, *&c.* violent and exorbitant Reſcouſes [d] of Perſons arreſted by Virtue of the King's Writs, Miſpriſion [e] of Treaſon, *Præmunire*, [f] Maim, and ſuch like heinous Offences, whereof no one who is notoriouſly Guilty, ſeems to be bailable by the Intent of this Statute; for notwithſtanding in the latter Part of it, it be ſaid generally, That thoſe who are accuſed of a Treſpaſs, for which a Man ſhall not loſe Life or Member, are repleviſable; yet upon the Conſtruction of the whole it ſeems reaſonable to qualify the Generality of that Expreſſion with this Limitation, that ſuch Accuſation ought to be either on a light Suſpicion; or if it be on plain and unqueſtionable Evidence, that the Offence ought to be inconſiderable, for if all Perſons whatſoever ſhall be repleviſable for Offences not touching Life or Member, let their Guilt be never ſo notorious, the abovementioned general unlimited Clauſe, that thoſe who are taken for open Offences ſhall be irrepleviſable, muſt be reſtrained to Felonies and Offences touching Member, which ſeems contrary to the moſt obvious reaſonable Purport of it, and alſo to common Practice, and that allowed general Rule, That Bail is only then proper where it ſtands indifferent whether the Party were Guilty or Innocent; *ſed quære.* Yet it ſeems to be in great meaſure left to the Diſcretion of the Perſon who has Power to admit others to Bail, to judge in what Caſes their Crime is ſo flagrant and enormous, that they ought not to have the Benefit of it. Supr. Sect. 44.

[a] Dalt. cap. 114.
[b] Bro. Mainpriſe, 62. 42 Aſſ. pl. 5.
[c] Coke Bail & Mainpriſe, Ch. 5. 27 Aſſ. pl. 12
[d] Keilw. 165. b. Fitz. Execution, 147. 13 H. 7. 21. b. Raſtal 380. pl. 6.
[e] H. P. C. 168.
[f] 6 H. 7. 1. b.

Of thoſe who are excluded by the Purview of the ſaid Statute, from the Benefit of a Replevin, in reſpect of the Heinouſneſs of the Crime alledged againſt them, there are four kinds.

1. *Thoſe who are taken for Arſon.*
2. *Thoſe who are taken for falſe Money.*
3. *Thoſe who are taken for falſifying the King's Seal.*
4. *Thoſe who are taken for Treaſon, which touches the King himſelf.*

Sect. 46. And all ſuch Perſons being expreſly declared to be irrepleviſable, it ſeems clear, That they can in no Caſe be delivered out of Priſon by the Sheriff, either by Virtue of the ſaid Writ of *Homine replegiando*, or without it: Yet if a Perſon at large be accuſed before a Sheriff, on a light Suſpicion of any of theſe, or of any other of the abovementioned Crimes, which always have been agreed to be irrepleviſable, as of Homicide, *&c.* it ſeems by no means to follow either from the Words or Intention of the Statute, That the Sheriff is bound to keep him in Priſon till he be delivered by due Courſe of Law; but in ſuch a Caſe it ſeems to be more reaſonable, that he take Surety of him to appear in a proper Court to anſwer ſuch Accuſation; for it ſeems extremely harſh, and contrary to the firſt Principles of the Law, which favours nothing more than the Liberty of the Subject, to put an Officer under a Neceſſity of depriving a Man of his Liberty upon every Accuſation of ſuch a Crime, be it never ſo weakly grounded. And the Words of the Statute, declaring Perſons to be irrepleviſable for ſuch Crimes, ſeem clearly applicable to ſuch only as are under an actual Impriſonment, and not to thoſe who are barely accuſed; for that none can be properly ſaid to be replevied, but thoſe who being actually impriſoned, are, upon finding Pledges, delivered out of Cuſtody; from which it follows, That Perſons not impriſoned are not within the Statute: Nay, the Law is ſo far from obliging a Sheriff to impriſon a Man on every Accuſation whatſoever of ſuch Crimes, that it ſubjects him, as well as any other Perſon, to an Action of Falſe Impriſonment, if he does it without a reaſonable Ground; as hath been more fully ſhewn in the Chapters concerning Arreſts. But if a Perſon be actually under an Arreſt, either of a Magiſtrate or private Perſon, for any of the abovementioned Crimes, it ſeems clear from the expreſs Words of the Statute, that the Sheriff cannot replevy him; and it ſeems, that at the Common Law he ought to have ſafely detained the Party ſo arreſted 'till he could have obtained his legal Deliverance, and that the Perſon ſo arreſted had no Remedy but by Indictment or Action of Falſe Impriſonment againſt thoſe who arreſted and delivered him to the Sheriff, on a groundleſs Suſpicion. But how far the Law may at this Day be altered in this Point, by the univerſal and allowed Practice of Sheriffs receiving no Perſon into their Cuſtody, for any Crime, without the Warrant of ſome Magiſtrate, ſhall be more fully conſidered in the next Chapter.

2 Inſt. 189. 40 Aſſ. 33. 2 H. H. P.C. 129, 134, 148. *Sect.* 47. It is certain, That the Court of King's Bench ſtill may, and always might, bail Perſons in Cuſtody for any of theſe Crimes, notwithſtanding this Statute; yet in Diſcretion it ſeldom uſes this Power but in very ſpecial Caſes, as ſhall be ſhewn in the following Part of this Chapter.

2 H. H. P. C. 134, 135. And now I am to conſider that Part of the Purview of the ſaid Statute, which ſhews what Perſons are repleviſable; for the better Underſtanding whereof, I ſhall endeavour to explain,

1. The Branch relating to Perſons accuſed as Principals.
2. That which concerns thoſe who are charged as Acceſſaries.

Sect. 48. As to the firſt Branch, Firſt, *Thoſe who are indicted of Larceny*
2 Inſt. 190. *by Inqueſts taken before Sheriffs, or Bailiffs, by their Office*, that is, before Sheriffs in their Torns, and Lords in their Leets, are expreſly declared to
S. P. C. 74. Letter C. H. P. C. 106. Dalt. cap. 114. 29 Aſſ. pl. 44. 16 Ed. 4. 5. pl. 4. Coke Bail & Mainpriſe, cap. 5. be repleviſable; and according to ſome Opinions, thoſe who are indicted or appealed in any other Court, of any other Felony, not expreſly declared by the Statute to be irrepleviſable, as Robbery or Burglary, *&c.* are repleviſable by the Sheriff, *ex officio*, without Writ, within the Equity of this Clauſe: Yet the Authorities which are brought to warrant this Opinion, relate only to the Bailment of Perſons by ſuperior Courts, upon Indictments or Appeals of ſuch Crimes before ſuch Courts, and do by no means prove that ſuch Perſons are repleviſable by the Sheriff *ex officio*, without Writ: And it is obſervable, that the Writs of Mainpriſe
Regiſter 270. b. 271. in the Regiſter, for Perſons indicted only of Treſpaſs, before Juſtices of Peace, expreſly declare, That ſuch Perſons cannot be delivered out of Priſon without the King's ſpecial Command; from whence it ſeems to follow, That ſuch Perſons are not within the common Benefit of a Replevin by the Sheriff, without ſome ſuch ſpecial Command. And if Perſons indicted of Treſpaſs only, before Juſtices of Peace, are not within the ordinary Remedy of a Replevin by the Sheriff without a Writ, ſurely it cannot be thought, that Perſons indicted of higher Crimes, and before Superior Courts, can be any way intitled to it: However, inaſmuch as the ſaid Statute of *Weſtminſter* 1. expreſly allows Perſons indicted of

Larceny before the Sheriff the ordinary Remedy of a Replevin, and exprefly excludes fome other particular Felonies, and fays nothing of others, it feems a reafonable Conftruction of the Statute, That the Sheriff might by Virtue of it, either with or without Writ, replevy thofe who were indicted before himfelf, or at a Court-Leet, of thofe other Felonies not exprefly excepted, as well as thofe indicted of Larceny only. And the Statute leaving fuch a Latitude to the Sheriff in Relation to the Perfons fo indicted before himfelf, or at a Court-Leet, it hath been ufual for fuperior Courts, (who though they be not within the Statute, have yet always had a great Regard to the Rules prefcribed by it) to ufe the fame Liberty in Relation to fuch Crimes, and fometimes greater, for fuch fpecial Reafons, and in fuch fpecial Cafes, as fhall be fet forth more at large in the following Part of this Chapter. Yet notwithftanding the Statute feems generally to allow the Benefit of a Replevin to all thofe who are indicted of Larceny, &c. without any Limitation; yet it hath been always conftrued to intend only, that fuch Perfons indicted of a Grand Larceny, as are of a good Reputation, fhall be replevifable; and therefore if there be ftrong Prefumptions of their Guilt, it feems that they ought not to be bailed; but this is in great Meafure to be left to Difcretion. Regifter 269. 2 Inft. 190. H. P. C. 100. 16 Ed. 4. 5. S. P. C. 74. c.

Sect. 49. Secondly, *Thofe who are imprifoned for a light Sufpicion*, are likewife declared by the Statute to be replevifable; yet notwithftanding the Words are general, it hath always been taken to be the Intent of them, That the Perfons fo imprifoned ought to be of a good Reputation: Alfo it feems clear, That the Statute means only fuch Perfons as are imprifoned for Crimes not exprefly excepted by it from the Benefit of a Replevin; and therefore that this Branch cannot extend to Perfons imprifoned for the Treafons mentioned in the Statute, Arfon, or Homicide, but only to thofe taken for Larceny, Robbery, Burglary and fuch like Felonies, &c. Regifter 83. b. 269. F. N. B. 250. C. 2 Inft. 190.

Sect. 50. Thirdly, Thofe who are imprifoned *for Petit Larceny, which does not amount to above the Value of* 12 d. are alfo declared by the Statute to be replevifable, *if they have not been accufed of fome other Larceny before:* And it feems to be agreed, That there is no Neceffity that fuch Perfons be of good Reputation; yet upon the Conftruction of the whole Statute, if fuch Perfons be taken with the Manner, or confefs the Fact, &c. or their Crime be otherwife open and manifeft, it feems that they ought not to be bailed; but if there be any Colour of Probability for their Innocence, it feems moft agreeable to the Intention of the Statute to bail them. 2 Inft. 190. Regifter 269. b. F. N. B. 250. C. Vide fupra, Sect. 45.

Sect. 51. Fourthly, *Perfons accufed of other Trefpafs for which a Man ought not to lofe Life or Member*, are declared by the Statute to be replevifable; yet perhaps the Generality of this Claufe is reftrained by that other Claufe which declares, That Perfons taken for open and manifeft Offences fhall not be replevied, as hath been more fully fhewn, *Sect.* 45.

Sect. 52. Fifthly, The Appellee of an Approver is alfo exprefly declared to be bailable after the Death of the Approver, unlefs he be a notorious Felon. But having already incidentally fhewn, *Sect.* 43. in what Cafes fuch an Appellee is replevifable, I fhall refer the Reader, for this Matter, to what is there faid concerning it.

Sect. 53. Secondly, As to the Branch concerning thofe who are charged as Acceffaries, which is in the following Words, *Thofe who are accufed of the Receipt of Thieves or Felons, or of Commandment, or of Force, or of Aid of Felony done, ſhall be repleviſable*, &c. it is obſervable, That notwithſtanding the Statute mentions only thoſe who are Acceſſary by receiving Felons, or by Commandment, Force or Aid, yet all thoſe who are acceſſary to a Felony any [a] other Way, as by Perſuaſion or any other Procurement, or Abetment, have always been taken to be within the Equity of it; and moſt [b] of the Books relating to this Matter ſeem generally to hold, That all Acceſſaries, whether to Homicide or any other Felony, are bailable 'till the Principal be convicted, or attainted; and that they are bailable even after ſuch Conviction or Attainder, upon their [c] pleading to the Indictment, and do not expreſs any Limitation or Reſtriction, that they be of good Fame, or but ſlightly ſuſpected, *&c.* And in the Caſe [d] of 25 *Ed.* 3. 44. *pl.* 14. wherein a Perſon appealed of Murder, as having holden the Deceaſed in his Arms while the other killed him, was not let to Mainpriſe, the Reaſon given for it by the Reporter is, becauſe the Defendant was in a Manner a Principal; for that otherwiſe being an Acceſſary only, he ought to have been let to Mainpriſe by the Intent of the Statute. Yet I find it made a *Quære* in the Year-Book of 21 [e] *Ed.* 4. Whether Acceſſaries are to be let to Bail of Courſe? And perhaps it may be more reaſonable to intend, in the above cited Caſe of 25 *Ed.* 3. That ſuch Perſon was denied the Benefit of Mainpriſe by Reaſon of the Notoriety of his Guilt; for it ſeems clear, both from the [f] *Regiſter*, [g] *Fitzherbert*, and [h] *Dalton*, That Acceſſaries to Felonies are not to be bailed unleſs they be of good Reputation; and if the Want of a good Reputation, which is at moſt but a very ſlight Inducement to preſume them guilty of a particular Crime, be a good Cauſe to exclude them from the Benefit of Mainpriſe, which is given them by the general Words of the Statute, it ſeems ſtrange, the ſtrong and unqueſtionable Evidence of their Guilt ſhould not much more exclude them from it; eſpecially conſidering, that it is an allowed Rule, [i] That Bail is only proper where it ſtands indifferent whether the Perſon accuſed were guilty or innocent. And ſince latter Statutes have, in many Caſes, excluded Acceſſaries before the Fact from the Benefit of Clergy, it ſeems abſurd to ſay, That Perſons notoriouſly guilty of being Acceſſary to the Crimes which exclude them from the Benefit of Clergy, ſhall be admitted to Bail; whereas if they had been committed to Priſon on the like Evidence of Guilt, as Principals, for Felonies within the Benefit of Clergy, or even for inferior Offences of an enormous Nature, they could not have had the like Privilege: And therefore ſince the general Words of the Statute concerning the Repleviſing of Acceſſaries, are agreed to receive the abovementioned Limitations, That they ought to be of a good Reputation, and alſo to plead firſt to the Indictment, if the Principal be attainted; why ſhould it not be reaſonable to admit this farther Reſtriction, That their Guilt be not notorious? Which ſeems admitted to be implied in moſt of the other Clauſes of the Statute, which yet are penned in as general Words as that relating to Acceſſaries. But this Matter ſeems at this Day to be put beyond all Queſtion, by 31 *Car.* 2. *cap.* 2. Par. 21. By which it is recited, *That many Times Perſons charged with Petit Treaſon, or Felony, or as Acceſſaries thereunto, are committed on Suſpicion only, whereupon they are bailable or not, according as the Circumſtances making out that Suſpicion, are more or leſs weighty*, &c. And thereupon it is enacted, *That no Perſon ſo charged, ſhall be removed or bailed by Virtue of that Act, in other Manner than he might before.* From which it ſeems clearly to follow, That where there are ſtrong Preſumptions of Guilt, againſt a Perſon ſo charged, he neither was bailable before that Statute, nor is now bailable by Virtue of it.

[a] Regiſter 270.
S. P. C. 71.
F. N. B. 250. E.
H. P. C. 100.
[b] S. P. C. 71.
Bro. Mainpriſe, 6, 11, 22, 54, 58.
H. P. C. 100.
2 H. H. P. C. 135.
Coke, Bail & Mainpriſe, Chap. 5.
Dyer 120. pl. 10.
25 Ed. 3. 42. pl. 14.
40 Ed. 3. 42. pl. 22.
50 Ed. 3. 15. a.
29 Aſſ. 44.
40 Aſſ. 8.
[c] S. P. C. 71.
H. P. C. 100.
2 H. H. P. C. 135.
Bro. Mainpriſe, 58, 64.
40 Ed. 3. 42. pl. 22.
43 Ed. 3. 17.
40 Aſſ. 8.
Cont. 27 Ed. 3. 94. pl. 3.
[d] Fitz. Coron, 135.
[e] 21 Ed. 4. 71.
Bro. Mainpriſe, 78.
[f] Regiſter 270.
[g] F. N. B. 250. E.
[h] Dalt. chap. 114.
[i] Supra. Sect. 40.

As to the second Point, *viz.* In what Cases Bail is grantable by a Justice of Peace, I shall endeavour to shew,

1. How far it is grantable by Construction of the Statutes and Commission, which give Justices of Peace a Jurisdiction over certain Crimes, without saying any Thing concerning the Power of granting Bail.
2. How far it is grantable by the Statutes specially relating to the Power of granting Bail.

Sect. 54. As to the first Point it seems, That where-ever Justices of Peace have Jurisdiction of a Crime, they may bail the Person indicted before them of such Crime, upon such Circumstances for which other Courts may bail the Person so indicted before them; for that it seems to be a good general Rule, That so far as any Persons are Judges of any Crime, so far they have Power of bailing a Person indicted before them of such Crime: And upon this Ground it seems clear, That any two Justices of Peace, whereof one is of the *Quorum*, may, of common Right, bail Persons indicted before the Sessions of Justices of Peace, for that any two such Justices may hear and determine the Indictment. [a] Also it hath been holden, That any one Justice of Peace hath the like Power in Relation to Persons so indicted, because every such Justice being a Judge of the Court which is to determine the Offence, seems consequently to have a discretionary Power of Judging whether it be bailable, and of admitting the Party to Bail. And this seems to be implied by the Statute of 1 *Ric.* 3. *cap.* 3. which giving one Justice of Peace Power of bailing Persons arrested for Felony, *in like Form as if such Persons had been indicted at Sessions*, clearly supposes, that if such Persons had been indicted at Sessions, they might have been bailed by any one Justice: And if any one Justice of Peace had such Power of bailing the Persons so indicted at Sessions, before the Statutes specially relating to the Power of Justices of Peace in granting Bail, it seems, That he still has the same Power in Relation to Persons so indicted of any bailable Crime under the Degree of Felony, because the said Statutes seem not to restrain him in any such Case, under the Degree of Felony, from any Power which he lawfully might claim before. Also it seems to be agreed, That any one Justice of Peace might always in his Discretion either bail or imprison one who has given another a dangerous Wound, according as it shall appear from the whole Circumstances, that the Party is most likely to live or die, for that every such Justice being a principal Conservator of the Peace, the Offence at present being only an enormous Breach thereof, and no Felony, seems properly to come under his Conusance.

H. P. C. 105, 106. Coke, Bail & Mainprise, Chap. 6. Lamb. 347, 348.

[a] See the Books above cited. Cromp. 197, 234, 235. H. P. C. 105.

2 H. H. P. C. 137.

B. 1. Chap. 63. Sect. 19.

Sect. 55. As to the second Point, *viz.* How far Bail is grantable by Justices of Peace, by Virtue of the Statutes specially relating to their Power of granting Bail, it is recited by 1 *R.* 3. *cap.* 3. *That divers Persons had been daily arrested and imprisoned for Suspicion of Felony, sometime of Malice, and sometime of a light Suspicion, and so kept in Prison, without Bail or Mainprise, to their great Vexation and Trouble: And thereupon it is enacted, That every Justice of Peace in every Shire, City or Town, may, by his or their Discretion, let such Prisoners and Persons so arrested to Bail or Mainprise, in like Form as though the same Prisoners, or Persons, were indicted thereof of Record, before the same Justices at their Sessions.* 2 H. H. P. C. 137.

Sect. 56. But it is recited by 3 *H.* 7. *cap.* 3. *That by Colour of the said Statute of* 1 R. 3. *divers Persons which were not mainpernable, were oftentimes let to Bail and Mainprise by Justices of Peace, against the due Form of Law,* 2 H. H. P. C. 137.

whereby

whereby many Felons had escaped, to the great Displeasure of the King, and Annoyance of his Liege People; and thereupon it is enacted, *That the Justices of Peace in every Shire, City, and Town, or two of them at least, whereof one to be of the* Quorum, *have Authority and Power to let any such Prisoners, or Persons mainpernable by Law, that have been imprisoned within their several Counties, City or Town, to Bail or Mainprise, unto their next general Sessions, or unto their next general Gaol-Delivery of the same Gaols, in every Shire, City, or Town, as well within Franchises as without, where any Gaols be, or hereafter shall be: And that the said Justices of Peace, or one of them, so taking any such Bail or Mainprise, do certify the same at the next general Sessions of the Peace, or the next general Gaol-Delivery of any such Gaol, in every such County, City or Town, next following after any such Bail or Mainprise so taken, on Pain to forfeit to the King for every Default thereupon recorded,* 10 l. *And that the aforesaid Act, giving Authority and Power in the Premisses, to any Justice of the Peace by himself, be in that Behalf utterly void, and of none Effect.*

2 H. H. P. C. 137. *Sect.* 57. And it is recited by 1 & 2 *Ph. & M.* 13. *That since the said Statute of* 3 H. 7. *one Justice of Peace, in the Name of himself, and one other of the Justices his Companion, not making the said Justice Party nor Privy unto the Case wherefore the Prisoner should be bailed, had oftentimes by sinister Labour and Means, set at large the greatest and notablest Offenders, such as be not replevisable by the Laws of this Realm; and yet the rather to hide their Affections in that Behalf, had signified the Cause of their Apprehension to be only for Suspicion of Felony, whereby the said Offenders had and did daily escape Punishment*, &c. And thereupon it is enacted, *That from the first Day of* April *then next coming, no Justice or Justices of Peace, shall let to Bail or Mainprise any such Person or Persons, who for any Offence or Offences, by them or any of them committed, be declared not to be replevised, or be forbidden to be replevised or bailed by the abovementioned Statute of* Westminster 1.

Sect. 58. And it is further enacted, *Par.* 3. *That any Person or Persons arrested for Manslaughter or Felony, or Suspicion of Manslaughter or Felony, being bailable by the Law, shall not be let to Bail or Mainprise by any Justices of Peace, if it be not in open Sessions, except it be by two Justices of Peace at the least, whereof one to be of the* Quorum, *and the same Justices to be present together at the Time of the said Bailment or Mainprise; which Bailment or Mainprise they shall certify in Writing subscribed or signed with their own Hands, at the next general Gaol-Delivery to be holden within the County where the said Person or Persons shall be arrested or suspected.*

Sect. 59. And it is farther enacted, *Par.* 4. *That the said Justices, or one of them, being of the* Quorum, *when any such Prisoner is brought before them for any Manslaughter or Felony, before any Bailment or Mainprise, shall take the Examination of the said Prisoner, and Information of them that bring him, of the Fact and Circumstances thereof, and the same, or as much thereof as shall be material to prove the Felony, shall put in Writing before they make the same Bailment; which said Examination, together with the said Bailment, the said Justices shall certify at the next general Gaol-Delivery, to be holden within the Limits of their Commission.*

Sect. 60. And it is farther enacted, *Par.* 5. *That the said Justices shall have Authority to bind all such by Recognizance or Obligation, as do declare any Thing material, to prove the said Offences or Felonies, to appear at the next general Gaol-Delivery to be holden within the County, City, or Town-Corporate where the Trial thereof shall be, and then and there to give Evidence against the Party at the Time of his Trial, and shall certify as well the same Evidence, as such Bond or Bonds in writing as he shall take, at or before the Time of his said Trial thereof to be had or made. And in Case any Justice of Peace of* Quorum *ſhall offend in any thing, contrary to the true Intent and Meaning of this Act; the Juſtices of Gaol-Delivery, where ſuch Offence ſhall happen to be committed, upon due Proof thereof, by Examination before them, ſhall for every ſuch Offence, ſet ſuch Fine on every of the ſame Juſtices, as the ſame Juſtices of Gaol-Delivery ſhall think meet,* &c.

Sect. 61. But it is provided, Par. 6. *That Juſtices of Peace, and Coroners, within the City of* London, *and the County of* Middleſex, *and in other Cities, Boroughs, and Towns Corporate, ſhall within their ſeveral Juriſdictions, have Authority to let to bail Felons and Priſoners, in ſuch Manner and Form as they had been before accuſtomed; and alſo ſhall take Examinations and Bonds, as is aforeſaid, upon every Bailment by them made, and certify every ſuch Bailment, Bond and Examination, at the next general Gaol-Delivery,* &c.

From theſe Statutes the following Particulars appear moſt obſervable.

Sect. 62. Firſt, That it ſeems clearly to be imply'd by the above mentioned Statute of 1 *R.* 3. 3. which authorized any one Juſtice of Peace to bail a Perſon on a ſlight Suſpicion of Felony, in like Manner as if ſuch Perſon had been indicted at Seſſions, That before that Statute, Juſtices of Peace could bail thoſe only for Felony, who had been indicted of it before them. And by Parity of Reaſon it ſeems alſo to follow, That they had no Power to bail Perſons for any other Crime before ſuch Indictment, unleſs it were an Offence directly tending to the Breach of the Peace, the Bailing of Perſons for which ſeems properly to come under their Conuſance as Conſervators of the Peace: And therefore it ſeems difficult to maintain the Power of one Juſtice of the Peace to bail a Perſon for any other Crime, unleſs it be by ſome Statute limited to the Conuſance of one Juſtice, or the Party have been indicted for it at Seſſions, becauſe the Commiſſion in giving a Juſtice a general Juriſdiction over any Crime, ſhall be conſtrued ſo far only to give him a Power to bail a Perſon accuſed of it, as it makes him a Judge of it, which he cannot be till it come regularly before him by Indictment; and the Statutes above mentioned ſpecially relating to the Power of Juſtices of Peace, in granting Bail, expreſly require the Conuſance of two Juſtices.

Coke, Bail and Mainpriſe, cap. 6. 2 H. H. P. C. 137, 138.

Supra Sect. 54.

Sect. 63. Secondly, That Juſtices of Peace have no Power to bail any Perſon not repleviſable by the above mentioned Statute of *Weſtminſter* 1. 15. from whence it ſeems to follow, That a Perſon under the actual Commitment or Arreſt of any other Magiſtrate, or even of a private Perſon, for any Crime declared to be irrepleviſable by that Statute, as Treaſon againſt the King's Perſon, Arſon, *&c.* cannot be delivered from his Impriſonment by the Bailment of any Juſtice of Peace. Yet if a Perſon at large be only accuſed of any ſuch Crime, on a ſlight Suſpicion, before a Juſtice of Peace, it ſeems that the Juſtice ought not to commit him, but to take Surety of him to appear before a proper Court, as hath been more fully ſhewn in Relation to the Sheriff, *Sect.* 46. And inaſmuch as the above mentioned Statute of 1 & 2 *Ph. & M.* 13. expreſly mentions the Bailing of Perſons for Manſlaughter, as well as for other Felonies, there can be no Doubt, but that Juſtices of Peace may, by Force thereof, ſafely bail any Perſon impriſoned on a ſlight Suſpicion of a Fact, clearly appearing to be no higher an Offence than Manſlaughter, and much more if it appear to amount to no more than Homicide by Miſadventure, or in Self-defence. Yet it ſeems to be agreed, That ſuch Juſtices muſt, at their Peril, take Care that the Offence in Truth amounted not to Murder; and that they ought in no Caſe to bail any Perſon who manifeſtly appears to

2 H. H. P. C. 138, 139, 140.

Vide Supra Sect. 33, 34.

1 Rol. Rep. 268. Dalt. cap 114. H. P. C. 99.

have

Lamb. 346, 347.

have been guilty of any of the Homicides above mentioned, either by his own Confeſſion, or the Notoriety of the Fact, not only becauſe the above mentioned Statute of *Weſtminſter* 1. 15. which is the Pattern preſcribed by 1 & 2 *Ph. & M.* for the Direction of Juſtices of Peace in Relation to bail, expreſly excludes all Perſons from the Benefit of it which are guilty of open and manifeſt Offences; but alſo becauſe the Statute of *Glouceſter*, *cap.* 9. is expreſs, That all Perſons who are guilty of Homicide, by Miſadventure or in Self-defence, ſhall be kept in Priſon 'till the next coming of the Juſtices Itinerant, or of Gaol-Delivery. [29]

Supra Sect. 44, 45. 2 Inſt. 314, 315.

Sect. 64. Thirdly, That the chief Import of theſe Statutes is to ſhew in what Manner Perſons are to be bailed by Juſtices of Peace, and not to declare what Perſons are bailable by them; in relation to which Matter, the old Rules of the Statute of *Weſtminſter* 1. are generally ſtill to be followed, which extending only to criminal Offences puniſhable in the ordinary way by Indictment before the Sheriff, *&c.* give no Power to bail Perſons taken on Proceſs in Civil Actions, or for Contempts to Superior Courts, as by Proceſs of Rebellion out of Chancery. And therefore by a reaſonable Conſtruction of all theſe Statutes, Juſtices of Peace have no Power in any ſuch Caſes to admit any Perſon to Bail.

Dalt. cap. 114. Cromp. 152. H. P. C. 105.

Sect. 65. As to the third Point, *viz.* Where Bail is grantable by the Juſtices of Gaol-Delivery, it ſeems to be clearly ſettled [a] at this Day, That ſuch Juſtices may bail any Perſon convicted before them of Homicide by Miſadventure, or in Self-defence, the better to enable him to purchaſe his Pardon: And if a Perſon convicted of Manſlaughter before ſuch Juſtices, purchaſe his Pardon, it ſeems, that they may [b] bail him, even after their Seſſions is determined, 'till the next Seſſions of Gaol-Delivery, that he may come in then and plead his Pardon, for that the Power of ſuch Juſtices ſeems [c] to continue for ſuch Purpoſes after their Seſſions. Alſo [d] if a Man be convicted of Manſlaughter before ſuch Juſtices, againſt plain Evidence, it is ſaid that they may bail him till the next Seſſions of Gaol-Delivery, in order to purchaſe his Pardon in the mean Time. But it ſeems, [e] That Juſtices of Peace have no Power to bail a Man in any of theſe Caſes, becauſe they are tied up for the moſt part to the Rules preſcribed by the above mentioned Statute of *Weſtminſter* 1. But this Statute not [f] extending to Juſtices of Gaol-Delivery, ſeems to leave them a diſcretionary Power in thoſe Caſes wherein it reſtrains the Sheriff from admitting Perſons to Bail. And therefore if a Defendant in an Appeal of Death, plead an Excommunication in Diſability of the Plaintiff, it ſeems to be holden by *Staundford*, [g] That ſuch Juſtices may bail the Defendant from Day to Day, till the Plaintiff ſhall be abſolved, for that otherwiſe the Defendant might lie in Priſon for ever, without any Opportunity of coming to his Trial. But it is obſervable, That the Books [h] which are cited for the Maintenance of this Opinion, ſpeak only of an Appeal of Robbery: Yet if Juſtices of Gaol-Delivery have ſuch Power of Bailing Perſons in the Caſe of Death, on the Circumſtances above mentioned, as it ſeems agreed in the Caſes above-cited that they have, I do not find any Reaſon why they may not as well upon other ſuch like Circumſtances, bail Perſons indicted or appealed before them of any other Crime, in ſuch Manner as the Court of King's Bench may do, as ſhall be more fully ſhewn under the next Point.

[a] Cromp. 154. a. 2 H. H. P. C. 129, 131. H. P. C. 101, 104, 105. Fitz. Coron. 361. Dalt. cap. 114. F. N. B. 246. C. S. P. C. 15. C. 16. D. Con. 25 Ed. 3. 42. pl. 27. S. P. C. 74. D. Fitz. Coron. 354. Mainpriſe, 1.
[b] Crompt. 153. b. Bro. Mainpriſe, 94. H. P. C. 101.
[c] Vide Supra cap. 6. ſect. 7.
[d] Cromp. 154. a.
[e] H. P. C. 104, 105. Vide Supra Sect. 63. Cont. Dalt. cap. 114.
[f] 2 Inſt. 185, 186.
[g] S. P. C. 72. F.
[h] Fitz. Mainpriſe, 6. 3 Aſſ. pl. 12. Salk. 61. ſeems contrary.

As to the Fourth Point, *viz.* Where Bail is grantable by the Courts of *Weſtminſter-Hall*, I ſhall endeavour to ſhew.

1. Where it is grantable by the Court of King's Bench.
2. Where by the other Courts of *Weſtminſter-Hall.*

As to the firſt of theſe Points I ſhall conſider,

1. Where Bail is grantable by the Court of King's Bench, to a Perſon impriſoned by the King's ſpecial Command, or by the Order of his P rvy Council.
2. Where to a Perſon committed by either Houſe of Parliament.
3. Where to one committed by the Court of Chancery.
4. Where to one committed by an Inferior Court of Record.
5. Where to one expreſly excluded by the above mentioned Statute of *Weſtminſter* 1. Chap. 15. from the common Benefit of a Replevin by the Sheriff.

Sect. 66. As to the firſt of theſe Particulars, *viz.* Where Bail is grantable by the Court of King's Bench to a Perſon impriſoned by the King's ſpecial Command, or by the Order of the Privy Council; I do not find but that where-ever [a] a Commitment by the Privy Council hath ſpecially expreſſed the Crime for which the Party hath been committed, this Court has always admitted him to Bail, on the like Circumſtances on which, in Diſcretion, it will grant Bail on other Commitments: [b] And where-ever it has appeared, that Perſons have been impriſoned by Colour of an uſurped Authority, pretended to be derived from any Patent whatſoever, contrary to Law, it ſeems that the ſaid Court hath always diſcharged the Perſons ſo impriſoned, without Bail. But there have been formerly many Opinions [c] That Perſons committed by the ſpecial Command of the King, or of his Privy Council, without expreſſing any other Cauſe of the Commitment, were not bailable by any Court whatſoever, without ſome Intimation of the King's Conſent to ſuch Bailment, by Letter from the Privy Council, or otherwiſe. And a Diſtinction [d] was taken by ſome between a Commitment by one of the Privy Council, and a Commitment by the whole Body; and that the former ought indeed to ſet forth ſome other Cauſe of the Commitment beſides the Command of the Perſon who made it; but that the latter needed not any.

[a] 5 Mod. 78. 1 Sid. 143. 1 And. 297, 298. 1 Leon. 70. Palm. 559.
[b] 1 Leon. 70. 1 And. 297.
[c] 33 H. 6. 28. b. 1 And. 298. 1 Rol. Rep. 134, 192. pl. 31, 32. 219. pl. 22. Con. Mo. 839. 1 And. 158. See the Arguments on the Habeas Corpus concerning Loans, 81, 82, &c.
[d] 1 Leon. 70, 71.

Sect. 67. But this Matter came afterwards to be very ſolemnly debated in the famous Caſe [e] of Sir *John Corbet* and others, who being impriſoned by a Warrant from the Privy Council, about the third Year of the Reign of King *Charles* the firſt, moved the Court of King's Bench to admit them to Bail upon their *Habeas Corpus*; whereupon it was returned; that they were detained in the Priſon of the *Fleet* by the ſpecial Command of the King, ſignified to the Warden by a Warrant of ſome of the Members of the Privy Council, in which Warrant no other Cauſe of the Impriſonment was contained but ſuch Special Command: And it was ſtrongly urged on the Behalf of the Priſoners, That ſuch Impriſonment is againſt the Statute of *Magna Charta*, *cap.* 29. which provides, *That no Freeman ſhall be taken or impriſoned, and that the King will not paſs upon him, nor condemn him, but by the Judgment of his Peers, or the Law of the Land*; and alſo againſt many other Statutes [f] made in Affirmance of *Magna Charta*, by which it is ordained, *That no Man ſhall be taken by Petition, or Suggeſtion, made to the King or to his Council, unleſs it be by Indictment or Preſentment, or by Proceſs by Original Writ; and that no Man ſhall be impriſoned*, &c. *without being brought to anſwer by due Proceſs of Law; nor be put to anſwer without Preſentment before Juſtices, or Matter of Record, or by due Proceſs, and Writ Original.*

[e] See the Arguments on the Habeas Corpus concerning Loans, & Ruſhworth's Collections, 1 Part. Fol. 458, &c.
[f] 25 Ed. 3. 4. 28 Ed. 3. 3. 42 Ed. 3. 3.

Original. And it was argued, That the Liberty of the Subject would be precarious, and lie at the King's Mercy, if Persons who happen to incur his Displeasure, for what perhaps the Law esteems no Crime, should by Means of such a Commitment be liable to be for ever imprisoned, without any Possibility of Redress; and that it seems inconsistent with natural Justice to expose a Man to so severe a Punishment for a supposed Crime alledged against him, without giving him an Opportunity of clearing himself by a lawful Trial. And it was farther urged, That, according to the Opinion of Sir *John Markham*, in the Time of King *Edward* the Fourth, the King could not so much as arrest a Man upon Suspicion of Treason or Felony, as any of his Subjects may; for that if the King should do Wrong, the Party could have no Action against him. Also it was insisted, That the Preamble of the Statute of *Westminster* 1. 15. which declares, That Persons imprisoned by the King's Command have always been taken to be irreplevisable, must be intended only of a Replevin by the common Writ *de Homine replegiando*, or by the Sheriff *ex officio*, without Writ, for that it speaks only of a Replevin by Sheriffs and others; and therefore shall not be taken to extend to superior Courts: And it was never thought, that the Court of King's Bench was restrained by it from Bailing Persons imprisoned for Homicide; and yet all such are equally declared by the Statute to be irreplevisable: Also many Precedents were alledged, whereby it appeared, That Persons committed by the King's special Command had been discharged upon Writs of *Habeas Corpus*.

1 H. 7. 4. b. 2 H. H. P. C. 131.

Sect. 68. But on the other Side it was argued, That such Commitments could not reasonably be intended to be against the Purview of the Statutes above-cited, inasmuch as the said Statute of *Westminster* 1. 15. which was made in the very next Reign after that in which the Statute of *Magna Charta* was made, it was declared to be a settled and undoubted Point, That Persons committed by the Command of the King (which, as it seems to be agreed, is to be understood of the King's special, absolute, and extrajudicial Command) are not replevisable: And it cannot be imagined that so high a Regard should be paid to such a Commitment, if it were thought to be illegal, and contrary to *Magna Charta*. And it was insisted, That Commitments of this Kind have often been allowed by the Courts [a] of Justice, and are mentioned by Authors [b] of the best Credit since the above-cited Statutes, without any the least Objection to their Legality, and as depriving the Party imprisoned by them from the common Benefit of the Writ of Replevin. And it was also strongly urged, That there are often secret Causes not fit to be divulged, which may make it necessary for the Safety of the State, in some particular Circumstances, to restrain some Persons from their Liberty for a certain Time, and that the King who is entirely entrusted with the Management of State-Affairs, shall be presumed always to act for the Publick Good; and that it is immodest for any of his Courts to question the Justice of his Proceedings of this Kind, which the Law seems wholly to have left to his Wisdom, or to suffer a Suggestion that he abuses his Prerogative to cover Oppression; and that the Subject is in no Danger of perpetual Imprisonment on this Account, for that the Court of King's Bench hath always used a discretionary Power over such Commitments, as well as all others, and therefore upon special Circumstances of Hardship, may admit Persons under such Commitments to Bail; but that where there was nothing extraordinary in the Case, it hath been the general Course of the Court not to do it without a special Order from the Council for it, as

Vide Supra Sect. 36.

[a] Vide Supra Sect. 66.
[b] S. P. C. 72, 73. F. N. B. 66. E.

Rushworth's Collections, Part 1. fol. 510.

appeared from the Examination of moſt of the Precedents relating to this Matter. And therefore in the Caſe abovementioned the Court of King's Bench was unanimous in Opinion, That Sir *John Corbet*, and the other Gentlemen ſo committed by the King's Special Command, as is abovementioned, had no Right, *prima facie*, to demand the Benefit of Bail, without the Conſent of the Council, and therefore remanded them. 1 Rol. Rep. 219. See the Arguments on the Habeas Corpus above mentioned, pag. 81.

Sect. 69. But this Matter being afterwards conſidered in Parliament, and it being the general Opinion, That the chief Reaſon why thoſe Gentlemen incurred the King's Diſpleaſure was their Refuſal to pay the Loans, which, as they inſiſted, were demanded of them without ſufficient Authority; and it being evident, That if there were no certain legal Remedy for the Liberty of the Subject againſt ſuch a Strain of the Prerogative, no Man could be ſafe in maintaining his Property, either in Parliament, or out of it, againſt a diſputed Demand from the Crown, but would be liable to a diſcretionary Impriſonment, and that under Colour of Law, without any certain Redreſs from the Law; it was thought neceſſary on this Occaſion to draw up the famous Petition of Right, which was afterwards aſſented to by the King, wherein, among other Things, the Lords and Commons complain to the King, *That againſt the Tenor of the above* [a] *cited Statutes, divers Subjects had then of late been impriſoned, without any Cauſe ſhewed; and when for their Deliverance they had been brought before Juſtices by Writs of* Habeas Corpus, *there to undergo and receive as the Court ſhould order; and their Keepers commanded to certify the Cauſes of their Detainer, no Cauſe had been certified, but that they were detained by his Majeſty's ſpecial Command ſignified by the Lords of his Privy Council, and yet were returned back to ſeveral Priſons, without being charged with any Thing to which they might make anſwer according to the Law: And thereupon the ſaid Lords and Commons, among other Things, humbly pray, That no Freeman, in any ſuch Manner as is before mentioned, be impriſoned, or detained,* &c. Ruſhworth's Collections, Part 1. 428, 473, 499, &c. Ruſhworth's Collections, Part 1. Fol. 613. [a] Supra Sect. 66.

Sect. 70. And it ſeems to have been generally agreed, ſince the Time of this Petition, That where-ever any Commitment by the Privy Council hath not expreſſed, with ſome convenient Certainty, the Crime alledged againſt the Party, he ought to be bailed upon his *Habeas Corpus.* Vide Cro. Car. 507, 579, 593.

Sect. 71. And for the greater Security of the Liberty of the Subject, againſt Commitments by the Command of the King, or of his Privy Council, it is farther provided and enacted, by 16 *Car.* 1. *cap.* 10. *Par.* 8. *That if any Perſon ſhall be committed, reſtrained of his Liberty, or ſuffer Impriſonment by the Command or Warrant of the King's Majeſty, in his own Perſon, or by the Command or Warrant of the Council-Board, or of any of the Lords or others of his Majeſty's Privy Council; That in every ſuch Caſe, every ſuch Perſon upon Damand or Motion to the Judges of the King's Bench or Common Pleas, in open Court, ſhall without Delay, upon any Pretence whatſoever, for the ordinary Fees uſually paid for the ſame, have forthwith granted unto him a Writ of* Habeas Corpus, *to be directed generally unto all and every Sheriff, Gaoler, Miniſter, Officer, or other Perſon in whoſe Cuſtody the Party committed or reſtrained ſhall be, and ſuch Sheriff,* &c. *ſhall, at the Return of the ſaid Writ, and according to the Command thereof, on due and convenient Notice thereof given unto him, at the Charge of the Party who requires or procures ſuch Writ, and on Security by his own Bond given, to pay the Charges of carrying back the Priſoner, if he ſhall be remanded by the Court,* &c. *which Charges ſhall be ordered by the Court, bring or Cauſe to be brought the Body of the Party before the Judges of the Court, from whence the ſame Writ ſhall iſſue, in open Court, and ſhall then likewiſe certify the true Cauſe of ſuch his Detainer or Impriſonment, and thereupon* 2 H. H. P. C. 144, 145.

See 1 Syd. 78. 1 Keb. 305. pl. 15, 17. *the Court within three Court-Days after ſuch Return made and delivered* [a] *in open Court ſhall proceed to examine and determine whether the Cauſe of ſuch Commitment, appearing upon the ſaid Return, be juſt and legal or not, and ſhall thereupon do what to Juſtice ſhall appertain, either by delivering, bailing, or remanding the Priſoner: And if any Thing ſhall be otherwiſe wilfully done, or omitted to be done by any Judge, Juſtice, Officer or other Perſon aforementioned, contrary to the true Meaning hereof, That then ſuch Perſon ſo offending ſhall forfeit to the Party grieved, his treble Damages,* &c.

Sect. 72. But it is provided, Par. 9. *That the above-recited Clauſe ſhall extend only to the Warrants and Directions of the Council-Board, and to the Commitments, Reſtraints and Impriſonments of any Perſon or Perſons, made, commanded or awarded, by the King's Majeſty, his Heirs or Succeſſors, in their own Perſon, or by the Lords and others of the Privy Council, and every one of them.*

Sect. 73. As to the ſecond Particular, *viz.* Where Bail is grantable by the Court of King's Bench, to a Perſon impriſoned by either Houſe of Parliament, There can be no Doubt but that the higheſt Regard is to be paid to all the Proceedings of either of thoſe Houſes, and that where-ever the contrary does not plainly and expreſly appear, it ſhall be preſumed that they act within their Juriſdiction, and agreeably to the Uſages of Parliament, and the Rules of Law and Juſtice: And therefore, where-ever it ſtands indifferent upon the Return of a *Habeas Corpus*, whether a Commitment by either of thoſe Houſes were ſtrictly legal or not, and the Parliament be ſtill ſitting, I can find no Precedent that the Priſoner hath been bailed by the Court of King's Bench. And it cannot but be expected, that thoſe Houſes would be apt to reſent an Attempt of this Kind, which might ſeem to carry with it an implicit Reflection on their Honour, as unjuſtly depriving a Subject of his Liberty, and putting him under a Neceſſity of demanding Juſtice from another Court, by unreaſonably refuſing to reſtore him to it; which ſurely ſhall never be intended, where their Proceedings are capable of a more favourable 1 Mod. 144, 145. Conſtruction. And therefore in the Lord *Shaftbury*'s Caſe, who, upon his *Habeas Corpus* in the King's Bench, was returned to have been committed by the Houſe of Lords for his high Contempt committed againſt that Houſe, the Court would not take Notice of any Exceptions againſt the Form of the Commitment, as that it was too general, and did not expreſs the Nature of the Contempt, or in what Place it was committed, *&c.* for that it ſhall be preſumed, That it was ſuch for which the Lords might lawfully make ſuch an Order, and no other Court ſhall preſcribe to them in what Form they ought to make it. But if it be demanded, in Caſe a Subject ſhould be committed by either of thoſe Houſes, for a Matter manifeſtly out of their Juriſdiction, what Remedy can he have? I anſwer, That it cannot well be imagined that the Law, which favours nothing more than the Liberty of the Subject, ſhould give us a Remedy againſt Commitments by the King himſelf, appearing to be illegal, and yet give us no Manner of Redreſs againſt a Commitment by our Fellow Subjects, equally appearing to be unwarranted. But as this is a Caſe, which, I am perſwaded, will never happen, it ſeems needleſs over nicely to examine it.

Sect. 74. However it ſeems agreed, That a Perſon committed for a Skin. 56, 163, 527. Contempt, by the Order of either Houſe of Parliament, may be diſcharged by the Court of King's Bench after a Diſſolution, or Prorogation of the Parliament, whether he were committed during the Seſſions, or afterwards; for that all the Orders of Parliament are determined by a

Diſſolution, or Prorogation; and all Matters before either Houſe muſt be commenced a-new at the next Parliament, except only in the Caſe of a Writ of Error: And if the Subject ſhould be deprived of his Liberty 'till the next Parliament, which perhaps may not meet again in many Years, no one could ſay when his Impriſonment would end.

1 Keb. 871, 887, 888. 1 Syd. 245. 1 Lev. 165. 1 Mod. 155, 157.

Sect. 75. But it is holden in *Shower's Reports*, That a Lord committed by the Houſe of Lords, on an Impeachment of Treaſon, and afterwards pardoned cannot be diſcharged by the Court of King's Bench, becauſe the Impeachment being in a Superior Court, the Pardon muſt be pleaded there; and the Commitment being by the Lords, the King's Bench cannot take Conuſance of it. Yet it ſeems to have been taken for granted in the Lord *Stafford*'s Caſe, That the Court of King's Bench may, in their Diſcretion, bail a Lord upon an Impeachment of High Treaſon, which in that Caſe they refuſed to do, not as a Matter out of their Power, but as a Thing which they were not bound to do, and improper on Conſideration of the whole Circumſtances. And though the Reaſons above 'cited from *Shower's Reports* ſeem proper to prove, That the Court of King's Bench cannot diſcharge a Priſoner from any Impeachment in Parliament whatſoever; yet they ſeem by no Means to prove, that they cannot bail him. But it is obſervable, That it doth not clearly appear, from either of the abovementioned Reports, whether any Parliament were ſitting at the Times of the Motions for ſuch Diſcharge and Bailment, or not; but it is certainly moſt likely to prevail in ſuch a Motion, when no Parliament is ſitting, nor likely ſoon to ſit, and after the Party hath been long in Priſon; becauſe, in ſuch a Caſe, if he ſhould not be bailed, he might be perpetually impriſoned for a Crime, without any Opportunity of making his ☞ Defence. [30]

Shower 100. Raym. 381. Skin. 56, 162, 163. Carth. 132, 133.

Sect. 76. As to the third Particular, *viz.* Where Bail is grantable by the King's Bench, to a Perſon committed by the Court of Chancery, little is ſaid in the Books, except in the Reign of King *James* the firſt, at the Time when Sir *Edward Coke* was Chief Juſtice, when this Matter was very much litigated, and occaſioned great Heats between the two Courts, and ſeveral Perſons committed to the *Fleet* by the Chancellor, were bailed by the Court of King's Bench, upon Exceptions to the Generality of the Form of the Commitments, as [a] not ſhewing the Time of the Commitment, or ſetting [b] forth only the Command of the Lord Chancellor as the Ground of the Impriſonment, without mentioning any Crime at all, or mentioning the Crime in [c] general Terms, as for a Contempt to the Court of Chancery, without ſhewing what the Contempt was, or at what Time committed: And one [d] *Glanvil*, who was generally committed by the Command of the Lord Chancellor, without ſetting forth any Cauſe of ſuch Command, ſeems to have been bailed upon Examination of the Merits of the Decree, for diſobeying whereof he was in Truth committed; whereby it appeared that the Decree related to a Matter before adjudged at the Common Law, which was thought contrary to the Purport of the [f] Statutes of 27 *Ed.* 3. 1. & 4 *H.* 4. 23. But this Proceeding being reſented by the Lord Chancellor, the ſaid *Glanvil* was afterwards recommitted by him for the ſame Matter, and yet was afterwards, on another *Habeas Corpus*, bailed the ſecond Time by the Court of King's Bench: But I have not met with any Precedent of this Kind of late Years; and how far the long Diſuſe of ſuch like Proceedings may have leſſened the Authority of the Caſes above mentioned, may deſerve to be conſidered. However, it cannot but be expected, That

[a] 1 Rol. Rep. 192. pl. 32. 218. pl. 19.
[b] Moore 839. 1 Rol. Rep. 219. pl. 21.
[c] 1 Rol. Rep. 192. pl. 31, 32. 218. pl. 19, 20. 219. pl. 23.
[d] 1 Rol. Rep. 111, 219. Moore 838. 2 Bulſt. 301. Cro. Jac. 343. like Caſe. 3 Bulſt. 115. 1 Rol. Rep. 277.
[f] Vide 1 Rol. Rep. 277. 3 Bulſt. 115. Daliſon 81. 3 Leon. 18.

That the Superior Courts will pay the highest Regard to one another's Prodeedings, and be ready to presume, That they are agreeable to Law, unless the contrary appear, or the Case be very particular and extraordinary, which may perhaps reasonably induce them, in some Circumstances, to make Exceptions from those general Rules, which in common Cases usually govern their Discretion. But what Case in particular may be said to be of so extraordinary a Nature, it would be needless and presumptuous for me to endeavour to examine. But as to the Case abovementioned, which was formerly so much litigated, concerning the Chancery's giving Relief against a Judgment of Law, since it seems to be settled at this Day, that the Chancery may, in some Cases, give Relief against the unequitable Use of such a Judgment, especially as to a Point not relievable by Law; whenever it stands indifferent, whether the Matter examined by Chancery, after a Judgment at Law, be of such a Nature as is proper for Relief in Chancery, or not; it is not probable, That any other Court of *Westminster-Hall* will easily presume that it is not, when the Chancellor, who is the proper Judge, hath determined that it is: And agreeably hereto it hath been adjudged, That a Commitment from Chancery, for Disobedience to a Decree, is good, without shewing what the Decree was.

Vaughan 130, 140. seems contrary.

Vide Book 1. Ch. 19. Sect. 17.

1 Mod. 155. Moore 840. pl. 1133.

Sect. 77. As to the fourth Particular, *viz.* Where Bail is grantable by the Court of King's Bench to one committed by an inferior Court of Record; it seems, That this Court, having the Supreme Controul of all inferior Courts, may, in Discretion, on Consideration of the whole Circumstances of any Case whatsoever, bail any Person who shall appear to have been unjustly or hardly deprived of his Liberty by any inferior Court. And therefore, where-ever it shall clearly and expresly appear, that a Person hath been committed by any such Court, for a Matter which either is in Truth no Crime at all, or if it be a Crime, is not within the Jurisdiction of such Court, there can be no Doubt but that it is a proper Motion to the King's Bench to bail him. But in what other Cases in particular one may hope for the like Success in a Motion of this Kind, it seems difficult to determine; for that every such Case depends upon its particular Circumstances, which have great Weight with the Court in its Determinations of this Kind, in which it is in great Measure left to its Discretion. And therefore, though perhaps it may bail a Man on a Commitment by a Mayor of a Town, or a Justice of Peace, or other inferior Magistrate, for a Contempt, without shewing the particular Nature of it; yet it cannot be expected, that it will with like Readiness bail a Man on such a general Commitment by a Court of a higher [a] Dignity, as a Court of *Oyer* and *Terminer*, or any other Court of *Westminster-Hall*; to the Honour of whose Proceedings the greatest Regard is always to be given; and on this Ground chiefly, as I suppose, where a Person on a *Habeas Corpus*, was returned to have been committed by an Order of the Exchequer, for not paying a Fine of 50 *l.* by the Ecclesiastical Commissioners imposed upon him, the Court of King's Bench [b] refused to bail him, though it was not shewn wherefore the said Fine was imposed. And as a great Regard is always paid to the Dignity of the Court by which the Party is committed; so is it likewise to the Notoriety of the Offence; and therefore, where a Person convicted of buying and selling old Money, before Justices of *Oyer* and *Terminer*, was committed in Execution for the Fine, by an Order of the Court, not strictly formal, yet the Court of King's Bench refused [c] to bail him, for this Reason chiefly, because he was in Execution, and his Commitment

Vaughan 157. Vide 6 Mod. 73, &c.

See Bushel's Case in Vaughan's Reports.

2 Bulst. 139, 140.

[a] See the precedent Section, and Cro. Jac. 219. and Vaughan 139, 140.

[b] Cro. Car. 579.

[c] 1 Sid. 144, 286, 320.

ment was defective only in Point of Form. Also where Persons taken in Execution for their Fines to the King, set on them by a Sessions of Justices of Peace, have not only brought their *Habeas Corpus*, but also their Writ of Error in the King's Bench, and assigned Errors, yet the Court has refused to bail them. But I take it for granted, in those Cases which are but briefly reported, That it appeared upon the whole Record, That such Fines were legally imposed. Also it seems, That the said Court has sometimes been induced to deny Persons committed by other Courts, by Warrants not strictly formal, the Benefit of Bail, for the Enormity, dangerous Tendency, or Obstinacy [a] of their Offence, which if it had been attended with less aggravating Circumstances might not have excluded them from it. Also the said Court, in determining whether it be proper to bail a Man committed by another Court, usually considers all the other Circumstances of the Case, as the Length [b] and Hardship [c] of the Imprisonment, and such like, in order to give such a Determination upon the whole, as may be most agreeable to the Honour and Prerogative of the Crown, and the Liberty and Safety of the Subject.

Salk. 348. 5 Mod. 19, 20, &c. Vide March 52, 53. 1 Sid. 288, 289. 1 Sid. 320. pl. 10. 144.

[a] 1 Bulst. from 48 to 54. 1 Rol. Rep. 220. pl. 14. 337. pl. 52. 411. pl. 54.

[b] 1 Rol. Rep. 218. pl. 19. 337. pl. 15. 2 Bulst. 140.

[c] Latch 12.

Sect. 78. But it seems to be agreed, That no one can in any Case controvert the Truth of the Return to a *Habeas Corpus*, or plead or suggest any Matter repugnant to it: Yet it hath been holden, That a Man may confess and avoid such a Return, by admitting the Truth of the Matters contained in it, and suggesting others not repugnant, which take off the Effect of them. And upon this Ground, where one *Swallow*, a Citizen of *London*, was committed for refusing to accept the Office of an Alderman of the said City to which he had been elected, and the Custom of the City justifying a Commitment for such a Refusal, and the Election and Refusal were set forth in the Return to the *Habeas Corpus*; he filed a Suggestion in the Crown-Office, That he was an Officer of the King's Mint, and that all such Officers were exempted from all City-Offices, both by Prescription and by the King's Charter; and thereupon the Patent of the Grant of his Office, and also the Patent of the Exemption being inrolled in the Court he was discharged.

1 Sid. 287, 288.

Sect. 79. Also the Court will sometimes examine by Affidavit, the Circumstances of a Fact on which a Prisoner brought before them by an *Habeas Corpus* hath been indicted, in order to inform themselves, on Examination of the whole Matter, whether it be reasonable to bail him or not. And agreeably hereto, where one *Jackson*, who had been indicted of Piracy before the Sessions of Admiralty, on a malicious Prosecution, brought his *Habeas Corpus* in the said Court in order to be bailed; the Court examined the whole Circumstances of the Fact by Affidavits, upon which it appeared, That the Prosecutor himself, if any one, was guilty, and carried on the present Prosecution to skreen himself; and thereupon the Court in Consideration of the Unreasonableness of the Prosecution, and the Uncertainty of the Time when another Sessions of Admiralty might be holden, admitted the said *Jackson* to Bail, and committed the Prosecutor till he should find Bail to answer the Facts contained in the Affidavits.

5 Mod. 323, 454, 455. 2 Jo. 222.

Trin. 4. Georg. 1.

Sect. 80. As to the fifth Particular, *viz.* Where Bail is grantable by the Court of King's Bench, to one excluded by the above mentioned Statute of *Westminster* 1. *chap.* 15. from the common Benefit of a Replevin by the Sheriff; It cannot be doubted, but that notwithstanding neither [d] the Judges of this, nor of any other Superior Court of Justice, are strictly

[d] 2 Inst. 185, 186, 189. 2 H. H. P. C. 129, 148. H. P. C. 104. Salk. 61.

within the Purview of that Statute; yet [a] they will always, in their Discretion pay a due Regard to the Rules prescribed by it, and not admit a Person to Bail who is expresly declared by it to be irreplevisable, without some particular Circumstance in his Favour: And therefore it seems difficult to find an Instance where Persons attainted [b] of Felony, or but convicted thereof by Verdict general or [c] special, or notoriously [d] guilty of Treason or Manslaughter, *&c.* by their own Confession or otherwise, have been admitted to the Benefit of Bail, without some special Motive to induce the Court to grant it: As where [e] a Person taken by a *Capias utlagatum*, on an Appeal of Felony by the Name of *J. S.* Gentleman, pleads that his Name is *J. S.* Yeoman, and not Gentleman, and so he is not the same Person who was outlawed, in which Case the Court in Discretion may bail him; for until the Plea is determined, it appears not whether he were the Person intended, or not. Or where [f] a Person outlawed alledges an Error in the Record, in which Case also the Court, *ex gratia*, may bail him, especially if the Error be apparent. Or where a Man is convicted [g] of Felony, upon Evidence by which it plainly appears to the Court that he is not guilty of it; in which Case even the Justices of Gaol-Delivery may bail him. Or where [h] it appears to the Court that the Prosecutor of an Indictment, or the Plaintiff in an Appeal, hath unreasonably delayed his Prosecution; as where two *Nihils* are returned upon two Writs of *Scire facias*, awarded against a Plaintiff in an Appeal removed by *Certiorari* into the King's Bench, and the Prisoner hath lain a long Time under Confinement. Or where [i] the Defendant in an Appeal hath pleaded an Excommunication in Disability of the Plaintiff; In which Case it is apparent that the Plaintiff cannot proceed at present; and if the Defendant should be kept in Prison till the Plaintiff be absolved, he might be a Prisoner for Life. Or where [k] it appears to the Court, That the Defendant may be in Danger of losing his Life, either by Famine, or a dangerous Distemper, *&c.* if he continue longer in Prison.

As to the second Point, *viz.* In what Cases Bail is grantable by the other Courts of *Westminster-Hall*: I shall consider,

1. How far it is grantable by such Courts, or Persons committed for Causes under the Degree of Treason or Felony.
2. How far to Persons committed for Treason or Felony.

Sect. 81. As to the first Point, *viz.* How far Bail is grantable by the said Courts, to Persons committed for Causes under the Degree of Treason or Felony, it seems, [l] That the Courts of Common Pleas and Exchequer, at any Time during Term, and the Court of Chancery, either in Term or Vacation, may award a *Habeas Corpus* by the Common Law, for any Person committed for any such Cause, and thereupon discharge him, if it shall clearly appear by the Return, That the Commitment was against Law (as being made by one who had no Jurisdiction of the Cause, or for a Matter for which by Law no Man ought to be punished) or bail him, if it shall be doubtful whether the Commitment were legal or not, *&c.* However it is certain at this Day, That by Force of the *Habeas Corpus* Act, Par. 3 & 10. set forth more at large *Sect.* 17 & 22. any of the said Courts, in Term-time, and any Judge of either Bench, or Baron of the Exchequer, being of the Degree of the Coif, in the Vacation,

[a] 3 Bulst. 113. 1 Rol. Rep. 168. Supra Sect. 33. Latch 12. S. P. C. 74, 75. Skin. 683. 5 Mod. 454, 455.
[b] Kelyng 90.
[c] Dyer 179. pl. 42. 1 Bulst. 87, 88.
[d] 1 Rol. Rep. 268. 3 Bulst. 113, 114. Vide supra Sect. 33.
[e] 5 H. 7. 16. pl. 7. 2 Inst. 188. H. P. C. 101. S. P. C. 74. Letter A.
[f] 19 H. 6. 2. a. S. P. C. 74. Letter A. 2 Inst. 188. 1 Sid. 316.
[g] Crompton's Justice 154. pl. 22.
[h] 5 Mod. 454, 455. 1 Sid. 78. 1 Bulst. 85. Palm. 558, 559. 1 Keb. 305, 306. 48 Ed. 3. 22. a.
[i] 3 Ass. pl. 12. 13 Ed. 4, 8. pl. 3. Bro. Mainprise, 48, 73. S. P. C. 72. Letter B.
[k] Latch 12. Cro. Jac. 356. Co. Lit. 289. a.
[l] 2 Inst. 53, 55, 615. 4 Inst. 290. 2 H. H. P. C. 147. Vaughan, 154, 155, 156, 157. 2 And. 297. Dalison 81. 3 Leon. 18. 2 Jo. 13, 14, 17. 2 Mod. 198. 306.

tion, may award a *Habeas Corpus* for any Prisoner whatsoever, who is bailable by the Intent of that Act, and thereupon bail him.

Sect. 82. As to the second Point, *viz.* How far Bail is grantable by the said Courts to Persons committed for Treason or Felony, it is observable, That the above mentioned Clauses of the said *Habeas Corpus* Act extend not to Persons committed for Treason or Felony, plainly and specially expressed in the Warrant of Commitment; neither do I find any printed Case, wherein Persons committed for such Crimes have been bailed either by the Courts of Common Pleas or Exchequer. However it is certain, That in some Cases Persons committed for Felony are bailable by the Court of Chancery. But our Law-Books being generally silent in Relation to these Matters I shall refer the Reader for the more accurate Knowledge of them, to Observation and Experience.

See Vaughan 156, 157. 2 Jo. 14. Regifter 271. a. b.

Sect. 83. As to the seventh general Point of this Chapter, *viz.* In what Form Bail is to be taken; it seems to be the Practice of the Court of King's Bench in admitting a Person to Bail, who is actually present [a] in Court, upon an Indictment or Appeal [b] of Felony, or other Crime, punishable with Loss [c] of Member, to take [d] a several Recognisance to the King in a certain Sum from each of the Bail, that the Prisoner shall appear at a certain Day, &c. and also, That the Bail shall be liable for the Default of such Appearance, &c. Body for Body. And [e] it seems to be left to the Discretion of Justices of Peace, in admitting any Person to Bail for Felony, to take the Recognisance either in a certain Sum, or else Body for Body. But [f] where a Person is bailed by the Court of King's Bench, before the Return of a *Capias* awarded against him for Felony, or (as it seems to be implied in the Book cited in the Margin that he may be,) or in any Court for a Crime of an Inferior Nature, it seems, That the Recognisance ought to be only in a certain Sum of Money, and not Body for Body. However it is certain [g] at this Day, That Persons bound Body for Body, are not liable on the Forfeiture of the Recognisance, to such Punishment to which the Principal is to be adjudged, if found Guilty, but only to be fined, &c.

2 H. H. P. C. 126, 127. [a] 1 Bulst. 45. [b] 2 Jon. 210. [c] Lev. 106. Contra 1 Sid. 211. [d] 4 Inst. 178. 1 Bulst. 45. 21 H. 7. 20. pl. 3. Con. 1 Sid. 210. Vide 2 Jo. 222. [e] H. P. C. 97. Crompt. Justice 335. a. 4 Inst. 178. Dalt. cap. 127. seems contrary. [f] 1 Bulst. 45. [g] 4 Inst. 178. S. P. C. 65.

Sect. 84. As to the eighth general Point of this Chapter, *viz.* What shall forfeit the Recognisance: If on a Bailment for Felony, the usual [h] Form, *ad Standum recto de felonia prædicta, & ad respondendum Domino Regi,* be made use of, and at the Trial the Party stand obstinately mute, it may reasonably be argued, that in Strictness the Recognisance is forfeited, for [i] that the Expressions above mentioned seem to import at least thus much, That the Prisoner shall make some Answer; and at the Common Law, before the Statute [k] of *Marlebridge, cap.* 28. if a Person under Bail had insisted on his Privilege as a Clerk, and refused to answer to the Crime alledged against him, his Sureties were to be amerced; and though the said Statute have in that Case excused the Bail, yet an obstinate Refusal to answer in other Cases may perhaps remain as it was at the Common Law. Mr. *Dalton* [l] indeed seems to be of another Opinion, because the Words above mentioned are always used of Course: But it seems strange, That Words should be looked on as idle and insignificant because they are most usual and proper. However, if late Practice and Experience have been agreeable to the above mentioned Opinion of Mr. *Dalton*, as I apprehend that they have, they will certainly be of great Force to maintain it: And indeed it must be confessed, That if a Man's Bail, who are his Gaolers of his own choosing, do as effectually secure his Appearance, and put him as much under the Power of the Court as if he had been in the Custody of the proper Officer, they seem to

Fitz. Mainprise, 13. 21 H. 7. 20. Pl. 3. H. P. C. 97. 2 H. H. P. C. 125. Contra Fitz. Mainprise, 12. [h] Dalt. cap. 127. S. P. C. 77. Letter C. 4 Inst. 178. [i] S. P. C. 77. C. [k] 2 Inst. 150. 4 Inst. 178. 2 H. H. P. C. 126. [l] Dalt. cap. 127.

to have anſwered the End of the Law, and to have done all that can be reaſonably required of them: But howſoever the Law may ſtand in Relation to this Caſe, it is certain, That if Perſons be bound by Recogniſance, that *J. S.* ſhall appear in the King's Bench the firſt Day of ſuch a Term, to anſwer to ſuch an Information againſt him, and not depart till he ſhall be diſcharged by the Court, and afterwards the Attorney
Queen and Redpath, 11 Ann. General enter a *Nolle proſequi* as to that Information, and exhibit another, on which the Defendant is convicted, and refuſes to appear in Court after perſonal Notice, the Recogniſance is forfeited; for being expreſs that the Party ſhall not depart till he be diſcharged by the Court, it cannot be ſatisfy'd unleſs he be forth-coming, and ready to anſwer to any other Information exhibited againſt him whilſt he continues not diſcharged, as much as to that which he was particularly bound to anſwer to. But in ſuch Caſe it ſeems, That the Recogniſance ſhall not be forfeited by the Party's not appearing in Court the firſt Day of every Term, after he hath pleaded to the Information, as it may be before he hath pleaded.

CHAP. XVI.

Of Commitments.

AND now I am to conſider in what Caſes, and in what Manner, Offenders are to be committed; for the better Underſtanding whereof I ſhall examine,

1. What Kinds of Offenders are to be committed.
2. By whom.
3. To what Priſon.
4. What is to be done previous to their Commitment.
5. What ought to be the Form of it.
6. At whoſe Charges they are to be ſent to Priſon.
7. To what Court the Commitment is to be certified.
8. By what Means the Party may be diſcharged from ſuch Commitment.

Sect. 1. As to the firſt Point, There is no Doubt but that Perſons
2 H. H. P. C. 123, 124. apprehended for Offences which are not bailable; and alſo all Perſons who neglect to offer Bail for Offences which are bailable, muſt be committed.

[a] 10 H. 4. 7. a. 7 Ed. 4. 20. a. 3 Ed. 4. 26. b. 27. a. 20 Ed. 4. 6. b. 10 Ed. 4. 17. b. 18. a. *Sect.* 2. And it is ſaid, That whereſoever a Juſtice of Peace is impowered by any Statute to bind a Perſon over, or to cauſe him to do a certain Thing, and ſuch Perſon being in his Preſence ſhall refuſe to be bound, or to do ſuch Thing, the Juſtice may commit him to the Gaol, to remain there till he ſhall comply.

5 H. 7. 4. b. 5. a. 2 H. 7. 3. b. 11 Ed. 4. 4. b. *Sect.* 3. As to the ſecond Point, *viz.* by whom ſuch Perſons are to be committed, it ſeems to be agreed by all the Old [a] Books, That whereſoever a Conſtable, or private Perſon, may juſtify the Arreſting another for a Felony or Treaſon, he may alſo juſtify the Sending or

bringing him to the common Gaol; and that every private Perſon has as much Authority in caſes of this Kind as the Sheriff, or any other Officer, and may juſtify ſuch Impriſonment by his [a] own Authority, but not by the Command of another. But [b] inaſmuch as it is certain, That a Perſon lawfully making ſuch an Arreſt may juſtify Bringing the Party to the Conſtable, in order to be carried by him before a Juſtice of Peace; and inaſmuch as the Statutes of 1 & 2 *Ph. & M.* 13. and 2 & 3 *Ph. & M.* 10. which direct in what Manner Perſons brought before a Juſtice of Peace for Felony ſhall be examined by him in order to their being committed or bailed, ſeem clearly to ſuppoſe, That all ſuch Perſons are to be brought before ſuch Juſtice for ſuch Purpoſe; and inaſmuch as the Statute of 31 *Car.* 2. commonly called the *Habeas Corpus* Act, ſeems to ſuppoſe, That all Perſons who are committed to Priſon, are there detained by Virtue of ſome Warrant in Writing, which ſeems to be intended of a Commitment by ſome Magiſtrate; and the conſtant Tenor of the late Books, Practice and Opinions, are agreeable hereto: It is certainly moſt adviſable at this Day, for any Private Perſon who arreſts another for Felony, to cauſe him to be brought, as ſoon as conveniently he may, before ſome Juſtice of Peace, that he may be committed or bailed by him.

[a] 5 H. 7. 4. b. 5. a. 2 H. H. P. C. 81. Fitz. Falſe Impriſ. 8.
[b] 9 Ed. 4. 26. b. 27. a. 10 Ed. 4. 17. b. H. P. C. 91, 112. 2 H. H. P. C. 120.
H. P. C. 91, 112. 2 H. H. P. C. 81. Dalt. cap. 118.

Sect. 4. But it is certain, [c] That the Privy Council, or any one or two of them, or a Secretary of State, may lawfully commit Perſons for Treaſon, and for other Offences againſt the State, as in all Ages they have done.

[c] 1 And. 298. Palm. 558. 1 Sid. 78. 1 Leon. 70, 71. Sir William Wyndham's Caſe, Trin. 2 Georg. 1. Sal. 347. 5 Mod. 78 to 85. Skin. 369, 596 to 600. Carth. 291.

As to the third Point, *viz.* To what Priſon ſuch Offenders are to be committed, I ſhall obſerve,

1. That the Priſon ought to be in the Realm of *England.*
2. That regularly it ought to be a Common Priſon.

Sect. 5. As to the firſt of theſe Particulars, it is enacted by 31 *Car.* 2. 12. *That no Subject of this Realm, being an Inhabitant, or Reſiant of this Kingdom of* England, *Dominion of* Wales, *or Town of* Berwick upon Tweed, *ſhall or may be ſent Priſoner into* Scotland, Ireland, Jerſey, Guernſey, Tangier, *or into Parts, Garriſons, Iſlands, or Places beyond the Seas, which then were, or at any Time hereafter ſhould be, within or without the Dominions of his Majeſty, his Heirs or Succeſſors; and that every ſuch Impriſonment is by the ſaid Statute enacted and adjudged to be illegal, and that every Subject ſo impriſoned, ſhall have an Action of Falſe Impriſonment,* &c. *and recover treble Coſts, and no leſs Damages than five Hundred Pounds againſt the Perſon making ſuch Warrant, who ſhall alſo incur a* Præmunire.

Sect. 6. As to the ſecond of the abovementioned Particulars, It is enacted by 14 *Ed.* 3. 10. as followeth, *In the right of the Gaols which were wont to be in Ward of the Sheriffs, and annexed to their Bailiwicks; it is aſſented and accorded, That they ſhall be rejoined to the Sheriffs, and the Sheriffs ſhall have the Cuſtody of the ſame Gaols, as before this Time they were wont to have; and they ſhall put in ſuch Under-keepers for whom they will anſwer.* And this is confirmed by 19 *H.* 7. *chap.* 10. Alſo it is recited by 5 *H.* 4. 10. *That divers Conſtables of Caſtles within the Realm, being aſſigned Juſtices of Peace by the King's Commiſſion, had by Colour of ſuch Commiſſion, uſed to take People to whom they bore evil Will, and impriſon them within the ſaid Caſtles, till they had made Fine and Ranſom with the ſaid Conſtables for their Deliverance.* And thereupon it is enacted, *That none be impriſoned by any Juſtice of the Peace, but only in the Common Gaol; saving to Lords and others which have Gaols their Franchise in this Case.*

Sect. 7. And it [a] seems, That the King's Grant since this Statute to private Persons to have the Custody of Prisoners committed by Justices of Peace, is void. And it is said, That none can claim a Prison as a Franchise, unless he have also a Gaol-delivery.

Sect. 8. It seems to be [b] agreed, That if a Person be arrested in one County, for a Crime done in it, and fly into another, and be re-taken there, he may be brought before a Justice of the County where the Offence was done, and be committed by him to the Gaol of such County. But it seems to be the stronger [c] Opinion, That if one who hath committed an Offence in one County, fly into another before he be taken, and be pursued and and arrested in such County, he ought to be brought before a Justice of the County where he is taken, and be committed by him to the common Gaol of the same County, [d] whether it lie in such County or another; [e] unless there be some special Reason to the Contrary, as an apparent Danger that the Party may be rescued from such Prison by Rebels, *&c.* And it seems to be laid down as a Rule, by some Books, [f] That any Offender may be committed to the Gaol next to the Place where he was taken, whether it lie in the same County or not.

Sect. 9. It is [g] said, That if a Constable bring a Felon to Gaol, and the Gaoler refuse to receive him, the Town where he is Constable ought to keep him till the next Gaol-Delivery. But [h] in other Cases it seems, That regularly no one can justify the Detaining a Prisoner in Custody out of the common Gaol, unless there be some particular Reason for so doing; as if the Party be so dangerously [i] sick that it would apparently hazard his Life to send him to the Gaol, [k] or there be evident Danger of a Rescous from Rebels, *&c.* Yet constant Practice seems to authorise a Commitment to a Messenger; and it is [l] said, That it shall be intended to have been made in order for the carrying of the Party to Gaol.

Sect. 10. As Prisoners ought to be committed at first to the proper Prison, so ought they not to be removed from thence, except in some special Cases. And to this Purpose it is enacted by 31 *Car.* 2. *chap.* 2. Par. 9. *That if any Subject of this Realm, shall be committed to any Prison, or in Custody of any Officer or Officers whatsoever, for any criminal, or supposed criminal Matter; that the said Person shall not be removed from the said Prison and Custody, into the Custody of any other Officer or Officers, unless it be by* Habeas Corpus, *or some other legal Writ; or where the Prisoner is delivered to the Constable, or other inferior Officer, to carry such Prisoner to some common Gaol; or where any Person is sent by Order of any Judge of Assise, or Justice of the Peace, to any common Workhouse, or House of Correction; or where the Prisoner is removed from one Prison or Place to another, within the same County, in order to a Trial, or Discharge by due Course of Law; or in case of sudden Fire, or Infection, or other Necessity; upon Pain that he who makes out Signs or Countersigns, or obeys or executes such Warrant, shall forfeit to the Party grieved one Hundred Pounds for the first Offence, two Hundred Pounds for the second,* &c.

Sect. 11. As to the fourth Point, *viz.* What ought to be done previous to the Commitment of such Offenders, it is enacted by 2 & 3 *Ph.* & *M.* 10. *That every Justice or Justices, before whom any Person shall be brought for Manslaughter, or Felony, or for Suspicion thereof, before he or they shall commit or send such Prisoner to Ward, shall take the Examination of such Prisoner, and Information of those that bring him, of the Fact and Circumstances thereof; and the same, or as much thereof as shall be material to prove the Felony,*

[a] See 1 And. 345. Cro. El. 829, 830. 9 Co. 119. b. Sal. 343. Far. 31.
[b] H. P. C. 93. 1 H. H. P. C. 580. 2 H. H. P. C. 94, 115. Dalt. cap. 118. Cromp. 172. b. 173. a.
[c] Dalt. cap. 118. Crompt. 72. b. H. P. C. 92, 93. 11 E. 4. 4. b. 5. a. 13 E. 4. 8. b. 9. a. Pl. Com. 37. a. Keilw. 45. b. Contra 2 Bulst. 264. 11 E. 4. 7. a. b.
[d] Keilw. 45. b. 11 E. 4. 5. a.
[e] 11 Ed. 4. 4 b. 5 a. 7. a. b.
[f] Keilw. 45. b. 22 Ed. 4. 34. b.
[g] H. P. C. 114. 10 H. 4. 7. pl. 2. Fitz. Escape, 8. Dalt. cap. 118. Bro. faux Imprisonment, 25.
[h] 2 H. H. P. C. 123. 20 Ed. 4. 6. b. Bro. faux Imprisonment, 21, 27. 11 Ed. 4. 7. a. b. 2 Ed. 4. 8. b.
[i] 2 H. H. P. C. 96, 119, 120.
[k] 2 H. H. P. C. 81. 11 Ed. 4. 4. b. 5. a.
[l] Sal. 347. See 5 Mod. 78 to 85. Skin. 599.

ſhall put in writing within two Days after the ſaid Examination, and the ſame ſhall certify in ſuch Manner and Form, and at ſuch Time, as they ſhould and ought to do, if ſuch Priſoner, ſo committed or ſent to Ward, had been bailed, or let to Mainpriſe, upon ſuch Pain as in 1 & 2 Ph. & M. 13. *is limited and appointed, for not taking or not certifying ſuch Examinations,* &c. And it is farther enacted, *That the ſaid Juſtices ſhall have Authority to bind all ſuch by Recognizance or Obligation, as do declare any thing material to prove the ſaid Manſlaughter, or Felony, to appear at the next General Gaol-Delivery to be holden within the County, City, or Town Corporate, where the Trial of the ſaid Manſlaughter, or Felony, ſhall be, then and there to give Evidence againſt the Party; and that the ſaid Juſtices ſhall certify the ſaid Bonds taken before them, in like manner as they ought to certify the Bonds mentioned in the ſaid former Act,* &c.

See Chap. 15. Sect. 60.

Sect. 12. It ſeems that a Juſtice of Peace ought not to detain a Priſoner by Virtue of this Statute, in order to examine him, any longer than is neceſſary for ſuch Purpoſe, for which it is ſaid, That the Space of three Days is a reaſonable Time.

Cro. E. 829, 830. 1 H. H. P. C. 586. 2 H. H. P. C. 120, 121.

As to the fifth Point, *viz.* What ought to be the Form of a Commitment, the following Rules are to be obſerved.

2 H. H. P. C. 122, 123.

Sect. 13. I. It muſt be in Writing, under the Hand and Seal of the Perſon by whom it is made and expreſſing his Office, or Authority, and the Time and Place at which it is made, and muſt be directed to the Gaoler, or the Keeper of the Priſon.

2 Inſt. 52, 591. Dalt. cap. 125. H. P. C. 94.

Sect. 14. II. It may be made either in the Name of the King, and only teſted by the Perſon who makes it, or it may be made by ſuch Perſon in his own Name.

Dalt. cap. 125.

Sect. 15. III. It may command the [a] Gaoler to keep the Party in ſafe and cloſe Cuſtody; for if every Gaoler be bound [b] by the Law to keep his Priſoner in ſuch Cuſtody, ſurely it can be no Fault in a *Mittimus* to command him ſo to do.

[a] Sir William Wyndham's Caſe, Trin. 2 Georg. 1.
[b] 8 Co. 100. 9 Co. 87. b. Dalt. cap. 118.

Sect. 16. IV. It ought to ſet forth the Crime alledged againſt the Party with convenient [c] Certainty, whether the Commitment be by the Privy [d] Council, or any other Authority; otherwiſe the Officer [e] is not puniſhable, by Reaſon of ſuch *Mittimus*, for ſuffering the Party to eſcape: And the Court before whom he is removed by *Habeas Corpus*, ought to diſcharge or bail him: And this doth not only hold where [f] no Cauſe at all his expreſſed in the Commitment, but alſo where it is ſo looſely ſet forth, that the Court cannot adjudge whether it were a reaſonable Ground of Impriſonment; as [g] where one was committed for manifold Contumacy to the High Commiſſion-Court, or for [h] refuſing to anſwer before them to certain Articles, or [i] for inſolent Behaviour and Words ſpoken at the Council-Table, *&c.* And it is holden by Sir [k] *Edward Coke*, in his ſecond Inſtitute, That a Commitment for High Treaſon, or Felony in general, without ſhewing the Species of the Offence, is not good; yet in [l] another Part of the ſame Book, ſuch general Commitments ſeem to be allowed by him to be good: And there are Precedents of Commitments for Felony in general, in good [m] Authors. And [n] it hath been reſolved, That Commitments for High Treaſon in general are good. [31]

[c] H. P. C. 94. Dalt. cap. 125. 2 Inſt. 52, 591.
[d] 16 Car. 1. cap. 10. Cro. Car. 133, 507, 579, 593. 2 And. 298. Contra 1 Ro. Re. 134. 1 Leon. 71. Ch. 15. Sect. 66 to 73.
[e] 2 Inſt. 591. H. P. C. 109, Infra cap. 17. Palm. 558.
[f] Cro. Car. 507, 579, 593. Barkham's & Lawſon's Caſe, Palmer 558.
[g] 1 Rol. Rep. 245.
[h] 1 Rol. Rep. 220, 245.
[i] Cro. Car. 133, 579. 2 Bulſt. 139, 140.
[k] 2 Inſt. 591. 5 Mod. 85.
[l] 2 Inſt. 52.
[m] 1 H. H. P. C. 595, 609. 2 H. H. P. C. 123. Crompt. 233. b. Dalt. cap. 125.
[n] 1 Sid. 78. 1 And. 298. 1 Keb. 305. Palmer 558. Sir William Wyndham's Caſe, Trin. 2 Geo 1.

Sect. 17.

Sect. 17. V. It is safe to set forth, That the Party is charged upon Oath; but this is not necessary, for it hath been [a] resolved, That a Commitment for Treason, or for Suspicion of it, without setting forth any particular Accusation, or Ground of the Suspicion, is good.

Sect. 18. VI. Every such *Mittimus* ought to have a lawful Conclusion, [b] *viz.* That the Party be safely kept till he be delivered by Law, or by Order of Law, or by due Course of Law; or that he be kept till farther [c] Order, (which shall be intended of the Order of Law,) or to the like Effect. And if the Party be committed only for want of Bail, it seems [d] to be a good Conclusion of the Commitment, that he be kept till he find Bail. But a Commitment, [e] till the Person who makes it shall take further Order, seems not to be good. And it seems, that the Party committed by such, or any other irregular *Mittimus*, may be bailed. [32] [33]

Sect. 19. As to the sixth Point, *viz.* At whose Charge Offenders are to be sent to Prison, it is enacted by 3 *Jac.* 1. 10. *That every Person and Persons, that shall be committed to the common or usual Gaol within any County or Liberty within this Realm, by any Justice or Justices of the Peace, for any Offence or Misdemeanor, having Means or Ability thereunto, shall bear their own reasonable Charges, for so conveying or sending them to the said Gaol, and the Charges also of such as shall be appointed to guard them to such Gaol, and shall so guard them thither. And if any such Person or Persons so to be committed, shall refuse at the Time of their Commitment and Sending to the said Gaol, to defray the said Charges, or shall not then pay or bear the same, that then such Justice or Justices of the Peace shall and may by Writing under his or their Hand and Seal, or Hands and Seals, give Warrant to the Constable or Constables of the Hundred, or Constable or Tythingman of the Tything or Township where such Person or Persons shall be dwelling and inhabit, or from whence he or they shall be committed, or where he or they shall have any Goods within the County or Liberty, to sell such, and so much of the Goods and Chattels of the said Persons, as by the Discretion of the said Justice, or Justices of the Peace, shall satisfy and pay the Charges of such his or their Conveying or Sending to the said Gaol; the Appraisement to be made by four of the honest Inhabitants of the Parish or Tything where such Goods or Chattels shall remain and be; and the Overplus of the Money which shall be made thereof, to be delivered to the Party to whom the said Goods shall belong.*

Sect. 20. And it is farther enacted, *That if the said Persons shall not have, or be known to have, any Goods or Chattels, which may be sold for the Purpose aforesaid, within the County or Liberty, an indifferent Assessment shall be made by the Constables and Church-Wardens, and two or three other the honest Inhabitants of the Parish, or Tything, where such Offenders shall be taken or apprehended, the said Taxation being allowed under the Hand of one or more Justice or Justices of the Peace, if there be such Constables or Church-Wardens there inhabiting; and in Default of them, by four of the principal Inhabitants of the said Parish, Township or Tything, where such Offenders shall be taken or apprehended: And if any so assessed shall refuse to pay their said Taxation, then the Justice or Justices of Peace by whom the said Offenders shall be committed to Prison, or any Justice of Peace near adjoining, shall and may give Warrant as aforesaid, to the Constable, Tythingman, or other Officer there, to distrain the Goods of any so assessed, which shall refuse to pay the same, and to sell the same; and that such Person or Persons so authorised, shall have full Power so to distrain, and by Appraisment of four substantial Inhabitants of the said Place, to sell a sufficient Quantity of the Goods and Chattels of the said Person so refusing, for the levying of the said Taxation; and if any Overplus of the Money come by the Sale thereof, the same to be delivered to the Owner.*

[a] Sir William Wyndham's Case, Trin. 2 Geo. 1. Dalt. cap. 125. Cromp. 233, b. 2 Inst. 52. Palm. 558, 559.
[b] 2 Inst. 52, 591. H. P. C. 94. Crompt. 233. b. Dalt. cap. 124.
[c] 1 Lev. 230. Contra Cro. Car. 558.
[d] 6 Mod. 73, 74.
[e] 1 H.H.P.C. 584, 595. 2 Inst. 52. 591. 1 Rol. Rep. 220. 1 Lev. 230. Cro. Car. 579. con. 3 Bulst. 48, 49. 1 Rol. Rep. 410.

Sect. 21. As to the seventh Point, *viz.* To what Court such Commitments are to be certified, it is enacted by 3 *H.* 7. 3. *That every Sheriff, Bailiff of Francise, and every other Person, having Authority or Power of keeping of Gaol, or of Prisoners for Felony, do certify the Names of every such Prisoner in their keeping, and of every Prisoner to them committed for any such Cause, at the next general Gaol-Delivery, in every County or Franchise where any such Gaol shall be, there to be calendered before the Justices of the Deliverance of the same Gaol, whereby they may, as well for the King as for the Party, proceed to make Deliverance of such Prisoners according to Law, on Pain to forfeit to the King for every Default there recorded, one hundred Shillings.*

Sect. 22. As to the eighth Point, *viz.* By what Means a Person under such a Commitment may be discharged, it seems, That a Person legally committed for a Crime, certainly appearing to have been done by some one or other, cannot be lawfully discharged by any one but by the King, till he be acquitted on his Trial, or have an *Ignoramus* found by the Grand Jury, or none to prosecute him, on a Proclamation for that Purpose by the Justices of Gaol-Delivery. But if a Person be committed on a bare Suspicion, without any Appeal or Indictment, for a supposed Crime, where afterwards it appears that there was none, as for the Murder of a Person thought to be dead, who afterwards is found to be alive; it hath been holden, That he may be safely dismissed without any farther Proceeding, for that he who suffers him to escape is properly punishable only as an Accessary to his supposed Offence; and it is impossible that there should be an Accessary where there can be no Principal; and it would be hard to punish one for a Contempt, in disregarding a Commitment founded on a Suspicion, appearing in so uncontested a Manner to be groundless.

Keilw. 34. 3 Inst. 209, 210. H. P. C. 94, 95. 1 H. H. P. C. 583.

Keilw. 34. H. P. C. 109, 110, 114.

CHAP. XVII.

Of Hindrances in bringing Offenders to publick Justice, &c.

HAVING shewn in what Manner Criminals are to be arrested bailed or committed, I am now to consider in what Manner they and their Assistants are punishable for an Hindrance in bringing them to publick Justice. And in Order hereto I shall examine,

1. How far they are punishable for an Offence of this Kind, before an Arrest made.
2. How far after an Arrest.

Sect. 1. As to the first Point, It is [a] certainly an Offence of a very high Nature to oppose one who lawfully endeavours to arrest another for Treason, or Felony. And some [b] have said, That the Person who so opposes an Arrest for Treason, whereof he knows the Party to have been guilty, is thereby guilty of the Treason; and that he who so opposes an Arrest for Felony, is an Accessary to the Felony. And if it be a ge-

[a] H.P.C. 116.
[b] S. P. C. 31. Letter B. Crompt. 38.b. 26 Ass. 47. Fitz. Justice of Peace, 114, 231. Contra H. P. C. 116. 1 H. H. P. C. 606. Fitz. Coron. 333. 2 Inst. 590.

a general [a] Rule, That whoever knowing a Person to have committed any such Crime, receives and comforts him, and endeavours to favour and aid him in the Making his Escape, thereby becomes a Principal in the Case of Treason, and an Accessary in the Case of Felony, though he use no Force in giving such Assistance to the Offender; it seems strange that he who so far takes Part with him as to fight in his Defence from Justice, should not be at least equally guilty. And therefore it seems reasonable to understand the Books above cited, which seem to contradict this Opinion, to intend no more than that it is not Felony in the Party himself, who is attacked in Order to be arrested, to save himself from the Arrest by such Resistance.

[a] H. P. C. 218, 219. 2 Inst. 183. Moor 8. pl. 29. S. P. C. 41. Letter E.

Sect. 2. [b] But if a Person, knowing another to have been guilty of such a Crime, barely receive him, and permit him to escape, without giving him any Manner of Advice, Assistance or Encouragement in it, as by directing him how to do it in the safest Manner, or furnishing him with Money, Provisions, or other Necessaries, it seems he is guilty of a high Misdemeanor only, but no capital Offence.

[b] S. P. C. 32. Letter I. 9 H. 4. 1. pl. 3. 26 Ass. 47.

H. P. C. 111, 271. *Sect.* 3. Also it is certain, That the Party himself who flies from such an Arrest, is not thereby guilty of a capital Offence, but only liable to forfeit his Goods, when such Flight is found against him, in such Manner as hath been already shewn, *Chap.* 9. *Sect.* 51. and shall be also more fully considered hereafter.

Sect. 4. How far a Vill, which suffers one who has been guilty of Homicide to escape, is liable to be amerced, hath been already shewn, *Chap.* 12. *Sect.* 2, 3.

Offences of this Kind, after an Arrest made, may be considered in Relation either,

1. To the Party under such an Arrest. Or,
2. To others.

Such Offences by the Party himself are either without or with Force.

Sect. 5. And first, As to such Offences by the Party himself, without Force, which seem properly to come under the Notion of Escapes, there is little remarkable in the Books; and therefore I shall content my self with taking Notice, That as all Persons are bound to submit themselves to the Judgment of the Law, and to be ready to be justified by it; whoever, in any Case, refuses to undergo that Imprisonment which the Law thinks fit to put upon him, and frees himself from it by any Artifice, before such Time as he is delivered by due Course of Law, is guilty of a high Contempt, punishable with Fine and Imprisonment. And if it be so great a Crime for one not arrested to fly, in Order to save himself from Imprisonment for a capital Offence, surely it must be at least as great a Crime, for one who is actually under the Custody of the Law for any such Crime, by any indirect Means to free himself from it. And some [c] have holden, That such an Escape amounts to Felony: But this Opinion seems to be over severe, and not to be maintained by the [d] Book cited to prove it.

H. P. C. 108. 2 Inst. 589, 590. Cro. Car. 210. 1 Ass. pl. 6.

[c] S. P. C. 31. Letter A.

[d] 2 Ed. 3. 2. pl. 4. Fitz. Coron. 149.

I

CHAP.

CHAP. XVIII.

Of breaking Priſon.

SUCH Offences by the Party himſelf, accompanied with Force, come under the Notion of Priſon-breaches; which I ſhall conſider,

1. As they ſtand by the Common Law.
2. On the Statute *de frangentibus Priſonam,* which was made in the firſt Year of King *Edward* 2.

Sect. 1. And firſt as to Priſon-Breaches, as they ſtood by the Common Law; it ſeems the better Opinion, [a] That all ſuch Offences were Felonies, if the Party were lawfully in Priſon for any Cauſe whatſoever, whether Criminal or Civil, and whether he were actually in the Walls of a Priſon, or only in the Stocks, or in the Cuſtody of any Perſon who had lawfully arreſted him; and it ſeems not to have been any Way material whether the Priſon did belong to the King, or to the Lord of a Franchiſe; not only for that every Perſon who is under a lawful Impriſonment, may properly enough be called the King's Priſoner; but alſo becauſe it is allowed, [b] That whoever breaks from any ſuch Impriſonment, ſince the Statute 1 *Edw.* 2. *de frangentibus Priſonam,* is guilty of Felony: From whence it ſeems clearly to follow, That he muſt have been in like Manner guilty before that Statute, the Purport whereof is not to make any Offences Felonies which were not ſo before, but only to reſtrain ſome of thoſe which were. And it [c] ſeems alſo to be clear, That the Confeſſion of ſuch Offence before the Coroner is not traverſable by the Common Law; which is not altered as to this Point by the Statute.

[a] Bracton, Lib. 3. ch. 9. Britton, fol. 17. S. P. C. 30. 2 Inſt. 589. H. P. C. 87. 1 H. H. P. C. 607. Contra S. P. C. 31. Letter D. 33. Letter H. 1 H. 7. 6. pl. 2. Bro. Coron. 130. Cro. Car. 210. 2 Inſt. 589.
[b] Vide infra Sect. 4.
[c] Vide ſupra Ch. 9. Sect. 49.

Sect. 2. And now I am to conſider theſe Offences, as they ſtand by the ſaid Statute, for the better Underſtanding whereof I ſhall firſt ſet down the Words of the Statute, and then endeavour to ſhew in what Manner they are to be underſtood.

Sect. 3. And firſt, the Words of the Statute are as follows, *De priſonariis priſonam frangentibus, Dominus Rex vult & præcipit, quod nullus de cætero, qui priſonam fregerit, ſubeat, judicium vitæ vel membrorum pro fractione priſonæ tantum, niſi cauſa, pro qua captus & impriſonatus fuerit, tale judicium requirat, ſi de illa ſecun dum legem & conſuetudinem terræ fuiſſet convictus, licet temporibus præteritis aliter fieri conſuevit.* For the better Underſtanding of the Conſtruction whereof, I ſhall conſider the following Points.

2 Inſt. 589. 1 H. H. P. C. 608.

1. What ſhall be ſaid to be a Priſon, within the Meaning of this Statute.
2. How far the Impriſonment ought to be well grounded.
3. What ſhall be ſaid to be a Breaking of Priſon.
4. For what Crime the Party ought to be impriſoned, to make the Offence of breaking the Priſon Felony, within the Intent of the Statute.

5. Whe-

5. Whether the Offence of breaking Priſon can ever amount to High Treaſon.
6. At what Time, and in what Manner, the Offender is to be proceeded againſt.
7. In what Manner he is to be indicted.
8. In what Manner thoſe are to be puniſhed for a Breach of Priſon, who are within the Benefit of the Statute.

Sect. 4. As to the firſt Point, *viz.* What ſhall be ſaid to be a Priſon [a] within the Meaning of the Statute; It ſeems clear, That any Place whatſoever, wherein a Perſon under a lawful Arreſt for a ſuppoſed Crime, is reſtrained of his Liberty, whether in the Stocks or Street, or in the common Gaol, or the Houſe of a Conſtable or private Perſon, or the Priſon of the Ordinary, is properly a Priſon within the Statute; for Impriſonment [b] is nothing elſe but a Reſtraint of Liberty.

[a] Fitz. Coron. 158, 290, 312, 48, 164, 250, 419. 22 Aſſ. pl. 85. Cro. Car. 210. 2 Inſt. 589, 590. H. P. C. 107. 1 H. H. P. C. 608, 609, 610. Dy. 99. pl. 60. Cromp. 38, 39.
[b] S. P. C. 30. D.

Sect. 5. As to the ſecond Point, *viz.* How far the Impriſonment ought to be well grounded, it is clear, [c] That if a Perſon be taken upon a *Capias* awarded on an Indictment or Appeal againſt him, for a ſuppoſed Treaſon, or Felony, he is within the Statute if he break the Priſon, whether any ſuch Crime were in Truth committed by him or any other Perſon or not; for that there is an Accuſation againſt him on Record, which makes his Commitment lawful, be he never ſo innocent, and the Proſecution never ſo groundleſs.

[c] 2 Inſt. 590. H. P. C. 109. 1 H. H. P. C. 610. Bro. Eſcape, 29.

Sect. 6. Alſo if an innocent Perſon be committed by a lawful *Mittimus* on ſuch a Suſpicion of a Felony, actually done by ſome other, as will juſtify his Impriſonment tho' he be neither indicted nor appealed, he is certainly [d] within the Statute if he break the Priſon, for that he was legally in Cuſtody, and ought to have ſubmitted to it till he had been diſcharged by due Courſe of Law.

See Book 1. Chap. 28. Sect. 11, 12.
[d] H. P. C. 109. 1 H. H. P. C. 610, 611. 2 Inſt. 590. Dy. 99. pl. 60. Cromp. 38. a.

Sect. 7. But if no [e] Felony at all were done, and the Party be neither indicted nor appealed, it ſeems clear, That no *Mittimus*, for ſuch a ſuppoſed Crime will make him guilty within the Statute by breaking the Priſon, for that his Impriſonment was unjuſtifiable.

[e] H. P. C. 109. 2 Inſt. 590, 591. Contra 2 Leon. 166.

Sect. 8. Alſo if a Felony were done, yet if there were no juſt Cauſe of Suſpicion, either to arreſt or commit the Party, it ſeems clear, That if his *Mittimus* be not in ſuch Form [f] as the Law requires, his breaking of the Priſon cannot be Felony, becauſe the Lawfulneſs of his Impriſonment in ſuch Caſe depends wholly on the *Mittimus*; which if it be not according to Law, the Impriſonment will have nothing to ſupport it. But if the Party were taken up for ſuch ſtrong [g] Cauſes of Suſpicion as will be a good Juſtification both of his Arreſt and Commitment, but happen to be committed by an informal Warrant, it ſeems, that it may be probably argued, That it will be Felony [h] in him to break the Priſon; for if by the ancient Common Law, any private Perſon might, of his own Authority, juſtify both an Arreſt and Commitment, for Treaſon or Felony, on a reaſonable Cauſe of Suſpicion, as it ſeems probable [i] from the Tenor of all the old Books that he might; and if the Neceſſity of a *Mittimus* [k] from a Magiſtrate, depend rather on the conſtant ſettled Practice of Juſtices of Peace than any direct Law, it ſeems difficult to maintain that a Slip in want of Form of ſuch a *Mittimus* ſhould make it lawful for the Priſoner to break the Priſon, whereas by the old Law it would have been Felony in ſuch a Caſe to have broken it, without any ſuch *Mittimus* at all. And on the other Side, if the Party be taken

[f] Vide Chap. 16. Sect. 13, 14, 15, 16, 17, 18.
[g] Vide ſupra Ch. 12. Sect. 8, 9, &c.
[h] Bro. Eſcape, 29. 42 Aſſ. 5. 1 H. H. P. C. 609, 610.
[i] Vide ſupra Ch. 12. & Ch. 16. Sect. 3.
[k] Vide 5 Mod. 30.

up for ſuch ſlight Cauſes of Suſpicion of a Felony actually done, as will
not in Strictneſs juſtify the Arreſt, yet if the Juſtice before whom he is Vide infra
brought think them of ſuch Weight as to require a Commitment, and do Sect. 15.
accordingly ſend the Party to Gaol by a regular *Mittimus*, it ſeems very
dangerous for him to break the Priſon; for the Practice of Juſtices of
Peace in making ſuch Commitments, being now grown into ſettled Law,
it ſeems reaſonable, that their *Mittimus* be a good Juſtification of the Im-
priſonment which it commands, for a Crime within their Juriſdiction re-
gularly brought before them; from whence it follows, That to break
from ſuch Impriſonment muſt be unlawful. And therefore, ſince it doth
not appear, that there hath been any direct Reſolution of theſe Points, per-
haps it may be reaſonable to underſtand, what is more generally ſaid by Sir
[a] *Edward Coke*, and Sir [b] *Matthew Hale*, in Relation to this Matter, accord- [a] 2 In. 591.
ing to the above mentioned Diſtinctions. [34] [b] H.P.C.109.

As to the third Point, *viz.* What ſhall be ſaid to be a Breaking of Pri-
ſon, within the Meaning of this Statute, the following Rules are to be
obſerved.

Sect. 9. I. There muſt be an actual [c] Breaking; for every Indictment [c] 2 Inſt. 590.
for this Offence, as a Felony, muſt have the Words *felonice fregit priſo-* H. P. C. 108.
nam, which ſeem neceſſarily to import the Uſe of ſome real Force or Vio- S. P. C. 31.
lence, and not ſuch only as may be implied by the Conſtruction of Law, Letter A.
in any Act done in Contempt of it; and therefore, if without any Ob-
ſtruction a Priſoner go out of the Priſon Doors, being opened by the Con- 1 H. H. P. C.
ſent or Negligence of the Gaoler, or otherwiſe eſcape without uſing any 611.
Kind of Force of Violence, he is guilty of a Miſdemeanour only, but not
of Felony, and the Gaoler is puniſhable in ſuch Manner as ſhall be ſet forth
more at large in the next Chapter.

Sect. 10. II. Such Breaking muſt be either by the Priſoner himſelf,
or by others through his Procurement, or at leaſt with his Privity;
for if the Priſon be broken by others, without his Procurement or Con-
ſent, and he eſcape through the Breach ſo made, it ſeems the better [d] [d] 2 Inſt. 589.
Opinion that he cannot be indicted for the Breaking, but only for the H. P. C. 108.
Eſcape. S. P. C. 30. Letter E.

Sect. 11. III. Such Breaking muſt not be neceſſitated by an inevitable Ac- 31. Letter B.
cident, happening without any Fault of the Priſoner; as where [e] the Priſon 1 H. H. P. C. 611.
is fired by Lightning, or otherwiſe, without his Privity, and he breaks it open Fitz. Coron.
to ſave his Life. 48. 1 H. 7. 6. a.

Sect. 12. IV. It ſeems, That no Breach of Priſon will amount to Felo- [e] 15 H. 7. 1, 2.
ny, unleſs the Priſoner eſcape; for if the Breaking of a Priſon by a Stranger, Pl. Com. 136.
in Order to free the Priſoners who are in it, be not Felony, unleſs the Pri- 2 Inſt. 590. H. P. C. 108.
ſoners go out of it, as it is ſaid [f] that it is not, it ſeems *a fortiori*, That 1 H. H. P. C.
ſuch a Breach by the Priſoner himſelf, who lies under ſo much ſtronger a 611.
Temptation to it, cannot be Felony unleſs he do eſcape. [f] Keilw. 87. a.

As to the fourth Point, *viz.* For what Crime the Party muſt be impriſoned,
to make his Breaking the Priſon Felony within the Meaning of the Sta-
tute, the following Rules are to be obſerved.

Sect. 13. I. It is not material, whether the Offence for which he
was impriſoned were capital at the Time of this Statute, or were made H. P. C. 108.
ſo by ſubſequent Statutes; for ſince all Breaches of Priſon were Felonies 1 H. H. P. C.
by the Common Law, which is reſtrained by the Statute in Reſpect only 611.

of Imprisonment for Offences not capital; when an Offence becomes capital, it is as much out of the Benefit of the Statute, as if it had always been so.

Sect. 14. II. The Offence for which the Party was imprisoned must be a Capital one at the Time of the Offence, and not become such by
[a] H. P. C. Matter subsequent; as where [a] *A.* is committed to a Prison for a dangerous
108, 219. Wound given to *B.* and breaks the Prison, and then *B.* dies: For though
2 Inst. 591. Pl. Com. 258. to some Intents such Offence be esteemed capital from the Time of the
b. 401. a. first Act, yet inasmuch as it was in Truth but a Trespass at the Time of
11 H. 4. 12. b. S. P. C. 33. A. the Breaking of the Prison, and it was then uncertain whether it would
1 H. H. P. C. ever become capital; and it becomes such afterwards *ab initio*, by Fiction
427, 591. only, for some special Purposes, and Fictions of Law are never carried farther than the Necessity of those particular Cases, which were the Cause of the inventing them, doth require; they shall never be construed to exempt a Person from the Advantage of a beneficial Law made in Favour of Life, who is clearly within the Letter, and doth not plainly appear to be out of the Meaning of it. However, it seems certain, That such an
11 H. 4. 12. b. Offender breaking Prison, while it is uncertain whether his Offence will
S. P. C. 35. Letter H. become capital, is highly punishable for his Comtempt, by Fine and Imprisonment, &c.

Sect. 15. III. If the Party be only arrested for, and in his *Mittimus* charged with a Crime which does not require Judgment of Life or Member, as Petit Larceny, or Homicide *se defendendo*, or by Misadventure, and
1 H. H. P. C. the Offence, in Truth, be no greater than the *Mittimus* doth suppose it to
609. H. P. C. 110. be, it is clear, from the express Words of the Statute, That a Breaking
2 Inst. 590. of the Prison cannot amount to Felony. And if the Offence for which the Party is committed, be supposed in the *Mittimus* to be of such a Nature as requires a capital Judgment, yet if in the Event it be found to be of an inferior Nature, and not to require such a Judgment, it seems difficult to maintain, That the Breaking of the Prison on a Commitment for it can be Felony; for the Words of the Statute are *Nisi Causa pro qua captus & imprisonatus fuerit, tale judicium requirit*; and here it appears, That the Offence, which is the Cause of his Imprisonment, doth not require such a Judgment; and it is hard to say, That a Mistake of the Nature of the Crime, by the Person who makes the Arrest or *Mittimus*, should so far prejudice the Party, as to make his Escape amount to Felony by Reason of such Mistake, which otherwise would have been but a Trespass. Also it seems to be agreed, That if a Person be committed for a supposed Felony, where no Felony hath been done, he is not guilty of Felony for breaking the Prison; from whence it clearly appears, That in that Case the Law doth not so far regard the Charge contained in the *Mittimus*, where there is no good Ground to support it, as in Respect thereof to exclude the Party from the Benefit of the Statute; and yet in that Case the Party is as much accused of a capital Offence as in the Case in Question; so that it is clear That the Law doth not so much respect the Heinousness of the Charge against the Party, as of the very Crime which is the Subject of the Charge: And this will farther appear, if it be considered, That the Accusation cannot be said to be the Cause which requires Judgment of Life or Member, but the Offence which supports the Accusation; and if there be no such Offence, there is, in Truth, no Cause which requires such a Judgment. On the other Side, if the Offence, which was the Cause of the Commitment, be in Truth of such a Nature as requires a capital Judgment, but in the *Mittimus* be supposed to be of an inferior Degree; it may probably be argued, That the Party's Breaking

ing of the Prison is Felony within the Meaning of the Statute; for the Cause of his Arrest and Commitment is the fact for which he was arrested and committed, and that does in Truth require Judgment of Life, tho' the Nature of it be mistaken in the *Mittimus*, which does no Way alter the Judgment of Law in Relation of the Guilt of it. But there appearing no express Resolution of these Points, and the [a] Authors who have expounded this Statute seeming rather to incline to a different Opinion, I shall leave these Matters to the Judgment of the Reader.

[a] 2 Inst. 590, 591. H. P. C. 109, 110.

Sect. 16. IV. It is not material, Whether the Party who breaks his Prison, were under an Accusation only, or actually attainted of the Crime charged against him; and yet the Words of the Statute are *si causa tale judicium requirit:* And it cannot be properly said, That the Offence of one attainted doth require such a Judgment, (for that there ought not to be a second Judgment against one already condemned) but only that it did require it; and it is a settled Rule, That all Statutes are to be construed strictly in Favour of Life, and that no parallel Case, which comes within the same Mischief, shall be construed to be within the Purview of it, unless it can be brought within the Meaning of the Words: Yet considering that the manifest Purport and Meaning of the Words of the Statute taken all together, is no more than this, That the Breaking of Prison shall not be a capital Offence; unless the Crime for which the Party was in Prison be also a capital Offence; and it is frequent, in the Construction of penal Laws, to bring Persons within the Purview of them by being within the Meaning of the Words, tho' not in strict Grammar properly within the very Letter; and it would be extremely harsh to imagine, that the Makers of the Statute could intend a greater Favour to Persons appearing to be guilty, and actually under the Condemnation of the Law, than to Persons under an Accusation only: There can be no Doubt, but that the Persons attainted, breaking Prison, are as much guilty within the Meaning of the above mentioned Exception as any others.

1 H. H. P. C. 609. S. P. C. 32. Letters A, B, C, D. See Book 1. Ch. 32. Sect. 2, 3, 4.

Sect. 17. As to the fifth Point, *viz.* Whether the Offence of breaking Prison can ever amount to High Treason; it seems clear, That a Person committed for High Treason becomes guilty of Felony only, and not of High Treason, by breaking the Prison and escaping singly, without letting out any other Prisoner; for that no Offence is to be construed High Treason, which is not either within the Purview of 25 *Ed.* 3. or of some subsequent Statute relating to Treason; but if other Persons committed also for High Treason escape together with him, and his Intention in breaking the Prison were to favour their Escape as well as his own, he seems to be guilty of High Treason in Respect of their Escape, for that there are no Accessaries in High Treason; and such Assistance given to Persons committed for Felony, will make him who gives it an Accessary to the Felony, and by the same Reason a Principal in the Case of High Treason. But this Offence coming more properly under the Notion of Rescous than of the Breaking of Prison, shall be more fully considered in the Chapter concerning Rescous.

Book 1. Ch. 17. Sect. 2. 2 Inst. 590. S. P. C. 32. Letter F. 1 H. 6. 5. b. 1 H. H. P. C. 137. H. P. C. 109.

Sect. 18. As to the sixth Point, *viz.* At what Time and in what Manner the Offender is to be proceeded against, it is said, That he may be arraigned for this Offence before he be convicted of the Crime for which he was imprisoned; for that it is not material whether he were guilty of such Crime or not, neither is he punishable as an Accessary in Respect thereof, but as a principal Offender in Respect of the Breach of

1 H. H. P. C. 611. H. P. C. 110, 116. 2 Inst. 592.

Prison it self; on which Account this Case differs from that of a Rescous or voluntary Escape, as shall be shewn more at large in the following Chapter. [35]

Fitz. Indictment, 30. 1 H. 7. 6. pl. 2.

Sect. 19. It seems clear, That the Sheriff's Return of a Breach of Prison, is not a sufficient Ground to arraign the Prisoner for it, unless he be also indicted.

H. P. C. 109. 2 Inst. 591. Fitz. Indictment, 18.

Sect. 20. As to the seventh Point, *viz.* In what Manner an Offender is to be indicted for a Breach of Prison, it is certain, That every Indictment of this Kind, to bring the Offender within the Intention of the Statute, must specially set forth his Case in such a Manner that it may appear that he was lawfully in Prison, and for such a Crime as requires Judgment of Life or Member; and that it is not sufficient to say in general, *Quod felonice fregit Prisonam.* And it seems, That the same Rules which are required for an Indictment of an Escape, set forth at large in the next Chapter, are generally to be observed in Indictments of breaking Prison.

Book 1. Ch. 20. Sect. 1. Ch. 59. Sect. 1. H. P. C. 116. S. P. C. 35. H. 11 H. 4. 12. b.

Sect. 21. As to the eighth Point, *viz.* In what Manner those are to be punished who are within the Benefit of the Statute, by being freed from that severe Judgment for the Breach of Prison, to which by the Common Law they would have been liable: There seems to be no Doubt, but that whoever breaks from any lawful Imprisonment is still punishable as for a High Misprision by Fine and Imprisonment; for that every capital Offence doth include in it a Misprision, and may be proceeded against as such only, if the King please; and it cannot be thought the Meaning of the Statute in ordaining, That such Offences shall not be punished as capital ones, to intend, That they shall not be punished at all.

CHAP. XIX.

Of Escapes suffered by Officers.

HAVING shewn in the precedent Chapters, how far the Party himself, under a lawful Arrest for a Crime charged against him, is punishable for unlawfully freeing himself from such Arrest, without waiting for his Deliverance by due Course of Law, I shall now in the second Place, consider Offences of this Kind in Relation to others. And

1. Such as are without Force.
2. Such as are accompanied with Force.

Such Offences, without Force, come under the Notion of Escapes, which are either,

1. By Officers. Or,
2. By Private Persons.

As to Escapes suffered by Officers, I shall endeavour to shew the following Particulars.

1. What shall be judged an Escape.
2. Where such Escape is to be esteemed voluntary, and where negligent.
3. Where the Prisoner may be re-taken after an Escape.
4. Whether the Escape is excused by such a Re-taking; or by killing the Prisoner, if he cannot be re-taken.
5. In what Manner the Officer suffering an Escape is to be indicted.
6. How an Escape is to be tried and adjudged.
7. How a voluntary Escape is to be punished.
8. How a negligent one.

As to the first Point, *viz.* What shall be adjudged an Escape, the following Rules are to be observed.

Sect. 1. I. There must be an actual Arrest, and therefore, If [a] an Officer having a Warrant to Arrest a Man, see him shut up in a House, and challenge him as his Prisoner, but never actually have him in his Custody, and the Party get Free, the Officer cannot be charged with an Escape.

Sect. 2. II. As there must be an actual Arrest, such Arrest must [b] also be justifiable, for if it be either for a supposed Crime, where no such Crime was committed, and the Party neither indicted nor appealed, or for such a slight Suspicion of an actual Crime, and by such an irregular *Mittimus* as will neither justify the Arrest nor Imprisonment, the Officer is not guilty of an Escape by suffering the Prisoner to go at large: And it seems to be a good general Rule, That where-ever an Imprisonment is so far irregular, That it will be no Offence in the Prisoner to break from it by Force, it can be no Offence in the Officer to suffer him to escape.

Sect. 3. III. As the Imprisonment must be justifiable, so must it be also for a criminal Matter; and some [c] are said to have holden, that no Escape is criminal, but where the Commitment is for Felony. However it is certain, that the Escape of one committed for Petit Larceny [d] only is criminal; and it seems most agreeable to the general Reason of the Law, That the Escape of a Person committed for any other Crime whatsoever should also be criminal. For surely, where-ever the publick Justice requires, That a Person be committed for a Crime; it likewise requires, That he be safely kept under such Commitment, and consequently may reasonably demand publick Satisfaction from the Officer to whose Custody he is committed, if he neglect to keep him as he ought.

Sect. 4. IV. As the Imprisonment must be justifiable, and for some Crime, so must its Continuance, at the Time of the Escape, be grounded on that Satisfaction which the publick Justice demands for such Crime; for if a Prisoner be acquitted, [e] and detained only for his Fees, it will not be criminal to suffer him to escape, though the Judgment were, That he be discharged paying his Fees; so that till they be paid, the first Imprisonment continued lawful, as before; for inasmuch as he is detained, not as a Criminal, but only as a Debtor, his Escape cannot be more criminal, than that of any other Debtor; yet if a Person convicted of a Crime, be condemned to Imprisonment for a certain Time,

[a] Coron. 76. 9 H. 4. 1. pl. 3. 27 Assis. pl. 1. Fitz. Coron. 249. Bro. Escape, 22.

[b] Fitz. Coron. 224. 1 H. H. P. C. 583, 584, 599. 42 Ass. pl. 5. Bro. Escape, 27, 29. 5 Mod. 414, 415, 416. Contra 2 Leon. 166. See Ch. 18. Sect. 5, 6, 7, 8.

[c] Fitz. Coron. 248. S. P. C. 33. Letter H.

[d] Fitz. Coron. 430, 431. S. P. C. 33. Letter H. 1 H. H. P. C. 592.

[e] Bro. Escape, 16. 21 H. 7. 7. S. P. C. 34. Letter F. 1 H. H. P. C. 594.

and alſo till he pay his Fees, and he eſcape after ſuch Time is elapſed, without paying them, perhaps ſuch eſcape may be criminal, for that it was Part of the Puniſhment, that the Impriſonment be continued till the Fees ſhould be paid; but it ſeems, that this is to be intended where the Fees are due to others as well as to the Gaoler, for otherwiſe the Gaoler will be the only Sufferer by the Eſcape, and it will be hard to puniſh him for ſuffering an Injury to himſelf only, in the Non-payment of a Debt in his Power to releaſe.

Sect. 5. V. It is an Eſcape, in ſome Caſes, to ſuffer a Priſoner to have greater Liberty than by the Law he ought to have; as to admit a Perſon to Bail, [a] who by Law ought not to be bailed, but to be kept in cloſe Cuſtody; or to permit [b] a Priſoner to go out of the Limits of the Priſon: Yet ſome [c] ſeem to have holden, that in this laſt Caſe it ſhall not be adjudged an Eſcape, unleſs the Priſoner be found to have had an Intention to eſcape; but it will be difficult to maintain, That the Offence of the Gaoler can depend on the Intention of the Priſoner.

Sect. 6. VI. If [d] the Gaoler ſo cloſely purſue the Priſoner, who flies from him, that he re-take him, without loſing Sight of him, the Law looks on the Priſoner ſo far in his Power all the Time as not to adjudge ſuch a Flight to amount at all to an Eſcape: But if the Gaoler once loſe Sight of the Priſoner, and afterwards re-take him, he ſeems in Strictneſs to be guilty of an Eſcape; and *à fortiori* therefore, [e] if he kill him in the Purſuit, he is in like manner Guilty, tho' he never loſt Sight of him, and could not otherwiſe take him, not only becauſe the King loſes the Benefit he might have had from the Attainder of the Priſoner, by the Forfeiture of his Goods, *&c.* but alſo becauſe the Publick Juſtice is not ſo well ſatisfied by the killing him in ſuch an extrajudicial Manner.

Sect. 7. VII. While the Privileges of Sanctuaries were allowed, if a Sheriff conducting a Priſoner to Gaol, had brought him in the Way, through the Limits of ſuch a Franchiſe, and the Priſoner had claimed the Privilege of it, and by that Means got free, it ſeems, [f] that the Sheriff was guilty of an Eſcape, for that it was his Fault, by bringing his Priſoner that way to Gaol, to give him an Opportunity of claiming the Franchiſe.

Sect. 8. VIII. Alſo while the Law allowed thoſe who had the Benefit of the Clergy, to free themſelves from Priſon in certain Caſes, by making their Purgation before the Ordinary, it was an Eſcape [g] in the Ordinary, to ſuffer ſuch Perſons to deliver themſelves by it, in ſuch Caſes in which they ought not to have been admitted to it.

Sect. 9. IX. If [h] a Priſoner be reſcued by Enemies, the Gaoler is not guilty of an Eſcape, as he would have been by the better Opinion, if he had been reſcued by Subjects, becauſe there is a legal Remedy againſt them. [36]

Sect. 10. As to the ſecond Point, *viz.* Where ſuch Eſcape is to be eſteemed voluntary, and where negligent, There [i] can be no Doubt, but that where-ever an Officer, who hath the Cuſtody of a Priſoner, charged with and guilty of a Capital Offence, doth knowingly give him his Liberty with an Intent to ſave him either from his Trial or Execution, he is guilty of a voluntary Eſcape, and thereby involv'd in the Guilt of the ſame Crime of which the Priſoner was guilty, and ſtood charged with. And it ſeems to be the Opinion of Sir *Matthew Hale*, [k] That in ſome Caſes an Officer may be adjudged guilty of ſuch Eſcape, who hath not ſuch Intent, but only means to give his Priſoner that Liberty which

See Fitz. Coron. 430. S. P. C. 34. Letter E.
[a] 25 E. 3. 39. pl. 22. 1 H. H. P. C. 596, 597. H. P. C. 113. Fitz. Eſcape, 4. Fitz. Coron. 246.
[b] Fitz. Coron. 242.
[c] Fitz. Coron. 431. S. P. C. 133. Letter E.
[d] Fitz. Coron. 236, 400. S. P. C. 33. Letters B, C. 1 H. H. P. C. 602. Bro. Eſcape, 14, 32, 49, 52. 10 H. 7. 25. b. 26. a. 6 H. 7. 11. b. 12. a.
[e] Fitz. Coron. 328, 346. S. P. C. 33. Letters B, C. See Book 1. Ch. 28. Sect. 11, 12.
[f] Bro. Eſcape, 38, 50. 2 H. 4. 15. pl. 14. Fitz. Coron. 222, 316. but 27 Aſſ. 54. and Bro. Eſcape, 24. ſeem contrary.
[g] Fitz. Coron. 16. 27 H. 6. 7. b. S. P. C. 33. Letters G, H. Vide 23 H. 8. 11.
[h] Bro. Eſcape, 10, 32, 52. 6 H. 7. 11. b. 12. a. 10 H. 7. 25. b. 26. a. 29 Aſſ. 34. 1 H. H. P. C. 596. Bro. Eſcape, 26. ſeems contrary.
[i] See Cro. Car. 492. S. P. C. 32. Letter I.
[k] H. P. C. 113.

which by the Law he hath no Colour of Right to give him; as where a Gaoler bails a Prisoner who is not bailable. [37] But it seems agreed, That a Person who hath Power to bail, is guilty only of a negligent Escape, by bailing one who is not bailable; neither can I meet with any Authority in other Books, to support the abovementioned Opinion, That the Bailing of one who is not bailable, by one who hath no Power to bail, must necessarily be esteemed a voluntary Escape; but the contrary Opinion seems more agreeable to the Purview of 5 *E.* 3. 8. set forth more at large in the subsequent Part of this Chapter: Also there are some Cases wherein an Officer seems to have been found [a] to have knowingly given his Prisoner more Liberty than he ought to have had, as to go out of the Prison on his Promise of Returning, or to go among his Friends, to find some who would warrant Goods to be his own, which he is suspected to have stolen, and yet seems to have been only adjudged guilty of a negligent Escape. But it must be confessed, That in these Cases, the Prisoner was only accused of Larceny; and it doth not appear, whether he were bailable or not, and generally the old Cases concerning this Subject, are so very briefly reported, that it is very difficult to make an exact State of the Matter from them; however thus much seems clear, That if in the Cases abovementioned, the Officer were only guilty of a negligent Escape, in suffering the Prisoner to go out of the Limits of the Prison, without any Security for his Return, he could not have been guilty in a higher Degree, if he had taken Bail for his Return; from which it seems reasonable to infer, That it cannot be in all Cases a general Rule, that an Officer is guilty of a voluntary Escape by bailing his Prisoner, whom he hath no Power to bail; but that the Judgment to be made of all Offences of this Kind, must depend on the Circumstances of the Case, as the Heinousness of the Crime with which the Prisoner is charged, the Notoriety of his Guilt, the Improbability of his returning to render himself to Justice, the Intention of the Officer, the Motives on which he acted, &c. [38]

Supra Sect. 5.

[a] Fitz. Coro. 242, 316, 431. S. P. C. 33.

Sect. 11. Neither is it a certain Rule, That an Officer, who unlawfully, knowingly, and willingly suffers a Capital Offender to escape, is in all Cases to be adjudged guilty of a voluntary Escape; for where an Ordinary suffered a Clerk attainted, being committed to his Custody, to free himself from Imprisonment, by making his Purgation, he might be truly said to have suffered such Prisoner to escape unlawfully, knowingly and willingly, and yet it seems, [b] that he was guilty only of a negligent Escape, for that he did not save the Prisoner from Execution, which was excused by the Privilege of the Clergy, but only from the Imprisonment.

[b] Fitz. Coro. 16, 370. Escape, 1. S.P.C. 34. G. 141. B. 15 H. 7. 9. pl. 8. 1 H. H. P. C. 593.

Sect. 12. As to the third Point, *viz.* In what Cases a Prisoner may be re-taken after an Escape; it seems to be clearly agreed, by all the Books, [c] That an Officer making a fresh Pursuit after a Prisoner, who hath escaped through his Negligence, may re-take him at any Time after, whether he find him in the same, or in a different [d] County. And it is said generally in some Books, [e] That an Officer who hath negligently suffered a Prisoner to escape, may re-take him where-ever he finds him, without mentioning any fresh Pursuit; and indeed, since the Liberty gained by the Prisoner is wholly owing to his own Wrong, there

[c] Fitz. Trespass, 94. Escape, 2. Coron. 236. Bro. Escape, 49, 32, 52. 1 H. H. P. C. 602. 13 Ed. 4. 9. 2 Ed. 4. 6. b.

[d] 33 H. 6. 52. b. 53. a. 3 Co. 44. b. 52. Bro. Escape, 4. Fresh Suit, 3, 5. Contra Keilw. 3. a.

[e] Fitz. Coron. 236, 400, 313, 335. S. P. C. 117. Letter C. Bro. Execution, 58, 151. 27 H. 8. 1. a. 13 H. 7. 1. b. F. N. B. 130.

seems

ſeems to be no Reaſon he ſhould take any manner of Advantage from it. But where a Gaoler hath voluntarily ſuffered a Priſoner to eſcape, it is ſaid by ſome, [a] That he can no more juſtify the Re-taking him, than if he had never had him in Cuſtody before, becauſe by his own free Conſent he hath admitted, that he hath nothing to do with him. And it ſeems to be holden by Sir *William Saundford*, [b] That after a Gaoler hath been fined for ſuffering a Priſoner negligently to eſcape, he cannot afterwards re-take him; [39] but the Book [c] on which alone he ſeems to ground his Opinion, doth not fully come up to it; for the Purport of it ſeems to be no more than this, That a Gaoler's Retaking of a Priſoner, after he hath been fined for an Eſcape, ſhall be to no Purpoſe, for that it is contrary to the Record, by which it appears, that the Priſoner hath been at large; by which it ſeems only to be intended, That a Gaoler, who hath been fined for an Eſcape, ſhall not avoid the Judgment of his Fine by re-taking the Priſoner: But I do not ſee how it can be collected from hence, that he cannot juſtify the Re-taking him.

[a] 2 Jon. 21, 22, 45. 3 Co. 52. b. Cro. Jac. 659. Quære 1 Danv. Abr. 633. pl. 4. 535. pl. 11.
[b] S. P. C. 33. Letter E.
[c] 13 E. 4. 9. Fitz. Eſcape, 2. Br. Eſcape, 35.

Sect. 13. As to the fourth Point, *viz.* How far an Eſcape is excuſed by re-taking the Priſoner, or by killing him, if he cannot be re-taken; perhaps it is the better Opinion, [d] That where-ever a Priſoner, by the Negligence of his Keeper, gets ſo far out of his Power that the Keeper loſes Sight of him, the Keeper is finable at the Diſcretion of the Court, notwithſtanding he re-took him immediately after; for it ſeems agreed, That this is to be adjudged a negligent Eſcape, which implies an Offence, and conſequently that it muſt be puniſhable. [40] It is true indeed, That in an Action againſt a Gaoler, for ſuffering one arreſted in a Civil Action to eſcape, it is a good Excuſe for the Gaoler, that before the Action brought he re-took the Priſoner upon freſh Suit, which is well maintained by ſhewing that he purſued him immediately after Notice of the Eſcape, though it were ſome Hours after it, and re-took him; but it does not from hence follow, that the like Excuſe will ſerve for the negligent Eſcape of a Criminal, becauſe this is an Offence againſt the Publick, but the other is only a private Damage to the Party: Neither will it be the like Hardſhip to the Officer to be expoſed to ſuch Puniſhment as the Court in Diſcretion ſhall think fit to impoſe upon him for the negligent Eſcape of a Criminal, as it would be to be liable to an Action of Eſcape, for ſuffering a Perſon in his Cuſtody, in a Civil Action, to eſcape; for that in the former Caſe the Court would moderate his Fine according to the Circumſtances of the whole Matter, and would certainly mitigate, if not wholly excuſe it, if he ſhould appear to have taken all reaſonable Care: But in the other Caſe, if he ſhould be liable to an Action, his Judgment would not lie in the Diſcretion of the Court, but he would be bound to pay the whole Debt, for which the Party was in his Cuſtody, if the Eſcape ſhould be adjudged againſt him. However it is certain, that it will be no Advantage to a Gaoler to re-take his Priſoner, after he has been fined for the Eſcape, as hath been ſhewn in the precedent Section; alſo it is clear, that he cannot excuſe himſelf by killing a Priſoner in the Purſuit, though he could not poſſibly re-take him; but muſt, in ſuch Caſe, be content to ſubmit to ſuch Fine as his Negligence ſhall appear to deſerve.

[d] S. P. C. 33. H. P. C. 114. ſeems contrary.
See the Books cited Sect. 6. 1 Rol. Abr. 808. 1 Danv. Abr. 633. pl. 4. 3 Danv. Abr. 119. pl. 1. Vide Stat. 8 W. 3. c. 27.
Vide ſupra, Sect. 6.

Sect. 14. As to the fifth Point, *viz.* In what Manner the Officer, ſuffering an Eſcape is to be indicted, it ſeems clear, That every Indictment for an Eſcape, whether negligent or voluntary, muſt expreſly ſhew, that the Party was actually [d] in the Defendant's Cuſtody for a Crime, Action, or Commitment for it; and that [e] it is not ſuffi-

[d] 27 Aſſ. pl. 9. 1 H. H. P. C. 599. Bro. Eſcape, 22. Fitz. Aſſiſe, 247.
[e] Salk. 272. 5 Mod. 414, 415.

cient to ſay, that he was in the Defendant's Cuſtody, and charged with ſuch a Crime; for that a Perſon in Cuſtody may be ſo charged, and yet not be in Cuſtody by Reaſon of ſuch Charge: And it ſeems alſo, That every ſuch Indictment muſt expreſly ſhew that the Priſoner went at large, which is moſt properly [a] expreſſed by the Words *exivit ad largum*. Alſo it ſeems neceſſary to ſhew the Time when the Offence was committed, for which the Party was in Cuſtody, not only [b] that it may appear, that it was prior to the Eſcape, but alſo [c] that it was ſubſequent to the laſt general Pardon. Alſo it ſeems clear, That every Indictment for a voluntary Eſcape, muſt alledge that the Defendant *felonice & voluntarie* A. B. *ad largum ire permiſit*; and muſt [d] alſo ſhew the Species of the Crime for which the Party was impriſoned; for it is not ſufficient to ſay in general, That he was in Cuſtody for Felony, *&c.* for that no one can be puniſhed in this Degree, but as involved in the Guilt of the Crime for which the Party was in his Cuſtody; and therefore the particular Crime muſt be ſet forth, that it may appear, that the Principal is attainted for the very ſame Crime, if it were Felony, or that it was in Truth committed, if High Treaſon. But it ſeems queſtionable, [e] whether ſuch Certainty, as to the Nature of the Crime, be neceſſary in an Indictment for a negligent Eſcape, for that it is not material in this Caſe, whether the Perſon who eſcaped were guilty or not.

[a] Bro. Eſcape, 52. 10 H. 7. 26. a.
[b] Contra 2 Leon. 166. Bro. Eſcape, 17. Cro. El. 752.
[c] Henly 13.
[d] Cro. El. 752. Hetley 73. S. P. C. 95. A. H. P. C. 110, 111, 206. 8 Ed. 4. 3. pl. 6.
[e] See Keilw. 192, 194.

Sect. 15. As to the ſixth Point, *viz.* In what Manner an Eſcape is to be tried and adjudged, it is to be obſerved, That where Perſons being preſent in a Court of Record, are committed to Priſon by ſuch Court, the Keeper of the Gaol is bound to have them always ready, whenever the Court ſhall demand them of him; and if he ſhall fail to produce them at ſuch Demand, the Court will adjudge him guilty of an Eſcape, without any farther Inquiry, unleſs he have ſome reaſonable Matter to alledge in his Excuſe, as that the Priſon was ſet on Fire, or broken open by Enemies, *&c.* for he ſhall be concluded, [f] by the Record of the Commitment, to deny that the Priſoners were in his Cuſtody: And ſome [g] have holden, That if a Gaoler ſay nothing in Excuſe of ſuch an Eſcape, it ſhall be adjudged voluntary; but I cannot find any Reſolution to this Purpoſe; and where it ſtands indifferent, whether an Eſcape be negligent or voluntary, it ſeems difficult to maintain that it ought to be adjudged a Crime of ſo high a Nature, without a previous Trial. [41]

S. P. C. 34, 35. Fitz. Coron. 466.
[f] 11 H. 6. 49. b. 12 H. 6. 2. b. 3. S. P. C. 35.
[g] S. P. C. 34. G. 39 H. 6. 33, 34.

Sect. 16. As to other Priſoners who are not ſo committed, but are in the Cuſtody of a Gaoler, Sheriff, Conſtable, or other Perſon, by any other Means whatſoever, it ſeems agreed, [h] That the Perſon who has them in Cuſtody is in no Caſe puniſhable for their Eſcape, except in ſome ſpecial Caſes, until it be preſented; for the better Underſtanding whereof I ſhall endeavour to ſhew,

[h] S. P. C. 35.

1. Before whom ſuch Preſentments are to be made.
2. In what Caſes they are traverſable.

Sect. 17. As to the firſt Point, It is enacted by the Statute of *Weſtminſter* 1. *Chap.* 3. *That nothing be demanded nor taken, nor levied by the Sheriff, nor by any other, for the Eſcape of a Thief, or Felon, until it be judged for an Eſcape by the Juſtices in Eyre; and that he who does otherwiſe, ſhall reſtore to him or them that have paid it, as much as he or they have taken or received, and as much alſo unto the King.*

[a] 27 Aſſ. pl. 1, 9. 21 Aſſ. pl. 12. S. P. C. 35. 2 Inſt. 166. 1 H. H. P. C. 600.

Sect. 18. It hath been adjudged, [a] That this Statute reſtrains not the Court of King's Bench from receiving ſuch Preſentments, for that its Juriſdiction includes in it that of Juſtices of Eyre, and this Court is it ſelf the Higheſt Court of Eyre.

Sect. 19. It is farther enacted, by 31 *Ed.* 3. 14. *That the Eſcape of Thieves and Felons, and the Chattels of Felons, and of Fugitives, and alſo Eſcapes of Clerks Convict, out of their Ordinary's Priſon, from thenceforth to be judged before any of the King's Juſtices, ſhall be levied from Time to Time, as they ſhall fall, as well of the Time paſt as Time to come.* By which it ſeems to be implied, That other Juſtices, as well as thoſe in Eyre, may take Cogniſance of Eſcapes; and it is certain, That Juſtices of Gaol-Delivery may puniſh Juſtices of Peace for a negligent Eſcape, in admitting Perſons to Bail, who are not bailable.

Vide Supra Ch. 6. S. 11, 12, 13, 14, 15. S. P. C. 35.

Sect. 20. And it is farther enacted by 1 *Ric.* 3. *Chap.* 3. *That Juſtices of Peace ſhall have Authority to inquire in their Seſſions, of all Manner of Eſcapes of every Perſon arreſted and impriſoned for Felony.*

S. P. C. 35. Letter F.

Sect. 21. As to the ſecond Particular, In what Caſes ſuch Preſentments are traverſable; It is laid down as a Rule, by Sir *William Staundford*, That where-ever an Eſcape is finable, the Preſentment of it is traverſable; but that where the Offence is amerciable only, there the Preſentment is of it ſelf concluſive; ſuch Amercements being reckoned among thoſe *minima de quibus non curat lex*; and this Diſtinction ſeems to be well warranted by the Old [b] Books; and in what Caſes Eſcapes are finable, and where amerciable only, ſhall be conſidered in the following Part of this Chapter, *Sect.* 31, 33, 35.

[b] 21 Aſſ. pl. 12. 27 Aſſ. pl. 9, 27. Fitz. Coron. 291, 328, 345. 346, 352. 1 H. H. P. C. 603. 2 H. H. P. C. 154. [c] S. P. C. 32. 1 H. P. C. 113. 1 H. H. P. C. 234, 590, 391. Bro. Coron. 112. 27 Aſſ. 62. 11 H. 4. 12. b. [d] H. P. C. 114, 115. 1 H. H. P. C. 593. Dy. 99. pl. 60. Fitz. Eſcap. 3. 27 Aſſ. pl. 62.

Sect. 22. As to the ſeventh Point, *viz.* In what Manner a voluntary Eſcape is to be puniſhed, it ſeems to be generally [c] agreed, That ſuch Eſcape amounts to the ſame Kind of Crime, and is puniſhable in the ſame Degree, as the Offence of which the Party was guilty, and for which he was in Cuſtody, Whether it be Treaſon, Felony or Treſpaſs; and whether the Perſon eſcaping were actually committed to ſome Gaol, or under an Arreſt only and not committed; and whether he were attainted, or only accuſed [d] of ſuch Crime, and neither indicted nor appealed: And it is ſaid to be no Excuſe of ſuch Eſcape, That the Priſoner had been acquitted on an Indictment of Death, and only committed till the Year and Day be paſſed, to give the Widow, or Heir of the deceaſed an Opportunity of bringing their Appeal. [42]

[e] Bro. Eſcape, 18, 23. 2 Ro. Re. 146. Fitz. Aſſiſe 252. 39 H. 6. 33, 34. Quære 27. Aſſ. pl. 27. 1 H. H. P. C. 594.

Sect. 23. Alſo ſuch an Eſcape, ſuffered by one who wrongfully takes upon him the Keeping of a Gaol, ſeems to be [e] puniſhable in the ſame Manner as if he were never ſo rightfully intitled to ſuch Cuſtody, for that the Crime is in both Caſes of the very ſame ill Conſequence to the Publick; and there ſeems to be no Reaſon that a wrongful Officer ſhould have greater Favour than a rightful, and that, for no other Reaſon but becauſe he is a wrongful one.

H. P. C. 114. [f] Salk. 272, 347, 348. Contra H. P. C. 114. 2 Inſt. 590, 591, 592. See Ch. 16. & Ch. 18. Sect. 5, 6, 7.

Sect. 24. Alſo if the Warrant of Commitment do plainly and expreſly charge the Party with Treaſon or Felony, but in ſome other Reſpect be not ſtrictly formal, yet it ſeems, That it may [f] be probably argued, That the Gaoler ſuffering an Eſcape, is as much puniſhable as if the Warrant were perfectly right; [43] for it would be highly inconvenient to ſuffer Gaolers to take Advantage of a Slip of this Kind in Commitments, which being generally made by Perſons of no great Knowledge in the Law, cannot be expected to be always agreeable to its Forms; and therefore if they be good in Subſtance, the publick Good ſeems to require, that the Gaoler be as much bound to obſerve them, as if they were never ſo exactly made.

Sect. 25. But it ſeems to be agreed, That no Eſcape can amount to a capital Offence, unleſs the Cauſe for which the Party was committed, [a] were actually ſuch at the Time of the Eſcape; and therefore, if a Gaoler ſuffer one to eſcape who is committed for having given a dangerous Wound to another, who afterwards dies of ſuch Wound, yet he is not guilty of Felony, for that the Offence of the Priſoner was but a Treſpaſs at the Time of the Eſcape; and though by a Fiction of Law it be afterwards, for ſome Purpoſes, eſteemed a Felony from the Time of the giving of the Wound, yet ſince it is, in Truth, no Felony till the Death of the Party, it ſhall be afterwards conſtrued ſuch in Reſpect of thoſe only who were privy to the Giving of the Wound.

[a] 2 H. P. C. 114, 219. See Ch. 16. Sect. 19. 11 H. 4. 12.b. 1 H. H. P. C. 591.

Sect. 26. Alſo it ſeems clear, That he who ſuffers another to eſcape who was in his Cuſtody for Felony, cannot be arraigned for ſuch Eſcape as for a Felony, until the Principal be attainted; for that he who ſuffers ſuch Eſcape, is by the better Opinion, not puniſhable in this Degree, but as an Acceſſary to the Felony; and it is a Rule, That no Acceſſary ought to be tried till the Principal be attainted, as ſhall be more fully ſhewn hereafter: Yet it ſeems certain, [b] That one accuſed of ſuch an Eſcape, may be indicted and tried for a Miſpriſion, before the Attainder of the principal Offender, for that whether ſuch Offender were guilty or innocent it was a high Contempt to ſuffer him to eſcape: And if the Commitment were for High Treaſon, and the Perſon committed actually guilty of it, it ſeems, That the Eſcape is immediately puniſhable as High Treaſon alſo, whether the Party eſcaping be ever convicted of ſuch ☞ Crime or not; [44] for that there are no Acceſſaries in High Treaſon, but all who are guilty of aſſiſting the Party guilty of ſuch Crime, in ſuch a Manner as would make them Acceſſaries to a Felony, are accounted Principals in the Treaſon, as ſhall be more fully ſhewn in the Chapter concerning Principal and Acceſſary.

1 H. H. P. C. 591, 598. H. P. C. 110, 215, 216. 2 H. H. P. C. 254. Fitz. Coron. 158. Quære 27 Aſſ. 62. Contra Crompton 58. [b] H.P.C.116. Fitz. Coron. 158. See Ch. 18. Sect. 21. H. P. C. 110. ſeems contrary. H. P. C. 116.

Sect. 27. Alſo it ſeems to be clear, That no one is puniſhable in this Degree for a voluntary Eſcape, but the Perſon only who is actually guilty of it; and therefore, that the principal Gaoler is only finable for a voluntary Eſcape ſuffered by his Deputy, for that no one ſhall ſuffer capitally for the Crime of another.

Salkeld 272. H. P. C. 113, 114. 1 H. H. P. C. 597, 598.

As to the eighth Point, *viz.* In what Manner a negligent Eſcape is to be puniſhed, I ſhall endeavour to ſhew,

1. How ſuch Eſcape is puniſhable by the Common Law.
2. How by Statute.

Sect. 28. As to the firſt Particular, I ſhall take it for granted at this Day, that whoever *de facto* occupies the Office of Gaoler is liable to anſwer for ſuch an Eſcape; and that it is no way material whether his Title to the Office be legal or not.

H. P. C. 114. 2 Rol. Rep. 146. Bro. Eſcape, 18, 23. Quære 27 Aſſ. 27.

Sect. 29. Alſo I take it to be the better Opinion, That [c] a Sheriff is as much liable to anſwer for an Eſcape ſuffered by his Bailiff, as if he had actually ſuffered it himſelf, and that [d] the Court may charge either the Sheriff or Bailiff for ſuch an Eſcape; and if a Deputy-Gaoler be not ſufficient to anſwer a negligent Eſcape, his Principal muſt anſwer for him: But

Vide ſupra Sect. 23. [c] Fitz. Coron 337. [d] Salk. 272. H. P. C 113. 1 H. H. P. C. 597, 604. 2 Levin 7

[a] 39 H. 6. 33, 34. 2 Rol. Abr. 155. Letters M, N. 3 Levin. 288. 2 Levin. 81. [b] Bro. Forfeiture of Offices, 27. 2 R. A. 155. Letter N.

But if the Gaoler who ſuffers an Eſcape, have an Eſtate [a] for Life, or Years, in the Office, I do not find it agreed how far he in Reverſion is liable to be puniſhed.

Sect. 30. It ſeems the better Opinion, That one negligent Eſcape will not amount to a Forfeiture of the Gaoler's Office, as one voluntary [b] one will; Yet if a Gaoler ſuffer many negligent Eſcapes, it is ſaid, that he puts it in the Power of the Court to ouſt him of his Office by its Diſcretion.

[c] 8 H. 5. 2. Fitz. Coron. 84, 292. [c] S. P. C. 35. H. Bro. Eſcape, 16. Raſtal's Ent. 583. b. [d] Fitz. Coro. 335. [e] 25 Ed. 3. 39. pl. 22. 27 Aſſ. pl. 9. S. P. C. 65. 26 Aſſ. pl. 51. H. P. C. 113. Fitz. Coron. 196, 291, 370. Graunt, 39. Eſcape, 4. See the Books ſupra Ch. 12. Sect. 2. [f] Fitz. Eſcap. 7. 40 Aſſ. pl. 42. [g] 3 H. 7. 15. pl. 30. 8 H. 5. 2. pl. 6. Fitz. Graunt, 37. [h] S.P.C. 35. K. H. P. C. 113. 1 H. H. P. C. 604. Fitz. Coron. 370. [i] S.P.C. 35. K. H. P. C. 113. 27 Aſſ. pl. 9. 40 Aſſ. pl. 42. 25 Ed. 3. 39. pl. 22. H. P. C. 113. Fitz. Coron. 454. [k] S.P.C. 33. K. Fitz. Coron. 422. [l] Fitz. Coro. 196. 26 Aſſ. pl. 51.

Sect. 31. It ſeems to be certain, That where-ever a Perſon is found guilty upon an Indictment, or Preſentment, of a negligent Eſcape of a Criminal actually in his Cuſtody, he ought to be condemned in a certain Sum to be paid to the King, which ſeems moſt properly to be called a Fine; but this doth not clearly appear from the old Books, for in ſome [c] of them it ſeems to be taken as a Fine, in others [d] as an Amercement, and in others it is ſpoken of generally, as an Impoſition of a certain Sum, and without any [e] Mention either of Fine or Amercement. But where the Books ſpeak of the Puniſhment of a Vill or Hundred, for ſuffering a Felon to eſcape without being arreſted, they ſeem always to take it as an Amercement, and not as a Fine: And where a Sheriff, having returned a *Cepi Corpus* into the King's Bench, on a *Capias* againſt a Man on an Indictment of Felony, does not bring him in at the Day, it ſeems [f] That he is, by the Courſe of the ſaid Court, to be amerced, not fined.

Sect. 32. It hath been holden, [g] That a negligent Eſcape may be pardoned by the King before it happens, but that a voluntary one cannot be ſo pardoned; but this ſhall be more fully conſidered in the Chapter concerning Pardon.

Sect. 33. And it ſeems, [h] That by the Common Law, the Penalty for ſuffering the negligent Eſcape of a Perſon attainted, was of Courſe 100 *l.* and for ſuffering ſuch Eſcape of a Perſon indicted and not attainted, was 5 *l.* [i] but if the Perſon eſcaping were neither attainted nor indicted, it ſeems, That it was left to the Diſcretion of the Court to aſſeſs ſuch a reaſonable Forfeiture as ſhould ſeem proper; and [k] if the Party had twice eſcaped, it ſeems, That the Penalties above mentioned were of Courſe to be doubled; yet it ſeems, That the Forfeiture was to be no greater for ſuffering [l] a Priſoner, committed on two ſeveral Accuſations to eſcape, than if he had been committed but on one.

Sect. 34. As to the ſecond Particular, *viz.* In what Manner Offences of this Kind are puniſhable by Statute, it is recited by 5 *Ed.* 3. *Ch.* 8. *That Perſons indicted of Felonies in Times paſt, had removed the Indictments before the King, and there yielded themſelves, and by the Marſhals of the King's Bench had been incontinently let to Bail, and after had done many evil Deeds,* &c. And thereupon it is enacted, *That ſuch Enditees and Appellees ſhall be ſafely and ſurely kept in Priſon, as belongeth to them, according to the Charge which the ſaid Marſhals ſhall have of the Juſtices; and if any Marſhal ſhall do otherwiſe, at the Complaint of every Man that will complain, the Juſtices ſhall do him Right during the Terms; and in the End of the Terms, upon their riſing, the ſaid Marſhals ſhall chooſe before the ſaid Juſtices, before they depart their Places, in what Town they will keep ſuch Priſoners at their Peril: And in the ſame Town they ſhall allow to them Houſes to keep ſuch Priſoners at their own Coſts and Charges; and there they ſhall keep them in Priſon, and ſhall not ſuffer them to go wandring abroad, neither by Bail nor without Bail. And if any ſuch Priſoner be found wandring out of Priſon, by Bail or without Bail, and that be found at the King's Suit, or at the Suit of the Party, the Marshals which shall be found thereof guilty, shall have half a Year's Imprisonment, and be ransomed at the King's Will; and the Justices shall thereof make Enquiry when they see Time; and as to the Marshals, it shall be done within the Verge that which Reason will. And in Case that the Marshals suffer by their Assent such Prisoners to escape, they shall be at the Law, as before the Time of the Statute they had been. And the King intendeth not by this Statute to lose the Escape, where he ought to have the same.*

Sect. 35. Also it is enacted by 19 *H.* 7. 10. *That every Sheriff have the Custody of the King's Common Gaols, during the Time of his Office, except all Gaols whereof any Person or Persons have the Keeping of Estate of Inheritance: And that all Letters Patents made for Term of Life, or Years, of the keeping of the said Gaols,* &c. *shall be annulled and void.* And then it is recited by the said Statute, *That divers Persons before that Time, for Treason and Felonies had been taken, some for Suspection of the same Deeds, and some upon Indictments, and thereupon brought to the same Gaols, and sometime remained in the Keeping of the Persons that so arrested them for the said Causes, and that such Persons, by Colour of Negligence, subtilly, and craftily, and oftentimes for Favour, Mede, Affection or Corruption, suffered the said Offenders to escape, as if it had been by Negligence, to the overt and express Impediment of Justice: And when such Escapes had been found before Justices having Authority to enquire thereof, and thereupon the Parties convicted, or yielded themselves to make Fine for the same, small Fines had been set in those Causes, to the little Dread and Fear and great Inboldning of the Offenders, by Means whereof, great and arrant Felons and heinous Murderers had escaped,* &c. And thereupon it is enacted, *That for every negligent Escape from any Sheriff, having the Keeping of any Gaol, or from any Constable of Castle, or other, being Keeper of any Gaols where such Prisoners accustomably have been, or shall be kept, of Persons indicted of High Treason being in their Keeping, that no less Fine be set or made for every such Escape, than* 100 *Marks, and more, by the Discretion of the Justice, that shall assess such Fines: And for every Escape of Persons escaping being in their keeping for Suspection of High Treason, no less Fine to be set or made than* 40 l. *and for every Escape of Persons indicted of Murder or Petit Treason,* 20 l. *at least, and more, by the Discretions of the Justices that shall assess such Fines: And for every Escape of Persons suspected of Murder or Petit Treason,* 10 l. *or more, by the Discretion of the Justices that shall assess such Fines: And for every Person escaping, being in their Keeping, indicted of Felony, other than Murder or Treason,* 10 l. *And for every Person suspected of Felony, other than Murder or Treason,* 100 *Shillings, or more, by the Discretion of the Justices, after the Manner and Quantity of their Demerits, saving to every Person such Right and Title to any such Escapes and Fines for the same, or to be quit of such Escapes, or of any other Ecapes, as they had, or ought to have had, at the Time of making of the said Act.*

CHAP. XX.

Of Efcapes fuffered by private Perfons.

HAVING in the precedent Chapter endeavoured to fhew the Nature of Efcapes fuffered by Officers, I am now in the fecond Place to confider the Nature of fuch Efcapes fuffered by private Perfons: But the
H. P. C. 112. Law being generally the fame in Relation to fuch Efcapes, as in Relation to thofe fuffered by Officers, I fhall refer the Reader, for the general Learning of this Kind, to what is faid in the former Chapter concerning Efcapes fuffered by Officers, and fhall content my felf in this Place with confidering the two following Particulars.

1. Where a private Perfon is to be adjudged guilty of fuch an Efcape.
2. In what Manner he is to be punifhed.

Sect. 1. As to the firft Point, it feems to be a good general Rule, That where-ever any Perfon hath another lawfully in his Cuftody, whether up-
[a] See Ch. 12. H. P. C. 112. 1 H. H. P. C. 595. on an Arreft made by himfelf or another, he is guilty [a] of an Efcape, if he fuffer him to go at large, before he hath difcharged himfelf of him by delivering him over to fome other who by Law ought to have the Cuftody of him.

Sect. 2. And therefore, if a private Perfon arreft another for Sufpicion of Felony, and deliver him into the Cuftody of another private
[b] H. P. C. 112. 44 Aff. pl. 12. Bro. Efcape, 31. 43 Ed. 3. 36. pl. 55. Fitz. Coron. 454. Efcape, 3. Perfon who receives him, and fuffers him to go at large, it is faid, [b] That both of them are guilty of an Efcape, the firft, becaufe he fhould not have parted with him, till he had delivered him into the Hands of a publick Officer; the latter, becaufe having charged himfelf with the Cuftody of a Prifoner, he ought, at his Peril, to have taken care of him.

Sect. 3. But if a private Perfon having made fuch an Arreft, have de-
[c] Fitz. Coron. 345. [d] Fitz. Coron. 328, 337. S. P. C. 34. D. livered over his Prifoner to the proper Officer (as the Sheriff, [c] or his Bailiff, [d] or a Conftable, [e]) from whofe Cuftody the Prifoner efcapes, the Party who made the Arreft is not chargeable with it.

Sect. 4. But if no Officer will receive fuch Prifoner into his Cuftody,
[e] H. P. C. 112. 1 H. H. P. C. 594, 595. [f] 10 H. 7. pl. 2. Fitz. Efcape, 8. H. P. C. 114. Fitz. Coron. 345. it feems [f] to be the fafeft Way to deliver him into the Cuftody of the Townfhip where the Perfon who arrefted him lives, or perhaps of that where the Arreft was made, which fhall be bound to keep him till the next Gaol-Delivery; but if fuch Townfhip refufe alfo to receive him, I do not fee how the Perfon who made that Arreft can difcharge himfelf of him before the next Gaol-Delivery, unlefs he can in the mean Time procure him to be bailed.

Sect. 5. Neither can fuch private Perfon excufe himfelf of the Efcape of fuch a Prifoner, by alledging, That he delivered him over to a Sheriff or other Officer, without fhewing to whom, in particular, by

Name, he so delivered him, that the Court may certainly know who is answerable for him.

Sect. 6. As to the second Point, *viz.* In what Manner a private Person is punishable for such an Escape, I shall take it for granted that if it were voluntary, he is punishable in the same Manner as an Officer, for which I shall refer the Reader to the former Chapter; and if it were negligent, he is punishable by Fine and Imprisonment, at the Discretion of the Court, as the Law is settled by 19 *H.* 7. 10. The Words whereof, so far as they relate to this Purpose, are as follows, *And if any Person hereafter have any Prisoner in his keeping, arrested for Suspection of Felony, Treason, or Murder, and that Person that is arrested, escape by negligent keeping, before that he be brought to the Gaol, that Person from whom he so escaped, shall forfeit for every Person that doth so escape, such Fine as shall be set by the Discretion of the Justices that shall have Authority to assess such Fines, as the Cause shall require, and the same Forfeiture to go to them that be intituled to have such Forfeitures at the Time of making the said Act.* H. P. C. 112. Bro. Coron 112. 27 Ass. 62.

CHAP. XXI.

Of Rescous.

THE Offence of a Stranger in forcibly freeing another from an Arrest, comes under the Notion of Rescous, which in most Instances is of the same Nature with the Offence of breaking Prison, which hath been already considered in the eighteenth Chapter; and therefore it seems sufficient for the Declaration of the Nature of this Crime, to shew, 1 H. H. P. C. 606.

1. In what Cases it agrees with the Offence of breaking Prison. And
2. In what it differs.

And first, This Offence agrees with that of breaking Prison in the following Particulars.

Sect. 1. I. Whatever is such a Prison, that the Party himself was, by the Common Law, guilty of Felony by breaking from it, in every such Case a Stranger was guilty of as high a Crime at least, in rescuing him from it. 2 Inst. 589. S. P. C. 30, 31. and the Cases cited. Ch. 18. Sect. 1 & 4.

Sect. 2. II. Where-ever [a] the Imprisonment is so far groundless, or irregular, or for such a Cause, or the Breaking of it is occasioned by such a Necessity, *&c.* that the Party himself breaking the Prison, is, either by the Common Law, or by the Statute *de frangentibus Prisonam*, saved from the Penalty of a capital Offender, a Stranger who rescues him from such an Imprisonment, is in like Manner also excused; *& sic è converso.* [a] See Ch. 18. S. P. C. 30, 31. H. P. C. 116.

Sect. 3. III. As the Party himself seems not to be guilty of Felony by breaking the Prison unless he go out of it; so neither is a Stranger unless the Prisoner actually go out of the Prison. Keilw. 87. a. Bro. Escape, 57.

Fitz. Enditement, 30. 1 H. 7. 6. pl. 2.

Sect. 4. IV. As the Sheriff's Return, that a Priſoner hath broken the Priſon, is not a ſufficient Ground to arraign him for ſuch Offence, unleſs he be indicted alſo for it; ſo neither is his Return of a Reſcous a good Ground for the Arraignment of the Reſcuer, unleſs he be indicted.

Vide ſupra, Ch. 18. Sect. 20. & Ch. 19. Sect. 14. Dyer 164. pl. 60.

Sect. 5. V. As an Indictment of breaking Priſon, and alſo an Indictment of Eſcape, muſt ſpecially ſet forth the Nature and Cauſe of the Impriſonment, and the ſpecial Circumſtances of the Fact in Queſtion, ſo alſo muſt an Indictment of Reſcous.

Vide ſupra, Ch. 18. Sect. 21.

Sect. 6. VI. As thoſe who break Priſon are ſtill puniſhable, as for a high Miſpriſion, by Fine and Impriſonment, in thoſe Caſes wherein they are ſaved from Judgment of Death, by the Statute *de frangentibus priſonam*, ſo alſo are thoſe who reſcue ſuch Priſoners in the like Caſes, in the ſame manner puniſhable.

2. The Offence of Reſcous differs from that of breaking Priſon in the following Particulars.

Vide ſupra, Ch. 18. Sect. 17. 1 H. H. P. C. 237.

[a] S. P. C. 11. C. 32. F. H. P. C. 109. Dalt. fol. 228. 1 Jo. 455. 1 H. 6. 5. b. Fitz. Coron. 2. Bro. Treaſ. 11.

[b] Cro. Car. 583.

[c] 1 H. 6. 5. b.

Sect. 7. I. Whereas a Perſon committed for High Treaſon, who breaks the Priſon and eſcapes, is guilty of Felony only, unleſs he lets others alſo eſcape whom he knows to be committed for High Treaſon, in which Caſe he is guilty of High Treaſon, not in reſpect of his own breaking of the Priſon, but of the Reſcous of the others: A Stranger [a] who reſcues a Perſon committed for and guilty of High Treaſon, knowing him to be ſo committed, is in all Caſes guilty of High Treaſon; and by ſome [b] he is in like manner guilty, whether he knew that the Priſoners were committed for High Treaſon or not; but this Opinion is not proved by the Authority of the Caſe [c] on which it ſeems to be grounded.

[d] Supra Ch. 18. Sect. 17.

[e] Vide ſupra, Ch. 19. H. P. C. 116. S. P. C. 43. Letter B. ſeems contrary.

Sect. 8. II. Whereas a Priſoner who breaks the Priſon, may be arraigned [d] for ſuch Offence before he be arraigned of the Crime for which he was impriſoned; he who reſcues one impriſoned for Felony cannot, according to the better [e] Opinion, be arraigned for ſuch Offence as for a Felony, till the principal Offender be firſt attainted; but if the Perſon reſcued were impriſoned for High Treaſon, the Reſcuer may immediately be arraigned, for that in high Treaſon all are Principals; alſo it ſeems, that he may be immediately proceeded againſt for a Miſpriſion only, if the King pleaſe.

CHAP. XXII.

Of Attachment.

HAVING ſhewn in what manner Offenders may be apprehended without Proceſs from a Court of Record, I am now to ſhew in what Manner they may be brought into Court by ſuch Proceſs, of which there are two Sorts.

1. Such as may be awarded by the Discretion of the Justices upon a bare Suggestion, or their own Knowledge, without any Appeal, Indictment, or Information.

2. Such as can be awarded only upon such Accusations.

Sect. 1. And first, I shall consider the Nature of the first of these, which is generally called an Attachment, and is properly grantable in Cases of Contempts, against which, for the most part all Courts of Record generally, but more especially those of *Westminster-hall*, and above all the Court of King's Bench, may proceed in a summary Manner according to their Discretion; and if they happen to be done by a Person present in the Court, and appear either from the Confession of the Party on his Examination upon Oath, or by the View or immediate Observation of the Judges themselves, the Court may immediately record the Crime, and commit the Offender, and also inflict such farther Punishment as shall seem proper: And if such Offences be done by a Person not present in Court, and be complained of by Affidavit, the Court will either make a Rule on the Party to attend at a certain Day, in Order to answer the Matter of the Complaint against him; or else will make a Rule upon him to shew Cause why an Attachment should not be granted against him; or else, if the Offence were of a very exorbitant Nature, as for Words of Contempt of the Court it self, will grant an Attachment on the first Complaint, without any such Rule to shew Cause; and the Party who is ordered to attend the Court in Pursuance of such Rule, ought regularly to appear in proper Person, and not by Attorney, as also must every one against whom an Attachment is granted; and if the Offence be of an heinous Nature, and the Person attending the Court upon such a Rule to answer it, or ppearing upon an Attachment, be apparently guilty, the Court will generally commit him immediately, in Order to answer Interrogatories, to be exhibited against him in Relation to such Contempt. But if there be any favourable Circumstances to extenuate or excuse the Offence, or if it appear doubtful whether the Party were guilty of it or not, the Court will generally in their Discretion, suffer the Party, having first given Notice of his Intention to the Prosecutor, to enter into a Recognisance to answer such Interrogatories; and if no such Interrogatories be exhibited within four Days after such Recognisance, will discharge the Recognisance upon Motion; yet if the Party do not make such Motion, and the Interrogatories be exhibited after the four Days, the Court will compel him to answer them: But in all the Cases abovementioned, if the Party fully purge himself upon Oath, in his Answer to such Interrogatories of the whole Matter charged upon him, the Court will discharge him of the Contempt, and leave the Prosecutor to proceed against him for the Perjury, if he thinks fit: But if the Party confess Part of the Contempts in his Answer to such Interrogatories, and deny others, the Court will not discharge him from the Contempts so denied, but will proceed farther to examine the Truth of them, and will inflict such Punishment as from the Whole shall appear reasonable; neither will the Court discharge the Party upon a shifting or evasive Answer to any material Part of the Charge against him, but will punish him in the same Manner as if he had confessed it.

Fitz. Corody 4.

Rastal 268. pl. 4, 5. Raym. 376. Cro.Car. 146.

1 Rol. Rep. 315.

Salk. 84.

3 H.7.6.pl.4. 22 Ed. 4. 33. b. 34.

6 Mod. 73.

6 Mod. 73.

The Queen and Barber, Mich. 11 Annæ. 6 Mod. 73. 2 Jon. 178.

2 Jo. 178.

But for the better Understanding in what Cases the Court may proceed in the Manner abovementioned against such Offenders, I shall endeavour to shew.

1. Where it may so proceed against the Ministers of the Court.
2. Where against others.

As to the first of these Points I shall consider,

1. Where it may so proceed against Sheriffs, Bailiffs of Franchises, and Sheriffs Bailiffs.
2. Where against Attornies, and others acting as such.
3. Where against other Officers.
4. Where against Jurors.

As to the first of these Points I shall endeavour to shew,

1. Where the Court may so proceed against Sheriffs, Bailiffs of Franchises, and Sheriffs Bailiffs, for not executing a Writ.
2. Where for doing it oppressively.
3. Where for not doing it effectually.
4. Where for making a false Return.

Sect. 2. As to the first Particular, *viz.* In what Cases the Court may proceed in the Manner abovementioned against Sheriffs, *&c.* for not executing a Writ; It seems clear from the general Reason of the Law, which gives all Courts of Record a Kind of discretionary Power over all Abuses by their own Officers, in the Administration or Execution of Justice, which bring a Disgrace on the Courts themselves, as not taking sufficient
Dy. 218. pl. 4. Care to prevent them; that where-ever it shall appear, That any such Officers have been guilty of any corrupt Practice in not serving any Writ, as where they refuse to do it, unless paid an unreasonable Gratuity from the Plaintiff, or receive a Bribe from the Defendant or give him Notice to remove his Person or Effects, in Order to prevent the Service of any Writ, the Court which awarded it may punish such Offences in such Manner as shall seem proper by Attachment, *&c.* as well as the Court of King's Bench, which has a general Superintendency over all Crimes whatsoever (as the Star-Chamber [a] had also formerly) but commonly leaves Of-
[a] 263, 264. fences of this Kind, in relation to Causes in other Courts to be punished
Noy 101. by such Courts to which they more immediately belong. But if there neither appear to have been any palpable Corruption in the Case, nor particular Obstinacy, as by disobeying a special Rule of the Court, in Relation to the Service of such Writ, nor other extraordinary Circumstances of
Hob. 264. Lasely versus Weston. wilful Negligence, the Judgment whereof is to be left to the Discretion of the Court, it seems not to be usual to grant an Attachment in such Cases,
See Fitz. Process, 13, 104. but to leave the Party to his ordinary Remedy against the Officer, which he may have either by serving him with Rules to return the Writ, *&c.* or by suing him for the Damage sustained by his Negligence, in an Action
[b] F. N. B. 38. C. 47. C. 265. F. Finch. 237. 5 Mod. 314, 315. Hob. 62, 263, 264. of Escape, or on the Case, or by taking out an *Alias* [b] and *Pluries*, which if the Sheriff do not execute, an Attachment, directed to the Coroners, goes against him of Course, unless he give a good Excuse for his not having done it.

Sect. 3. As to the second Particular, *viz.* Where the Court may proceed in the Manner abovementioned, against a Sheriff, or Bailiff, *&c.* for an oppressive Practice in the Execution of a Writ; it is every Day's Practice to grant Attachments for Misdemeanours of this Kind, as for using needless Force, Violence and Terror, in making an Arrest, or by breaking open Doors where by Law it is not justifiable, and there is no plausible Excuse for doing it, or treating the Persons arrested basely and inhumanly, or keeping them in Custody till they consent to pay Money for their Deliverance, or making an Arrest without due Authority, as by Force of a blank [a] Warrant, filled up with the Name of a special Bailiff by the Party himself, or Bailiff, without the Privity or subsequent Agreement of the Sheriff; yet I have sometimes known Attachments of this Kind denied, in Respect of the common Use of the Practice, which by Experience hath been found to be almost necessary in some Cases to prevent the Defendant's having Notice of the intended Arrest, and therefore, if it shall appear to the Court, that there was any such reasonable Cause for such a Proceeding, it will be a great Inducement to excuse, if not wholly to dispense with it.

11 H. 6. 42. b. 43. a.

[a] Noy 101. Moor 770. pl. 1064. 2 Rol. Abr. 278. H.

Sect. 4. As to the third Particular, *viz.* Where the Court may proceed in the Manner abovementioned, against a Sheriff, or Bailiff, &c. for not executing a Writ effectually; it seems clear, That where any such Officer is guilty of a corrupt Practice in depriving the Party who sues out a Writ of that Benefit and Advantage which he ought to have from the Execution of it, he is liable to be punished in the Manner abovementioned, as if he levy the Debt by Virtue of an Execution, and keep the Money in his own Hands, and imbezil it: But unless there appear some gross and palpable Corruption in a Sheriff neglecting to return a Writ which hath been executed by him, or to bring in the Body or Money, &c. according to his Return, the Court will hardly grant an Attachment against him immediately, but will rather proceed against him by Rules to return the Writ, &c. and if he do not obey them, will increase the Amercements upon him till he do, or perhaps grant an Attachment for the Contempt: And [b] if the Sheriff return, That he sent the Process to the Bailiff of a Liberty, who hath given him no Answer, a *Non omittas* shall be awarded to the Sheriff: And if he return, That he sent the Process to such Bailiff, who hath returned a *Cepi Corpus*, or such like Matter, and the Bailiff bring not in the Body or Money, &c. at the Day, by the better [c] Opinion the Bailiff shall be amerced, and a Writ [d] shall issue to the Sheriff, to distrain the Bailiff to bring in the Body, &c.

[b] Fitz. Process, 13, 32.

[c] Rastal 109. Capias, pl. 20, 189. pl. 20, 21, 22. 670. pl. 2. 36 H. 6. 1. Contra Bro. Process, 25. Fitz. Return de Vicont. 35. 3 H. 7. 11. 47 Ass. pl. 6.

Sect. 5. As to the fourth Particular, *viz.* Where the Court may proceed in the Manner abovementioned, against a Sheriff, &c. for making a false Return to a Writ: There seems [e] to be no Doubt, but that whereever any such Officer endeavours to impose upon a Court, by making a Return to a Writ of a Matter known by him to be false, he is, in Strictness, liable to be punished in this Manner for his Contempt: Yet it seems, That the Court will not easily be prevailed on to proceed in this Manner for a bare false Return, but will rather leave the Party injured by it to his Remedy by an Action on the Case, unless there be some extraordinary Circumstances of Hardship or Oppression, as where [f] an Officer who had arrested one on a *Capias*, returned, That he had taken him, but that the Party was so sick, that he could not bring in his Body at the Day for Fear of endangering his Life, where in Truth the Party had been all the while in good Health, and was only detained under such Pretence, in Order to extort Money from him, &c.

[d] Fitz. Process, 12, 14, 104, 122, 132, 135, 225. Execution, 101. Return de Vicont. 35. 27 Ed. 3. 83. pl. 8. 27 Ed. 3. 77. pl. 9. Rastal, 109. Capias, pl. 20. Bro. Process, 25, 48, 113, 115. Bro. Return, 96, 99. 5 Ed. 4. pl. 14. 11 H. 4. 43. pl. 13. 38 Ed. 3. 1. b. 39 Ed. 3. 3. 8 H. 5. 2. pl. 8.

[e] Fitz. Process, 5. Bro. Surmise, 19. Retorn de brief, 100. Rastal, Habeas Corpus, 7.

[f] 11 H. 6. 42. b. 43.

As to the ſecond Point, *viz.* In what Caſes the Court may proceed in the Manner abovementioned, againſt Attornies, and others acting as ſuch, I ſhall endeavour to ſhew,

1. Where it may ſo proceed againſt them, for appearing for a Perſon without ſufficient Authority.
2. Where for Injuſtice to their Clients.
3. Where for other Contempts to the Court, or diſhoneſt Practice.

Sect. 6. As to the firſt of theſe Particulars, *viz.* Where the Court may proceed, in the Manner abovementioned, againſt Attornies and others acting as ſuch, for appearing for any Perſon without ſufficient Authority; There is no Doubt [a] but that it may ſo proceed againſt them, for taking upon them to proſecute or defend a Suit for another, without any Manner of Directions from him; alſo if they have in Truth a Warrant from the Party, but do not cauſe it to be recorded before Judgment, it ſeems, [b] That they are in Strictneſs liable to an Attachment, for that the Court takes no judicial Notice of any ſuch Warrant not of Record; yet [c] if in ſuch Caſe it appear, upon Examination, that the Warrant of Attorney happened not to be recorded, through the Negligence of the Officer, or ſome ſuch like Accident, attended with no corrupt Practice in the Attorney, it ſeems, That the Court would never eaſily be prevailed on to proceed in this Manner againſt the Attorney; and much leſs at this Day, ſince he is liable by Statute to a certain pecuniary Forfeiture for every Offence of this Kind.

[a] 38 Ed. 3. 8. b. 41 Ed. 3. 1. pl. 3. Raſtal 582. pl. 28. 16 Ed. 4. 5. b.
[b] Raſtal 96. pl. 3.
[c] Fitz. Judgment, 96. 41 Ed. 3. 1, pl. 3. 38 Ed. 3. 8. b. 4 Ed. 4. 13. pl. 31. 16 Ed. 4. 5. b. Raſtal 582. pl. 28.

Sect. 7. For it is enacted by 32 *H.* 8. 30. made perpetual by 2 *Ed.* 6. 32. and by 18 *El.* 14. and 4 & 5 *Annæ*, 16. *That the Plaintiff's Attorney ſhall file his Warrant the ſame Term he declares, and the Defendant's Attorney the ſame Term he appears, on Pain of Forfeiting ten Pounds, and alſo ſuffering ſuch Impriſonment, as by the Diſcretion of the Juſtices of the Court, where any ſuch Default ſhall fortune to be, ſhall be thought convenient.*

Coke's Entries 167.

Sect. 8. And it ſeems, That ſince theſe Statutes, it hath not been uſual to grant Attachments in theſe Caſes, without ſome apparent Circumſtances of Fraud, or other Corruption.

Vide Dyer 180. pl. 48. Raſtal 289. pl. 2.

Sect. 9. But howſoever a regular Attorney may be excuſed from an Attachment, for not having recorded his Warrant, thoſe have no Reaſon to expect the like Favour from the Court, who take upon them to appear for others as Attornies, without having been admitted and ſworn as ſuch, for theſe are liable to an Attachment for every Appearance, whether their Warrant were recorded or not. [45] ☞

Sect. 10. As to the ſecond Particular, *viz.* Where the Court may proceed in Manner abovementioned againſt Attornies, and others acting as ſuch, for Injuſtice to their Clients; It is every Day's Practice to move for it againſt them, for baſe and unfair Dealing towards their Clients in the Way of Buſineſs, as for protracting Suits by little Shifts and Devices, and putting the Parties to unneceſſary Expences in Order to raiſe their Bills, or demanding Fees for Buſineſs which never was done, or for refuſing to deliver up to their Clients Writings with which they had been intruſted in the Way of Buſineſs, or Money which has been recovered and received by them to their Clients Uſe, and for other ſuch like groſs and palpable Abuſes: But the Court will ſeldom grant an Attachment for the Detainer of ſuch Writings or Money, without firſt making a Rule on the Attorney, to deliver them to the

Raſtal 93. pl. 3.

See 4 H. 4. Ch. 18. 3 Ja. 1. 7.

the Party; alſo it will juſtify an Attorney's Detaining ſuch Writings or Money for his Security till he be paid all his juſt Fees; nor will it ever interpoſe in this Manner as to any Writings or Money received by an Attorney on any other Account, except only in his Way of Buſineſs as an Attorney, but will leave the Party to his ordinary Remedy by Action. Salk. 87. pl. 5.

Sect. 11. As to the third Particular, *viz.* Where the Court may proceed in the Manner above mentioned againſt Attornies, and others acting as ſuch, for other Contempts to the Court, or diſhoneſt Practice, it ſeems, That it may not only proceed in ſuch Manner againſt them for Diſobedience of its Rules, after Notice given them of ſuch Rules, either expreſly or impliedly; but alſo, for any ſuch ill Practice as is againſt the known and obvious Rules of Juſtice and common Honeſty; as for Forging [a] a Writ, or any other Matter of Record, [b] or but attempting to do it; or for taking out a *Capias*; [c] which has no Original to warrant it; or for receiving [d] Money of the Client for ſuing out an Original, and alſo for the Fine due thereon to the King, where, in Truth, no Original has been ſued out, nor any Fine paid to the King; or for endeavouring to impoſe upon the Court, as [e] by cauſing an Action to be brought againſt one in it by Colluſion, without any juſt Ground, in order thereby to intitle the Party to the Privilege of the Court, and afterwards, upon the Examination of the Matter in Court, giving a falſe Account of it; or [f] for giving Directions to a Sheriff concerning what Perſons he ſhould return on a Panel; and for other Miſdemeanors of the like Nature.

[a] Cro. Car. 74. Dyer 241. pl. 50. 244. pl. 58. [b] Fitz. Attachment, 7. [c] 20 H. 6. 37. a. Fitz. Attachment, 3. [d] Cro. Car. 74. [e] 16 Ed. 4. 5. Bro. Privilege, 43. [f] Moore 882. pl. 1237.

Sect. 12. As to the third Point, *viz.* Where the Court may proceed in the Manner abovementioned, againſt other Officers of the Court; There being ſcarce any Thing of this Kind to be met with in the Books, I ſhall only obſerve, that it ſeems clear, from the general Reaſon of the Law, which gives all Courts of Record a Kind of diſcretionary Power in the Government of their own Officers, that any ſuch Court may proceed in ſuch Manner againſt any ſuch Officer, not only for refuſing to execute its Commands, or for executing them irregularly, remiſly, [g] or oppreſſively, but alſo for all Kinds of Oppreſſion or Injuſtice done by them in the Execution of their Offices, or by Colour of them.

Vide ſupra, Sect. 1. Fitz. Office del Court, 12. Raſtal 329. pl. 8. 268. pl. 5. Dy. 218. pl. 4. [g] Fitz. Treſpaſs, 73. 33 H. 6. 55. b. 56. a.

Sect. 13. As to the fourth Point, *viz.* In what Caſes the Court may proceed in the Manner abovementioned, againſt Jurors, It is obſervable, that Jurors may be conſidered either in a Miniſterial Capacity, *viz.* as Perſons bound to attend the Court, in order to perform the Duty for which they are returned, until they ſhall be diſcharged; or in a Judicial Capacity, *viz.* as Judges of the Fact which is to be tried or inquired by them; and therefore, for the better Underſtanding of this Matter, I ſhall conſider,

1. How far Jurors are puniſhable in the Manner abovementioned, in their Miniſterial Capacity.
2. How far in their Judicial.

As to the firſt Particular, it ſeems clear, That Jurors are puniſhable in the Manner abovementioned in their Miniſterial Capacity, in the following Inſtances.

Sect. 14. I. For making Default; as where more than one of the Perſons returned on a Jury, do appear; but not a ſufficient Number to take an Enqueſt, 48 Ed. 3. 30.

Enqueſt, and ſome [a] of the others come within View of the Court, or into the ſame Town [b] in which the Court is holden, but refuſe to come into the Court to be ſworn; in which Caſes, upon Proof of ſuch Matter, the Court [c] may, at the Prayer of the Party, order the Jurors who appeared, to inquire what is the Yearly Value of ſuch Defaulters Lands, and after ſuch Inquiry made, either ſummon them to appear, on Pain of forfeiting ſuch Sum as their Lands have been found to be worth by the Year, or ſome leſſer [d] Sum, or impoſe [e] a Fine of the like Sum upon them, without any farther Proceeding. But it ſeems, [f] That ſuch Juror ſhall be liable to loſe his Iſſues only for ſuch Default, and not the yearly Value of his Lands, unleſs the Party pray it: But a Juror [g] who hath actually appeared, and after makes Default, is ſaid to be ſubject to ſuch Forfeiture of the yearly Value of his Lands, whether the Party pray it or not, becauſe his Contempt appears to the Court by its own Record; yet [h] even in this Caſe the Court, in Diſcretion, will ſometimes only impoſe a ſmall Fine. Alſo it is ſaid, That no Juror ſhall be ſubject to ſuch Penalty, where [i] the Inqueſt could not be taken, if he had appeared; as where but five of the Jurors ſummoned on an Aſſiſe, have had a View of the Land. Alſo it ſeems, [k] That a Juror who makes Default without ever coming into the Town wherein the Court is holden, is liable only to loſe his Iſſues, or to be amerced, but not to be fined: And it is ſaid, That he ſhall neither [l] be fined nor amerced, if the Defendant be eſſoined on the Day on which the Jury was to appear, for that his Appearance in ſuch Caſe would be to no Purpoſe; and it ſeems [m] queſtionable whether a Juror be amerciable for not appearing at the Return of a *Sicut alias Venire facias*, where the firſt *Venire* was not ſerved; neither doth a Juror ſeem to be amerciable at all, at the Day of the Return of the firſt *Venire* [n] *facias*, except before Juſtices errant, or of Oyer and Terminer, *&c.*

Sect. 15. II. For refuſing to be ſworn when they do appear; for which, as it ſeems, [o] every Court of Record may of common Right impoſe ſuch a reaſonable Fine on any one returned on a Grand or Petit Jury, as ſhall ſeem convenient.

Sect. 16. III. For refuſing [p] to give any Verdict at all.

Sect. 17. IV. For endeavouring to impoſe upon the Court; as where [q] a Petit Jury offer a Verdict to the Court, as agreed to by their whole Number, where, in Truth, ſome of them have not agreed to it; or where [r] they agree upon two Verdicts, and firſt to offer one of them to the Court, and to ſtand to it, if the Court ſhall expreſs no Diſſatisfaction to it; but if the Court ſhall diſlike it, then to give the other.

Sect. 18. V. For miſbehaving themſelves after their Departure from the Bar; as where they [s] do not all keep together till they have given their Verdict; or where any [t] of them carry any Thing eatable with them in their Pockets; or eat [u] or drink, or otherwiſe refreſh themſelves without Leave from the Court, before they have given their Verdict, though they were agreed [x] on it, and were alſo all the Time in the Cuſtody of the Bailiff appointed to take Care of them.

[a] Raſt. 267. b. pl. 2. 268. a. pl. 3.
[b] Raſt. 267. b. pl. 1. 30 Aſſ. pl. 3, 42. 48 Ed. 3. 30. Bro. Jurors, 25, 26. 20 Aſſ. pl. 11.
[c] Raſt. 267. b. pl. 12. 268. a. pl. 3. 4 Ed. 4. 37. a. 9 H. 4. 5. a. 20 Aſſ. pl. 11. 8 Co. 41. a
[d] Raſt. 267. b. pl. 2.
[e] Raſt. 267. pl. 2. 268. pl. 3.
[f] Fitz. Peine, 1, 2. 30 Aſſ. 42. 4 H. 6. 7. a. 4 Ed. 4. 36. b. 37. a. 36 H. 6. 27. a. Bro, Jurors, 15, 18, 26. Enqueſt, 42.
[g] Fitz. Challenge, 47. 36 H. 6. 27. a.
[h] Fitz. Office de Court, 12.
[i] Fitz. Peine, 3. 9 H. 4. 5. a.
[k] 10 E. 4. 19.
[l] 10 E. 4. 19. 30 Aſſ. pl. 17. Quære 48 E. 3. 12. a. 12 Aſſ. pl. 14. Fitz. Aſſiſe, 65.
[m] 1 H. 7. 8. a.
[n] Fitz. Aſſ. 136, 466. 11 Aſſ. pl. 7. Bro. Amercement, 68. See the Chapter of Proceſs againſt Jurors.
[o] 2 Inſt. 142, 143. 44 Ed. 3. 19. b. 8 Co. 38. b. 7 H. 6. 12. b.

[p] Vaughan 152. Noy 49. 3 Bulſt. 173. 9 H. 6. 44. b. [q] 29 Aſſ. pl. 27. Bro. Jurors, 28. 40 Aſſ. pl. 10. 1 Rol. Abr. 219. pl. 4. [r] Cro. El. 779. [s] 14 H. 7. 29. b. 30. Vaughan 151. [t] Dyer 78. pl. 41. [u] Dyer 218. pl. 4. Vaughan 152. Cro. Jac. 21. Fitz. Examination, 17. Bro. Jurors, 13. [x] Raſt. 268. pl. 4, 5.

Sect. 19. VI. For sending [a] for, or receiving Instructions from either of the Parties concerning the Matter in Question, and therefore [b] much more for receiving a Bribe.

[a] Rast. 329. b. pl. 8. Hob. 114. Fitz. Exami. 17.
[b] 40 Ass. 43.

Sect. 20. As to the second Particular, *viz.* How far Jurors are punishable in the Manner abovementioned, in their Judicial Capacity, it seems to be the current Opinion of the old Books, that Jurors are not subject to any Prosecution for a false Verdict, except by way of Attaint: And there seem to be very few ancient Precedents, for the Punishment either of a Grand or Petit Jury, meerly for giving a Verdict against Evidence, or the Direction of the Court either in a Criminal or Civil Matter. It is said [c] indeed in *Fitzherbert*'s Abridgment of a Case in the Time of King *Richard* II. That the Judge told the Jury, upon their Acquitting a common Thief of an Indictment, that they should be bound to their Behaviour for their Lives: But this was only the sudden Opinion of a Judge; and it doth not appear, that the Jurors were afterwards actually so bound in Pursuance of the said Opinion; and *Fitzherbert* makes a *Quære* in his Abridgment of the Case, by what Law they could be so bound: And as to those three [d] other Cases in the Time of King *Edward* III. wherein it is said, That a Juror was committed for refusing to agree with the other eleven, it may be answered, That it is said [e] in the first of those Cases, *That such Juror stay'd his Companions a Day and a Night, without agreeing with them, and this without Reason*; from whence it is reasonable to intend, That there might be some Circumstances of Misbehaviour, as an obstinate perverse Resolution, Right or Wrong, to find a Verdict one Way, and not to consult with the other Jurors, nor hear their Reasons, &c. And in the last of the [f] said Cases it is said, that the Juror committed by the Justices of Assise, for refusing two Days and a Night to agree with his Companions, and saying, that he would rather die in Prison than agree with them, was afterwards discharged by the Justices of the Common Bench, upon the Adjournment of the Assise thither. And it was Part [g] of the Charge against *Empson*, who was indicted in the Beginning of the Reign of King *Henry* VIII. for a great Complication of Offences, That he had committed a Jury to Ward, and bound them to appear before the King and his Council, and afterwards, on their Appearance, fined them (though with the Concurrence of the rest of the Council) in the Sum of 8 *l.* a-piece, for refusing to find a Person guilty of an Indictment of Larceny, upon sufficient Evidence; yet it is said in *Dalison*'s [h] Reports of Cases, in the third and fourth Years of *Philip* and *Mary*, That it was agreed, that Justices of Assise, Oyer and Terminer, Gaol-Delivery, or Peace, have no Power indeed to assess Fines on Jurors who make a false Oath before them, but that they may give them a Day before themselves, or the King's Council; by which it seems to be implied, That such Jurors were then thought to be some way or other punishable by such Judges, or at least by the King's Council; for otherwise it would be to little Purpose to bind them to appear before them. Also it seems to be holden by Sir *Edward Coke*, [i] That though a Jury be no way punishable for Convicting a Man upon an Indictment against Evidence, yet they might be charged in the Star-Chamber for their Partiality in finding a manifest Offender not guilty: And about [k] the latter End of the Reign of Queen *Elizabeth*, a Jury was committed and fined, and bound to the Good Behaviour, for finding one *Wharton* guilty of Manslaughter only, against clear Evidence and the Direction of the Court, upon an Indictment of Murder: And it is said in *Palmer*'s [l] Reports, That Jurors, who go against

See Book 1. Ch. 72. Sect. 4.
2 H. H. P. C. 160, 161, 310 to 313.
[c] Fitz. Coron. 108. Vaughan 152.
[d] Fitz. Imprisonment, 4. Judgment, 89. Verdict, 40.
[e] 8 Ass. pl. 35. Vaughan 151. 2 Jon. 16, 17.
[f] 41 Ass. pl. 11. 41 Ed. 3. 31. Vaugh. 151. 2 Raymond 88, 89.
[h] Dalison 18.
[i] 12 Co. 23, 24.
[k] Yelv. 23. Noy 48, 49.
[l] Palmer 35?.

against the Directions of the Court are to be fined: And there are several Instances in the Beginning of the Reign of King *Charles* II. wherein it was resolved, that both Grand [a] and Petit [b] Juries were finable by the Justices of Gaol-Delivery, for going against plain Evidence, and the Directions of the Court; but these Proceedings were always thought grievous, and were complained [c] of in the House of Commons; and this Question was at last fully considered and debated in *Bushel*'s Case, who having been committed by the Justices of Oyer and Terminer at the *Old Baily*, brought his *Habeas Corpus* in the Court of Common Pleas; to which it was returned, That he was committed for the Fine of forty Marks, imposed on him for having, with other Jurors, acquitted certain Defendants of an Indictment for an unlawful Assembly, against full and manifest Evidence, and against the Direction of the Court in Matter of Law; and upon this Return he was discharged, and the Return was adjudged insufficient, for not setting forth particularly [d] so much of the Evidence that it might appear that it was full and manifest; and likewise [e] for not setting forth, That the Defendant did know, and believe it to have been full and manifest; and also, [f] for not shewing what the Direction of the Court was, and in what Manner the Defendant found against it. And it was also resolved, [g] That Petit Jurors are in no Case finable for giving a Verdict against the Evidence delivered in Court, whether they be liable to an Attaint for such Verdict or not, not only for that the Jury are by Law the proper Judges of Matter of Fact, as the Judges are of Matter of Law, and therefore ought to be free in their Judgment of it, without being over-ruled by the Judges, who, strictly speaking, have no more to do with the Judgment of the Fact, than the Jurors have with the Judgment of the Matter of Law; neither is it possible that a Judge can certainly know that a Juror acts corruptly in giving his Verdict contrary to the Strength of the Evidence delivered in Court; for he may be influenced by his own personal Knowledge of the Truth of the Fact, of the Credit of the Witnesses, the Reputation of the Parties, and many other Circumstances unknown to the Judge, and well known to the Jury; for which Cause the Law provided, That all Issues should be tried by the Neighbourhood of the Place in which they are supposed to arise, because Neighbours are presumed to have better Knowledge than others of what concerns their Neighbours. And for these Causes, and other such like, the Court of King's Bench granted an Information against a Town-Clerk, for publishing an Order of the Court against Jurors, who had found a Person guilty of Manslaughter only, upon an Indictment of Murder, by which Order the said Jurors were declared to be justly suspected of Bribery, and declared uncapable of holding an Office, *&c.*

[a] 1 Syd. 229, 230. 2 Keb. 180.
[b] 1 Sid. 272, 273. Raym. 88, 89, 138. 1 Keb. 769. 938. 2 Keb. 404.
[c] 1 Syd. 338. 2 Keb. 180, 181.
[d] Vaughan 142. 2 Jon. 16, 17.
[e] Vaughan 142. 2 Jon. 16, 17.
[f] Vaughan 143.
[g] Vaughan 144, 145. 3 Keb. 352. 2 Jon. 16. Vide Hob. 114. Contra 3 Keb. 352.

Hilary 10 Ann. Queen & Wakefield.

Sect. 21. Yet if it shall plainly appear in any Case, that Jurors are perfectly satisfied of the Truth of a Fact, whereupon they declare to the Court, that they find it in such a particular Manner, and the Court directly tell them, That upon the Fact so found, as they have agreed it to be, the Judgment of the Law is such or such, and therefore, that they ought to give a Verdict accordingly, yet they obstinately insist upon a Verdict contrary to such a Direction; it seems agreeable to the general Reason of the Law, that the Jurors are finable by the Court in such a Case, unless an Attaint lies against them; for otherwise they would be dispunishable for so palpable a Partiality, in taking upon them to judge of Matters of Law, which they have nothing to do with, and are presumed to

2 Jon. 15, 16. Vaughan 144, 145. Palm. 363.

to be ignorant of, contrary to the exprefs Direction of one who by the Law is appointed to direct them in fuch Matters, and is to be prefumed of Ability to do it.

Sect. 22. Alfo if a Judge, for the better Direction and Information of a Jury, fhall ask them their Opinions concerning fuch a particular Fact, and they fhall refufe to anfwer him, and obftinately infift to deliver in their Verdict as they think fit, contrary to his Direction, it feems queftionable, whether they may not be fined in fuch a Cafe alfo, unlefs an Attaint lie againft them; for that it is the Duty of Jurors to take the Advice and Information of the Court, in Order to be governed by it as far as fhall be confiftent with their Confciences. Bracton 288. b. 289. 2 Jon. 15, 16. Vaughan 144.

Sect. 23. Alfo if a Jury fhall refufe to find an Office for the King, upon full Evidence it hath been holden, That they may be fined, for that in fuch Cafe they are not liable to an Attaint, and their Finding does not determine any Man's Right, and the King, in many Cafes, hath no other Remedy; yet it feems queftionable, how far at this Day thefe Reafons may be thought conclufive; and it feems, that they hold as ftrongly for the Punifhment of Grand Jurors refufing to find an Indictment of High Treafon; and yet it will be hard to maintain, That fuch Jurors are any Way punifhable for fuch a Refufal. Moor 730. 3 Leon. 148. Vaughan 153. 9 H. 6. 44. b.

Sect. 24. But if a Petit Jury in a Leet, conceal a Matter prefentable by them, it is a good Cuftom that they may be amerced for fuch Concealment, being found by the Grand Jury; and by 3 *H.* 7. 1. fet forth more at large, Book 1. Ch. 59. S. 1. *If an Inqueft conceal any Matter inquirable before Juftices of Peace, another Inqueft may be impanelled to inquire of fuch Concealments, and the Concealers may be amerced by the Difcretion of fuch Juftices.* 9 H. 6. 44. b.

Having fhewn in what Cafes the Minifters of the Court are punifhable in the Manner above mentioned, I am now to fhew, in what Cafes others may be fo punifhed; and for this Purpofe I fhall endeavour to fhew,

1. Where inferior Judges are punifhable in fuch Manner.
2. Where Counfellors.
3. Where Gaolers.
4. Where any Perfon whatfoever.

As to the firft Point, I fhall endeavour to fhew, where inferior Judges are in fuch Manner punifhable,

1. For proceeding without Jurifdiction.
2. For proceeding unjuftly, oppreffively or irregularly.
3. For refufing to do Juftice.
4. For Contempts of fuperior Courts.

Sect. 25. As to the firft of thefe Particulars, *viz.* In what Cafes inferior Judges are punifhable in the Manner above mentioned, for proceeding without Jurifdiction; it feems, [a] That the Court of King's Bench having a general Superintendency over all inferior Courts may in Strictnefs award an Attachment againft any fuch Court ufurping a Jurifdiction no Way belonging to it, and putting the Subject to unneceffary Vexation by Colour of a Judicial Proceeding wholly unwarranted [a] 41 Aff. pl. 30. Salk. 201. 1 Keb. 484. Palm. 564. Far. 1, 38, 84, 85.

by Law, and therefore [a] prohibited by it; yet in theſe Caſes it ſeems to be rather the more uſual [b] Way, firſt to award a Writ of Prohibition to ſuch Court, and afterwards an Attachment upon its Proceeding after ſuch Prohibition, and not to grant a Rule to ſhew Cauſe why an Attachment ſhould not go in the firſt Inſtance, unleſs there be ſome extraordinary Circumſtances in the Caſe; as where [c] the Steward of a Leet is guilty of a double Uſurpation, as of holding Plea of a Matter which aroſe out of his Precinct, and which, if it had ariſen within his Precinct, would not have been within the Juriſdiction of his Court; or where [d] the Judge of an inferior Court refuſes to receive a Plea that the Cauſe of Action aroſe out of his Juriſdiction; or where [e] any Judge takes Cogniſance of a Cauſe to which he himſelf is a Party; or where the Judge of a Court-Baron is privy to a Practice of ſplitting [f] a Cauſe of Action for more than forty Shillings into leſſer Sums, in Order to bring it within the Juriſdiction of the Court; but in this laſt Caſe, there ſeem to be more Inſtances [g] of Prohibitions than Attachments; and in the Caſes above mentioned, and all others of the like Nature, it ſeems to lie wholly in the Diſcretion of the Court to grant either.

Sect. 26. As to the ſecond Particular, *viz.* In what Caſes inferior Judges are puniſhable in the Manner above mentioned, for acting unjuſtly, oppreſſively or irregularly; it is not eaſy to meet with Caſes of this Kind in the Books, there being ſeldom any Thing in them ſo remarkable as to be thought worth reporting; but it ſeems to be a common Practice, to grant Attachments againſt the Judges of ſuch Courts for any Practice contrary to the plain Rules of natural Juſtice, though it have been never ſo long uſed in ſuch Courts; as for denying a Defendant a Copy of the Declaration againſt him, and going on to Trial, or giving Judgment againſt him, without giving him any Manner of Notice, or Time to make his Defence; or for taking of unreaſonable [h] Diſtreſſes, either on meſne Proceſs, or Execution; or for compelling [i] a Defendant to give exorbitant Bail; or for proceeding contrary to the Prohibition [k] of a Statute, as [l] by amercing a Clergy-Man according to his Spiritual Benefice; or by aſſeſſing [m] an Amercement without any Affeerment by the Tenants of the Manor; or by [n] taking Money of a Plaintiff or Defendant for vicious Pleading.

Sect. 27. As to the third Particular, *viz.* In what Caſes inferior Judges are puniſhable in the Manner above mentioned, for refuſing to do Juſtice; It ſeems clear, from the general Reaſon of the Law, and the common Practice of the Court of King's Bench in Caſes of this Nature, That the ſaid Court may in its Diſcretion, award an Attachment againſt any ſuch Judge, obſtinately and perverſely, and without any Colour of a reaſonable Excuſe, refuſing to proceed at all, or to give Judgment, or award Execution, in a Matter brought regularly before him; for all ſuch Delays of Juſtice are not only grievous to the Suitor, but bring a Diſgrace upon the Law itſelf: Yet if there be no extraordinary Circumſtances in any ſuch Delay, to bring the Judge under a reaſonable Suſpicion of Corruption, it ſeems the more uſual Method to take out a Writ to ſuch Judge, commanding him to do the Thing, of the Delay whereof you complain; and if ſuch Writ be not obeyed, to take out an *Alias & Pluries*, or to take [o] out the *Alias & Pluries* together with the firſt Writ; and thereupon, if the Judge refuſe to comply, to take out an Attachment againſt him at the Suit of the King and of the Party, which may either be returnable into the Court of King's Bench, or

[a] Vide 19 H. 6. 54. b. 9 H. 6. 61. F.N.B. 270. c.

[b] Regiſter 145, 146. F. N. B. 239. H. 240. B. 1 Syd. 464. 6 Mod. 90. 2 Inſt. 312. 2 Rol. Abr. 317. Letter I.

[c] 41 Aſſ. 30. Fitz. Leet, 9. Bro. Leet, 18, 31.

[d] Vaughan and Hodges Paſchæ 11 Annæ.

[e] Salk. 201. pl. 3. 396. pl. 1. Far. 1, 2.

[f] Palmer 564. 1 Keb. 484.

[g] 19 H. 6. 54. 2 Rol. Ab. 317. I. pl. 1. 6 Mod. 90. 2 Keb. 617. 1 Ventris 65, 73. 1 Keb. 484. 1 Sid. 464.

[h] Salk. 201. 3 Keb. 92.

[i] 2 Jon. 178.

[k] F. N. B. 76. D. 160. B. 165. C. 166. D. 270. C. 9 H. 6. 61. 19 H. 6. 54.

[l] F. N. B. 76. B, C, D.

[m] F. N. B. 76. D.

[n] F. N. B. 270. A, B, C. 2 Inſt. 122. Fitz. Attachment, 8.

[o] F. N. B. 68. E. Infra Sect. 34.

at the Party's Election into the Court of Common Pleas, except in some special [a] Cases; and this seems [b] to be the proper Remedy to compel the Lord of a Manor to hold a Court for the determining of a Writ of Right Patent, or a Writ [c] of Right Close; or to compel the Judge of any inferior Court, whether of Record [d] or not, to proceed [e] in a Plea, or to give Judgment, [f] or to award Execution. [g]

Sect. 28. As to the fourth Particular, *viz.* In what Cases inferior Judges are punishable in the Manner above mentioned, for Contempts of superior Courts: There is no Doubt but that Justices [h] of Peace, or Commissioners [i] of Sewers, may be so punished for proceeding in any Matter before them, after a *Certiorari* delivered to them, or the Judge of a Spiritual [k] or Civil [l] Law Court, for proceeding in a Cause, after Notice of a Rule to shew Cause why a Prohibition should not go, or a Judge of any inferior Common Law Court, for proceeding in a Cause after a *Habeas Corpus*, or Writ of Error allowed; or a Sheriff, [m] for proceeding in Replevin, or other Cause, in the County-Court, after a *Supersedeas*, *Pone* or *Recordare*. Also a Rule [n] has been granted to shew Cause why an Attachment should not go against the Steward of a Wapentake for proceeding after a Tolt, though this be only a Contempt to the County-Court.

Sect. 29. Also Justices of Peace may be punished in the Manner above mentioned, for acting in a contemptuous Manner against the Determination of the Court of King's Bench; as where an Order of Settlement, specially setting forth the Circumstances of the Case, is removed into the said Court, and quashed there, by the Judgment of the Court, upon the Merits; and yet the Justices of Peace afterwards make another Order to remove the same Person to the same Place, for the very same Cause, without regarding the Judgment of the Court though it were well known to them, and insisted on by the Parties.

Sect. 30. As to the second Point, *viz.* In what Cases Counsellors are punishable in the Manner above mentioned, it seems clear, That notwithstanding they are neither Officers of any Court, nor Invested with any Judicial Office, but barely practise as Counsellors, yet [o] inasmuch as they have a special Privilege to practise the Law, and their Misbehaviour tends to bring a Disgrace upon the Law it self, they are punishable for any foul Practice as other Ministers of Justice are.

Sect. 31. As to the third Point, *viz.* In what Cases Gaolers are punishable in the Manner above mentioned, it seems clear, That they are not only punishable in this Manner, as all other Officers are, by the Courts to which they more immediately belong, for any gross Misbehaviour in their Offices, or Contempts of the Rules of such Courts, but they are also punishable by any other Courts for disobeying Writs of *Habeas Corpus* awarded by such Courts, and not bringing up the Prisoner at the Day prefixed by such Writs. Also it seems clear, [p] That it is no Excuse for not obeying a Writ of *Habeas Corpus ad subjiciendum*, that the Prisoner did not tender the Fees due to the Gaoler: Also [q] it seems to be the better Opinion, That the Want of such a Tender is no Excuse for not obeying a Writ of *Habeas Corpus ad faciendum & recipiendum*; however [r] it it certain, That if the Gaoler bring up the Prisoner by Virtue of such *Habeas Corpus*, the Court will not turn him over till the Gaoler be paid all his Fees, [s] nor, as some [t] say, till he be paid all that is due to him for the Prisoner's Diet, for that a Gaoler is compellable [u] to find his Prisoner Sustenance; but this is denied by others. [x]

[a] F. N. B. 62. O. 230. E. 63. B. 67. B. 13. H. 14. A.
[b] F. N. B. 3. E. 13. A.
[c] F. N. B. 12. E.
[d] Rastal's Entries, 83. b. pl. 4. F. N. B. 20. B. 153. D. 243. D.
[e] F. N. B. 12. E. 13. A. Rast. Ent. 83. B. pl. 4.
[f] F. N. B. 153. B. C. 243. D.
[g] F. N. B. 20. A. B.
[h] Moor 677. pl. 921. Yelv. 32. 1 Keb. 93.
[i] 1 Mod. 44.
[k] 2 Jon. 47.
[l] 1 Ro. R. 315.
[m] F. N. B. 13. B. 14. A. Fitz. Replevin, 31. 43 Ed. 3. 25. Fitz. Process, 168. Action sur le Case, 39.
[n] Burgh & Blunt. Hil. 3 Geor. 1.
[o] 6 Mod. 137. See Book 1. Ch. 83. S. 27.
[p] 1 Keb. 272. pl. 57.
[q] March 89. 1 Keb. 280. pl. 79. 2 Jon. 178. Contra 1 Keb. 566. pl. 11.
[r] 2 Jon. 178.
[s] 2 Rol. Abr. 32. B.
[t] 1 Rol. Rep. 338, 339. Contra 2 Rol. Abr. 32. B.
[u] Co. Lit. 295. a. 9 Co. 87. b.
[x] Pl. Com. 68. a. 2 Rol. Ab. 32. B.

Sect. 32. Also it seems, That the Court of King's Bench, which has a general [a] Superintendency over all Persons who are in any Respect Ministers of Justice, may award an Attachment against any Gaoler using a Prisoner barbarously and inhumanly; yet it is said, [b] That a Gaoler is no Way punishable for keeping a Debtor in Irons. And it seems agreed at this Day, That a Gaoler shall not be punished in the Manner above mentioned, for the bare Escape of a Person in his Custody by Civil Process; but that the Party grieved by such Escape ought to take his Remedy by Action.

Sect. 33. As to the fourth Point, *viz.* In what Cases any Person whatsoever is punishable in the Manner above mentioned; it seems, That even Peers of the Realm, whether Spiritual or Temporal, are liable to such punishment for some Contempts, as for rescuing [c] a Person arrested by due Course of Law, or for proceeding in a Cause against [d] the King's Writ of Prohibition, or for disobeying other [e] Writs, wherein the King's Prerogative, or the Liberty [f] of the Subject are nearly concerned; but it doth [g] seem clear, that it is a certain general Rule, That a Peer is punishable in this Manner for Disobedience of all Writs whatsoever; and it seems [h] certain, That no Peer is liable to an Attachment for not appearing on a Jury; therefore it seems, That what is said [i] in some Books in general, That an Attachment lies against Peers for Contempts, ought to be understood of such only as are of an enormous [k] Nature, as those above mentioned, and others [l] of the same Kind, about which it is difficult to lay down any certain particular Rules; however it is certain, that all other Persons are liable to an Attachment for Contempts, all the particular Instances whereof it would be endless to enumerate, and therefore I shall only take Notice of the most remarkable, which seem reducible to the following Heads.

1. Contempts of the King's Writs.
2. Contempts in the Face of a Court.
3. Contemptuous Words or Writings, concerning the Court.
4. Contempts of the Rules or Awards of the Court.
5. Abuses of the Process of the Court.
6. Forgeries of Writs, and other Deceits of the like Kind, tending to impose on the Court.

Sect. 34. As to the first Particular, *viz.* Where Persons are punishable in the Manner above mentioned for Contempts of the King's Writs; it seems that it may reasonably be argued, That all such Writs, being in the King's Name, and importing some lawful Command or Prohibition from him, which every Subject is in Duty bound to obey, every Disobedience [m] of any of them being a Contempt of the King's Authority, is, in Strictness, punishable in the Manner above mentioned, if the Court in Discretion shall think fit so to proceed: Yet it doth not seem to have been usual for the Court to proceed in this Manner for a bare Nonfesance, in not performing the Command of the first Writ in any Case whatsoever. But [n] it seems clear, That an Attachment lies of Course for the Nonperformance of the Demand of a *Pluries*, which may in some Cases, if not in all, be taken out together with the *Alias*, at the same Time with the first Writ: Also it seems, That the Court may in any special Case, in which it shall seem proper, make a Rule to compel the Party to whom the first Writ is directed, to execute it; and

[a] 6 Mod. 137.
[b] 2 Inst. 381. 2 Rol. Ab. 806. C. 1. 807. pl. 2. 3 Co. 44.
[c] Fitz. Process, 114, 161. Retorn de vicount, 74. 1 H. 5. 14. a. Dyer 212. pl. 36. 27 H. 8. 22. b. Crompton Jur. 14. a.
[d] 21 Ed. 3. 3. pl. 7.
[e] 2 R. A. 228. Letter A. 234. pl. 3. 8 Ed. 4. 17. a. Vide 25 Ed. 3. Ch. 6. F. N. B. 47. c. Fitz. Quare non admisit, 7. Bro. Contempt, 5. 8 Co. 60.
[f] 11 H. 4. 15. b. Fitz. Withernam, 4.
[g] 21 Ed. 3. 3. pl. 7. F. N. B. 33. E.
[h] Dyer 319. pl. 98.
[i] Fitz. Process, 198. Cro. El. 170. 2 Rol. Ab. 234. pl. 3. Bro. Contempt, 3, 19. 6 Co. 54. a. Finch 355.
[k] Dyer 315. pl. 98. Hob. 61. 21 Ed. 3. 59. b. Rastal 313. pl. 19, 20. 29 Ass. pl. 33.
[l] Cro. El. 170, 503. 1 Rol. Abr. 220. pl. 12. 221. pl. 13. 3 Inst. 142.
[m] 1 Mod. 44. 5 Mod. 314, 315. Fitz. Quare non admisit, 7.
[n] Fitz. Suggestion, 25. 43. Ass. 39. Rastal 457. pl. 7. Finch 237. 11 H. 4. 86. Fitz. Count. 34. Suggestion, 25. F. N. B. 63. E. Supra Sect. 27

if ſuch Rule ſhall be diſobeyed, there can be no Doubt but that the Court may proceed againſt ſuch Diſobedience in the ſame Manner as they uſually do againſt the Diſobedience of any other Rule: Alſo it ſeems [a] to be common Practice to grant Attachments upon Affidavits of Contempts to the King's Writs, by acting contrary to the Purport of them. Alſo there can be no Doubt, but that if a Sheriff ſhall in any Caſe return to the Court, That a Perſon arreſted, [b] or Goods ſeiſed, [c] or Poſſeſſion of Lands delivered [d] by him, by Virtue of the King's Writ, were reſcued or violently taken from him, *&c.* the Court may award an Attachment againſt the Reſcuers. Alſo it is certain, That the Court hath, in ſome Caſes, awarded an Attachment upon Affidavits of a Reſcous, where the Officer hath not returned one; yet this was anciently [e] looked on as irregular, and of late the Court has refuſed to grant an Attachment in any Caſe for a Reſcous, unleſs the Officer will return it; for that it hath been found by Experience, that Officers will often take upon them to ſwear a Reſcous, where they will not venture to return one.

[a] F. N. B. 165. B. 166. B, C, D, 270. C. 173. E. 174. A, B. 175. B. Fitz. Suggeſtion, 9. 8 Co. 60. Supra Sect. 33. [b] Fitz. Attachment, 1. Proceſs, 56. Fitz. Retorn de vicount, 74. 37 H. 6. 27. b. Dy. 212. pl. 36. 2 Jon. 39. [c] Fitz. Attachment, 5. 38 Ed. 3. 9. b. [d] Salk. 321. pl. 7. 6 Mod. 27. [e] Fitz. Suggeſtion, 25.

Sect. 35. As to the ſecond Particular, *viz.* Where Perſons are puniſhable in the Manner above mentioned, for Contempts in the Face of the Court; it ſeems clear, that all Perſons are puniſhable in this Manner, not only for making an actual Breach of the Peace, but alſo for any heinous Miſdemeanor in the Face of the Court; as [f] for giving falſe, trifling, and contradictory Anſwers upon an Examination in Court concerning one's Ability to be Bail for another, in an Action depending in the Court, or concerning any other ſuch like Matter in Queſtion before the Court, and to be determined by the Examination of the Parties; or [g] for any contemptuous Behaviour towards any Judge in the Face of the Court, as by charging him with Injuſtice, and praying for an Information againſt him, *&c.*

[f] Cro. Car. 146. 7 H. 6. 25. pl. 10. [g] Raym. 375.

Sect. 36. As to the third Particular, *viz.* Where Perſons are puniſhable in the Manner above mentioned, for contemptuous Words or Writings, concerning the Court; it ſeems needleſs to put any Inſtances of this Kind, which are generally ſo obvious to common Underſtanding, and therefore I ſhall only obſerve, That ſometimes Attachments have been granted for contemptuous Words concerning the Rules of the Court, without making any Rule to ſhew Cauſe why ſuch Attachments ſhould not be granted, becauſe it would be vain to ſerve him with a ſecond Rule who has deſpiſed the firſt.

Salk. 84.

Sect. 37. As to the fourth Particular, *viz.* Where Perſons are puniſhable in the Manner above mentioned, for Contempts of the Rules or Awards of the Court; There is nothing more frequent than to proceed in this Manner for Contempts of this Kind; as where [h] a Defendant in an Action of Account being adjudged to account before Auditors, refuſes to do it, unleſs they will allow ſuch an Acquittance, which was diſallowed by the Court before; or [i] where one who has ſubmitted to an Arbitration by Rule of Court, being afterward perſonally ſerved with a Copy of the Award, and required to perform it, refuſes to do it; or where one refuſing to pay the Coſts taxed by the Maſter, for that ſuch a Taxation is, in Judgment of Law, a Taxation by the Court: But it ſeems, That generally an Attachment is not grantable for Diſobedience of any Rule, unleſs the Party have been perſonally ſerved with it; nor for Diſobedience of a Rule, at *Niſi Prius*, unleſs it be

43 Aſſ. pl. 33. [h] Fitz. Impriſonment, 18. and Vide Fitz. Accompt, 23, 84, 109, 112. 29 Ed. 3. 35. b. [i] 1 Mod. 21. Salk. 71. pl. 4. 83. pl. 1. Far. 8. Vide 9 & 10 Gul. 3. 15.

Salk. 84.

be made a Rule of Court, not for Diſobedience of a Rule made by a Judge at his Chamber, unleſs it be entred.

Sect. 38. As to the fifth Particular, *viz.* Where Perſons are puniſhable in the Manner above mentioned, for Abuſes of the Proceſs of the Court: There are ſo many Inſtances of this Kind that it would be in vain to go about to enumerate them all, and therefore I ſhall only take Notice of ſome of the Principal of them, as,

Hob. 264.

Sect. 39. Firſt, the Taking out ſuch Proceſs without any Colour of Right to it; as where one ſues out Execution without any Judgment to warrant it, &c. or where a Woman brings an Appeal [a] of the Death of her Husband, whom ſhe knows to be alive.

[a] 8 H. 4. 17. Fitz. Coron. 73.

Sect. 40. Secondly, The making uſe of ſuch Proceſs as a Stale to help the Juriſdiction of an inferior Court; as where on arreſts another by a *Latitat*, in order by that Means to bring him within the Limits of an inferior Court, and when he has got him there, drops the *Latitat* and proceeds in the inferior Court.

Styles Rep. 239, 343.

Sect. 41. Thirdly, making uſe of ſuch Proceſs in a vexatious Manner; as where a Perſon who has brought an Action in one Court, does afterwards ſue the ſame Defendant, for the very ſame Cauſe, in another Court, while the firſt Action is ſtill depending, in which Caſe the Defendant ſeems to have an Election either to move for an Attachment, [b] or to bring an Action [c] on the Caſe for ſuch a vexatious Proceeding againſt him.

[b] Fitz. Corpus cum Cauſa, 3. 14 H. 7. 6. b. 7. a. 6 Co. 60. a. Savil 14.

[c] 7 H. 6. 45. a.

Sect. 42. Fourthly, Making uſe of ſuch Proceſs any other way to ſerve the Purpoſes of Oppreſſion or Injuſtice; as where [d] one arreſts another at my Suit, without my Privity, in order to make ſome undue Advantage of him, &c.

[d] Hob. 264. Dyer 249. pl. 84. Vide 8 El. 2.

Sect. 43. As to the ſixth Particular, *viz.* Where Perſons are puniſhable in the Manner above mentioned for forging of Writs, and other Deceits of the like Kind, tending to impoſe on the Court; nothing can be more frequent than to proceed in ſuch Manner for Offences of this Kind, as for altering [e] the *Teſte* of Writs, or for filling [f] them up after they are ſealed, or [g] for bringing groundleſs Actions, in Order to intitle the Parties to the Privilege of the Court, or for getting [h] Judgment in Ejectment, by Affidavit of the Service of a Declaration on one who was procured to perſonate the Tenant, or for any ſuch like Practices.

[e] Dyer 241. pl. 50. 244. pl. 58.

[f] 6 Mod. 310.

[g] Dyer 245. pl. 61. Bro. Privilege, 43.

[h] 6 Mod. 16. Savil 31.

CHAP.

CHAP. XXIII.

Of Appeal.

BEFORE we examine the Nature of ſuch Proceſs, as is grounded on an Appeal, Indictment, or Information, it may not be improper, firſt to conſider the Nature of each of theſe in Particular. And firſt of Appeals, of which there are two Sorts,

1. By an Innocent Perſon.
2. By an Offender confeſſing himſelf Guilty, who is commonly called an Approver.

Sect. 1. And Firſt, Of an Appeal by an Innocent Perſon, which is the Party's private Action; proſecuting alſo for the Crown, in Reſpect of the Offence againſt the Publick, which he may do two ways.

Finch of Law 310, 311. Plow. Com. 476.

1. By Writ.
2. By Bill.

Sect. 2. As to the Writ of Appeal, I ſhall only take Notice in this Place, That it is an Original iſſuing out of Chancery, and returnable in the King's Bench only; and for the Form of it, I ſhall refer the Reader to the later Part of this Chapter, wherein I ſhall endeavour to ſhew for what Defects it may be abated.

Sect. 3. Alſo I ſhall refer the Reader to the ſame Place, for the Form of a Bill of Appeal, and ſhall not here take any farther Notice of it, than by obſerving that it muſt contain greater Certainty than a Writ of Appeal, and is in the Lieu both of the Writ and Declaration, and ſhewing before what Courts, and againſt whom it may be proſecuted.

Sect. 4. And firſt, there is no Doubt [a] but that any Appeal may be ſued by Bill in the King's Bench againſt any Perſon *in cuſtodia Mareſchalli*, either by an actual Commitment, or by having Bail filed for him in that Court; but [b] not againſt one who is mainpriſed *de die in diem*, for that ſuch an one cannot be ſaid to be *in cuſtodia Mareſchalli*. And it hath been reſolved, [c] That if the Appellee be arraigned and tried the ſame Term, there is no Neceſſity to file the Bill againſt him. [46] Alſo [d] it ſeems clear, That if a Defendant appear in the ſaid Court on a void Writ of Appeal, he may be committed to the Marſhalſey, and then declared againſt *in cuſtodia Mareſchalli*; but where a Defendant appears on a Writ not void, but voidable only, as for the Want of an Addition, *&c.* it was once [e] holden, That he could not be committed, nor declared againſt *in cuſtodia Mareſchalli*; but ought to be diſcharged. But the contrary hereto ſeems to be now ſettled in the Caſe of *Reeves* [f] againſt *Trundal*, who appearing in the Court on a Writ of Appeal of Death, demanded Oyer of

[a] Cro. El. 605, 695. Skin. 634. S. P. C. 64. Letters C, D. H. P. C. 179. 17 Aſſ. pl. 5. 17 Ed. 3. 13. pl. 40.
[b] 4 Inſt. 180. 1 Bulſt. 74.
[c] 1 Jo. 425. Cro. Car. 532. 1 Rol. Ab. 536. K.
[d] Cro. El. 694, 695.
[e] Cro. El. 605, 695.
[f] Paſchæ, 3. Georg. 1.

Like Caſe between Smith and Bowen, Mich. 7. Annæ.

of the Writ, and pleaded in Abatement the want of an Addition; and thereupon the Court abated the Writ, and ſuffered him to be arraigned by Bill *in cuſtodia Mareſchalli:* And ſurely this cannot but ſeem more reaſonable than to ſuffer a Priſoner under ſo heavy an Accuſation, to which he is ſtill liable, to go at large without a Trial; neither do I find any Reaſon given why a Priſoner appearing on a voidable Writ, ſhould have a greater Advantage than on a void one.

Keilw. 152. b. pl. 4.

Sect. 5. Secondly, It is alſo holden, that an Appeal may be commenced before Juſtices in Eyre, which, as I ſuppoſe, muſt be intended of an Appeal by Bill, for that all Writs of Appeal muſt be returnable in the King's Bench.

2 Inſt. 418, 420.

Sect. 6. Thirdly, Alſo it ſeems clearly to follow, from the Purport of the Statute of *Weſtminſter*, 2. Ch. 29. That Bills of Appeal may be commenced and determined before Juſtices, ſpecially aſſigned, in ſpecial Caſes, and for certain Cauſes, to hear and determine them.

[a] Bro. Appeal, 11, 19, 51, 123. Dyer 201. pl. 67. S. P. C. 64. Letter C. H. P. C. 179. 2 H. H. P. C. 35.

Sect. 7. Fourthly, It is certain, [a] that Commiſſioners of Gaol-delivery may receive a Bill of Appeal againſt any Priſoner of the Gaol which they are authoriſed to deliver. Alſo it is generally holden, That they may receive ſuch a Bill againſt a Perſon who has been let to Bail by them, but not againſt one who has been let to Mainpriſe. And it hath been reſolved, That if Part of the Accomplices to the ſame Felony be in the Priſon which ſuch Juſtices are to deliver, and the others be not in it, the Juſtices ſhall receive an Appeal againſt them all, which, after the Trial of thoſe that are in the Priſon, ſhall be removed into the King's Bench, where the others ſhall be proceeded againſt. But theſe three laſt Points, having been already more largely conſidered, Chap. 6. Sect. 5. I ſhall refer the Reader to what is there ſaid concerning them.

Vide Supra fol. 28, 29, 30. Dy. 99. pl. 62.

Sect. 8. Fifthly, It ſeems to follow, from the Purport of the Statutes which have been generally conſtrued to authorize Juſtices of Aſſiſe to deliver Gaols without any ſpecial Commiſſion of Gaol-delivery, that they may receive Bills of Appeal in the ſame manner as Commiſſioners of Gaol-delivery may.

[b] Coro. 95. [c] Vide S. P. C. 65. Letter A. 2 Inſt. 420. H. P. C. 179. 2 H. 4. 19. pl. 12. Bro. Appeal, 18. [d] 44 Ed. 3. 44. pl. 57. See Bro. Appeal, 11. [e] See Ch. 9. Sect. 39, 40, 41. 2 H. H. P. C. 67, 68.

Sect. 9. Sixthly, It ſeems to be holden in *Fitzherbert*'s Abridgment, [b] That Juſtices of Peace have Power to receive Appeals by Virtue of 34 *Ed.* 3. 1. which enacts, That they ſhall hear and determine all manner of Felonies and Treſpaſſes in the ſame County, *&c.* But there is much greater Authority [c] for the contrary Opinion; and the Caſe in the [d] *Year Book*, in the Abridgment whereof the ſaid Opinion of *Fitzherbert* is inſinuated, is plainly miſtaken, for that it makes no Manner of Mention of Juſtices of Peace, but only of Juſtices of Gaol-delivery; to which may be added, That the above mentioned Statute of 34 *Ed.* 3. 1. which empowers Juſtices of Peace to hear and determine Felonies, *&c.* is expreſs, That they ſhall have Power ſo to do at the King's Suit, which muſt be either taken to exclude the Suit of the Party, or to ſignify little or nothing.

[f] See Ch. 9. Sect. 42. [g] H. P. C. 180. S. P. C. 65. a. 1 Inſt. 74. a. b. Vide infra Sect. 28.

Sect. 10. Seventhly, it is certain, That an Appeal may be commenced [e] by Bill, before the Sheriff and Coroner, and removed [f] from them into the King's Bench, by *Certiorari*, as hath been more fully ſhewn, Chap. 9.

Sect. 11. Eighthly, It ſeems to be agreed, [g] That an Appeal by the Courſe of the Civil Law, in Nature of a Bill of Appeal by the Common Law, may be ſued before the Conſtable and Marſhal for ſome

Felonies done out of the Realm, in Relation whereunto it is enacted by 1 *H.* 4. 14. as followeth, *For many great Inconveniences and Mischiefs that often have happened by many Appeals made within the Realm before this Time, it is ordained from henceforth, That all Appeals to be made of things done within the Realm, shall be tried and determined by the good Laws of the Realm: And that all Appeals to be made of Things done out of the Realm, shall be tried and determined before the Constable and Marshal of* England *for the Time being.*

Sect. 12. In the Construction of this Statute, it seems to have been agreed, [a] That if any of the King's Subjects kill any other of his Subjects in any foreign Realm, the Wife, or Heir of the deceased may have an Appeal of his Death, before the Constable and Marshal, who shall proceed according to the Civil [b] Law, and give Sentence by the Testimony of Witnesses, or Combat: From whence it follows, [c] That no such Sentence can corrupt the Blood of the Appellee, for that such Corruption can only be caused by a Judgment by Course of the Common Law. Also [d] it seems to be clear, That no such Appeal can be prosecuted before the Marshal alone without a Constable.

Sect. 13. It hath been holden, [e] That if a Man die in *England*, of a Wound given him in a foreign Realm, he may be appealed by the Intent of this Statute, before the Constable and Marshal, for that it is certain, ☞ That he cannot be tried by the Common Law; [48] and it cannot be thought the Meaning of the Statute in restraining the Civil Law, in Cases within the Conusance of the Common, to restrain it also in Cases which the Common Law had nothing to do with, and which were properly cognisable by the Civil Law, and by that only; for the only End of such a Construction would be to cause a Failure of Justice.

Sect. 14. It is farther enacted by the said Statute of 1 *H.* 4. 14. *That no Appeals be from thenceforth made, or in any wise pursued in Parliament, in any Time to come.*

[a] S. P. C. 65. Letter B. 1 Inst. 74. a. 13 H. 4. 5. a.
[b] 4 Inst. 155. 1 Inst. 74, 391. b. Supra Ch. 4. Sect. 10. Bro. Jurisdict. 103.
[c] See Book 1. Ch. 37. Sect. 8. and Ch. 4. of this Book Sect. 10. and 1 Inst. 391. a.
[d] See Ch. 4. Sect. 8. Letter F. Hutt. 3. 1 Inst. 74. b.
[e] S. P. C. 65. Letter B. 1 Inst. 74. b. B. 1. Ch. 31. Sect. 11.

Appeals considered, as to the Matter of them, are of two Kinds.

1. Not Capital.
2. Capital.

Sect. 15. And first, of those not Capital, whereof there were anciently several Kinds, as Appeals *de pace, de plagis*, and *de Imprisonamento*, as well as Appeals of *Mayhem*; but the former of these having been out of Use, and turned to Actions of Trespass, for these many hundred Years, I shall only consider the Nature of an Appeal of *Mayhem*; for the better Understanding whereof I shall endeavour to shew,

Fleta, Lib. 1. chap. 41. Bract. Lib. 3. chap. 25. 4 Inst. 182. 1 Inst. 126. b.

1. Of what *Mayhems* it lies.
2. What ought to be the Form of the Writ, Bill and Declaration.
3. What Defence may be made by the Appellee.
4. How the *Mayhem* shall be tried, and where the Trial shall be peremptory.

Sect. 16. As to the first Point, *viz.* Of what *Mayhems* an Appeal lies; I shall take it for granted, That notwithstanding every [f] Hurt whatsoever done to a Man's Body, whereby he is less able in Fighting, may perhaps, properly enough, in a large Sense, be called a *Mayhem*, and [g] will certainly subject the Person who occasioned it to the Payment

[f] See B. 1. Ch. 44.
[g] 2 Jo. 203. Hob. 134.

of Damages in an Action of Trespass by the Party grieved, whether it were malicious, or happened through Accident or Misadventure; yet [a] an Appeal of *Mayhem* cannot be maintained for any such Hurt, unless it were accompanied with some evil Intention in the Person who caused it; for surely the Law, in requiring that the Word Felony be made use of in every such Appeal, (as will be more fully shewn under the next Point) cannot imply less than that the Fact must be attended with some odious Circumstances. Yet it seems clear, That if a Man striking at another with such an evil Intent, as would subject him to an Appeal of *Mayhem*, if the Person struck at should be maimed, shall happen to miss him, and strike a third Person, and maim him, he his liable [b] to an Appeal of *Mayhem* at his Suit, whether he had any Kind of Ill Will against him or not.

[a] 13 H. 7. 14. pl. 5.

[b] Bro. Appeal, 157. 13 H. 7. 14. pl. 5. See B. 1. Ch. 31. Sect. 41.

As to the second Point, *viz.* What ought to be the Form of the Writ, Bill and Declaration, I shall only take Notice in this Place,

Sect. 17. First, That the Word *Mayhemiavit* [c] is so necessary in every such Writ, Bill and Declaration, that it can be supplied by no other Word of the like Sense, nor by any Circumlocution whatsoever.

Sect. 18. Secondly, That in every such Writ, Bill or Declaration, the *Mayhem* must [d] be laid to have been done *felonice*, and yet the Defendant is not at this Day subject to the Loss of Member from such an Appeal, as anciently [e] he was, in which Respect the Law seems to have required the Use of the Word *felonice*.

Sect. 19. Thirdly, [f] That it is in the Election of the Plaintiff to declare against him who actually gave the Wound, as the principal Offender, and against those who abetted him, as Accessaries; or else to declare against them all as Principals.

Sect. 20. Fourthly, That if a Man bring a Writ of Appeal of *Mayhem*, and count of Battery, he abates the Writ, because the Writ supposes no Battery, and therefore is not pursued by such a Declaration as it ought to be. But for other Particulars relating to the Form of Appeals, I shall refer the Reader to the Books [g] of Entries.

Sect. 21. As to the third Point, *viz.* What Defence may be made by the Appellee; being able to find little or nothing Particular concerning Pleas in Abatement by such an Appellee, I shall refer the Reader for that Matter, to what is said concerning Pleas in Abatement of Appeals in general, in the latter Part of this Chapter, and only take Notice in this Place of the following Particulars.

[c] 1 Inst. 126. b.

[d] 1 Inst. 127. a. Bro. Appeal, 72, 86, 143.

[e] See B. 1. Ch. 44. Sect. 3. 1 Inst. 127. a. Pulton 17. a.

[f] 41 Ass. 16. 40 Ass. 9. Fitz. Trespass, 199. Coron. 11, 228. S. P. C. 44. Letter F. Contra Bro. Appeal, 60, 154. Fitz. Coron. 60, 110.

[g] Coke's Entries 50, 51. Rastal's Entries 45, 46.

1. Where a Recovery in another Action may be pleaded in Bar of an Appeal of *Mayhem*.
2. Where and in what Manner *son Assault demesne*, and other Matters of the like Nature may be so pleaded.
3. Whether an Arbitrament, or an Accord with Satisfaction, may be so pleaded.
4. What Kind of Release may be so pleaded.
5. Where a Nonsuit in a former Action.
6. That [h] an Appellee cannot wage his Law.

[h] 1 Inst. 295. a. Vide 48 Ed. 3. 6. Fitz. Ley, 36.

Sect. 22. As to the first of these Particulars, *viz.* Where a Recovery in another Action may be pleaded in Bar of an Appeal of *Mayhem*;

It ſeems clear, That notwithſtanding a Recovery [a] in an Appeal of *Mayhem* cannot be pleaded in Bar of an Action of Treſpaſs for the Battery with which the *Mayhem* was accompanied, becauſe [b] in ſuch an Appeal the *Mayhem* only is conſidered diſtinct from the Battery; yet [c] a Recovery in an Action of Treſpaſs, for an Aſſault, Battery and Wounding, may be pleaded in Bar of an Appeal of *Mayhem*, appearing by proper Averments to be brought for the ſame Treſpaſs; for it ſhall be intended that the Jury in giving Damages for the Wounding, included the Maim, and no Man ſhall be liable to double Vexation for one and the ſame Thing; yet [d] in ſuch a Caſe if the Appellee ſhall make it appear, by a ſpecial Replication, that the Maim hath been occaſioned ſince the Verdict in the Action of Treſpaſs, by ſome ſubſequent Mortification, Dryneſs or Shrinking of the Part, by Reaſon of the Wound, perhaps he may avoid ſuch Plea by ſuch ſpecial Matter; but the Court will not intend it unleſs it be ſpecially ſhewn.

[a] 22 Aſſ. pl. 82. Fitz. Coron. 110, 182. 4 Co. 43. 43 Aſſ. 39.
[b] Bro. Appeal, 60.
[c] 4 Co. 43. a. 1 Leon. 318, 319. 43 Aſſ. pl. 3.
[d] 1 Leon. 318, 319.

Sect. 23. As to the ſecond Particular, *viz.* Where, and in what Manner *ſon Aſſault Demeſne*, and other Matters of the like Nature, may be pleaded in Bar of an Appeal of *Mayhem*; It ſeems clear, that it is a good Plea in Bar of ſuch an Appeal, That [e] the Plaintiff firſt aſſaulted the Defendant, and would have beaten and killed him, unleſs he had defended himſelf againſt him, *&c.* Or that [f] the Plaintiff firſt aſſaulted the Defendant, who fled from Place to Place, till he was reduced to a Neceſſity of fighting, *&c.* And in ſome Books [g] it ſeems to be holden in general, That *ſon Aſſault Demeſne* may be pleaded in Bar of any ſuch Appeal without any ſuch ſpecial Circumſtances in Favour of the Defendant: Yet how far a trifling Aſſault may juſtify a grievous *Mayhem*, as the Cutting off of a Leg or Hand, *&c.* unleſs it happened accidentally in the Scuffle, without any barbarous Intention, may well deſerve to be conſidered. However [h] it ſeems clear, That if the Maim in the Declaration be laid in *A.* and the Defendant juſtify the ſame Maim, by Reaſon of an Aſſault made upon him by the Plaintiff in *B.* he needs not traverſe the Maiming of the Plaintiff in *A.* or in any other Place, for it is apparent, that the ſame Maim could not be given but in one and the ſame Place, and therefore being juſtified in any one Place it is well anſwered. Alſo it ſeems [i] clear, That a Man cannot juſtify the Maiming another in Defence of his Poſſeſſions, but only in the Defence of his Perſon. Alſo it is certain, [k] That a Defendant cannot give in Evidence on the general Iſſue, that the Plaintiff firſt aſſaulted him, but muſt ſpecially plead it.

[e] 2 Rol. Ab. 547. Lett. F. Raſt. Ent. 45.
[f] 2 Rol. Ab. 112. Lett. B. 25 Ed. 3. 42. pl. 21. See B. 1. Ch. 60. Sect. 23.
[g] 27 Ed. 3. 94. pl. 1. 41 Aſſ. pl. 21. Fitz. Coron. 142. 1 Keb. 921. 1 Sid. 246.
[h] 41 Aſſ. pl. 21. Bro. Viſne, 74. Bro. Traverſe, 173.
[i] 2 Rol. Abr. 548. pl. 5. 2 Inſt. 316.
[k] 2 Inſt. 282, 283. 2 Inſt. 316.

Sect. 24. As to the third Particular, *viz.* Where an Arbitrament, or Accord with Satisfaction, may be pleaded in Bar of an Appeal of *Mayhem*; it clearly ſeems to be admitted in the Pleadings, [l] in ſome Books, and is ſaid [m] to have been adjudged in a Roll, not printed, That notwithſtanding every ſuch Appeal muſt ſuppoſe the Fact to have been done feloniouſly, yet inaſmuch as at this Day it ſubjects not the Appellee to the Loſs of Member, but only to Damages, *&c.* as an Action of Treſpaſs doth, it may be well barred either by Arbitrament, or an Accord with Satisfaction executed.

[l] 35 H. 6. 39. b. 30. a. 6 H. 7. 1. pl. 1. Fitz. Coron. 63. 6 Co. 44. a.
[m] 9 Co. 78. b.

Sect. 25. As to the fourth Particular, *viz.* What Kind of Releaſe may be pleaded in Bar of an Appeal of *Mayhem*; There can be no Doubt, but that a Releaſe of all Manner of Appeals, [n] or a Releaſe of all Manner of Actions, or a Releaſe of all Manner of Demands, [o] might always be pleaded in Bar of ſuch an Appeal; and that a Releaſe of all

[n] Lit. Sect. 501.
[o] Lit. Sect. 508.

Manner

[a] 1 Inſt. 288. 1 Inſt. 288.

Manner of Actions [a] perſonal may alſo be pleaded in Bar of it at this Day, becauſe the Appellant ſhall recover in it nothing but Damages; but while it ſubjected the Appellee to the Loſs of Member, it ſeems queſtionable, whether it could be barred by a Releaſe of Actions perſonal, becauſe it ſeems to have been then eſteemed an Action of a higher Nature, and not properly to come under the Notion of a perſonal Action.

[b] 43 Aſſ. pl. 39. 40 Aſſ. pl. 1. 1 Inſt. 139. a. Fitz. Coron. 214. [c] 43 Aſſ. pl. 39. Bro. Appeal, 138. [d] Bro. Appeal, 60. Fitz. Coron. 116, 182. Vide ſupra, Sect. 22. [e] Bro. Appeal, 138. Fitz. Ley 36. [f] 1 Inſt. 139. a.

Sect. 26. As to the fifth Particular, *viz.* Where a Nonſuit in a former Action may be pleaded in Bar of an Appeal of *Mayhem*; It ſeems clear, [b] That a Nonſuit in any ſuch Appeal, after the Plaintiff hath appeared to it, may be pleaded in Bar of any other. Alſo [c] it ſeems to have been adjudged, That it may alſo be pleaded in Bar of an Action of Treſpaſs brought for the ſame Maim, and alſo for the Battery with which it was accompanied; yet howſoever the Law may ſtand in Relation to this Matter; if ſuch Action be brought for the Battery only, without mentioning the *Mayhem*, I ſee not how it can be barred by ſuch a Nonſuit, becauſe it is generally holden, That in an Appeal of *Mayhem* no Conſideration [d] can be had of the Battery, but only of the *Mayhem*; and if ſo, it ſeems ſtrange, that a Nonſuit in ſuch an Appeal ſhould bar an Action of a different Nature, brought for a Matter which the Appeal had nothing to do with. However [e] it ſeems clear, That a Nonſuit in an Action of Treſpaſs is no Bar of an Appeal of *Mayhem.* Alſo I take it for granted, That a Nonſuit in an Appeal of *Mayhem*, before the Plaintiff hath appeared to it, is not [f] a Bar of any other Appeal or Action, becauſe the Writ, for what appears to the contrary, might be purchaſed by a Stranger, in the Name of the Plaintiff.

[g] 28 Aſſ. pl. 5. 8 H. 4. 21. pl. 1. 2 Rol. Abr. 578. Letter F. [h] 28 Aſſ. pl. 5. Raſt. Ent. 46. pl. 5, 6. 28 Ed. 3. 94. pl. 1. [i] 6 H. 7. 1. pl. 1. 21 H. 7. 33, pl. 30. 21 H. 7. 40. pl. 58. 41 Aſſ. pl. 27. [k] 22 Aſſ. pl. 82. Vide 21 H. 7. 33. pl. 30. [l] 2 Inſt. 313. [m] 6 H. 7. 1. pl. 1. 28 Aſſ. pl. 5. 21 H. 7. 33. pl. 30. 37 Aſſ. pl. 9. 26 Aſſ. pl. 32.

Sect. 27. As to the fourth Point, *viz.* How the *Mayhem* ſhall be tried, and where the Trial ſhall be peremptory; There is no [g] Doubt but that if the Defendant put it in Iſſue whether the Plaintiff were maimed or not, and pray that the Part which was hurt be viewed by the Court, in Order to have it adjudged on ſuch View, whether there be any *Mayhem* or not, the Court may take a View of the Part, and on ſuch View, determine the Matter; or if there remain a Doubt upon the View, may [h] award a Writ to the Sheriff to return ſome able Phyſicians and Surgeons, for the better Information of the Court. But it ſeems, that the Court cannot proceed to ſuch a Trial by their View, unleſs the Defendant pray it: And in ſuch Caſe it ſeems, [i] That they are not bound to try it in ſuch Manner, but may order a Trial by a Jury, at which it is ſaid, [k] That they may, if they think fit, order that the Jury ſhall have a View of the Wound: And becauſe the Court hath ſuch a diſcretionary Power in Relation to ſuch View, it hath been reſolved, [l] that the Plaintiff in the Appeal muſt appear in proper Perſon, and not by Attorney, becauſe that would put the View out of the Power of the Court. And it ſeems to be agreed, [m] That an Adjudication made upon ſuch View is peremptory and concluſive to each Party.

Sect. 28. It ſeems to be holden, That the Defendant, in an Appeal of Maim, may in ſome Caſes wage Battel; but I find no Inſtance in which Battel hath been actually waged in ſuch an Appeal.

Secondly of Capital Appeals there are two Kinds.

1. Of Treaſon.
2. Of Felony.

Sect. 29. And first of Appeals of Treason, which, as it is said, [a] might be sued anciently not only before the Parliament, but also before other Courts of Common Law, as well as before the Constable and Marshal, and were determinable by Battel, Verdict, or otherwise, according to the Course of the several Courts before which they were commenced. But it is certain, That such Appeals before the Parliament are taken away by 1 *H.* 4. 14. set forth more at large in the fourteenth Section of this Chapter. But I do not see any Reason why Appeals of Treason, done in the Realm, before other Courts of Common Law, which had before Jurisdiction thereof, should be construed to be taken away by that Statute, which by ordaining, *That Appeals of Things done within the Realm, shall be tried and determined by the good Laws of the Realm*, cannot be intended to restrain any Appeal determinable wholly by those Laws, as all the Appeals before the Courts of Common Law seem always to have been. However, since there has been no Instance of any such Appeal, before any Court of Common Law, either since the making of the said Statute, nor for many Years before, the Law relating to such Appeals seems wholly obsolete at this Day. [49] But as for Appeals before the Constable and Marshal, of Treasons done out of the Realm, it seems clear, that the Law in Relation to them is still in Force, as it always hath been; for the said Statute of 1 *H.* 4. 14. by ordaining, *That Appeals of Things done out of the Realm, shall be tried and determined before the Constable and Marshal*, seems clearly rather to affirm than weaken their Jurisdiction in Relation to such Treasons. Also it hath been adjudged, that the Statutes which ordain, That Treasons done out of the Realm shall be tried in the King's Bench, *&c.* do not take away the Jurisdiction of the Constable and Marshal, in Relation to Appeals of such Treasons, as hath been more fully shewn Chap. 4. Sect. 10. And agreeable hereto, an Appeal of Treason, supposed to have been committed beyond Sea, was actually commenced in the seventh Year of the Reign of King *Charles* the First, by *Donald* Lord *Rea*, against *David Ramsey*, Esq; before the Constable and Marshal, who, for want of sufficient Proof to clear the Truth of the Accusation, actually awarded, That a Duel should be fought between the said Appellant and Appellee, for the final Determination of the Matter.

[a] 3 Inst. 132. Bract. 118, 119. Fleta Lib. 1. Ch. 21. S. P. C. 78. Letter C. Contra Bro. Appeal, 46. 1 H. H. P. C. 349. 2 H. H. P. C. 150.*

4 Inst. 124. H. P. C. 180. seems contrary.

Rushworth's Collect. Part 2 Vol. 1. from fol. 112 to 128.

Of Appeals of Felony there are four principal Kinds.

1. Of Death.
2. Of Larceny.
3. Of Rape.
4. Of Arson.

But before I examine the Nature of each of these in Particular, I shall premise some Things in general concerning what Persons are capable of bringing them; as,

Sect. 30. First, That [b] the Infancy, Old Age, or other Imbecillity of the Plaintiff, is no good Objection against his bringing an Appeal, tho' it take from the Defendant the Benefit of waging Battle, and in that Respect put him in a worse Condition than he would be in, if the Appeal were brought by a Person capable of fighting; for inasmuch as the Defendant has proper Means for his Acquittal, by putting himself upon a Trial

[b] Moor 461. pl. 646. H. P. C. 183, 184. Keilw. 120 a. S. P. C. 60. Letter D. See the Books under cited. Con. 45 Ed. 3. 25. pl. 36. 41 Ass. pl. 14.

Trial by his Country, and the Imbecillity of the Plaintiff is wholly owing to the Act of God, and no ways leſſens the Injury complained of by him, it is not reaſonable he ſhould ſuffer any Diſadvantage from it. And agreeably hereto it ſeems to have been ſettled [a] of late Times, contrary to the numerous Authorities [b] in the Old Books, That the Parol ſhall not demur in an Appeal for the Nonage of the Plaintiff. Yet it is certain, [c] That an Infant muſt proſecute ſuch Suit by a Guardian; and it is ſaid, [d] That he ſhall be nonſuited for the Non-appearance of ſuch Guardian, upon Demand, at any Day whereon he is demandable, notwithſtanding an Allegation that he was not able to come by Reaſon of Sickneſs, or other ſuch like Excuſe. And there [e] is a Caſe wherein the Court refuſed to inlarge the Day of ſuch Guardian's Appearance upon a Surmiſe of his Sickneſs. But notwithſtanding the Guardian be ſo neceſſary in the Proſecution of ſuch a Suit, yet if the Infant come into Court, and ſay he will relinquiſh it, and yet the Guardian will proſecute it; the Court may, [f] in Diſcretion, diſcharge ſuch Guardian, and aſſign another, for it is not reaſonable that an Infant be bound to continue a Suit againſt his Will, which demands nothing but Revenge, and will be chargeable to him.

Sect. 31. Secondly, [g] That a Woman may ſue any other Appeal except that of the Death of an Anceſtor; for that the Statute of *Magna Charta*, 34, which ordains, *That no Man ſhall be impriſoned on the Appeal of a Woman, for the Death of any one but her own Huſband*, reſtrains not any other Appeal whatſoever.

Sect. 32. Thirdly, That an Ideot, [h] or Perſon born Deaf and Dumb, or one attainted [i] of Treaſon or Felony, or but outlawed [k] in a Perſonal Action (ſo long as ſuch Attainder or Outlawry continues in force) cannot bring any Appeal whatſoever.

And now I am more particularly to conſider the Nature of an Appeal of Death in particular, for the better Underſtanding whereof, I ſhall examine the following Points.

1. Within what Time it muſt be brought.
2. In what County.
3. By whom.

Sect. 33. As to the firſt Point, *viz.* Within what Time an Appeal of Death muſt be brought, it is enacted by the Statute of *Glouceſter*, Ch. 9. *That an Appeal*, [l] (which from the Purport of the whole Statute hath been conſtrued [i] to be meant only of an Appeal of Death) *ſhall ſtand in Effect, and ſhall not be abated for Default of freſh Suit, if the Party ſhall ſue within the Year* [m] *and the Day after the Deed done.* And it hath been holden, [n] That the Computation of ſuch Year and Day is to be made from the Time of the Wound which occaſioned the Death, and not from the Time of the Death; and this Opinion ſeems ſomewhat to be favour'd by the Letter of the Statute, which is, That the Party ſhall ſue within the Year and Day after the Deed done, but no Deed is done at the Time of the Death, but at the Time of the Wound; yet the contrary Opinion is ſettled [o] to be Law, and is certainly moſt agreeable to the Intent of the Statute, the plain Import whereof ſeems to be, That the Appellant ſhall not be adjudged to have made Default of freſh Suit, unleſs he have been negligent a Year and a Day; but negligent he could

[a] 27 H. 8. 11 pl. 25. Keilw. 120. pl. 66. S.P.C. 60. D. H. P. C. 183. Smith and Bowen, Mich. 7 Annæ. 2 Inſt. 320.
[b] 32 Aſſ. pl. 8. Dyer 137. pl. 24. 11 H. 4. 94. pl. 56. 13 Aſſ. pl. 10. 17 Ed. 4. 2. pl. 4. Bro. Appeal, 116. Fitz. Age 57, 83. 21 Aſſ. pl. 4. 27 Ed. 3. 83. pl. 2. 21 Ed. 3. 23. pl. 16.
[c] 27 H. 8. 11 pl. 25.
[d] Noy 88. Latch 173.
[e] Noy 88. Latch 173.
[f] 1 Rol. Abr. 288. D. Style 456. Vide Salk. 176, 177.
[g] Co. Lit. 25. b. 2 Inſt. 68. Fitz. Coron. 357. S. P. C. 60. F. H. P. C. 184.
[h] H. P. C. 183. S. P. C. 60. D. 98. C.
[i] 11 Aſſ. pl. 27.
[k] 17 Aſſ. pl. 26. Bro. Appeal, 118, 146. Fitz. Utlagary, 47.
[l] S. P. C. 62. Letter B. Infra Sect. 48.
[m] Bro. Appeal, 37. 22 Ed. 4. 39. b.
[n] S. P. C. 63. Letter A.
[o] 4 Co. 42. b. 2 Inſt. 320. 3 Inſt. 53. 1 H. H. P.C. 427.

I not

not be as to the bringing an Appeal before the Party was actually dead, because till then no Appeal lay. And agreeably hereto it seems also to be settled, [a] That if a Person become Accessary after the Death, by receiving the Offender, an Appeal lies against him, at any Time within the Year and Day after such Receipt, because till then the Appellant could not possibly be guilty of any Negligence as to the Bringing of an Appeal against the Receiver. Also if an Appeal had been abated by the Demise of the King, before 1 *Ed.* 6. Ch. 7. (by which this Mischief is provided against) it seems [b] clear, That the Appellant might have sued a Re-attachment against the Appellee, within the Year and Day after such Demise, for that he was in no Default, and otherwise would have been without Remedy.

Sect. 34. It seems, That the Year and Day in any of the Cases above-mentioned, are to be computed from the Beginning of the Day, on which the Death, or Receipt, *&c.* happened, and not from the precise Minute, or Hour, because regularly the Law makes no Fraction of a Day; and therefore [c] if the Party dye at any Time the first Day of *January*, the Year shall end the first Day of *January* following.

Sect. 35. As to the second Point, *viz.* In what County an Appeal of Death must be brought, I shall take it for granted, That it is a local [d] Action, and consequently cannot be brought in a foreign County. But if a Person happen to dye in one County of a Wound received in another, it is said, [e] That the Appellant had, by the Common Law, his Election to bring his Appeal in either County, and that in every such Case the Trial ought [f] to be at the Bar, and by a Jury returned [g] from the Body of each of those Counties. But since the making of 2 & 3 *Ed.* 6. 24. by which it is enacted, *That in such Cases, the Party to whom Appeal of Murder shall be given by the Law, may commence, take, and sue Appeal of Murder in the same County where the Person feloniously stricken, or poisoned, shall dye,* &c. I take it for granted, That such an Appeal, in the County wherein the Party died, may be tried by a Jury of such County without the Joinder of any other.

I shall not in this Place examine in what County Accessaries to Murder are to be appealed or tried, but shall refer the Consideration thereof to the Chapter concerning the Arraignment of the Principal and Accessary.

As to the third Point, *viz.* By whom an Appeal of Death is to be brought, I shall endeavour to shew,

1. Where it may be brought by a Wife.
2. Where by an Heir.

1. As to an Appeal by a Wife, the following Particulars seem most observable.

Sect. 36. First, She must be able to prove, not only that she was wholly Innocent herself of the Death complained of, but also that she was the lawful Wife of the Deceased, at the Time of his Death; for it seems to be clearly settled, [h] That *N'unques accouple in loial matrimonie* is a good Plea in such an Appeal, and triable by the Bishop's Certificate, who, if the Marriage were unlawful, by Reason of a Precontract, or Consan-

[a] 26 Aff. pl. 52. 3 Inst. 53. S. P. C. 63. Letter B. 2 Inst. 320.

[b] 2 H. 7. 10. pl. 5. Bro. Appeal, 81. 10 Ed. 4. 13. pl. 7. Fitz. Re-attachment, 8. 7 Co. 30.

[c] Vide 5 Co. 1. Co. Lit. 130. b. 255. A. Contra 3 Inst. 53.

[d] 18 Ed. 3. 32. pl. 6. S. P. C. 63. D. Fitz. Forfeiture, 14. Dyer 18. pl. 50, &c.

[e] 2 H. H. P. C. 163. 3 H. 7. 12. pl. 4. 4 H. 7. 18. pl. 10. Fitz. Coron. 50, 60. But the Preamble of 2 & 3 Ed. 6. 24. seems contrary.

[f] Dy. 46. pl. 8.

[g] 3 H. 7. 12. pl. 4. Finch 410, 411. Dy. 46. pl. 8.

Vide infra Sect. 59. & 60.

[h] 2 Inst. 68. 28 Ed. 3. 91. pl. 4. 50 Ed. 3. 15. 27 Aff. pl. 3. 11 H. 4. 14 a. b. S. P. C. 59. A. B. H. P. C. 181. 1 Inst. 33. b.

Consanguinity, or otherwise, ought to certify against the Appellant. Also it is laid down as a Rule in the Old Books, [a] That a Wife may have an Appeal of the Death of her Husband *inter brachia sua interfecti & non aliter*. By which Words, *inter brachia sua*, according to Sir *Edward Coke*, [b] it is to be understood, That the deceased had the Wife lawfully in Possession at his Death; and if this be the Meaning of them, thus much at least seems to follow, That if the Husband were divorced from the Wife at his Death, though by a voidable Sentence, she cannot maintain an Appeal. Yet it is generally holden, That a Wife who hath eloped from her Husband may have an Appeal of his Death, as shall be more fully shewn in the next Section. And *Staunford* [c] seems to understand the Import of the Expression abovementioned to be this, That the Wife ought to have had the Deceased in her View, and to have been present at his Death, which is most certainly not necessary at this Day. But finding little more said concerning this Matter in any other Modern Book, I shall leave the farther Consideration thereof to others.

Sect. 37. Secondly, In some Cases a Woman may have an Appeal of the Death of her Husband, where she cannot claim Dower of his Lands; as where the Husband was attainted [d] of High Treason at the Time of his Death; for after the Attainder he was still her Husband as much as before, and [e] it is the Loss of her Husband which is the Cause of the Appeal. Also where a Woman elopes from her Husband, it is said, that she may have an Appeal [f] of his Death, though not a Writ of Dower; for by the Common Law she might have had both; and the Statute of *Westminster* 2. Ch. 34. which takes from her the latter, leaves the other as before.

Sect. 38. Thirdly, If such Appellant take another Husband either before, or pending the Appeal, she puts [g] an End to it for ever; for being given her only from a Regard to her Widowhood, it cannot but cease when that determines, and being once barred, it is barred for ever. And on this ground it seems also to be certain, [h] That if she marry after Judgment in Appeal, she cannot pray Execution. However it seems clear, That in such a Case the Appellee shall not [i] be discharged without the King's Pardon: But I do not find it settled [k] what ought to be done with the Appellee in such a Case. But thus much seems to be certain, That the King cannot proceed against him by way of Indictment, because he is attainted already; and therefore it may probably be argued, That the Court may award Execution against him, either *ex Officio*, or at least at the Demand of the King; for otherwise he would save his Life by Reason of the Attainder by which he is adjudged to lose it.

Secondly, as to the Appeal of Death by an Heir, the following particulars seem most remarkable.

Sect. 39. First, if the deceased had a Wife at the Time of his Death, and such Wife where wholly innocent of it, she [l] only, and not the Heir, hath a Right to the Appeal; and whether she bring one, or wholly neglect it, and though she dye or marry within the Year and Day, the Heir cannot bring an Appeal; and the Reason hereof, according to *Keilway*, [m] is this, That the Appeal being once out of the Blood, shall

[a] Bract. Lib. 3. cap. 29. Fleta Lib. 1. cap. 35. S. P. C. 58. C.
[b] 2 Inst. 68, 217.
[c] S. P. C. 59.
[d] 27 Ass. pl. 41. 35 H. 6. 57. b. 58. Bro. Appeal, 131. Fitz. Coro. 21. Co. Lit. 33. b. 7 Co. Calvin's Case, 13. b. S. P. C. 59.
[e] Bro. Appeal. 148.
[f] Bro. Appeal, 17. 1 Inst. 33. b. S.P.C. 59. C. Contra. 2 Inst. 317.
[g] H. P. C. 181. S. P. C. 59. Letter B. 2 Inst. 69. 20 H.6.43.b. Bro. Appeal, 148.
[h] 11 H. 4. 48. b. Bro. Appeal, 109, 112, 148. con. 21 E. 4. 73. b. See also the Books above cited.
[i] Bro. Appeal, 27. 3 Inst. 209, 210. 2 H. 7. 10. pl. 5. 8 H. 4. 22. pl. 7. Fitz. Scire facias, 41. 38 H. 6. 13. pl. 26. 9 H. 7. 5. b. S. P. C. 166. Letter A.
[k] 2 Leon. 83. Vide. 21 Ed. 4. 72. b. 73.
[l] Keilw. 120. pl. 65. H. P. C. 181, 182. S. P. C. 59. E. 20 H. 6. 43.
[m] Keilw. 120. pl. 65.

not return to it again: Yet [a] if the Wife herself had a Share in the Guilt, the Heir may have an Appeal against her. But if the Petit Treason be pardoned by the Parliament, it seems, [b] That the Heir can bring no Appeal; for he cannot bring it for the Murder only, because the Petit Treason includes in it Murder and more, and being the greater Offence drowns the less, and therefore the Pardon of it seems to pardon the Murder also.

Sect. 40. Secondly, Every such Appellant must be Heir [c] general to the deceased, by the Course of the Common Law, unless [d] the Heir general had himself a Share in the Guilt, in which Case the next Heir shall have an Appeal against him. But a Father cannot [e] have an Appeal of the Death of his Son, because he cannot be his Heir. Neither [f] can any one bring an Appeal of the Death of a Person attainted of Treason or Felony, except his Wife, because he can have no Heir. Neither shall a special [g] Heir, by the Custom of Borough-English, or otherwise, have an Appeal of the Death of his Ancestor, because he is not his next general Heir; and yet he is inheritable to such of his Lands to which the Custom extends, *&c.* And for the like Reason, if the deceased, at the Time of his Death, had two Sons, the elder whereof is attainted of Treason or Felony, neither [h] of them can have an Appeal; not the Elder, because of the Attainder; not the Younger, because he cannot be Heir to his Father while he has an Elder Brother; who, though he be looked upon as dead in Law to some Purposes, is yet in Truth alive, and capable of forfeiting all the Privileges belonging to the Heir, though not of taking Benefit from any of them. But notwithstanding a younger Son cannot bring an Appeal of the Death of the Father, while there is an Elder Son of the same Father living; yet if the eldest Son be by one Venter, and the Middle and Younger Son by another, and the Middle Son be killed, the Youngest only shall have an Appeal of his Death, because he only is his Heir, as being of the whole Blood with him: And therefore, [i] it is no good Plea to an Appeal for the Death of a Brother, That the Appellant has *J. S.* an Elder Brother living, without shewing, that *J. S.* was of the whole Blood to the deceased.

Sect. 41. Thirdly, If an Appeal be once commenced by an Heir, who dies hanging the Suit, it seems to be agreed, [k] by almost all the Books, That no other Heir can afterwards proceed in such Appeal, or commence a new one; for that this is a Personal Action, given to the Heir in Respect to his immediate Relation to the Person killed, at the Time of his Death, and like other Personal Actions, shall die with the Person. But some [l] have holden, That if the first Heir die within the Year and Day, without commencing an Appeal, the next Heir may bring one. But this is made a Doubt by others, [m] and the Generality [n] of the Books seem to favour the contrary Opinion, as being more agreeable to the Reason of the Case abovementioned, and the general Tenor of the Law in Relation to Appeals, which in no Case that I know of, will suffer the Right of bringing one to be transferred from one to another; and therefore, as in Case [o] where the deceased hath a Wife at the Time of his Death, who dies within the Year and Day, the Heir hath no Right to an Appeal; so if he have an Heir at his Death, in whom the Right of the Appeal is vested, and such Heir die within the Year

[a] Cro. Car. 531, 532. 1 Jon. 425. 18 Ed. 4. 1. pl. 3. Fitz. Coron. 459. H. P. C. 181, 182. S. P. C. 59. D.

[b] Dy. 50. pl. 4. 1 Leon. 326.

[c] 27 Ed. 3. 83. pl. 2. Fitz. Coron. 322. H. P. C. 182. S. P. C. 59. F. 27 Ass. pl. 25.

[d] H. P. C. 182. Fitz. Coron. 459. S. P. C. 60. Letter B.

[e] Fitz. Coron. 41.

[f] Bro. Appeal, 116, 131. 2 Ass. pl. 3.

[g] S. P. C. 59. F. H. P. C. 182.

[h] S. P. C. 60. Letter A. 1 Inst. 8. a. 13. a. 20 H. 6. 43. b. Fitz. Coron. 235. But Fitz. Coron. 322. seems contrary.

[i] 7 Ed. 4. 15. pl. 3. Fitz. Coro. 28. Bro. Appeal, 94. S. P. C. 60. E.

[k] 11 H. 4. 11. b. 12. a. 9 H. 7. 5. b. 16 H. 7. 15. pl. 14. S. P. C. 59. G. H. P. C. 182. Bro. Appeal, 30, 88, 104, 141, 144.

[l] 16 H. 7. 15. pl. 14. Bro. Appeal, 156. 11 H. 4. 11. b.

[m] S. P. C. 59. G. Dy. 69. pl. 31.

[n] 20 H. 6. 43. b. 11 H. 4. 12. a. H. P. C. 182. Bro. Appeal, 30, 88, 104, 141, 144.

[o] Supra Sect. 39.

[a] H.P.C. 182. 13 H. 4. 6. pl. 14. 11 H. 4. 11. b. [b] S.P.C. 59. I. [c] 38 H. 6. 13. pl. 26. 9 H. 7. 5. b. 6. a. 16 H. 7. 15. pl. 14. 11 H. 4. 11. b. 12. a. Bro. Appeal, 141, 144, 156. [d] 2 Leon. 83. seems contrary.

and Day, it seems, That no other Heir shall have an Appeal. Yet it is holden, [a] by Sir *Matthew Hale*, and some others, That if the first Heir get Judgment in an Appeal of Death, and die, his Heir may sue Execution. But this is doubted of by Sir *William Staundford*, [b] and seems contrary to many [c] of the old Books, and not easily reconcileable with the Reason of the Cases abovementioned. But whether in this Case the Court may [d] not award Execution, either *ex Officio*, or at the Demand of the King, may deserve to be considered, for the Reasons given *Sect.* 38. Also if a Person who is killed have no Wife at the Time of his Death, and no Issue but Daughters, and all those Daughters die within the Year and Day, it may reasonably be argued, That the Heir Male may have an Appeal, because the Right of bringing one never vested in any other before. But finding this Case in none of the Books, I shall leave it to be more fully considered by others.

[e] Fitz. Office de Court, 7. 10 Ed. 4. 7. pl. 18. [f] 2 Inst. 68. 1 Inst. 25. [g] H.P.C. 182, 183. 2 Inst. 68. Fitz. Coron. 385. the contrary adjudged by all the Judges in the Exchequer-Chamber, but one. 20 H. 6. 43. Quære 17 Ed. 4. 1. pl. 1. 1 Inst. 25. S. P. C. 58. B, C. Bro. Appeal, 104. [h] 21 E. 3. 23. pl. 16. 45 Ed. 3. 25. pl. 36. 27 Aff. pl. 25. S. P. C. 81. Letter A. 1 Bulst. 71, 75. H. P. C. 187.

Sect. 42. Fourthly, Every such Appellant must not only be Heir general to the deceased, but also Heir Male; and this depends upon *Magna Charta*, Ch. 35. by which it is enacted, *That no one shall be taken or imprisoned on the Appeal of a Woman for the Death of any one but her own Husband.* And the Judges are so far bound to take Notice of this Statute, That if a Woman bring an Appeal of the Death of her Father, or of any other but her Husband, they ought [e] *ex Officio*, to abate the Writ, though the Defendant take no Exeption to it. But it is said, [f] That by the Common Law an Heir Female might have brought an Appeal of the Death of her Ancestor, as well as an Heir Male. And it [g] seems to be the better Opinion at this Day, That the Heir Male of the deceased, who derives his Blood through a Female, may have an Appeal, as the Uncle being Heir on the Part of the Mother, or the Grandson by a Daughter, *&c.* and yet the Mother in the first Case, and the Daughter in the second, could have had no Appeal; for inasmuch as by the Common Law, such Mother and Daughter had not only a Right to bring such Appeal, but also to have such Right derived through them to others, it seems hard to construe the Statute by depriving them of the former to take from them the other also; especially considering, That an Heir Male, who derives his Blood through Females, seems no Way less worthy to bring an Appeal, than if he had derived it through Males; and all Statutes whatsoever, which are made in Abridgment of any Right of the Subject, ought to be strictly construed.

Sect. 43. Fifthly, In every such Appeal, by one, as Heir to the deceased, it must specially [h] appear by the Writ, or at least by the Count, in what Manner he is so.

And now I am come to an Appeal of Larceny, for the better Understanding whereof I shall consider,

1. By whom it may be brought.
2. Against whom.
3. In what County.
4. Within what Time.
5. Where there shall be a Restitution of the Goods stoln.

As to the first Point, *viz.* by whom an Appeal of Larceny may be brought, the following Particulars seem most remarkable.

Sect. 44. Firſt, There is no Neceſſity that the Appellant have the abſolute Property of the Goods ſtoln; for it ſeems agreed, That a Carrier, or even a Servant, [a] to whom Goods are delivered to be carried to a certain Place, or Churchwardens [b] having Poſſeſſion of the Goods of a Church, or in general, any Perſon whatſoever, [c] who is ſo far intruſted with the Goods of another as in Judgment of Law to have the Poſſeſſion, and not the bare Charge of them, may have an Appeal of Larceny againſt any one who ſhall ſteal them, for that they have a ſpecial Kind of Property in them againſt all Strangers: And it ſeems that they may either bring a general [d] Appeal as for their own Goods, or a ſpecial [e] one for the Goods of *J. S.* in their Cuſtody. Alſo it is ſaid, That a Perſon who hath been robbed of his Goods, ſtill continues to have ſo far the Poſſeſſion as well as the Property of them, that he may bring an Appeal of Larceny againſt any one who ſhall ſteal them from the Robber, as ſhall be more fully ſhewn in the next Section. But it ſeems [f] clear, That no one can maintain ſuch an Appeal who has the bare Charge of Goods without a Poſſeſſion, as a Butler or Cook, who in my own Houſe have the Charge of my Goods, for that in ſuch a Caſe the whole Poſſeſſion, as well as the abſolute Property, in the Judgment of Law always continues in me. Alſo it is certain, That a Villein cannot [g] have an Appeal of Larceny againſt his Lords, for any of his Goods taken by the Lord, becauſe [h] the Lord by ſeizing them makes them his own. But it is agreed, [i] That a Villein may have an Appeal of Death or of Rape againſt his Lord. Alſo it ſeems clear at this [k] Day, That any Tenant who is not a Villein, may have an Appeal of Larceny againſt his Lord.

Sect. 45. Secondly, There is no Neceſſity that the Wrong for which ſuch an Appeal is brought, were immediately done to the Perſon of the Appellant; for if a Servant be robbed of the Maſter's Goods in his Cuſtody, the Maſter [l] may bring the Appeal as well as the Servant, and in ſuch Caſe he who firſt commences it ſhall prevent [m] the other. Alſo if one be robbed of Goods wherein another is jointly intereſted with him, and die, the Survivor [n] may bring an Appeal. Alſo if I be robbed by *A.* who afterwards is robbed of the ſame Goods by *B.* it is ſaid, [o] That I may have an Appeal of Larceny againſt *B.* becauſe *A.* claiming no Property, but taking the Goods merely as a Felon, had, in Judgment of Law, neither any Property nor Poſſeſſion in them, but the ſame wholly continued in me. But if the Goods had been taken from me by a Treſpaſſer, under the Pretence of ſome Title, and ſuch Treſpaſſer had been robbed of them, It ſeems that I could have no Appeal for them. Neither can an Executor [p] bring an Appeal for a Larceny from the Teſtator, becauſe ſuch Larceny, at the Time when it was committed, was no Injury to the Executor, but to the Teſtator only; and therefore the Appeal for it being a mere perſonal Action, and wholly veſted in the Teſtator, there is no Doubt but that it dies with him, as all other Actions for mere Torts do.

[a] Fitz. Coro. 100. Latch 127. S. P. C. 60. F.
[b] 11 H. 4. 12. pl. 25. 12 H. 7. 27. b. 28, 29. 37 H. 6. 30, 31.
[c] 2 Ed. 4. 15. b. 2 Ric. 3. 22. pl. 53. 3 H. 7. 12. pl. 9. 5 H. 7. 18. pl. 11. 21 H. 7. 14. pl. 23. Bract. Lib. 3. chap. 26. See B. 1. Ch. 33. Sect. 3. S. P. C. 60. F.
[d] Keilw. 70. pl. 7.
[e] Bract. Lib. 3. chap. 26. Fitz. Coron. 100. 11 H. 4. 12. Bro. guard d'Egliſe, 6. Bro. Coron. 142. Bro. Appeal, 91.
[f] 3 Inſt. 108. See B. 1. Ch. 33. Sect. 6.
[g] H. P. C. 184. S. P. C. 60. F. Fitz. Coron. 17. Bro. Coron. 216. Bro. Appeal, 34.
[h] Lit. Sect. 177.
[i] Lit. Sect. 189, 190. H. P. C. 184.
[k] S. P. C. 62. Letter A.
[l] H. P. C. 184.
[m] Latch 127.
[n] H. P. C. 184. S. P. C. 61. Fitz. Coron. 392.
[o] H. P. C. 184. S. P. C. 61. Fitz. Coron. 39, 79. 13 Ed. 4. 3. pl. 7. Keilw. 160. b. Bro. Appeal, 100. 4 H. 7. 5. b. See B. 1. Ch. 33. Sect. 9.
[p] H. P. C. 184. S. P. C. 60. F.

Sect. 46. As to the ſecond Point, *viz.* Againſt whom an Appeal of Larceny may be brought; having incidentally ſhewn what is moſt conſiderable relating to this Point under the former, I ſhall only take Notice in this Place, That this, or any other Appeal lies againſt an Infant, [a] as well as againſt a Perſon of full Age, and againſt a Feme Covert, [b] in the ſame Manner as if ſhe were ſole, without taking Notice of the Huſband.

Sect. 47. As to the third Point, *viz.* In what County ſuch Appeal is to be brought; There is no Doubt, but that, like all other [c] Appeals, it is a local Action, and muſt be brought in the County where the Felony complained of was done. Yet if one rob me in the County of *A.* and afterwards carry my Goods into the County of *B.* I have my Election [d] either to bring an Appeal of Robbery in the County of *A.* or an Appeal of Larceny in the County of *B.* becauſe the Poſſeſſion as well as Property of the Goods continued in me, in Judgment of Law, after the Robbery; and therefore, in what Place ſoever the Robber keeps them from me, he feloniouſly injures me in the Poſſeſſion as well as Property of them, and conſequently may properly enough be ſaid to ſteal them from me: Yet he ſhall be appealed for the Robbery in the firſt County only, [e] for there only he was guilty of a Taking from the Perſon, without which there can be no Robbery. Alſo [f] if one take me from the County of *A.* into the County of *B.* and there rob me, he ſhall be appealed for the Robbery in the County of *B.* only, for he was guilty only of a Treſpaſs in the County of *A.* But [g] if one bring my Goods into the County of *B.* by Reaſon of a Menace in the County of *A.* it may be queſtioned which is the proper County for the Bringing of the Appeal.

Sect. 48. As to the fourth Point, *viz.* Within what Time an Appeal of Larceny is to be brought; It ſeems to be agreed [h] at this Day, That it may be ſued at any Time, as well after as within the Year and Day, if the Plaintiff have made freſh Suit; for that the Statute of *Gloceſter*, Chap. 9. which requires, That an Appeal be brought within the Year and Day, hath been conſtrued [i] to intend no other Appeal but that of Death; and the Common Law ſeems to have limited no certain Time for the Bringing of an Appeal, but to have ſuffered it to be brought at any Time by one who had made freſh Suit; the Nature whereof ſhall be more fully conſidered in the fiftieth Section. But it ſeems, That one who has been guilty of a groſs Neglect in purſuiug the Offender, may be barred of ſuch an Appeal, as well within the Year and Day as after; for that the Common Law ſeems [k] in all Appeals to have required, that the Appellant ſhould have made freſh Suit; and the ſaid Statute of *Gloceſter*, which takes away the Neceſſity of it in Appeals of Death brought within the Year and Day, extends not to other Appeals.

Sect. 49. As to the fifth Point, *viz.* In what Caſes there ſhall be a Reſtitution of the Goods ſtoln, I ſhall premiſe, That until [l] ſuch Goods are ſeiſed to the Uſe of the King, or of ſome other Perſon claiming them under the Crown, as being Waifs, or the Goods of a Felon, *&c.* the rightful Owner, without any freſh Suit or Appeal, may ſeize them where-ever he finds them; but they ſhall not be reſtored to them after ſuch Seizure by others, without bringing his Appeal, *&c.* And for the better Underſtanding in what Caſes a Reſtitution of the Goods ſo ſeized ſhall be awarded on ſuch an Appeal, I ſhall examine the following Particulars.

[a] S.P.C. 62. a. H. P. C. 185.
[b] Bro. Coron. 60. 15 Ed. 4. 1. pl. 2.
S.P.C. 62. A. H. P. C. 185. Vide Fitz. Coron. 17.
[c] Supra Sect. 35. 11 H. 4. 93. pl. 53. Fitz. Coron. 437. Bro. Appeal, 35. Dy. 38, 39, 40.
[d] 7 H. 4. 43. pl. 9. Dy. 39. pl. 56, 40. pl. 66. 4 H. 7. 5. b. 6. a. S.P.C. 63. G. 26 Aſſ. pl. 32. 7 Co. 2. a. Fitz. Coron. 62, 79. Fitz. Aſſiſe, 446. Bro. Appeal, 35. B. 1. Ch. 33. Sect. 9.
[e] H.P.C. 184. 7 Co. 2. a. Contra Keilw. 160. b.
[f] S. P. C. 63. Letter F. Infra Sect. 71.
[g] S. P. C. 63. Letter F.
[h] H.P.C. 185. S. P. C. 62. Letter B. 165. D. Bro. Appeal, 37, 62. 7 H. 4. 44. pl. 9. Contra 22 Aſſ. pl. 97.
[i] Supra Sect. 33.
[k] 2 Inſt. 319.
[l] 21 Ed. 4. 16. pl. 7. Fitz. Eſtray, 2. Avowry, 151. S. P. C. 186. 5 Co. 109. 1 H. H. P. C. 541.

1. Whether it neceſſarily require a freſh Suit.
2. What ſhall be eſteemed a freſh Suit.
3. By whom, and in what Manner, ſuch freſh Suit ſhall be inquired and adjudged.
4. How far the Appeal muſt be proſecuted.
5. Whether the Appellant's Title to ſuch Reſtitution ſhall be preferred to any ſubſequent Title claimed in the Goods.
6. Whether there ſhall be ſuch a Reſtitution on any other Proſecution beſides that of Appeal.
7. Whether there ſhall be a Reſtitution to any Goods not mentioned in the Appeal.

Sect. 50. As to the firſt Particular, *viz.* Whether ſuch Reſtitution neceſſarily require a freſh Suit; It ſo fully appears to do ſo by almoſt all the Books [a] relating to this Matter, that it ſeems needleſs to cite Authorities to prove it.

Sect. 51. As to the ſecond Particular, *viz.* What ſhall be eſteemed a freſh Suit; It ſeems to have been anciently holden, [b] That to make a freſh Suit, the Party ought to have raiſed a Hue and Cry with all convenient Speed, and alſo to have taken the Offender: But at this Day it ſeems to be ſettled, [c] That if the Party have been guilty of no groſs Neglect, but have uſed all reaſonable Care and Diligence in inquiring after, purſuing and apprehending the Felon, he ought to be allowed to have made ſufficient freſh Suit, whether any Hue and Cry were levied or not, and whether ſuch Offender were taken by Means of ſuch Purſuit, or without any Aſſiſtance from it.

Sect. 52. As to the third Particular, *viz.* By whom, and in what Manner, ſuch freſh Suit ſhall be inquired and adjudged; It ſeems, [d] That it is uſual and proper to make ſuch Inquiry by the ſame Jury that tries the principal Matter; and it is certain, That upon the Finding of the freſh Suit by ſuch Jury, the Court may award a Reſtitution: And in ſuch Caſes wherein the Appellee is condemned without any Trial, as where he is convicted by his own Confeſſion, or outlawed, or ſtands mute, &c. it ſeems, That the Court may make ſuch Inquiry, by any [e] Inqueſt of Office, returned for ſuch Purpoſe, and on their finding the freſh Suit award a Reſtitution: But in either Caſe ſuch Inqueſt is but an Inqueſt [f] of Office, and perhaps is not abſolutely neceſſary, but required chiefly for the Satiſfaction of the Conſcience of the Judges, in a Matter which, if they think fit, they may, by the Purport of ſome Authorities, [g] examine themſelves, as they generally may, (according to ſome [h] Opinions) any Matters whatſoever inquirable by an Inqueſt of Office, eſpecially [i] if the Parties intereſted in the Thing in Queſtion be willing that they ſhould do ſo: And agreeably hereto it is holden, in the beſt Authors, [k] That the Judging of freſh Suit lies in the Diſcretion of the Court; and there is a Caſe [l] wherein a Writ of Reſtitution of the Goods ſtoln was actually awarded, without making any Inquiry of the freſh Suit; but in the Book wherein this Caſe is reported, it is made a *Quære*, whether ſuch Inquiry ought not to be made at the Return of ſuch Writ.

Sect. 53. As to the fourth Particular, *viz.* How far the Appeal muſt be proſecuted in Order to intitle the Appellant to a Reſtitution,

[a] See the Authorities cited to the three next Sections.

[b] Fitz. Coron. 319, 379, 392. 1 H. H. P. C. 540. S. P. C. 62, 165. 2 Rich. 3. 13. a.

[c] Bro. Freſh Suit, 1, 6. 7 H. 4. 44. pl. 9. S. P. C. 62. Letter B. 165. D. Quære Hetley 64, 65.

[d] 4 Ed. 4. 11. b. S. P. C. 166. Letter B.

[e] 8 H. 4. 1. pl. 2. 7 H. 4. 31. pl. 16. 2 Rich. 3. 13. pl. 31. 10 H. 4. 5. pl. 18. Contra S. P. C. 165. Letter B.

[f] S. P. C. 166. Letter B. and ſee the Books cited to the other Points of this Section, and Raſt. Ent. 52, 53.

[g] Vide Fitz. Coron. 379, 392.

[h] 14 H 4. 9. b. 3 H. 6. 29. b. 8 H. 6. 5. a. Yel. 152. 1 Brownl. 214. 1 Sid. 442. pl. 15. Contra Latch 213. 3 Leon. 150, 213.

[i] Cro. Jac. 415. pl. 3. 2 Saund. 106, 107.

[k] H. P. C. 185. S. P. C. 62. Letter B.

[l] 21 E. 4. 16. pl. 7. Fitz. Coron. 42. Bro. Freſh Suit, 4. Vide S. P. C. 166. Letter A. 2 Leon. 108.

it seems, That anciently the Appellant could in no Case be intitled to a Restitution, unless [a] the Appellee were attainted at his Suit; and therefore if several Appeals were commenced against the same Person by several Plaintiffs, and the Appellee were attainted at the Suit of one of them, no [b] other could have a Restitution, because the Appellee [c] being once attainted, could not be afterwards attainted again: But [d] it seems to be settled at this Day, That there is no such Necessity that the Appellee be attainted at the Suit of the Appellant; and therefore in the Case abovementioned, after such Attainder at the Suit of one Appellant, it shall be inquired by an Inquest of Office, Whether the Appellee were guilty of the Facts complained of in the other Appeals, and made fresh Suit, &c. and upon such Matter found by such Inquest, a Restitution shall be awarded, &c. Also [e] if an Appellee die in Prison, it seems, That the like Inquiry shall be made by Inquest of Office, and thereupon a Restitution awarded, &c. And [f] if an Appellee be outlawed, or have the Benefit of his Clergy before Conviction, or stand mute, or challenge peremptorily above twenty Jurors, or break from Prison, perhaps a Restitution shall be awarded upon such an Inquest's Finding the fresh Suit, without any farther Inquiry whether the Appellee were guilty or not; because by refusing to take his Trial, he tacitly seems to admit himself guilty. Also if one bring an Appeal against two, whereof one is attainted, and the other acquitted; yet [g] it seems, he shall have a Restitution. But [h] if both the Appellees had been acquitted, it seems, That the Appellant should never have his Goods again, though it were expresly found that they were his Goods, but he shall forfeit them to the King for his false Appeal. But *Quære* if this ought not to be understood of such Goods only [i] as were before seised to the King's Use, as having been waived, &c.

Sect. 54. As to the fifth Particular, *viz.* Whether the Appellant's Title to such Restitution, shall be preferred to any subsequent Title gained in the Goods; It seems clear, That the Appellant's Title to such Restitution shall not [k] be barred by any Seisure of such Goods, as being Waifs, or Estrays, or the Goods of Felons, &c. nor [l] even by a Sale of them, *bonâ fide*, made in Market overt, &c. And by the like Reason it is certain, that the Prosecutor of an Indictment, since 21 *H.* 8. 11. set forth more at large in the next Section, shall not be barred of his Restitution by any such Seisure, or Sale, &c.

Sect. 55. As to the sixth Particular, *viz.* Whether there shall be a Restitution of the Goods stoln, upon any other Prosecution besides that of Appeal; It seems to be clearly agreed, [m] That by the Common Law it could not be had upon any other Prosecution whatsoever: But to remedy this Inconvenience, it is enacted, by 21 *H.* 8. 11. *That if any Felon or Felons, do rob, or take away any Money, Goods or Chattels, from any of the King's Subjects, from their Persons or otherwise, within this Realm, and thereof the said Felon or Felons be indicted, and after arraigned of the said Felony, and found guilty thereof, or otherwise attainted by Reason of Evidence given by the Party so robbed, or Owner of the said Money, Goods or Chattels, or by any other by their Procurement; that then the Party so robbed, or Owner, shall be restored to his said Money, Goods and Chattels; and that as well the Justices of Gaol-Delivery, as other Justices, after whom any such Felon or Fe-*

[a] 44 Ed. 3. 44. pl. 57. Fitz. Coron. 95, 162, 318, 319. Avowry, 151. S. P. C. 165. Letter D. 166.
[b] Fitz. Coro. 95.
[c] Vide infra in the Chapter concerning Judgment. Contra 4 E. 4. 11. b.
[d] S. P. C. 166. 7 H. 4. 31. pl. 16. Fitz. Coron. 81, 194, 379, 380.
[e] Fitz. Coron. 379. Forfeiture, 15. S. P. C. 166.
[f] 1 H. H. P. C. 540. 21 Ed. 4. 16. pl. 7. 10 H. 4. 5. pl. 18. 40 Ass. 39. 2 R. 3. 13. pl. 31. 8 H. 4. 1. pl. 2. 26 Ass. 32. Fitz. Coron. 42, 71, 194, 217, 379, 466. S. P. C. 166. 2 Leon. 108.
[g] S. P. C. 166.
[h] Fitz. Coron. 367, 368. 5 Co. 110. a.
[i] Vide supra, Sect. 48.
5 Co. 110. a. S. P. C. 186. Contra 3 Inst. 227.
[k] S. P. C. 186. 5 Co. 109. 21 Ed. 4. 16. pl. 7. Keyling 35, 47. See the Books cited Sect. 49. Quære Hetley 64, 65. Fitz. Avowry, 151. Coron. 71, 318, 319. Bro. Appeal, 24.
[l] Keyling 34, 47. Quære Moor 360. Popham 84. 1 And. 344. 1 H. H. P. C. 543, 544.
[m] 4 H. 7. 5. pl. 1. Fitz. Coron. 62, 460. S. P. C. 66. Letter E. 165, 167. Letter A. H. P. C. 212. Latch 144. 1 H. H. P. C. 542.

lons shall be found guilty, or otherwise attainted, by Reason of Evidence given by the Party so robbed, or Owner, or by any other by their Procurement, have Power by the said Act to award, from Time to Time, Writs of Restitution for the said Money, Goods and Chattels, in like Manner as though any such Felon or Felons were attainted at the Suit of the Party in Appeal.

Sect. 56. Sir *William Saundford*, [a] in his Construction of this Statute, seems to incline to an Opinion, That the Party may have a Restitution by Virtue of it without making any fresh Suit; and this seems to be agreeable to Practice, and the Purport of the first Part of the Statute, which seems to require no more in Order to intitle the Party to a Restitution, than that the Indictee be found guilty, or otherwise attainted by his Evidence, *&c.* Yet if it shall plainly appear to the Court, That the Party hath been guilty of gross Neglect in prosecuting the Offender, it may reasonably be argued, That he is not intitled to a Restitution; for the latter Part of the Statute, by ordaining, That Writs of Restitution shall be awarded as though the Felon had been attainted in an Appeal, seems to imply, That it is a sufficient Favour, within the Intentions of the Makers of the Statute, to the Prosecutor of an Indictment, to give him a like Remedy for a Restitution of his Goods, as the Common Law gave to the Plaintiff in an Appeal; but it is certain, [b] That the Plaintiff in an Appeal, who appears to have been guilty of such a Neglect, cannot demand a Restitution by the Common Law. And the Construction I would contend for will appear the more reasonable, if it be considered, that it hardly can be imagined to be the Intention of the Makers of the Statute, to give the Party a greater Benefit from a Conviction grounded on his own Evidence, as a Conviction on an Indictment may be, than from a Conviction on the Evidence of others, as a Conviction in Appeal must be. However, if it shall appear to the Court, upon the Evidence at the Trial or otherwise, That the Party has been reasonably diligent in prosecuting the Offence, I readily grant, That the Justices may, if they think fit, in their Discretion award a Restitution, without making any Inquiry concerning the fresh Suit; but this seems to be no more than they may also do in Appeal, if they think fit, as I have already more fully endeavoured to shew in Section 52.

[a] S. P. C. 167. 1 H. H. P. C. 545.

[b] Supra Sect. 50, 51, 52.

Sect. 57. As to the seventh Particular, *viz.* Whether there shall be a Restitution to any Goods not mentioned in the Appeal; There is no [c] Doubt, but that if a Man be robbed of several Goods by the same Person, either at the same or different Times, and such Goods be seised as Waifs, *&c.* and afterwards the Party, in his Appeal for the Robbery, mention some of those Goods only, and omit the rest, and the Appellee be convicted, *&c.* the Appellant shall be restored to such of the Goods only as were mentioned in the Appeal, and the rest shall be confiscated, not only in Respect of that Favour which the Law presumes that the Appellant beareth to the Felon, in making the Charge against him easier than it ought to have been, which might possibly have given him an Opportunity to have escaped, but also because, as it seemeth, the Restitution ought regularly to be grounded on the Record of the Appeal; and by that no other Goods can appear to have been stoln than what are mentioned in it: But whether an Appellant, who had, before his Appeal brought, lawfully regained the Possession of his Goods stoln, shall forfeit to the King such of them as he leaves out of his Appeal, doth neither clearly appear from the principal [d] Case concern-

[c] Fitz. Coron. 100. H. P. C. 184. 3 Inst. 227. 5 Co. 110. a. S. P. C. 186. 1 H. H. P. C. 538.

Vide supra, Sect. 49, 54.

[d] Fitz. Coron. 100.

concerning this Matter, nor from any of the Books above cited, which ſeem chiefly to rely on the Authority of it. But there is a ſpecial [a] Caſe wherein the Appellant ſhall recover Things which were neither ſtoln from him, nor mentioned in his Appeal; as where the Appellee ſells [b] the Things ſtoln, or exchanges [c] them for ſome other Thing, before the Appeal brought, and the Money taken on the Sale, or Thing given in Exchange, are ſeiſed to the King's Uſe, *&c.* in which Caſe they ſhall be delivered to the Appellant, on the Conviction of the Appellee, though they were never in his Poſſeſſion before; for he appears to be in no Manner of Fault, and there is no Reaſon that he ſhould be prejudiced by the Act of the Felon. And I take it for granted, That in all theſe Caſes the Law is the ſame at this Day in Relation to a Reſtitution, by Force of the above cited Statute of 21 *H.* 8. to the Proſecutor of an Indictment.

[a] Vide Fitz. Coron. 323. Bro. Reſtitution, 22. Property, 34. 2 Bulſt. 310.
[b] Noy 128.
[c] Cro. El. 661.

And now I am come to an Appeal of Rape, for the better Underſtanding of the Nature whereof, I ſhall conſider,

1. By whom, and in what Manner it may be brought.
2. In what County.
3. Within what Time.

Sect. 58. As to the firſt Point, *viz.* By whom, and in what Manner an Appeal of Rape may be brought; It ſeems, [d] That by the Common Law, it might be brought by any Woman who had been raviſhed, againſt the Raviſher, whether ſuch Perſon raviſhed were the Nief [e] of the Raviſher, or a Free Woman, and whether ſhe were a Virgin, Wife or Widow; neither [f] do I find that ſhe could be barred of her Appeal at the Common Law, for conſenting after the Rape, to the Raviſher, as ſhe may [g] be at this Day, by Force of the Statutes of *Weſtminſter* 2. 34. & 6 *Ric.* 2. 6. But it ſeems that a Woman lawfully married, can neither [h] by the Common Law, nor by Force of any Statute, bring ſuch an Appeal without her Husband, as one married *de facto* only, and not *de jure*, perhaps may.

Sect. 59. But howſoever the Common Law might ſtand in Relation to Appeals of Rape, it ſeems, That they were wholly taken away by the Statute of *Weſtminſter* 1. 13. by which the Offence of Rape was reduced to a Treſpaſs only, and conſequently puniſhable only by an Action, or Indictment of Treſpaſs: But afterwards, Appeals of Rape were given again by the Statute of *Weſtminſter* 2. 34. by which it is enacted, *That if a Man from thenceforth do raviſh a Woman married, Maid or other, where ſhe did not conſent, neither before nor after, he ſhall have Judgment of Life and Member. And likewiſe where a Man raviſheth a Woman married, Lady, Damſel or other, with Force, altho' ſhe conſent after, he ſhall have Judgment as before is ſaid, if he be attainted at the King's Suit, and there the King ſhall have the Suit.*

Sect. 60. It ſeems to be ſo clear, [i] That this Statute impliedly gives an Appeal to the Woman who does not conſent to the Raviſher, that it ſeems needleſs to endeavour to prove it; but it is obſervable, [k] That the Statute does not reſtore the old Common Law in Relation to ſuch Appeals, as it would have done, if it had only repealed the abovementioned of *Weſtminſter* 1. 13. but makes a new Law in Relation to them;

[d] Bracton 147, 148. Fleta, Lib. 1. Chap. 25. Sect. 14. 2 Inſt. 180. See Book 1. Ch. 41. Sect. 7. Contra 2 Inſt. 433. 1 Inſt. 123. b.
[e] Littleton, Sect. 190. Contra Fitz. Coron. 17. S. P. C. 98. b.
[f] Vide Bract. 147. S. P. C. 61. 148. Letter A.
[g] Vide 2 Inſt. 433, 434. 1 H. H. P. C. 632. Infra Sect. 59, 60, 61.
[h] 8 H. 4. 21. pl. 2. 11 H. 4. 14. S. P. C. 98. b.
[i] 47 Aſſ. 6. Littleton, Sect. 190. 2 Inſt. 433. S. P. C. 6, 81. Contra Fitz. Utlagary, 49. Bro. Coron. 169.
[k] Vide ſupra, Ch. 10. Sect. 52.

from whence it follows, That all Appeals of Rape at this Day, must [a] conclude *contra formam Statuti*.

Sect. 61. It is farther enacted, by 6 *Rich.* 2. 6. in the following Words, *Against the Offenders and Ravishers of Ladies, and the Daughters of Noblemen, and other Women in every Part of the Realm, in these Days offending more violently, and much more than they were wont: It is ordained and stablished, That wheresoever, and whensoever such Ladies, Daughters and other Women aforesaid be ravished, and after such Rape do consent to such Ravishers, That as well the Ravishers as they that be ravished, and every of them, be from thenceforth disabled, and by the same Deed be unable to have or challenge all Inheritance, Dower or joint Feoffment after the Death of their Husbands and Ancestors. And that incontinently in this Case, the next of the Blood of those Ravishers, or of them that be ravished, to whom such Inheritance, Dower or joint Feoffment ought to revert, remain or fall after the Death of the Ravisher, or of her that is so ravished, shall have Title; That is to say, after the Rape to enter upon the Ravisher, or her that is ravished, and their Assigns, and Land-Tenants, in the same Inheritance, Dower or joint Feoffment, and the same to hold in State of Inheritance: And that the Husbands of such Women, if they have Husbands, or if they have no Husbands in Life, that then the Fathers, or other next of their Blood, have from thenceforth the Suit to pursue, and may sue against the same Offenders and Ravishers in this Behalf, and to have them thereof convict of Life, and of Member, although the same Women after such Rape, do consent to the said Ravishers. And the Defendant in this Case shall not be received to wage Battel, but the Truth of the Matter shall be tried by Inquisition of the Country. Saving always to our Lord the King, and to other Lords of the Realm, all their Escheats of the said Ravishers, if peradventure they be thereof convict.*

[a] 9 Ed. 4. 26. a. Fitz. Enditement, 18. Dyer 202. pl. 68. Vide infra Sect. 70.

In the Construction of this Statute the following Points have been holden.

Sect. 62. First, That [b] in an Appeal brought upon it by a Husband for the Rape of his Wife, it is a good Plea, That the Appellant and Woman ravished were never lawfully married, which shall be tried by the Bishop's Certificate, who, if the Marriage were unlawful by Reason of a Precontract, &c. ought to certify against the Appellant.

Sect. 63. Secondly, That there is no [c] Necessity to alledge, That the Woman did consent to the Ravisher, in a Count which rehearses the Statute, and concludes that the Rape was against the Form of it; which implies, that the Woman consented, &c.

Sect. 64. Thirdly, That [d] if a Woman who hath neither Husband nor Father, be ravished by her next of Kin, and consent to him, the next of Kin to the Ravisher shall have the Appeal.

Sect. 65. Fourthly, That [e] whosoever happens at the Time to be next Heir to the Person so ravished, and consenting, &c. shall have the Appeal, and also enter [f] into the Lands of the Person ravished, and retain them against any other who shall afterwards happen by Matter *ex post facto* to become Heir; and therefore where a Woman having Issue only a Daughter, consents to a Ravisher, and the Daughter enters, and then a Son is born to such Woman, the Daughter shall retain the Lands, because she took them by Virtue of a Title given by the Statute which first vested in her as a Purchaser, and never was in any Ancestor.

[b] 11 H. 4. 13. 14. Fitz. Coron. 86, 228. Bro. Parliament, 89.

[c] 11 H. 4. 14. Fitz. Coron. 86, 228. S. P. C. 81. Letter C. Dy. 312. pl. 86, 202. pl. 68.

[d] 2 Inst. 434. Vide supra Sect. 39, 40. 1 H. H. P. C. 632.

[e] S. P. C 61. b.

[f] Fitz. Assise, 27. 5 Ed. 4. 6. a 9 H. 7. 25. a. Long quinto Ed. 4. 60, 61. 1 Co. 95. a 98. 137. b. 3 Co. 61. a 62. a. Pl. Com. 56. b 1 H. H. P. C. 631.

[a] Long quinto, Ed. 4. 58, 59, 60. Bro. Entry Congeable, 94. 5 Ed. 4. 5. pl. 24. Fitz. Aſſiſe, 27.

Sect. 66. Fifthly, That [a] the next in Remainder or Reverſion, to whom the Lands of the Woman who conſents to a Raviſher would come if ſhe were dead, ſhall enter and retain her Lands by Virtue of the Statute, provided he be of Kin to her, albeit another Perſon be nearer; yet it ſeems, That the Perſons ſo intitled to the Lands cannot have an Appeal of Rape, where there is another nearer of Kin; for tho' the Clauſe relating to the Entry into the Lands ſeems to intitle ſuch of the next of Kin, to whom the Inheritance would fall after the Death of the Party, whether they be abſolutely neareſt or not; yet the Clauſe relating to the Appeal ſeems to extend to none but the Husband, or Father, or very next of Kin.

[b] Long quinto, Ed. 4. 58. Pl. Com. 42, 43.

Sect. 67. Sixthly, That it is not [b] ſufficient in ſetting forth the Title of the Perſon claiming the Lands by Virtue of the Statute, to ſay in general, That he is next of Blood to whom the Inheritance would fall, *&c.* without ſhewing ſpecially in what Manner he is ſo, *&c.*

[c] Long quinto, Ed. 4. 59, 60, 61. Bro. Entry Congeable, 64. 5 Ed. 4. 5. pl. 24.

Sect. 68. Seventhly, That it is not [c] concluſive Evidence to prove the Woman's Conſent to the Raviſher, to ſhew, That ſhe lived with him ſome Years as his Wife, and had a Child by him, if all the Time ſhe was under his Power, and never at her Liberty.

[d] Pl. Com. 364. See 1 Danv. Abr. 698. pl. 12. 669. 700. Letter B. 1 Inſt. 79.

Sect. 69. Eighthly, That [d] if the Party raviſhed and conſenting to the Raviſher, be under the Age of twelve Years, ſhe ſhall not loſe her Lands by the Intent of the Statute, for that the Conſent of a Woman under that Age is looked upon as given by one uncapable of Diſcretion, and therefore is not regarded by the Law.

[e] S. P. C. 61. Letter C. See 1 H. 6. 1. pl. 1. Bro. Rape, 4.
[f] S. P. C. 81. Letter C. See 1 H. 6. 1. pl. 1. Bro. Rape, 4.
[g] Vide 5 H. 7. 17. pl. 10.
[h] Supra Sect. 59, 60.
[i] 5 H. 7. 17. pl. 10. Cro. Car. 564. 6 Mod. 140.

Sect. 70. Ninthly, That [e] in Appeals brought on this Statute, the Count ought to rehearſe it: But I do not find any Reſolution cited to maintain this Opinion. It is true indeed, That in the Year-Book of 11 *H.* 4. 13, 14. the Statute is recited in an Appeal grounded on it: But it is not there ſaid to be neceſſary to be ſo recite; neither do I find any Reaſon given why an Appeal may not as well be grounded on this Statute without reciting it, as on the Statute of *Weſtminſter* 2. 34. as [f] it is agreed that it may be: If it be ſaid, [g] That the Common Law gave the ſame Appeal as is given by the Statute of *Weſtminſter* 2. and therefore there is no Need to recite it; but that there never was ſuch an Appeal at the Common Law as is given by the Statute of *Rich.* 2. and therefore the Appeal grounded on it ought to recited it; it may be anſwered, That the ſaid Statute of *Weſtminſter* [h] does not revive the old Common Law in Relation to ſuch Appeals, but makes a new Law in Relation to them; ſo that Appeals brought upon it, do altogether as much depend upon it, as thoſe brought on the Statute of *Rich.* 2. do on that. Neither [i] does there appear to be any ſuch Rule, That in Indictments, or Actions grounded on Statutes which give a Remedy in Caſes which were no Way provided for by Law, there is a Neceſſity to recite ſuch Statutes; and indeed at beſt it ſeems but Surplus to recite what the Court is bound *ex Officio* to take Notice of.

[k] Supra Sect. 35, 47.
[l] 3 H. 7. 12. pl. 4. Fitz. Viſne, 28. Bro. Appeal, 83. S. P. C. 63. Letters E, F. H. P. C. 186.

Sect. 71. As to the ſecond Point, *viz.* In what County an Appeal of Rape may be brought; There is no Doubt, but that this, like all other [k] Appeals, is a local Action, and conſequently ought to be brought in the County wherein the Felony was done. And therefore if a Man take a Woman by Force in one County, and carry her into another, and there raviſh her, the Appeal [l] ſhall be brought only in the County wherein the Rape was committed; for the Taking in the other was no more than a Trespass, and needs not be taken Notice of at all in the Appeal of the Rape; and if it be, is only looked upon as Surplus.

Sect. 72. As to the third Point, *viz.* In what Time an Appeal of Rape may be brought; It seems, That at this Day it may be brought in any reasonable [a] Time, the Judgment [b] whereof lies in the Discretion of the Court, for that at the Common Law there was no certain Time limited for the Bringing of it; and the Statute of *Westminster* 1. 13. by which the Offence of Rape was turned into a Trespass, and forty Days limited for the Suit of the Person ravished, is repealed; and the Statute of *Gloucester* 9. which requires that Appeals be brought within the Year and Day, extends only to Appeals of Death; and the Statute of *Westminster* 2. 34. which makes Rape a Felony again, limits no Time for the Bringing of it, but leaves it to the Construction of Law, which shall be agreeable to the ancient Rules of Law in such Points, wherein the Statute is silent.

[a] S. P. C. 63. Letter C. H. P. C. 186. 1 H. H. P. C. 632, 633.
[b] Vide supra Sect. 51, 52. Littleton, 69. 2 Inst. 56. Supra, Sect. 33, 48.

Sect. 73. And now I am come to an Appeal of Arson; [c] but the Learning relating to it seeming to be altogether obsolete at this Day, I shall refer the Reader to the Old [d] Books for it.

[c] 1 Inst. 288. a.
[d] Fleta lib. 1. chap. 37. Bract. lib. 3. chap. 27.

Having thus endeavoured to shew in what Courts Appeals may be brought, and the several Kinds of them, and examined the Particulars which seemed most properly to come under the Consideration of each Kind, I shall now proceed to examine some other Matters concerning them, wherein I shall consider them all together. As,

1. In what Cases the Appellant and Appellee are to appear in proper Person, and where by Attorney or Guardian.
2. How the Appellant ought to declare.
3. How he may be nonsuited.
4. For what Faults the Writ may be abated.
5. What may be pleaded in Bar of an Appeal.
6. Where the Appellant and his Abettors shall render Damages to the Appellee for a false Appeal.
7. Where the Appellant is to be fined.

Sect. 74. As to the first Point, *viz.* In what Cases the Appellant and Appellee are to appear in proper Person, and where by Attorney, or Guardian: It seems, That by the Common Law neither [e] Plaintiff nor Defendant in any Appeal whatsoever, whether of Felony or Mayhem, [f] could make an Attorney, but must appear either by Guardian [g] or in proper Person, on every [h] Day of Continuance, except in some special Cases; as where the Defendant being convicted in an Appeal of Felony prayed the Benefit of his Clergy, and the Plaintiff replied, that he had been twice married, in which Case he might [i] be admitted to go on with the Suit by Attorney, because he had nothing more to do but to get a Certificate of the Bigamy from the Bishop, which, as it was [k] said any Stranger might procure as well as the Plaintiff. *Sed quære*; for it is said, [l] That none can demand Execution but the Plaintiff, and that the Plaintiff cannot do it but in proper Person; from whence it seems reasonable to argue, That he ought in all other Cases, as well to carry on his Suit in proper Person. But it seems [m] clear, That after a Defendant is acquitted, he may appear by Attorney for the Recovery of his Damages against the Abettors, *&c.* And it is enacted [n] by 3 *H.* 7. 1. *That*

[e] 2 Inst. 313. Carth. 55, 56. 3 Mod. 268. Salk. 59, 62, 64. Bro. Attorney, 64, 78. 2 Ri. 3. 13. pl. 38. Bro. Appeal, 112. Rastal's Entries, 47.
[f] 2 Inst. 313. F. N. B. 27. F. Contra Fitz. Attorney, 104. 21 H. 7. 39. pl. 54.
[g] Supra Sect. 30.
[h] 1 H. 7. 27. pl. 3. Fitz. Utlagary, 34.
[i] 40 Ass. 17. Fitz. Attorney, 39, 90. 40 Ed. 3. 42. pl. 23. S. P. C. 135. Vide Fitz. Coron. 13.
[k] 11 H. 4. 11. b. S. P. C. 135. Fitz. Coron. 13.
[l] 21 Ed. 4. 72, 73.
[m] 8 Ed. 4. 3. pl. 5. Fitz. Attorney, 24.
[n] F. N. B. 26.

That the Appellant in any Appeals of Murder or Death of a Man, where Battel by the Courſe of Common Law lies not, may make Attorney and appear in the ſame, in the ſaid Appeals after they be commenced, to the End of the Suit and Execution of the ſame. But [a] if a Defendant or Plaintiff appear and plead by Attorney where they ought not, and the Court receive the Plea and adjourn the Cauſe; it ſeems, That the Appeal is diſcontinued, becauſe ſuch Appearance was meerly void in Law. [50]

[a] Salk. 59, 62. Carth. 56. Skin. 670.

As to the ſecond Point, *viz.* In what Manner the Appellant ought to declare; I ſhall refer the Reader for Precedents of Counts in Appeal, to *Staundford*'s [b] *Pleas of the Crown*, and the Books [c] of *Entries*, and ſhall in this Place conſider only the following Particulars,

[b] S. P. C. 78. 79.
[c] Raſtal's & Coke's Entries, Titles Appeal & Mort. Tremaine 15 to 33.

1. In what Manner ſuch Count muſt purſue the Writ.
2. How it ought to ſet forth the Subſtance and Matter of Fact.
3. How the Circumſtances of Time and Place.
4. Whether one and the ſame Count ought to be againſt thoſe who do not appear as well as againſt thoſe who do appear, and againſt the Acceſſaries as well as the Principals.

Sect. 75. As to the firſt Point, *viz.* In what Manner the Count in Appeal muſt purſue the Writ; I ſhall take it for granted, That this, like all other Counts in other Actions, muſt in Subſtance [d] agree with the Writ, which ſhall be abated, if the Count vary from it in any material Point. And therefore in a Common Appeal of Death, if the Appellant declare, That the Appellee traiterouſly killed the Perſon deceaſed, as he was going to ſuccour the King in his Wars, the Writ ſhall be abated [e] becauſe that contains no Charge of Treaſon. So alſo if the Plaintiff, in an Appeal of Mayhem, declares, That the Appellee beat as well as maimed him, the Writ ſhall be abated [f] becauſe that mentions not any Battery.

[d] Finch of Law 357.
[e] Bro. Appeal, 12. 45 Ed. 3, 25. pl. 36. 21 Ed. 3. 23. pl. 16. S. P. C. 78. Letter C.
[f] Fitz. Coro. 110. Supra Sect. 20.

As to the ſecond Point, *viz.* In what Manner the Count in Appeal ought to ſet forth the Subſtance and Manner of the Fact, I ſhall obſerve the following Particulars.

Sect. 76. I. That where ſeveral are preſent at the Fact, and one only actually does it, and the others abet and encourage him, it is in the Election of the Plaintiff, either to ſuppoſe [g] in his Declaration, That every one of them did the Fact, becauſe in ſuch a Caſe the Act of one is, in the Judgment of the Law, the Act of all; or to ſhew the ſpecial [h] Manner of the Caſe as in Truth it was, and ſet forth the Fact to have been done only by the Perſon who did it, and the others to have been his Abettors, *&c.*

Sect. 77. II. That no *Periphraſis*, [i] or Circumlocution whatſoever, will ſupply the Want of thoſe Words of Art, which the Law hath appropriated for the Deſcription of the Offence; from whence it follows, That an Appeal of Death cannot [k] amount to a Charge of Murder without the Word *Murdravit*, let it be never ſo exact and particular in ſetting forth the Malice and all other Circumſtances of the Killing; neither

[g] 11 H. 4. 13. b. 4 H. 7. 18. pl. 10. S. P. C. 44. Letter B. 80. Letters C, D. Supra Sect. 19. H. P. C. 187. Bro. Rape, 2, 3. See the Chapter of the Arraignment of Principal & Acceſſary.
[h] 4 Co. 41. Fitz. Coro. 97, 216. 40 Aſſ. 25. 44 Ed. 3. 38. pl. 31. Raſtal's Entries 43. b. 45. pl. 1. 46. pl. 2. 47. pl. 3. Coke's Entries 57. &c.
[i] 5 Co. 121. b. [k] Dyer 261. pl. 26. Far. 16. Cro. Jac. 20. Salk. 377. 9 Ed. 4. 26 b.

[a] can an Appeal of Rape be ſufficient without the Word *Rapuit*; nor [b] an Appeal of Larceny without the Word *Cepit*; nor [c] an Appeal of Mayhem without the Word *Mayhemiavit*; nor any [d] of the Appeals above mentioned without the Word *Felonicè*.

Sect. 78. III. That in every Appeal of Larceny [e] it muſt expreſly appear whoſe the Goods were that were ſtoln, and in every Appeal of Death, [f] who the Perſon was that was killed; becauſe otherwiſe it cannot appear that the Plaintiff is intitled to the Appeal; yet an Indictment *de morte* [g] *cujuſdam ignoti*, or for feloniouſly ſtealing [h] the Goods *cujuſdam ignoti*, is good; for it is ſufficient, That the Perſon injured was under the Protection of the Law.

Sect. 79. IV. That in an Appeal of Rape the Fact ſeems to be ſufficiently [i] declared, by ſhewing, That the Defendant *felonicè rapuit* the Woman, without adding the Words *carnaliter cognovit*, or any others tantamount, or firſt ſhewing the particular Manner of the Terror or Violence, and then concluding, That the Defendant *ſic felonicè rapuit*. Alſo it ſeems, [k] That the like general Manner of ſetting forth the Fact, is ſufficient in an Appeal of Larceny; but it ſeems to be uſual, in Appeals of Larceny, to ſet forth the Price of the Things ſtoln; but whether this be neceſſary for any other Purpoſe than to ſhew, That the Crime amounts to Grand Larceny, and to aſcertain the Goods, in Order thereby the better to intitle the Appellant to a Reſtitution, I leave to be conſidered. But [l] in an Appeal of Mayhem it ſeems neceſſary; Firſt, To ſet forth particularly in what Manner the Hurt was done, and the Conſequences following it, and then to conclude, That the Defendant *ſic felonicè mayhemiavit* the Appellor. Alſo it ſeems clear, [m] That in an Appeal of Death it is neceſſary, not only from the Statute of *Gloceſter* [n] Ch. 9. which requires, That an Appeal of Death ſhall declare the Deed; but alſo from the Common Law, firſt, To ſet forth in the Count all the ſpecial Circumſtances of the Fact, and [o] then to conclude, That the Appellee *ſic felonicè murdravit* the Party; and this being the Appeal moſt in Uſe at this Day, it may not be improper to ſet down theſe following Rules concerning this Matter.

Sect. 80. I. That every ſuch Count ought to ſet forth in what Part [p] of the Body the Wound was given; in which Reſpect, the ſame Certainty ſeems to be required in Appeals as in indictments; and therefore, if the Count ſay only, that the Wound was given *circa pectus*; it ſeems to be vicious, as it hath been reſolved, [q] That an Indictment in the like Manner uncertain is, becauſe it doth not aſcertain the Part wounded, which, for what appears, might have been the Neck, Arm or Belly; and for the like Reaſon ſuch Count ſeems alſo to be vicious, if it ſay, That the Wound was in the Hand, or Leg, or Arm, without [r] ſhewing whether it were the right or left; neither [s] is ſuch an Uncertainty holpen by laying other Wounds with ſufficient Certainty, if there be a general Concluſion that the Party died of the Wounds above mentioned; becauſe the Death being as much imputed to the Wound that is inſufficiently laid, as to the others, it appears not but that it might be chiefly owing to that which is inſufficiently laid, and therefore the Whole is inſufficient. But it hath been reſolved, That it is ſufficient in an Indictment of Death, and therefore it ſeems alſo to be ſufficient in an Appeal, to ſhew, That the Wound

[a] S. P. C. 82. Letter B. 24. Letter D. 96. Letter D. 9 Ed. 4. 26. 20 H. 7. 7. a. 1 Inſt. 124. a.
[b] Fitz. Endictment, 2, 8. S. P. C. 96. Letter B. H. P. C. 207.
[c] Supra, Sect. 17.
[d] S. P. C. 94, 96. Letter C. H. P. C. 206, 207. 20 H. 7. 7. a. 1 Bulſt. 93. Cro. Jac. 20. Dyer 202. pl. 67. Quære 1 H. 6. 1. pl. 1. Contra Fitz. Endictment, 26. Dy. 69. pl. 28.
[e] Raſtal's Entries, 53. b. 54, 55.
[f] Fitz. Endictment, 10. S. P. C. 95. Letter G. 181. b. 22 Aſſ. 94.
[g] H. P. C. 207. 22 Aſſ. 94. Fitz. Coro. 159. S. P. C. 94. Letter G. 181. b. 1 Aſſ. pl. 7. Dy. 99. pl. 61.
[h] Fitz. Enditement, 9, 12. H. P. C. 207. 1 H. H. P. C. 512. 2 H. H. P. C. 181. S. P. C. 95. Letter G. 181. b. Dy. 99. pl. 61. Keilw. 25. b. Moor 466. 18 Aſſ. pl. 15. Contra 9 H. 6. 45. b.
[i] Dy. 202. pl. 67. 11 H. 4. 13. Fitz. Coron. 86. S. P. C. 81. Letter C. H. P. C. 187.
[k] See Raſt. Ent. 53. b. 54, 55.
[l] See Raſtal's Entries 45, 46. and Coke's Entries 50. b. 51, 52, 53.
[m] See Raſtal's Entries 46. b. 47, &c. Coke's Entries 53. b. 54. &c. Salkeld 377. Far. 16.
[n] 2 Inſt. 318, 319. 2 Lev. 140, 141. 5 Co. 120, 121, 122.
[o] 4 Co. 47. a.
[p] 2 Inſt. 318.
[q] 4 Co. 40. b. 5 Co. 121. b. 2 H. H. P. C. 186.
[r] 5 Co. 121. b.
[s] 4 Co. 40. b.

[a] 4 Co. 41. pl. 4. Skin. 443, 553. Carth. 332. 5 Co. 121. b. Cro. Jac. 95. pl. 23. Con. Cro. El. 137. pl. 10.
[b] 4 Co. 41. pl. 4. H. P. C. 207.

was given in the left [a] Part of the Belly, or in the left Part of the Side, or in the left Hand, or in the left Arm, or in the Face, or in the Breaſt, or in the Belly, or even in the Forepart of the Body, in which Caſe the Word *Body* ſhall be underſtood of the Trunk of the Body, between the Neck and Thighs. And it hath been reſolved, [b] That where there is ſuch a ſufficient Certainty, the Addition of a farther uncertain or unintelligible Deſcription, will do no Hurt; as where a Wound is laid *in ſiniſtra parte ventris circa umbilicum*, *&c.* in which Caſe the laſt Words ſhall be rejected as abundant and Surplus.

[c] S. P. C. 79. Letters C, D. 2 Inſt. 318. 4 Co. 40. b. 5 Co. 122. a.
[d] S. P. C. 79. Letters C, D.
[e] 5 Co. 121. b. 122. a.
[f] 2 Inſt. 318. 5 Co. 122. a. 4 Co. 41. b. 42. a.

Sect. 81. II. Such Count ought alſo [c] to ſhew the Length and Breadth of the Wound, that it may appear to the Court that it was mortal; but it is ſaid, [d] That anciently this was not required: And if a Man be ſhot, or run through the Body, with a Bullet, or Sword, *&c.* it ſeems [e] ſufficient to ſay, That the Defendant, with Malice, *&c.* ſtruck the Perſon killed in ſuch a Part of his Body, and gave him in ſuch Part *mortale vulnus penetrans in & per corpus*, *&c.* for this ſufficiently ſhews, That the Wound was mortal. Alſo in ſome Caſes it is impoſſible to ſhew the Length and Breadth of the Wound where a Limb is cut off, and [f] therefore it is plain, That in ſuch Caſes it cannot be required.

[g] Palm. 282. 3 Mod. 202.
[h] 5 Co. 122. 2 H. H. P. C. 184. 1 Bulſt. 124.
[i] Cro. Jac. 635. See H. P. C. 207. and Yel. 28.
[k] 5 Co. 122. Vide Dy. 99. pl. 63.
[l] 4 Co. 44. b. 3 Mod. 202.
[m] 4 Co. 44. b.

Sect. 82. III. It is not ſafe, [g] in any ſuch Count to omit the Word *percuſſit*, where the Fact will bear it; and by the Authority of ſome [h] Books this cannot be ſupplied, in ſuch Caſes, by the Words *dedit mortale vulnus*, *&c.* nor by any other: Yet in *Croke's* [i] *Reports* this Opinion ſeems to be queſtioned, neither do I find any Reaſon given why the Word *percuſſit* ſhould be of ſuch abſolute Neceſſity, for it is not ſo much as pretended in *Long's* [k] Caſe, which ſeems to be the chief Foundation of this Opinion, That this is a Word of Art appropriated to this Uſe; but all that ſeems there contended for is, That where the Death was occaſioned by any external Violence, coming under the Notion of Striking, it muſt expreſly appear, That a Stroke was given. Nor does the Law admit of a leſs exact Certainty, as to the Setting forth the Fact, where the Death was occaſioned by any other Means, as by Poiſon, *&c.* for it hath been reſolved, [l] That an Indictment (which in this Reſpect ſeems not to differ from an Appeal) ſetting forth, That *J. S.* perſuaded the Perſon deceaſed to take a certain poiſonous Potion under a Notion of a Medicine, and that the deceaſed, *Neſciens præd' potum cum veneno fore intoxicatum, ſed fidem adhibens dictæ perſuaſioni dicti* J. S. *recepit & bibit*, is inſufficient, becauſe it doth not expreſly ſay, That the Party received and drank the Poiſon. And it was alſo reſolved, That the Want of ſuch Certainty is not ſupplied by theſe Words immediately following, *Per quod idem* N. *immediate poſt receptionem veneni prædicti per tres horas immediate ſequentes languebat & obiit*, *&c.* and yet there cannot well be a ſtronger Implication that the Poiſon was taken and drank by him; for it being the ſtrict [m] Rule of Law in theſe Caſes to have the Subſtance of the Fact expreſſed with preciſe Certainty, the Judges will ſuffer no argumentative Certainty whatſoever to induce them to diſpenſe with it. For if they ſhould once be prevailed with to do it in one Caſe, the like Indulgence would be expected from them in others nearly reſembling it, and then in others reſembling thoſe, and no one could ſay where this might end; which could not but endanger the Subverting of one of the moſt fundamental Principles of the Law, by giving Room to Judges by Arguments from what the Jury have found, to convict a Man of a Fact which they have not found.

Sect. 83. IV. Such Count ought [a] alſo expreſly to ſhew that the Party died of the Hurt ſpecially ſet forth; and it hath been reſolved, [b] That an Indictment, and from the ſame Reaſon it ſeems that an Appeal, ſetting forth that the Defendant choaked the deceaſed, *qua ſuffocatione obiit*, inſtead of *de qua ſuffocatione*, *&c.* is erroneous; yet where the Death was cauſed by divers Poiſons, or Wounds, *&c.* the Count may ſay in general that the Party died of the ſeveral Poiſons or Wounds above mentioned, without [c] ſaying, That he died of any one of them in particular; for perhaps the Truth of the Caſe might be, That none of them alone, but all together cauſed the Death. Or [d] the Count in ſuch Caſe perhaps may ſay, That the Party died of the firſt Poiſon or Wound, and that he would have died of the ſecond, if he had not died of the firſt, and alſo that he would have died of the third, if he had not died of the two firſt.

[a] 2 Inſt. 318.
[b] 1 Rol. Rep. 137. pl. 20.
[c] 3 Inſt. 50. 135. Quære 4 Co. 40. b.
[d] 44 Ed. 3. 38. pl. 31. 40 Aſſ. pl. 25. S. P. C. 80. Letter C. 4 Co. 40. b.

Sect. 84. V. If the Killing were with a Weapon, the Count muſt [e] ſhew with what Weapon in particular, and yet if upon the Evidence it ſhall appear that the Killing was not by ſuch Weapon, but by ſome other, the Variance [f] is immaterial, and the Appellee ought to be convicted, as ſhall be ſhewn more at large under the Chapter of *Evidence*. And if the Killing were not by a Weapon, but by ſome other Means, as by poiſoning, drowning, ſuffocating, burning, or the like, the Count [g] muſt ſet forth the Circumſtances of the Fact as ſpecially as the Nature of it will admit. But in ſuch Caſes, where no Weapon was uſed, it cannot but be abſurd to require the Mention of one in the Appeal, and therefore the Statute of *Glouceſter*, Ch. 9. which directs generally, That in all Appeals of Death the Weapon muſt be ſet forth, is to be intended only [h] of ſuch Killing in which a Weapon was uſed: For the Law is ſo far from requiring it in other Caſes, that it will not ſuffer an Appeal of Killing by a Weapon to be maintained by Evidence of Killing by any other Means in which no Weapon was uſed; neither will it ſuffer an Appeal of Killing by any of thoſe Means without the Help of a Weapon, to be maintained by Evidence of Killing by a Weapon, as ſhall alſo be ſhewn more at large in the Chapter above referred to.

[e] Raſtal's Entries 46. pl. 2. 47. pl. 3, 4. 49. pl. 6. 51. pl. 11. 2 Inſt. 318. 3 Mod. 158. See the Stat. of Glouceſt. chap. 9.
[f] 2 Inſt. 319. H. P. C. 265. 9 Co. 67.
[g] 2 Inſt. 318, 319.
[h] 2 Inſt. 318, 319.

Sect. 85. It hath been adjudged, [i] That the Words *vi & armis* are not neceſſary in ſuch Appeal, becauſe they are ſo fully implied.

[i] Smith and Bowen, Mich. 7 An.

Sect. 86. As to the third Point, *viz.* In what Manner the Count in Appeal muſt ſet forth the Circumſtances of Time and Place, it is enacted by the Statute of *Gloceſter*, Ch. 9. *That if an Appeal declare the Deed, the Year, the Day, the Hour, the Time of the King, and the Town where the Deed was done, and with what Weapon, the Appeal ſhall ſtand in Effect*, &c. And tho' this more particularly relates [k] to Appeals of Death, yet it ſeems alſo to be generally a good Rule as to the Circumſtances of Time and Place in other Appeals; and therefore I ſhall conſider them all together, and firſt premiſe, [l] That no Omiſſion of any of theſe Circumſtances, where the Law requires them to be expreſly ſet forth, can be aided by the Conviction of the Defendant; and then for the better Underſtanding in what Caſes the Law requires them to be expreſly ſet forth, I ſhall endeavour to ſhew what Certainty the Count in every Appeal ought to ſhew.

[k] 2 Inſt. 317.
[l] 1 R. A. 781. Letter N.

1. The Hour.
2. The Day.
3. The Year and Time of the King.
4. The Place where the Deed was done.

Sect. 87. As to the first of these Particulars, *viz.* With what Certainty the Count in Appeal ought to set forth the Hour, it is observable that all [a] the Precedents of such Counts (excepting only, one [b]) in Appeals of Larceny in *Rastal*'s Entries, which seems to be the only Book of Authority in which any such Counts are to be found; and also all the Precedents in *Coke* and *Rastal* of such Counts in Appeals of [c] *Mayhem*, take Notice of the Hour, as well as those in Appeals of Death; [d] and therefore certainly it is not safe wholly to omit it; yet it hath been holden, [e] That such an Omission is not fatal, even in an Appeal of Death, because the Common Law did not require the Mention of the Hour and the Statute above mentioned is in the Affimative. Yet if the Hour as well as Day be set forth in the Allegation of the Offence of the Principal, it is said to be fatal to mention the Day only in the Allegation of the Offence of the Accessary. But it seems that there is no Necessity in any Case precisely to alledge, That the Fact was done at such an Hour, but that it is sufficient to say, That it was done about such Hour, as appears from every [f] one of the Precedents in *Coke* and *Rastal*, in which the Hour is mentioned, and also from other [g] good Authorities; yet we find the contrary Opinion holden by three Judges against two in *Bulstrode*'s [h] Reports. But it seems [i] certain that a Mistake of the Hour will not be material upon Evidence.

Sect. 88. As to the second of the above mentioned Particulars, *viz.* With what Certainty the Count in Appeal ought to set forth the Day, There can be no Doubt but that every such Count must set forth the Day on which the Fact was done, as appears from all the Precedents cited in the foregoing Section; and also from the Common Form of all other Declarations in all Actions whatsoever, as well of Indictments, for which it is needless to cite Authorities. And if the Fact happened in the Night, it seems [k] most proper to alledge it *in nocte ejusdem diei.* But it is said not to [l] be sufficient to alledge the Fact done about such a Day, or between such a Day and such a Day, but that the very Day must be precisely set forth. And it seems to be insufficient to alledge [m] it on the Feast-Day of such a Saint, without an Addition, if there be another Saint of the same Name, as on St. *John*'s Day, without shewing which Saint is meant, *viz.* the Baptist or Evangelist. Also [n] it seems to be erroneous to set forth the Fact on an impossible Day, as on the thirty-first of *June*, or thirtieth of *February*, for this is of no more Effect than to mention no Day at all. Also it seems clear that an Appeal of Death must not only set forth the Day when the Hurt was given, but also the Day when the Party died of it, as appears from all the Precedents [o] of this Kind both in *Coke* and *Rastal*; and also from the manifest Reason of the Thing, [p] that it may appear that the Party died within the Year and Day after the Stroke, in which Case [q] only the Law intends that the Death was occasioned by it. And it is [r] said not to be sufficient to alledge, That the Defendant assaulted the Party at a certain Day, and feloniously struck him, without expresly adding, That he struck him *adtunc & ibidem*; and yet both Sentences being joined with the Copulative, it is the most natural Import of the whole, That the Stroke and Assault were both at the same Time, *&c.* and such Certainty seems to be sufficient in Declarations [s] in civil Actions, and even in Indictments [t] of Trespasses. But in Indictments and Appeals of Death a more express Certainty is said to be required, because the Stroke which caused the Death, being a Crime

[a] Rast. Ent. 53. pl. 1, 2, 3. 54. pl. 4, 5.
[b] Rast. Ent. 55. pl. 6.
[c] Coke Ent. 50. b. 51. pl. 2. 52. pl. 3. Rast. Ent. 45. pl. 1, 2, 3, 4.
[d] Co. Ent. 53. pl. 4. 56. pl. 5. 57. pl. 6. 59. pl. 7. Rast. Ent. 43. b. 46. pl. 31. 47. pl. 3, 4. 48. b. 49. pl. 6. 50. pl. 10. &c.
[e] S.P.C. 80. b. 1 Bulst. 82. H. P. C. 187.
[f] Co. Ent. 50. b. 51. pl. 2. 52. pl. 3. 53. pl. 4. 56. pl. 5. 57. pl. 6. 59. pl. 7. Rast. Ent. 43. b. 45. pl. 1, 2, 3, 4. 46. pl. 2. 47. pl. 3, 4. 48. b. 49. pl. 6. 50. pl. 10. 57. pl. 11. &c.
[g] 2 Inst. 318. Salk. 59. pl. 2. Skin. 443, 553. 4 Mod. 292. Carth. 17, 333. Tremaine 15, 21.
[h] 1 Bulst. 77, 80, 81, 82, 83. Vide 3 Mod. 158.
[i] H. P. C. 264. 2 Inst. 318.
[k] 2 Inst. 318.
[l] 2 Inst. 318.
[m] Bro. Indict. 47. 3 H. 7. 5. pl. 2.
[n] Moor 555. pl. 723.
[o] See Citations in the precedent Section.
[p] 2 Inst. 318. Bro. Indictment, 41.
[q] B. 1. Ch. 31. Sect. 9, 10.
[r] Dy. 28. as in the Margin. Dy. 8. pl. 28. See B. 1. Ch. 64. Sect. 42. Keilw. 100. Quære. See B. 1. Ch. 64. Sect. 42. 1 Rol. Rep. 295.
[s] Cro. Jac. 362, 443.
[t] Cro. Ca. 271, 525. Cro. Jac. 41.

of a different Nature, and much higher than the Assault, may be well enough intended to have happened at a different Time; and therefore the precise Time of each must be certainly expressed. And even this may be vitiated by a Repugnancy in the Conclusion; for if the Assault and Stroke be alledged in the Premisses on the tenth of *December*, and the Death subsequent on the twentieth of *December* following, and then it be alledged in the Conclusion, that the Defendant in such Manner feloniously murder'd the Party on the tenth of *December* aforesaid, the whole is naught for the Repugnancy; [a] because the Party could not be said to have been murdered, 'till he was dead: And tho' to some Purposes by a Fiction of Law the Offence of the Defendant after the Death of the Party, is punish'd as a Felony from the Time of the Stroke; yet in Truth and Propriety of Speech (which must be observed in legal Proceedings) it is not a Felony but only a Trespass 'till the Death; yet if in such Conclusion it had been alledged that the Defendant in such Manner feloniously murdered the Party on the twentieth of *December* aforesaid, it had been sufficient. But it is said [b] to be the better Way to conclude generally, That the Defendant in such Manner feloniously murdered the Party. And it is certain [c] that a Mistake of the Day will not be material upon Evidence.

[a] 4 Co. 42. 47. H. P. C. 207. 2 Inst. 318. Noy 45. Hetley 35. Dy. 50. pl. 9, 10. Quære Cro. El. 739. pl. 12.
[b] 4 Co. 42. 47. 2 Inst. 318.
[c] H. P. C. 264. 2 Inst. 318.

Sect. 89. It hath been holden that an Allegation of the Day, *prima facie* somewhat uncertain, may be holpen by the apparent Sense of the whole; as where [d] it is alledged, That the Principal such a Day made the Assault and gave the Stroke, and that the Party died on such a subsequent Day, *&c.* and that *A. B.* was *adtunc & ibidem abettans* the said Principal to do the Felony and Murder aforesaid; in which Case it is said that the Words *adtunc & ibidem*, from the manifest Import of the whole, shall be referred to the Time of the Stroke; because by that only the Felony, which *A. B.* is charged to have abetted, was done. Yet if *A. B.* had been said to have been present at the Time of the Felony and Murder aforesaid, *scilicet* on the Day of the Stroke, *tunc & ibidem* abetting the Felony and Murder aforesaid, *&c.* it seems [e] that the Appeal is insufficient as to the said *A. B.* for the Repugnancy; because he is expresly alledged to have been present, and to have abetted the Principal, at the Time of the Felony and Murder, which must be taken for the Time of the Death, by which the Offence, which was before but a Trespass, became Felony and Murder, but by being present at the Time of the Death, it is impossible he could abet a Stroke given so long before; and therefore it is repugnant and inconsistent in such a Manner to alledge it. Nor is such a Repugnancy any way holpen by the subsequent Allegation of the very Day of the Stroke, coming after the Word *Scilicet*, for it is apparent that the Time of the Felony, could not be on the Day of the Stroke, and therefore it rather adds to than helps the Fault to alledge that it was. But [f] the best Way of alledging such Abetment had been to have set forth, That the said *A. B.* was *præsens, auxilians, &c. ad feloniam & murdrum prædictum in forma prædicta faciend'*.

[d] Vide Dyer 164. 60. b. Cro. El. 176. Quære Cro. El. 739. pl. 12.
[e] 4 Co. 42.
[f] 4 Co. 42.

Sect. 90. As to the third Particular, *viz.* With what Certainty the Count in Appeal ought to set forth the Year and Time of the King, there can be no Doubt but that every such Count must expresly set forth in what Year the Fact was done, as appears from the known Form of all other Counts, and also of Indictments. And in an Appeal of Death it is certainly necessary [g] to set forth not only the Year in which the Stroke was given, but also that in which the Death happened, that it may appear that the Death happened within the Year and Day after the Stroke. But it seems clear from all the Precedents, that it is sufficient to shew in what

[g] 2 Inst. 318, 319. Bro. Indictment, 41. Book 1. Ch. 31. S. 9, 10.

Year of the King's Reign the Fact was done, and the Death happened, without ſhewing the Year of the Lord. Alſo it hath been adjudged, [a] that it is ſufficient to alledge the Fact in ſuch a Year of ſuch a King, without ſaying it was in ſuch a Year of his Reign, becauſe it is clearly implied.

Sect. 91. As to the fourth Particular, *viz.* With what Certainty the Count in Appeal ought to ſet forth the Place where the Deed was done, there can be no Doubt but that every Count in an Appeal of Death muſt ſhew [b] the Place where the Death happened, as well as that where the Hurt was given, and this with the ſame [c] preciſe Certainty and Freedom from Repugnancy [d] as is required in Relation to the Time of the Death and Hurt, for which I ſhall refer the Reader to the 89th and 90th Sections of this Chapter, wherein what is ſaid in Relation to the Time of the Hurt and Death is equally applicable to the Place. Alſo it ſeems that a Miſtake of the Place is not [e] material upon Evidence upon not Guilty pleaded, any more than a Miſtake of the Time, provided the Fact be proved at ſome other Place in the ſame County.

Sect. 92. But it ſeems to be not only neceſſary in an Appeal of Death to alledge ſome Place both of the Death and Hurt, and in every Count in every other Appeal to alledge ſome Place, where the Fact was committed, but alſo that ſuch Allegation be in proper Place; for the better Underſtanding whereof I ſhall premiſe, that if the Truth will bear it, it is ſafeſt [f] to lay it in a Town, as the Statute of *Glouceſter* abovementioned directs; but if it were done out of a Town, it ſeems that you may lay it in any other Place from whence a Viſne may come; in Relation to which Matter the Law being in great Meaſure ſuperſeded in civil Actions by the Statute *For the Amendment of the Law*, and chiefly in Uſe in criminal Cauſes, it may not be improper in this Place more fully to conſider it, and for that Purpoſe I ſhall lay it down as a good general Rule, That a Viſne may come from any Place, which is of ſo ſmall a Compaſs, that all who live in or near it may reaſonably be preſumed to have ſome Knowledge of the Perſons living in it, and therefore are eſteemed the moſt proper Judges of the Facts done within its Limits, as being moſt likely to be proved by Witneſſes, and charged upon Perſons with whoſe Integrity and Reputation they are beſt acquainted. And upon this Ground it hath been adjudged, that a Viſne may come not only from a Town, but from [g] a Ward, a [h] Pariſh, Hamlet, [i] Burgh, Manor, [k] Caſtle, [l] or even from a Foreſt, [m] or other Place known [n] out of a Town. Alſo it ſeems [o] clear that whenſoever a Place is generally alledged in Pleading, the Law will intend it to be a Vill unleſs it be mentioned with ſome Addition which ſhews the contrary; or [p] be alledged within a City or Vill, in which Caſe it would be abſurd to take it for a Vill of it ſelf; yet [q] if in Truth there be no ſuch Town, nor Hamlet, nor Place known out of a Town; or [r] if a Fact alledged in a Foreſt, were done in ſome Vill in the Foreſt not mentioned in the Record, the Defendant may plead it in Abatement. Alſo if a Fact done in a Vill within a Pariſh, which contains divers Vills, be in the Count in an Appeal alledged generally in the Pariſh, [r] or a Fact done in a City, which contains divers Pariſhes, be in the Count in an Appeal alledged generally in the City, it ſeems [s] that the Defendant may plead ſuch Matter in Abatement; for otherwiſe he could take no Advantage of the Inſufficiency of the Allegation, becauſe the Place named, as it ſtands

[a] Lev. 140. See 1 Sid. 140.
[b] Hetl. 35. Cro. El. 137. pl. 10. 738. pl. 11. 739. pl. 12.
[c] Dy. 68. pl. 28.
[d] Noy 45. Dy. 50. pl. 9, 10. Cro. Eliz. 196. pl. 13.
[e] H. P. C. 264, 265. Salk. 288.
[f] Fitz. Coro. 80. 2 Inſt. 319. 3 Mod. 158. 4 Mod. 290. Salk. 59, 60.
[g] Yel. 159. 1 Sid. 178. Cro. Jac. 222.
[h] 6 Co. 14. Co. Lit. 125. Salk. 60.
[i] Co. Lit. 125. b. Cro. El. 866. 1 Sid. 326.
[k] 2 Rol. A. 612. pl. 6, 7. 613. pl. 1. 614. pl. 8. 618. pl. 2. Co. Lit. 125. Cro. Jac. 405.
[l] 2 Rol. A. 618. pl. 1. 621. pl. 21. Co. Lit. 125. b.
[m] Cro. El. 200. pl. 26. 1 Sid. 326. 2 Rol. A. 621. pl. 26. Bro. Appeal, 19. Vide Co. Lit. 125. b. Con. Bro. Appeal, 127.
[n] 6 H. 7. 3. pl. 1. Co. Lit. 125. a. b. 2 Inſt. 319. 1 Sid. 326.
[o] Bro. Pleadings, 61. Co. Lit. 125. b. 2 Rol. A. 54. pl. 30, 31, 32. 1 Sid. 88. con. 1 Sid. 326. Carth. 333. Skin. 554.
[p] Cro. El. 732. 1 Sid. 326.
[q] Bro. Pleadings, 61. 6 H. 7. 3. pl. 1. 2 Rol. A. 621. pl. 26. 7 H. 4. 27. a. See 2 Rol. A. 616. pl. 2, 3, 4, 5, 6, 7. 1 Sid. 88.
[r] Cro. El. 200. 7 H. 4. 27. a. 2 Rol. A. 621. pl. 26.
[s] See the Caſes cited under Letter o. 7 H. 4. 27. a. Salk. 59, 60. Co. Lit. 125. b. 4 Co. 14. b. 2 Inſt. 319.

on the Record, muſt, till the contrary be ſhewn, be intended to contain no more than one Town, or Pariſh, on which Suppoſition a Viſne may well come *de vicineto* [a] *civitatis*, which does not exclude the City, but takes in the City and its Neighbourhood within its Juriſdiction, whether ſuch City be within a County, [b] or be a County of it ſelf; excepting only the City of [c] *London*, from whence it ſeems that no Viſne can come, not only by Reaſon of the Largeneſs of its Extent, but alſo becauſe it hath been the conſtant Uſage of Pleading to ſhew the Ward and Pariſh in which a Fact alledged [d] in *London*, was done.

Sect. 93. It hath been alledged that no [e] Viſne can come from the *Wild* of *Suſſex*, not only by Reaſon of the Largeneſs of its Extent but alſo becauſe it ſhall be taken for a Wood without Inhabitants; and therefore it would ſeem inconſiſtent to award the Return of a Jury from it. And yet it hath been holden [f] that a Viſne may come from a Park; alſo it ſeems to be the general Opinion, That a Viſne may come from a Foreſt, as hath been more fully ſhewn in the Precedent Section, from whence it may plauſibly be argued, that it may come as well from ſuch a *Wild*, ſuppoſing it to be a Wood. Alſo it ſeems [g] to be queſtionable whether a Viſne may not come from a Walk in a Foreſt, being alledged as a Place in which a Fact was done; but it ſeems clear that no Viſne can come from it, if it be alledged only as a Liberty, for that no Viſne can come from a Thing incorporeal, [h] but only from a Place. Alſo it hath been holden that no Viſne [i] can come from the Site of a Manor, perhaps for this Reaſon, becauſe it doth not properly ſignifie a Place, but rather the Limits and Situation of a Place.

Sect. 94. As to the fourth Point, *viz.* Whether one and the ſame Count in Appeal ought to be againſt thoſe who do not appear, as well as againſt thoſe who do appear, and againſt the Acceſſaries as well as the Principals. It is ſaid [i] by Sir *Matthew Hale*, That in an Appeal againſt *A. B.* and *C.* if *A.* only appear, yet the Plaintiff ought to count againſt them all, by the better Opinion. And the like ſeems alſo to be holden by Sir *William Staunforde* [k] and *Brook* [l]; yet the Point adjudged in the Principal [m] Caſe, which ſeems to be the chief Foundation of theſe Opinions, ſeems to be no more than this, That where an Appellant hath had Judgment and Execution in one Appeal, he ſhall not afterwards have another againſt Perſons not named in the firſt. And all the Precedents that I can find, either in *Coke* [n] or *Raſtal*, [o] of Counts in Appeals, wherein ſome of the Defendants have not appeared, do indeed mention the Perſons abſent, as well as thoſe preſent, and ſhew in what Manner they were guilty, yet are all of them expreſs that the Appellant *inſtanter appellat* thoſe that appear only; and that he would in like Manner appeal thoſe that are abſent, if they were preſent; by which it ſeems clearly to be implied, That when they ſhall appear, there ſhall be another Declaration againſt them, and that the preſent Declaration is eſteemed only as a Declaration againſt thoſe that do appear. Neither do I find any Difference in the Precedents abovementioned, as to the Form of ſuch Counts in Relation to this Matter, where the Perſons not appearing are Acceſſaries, from that wherein they are Principals. But whether the Omitting of a Perſon in one Appeal be always a good Bar to the charging of him in another, ſhall be conſidered in the following Part of the Chapter, wherein I ſhall treat of the Nature of Pleas in Bar to Appeals.

Sect. 95. As to the third Point, *viz.* How the Appellant may be nonſuited, it is generally holden in ſome Books, [p] that by the Common Law,

[a] 2 Rol. A. 622. pl. 31, 32, 35, 36, 37, 38, 623. pl. 41, 42. 8 H. 5. 10. pl. 20. Cro. Jac. 307, 308. 2 H. H. P. C. 262. Con. S. P. C. 155. b.
[b] See the Authorities cited under Letter m.
[c] 1 Sid. 178. pl. 10. Cro. Jac. 307, 308. 2 Rol. A. 622. pl. 39. Cro. Jac. 150. pl. 10. Quære Cro. El. 732. Con. S. P. C. 154. Letter C. 2 Rol. A. 617. E. 1.
[d] Cro. El. 732.
[e] 1 Sid. 88. 2 Rol. A. 617. pl. 2. Hob. 266.
[f] 1 Sid. 327.
[g] 2 Lev. 307. Contra 1 Sid. 326. 1 Sid. 327.
[h] 1 Sid. 326.
[i] 2 Rol. A. 618. pl. 3. H. P. C. 188.
[k] S. P. C. 65. Letter C.
[l] Brook, Appeal, 28.
[m] 9 H. 4. 1. pl. 7. See 4 Co. 47. Dyer 120. pl. 10.
[n] Coke's Entries 50. b.
[o] Raſtal's Entries 46. pl. 2. 47. pl. 4. 50. pl. 10. 51. pl. 11, 13, 15, 53. pl. 2, 3, 54. pl. 4. See 47 Aſſ. pl. 6.
[p] Bro. Nonſuit, 44. Co. Lit. 139. b. 1 Rol. A. 131. E. pl. 3, 4, 5. 132. pl. 6, 7, 8, 9, 10. 3 Ed. 4. 11. b. Contra Fitz. Nonſuit, 15, 34. Quære Bro. Nonſuit, 6. 20 H. 6. 44. pl. 30. 2 Bulſt. 19.

if a Plaintiff in any Action whatsoever be demanded at any Day of Continuance before Judgment, and do not appear, either in [a] proper Person, or by Attorney or Guardian, as the Law requires, he shall be nonsuited, whatsoever [b] Excuse he may have for his Absence. But it is enacted by 2 *H.* 4. 7. *That if the Verdict pass against the Plaintiff, the same Plaintiff shall not be nonsuited.* And since the Statute it hath been adjudged, [c] that if a Defendant in an Appeal of Murder be found guilty of Manslaughter only, the Appellant cannot be nonsuited; but it doth not appear whether this Resolution be grounded on the said Statute, or on the Common Law; for it seems difficult to maintain that such a Verdict which finds the Substance of the Fact, shall be said to pass against the Appellant, in which Case only the Nonsuit is taken away by the Statute. And therefore perhaps a Nonsuit in this Case may not be suffered by the Common Law, which seems not to have permitted a Nonsuit after a full Verdict, except in such Cases only whereupon some Doubt remained with the Court, as may be reasonably argued from the Authorities above cited under Letter b. But it seems that an Appellant may be nonsuited after a special [d] Verdict, or after a Demurrer [e] and Argument thereupon.

Sect. 96. As to the fourth Point, *viz.* For what Faults the Writ may be abated, [51] I shall premise that in Order to take Advantage of a Defect in the Writ it self, the Appellee [f] ought to demand Oyer of it, which he must do in open [g] Court. And for the better Understanding for what Faults such Writ shall be abated, I shall consider the following Particulars.

1. Where it may be abated by the Court *ex Officio.*

2. Where upon the Exception, or Plea of the Party, but not without such Exception or Plea.

3. What Defects of this Kind may be amended, which without such Amendment might abate the Writ.

As to the first Particular it seems, that the Writ may be abated by the Court *ex Officio,* [h] for the following Faults, whether the Party take Notice of them or not; as,

Sect. 97. I. [i] Where a Writ or Declaration wants those Words of Art which are appropriated by Law for the Description of the Offence; as where an Appeal of Burglary [k] has the Word *Burgaliter* instead of *burgulariter*, or *burglariter*; or an Appeal of Rape wants the Word *Rapuit,* [l] or any Appeal wants the Word *Felonice.* [m]

Sect. 98. II. Where the Declaration varies from the Writ; as [n] by laying the Offence in the Reign of a present King, where the Writ supposed it to have been in the Reign of a former King. Or by giving the Defendant a Name different from that in the Writ; as where the Writ [o] calls him *A. B.* of *C.* Alderman, and the Declaration *A. B.* of *C.* Esquire. Or where the Declaration is otherwise [p] defective in not pursuing the Writ, or in not setting forth both the Substance [q] and Circumstances [r] of the Fact with that Certainty which the Law requires: Or in [s] laying the Offence in a different County, from that in which the the Writ was brought.

Sect. 99. III. Where [t] the Declaration, doth not conclude *contra formam Statuti* in such Cases where by Law it ought.

Sect. 100. IV. Where the Sense is defective for want of a material Word in the Writ; as [u] if the Conclusion be *ibi hoc breve, &c.* without the Word *habeas*; Or where there is a false Concord in the Writ, as *hos* [x] or *hanc breve*; or the singular [y] Number instead of the Plural; or (as some [z] seem to hold generally) any other false *Latin*; or even the Use

[a] Vide supra Sect. 74.
[b] Noy 88. Latch 173. Vide supra Sect. 30.
[c] Moor 407. pl. 546. Cro. El. 465.
[d] 2 Jon. 1.
[e] Co. Lit. 139. b. 2 Jones 1. See 20 H. 6. 44. pl. 30. and the Authorities cited under Letter e.
[f] 2 Bulst. 19. 3 Bulst. 243.
[g] Between Widdrington and Charlton agreed Mich. 10 Annæ.
[h] Finch of Law 226. 2 Danv. Abr. 252. Supra, Sect. 42.
[i] Vide supra Sect. 77.
[k] 4 Co. 39.
[l] Supra, Sect. 77.
[m] Supra, Sect. 18, 77.
[n] Fitz. Brief 219, 231.
[o] Yel. 120.
[p] Supra, Sect. 75.
[q] Supra, Sect. 76, &c.
[r] Supra, Sect. 86, &c. Cro. El. 196.
[s] Supra, Sect. 35, 47, 71. Bro. Appeal, 38.
[t] Supra, Sect. 60.
[u] Fitz. Coro. 121. S. P. C. 82. Letter A.
[x] 9 H. 7. 16. pl. 8.
[y] 10 Ed. 3. 1. pl. 2. [z] H. P. C. 189. S. P C. 82. Letter A. 5 Co. 121.

of a Word which is not *Latin*, tho' [a] by the Change or Addition of a Letter it might be made so. But it seems that such Faults in the Declaration are not fatal if the Writ or Bill on the File be right, as shall be shewn more at large in the following Part of this Chapter.

[a] 2 H. 4. 8. pl. 35.

Sect. 101. V. Generally where the Writ, or Declaration are any otherwise defective in not observing the legal Form, as [b] where in a Writ of Appeal sued by Husband and Wife, the Conclusion is in the Name of the Wife only: Or where the Writ omits [c] either the Name of Baptism or Surname of the Appellant or Appellee, being under the Degree of Nobility, which alone can give so high [d] a Name of Dignity as to supply the want of a Surname.

[b] Fitz. Brief, 252.

[c] Finch of Law 253. 27 H. 6. 3. pl. 24. 2 Inst. 665.

[d] Finch 252. 8 Ed. 4. 24. pl. 2. 2 Inst. 666. 25 Ed. 3. 39. pl. 6.

As to the second Particular, *viz.* Where the Writ may be abated upon the Plea or Exception of the Party, but not without such Plea or Exception, I shall endeavour to shew,

1. Where it may be so abated for the want of fifteen Days between the *Teste* and the Return of the Writ.
2. Where for a *Misnosmer* or wrong Addition.
3. Where for a Defect in the Addition of the Appellant or Appellee.
4. Where for the Multiplicity of Action.
5. Where for making of *J. S.* a Defendant, when there is no such Person.
6. Whether the Defendant may have more than one of such Pleas or Exceptions.

Sect. 102. As to the first Point, *viz.* Where a Writ of Appeal may be abated upon the Exception or Plea of the Party for the want of fifteen Days between its *Teste* and Return. If the Party, before he hath pleaded in chief, do specially shew to the Court such a Defect in the Writ, the later Authorities [e] seem to incline that it ought to be abated, because the Writ is the Foundation of the whole Proceeding, and the Law seems to be in nothing more curious than in strictly keeping up its legal Forms. Yet it hath been resolved, [f] that such a Defect is salved by the Party's Coming in and pleading in chief without taking Advantage of it: Also it hath been adjudged, That where the Original is right, all Defects in the Mesne Process are salved by the Party's Appearance, as shall be shewn more at large in the Chapter concerning Process.

[e] Salkeld 63. pl. 4. Vide 2 Inst. 667. Cro. Jac. 424. pl. 8. 1 Ventris 7. 1 Sid. 406. Cont. 12 Ed. 4. 11. Bro. Error, 169.

[f] Salkeld 63. pl. 4.

Sect. 103. As to the second Point, *viz.* Where a Writ of Appeal may be abated, upon the Exception or Plea of the Party, for a *Misnosmer* or wrong Addition, it seems to be agreed, [g] that if there be a Mistake in the Writ or Declaration as to the Name of Baptism [h] or Surname [i] of the Appellant [k] or Appellee; or [l] as to the Town, Parish or County, Estate, Degree or Mystery, whereof they are said to be, as where [m] one who is neither by Birth, Office, Creation or Reputation an Esquire, or Gentleman, is named with either of those Additions; or where a Gentleman by Birth, who follows a Trade or Husbandry, is named [n] with the Addition of the Trade or Husbandry, and not of Gentleman; or where a Peer, who has more than one Name of Dignity, is not named [o] by the most Noble; or where a Gentleman or Gentlewoman [p] is named Spinster; or a Yeoman [q] is named Gentleman; or [r] if there be no such Town, Parish, nor Hamlet, nor Place known out of a Town, as that whereof either the Appellant or Appellee are said to be; and the Appellee before [s] Imparlance plead such Matter in Abatement, and thereon Issue is joined and found for him,

[g] Finch 363. 364.

[h] 9 H. 5. 1. pl. 3.

[i] H. P. C. 243. Rastal's Entries 49, 51, b. 54. pl. 4. See the Chapter concerning Pleas to Felony.

[k] 9 H. 5. 1. pl. 3.

[l] Bro. Appeal, 44. Rastal's Entr. 108. 11 H. 6. 11. pl. 25. 35 H. 6. 55. 10 Ed. 4. 12. pl. 10. 2 Inst. 667, 668. [m] 2 Inst. 668. 6 Co. 67. [n] 14 H. 6. 15. pl. 51. 2 Inst. 668, 669. [o] 2 Inst. 669. [p] 2 Inst. 668. [q] 5 H. 7. 16. pl. 7. 10 Ed. 4. 16. pl. 19. Rastal's Entries 108. Theloal, lib. 11. Chap. 4. Sect. 19. [r] 3 Mod. 267. Salkeld 59. [s] Finch 434. 21 Ed. 4. 7. 24 b.

the

the Writ ought to be abated. And it seems [a] also to have been holden, that if the Appellant after Imparlance confess that he hath brought his Appeal by a wrong Name, the Writ shall be abated: But it is said [b] to be no Fault to give an Esquire the Addition of Gentleman, *& sic è converso.* Also if one [c] who is usually known and called by the Surname of *B.* be so named in the Appeal, and the Appellee plead that his Name is *C.* and not *B.* and the Appellant reply that the Appellee is, and at the Time of the Purchase of the Original, was as well known by the Name of *B.* as by the Name of *C.* and this be confessed and found for him, it avoids the Plea of the Misnosmer. And if one who hath his usual Abode at *B.* and hath been sometime seen at *C.* be named of *C.* in an Appeal, it hath been questioned [d] whether this be such a Fault as will abate the Writ; because sometimes Appellees may not have any known Dwelling; but if that happen to be the Case, surely it is safest to reply it, and then there seems to be little Doubt but it may make good the Naming of the Party of any Place wherein he has at any Time been. And if a Place where he dwells, and is a House-Keeper, and also another Place where he keeps his Wife and Family be well known, it seems that the Writ may name him of either of such Places, or perhaps of both of them, but is abateable unless it name him of one of them.

[a] 9 H. 5. 1. pl. 3. Bro. Appeal, 38.
[b] Bro. Addition, 44.
[c] Rastal's Entries 50. pl. 10. 54. pl. 4.
[d] 1 Sid. 325. Vide 10 Ed. 4. 12. pl. 10. 4 H. 6. 4. pl. 9.

Sect. 104. As to the third Point, *viz.* Where a Writ of Appeal may be abated by the Exception or Plea of the Party, for a Defect in the Addition of the Appellant or Appellee, it seems that the Common Law in no Case [e] requires any other Description of an Appellant or Appellee, but by their Name of Baptism and Surname, unless they be of the Degree of a Knight, [f] or of some higher Dignity; in which Cases, whether the Name of Dignity be ancient, or (as some say [g]) of a new Creation, as that of Baronet, *&c.* it ought to be added to the Name of Baptism and Surname; and if it be of the Degree of Nobility, it ought [h] to supply the Place of the Surname. And it seems that the Law was [i] so curious in this Particular, that if a Plaintiff in any Action gained a new Name of Dignity hanging a Writ, he made it abateable; but this Inconvenience is remedied by 1 *Ed.* 6. 7. Sect. 3. by which it is enacted, *That if any Plaintiff in any Manner of Action shall be made a Duke, Archbishop, Marquess, Earl, Viscount, Baron, Bishop, Knight, Justice of either Bench, or Serjeant at Law, depending the same Action, that such Action for such Cause shall not be abateable or abated.* But it hath been holden [k] that the Dignity of a Baronet is not within this Statute, because there was no such Dignity at the Time of the making of it.

Sect. 105. To prevent [l] the Inconvenience of troubling one Person for another, which cannot but often happen if there be no other additional Description of the Defendant, it is enacted, by 1 *H.* 5. Chap. 5. *That in every original Writ of Actions personal, Appeals, and Indictments and in which the Exigent shall be awarded, to the Names of the Defendants in such Writs Original, Appeals and Indictments, Additions shall be made for their Estate or Degree, or Mystery, and of the Towns or Hamlets, or Places and Counties of the which they were or be, or in which they be or were conversant. And if by Process upon the said Original Writs, Appeals or Indictments, in the which the said Additions be omitted, any Outlawries be pronounced, that they be void, frustrate and holden for none. And that before the Outlawries pronounced, the said Writs and Indictments shall be abated by the Exception of the Party, wherein the said Additions be omitted.*

[e] 2 Inst. 665. 666. 11 H. 4. 40. pl. 3. 11 H. 6. 11. pl. 25. 10 Ed. 4. 16. pl. 19.
[f] 11 H. 4. 40. pl. 3. 14 H. 6. 14. b.
[g] Hob. 129. 2 Rol. A. 469. pl. 10. 2 Inst. 666, 667. Contra Latch 169.
[h] Supra Sect. 101.
[i] 32 H. 6. 29. b. Contra 24 E. 3. 25. pl. 14. 26 pl. 21. 25 Ed. 3. 83. pl. 6.
[k] 1 Sid. 40. Littleton's Rep. 81. Cro. Ca. 104.
[l] 21 E. 4. 72. 2 Inst. 870. 2 H. H. P.C. 176, 177.

Sect. 106. For the better Explication of this Statute, so far as it relates to the Subject of this Treatise, I shall first premise, that [a] generally such Additions in *English* are as good as in *Latin*; and where there are several Defendants of different Names and the same Addition, it is [b] safest to repeat the Addition after each of their Names, applying it particularly to every one of them; and where a Father hath the same Name and the same Addition with a Defendant being his Son, the Writ is [c] abateable unless it add the Addition of *Puisne* to the other Additions; but where the Father is the Defendant, it is said that there is no need of the Addition of *Eigne*. [d] And if the Son be *in Custodia Mareschalli*, and so declared against, it is said that the Count is good without the Addition of *Puisne*, unless the Father of the same Name and Additions be also in the Custody of the Marshal. And for the better Understanding of the Nature of the several Additions required by the Statute abovementioned, I shall endeavour to shew,

[a] 1 Sid. 101. 1 Keb. 12.
[b] Bro. Additions, 3.
[c] 37 H. 6. 29. pl. 10. 39 H. 6. 46. 4 Ed. 3. 31. pl. 11.
[d] Salkeld 7.

1. What is a sufficient Addition of the Estate or Degree.
2. What of the Mystery.
3. What of the Town, Hamlet, Place, or County, of the Appellee.
4. How the Defect of an Addition may be salved.

Sect. 107. As to the first Particular, *viz.* What is a sufficient Addition of the Estate or Degree of the Appellee, I shall observe; First, That it is necessary to shew the present Estate or Degree of the Appellee [e] at the Time of the Writ, in which Respect this Addition, and also the Addition of the Mystery differs from that of the Place, which is sufficiently set forth by naming the Appellee late of such a Place.

Sect. 108. Secondly, that such Addition must be expressed in such a Manner that it may plainly appear to refer to the Appellee; for it hath been resolved, that to name the Appellee Son of *A.* of *B.* Butcher, is insufficient, because Butcher refers to *A.* rather than to the Appellee.

[e] 9 Ed. 4. 2. pl. 8. 22 Ed. 4. 13. pl. 35. 21 H. 6. 3. pl. 4. 2 Inst. 670.

Sect. 109. Thirdly, That [f] a Bishop of an *Irish* Diocese may be as well described by the Addition of his Bishoprick, as an *English* Bishop may by the Addition of an *English* one; (as it seems to be admitted in the Year-Book of 21 *H.* 6. 3. pl. 4.) But it seems [g] clear, That no one can be well described by the Addition of a temporal Dignity in *Ireland*, or any other Nation besides our own, because no such Dignity can give a Man a higher Title here than that of Esquire.

[f] See Thelo. Lib. 6. cap. 15. sect. 8.
[g] 2 Inst. 667.

Sect. 110. Fourthly, That the Degree of a Serjeant [h] at Law is a good Addition, from whence it may reasonably be argued that a Degree in either University is also a good Addition, as it is holden by Sir *Edward* [i] *Coke* without Question; yet this is made a *Quære* by *Theloal*, [k] and it is holden in the Year-Book of 35 *H.* 6. 55. and admitted by Sir *Edward Coke* in the very Place above-cited, That a Doctor in Divinity may have the Addition of Clerk, which seems not easily reconcileable with the Opinion that the Degree of a Doctor is a good Addition; for if it were, why should not the Writ be abateable for having the Addition of Clerk instead of it, contrary to the allowed Rule [l] in other Cases, that the most worthy Addition is to be used?

[h] Theloal, Lib. 6. Ch. 15. Sect. 12.
[i] 2 Inst. 668.
[k] Theloal, Book 6. Ch. 15. Sect. 13.
[l] Vide supra Sect. 102.

Sect. 111. Fifthly, That *Generosus* [m] or *Armiger* [n] are either of them, good Additions for the Estate and Degree of a Man; *Generosa* [o] for that of

[m] 2 Inst. 667. 668. Bro. Addition, 44, 50.
[n] 2 Inst. 667. Bro. Addition, 44. 50.
[o] 2 Inst. 668.

a Woman

a Woman; and Yeoman [a] and Labourer [b] are alſo good Additions for the Eſtate and Degree of a Man, but not for that of a Woman; and Widow [c] or Single [d] Woman, or as ſome [e] ſay, Wife of *J. S.* are all of them good Additions of the Eſtate and Degree of a Woman, but no ſuch like Addition is good for the Eſtate and Degree of a Man. And Spinſter [f] is a good Addition for the Eſtate and Degree of a Woman, and perhaps alſo for that of a Man.

Sect. 112. Sixthly, That Burgeſs [g] and Citizen, and Servant, [h] are all of them too general, and therefore not good Additions of the State or Degree either of Man or Woman.

Sect. 113. As to the ſecond Particular, *viz.* What is a ſufficient Addition of the Myſtery of an Appellee; having firſt premiſed that the Word *Myſtery* [i] includes all lawful Arts, Trades and Occupations; and [k] that if one under the Degree of a Gentleman have divers of ſuch Arts, Trades or Occupations, he may be named by any of them, I ſhall endeavour to ſhew,

1. What Additions of this Kind are clearly good.
2. What are clearly inſufficient.
3. What are queſtionable.

Sect. 114. And firſt, the following Additions of this Kind clearly ſeem to be good, as Husband-man, [l] Merchant, [m] Broker, [n] Taylor, [o] Point-maker, [p] Smith, [q] Miller, [r] Carpenter, [s] Cook, [t] Brewer, [u] Baker, [x] Butcher, [y] Pariſh-Clerk, [z] Mercer, [aa] Fiſh-Monger, [bb] Dyer, [cc] School-Maſter, [dd] Scrivener, and ſuch like.

Sect. 115. Secondly, The following Additions of this Kind clearly ſeem to be inſufficient, as Maintainer, [ee] Extortioner, [ff] Thief, [gg] Vagabond, [hh] Heretick, [ii] common Informer, and ſuch like.

Thirdly, The following Additions of this Kind ſeem to be queſtionable, as,

Sect. 116. Firſt, Farmer, which by the better [kk] Opinion ſeems to be an inſufficient Addition, becauſe if any Myſtery be implied in the Notion of it, it is that of Husbandry, of which Husbandman is the proper Addition.

Sect. 117. Secondly, Chamberlain, Butler, and Pantler, which are holden [ll] to be inſufficient Additions, becauſe they denote only a ſpecial Kind of Officer, or Servant, and imply nothing, which in the common Underſtanding of the Words comes under the Notion of a Myſtery. And from this Ground it ſeems to follow, that neither Groom [mm] nor Page are good Additions; and yet in ſome [nn] of the old Books they ſeem to have been ſo admitted.

Sect. 118. Thirdly, Hoſteler, which hath been holden [pp] to be a good Addition, and ſeems properly enough to come under the Notion of a Myſtery. And tho' it hath been reſolved, [qq] That any one who keeps an Inn may be ſued by the Addition of a Labourer, upon the Cuſtom of the Realm, for want of due Care of the Goods of his Gueſts; becauſe whoever keeps a common Inn, is in that reſpect liable to anſwer for ſuch Defects, by whatſoever Addition he may be ſtyled; yet this does by no

[a] 2 Inſt. 668. Bro. Addition, 3, 47, 50.
[b] Bro. Addition, 5, 39.
[c] Fitz. Addition, 5. Bro. Addition, 64, 66. Theloal, Lib. 6. cap. 15. Sect. 4.
[d] Fitz. Addition, 5. 14 Ed. 4. 7. pl. 12. Bro. Addition, 64, 66. Theloal, lib. 6. cap. 15. Sect. 4.
[e] 1 H. 4. 5.b. 4 H. 6. 4. pl. 9. Quære Cro. E. 198. Dy. 47. pl. 2, 3, 4.
[f] Dyer 46. pl. 2, 3. 47. pl. 5. 88 pl. 107. 1 Sid. 247.
[g] 2 Inſt. 668.
[h] 2 Inſt. 668. Bro. Addition, 42, 50, 55. 56. con. Bro. Addition, 5.
[i] 2 Inſt. 668. 669.
[k] Bro. Addition, 44. 2 Inſt. 668.
[l] Bro. Addition, 44, 50.
[m] Bro. Addition 40, 50, 66.
[n] 9 H. 6. 65. pl. 19. Theloal. lib. 6. ca. 15. Sect. 5.
[o] Bro. Addition, 15, 39.
[p] 7 H. 6. 1. pl. 7.
[q] 21 H. 6. 54. pl. 9. 22 H. 6. 53. a.
[r] Bro. Additions, 39, 51.
[s] Bro. Additions, 15, 22, 39.
[t] 14 H. 6. 15. pl. 51. Theloal, lib. 6. cap. 15. Sect. 6.
[u] Fitz. Utlagary, 32, 37. 5 H. 5. 7. pl. 16.
[x] 6 Ed. 4. 3. pl. 10.
[y] Bro. Additions, 42.
[z] Bro. Additions, 52, 62.
[aa] 2 Inſt. 668.
[bb] 19 H. 6. 51. pl. 9.
[cc] 5 H. 5. 7. pl. 16.
[dd] 2 Leon. 186.
[ee] 9 H. 6. 65. pl. 19. 2 Inſt. 668. 22 Ed. 4. 1. pl. 1. 2 Inſt. 668.
[ff] 9 H. 6. 65. pl. 19.
[gg] 22 Ed. 4. 1. pl. 1. 2 Inſt. 668.
[hh] 22 Ed. 4. 1. pl. 1.
[ii] 1 Rol. Rep. 190.
[kk] Theloal, lib. 6. cap. 15. Sect. 9. 2 Inſt. 668. Bro. Addition, 10. 28 H. 6. 4. pl. 18.
[ll] Bro. Addition, 50, 58. 2 Inſt. 668. Theloal, lib. 6. cap. 15. Sect. 10.
[mm] 2 Inſt. 668.
[nn] Bro. Addition, 50, 58. Fitz. Coro. 43. 21 Ed. 4. 71.
[pp] Bro. Addition, 35. 21 H. 6. 50. pl. 3.
[qq] 22 H 6. 21. Theloal, lib 6. cap. 5.

Means prove ſuch Perſon may not as well be ſued by the Addition of Hoſteler, but only that he may be ſued as well under any other Addition.

As to the third Particular, *viz.* What is a good Addition of the Town, Hamlet, Place, or County of the Appellee, I ſhall obſerve,

Sect. 119. Firſt, That it is a good Addition of this Kind to Name the Appellee late [a] of ſuch a Town, in which Reſpect this Addition differs from that of the Eſtate, Degree or Myſtery. And it is ſaid that if a Defendant be named of *A.* and late of *B.* it is ſufficient to prove either Addition.

Sect. 120. Secondly, That the conſtant Courſe of Precedents hath made it a ſufficient Addition of this Kind, to name the Defendant of a City which is a County [b] of it ſelf, as *de Londino* [c] *De Norwico, &c.* without more, by which it ſhall be intended that he lives in the County as well as City of *London* and *Norwich, &c.* unleſs he ſhew the contrary, tho' Part of each of theſe Cities lie out of their Counties. However it is certain, that it is not ſufficient to name a Defendant *Londini* [d] or *Briſtoliæ, &c.* becauſe that imports only that he belongs to ſuch Town, and not that he reſides there. Alſo it ſeems clear, [e] That it is not ſufficient to name a Defendant of any Town which is not a County of it ſelf, without ſhewing in what County it lies. Alſo if [f] a Man be named of a Pariſh which contains more Towns, or Hamlets, or Places known out of any Town, or Hamlet, the Defendant may plead ſuch Matter in Abatement, becauſe ſuch an Addition does not purſue the Statute; but a Pariſh ſhall be intended to contain no more than one Town, unleſs the Contrary be ſhewn.

Sect. 121. Thirdly, That if there be two Towns in a County of the ſame principal Name, with different Additions to diſtinguiſh them from one another, as *Great Dale*, and *Little Dale*, or *Upper Dale*, and *Lower Dale*, and the Defendant be named only of the principal Town without any Addition, as of *Dale* only, the Defendant may plead [g] that there are two *Dales* in the ſame County called *Great Dale* and *Little Dale*, and none without an Addition, *&c.* Or according to ſome Opinions [h] either in this Caſe where there are two different Towns called *Dale*, or even where there is but one Town, ſometimes called *Southdale*, and ſometimes *Northdale*, but never ſimply *Dale* without an Addition, the Defendant may plead that there is no ſuch Town as *Dale*, in the ſame County, becauſe Parcel of a Name cannot be ſaid to be the Name. But if there be two Towns of the ſame Name in a County without any Addition to diſtinguiſh them, as it ſometimes happens where they lie at a Diſtance from one another, I do not find any Authority that it is not ſufficient in ſuch Caſe to name the Defendant generally of either of ſuch Towns, without adding any Thing to diſtinguiſh it from the other.

Sect. 122. Fourthly, That if an Appellee live in a Hamlet of a Town, it is ſaid [i] to be in the Election of the Appellant to name him either of the Hamlet or of the Town; but it ſeems that this is to be intended only of ſuch Hamlets which are ſo far eſteemed to be Parts of a Town, that thoſe who live in them are in common Speech indifferently ſtiled ſometimes of the Hamlet and ſometimes of the Town; for I ſee not how the Addition of the Town can be proper, where the Party lives in a Place known by a diſtinct Name, and not Parcel of it.

Sect. 123. Fifthly, That if an [k] Appellee live in a Place known by a ſpecial Name, and lying out of any Town or Hamlet, he may be well

[a] Vide ſupra, Section 107. 21 Ed. 4. 15. pl. 1. 19 H. 6. 66. pl. 6. 1 Ed. 4. 1. pl. 3. 1 Ed. 4. 2. pl. 6, 7. Dyer 213. pl. 44. &c. 9 H. 6. 66. pl. 6. Theloal, lib. 6. cap. 14. Sect. 17.

[b] 2 Inſt. 669.

[c] 4 Ed. 4. 16. pl. 30. 21 Ed. 4. 15. pl. 1. 27 H. 6. 4. pl. 26. 35 H. 6. 12. pl. 21.

[d] 35 H. 6. 12. pl. 21. 7 H. 6. 1. pl. 7. 4 Ed. 4. 10. pl. 13.

[e] Cro. Jac. 167.

[f] 2 Inſt. 669. Vide ſupra, Sect. 92, 103. Theloal, Lib. 6. cap. 14. Sect. 20. 35 H. 6. 30. pl. 37.

[g] 7 H. 6. 39. a. b. 19 H. 6. 35. pl. 77. 8 H. 5. 8. pl. 8. 21 Ed. 4. 51. 10 H. 7. 4. pl. 5. 10 H. 6. 5. pl. 16. Raſtal's Entries 47. a.

[h] 3 H. 6. 8. pl. 8. 14 H. 6. 23. pl. 68. Theloal, Lib. 6. cap. 14. Sect. 23. Contra 7 H. 6. 45. pl. 285

[i] Theloal. Lib. 6. cap. 14. Sect. 14. 2 Inſt. 669. 35 H. 6. 30. pl. 37. 14 H. 6. 23. pl. 68. 2 Inſt. 669.

[k] 2 Inſt. 669. 21 Ed. 4. 37. pl. 1. Fitz. Brief, 467. 7 H. 4. 27. a.

named of ſuch Place; but if he live in any Place known within a Town or Hamlet, it is ſaid to be ſafeſt to name him of the Town or Hamlet.

2 Inſt. 669. 3 H. 6. 31. pl. 21. 2 Theloal, Lib. 6. cap. 14. Sect. 6, 7, 9.

Sect. 124. Sixthly, That the Addition of the Place of Habitation of a Wife is ſufficiently ſhewn by ſhewing that of the Huſband, becauſe it ſhall be intended that the Wife lives where the Huſband does.

[a] 35 H. 6. 12. pl. 21. Bro. Error, 69. Cro. Jac. 610. 2 Rol. Rep. 225. 1 Rol. A. 780. pl. 5. 2 Inſt. 670. 7 H. 6. 39. a. b. ſeems contrary. [b] 1 Sid. 247. 1 Keb. 885. [c] Paſch. 3 Georgii 1.

Sect. 125. As to the fourth Particular, *viz.* How the Defect of an Addition may be ſalved; it hath been adjudged, [a] That if an Appellee named with an inſufficient Addition, or without any, appear and plead to the Appeal, he cannot afterwards take Advantage of the Defect of the Addition, becauſe by his Appearance and Plea he admits himſelf to be the Perſon intended. And ſome have holden, [b] That the Party by his bare Appearance ſalves the Want of an Addition, or a bad one; but this ſeems Contrary to almoſt all the Authorities above cited in Relation to this Matter, which ſeem to admit that the Party before other Matter pleaded may take Advantage either of the Want of an Addition or of a bad one. And accordingly it was lately [c] adjudged in an Appeal of Death between *Reeve* and *Trundal*, that the Want of an Addition of the Appellee was a good Plea in Abatement, and the Writ of Appeal was abated by ſuch Plea.

[d] S. P. C. 82. Letters C, D. H. P. C. 189. Bro. Brief, 192. Cro. El. 695. Fitz. Brief, 548, 774. [e] 10 H. 4. 4. pl. 13. S. P. C. 82. Letter D. Fitz. Coron. 269, 465. See 4 Ed. 3. 9. pl. 21. [f] Supra, Ch. 9. Sect. 39, 40, 41. [g] S. P. C. 82. Letter D. [h] Fitz. Coron. 4. [i] Bro. Appeal, 44. [k] H. P. C. 189. [l] 7 H. 7. 6. pl. 10. Fitz. Brief, 192. Bro. Appeal, 87. S. P. C. 82. Letter C. 2 H. H. P. C. 149. *

Sect. 126. As to the fourth Point abovementioned, *viz.* Where a Writ of Appeal may be abated upon the Exception or Plea of the Party for the Multiplicity of Action, it ſeems [d] clear, That after an Appellant hath appeared on a Writ of Appeal, or even on a Bill of Appeal removed into the Court of King's Bench from before the Sheriff and Coroners by *Certiorari*, if he commence a new Appeal for the ſame Matter, the Appellee may plead in Abatement that ſuch prior Appeal is ſtill depending, &c. But it ſeems [e] clear, That it is no Plea in Abatement of a Writ of Appeal, that the Appellant hath brought a Bill of Appeal for the ſame Matter before the Sheriff and Coroners, becauſe ſuch Bill is not of ſo high a Nature as a Writ of Appeal, but is ſaid to be only in Nature of a Plaint till it be removed into the King's Bench, which ſeems [f] to depend on the Statute of *Magna Charta* 17. ſince which Statute the Sheriff and Coroner cannot proceed to Trial upon a Bill of Appeal, as perhaps they might have done by the Common Law. But after ſuch Bill of Appeal before the Sheriff and Coroners is removed into the King's Bench, if the Plaintiff bring a Writ of Appeal for the ſame Matter, it is holden [g] by *Staundforde*, and ſeems to be admitted in the Year-Book of 4 *H.* 6. 14, 15. and both by *Fitzherbert* [h] and *Brook* [i] in their Abridgments of the ſaid Year-Book, that the Appellee may plead in Abatement that ſuch Bill of Appeal is depending, becauſe after it is removed into the King's Bench, it is of as high a Nature as a Writ of Appeal. Yet Sir *Matthew Hale* [k] ſeems to be of Opinion that ſuch Bill ſo removed is not pleadable in Abatement 'till the Plaintiff hath appeared thereon; perhaps for this Reaſon, that before the Plaintiff hath appeared, it doth not appear of Record that he hath proſecuted the Suit in the King's Court, becauſe the *Certiorari* might have been taken out by a Stranger. Upon which Ground it ſeems to have been reſolved [l] that it is no good Plea in Abatement of an Appeal, that the Plaintiff hath purchaſed another Writ of Appeal returnable at ſuch a Day, &c. and that ſuch Writ was delivered of Record to the Sheriff, becauſe it might be for what appears upon the Record, That the firſt Appeal was ſo far proſecuted by a Stranger; but in the ſame Caſe it is admitted that ſuch prior Appeal depending will abate the ſecond, where it appears on Record that the ſame Plaintiff hath appeared and ſued it, as in praying of Proceſs, &c.

Sect. 127. As to the fifth Point, *viz.* Where a Writ of Appeal may be abated for the making of *J. S.* the Defendant, where there is no such Person, it seems clear, [a] That if there be divers Defendants in an Appeal, and one of them who does not appear be misnamed either as to the Surname, or Name of Baptism, or be described by a wrong Addition, or were dead before the Writ purchased, any of the Defendants who do appear may plead, That whereas the Appeal is sued out against *A. B.* of *C.* in the County of *D.* Yeoman, there was not at the Time of the Purchase of the Writ, nor hath been since, any such Person as *A. B. in rerum natura*, as by the Writ is supposed, whereon if Issue be joined, if the Appellant cannot prove that there now is, or was at the Time when the Writ was purchased, such a Person of such Name and Addition as by the Writ are supposed, it seems that the Verdict ought to go against him, whereupon the Writ shall be abated as to all the Defendants. But it is not [b] adviseable in such a Case to plead that there was not at the Time of the Purchase of the Writ, &c. any such Person as *A. B.* of *C.* in the County of *D.* Yeoman, because it implies a Negative pregnant. Also if a Defendant misnamed or described by a wrong Addition do appear, it seems to be agreed [c] that no other Defendant besides himself can plead the *Misnosmer* or wrong Addition. But I do not find it to be agreed [d] That such a Plea by one Defendant shall abate the Writ as to any other besides himself; but if such Matter when pleaded by another on the Non-appearance of the Defendant, will abate the Writ as to all, it seems, difficult to give a Reason why it should not have the like Effect when pleaded by the Party himself.

Sect. 128. As to the sixth Point, *viz.* Whether the Appellee may have more than one such Plea or Exception, there seems to be no Doubt but that if a Defendant in an Appeal, or even in an Indictment of Felony, think it proper to make Use of never so many Pleas or Exceptions of this Kind, requiring all of them the same kind of Trial, he may take Advantage of them all, [e] unless [f] they be repugnant to one another. Also it seems to be the better Opinion, [g] That he shall have the like Advantage, where such Pleas or Exceptions do not all of them require the same Kind of Trial, but some of them are triable by Matter of Record, and others by the Country. And if such Pleas or Exceptions be all of them triable by the Country, it seems to have [h] been generally agreed, That the Defendant must at the same Time plead also with them all his Matters in Bar, if he have any such, and also plead over to the Felony, (unless where he hath admitted the Fact by the Matter pleaded in Bar,) But if the Plea in Abatement be triable by Matter of Record, it is holden in some Books, [i] that the Defendant is not bound to plead over to the Felony, till such Plea in Abatement be found against him. But [k] the greater Number of Precedents, and constant Practice of late seem to be otherwise. However it seems clear, [l] That whatsoever Matters are pleaded in Abatement of an Appeal, or Indictment of Felony, and found against the Defendant, yet he may afterwards plead over to the Felony.

☞ [52] And in these Respects such an Appeal and Indictment differ from Appeals [m] of *Mayhem* and all civil Actions whatsoever, except only Assizes of Mortdancestor [n], Novel [o] Disseisin, Nusance [p], and *Juris utrum*; [q] for it seems to be a settled Rule, that in Appeals of *Mayhem* and all other civil Actions,

[a] Dyer 348. pl. 14. H. P. C. 189. S. P. C. 82. Letter E. Rastal's Entries 49. a. 52. a. Fitz. Coron. 15, 43, 64. 26 H. 6. 6. pl. 6. 21 H. 7. 34. pl. 35. 7 H. 4. 27. pl. 4.

[b] Bro. Appeal, 111. 6 H. 7. 7. pl. 2. 21 E. 4. 71, 72.

[c] S. P. C. 82. Letter E. See the Books above cited.

[d] 21 H. 7. 31. pl. 13. 5 Ed. 4. 3. pl. 14. 7 H. 4. 27. pl. 4. S. P. C. 82. Letter E.

[e] Finch of Law 363, 364, 385. 4 H. 6. 15. b. 16. a. Bro. Appeal, 44.

[f] S. P. C. 82. Letter E.

[g] Finch of Law 364. Quære 4 H. 6. 16. a. Bro. Appeal, 44.

[h] Finch of Law 363, 364, 385. 21 Ed. 4. 71. pl. 56. Reeves and Trundal. Paschæ 3 Georgii 1. Dy. 88. pl. 107. Rastal's Entries 49. a. b 3 Mod. 266, 267. 27 Ass. pl. 3. Quære 6 H. 7. 7. pl. 2. Shower's Reports 47.

[i] Bro. Appeal, 48, 66. 1 H. 6. 1. pl. 1.

[k] Cro. El. 695. 10 H. 4. 4. pl. 14. 4 H. 6. 15. b. 1 H. 6. 1. pl. 1. Rastal's Entries 47. a.

[l] Finch of Law 363, 364, 385. 27 Ass. pl. 3. 1 H. 6. 1. pl. 1. 2 H. H. P. C. 239.

[m] Cro. El. 495. pl. 14. Popham 115. Owen 59, 60. Moor 457. pl. 628. Noy 36.

[n] Finch of Law 385, 418. 40 Ed. 3. 29. b. 39 Ass. pl. 13.

[o] 1 Ed. 3. 11. pl. 33. Dy. 310. pl. 82. 4 H. 6. 16. a. 1 Jon. 413. S. P. C. 82. Letter E. Cro. Ca. 520. Finch of Law 363, 364, 385.

[p] Finch of Law 363, 385.

[q] 40 Ed. 3. 29. b. Finch of Law 363, 385.

Actions, those abovementioned only excepted, if a Plea in Abatement, triable by the Country, [a] be found against the Defendant, he shall not [b] be suffered afterwards to plead any new Matter, but final Judgment shall be given against him. Also it seems to be agreed [c] that in all other Actions, except those abovementioned, if a Defendant together with a Plea in Abatement plead also a Plea in Bar, or the general Issue, he waives the Plea in Abatement; and the Plea in Bar or general Issue only shall be tried.

Sect. 129. And now I am in the third Place to consider, what Faults of this Kind are amendable, which without such Amendment would abate the Writ. It is to be observed, that Appeals are expresly excepted out of 8 *H.* 6. 12. which is the principal Statute of Amendments: Also it seems [d] to be generally taken for granted, that no criminal Prosecution whatsoever is within any other Statute of Amendments, or any of the Statutes of *Jeofails*; from whence it follows that no Defect is amendable in an Appeal, but such only as is amendable by the Common Law. And therefore it seems to be the better Opinion, that no false [e] *Latin* in a Writ or Bill of Appeal, nor Omission of a Word, [f] nor even of a Letter, [g] nor other Defect or Variance [h] from the proper legal Form, can be amended, because no such Fault is amendable by the Common Law, without the Consent [i] of the Parties, except only in Actions wherein the King [k] is a Party. It seems indeed to be generally holden in some Books, [l] that such Faults in a Writ are amendable where the *Cursitor* varies from his Instructions, in the Names or [m] Additions of the Parties, or other like Matters which he must take from his Instructions. But what is said in such Books in Relation to this Matter seems to be intended of such Writs only as are within the Purview of the Statutes of Amendments, and therefore cannot be applied to Appeals; yet it seems that a Misprision in the Count is amendable by the Common Law, as well in an Appeal as in any other Action, before it is entered on the Record; and so it seems that the Year [n] Book of 7 *H.* 4. 27. is to be intended, in which a Mistake in the Declaration in laying the Fact in an improper *Visne*, was suffered to be amended. Also it seems that after the Count is entered on the Record, a Variance in it from the Writ, if a meer Misprision, may be amended by it, as it seemed to be agreed in an Appeal of Death between *Smith* and *Bowen*, [o] wherein the Word *Murdrum* in the Count on the Record was adjudged to be amendable by the Word *Murdrum* in the Bill on the File.

As to the fifth general Point, *viz.* What may be pleaded in Bar of an Appeal, having already in the former Part [p] of this Chapter endeavour'd to shew whatmay be pleaded in Bar of an Appeal of *Mayhem*, and intending in the latter Part of the Book to consider the Learning relating to Pleas in Bar of criminal Prosecutions in general, I shall in this Place only examine the Nature of Pleas in Bar of Appeals of Felony in particular, and for that Purpose having premised that, by the better Opinion [q] at this Day, no special Plea in Justification of the Killing shall be admitted in an Appeal of Death, but that in every such Case the general Issue is to be pleaded, I shall consider,

1. What Pleas will be good Bars of an Appeal of Felony by shewing that the Plaintiff had never any Right to bring it.
2. Whether a *Retraxit* on Nonsuit in a former Appeal of this Kind will be good Bars of another.
3. Whether a Discontinuance.

[a] Vide Cro. El. 803. pl. 34. Dyer 228. pl. 45. Yelv. 36.
[b] 1 Sid. 252. pl. 22. 1 Lev. 163. 1 Inst. 33. Yelv. 112. Aleyn 65, 66.
[c] Cro. El. 495. Owen 59. Noy 36. Moor 457. Popham 115. Vide Thelo. Lib. 15. cap. 5.
[d] Vide Salkeld 51. 6 Mod. 269. 1 Bulst. 142, 144.
[e] 9 H. 7. 16. pl. 8. 1 Bulst. 142, 144. 4 H. 6. 16. pl. 16. Bro. Amend. 62.
[f] Fitz. Coron. 121. 13 Aff. pl. 10.
[g] Fitz. Amendment, 68.
[h] Fitz. Variance, 59. 8 Co. 156. b. 4 H. 6. 16. pl. 16.
[i] Fitz. Amendment, 63.
[k] 8 Co. 156. b. 4 H. 6. 16. pl. 16. 40 Aff. pl. 26.
[l] Moor 866. pl. 1196. 1 Rol. 138. pl. 13. Cro. El. 644. pl. 49. Quære Hob. 128.
[m] 2 Ventris 46, 49, 130, 152. 1 Sid. 412. pl. 8. Hob. 118. Hutton 56, 57. Cro. Car. 74. Littleton's Rep. 50.
[n] Fitz. Coron. 80.
[o] Mich. 7 Annæ.
[p] Sect. 22, 23, 24, 25, 26.
[q] See Book 1. Chap. 28. Sect. 3.

4. Whether an Abatement of a former Appeal.
5. Where the Bringing of an Appeal of this Kind againſt one Perſon ſhall be a Bar of any ſubſequent Appeal againſt any other Perſon not named in the firſt.
6. Where a Releaſe will be a good Bar of an Appeal of this Kind.
7. Where the Appellant may be barred as to one Appellee, and continue his Suit againſt the reſt.
8. Whether any, and which of theſe Pleas, are conſiſtent with the general Iſſue.

Sect. 130. As to the firſt Particular, *viz.* What Pleas will be good Bars of ſuch an Appeal by ſhewing that the Plaintiff had never any Right to bring it, it ſeems to be a good general [a] Rule, That any Plea of this Kind is good which ſhews that the Plaintiff wants any of thoſe Requiſites which the Law makes neceſſary to intitle him to the Appeal. And therefore in an Appeal of Death by a Woman it is a good Plea, that [b] ſhe was never lawfully married to the Deceaſed; or [c] that ſhe hath not continued a Widow ſince his Death, but hath taken another Huſband. Alſo in an Appeal of Death by one as Heir, it is a good Plea, that *A. B.* at the Time [d] of the Writ was and ſtill is Heir of the Deceaſed; or [e] that one of the Defendants was the Wife of the Deceaſed, and made a Defendant by Covin to exclude her from her Appeal; or that the Plaintiff is a Baſtard [f] and not legitimate. And where one brings an Appeal as Brother and Heir, it is a good Plea, That he is not [g] Brother and Heir as by his Writ and Declaration he hath ſuppoſed, or [h] that he hath an Elder Brother by the ſame Father and Mother ſtill alive; or where one brings an Appeal as Couſin and Heir, *viz.* Brother of *A. B.* Father of the deceaſed, it is a good Plea, That he is not Couſin [i] and Heir, *viz.* Brother of *A. B.* Father of the deceaſed, *&c.* as by his Writ and Declaration he hath ſuppoſed. Alſo [k] it is a good Plea in any Appeal of Death, that the Plaintiff hath ſlipt his Time in not bringing the Appeal within the Year and Day after the Death of the Perſon ſuppoſed to have been killed. Alſo it is a good [l] Plea in an Appeal of Robbery, That the Plaintiff is a Villein to the Defendant. And it is a good [m] Plea in an Appeal of Rape by a Man and a Woman, That the Plaintiffs were never lawfully married. And [n] it is a good Plea in Bar of any Appeal of Felony, That the Plaintiff is an Ideot, or that he was born deaf and dumb. Alſo it is ſaid by Sir *William Staundford*, [o] that it is a good Plea in Bar of any ſuch Appeal, That the Plaintiff is attainted of Treaſon or Felony; however [p] it ſeems that ſuch Attainder is no perpetual Bar, but only during the Time it continues in Force.

Sect. 131. As to the ſecond Particular, *viz.* Where a *Retraxit* or Nonſuit in a former Appeal of this Kind will be good Bars of another; I take it to be clear, [q] that a *Retraxit* of any ſuch Appeal is a Bar of all ſubſequent Appeals of the ſame Kind; for it ſeems to be a general ſettled Rule, That a *Retraxit* of any Action whatſoever is a Bar of all others of the like or inferior Nature. Alſo it ſeems to be certain, That a Nonſuit on a Bill [r] of Appeal, whether commenced in the Court of King's Bench, or before Juſtices [s] of Gaol-Delivery, or before the Sheriff [t] and Coroners, or a Nonſuit after [u] Declaration on a Writ of Appeal, is a Bar of all other Appeals of the ſame Kind; becauſe no ſuch Bill or Declaration ſhall be received, unleſs [x] the Appellant have firſt appeared in proper Perſon; and it ſeems to be agreed by all the Books, That a Non- ſuit

[a] S. P. C. 98. H. P. C. 190.
[b] Supra Sect. 36. S. P. C. 98.
[c] Supra Sect. 38. S. P. C. 98.
[d] Raſtal's Entries 50. pl. 8.
[e] Raſtal's Entries 50. pl. 9.
[f] Raſtal's Entries 49. a.
[g] Raſtal's Entries 49. a: b.
[h] Supra Sect. 40. Letter i.
[i] Raſtal's Entries 49. a.
[k] S. P. C. 98.
[l] Supra Sect. 44. Letter h. S. P. C. 98.
[m] Supra Sect. 62. S. P. C. 98. Letter B.
[n] Surpa Sect. 32. S. P. C. 98. Letter C.
[o] S. P. C. 98. Letter C.
[p] Supra Sect. 32.
[q] 1 Inſt. 138. b. 139. a. H. P. C. 190. 8 Co. 58, 62.
[r] S. P. C. 148. Letters A, B.
[s] 10 H. 4. 4. pl. 14.
[t] S. P. C. 148. Letters A, B. 22 Aſſ. pl. 97.
[u] H. P. C. 190. S. P. C. 148. Lettters A, B. Cro. El. 605.
[x] Salkeld 64. Vide F. N. B. 26. Letter P.

suit after such an Appearance is peremptory. Also it is holden generally in some Books, [a] That a Nonsuit after Appearance is a peremptory Bar to the Appellant, without adding that he must also have declared; from whence, and also from the general Reason of the Thing, it may be reasonably argued, That if it any way appear on Record that the Appellant who was nonsuited in a former Appeal, did actually appear and prosecute such Appeal, as by praying [b] of Process on it, *&c.* he shall be barred in any other Appeal of the same Kind. But it seems [c] that the bare Taking out of a Writ of Appeal, and causing it to be delivered of Record to the Sheriff, and a Nonsuit upon it, is no Bar of a second Appeal, because it doth not appear of Record, but that it might be done by a Stranger; and notwithstanding some Books [d] seem to hold generally, that any Nonsuit in Appeal is peremptory, yet it seems to be in great Measure settled [e] at this Day, that such Nonsuit ought to be after an Appearance in proper Person of Record.

[a] 22 Ass. pl. 97. 47 Ed. 3. 16. pl. 27. Bro. Appeal, 28, 71. Fitz. Coron. 184. 1 Inst. 139. a. Vide 4 H. 6. 16. a. Supra Sect. 26. 9 H. 4. 2. b. 3. a. 47 Ass. pl. 7.

[b] Vide 7 H. 7. 6. pl. 10.

[c] S. P. C. 148. Letter A. 7 H. 7. 6. pl. 10. 1 Sid. 32.

[d] 27 Ass. pl. 7. Cro. El. 605. Vide 4 H. 6. 16. a. 1 Sid. 32.

[e] See the Books cited to the other Points of this Section.

Sect. 132. As to the third Particular, *viz.* Whether a Discontinuance of a former Appeal of this Kind will be a good Bar of another, it is holden [f] by the Reporter of the Year Book of 16 *Ed.* 4. That a Discontinuance of one Appeal is a Bar of any other, because the Life of the Appellee was once put in Jeopardy by the first Appeal; but this Reason proves as strongly that the Abatement of an Appeal where the Writ was good shall be a Bar of another; for by an Appeal so abated the Life of the Appellee is as much put in Jeopardy as by an Appeal that is discontinued; and yet it seems to be agreed at this Day, that such an Abatement of an Appeal cannot regularly be a Bar of another, as shall be more fully shewn in the next Section. Nor can I find it any where adjudged, That the Discontinuance of one Appeal is a Bar of another. It is true indeed, that in *Bradley* [g] and *Bank*'s Case, the Appellee was totally discharged upon a Discontinuance. But the Reason hereof seems to have been, not that the Discontinuance would be of it self a Bar to any other Appeal, but because the Year and Day were passed, and consequently there could be no other Appeal; and the Appellee had also been before convicted on an Indictment, and had his Clergy, and consequently could not be proceeded against at the Suit of the King. However, granting the Opinion aforementioned to be Law, that the Discontinuance of one Appeal shall be a good Bar of any other; surely it is to be intended of such a Discontinuance only, as happens after the Appearance of the Appellant, for the Reasons given in the precedent Section, in Relation to a Nonsuit.

[f] 16 E. 4. 11. pl. 7. Bro. Appeal, 103. Vide S. P. C. 59. G.

[g] 1 Bulst. 141. Cro. Jac. 283. 284. Yelv. 204.

Sect. 133. As to the fourth Particular, *viz.* Whether an Abatement of a former Appeal of this Kind will be a good Bar of another, it seems clear, that if an Appeal by a Wife abate by her taking another Husband, or an Appeal by an Heir abate by his Death, there can be no [h] other Appeal. But the Reason hereof seems not so much to depend on the Abatement, as on the Marriage in the first Case, and the Death in the second; which, as it seems the better [i] Opinion, would of themselves have abated a subsequent Appeal, whether any had been brought before or not. Yet I find it holden generally in some [k] of the Old Books, that an Appeal once determined, cannot revive; and in [l] others, that where an Appeal of Mayhem, which in this Respect seems not to differ from other Appeals, is abated without the Default of the Party, he may have a new one, by which it seems to be implied, that if it abated by his Default he cannot have a new one; and this Opinion seems also to be confirmed by some other

[h] Vide S. P. C. 147. Letter E. H. P. C. 200.

[i] Vide supra Sect. 38, 39, 41.

[k] 6 H. 4. 6. pl. 29. Bro. Appeal, 10.

[l] 50 Ed. 3. 1. pl. 2. Bro. Appeal, 16.

other [a] Old Books, but it is denied [b] by others. However I take it to be ſettled [c] at this Day, that where there continues to be a Plaintiff, not diſabled to proſecute, he ſhall not be barred in a ſecond Appeal by an Abatement of the firſt.

Sect. 134. As to the fifth Particular, *viz.* Where the Bringing of an Appeal of this Kind, againſt one Perſon will be a Bar of any ſubſequent Appeal againſt any other Perſon not named in the firſt; it is ſaid, [d] that anciently one might have had two Appeals for the ſame Fact, one againſt the Principal, the other againſt the Acceſſary. And even at this Day, if one be robbed of the ſame [e] Goods, at ſeveral Times, or receive different [f] Maims, whether at the ſame or at ſeveral Times; or a Woman be raviſh'd more than once, whether by the ſame or by different Perſons, it ſeems clear that ſeveral Appeals lie for each diſtinct Offence. But it ſeems to be generally [g] agreed at this Day, that after one hath brought an Appeal of Felony againſt one Perſon, who is thereon attainted and hanged; he may be barred by it in any ſubſequent Appeal, for the very ſame Crime, againſt any other Perſon not named in the firſt; whether ſuch ſubſequent Appeal, againſt the Perſon ſo omitted in the firſt, be brought againſt him as Principal, or as Acceſſary [h] before the Fact, or even as Acceſſary after the Fact, unleſs where he happens to be ſo Acceſſary after the firſt Appeal was commenced; in which Caſe it is certain that he is liable to ſuch ſecond [i] Appeal, becauſe it was impoſſible to charge him in the firſt. But otherwiſe, after an Attainder had on the firſt Appeal, the Law ſeems to diſallow the Bringing of a ſecond; for this Reaſon, that where an Appellant has ſo far had his Revenge in one Appeal, he ſhall not be indulged in the Bringing of another, which his own Laches only made neceſſary. Alſo it ſeems to be [k] clear, that if one bring an Appeal of Felony againſt another, who is either acquitted by Verdict, or otherwiſe finally diſcharged by any other Matter, which will peremptorily bar any other Appeal againſt him by the ſame Appellant, for the ſame Fact, the Appellant may alſo be barred in any other Appeal for the ſame Fact againſt any [l] other Perſon whatſoever; perhaps for this Reaſon, that he who appears to have brought an ill grounded Action of ſo high a Nature, or to have ſo far made Default in the Proſecution of ſuch an Action, as to be for ever barred from bringing another againſt the ſame Defendant, ſhall not be thought worthy to bring another againſt any other Perſon whatſoever. But I cannot be ſatisfied with the Reaſon which ſome of the Books ſeem to give why all the Defendants muſt be named in one Appeal; which is this, that the Statute of *Magna Charta* 34. by which it is provided, *That none ſhall be impriſoned upon the Appeal of a Woman, for the Death of any other than her own Huſband*, ſpeaks only of Appeal in the ſingular Number; from whence it is ſaid to be collected, that all the Defendants muſt be named in one Appeal. But by what Kind of Argument this Collection is made, I do not find, nor do I ſee why twenty Appeals brought by the ſame Woman, if the Law would permit ſo many, are not as much within the Letter and Meaning of the Statute as one Appeal. And where the Law does permit the Bringing of a ſecond Appeal againſt the ſame Perſon, as it is clear that in ſome Caſes it does, it may reaſonably be argued, that he may as well bring it againſt others alſo; As [m] where the firſt is abated, and there ſtill continues to be a Plaintiff not diſabled to proſecute, [n] and in ſome other Caſes: For if an Appellant be not barred by the Abatement of his firſt Appeal, from bringing a ſecond againſt thoſe who had Vexation by the firſt, and were legally diſcharged from it, why ſhould he be barred by it, as to thoſe who were not concerned in it?

[a] 9 H. 5. 1. pl. 3. Bro. Appeal, 38, 44. 4 H. 6. 16. a.

[b] Bro. Appeal, 53, 118, 146. 13 Aſſ. pl. 10.

[c] Vide ſupra Sect. 4.

[d] S. P. C. 65. Letter C.

[e] S. P. C. 65. Letter D.

[f] 9 H. 4. 2. a. 11 H. 4. 14. a. Bro. Appeal 28.

[g] Bro. Appeal 32. 11 H. 4. 13. b 14. a.

[h] H.P.C. 190 S. P. C. 65, 98. Letter C. Bro. Appeal, 14, 28. 4 Co. 47. b. Vide ſupra Ch. 6. Sect. 5.

[i] Keilw. 83. a. ſeems contrary as to Appeals of Robbery.

[k] 28 Ed. 3. 90. pl. 138. 26 Aſſ. pl. 42. Keilw. 83. a. 4 Co. 44. a. 48. a.

[l] 47 Ed. 3. 16. pl. 27. Fitz. Coron. 104. 9 H. 4. 2. a. H. P.C. 188, 190. S. P. C. 98. Letter C. 47 Aſſ. pl. 7.

[m] 28 Ed. 3. 90. pl. 138. 4 Co. 48.

[n] See the precedent Section.

Sect. 135. As to the sixth Particular, *viz.* Where a Release will be a good Bar of an Appeal of this Kind, it seems clear, That a Release of all manner of Actions, or of all Actions [a] Criminal, or of all Actions [b] Mortal, or of all Actions concerning *Pleas of the Crown*, or of all [c] Appeals, or of all [d] Demands, will be a good Bar of any such Appeal. But it [e] seems that a Release of all Actions Personal will not bar such an Appeal, because that an Appeal in which the Appellee is to have Judgment of Death, is higher than an Action Personal, and not properly called an Action Personal. Also it seems [f] clear, That whatsoever the Nature of the Release may be, it shall not wholly discharge the Appeal, unless it were made before it was commenced; for if it be subsequent to the Appeal, it shall only discharge it as to the Suit of the Plaintiff, and after Judgment given for such Discharge, he shall be arraigned on the Appeal at the King's Suit, as shall be shewn more at large in the Chapter of Indictments. Also it is [g] certain, That no Release shall discharge a Person attainted, without the King's Pardon.

Sect. 136. As to the seventh Particular, *viz.* Where the Appellant may be barred as to one Appellee, and continue his Suit against the Rest, it [h] seems, that if he be barred by a Release given, or *Retraxit* entred as to one, or by being vanquished in Battle by one, yet he may continue his Suit against the Rest, because he is to have a several Execution against every one of them. Yet in an Appeal against divers, whether they plead the same or several Issues, it hath been adjudged, [i] that a Nonsuit against one, at the Trial of any one of the Issues, is a Nonsuit as to all, of which this seems to be the best Reason, That [k] such a Nonsuit operates in Nature as a Release of the whole. But whether [l] the Discontinuance of an Appeal, as to one Appellee, shall have the like Construction as to all, may deserve to be considered.

Sect. 137. As to the eighth Particular, *viz.* Whether any, and which of the Pleas abovementioned are consistent with the general Issue, it seems agreed at this Day, That if the Defendant in an Appeal of Death, by a [m] Wife, plead *Nunques accouple in loial Matrimony*; [n] or in an Appeal of Death by one as Heir, plead that the Appellant is a Bastard, [o] or that he hath an elder Brother of the whole Blood alive, or in [p] any Appeal of Death, plead that the Person supposed to have been killed, was dead above a Year before the Purchase of the Writ, or that [q] the Appellant hath formerly brought an Appeal for the same Fact against another Person, who was thereon attainted and hanged, or generally [r] any other Plea not amounting to an implied Confession of the Fact, as a Release, *&c.* Whether it be triable by Matter [s] of Record, or by *Pais*; and whether it [t] deny that the Appellant had ever any Right to the Appeal, or admit that he once had a Right, but shew that he is now barred; he may together, with such Plea in Bar, plead also Not guilty to the Felony. And if such Plea be triable by the Common Law, unless the Appellant reply both to that, and also to the Plea of Not guilty, he discontinues the Appeal; but [u] if it be not triable by the Common Law, the Defendant needs only to reply to it, and not to the Felony, till after such Plea has been tried. But it is holden in many Books [x] of good Authority, That a Man shall not be admitted to plead a Release, and the general Issue also, because it is repugnant at the same Time to insist that the Crime is re-

[a] Littleton, Sections 500, 501.
[b] 1 Inst. 287. b. 288. a.
[c] Littleton, Section 501.
[d] Littleton, Section 508.
[e] Littleton, Sections 500, 501. Contra Fitz. Release, 46. Quære Bro. Appeal, 29. 21 Ed. 4. 72. 9 H. 4. 2. pl. 8. Vide supra Section 25.
[f] Fitz. Coron. 12. S. P. C. 148. Letter B. H. P. C. 200. Rastal's Entries 43. pl. 8. 48. a.
[g] Supra Sect. 38, 42.
[h] H. P. C. 190. 21 Ed. 4. 72. a. b. 2 R. 3. 9. pl. 18. Bro. Appeal, 111, 120.
[i] Cro. El. 460. pl. 6. Dyer 120. pl. 11. 7 H. 6. 27. pl. 19. 27 Ed. 3. 87. pl. 45. 2 Roll's Ab. 133. Letter H. 1 Inst. 139. 1 Sid. 378. pl. 7. Bro. Discontinuance de process, 20.
[k] Hob. 180.
[l] Vide 7 H. 6. 27. pl. 19. 30 Ass. pl. 36. 39 Ed. 3. 3. a. 38 Ass. pl. 17. 27 Ed. 3. 87. pl. 45.
[m] 3 Leon. 268. Cro. El. 223.
[n] 7 Ed. 4. 15. pl. 3. Quære 14 Ed. 4. 7. pl. 10.
[o] Rastal's Entries 49. pl. 5. 7 Ed. 4. 15. pl. 3. Quære 14 Ed. 4. 7. pl. 10. 21 H. 6. 29. a.
[p] 22 Ed. 4. 39 b.
[q] 9 H. 4. 2. pl. 7.
[r] 21 H. 6. 29. a. 22 Ed. 4. 39. b. 40. Rastal's Entries 49. pl. 6, 7. 50. pl. 8. 583. b. 584. S. P. C. 98. Letter D. Keil. 188, 189.
[s] 21 H. 6. 28, 29. 4 H. 7. 5. pl. 1. 9 H. 4. 2. pl. 7. 35 H. 6. 57. pl. 2. 8 Ed. 4. 3. pl. 6. Con. Bro. Appeal, 14, 48. 4 H. 7. 5. b. 6. a.
[t] 7 Ed. 4. 14. pl. 3. 21 H. 6. 29. a.
[u] Cro. El. 223. 3 Leon. 268.
[x] S. P. C. 68. Letter D. Finch 385, 386. H. P. C. 190, 191. Hob. 170, 171.

leaſed, and [a] yet that there was no ſuch Crime committed to be releaſed. But I do not find this Point any where adjudged; and as to the Argument above mentioned, from the Repugnancy of the Plea of a Releaſe, to the general Iſſue, it may be anſwered, That a Man may reaſonably take a Releaſe to free himſelf from Trouble, from the Suſpicion of a Crime, of which he would by no Means own himſelf guilty; and in Appeals of Death after a Plea of [b] *Autrefoits convict* by Verdict, and even after the Plea of [c] *Autrefoits convict* by Confeſſion, and Clergy thereon had, the general Iſſue has been received; and yet ſuch Pleas as much imply a Confeſſion of the Fact, as the Plea of Releaſe. And in *Smith*'s Caſe, who was indicted of High Treaſon in the Beginning of his late Majeſty's Reign, for the Murder of Colonel *Parks*, after a Plea of a Pardon, the general Iſſue was received. However, I do not find it any where holden, That the Plea of a Releaſe may not be pleaded, if the Defendant think fit, without Pleading the general Iſſue. Alſo it ſeems queſtionable, [d] Whether any other Plea in Bar, whether triable by Matter of Record, or by *Pais*, may not alſo be received without Pleading the general Iſſue, as it ſeems clear, that in ſome Caſes it may, [e] as where it declines the Juriſdiction of the Court, [f] or would be prejudicial to the Defendant by infranchiſing the Plaintiff, as where a Villein brings an Appeal of Robbery againſt his Lord, who pleads the Villenage in Bar, in which Caſe he ſhall not be compelled to plead not guilty, becauſe that would amount to an Infranchiſement of the Plaintiff; by ſuppoſing that the Fact, if committed, needs a Defence which it cannot do unleſs the Plaintiff have a Property, which if he be a Villein, he cannot have againſt his Lord. Alſo it ſeems clear, that [g] if any of the Bars above mentioned, except that of a Releaſe, be ſuffered to be pleaded without the general Iſſue, and be found againſt the Defendant, they do not conclude him from pleading the general Iſſue afterwards; and as to the Plea of a Releaſe, whether that being pleaded without the general Iſſue, and found againſt the Defendant, do conclude him at this Day to plead the general Iſſue afterwards, may deſerve to be conſidered for the Reaſons above mentioned. [h] But it ſeems, That if a Demurrer to the Court be adjudged againſt an Appellee, he ſhall not be admitted to plead either in Bar, or the general Iſſue, but ſhall be condemned, as ſhall be ſhewn more at large in the Chapter of Demurrers.

Sect. 138. As to the ſixth general Point, *viz.* Where the Appellant ſhall render Damages to the Appellee for a falſe Appeal, having premiſed that by the Common Law a Defendant may [i] recover Damages for a falſe and malicious Appeal, againſt the Appellant and his Abettors, by a Writ of Conſpiracy, or an Action on the Caſe, in the Nature of ſuch Writ, as hath been more fully ſhewn in Book 1. [k] I ſhall here endeavour to ſhew in what Caſes, and in what Manner he may, if he chuſe rather ſo to proceed, recover ſuch Damages by the Statute of *Weſtminſter* 2. 12. which was made for his ſpeedier Remedy, and is enacted as followeth.

Sect. 139. *Foraſmuch as many through Malice intending to grieve others, do procure falſe Appeals to be made, of Homicides and other Felonies, by Appellors, having nothing to ſatiſfie the King for their falſe Appeal, nor to the Parties appealed for their Damages: It is ordained, that when any being appealed of Felony, ſurmiſed upon him, doth acquit himſelf in the King's Court in due Manner, either at the Suit of the Appellor, or of our Lord the King, the Juſtices be-*

[a] Hob 270, 271.
[b] 1 Bulſt. 141. Yelv. 204. Cro. Jac. 283.
[c] 4 Co. 45. 1 And. 68.
[d] Finch 385. S. P. C. 151. Letter A. 22 Ed. 4. 39. b. 40. Shower's Reports 47.
[e] Widdrington and Charlton, Trin. 11 An. 50 Ed. 3. 15. 28 Ed. 3. 91. pl. 4. 27 Aſſ. pl. 41. 35 H. 6. 57. pl. 2. 8 Ed. 4. 3. pl. 6.
[f] Keil. 175. pl. 10. 91. pl. 1. 186. pl. 3. Raſtal's Entries 54. a.
[g] 18 Ed. 3. 32. pl. 4. Carth. 56. H. P. C. 191. S. P. C. 98. Letter D. Vide Lettleton, Section 192, 193, 194, 208.
[h] 14 Ed. 4. 7. pl. 10. 50 Ed. 3. 15. 16. a. 28 Ed. 3. 91. pl. 4. S. P. C. 98. Letter D. Fitz. Coro. 429. 27 Aſſ. pl. 3. Contra 7 Ed. 4. 15. pl. 3. Keilw. 100. H. P. C. 190, 191. Finch 385, 386. H. P. C. 243. 14 Ed. 4. 7. pl. 10. Keilw. 100.

[i] 2 Inſt. 383. Keilw. 27. a. S. P. C. 167. b.

[k] Book 1. Ch. 72. Sect. 2 and 3.

fore whom the Appeal ſhall be heard and determined, ſhall puniſh the Appellor, by a Year's Impriſonment; and the Appellor ſhall nevertheleſs reſtore to the Parties appealed their Damages, according to the Diſcretion of the Juſtices, having Reſpect to the Impriſonment or Arreſtment, that the Party appealed hath ſuſtained by Reaſon of ſuch Appeals, and to the Infamy that they have incurred by the Impriſonment, or otherwiſe; and ſhall nevertheleſs make a gievous Fine unto the King. And if peradventure ſuch Appellor be not able to recompence the Damages, it ſhall be inquired by whoſe Abetment, by Malice, the Appeal was commenced, if the Party appealed deſire it. And if it be found by the ſame Inqueſt, that any Man is Abettor thro' Malice, he ſhall be diſtrained by a judicial Writ at the Suit of the Party appealed to come before the Juſtices. And if he be lawfully convict of ſuch malicious Abetment, he ſhall be puniſhed by Impriſonment and Reſtitution of Damages, as before is ſaid of the Appellor.

And for the better Underſtanding this Statute, I ſhall endeavour to ſhew how the ſeveral Parts of it have been expounded.

Sect. 140. And firſt, Whereas the Words of the Preamble are, *That many through Malice procure falſe Appeals to be made by Appellors, having nothing*, &c. And in the Purview it is ſaid, *That it ſhall be inquired by whoſe Abetment, by Malice, the Appeal was commenced*, &c. *And if it be found that any Man is an Abettor, through Malice*, &c. In all which Places the Malice is expreſly referred to the Procurers and Abettors only, and in no Part of the Statute to the Appellant, it is holden by [a] ſome, That where-ever an Appellee is acquitted of an Appeal of Felony, he ſhall recover Damages by Force of this Statute againſt the Appellant, except only where he hath been indicted of the ſame Felony before. And it muſt be confeſſed, that in the [b] Reports and Entries [c] relating to this Matter, Damages ſeem generally of Courſe to have been awarded againſt the Appellant, on the Acquittal of the Appellee in all other Caſes, without any finding that the Appeal was malicious. Ye it is holden by [d] others, That the Appellant is no more within the Intent of the Statute, than his Abettors, unleſs his Appeal were grounded on Malice. And if it be conſidered, that where the Appellant is to render Damages by Force of the Statute, he is alſo, by the expreſs Words of it, to have a Year's Impriſonment, and to be grievouſly ranſomed to the King; ſurely it cannot be imagined that the Makers of the Statute intended in any Caſe to expoſe him to ſo ſevere a Puniſhment for a legal Proſecution, which he has reaſonable Evidence to induce him to commence, though it may not be ſufficient to induce a Jury to convict the Defendant. Neither do I ſee any Reaſon why the Bringing an Appeal againſt one who hath been before indicted, by a ſufficient Indictment [e] of the very ſame [f] Crime, which is agreed [g] not to be within the Meaning of the Statute, ſhould be the only excepted Caſe; eſpecially conſidering that any other Caſe, wherein the Appellant plainly appears to proceed on a probable Ground of Suſpicion, is within the Reaſon given in many Books [h] for the Favour ſhewn to the Appellant, where the Appellee has been indicted before; which is this, that the Appellant had Cauſe and Evidence to purſue the Appeal, and it appears to the Court that it was not meerly founded on Malice. And this is alſo one of the Reaſons given in the [i] Books, why the Appellant is not to render Damages, by the Intent of the Statute, where the Appellee in an Appeal of Murder is found guilty of Homicide *ſe defendendo* only. And as to the general Expreſſions of

[a] 1 Inſt. 139. b. 2 Inſt. 384. Vide Littleton, Section 208. 22 Aſſ. pl. 39. 26 H. 8. 3. pl. 14.
[b] See the Books cited under this and the following Sections.
[c] Raſtal's Entries 56. pl. 2.
[d] S. P. C. 168. Letter B. See L. Quinto, Ed. 4. 126. a. 40 Ed. 3, 42. pl. 24.
[e] 20 Ed. 4. 6. pl. 5. 2 Inſt. 384.
[f] 26 H. 8. 3. pl. 14. 33 H. 6. 1. pl. 6. 40 Ed. 3. 42. 24. 14 H. 7. 2. pl. 8. 40 Aſſ. pl. 18.
[g] 22 Aſſ. pl. 39. 26 H. 8. 3. pl. 14. 33 H. 6. 1. pl. 6.

40 Ed. 3. 42. pl. 24. 14 H. 7. 2. pl. 8. 20 Ed. 6. pl. 5. 40 Aſſ. pl. 18. Fitz. Damages, 67. [h] 40 Ed. 3. 42. pl. 24. 14 H. 7. 2. pl. 8. [i] 21 Aſſ. pl. 77. 2 Inſt. 384.

2 the

the Books above mentioned, in which Damages ſeem of Courſe to be awarded againſt the Appellant, without any Inquiry, whether his Appeal were malicious or not; it may be anſwered, That the Books ſpeak as generally in Relation to the Recovery of the Damages againſt the Abettors; and yet it ſeems [a] plain from the whole Purport of the Statute, that they are not within the Purview of it, unleſs their Abetment were founded on Malice. And ſome [b] ſeem to have gone ſo far as to hold, that the Heir who abets his Mother in bringing an Appeal for the Death of his Father, can be in no Caſe within the Statute, by Reaſon of ſuch Abetment; becauſe Nature and Duty oblige him, in ſuch a Caſe, to abet his Mother. But this Reaſoning, if ſtrictly examined, ſeems to prove no more than this, That in ſuch a Caſe the Heir ſhall *prima facie* be intended to have abetted the Appellant, rather out of Duty than Malice, and that therefore he ſhall not be taken to be within the Purview of the Statute, without very ſtrong Evidence of his Malice. But ſurely it cannot be denied, That in ſome Caſes it may be notorious, That an Heir abets ſuch an Appeal, not out of Duty but Malice; as where he himſelf, without the leaſt probable Ground of Suſpicion, is the firſt Promoter of the Proſecution; or where he cauſes it to be carried on by violent and unfair Methods, not for the Sake of Juſtice but Oppreſſion, in which Caſes it ſeems harſh to ſay, That he is not as well within the Meaning as Letter of the Statute.

[a] 2 Inſt. 384. S. P. C. 168. Letter B. Pl. Com. 88. b. ſeems contrary. Vide Dy. 120. pl. 10.

[b] Fitz. Champerty, 10. Pl. Com. 88. b. 2 Inſt. 384.

Sect. 141. Secondly, In the Conſtruction of the Words *Homicides and other Felonies*, in the Preamble of the Statute, it hath [c] been adjudged that the Purview of it extends to Rape, which was made a Felony by another [d] Branch of the ſame Statute; and it is [e] holden, both by *Coke* and *Staundforde*, That, it in like Manner extends to Offences made Felonies by any ſubſequent Statute.

[c] Fitz. Coro. 275, 381. Pl. Com. 124. b.

[d] Supra, Sect. 59, 60.

[e] 2 Inſt. 384. S. P. C. 198. Letter D.

Sect. 142. Thirdly, In the Conſtruction of theſe Words, *When any being appealed of Felony ſurmiſed upon him, doth acquit himſelf in the King's Court in due Manner, either at the Suit of the Appellor, or of our Lord the King*; it ſeems to have been generally agreed, That no Acquittal is within the Intention of the Statute, [f] unleſs it be had on an Appeal, (either at the Suit of the Party, or of the King, after a Nonſuit of the Party,) and be of ſuch a Nature as [g] finally to bar all other Proſecutions for the ſame Felony, whether at the Suit of the King, or of the ſame, or any other Party. And therefore it ſeems clear, That no Damages ſhall be recovered on the [h] Abatement of an Appeal, nor on the bare [i] Nonſuit of the Appellant, nor where the Appellant is barred, either by a [k] Demurrer, or by a [l] Plea, ſhewing that he is not intitled to the Appeal, nor on any Acquittal on an inſufficient [m] Original; becauſe in all theſe Caſes the Appellee is liable to another Proſecution for the ſame Felony. And if a Perſon appealed of Murder, be found guilty [n] of Homicide by Miſadventure, or *Se defendendo*, which will be a Bar of any other Proſecution for the ſame Killing; yet it hath been reſolved that he ſhall not recover Damages, not [o] only becauſe it appears that the Appeal was not groundleſs, but alſo becauſe the Appellee is not totally acquitted. But it is [p] clear, That the Appellee is intitled to his Damages, where he is acquitted on an Appeal at the Suit of the King, after a Nonſuit of the Plaintiff, where he vanquiſhes [q] the Appellant in a Trial by Battle. Alſo if two be appealed, the one as Principal, and the other as Acceſſary; and the Jury being

[f] S. P. C. 169. Letter B. 2 Inſt. 385. Vide 14 H. 7. 2. pl. 8.

[g] S. P. C. 169.

[h] 4 Co. 47. b. S. P. C. 169. Letter A. 9 H. 4. 2. b. Vide 9 H. 5. 1. pl. 3.

[i] 2 Inſt. 385. Fitz. Conſpiracy, 25. But 33 H. 6. 1. pl. 6. Fitz. Coro. 102. 48 Ed. 3. 22. pl. 2. ſeem doubtful in this Caſe.

[k] 2 Inſt. 385. Fitz. Coro. 12. S. P. C. 169. Letter A.

[l] 27 Aſſ. pl. 25. 2 Inſt. 385. S. P. C. 169. [m] 4 Co. 45. a. 47. a. Fitz. Coro. 444. 9 H. 5. 2. S. P. C. 169. [n] 22 Aſſ. pl. 77. 2 Inſt. 385. S. P. C. 199. [o] Vide ſupra, Sect. 138. pl. 8. [p] 41 Aſſ. & 24. Fitz. Coro. 275, 381. Damages, 77. [q] Fitz. Coro. 98. S. P. C. 169. Letter E.

ing charged on the Acceſſary, as well as the Principal, do acquit the Principal; it ſeems to be [a] agreed, that the Acceſſary ſhall recover Damages, by the Intent of the Statute, without any expreſs Verdict concerning him, becauſe he is impliedly acquitted by the Acquittal of the Principal; for it is impoſſible, that there ſhould be an Acceſſary where there is no Principal. And this Reaſon ſeems to hold as ſtrongly for the Damages, where the Acceſſary doth not appear on the Trial or Acquittal of the Principal; becauſe in ſuch Caſe the Acquittal of the Principal is as [b] much an Acquittal of the Acceſſary, as where he doth appear. But it is holden [c] by Sir *Edward Coke*, That ſuch an Acceſſary ſhall not recover Damages, becauſe no Jury can be returned to aſſeſs them; and Sir *William Staundford* [d] ſeems to be of Opinion, that ſuch an Acceſſary ſhall not recover Damages, unleſs he be expreſly acquitted by Verdict, after the Acquittal of the Principal. Yet whether [e] the Juſtices themſelves may not, in a Caſe of this Nature, if they think fit, aſſeſs the Damages, without any Jury, or elſe aſſeſs them by an Inqueſt of Office, may deſerve to be conſidered. Alſo it ſeems to be to little Purpoſe to require an actual Acquittal of a Perſon, where it appears by the Acquittal of another, that he could not be guilty. However it ſeems clear, That a Perſon appealed as Acceſſary to two Principals, ſhall not [f] recover Damages by the Acquittal of one of them; becauſe for what appears he might be acceſſary to the other. Neither [g] ſhall he recover Damages where he is diſcharged by the Death of the Principal, before his Attainder, becauſe it doth not appear but that he might have been guilty.

[a] S. P. C. 168. F. 169. 2 Inſt. 385. 33 H. 6. 1. pl. 6.
[b] 33 H. 6. 1. pl. 6.
[c] 2 Inſt. 385.
[d] S. P. C. 168. Letter F. Vide 41 Aſſ. pl. 24.
[e] Vide ſupra Sect. 52, 53.
[f] 2 Inſt. 385. Dyer 120. pl. 11. Fitz. Coro. 463.
[g] S. P. C. 173. Letter A.

Sect. 143. It ſeems at this Day, that if a Defendant, appearing upon erroneous Proceſs to a good Appeal, be acquitted, he ſhall recover Damages by the Intent of the ſaid Clauſe, becauſe ſuch an Acquittal is a good Bar of any other Proſecution for the ſame Felony, and the Life of the Appellee was put in Danger by the [h] Appeal. But there were formerly ſome Opinions, That the Appellee in ſuch a Caſe ſhould not recover Damages, becauſe his Life was not in Danger at the Time of the Trial, for that he might have taken Advantage of the Error in the Proceſs: But granting it to be a good Rule, That the Defendant ſhall not recover Damages where his Life is not in Danger at the Time of the Trial, which yet I find not confirmed by any Authority, beſides the Year-Book of 9 *H.* 5. 2. it may be anſwered, That in the Caſe in Queſtion the Defendant's Life is in Danger at the Time of the Trial, becauſe the Error in the Proceſs is ſalved by his Appearance, as ſhall be ſhewn more at large in the Chapter concerning Proceſs.

33 H. 6. 1. pl. 6.
[h] 9 H. 5. 2. 2 Inſt. 386. Quære S. P. C. 169. b. Fitz. Coro. 444. Yelv. 204. Cro. Jac. 284. 4 Co. 45. a.

Sect. 144. If a Perſon who has taken a Releaſe, or prayed the Benefit of Clergy, waive ſuch Releaſe, or Benefit of Clergy, and put himſelf on his Trial and be acquitted; it is ſaid, [i] that he ſhall recover his Damages, notwithſtanding the Objection that the Taking ſuch Releaſe, or making ſuch Prayer, ſeem to carry with them an implied Confeſſion of Guilt.

[i] S. P. C. 169, 173. Letter A. Vide Fitz. Coro. 386. & 33 H. 6. 1. pl. 6. Supra, Sect. 135.

Sect. 145. Where-ever any Perſon is ſo far acquitted on an Appeal carried on at the Suit of the Party, as to be intitled to his Damages, [k] he ſhall have Judgment for them without any Proceſs to bring in the Party to anſwer to the Damages, becauſe he is ſtill in Court; but where he is ſo acquitted on an Appeal carried on at the Suit of the King after a Nonſuit of the Party, he ſhall not recover Damages, without a *Scire facias*, to bring in the Party, becauſe he was out of Court by the Nonſuit.

[k] S. P. C. 169. Letter C.

Fourthly, In the Conſtruction of theſe Words, *The Juſtices before whom the Appeal ſhall be heard and determined, ſhall puniſh the Appellor by a Year's Impriſonm. and the Appellor ſhall nevertheleſs reſtore to the Parties appealed their Damages, according to the Discretion of the Justices, having Respect to the Imprisonment or Arrestment, that the Party appealed hath sustained by Reason of such Appeals, and to the Infamy that they have incurred by the Imprisonment, or otherwise*, &c. the following Points have been holden.

Sect. 146. First, That Justices of *Nisi prius* [a] have no Power to give Judgment for such Imprisonment or Damages, upon an Acquittal before them, whether before or since the Statute of 14 *H.* 6. by which it is enacted, *That such Justices shall have Power in all Cases of Felony or Treason, to give their Judgments, as well where a Man is acquitted, as where he is attainted.* For [b] the Words above mentioned in the Statute of *Westminster* 2. are to be intended of such Justices only before whom the whole Plea of the Appeal is heard and determined, and therefore in Strictness can extend to the Justices of the King's Bench only, where the Appeal is commenced before them (for that the whole Appeal is in such Case heard and determined before them, either in Person, or else by others delegated by, and representing them,) and not to the Justices of *Nisi prius*, who have nothing to do with the Appeal before the Trial, nor any Original Power to try it. And the Statute above mentioned of 14 *H.* 6. hath been construed to intend only to enable Justices of *Nisi prius* to give the Principal Judgment, and not to transfer to them from the Court of King's Bench, a Power in collateral Matters. Yet [c] Justices of *Nisi prius* have by Usage not now to be disputed, gained a Power to assess the Damages, and to inquire of the Sufficiency of the Plaintiff to answer them, and also of the Abettors. But I do not find that they have ever given Judgment for the Damages. Yet there is no Doubt [d] but that, if such Justices be also Justices of Assise, and as such have an Appeal commenced before them, they may, as Justices of Assise, upon the Acquittal of the Appellee, not only inquire of the Damages, *&c.* but also give Judgment for them, both by the Letter and Meaning of the Statute.

Sect. 147. Secondly, That if a Jury give too small Damages to the Appellee, the Court may increase [e] them; from which it seems to follow, That if a Jury give too large Damages, the Court may abridge them. And surely no less can be implied by the Statutes ordering, That the Damages shall be given according to the Discretion of the Justices, Respect being had to the Imprisonment, *&c.* And this Construction also seems agreeable to the Rules of Law in other Cases, by which the Court is said [f] to have a general discretionary Power, except in some special Cases, as Local [g] Trespasses, *&c.* either to increase or abridge the Damages found by an Inquest of Office; and where a Jury which hath acquitted an Appellee inquires afterwards of the Damages, it seems in Respect of such Inquiry to be no more than an Inquest of the Office, tho' it were returned to try the Cause.

Sect. 148. Thirdly, That if there be several Appellees, and all of them acquitted, the Damages ought to be severally [h] assessed as to every one of them; and this doubtless is agreeable both to the Letter and Meaning of the Statute, which provides that in the giving the Damages, Respect shall be had to the Imprisonment and Infamy, and other Damage sustained by Reason of the Appeal; and these being several, and receiving different Aggravations from the different Circumstances of the Person's particular Case, it cannot but be reasonable, That the Damages be assessed severally also.

[a] 10 Ed. 4. 14. pl. 12. 22 Ed. 4. 19. pl. 44. S. P. C. 169. Letter D. 2 Inst. 386.
[b] S. P. C. 169. Letter D.
[c] 4 Co. 93. b. 2 Inst. 386. Dyer 120. pl. 10, 11, 12, 13. Bro. Appeal, 113. Fitz. Coro. 463. 8 H. 5. 6. pl. 26.
[d] 22 Ed. 4. 19. pl. 44. Bro. Appeal, 113.
[e] Cro. El. 223. Vide 2 Inst. 387. 42 Aff. pl. 19. seems to be contrary.
[f] 3 H. 6. 29. b. 14 H. 4. 9. b. 8 H. 4. 23. pl. 9. 3 H. 4. 4. pl. 16. 7 H. 6. 31. pl. 16. 19 H. 6. 31. pl. 16. 19 H. 6. 10. pl. 28. Bro. Abridgment, 36. Vide 27 H. 8. 2. pl. 8 & supra, Sect. 52.
[g] 27 H. 8. 2. pl. 8. 19 H. 6. 42. pl. 86. 19 H. 6. 10. pl. 28. Vide 3 H. 6. 29. b.
[h] S. P. C. 170. Letter A. Dyer 120. pl. 10. 11 H. 4. 16. b. 12 Co. 126. 2 Inst. 386. 41 Aff. pl. 24. Fitz. Damage 77. 8 H. 5. 6. pl. 26.

Sect. 149. Fourthly, That a Monk or Feme Covert, being appealed without the Abbot, or Husband, cannot have a Judgment for the Damages on their Acquittal, becauſe they are diſabled by the Law to recover any Damages without the Abbot or Husband; and the general Words of a Statute ſhall not be conſtrued to enable Perſons in a Point, wherein the Common Law hath diſabled them. But the Authority of this Opinion, as to a Wife, is queſtioned by [a] *Hobart*, neither do any of thoſe [b] who ſeem to give it greater Weight, bring any other Proof of it, than a Note in *Fitzherbert*'s Abridgment, of a Reſolution to ſuch Purpoſe, in the Time of *Edward* 3. as to the Caſe of a Monk, and an Aſſertion, that the Law is the ſame in the Caſe of a Wife: Againſt which it may be plauſibly argued, That ſince the Impriſonment and Infamy ſuſtained by a Feme Covert, in a malicious Appeal againſt her, are far from being leſs grievous in Reſpect of her Coverture, and are a good [c] Ground of a Writ of Conſpiracy at the Common Law, brought by the Husband and Wife; and ſince the Wife may take any thing to the Benefit of her Husband, and it appears to the Court that the Appellant by his own Act, without any Default either in the Husband or Wife, gives them a good Title to the Damages; and ſince no expreſs Judgment can be given for the Husband, being not a Party to the Record, and it is moſt for his Advantage, as well as his Wife's, that a preſent Judgment be given: It may perhaps be thought no unreaſonable Conſtruction of the Statute, that in this particular Caſe Judgment ſhould be given for the Wife to recover the Damages, which would as much enure, for the Benefit of her ſelf and her Husband, as an expreſs Judgment for them both on a Writ of Conſpiracy.

[a] Hobart 98.
[b] 2 Inſt. 385. 11 Co. 77. b. 9 Co. 73. a. 1 Rol. Rep. 170. S. P. C. 170. Letter B. Fitz. Coro. 276.
[c] 2 Inſt. 386. 24 Ed. 3. 73. pl. 90. 1 Inſt. 132. b.

However, It is certain, [d] That if the Husband and Wife are both of them appealed and acquitted, they ſhall have a joint Judgment for the Damage done to the Wife, for which the Wife alone ſhall ſue Execution, if the Husband die without ſuing it, and the Husband alone ſhall have Judgment for the Damage done to himſelf.

[d] Fitz. Judgment, 108. 2 Inſt. 385, 386. 11 H. 4. 16. b. 17. a. S. P. C. 170. Letter B.

Fifthly, In the Conſtruction of the Words, *And if peradventure the Appellor be not able to recompence the Damages, it ſhall be inquired by whoſe Abetment, by Malice, the Appeal was commenced, if the Party appealed deſire it. And if it be found by the ſame Inqueſt, that any Man is Abettor thro' Malice, he ſhall be diſtrained by a judicial Writ, at the Suit if the Party appealed to come before the Juſtices*, &c. The following Points have been holden.

Sect. 150. Firſt, That [e] the Abettors are in no Caſe liable to render Damages, where the Appellant himſelf is not liable, tho' never ſo ſufficient; and this is confirmed by Experience, and the manifeſt Purport of the Statute, which by directing that the Abettors be inquired of, where the Appellant appears inſufficient to anſwer the Damages, plainly intimates that they are to be inquired of in ſuch Caſes only, wherein the Appellant muſt have anſwered them, if he had been able; and agreeably hereto it ſeems to be ſettled, [f] That a Releaſe of Damages to the Appellant will diſcharge the Abettors, if they can produce it.

[e] S.P.C. 170. Letter D. 171. Letter A. 2 Inſt. 386.
[f] 20 H. 7. 7. b.

Sect. 151. Secondly, That [g] unleſs the Appellant be found by the Jury to be inſufficient, the Abettors ſhall not be inquired of; and yet the Statute doth not expreſly direct that the Jury ſhall inquire of the Sufficiency of the Appellant. But it being the general Method of the Law in other Caſes of like Nature, to make an Inquiry by a Jury, it is certainly a reaſonable Conſtruction of the general Words of the Statute, that ſuch Inquiry may be made in the preſent Caſe. Yet, whether the Juſtices themſelves may not, if they think fit, make ſuch Inquiry without a Jury,

[g] 2 Inſt. 386.

it being but an Inquiry of Office, may deserve to be considered for the Reasons in the 52 and 147 Sections of this Chapter. However there can be no Doubt but that the Insufficiency of the Appellant must appear by one or the other of these Inquiries, before the Abettors can be inquired of.

Sect. 152. Thirdly, That [a] the Abettors may traverse the Jury's Finding the Appellant to be insufficient, or that they abetted him, *&c.* For it is hard that a Man should be concluded by any Matter whatsoever, found to his Prejudice in an Action, to which he is no way Privy. Also it is holden by [b] *Staundförde*, That if a Jury on the Acquittal of one Defendant find that there were no Abettors, yet they may afterwards on the Acquittal of another Defendant find that there were Abettors, because there is no Reason that the first Inquest shall bind one who is not Privy to it, and has no Remedy against it. But the contrary hereto is holden in the Book of [c] Assizes, where the Court refused to inquire of the Abettors, on the Acquittal of a Defendant, because it had been found on the Acquittal of another, that there were no Abettors; but this Case, if thoroughly examined, seems repugnant to it self; for the Jury were permitted on the second Acquittal to tax the Damages, which yet are said to have been taxed before; but to what Purpose should this be done, unless it were first found that the Appellant was sufficient or else that there were Abettors, which could not but control the first Finding; as also the second Taxation of the Damages must do, unless it were wholly the same with the first.

Sect. 153. Fourthly, That [d] if the Appellant be found sufficient to render Part of the Damages, and not the Whole, Judgment shall be given against the Abettors for the Whole, and not for Part against them, and for the other Part against the Appellant; for that these Words of the Statute, *If peradventure the Appellor be not able to recompence the Damages*, must be understood of all the Damages.

Sect. 154. Fifthly, That [e] the Appellee after his Acquit l may sue for the Damages by Attorney.

Sect. 155. Sixthly, That [f] though the Statute expresly give only judicial Process for the Recovery of the Damages against the Abettors, yet the Appellee may, if he think fit, take out an Original Writ of Abetment, grounded on the Statute, and therein count to greater Damages than were found by the Jury; which in Respect of such Finding, being but in Nature of an Inquest of Office, shall not conclude the Appellee.

Sect. 156. Seventhly, That [g] if the Appellee chuse rather to proceed for the Recovery of his Damages by judicial Process, than by Original; it is safest for him to make Use of a Distress, which is given by the express Words of the Statute; yet there is a Note [h] of an Old Case, wherein a *Venire facias* was first awarded; but it is [i] questionable, whether this be justified by the Statute or not.

Sect. 157. Eighthly, That [k] it is Time enough for the Appellee to shew the Time and Place of the Abetment, when the Abettors appear upon such Process; and by such shewing he supplies the Omission of the Jury in not finding any Time or Place, on their Inquiry of the Abetment, *&c.*

Sect. 158. Ninthly, That [l] the Nonsuit of an Appellee, either in an Original Writ, or Process against the Abettors whether before or after Appearance, is no Bar of a second Writ or Process.

[a] S. P. C. 171. Letter A. Quære 8 Ed. 4. 3. pl. 5. 12 Co. 126. 2 Inst. 386. Rastal's Entries 44. Bro. Appeal, 96.

[b] S. P. C. 170. Letter F.

[c] 41 Ass. 24.

[d] 12 Co. 126. S. P. C. 170. Letter D. 8 Ed. 4. 3. pl. 5. 8 H. 5. 6. pl. 26. 26 H. 8. 3. pl. 14. 2 Inst. 386. Fitz. Coro. 29. 386, 463. Bro. Appeal, 96. Contra 41 Ass. pl. 8. Fitz. Coro. 219. Bro. Appeal, 74.

[e] Fitz. Coro. 13.

[f] Fitz. Action sur le Statute, 28. 2 Inst. 386, 387. S. P. C. 171. Letter D. 1 Inst. 139.

[g] S. P. C. 171. Letter B. 2 Inst. 386, 387.

[h] Fitz. Coro. 102.

[i] S. P. C. 171. Letter B. 2 Inst. 386, 387.

[k] S. P. C. 171. Letter A. 2 Inst. 386. Fitz. Coron. 45.

[l] S. P. C. 171. Letter C. 1 Inst. 139. Fitz. Coron. 386.

Sect. 159. As to the ſeventh general Point, *viz.* Where the Appellant is to be fined, there can be no Doubt but [a] that by the expreſs Words of the above expounded Statute of *Weſtminſter* 2. 18. Where-ever the Appellant, or his Abettors, are by the Purport thereof to render Damages to an Appellee, they are alſo to be fined to the King, and impriſoned for a Year. Alſo it ſeems clear from the general Purport of the [b] Books, that an Appellant appearing to have brought an ill grounded Appeal, whether of Felony or [c] Mayhem, ſhall be fined, in many Caſes wherein he is not liable to render Damages by the Statute above mentioned; as where he is [d] Nonſuit, either againſt all, or Part [e] of the Appellees only, whether after, or, as ſome [f] have holden, before Appearance, or where the Writ abates thro' the [g] Default of the Appellant in wilfully ſuing by a [h] wrong Name, or a [i] vitious Writ, *&c.* and even a *Feme Covert*, [k] ſuing an Appeal known by her to be groundleſs, as for the Death of a Huſband whom ſhe knows to be alive, ſhall be fined. But it is certain that where a Writ abates by the Act [l] of God, or for any other Cauſe, no way imputable to the Appellant, he ſhall neither be fined nor amerced. Alſo it is certain, that an Infant is in no Caſe to be fined for a falſe Appeal, but ſome [m] have holden that he may be amerced, which is contradicted by others, who ſay, [n] That an Infant can in no Caſe be amerced.

[a] S.P.C. 170. Letter C. Fitz. Fines, 2. 1 Aſſ. pl. 9. 22 Aſſ. pl. 39. 8 H. 4. 17. pl. 2.
[b] See the Books cited the following Part of this Section. Fitz. Coro. 137. 8 Co. 60. a. S.P.C. 170. Letter C. ſeems contrary.
[c] 40 Aſſ. pl. 1. Fitz. Cor. 214.
[d] Fitz. Fines, 49. 41 Aſſ. pl. 8. Fitz. Coro. 219. Damages, 77.
[e] 22 Aſſ. pl. 82. Fitz. Coro. 182.
[f] Fitz. Fines, 107.
[g] 8 Co. 60. a.
[h] 9 H. 5. 1. pl. 3. Fitz. Fines, 28. Bro. Fines, 16.
[i] Fitz. Coro. 121.
[k] Bro. Appeal, 25. 8 H. 4. 17. pl. 2.
[l] Fitz. Brief, 612.
[m] Bro. Fines for Contempt, 37. 41 Aſſ. pl. 14.
[n] Co. Lit. 127. Cro. Ca. 161. Vide 1 Danvers's Abridgment 462. L. pl. 1, 2, 463. pl. 8, 9, 10, 13.

CHAP. XXIV.

Of Approver.

Sect. 1. HAVING gone through the ſeveral Kinds of Appeals by innocent Perſons, I am now in the ſecond Place to conſider the Nature of an Appeal by an Offender, confeſſing himſelf to be guilty, who is commonly called a Prover or [a] Approver in *Engliſh*, or *Probator* in *Latin*; becauſe he muſt at his Peril prove his Appeal in every Point, and for ſo doing is pardoned of Courſe. And for the better Underſtanding the Nature of ſuch Appeal, I ſhall examine the following Particulars.

[a] S.P.C. 142. 3 Inſt. 129. H.P.C. 192. 2 H.H.P.C. 225, 226.

1. When a Man may be ſaid to become an Approver.
2. Who may be admitted to be Approvers, and who not.
3. In what Caſes.
4. Of what Offences.
5. Againſt what Offenders.
6. Before what Juſtices.
7. How they are to be ordered and demeaned, both before and after the Appeal.

8. What Process is to be awarded against the Appellees.
9. In what Manner the Court is to proceed upon, and after the Trial.
10. How the Approver is to be rewarded for making good his Appeal.

Sect. 2. As to the first Point, *viz.* When a Man may be said to become an Approver, it seems [a] agreed, That a Man is then properly an Approver, when being indicted of Treason or Felony, before competent Judges, and in Prison for the same, and capable of being an Approver, he confesses the Indictment, and is sworn to reveal all the Treasons and Felonies he knows, and then before a Coroner enters his Appeal against all that were Partners with him in the Crime in the Indictment, being at the Time of the Appeal within the Realm.

As to the second Point, *viz.* Who may be admitted to be Approvers, and who not, I shall observe,

Sect. 3. First, That [b] a Peer of the Realm cannot be an Approver.

Sect. 4. Secondly, That [c] neither a Person attainted of Treason, or Felony, nor even one outlawed in a Personal Action, as some [d] say, can be an Approver, because by his Attainder or Outlawry, he is out of the Law, and his Accusation shall not be of such Credit, as to put any Person upon his Trial.

Sect. 5. Thirdly, That [e] an Ideot, or Person born deaf and dumb, or any one that is *Non compos* at the Time, or an Infant under the Age of Discretion, cannot be an Approver, because no such Person ought to be admitted to take the Oath before the Coroner, without which there can be no Approvement.

Sect. 6. Fourthly, That it is holden both by [f] *Staundforde*, [g] *Coke*, and [h] *Hale*, That no Woman, nor Infant, can be an Approver, but it is observable that the Opinions of *Staundforde* and *Coke* seem chiefly to be grounded on this Foundation, that the Appellee may have such like Exceptions against Approvers, as the Defendant may have in an Appeal brought by a lawful Person, and therefore may except that the Approver is within Age, or a Woman, &c. because such Persons cannot wage Battle; but it being settled at this Day, that these are no good Exceptions to an Appeal brought by a lawful Person, as hath been more fully shewn in the precedent [i] Chapter, it seems to be justly questionable, whether they are now to be admitted as good Exceptions to an Appeal, by an Approver. To which may be added, that in the Opinion of [k] *Hale*, contrary to that of [l] *Staundforde* and [m] *Coke*, a Man above the Age of seventy, or maimed, may be an Approver, though he cannot wage Battel; from whence it follows clearly, that in the Judgment of *Hale*, there is no Necessity that an Approver ☞ should be able to wage Battel. [53]

Sect. 7. Fifthly, That it seems to be [n] agreed, That a Person in holy Orders cannot be an Approver, because it is a Rule, that no Member of the Clergy can sue any Appeal whatsoever, in a Matter or Cause of Death.

As to the third Point, *viz.* In what Cases one may be admitted to be an Approver, I shall observe,

Sect. 8. First, That no [o] one shall be admitted to be an Approver, till he hath confessed the Crime charged against him in his Indictment.

Sect. 9. Secondly, That it is holden [p] in some Books, that he that hath once pleaded Not guilty, cannot be an Approver, but shall be hanged, because he is found false, and his Confession contradicts his former Plea; yet the contrary hereto is holden by [q] others, and [r] *Staundforde* admits that the Court

[a] H. P. C. 192. 2 H. H. P. C. 227, 229. 3 Inst. 129, 130
[b] 3 Inst. 129. H. P. C. 192.
[c] 3 Inst. 129. H. P. C. 192. S. P. C. 146. Letter C. Bro. Coro. 81, 211. Fitz. Coro. 112, 127, 167, 387, 443, 445. 11 Ass. pl. 27. 17 Ass. pl. 4.
[d] Bro. Appeal, 57. Supra Ch. 23. Sect. 32. Fitz. Coro. 175.
[e] 3 Inst. 129. S. P. C. 147. H. P. C. 192. Vide supra Ch. 23. S. 32.
[f] S. P. C. 147. Letter D.
[g] 3 Inst. 129.
[h] H. P. C. 192. 2 H. H. P. C. 233.
[i] Sections 30 and 31.
[k] H. P. C. 192.
[l] S. P. C. 147. Letter D.
[m] 3 Inst. 129.
[n] S. P. C. 147. Letters A, B, D. H. P. C. 192. 3 Inst. 139.
[o] Fitz. Coro. 50, 231, 441.
[p] 3 Inst. 129. H. P. C. 193. S. P. C. 144. Letter B. 145. a. Fitz. Coro. 440. 21 Ed. 3. 18. pl. 25. 19 H. 6. 47. pl. 103.
[q] Finch 387. 12 Ed. 4. 10. pl. 26. Vide 2 H. 7. 3. a.
[r] S. P. C. [illegible]

Court of Grace may admit ſuch Perſons to be Approvers, and this is as much as can be contended for in any other Caſe; for it ſeems [a] agreed, That the Court is not bound of Right, to admit any Perſon whatſoever to be an Approver. [54]

Sect. 10. Thirdly, That it is [b] agreed, That any one indicted of Treaſon or Felony may be an Approver, but that unleſs the Crime with which a Perſon is charged, amount either to Felony or Treaſon, he cannot be an Approver.

Sect. 11. Fourthly, That it is alſo [c] agreed, That no Perſon accuſed of Treaſon or Felony, can be an Approver, unleſs he be actually indicted for it; becauſe his Confeſſion amounts not to a Conviction until he be indicted, and conſequently puts it not in the Power of the Court to give Judgment againſt him, when his Appeal ſhall be rejected or falſified, as every Approvement ought to do.

Sect. 12. Fifthly, That it ſeems alſo to be generally [d] agreed, That if a Perſon indicted be alſo appealed of the ſame Felony, he can no longer be an Approver, the Reaſon whereof ſeems to be, that though the King may in his Diſcretion, by admitting a Perſon to be an Approver, reſpite the Judgment and Execution of one proſecuted by Indictment, which is his own Suit, yet he cannot delay them in an Appeal, which is the Suit of the Party, and *à fortiori* therefore it follows, That [e] if a Perſon be appealed only, and not indicted, he cannot be an Approver.

Sect. 13. Sixthly, That notwithſtanding the Appeal of an Approver may in ſome Reſpects be looked upon as the Suit of the King, and equivalent to an Indictment, yet the Appellee [f] of an Approver cannot become an Approver himſelf, not only becauſe it would falſifie the Appeal of the firſt Approver, in ſuppoſing that he had omitted ſome of his Partners, but alſo becauſe it would cauſe an infinite Delay; for the Appellee of ſuch an Approver might as well become an Approver of others, and ſo on.

Sect. 14. As to the fourth Point, *viz.* Of what Offences a Perſon may be admitted to approve another, it ſeems [g] agreed, That no one can approve another of any other Offence, but the very Crime contained in the Indictment, and therefore that he cannot approve a Man of a Crime of a different [h] Nature, nor even of being Acceſſary [i] before or [k] after to the ſame Crime, becauſe no Man can abet, or receive himſelf. But it ſeems alſo to be agreed, That inaſmuch as the Oath of an Approver is [l] general, to diſcover all the Treaſons and Felonies he knows, if he accuſe any Perſons of Crimes of a different Nature from his own, whether in the ſame, or a foreign [m] County, his Accuſation will be a reaſonable Ground to carry on a Proſecution againſt them for ſuch Crimes, though it [n] be not of it ſelf of Force ſufficient to put them on their Trials.

Sect. 15. As to the fifth Point, *viz.* againſt what Offenders a Perſon may be admitted to become an Approver, it ſeems [o] clear, That a Man may be an Approver againſt any Perſon whatſoever within the Realm, whether he live in the ſame or a foreign County, provided he be named of the County wherein he dwells. But it is ſaid, That if it appear either by the [p] Confeſſion of the Approver, or the Return [q] of the Sheriff, or the Teſtimony [r] of Perſons of Credit in the County, that [s] there are no ſuch Perſons, as ſome of thoſe named in the Appeal, *in rerum natura*, or within the [t] Realm, or even [u] within the County, whereof they are named in the Appeal, the Approver ſhall be hanged, unleſs the [x] Court in Mercy will ſpare him, becauſe his Appeal in reſpect of ſuch Perſons appears to be falſe, or to no Purpoſe.

[a] 3 Inſt. 129. H. P. C. 194. 2 H. H. P. C. 226. 21 H. 6. 34.
[b] 19 H. 6. 47. pl. 103. 3 Inſt. 129. 21 Ed. 3. 18. pl. 24. Finch 387. Fitz. Coron. 231, 448. Bro. Coro. 41. 2 H. H. P. C. 227.
[c] 3 Inſt. 129. H. P. C. 193. 2 H. H. P. C. 228. S. P. C. 143. b. Fitz. Coro. 231. ſeems contrary.
[d] 3 Inſt. 129. Finch 387. H. P. C. 193. 2 H. H. P. C. 228. S. P. C. 147. Letter B. 181 Letter C.
[e] 2 Rich. 3. 22. pl. 53. 11 H. 7. 5. pl. 22. Bro. Coro. 228. Fitz. Coro. 442. 40 Aſſ. pl. 39. ſeems contrary.
[f] Fitz. Coro. 113. S. P. C. 147. Letter B. 2 H. H. P. C. 228. 11 H. 4. 93. pl. 54. ſeems contrary.
[g] S. P. C. 143. Letter A. 2 H. H. P. C. 227. H. P. C. 194. 3 Inſt. 129, 130. 2 Inſt. 629. Finch 387.
[h] Fitz. Coro. 127, 217. 40 Aſſ. pl 39. 11 H. 4. 93. pl. 54.
[i] 27 Aſſ. pl. 69. 13 Ed. 4. 14. pl. 8. Fitz. Coro. 35, 208. Bro. Coro. 154.
[k] Fitz. Coro. 126.
[l] 2 Inſt. 629. H. P. C. 194. 12 Ed. 4. 10. pl. 26. Fitz. Coro. 37, 387.
[m] Fitz. Coro. 437.
[n] Fitz. Coro. 126, 127, 387.
[o] Fitz. Aſſiſe, 446. Fitz. Coro. 460. S. P. C. 154.
[p] S. P. C. 145. Letter F. 1 Ed. 4. 16. pl. 4. Fitz. Coro. 153.
[q] H. P. C. 194. 21 H. 6. 34. pl. 1.
[r] H. P. C. 195. S. P. C. 145. Fitz. Coro. 133.
[s] Bro. Coro. 49. 21 H. 6. 34. pl. 1. H. P. C. 195.
[t] 1 Ed. 4. 16. pl. 4. 1 Aſſ. pl. 2. S. P. C. 145.
[u] Fitz. Coro 46.
[x] S. P. C. 145

Sect. 16. As to the ſixth Point, *viz.* Before what Juſtices a Perſon may be admitted to be an Approver, it ſeems to be a ſettled [a] Rule, That a Man may be an Approver before any Juſtices, who have Power to aſſign a Coroner to take the Appeal; and for this Reaſon it ſeems to be [b] agreed, That one may be an Approver before the Juſtices of the King's Bench, and Juſtices of Gaol-Delivery, and Juſtices in Eyre. And upon this Ground it is holden in Sir *Edward Coke*'s *third* [c] *Inſtitute*, and alſo in Sir *Matthew Hale*'s [d] *Pleas of the Crown*, under the Chapter of Approver, That ☞ a Man may be an Approver before Juſtices of *Oyer and Terminer*. [55] But the Foundation of this Opinion ſeems to be overthrown by what is ſaid by both theſe [e] Authors in other Places, wherein it is holden that Juſtices of *Oyer and Terminer* cannot aſſign a Coroner, becauſe it is not within their Commiſſion: And it ſeems to be a [f] general Rule, that thoſe only can receive the Appeal of an Approver who can aſſign a Coroner to take it; and therefore it ſeems to be agreed, That neither a [g] Court-Baron, nor [h] Juſtices of Peace, nor any other ſpecial [i] Juſtices, can receive ſuch Appeal, unleſs their Commiſſion extend to it. And for the like Reaſon it ſeems to be the Opinion of [k] Sir *Edward Coke*, that the Lord High Steward of *England* cannot receive ſuch an Appeal; but this is contradicted by [l] Sir ☞ *Matthew Hale*. [56]

As to the ſixth Point, *viz.* In what Manner an Approver is to be ordered and demeſned, both before and after the Appeal, the following Particulars ſeem moſt remarkable.

Sect. 17. Firſt, That it ſeems to be [m] agreed, That where-ever a Perſon indicted of Treaſon or Felony confeſſes the Indictment, whether he appealed others or not, he puts it entirely in the Diſcretion of the Court, either to give Judgment, and award Execution againſt him, or to reſpite them till he ſhall have made good his Appeal.

Sect. 18. Secondly, That [n] whenever a Perſon is admitted to become an Approver, the Court ſhall aſſign a Coroner to receive his Appeal, and ſhall take an Oath from him to diſcover all the Treaſons and Felonies that he knows.

Sect. 19. Thirdly, That [o] the Court which admits a Man to become an Approver, ought to limit him a certain Number of Days, to make his Appeal in, during which it is holden by [p] ſome, That he is to have a Penny a-day as his Wages from the King; but by [q] others, That he ought not to have it till he has made good his Appeal, by convicting the ☞ Appellees. [57]

Sect. 20. Fourthly, That the Approver during all the Time aſſigned him for making his Appeal, ought [r] to be at his Liberty, and out of Priſon; for [s] he may diſavow an Appeal made by Dureſs of Impriſonment; but if he alledge that an Appeal was extorted from him by ſuch Dureſs, and ſuch Allegation be found to be falſe, either by the Examination of the Coroner, or by an Inqueſt of Office, the Approver ſhall be hanged.

Sect. 21. Fifthly, that [t] the Approver ought to make his Appeal before the Coroner, on every one of the Days limited for the Making of it; for if he fail on any one of them, and the Coroner record ſuch Failure, Judgment ſhall be given againſt him.

[a] 3 Inſt. 130. S. P. C. 143. Letter C. H. P. C. 194.
[b] 3 Inſt. 130. S. P. C. 143. Letter C. H. P. C. 194. 2 H. H. P. C. 229. Fitz. Aſſiſe, 446.
[c] 3 Inſt. 130.
[d] H. P. C. 194.
[e] 4 Inſt. 165. H. P. C. 162. 2 H. H. P. C. 31, 229.
[f] H. P. C. 194. 3 Inſt. 130. S. P. C. 143. Letter C.
[g] H. P. C. 194. S. P. C. 144.
[h] 9 H. 4. 1. pl. 1. 2 H. 4. 19. pl. 12. 10 Co. 76. b. Bro. Appeal, 18. H. P. C. 194. 2 H. H. P. C. 229.
[i] S. P. C. 144.
[k] 3 Inſt. 130.
[l] H. P. C. 194.
[m] 21 H. 6. 34. pl. 1. 19 H. 6. 35. pl. 74. Bro. Coro. 48, 49. Fitz. Coro. 66, 67, 447. H. P. C. 194. 2 H. H. P. C. 226. 3 Inſt. 129.
[n] H. P. C. 194. 2 Inſt. 629. S. P. C. 143. Letter A. Fitz. Coro. 37. 12 Ed. 4. 10. pl. 26.
[o] H. P. C. 195. 2 H. H. P. C. 229, 230. S. P. C. 145. Letter C. 12 Ed. 4. 10. pl. 26. Fitz. Coro. 37, 439. 26 Aſſ. pl. 19.
[p] Fitz. Coro. 439. H. P. C. 194. S. P. C. 145. Letter B. Bro. Coro. 34. 11 H. 4. 93. pl. 54.
[q] 21 H. 6. 34. pl. 1.
[r] H. P. C. 195. Fitz. Coro. 439. S. P. C. 145. Letter D.
[s] Fitz. Coro. 118, 169, 255. 12 Aſſ. pl. 29. S. P. C. 145. Letter D.
[t] H. P. C. 195. Bro. Coro. 99. 26 Aſſ. pl. 19. S. P. C. 145. Letter A.

And

And ſo ſhall it be [a] alſo; If after he have formed his Appeal before the Coroner, he make the leaſt Variation in his repeating it before the Court, and the Coroner record ſuch Variation.

Sect. 22. As to the ſeventh Point, *viz.* What Proceſs is to be awarded againſt the Appellees, it ſeems [b] agreed, That the Coroner may award Proceſs to the Sheriff, againſt any Appellee in the ſame County, till it come to the Exigent; but it is certain, that [c] he cannot award it to any other Officer, except the Sheriff, nor to any Sheriff out of his own County: And it ſeems [d] queſtionable, whether he be not reſtrained by the Statute of *Magna Charta*, Ch. 17. to award the Exigent to the Sheriff of his own County. But it ſeems [e] agreed, that the Juſtices of the King's Bench, or Juſtices in Eyre, might by the Common Law as well award Proceſs of Outlawry, as any other Proceſs, againſt Appellees in any County whatſoever.

And it is [f] certain, That Juſtices of Gaol-Delivery may award Proceſs into any County, to apprehend and try them by Force of 28 *Ed.* 1. commonly called the Statute *de Appellatis*; but whether this Statute do impower ſuch Juſtice to award Proceſs of Outlawry into a Foreign County, may deſerve to be conſidered. [58]

a H.P.C.195. 2 H. H. P. C. 230. S. P. C. 145. Letter E. 26 Aſſ. pl. 19. b H.P.C.196. 2 H. H. P. C. 231. S. P. C. 146. c Fitz. Coro. 462. 2 H. H. P. C. 231. 29 Ed. 3. 42. d Supra ch. 9. Sect. 41, 43. e H.P.C. 196. S.P.C. 146. Fitz. Coro. 460. f H.P.C.196. 2 H. H. P. C. 37, 231. S. P. C. 146.

As to the eighth Point, *viz.* In what Manner the Court is to proceed upon, and after the Trial, I ſhall obſerve.

Sect. 23. Firſt, That it is in the Election [g] of the Appellee, either to put himſelf upon his Country, or to wage Battel with the Approver.

Sect. 24. Secondly, That let there be never ſo many Appellees, if they wage Battel, the Approver muſt fight them [h] all. But on the Contrary, it ſeems to be generally [i] agreed, That if a Perſon appealed by ſeveral Approvers of one and the ſame Felony, vanquiſhes any one of them, he ſhall be acquitted againſt them all, and all of them ſhall be condemned, in the ſame Manner as if every one of them had been actually vanquiſhed. But if an Approver having appealed ſeveral of the ſame Crime, be vanquiſhed by one of them, it ſeems to be [k] holden, that his Appeal is ſtill in force againſt the Reſt; but the Note in [l] *Fitzherbert's Abridgment*, which ſeems to be the Foundation of this Opinion, ſeems rather to be intended of an Appeal by an innocent Perſon, than of an Appeal by an Approver, in Relation to whom it ſeems to be a general Rule, that being once falſified as to any one of the Appellees, he ought to be condemned, as hath been more fully ſhewn in the 9th and 15th Sections of this Chapter.

Sect. 25. Thirdly, That if the King pardon the Approver or Appellee, hanging the Appeal, the Approvement [m] ceaſes, and the Appellee ſhall be diſcharged; for in the firſt Caſe, by the Pardon the Felony is extinct, and a Man can no longer be an Approver, than while he is under the Guilt of the Crime, whereof the Approvement is made, and liable to be condemned by the Court, whenever his Appeal ſhall be falſified, &c. And in the ſecond [n] Caſe, it cannot be doubted but that the King's Pardon will diſcharge the Appellee, becauſe an Approvement is rather the Suit of the King, than of the Party.

Sect. 26. Fourthly, That whether the Appeal of an Approver be falſified by the [o] Confeſſion or Vanquiſhment [p] of the Approver, or verified by the Conviction or Vanquiſhment of the Appellee; yet if the Offence be within the Benefit of Clergy, neither the Approver in the firſt Caſe, nor the Appellee in the ſecond, are excluded from it, any more than in the Caſe of an Indictment.

g H.P.C. 196. S. P. C. 142. Letter D. 3 Inſt. 130. 47 E. 3. 5. pl. 10. h S. P. C. 180. Letter E. 2 H. H. P. C. 233, 234. H. P. C. 196. 47 Ed. 3. 5. pl. 10. 19 H. 6. 35. pl. 74. 3 Inſt. 130. i H. P.C.196. S. P. C. 74. Letter B. 106 Letter D. 149 Letter B. 180 Letter E. 11 H. 4. 93. pl. 49. 21 H. 6. 34. b. 35. a. Bro. Coro. 31, 49. 3 Inſt. 130. Fitz. Coro. 143. 7 Ed. 3. 12. pl. 29. k S. P. C. 108. Letter E. l Fitz. Coro. 98. m 47 Ed. 3. 16. pl. 26. 47 Ed. 3. 5. pl. 10. Fitz. Coro. 103. H. P. C 201. 3 Inſt. 130. S. P. C. 149. Letter B. n H. P. C. 201. Bro. Coro. 49. 21 H. 6. 35. o Fitz. Coro. 128, 369. Fitz. Aſſiſe, 421. H. P. C. 197. Contra 21 Ed. 3. 17. pl. 21. Bro. Coro. 38. Fitz. Coro. 447. p Bro. Clergy, 5, 26. 11 H. 4. 93. pl. 49.

Sect. 27. As to the ninth Point, *viz.* How the Approver is to be rewarded for making good his Appeal; it is said, [a] That if an Approver convict all the Appellees, whether by Battel or Verdict, the King, *ex merito justitiæ*, ought to pardon him as to his Life, and also give him his Wages [b] from the Time of the Appeal to the Time of his Conviction. But [c] it seems, That anciently he ought not to be suffered to continue in the Kingdom. And it is recited by 5 *H.* 4. *ch.* 2. *That divers notorious Felons, for Safeguard of their Lives, had become Provors, to the Intent, in the mean Time, by Brocage, and great Gifts to pursue and have their Pardons, and then after their Deliverance, had become more notorious Felons than they were before*; and thereupon it is enacted, *That if any Person pray or pursue, or cause to be prayed or pursued for any such Felon so attainted by his own Confession, to have any Charter of Pardon, the Name of him that pursues such Charter be put in the same Charter, making Mention that the same Charter is granted at his Instance. And if he to whom such Charter is granted become a Felon again, the Party who pursued the Charter shall forfeit* 100 l.

[a] H.P.C.197. 2 H. H. P. C. 233. S. P. C. 142. Letter D. 3 Inst. 129, 130. Contra 19 H. 6. 35. pl. 74. Fitz. Cor. 6.

[b] Vide supra sect. 19.

[c] S. P. C. 142. Letter D.

CHAP. XXV.

Of Indictment.

Sect. 1. AN Indictment is an Accusation, at the Suit of the King, by the Oaths of twelve Men of the same County wherein the Offence was committed, returned to inquire of all Offences in general in the County, determinable by the Court into which they are returned, and finding a Bill brought before them to be true; but when such Accusation is found by a Grand Jury, without any Bill brought before them, and [d] afterwards reduced to a formed Indictment, it is called a Presentment, and when it is found by Jurors returned to inquire of that particular Offence only which is indicted, it is properly called an Inquisition. And for the better Understanding the Nature of such Proceedings, I shall consider the following Particulars,

[d] Lamb. B. 4. ch. 3.

1. Whether a Grand Jury may find Part of a Bill brought before them true, and Part false.
2. Whether an Indictment be merely the Suit of the King.
3. What Matters are indictable.
4. Where a Man may be tried at the Suit of the King for a capital Offence, without any Indictment.
5. Whether a Man may be arraigned on an Indictment while an Appeal is depending against him for the same Offence.
6. Who may and ought to be Indictors, and in what Manner they are to be returned.
7. Within what Place the Offences inquired of must arise.
8. What ought to be the Form of the Body of an Indictment.
9. What ought to be the Form of the Caption of it.
10. Upon what Proof it may be found.

11. In what Caſes it may be quaſhed.
12. What may be pleaded to it, and in what Manner.

Sect. 2. As to the firſt Point, *viz.* Whether a Grand Jury may find Part of the Bill brought before them true, and Part falſe, it ſeems to be generally agreed, That they muſt either find *Billa Vera*, or *Ignoramus*, for the Whole; and that if they take upon them to find it ſpecially, or conditionally, or to be true for Part only, and not for the reſt, the Whole is void, and the Party [a] cannot be tried upon it, but ought to be indicted anew; and accordingly it hath been reſolved, That if a Grand Jury indorſe a Bill of Murder, [b] *Billa vera ſe defendendo*; or *Billa vera* for Manſlaughter, [c] and not for Murder; or if they indorſe a Bill upon the Statutes of News, *Billa vera*, [d] but whether *Iſta verba prolata fuerunt malicioſe, ſeditioſe, vel econtra ignoramus*; or if they indorſe an Indictment of Forcible Entry, and Forcible Detainer, *Billa vera* [e] as to the Forcible Entry, and *Ignoramus* as to the Forcible Detainer; or if they indorſe, [f] That if the Freehold were in *J. S.* or the Poſſeſſion were in *J. S.* then they find *Billa vera*, the Whole is void.

Sect. 3. As to the ſecond Point, *viz.* Whether an Indictment be merely the Suit of the King; it is every Day's Practice, That it is ſo far eſteemed the King's Suit, that the Party who proſecutes it is a good Witneſs to prove it: Alſo it ſeems to be agreed, [g] That no Damages can be given to the Party grieved upon an Indictment, or any other criminal Proſecution, [h] notwithſtanding the King, by his Commiſſion erecting a New Court, expreſly direct, That the Party ſhall recover his Damages by ſuch a Proſecution. Alſo, where by Statute Damages are given to the Party grieved by the Offence intended to be redreſſed, it [i] ſeems that they cannot be recovered on an Indictment grounded on ſuch Statute, unleſs ſuch Method of recovering them be expreſly given by the Statute; but that they ought to be ſued for in an Action on the Statute, in the Name of the Party grieved. But it ſeems [k] certain, That the Court of King's Bench, having the King's Privy Seal for that Purpoſe, may give to the Proſecutor the third Part of the Fine aſſeſſed on a Criminal Proſecution, for any Offence whatſoever. Alſo, it is every Day's Practice of that Court, to induce Defendants to make Satisfaction to Proſecutors for the Coſts of the Proſecution, and alſo for the Damages ſuſtained by the Injury whereof the Defendants are convicted, by intimating an Inclination on that Account to mitigate the Fine due to the King.

[a] 2 Rol. Rep. 52. 3 Bulſt. 206. 1 Rol. Rep. 407, 408.
[b] 2 Rol. Rep. 52. Powel's Caſe.
[c] 3 Bulſt. 206. 1 Rol. 408. 1 Sid. 230.
[d] Leon. 287.
[e] Yelv. 99. 1 Sid. 414. Vide B. 1. c. 64. ſect. 40. Cro. Jac. 151. Con. 1 Sid. 99.
[f] Yelv. 15.
[g] 1 Rol. Abr. 220. Letter B. 2 Rol. Abr. 83. Letter P. Cro. Car. 531, 558.
[h] Cro. Car. 558. Vide ſupra Ch. 1. Sect. 3, 4, 6, 7, 8.
[i] 1 Rol. Abr. 220. Letter B. 1 Jon. 380. Cro. Car. 448.
[k] 1 Keb. 487. pl. 30.

Sect. 4. As to the third Point, *viz.* What Matters are indictable: There can be no Doubt, but that all Capital Crimes whatſoever, and alſo all Kinds of inferior Crimes of a publick Nature, as Miſpriſions, and all other Contempts, all Diſturbances of the Peace, all Oppreſſions, and all other Miſdemeanors whatſoever of a publickly evil Example againſt the Common Law, may be indicted; but no Injuries of a [l] private Nature, unleſs they ſome Way concern the King. Alſo it ſeems to be a good general Ground, That where-ever the Statute prohibits a Matter of a publick Grievance to the [m] Liberties and Security of a Subject; or commands a Matter of publick [n] Convenience, as the repairing of the Common Streets of a Town, an Offender againſt ſuch Statute is puniſhable, not only at the Suit of the Party aggrieved, but alſo by Way of Indictment for his Contempt of the Statute, unleſs ſuch Method of Proceeding do manifeſtly appear to be excluded by it. Yet if the Party offending have been fined to the King in the Action brought by the Party, as it is ſaid [o] that he may in every Action for doing a Thing prohibited by Statute, it ſeems

[l] 27 Aſſ. pl. 20. Bro. Indictment, 16. Preſentment, 26.
[m] 2 Inſt. 55, 163. Cro. Jac. 577.
[n] 1 Mod. 34. 1 Sid. 209.
[o] 8 Co. 60. b. 2 Inſt. 131.

ſeems queſtionable, whether he may afterwards be indicted; becauſe that would make him liable to a ſecond Fine for the ſame Offence. Alſo, if a Statute extend only to private [a] Perſons, or if it extend to all Perſons in general, but chiefly concern Diſputes of a private Nature, as thoſe relating to [b] Diſtreſſes made by Lords on their Tenants, it is ſaid that Offences againſt ſuch Statute will hardly bear an Indictment. Alſo, where a Statute makes a new Offence, which was no Way prohibited by the Common Law, and appoints a particular Manner of proceeding againſt the Offender, as by Commitment, or Action of Debt, or Information, &c. without mentioning an Indictment, it ſeems to be [c] ſettled at this Day, that it will not maintain an Indictment, becauſe the Mentioning the other Methods of proceeding only, ſeems impliedly to exclude that of Indictment. [59] [d] Yet it hath been adjudged, That if ſuch a Statute give a Recovery by Action of Debt, Bill, Plaint, or Information, or otherwiſe, it authoriſes a Proceeding by Way of Indictment. [e] Alſo, where a Statute adds a farther Penalty to an Offence prohibited by the Common Law, there can be no Doubt but that the Offender may ſtill be indicted, if the Proſecutor think fit, at the Common Law. And if the Indictment for ſuch Offence conclude *contra formam Statuti*, and cannot be made good as an Indictment upon the Statute, it ſeems [f] to be now ſettled, That it may be maintained as an Indictment at Common Law, as will be more fully ſhewn in the following Part of this Chapter.

As to the fourth Point, *viz.* Where a Man may be tried at the Suit of the King for a capital Offence without any Indictment, I ſhall endeavour to ſhew,

1. Where one may be ſo tried as having been taken with the Manner.
2. Where one may be ſo tried upon a Verdict.
3. Where upon an Appeal not proſecuted.
4. Whether one may be ſo tried upon a Sheriff's Return.

Sect. 5. As to the firſt Point, *viz.* Where one may be ſo tried as having been taken with the Manner: [g] It is ſaid, That anciently if one guilty of Larceny had been freſhly purſued and taken with the Manner, and the Goods ſo found upon him had been brought into the Court with him, he might be tried immediately without any Indictment; and this is ſaid to have been the proper Method of proceeding in ſuch Manors which had the Franchiſe of Infangthefe, but ſeems to be altogether obſolete at this Day. [60]

Sect. 6. As to the ſecond Point, *viz.* Where one may be ſo tried upon a Verdict: It is [h] ſaid, That in an Action of Treſpaſs in the King's Bench, *De muliere abducta cum bonis viri*, if the Defendant be found guilty of having carried away the Woman and Goods with Force, and feloniouſly; or [i] in a common Action of Treſpaſs in the ſaid Court, for Goods carried away, if it be found that the Defendant feloniouſly ſtole them, he ſhall be put to anſwer the Felony without any farther Accuſation; for ſuch a Charge by the Oath of twelve Men, on their Inquiry into the Merits of a Cauſe, in a Court which has Juriſdiction over the Crime, is equivalent to an Indictment; and the King being always in Judgment of Law preſent in Court, may take Advantage of any Matter therein properly diſcloſed for his Benefit. But ſuch a Verdict in a Court which has [k] no Juriſdiction over criminal Matters, ſeems to be of little Force, becauſe ſuch Court has nothing to do with ſuch Matters. And it ſeems,

[a] 1 Sid. 209. 2 Mod. 34.
[b] 1 Mod. 71, 288.
1 Lev. 299. Raym. 205. 1 Vent. 104. 2 Inſt. 131, 132.
[c] Bond's Caſe, Michaelmas 3 Georgii 1. Shower 398, 399. 3 Keb. 34, 273. Cro. Jac. 643, 644. 3 Mod. 79. 4 Mod. 144. Carth. 263. Palmer 388. 1 Sid. 434, 439. 6 Mod. 86. 2 Rol. Rep. 247, 248, 398.
[d] Dominus Rex verſus Dixon, Trin. 3 Georg. 1.
[e] 3 Mod. 118. 1 Sid. 192. ſeem contra.
[f] The Caſe of the County of the City of Norwich, adjudged Paſch. 3 Georgii 1. 2 H. H. P. C. 171. contra.
[g] Vide ſupra Ch. 15. Sect. 41. 7 H. 4. 43. pl. 9. 26 Aſſ. pl. 32. 1 Ed. 3. 13. pl. 6. S. P. C. 28, 29, 148. Letter C. 179. Letter B. H. P. C. 198. 2 H. H. P. C. 156, 149*. Bro. Appeal, 130. 1 Aſſ. pl. 5. Fitz. Coron. 156, 357.
[h] H. P. C. 199. 2 H. H. P. C. 150*, 151*. S. P. C. 94. Letter B. 95. Fitz. Coron. 122. Fitz. Utlagary, 49. 13 Aſſ. pl. 5. Bro. Coron. 77.
[i] H. P. C. 199. S. P. C. 94. Letter B. Fitz. Indictm. 31.
[k] S. P. C. 94. Letter B. Fitz. Indictment, 31.

That

[a] That even in the King's Bench, if on any Indictment whatſoever, except only an Inquiſition of Death found before a Coroner on View, a Perſon not mentioned in it be found guilty of the Crime whereof others are indicted, yet ſuch Finding ſhall not ſerve for an Indictment againſt him, becauſe it was wholly extrajudicial. [b] But ſuch Finding of others guilty, whether in the King's Bench, or other Court of Criminal Juriſdiction, upon an Inquiſition of Death, found before a Coroner on View, is of greater Force, becauſe the Jury acquitting the Party ſo indicted, [c] ought to inquire what other Perſon did the Fact; becauſe it appears by a Record of the higheſt Credit, That a Perſon is killed. [d] Alſo, if a Perſon be declared againſt in a proper Court, for having been guilty of a Miſdemeanor, *ſimul cum A. B. & C.* and thereupon the Jury find *A. B.* and *C.* guilty; it ſeems that ſuch Verdict will ſerve for an Indictment againſt them, becauſe it was not wholly extrajudicial.

As to the third Point, *viz.* Where one may be ſo tried upon an Appeal not proſecuted, the following Particulars ſeem moſt remarkable.

Sect. 7. Firſt, That an Appeal by an innocent Perſon, and an Appeal by an [e] Approver, are equally favoured in this Reſpect.

Sect. 8. Secondly, That regularly where a Perſon is indicted and appealed of the ſame [f] Crime, and the Appeal is not proſecuted, he ſhall not [g] be arraigned upon the Indictment, but upon the Appeal.

Sect. 9. Thirdly, [h] That if an Appellant be nonſuit in an Appeal by Writ, before he hath declared, the Appellee cannot be arraigned at the King's Suit on the Writ of Appeal; not only becauſe it contains no Certainty of the Circumſtances of the Fact, which it is the proper [i] Office of the Declaration to aſcertain; but alſo becauſe, for what appears to the contrary by the Record, the Writ might [k] have been purchaſed by a Stranger. And therefore in ſuch Caſe it ſeems to be in the Diſcretion [l] of the Court, either to diſmiſs the Appellee, or to bail him, 'till it ſhall appear, Whether there will be any other Proſecution againſt him. But if an Appellant, by Writ, be nonſuit after Declaration, or any Appellant by Bill or Approver, be nonſuit, it ſeems, [m] That regularly the Appellee ſhall be arraigned at the King's Suit, on the Bill or Declaration; becauſe they muſt be as certain as an Indictment, and cannot be commenced but in Perſon.

Sect. 10. Fourthly, That it ſeems to be a ſettled Rule, That whereever an Appeal is once well commenced, and afterwards ſo far determined, without a full Acquittal, That neither the ſame, nor any [n] other Plaintiff, can ever bring another Appeal againſt the ſame Appellee, he may be arraigned upon the Bill or Declaration, at the Suit of the King; as where an Appellant, having a good Title to the Appeal, makes a Releaſe [o] to the Appellee, hanging the Action, or ſuffers a [p] Nonſuit, or [q] *Retraxit*, or [r] demurs to a good Plea or Iſſue, tendered by the Appellee, which Demurrer is adjudged againſt him; or where ſuch an Appellant or Approver [s] confeſs their Appeal to be falſe, [t] unleſs they make ſuch Confeſſion in the Field, upon a Trial awarded by Battel; for ſuch Confeſſion amounts to a Vanquiſhment of the Appellant or Approver, and conſequently is a full Acquittal of the Appellee; after which his Life ſhall not be brought

[a] 13 Ed. 4. 3. pl. 7. Fitz. Coron. 39.
[b] 13 Ed. 4. 3. pl. 7.
[c] Supra Ch. 9. Sect. 33.
[d] Bro. Indict. 13. 26 Aſſ. pl. 62.
2 H. H. P. C. 149*, 150*.
[e] S. P. C. 147. Letter E. 148. H. P. C. 199, 200. Bro. Appeal, 53. Bro. Coron. 3, 16, 49.
[f] H. P. C. 199. 31 H. 6. 11. pl. 6. Fitz. Coro. 18. S. P. C. 107. Letter A.
[g] H. P. C. 199. 2 H. H. P. C. 221. S. P. C. 107. Letter E. 33 H. 6. 1. pl. 6. 4 Ed. 4. 10. pl. 14. Bro. Appeal, 92, 149. S. P. C. 147. Letter A. Fitz. Coron. 114.
[h] S. P. C. 148. Letters A, B, C. H. P. C. 199, 200. Bro. Appeal, 67, 130. Fitz. Coron. 156, 198, 357, 384.
[i] See Ch. 23. Sect. 86, 87, &c.
[k] See Ch. 23. Sect. 26, 131.

[l] S. P. C. 148. Letter C. Bro. Appeal, 67, 130. 27 Aſſ. pl. 7. 1 Aſſ. pl. 5. Fitz. Coro. 156, 198, 357. [m] S. P. C. 148. H. P. C. 199, 200. Bro. Appeal, 67. [n] S. P. C. 148. Bro. Appeal, 118. Fitz. Coron. 369. Vide Bro. Coron. 35. 9 H. 5. 2. pl. 7. [o] S. P. C. 148. Letter B. H. P. C. 200. Bro. Appeal, 27. Fitz. Coron. pl. 12. [p] H. P. C. 199. S. P. C. 147. Letter E. Cro. Eliz. 460. Fitz. Coron. 25, 381. Bro. Niſi prius, 28. Fitz Utlagary, 47. [q] S. P. C. 147. Letter E. 148. Letter B. [r] Dyer 120. pl. 13. [s] S. P. C. 148. Letter B. Fitz. Coron. 103. 3 H. 6. 50. pl. 16. 13 Aſſ. pl. 10. H. P. C. 200. 47 Ed. 3. 5. pl. 10. Bro. Coron. 3, 16, 49, 78. Bro. Appeal, 53. [t] 21 H. 6. 34. pl. 1. S. P. C. 148. Letter B. H. P. C. 200.

again into Danger for the ſame Crime. And this ſeems to be the only Reaſon why after ſuch a Vanquiſhment, or a Verdict in his Favour, an Appellee ſhall be diſcharged, as well againſt the Suit of the King, as that of the Party. But it ſeems, That in all other Caſes whatſoever, an Appellee, in an Appeal well commenced, being wholly diſcharged of the Suit of the Party, may be arraigned upon the Appeal, at the Suit of the King, whether ſuch Diſcharge were merely owing to the Act of the Party, as in the Caſes abovementioned, or to the Act of the Court; as [a] where an Approver is adjudged to be hanged before he hath perfected his Appeal; or partly to the Act of Law, and partly to the Act of the Party, as [b] where an Appeal by a Woman for the Death of her firſt Huſband, is abated by her marrying a ſecond; or where an Appellee is diſcharged of an Appeal, for not [c] having been made a Defendant in a former Appeal, brought by the ſame Appellant for the very ſame Fact; or whether ſuch Diſcharge be merely owing to the Act of God; as [d] where an Appellant dies a natural Death, while his Appeal is depending. It ſeems indeed to be holden in the Year-Book [e] of 4 *H.* 6. as a general Rule, that where-ever a Writ is abated, the Declaration depending upon it is determined alſo, and conſequently, that the Appellee cannot be arraigned upon it; but to this it may be anſwered, that in the very ſame Place it is allowed, that after a Nonſuit in an Appeal, the Appellee may be arraigned at the Suit of the King; and it ſeems difficult to give a Reaſon, why a Writ is not as much determined upon a Nonſuit, as upon an Abatement; to which may be added, that the Point adjudged, which was this, That where a Writ abates for a Miſnoſmer, the Defendant ſhall not be arraigned at the Suit of the King, ſeems plainly to go on this Ground, That where a Suit is ill commenced, the King ſhall not have a greater Advantage from it than the Party might have had; and therefore the Opinion abovementioned, being alſo contradicted by the beſt [f] Authorities, ſeems to be of little Weight.

Sect. 11. Fifthly, That where-ever [g] an Appeal abates for an Inſufficiency of the Writ, or is barred for want of a good Title in the Appellant; or for any other Matter which ſhews it was ill commenced, the Defendant ſhall not be arraigned upon it at the Suit of the King, becauſe it never had a good Foundation, and cannot give a greater Advantage to the King than to the Party himſelf who ſued it; and therefore it ſeems to be agreed, That if an Appeal be abated for want of Form apparent in the Writ, as [h] for the Omiſſion of the Word *Habeas*, or for falſe [i] *Latin*, or for any other [k] apparent Defect; or if it be abated for a Defect not apparent of it ſelf, but diſcloſed by the Pleadings of the Parties, as for a [l] Miſnoſmer, or wrongful Addition, or any ſuch like Inſufficiency; or if it be abated on Account of the Diſability of the Appellant, as by the Plea of Outlawry [m] for Felony or Treſpaſs; or if it be put without Day upon a Plea of Excommunication of the Appellant; or [n] if it be barred by a Releaſe made before the Commencement of the Suit, or by Reaſon that the Time for bringing it was elapſed [o] before it was commenced, or becauſe the Appellant appears to have never had any Right to bring it; as where in an Appeal by one as Wife, it is found that ſhe was [p] never lawfully married to the Deceaſed; or in an Appeal by one as Heir [q] to

[a] S. P. C. 147. Letter E. 21 Ed. 3. 17. pl. 20.
[b] S. P. C. 147. Letter E. H. P. C. 200.
[c] 47 Ed. 3. 16. pl. 27. Fitz. Coro. 104.
[d] S. P. C. 147. Letter E. 47 Ed. 3. 5. pl. 10.
[e] 4 H. 6. 16. Bro. Appeal, 44.
[f] S. P. C. 147. Letter E. H. P. C. 200.
[g] Bro. Appeal, 5. Fitz. Coro. 68. Bro. Coro. 35. Contra 41. Aſſ. pl. 14. Fitz. Age, 74.
[h] Fitz. Coro. 121. S. P. C. 149. Letter A. 13 Aſſ. pl. 10. Bro. Appeal, 53.
[i] H. P. C. 200.
[k] Bro. Coro. 78. S. P. C. 148. Letter C.
[l] Bro. Appeal, 44. Fitz. Coro. 12, 103. 4 H. 6. 15, 16. S. P. C. 148. Letter C. H. P. C. 200.

[m] S. P. C. 149. Letter A. H. P. C. 200. Fitz. Utla. 47. Bro. Appeal, 57, 118, 146. 17 Aſſ. pl. 26. Fitz. Coro. 175. [n] S. P. C. 148. Letter B. Fitz. Coro. 12. H. P. C. 200. Vide ſupra Sect. 10. [o] S. P. C. 149. Letter A. H. P. C. 200. [p] S. P. C. 149. Letter A. H. P. C. 200. Fitz. Coro. 3. [q] S. P. C. 149. Letter A. 27 Aſſ. pl. 25. Bro. Appeal, 68. H. P. C. 200. Fitz. Coro. 201, 384. Contra Bro. Appeal, 53. 13 Aſſ. pl. 10.

his Father, it is found that he hath an elder Brother alive by the ſame Father, &c. the Appellee ſhall not be arraigned upon the Appeal, at the Suit of the King, but ſhall be wholly diſcharged of it. But where an Appeal is put without Day on the Plea of [a] Excommunication, the Appellee ſhall be mainpriſed from Day to Day till the Plaintiff be abſolved; and notwithſtanding it ſeems to be holden generally in ſome [b] Books, That where an Appeal is abated for any of the Inſufficiencies abovementioned, or barred, the Appellee ſhall be ſet at large, and be diſcharged, as well againſt the King as the Party; yet [c] ſurely this muſt be underſtood only of ſuch Caſes wherein it appears, That neither any Indictment is preferred, or intended to be preferred by the King, nor any other Appeal preferred, nor intended to be preferred by the ſame or ſome other Party; for otherwiſe ſurely it cannot but be intended, that it muſt be in the Diſcretion of the Court, upon Conſideration of the Circumſtances of the Caſe, either to commit or bail the Appellee for a reaſonable Time, in Order to anſwer ſuch further Proſecution, or [d] to bind him to his Good Behaviour for a certain Time, &c.

Sect. 12. Sixthly, That whatſoever may be pleaded by an Appellee either in Bar or Abatement of an Appeal, while it is carried on at the Suit of the Party, may [e] as well be pleaded by him, when it is proſecuted at the Suit of the King; as [f] that the Appellant ſuing an Appeal of Death, as Wife to the Deceaſed, was never married to him, or [g] that ſhe is outlawed, &c. which depends upon the Reaſon taken Notice of in the precedent Sections, *viz.* That an Appeal ſhall not give the King a greater Advantage than the Party himſelf who ſued it.

Sect. 13. Seventhly, That [h] where-ever an Appellee is arraigned upon the Suit of the King, he may plead the King's Pardon, in the ſame Manner as if he had been arraigned upon an Indictment: But if an Appellee, who by pleading ſuch a Pardon diſcharges himſelf of an Appeal at the Suit of the King, be alſo indicted, it is adviſeable [i] to take Care at the ſame Time when he is in ſuch Manner diſcharged of the Appeal, to have a Ceſſer of Proceſs entered on the Indictment, to prevent the Vexation of a cauſeleſs Proſecution upon it.

Sect. 14. As to the fourth Point, *viz.* Whether one may be tried at the Suit of the King for a capital Offence, without any Indictment upon a Sheriff's Return, it ſeems to be generally agreed, [k] That neither the Sheriff's Return of a Reſcous or Eſcape, or of any other Matter, nor any other Record whatſoever, except only an Appeal or Indictment, or ſomething equivalent thereto, as the Verdict of twelve Men, finding a Man guilty in ſuch Manner as is above ſet forth in the ſixth Section of this Chapter, can at this Day put a Man upon his Trial for a capital Offence, as being contrary not only to the Common Law, but to [l] *Magna Charta*, and other [m] Statutes made in Affirmance of it.

Sect. 15. As to the fifth general Point of this Chapter, *viz.* Whether a Man may be arraigned on an Indictment, while an Appeal is depending againſt him for the ſame Offence, it ſeems [n] that it was the Common Practice before the Statute of 3 *H.* 7. 1. whether any Appeal were depending or not, not to try any Man upon an Indictment of Murder, before the Year and Day were paſſed, leſt thereby the Suit of the Party ſhould be prevented. And if ſuch Regard were had to an Appeal where none was depending, it cannot be thought but that much [o] greater was

[a] S. P. C. 149. Letter A. 13 Ed. 4. 8. pl. 3. 3 Aſſ. pl. 12. Fitz. Mainpriſe, 6. [b] 18 Ed. 3. 35. pl. 15. Bro. Appeal, 146. 11 Aſſ. pl. 27. 17 Aſſ. pl. 26. Fitz. Utlagary 47. Fitz. Coro. 12, 68, 167, 175, 201, 384. Bro. Nonab. 23. [c] H.P.C. 200. Vide S. P. C. 149. Letter A. Bro. Appeal, 67, 130. Fitz. Coro. 156, 198, 357. Fitz. Error, 52. 27 Aſſ. pl. 7. 1 Aſſ. pl. 5. 32 Aſſ. pl. 8. 7 H. 7. 5. pl. 7. [d] Fitz. Coro. 387. S. P. C. 149. Letter D. [e] S.P.C. 172. Letter B. Quære Fitz. Coro. 452. [f] Fitz. Coro. 3. [g] 21 Ed. 3. 17. pl. 20. Bro. Coro. 37. [h] Fitz. Monſtrans de faits 128. H.P.C. 201. S. P. C. 104. Letter A, B. Fitz. Coro. 25. 11 H. 4. 41. pl. 6. Vide ſupra Ch. 24. Sect. 25. [i] S.P.C. 104. H. P. C. 201. 4 Ed. 4. 10. pl. 14. Fitz. Coro. 25. [k] 2 H.H.P.C. 151 *. H. P. C. 201. 2 Inſt. 50. S. P. C. 31. Letter C. 94. Letter B. 95. 2 Ed. 3. 1. pl. 4. 1 H. 7. 6. pl. 2. Fitz. Coro. 48, 149. Bro. Coro. 130. Vide ſupra Ch. 19. Sect. 15. [l] 9 H. 3. ch. 29. [m] 25 Ed. 3. de proditionibus, cap. 4. 28 Ed. 3. 3. 37 Ed. 3. 18. [n] See the Preamble of 3 H. 7. 1. S. P. C. 107. Letter A. Fitz. Coro. 44, 82. 7 H. 4. 36. a. [o] 44 Ed. 3. 38. pl. 35. 31 H. 6, 11. pl. 6. 21 Aſſ. pl. 4. 21 Ed. 3. 23. pl. 16. Fitz. Coro. 18, 114. Fitz. Reſponder 36.

had to one actually depending whether before or after the Year and Day were paſſed, [a] Yet it ſeems that the Court was never in any Caſe peremptorily bound to ſuſpend the Proceedings on an Indictment in reſpect of an Appeal, but might always in Diſcretion, whenever it ſhould ſeem proper, proceed on an Indictment, hanging an Appeal. And accordingly we find, that in many Inſtances [b] in the Old Books, when it is was holden, That in an Appeal by an Infant, the Parol ſhould [c] demur till his full Age, the Court have proceeded to try a Man upon an Indictment, while an Appeal by an Infant was depending againſt him, to prevent the Delay, which could not but be occaſioned, if the Proceedings ſhould be deferred till the Appellant ſhould come to full Age. Alſo [d] where a Writ of Appeal of Robbery hath been ſued out againſt a Perſon under an Indictment for the ſame Robbery, and ready to be tried, the Court have refuſed to put off the Trial of the Indictment in reſpect of ſuch Writ of Appeal; becauſe before the Appellant hath declared, it doth not judicially appear, that both the Indictment and Appeal are for the very ſame Fact. But if there were no ſuch ſpecial Reaſon to induce the Court to proceed upon an Indictment while an Appeal is depending, it ſeems to have been the general [e] Practice to ſuſpend the Proceedings on the Indictment till the Appeal were determined.

As to the ſixth general Point of this Chapter, *viz.* Who may be, and ought to be Indictors, and in what Manner they are to be returned, I ſhall endeavour to ſhew,

1. How theſe Matters ſtand by the Common Law.
2. How by Statute.

Sect. 16. As to the firſt Particular, it ſeems clear, That by the Common Law every Indictment muſt be found by twelve [f] Men at the leaſt, every [g] one of which ought to be of the ſame [h] County, and returned by the Sheriff, or other proper Officer, without the Nomination of any other Perſon whatſoever; and ought alſo to be a Freeman, and a lawful liege Subject; and conſequently neither under an [i] Attainder of any Treaſon or Felony; nor a [k] Villein, nor Alien, nor outlawed, whether for a criminal Matter, or, as [l] ſome ſay, in a perſonal Action. And from hence it ſeems clear, that if it appear by the Caption of an Indictment, or otherwiſe, that it was found by [m] leſs than twelve, the Proceedings upon it will be erroneous. [n] Alſo, it ſeems that any one who is under a Proſecution for any Crime whatſoever, may, by the Common Law, before he is indicted, challenge any of the Perſons returned on the Grand Jury; as being outlawed for Felony, &c. or Villeins, or returned at the Inſtance of a Proſecutor, or not returned by the proper Officer, &c.

Sect. 17. Alſo many Indictments in inferior [o] Courts have been [p] quaſhed for want of the Words *Proborum & legalium hominum*, in the Caption of the Indictment, ſetting forth by what Perſons it was found; [q] but this is ſaid to be no Exception to an Indictment found in the Court of King's Bench, or Grand Seſſions, or Counties Palatine, and hath been often [r] overruled, as to Indictments in other Courts, becauſe all Men ſhall be intended to be honeſt and lawful, till the contrary appear.

[a] 4 Co. 45. b. 47. 7 H. 4. 34. pl. 22, 35. pl. 4. 21 H. 6. 28, 29. Fitz. Conſpir. 6. Fitz. Coro. 82. Quære Fitz. Coro. 114. Bro. Appeal, 41.
[b] Fitz. Coro. 278, 279. 32 Aſſ. pl. 8. 41 Aſſ. pl. 14. Bro. Appeal, 75. Quære Fitz. Coro. 114. 21 Ed. 3. 23. pl. 16. Bro. Appeal, 105, 119.
[c] 13 Aſſ. pl. 10. Fitz. Age 41, 57. 17 Ed. 4. 2. pl. 4. Bro. Appeal, 105. Vide ſupra Ch. 23. Sect. 30.
[d] 31 H. 6. 11. pl. 6. Fitz. Coro. 18.
[e] Dyer 296. pl. 20. See the Books cited to the other Parts of this Section.
[f] Cro. Eliz. 654. 3 Inſt. 30. 2 Inſt. 387.
[g] See the Preamble of 11 H. 4. 9. 3 Inſt. 32, 33, 34. 12 Co. 99.
[h] 2 Rol. Rep. 82.
[i] 3 Inſt. 32.
[k] Popham 202. 1 Inſt. 156. b.
[l] 2 H.H.P.C. 155*. 3 Inſt. 32. 21 H. 6. 30. pl. 17. Vide Fitz. Proceſs, 208. Quære Cro. Car. 134, 147. 1 Jon. 198, 199.
[m] Cro. Eliz. 654. pl. 16.
[n] 11 H. 4. 41. pl. 8. Bro. Coro. 189. Bro. Indict. 2. 21 H. 6. 30. pl. 17. Quære Cro. Car. 134, 135, 147.
[o] 1 Keb. 629. pl. 112. 2 Keb. 471. pl. 63.
[p] Cro. Eliz. 751. pl. 7. Cro. Jac. 635. Palm. 282, 389. 2 Rol. Rep. 400. 2 Rol. Ab. 82. pl. 7. 3 Mod. 122. Poph. 202.
[q] 1 Keb. 629. pl. 112. 2 Keb. 471. pl. 63. 1 Lev. 208.
[r] 2 Keb. 135, 284. 1 Keb. 50. pl. 5. Cro. Jac. 41. 1 Sid. 106, 367. Quære 2 Rol. Ab. 82. pl. 8.

Sect. 18.

[a] 11 H. 4. 41. pl. 8. Fitz. Indict. 25. Coron. 89. Bro. Indict. 2. Vide infra Sect. 27.
[b] S. P. C. 88. 12 Co. 99. H. P. C. 202. 3 Inſt. 32. 33, 34. Vide Cro. Ca. 134, 135.

Sect. 18. It is reſolved in the [a] Year-Book of 11 *H.* 4. by the Advice of all the Juſtices, That one outlawed on an Indictment of Felony, may plead in Avoidance of it, that one of the Indictors was outlawed for Felony, *&c.* But it ſeems to be the general [b] Opinion, That this Reſolution is rather grounded on the Statute of 11 *H.* 4. *ch.* 9. which was made in the ſame Term, in which this Reſolution was given, than on the Common Law; becauſe it appears by the very ſame Year-Book, that when this Plea was firſt propoſed it was diſallowed; from whence, as I ſuppoſe, it is collected, that the ſubſequent Reſolution was founded on the Authority of the ſaid Statute, which may be intended to have been made after the Plea was diſallowed, and before the ſubſequent Reſolution, by which it was adjudged good. Yet, conſidering that the ſaid Reſolution was given in the Beginning of *Hillary* Term, and that the Parliament which made the ſaid Statute was not holden before the Beginning of the ſame Term; and therefore it is not likely that the ſaid Statute was ſo ſoon made; and alſo conſidering, that the ſaid Reſolution was given by Advice of all the Judges, who ſeem to have been conſulted about the Validity of the Plea abovementioned at the Common Law, and takes no Manner of Notice of any Statute, but only of the Law in General, it may deſerve a Queſtion, Whether ſuch Plea be not good at the Common Law?

Vide 2 Rol. Abr. 647, 648. Cro. Eliz. 413. Cro. Jac. 672.

Sect. 19. I do not find it any where holden, that none but Freeholders ought to be returned on a Grand Jury; [61] but how far the Law is in this Reſpect altered by Statute, ſhall be ſhewn in the twenty-firſt Section.

[c] 2 Inſt. 448.
[d] Regiſt. 180. b. F. N. B. 166. D. Vide 2 Inſt. 447, 448.
[e] Regiſt. 178. F. N. B. 165. Vide 2 Inſt. 561.

Sect. 20. As to the ſecond Particular, *viz.* How the Matters abovementioned ſtand by Statute, it is enacted by the Statute of *Weſtminſter* 2. 28. *That old Men above the Age of ſeventy Years, Perſons perpetually ſick, or infirm at the Time of the Summons, or not dwelling in the County, ſhall not be put in Juries, or leſſer Aſſiſes.* And the Equity thereof, and the Reaſon of the Thing, ſeem plainly ſo far to extend to Grand Juries, that if it ſhall appear, that any of the Perſons abovementioned be returned on a Grand Jury, the Court, into which they are returned, will eaſily excuſe their Non-appearance. But it ſeems clear, [c] that any ſuch Perſons being returned on a Grand Jury, may lawfully ſerve upon it, if they think fit; neither do I find that they can have an Action on the ſaid Statute for being ſo returned; for the Writ [d] in the Regiſter grounded on, and reciting the Statute, mentions the Prohibition of it to be, that Men above the Age of ſeventy Years ſhall not be put *in Aſſiſis, juratis, vel recognitionibus aliquibus*, which Expreſſions ſeem proper for Petit Juries only; whereas the [e] Writ grounded on the Statute of *Articuli ſuper chartas*, ſet forth at large in the twenty-firſt Section, recites the Prohibition thereof to be, that none of the Perſons in the Writ mentioned ſhall be put *in inquiſitionibus nec juratis*, which Expreſſion ſeems to be of a larger Extent, and to take in Grand as well as Petit Juries; by which it ſeems clearly to be implied, that in the Judgment of thoſe who formed the ſaid Writ, the Statute laſt mentioned is more general than the former.

Sect. 21. It is farther enacted by the abovementioned Statute of *Weſtminſter* 2. 38. *That none ſhall be put in Aſſiſes or Juries, though they ought to be taken in the proper County, who have leſs Tenements than to the Value of twenty Shillings yearly.* And it is required by the Statute of 21 *Ed.* 1. commonly called the Statute *De his qui ponendi ſunt in Aſſiſis, That they ſhould have Tenements to the Value of* 40 s. *yearly; Provided, That before Juſtices in Eyre for Common Pleas in their Eyres, and alſo in Aſſiſes, and Juries, which shall be taken in Cities and Burghs, and other trading Towns, the same may be done as was accustomed:* And this Exception is likewise mentioned in the [a] Writ in the Register, which seems to be grounded on both these Statutes; by which it appears, That neither by the Common Law nor by these Statutes there was any Necessity in Proceedings before Justices in Eyre, *&c.* That Petit Jurors should be Freeholders; and if so, it seems probable that there is no greater Necessity that Grand Jurors making an Inquiry before them should be Freeholders; and if a Grand Juror before such Justices need not to be a Freeholder, why should there be a greater Necessity that a Grand Juror before other Justices should be a Freeholder? And it is farther remarkable, that the abovementioned Writ in the Register, which seems to be grounded on these Statutes, mentions only Persons put *in assisis, juratis vel recognitionibus aliquibus:* To which may be added, that the [b] several subsequent Statutes, which require that none but Freeholders or Copyholders of Lands of such a Value shall be returned on Juries, expresly extend only to Juries returned for the Trial of Issues, except only the [c] Statutes concerning Indictments in the Sheriff's Torn, which require, that every Juror finding such Indictment shall have 20 *s.* yearly of Freehold, or 26 *s.* of Copyhold, and also except 3 *H.* 7. 1. which requires that every Juror of an Inquest by which Justices of Peace shall inquire of Concealments by other Inquests shall have Tenements of the yearly Value of 40 *s.* and also except 33 *H.* 6. 2. which requires that every Indictment in the County Palatine of *Lancaster*, of Persons supposed by the same Indictment to live in some other County, and also every Indictment in any other County, of Persons in the same Indictment, supposed to live in the said County of *Lancaster*, shall be taken by such Jurors only as have Lands to the yearly Value of one hundred Shillings: All which seems to make it doubtful, Whether there be any Necessity either by the Common Law or Statute, That a Grand Juror in any other Case must be a Freeholder.

[a] Register 181. a. F.N.B. 166 D. Vide 2 Rol. Ab. 647, 648. Cro. El. 413.

[b] 2 H. 5. Stat. 2. cap. 3. 35 H. 8. c. 6. 27 El. c. 6. 4 & 5 Gul. & Mar. c. 24. 7 & 8 Gul. 3. 32. 3 Geo. 2. c. 25.

[c] Vide supra cap. 10. Sect. 65, 66, 67, 68.

Sect. 22. It is enacted by 28 *Ed.* 1. commonly called the Statute of *Articuli super Chartas, cap.* 9. *That no Sheriff, nor Bailiff shall impanel in Inquests, nor in Juries over many Persons, nor others, nor otherwise than as is ordained by Statute: And that they shall put in those Inquests and Juries, such as be next Neighbours, most sufficient, and least suspicious.* And the like is enacted almost in the very same Words by 42 *Ed.* 3. 11. And it is farther enacted by the said Statute of *Articuli super Chartas, That he who doth contrary, and is attainted thereupon, shall pay unto the Plaintiff his Damages double, and shall be grievously amerced to the King.* And the said Statute of *Articuli super Chartas*, is said by Sir *Edward Coke*, to extend to all Suits or Proceedings, either criminal or civil, Real, Personal, or mix'd, Publick or Private, Assises or Enquests; and surely that Part of it which ordains, that the most sufficient and least suspicious shall be returned on all Juries, is so agreeable to common Right and natural Justice, that it cannot but be thought to be in Affirmance of the Common Law, and equally to extend to Grand and Petit Juries, and consequently if any Officer shall be wilfully guilty of an Offence against it in the Return of any Jury, he cannot but be punishable for his Contempt, at the Suit of the King. And it is enacted by 23 *E.* 3. 6. *That Justices of Assises shall have Commissions sufficient to inquire in their Sessions of Sheriffs,* &c. *for putting into Panels Jurors suspect and of evil Fame.* And it is farther enacted by 34 *Ed.* 3. 4. *That all Panels shall be made of the next People, which shall not be suspect nor procured. And that the Ministers which do against the same, shall be punished before the Justices who take the Inquest, according to the Quantity of their Trespass,* 2 Inst. 561.

as well against the King as against the Party for the Quantity of the Damage which he hath suffered in such Manner; and both these Statutes seem equally to extend to the undue Return of Grand and Petit Juries. But it is observable, that the Clause of the above recited Statute of *Articuli super Chartas*, which ordains that the Sheriff, *&c.* shall render double Damages, extends only to Juries returned in Suits between Party and Party; because it says, that he shall render them to the Plaintiff, which is a Denomination never given to the King or Prosecutor, where the Proceeding is by Way of Indictment; and accordingly we find that the Writs in the

[a] Regist. 178. F. N. B. 165. [a] Register grounded on this Statute expresly relate to Suits between Party and Party.

Sect. 23. But the principal Statutes relating to the Return of Grand Juries, are 11 *H.* 4. 9. and 3 *H.* 8. 12. the first whereof is as followeth, *Because, that now of late Enquests were taken at* Westminster, *of Persons named to the Justices, without due Return of the Sheriff, of which Persons some were outlawed before the said Justices of Record, and some fled to Sanctuary for Treason, and some for Felony, there to have Refuge, by whom, as well many Offenders were indicted, as other lawful liege People of our Lord the King, not guilty, by Conspiracy, Abetment, and false Imagination of other Persons, for their special Advantage and singular Lucre against the Course of the Common Law used and accustomed before this Time: Our said Lord the King, for the greater Ease and Quietness of his People, will and granteth, that the same Indictment so made, with all the Dependance thereof, be revoked annulled, void, and holden for none for ever: And that from henceforth no Indictment be made by any such Persons, but by Enquests of the King's lawful liege People, in the Manner as was used in the Time of his noble Progenitors, returned by the Sheriffs, or Bailiffs of Franchises, without any Denomination to the Sheriffs, or Bailiffs of Franchises before made by any Person, of the Names, which by him should be impanelled, except it be by the Officers of the said Sheriffs or Bailiffs of Franchises sworn and known to make the same, and other Officers to whom it pertaineth to make the same according to the Law of* England: *And if any Indictment be made hereafter in any Point to the contrary, that the same Indictment be also void, revoked, and for ever holden for none.*

In the Construction of this Statute the following Points have been resolved,

[b] 12 Co. 98, 99. 3 Inst. 33. [c] Supra cap. 5. Sect. 33. *Sect.* 24. [b] First, That where a Person not returned by the Sheriff on a Grand Jury procures his Name to be read among those of others who were actually returned, whereupon he is sworn of the Grand Jury, *&c.* he may be indicted, either in the King's Bench [c] or before Justices of *Oyer* and *Terminer*, for his Contempt of the Statute; and being found guilty, may be fined and imprisoned; and yet the Statute doth not expresly provide that any such Person shall be any Way punished, but only that the Indictment should be void, *&c.*

[d] 12 Co. 98. 3 Inst. 33. Cro. Ca. 134. [e] 1 Jon. 198, 199. Cro. Ca. 134, 147. *Sect.* 25. [b] Secondly, That Indictments of Offences not capital are as much within the Statute as Indictments of Treason or Felony; and also Indictments before Justices of Peace as much as Indictments before superior Justices; but it hath been [e] questioned whether a Coroner's Inquest be within the Purview of it.

[f] H. P. C. 202. 3 Inst. 34. Cro. Ca. 134, 147. 1 Jon. 198, 199. *Sect.* 26. Thirdly, That a Person arraigned upon any Indictment taken contrary to the Purview of the Statute, [f] may plead such Matter in Avoidance of the Indictment, and also plead over to the Felony.

Sect. 27. Fourthly, That a Person outlawed upon any such Indictment without a Trial, may also shew in Avoidance of the Outlawry, that the Indictment was taken contrary to the Purview of the Statute, as seems fully to appear from the [a] abovementioned Year-Book of 11 *H.* 4. 41. But if a Person, who is tried upon such an Indictment, takes no such Exception before his Trial, it may be [b] doubtful whether he may be allowed to take such Exception afterwards, because he hath slipp'd the most proper Time for it; except it can be verified by the Records of the same Court wherein the Indictment is depending, as by an Outlawry in such Court of one of the Indictors, &c. in which Case it is [c] said, That any one, as *amicus Curiæ*, may inform the Court of it.

[a] Supra Sect. 17.
[b] 3 Inst. 34. Bro. Indict. 2.
[c] 3 Inst. 34.

Sect. 28. [d] Fifthly, That if any one of the Grand Jury who find an Indictment be within any one of the Exceptions in the Statute, he vitiates the Whole, tho' never so many unexceptionable Persons joined with him in finding it.

[d] 11 H. 4. 41. pl. 8. H. P. C. 202. S. P. C. 88. 3 Inst. 33.

Sect. 29. Sixthly, That if a Prisoner indicted of Felony offer to take any such Exception, he shall upon his Prayer have [e] Counsel assigned him for his Assistance in it.

[e] Cro. Ca. 134, 147. 1 Jon. 198. 3 Inst. 34.

Sect. 30. [f] Seventhly, That the Court needs not admit of the Plea of the Outlawry of an Indictor, in Avoidance of any such Indictment, unless he who pleads it, have the Record ready.

[f] Cro. Ca. 147.

Sect. 31. It seems somewhat questionable, [g] whether Outlawry in a personal Action be within the Purview of the Statute.

[g] Jon. 198, 199. Cro. Ca. 134, 147.

Sect. 32. It is recited by the abovementioned Statute of 3 *H.* 8. 12. *That many Oppressions had been, by the untrue Demeanor of Sheriffs and their Ministers, done to great Numbers of the King's Subjects, by Means of returning, at Sessions holden for the Bodies of Shires, the Names of such Persons, as for the singular Advantage of the said Sheriffs and their Ministers, would be wilfully forsworn and perjured, by the sinister Labour of the said Sheriffs and their Ministers: By Reason whereof many substantial Persons, (the King's true Subjects) had been wrongfully indicted of divers Felonies and other Misbehaviour by their Covin and Falsehood: And also sometimes by Labour of the said Sheriffs, divers great Felonies had been concealed, and not presented by the said Persons, by the said Sheriffs and their Ministers partially returned, to the Intent to compel the Offenders to make Fines and give Rewards to the said Sheriffs and their Ministers.*

Vide supra Sect. 16. 2 H. H. P. C. 155 *.

And thereupon it is enacted, *That all Panels to be returned, which be not at the Suit of any Party, that shall be made, and put in by every Sheriff and their Ministers afore any Justice of Gaol-Delivery, or Justices of Peace whereof one to be of the* Quorum, *in their open Sessions, to enquire for the King, shall be reformed by putting to, and taking out of the Names of the Persons, which so be impanelled by every Sheriff and their Ministers, by the Discretion of the same Justices, before whom such Panels shall be returned. And that the same Justice and Justices shall command every Sheriff, and their Ministers in his Absence, to put other Persons in the same Panel by their Discretions: And that the same Panels so reformed by the said Justices be good and lawful. And that if any Sheriff, or any their Minister, at any Time do not return the same Panels so reformed, that then every such Sheriff and Minister so offending shall forfeit for every such Offence* 20l. &c.

Sect. 33. It hath been resolved that this Statute doth not take away the Force of the above-recited Statute of 11 *H.* 4. in any Point wherein it doth not expresly vary from it; from whence it follows, that if any of the Jurors who find an Indictment be outlawed, or returned by a Sheriff or Bailiff, at the Nomination of any other Person, the Indictment may be avoided in the

H. P. C. 202. 2 H. H. P. C. 156. * 3 Inst. 33. Contra S. P. C. 88.

ſame Manner as before, by Force of 11 *H.* 4. except ſuch Nomination be made by the Juſtices authorized by 3 *H.* 8. to reform that Penal.

Sect. 34. As to the ſeventh general Point of this Chapter, *viz.* Within what Place the Offences inquired of muſt ariſe, notwithſtanding it were anciently [a] holden, That if one who had committed a Robbery in the County of *A.* were taken with the Manner in the County of *B.* he might be put to anſwer in the County of *B.* (by which I ſuppoſe it is intended that he might be put to anſwer on an Indictment found in the County of *B.*) and then tried by a Jury from the County of *A.* Yet it ſeems to be generally [b] agreed at this Day, that by the Common Law, no Grand Jurors can indict any Offence whatſoever, which doth not ariſe within the Limits of the Precinct for which they are returned: And upon this Ground it hath been reſolved to be a fatal Exception to an Indictment, that it doth not appear by it that the Offence aroſe within the [c] County, or [d] Riding, or [e] other ſpecial Diviſion, or [f] Precinct, for which the Jury which found it was returned. And *à fortiori* therefore it muſt be a [g] good Exception, that it expreſly appears by the Indictment that the Offence aroſe in a County, *&c.* different from that for which the Jury was returned. And it is [h] holden, that even the Finding of a collateral Matter expreſly alledged in the Indictment to have happened in a different County, is void. But [i] ſome have holden, That if the County be expreſſed in the Margent of an Indictment, the Vill or Vills, in which the Offence is laid, ſhall be intended to be in the ſame County. But the greater [k] Number of Authories require a greater Certainty, as by expreſly alledging ſuch Vill or Vills in the County named in the Margent, or *in comitatu prædicto*, which ſeems to be ſufficient where but one County is named before; but to be [l] uncertain where a County is named in the Body of the Indictment different from that in the Margent. But it ſeems from the Authority of [m] *Baud*'s Caſe, that if a Fact be alledged in *B. juxta D. in Comitatu E.* being the ſame County for which the Jury is returned, the County is ſet forth with ſufficient Certainty, becauſe *B.* ſhall be intended to be in the ſame County with *D.* Alſo if one be indicted for a Reſcous from an Arreſt in the County of *B.* it hath been [n] holden, that it is needleſs to expreſs the County wherein the Reſcous was done with greater Certainty, becauſe it ſhall be intended to have been in the ſame County wherein the Arreſt was; *à* [o] *fortiori* therefore, if a Fact be alledged at *B.* in the Pariſh of *C.* in the County of *D.* it cannot but be intended that *B.* as well as *C.* is in the County of *D.*

Sect. 35. But of whatſoever Nature an Offence indicted may be, whether local or tranſitory, as ſeditious Words, or Battery, *&c.* it ſeems to be [p] agreed, That if upon Not guilty pleaded it ſhall appear, that it was committed in a County different from that in which the Indictment was found, the Defendant ſhall be acquitted, as ſhall be ſhewn more at large in the Chapter concerning Evidence.

Sect. 36. And therefore at the Common Law, if a Man had died in one County of a Stroke received in another, it ſeems to have been the more [q] general Opinion, that regularly the Homicide was indictable in neither of them, becauſe the Offence was not compleat in either, and no Grand Jury could inquire of what happened out of their own County. But this Inconvenience is remedied by 2 & 3 *Ed.* 6. 24. by which it is enacted, *That where any Perſon ſhall be feloniouſly ſtricken, or poiſoned in one County, and die of the ſame Stroke or Poiſoning in another County, that then an Indictment thereof found by Jurors of the County, where the Death ſhall happen, whether it ſhall be found before the Coroner, upon the ſight of ſuch dead*

[a] 26 Aſſ. pl. 32. Fitz. Coro. 194. Vide ſupra Sect. 5.

[b] 3 Inſt. 49. H. P. C. 203.

[c] 1 Bulſt. 203, 205. Cro. El. 137. pl. 8. Dy. 69. pl. 29. 2 Keb. 302. pl. 94.

[d] Cro. Jac. 276.

[e] Cro. Jac. 276.

[f] Keilw. 89. 33 pl. 6.

[g] Stedman's Caſe, Cro. El. 137.

[h] Cro. Jac. 17.

[i] 1 Bulſt. 203. 1 Sid. 312. Keilw. 33. pl. 6. Cro. Jac. 167.

[k] 1 Sid. 345, 346. Cro. El. 606. pl. 4. 677. pl. 6. 738. pl. 10. 751. pl. 7. Vide Cro. Jac. 96, 276. 2 Keb. 302. pl. 94.

[l] Cro. El. 100. pl. 5. 184. pl. 1. 436. pl. 51.

[m] Cro. Jac. 41.

[n] Cro. Jac. 345. Vide Fitz. Coro. 45. Attachm. 1. Retorn de Viſcount, 32. Bro. Retorn de Brief, 97. 3 H. 7. 11. pl. 3. 5 H. 7. 17. b. 18. a. 10 Ed. 4. 15. pl. 13. Dy. 69. pl. 29.

[o] Cro. El. 108. pl. 3.

[p] H. P. C. 203. Kelynge 15.

[q] Vide B. 1. Ch. 31. S. 13. 6 H. 7. 10. pl. 7. 10 H. 7. 28. pl. 20. Fitz. Indictment, 23. See the Preamble of 2 & 3 Ed. 6. 24. Contra Fitz. Coro. 373. Indictment, 24. 7 H. 7. 8. pl. 1. 10 H. 7. 20. pl. 8. Fitz. Cor. 446.

Body; or before the Justices of Peace, or other Justices or Commissioners, which shall have Authority to inquire of such Offences, shall be as good and effectual in the Law, as if the Stroke or Poisoning had been committed and done in the same County where the Party shall die, or where such Indictment shall be so found.

Sect. 37. And it seems that by the Common Law, if a Fact done in one County prove a Nusance to another, it may be indicted in [a] either County. [a] H.P.C. 20 3 Fitz. Bar. 279. Assise 446. 19 Ass. pl. 6.

Sect. 38. Also by the Common Law, if one guilty of Larceny in one County carry the Goods stoln into another, he [b] may be indicted in either, as hath been more fully shewn in the first [c] Book. [b] Keilw. 160. b. 4 H. 7. 5. b. Fitz. Cor. 62. [c] Ch. 33. S. 9.

Sect. 39. Also if a Man marry two Wives, the first in a foreign Country, and the second in *England*, it is [d] holden that he may be indicted and tried for it in *England* upon the Statute of 1 *Jac.* 1. 11. which makes it Felony; because the second Marriage alone was criminal, and the first had nothing unlawful in it, and was merely of a transitory Nature: But where the second Marriage is in a foreign Country, it hath been holden, That the Party is not triable on the Statute above mentioned; but this seems contrary to the Purview of it, as hath been more fully shewn in *Book* 1. *Chap.* 43. *Sect.* 7. [d] 1 Sid. 171. Kelynge 79, 80.

Sect. 40. Also if a Woman be taken with Force in one County, and carried into another, and there married, the Offender may be indicted and tried in the second County, upon the Statute of 3 *H.* 7. 2. against Forcible Marriage, because the Continuance of the Force in such County amounts to a Forcible Taking within the Statute. But if an Offence in stealing, taking away, withdrawing, or avoiding a Record, against the Purport of 8 *H.* 6. 12. be committed partly in one County and partly in another, so as not to amount to a compleat Offence within the Statute in either, it is said that the Party cannot be indicted for a Felony in either, but only for a Misprision. Book 1. Ch. 42. Sect. 19. Book 1. Ch. 45. Sect. 6.

Sect. 41. It is enacted by 26 H. 8. 6. *For the Punishment and speedy Trials, as well of the Counterfeiters of any Coin current within this Realm, washing, clipping, or minishing of the same, as of all and singular Felonies, Murders, wilful burning of Houses, Manslaughters, Robberies, Burglaries, Rapes, and Accessaries of the same, and other Offences feloniously done, within any Lordship Marcher of* Wales, *that the Justices of the Gaol-Delivery, and of the Peace, and every of them for the Time being in the Shire or Shires of* England, *where the King's Writ runneth, next adjoining to the Lordship Marcher, or other Places in* Wales, *where such counterfeiting, washing, clipping, or minishing of any Coin current within this Realm, or Murder shall be committed; or where any other Felonies or Accessaries shall be committed, shall have full Power at their Sessions and Gaol-Delivery, to enquire by Verdict of twelve Men of the same Shire or Shires next adjoining, within* England, *where the King's Writ runneth, there to cause all such Counterfeiters, Washers, Clippers of Money, Felons, Murderers, and Accessaries to the same, to be indicted according to the Laws of this Land, in like Manner and Form, as if the same Petit Treasons, Murders, Felonies, and Accessaries to the same, had been done within any of the said Shires within the said Realm: And also to hear, determine, and judge the same, according to the Laws of the Realm.*

Sect. 42. And it seems generally to have been [e] holden, That the Power given by this Statute to the Justices of Gaol-Delivery and of Peace, in the adjoining *English* Counties, in Relation to the Offences therein mentioned, is not repealed by 34 & 35 *H.* 8. 26. which impowers the Justices of the Grand Sessions in *Wales* to take Indictments of such Offences. But it hath been [f] resolved that an Acquittal on an Indictment [e] 1 Mod. 64, 68. 2 Keb. 685. Cro. Car. 247, 331. 1 H. H. P. C. 157. See Book 1. Ch. 31. Sect. 14. [f] 1 Lev. 118.

ment at the Grand Sessions is a good Bar of an Indictment for the same Crime in an *English* County.

Sect. 43. It is enacted by 28 *H.* 8. 15. which hath been more fully set forth and expounded in *Book* 1. *Ch.* 37. *That Treasons, Felonies and Robberies*, &c. *upon the Sea*, &c. *shall be inquired*, &c. *in such Places in the Realm as shall be limited in the King's Commission*, *in like Manner as if such Offences had been committed on the Land.*

[a] Book 1. Ch. 37. Sect. 11. Quære Moor 121. pl. 265.

Sect. 44. It hath been [a] resolved, That this Statute extends not to Offences done in Creeks or Ports within the Body of a County, because such Offences were always cognisable by the Common Law.

[b] 3 Inst. 11, 112. 4 Inst. 124.

Sect. 45. Also it hath been [b] resolved, That the Force of this Statute, in Relation to Treasons done upon the Sea, is not taken away by 35 *H.* 8. 2. more fully set forth in the forty-seventh Section.

[c] Yel. 134, 135. 13 Co. 51, 52. Noy 131. Contra H. P. C. 77. 3 Inst. 112. Book 1. Ch. 37. Sect. 7.

Sect. 46. It was made a [c] Doubt upon this Statute, Whether one who was an Accessary at Land to a Felony at Sea, were triable by the Admiral, within the Purview of it; but this is settled by [d] 11 & 12 *W.* 3. *c.* 7. which enacts, that Accessaries to Piracy before or after, in such Manner as is set forth more at large in that Statute, shall be inquired of, tried, and adjudged according to the said Statute of 28 *H.* 8. 15. [62]

[d] Book 1. Ch. 37. Sect. 15.

[e] Book 1. Ch. 37. Sect. 12.

Sect. 47. It is farther [e] enacted by the said Statute of 11 & 12 *W.* 3. *c.* 7. That all Piracies and Felonies upon the Sea, *&c.* may be tried at Sea, or upon the Land, in his Majesty's Plantations, in such Manner as hath been more fully set forth in the first Book.

[f] 19 E. 4. 6. b. See the Preamble of 35 H. 8. 2.

[g] Vide supra Ch. 4. Sect. 9. and Ch. 23. Sect. 29. Dyer 131. pl. 75.

[h] 1 Inst. 261.

[i] H. P. C. 204. 3 Inst. 11.

[k] Contra Dyer 131. pl. 75. and 11 Co. 63. a. 1 And. 262.

Sect. 48. It seems to have been a great [f] Doubt before the making of the Statute of 35 *H.* 8. 2. in what Manner and in what Place High Treason done out of the Realm was to be tried; for some seem to have holden, That it was triable only upon an [g] Appeal before the Constable and Marshal; others, that it might be tried upon an Indictment, laying the Offence in [h] any County where the King pleased; and others, that it was triable by Way of Indictment in that County [i] only wherein the Offender had lands: But surely it [k] cannot reasonably be doubted, but that it was triable some Way or other, for it cannot be imagined that an Offence of such dangerous Consequence, and expresly within the Purview of 25 *Ed.* 3. should be wholly dispunishable, as it must have been, if it were no Way triable.

Sect. 49. *But for a plain Remedy, Order, and Declaration of this Matter*, it is enacted by 35 *H.* 8. 2. *That all Manner of Offences, being then already made or declared, or after to be made or declared, by any of the Laws and Statutes of this Realm, to be Treasons, Misprisions of Treasons, or Concealments of Treasons, and done, perpetrated, or committed by any Person or Persons, out of this Realm of* England, *shall be from thenceforth inquired of, heard and determined before the King's Justices of his Bench, for Pleas to be holden before himself, by good and lawful Men of the same Shire, where the said Bench shall sit and be kept; or else before such Commissioners, and in such Shire of the Realm, as shall be assigned by the King's Majesty's Commission, and by lawful Men of the same Shire, in like Manner and Form to all Intents and Purposes, as if such Treasons, Misprisions of Treasons, or Concealments of Treasons, had been done, perpetrated, and committed within the same Shire, where they shall be so inquired of, heard and determined, as is aforesaid.*

In the Construction of this Statute the following Points have been resolved,

Sect. 50. First, That if the Court of King's Bench, or Commissioners appointed in Pursuance of the Statute, after having taken an Indictment of a foreign Treason, remove into a different County from that in which the Indictment was found, the [a] Trial shall be by Jurors returned from the first County; and this is most agreeable to the general Course of the Common Law; which [b] requires, That Indictments shall be tried by Jurors of the same County in which they were found.

Sect. 51. Secondly, That the Commissioners and County for the Trial of such Treasons, are [c] sufficiently assigned by the King in Pursuance of this Statute, by his either writing his Name to the Commission that appoints them, or signing the Warrant to the Lord Keeper for the Commission.

Sect. 52. Thirdly, That a Treason done by an [d] *Irishman* in *Ireland*, is triable in *England* according to the Purview of this Statute; for *Ireland* being out of the Realm of *England*, a Treason committed [e] in it is certainly within the Letter of the Act; and nothing within the Letter of a Statute made for enlarging the Jurisdiction, and supplying the Defects of the Common Law, shall easily be construed out of the Meaning of it. And therefore it seems reasonable, that any Offence which by 25 *Ed.* 3. or any other subsequent Statute, either expresly extending to, or [f] received in *Ireland*, is equally Treason in *Ireland* and *England*, may be tried here by Virtue of this Statute. But if an Offence be made Treason by an *Irish* Statute, which is not Treason in *England*, I see not how it can be tried here; since being neither made nor declared to be Treason by any Law or Statute of this Realm, it is not within the Description of the Offences provided for by 35 *H.* 8. To which may be added, that Offences beyond Sea, to be tried here by Virtue of that Statute, are to be inquired of and determined in like Manner as if they had been committed in such Shire wherein they shall be inquired of and determined; but if an Offence which is Treason in *Ireland* and not in *England*, had been committed in any *English* County, it is manifest that it could not be punished as Treason. Also it hath been [g] resolved, That no Treason committed in *Ireland* by an *Irish* Peer, is triable in *England*, because he is intitled to a Trial by his Peers, which cannot be had in *England*. [63]

Sect. 53. Fourthly, That this Statute is not [h] repealed by 1 & 2 *Ph.* & *Mar.* 10. which enacts, *That all Trials hereafter to be had, awarded or made, for any Treason, shall be had and used according to the Common Laws of the Realm, and not otherwise.* For it is the manifest Purport of this Statute to restore the ancient Course of the Common Law as to the Trial of Treasons, in which great Innovations had been made by Statutes in the Reigns of King *Henry* VIII. and *Edward* VI. but it cannot be thought agreeable to the Intention of it to abrogate any Statute, which in a doubtful Case settled and confirmed the Jurisdiction of the Common Law, and gave a Method of Trial as agreeable as possible to its usual and ordinary Manner of Proceeding.

Sect. 54. It was a great Doubt at the Common Law, [i] Whether an Accessary in one County to a Felony in another, were indictable in either. But this is remedied by 2 & 3 *Ed.* 6. 24. by which it is enacted, That such an Accessary may be indicted and tried in the same County wherein he was Accessary. But intending more fully to treat of this Matter in the Chapter concerning the Arraignment of the Principal and Accessary, I shall refer the Reader thither for the farther Consideration of it.

[a] H.P.C. 204. 3 Inst. 34.

[b] S.P.C. 90. Letter B. Vide Dyer 286. pl. 45.

[c] H.P.C. 16, 205. 3 Inst. 11.

[d] 3 Inst. 11. 1 And. 262, 263. H.P.C. 16, 205. 1 H.H.P.C. 155. 11 Co. 63. a. Vide 3 Keb. 560, 566. Warner's Case.

[e] See B. 1. Ch. 17. Sect. 67.

[f] 1 And. 263. 1 Sid. 357. pl. 11.

[g] Dyer 360. pl. 6. Vide 1 And. 262.

[h] 11 Co. 63. Co. Lit. 261. b. 1 H.H.P.C. 284. H.P.C. 205. 3 Inst. 24. 1 And. 262. S.P.C. 90. Letter B. Dyer 131. pl. 75. 286. pl. 45. 298. pl. 29. 300. pl. 38.

[i] Keilw. 67. Dyer 38.

As

As to the eighth general Point of this Chapter, *viz.* What ought to be the Form of the Body of an indictment, I ſhall endeavour to ſhew:

1. What ought to be the Form of the Body of an Indictment at Common Law.
2. What of an Indictment upon a Statute.

As to the firſt of theſe Particulars I ſhall endeavour to ſhew,

1. How the Body of an Indictment at Common Law, ought to ſet forth the Subſtance and Manner of the Fact.
2. How the Perſons mentioned or referred to in it.
3. How the Thing wherein the Offence was committed.
4. How the Circumſtances of Time and Place.
5. Where it may be vitiated by falſe, or improper *Latin*, or the Uſe of *Engliſh* inſtead of *Latin*.
6. Where the Offence indicted may be laid jointly, and where ſeverally, and where both jointly and ſeverally, and where the Offences of ſeveral Perſons may be laid in one Indictment.
7. Whether the Words *Vi & Armis* be in any Caſe neceſſary.
8. Whether it be neceſſary to lay the Offence *contra pacem.*
9. Whether it be neceſſary to lay it *contra coronam & dignitatem Regis.*
10. Whether it be neceſſary to lay it *in contemptum Regis.*
11. Whether it be neceſſary to lay it *illicitè.*
12. Whether a Defect in any of theſe Particulars be amendable.

As to the firſt Point, *viz.* How the Body of an Indictment at Common Law ought to ſet forth the Subſtance and Manner of the Fact, I ſhall endeavour to ſhew:

Firſt, In what Manner it ought to ſet them forth in Relation to the Offence of the Principal.

Secondly, In what Manner in Relation to the Offence of the Acceſſary.

As to the firſt of theſe Particulars, *viz.* In what Manner the Body of an Indictment at Common Law, ought to ſet forth the Subſtance and Manner of the Fact, in Relation to the Offence of the Principal, I ſhall obſerve,

Sect. 55. Firſt, That no Periphraſis or Circumlocution whatſoever will ſupply thoſe Words of Art which the Law hath appropriated for the Deſcription of the Offence, as [a] *Murdravit* in an Indictment of Murder; [b] *Cepit*, in an Indictment of Larceny; [c] *Mayhemiavit*, in an Indictment of Maim; [d] *Felonicè*, in an Indictment of any Felony whatever; [e] *Burglariter* or *Burgulariter*, or elſe *Burgalariter*, in an Indictment of Burglary; [f] *Proditoriè*, in any Indictment of Treaſon; [g] *Contra ligeantiæ ſuæ debitum*, in an Indictment of Treaſon againſt the King's Perſon.

Sect. 56. Secondly, That in an Indictment, as well as in an [h] Appeal of Rape, the Fact ſeems to be ſufficiently aſcertained by the Words *Felonice rapuit*, without adding *carnaliter cognovit*, or firſt ſetting forth the ſpecial Manner of the Terror or Violence, and then concluding that the

2 H. H. P. C. 169, 172, 184, 187.
[a] Supra Ch. 23. Sect. 77. Dyer 304. pl. 56. Bro. Indict. 7. Cro. El. 920.
[b] Fitz. Coron. 119. Indictm. 2, 8. Bro. Coro. 76. 22 Aſſ. pl. 32. 2 Ed. 3. 1. pl. 3. Supra Ch. 23. Sect. 77.
[c] Supra Ch. 23. Sect. 77.
[d] 2 Ed. 3. 1. pl. 3. 2 Ed. 3. 18. pl. 1. Fitz. Indictment, 3. Supra Ch. 23. Sect. 77. Bro. Indictment, 36. Bro. Appeal, 48. 18 Ed. 4. 10. pl. 28. Cro. El. 193. pl. 7. 4 Co. 41. b. 5 Co. 121. b. See 9 Co. 69. a.
[e] Daliſon 22. 4 Co. 39. b. H. P. C. 207. 5 Co. 121. b. Cro. El. 920.
[f] H. P. C. 11. 3 Inſt. 15. Fitz. Coro. 55. S. P. C. 3. Letter A. 3 H. 7. 10. pl. 2. Carth. 319.
[g] 3 Lev. 396. Calvin's Caſe, 5, 6, 10. Skin. 442. Carth. 319.
[h] Supra Ch. 23. Sect. 79. Letter I. Fitz. Indictment, 18. 9 Ed. 4. 26.

Defendant *ſic felonicè rapuit, &c.* Alſo it ſeems, That the like general Manner of ſetting forth the Offence, which is ſufficient in an [a] Appeal of Larceny, will alſo be ſufficient in an Indictment.

Sect. 57. Thirdly, That in other Caſes it is [b] generally a good Rule in Indictments as well as Appeals, That the ſpecial Manner of the whole Fact ought to be ſet forth with ſuch Certainty, that it may judicially appear to the Court, That the Indictors have not gone upon inſufficient Premiſſes. And upon this Ground it ſeems to be agreed, That an Indictment finding that a Perſon hath feloniouſly broken Priſon without ſhewing the Cauſe of his Impriſonment, *&c.* by which it may appear that it was of ſuch a Nature, that the Breaking might amount to Felony, is [c] inſufficient. Alſo [d] Indictments againſt Perſons for refuſing to be ſworn Conſtables, after they had been *legitimo modo electi*, have been quaſhed for not ſhewing the Manner of the Election, that it might appear to have been ſuch as obliged the Defendants to have undertaken the Office. Alſo it hath been [e] adjudged, That an Indictment of Burglary is inſufficient without the Word *Noctanter.* Alſo it ſeems to be [f] agreed, That an Indictment charging a Man with a Nuſance in reſpect of a Fact, which is lawful in itſelf, as the Erecting of an Inn, *&c.* and only becomes unlawful from Particular Circumſtances, is inſufficient, unleſs it ſet forth ſome Circumſtances which make it unlawful: But it is ſaid that this is needleſs where the Thing indicted is unlawful in its own Nature, as the Keeping of a Bawdy-Houſe, *&c.* Alſo it hath been [g] adjudged, That an Indictment for traiterouſly coining *Alkemy* like to the King's Money, without ſhewing what Money, is inſufficient; of which this ſeems to be the plaineſt Reaſon, That it appears not whether it were made like to the King's gold or ſilver Coin, or only like to that in Braſs or Copper, *&c.* and if it were made like to that of the latter Kind only, it [h] ſeems that the Offence could not amount to Treaſon. Alſo it [i] ſeems, That an Indictment of Perjury, not ſhewing in what Manner and in what Court the falſe Oath was taken, is inſufficient, becauſe for what appears it might have been extrajudicial, *&c.* Alſo it ſeems clear, That it is neceſſary both in Indictments and [k] Appeals of Mayhem and Murder, to ſet forth particularly in what Manner the Hurt was given, and that an Omiſſion thereof is not holpen by a general Concluſion, that the Defendant *ſic felonicè Mayhemiavit* or *Murdravit, &c.* But having already ſhewn in the Chapter of Appeals, with what Certainty the Count in an Appeal of Death, muſt ſet forth the ſpecial Manner of the Fact, as by ſhewing in what [l] Part of the Body the Wound was given, and the [m] Length and Breadth of ſuch Wound; and [n] that the Party died of it; and with what [o] Weapon it was given; and that the Word [p] *Percuſſit* cannot ſafely be omitted where the Truth of the Fact will bear it, I ſhall refer the Reader to the ſaid Chapter of Appeals, for the Learning relating to theſe Points. It hath been [q] adjudged, That an Indictment of Extortion charging *J. S.* with the Taking of 50 *s.* as Bailiff of an Hundred, *colore officii*, without ſhewing for what he took it, is good at leaſt after Verdict, for perhaps he might claim it generally as being due to him as Bailiff, in which Caſe the Taking could not be otherwiſe expreſſed. But this ſeems to be a ſpecial Caſe.

Sect. 58. Fourthly, That an Indictment charging a Man disjunctively is void, as where it finds that A. *Murdravit* B. *vel Murdrari cauſavit*, or that A. *Verberavit* B. *vel Verberari cauſavit*; or that A. [r] *Fabricavit talem cartam vel fabricari cauſavit*, for here are diſtinct Offences, and it appears not of which of them the Indictors have accuſed the Defendant.

[a] Supra Ch. 23. Sect. 79. Letter k

[b] Cro. El. 147. pl. 11. 201. pl. 30. 9 Ed. 4. 26. 2 H. H. P. C. 184, 185, 186.

[c] Bro. Indictment, 7. 9 Ed. 4. 26.

[d] Aleyn 78, 79. 1 Mod. 24. 5 Mod. 96, 129.

[e] Supra Ch. 10. Sect. 46.

[f] Cro. El. 583, pl. 12. 2 Rol. Rep. 345. Palm. 368. 374.

[g] Fitz. Indictment, 10. S. P. C. 95. Letter D. H. P. C. 206. Vide 2 Roll. Rep. 12.

[h] Book 1. Ch. 17. Sect. 57.

[i] Cro. El. 137.

[k] Supra Ch. 23. Sect. 79. 2 Lev. 140, 141. Salk. 377. Far. 16. Kelynge 124.

[l] Supra Ch. 23. Sect. 80.

[m] Supra Ch. 23. Sect. 81.

[n] Supra Ch. 23. Ch. 83.

[o] Supra Ch. 23. Sect. 84.

[p] Supra Ch. 23. Sect. 82.

[q] 1 Sid. 91.

[r] 5 Mod. 137, 138. 1 Salk. 342, 371. pl. 8.

Sect. 59. Fifthly, That [a] regularly every Indictment muſt either charge a Man with ſome particular Offence, or elſe with ſeveral of ſuch Offences, particularly and certainly expreſſed, and not with being an Offender in general; for no one can well know what Defence to make to a Charge ſo uncertain, or to plead it either in Bar or Abatement of a ſubſequent Proſecution; neither can it appear that the Facts given in Evidence againſt a Defendant on ſuch a general Accuſation, are the ſame of which the Indictors have accuſed him; neither can it judicially appear to the Court, what Puniſhment is proper for an Offence ſo looſely expreſſed. And upon this Ground it hath been adjudged, That an Indictment is inſufficient which only charges a Man in general, with having [b] ſpoken divers falſe and ſcandalous Words againſt *J. S.* being Mayor of ſuch a Place; or with being a [c] common Defamer, Vexer, and Oppreſſor of many Men; or with being a common [d] Diſturber of the Peace, and having ſtirred up divers Quarrels as well among his Neighbours as other of the King's Subjects at ſuch a Place, to the great Loſs and Diſturbance of his Neighbours aforeſaid, and other the King's Subjects, *&c.* or with being a [e] common Oppreſſor and Diſturber of the Peace; or with having been and ſtill continuing to be a Man of evil [f] Behaviour; or with being a [g] common Deceiver of the King's People; or with being a [h] common Publiſher of the King's Secrets, and of his Own, and of divers other Perſons impanelled together with him to inquire for the Body of the County of divers Felonies againſt his Oath, *&c.* or with being a [i] common Foreſtaller; or with being a [k] common Thief; or being a [l] common Evil-doer; or with being a common [m] Champertor; or with being a common [n] Conſpirator, and ſuch like. It is holden indeed in a Note in *Fitzherbert's Abridgment*, That an Indictment for Confederacy in general is good, but this is made a *Quære* by the Reporter of the [o] Year-Book, from which the ſaid Note in *Fitzherbert* is taken, and is denied to be Law both by [p] *Brook* and [q] *Rolle*, nor do I any where find the leaſt Reaſon offered to diſtinguiſh this from the other Caſes above mentioned. Alſo it is holden by Sir *Edward* [r] *Coke*, That the ancient Form of Indictments charging Men with having as Hereticks and Traitors, and Infeſters of the Highways, conſpired and confederated, *&c.* to deſtroy the Catholick Faith, and having daily publiſhed falſe and ſeditious Writings, *&c.* were utterly inſufficient, and yet ſuch Indictments ſeem to have been [s] frequent; as were alſo Indictments charging Men in general, as *Inſidiatores viarum, & depopulatores agrorum,* which [t] Words took the Benefit of Clergy from the Perſons indicted, before the Statute of 4 *H.* 4. 2. by which it is enacted, That theſe Words ſhall no more be put into Indictments, nor if they be, ſhall have ſuch Effect as to take from the Perſons indicted the Benefit of Clergy; [u] and this Statute in this Reſpect ſeems to be in Affirmance of the Common Law, which ſeems generally to diſallow of ſuch uncertain Indictments, as appears from the Reaſons and Authorities above ſet forth. Yet it hath been adjudged, That a Man may be generally indicted as a common Barrator againſt the [x] Form of the Statute, and [y] againſt the Peace, without ſhewing any of the particular Facts in the Indictment, by which he appears to have been ſo; for Barratry is an Offence of a [z] complicated Nature, conſiſting in the Repetition of divers Acts in Diſturbance of the common Peace, all of which it would be too prolix to enumerate in the Indictment; and therefore [aa] Experience hath ſettled it to be ſufficient to charge a Man generally as a common Barrator, (which is a [bb] Word of Art appropriated to

[a] Vide 1 Lev. 203. 1 Keb. 278. 2 H. H. P. C. 182. Shower 389, 390.
[b] 1 Roll. Re. 79. 2 Roll. Ab. 79. pl. 11.
[c] 2 Roll. Ab. 79. pl. 1, 2. 1 Mod. 71.
[d] 2 Rol. Ab. 79. pl. 10.
[e] 1 Mod. 71, 288. 1 Lev. 299. Raym. 205. 1 Vent. 104.
[f] 2 Roll. Ab. 79. pl. 12.
[g] 6 Mod. 311.
[h] Moor 302. pl. 451.
[i] Fitz. Action ſur le Stat. 26. 29 Aſſ. pl. 45. Moor 302. pl. 451.
[k] 2 Roll. Ab. 79. pl. 5. Moor 302. pl. 451. 22 Aſſ. pl. 73.
[l] 22 Aſſ. pl. 73.
[m] 29 Aſſ. pl. 45.
[n] 29 Aſſ. pl. 45.
[o] 22 Aſſ. pl. 45.
[p] Bro. Indictment, 12.
[q] 2 Roll. Ab. 79. pl. 8.
[r] 3 Inſt. 41.
[s] 3 Inſt. 41.
[t] 11 Co. 29. a. H. P. C. 206. 1 H. H. P. C. 571. 2 H. H. P. C. 333.
[u] Vide 3 Inſt. 41. Lambard, Book 4. Ch. 5. Fol. 404.
[x] Book 1. Ch. 81. Sect. 10.
[y] Cro. Jac. 527. 2 Roll. Ab. 82. pl. 5.
[z] Book 1. Ch. 81. 8 Co. 36. b. 37.
[aa] 2 Roll. Ab. 79. pl. 3. Cro. Jac. 527. 2 Keb. 409. pl. 33.
[bb] Book 1. Ch. 81. Sect. 10. 2 Lev. 208.

this Purpose,) and before the Trial to give the Defendant a [a] Note of the particular Matters which you intend to prove against him. Also it is [b] holden, That there is no Need to name any particular Place where the Defendant was a Barrator, because he shall be supposed to have been guilty in divers Places, and the *Venire* is most proper from the Body of the County. Also it is said that there is no Need in the Conclusion of such an Indictment, to lay the Offence *ad nocumentum omnium ligeorum, &c.* but that [c] *Diversorum* is sufficient in such an Indictment as well as in an Indictment of a common Scold, *&c.* because it appears from the Nature of the Thing, that it could not but be a common Nusance. Also it seems to be [d] agreed, That an Indictment against one as a common Scold, is good without setting out the Particulars, for the same Reasons that such Indictment of Barratry is good.

[a] Book 1. Ch. 81. Sect. 13.
[b] Vide B. 1. Ch. 81. Sect. 11.
[c] 2 Keb. 409. pl. 33. See Book 1. Ch. 75. Sect. 5.
[d] 6 Mod. 311. Book 1. Ch. 75. Sect. 5.

Sect. 60. Sixthly, That the Charge must be laid positively, and not by way of [e] Recital, as with a *Quod cum, &c.* and that the Want of a direct Allegation of any Thing Material in the Description of the Substance, Nature, or Manner of the Crime, [f] cannot be supplied by any Intendment or Implication whatsoever: And upon this Ground it seems to be [g] generally holden, That an Indictment of Death having the Words *Felonicè murdravit, &c.* cannot amount to an Indictment of Murder, without the Words *Ex malitia præcogitata*; and yet by the Word *Murdravit* it expresly charges the Party with Murder, and it is impossible that there could be a Murder, and no Malice prepense. Also it seems to be generally agreed, That no Indictment of Death can be good without an express Allegation, that the Deceased both received the Hurt which is laid as the Cause of his Death, and also that he died of the Hurt so received; and that the Want thereof cannot be made good by any Implication whatsoever, as hath been more fully shewn, *Ch.* 23. *Sect.* 82, 83. Also it hath been [h] adjudged, That an Indictment against *J. S.* for feloniously breaking such a Prison, and commanding *J. N.* who was therein imprisoned for Felony to escape, is not a good Indictment for a felonious Breaking, without expresly shewing that *J. S.* did escape; and yet the Breaking is expresly laid to be felonious, and it is impossible that it could be so, unless the Party did escape. But it will be needless to enumerate any more Instances of this Kind, which are so very frequent, that there is scarce any Case which mentions Exceptions taken to Indictments, without having some or other grounded on this Rule, That in an Indictment nothing material shall be taken by Intendment or Implication. Yet the Law will not admit of too great a Nicety of this Kind, for it hath been adjudged, That if in the first Part of an Indictment of Death, the Assault be laid with Malice prepense, *&c.* there is no [i] Need to repeat it in the following Clause, which shews the Giving of the Wound, being joined with a Copulative to the precedent Sentence, and laid at the same Time and Place with the Assault. Also it hath been [k] adjudged, that where an Indictment sets forth, That *J. S.* was lawfully arrested by Virtue of a Plaint before such a Sheriff, *&c.* it shall be intended that there was a good Warrant. Also it hath been [l] adjudged, That where a Warrant is alledged, authorizing the Arrest of *J. S.* within the Liberties of *London*, and the Indictment lays the Execution of it in such a Parish and Ward in *London*, without expresly laying the Parish and Ward within the Liberties of *London*, yet the Indictment is good; for the Court will not admit of such a strained Exception, that a Parish in *London* may be out of the Liberties of *London*.

[e] Salk. 371. pl. 6.
[f] S. P. C. 96. Cro. Jac. 20. 4 Co. 42. 5 Co. 120. b.
[g] Dyer 99. pl. 63. & 65. H. P. C. 231. 2 H. H. P. C. 187. Vide 2 Lev. 140, 141. 4 Co. 41. b. Contra Dyer 68. pl. 28.
[h] Keilw. 87. Vide supra Ch. 18. Sect. 12.
[i] 4 Co. 41. b.
[k] Cro. Jac. 473.
[l] 9 Co. 67. 5 Co. 120.

[a] Cro. Jac. 610. 2 Mod. 128. 2 Rol. Rep. 226. Moore 606. 2 Lev. 229. Contra 2 Rol. Rep. 226. Quære Ray. 378. 1 Keb. 852.

[b] Book 1. Ch. 64. Sect. 38. Cro. Jac. 610. 2 Rol. Rep. 226. 2 Lev. 229. 2 Mod. 129.

Sect. 61. Alſo it hath been [a] adjudged, That where an Indictment finds that *J. S. exiſtens* of ſuch or ſuch a Degree or Trade, &c. as brings him within the Purview of the Law whereon the Indictment is founded, committed ſuch a Fact, it ſhall be intended that he was of ſuch Degree, &c. at the Time of the Fact, without any expreſs Allegation to that Purpoſe, becauſe that is the moſt natural Conſtruction of the Participle *exiſtens*, going before the Verb to which it is the nominative Caſe; [b] yet where an Indictment of Forcible Entry, finds that *A.* diſſeiſed *B.* of ſuch Land *exiſtens liberum tenementum* of *B.* it ſeems agreed, That the Indictment is inſufficient, becauſe it ſtands indifferent, according to the common Rules of Conſtruction, whether the Land were the Freehold of *B.* at the Time of the Diſſeiſin, or at the Time of the Finding of the Indictment, the Word *exiſtens* not being the nominative Caſe to the Verb, but applied to the Thing which was the Subject of the Action. But I cannot find any certain general Rule, whereby it may be known in what Caſes an Exception of this Kind ſhall be taken to be ſo over nice, that the Court will not regard it. All therefore that I ſhall add on this Head is this, That as on the one Hand the Law will not ſuffer a Man to be condemned of any Crime whereof the Jury have not expreſly found him guilty, by any Argument or Implication from what they have ſo found; ſo on the other Hand it will not ſuffer a Criminal to eſcape on ſo trifling an Exception, which it would be abſurd and ridiculous to take Notice of; for *nimia ſubtilitas in jure reprobatur*. But the Judgment hereof cannot but be in a great Meaſure left to the Diſcretion of the Judges, who from the Circumſtances of each particular Caſe, the Compariſon of Precedents, and the plain Reaſon of the Thing, ſeem always to have endeavoured to have gone within theſe Rules as nearly as poſſible.

[c] 3 Mod. 104.

[d] See Book 1. Ch. 64. Sect. 39.

[e] Supra Ch. 23. Sect. 88. and 89. 2 H. H. P. C. 188.

[f] 2 Rol. Abr. 81 pl. 5.

Sect. 62. Seventhly, That it is a certain Rule, That where one material Part of an Indictment is repugnant to another, the Whole is void, for the Law will not admit of ſuch Nonſenſe and Abſurdities in legal Proceedings, which, if ſuffered, would ſoon introduce Barbariſm and Confuſion; alſo it takes off much from the Credit of an Indictment, that thoſe by whom it is found, have contradicted themſelves. And upon this Ground it hath been adjudged, That if an Indictment [c] charge the Defendant with having forged a certain Writing by which *A.* was bound to *B.* which is impoſſible, if the Writing were forged; or if an Indictment of Forcible Entry ſet forth, That the Defendant diſſeiſed *J. S.* of Lands, wherein it appears by the Indictment it ſelf that he had no Freehold whereof he could be diſſeiſed; or that the Defendant entred peaceably on *J. S.* and then and there Forcibly diſſeiſed him; or that he diſſeiſed him of Land then being and ever ſince continuing to be his Freehold; [d] every ſuch Indictment is void, for its manifeſt Inconſiſtency and Repugnancy. And upon the like Reaſon it hath been adjudged, That an Indictment of Death, laying the Stroke at *A.* and the Death at *B.* or the Stroke on the firſt of *May*, and the Death on the Tenth, and then concluding that the Defendant in ſuch Manner murdered the Party at *A.* aforeſaid, or on the firſt of *May* aforeſaid, is inſufficient for the Repugnancy, as hath been more fully ſhewn in the [e] Chapter of Appeals, becauſe it ſuppoſes the Murder to have been committed at a Place in the firſt Caſe, and on the Day in the ſecond; in which it appears by the Indictment it ſelf, That the Party was not killed but only wounded. Alſo it hath been [f] adjudged, That an Indictment for ſelling Iron with falſe Weights and Meaſures, is void, not only becauſe it is abſurd to ſuppoſe that Iron could be ſold by by Meaſure, but alſo becauſe it is repugnant and inconſiſtent that it ſhould be ſo ſold at the ſame Time when it was ſold by Weight. Alſo if an Indictment at a Seſſions holden the 13th of *January*, 30 *Car.* 2. find that the Defendant has been abſent from Church ſix Months from the firſt of *January*, 30 *Car.* 2. it is [b] agreed, That it is void for the Impoſſibility, for there are but eleven Days between the firſt of *January*, and the Holding of the Seſſions. Alſo if an Indictment charge a Man with having feloniouſly done a Fact, which appears upon the Face of the Indictment to have been but a Treſpaſs, as with feloniouſly cutting down and carrying away Trees, the Court will [c] not arraign him; yet where the Senſe appears plain, the Court will often diſpenſe with a ſmall Impropriety in the Expreſſion, as where one is indicted for having mowed *unam acram fœni*, which is [d] ſaid to be ſufficient, and yet that which was mowed, could not at the Time of the Mowing be in Strictneſs called Hay, but Graſs only.

[b] Raym. 434. Par. Caſe. 3 Keb. 653. pl. 8.
[c] 12 Aſſ. pl. 32 Fitz. Coro. 171. Indictment 9. Bro. Coro. 76. Book 1. Ch. 33. Sect. 21.
[d] 2 Rol. Abr. 81. pl. 1. Parallel Caſes 2 Rol. Ab. 81. pl. 2. 3. Vide 18 Aſſ. pl. 15.

As to the ſecond Particular, *viz.* In what Manner the Body of an Indictment at Common Law muſt ſet forth the Subſtance and Manner of the Fact, in Relation to the Offence of the Acceſſary, I ſhall obſerve,

Sect. 63. Firſt, That a Repugnancy in ſetting forth ſuch Offence is equally fatal as in ſetting forth that of the Principal; and therefore if an Indictment of Death which lays the Stroke on one Day, and the Death on a ſubſequent one, charge the Acceſſaries with having abetted the Fact, at the Time of the Felony and Murder only, it is inſufficient, as hath been more fully ſhewn in the [e] Chapter of Appeals, becauſe it appears by the Indictment it ſelf, That the Time of the Death, and conſequently of the Murder, was ſubſequent to that of the Stroke, and therefore it is repugnant to alledge that the Defendant abetted the Stroke by being preſent at the Time of the Death.

Sect. 64. Secondly, That where ſeveral are preſent, and abet a Fact, and one only actually does it, an [f] Indictment may, in the ſame Manner as an [g] Appeal, either lay it generally, as done by them all, or ſpecially, as done only by the one and abetted by the reſt. But it hath been reſolved, That if an Indictment barely charge a Man with having been preſent when a Murder was committed, it is [h] void, becauſe a Man may be innocently preſent, and ſhall not be preſumed to have been a Party, where no Circumſtance is found that makes him ſo.

Sect. 65. Alſo it hath been [i] adjudged, That an Indictment of *J. S.* as Acceſſary to four, by theſe Words, that *J. S. ſciens ipſos quatuor homines feloniam prædictam feciſſe apud D. felonicè receptavit*, is naught for not ſaying *eos receptavit*, for it doth not appear how many of them the Indictors have found him to have received, whether all four, or three, or two, or but one.

Sect. 66. It hath been [k] holden, That an Indictment charging a Conſtable with having voluntarily and feloniouſly ſuffered a Perſon, arreſted by him upon Suſpicion of Felony, to eſcape, without ſhewing what the Nature of the Felony was, and that it was actually committed, is void for the Uncertainty, not only becauſe it appears not but that the Offence of which the Party was ſuſpected, was never actually committed; in which Caſe the Eſcape could [l] not be criminal; but alſo becauſe it appears not what the Felony was, and unleſs the Arreſt were for a Felony, the Eſcape could not be felonious. But it is ſaid, That an Indictment for knowingly receiving Perſons outlawed for, or convicted of Felony, or for knowingly ſuffering ſuch Perſons to eſcape, [m] may be good without ſhewing what the

[e] Ch. 23. Sect. 88, 89. Supra ſect. 64.
[f] H. P. C. 265, 266. 9 Co. 67. Plowd. Com. 97. 1 H. H. P. C. 437.
[g] Supra Ch. 23. ſect. 76.
[h] 14 H. 7. 31. pl. 7. Bro. Indictment, 5.
[i] 30 H. 6. 2. pl. 10. Fitz. Indictment, 13. S. P. C. 95. Letter B. H. P. C. 206.
[k] Cro. El. 752. pl. 10. Hetley 53. 8 Ed. 4. 3. pl. 6. H. P. C. 206. S. P. C. 95. Letter A. Fitz. Indictment, 16. Vide Fitz. Coro. 55, 76.
[l] Supra Ch. 12 Sect. 16, 17. Ch. 18. Sect. 7. Ch. 19. Sect. 2, 3.
[m] 8 Ed. 4. 3. pl. 6. Fitz. Indictment, 16. Quære Keilw. 194. a.

Felony was, or that it was actually committed, if the Record of the Outlawry or conviction be ſet forth with convenient Certainty: And the moſt plauſible Reaſon of this Opinion ſeems to be this, That it may be ſufficiently made out by ſuch Record, of what Kind the Felony was, and alſo that it was actually committed, *&c.* It is holden indeed by Sir *William* [a] *Staundford*, That ſuch a general Indictment for receiving a Perſon outlawed for Felony in the ſame County wherein he dwells is good, but not if it were in another, becauſe a Man is bound at his Peril to take Conuſance of an Attainder of Felony in his own County, but not in another. But I much queſtion the Authority of this Diſtinction, ſince, as the Law ſeems now to be [b] holden, a Man is no more bound to take Conuſance of ſuch an Attainder in his own County, than in any other.

Sect. 67. It hath been [c] holden, That an Indictment finding that *J. S. ſcienter receptavit* ſuch a one, being a Felon is not good, for this Reaſon among others, becauſe it doth not expreſly find, that *J. S.* knew the Perſon ſo received by him to have been a Felon. But this is contradicted by other [d] Authorities, by which it is holden, That the Word *ſcienter* in ſuch a Caſe ſhall be conſtrued to go thro' the whole Sentence.

As to the ſecond Point, *viz.* In what Manner the Body of an Indictment at Common Law muſt deſcribe the Perſons mentioned in it, I ſhall endeavour to ſhew,

1. In what Manner it muſt deſcribe the Defendant.
2. How other Perſons mentioned or referred to in the Indictment.

Sect. 68. As to the firſt Particular, it is ſaid, That an Indictment that the King's Highway in ſuch a Place is in Decay, thro' the Default of the Inhabitants of ſuch a Town, is [e] good without naming any Perſon in certain: Alſo it is ſaid, [f] That no Indictee can take any Advantage of a miſtaken Surname in the Indictment, either by Plea in Abatement, or otherwiſe, notwithſtanding ſuch Surname hath no Manner of Affinity with his true one, and he was [g] never known by it; and in this Reſpect, an Indictment differs from an Appeal, whereof it is [h] certain that a Miſnoſmer of a Surname may be pleaded in Abatement, as well as any other Miſnoſmer whatſoever. [64]

Sect. 69. But I do not find but that every other Miſnoſmer of the Defendant, except that of the Surname, and alſo every defective Addition, are as fatal in an Indictment as an Appeal; for it ſeems generally to be [i] holden, That a Miſnoſmer of the Defendant's Name of Baptiſm may be pleaded in Abatement of an Indictment. Alſo it hath been [k] adjudged to be a good Plea in Abatement of an Indictment againſt one by the Name of Sir *J. S.* Knight, that he is a Baronet, and no Knight. Alſo it hath been [l] holden, That it is a good Plea in Abatement of an Indictment againſt Garter King at Arms, that he is not called Garter in the Indictment, becauſe it is a Name of Dignity, being given him by the Words *creamus, coronamus,* and *nomen imponimus*; and from the Reaſon of this Caſe, it ſeems plainly to follow, That the Omiſſion of any other Name of [m] Dignity may be pleaded in Abatement of an Indictment: [n] And if ſo, why ſhould not the Omiſſion of the Defendant's Name of Baptiſm be equally fatal?

Sect. 70. It ſeems to be agreed, That notwithſtanding an Indictment be the Suit of the King, yet being within the expreſs Letter of the Statute of 1 *H.* 5. 5. concerning Additions, ſet forth more at large in the Chapter of

[a] S. P. C. 96. Letter G. Vide Fitz. Coro. 377. Dy. 355. pl. 36. [b] H. P. C. 218. [c] 7 H. 6. 42. b. Bro. Indictment, 4. Fitz. Indictment, 11. 3 Keb. 760. pl. 45. S. P. C. 96. Letter G. [d] 2 Lev. 208. 8 Ed. 4. 3. pl. 6. 1 D'Anv. Abridg. 19. pl. Letter H. [e] 2 R. A. 79. L. [f] 1 H. 5. 5. pl. 8. H. P. C. 243. S. P. C. 181. Letter D. Fitz. Miſnoſmer, 9. Vide 3 H. 6. 25, 26. Theloal, lib. 11. cap. 5. Sect. 14. [g] Quære Kelyng 11, 12. [h] 1 H. 5. 5. pl. 8. Raſt. Ent. 50. pl. 10. 54. pl. 4. H. P. C. 243. 2 H. H. P. C. 175, 176. S. P. C. 181. Letter D. Supra Ch. 23. Sect. 102. [i] Theloal, lib. 11. Ch. 5. Sect. 12. 11 H. 4. 41. pl. 7. Fitz. Coro. 88. Miſnoſmer, 18. H. P. C. 243. Contra 3 H. 6. 26. a. Bro. Miſnoſmer, 6. [k] Cro. Ca. 371. 1 Jon. 346. [l] 2 Leon. 248, 249. Quære Cro. El. 542. pl. 8. [m] Vide ſupra Ch. 23. Sect. 103, 104. Shower 392, 393. Skin. 517. 2 H. H. P. C. 240. Trem. 12. Carth. 299. [n] Vide Ch. 23. Sect. 103. Keilw. 25. b. 26. a. Quære Palm. 195.

of [a] Appeals, it [b] cannot be conſtrued to be out of the Meaning of it. From whence it follows, That the Want of a ſufficient Addition, within that Statute is as good an [c] Exception to an Indictment, if [d] Proceſs of Outlawry lie on it, as it is to an Appeal. Alſo it hath been adjudged, That it is a [e] fatal Fault to apply ſuch Addition to the Name which comes under the *Alias dictus* only, and not to the firſt Name: But it is ſaid not to be material [f] whether any Addition be put to the Name which comes under the *Alias dictus* or not, becauſe what is ſo expreſſed is not material. But it is ſo great a Fault to put no Addition to the firſt Name, that where ſeveral are indicted, ſuch an Omiſſion, in Reſpect of one of them, makes the Indictment [g] vicious as to all. [65] And it may be probably argued, that there is the ſame Reaſon for the like Fault in an Appeal againſt divers, to abate it alſo as to all, but I do not find this Point [h] expreſly agreed. But it ſeems clear, That generally the Law is the ſame in Relation to Additions in Indictments and Appeals. Having therefore already treated in the Chapter of Appeals of the general Learning relating to this Subject, and ſhewn that an Addition in [i] *Engliſh* is as good as in *Latin*; and that where ſeveral Defendants have the ſame Addition, it is [k] ſafeſt to repeat it after each of their Names; and that the Son being of the ſame Name and Addition with the Father, ought to be diſtinguiſhed with ſome [l] farther Deſcription; and having alſo ſhewn what is a ſufficient Addition of the [m] Eſtate, or Degree, or [n] Myſtery, and alſo of the [o] Town, Hamlet, Place and County of the Defendant: And alſo how the Defect of an Addition may be [p] ſalved by the Appearance and Plea of the Defendant, I ſhall refer the Reader for all theſe Particulars to the Chapter of Appeals.

Sect. 71. As to the ſecond Particular, *viz.* In what Manner the Body of an Indictment at Common Law muſt deſcribe the other Perſons beſides the Defendant mentioned or referred to in it: It is certainly ſafeſt to deſcribe them with convenient Certainty, which will hardly be diſpenſed with except in ſpecial Caſes, and for ſpecial Reaſons. For thoſe general Indictments which [q] anciently ſeem to have been allowed for ſuffering divers Bakers to bake, *&c.* againſt the Aſſiſe, *&c.* nor for diſtraining divers Perſons without Cauſe, *&c.* have by the later [r] Authorities been holden inſufficient for their Uncertainty in not naming ſome Perſons in particular who were ſo ſuffered to bake, or diſtrained, without which the Court cannot ſo well know what Fine will be proper; nor can the Defendant be ſo well enabled to make his Defence, nor to plead the Indictment to a ſubſequent Proſecution. And for the ſame Reaſons among others, an [s] Indictment for taking divers Sums of divers Perſons for ſuch a Toll at ſuch a Rate, without naming any Perſons in particular, hath been adjudged naught. Yet where in common Preſumption it may be very difficult, if not impoſſible, to know the Names of the Perſons referred to in an Indictment, it [t] may be good without naming any of them; [u] as where one is indicted for having knowingly received and harboured divers Thieves, to the Jurors unknown; in which Caſe, ſuch a general Charge is maintainable from the Neceſſity of the Thing; for otherwiſe a notorious Offender of this Kind might be wholly diſpuniſhable, for Want of the Jurors knowing the Names of the Perſons ſo received, and yet might be publickly known to carry on ſuch a Practice, to the common Nuſance of the Country; in which Reſpect it cannot but be reaſonable in ſuch a Caſe to puniſh him, tho' not as an Acceſſary to the Thieves, without ſhewing that he had received ſome of them in particular. And for the like Reaſon, if

[a] Supra Ch. 23. Sect. 105.
[b] Bro. Addition, 50. Long quinto Ed. 4. 33, 34. Finch 234.
[c] Bro. Additions, 23, 41. 2 Leon. 183. Shower 392, 393. 9 Ed. 4. 48. pl. 2. Dyer 46. pl. 2, 3, 4.
[d] Cro. El. 32. pl. 9. 148. pl. 16. Cro. Ja. 531.
[e] S. P. C. 68. 2 H. H. P. C. 177. 2 Leon. 183. 30 H. 6. pl. 2. Cro. El. 583. pl. 12. Vide Dy. 88. pl. 107. 1 Ed. 4. 1. pl. 3.
[f] 30 H. 6. pl. 2. S. P. C. 68. Fitz. Proceſs, 103. 1 Ed. 4. 1 pl. 3.
[g] 1 Bulſt. 183.
[h] Vide ſupra ch. 23. ſect. 127. Fitz. Count, 18.
[i] Supra ch. 23. ſect. 106.
[k] Supra ch. 23. ſect. 106.
[l] Supra ch. 23. ſect. 106.
[m] Supra ch. 23. ſect. 107. to 113.
[n] Supra ch. 23. ſect. 113 to 118.
[o] Supra ch. 23. ſect. 118 to 124.
[p] Supra ch. 23. ſect. 124.
[q] 38 Aſſ. pl. 11, 12. Bro. Preſentment, 27.
[r] Bro. Indictment, 21. 2 Rol. Ab. 80. pl. 1, 2.
[s] Shower 389, 390.
[t] Pl. Com. 85. b. 129. a.
[u] 2 Lev. 208.

if a [a] Stranger unknown to the Country be found ſlain, or if the dead Body of a Perſon who was well known, be disfigured in ſuch a Manner by its Wounds, that no one can diſcover whoſe it was, it is certain that an Indictment againſt the Offender, for having killed *quendam ignotum*, will be good. [b] And upon the ſame Ground, if a Stranger unknown to the Country be robbed, and will not come in to proſecute, nor diſcover his Name; it ſeems clear, That an Indictment againſt the Offender for having robbed *quendam ignotum* is good. And if Goods be found upon one notoriouſly ſuſpected of Felony, of which he can give no Manner of Account, as where a Highwayman is apprehended with his Pockets full of Watches and Rings; it ſeems, That he may either be indicted for ſtealing ſuch Watches and Rings, being the Goods *quorundam ignotorum*, or, as ſome [c] ſay, for ſtealing them generally. Alſo in the Indictment of the Regicides for the Murder of King *Charles* I. it was [d] agreed, That the Fact was well laid, as done *per quendam ignotum*, with a Vizor on his Face. And if one ſteal the Goods of an Abbey, *&c.* during a Vacancy, he may be indicted for ſtealing [e] *Bona Eccleſiæ*, and yet the Church can have no Property. But theſe ſeem to be ſpecial and extraordinary Caſes, depending on particular Reaſons, and grounded on manifeſt Neceſſity, without which, it ſeems, that ſuch Indictments cannot be maintained: For it ſeems to be taken as a Ground in [f] many Books, That regularly the Perſons offended, as well as the Defendant, ought to be certainly deſcrib'd in every Indictment. And agreeably hereto it hath been [g] adjudged, That an Indictment for ſtealing *quandam peciam panni linei cujuſdam J. S.* without adding *de bonis & catallis cujuſdam J. S.* is inſufficient, becauſe it doth not expreſly appear to whom the Goods ſtolen did belong. Alſo it was anciently [h] holden, That where one is indicted for the Death of a Perſon unknown, the Inqueſt ought to tell his Name to the Court; but ſurely this muſt be intended where they have ſome Means to know it. However, from the Whole thus much ſeems plainly to follow, That where-ever the Perſon injured is known to the Jurors, his Name ought to be put into the Indictment. And therefore as I take it, thoſe [i] Books which ſeem generally to allow of Indictments of killing, or robbing Perſons unknown, are to be underſtood with this Limitation, That ſuch Indictments are then good when the Party is in Truth unknown to the Jurors. And agreeably hereto, others [k] who ſpeak more fully of the Matter ſeem plainly to go upon the Neceſſity of the ſeveral Caſes. And the Want of ſuch Neceſſity ſeems probably to have been the beſt Reaſon why Indictments not ſhewing to whom the Wrong was done, were diſallowed in ſome of the old [l] Books. However, it is certain, That an Appeal for the Death or Robbery of a Perſon unknown, is in no Caſe good, as hath been more fully ſhewn in the [m] Chapter of Appeals.

Sect. 72. It hath been [n] adjudged, That an Indictment of an Aſſault on *John* Pariſh-Prieſt of *D.* in the County of *C.* is good, without mentioning his Surname, for if a wrongful Surname of the Defendant himſelf will not vitiate an Indictment, as hath been more fully ſhewn, *Sect.* 69. ſurely *a fortiori* the Omiſſion of the Surname of any other Perſon will not vitiate it; eſpecially where ſuch Perſon is otherwiſe deſcribed with ſuch Certainty, that it is impoſſible to miſtake him for any other. But if an Indictment for a Wrong done to a Perſon well known deſcribe him only by

[a] 1 Ed. 3. 20. pl. 26. 1 Aſſ. pl. 7. Fitz. Coro. 159. 23 Aſſ. 94. Fitz. Indictment, 10. S. P. C 95. Letter G. 2 H. H. P.C. 181. Pl.Com.85.b. b. 129. a. 9 H. 6. 45.b. Dy.99.pl.61. 285. pl. 38. Vide Fitz.Coro. 146, 183. Noy 85. Supra Ch. 23. Sect. 78.
[b] Fitz. Indict. 12, 17. 9 Ed. 4. b. S. P. C. 95. Letter G. 2 H.H. P. C. 181. Dy.99.pl.61. Keilw. 25. Supra Ch. 23. Sect. 78. Bro. Indictment, 11. Pl. Com. 85. b. 129. a. 18 Aſſ. 15. ſeems contrary.
[c] Fitz. Indict. 9, 26. S. P. C. 95. Letter G. Contra Fitz. Indict. 27. Bro. Indict. 20. 30 Aſſ. pl.37.
[d] Kelinge 10.
[e] 7 Ed.4. 14. pl. 1. Fitz. Indictment, 15. S. P. C. 95.
[f] Lamb. B. 4. Ch. 5. Dalt.Ch.131. S. P. C. 95. Letter G.
[g] Cro.El.489. 490.
[h] 1 Ed. 3. 20. pl. 26. 1 Aſſ. pl. 7. Fitz. Coro. 159, 183. Vide Bro. Indict. 10.
[i] H.P.C.207. Dy. 285. pl. 38.
[k] S. P. C. 95. Letter G. Pl. Com. 85. b. 129. a. Keilw. 25. 9 H. 6. 45. b. Vide Dyer 99. pl. 61. Dalton ch. 131.
[l] Fitz. Indict. 27. 30 Aſſ. pl. 37. 18 Aſſ. pl. 15. 2 Leon. 39.
[m] Supra ch. 23. ſect. 78.
[n] Keilw. 25. Dy. 285. pl. 38.

his Name of Baptiſm, without ſome Addition to diſtinguiſh him from others of the ſame Name, it ſeems [o] queſtionable, Whether it be not inſufficient for the Reaſons given in the foregoing Section? it is [a] ſaid, indeed, in a ſhort Note of a Caſe in *Moor's* Reports, That an Indictment againſt one *Cole, quod burglariter domum cujuſdam Ricardi fregit*, was adjudged good, without the Surname; and it not being there mentioned, that there was any other Deſcription of the Party but by his Name of Baptiſm, it may be argued that that alone is ſufficient: But to this it may be anſwered, That the only Point taken Notice of as adjudged, is that the Surname is not neceſſary, and perhaps in the Record at large there might be ſome Addition: But granting that there was none, yet the Authority of this Caſe is the leſs to be regarded, becauſe of the Books cited to ſupport it, [b] two ſeem to be directly againſt it; and the [c] third, which is moſt to the Purpoſe, only proves that an Indictment for ſtealing the Goods *cujuſdam ignoti* is good, which ſeems by no means to come up to the Point in Queſtion, as hath been more fully ſhewn in the precedent Section. Yet however the Law may ſtand in relation to ſuch an Uncertainty, it ſeems to be [d] agreed, That a Repugnancy or Abſurdity in the Deſcription of the Perſon injured will vitiate an Indictment, as where one is indicted for ſtealing *bona prædict' J. S.* where no *J. S.* was mentioned before, for tho' in Civil Actions, the Word *prædict'* hath been ſometimes [e] rejected, as Surplus and void, where it could be referred to [f] no certain Antecedent, yet this may perhaps chiefly depend on the Statutes of *Jeofailes*, which in many Caſes help Defects in Form in Civil Actions, but extend not to criminal Caſes, wherein the greateſt Exactneſs is required; and if an Award may be defeated by appointing a [g] Payment on a certain Day before-mentioned, where no ſuch Day was mentioned before, it cannot well be imagined that the like Inconſiſtency will be leſs fatal in a criminal Proceeding.

Sect. 73. It hath been [h] adjudged not to be neceſſary in an Indictment of Death to alledge, that the Perſon killed was in the Peace of God, and of our Lord the King, *&c.* tho' ſuch Words are commonly put into Indictments, for they are not of Subſtance, and perhaps the Truth might be that the Party was at the Time actually breaking the Peace.

Sect. 74. As to the third Point, *viz.* In what Manner the Body of an Indictment at Common Law muſt deſcribe the Thing wherein the Offence was committed, it ſeems clear that no Indictment can be good which wants a convenient Certainty of this Kind: And therefore it is [i] ſaid, That an Indictment for forging a Leaſe of certain Lands, without naming ſome one certain Parcel, is inſufficient. Alſo it ſeems to be agreed, That an [k] Indictment for ſtealing *bona & catalla J. S.* without any farther Deſcription of them is void for its Uncertainty, for the like Reaſons for which Indictments charging a Man with being an Offender in general are void, and hath been more fully ſet forth in the fifty-ninth Section: And upon the like Ground it hath been [l] adjudged, that an Indictment for a Treſpaſs in two Cloſes of Meadow or Paſture; or for diverting *quandam* [m] *Partem aquæ* running from ſuch a Place to ſuch a Place, without any farther Deſcription; or for ingroſſing [n] *magnam quantitatem ſtraminis & fœni*, or [o] *diverſos cumulos tritici*, without ſhewing how much of each; or for carrying away *duas* [p] *centenas caſèi*, without adding the Words, *libras* or *uncias*, or ſome other Subſtantive to *centenas*; or for erecting ſeveral [q] Cottages *contra formam ſtatuti*, without ſhewing how many, *&c.* are inſufficient for their Uncertainty. As to the [r] Caſe of the King againſt *Wetwang*, wherein the Court diſallowed an Exception to the Generality

[o] Vide Dalton ch. 131. Lambard, Book 4. ch. 5. 2 H. H. P. C. 182.
[a] Moore 466. pl. 662.
[b] 18 Aſſ. pl. 15. Fitz. Indictment, 27.
[c] 9 Ed. 4. 1. b.
[d] Lambard, Book 4. ch. 5. Folio 495. 9 Ed. 4. 1. b. Fitz. Indictment, 17. Bro. Indictment, 6. S. P. C. 95. b. Vide Cro. Ca. 465.
[e] 3 Levinz. 436. Cro. El. 709. pl. 31.
[f] Vide Cro. Ja. 549, 550. pl. 11. 585, 586. pl. 7. 618. pl. 8. Yelv. 76. 111. Cro. Eliz. 658. pl. 2.
[g] Cro. Ja. 149. pl 8. 1 Rol. A. 254. pl. 15. 263. pl. 6. Yelv. 97, 98.
[h] 4 Co. 41. b.
[i] Hob. 272.
[k] Dalton, ch. 131. Lamb. B. 4. ch. 5. fo. 496. 2 H. H. P. C. 182.
[l] 2 Rol. Ab. 81. pl. 4. 5 Mod. 138. Dalt. ch. 131. Parallel Caſes B. 1. ch. 64. Sect. 37.
[m] 2 Rol. Ab. 80. pl. 14. 2 Bulſ. 119. Parallel Caſes. B. 1. ch. 76. Sect. 88.
[n] Cro. Ca. 380, 381. Vide 2 Bulſ. 317. Shower 389, 390.
[o] 1 Rol. R. 134, 135.
[p] Cro. El. 754.
[q] 2 Rol. A. 80. pl. 13.
[r] 2 Keb. 178. 1 Lev. 203.

of an Indictment for taking *quosdam pisces*, without ſhewing how many, it may be anſwered, that this was contrary to the Opinion of Mr. Juſtice *Twiſden*, and was only the ſudden Opinion of two of the other Judges; neither does it appear that the Indictment was adjudged good, but only that the Court refuſed to quaſh it, and ordered the Defendant to plead to it. However, it ſeems clear from conſtant Experience, [a] That if an Indictment be uncertain as to ſome Particulars only, and certain as to the reſt, it is void only as to thoſe which are uncertainly expreſſed, and good for the Reſidue.

Sect. 75. If the Indictment be for a Larceny or Treſpaſs on a living Thing, as an Ox, Sheep, or Horſe, *&c.* it ſeems to be holden by [b] *Lambard* and [c] *Dalton*, that it is moſt proper to expreſs to whom the Property of it belonged, by calling it reſpectively the Ox, Sheep, or Horſe of the Party injured, without uſing the Words *bona* or *catalla*: But that it is proper to uſe theſe Words, where the Thing taken was not a living Creature. Alſo it is holden by [d] *Lambard*, that it is proper to ſhew the Worth of all living Things, and alſo of ſuch dead Things as are ſold by Weight or Meaſure, by expreſſing that they are of ſuch a Price, and the Worth of other dead Things, by expreſſing that they are of ſuch a Value; yet no Inſtance is produced where any Indictment has been diſallowed in either Caſe for a Variance from theſe Rules. And as to the firſt of them it is farther obſervable, that the [e] Precedents in *Crompton* of Indictments for ſtealing of Horſes, and Oxen, expreſly alledge the Horſe and Ox ſtol'n *de bonis & catallis cujuſdam J. S.* &c. Alſo an Appeal of ſtealing Sheep in [f] *Raſtal's Entries* expreſly alledges them *de bonis & catallis* of the Appellant. And as to the ſecond of the Rules above-mentioned, it is obſervable that the Directions in the [g] Regiſter concerning this Matter, which ſeem to be the chief Foundation of the ſaid Rule are thus expreſſed, that in a Writ of Treſpaſs of immoveable Chattels, the Writ ſhall ſay, *Tants de chateux ad valentiam X. S.* But if it be brought of a moveable Chattel, it ſhall ſay *precii X. S.* and *non ad valentiam.* Yet it appears by the Regiſter it ſelf, that even in Writs of Treſpaſs concerning which theſe Directions are given, the Worth of the Things taken away is ſometimes omitted for the [i] Whole, and ſometimes for [k] Part. And it is ſaid to have been [l] adjudged, That ſuch Writs are good notwithſtanding ſuch Omiſſions. Alſo where Things moveable and immoveable are mentioned together in the ſame Writ, the Worth of all of them together is ſometimes [m] expreſſed under the Words *ad valentiam, &c.* And ſometimes the Worth of moveable Chatels, as that of [n] Corn in a Granary, *&c.* of [o] Wine in a Veſſel, and of [p] Wool, is expreſſed under the Words *ad valentiam*: From all which it ſeems to [q] appear, That the ſaid Directions are not neceſſary to be obſerved, even in Writs of Treſpaſs, concerning the Form whereof they are expreſly given, and that it is not material whether the Words *ad valentiam* or *precii* are uſed, or whether any Value be ſet on the Things taken away or not. And if ſo, why ſhould it be a greater Fault not to obſerve the ſaid Directions in Indictments, which are [r] not tied to the ſtrict Forms of Writs? Therefore from the whole, it ſeems [s] queſtionable, whether it be needful to ſet forth the Value of the Goods in an Indictment of

[a] Vide Poph. c. 208.
[b] Lambard, B. 4. ch. 5. fol. 496.
[c] Dalt. ch. 131.
[d] Lambard, B. 4. ch. 5. fol. 497, 498. 2 H. H. P. C. 187. Vide Cro. Ja. 130.
[e] Crompton de pace, 247, 248.
[f] Raſt. Entr. 55. pl. 6.
[g] Regiſter 93. b.
[i] Vide Regiſter 93. b. in the Writ de warrena fugata, &c. and that de parco fracto, and 94. a. in the Writ de equo & catallis arreſtatis, 94. b. in the Writ de averiis imparcatis, &c. and in that de tranſgreſſione facta uxori, &c. and 96. b. in that de equo percuſſo & 97. a. in that de ovibus fugatis, &c.
[k] Regiſt. 93. b. in the Writ de clauſo fracto, arboribus ſuccifis, 94. b. in the Writ de domo fracta, &c. and in the Writ de Jumento, &c. fugatis, and in that de equis imparcatis, and 95. b. in that de palis, &c. and in that de piſcaria piſcata, &c. and in that de domo fracta, &c. and 96. a. in that de ovibus tonſis, &c. and 96. b. in that de warrena fugata, &c. and 97. a. in that de porcis fugatis, &c.
[l] Regiſter 97. b. Vide Cro. Ja. 130. 1 Sid. 39, 150.
[m] Regiſter 94. a. in the Writ de piſcaria piſcata, &c. and 95. b. in that de piſca' piſcata, &c. and in that de domo fracta, &c. and 96. de excluſis ſtagni.
[n] Regiſter 95. b. in the Writ de bladis inundatis, &c. and 96. a. in that de clauſo fracto, &c.
[o] Regiſter 95. b. in the Writ de vino, &c.
[p] Regiſter 96. and in the Writ de ovibus tonſis, &c.
[q] Vide F. N. B. 88. Letter M. Cro. Ja. 130. 1 Sid. 39, 150, 121, 15. 2 H. H. P. C. 183.
[r] Q. Dy. 4. 26. b.
[s] See Dalton, ch. 131. Lambard, B. 4. ch. 5. fol. 496, 497. 2 H. H. P. C. 183.

Treſpaſs for any other Purpoſe than to aggravate the Fine, and whether it be neceſſary in an Indictment of Larceny for any other Purpoſe than to ſhew that the Crime amounts to grand Larceny, and to aſcertain the Goods thereby the better to intitle the Proſecutor to a [a] Reſtitution.

As to the fourth Point, *viz.* in what Manner the Body of an Indictment at Common Law muſt ſet forth the Circumſtances of Time and Place, I ſhall endeavour to ſhew,

1. How it ought to ſet forth the Circumſtance of Time.
2. How that of Place.

Sect. 76. And firſt as to the Circumſtance of Time, I find it no where holden, That it is neceſſary to mention the Hour in an Indictment. But on the contrary, it is ſaid, [b] That if there be any Neceſſity for it in an Appeal, which yet is [c] queſtionable, it is from the Statute of *Glouceſter*, and not from the Common Law; and therefore I ſhall take it for granted, That it is not neceſſarily required in an Indictment; ſince it is certain, That there is no Statute that makes it ſo, and the Common Law ſeems to have required no greater Certainty in an Indictment than in an Appeal.

Sect. 77. But it is laid down as an undoubted Principle in all the Books [d] that treat of this Matter, That no Indictment whatſoever can be good, without preciſely ſhewing a certain Year and Day of the material Facts alledged in it. Alſo it hath been [e] adjudged, That the Sheriffs Return of a Reſcous, without ſhewing the Year and Day, is inſufficient, becauſe ſuch a Return is in Lieu of an Indictment. Alſo it is taken for granted in [f] *Dyer*, That an Indictment of Reſcous is not good, without expreſly ſhewing the Day and Year both of the Arreſt, and alſo of the Reſcous, and that the Time of the latter is not ſufficiently ſhewn, by [g] ſhewing that of the former. And where an Indictment of Reſcous ſet forth, That *J. S.* committed ſuch a Felony ſuch a Day, and Year, and Place, *per quod* A. B. *prædictum* J. S. *cepit & arreſtavit, & in ſalva cuſtodia ſua adtunc & ibidem eundem* J. S. *habuit & cuſtodivit*, it is made a [h] *Quære*, Whether the Indictment be not inſufficient, becauſe no Time of the Arreſt is alledged in the ſame Sentence with it; and it is doubtful whether the Time of the Cuſtody which is alledged in the next Sentence, by Force of the Copulative be applied alſo to the Arreſt or not, and *Dyer* ſeems rather to incline to the contrary Opinion. However, it is certain, That if an Indictment lay the Offence on an [i] uncertain or impoſſible Day, as where it lays it on a [k] future Day, or lays one and the ſame Offence at [l] different Days, or lays it on ſuch a Day which makes the Indictment [m] repugnant to it ſelf, it is void. Alſo it hath been adjudged, That no [n] Defect of this Kind can be helped by the Verdict. Alſo it is ſaid, That an Indictment of Death laying an Aſſault at a certain Time and Place is [o] not ſufficient without repeating the Time and Place in the Clauſe of the Stroke, and the like Rule ſeems alſo to hold as to Indictments of other Felonies, in which reſpect ſuch Indictments differ from Indictments of Treſpaſs. Alſo it is [p] certain, That an Indictment of Death ought as well to ſet forth the Year and Day of the Death as of the Stroke, that it may appear that the Party died within the Year and Day. But theſe Matters having been more fully conſidered in the Chapter of Appeals, I ſhall refer the Reader thither for the better Underſtanding of them.

Sect. 78. It ſeems to be [q] generally agreed, That the Words *adtunc & ibidem* in the ſubſequent Clauſes of an Indictment are of the ſame Effect as if the Year and Day mentioned in the former Part of it had been expreſly

[a] Supra ch. 23. ſect. 55, 56, 57.
[b] S. P. C. 80.
[c] Supra ch. 23. ſect. 87. 1 Bulſt. 203.
[d] S. P. C. 95. Letter A. Lambard, B. 4. ch. 5. Dalt. ch. 131. Fitz. Indict. 28. Dyer 164. pl. 60. H. P. C. 206. 2 H. H. P. C. 177, 178. 8 H. 5. 8. pl. 4.
[e] Fitz. Coro. 45. Attach. 1. Bro. Return de brief, 97. 3 H. 7. 11. pl. 3.
[f] Dyer 164. pl. 60. Vide Fitz. Return de Viſcount, 32. Dy. 69. pl. 29. 10 Ed. 4. 15. pl. 13. Quære 5 H. 7. 17. b. 18. a.
[g] Yet the contrary is adjudged 2 Bul. 208. Cro. Ja. 345.
[h] Dy. 164. pl. 60.
[i] Supra ch. 23. ſect. 88. Moor 555. pl. 753.
[k] Raſt. Entries 263. pl. 5.
[l] 2 H. 7. 7. pl. 22.
[m] Supra ſect. 64. & ch. 23. ſect. 88, 89.
[n] 1 Rol. Ab. 781. N. 1.
[o] Supra ch. 23. ſect. 88. Hetley 35. 119, 120. 5 H. 7. 17. b. 18. a. 1 Bulſt. 203, 204.
[p] Supra ch. 23. ſect. 90.
[q] Dy. 28. pl. 6. 2 H. H. P. C. 178, 179. Vide Keilw. 100. ſupra ch. 23. ſect. 88. 4 Co. 41 b. Quære Dyer 164. pl. 60

preſly repeated. Alſo it hath been [a] adjudged, That an Indictment laying the Offence on the *Thurſday* after the Day of *Pentecoſt* in ſuch a Year is good: And from the like Ground it ſeems to follow, That an Indictment laying it on the [b] *Utas* of *Eaſter*, &c. (which ſhall be taken for the very eighth Day after the Feaſt,) or on the Tenth of *March* [c] laſt (if it may be aſcertained by the Style of the Seſſions before which the Indictment was taken) is as good as if it had ſhewn the Day and Year by expreſly naming ſuch a Day of ſuch a Month, &c.

Sect. 79. And where an Indictment charges a Man with a bare Omiſſion, as the not ſcouring ſuch a Ditch, &c. it is [d] ſaid, That it needs not ſhew any Time.

Sect. 80. It is moſt [e] regular to ſet forth the Year by ſhewing the Year of the King, yet this may be diſpenſed with for ſpecial Reaſons, if the very Year be otherwiſe ſufficiently expreſſed, for that only is material; and therefore in the [f] Caſe of the Regicides no Year of any King was laid for the King's Murder, but the compaſſing of his Death was laid in the twenty-fourth Year of King *Charles* the Firſt, and the Murder was laid on the thirtieth Day *ejuſdem menſis Januarii*, becauſe if the Reign of either King had been expreſſed, it might have cauſed a Diſpute Whether that or the other would have been more proper.

Sect. 81. It is [g] agreed, That a Miſtake in not laying an Offence on the very ſame Day on which it is afterwards proved upon the Trial, is not material upon Evidence.

Sect. 82. If an Indictment charge a Man with having done ſuch a Nuſance ſuch a Day and Year, &c. and on divers other Days, it is void [h] only as to the Facts on thoſe Days which are uncertainly alledged, and effectual for the Nuſance on the Day ſpecified; but if it charge a Man generally with ſeveral Offences at ſeveral Times, without laying any one of them on a certain Day, [i] as with extorting divers Sums of divers Subjects for a Paſſage over ſuch a Ferry, &c. [66] between ſuch a Day and ſuch a Day, it hath been adjudged, That it is wholly void. Yet it hath been ſolemnly reſolved, That a Conviction of [k] Deer-ſtealing ſetting forth the Offence between the Eighth and Twelfth of *July*, &c. is ſufficient.

Sect. 83. As to the ſecond Particular, *viz.* How an Indictment at Common Law muſt ſhew the Place where the Offence was done, it ſeems agreed by all the [l] Books, That no Indictment can be good without expreſly ſhewing ſome Place wherein the Offence was committed; which muſt [m] appear to have been within the Juriſdiction of the Court in which the Indictment is taken, and muſt alſo be alledged in ſuch a Manner as is perfectly free from all [n] Repugnance and Inconſiſtency; for if one and the ſame Offence be laid at two [o] different Places, or at the Town of *B.* [p] aforeſaid, where no ſuch Town was mentioned before; or if in an Indictment of Murder, the Stroke be laid at *A.* and the Death at *B.* and then it is [q] concluded that the Defendant *Sic felonicè murdravit* the Perſon deceaſed at *A.* the Indictment is void. And ſo it is alſo, if it do [r] not lay a Place both of the Stroke and Death; or if the Place or Places ſo alledged, be not ſuch from whence a [s] Viſne may come. Yet it hath been adjudged, That a Fact laid in a Pariſh of *London*, with ſome other Addition, as in the Pariſh of St. [t] *Michael* in *Woodſtreet*, *London*, or in the Pariſh of St. [u] *Lawrence Jury*, is good, without ſhewing the Ward in which

[a] 7 H. 6. 39. pl. 4. Fitz. Error, 17. Plow. Com. 122. b.
[b] Lamb. B. 4. ch. 5. fol. 491.
[c] Lamb. B. 4. ch. 5. fol. 491.
[d] Book 1. ch. 10. ſect. 5. Lamb. B. 4. ch. 5. fol. 492.
[e] Supra ch. 43. ſect. 90. 1 Lev. 113. 1 Salk. 195.
[f] Keling. 11.
[g] Supra ch. 23. ſect. 87, 88, 91. 3 Inſt. 230. 2 H. H. P. C. 179.
[h] Rex v. Dixon, Trin. 2 Georg. 1. Vide ſupra ſect. 74.
[i] Shower 389, 390.
[k] Dom. Reg. verſus Simpſon, adjudged Trin. 13 Annæ.
[l] 25 Ed. 3. 43. pl. 36. Fitz. Indictment, 1. Suggeſtion, 7. 4 H. 7. 8. pl. 7. 2 H. H. P. C. 180. Kelw. 98. pl. 8. 1 Bulſt. 124. See the Books cited ſect. 70. under the Letters, d, e, f, g, h.
[m] Vide Keilw. 33. pl. 6. 89. pl. 9. Cro. El. 448.
[n] Vide ſupra ſect. 62. and 77. & ch. 23. ſect. 88, 89, 91.
[o] 2 H. 7. 7. pl. 22.
[p] Cro. Ca. 465. Vide ſupra ſect. 74.
[q] See ch. 23. ſect. 88, 89, 91.
[r] Supra ch. 23. ſect. 92. Hetley 35. 118, 119. Dyer 68. pl. 28.
[s] Supra ch. 23. ſect. 92, 93.
[t] 9 Co. 66. b. Contra Cro. El. 732. Supra ch. 23. ſect. 92.
[u] 7 H. 6. 36. pl. 42.

the Pariſh lies. But theſe Matters having been more fully treated of in the [a] Chapter of Appeals, and alſo in the foregoing Part of this [b] Chapter, relating to the Certainty of the Time of the Offence, I ſhall refer the Reader thither, for the fuller Conſideration of them.

[a] Ch. 23. Sect. 88, 89, 91, 92, & 93. [b] Supra Sect. 76, 77, 78.

Sect. 84. It ſeems, That there is no Need in an Indictment on a Statute, ſetting forth the Deſcription which brings the Defendant within the Purview of it, to ſet forth any Place where thoſe Things happened, which brought him within ſuch Deſcriptions; and therefore where a Statute makes it High Treaſon for a Perſon born within the Realm, and in Popiſh Orders, to come into, or remain in the Kingdom, *&c.* there is no Need in an [c] Indictment on ſuch Statute to ſhew in what Place the Defendant was born or ordained. Alſo it ſeems to be [d] agreed, That a Miſtake of the Place in which an Offence is laid, will not be material upon the Evidence on Not guilty pleaded, if the Fact be proved at ſome other Place in the ſame County. But if there be no ſuch Place in a County as that wherein an Offence is laid in an Appeal or Indictment, all Proceſs on ſuch Indictment or Appeal is made void by the Statute of 7 *H.* 5. and 9 *H.* 5. 1. and 18 *H.* 6. 12. By the laſt of which Statutes it is recited, *That in the Parliament holden in the ninth Year of* H. 5. *it was ordained, For that many People of Malice cauſe often the King's liege People to be appealed or indicted in diverſe Counties of Treaſons or of Felonies, ſuppoſing by the ſaid Indictments or Appeals, that the ſaid Treaſons or Felonies were done in a certain Place in ſuch a County,* &c. *where no ſuch Place is in the ſame County, that the Proceſs of the ſame ſhall be void; and that the Indictors, Procurators and Conſpirators ſhall be puniſhed by Fine,* &c. *by the Diſcretion of the Juſtices, and alſo liable to Writs of Conſpiracy, and by the preſent Statute the above recited Statute is made perpetual.*

[c] Poph. 93, 94. B. 1. Ch. 17. Sect. 79, 80, 81, 82. [d] Vide ſupra Sect. 81. & Ch. 23. Sect. 91. Kelyng. 15. Salk. 288. H. P. C. 264, 265.

Sect. 85. It is obſervable, That the Statute made in the ninth Year of *H.* 5. herein referred to, ſeems to be wholly omitted by *Keble* and *Pulton*, who have no other Statute concerning this Matter made in the ninth Year of *Henry* V. excepting the firſt, which only confirms a Statute made in the ſeventh Year of the ſame King concerning Appeals and Indictments; and there is no other Statute whatſoever in the ſeventh Year of that King mentioned in *Keble* or *Pulton*, but only one which requires the Juſtices before the Award of any Exigent to inquire by Inqueſt of Office, Whether there be any ſuch Place in the County as that wherein an Offence is laid in an Appeal or Indictment. But this Statute ſeems only to extend to the County of *Lancaſter*, for it is directed to the Chancellor of that County, and recites, That Perſons had been indicted and appealed in Places falſly alledged in the ſaid County, and in the enacting Part ſpeaks only of Juſtices who had Power to determine Felonies in the ſaid County, and in the latter expreſly commands the ſaid Chancellor to cauſe it to be proclaimed in the ſame County, but mentions no other. From all which I ſee not how it can extend to any other County, and yet *Wingate* in his [e] Abridgment makes it equally extend to all Counties. However, [f] *Raſtal* in his Collection of Statutes ſeems to have ſet down the very Statute which is referred to by the above recited Statute of 18 *H.* 6. 12. and this is certainly [g] ſtill in Force.

[e] Wingate's Abridgment of the Statutes under the Title of Conſpiracy, Sect. 3. [f] Raſt. Statutes, Conſpiracy, 3. [g] Lamb. B. 4. ch. 5. f. 493. F. N. B. 115. G.

As to the fifth Point, *viz.* Where the Body of an Indictment may be vitiated by falſe or improper *Latin*, or the Uſe of *Engliſh* inſtead of *Latin*; I ſhall endeavour to ſhew,

1. Where falſe *Latin* will vitiate an Indictment.
2. Where a Word which is not *Latin*.
3. Where ſuch Faults are holpen by an *Anglicè*.

Sect. 86. As to the firſt of theſe Particulars, it ſeems to be holden generally in ſome [a] Books, that no falſe *Latin* will vitiate an Indictment, and it ſeems to be holden by my Lord [b] *Coke*, That an Indictment ſhall not be quaſhed for any falſe Concord between the Subſtantive and Adjective, as *præfatæ Regi*, or *Præfato Reginæ*, becauſe tho' the Expreſſions be incongruous, yet they are *Latin* and ſignificant; neither do I find this Opinion denied by any other Authority, and therefore I leave it to be conſidered, Whether it may not ſtill be maintained, eſpecially [c] conſidering, That the Senſe appears as fully, clearly and expreſly from ſuch *Latin* as if it had been never ſo properly expreſſed. And it ſeems alſo, That the like Reaſon may be given for the Caſe in [d] *Yelverton*, wherein an Indictment of forcible Entry, finding that the Defendant *unum meſuagium ingreſſum fecit*, without adding the Word *in* before *meſuagium*, was adjudged good; but it is ſaid in the Book, That this is not falſe, though it be not fine *Latin*; by which it ſeems to be implied, That if it had been falſe *Latin*, it might have vitiated the Indictment. However, it ſeems to be ſettled at this Day, That an Indictment againſt two or more, laying the Fact charged againſt them in the ſingular Number, is inſufficient, as where it finds, That *A.* and *B. inſultum* [e] *fecit*; the Reaſon whereof perhaps may be this, That it appears ſomewhat doubtful upon the Face of the Indictment whether the Jurors intended to charge more than one, becauſe the Fact is laid in the ſingular Number, which it ſeems abſurd to apply to more than one, and therefore the Indictment is inſufficient for its Uncertainty. As to [f] *Fulwood*'s Caſe, wherein *Croke* reports the contrary to have been reſolved, it is certain, That the Verb in the Record is in the plural Number. And as to the [g] Caſes wherein Faults of this Kind have been amended in original Writs, as *teneat conventionem* for *teneant*, and ſuch like; it may be anſwered, That thoſe Amendments were made by Virtue of the Statutes of [h] Amendments, which extend not to criminal Proceedings. And as to the Caſe in [i] *Bulſtrode*'s Reports, wherein it is ſaid to have been reſolved, That an Indictment of Felony againſt more than one in the ſingular Number was amended, and thereupon the Defendants were adjudged to be hanged; it may be anſwered, That it doth not appear in what Part of the Indictment the ſingular Number was put for the plural; neither is the ſaid Reſolution, in whatſoever Senſe it be taken, reconcileable with the later Authorities, as ſhall be more fully ſhewn under the twelfth Point. But it is [k] ſaid, That a Fault of this Kind is made good by the Grand Jury's finding the Indictment *Billa vera* againſt one of the Defendants only; the Reaſon whereof perhaps may be this, That the Uncertainty of the Indictment is ſupplied by ſuch an Indorſement. But this ſeems contrary to the Authorities relating to this Matter cited in the ſecond Section. Alſo it hath been [l] adjudged, That where a Bill of Indictment lays the Fact in the plural Number againſt two, and it is found *Billa vera* as to one of them only, it is good; and yet the Verb in the plural Number in the Record muſt, after ſuch a Finding, be applied only to one Perſon; but to this it may be anſwered, That there is no Uncertainty either in the Bill or Indorſement. Alſo it hath been [m] adjudged, That the Word *Solvet* inſtead of *Solvat*, is not fatal in a Judgment; but that a new one ſhall be given.

[a] 5 Co. 121. a. Cro. Ca. 465.
[b] 5 Co. 121. b. Vide Cro. El. 108. pl. 3. 2 H. H. P. C. 169.
[c] Vide Cro. El. 108. pl. 3.
[d] Yelv. 27, 28.
[e] Dominus Rex verſus Dobſon, Term. Hill. 3 Georgii 1. 2 Keb. 51. pl. 9. Vide Cro. Ca. 465, 573. Cro. El. 754. pl. 15.
[f] Cro. Ca. 489.
[g] 2 Vent. 173. Yelv. 224, 225. 2 Saund. 38. Cro. Ja. 306, 369.
[h] Salk. 51, 52. 6 Mod. 268.
[i] 2 Bulſt. 35.
[k] 2 Keb. 51. pl. 9.
[l] Cro. Ca. 464, 465.
[m] 1 Sid. 219.

Sect. 87. As to the second Particular, *viz.* Where the Use of a Word which is not *Latin* will vitiate an Indictment, it seems generally [a] agreed, That an Indictment wholly in *English* is void, which seems to depend upon the Statute of 36 *Ed.* 3. 15. *By which 'tis enacted, That all Pleas which be pleaded in any of the King's Courts shall be entered and enrolled in Latin.* And from hence it seems clearly to follow, That if any material Part either of the Body or Caption of an Indictment be expressed in a Word which is not *Latin*, as by the Word [b] *erectaverunt*, instead of *erexerunt*, or [c] *brachia sua dextra*, instead of *brachio*, or [d] *præsentant' existit* instead of *præsentat'*, the Indictment is insufficient; (except in some special Cases herein after set forth) for no one can say, That the bare giving a *Latin* Termination to a Word unknown in that Language, can make it become *Latin*; and if the Want of one material Word may be supplied, why not the Want of two, and so on? It hath indeed been [e] holden, That a Fault of this Kind, as *imaginavit*, for *imaginatus est*, *avæ* for *aviæ* is amendable in an original Writ, which yet is denied by others, if it be in a [f] Substantial Part. However, it seems certain, That such Amendment must depend upon the Statutes of Amendments, which extend [g] not to criminal Proceedings. Also it seems, That it is no less a Fault to make Use of a Word which is proper *Latin* in another Sense, whether entirely different, or of a much larger Extent, than that in which it is used, as of the Word [h] *collis* for *colli*, or [i] *mala ars* for *veneficium*. Also it seems agreed, That an Abbreviation not justified by legal Usage, as [k] *Dno* without a Dash, for *Domino*, [l] *R. Rs.* for *Regni Regis*; or the Expression of a Number in any Figures that are not [m] *Roman*, is equally fatal as it would have been wholly to have omitted what you endeavour in such Manner to express. Also it hath beeh [n] adjudged, That an Inquisition finding that *J. S. seipsum emersit, &c.* is insufficient; because *emergo* doth not signify to put into, but rise out of the Water. [o] Also it is said, That an Indictment has been quashed for the Words *Pace Regia*, instead of *Pace Regis*; but it appears not what was the Nature of the Indictment, nor in what Part of it these Words were used, and therefore I would suppose it to have been in such Part of some Indictment wherein those Expressions are so material that they cannot be rejected as Surplus and immaterial; for it seems to be a settled Rule, That nothing which may be so rejected shall vitiate an Indictment; as where the Year of the Lord is written in common [p] Figures, but the Year of the King is well expressed, or where an Indictment is said to be taken before *J. S.* and *J. N.* [q] *duo Justiciariis, &c.* Also it seems, That the Use of a Word which is not proper *Latin*, as of the [r] Word *contrafacere*, for counterfeiting, may be made good by Precedents. And there can be no Doubt but that [s] Terms of Art, which are necessary in all Indictments, as *Felonia*, *Murdrum*, *Burglaria*, and such like are good, tho' they be not good classical *Latin*; for they are of such a complex and peculiar Signification as no proper *Latin* Word will come up to. Also it hath been [t] adjudged, That a literal Translation of a Statute into *Latin* is sufficient, if intelligible, let it be never so unelegant, as where it sets forth that the Defendant *super caput suum proprium* did forge, Meaning, That he did it of his own Head.

Sect. 88. As to the third Particular, *viz.* What Faults of this Kind are holpen by an *Anglicè*: It seems to be holden generally in some Books, That the Use of a Word which is either not *Latin* at all, or not *Latin* in the Sense in which it is used, may in many Cases be holpen by an *Anglicè*,

as

2 H. H. P. C. 169, 170.
[a] Cro. El. 85. pl. 4. Quære 3 Keb. 637.
[b] Cro. El. 231. pl. 22.
[c] Cro. El. 137. pl. 10.
[d] 1 Sid. 175. Salk. 370. pl. 2.
[e] 8 Co. 159.b. 2 Bulst. 35. Moore 5. pl. 17. N. Bend. 33. pl. 53. 1 And. 24.
[f] 1 Lev. 1, 2. 5 Co. 45. Cro. El. 462.
[g] 1 Salk. 51, 52. 6 Mod. 268. Vide supra Sect. 86.
[h] 1 Bulst. 109.
[i] Noy 85. 1 Jon. 144. Latch 156.
[k] 1 Sid. 175.
[l] 1 Sid. 140.
[m] 1 Salk. 195. 1 Sid. 40. pl. 6. 3 Keb. 301. 2 Lev. 102. 1 Mod. 78.
[n] 2 Lev. 140. 3 Mod. 100. B. 1. Ch. 27. Sect. 15.
[o] 1 Sid. 140.
[p] 1 Salk. 195. 1 Mod. 78.
[q] Cro. El. 108. pl. 3.
[r] 2 Jon. 49, 50.
[s] Dalt. ch. 131. 10 Co. 133.
[t] 2 Lev. 221.
2 H. H. P. C. 169.

as [a] *erectaverunt, anglicè* did erect; [b] *Retes, anglicè* Nets; [c] *Pellices, anglicè* Skins; *Ollis* [d] *æriis, anglicè* braſs Pots. But to this it may be anſwered, That as to the three firſt of theſe Inſtances, what is ſaid concerning this Matter is only ſpoken of by the By, and did not come into Judgment; and as to the laſt of them it may be ſaid, That it doth not concern a criminal Proceeding, but a civil Action, and that after a Verdict: And if the Purport of it be, that an *Anglice* helps the Uſe of a Word that is not *Latin* in an Action of Trover, tho' Damage be expreſly given for it, it is contradicted by many other expreſs [e] Reſolutions, in which it ſeems to have been taken as a ſettled Rule, That where Damages are expreſly given for a Thing expreſſed by a Word that is not *Latin*, it is no Way helped by an *Anglicè*. Alſo it hath been [f] adjudged, That an Indictment for taking *octo diſcas, Anglicè* Diſhes, is inſufficient; and this is agreeable to what is laid down as a ſettled Rule in many [g] Books, *viz.* That where there is a proper *Latin* Word for the Thing intended to be expreſſed, no *Anglicè* will help an improper one, as it will do where there is [h] no proper *Latin* Word, becauſe in ſuch a Caſe there is ſuch a Neceſſity either to uſe a feigned one or none at all. Alſo it hath been adjudged, That where there is a proper *Latin* Word, an *Anglicè* cannot make good the Uſe of any other either in a more [i] ſpecial or [k] extenſive Signification than the *Latin* Language will bear, as to make the Words [l] *malas artes* ſignify Witchcraft, or [m] *Riſcus* a Box full of Linen, or [n] *fulcrum tecti*, a Field Bed with a Teſter and Curtains; in which Caſes the Judges will take [o] no Manner of Notice of what comes under the *Anglicè* beyond the ſtrict Signification of the *Latin*. [67]

Sect. 89. As to the ſixth Point, *viz.* Where the Offence indicted may be laid jointly, and where ſeverally, and where both jointly and ſeverally, and where the Offences of ſeveral Perſons may be laid in one Indictment; it ſeems certain at this Day, That notwithſtanding the Offence of ſeveral Perſons cannot but in all Caſes be ſeveral; becauſe the Offence of one Man cannot be the Offence of another, but every one muſt anſwer ſeverally for his own Crime; yet if it wholly ariſe from any ſuch joint Act, which in it ſelf is criminal, without any Regard to any particular perſonal Default of the Defendant, as the joint [p] Keeping of a Gaming-Houſe, or the [q] unlawful Hunting and Carrying away of a Deer, or [r] Maintenance or [s] Extortion, *&c.* The Indictment or Information may either charge the Defendants jointly and ſeverally, as thus: *Quod* [t] *cuſtodiverunt, & uterq; eorum cuſtodivit*; or, *quod* [u] *aſportaverunt, & eorum uterq; aſportavit*; or may charge them jointly only, without charging them [x] ſeverally, becauſe it ſufficiently appears from the Conſtruction of Law, That if they joined in ſuch Act, they could not but be each of them guilty; and from hence it follows, That on ſuch Indictment or Information [y] ſome of the Defendants may be acquitted, and others convicted; for the Law looks on the Charge as ſeveral againſt each, tho' the Words of it purport only a joint Charge againſt all. But where the Offence indicted doth not wholly ariſe from the joint Act of all the Defendants, but from ſuch Act joined with ſome perſonal and particular Defect or Omiſſion of each Defendant, without which it would be no Offence; as the Following a joint Trade without having ſerved a ſeven Years Apprenticeſhip required by the Statute, in which Caſe it muſt be the particular Defect of each Trader which muſt make him guilty, and one of them may offend againſt the Statute, and the others not, the Indictment or Information [z] muſt charge them ſe-

[a] Cro. El. 231.
[b] Keilw. 100. 3 Bulſt. 178. ſeems contrary.
[c] 1 Sid. 318.
[d] Cro. Ja. 129.
[e] 1 Lev. 99, 129, 204. 1 Sid. 98, 318. Raym. 15. 3 Lev. 336. 10 Co. 130, 133.
[f] 2 Keb. 779. pl. 4.
[g] Noy 85. Latch 156. March 16, 60. 1 Jon. 144. 10 Co. 133. Vide 1 Lev. 204. 1 Sid. 318. Yelv. 68.
[h] 10 Co. 133. Noy 85. Latch 156. March 16. 1 Sid. 81. 1 Jon. 144.
[i] Noy 85. 1 Sid. 60, 81.
[k] Cro. Ja. 664, 665.
[l] Noy 85. Latch 156. 1 Jon. 144.
[m] Cro. Ja. 664, 665. 2 Rol. Rep. 254, 255.
[n] 10 Co. 130, 132, 133.
[o] Cro. Ja. 664, 665. 2 Rol. Rep. 254, 255. 10 Co. 130, 132, 133.
[p] Dominus Rex verſus Dixon & uxorem, adjudged Trin. 2 Georgii 1. 2 H. H. P. C. 174.
[q] Dominus Rex verſus Hawkins, adjudged Mich. 5 Georgii 1.
[r] 1 Vent. 302.
[s] Salk. 382. pl. 32.
[t] Dominus Rex verſus Dixon & uxorem, adjudged Trin. 2 Geo. 1.

[u] Dominus Rex verſus Hawkins, adjudged Mich. 3 Geo. 1. [x] Domina Regina verſus Williams, adjudged Mich. 10 Annæ. Bear & White, 4 Guliel. 3. Cro. Car. 380, 381. 2 Rol. Ab. 707. pl. 45, 48. 708. pl. 52. Contra 2 Rol. Rep. 345. Palmer 367, 368. [y] 2 Rol. Ab. 707. pl. 45, 48. 708. pl. 52. Bear & White, 4 Guliel. 3. [z] 2 Rol. Ab. 81. pl. 6. 5 Mod. 180. 2 H. H. P. C. 174.

verally and not jointly; for it is absurd to charge them jointly, because the Offence of each Defendant arises from a Defect peculiar to himself. And for the like Reason a joint Indictment against several for not [a] repairing the Street before their Houses hath been quashed. But I do not find it settled in what Cases several Offences of several Persons may be join'd in one Indictment; for in some [b] Books Indictments against several for several Offences, as for Recusancy, [c] following a Trade without having served an Apprenticeship, not [d] repairing the Streets, *&c.* are mentioned without any Exception on this Account: And it is holden, That one Indictment against two Justices for not [e] inquiring of a Riot, and an Indictment against two Perrsons for speaking of the same [f] Words, may be maintained; and yet it is [g] agreed, That one Action lies not against several for the same Words. Also in [h] *Rolle*'s Reports on Indictment against several for having Inmates in their Houses is said to have been quashed; because it was but one joint Indictment against them all, whereas there ought to have been several Indictments against them. Also in the sixth [i] Modern Reports, an Indictment against several for the Neglect of a Day of Fasting appointed by Proclamation, is said to have been quashed for the like Reason. And this is certainly the most agreeable to the Rule of bringing Actions upon penal Statutes, wherein several Offences shall not be joined, except it be in Respect of some one Thing to which all of them have a Relation; as where several [k] join in a Suit in the [l] Admiralty for a Contract on Land, or in procuring or giving an untrue Verdict, or are privy to one another [m] in Maintenance of the same Cause.

Sect. 90. As to the seventh Point, *viz.* Whether the Words *vi & armis* be in any Case necessary in the Body of an Indictment at Common Law; it is taken for granted in some [n] Books, That they were necessary at Common Law in all Indictments for Offences which amount to an actual Disturbance of the Peace, as Rescouses and Assaults, and such like; yet I do [o] not find it agreed, That they were ever necessary in such Indictments, wherein it would seem absurd to put them in, as in Indictments for [p] Conspiracies, [q] Cheats, Slanders, Escapes, and such like; or [r] Nusances committed in a Man's own Ground. However, there can be no Doubt but that the Omission of them in Indictments of this Kind, is made good by the Statute of 37 *H.* 8. 8. by which it is recited, *That in all Indictments of Felony and Trespass, and divers others, it was common to use the Words* vi & armis, *and in divers of them to declare the Manner of the Force and Arms, that is to say,* vi & armis videlicet, baculis, cultellis, arcubus & sagittis, *or other such like Words; where of Truth the Parties indicted had no such Weapons at the Time of the Offence, yet for Lack of such Words the said Indictments were taken as void, and had been avoided by Writ of Error or Plea,* &c. and thereupon it is enacted, *That these Words* vi & armis, videlicet, cum baculis, cultellis, arcubus & sagittis, *or other such like, shall not of Necessity be put in any Indictment or Inquisition: Nor shall the Parties indicted have any Advantage by Writ of Error or Plea or otherwise, to avoid any such Indictment or Inquisition for the Want of these or the like Words: But that the same Inquisitions and Indictments, and every of them, lacking the said Words, or any of them, shall be adjudged as effectual to all Intents, Constructions and Purposes, as the same Inquisitions and Indictments having the same Words in them.*

Sect. 91. But notwithstanding this Statute seems to be so express as to all Indictments, yet it is [s] holden in many Books, That Indictments of Trespass, and such like, are still insufficient without the Words *vi & armis*, and many Indictments have accordingly been quashed for want of them, where they are not implied in some others, as [t] *rescussit*, or [u] *manu forti*

[a] 2 Rol. Ab 81. pl. 7.
[b] 1 Leon. 241.
[c] 2 Rol. Ab. 81. pl. 6. Salk. 382. 1 Vent. 302.
[d] 2 Rol. Ab. 81. pl. 7
[e] Stile's Rep. 245.
[f] Stile's Rep. 312.
[g] Cro. Ja. 647. 1 Rol. Ab. 781. O. pl. 1. Palm. 313. 1 Bulst. 15.
[h] 2 Rol. Rep. 164.
[i] 6 Mod. 210.
[k] Brook, Joinder in Action, 5, 47, 100, 108. F. N. B. 171. Letters D, E. Fitz. Decies tantum, 1, 4, 6, 8, 9.
[l] Quære Dy. 159. pl. 39.
[m] Brook, Maintenance, 26, 52.
[n] Cro. Jac. 473. Skin. 426. 2 H. H. P. C. 187. 2 Lev. 221. See the Books cited in the next Section. Quære supra Ch. 23. Sect. 85.
[o] Yet see the Preamble of 37 H. 8. 8.
[p] 1 Lev. 125, 126. Dalt. ch. 131.
[q] 1 Keb. 562. Dalt. ch. 131
[r] Poph. 206. Cro. Ca. 377.
[s] S. P. C. 94. 2 Lev. 221. 1 Sid. 140. 1 Bulst. 205 1 Lev. 126 1 Keb. 101. 2 Keb. 154. Vide Poph. 206. Cro. Ca. 377, 378.
[t] Cro. Ja. 345 2 Bulst. 208 2 H. H. P. C 187.
[u] B. 1. Ch. 64. sect. 44. Dalt. ch. 131

forti, &c. But it ſeems difficult to aſſign any Reaſon for theſe Opinions, unleſs it be, That becauſe the enacting Part of the Statute ſays, That the Words *vi & armis, videlicet cum baculis, cultellis, &c.* are not neceſſary, *&c.* the Meaning was only to take away the Neceſſity of thoſe ſuperfluous Words *baculis & cultellis, &c.* but not of the Words *vi & armis*, where they are proper and pertinent; but to this it may be anſwered, That the Preamble ſeems to complain of the Opinion, that the Words *vi & armis*, whether put by themſelves, or uſed with thoſe other Words, were in any Caſe thought neceſſary in Indictments; and it is moſt natural ſo to explain the enacting Part of a Statute as to make it extend to all the Miſchiefs complained of in the Preamble; beſides, the enacting Part of the Statute is expreſs, *That Indictments without theſe Words* vi & armis, videlicet, baculis, cultellis, arcubus & ſagittis, *or any of them, ſhall be as effectual as if they had them compriſed in them*; and ſurely the Words *vi & armis* cannot but be comprehended under theſe Words, *or any of them*. It is ſaid [a] indeed in *Levinz*'s ſecond Reports, That the Words *vi & armis* are ſtill neceſſary, becauſe without them there can be no *Capiatur* entered, nor Fine to the King; but this is in Effect to contradict the Statute which ſays, That an Indictment without thoſe Words ſhall be as effectual to all Intents, Conſtructions and Purpoſes, as an Indictment with them. Beſides, will any one ſay, That there can be no *Capiatur* nor Fine to the King upon Indictments of Cheats, Conſpiracies and ſuch like? Wherein yet it ſeems to be agreed, That thoſe Words are not neceſſary. And agreably hereto, the Court of King's Bench has [b] often refuſed to quaſh Indictments of Treſpaſs for the Want of thoſe Words. However, it is certainly ſafe and adviſeable to make Uſe of them where they are proper and pertinent, if it be to no other Purpoſe than to aggravate the Offence.

Sect. 92. As to the eighth Point, *viz.* Whether it be neceſſary in the Body of an Indictment at Common Law to lay the Offence *contra pacem*; inaſmuch as all Offences whatſoever which are ſubject to a publick Proſecution ſeem in general to be ſo, as they are Breaches of the Law, and in that Reſpect tend to the Diſturbance of the quiet and peaceable Government of the King over his People; it ſeems to be a good general [c] Rule, That no Indictment or Information, for an Offence, Capital or not Capital, againſt the Common Law or Statute, can be good, except it expreſly ſuppoſe ſuch Offence to have been done againſt the Peace of the King or King's, in whoſe Reign or Reigns it was committed. And accordingly I find, that every Precedent of an Indictment in *Coke*'s Entries, whether for [d] Treaſon, or [e] Felony, or [f] inferior Offences, expreſly lays the Offence againſt the Peace of the King, except only in four Inſtances whereof the one is of an Indictment for a [g] Nuſance for not repairing the Highway, which if it may be maintained, ſeems to depend chiefly on this Reaſon, That the Offence is of ſuch a Nature, that a Man may be as well guilty of it in his own Ground as in that of another; and therefore it hath been [h] holden, That it needs not be laid againſt the Peace, becauſe the Laying it in ſuch a Manner may ſeem to imply ſomewhat of Force or Treſpaſs againſt the Perſon or Poſſeſſion of another; but it ſeems difficult to reconcile this Opinion with thoſe many Reſolutions taken Notice of in the following Part of this Section, by which Indictments, for want of theſe Words, *contra pacem*, have been adjudged inſufficient, where the Offences could on no other Account be ſaid to be againſt the Peace, than as they were Breaches of the Law, as all Nuſances certainly are. And one [i] other of the ſaid Inſtances in *Coke*'s Entries is, of an Indictment of *Homicide* by Miſadventure, and one other [k] of an Indictment of *Homicide* in Self-De-

[a] 2 Lev. 221.
[b] Cro. Ja. 472, 473. Vide Cro. Ja. 345. 2 Bulſt. 208. Dalt. ch. 131. Lamb. B. 4. ch. 5. f. 502, 503.
[c] 3 Keb. 490. pl. 45. 1 Keb. 789. pl. 43. 2 Bulſt. 258. 2 H. H. P. C. 188. See the Caſes cited in the following Part of this Section, and Cro. El. 186. pl. 10. 6 Mod. 128.
[d] Co. Ent. 360. pl. 14, 15. 361. pl. 16.
[e] Co. Ent. 351. pl. 1. 352. pl. 2. 355. pl. 7, 8. 356. pl. 9. 358. pl. 11, 12. 359. pl. 13.
[f] Co. Ent. 352, 353, 361. pl. 17. 362. pl. 18.
[g] Co. Ent. 358. pl. 10. See Raſt. Ent. 263. pl. 7.
[h] 2 Rol. Ab. 82. pl. 9. 83. pl. 5, 6. Contra Cro. Ca. 584.
[i] Co. Ent. 253. pl. 4.
[k] Co Ent. 254. pl. 5.

fence; but these Precedents if they may be maintained, seem to depend chiefly on this Reason, That such Offences are supposed to be owing rather to the Misfortune than Fault of the Party. And the [a] fourth of the said Instances, is of an Indictment of Perjury on the Statute; which concludes *in Contemptum Reginæ, &c. & contra formam Statuti*, without adding *contra pacem*. But [b] *Rastal*'s Precedents, both of Indictments of Felony, and of inferior Offences do as often omit the Words *contra pacem*, as make use of them. However, certainly the much greater Number of Precedents expresly conclude *contra pacem*, and the Authority of these is much strengthened by those many Cases in the Reports, wherein Indictments and Informations appear to have been quashed for Want of the Words *contra pacem*; as Indictments and Informations for [c] Barratry, [d] Forgery, [e] Retaining a Servant without a Testimonial from his last Master, [f] following a Trade without having served an Apprenticeship, [g] erecting a Cottage, [h] Assault and Battery, *&c.* But it seems clear from all the Precedents, That neither an Information [i] *qui tam*, on a penal Statute, nor an Information by the King for an [k] Intrusion, or other [l] Wrong of a Civil Nature done to his Lands, Goods or Revenues, need the Words *contra pacem*.

Sect. 93. If the Offence indicted be expresly laid partly in the Reign of one King, and partly in the Reign of another, as where *J. S.* is indicted for having erected a Wear in the Time of Queen *Elizabeth*, and continued it in the Time of King *James*, and thereupon the Indictors conclude, That so the Wear was erected and continued *contra pacem Regis, &c.* without adding *contra pacem nuper Reginæ*, the Indictment is [m] insufficient, because it appears, That the Commencement of the Wrong, which is as much indicted as the Continuance, was in the Reign of Queen *Elizabeth*, and consequently, if a Crime, must have been against the Peace of her Reign. But if the Indictors had concluded only, That *J. S.* so continued the Wear *contra pacem Domini Regis, &c.* and had laid the Erection of it by Way of Recital, or Inducement only, it is [n] said, that the Indictment had been good, because it should be taken as an Indictment for the Continuance only.

Sect. 94. As to the ninth Point, *viz.* Whether it be necessary in the Body of an Indictment at Common Law, to lay the Offence *contra coronam & dignitatem Regis*, it is observable, That all the Precedents of Indictments in *Coke*'s Entries, cited in the ninety-fourth Section, which lay the Offence *contra pacem*, lay it also, *contra coronam & dignitatem, &c.* Yet not one of [o] *Rastal*'s Precedents doth so; neither do I find any one Case wherein an Indictment against which no other Exception could be taken, has been adjudged [p] insufficient for the Want of these Words. But on the contrary I find it expresly resolved in [q] *Holbrook*'s Case, That an Indictment of a Riot is good without them. [68]

Sect. 95. As to the tenth Point, *viz.* Whether it be necessary in the Body of an Indictment at Common Law, to lay the Offence *in contemptum Regis*; it is so laid in some Indictments of inferior Crimes in [r] *Coke* and *Rastal*, and in others [s] not. Also it is so laid, with the Addition of the Clause *contra leges suas*, in every Information of Intrusion upon the King's Lands in [t] *Coke* and [u] *Rastal*, and also in an Information in [x] *Coke* for a Trover and Conversion of the King's Goods. But in [y] two Informations for Mines claimed by the King, which are the only Precedents I find of this

[a] Co. Ent. 363. pl. 19.
[b] Rast. Ent. 263.
[c] 2 Rol. Ab. 82. pl. 5. Cro. Jac. 527. pl. 4.
[d] 2 Rol. Ab. 82. pl. 11.
[e] 1 Mod. 78.
[f] 3 Keb. 790. pl. 45. 1 Keb. 501. pl. 58. 848. pl. 48. 6 Mod. 128.
[g] 1 Keb. 474. pl. 91.
[h] 2 Keb. 36. pl. 72. Vide 2 Keb. 779. pl. 7. Yelv. 66.
[i] Rast. Ent. 409. pl. 2. 1 Keb. 860. pl. 70. Co. Ent. from 364 to 372. 393. pl. 17.
[k] Rast. Ent. 412. pl. 4. Co. Ent. from 372 to 390.
[l] Rast. Ent. 410. pl. 3. Co. Ent. 390. pl. 16.
[m] Yelv. 66. Vide 4 H. 6. 4. pl. 7. 2 H. H. P.C. 188, 189. Fitz. Brief, 25.
[n] Yelv. 66. 4 H. 6. 4. pl. 7. Fitz. Brief, 25.
[o] See Rast. Ent. 263.
[p] See 2 Bulst. 258. Aleyn 49, 50.
[q] 2 Ro. Ab. 82. pl. 1.
[r] Co. Ent. 353, 363. pl. 19. Rast. Ent. 263. pl. 9.
[s] Co. Ent. 362. pl. 17, 18. Rast. Ent. 263. pl. 6, 7, 11.
[t] Co. Ent. 372. pl. 10. 376. pl. 11. 379. pl. 12. 381. pl. 13. 385. pl. 14. 387. pl. 15. 1 Co. 16. b. 26. b.
[u] Rast. Ent. 412. pl. 4.
[x] Co. Ent. 390. pl. 16.
[y] Rast. Ent. 410. pl. 3. Plow. Com. 310.

this Kind, the ſuppoſed Injury is laid only *ad damnum Regis*, without either of the ſaid Clauſes; neither do I find either of them in any Indictment of Treaſon or Felony, nor in any Information *qui tam* in *Coke* or *Raſtal*; and tho' it ſeems to be admitted in the Year-Book of [a] 4 *H.* 6. that in an Action on a Statute it is neceſſary to conclude, *in contemptum Domini Regis*, yet in [b] *Lutwych's Entries* it is oftner omitted than uſed, and no Exception appears to have been taken for the Omiſſion.

Sect. 96. As to the eleventh Point, *viz.* Whether it be neceſſary in an Indictment at Common Law to lay the Offence *illicitè*, I cannot find this Word uſed in any one of *Coke's* or *Raſtal's* Precedents of Indictments; neither do I find any clear and expreſs [c] Authority, that it is in any Caſe neceſſary in an Indictment at Common Law; but on the contrary I find it expreſly [d] adjudged, That it is not neceſſary in an Indictment of a Riot, becauſe the Act it ſelf contained in the Indictment ſo plainly appears to be unlawful. But where a Statute uſes the Word unlawfully in the Deſcription of an Offence, it is certain that an Indictment grounded on it muſt uſe the Word *illicitè*, or ſome other tantamount.

Sect. 97. As to the twelfth Point, *viz.* Whether a Defect in any of the Particulars above-mentioned be amendable; I take it to be [e] ſettled, That no criminal Proſecution is within the Benefit of any of the Statutes of Amendments; from whence it follows that no Amendment can be admitted in any ſuch Proſecution, but ſuch only as is allowed by the Common Law. And agreeably hereto I find it laid down as a [f] Principle in ſome Books, That the Body of an Indictment removed into the King's Bench from any inferior Court whatſoever, except only thoſe of *London*, can in no Caſe be amended; but it is [g] ſaid, That the Body of an Indictment from *London* may be amended, becauſe by the City-Charter a Tenor of the Record only can be removed from thence. [h] And it ſeems, That by the Courſe of the King's Bench, a Rule may be made on any Coroner to amend even the Body of his Inqueſt by his Notes in a meer Matter of Form. But I do not find it any where holden, That this can be done after it is filed, by which it becomes a Record of the Court; and then the ſame Objection ſeems to lie againſt the Amendment of it, as of an Indictment. But it ſeems to be [i] agreed, That the Caption of an Indictment from any Place may upon Motion be amended by the Clerk of the Aſſiſes or of the Peace, ſo as to [k] make it agree with the original Record at any Time during the ſame Term in which it came in, [l] but not in a ſubſequent Term. But I have known it holden, That the Caption of an Inquiſition cannot be amended at any Time after it is filed, any more than the Body; the Reaſon whereof perhaps may be this, That the Caption being Part of, and drawn at the ſame Time with the Inquiſition, greater Exactneſs is required in it than in that of an Indictment, which is left as a Thing of Courſe to be drawn up by the Clerk of the Court, when Occaſion ſhall require. Alſo by the Opinion of two Judges againſt that of two, the Want of Continuances in the Record of an Attainder of Felony [m] cannot be amended by the Certificate of the Clerk of the Aſſiſes, eſpecially if the King ſignify his Pleaſure, that he doth not deſire any Amendment. And it ſeems to be [n] ſettled at this Day, that no Diſcontinuance is amendable in any criminal Proſecution, [o] without Conſent. But it hath been [p] adjudged, That a meer Miſpriſion in the Joining of an Iſſue in a criminal Proſecution, as where the Word *ſimiliter*, &c. is omitted, may be

[a] 4 H. 6. 4. pl. 7. Fitz. Brief, 25.
[b] Lutw. 132, 133, 134, 135, 139, 165, 167.
[c] See 1 Keb. 859. pl. 68. 2 Keb. 715. pl. 99.
[d] 2 Rol. Ab. 82. pl. 4.
[e] 1 Jon. 421. 1 Salk. 51, 52. 6 Mod. 268, &c. Vide ſupra Ch. 23. Sect. 129. 1 Sid. 66. pl. 39.
[f] 1 Keb. 252. pl. 20. 2 Keb. 580. pl. 112. 1 Sid. 155. pl. 5. Vide 1 Keb. 45. pl. 120. 2 Keb. 141. pl. 13. 142. pl. 15. Contra 2 Bulſt. 35.
[g] 1 Keb. 252. pl. 20. 1 Sid. 155. pl. 5. 229, 230. 1 Keb. 571. pl. 26. Vide Hob. 135.
[h] See B. 1. Ch. 27. Sect. 16.
[i] 1 Saund. 249. 1 Sid. 175. pl. 7. 1 Keb. 656. pl. 36. 3 Mod. 167.
[k] Cro. Jac. 276, 277. Vide 1 Sid. 155.
[l] 1 Sid. 155. pl. 5. 1 Keb. 45. pl. 120. 656. pl. 36. 1 Sid. 175. pl. 7. 12 H. 7. 25. pl. 3. 10 Ed. 4. 15. pl. 15.

[m] 1 Rol. Ab. 196. A. 1 Jon. 420. [n] Salk. 51, 52. 6 Mod. 268. Bro. Amendment, 10, 17, 66, 92. Fitz. Amendment, 59. 29 E. 3. 32. Diſcontinuance de proceſs, 47. [o] 21 H. 7. 40. pl. 65. Fitz. Amendment, 78. [p] Cro. Jac. 502, 529, 530. 2 Rol. Rep. 59.

amended at any Time. Alſo it hath been [a] adjudged, That the Direction of a *Venire, Vicecomitibus* of ſuch a Place, which is returned by *J. S. vicecomite*, may be amended on the Oath of *J. S.* that there is but one Sheriff of the Place, which is himſelf. Alſo it is every Day's Practice to amend [b] criminal Informations, and the Pleadings thereon by Rule of Court, while all is in Paper. And [c] *Quære* if the Record may not be ſo amended by the Paper-Book at any Time before Judgment?

Sect. 98. It ſeems to have been anciently the common Practice where an Indictment appeared to be ſufficient, either for its Uncertainty, or the Want of proper legal Words, not to put the Defendant to anſwer it; but if it were found in the ſame County in which the Court ſat, to award Proceſs againſt the Grand Jury, to come into Court and [d] amend it. And it ſeems to be the common Practice at [e] this Day, while the Grand Jury who found a Bill, is before the Court to amend it by their Conſent in a Matter of Form, as the Name or Addition of the Party, &c.

Sect. 99. And now I am in the ſecond Place to ſhew what ought to be the Form of the Body of an Indictment upon a Statute; for the better Underſtanding whereof, having premiſed, that the ſame Rules which have been already laid down concerning Indictments at Common Law, are generally applicable to Indictments on Statutes, I ſhall in this Place conſider ſuch Matters only as more peculiarly belong to the Form of the Body of an Indictment upon a Statute, under the following Particulars:

1. Whether it be neceſſary that ſuch Indictment recite the Statute whereon it is grounded.
2. What Miſ-recitals of ſuch Statutes are fatal.
3. How far it is neceſſary to bring the Offence indicted within the very Words of the Statute.
4. Whether an Indictment grounded on a Statute, which will not maintain it, may be made good, as an Indictment at Common Law.
5. How far it is neceſſary to conclude *contra formam Statuti.*

[a] 1 Keb. 900. pl. 71. 901. pl. 75. 1 Sid. 244. Vide 8 Co. 156. b. 3 Lev. 430.
[b] 1 Salk. 47. pl. 1, 2, 3.
[c] Salk. 47. pl. 2, 3. Salk. 56. pl. 10. Vide 1 Keb. 452. pl. 45. Cro. Ca. 144. 1 Lev. 189. 3 Lev. 430.
[d] 22 Aſſ. pl. 73. 2 Ed. 3. 1. pl. 3. 8 H. 5. 8. pl. 4. S. P. C. 97. Letter A. Fitz. Indictment, 2, 3, 27. Vide 25 E. 3. 43. pl. 36. Bro. Indictment, 12.
[e] Kelynge 37.

Sect. 100. As to the firſt Particular, *viz.* Whether it be neceſſary that ſuch Indictment recite the Statute whereon it is grounded; I take it to be [f] ſettled, that there is no Neceſſity in any Indictment or Information on a [g] publick Statute, to recite ſuch Statute, whether the Offence be ſuch only becauſe prohibited, or be an Evil in its own Nature, and whether it be prohibited by more than one Statute, or by one only; for the Judges are bound *ex officio* to take Notice of all publick Statutes, [h] and where there are more than one by which an Indictment or Information may be maintained, they will go upon that which is moſt for the King's Advantage.

As to the ſecond Particular, What Miſ-recitals of ſuch Statutes are fatal, I ſhall endeavour to ſhew:

1. Whether all Miſ-recitals of the ſubſtantial Part of the Statute are fatal.
2. What Miſ-recitals of the Place or Time at which the Parliament was holden.
3. Whether a Miſ-recital of the Title of a Statute.
4. What other Miſ-recitals are fatal.

[f] 5 H. 7. 17. b.
[g] Fitz. Action ſur le Statute, 7. 20. 2 Rol. A. 79. pl. 8. Plowd. Com. 1, 79, &c. 1 H. 6. 1. pl. 2. 4 Co. 48. a. Cro. El. 236. pl. 1. Cro. Ca. 229. Dyer 155. pl. 19. 346. pl. 9. Bro. Action ſur le Stat. 4. Parliam. 15. but Cro. El. 187. pl. 12. 47 Ed. 3. 10. pl. 7. Dyer, 159. pl. 37. Bro. Parliament, 75. Bro. Champerty, 1. Show. 337. F. N. B. 55. C. ſeem contrary. Quære 6 Mod. 140, 141. Moor 468. pl. 669. Moor 699. pl. 972. 4 Co. 13. 76. Bro. Avowry, 5. Bro. Parliament, 15, 32. 2 H. H. P. C. 172, 192.
[h] Dyer 155. pl. 19. Dyer 346. pl. 9. 5 H. 7. 17. b. 6 Mod. 140. Vide Cro. El. 187. pl. 12.

Sect. 101. As to the first of these Particulars, it seems to be settled, That notwithstanding there be no Necessity to recite a publick Statute; yet if the Prosecutor take upon him to do it, [a] and materially vary from a substantial Part of the Purview of the Statute, and conclude *contra formam Statuti prædicti*, he vitiates the Indictment, [69] because it judicially appears to the Court, that there is no such Foundation for the Prosecution, as that whereon it is expresly grounded; as where in an [b] Indictment with such a Conclusion on the Statutes which prohibit Entries with strong Hand, the Word *Vi* is put for *manu forti*; or where the Word [c] *nuncia* is put for *mendacia* in such an Indictment on the Statutes against the Tellers of Lies of great Men; [d] or where the Verb in a Statute which expresses the Principal Act wherein the Offence consists, is expressed in such an Indictment on such a Statute, by a Word which is neither classical nor legal *Latin*; [e] or where a Statute in describing the Courts wherein it prohibits Persons to bring Actions in other Names without their Privity, calls them Courts wherein Pleas are holden in Actions personal, *&c.* and you in reciting it in such an Indictment call them Courts wherein Pleas are holden in any Actions.

Sect. 102. Yet it seems that the following Mis-recitals of the substantial Part of the Purview of a Statute in any Indictment are not fatal, as the Omission of a synonymous Word, having no other Meaning than what is fully expressed in the Words which are recited; or the Joining of Words which are either wholly synonymous, or much of the same Sense, as signifying such Things as generally include one another, (as [g] the Words *malitiosè & contemptuosè, &c.*) with a Copulative, where the Statute uses a Disjunctive, or the Using the singular Number for the Plural, or the Plural for the singular, where the Sense is the same; as where in [h] reciting a Statute speaking of Suits in any Courts, you Use the Words *in aliqua Curia*; or where in reciting the Statute against disturbing Persons in their open Preaching, you use the [i] Words *in apertis prædicationibus.*

Sect. 103. Also it [k] seems that no Advantage can be taken of a Variance from any Part of a private Statute, without shewing it to the Court in a proper Manner, because otherwise such a Statute shall be taken to be as it is recited.

Sect. 104. As to the second of the Particulars above mentioned, *viz.* What Mis-recitals of the Place or Time at which the Parliament was holden, are fatal, [l] it seems to be generally agreed, That a Mis-recital of the Place or Day at which the Parliament was holden, vitiates an Indictment. [m] As if a Parliament was first holden on the twenty-eighth of *April* in the thirty-second Year of *Henry* VIII. and afterwards holden by Prorogation on the twelfth of *April* the next Year, and a Statute then made, be recited as made at a Parliament holden on the twenty-eighth of *April* in the thirty-second Year of *Henry* VIII. Or if a Parliament be summoned to meet on the twenty-third of *January* in such a Year, and before the Meeting be prorogued to the twenty-fifth, and then holden, and a Statute made by such Parliament be [n] recited as made in a Parliament holden on the twenty-third; or if a Parliament first holden in one Year be continued by Prorogation to another, and then sit again, and a Statute made at such Sessions be [o] recited as made in a Parliament holden or begun at such second Year, (which is all one,) instead of saying that it was made at a Sessions of Parliament then holden, and the Indictment conclude *contra formam Statuti prædicti*, the Variances in Strictness are fatal; for the Court will not make any Case better than the Record has made it; and therefore where that expresly grounds it on the Act of

[a] Pl. Com. 79. 83. b. 84. Cro. El. 236. 245. pl. 4. Palm. 565. 4 Co. 48. See the three next Sections. 1 Ro. Rep. 50. Cro. Car. 135. 136. 2 H. H. P. C. 172. 1 Jon. 194.
[b] Cro. El. 93. pl. 2. 2 Bulst. 258.
[c] 4 Co. 12. b. 13. Cro. Ca. 135.
[d] 2 Jon. 49, 50. 3 Keble 661. pl. 11.
[e] Cro. El. 236.
[f] Cro. Ja. 362. See the 108th Section.
[g] 2 Bulst. 47, 49, 50, 51, 52, 53.
[h] Cro. Car. 522, 523.
[i] 2 Bulst. 47, &c.
[k] 4 Co. 13. 1 Sid. 356.
[l] Bro. Parliament, 87. Bro. El. 853. pl. 12.
[m] Plow. Com. 79, 83, 84. Cro. Ca. 136. 232. 3 Keb. 468. pl. 55. 2 Jon. 50. Hob. 310. Cro. Ja. 139. Cro. El. 245. pl. 4. But this is made a Quære by Coke in 2 Bulst. 53.
[n] Dyer 203. pl. 72, 73. Hetly 129.
[o] Cro. Ja. 111. pl. 9. 139. Lutw. 140. 4 Inst. 27. Vide 1 Brown. 100. Yelv. 127. Dyer 95. pl. 36, 37, 38. 171. pl. 6. Skin. 110, 111.

of a ſuppoſed Parliament, where there was no ſuch Act, the Court will not find one out to make it good. Alſo it hath been [a] adjudged, That a Repugnancy in ſetting forth the Time when a Parliament was holden, is fatal, as if a Statute be recited as made on ſuch a Day, in the firſt and ſecond Years of ſuch a King, for it is impoſſible that one and the ſame Day ſhould be in two Years. Alſo it is holden in [b] *Croke*'s Reports, That an Indictment was diſcharged for not ſhewing in what County a Parliament was holden; but no Reaſon is given for this Opinion, [c] and it hath been adjudged, That the total Omiſſion of the Day when the Parliament was holden, is no Fault in the Recital of a Statute. Alſo it ſeems to be [d] agreed, That a Miſtake in ſuppoſing a Statute to have been made at a Parliament holden in ſuch a Year, when in Truth it was then holden by Prorogation, may be help'd by the conſtant Courſe of Precedents upon ſuch Statute. Alſo it ſeems to be [e] agreed, That not only a Miſ-recital of the Day whereon the Parliament was holden, but even a Miſrecital of the Purview of a Statute may be ſalved by a general Concluſion *contra formam Statuti*, without adding *prædicti*, *&c.* [f] But I do not find it ſettled, Whether a Fault of this Kind can be help'd by the Defendant's Admittance, that there is ſuch a Statute as is ſuppoſed; and it will be difficult to maintain that the Party's Admittance of what the Court judicially knows to be contrary to the Truth, can make good any Judgment.

[a] Moore 302. pl. 452.

[b] Cro. El. 106. pl. 21.

[c] Dyer 203 pl. 74.

[d] Yelv. 127. Brownl. 100. 2 Keb. 34. pl. 68. Dyer 171. pl. 6.

[e] Cro. Car. 232, 233. Palm. 565. Raym. 191. 192. 3 Keb. 647, 648. Lutw. 140.

[f] Affirmed Cro. Jac. 139. Denied Cro. El. 236.

Sect. 105. As to the third of the Particulars above-mentioned, *viz.* Whether the Miſ-recital of the Title of a Statute be fatal; it is [g] ſaid to have been holden by Sir *Matthew Hale*, That the Miſ-recital of the entitling of an Act will not vitiate a Replication, becauſe it is not Matter of Subſtance; and a Judgment is [h] ſaid to have been lately given in the Court of Common Pleas agreeable to this Opinion; but the contrary is [i] ſaid to have been ſince adjudged in the Court of King's Bench.

[g] Hardreſs 324.

[h] 6 Mod. 62.

[i] 6 Mod. 62.

Sect. 106. As to the fourth of the Particulars above-mentioned, *viz.* What other Miſ-recitals of a Statute are fatal; [k] it is ſaid to have been often adjudged, That a Variance in reciting a Statute to commence after the Making, where the Statute is expreſs, that it ſhall commence after the End of the Seſſions, is fatal. But I take it to be a ſettled Rule, That a Variance no Way altering the Senſe of the Statute does [l] no Hurt; as where in the Recital of an Oath preſcribed by Statute, the Words *Sea of Rome* are put for *See of Rome:* and *I do declare in Conſcience*, inſtead of *I do declare in my Conſcience*. Alſo it ſeems to be [m] agreed, That a Variance from an immaterial Part of a Statute does no Hurt, [n] and therefore that where a Statute contains ſeveral Branches relating to ſeveral diſtinct Matters, an Omiſſion of ſuch Branches as no way relate to the Offence indicted does no Hurt, becauſe they are nothing to the preſent Purpoſe. Alſo it hath been adjudged, That every Miſ-recital even of ſuch Branch is not fatal; as if it vary only in ſuch a Part of the Deſcription of the Offence, as is put in only by Way of Flouriſh, and *ex abundanti*, and makes no neceſſary Ingredient in the Offence prohibited, nor needs any Proof; as if in a Proſecution on the Statute of 12 *R.* 2. the [o] Recital be that none ſhall deviſe, ſpeak, or tell any falſe News, Lies, or other ſuch falſe Things, *&c. unde diſcordia aut aliqua lis* (*Anglicè* Debates) *inter magnates, vel inter magnates & communitatem dicti Regni oriri poſſint*; where the Words of the Statute are, *That none ſhall deviſe, ſpeak, or tell any falſe News, Lies, or other ſuch falſe Things*, &c. *whereof Diſcord or any Slander might riſe within the ſaid Realm*; for the firſt Words, *viz. That none ſhall deviſe*, &c. *any falſe News, Lies, or other ſuch falſe Things*, &c. are only material.

[k] 2 Rol. Abr. 465. Letter B.

[l] 1 Vent. 172. Skin. 11, 52.

[m] Cro. El. 186. pl. 10. 4 Co. 48. Palm. 565. Cro. Ca. 135, 136, 564. 1 Jon. 194.

[n] Plowd. Com. 65, 105. a. Dyer 103. pl. 7. Hob. 226. 3 Keb. 662.

[o] Cro. Car. 135, 136. Palm. 565. 1 Jon. 194.

material. Indeed, as this Caſe is reported by *Croke*, there is a Miſ-recital even in this Part, for inſtead of *other falſe Things*, the Recital is ſaid to mention *other Things* generally, omitting the Word *falſe*; but I ſuppoſe that this is a Miſtake of the Printer, and that there is no ſuch Variance in the Record of the Caſe, becauſe no Exception is reported to have been taken to it.

Sect. 107. But if a Miſ-recital of ſuch a Part of the Purview of a Statute be not fatal, it ſeems *à fortiori* to follow, That a Miſ-recital of the Preamble is not material, where the ſubſtantial Part of the Purview is well recited. And upon this Reaſon chiefly, as I ſuppoſe, it hath been adjudged, That if in an Action on the [a] Statute of Hue and Cry for a Robbery, the Declaration recite the Preamble to ſpeak of the Burning of Houſes, where the Statute mentions Arſons generally, without any particular Mention of the Arſon of Houſes; or in an Action for the Slander of an Earl, on 2 *R.* 2. 5. if the Declaration in reciting the Preamble mention only what relates to Earls, &c. and omit the Clauſe concerning the other great Officers, [b] yet the Plaintiff may have Judgment eſpecially after Verdict. And theſe Reſolutions ſeem to weaken the Authority of *Parker*'s Caſe reported by [c] *Hutton*, wherein it was ſaid to have been holden by three Judges againſt the Opinion of *Hobart*, that the Putting of the Word *indicari* for *indictari* in the Recital of the Preamble of the ſaid Statute of Hue and Cry, in a Writ grounded thereupon, is fatal.

[a] Vide 3 Keb. 647. pl. 68. 661, 662. 2 Jon. 51.
[b] 2 Jon. 49, 50, 51. 3 Keb. 647. pl. 68. 3 Keb. 661, 662. Vide Cro. Jac. 139.
[c] Hutton 56, 57. 3 Keb. 648, 662. 2 Jon. 50, 51.

Sect. 108. If an Indictment on 8 *H.* 6. in reciting that Part of the Statute which declares in what Actions the Party grieved ſhall recover his Damages, after having mentioned Recoveries by Verdict, omit the [d] Words *or in any other Manner*; or uſe the [e] Words *Aſſiſum novæ diſſeiſinæ* for *Aſſiſam novæ diſſeiſinæ*; [f] or recite the Statute, as giving the Fine on a Recovery by Action *dicto domino Regi*, where there is nothing to make good the Word *dicto*, [g] or recite the Statute relating to the Bringing an Action to be, *if the Party after ſuch Entry make any Feoffment*, &c. where the Words are, *if after ſuch Entry any Feoffment be made*, or [h] recite it to be, *if any Perſon be put out and diſſeiſed* in the Conjunctive, where the Words of the Statute are, *if any Perſon be put out or diſſeiſed* in the Disjunctive, the Variances have been adjudged fatal. Yet [i] it hath been holden, That the laſt of theſe is an immaterial Variance, becauſe tho' the Words above-mentioned be disjunctive in the Statute, they have always been expounded in the Copulative. Alſo it may be queſtioned how far the reſt of theſe Authorities may be Law at this Day, ſince of [k] late the Court has not been ſo ſtrict in Recitals as formerly; and if an Indictment fully recite a Statute ſo far as it concerns Indictments, a Miſpriſion in what concerns other Matters ſeems to be much helped by the Authorities of the Caſes above cited.

[d] Cro. El. 186. pl. 10.
[e] Cro. El. 93. pl. 2.
[f] 1 Bulſt. 218.
[g] Cro. El. 307. pl. 10. Parallel Caſe, Cro. El. 697. pl. 10.
[h] Cro. El. 96. pl. 9. vide Cro. El. 697. pl. 10.
[i] Cro. El. 307. pl. 10.
[k] 3 Keb. 662.

Sect. 109. It hath been [l] adjudged, That a total Omiſſion of the Clauſe of a Statute which ordains what the Party ſhall forfeit, does no Hurt. Yet if the Statute be wholly miſ-recited in ſuch Clauſe, as if the Words [m] *admitteret* or *forisfaceret* be uſed in ſuch Clauſe for *amitteret* and *forisfaceret*, the Exception for the Variance ſeems to have greater Weight. Yet if the Word miſ-recited be ſynonymous with the other which is rightly recited, and the [n] whole Purport of both as fully expreſſed in one Word, which is properly recited, as if both had been uſed, as it certainly is in the Caſe above-cited, wherein the Word *forisfaceret* is rightly recited, and the Word *admitteret* miſ-recited, it may perhaps be queſtioned whether ſuch an Exception would be fatal at this Day, eſpecially conſidering that it is in a

[l] 20 H. 6. 31, 32. which ſeems miſtaken in the Abridgments. Fitz. Brief, 86. Bro. Champerty, 1. Vide Plowd. Com. 84. b. Dyer 160. pl. 40.
[m] Cro. Jac. 133. pl. 5.
[n] Vide Cro. Jac. 362.

Part of the Statute which might as well have been omitted in the Recital; and there is no Variance but from a Word wholly nugatory and superfluous, and the Sense would be compleat by rejecting the Word mistaken, as Surplus and insensible. But if in the Mis-recital of such a Clause, there be such a Variance as carries with it a plain material Repugnancy to the Intent of the Statute, [a] as where the Words, *whoever shall do the same, shall incur the Pain*, &c. are thus recited, *whoever shall do the contrary, shall incur the Pain*, &c. I do not well see how any Thing can be said to make it good; for it is a general Rule, that [b] Repugnancies in Indictments are fatal and the Prosecutor himself declares, That not those who do the Thing indicted, but those who do it not are within the Penalty of the Statute.

Sect. 110. As to the third Particular, *viz.* How far it is necessary to bring the Offence indicted within the very Words of the Statute; I take it for a general Rule, that [c] unless the Statute be recited, neither the Words *contra* [d] *formam Statuti*, nor any *Periphrasis*, Intendment or [e] Conclusion will make good an Indictment, which does not bring the Fact prohibited or commanded, in the doing or not doing whereof the Offence consists, within all the material Words of the Statute. And upon this Ground it hath been resolved, that an Indictment of Rape finding that the Defendant such a Day and Place, *&c.* A. B. *felonicè cepit, & eam adtunc & ibidem carnaliter cognovit, &c. contra voluntatem suam, &c.* is not [f] sufficient without the Word *Rapuit*; because that is the Word used by the Statute which makes the Offence Felony. Also it hath been [g] adjudged, That Indictments for Perjury on 5 *El.* 9. omitting the Words *voluntariè & corruptè*, in setting forth the Swearing; and Indictments for striking in a Church on 5 & 6 *Ed.* 6. 4. [h] omitting the Words *to the Intent to strike*, &c. and Indictments for aiding the Procurers of the Pope's Bulls on 13 *El.* 4. [i] omitting the Words *To the Intent to set forth*, &c. *the usurped Power*, &c. and Indictments for Forestalling on 5 & 6 *Ed.* 6. 14. setting forth, That the Defendant bought certain Goods of *J. S.* which he was about to sell at such a Market; but [k] not expresly alledging, that *such Goods were then coming to such Market to be sold*; and [l] Indictments for ingrossing on the same Statute, setting forth, That the Defendant bought so much Corn, *&c.* without alledging, that *he ingrossed it*, &c. *by buying*, &c. and [m] Indictments for Treason in Compassing the King's Death, on 25 *E.* 3. having neither the Word *Compass* nor *Imagine*, *&c.* cannot be taken as Indictments on such Statutes. And the like hath been adjudged in many other [n] Cases.

Sect. 111. Neither doth it seem to be always sufficient to pursue the very Words of the Statute, unless by so doing you fully, directly and expresly alledge the Fact in the doing or not doing whereof the Offence consists, without any the least Uncertainty or Ambiguity; for it hath been [o] adjudged, that an Indictment for Perjury on 5 *El.* 9. setting forth, That the Defendant *tacto per se sacro evangelio falso deposuit, &c.* is not good without directly shewing that he was sworn. Also it hath been [p] adjudged, that an Information on 18 *H.* 6. 17. for not abating so much of the Price of Wine sold as the Vessels wanted of the Statute-Measure, is insufficient, if it do not expresly shew how much they wanted. Also it is said, That an Indictment on the Statute of Usury setting forth, that the Defendant took more than five in the Hundred, is not good, without shewing in particular how much.

[a] 4 Co. 12. b. 13. a.
[b] Supra Sect. 62, 63.
[c] Cro. El. 535. 67.
See the Books cited to the latter Part of this Section. Cro. El. 749. pl. 2. seems contrary.
[d] Dy. 363. pl. 25. 2 H. H. P. C. 170, 171. 2 Ro. Re. 227, 263. 2 Leon. 211. 11 Co. 58. a.
[e] Cro. El. 147. pl. 11. Cro. El. 201. pl. 30. 2 Leon. 211.
[f] 9 Ed. 4. 26. Bro. Indictment, 7. Vide supra ch. 23. Sect. 77.
[g] Cro. El. 147. pl. 11. Cro. El 201. pl. 30. 2 Leon. 211. Vide Coke's Entries 367, 368.
[h] Cro. El. 231. pl. 23. 2 Leon. 188. Noy 171.
[i] Dy. 363. pl. 25.
[k] 1 Rol. Rep. 421. See Book 1. Ch. 80. Sect. 12, 13.
[l] 2 Leon. 39. See Book 1. Ch. 80. Sect. 15 & 20.
[m] Kelyng. 8. B. 1. Ch. 17. Sect. 8.
[n] 11 Co. 58. a. Dyer 346. pl. 9. 2 Ro. Re. 227, 263. Sup. Sec. 104. 2 Rol. Ab. 81. pl. 15. 9 Ed. 4. 26, 27.
[o] Cro. El. 105. pl. 17. See 9 Ed. 4. 26.
[p] 2 Leon. 38, 39.

Sect. 112. As to the Deſcription of the Perſon of the Defendant, in order to bring him within the Purview of a Statute, which extends only to ſuch Kind of Perſons as are ſpecially mentioned in it; it is a good [a] general Rule, That every Indictment muſt bring the Defendant within all the Deſcriptions mentioned in the Body of the Act, except they are ſuch as carry with them the bare Denial of a Matter, the Affirmation whereof is a proper and natural Plea for the Defendant; as where it is enacted, That all Perſons having no Reaſonable Excuſe to be abſent, ſhall go to their Pariſh-Church, *&c.* in which Caſe it is ſaid, that it is not neceſſary to ſhew, that the Defendant had no reaſonable Excuſe, for this will come moſt properly in Queſtion from the Plea of the Defendant. Alſo it ſeems that there is no Need in deſcribing the Defendant to ſet forth the Place where the Thing happened, which brought him within the Deſcription, as hath been more fully ſhewn in the 84th Section. Alſo it hath been adjudged, That it is [b] ſufficient in deſcribing the Defendant to ſay, That he *exiſtens* ſo and ſo, as the Statute mentions, did the Fact, without alledging that he was ſo at the Time of the Fact; for that ſhall be intended, as hath been more fully ſhewn in the ſixty-firſt Section.

[a] Poph. 93, 94. See Book 1. Ch. 10. Sect. 2. 2 Leon. 5. Quære 2 Keb. 582. pl. 18.

[b] Moor 606. pl. 838. Cro. Jac. 610. 2 Leon. 5. 2 Lev. 229. 2 Ro. Re. 226. contra 2 Ro. Re. 263. Quære Raym. 378. 1 Keb. 852. pl. 55.

Sect. 113. It ſeems [c] agreed, that there is no Need to alledge in an Indictment, that the Defendant is not within the Benefit of the Proviſoes of a Statute whereon it is founded; and this hath been [d] adjudged, even as to thoſe Statutes which in their Purview expreſly take Notice of the Proviſoes, as by ſaying, that none ſhall do the Thing prohibited, otherwiſe than in ſuch ſpecial Caſes, *&c.* as are expreſſed in the Act. But as I take it, a Conviction on a Penal Statute ought expreſly to ſhew, that the Defendant is not within any of its Proviſoes; for ſince no [e] Plea can be admitted to ſuch a Conviction, and the Defendant can have no Remedy againſt it, but from an Exception to ſome Defect appearing in the Face of it, and all the Proceedings are in a ſummary Manner, it is but reaſonable that ſuch a Conviction ſhould have the higheſt Certainty, and ſatisfy the Court, That the Defendant had no ſuch Matter in his Favour as the Statute itſelf allows him to plead.

[c] Poph. 93, 94. 1 Jon. 157. 1 Lev. 26. Vide Savil 32. pl. 73. 2 H. H. P. C. 170, 171.

[d] Poph. 93, 94.

[e] Quære 1 Salk. 181, 182.

Sect. 114. It ſeems to be laid down as a general Rule in [f] *Savil*'s Report, which is alſo confirmed by the Year-Book of 11 *H.* 4. 14. That if the Statute whereon an Indictment is grounded be particularly recited; the the general Concluſion, *contra formam Statuti*, after the Allegation of the Fact, will ſupply an Omiſſion in it of a Circumſtance mentioned in the Statute, which would be fatal without ſuch a Recital and Concluſion; for ſince the Statute is particularly recited, and the Defendant charged with having done the Offence againſt the Form of it; and it is impoſſible that he could ſo have done, if any Circumſtance expreſly required by the Statute had been wanting; it ſeems that the Offence may properly enough be ſaid to be as fully ſet forth in the very Words of the Statute, as if ſuch Words had been repeated in the Allegation of the Offence, according to the common Rule, that *Verba relata hoc maximè operantur per referentiam ut in eſſe videantur.* Neither do I find this contradicted by any of the Reſolutions in the precedent Sections; for it does not appear that there was ſuch a Recital and concluſion in any of the Indictments therein referred to. Yet notwithſtanding the Omiſſion of a Circumſtance mentioned in a Statute, may perhaps in ſuch Manner be holpen; it ſeems that the Want of a certain Deſcription of the Time or Place, or Things or Perſons concerned, or of the Concluſion *contra pacem*, or of an expreſs and direct Allegation of the Fact it ſelf, cannot be ſo ſupply'd; for ſuch Omiſſions [g] vitiate an Indictment drawn in the very Words of the Act.

[f] Savil 33. pl. 78. Vide ſupra ch. 23. Sect. 63. 2 Ro. Rep. 227. S. P. C. 81. C.

[g] 2 Rol. Rep. 226. ſeems contrary.

Sect. 115.

Sect. 115. As to the fourth Particular, *viz.* Whether an Indictment grounded on a Statute which will not maintain it, may be made good as an Indictment at Common Law; it seems formerly to have been [a] generally taken for granted, that no Indictment whatsoever which is grounded on a Statute, and concludes *contra formam Statuti*, and cannot be made good by any Statute, can be maintained as an Indictment of an Offence at Common Law; the chief Reason whereof seems to be this, That it appears that the Prosecution is intended to be grounded on a Foundation which will not support it. But the contrary seems to have been adjudged in [b] *Page*'s Case, wherein it was resolved, That if Persons be indicted specially on the Statute of Stabbing, and the Evidence be not sufficient to bring them within the Statute, they may be found guilty of general Manslaughter at Common Law, and that the Words *contra formam Statuti* shall be rejected as senseless, where the Offence is prohibited by the Common Law only. And the same hath been since [c] adjudged as to other Statutes; and as I took it, was lately agreed in an Information against the City of [d] *Norwich.*

Sect. 116. As to the fifth Particular, *viz.* How far it is necessary for an Indictment on a Statute, to conclude *contra formam Statuti*, it seems that Judgment on a Statute shall in no Case be given on an Indictment, which does not so conclude; for granting that such Judgment may in some Cases be given in an Action brought at Common Law, without Reference to any Statute, as it is [e] said, that Judgment on 8 *H.* 6. 9. may be given on the old Common Law Writ of Assise of Novel Disseisin, yet it will not follow, That such a Judgment can in any Case be given on an Indictment drawn as for an Offence at Common Law, without any Reference to Statute. For as to the said Case of an Assise of Novel Disseisin, it may be said that the Statute of 8 *H.* 6. expressly says, That the Party may recover by such Writ; and therefore since there is no special Writ of this Kind formed upon the Statute, and the Party has [f] no Authority to make out a Writ himself in a new Form, it is reasonable that he may recover by the old Writ. But it [g] seems that Judgment on this Statute cannot be given on an Action of Trespass in the Common Law Form, because there is a special Writ of Trespass in the [h] Register grounded on the Statute; and it seems to be [i] agreed, that where there is a special Writ grounded on a Statute, Judgment shall never be given on such a Statute in an Action brought at Common Law. And in like Manner, since every one who prosecutes an Indictment is at Liberty to draw it as he pleases, so that he observes the general Rules of Law concerning Indictments; it seems to be [k] taken as a common Ground, That a Judgment by Statute shall never be given on an Indictment at Common Law, as every Indictment which doth not conclude *contra formam Statuti*, shall be taken to be. And therefore [l] if an Indictment do not conclude *contra formam Statuti*, and the Offence indicted be only prohibited by Statute and not by Common Law, it is wholly insufficient, and no Judgment at all can be given upon it: But if the Offence were also an Offence at Common Law, I take it to be in a great Measure settled at this Day, that [m] Judgment may be given as for an Offence at Common Law, tho' the Indictment conclude *contra formam Statuti*, as ☞ hath been more fully shewn in the precedent Section. [70]

[a] Cro. El. 231. pl. 23. Cro. El. 307. pl. 10. Cro. El. 697. pl. 10. 2 Leon. 188. Noy 171, 172. 5 Co. 99. 2 Rol. Re. 263. Cro. Ca. 465. 2 Keb. 36. pl. 73. 2 Keb. 566. pl. 70. Vide 6 Mod. 17. the same may be collected from 2 Rol. Ab. 82. pl. 2, 3. and 1 Jon. 379. 2 H. H. P. C. 170.

[b] H. P. C. 58. 2 H. H. P. C. 191. Aleyn 43, 44. B. 1. Ch. 30. Sect. 9.

[c] 1 Sid. 420. 2 Keb. 138. pl. 5. Vide 1 Salk. 212.

[d] The King against the City of Norwich, adjudged Hilar. 5 Georgii 1.

[e] 9 H. 6. 2. pl. 5. Bro. Action sur le Statute, 6.

[f] 2 Inst. 407.

[g] Vide 2 Inst. 200. Bro. Parliament, 75.

[h] Register 289. a.

[i] 9 H. 6. 2. pl. 5. 56. pl. 42. 19 H. 6. 54. b. 47 Ed. 3. 10. pl. 7. 8 H. 4. 13. b. 2 Ed. 4. 9. pl. 5. Bro. Action sur le Statute, 6, 10. Parliam. 75. Fitz. Judgment, 10. Cessavit, 18. Attachment sur Prohibition, 1, 3. Bendloe 57. pl. 92. Cro. El. 759. 760.

[k] See the Authorities cited to the other Parts of this Section.

[l] 2 Rol. Re. 38. 1 Saund. 249. 1 Sid. 409. 2 Keb. 506. pl. 79. 1 Salk. 370. pl. 3.

[m] See the precedent Section. 2 Keb. 477. pl. 7. 1 Sid. 409. 1 Saund. 249, 250. 9 H. 6. 56. pl. 42. Fitz. Attachment sur Prohibition, 1, 3. But 2 Rol Ab. 82. pl. 2, 3. 2 Keb. 566. pl. 70. 1 Jo. 379, 380. seem contrary.

Sect. 117.

Sect. 117. If there be more than one Statute concerning the ſame Offence, and the firſt of them were never diſcontinued, and the latter [a] only continue the former without making any Addition to it; or only [b] qualify the Method of Proceeding upon it, without altering the Subſtance of its Purview; it ſeems agreed, That it is ſafe in an Indictment on any ſuch Statute to conclude *contra formam Statuti*; and it hath been [c] holden, That a Concluſion *contra formam Statutorum*, will in ſuch Caſes vitiate the Proſecution; but where a Statute hath been wholly diſcontinued, and is afterwards revived, there [d] ſeem to have been ſome Opinions, That a Proſecution on it ought to conclude *contra formam Statutorum*. Alſo where the ſame Offence is prohibited by ſeveral independent Statutes there are ſome [e] Authorities, that you muſt either conclude *contra formam Statutorum*, or *contra formam* of the particular Statutes naming them, and that if you barely conclude *contra formam Statuti*, the Indictment will be inſufficient, for not ſhewing on which of the Statutes it was taken. But there are alſo ſtrong [f] Authorities for the contrary Opinion, which is alſo moſt agreeable to [g] Precedents; to which may be added, That if it be a good Objection to ſuch an Indictment, concluding *contra formam Statuti*, that it appears not on which of the Statutes the Proſecution is grounded, the ſame Objection may as well be made to an Indictment concluding *contra formam Statutorum*; for it no more appears from ſuch a Concluſion on what Statute the Proſecution is grounded, than from the Concluſion *contra formam Statuti*; and yet it ſeems to be [h] generally admitted, That a Concluſion *contra formam Statutorum* is good where the Indictment is for an Offence prohibited by ſeveral Statutes. Alſo where ſuch an Indictment concludes *contra formam Statuti*, without ſhewing what Statute is [i] intended, why may it not be ſaid that ſuch Statute ſhall be taken as is moſt for the King's Advantage, as well as where the Indictment concludes *contra formam Statutorum*, in which Caſe it ſeems to be admitted, that it ſhall be ſo taken. But where a later Statute ordains, That a former Statute ſhall be executed in a new Caſe not mentioned in the former, as 8 *H.* 6. 9. does, that 15 *Ric.* 2. 2. ſhall be executed in the Caſe of a forcible Detainer, which is not mentioned in 15 *Ric.* 2. or where a new Statute adds a new Penalty to an Offence prohibited by a former Statute, as [k] 23 *Eliz.* doth that of 20 *l.* for a Month's Abſence from Church contrary to the Tenor of 1 *Eliz.* it ſeems that it may with greater Reaſon be argued, That if the Indictment conclude *contra formam Statuti*, it will be [l] inſufficient, becauſe it may ſeem, that the Offence is not puniſhable by any one Statute only. Yet conſidering that the Precedents in theſe Caſes generally conclude *contra formam Statuti*, and the Proſecution in Truth depends on the Addition made by the later Statute, which ſeems of it ſelf alone ſufficient to ſupport it, it may be reaſonably argued, and ſeems agreeable to the later [m] Opinions, that ſuch a Concluſion may be allowed in theſe Caſes alſo. However it ſeems ſafe in any of the Caſes abovementioned, to conclude *contra formam* [n] *Statut'*, which ſhall ſtand either for *Statuti* or *Statutorum*, or be rejected in ſuch manner as will beſt maintain the Indictment.

Sect. 118. As to the ninth general Point of this Chapter, *viz.* What ought to be the Form of the Caption of an Indictment, I ſhall take it for granted, that every ſuch Caption is erroneous, which doth not ſet forth with proper Certainty, both the Court in which, and the Jurors by whom, and alſo the Time and Place at which the Indictment was found; for the better Underſtanding whereof I ſhall endeavour to ſhew what Certainty of this Kind is neceſſary.

[a] Cro. E. 750. pl. 6. Owen 135. 1 Lut. 221. 2 H. H. P. C. 173.
[b] Yelv. 116. Cro. Jac. 187. pl. 9.
[c] Yelv. 116. See Cro. Jac. 187. pl. 9.
[d] Owen 135. 1 Lutw. 221. 2 H. H. P. C. 173.
[e] Cro. El. 760. pl. 6. 187. pl. 12. 2 Leon. 5. Cro. Jac. 142. pl. 19. Aleyn 49, 50. 2 Bulst. 258. Dalt. Ch. 131.
[f] Crompt. 104. pl. 49. 5 H. 7. 17. b. Cro. El. 186. pl. 10. 4 Co. 48. a.
[g] Vide 2 Rol. Ab. 79. pl. 3. 82. pl. 5, 6. Dalton Ch. 129. Aleyn 50. B. 1. Ch. 81. Sect. 10.
[h] Dyer 155. pl. 15. Cro. El. 750. pl. 6. Aleyn 49, 50. Lamb. B. 4. Ch. 5.
[i] Dyer 155. pl. 15. 347. pl. 9. 2 Rol. Re. 227. 5 H. 7. 17. b. Owen 135. Supra Sect. 90. Contra 2 Leon. 5. 2 Rol. Re. 65.
[k] Vide Cro. Jac. 142. Cro. El. 750. pl. 6. 2 Leon. 5.
[l] Aleyn 49, 50.
[m] Vide 1 Mod. 191. 3 Lev. 61. 1 Lutw. 212.
[n] Aleyn 50. 6 Mod. 140. 2 H. H. P. C. 165, 166, &c.

1. In Respect of the Court, before which.
2. Of the Jurors, by whom.
3. Of the Time: And,
4. Of the Place, at which the Indictment was found.

Sect. 119. As to the first of these Particulars, it is certain, that every such Caption must shew that the Indictment was taken before such a Court as had Jurisdiction over the Offence indicted; and therefore if it set forth, that any Indictment whatsoever was taken before *J. S.* [a] Steward, without shewing to whom he was Steward, or in what Court; or that an Inquisition of Death, upon View of the Body, was taken before *J. S.* [b] Mayor of *London*, or before *J. S.* Steward to [c] such a Person, and in such a Court without adding, that he was a Coroner; or if it expresly call him Coroner, but do not also shew that he was such for the [d] District in which the Inquisition was taken, it is insufficient. But it hath been [e] adjudged, that it is sufficient to set forth, that it was taken before *J. S.* a Coroner in the County, without saying, that he was a Coroner for the County, for that cannot but be intended.

Sect. 120. Where [f] the Caption of an Indictment alledges it taken at the General Sessions of the Peace of such a County or Burgh, it doth not seem necessary to add, that such Sessions was holden for such County or Burgh, because it could not but be so holden, if it were the General Sessions of such County or Burgh; but if it had been only described as a General Sessions holden in such County or Burgh, it is said [g] to be a fatal Exception, that it is not expresly alledged as holden for such County or Burgh; but [h] *Quære*, if this be not helped by putting the County in the Margin.

Sect. 121. There are some [i] Authorities, that if the Caption of an Indictment before Justices of Peace take no Notice of their Commission to hear and determine Felonies, *&c.* which is generally done by the Clause *nec non ad diversas Felonias, &c.* it is insufficient: But having already more fully considered this Matter, *Ch.* 8. *Sect.* 33. I shall refer the Reader to what is there said concerning it.

Sect. 122. There are also several Authorities, that the Caption of an Indictment before Justices of Peace is insufficient, unless either the Words [k] *Domini Regis*, or [l] *Publicæ*, be added after *Pacis*; and it hath been sometimes holden, that even the Words *Domini Regis* are not sufficient without the Word [m] *nunc*, or some other, to shew whether it were the Peace of the present King, or of some of his Predecessors. And the chief Ground of these Opinions seems to be the Statute of 27 *H.* 8. 24. *Sect.* 4. by which it is enacted, *That in every Writ and Indictment that shall be made within any County-Palatine or Liberty, whereby any Thing shall be supposed to be done against the King's Peace, it shall be supposed to be done against the King's Peace, his Heirs and Successors, and not against the Peace of any other Person whatsoever, any Statute, Grant, or Usage, to the Contrary notwithstanding.* From whence, I suppose, it may have been collected, that by Parity of Reason, Justices of Peace ought to be styled, in legal Proceedings, Justices of the King's Peace, that it may appear that the Peace of no other Person, but of the King, is intended. But since this is not expresly required by the said Statute; and it cannot but be intended, (especially at this [n] Day, when none but the King can appoint Justices of Peace,) that all Justices of Peace must be Justices of the publick Peace, or of the King's Peace, which is the same Thing; and accordingly Exceptions for the want of

[a] 22 Ed. 4. 19. b. Bro. Battail, 7. Indictment, 46.
[b] 22 Ed. 4. 13. a. H. P. C. 207. S. P. C. 96. F.
[c] 22 Ed. 4. 12. b.
[d] Cro. Eliz. 193. pl. 7. 2 Ro. Rep. 82. 22 Ed. 4. 19. b. Bro. Bat. 7. Indictment, 46.
[e] Pl. Com. 77. a. 76. b. 4 Co. 41. b.
[f] 1 Sid. 247. pl. 11.
[g] 1 Keb. 329. pl. 66, 668. pl. 59. 1 Lev. 304. 2 Keb. 133. pl. 99. 2 Keb. 128. pl. 83. 141. pl. 11. 1 Keb. 635. pl. 126. seems contrary.
[h] Cro. Eliz. 490.
[i] S. P. C. 96. Letter E. H. P. C. 207. 2 Keb. 160. pl. 46. Bro. Indictment, 32. But this is left as a Quære, 22 Ed. 4. 12. b. 13. a. Bro. Error, 186. See Bro. Indictment, 50.
[k] 1 Lev. 175. 2 Keb. 647. pl. 84. 1 Sid. 247. pl. 11, 422. pl. 13.
[l] 1 Keb. 37. pl. 101. 1 Sid. 422. pl. 13.
[m] 1 Sid. 422. pl. 13. 2 Keb. 582. pl. 117.
[n] Vide Ch. 5. Sect. 1.

theſe Words have been often [a] over-ruled; I take them to be obſolete at this Day, as it ſeemed to be lately ſettled between the [b] King and *Hawkins* on a Conviction of Deer-ſtealing.

Sect. 123. But it ſeems generally agreed, [c] That if the Caption of an Indictment, at a Seſſions of the Peace, do not mention before whom it was holden, or if it ſet it forth [d] generally as holden before Juſtices, without ſhewing any Thing of the Nature of their Commiſſion, or as holden before Juſtices [e] of the Peace, &c. without naming any of them, or ſhewing for what Place they were Juſtices, or if it [f] deſcribe them as Juſtices *ad pacem in comitatu prædict', conſervand'*, omitting the Word *aſſignat'*, it is inſufficient. [g] Yet it hath been adjudged, that it is not neceſſary for the Caption of an Indictment taken at a General Seſſions of the Peace, to ſtyle any of the Juſtices of the *Quorum*, becauſe it ſufficiently ſhews that one or more of them were ſuch, by ſhewing, That the Seſſions was a General one.

Sect. 124. It hath been adjudged, [h] that the Caption of an Indictment, ſetting it forth as taken *ad magnam curiam cum leta tentam*, is inſufficient; the chief Reaſon whereof ſeems to be this, that ſuch a Caption rather imports, that the Indictment was taken at the Court which had no Juriſdiction to take it, than at the proper one; for it ſeems to be expreſs, that it was taken at the Court-Baron, and mentions nothing in Relation to the Court-Leet, but that it was holden together with the Court-Baron. And agreeably hereto it is ſaid in the Year-Book of 10 *Edw.* 4. 15. that if the Caption had been *ad magnam Curiam & ad letam*, it had been ſome Senſe, but that *cum leta* bears no Senſe. From whence it may be argued, that if a Caption ſet forth an Indictment as taken at a Court-Baron and Court-Leet, it may be good, becauſe the Court-Baron having no Manner of Juriſdiction in criminal Matters, and the Court-Leet having ſuch Juriſdiction, it may well be [i] intended that the Indictment was taken at the Court-Leet, and not at the Court which had nothing to do with it. *A fortiori* therefore, if an Indictment be ſet forth as taken *ad viſ. franci pleg. cum cur' baron' tent'*, it ſhall be intended to have been taken at the Court-Leet; as it is [k] ſaid to have been holden by the late Chief Juſtice *Holt*, who yet ſeemed to be of Opinion, That if a Court-Baron had a Juriſdiction of ſuch Matters as well as a Court-Leet, but in a different Manner, ſuch a Caption would have been inſufficient, for not ſhewing more expreſly at which of the Courts the Indictment was taken.

Sect. 125. It hath been adjudged, [l] that the not ſetting forth in the Caption of an Indictment taken at a Leet, whether the Court were holden by Grant or Preſcription, is holpen by the Multitude of Precedents.

Sect. 126. As to the ſecond Particular, *viz.* What Certainty is neceſſary in the Caption of an Indictment in reſpect of the Jurors by whom it was found, it ſeems agreed, That no Caption of an Indictment whether found at a [m] Court-Leet, or other inferior Court, can be good, without expreſly ſhewing, that the Jurors who found it were of the [n] County, City, or Burgh, or other Precinct, for which the Court was holden, and that they were at leaſt [o] twelve in Number, and [p] alſo, that they found the Indictment upon their Oaths. Alſo, Indictments have been [q] quaſhed for an Omiſſion of the Names of the Jurors in the Caption; but there is a [r] Precedent in *Saunders*'s Reports of a Caption, ſetting

[a] 2 Keb. 385. pl. 58.
[b] 1 Sid. 247. pl. 11. It is made a Quære, 1 Keb. 656. pl. 36. 1 Sid. 175. pl. 7.
[b] Adjudged, Term. Mich. 3 Georgii 1.
[c] 1 Mod. 24. 2 Keb. 580. pl. 112. Cro. Eliz. 738. pl. 10.
[d] 1 Bulſt. 203.
[e] 2 Keb. 128. pl. 83. Cro. Eliz. 738. pl. 10. Vide Keilw. 192. b. 194. a. 2 Keb. 385. pl. 58. 22 Ed. 4. 19. b. Bro. Battail, 7. Indictment, 46.
[f] 1 Saund. 263.
[g] 1 Sid. 367. 3 Mod. 152. 2 Keb. 366. pl. 19.
[h] 10 Ed. 4. 15. pl. 15. Bro. Indictment, 34. Fitz. Indictment, 20. S. P. C. 95. Letter C. H. P. C. 206. 2 Keb. 139. pl. 7.
[i] 1 Salk. 195. Supra Ch. 11. Sect. 6.
[k] 1 Salk. 195.
[l] 1 Salk. 200.
2 H. H. P. C. 167.
[m] 6 H. 4. pl. 4.
[n] Raym. 434. Cro. Eliz. 677. pl. 6. 2 Keb. 160. pl. 46. 3 Keb. 807. pl. 17. Vide ſupra Sect. 33.

[o] Cro. Eliz. 654. pl. 16. Vide ſupra Sect. 15. 6 H. 4. pl. 4. 41 Ed. 3. 31. pl. 36. [p] 2 Keb. 676. pl. 54. 1 Sid. 140. 3 Mod. 201. 1 Keb. 629. pl. 112, 329. pl. 66. See the Caſes cited to Letters, a, b, c, d, e, f, g. and 1 Salk. 371. pl. 7. [q] 2 Rol. Ab. 82. pl. 10. 2 Keb. 470 pl. 61. 6 H. 4. pl. 4. Qu. 2 R. 3. 11. pl. 25. Vide Raſt. Ent. 553, 606. [r] 1 Saund. 249. Vide 13 H. 7. 20. a. 2 Keb. 366.

forth, that the Indictment was taken by twelve Men, *&c.* without naming them, and yet no Exception appears to have been taken on this Account. Alſo many Indictments taken in inferior [a] Courts, have been quaſhed for want of the Words *proborum & legalium hominum* in the Caption; but this Exception hath been often over-ruled, as hath been more fully ſhewn in the ſixteenth Section of this Chapter. Alſo many Indictments in ſuch Courts have been quaſhed for Want of the Words [b] *jurat' & onerat'*, in the Caption; and alſo for Want of the Words [c] *adtunc & ibidem*, before the Words *jurat. & onerat'*; and alſo for [d] want of the Words *ad inquirendum pro dicto Domino Rege & pro corpore comitatus*; and alſo for want of the Words [e] *ſuper ſacramentum ſuum dicunt*, after the Words *jurat. & onerat'*; and alſo for expreſſing the [f] Oath to have been to inquire *pro corpore civitatis prædictæ*, where the Offence aroſe in, and the Seſſions was holden for a Burgh, *&c.* But it is [g] ſaid, that in the Caption of an Indictment taken in the King's Bench, or at the [h] Grand Seſſions, the Words *ſuper ſacramentum ſuum dicunt*, ſupply the Want of the Words *jurat. & onerat'*, *&c.* Alſo, it is ſaid to have been [i] adjudged, that the Words *jurat. & onerat. ad inquirend. pro Domino Rege & corpore comitatus* are ſufficient, without the Word *pro* before *corpore*; and that the Addition of the Words *ad largum* after *inquirend.* does no [k] Hurt; and that there is no Need of the Words *ad inquirendum pro corpore comitatus* in an [l] Inquiſition taken for a particular Purpoſe; and that the Omiſſion of the Word [m] *onerat.* is not fatal, if there be the Word *jurat'*, for that fully implies it.

Sect. 127. As to the third Particular, *viz.* What Certainty is neceſſary in the Caption of an Indictment, in reſpect of the Time when it was found? It ſeems [n] agreed, that ſuch Caption muſt ſet forth a certain Day and Year when the Court was holden, before which the Indictment was found, and muſt record it as then found in the [o] Preſent Tenſe, and not in the Preterperfect; for it hath been [p] adjudged, that if it deſcribe the Seſſions at which the Indictment was taken, as holden *die Martis & die Mercurii*; or as holden on ſuch a Day in ſuch a Year of the King, without [q] aſcertaining what King; or if it ſet forth the Style of the Day or Year in any [r] Figures but *Roman*, it is inſufficient. But it ſeems to be [s] agreed, That it is ſufficient to expreſs the Year of the King, without adding that of the Lord: Alſo it ſeems, that [t] *extitit præſentatum* for *exiſtit* is made good by the Multitude of Precedents.

Sect. 128. As to the fourth Particular, *viz.* What Certainty is neceſſary in the Caption of an Indictment in reſpect of the Place where it was found? It ſeems agreed, That if ſuch Caption either ſet forth no [u] Place at all where the Indictment was found, or do not [x] ſhew with ſufficient Certainty, that the Place ſet forth is within the Juriſdiction of the Court before which it was taken, as where it ſets forth the Indictment as taken at a Seſſions of the Peace holden for ſuch a County, at *B.* [y] without ſhewing in what County *B.* is, otherwiſe than by putting the County into the Margin, it is inſufficient: Alſo if an Act of Parliament, whether it be in Print or not, appoint, that the Quarter-Seſſions of ſuch a County ſhall be holden at ſuch a Place only, and not elſewhere, except for Cauſe of the Plague, *&c.* it ſeems, [z] that the Caption of every Indictment taken at any ſuch Seſſions, is inſufficient, unleſs it expreſly ſhew, that it was holden at ſuch Place. But it hath been [aa] adjudged, That the Cap-

[a] 1 Keb. 629. pl. 112. 2 Keb. 471. pl. 63. 2 Rol. Abr. 82. pl. 8. 2 Keb. 366. pl. 19.
[b] 1 Keb. 101. pl. 100. 524. pl. 14. 629. pl. 112. 852. pl. 55. 2 Keb. 367. pl. 20. Vide 3 Keb. 128. pl. 50. Contra 2 Keb. 59. pl. 28. 2 Jo. 180.
[c] 1 Mod. 26. 2 Keb. 583. pl. 121, 610. pl. 47.
[d] 2 Keb. 471. pl. 63. Show. 272. 6 Mod. 95, 180.
[e] 1 Sid. 140. 1 Keb. 498. pl. 51.
[f] 1 Saund. 249.
[g] 1 Keb. 629. pl. 112.
[h] 2 Keb. 471. pl. 63.
[i] 6 Mod. 180.
[k] 1 Sid. 140.
[l] 1 Show. 272. 6 Mod. 95.
[m] Dom. Rex verſus Gravenor, adjudged Hil. 3 Georg. 1.
[n] Vide 1 Bulſt. 203. Supra Ch. 10. Sect. 9.
[o] 1 Sid. 229. 230. 1 Keb. 37. pl. 101. 823. pl. 114. Vide 1 Mod. 81. 2 Saun. 393. 1 Vent. 170.
[p] 4 Co. 48. a.
[q] 2 Keb. 582. pl. 117, 118. Vide ſupra Sect. 87.
[r] 2 H.H.P.C. 170. 1 Mod. 78. 2 Keb. 128. pl. 83.
[s] Vide ſupra Sect. 80. and Ch. 23. Sect. 90.
[t] 1 Sid. 140, 368. 1 Keb. 37. pl. 101. 2 Keb. 367. pl. 20. 5 Co. 120. Fitz. Indictment, 20. Bro. Indictment, 34. 10 Ed. 4 15. pl. 15.
[u] Dyer 69. pl. 29.
[x] Cro. Jac. 276, 277.
[y] Cro. Eliz. 137. pl. 9, 606. pl. 4. 738. pl. 10, 751. pl. 7.
[z] Dyer 135. pl. 14.
[aa] 5 Co. 120. b. 121. Vide Poph. 208. Cro. Eliz. 490.

tion

tion of an Inquiſition as taken at *B.* before *J. S.* Coroner of the King's Liberty of *B.* aforeſaid, is good, without expreſly ſhewing that *B.* is within the Liberty of *B.* for it cannot but be intended.

Sect. 129. As to the tenth general Point of this Chapter, *viz.* Upon what Proof, and within what Time after the Offence, an Indictment may be found? It [a] ſeems, that before 1 *Ed.* 6. no certain Number of Witneſſes was required upon the Indictment or Trial of any Crime whatever; for it ſeems to be generally [b] agreed, that the Statutes of 1 and 2 of *Philip* and *Mary*, 10 & 11. in reſtoring the Order of Trial by the Courſe of the Common Law, took away the Neceſſity of two Witneſſes in all Caſes within thoſe Statutes; from whence it plainly ſeems to follow, that they were not required by the Common Law. It is holden [c] indeed by ſome, that by the ancient Common Law one Witneſs was not ſufficient to convict any Perſon of High Treaſon; and this is ſaid to be grounded on the Law of God, expreſſed both in the Old and New Teſtament. But granting that one Witneſs was not ſufficient for a Conviction, it doth not follow but that he might be ſufficient for an Indictment. [71] Alſo, however the Law might have ſtood in Relation to theſe Matters before the Conqueſt, it ſeems to have been wholly altered long before the Statute of *Ed.* 6. And I rather incline to this Opinion, ſince I find it ſo little ſupported by the Generality of the Authorities cited by Sir *Edward Coke* for the Proof of the contrary, which wholly relate either to the Proof of an Eſſoin, or of a Summons [d] in a real Action, or [e] of the Default of Perſons ſummon'd on a Jury, or [f] other Matters rather leſs to the Point. And as to the abovecited Paſſages of Scripture it may be anſwered, that thoſe in the Old Teſtament concern only the judicial Part of the *Jewiſh* Law, which being framed for the Particular Government of the *Jewiſh* Nation, doth not bind us any more than the Ceremonial; and that thoſe in the New Teſtament contain only prudential Rules for the Direction of the Government of the Church, in Matters introduced by the Goſpel, and no way control the Civil Conſtitutions of Countries. To which may be added, That whatſoever may be ſaid either from Reaſon or Scripture for the Neceſſity of two Witneſſes in Treaſon, holds as ſtrongly in other Capital Cauſes, and yet it is not pretended, that there is or ever was any ſuch Neceſſity in relation to any other Crime but Treaſon.

[a] Vide 3 Keb. 68. pl. 7. Bro. Coro. 220. 2 Jo. 233.
[b] Bro. Coro. 220. S. P. C. 164. Dyer 132. pl. 75. 1 Jon. 233. Kel. 18, 49. Vide 3 Inſt. 24, 25, 26. H. P. C. 208, 262.
[c] 3 Inſt. 26, Raym. 408.
[d] Bract. 354. b.
[e] 35 H. 6. 46. b. 47. a.
[f] 48 Ed 3. 30. pl. 17. 15 Ed. 4. 1.

Sect. 130. But it is enacted by 1 *Ed.* 6. 12. *par.* 22. *That no Perſon or Perſons, after the firſt Day of* February *then next to come, ſhall be indicted, arraigned, condemned, or convicted for any Offence of Treaſon, Petit Treaſon, or Miſpriſion of Treaſon,* &c. *unleſs the ſame Offender or Offenders, be accuſed by two ſufficient and lawful Witneſſes, or ſhall willingly without Violence confeſs the ſame.*

Sect. 131. Alſo it is further enacted by 5 & 6 *Ed.* 6. 11. *par.* 8. *That no Perſon or Perſons after the firſt Day of* June *then next coming, ſhall be indicted, arraigned, condemned, convicted or attainted, for any of the Treaſons in the Act mentioned, or for any other Treaſons that then were, or after ſhould be, which ſhould after be perpetrated, committed, or done, unleſs the ſame Offender or Offenders, be thereof accuſed by two lawful Accuſers; which ſaid Accuſers at the Time of that Arraignment of the Party accuſed, if they be then living, ſhall be brought in Perſon before the Party ſo accuſed, and avow and maintain what they have to ſay againſt the ſaid Party, to prove him guilty of the Treaſons or Offences contained in the Bill of Indictment laid againſt the Party arraigned, unleſs the ſaid Party arraigned ſhall willingly, without Violence, confeſs the ſame.*

Sect. 132. But it is enacted by 1 & 2 *Ph. & Ma.* 10. *That all Trials after that Statute to be had, awarded, or made for any Treason, ſhall be had and uſed only according to the due Order and Courſe of the Common Law.*

Sect. 133. Alſo it is enacted by 1 & 2 *Ph. & Ma.* 11. *That all and every Perſon and Perſons who ſhall be accuſed or impeached of any of the Offences contained in that Statute, or of any other Offence or Offences concerning the Impairing, Counterfeiting or Forging of any Coin Current within this Realm, ſhall and may be indicted, arraigned, tried, convicted or attainted by ſuch like Evidence, and in ſuch Manner and Form as has been uſed and accuſtomed within the Realm, at any Time before the firſt Year of the Reign of King* Edw. 6.

Sect. 134. It is further enacted by 7 *W.* 3. 3. *That after the 25th Day of* March *in the Year* 1696, *no Perſon or Perſons whatſoever ſhall be indicted, tried or attainted of High Treaſon, whereby any Corruption of Blood may, or ſhall be made to any ſuch Offender or Offenders, or to any the Heir or Heirs of any ſuch Offender or Offenders, or of Miſpriſion of ſuch Treaſon, but by and upon the Oaths and Teſtimony of two lawful Witneſſes, either both of them to the ſame Overt-Act, or one of them to one, and the other of them to another Overt-Act of the ſame Treaſon, unleſs the Party indicted and arraigned, or tried, ſhall willingly, without Violence, in open Court confeſs the ſame, or ſhall ſtand mute, or refuſe to plead; or in Caſes of High Treaſon, ſhall peremptorily challenge above the Number of thirty five of the Jury.*

Sect. 135. And it is further enacted by the ſaid Statute, *That no Perſon or Perſons whatſoever, (ſuch only excepted as ſhall be guilty of deſigning, endeavouring, or attempting any Aſſaſſination on the Body of the King, by Poiſon, or otherwiſe,) ſhall be indicted, tried or proſecuted for any ſuch Treaſon as aforeſaid, or for Miſpriſion of ſuch Treaſon, that ſhall be committed or done within the Kingdom of* England, *Dominion of* Wales, *or Town of* Berwick *upon* Tweed, *unleſs the ſame Indictment be found by a Grand Jury, within three Years next after the Treaſon or Offence done and committed.*

Sect. 136. But it is provided, *That nothing in this Act ſhall any Ways extend to any Impeachment, or other Proceedings in Parliament, nor to any Indictment of High Treaſon, nor to any Proceeding thereupon, for counterfeiting his Majeſty's Coin, his Great Seal or Privy Seal, his Sign Manual, or Privy Signet.*

Upon theſe Statutes the following Particulars ſeem moſt remarkable.

Sect. 137. *Firſt*, That where the Statute of 1 *Ed.* 6. requires, That the Party be accuſed by two lawful Witneſſes; and that of 5 & 6 *Ed.* 6. That he be accuſed by two lawful Accuſers; they both mean the very [a] ſame Thing, becauſe the Common Law admits of no other Accuſers but Witneſſes.

Sect. 138. *Secondly*, That according to the general [b] Opinion, it is not required either by the 1ſt, or 5 & 6 *Ed.* 6. That ſuch Accuſers or Witneſſes be preſent with the Indictors in Perſon, but that they may ſend their Accuſation to the Indictors in Writing under their Hands, which will be ſufficient even after their Death. Alſo it is obſervable, That the Books which ſpeak of this Matter do not expreſly ſay, that ſuch Accuſation muſt be upon Oath, but ſurely this cannot but be intended; for how can any Accuſer be ſaid to be a lawful Witneſs, if he be not upon his Oath? But this is cleared by 7 *W.* 3. as to the Treaſons within that Statute; for it expreſly provides, That no Perſon ſhall be indicted thereof, but by and upon the Oath and Teſtimony of two lawful Witneſſes.

[a] Bro. Coro. 220. 3 Inſt. 25, 26. H. P. C. 208.

[b] 1 H. H. P. C. 301. S. P. C. 164. Bro. Coro. 220. H. P. C. 208. But 3 Inſt. 25, 26, ſeems contrary.

[a] 3 Inst. 25, 26. [b] H.P.C. 208. 1 H. H. P. C. 306. Contra Dyer 99. pl. 68. Vide S. P. C. 164. Bro. Coro. 220.

Sect. 139. *Thirdly,* By the Judgment both of [a] *Coke* and [b] *Hale,* one who can only witness by Hearsay what he has heard a good Witness say, is not a lawful Accuser within any of these Statutes; [72] for if this were to be allowed, nothing would be more easy than in any Case, where there is one Witness, to get a second, which would totally elude the Provision of the Statutes in requiring two lawful Witnesses, *&c.*

[c] 2 And. 66, 67. 3 Inst. 25.

Sect. 140. *Fourthly,* That the Words, *unless the Party shall willingly, without Violence, confess the same,* in the 1st, and 5 & 6 *Ed.* 6. are to be understood [c] where the Party accused upon his Examination, before his Arraignment, willingly confesses the same without Torture: But it is observable, that 7 *W.* 3. is thus expressed, *Unless the Party indicted and arraigned, or tried, shall willingly, without Violence, in open Court confess the same.*

[d] Raym. 407, 408. Kel. 9.

Sect. 141. *Fifthly,* That one Witness to one, and another Witness to another Overt-Act of the very same [d] Treason, have been construed to be sufficient, within the Statutes of the 1st, and 5 & 6 *Ed.* 6. and the express Words of 7 *W.* 7. are agreeable hereto.

[e] S. P. C. 90, 164. 3 Inst. 24, 25, 26, 27. Bro. Coro. 220.

Sect. 142. *Sixthly,* That the Statute of 1 & 2 *Ph.* & *Ma.* 10. by enacting, That all Trials of Treason shall from thenceforth be according to the Course of the Common Law, doth not [e] take away the Necessity of two Witnesses upon an Indictment, required by the 1st, and 5 & 6 *Ed.* 6. because the Indictment is no Part of the Trial, but is more properly the Accusation to be tried.

[f] Bro. Coro. 220. 3 Inst. 24.

Sect. 143. *Seventhly,* [f] That the said Statute of 1 & 2 *Ph.* & *Ma.* doth not extend to Misprision of Treason; but this is expresly provided for by 7 *W.* 3. as to such Treasons as are within that Statute, and therefore there must be two Witnesses to the Indictment, as well as Trial of every such Misprision.

[g] Bro. Coro. 220. 3 Inst. 24.

[h] Vide supra sect. 140.

Sect. 144. *Eighthly,* That [g] Petit Treason is within the 1st, and 5 & 6 *Ed.* 6. and 1 & 2 *Ph.* & *Ma.* 10. but not within the 7th of *W.* 3. from whence it follows, That two Witnesses are required to the Indictment, and not to the Trial of it, and that two Witnesses are not necessary even upon the Indictment, if [h] the Party, upon his Examination, confess it.

[i] 2 Jo. 233. Vide Bro. Coro. 220. 3 Keb. 68. pl. 7.

Sect. 145. *Ninthly,* That the Statute of 1 & 2 *Ph.* & *Ma.* 11. which enacts, That all Persons accused of any Offences concerning the Impairing, Counterfeiting or Forging the Coin, shall be indicted and tried as at the Common Law, hath been construed [i] to extend to Clipping, and all other Offences in impairing the Coin, which have been made Treasons since the said Statute of 1 & 2 *Ph.* & *Ma.* From whece it may be probably argued, That the Statute of 7 *W.* 3. by expresly providing, That nothing therein shall extend to High Treason for counterfeiting the Coin, intended in like Manner, that it should not extend to any other High Treason concerning the Coin.

[k] State Trials Vol. 4. Page 135. 1 Sid. 54. pl. 19. 247. pl. 11. 2 Keb. 128. pl. 83. 1 Keb. 45. pl. 120. Cro. Car. 584. Palm. 389. Salk. 372. pl. 11. State Trials, Vol. 4. Pag. 134.

Sect. 146. As to the eleventh general Point of this Chapter, *viz.* In what Cases an Indictment may be quashed: I take it to be [k] settled, That by the Common Law the Court may, in Discretion, quash any Indictment, for any such Insufficiency, either in the Caption, or Body of it, as will make any Judgment whatsoever, given upon any Part of it against the Defendant, erroneous; yet it seems, That Judges are in no Case bound, *ex debito justitiæ,* to quash an Indictment, but may oblige the Defendant either to plead or to demur to it: And this they generally do where it is for a Crime of an enormous or publick Nature, as Perjury, Forgery, Sedition, Nusances to the Highways, and other Offences of the like Nature. [a] Neither will the Court quash an Indictment removed by *Certiorari*, if a Recognisance for the Trial of it hath been forfeited. [a] Salk. 380. pl. 26.

Sect. 147. Also it is enacted by 7 *W.* 3. 3. *That no Indictment for High Treason, or Misprision thereof, (except only Indictments for counterfeiting the King's Coin, Seal, Sign or Signet,) nor any Process or Return thereupon, shall be quashed on the Motion of the Prisoner, or his Counsel, for miswriting, misspelling, false or improper* Latin, *unless Exception concerning the same be taken and made in the respective Court, where such Trial shall be, by the Prisoner, or his Counsel assigned, before any Evidence given in open Court upon such Indictment; nor shall any such Miswriting, Misspelling, false or improper* Latin, *after Conviction on such Indictment, be any Cause to stay or arrest Judgment thereupon: But nevertheless, any Judgment given upon such Indictment shall and may be liable to be reversed upon a Writ of Error, in the same Manner, and no other than as if this Act had not been made.*

Sect. 148. It hath been settled [b] in the Construction of this Statute, that no such Exception can be taken, after Plea pleaded. [b] State Trials Vol. 4. Page 135, 329.

Sect. 149. It is said [c] in *Siderfin*'s Reports, That the Court never [d] quasheth an Information exhibited by a common Person, but that it will quash an Information exhibited by the Attorney General, or by the Master of the Crown-Office, upon Motion, if there be Cause: But this was denied in one [e] *Nixon*'s Case, wherein the Court seemed to be agreed, That they never have, or will quash any Information whatsoever. [c] 1 Sid. 152. Vide 1 Sid. 54. pl. 19. [d] Cont. 1 Keb. 255. pl. 28. [e] King versus Nixon, Trin. 5 Georgii 1. Vide Salk. 372. pl. 11.

Sect. 150. As to the twelfth general Point of this Chapter, *viz.* What may be pleaded to an Indictment, and in what Manner: Having already shewn in this Chapter how a Defendant may plead [f] to an Indictment, That the Indictors were returned contrary to the Purview of 11 *H.* 4. 9. And having also [g] shewn, how he may plead a Misnosmer, or wrongful Addition; and intending in the following Part of the Book to shew, how he may plead a former Acquittal, Conviction or Attainder, or a Pardon or other special Plea, or the general Issue; I shall in this Place only take Notice, That the Defendant may plead any Plea in Abatement of an Indictment of Felony; and also plead over in Bar, and take [h] the general Issue also, in the same Manner as an Appellee may do, as hath been more fully shewn, *Ch.* 23. *Sect.* 127, 138. [f] Supra Sect. 25. [g] Supra Sect. 70, 71, 72. Vide Ch. 23. Sect. 103. [h] Finch 385. H. P. C. 202, 249, 254.

CHAP. XXVI.

Of Information.

INformations are of two Kinds:

First, Such as are merely at the Suit of the King.

Secondly, Such as are partly the Suit of the King, and partly the Suit of the Party.

And

And firſt, for the better Underſtanding the firſt of theſe, I ſhall endeavour to ſhew,

1. In what Caſes they lie.
2. What ought to be the Form of them.
3. How the Law concerning them hath been altered by Statute.

Sect. 1. As to the firſt of theſe Particulars, *viz.* In what Caſes ſuch Informations lie: It hath been holden, That the King ſhall put no [a] one to anſwer for a Wrong done principally to another, without an Indictment or Preſentment, but that he may do it for a Wrong done principally to himſelf. But I do not find this Diſtinction confirmed by Experience, for it is every Day's Practice, agreeable to numberleſs Precedents, to proceed by Way of Information, either in the Name of the Attorney General, or of the Maſter of the Crown-Office, for Offences of the former Kind, as for [b] Batteries, [c] Cheats, Seducing [d] a young Man or Woman from their Parents in Order to marry them againſt their Conſent, or for any other wicked Purpoſe; Spiriting [e] away a Child to the Plantations, Reſcuing [f] Perſons from legal Arreſts, [g] Perjuries and Subornations thereof, [h] Forgeries, Conſpiracies, (whether to accuſe [i] an innocent Perſon, or to impoveriſh [k] a certain Set of lawful Traders, *&c.* or to [l] procure a Verdict to be unlawfully given, by cauſing Perſons bribed for the Purpoſe, to be ſworn on a *Tales*,) and other ſuch like Crimes done principally to a private Perſon, as well as for Offences done principally to the King, as for [m] Libels, ſeditious Words, [n] Riots, falſe News, [o] Extortions, Nuſances, (as in not [p] Repairing Highways, or Obſtructing [q] them, or Stopping [r] a Common River, *&c.*) Contempts, as in Departing [s] from the Parliament without the King's Licence, Diſobeying [t] his Writs, Uttering [u] Money without his Authority, Eſcaping [x] from a legal Impriſonment on a Proſecution for a Contempt, neglecting to keep Watch and Ward, Abuſing [y] the King's Commiſſion to the Oppreſſion of the Subject, making a Return to a *Mandamus* of Matters [z] known to be falſe; and in general, any other Offences againſt the Publick Good, or againſt the firſt and obvious Principles of Juſtice, and Common Honeſty. [73]

Sect. 2. Alſo it ſeems, [aa] That of Common Right ſuch an Information, or an Action in the Nature thereof may be brought for Offences againſt Statutes, whether they be mentioned by ſuch Statutes or not, unleſs other Methods of proceeding be particularly appointed, by which all others are impliedly excluded.

Sect. 3. But I do not [bb] find it any where holden, That ſuch an Information will lie for any Capital Crime, or for Miſpriſion of Treaſon.

Sect. 4. As to the ſecond Particular, *viz.* What ought to be the Form of ſuch Informations: Having already in the Chapter of *Indictments* incidentally ſhewn the Principal Points relating to this Matter, I ſhall only take Notice in this Place, That ſeeing an Information differs from an Indictment in little more than this, that the one is found by the Oath of twelve Men, and the other is not ſo found; but is only the Allega-

[a] Thelo. B. 1. Ch. 4. Sect. 9, 10, 11, 12, 13, 14. Finch 336. Fitz. Action ſur le Statute, &c.
[b] See the Preamble of 4 & 5 Will. & Ma. infra Sect. 5. Show. 116, 117, 118.
[c] Show. 110, 116, 117. 1 Sid. 431. Far. 40. Skin. 108, 109.
[d] Cro. Car. 557, 558. March 52, 53. 3 Keb. 101. 1 Lev. 257. 1 Sid. 387. 5 Mod. 221, 222. Far. 39. Carth. 384. Skin. 81. 2 Keb. 432. Raym. 473.
[e] Raym. 474. Skin. 47.
[f] Raym. 231. Show. 109, 110, 113. Cro. Car. 579.
[g] Raym. 202. 5 Mod. 342, Far. 100, 101. Salk. 78.
[h] Show. 111.
[i] Raym. 417.
[k] 1 Sid. 174.
[l] See the Precedent of ſuch an Information, 1 Saund. 300, 301.
[m] Raym. 201. Show. 118, 119. Carth. 14, 15.

[n] 5 Mod. 459. Cro. Car. 252. Show. 106. Skin. 116. [o] Raym. 216. Carth. 226. [p] Raym. 384. Show. 110, 111, 112, 116. 1 Sid. 140. [q] Show. 112, 116. [r] Show. 114, 118. [s] Ibid. [t] Cro. Car. 253. [u] Raym. 185. [x] Cro. Car. 209. [y] Show. 116. [z] Salk. 374. pl. 16. [aa] Show. 111, 115, 116, 117. 3 Mod. 117. 2 And. 128. Raſt. Ent. 686. b. Vitail, 1. Vide 3 Leon. 237. & ſupra Ch. 25. Sect. 4. 2 And. 127, 128. [bb] Vide Show. 109, 110. 2 H. H. P. C. *151.

tion of the Officer who exhibits it, whatsoever Certainty is requisite in an Indictment, the same at least is necessary also in an Information, and consequently, as all the material Parts of the Crime must be precisely found in the one, so must they be precisely alledged in the other, and not by Way of [a] Argument or Recital. Yet it hath been adjudged, That where an Information of Perjury was drawn in this Manner, *Memorandum quod* A. B. *&c. dat Curiæ hic intelligi & informari quod Termino Sancti Hill', &c. in Rotulis continetur sic, viz.* That such an Action was brought, and a Trial had thereon, *&c. Et quod* the Defendant, at such Trial, took such an Oath, which was false, *&c.* without adding before such Mention of the false Oath, *Et ulterius dat Cur. hic intelligi*; yet, by Reason of the late Precedents the Information is as [b] sufficient, at least after Verdict, as if those Words had been added; and it must be confessed, That this is the most reasonable Construction, for how can it be intended that it could be contained in the Record of the Trial, That such an Oath was taken at it, or that it was false?

[a] Salk. 378

[b] Raym. 34, 35.

Sect. 5. As to the third Particular, *viz.* How the Law concerning such Informations hath been altered by Statute? It is recited by 4 & 5 *Wil. & Ma.* 18. *That divers malitious and contentious Persons had more of late, than in Times past, procured to be exhibited and prosecuted Informations in their Majesties Court of King's Bench at* Westminster, *against Persons in all the Counties of* England, *for Trespasses, Batteries, and other Misdemeanors, and after the Parties so informed against had appeared to such Informations, and pleaded to Issue, the Informers had very seldom proceeded any further, whereby the Persons so informed against had been put to great Charges in their Defence; and altho' at the Trials of such Informations Verdicts had been given for them, or a* Nolle Prosequi *entred against them, they had no Remedy for obtaining Costs against such Informers.* And thereupon it is enacted, *That after the first Day of* Easter-Term *in the Year* 1693, *the Clerk of the Crown, in the said Court of King's Bench, for the Time being, shall not without express Order, to be given by the said Court, in open Court, exhibit, receive, or file any Information for any of the Causes aforesaid, or issue out any Process thereupon, before he shall have taken, or shall have delivered to him a Recognizance from the Person or Persons procuring such Information, to be exhibited with the Place of his, her, or their Abode, Title or Profession, to be entered to the Person or Persons against whom such Information or Informations, is, or are to be exhibited, in the Penalty of twenty Pounds, that he, she, or they will effectually prosecute such Information or Informations, and abide by, and observe such Orders, as the said Court shall direct; which Recognizance the said Clerk of the Crown, and also every Justice of the Peace of any County, City, Franchise, or Town corporate, (where the Cause of any Information shall arise,) are by the same Statute impowered to take: After the Taking whereof by the said Clerk of the Crown, or the Receipt thereof, from any Justice of the Peace, the said Clerk of the Crown shall make an Entry thereof upon Record, and shall file a* Memorandum *thereof in some publick Place in his Office, that all Persons may resort thereunto without Fee; and in case any Person or Persons against whom any Information or Informations for the Causes aforesaid, or any of them, shall be exhibited, shall appear thereunto, and plead to issue, and that the Prosecutor or Prosecutors of such Information or Informations, shall not at his and their own proper Costs and Charges, within one whole Year next after Issue joined therein, procure the same to be tried; or if upon such Trial a Verdict pass for the Defendant or Defendants, or in Case the same Informer or Informers procure a* Nolle Prosequi *to be entred; then, in any of the said Cases the said Court of King's Bench is authorised to award the said Defendant or Defendants, his, her, or their Costs, unless the Judge, before whom such In-*

formation ſhall be tried, ſhall at the Trial of ſuch Information, in open Court, certify upon Record, That there was reaſonable Cauſe for exhibiting ſuch Information; and in caſe the ſaid Informer or Informers ſhall not within three Months next after the ſaid Coſts taxed, and Demand made thereof, pay to the ſaid Defendant or Defendants the ſaid Coſts, then the ſaid Defendant and Defendants ſhall have the Benefit of the ſaid Recognizance, to compel them thereunto.

Sect. 6. But it is provided, *That nothing hereof ſhall extend, or be conſtrued to extend, to any other Information than ſuch as ſhall be exhibited in the Name of their Majeſties Coroner, or Attorney, in the Court of King's Bench, for the Time being (commonly called the Maſter of the Crown Office.)* From whence it follows, That Informations exhibited by the Attorney General remain as they were at the Common Law.

For the better Underſtanding this Statute, I ſhall endeavour to ſhew,

1. Whether it extend to all Kinds of Informations.
2. In what Caſes the Court will order an Information to be filed.
3. How the Party may be relieved againſt Proceſs iſſued againſt him, before any Recognizance given.
4. Where the Defendant ſhall have Coſts.

Sect. 7. As to the firſt of theſe Particulars: It ſeems clear, That this Statute extends to all Informations whatſoever exhibited by the Maſter of the Crown-Office; and tho' it may be objected, That an Information in the [a] Nature of a *Quo Warranto*, being a proper Means to try a Right is not within the Meaning of the Statute, which mentioning *Treſpaſſes, Batteries, and other Miſdemeanors*, may be reaſonably conſtrued to intend ſuch other Miſdemeanors only as are of an inferior Nature, like to thoſe ſpecified, which are generally wrangling and frivolous ones; yet ſeeing this is a remedial Law, and therefore ought to be largely conſtrued, and ſuch Informations may be as vexatious as any other, and always ſuppoſe an Uſurpation of ſome Franchiſe, and every ſuch Uſurpation is certainly a Miſdemeanor, it hath been ſettled that this Statute doth extend to them.

[a] Salk. 376. pl. 19. Carth. 504.

Sect. 8. As to the ſecond Particular, *viz.* In what Caſes the Court will order an Information to be filed: It ſeems to have been the general Practice not to make ſuch an Order, without firſt making a Rule upon the Perſon complained of to ſhew Cauſe to the contrary; which Rule is never granted, but upon Motion made in open Court, and grounded upon Affidavit of ſome Miſdemeanor, which if true, doth either for its Enormity, or dangerous Tendency, or other ſuch like Circumſtances, ſeem proper for the moſt publick Proſecution. And if the Perſon upon whom ſuch a Rule is made, having been perſonally ſerv'd with it, do not, at the Day given him for that Purpoſe, give the Court good Satisfaction, by Affidavit, that there is no reaſonable Cauſe for the Proſecution, the Court generally grants the Information; and ſometimes upon ſpecial Circumſtances, will grant it againſt thoſe who cannot be perſonally ſerv'd with ſuch Rule, as if they purpoſely abſent themſelves, *&c.*

Sect. 9. But if the Party on whom ſuch a Rule is made, ſhew to the Court a reaſonable Cauſe againſt ſuch Proſecution; as that he has been before indicted for the ſame Cauſe, and acquitted; or that the Intent of the [b] Proſecution is to try a Civil Right, as the Title to Land, *&c.* which is not yet determined; or that the Complaint is trifling, vexatious, or oppreſſive; or if he can ſhew to the Court (in Anſwer to a Motion for

[b] Cro. Jac. 212.

an Information, in the Nature of a *Quo Warranto*) that his Right to the Franchise in question had been already determined on a *Mandamus*; or that it hath been acquiesced in many Years, without any Dispute; or that it depends on the Right of those who voted for him, which hath not been yet tried; or that the Franchise no way concerns the Publick, (as all those which relate to the Government of a Corporation, or the Election of Members of Parliament, and Fairs, and Markets, *&c.* are said to do) but is wholly of a private [a] Nature, as a Cony-warren, *&c.* Or that the Election, by which he claims, is agreeable to Charter; or that he has never acted under it; the Court will not grant the Information, unless there be some particular and extraordinary Circumstances in the Case, the Determination whereof being wholly left to the Discretion of the Court, cannot well come under any certain stated Rules.

[a] Vide Salk. 374. pl. 15.

Sect. 10. As to the third Particular, *viz.* How the Party may be relieved against Process issued against him, before any Recognizance given according to the Statute? It seems that he may move the Court [b] to set it aside, as having issued contrary to the Directions of the Statute.

[b] Salk. 376, pl. 19.

As to the fourth Particular, *viz.* Where the Defendant shall have Costs, I shall observe,

Sect. 11. *First*, That if the Information be tried at Bar, the Defendant can have no Costs within this Statute; for the Words are, [c] *That the Court is authorised to award Costs,* &c. *unless the Judge, before whom the Information shall be tried, shall at the Trial, in open Court, certify upon Record, that there was a reasonable Cause for exhibiting such Information.* Which is most naturally to be understood of a Trial, at *Nisi Prius*; and it would be absurd to suppose, That the Statute intended that the Justices of the King's Bench, at a Trial before themselves, should make a Certificate to themselves: To which may be added, That where a Cause is of such Consequence as to be tried at the Bar, it may reasonably be intended to be out of the Purview of the Statute, which was chiefly designed against trifling and vexatious Prosecutions.

[c] Clerk's Case Far. 47.

Sect. 12. *Secondly*, That if there be several Defendants, and any one of them found guilty, those who are acquitted cannot have [d] Costs within this Statute; and this is agreeable to the Construction made of the Statutes which give Costs to Defendants in civil Actions, by Force whereof no Defendant in such like Case, could recover Costs before the Statute of 8 *&* 9 *Will.* 10.

[d] Salk. 194, pl. 5.

Sect. 13. *Thirdly*, That it hath been adjudged in the Construction of these Words, *The Court of King's Bench is authorised to award to the Defendant his Costs, where the Judge who tries an Information, does not at such Trial certify, That there was a reasonable Cause for the Information* [e]. That the said Court is bound of Right, in every such Case, to award them, whether the Acquittal were upon the Merits, or only from a Slip in Point of Form, and howsoever notorious the Offence might be; for where a Court is authorized by Statute, to do a Matter of Justice to the Party, upon certain Circumstances, it has no discretionary Power of considering, whether it ought to do it, or not, when a Case appears to be within those Circumstances. To which may be added, That the Statute being general as to all Cases, wherein the Judge, who tries the Information, doth not certify a reasonable Cause, seems to imply, That it shall be left to such Judge only for this Purpose to consider, whether the Prosecution were reasonable or not, and it is the Prosecutor's Folly not to apply to him.

[e] Dom. Regina versus Davis, adjudged Mich. 10 Annæ. Vide 2 Chancery Cases 191.

Sect. 14. It is further enacted by 9 *Annæ*, 20. *That in case any Person or Persons shall usurp, intrude into, or unlawfully hold and execute the Office or Franchise of Mayor, Bailiff, Portreeve, or other Office within a City, Town corporate, Borough, or Place in* England *or* Wales, *it shall and may be lawful, to and for the proper Officer of the Court of Queen's Bench, the Court of Sessions of Counties Palatine, or the Court of Grand Sessions in* Wales, *with the Leave of the said Courts respectively, to exhibit one or more Information or Informations, in the Nature of a* Quo Warranto, *at the Relation of any Person or Persons, desiring to sue, or prosecute the same, and who shall be mentioned in such Information or Informations, to be the Relator or Relators against such Person or Persons so usurping, intruding into, or unlawfully holding and executing any of the said Offices or Franchises, and to proceed therein in such Manner as is usual in Cases of Informations, in the Nature of a* Quo Warranto; *and if it shall appear to the said respective Courts, that the several Rights of divers Persons to the said Offices or Franchises may properly be determined on one Information, it shall and may be lawful for the said respective Courts to give Leave to exhibit one such Information against several Persons, in order to try their respective Rights to such Offices or Franchises, and such Person or Persons, against which such Information or Informations, in the Nature of a* Quo Warranto, *shall be sued or prosecuted, shall appear and plead as of the same Term or Sessions in which the said Information or Informations shall be filed, unless the Court, where such Information shall be filed, shall give further Time to such Person or Persons, against whom such Information shall be exhibited, to plead; and such Person or Persons who shall sue or prosecute such Information or Informations in the Nature of a* Quo Warranto, *shall proceed thereupon, with the most convenient Speed that may be.*

Sect. 15. And it is further enacted and declared, *That in case any Person or Persons, against whom any Information or Informations, in the Nature of a* Quo Warranto, *shall, in any of the said Cases, be exhibited in any of the said Courts, shall be found or adjudged guilty of an Usurpation, or Intrusion into, or unlawfully holding and executing any of the said Offices or Franchises, it shall and may be lawful to and for the said Courts respectively, as well to give Judgment of Ouster against such Person or Persons, of and from any of the said Offices or Franchises, as to fine such Person or Persons, respectively for his or their usurping,* &c. *And also to give Judgment that the Relator or Relators, in such Information named, shall recover his or their Costs of such Prosecution; and if Judgment shall be given for the Defendant or Defendants in such Information, he or they, for whom such Judgment shall be given, shall recover his or their Costs therein expended against such Relator or Relators, such Costs to be levied by* Capias ad Satisfaciendum, Fieri Facias, *or* Elegit.

Sect. 16. And it is further enacted, *That the Statute for the Amendment of the Law, and all the Statutes of* Jeofails *shall be extended to Informations, in Nature of a* Quo Warranto, *and Proceedings thereon, for any the Matters in the said Act mentioned.*

And now I am in the second Place to consider the Nature of such Information, as is partly the Suit of the King, and partly the Suit of the Party, which is commonly called an Information *qui tam*, and this having a great Affinity with Actions on Statutes, I shall consider them together, and endeavour to shew,

1. In what Cases they lie.
2. What ought to be the Form of them.
3. In what Courts they may be brought.
4. In what County.
5. Within what Time.

 6. Who

6. Who are diſabled to bring them.
7. Whether there may be a Nonſuit in them?
8. Whether the Informer or Defendant may appear by Attorney?
9. In what Caſes there ſhall be Coſts.
10. Whether the Defendant may wage his Law, or take Advantage of a Protection?
11. In what Manner the Defendant is to plead to ſuch an Information or Action.
12. By whom the Replication ſhall be made.
13. In what Manner the Iſſue ſhall be joined, and where it ſhall be tried.
14. Where the Verdict may be found as to Part of the Information againſt the Informer, and as to other Part for him.
15. What Judgment on ſuch an Information or Action is good.
16. Whether the Penalty of a penal Statute may be compounded or granted over?

Sect. 17. As to the firſt of theſe Particulars, *viz.* In what Caſes an Information or Action *qui tam* will lie; I [a] take it for granted, that they lie on no Statute which prohibits a Thing as being an immediate Offence againſt the Publick Good in general, under a certain Penalty, unleſs the Whole, or Part of ſuch Penalty be expreſly given to him who will ſue for it; becauſe [b] otherwiſe it goes to the King, and nothing can be demanded by the Party. But where ſuch Statute gives any Part of ſuch Penalty to him who will ſue for it by Action or Information, *&c.* I take it to be ſettled at this Day, That any one may bring ſuch Action, or Information, and lay his Demand [c] *tam pro Domino Rege quam pro ſeipſo.* [d] Alſo where a Statute prohibits, or commands a Thing, the Doing or Omiſſion whereof is an immediate Damage to the Party, and alſo highly concerns the Peace, Safety, or good Government of the Publick or the Honour of the King, or of his Supreme Courts of Juſtice; as the Statutes of the [e] Scandal of Great Men, of [f] Hue and Cry, and thoſe that reſtrain certain Suits in the [g] Civil or Canon Law Courts, or even in inferior [h] Common Law Courts, it ſeems to have been the general Opinion, that the Party grieved may, and it is holden [i] by ſome that he ought to bring his Action on ſuch Statute *tam pro Domino Rege quam pro ſeipſo.* And it ſeems to be taken [k] as a Ground in ſome Books, That where-ever the King is to have a Fine on an Action on a Statute, the Action muſt be ſo laid; but not where the Defendant is only to be amerced. But I much queſtion, Whether this be a good general ſettled Rule in Relation to this Matter; ſince in an Action on the Statutes of Hue and Cry, the Defendant ſhall [l] only be amerced; and yet ſuch Action may certainly be laid *tam pro Domino Rege quam pro ſeipſo.* Alſo in Actions, which by the Common Law a Man may bring *tam pro Domino Rege quam pro ſeipſo*, as in thoſe for Injuries to the Party, mixed with a high Contempt to the King, (as where a [m] Judge refuſes to allow the Benefit of the King's Pardon to a Priſoner, unleſs he will give him ſuch a Bribe; or where one makes a [n] Reſcous of one taken on a *Capias Utlagatum*, at the Suit of the Party, or the Sheriff ſuffers one taken on ſuch a *Capias* to [o] eſcape) the Plaintiff is [p] ſaid to have his Election to lay his Action this Way, but not to be compelled ſo to do. To which may be added, that the Plaintiff cannot ſo lay his Action for a Common Treſpaſs at Common Law, and yet therein the Defendant is to be fined.

[a] 2 And. 127, 128.
[b] 2 And. 128. 2 Jon. 234. Vide 1 And. 139, 140.
[c] Vide Co. Ent. 375, 376, 377.
[d] 1 Lutw. 133, 134, 138, &c. Dy. 95. pl. 36. 346. pl. 9. 1 And. 139, 140. Long quinto Ed. 4. 117. b. 118. a.
[e] 4 Co. 13. a. 12 Co. 134.
[e] 4 Co. 13. a. 12 Co. 134. Hetl. 122. Quære 1 Sid. 233. 1 Lev. 148.
[f] Raſt. Ent. 406, 407. Co. Ent. 348, &c.
[g] Raſt. Ent. 226. Diſmes 23. b. pl. 1. 24. a. pl. 2. Cro. Jac. 134. Dy. 159. b. 1 Ro. Re. 203.
[h] Raſt. Ent. 433. pl. 1, 2.
[i] 4 Co. 13. a.
[k] Cro. Ja. 134. Hetl. 121. Vide Moor 911. pl. 1285.
[l] Cro. Ja. 350.
[m] 1 Rol. Ab. 1. A. pl. 1.
[n] 1 Rol. Ab. 1. A. pl. 2.
[o] 1 Rol. Re. 78. pl. 19. Cro. Jac. 360, 361, 532, 533. Cro. Eliz. 877. Parallel Caſes, Noy 22. 2 Rol. Ab. 93. pl. 14. 41 Aſſ. pl. 12. 27 Aſſ. pl. 49.
[p] Cro. Jac. 619. pl. 5.

Neither does the Opinion I would contend againſt, ſeem to be confirmed by the conſtant Courſe of Precedents; but on the contrary, many of thoſe on the Statutes againſt [a] Forcible Entries, and on the Statutes againſt [b] illegal Diſtreſſes do not lay the Action *tam pro Domino Rege quam pro ſeipſo*; and yet there are [c] Authorities in this laſt Caſe, as well as in the former, that the Defendant is liable to be fined. But the Caſe of an [d] Action on 2 & 3 *Ed.* 6. 13. wherein it ſeems clear that it is not neceſſary to lay the Action *tam pro Domino Rege quam pro ſeipſo*, does not ſeem to come up to the Point; becauſe it is generally holden, that the Defendant is only amerceable in ſuch Action, being in Nature of an Action of Debt, and not finable, as it is ſaid [e] that he may be in an Indictment or Information grounded on the [f] Contempt of the Statute.

Sect. 18. As to the ſecond Particular, *viz.* What ought to be the Form of ſuch Information or Action: Having in the precedent Chapter *Sect.* 92. endeavoured to ſhew that there is no need that ſuch Information or Action conclude *contra pacem*; and in *Sect.* 95. Whether it be neceſſary for them to conclude *in contemptum Regis*; and in *Sect.* 100. That they need not recite the Statute whereon they are grounded; and in *Sections* 101, 102, &c. What Miſ-recitals of a Statute will be fatal; and in *Sect.* 110, 111, &c. How far it is neceſſary to bring the Caſe within the very Words of the Statute; and in *Sect.* 116, 117. How far it is neceſſary to conclude *contra formam Statuti*; and in *Sect.* 115. In what Caſes one may have Judgment on a Statute, in an Action brought at Common Law; I ſhall in this Place obſerve only theſe following Particulars:

Sect. 19. *Firſt*, If an Information contain ſeveral Offences againſt a Statute, and be well laid as to ſome of them, but defective as to the reſt, the Informer may have Judgment for ſo much as is well laid. [g] As where the Words of the Statute are fully purſued in the Deſcription of ſome of the Offences and not of others; [h] or where ſome of the Times that the Defendant hath offended againſt the Statute are expreſſed with convenient Certainty, and others not; as where it is alledged that the Defendant, for eleven Months, and more, from 10 *September* in ſuch a Year unto 9 *September* in the Year following, uſed a Trade, without having been an Apprentice, &c. or was abſent from Church, &c. in which Caſes Judgment ſhall be given for the eleven Months. But if the whole Time be expreſſed inconſiſtently; as that the Defendant was an Offender eleven Months, from the firſt of *November* in ſuch a Year to the firſt of *Auguſt* following, the whole is void for the Repugnancy, as hath been more fully ſhewn, *Ch.* 25. *Sect.* 62.

Sect. 20. *Secondly*, It ſeems to be ſettled at this Day, That it is in the Election of him who brings an Action on a penal Statute, which gives one Moiety of the Forfeiture to the King, and another to the Informer, either to have a Writ againſt the Defendant, *Quod reddat* [i] *Domino Regi & A. B. qui tam, &c. quas eis debet*; or to have it in this Form, *Quod reddat A. B. qui tam, &c. quas ei debet.* Alſo it ſeems to be ſettled, That whether the Writ be in the one Form, or the other, it is well purſued by a Declaration in the Name of the Plaintiff only. [k] Alſo it ſeems to be doubtful, whether there be any Neceſſity that either the Writ, or Count, in any ſuch Action, do expreſs that it is brought by or for the King, as well as the Party, as hath been more fully ſhewn in the 17th *Section*; and there is a [l] Precedent of ſuch an Action brought in the King's Name by *A. B. qui pro ſeipſo in hac parte ſequitur.* But it ſeems [m] agreed, that

[a] Co. Ent. 44. b. 146. a. Precedents both Ways.
[b] Raſt. Ent. 226. b. pl. 1. 2 Inſt. 132, 133.
[c] Co. Ent. 45. b. 35 H. 6. 6. 2 Inſt. 131. 1 Rol. A. 222. pl. 12, 13. Quære Dy. 177. 1 Danv. 460. pl. 12. Cro. Ca. 559, 560.
[d] Moore 911. pl. 1285. 2 Rol. Abr. 223. pl. 17. Cro. El. 621. Hetl. 121, 122.
[e] Moor 911. pl. 1285. Vide Cro. Ja. 538, 631.
[f] Vid. Sav. 62.
[g] Cro. Jac. 104.
[h] 1 Sid. 368. 2 Keb. 366, 367. 2 Rol. A. 696. pl. 7. Cro. Jac. 529, 530. Cro. El. 835.
[i] 1 Jon. 261, 262. Cro. Ca. 256. Pl. Com. 77, 78. Dy. 95. pl. 36. 3 Lev. 374, 375. Quære Daliſ. 66, 67. Moor 64, 65. Bro. Act. ſur le Statute, 4. 27 H. 8. 23. pl. 20. pl. 5.
[k] Bro. Act. popular, 5. Long quinto Ed. 4. 117. b. 118. a. See Raſt. Ent. 686. Vit. 1. 427. pl. 4. 428.
[l] Raſt. Ent. 427. pl. 3.
[m] Jo. 261, 262. Cro. Ca. 256. Co. Entr. 371. b.

every Information must be in this Form, That the Informer *tam pro Domino Rege quam pro seipso sequitur*, even where it is brought on a Statute which gives one third Part of the Penalty to a third Person. But I find some Difference as to the Forms of such Informations, as to some other Respects; for sometimes they say, [a] that the Action accrues to the Informer *qui tam*, *&c.* to demand the Sum forfeited, for the King and himself; and [b] sometimes that it accrues to the King, and to the Informer, *qui tam*, *&c.* and [c] sometimes, that it accrues to the King, and to *J. S. &c.* (*viz.* where the Statute divides the Penalty into three Parts, *&c.*) and also to the Informer, *qui tam*, *&c.* and sometimes they have no [d] Clause at all of this Kind. And [e] *Quære*, If it be not fatal to have any such Clause where the Penalty is not recoverable by the Information, but requires a subsequent one, grounded on the Conviction? Also, sometimes such Informations pray Process against the Defendant, to bring him in to [f] Answer to the Informer, *qui tam*, *&c.* only; sometimes [g] to answer *tam Domino Regi quam A. B. qui tam*, *&c.* and [h] sometimes to answer *de & super præmissis* generally, without expressing to whom.

Sect. 21. *Thirdly*, Regularly it is safest for every such Information, or Action, to demand the very Sum due to the Informer, and neither more or less; for it hath been adjudged, [i] That if an Action on a Statute demand the whole Forfeiture for the Informer, where the Statute gives Part of it to the King, it is insufficient: Also it hath been holden, [k] That if the Information make no Demand at all, or demand more or less for the Party than appears to be his Due, it is insufficient as to him; yet [l] perhaps it may be good as to the Share of the Forfeiture given to the King. Also it hath been [m] adjudged, That it is sufficient to demand the Share due to the Informer, without making any Mention of that due to the King: Also, [n] where the *quantum* of the Forfeiture depends upon the Finding of the Jury, as it does on the Statute of *Forestalling*, it hath been adjudged sufficient to leave a Blank for the Sum. Also it hath been [o] adjudged, That a Popular Action may conclude *ad grave damnum*, without adding *of the Plaintiff*; because every Offence, for which such Action is brought, is supposed to be a general Grievance to every Body.

Sect. 22. *Fourthly*, It is enacted by 18 *Eliz.* 5. *Par.* 1. *That none shall be admitted or received to pursue against any Person or Persons, upon any penal Statute, but by Way of Information or Original Action, and not otherwise.* And it hath been adjudged, That no Popular Action, since this Statute, can be brought on a former Statute, either by [p] Bill in the King's Bench, or by [q] Plaint in an Inferior Court, but only by Original Writ, or Information; whether the Statute on which such Action is grounded, [r] inflict a Penalty generally, without saying how it shall be recovered, or expresly give a Recovery by Bill or Plaint, *&c.* (as that of 4 & 5 *Ph. & M.* against [s] making Kerseys, without having served an Apprenticeship; and that of 5 *Eliz.* 4. against [t] following any other Trade without having served an Apprenticeship.) Yet the contrary hath been since expresly adjudged [u] as to such former Statutes as expresly give a Recovery by Bill or Plaint, because the Statute of 18 *Eliz.* doth not mention original Writs, but original Actions; and a Suit by Bill or Plaint is an [x] original Action in the Court in which it is commenced, and therefore may reasonably seem to be only within the Intent of the Statute, where it is removed into a Superior Court, and there proceeded upon. And if this be

[a] Co. Ent. 370. b. Rast. Ent. 430. pl. 13, 14. 431. b. pl. 15. 463. b. 5.
[b] Co. Ent. 369. a. 366. a. b. 365. a. Rast. 208. b.
[c] Co. Ent. 371. b. Vide 2 Keb. 820. 2 Mod. 100.
[d] Co. Ent. 370. a. 364. a. b.
[e] 1 Lutw. 162. Vide supra B. 1 Ch. 8. Sect. 10.
[f] Co. Ent. 364. b.
[g] Co. Ent. 370. a. 369. a. 365. a. 366. a. b.
[h] Co. Ent. 371. b. 372. a.
[i] Bro. Action sur le Statute, 4. 27 H. 8. 23. pl. 20. Vide Hob. 245.
[k] Hob. 245. Vide Cro. Ca. 330, 331.
[l] Cro. Ca. 330, 331.
[m] 1 Jon. 156, 157.
[n] 1 Jo. 156, 157.
[o] Bro. Action Popular, 2.
[p] Cro. Eliz. 76, 77. Mo. 247. pl. 390. 3 Inst. 194.
[q] Cro. Eliz. 544. pl. 14.
[r] 23 H. 6. 10. Cro. El. 76, 77. Mo. 247. pl. 390. 3 Inst. 194.
[s] 4 & 5 Ph. & M. 5. par. 32, 33, 34. 6 Co. 19. b. Mo. 412. pl. 565.
[t] 5 El. 4. par. 31, 39. Cro. El. 544. pl. 14. Noy 60.
[u] 1 Rol. Abr. 537. pl 8, 9.
[x] Vide 2 Danv. Abr. 279, 280. 3 Leon. 237.

the

the Meaning of the Statute, I ſee not how any Suit whatever, by Bill or Plaint on any penal Statute, can be within the Purview of it, while ſuch Bill or Plaint continue in the Court in which they were commenced, whether the Statute on which they are brought do expreſly mention them, or leave the Method of ſuing to the general Conſtruction of Law. To which may be added, That the Statute 21 *Jac.* 1. 4. *Par.* 1. ſeems to ſuppoſe, that Actions on penal Statutes may indifferently be brought by Writ, Plaint, Bill, or Information; for the Words are, *That all Offences hereafter to be committed againſt any penal Statute, for which any Common Informer or Promoter may lawfully ground any Popular Action, Bill, Plaint, Suit, or Information, before Juſtices of Aſſiſe,* &c. *ſhall be commenced,* &c. *by way of Action, Plaint, Bill, Information, or Indictment in the proper County, before the Juſtices of Aſſiſe, &c.* However it ſeems clear, [a] That no Suit, by Bill or Plaint, by a Party grieved, ſuing upon a Clauſe, either expreſly or impliedly relating to himſelf only, is within the ſaid Statute of 18 *El.* For it is expreſly provided, *Par.* 6. *That it ſhall not reſtrain any certain Perſon, Body Politick or Corporate, to whom, or to whoſe Uſe, any Forfeiture is limited by any Statute, and not generally to any Perſon that will ſue; but that every ſuch Perſon may ſue as before.* [b] But where the Party particularly grieved by an Offence againſt a Statute, ſues for a Forfeiture generally limited to any one who will ſue for it, he ſeems to be as much within the Reſtraint of the ſaid Statute, as if he were not the Party grieved.

[a] Cro. El. 434. pl. 45, 645. pl. 53. Vide Cro. El. 76, 77. 3 Leon. 237.

[b] Cro. El. 76, 77. Vide 3 Leon. 237.

Sect. 23. *Fifthly,* [c] In an Action on a Statute, which requires ſome Officers at one certain Time after their Admiſſion, and others at another, to qualify themſelves by certain Acts, it is ſafeſt, expreſly to ſhew the Time when the Defendant was admitted to his Office, and that he neglected to qualify himſelf in the Time limited; and alſo, That he actually exerciſed his Office after ſuch Neglect.

[c] Lutw. 162.

Sect. 24. *Sixthly,* It is ſaid, [d] That the Fact is ſufficiently alledged after a *quod cum* in an Action on a Statute, but not in an Information.

[d] Show. 337.

Sect. 25. As to the third Particular, *viz.* In what Courts ſuch an Information or Action may be brought: Having already, *Ch.* 5. *Sect.* 33. endeavoured to prove, that where a Statute appoints that a Penalty ſhall be recovered in any of the King's Courts of Record, the Offence may be indicted before Juſtices of *Oyer* and *Terminer,* tho' not in a Court-Leet, or of [e] Pie-powders, or ſuch others, inſtituted for ſpecial Purpoſes; and intending under the next Particular, incidentally to conſider what Suits may be brought in the Courts of *Weſtminſter-Hall,* on penal Statutes; I ſhall only take Notice in this Place, That where a Statute limits Suits by an Informer *qui tam* to other Courts, yet any [f] one may, by Conſtruction of Law, exhibit an Information in the Exchequer for the whole Penalty for the Uſe of the King.

Contra Hut. 99. 1 Jo. 193. Lit. 163. Vide Cro. Ca. 112. 1 Vent. 8.

[e] Cro. El. 530. pl. 59. 6 Co. 20. a.

[f] 2 And. 127, 128. Cro. Jac. 178, 179.

Sect. 26. As to the fourth Particular, *viz.* in what County ſuch Information or Action may be brought: It is enacted by 31 *El.* 5. *That in any Declaration, or Information,* ([g] *not being exhibited by ſuch Officers of Record, as had in Reſpect of their Offices, before the Time of the ſaid Statute, lawfully uſed to exhibit Informations, or ſue upon penal Laws; and not* [h] *concerning Champerty, buying of Titles, or Extortion, or the King's Cuſtoms,* &c. *or Uſury, or Foreſtalling,* &c.) *the Offence againſt any penal Statute ſhall not be laid to be done in any other County but where the Matter alledged to be the Offence, was in Truth done: And that the Defendant may traverſe, and alledge, That the Offence ſuppoſed to be committed, was not committed in the County*

[g] Parag. 3.

[h] Parag. 4. B. 1. Ch. 80. Sect. 47.

where it is alledged; which being tried for the Defendant, or if the Plaintiff be thereupon nonſuit, the Plaintiff ſhall be barred in that Action or Information.

Sect. 27. It is further enacted, *Par.* 7. *That all Suits for uſing unlawful, or not uſing lawful Games, or for not having Bows or Arrows, or for uſing a Trade without having been brought up in it, ſhall be ſued and proſecuted in the General Quarter-Seſſions of the Peace, or Aſſiſes of the ſame County, where the Offence ſhall be committed, or otherwiſe enquired of, heard and determined in the Aſſiſes, or General Quarter-Seſſions of the Peace of the ſame County where ſuch Offence ſhall be committed, or in the Leet within which it ſhall happen and not in any wiſe of the ſame County, where ſuch Offence ſhall happen, or be committed.*

In the Conſtruction of this Statute, the following Particulars ſeem moſt remarkable:

Sect. 28. *Firſt*, That it hath been adjudged, That the Defendant can have no Advantage of the above-recited Clauſe, which appoints, That all Offences againſt penal Statutes ſhall be laid in the proper Counties, but [a] only by way of Plea; and this Conſtruction ſeems very agreeable to the Purport of the ſaid Clauſe; the Words whereof are, *That the Defendant may traverſe the County*, &c. *which being tried for him, or if the Plaintiff be thereupon nonſuit, the Plaintiff ſhall be barred*, &c. But *this Point is otherwiſe ſettled by* 21 Jac. 1. 4. *Par.* 3.

[a] 2 And. 180, the contrary adjudged. Cro. El. 735, 736.

Sect. 29. *Secondly*, That the ſaid Clauſe extends [b] not to any Suit by a Party grieved, or by the [c] Attorney General, but only to thoſe brought by common Informers.

[b] Cro. El. 645. pl. 53.
[c] 1 Vent. 8. Cro. Ja. 178.

Sect. 30. *Thirdly*, That the laſt recited Clauſe, concerning Suits for uſing a Trade without having been brought up in it, *&c.* which are appointed to be brought at the Aſſiſes, or Seſſions, in the proper County, and not in any wiſe out of the County, reſtrains not an Information in the [d] King's Bench, or Exchequer, for ſuch Offence happening in the ſame County where thoſe Courts are ſitting; for the negative Words of the Statute are not, That ſuch Suits ſhall not be brought in any other Court, but, That they ſhall not be brought in any other County; and the Prerogative of theſe High Courts ſhall not be reſtrained without expreſs Words. But where the Offence is in a different County, ſuch Suits, in thoſe, or any other Courts, out of the proper County, ſeem to be within the expreſs [e] Words of the Statute; Yet it was long a very great [f] Queſtion, Whether an Action of Debt or Information, in the Courts of *Weſtminſter-Hall*, were not to be conſtrued to be out of the Meaning of them: But this Point is now ſettled in the Conſtruction of the Statute of 21 *Jac.* 4. as ſhall be more fully ſhewn hereafter.

[d] Cro. Jac. 178, 179. Salk. 373. Hob. 184.
[e] Vide Hob. 184, 327. Cro. Jac. 85.
[f] 1 Keb. 584. pl. 46. 2 Keb. 99. pl. 23. 125. pl. 77. 3 Keb. 247. pl. 67. 448. pl. 8. 1 Sid. 303, 400.

Sect. 31. It is enacted by the ſaid Statute of 21 *Jac.* 1. 4. *That all Offences to be committed againſt any penal Statute, for which any Common Informer or Promoter may lawfully ground any Popular Action, Bill, Plaint, Suit or Information before Juſtices of Aſſiſe, Juſtices of* Niſi Prius *or Gaol-Delivery, Juſtices of* Oyer *and* Terminer, *or Juſtices of Peace, in their General or Quarter-Seſſions, (except Offences againſt the Statutes concerning* [g] *Recuſancy*, &c. *or Maintenance*, &c. *or the King's Cuſtoms*, &c. *or tranſporting Gold, or Silver, or Munition, or Wool, or Leather*, &c.) *ſhall be commenced, ſued, proſecuted, tried, recovered and determined, by Way of Action, Plaint, Bill, Information or Indictment before the Juſtices of Aſſiſe, Juſtices of* Niſi Prius, *Juſtices of* Oyer *and* Terminer, *and Juſtices of Gaol-Delivery, or before the Juſtices of the Peace of every County, City, Borough or Town Corporate, and Liberty, having Power to enquire of, hear and determine the ſame, in*

[g] Vide Hob. 251. & B. 1. ch. 10. S. 5. Raym. 394.

 Eng-

England *or* Wales, *wherein ſuch Offences ſhall be committed, in any of the Courts, Places of Judicature, or Liberties aforeſaid, reſpectively, only at the Choice of the Parties who ſhall commence Suit, or proſecute for the ſame, and not elſewhere, ſave only in the ſaid Counties, or Places uſual for thoſe Counties, or any of them; And that the like Proceſs in every Popular Action, Bill, Plaint, Information or Suit, to be commenced, ſued or proſecuted, by Force of, or according to the Purport of this Act, be had and awarded, to all Intents and Purpoſes, as in an Action of Treſpaſs* Vi & Armis *at Common Law. And that all, and all Manner of Informations, Actions, Bills, Plaints, and Suits whatſoever, to be commenced, ſued, proſecuted, or awarded, either by the Attorney General, or by any Officer whatſoever, or by any Common Informer, or other Perſon whatſoever, in any of his Majeſty's Courts at* Weſtminſter, *for, or concerning any the Offences aforeſaid, ſhall be void.*

Sect. 32. And it is farther enacted, *That if on the General Iſſue the Offence be not proved in the ſame County in which it is laid, the Defendant ſhall be found not Guilty*, as ſhall be more fully ſhewn under the eleventh Particular.

Sect. 33. Alſo it is farther enacted, *That no Officer ſhall receive, file, or enter of Record, any Information, Bill, or Plaint, Count or Declaration, grounded on the ſaid penal Statutes, or any of them, which by this Act are appointed to be heard and determined in their proper Counties, until the Informer or Relator hath firſt taken a Corporal Oath before ſome of the Judges of that Court, that the Offence or Offences laid in ſuch Information*, &c. *was, or were not committed in any other County than where, by the ſaid Information*, &c. *the ſame is, or are ſuppoſed to have been committed*, &c. *the ſame Oath to be there entred of Record.*

[a] 1 Salk. 372, 373. Carth. 465. 5 Mod. 425. 2 Lev. 204. 3 Inſt. 192, 193. See the contrary adjudged 1 Vent. 8. 1 Lev. 249. 3 Lev. 71. 3 Keb. 804. pl. 7. 2 Keb. 401, 447, 458. 1 Sid. 303, 400. See the ſame Caſe doubted 1 Vent. 364. 2 Lev. 204. Latch 192. Sup. Sect. 30. 1 Sid. 359, 360. 1 Lut. 165. 2 Keb. 340. pl. 10. Raym. 394.
[b] 1 Jon. 193. Sup. Sect. 30.
[c] 1 Salk. 373. pl. 14.
[d] 1 Salk. 372, 373. Carth. 465, 466.

In the Conſtruction of this Statute, I ſhall obſerve the following Particulars:

Sect. 34. *Firſt*, That as the Law is now [a] ſettled, no Action of Debt, or Information, or other Suit whatever can be brought in any Court of *Weſtminſter-Hall*, on any penal Statute, made before the ſaid Statute of 21 *Jac.* for any Offence not therein excepted, for which the Offender may be proſecuted in the Country, [b] unleſs ſuch Offence ſhall be committed in the ſame County in which ſuch Court ſhall ſit; and ſurely this cannot but be thought moſt agreeable to the Meaning as well as the Letter of the ſaid Statute; the whole Proviſion whereof would be to little Purpoſe, if ſuch Suits ſhould be conſtrued out of it. And as to the Objection, That if all Suits on penal Statutes ſhould be wholly taken from the Superior Courts, all Offences againſt them would become diſpuniſhable by the Offender's Removing himſelf out of the County wherein he committed them; becauſe the Courts in the Statute mentioned, have no Juriſdiction out of the Counties wherein they ſit; it hath been [c] anſwered, That Proceſs of Outlawry will lie againſt ſuch Offenders, by Virtue of the above-recited Clauſe of the ſaid Statute, which gives the like Proceſs in all Suits proſecuted according to the Purport of it, as in Actions of Treſpaſs at the Common Law.

Sect. 35. *Secondly*, That [d] where a Subſequent Statute gives an Action of Debt, or any other Remedy, for the Recovery of a Penalty in any Court of Record generally, it ſo far impliedly repeals the Reſtraint of 21 *Jac.* and conſequently leaves the Informer at his Liberty to ſue in the Courts of *Weſtminſter-Hall*.

Sect. 36. *Thirdly*, That the Statute of 21 *Jac.* gave [a] no Jurisdiction to the Courts therein mentioned, over any Offences, in Relation to which they had none before; and [b] therefore that Suits for such Offences must be brought in the Courts of *Westminster-Hall* in the same Manner as before.

Sect. 37. *Fourthly*, That [c] the said Statute hinders not the Removal of any Indictment into the King's Bench by *Certiorari*; after which it may be either tried there, or in the Country by *Nisi prius.*

Sect. 38. *Fifthly*, That [d] it hath been adjudged, That an Officer by receiving an Information without such a previous Oath, That the Offence arose in the same County in which it is laid, doth not make the Proceedings upon it erroneous; for the Act is only directory to the Officer, but doth not intend that such Oath should be made Parcel of the Record; and therefore the Omission of it cannot be assigned for Error; and yet the Act is express, That such Oath shall be entered of Record. But *Quære*, If the Court may not properly be [e] moved to set aside such Process, as having issued contrary to the Directions of the Statute?

Sect. 39. *Sixthly*, That no [f] Suit by a Party grieved is within the Restraint of the Statute.

Sect. 40. As to the fifth Particular, *viz.* Within what Time such Information or Action may be brought: It is to be observed, That all Popular Actions were limited to a certain Time by 7 *H.* 8. 3. But this [g] Statute being repealed by 31 *Eliz.* 5. I shall take no farther Notice of it.

Sect. 41. But it is enacted by the said Statute of 31 *El.* 5. *Par.* 5. *That all Actions, Suits, Bills, Indictments, or Informations which shall be brought for any Forfeiture upon any Statute penal, made or to be made, whereby the Forfeiture is or shall be limited to the Queen, her Heirs or Successors only, shall be brought within two Years after the Offence committed; and not after two Years. And that all Actions, Suits, Bills, or Informations, which shall be brought for any Forfeiture, upon any penal Statute, made, or to be made, except the Statutes of Tillage, the Benefit and Suit whereof is, or shall be by the said Statute, limited to the Queen, her Heirs or Successors, and to any other that shall prosecute in that Behalf, shall be brought by any Person that may lawfully sue for the same, within one Year next after the Offence committed, and in Default of such Pursuit, that then the same shall be brought for the Queen's Majesty, her Heirs or Successors, any Time within the two Years after that Year ended. And if any Action, Suit, Bill, Indictment, or Information, shall be brought after the Time so limited, the same shall be void. And it is provided, That where a shorter Time is limited by any penal Statute, the Prosecution must be within that Time.*

Sect. 42. Also it is enacted by 18 *El.* 5. *Par.* 1. *That upon every Information which shall be exhibited on any penal Statute, a Special Note shall be made of the very Day, Month, and Year of the exhibiting thereof into any Office, or to any Officer, which lawfully may receive the same, without any Antedate thereof to be made; and that the same Information be accounted and taken to be of Record, from that Day forward and not before: And that no Process be sued out upon such Information, until the Information be exhibited in Form aforesaid,* &c. *and that every Clerk making out Process contrary to this Act, shall forfeit* 40 s. &c.

Sect. 43. It is farther enacted by 21 *Jac.* 1. 5. *That no Officer shall receive, file, or enter of Record, any Information, Bill, Plaint, Count, or Declaration, grounded on any penal Statute (being* [h] *within the Provision of the said Statute of* 21 Jac.) *until the Informer or Relator hath first taken a corporal Oath, before some of the Judges of the Court, that he believes in his Conscience, the Offence*

[a] 1 Vent. 8. Cro. Ca. 112. Hutt. 98, 99.

[b] Cro. Ca. 112. Lit. Rep. 163. Hutt. 98, 99. Vide 2 Keb. 106. pl. 42.

[c] 1 Jon. 193.

[d] Cro. Ca. 316. Vide 4 Inst. 272. 2 Inst. 193.

[e] Vide Salk. 376. pl. 19. Supra Sect. 10.

[f] Cro. El. 645. Noy 71. Shower 354. 3 Leon. 237.

[g] Vide Bro. Action Popular, 6.

[h] For this Matter see the 38th Sect.

ſence was committed within a Year before the Information or Suit, within the County where the ſaid Information was commenced, &c.

In the Conſtruction of theſe Statutes, I ſhall obſerve the following Particulars;

[a] Hob. 270.

Sect. 44. *Firſt*, That [a] if an Offence prohibited by any penal Statute, be alſo an Offence at Common Law, the Proſecution of it, as of an Offence at Common Law, is no way reſtrained by any of theſe Statutes.

[b] Shower's Rep. 353, 354.

Sect. 45. *Secondly*, That if a Suit on a penal Statute be brought after the Time limited, the Defendant needs not plead the Statute, but [b] may take Advantage of it on the General Iſſue.

[c] Cro. Ca. 331. Cro. Jac. 366. Vide Dalif. 60. pl. 13.

Sect. 46. *Thirdly*, That if an Information *qui tam* be brought after the Year on a penal Statute, which gives one Moiety to the Informer, and the other to the King, it is naught only [c] as to the Informer, but good for the King.

[d] Supra Sect. 38.

Sect. 47. *Fourthly*, That the Party grieved is [d] not within the Reſtraint of theſe Statutes, but may ſue in the ſame Manner as before.

[e] Show. Rep. 353, 354.

Sect. 48. *Fifthly*, That it ſeems not [e] to be ſettled, Whether the Suing of a *Latitat* within the Year be a ſufficient Commencement of a Suit on a penal Statute, to avoid the Limitation of theſe Statutes?

[f] Show. 353, 354.

Sect. 49. *Sixthly*, That it [f] ſeems alſo to be queſtionable, Whether a Suit by a Common Informer, on a penal Statute, which firſt gives an Action to the Party grieved, and in his Default, after a certain Time, to any ony one who will ſue, be within the Reſtraint of theſe Statutes?

Sect. 50. *Seventhly*, That it ſeems queſtionable, Whether the Clauſe in 31 *El.* 5. *Par.* 4. by which it is enacted, *That nothing in the ſaid Act contained ſhall extend to Champerty, King's Cuſtoms, or Foreſtalling,* &c. *but that every ſuch Offence may be laid in any County; any Thing in the ſaid Act to the contrary notwithſtanding,* do except the ſaid Offences, out of the above-recited Clauſe, relating to the Time within which Suits on penal Statutes muſt be brought? For the Words above-mentioned, *viz. But that every ſuch Offence may be laid in any County*, ſeem to reſtrain the Generality of the precedent, which ſay, *That nothing in the Act contained ſhall extend to ſuch Offences.*

Sect. 51. As to the ſixth Particular, *viz.* What Perſons are diſabled to bring ſuch an Information or Action: It is enacted by 31 *El.* 5. *Par.* 1. *That no Perſon, other than the Party grieved, ſhall be received to inform, or ſue upon any penal Statute, that before that Time hath been for any Miſdemeanor, by any Order of any the Queen's Majeſty's Courts, ordered not to follow or purſue any Suit upon any penal Statute.*

[g] Co. Lit. 139. b. Fitz. Nonſuit, 13. Bro. Nonſuit, 68. Preroga. 116.
[h] Co. Lit. 139. b. Bro. Nonſuit, 68. Preroga. 116.

Sect. 52. As to the ſeventh Particular, *viz.* Whether there may be a Nonſuit in ſuch an Information or Action? It ſeems agreed, That notwithſtanding the King [g] cannot be nonſuit in any Information or Action wherein he himſelf is the ſole Plaintiff; yet any [h] Informer *qui tam*, or [i] Plaintiff in a Popular Action, may be nonſuit, and thereby wholly [k] determine the Suit, as well in Reſpect of the King as of himſelf: Alſo it ſeems agreed, [l] That the Attorney General may enter a *Nolle Proſequi*, (which, as [m] ſome ſay, has the Effect of a Nonſuit) to any Information or Action brought by the King only.

[i] Bro. Nonſ. 35. [k] 37 H. 6. 5. a. Bro. Nonſuit, 35 [l] Lit. 139. b. [m] Co. Litt. 139. b. Vide 1 Sid. 420. Quære Salk. 21, pl. 11.

Sect. 53. As to the eighth Particular, *viz.* Whether the Informer or Defendant may appear by Attorney? It seems agreed, That after [a] Plea pleaded to an Indictment, Information or Action, for any Crime whatsoever, under the Degree of [b] Capital, the Defendant might always, by the Favour of the Court, be permitted to appear by Attorney: Also it seems, That generally the Court might always dispense with the personal Appearance of the Defendant, even before [c] Plea pleaded, [d] except in such Cases, wherein a personal Appearance is required by some Statute, as it is in [e] *Præmunire*, *&c.* in which Cases it seems generally agreed, That an Appearance by Attorney cannot be admitted, without some special Writ or Grant to that Purpose, whether the Defendant be a Peer [f] or Commoner. It is said indeed, in *Rolle*'s *Rep.* That Sir [g] *Anthony Mildmay* was suffered to plead a Pardon to a *Præmunire* by Attorney, and no Mention is made of any such Writ or Grant: But I presume that there was a Clause to this Effect in his Pardon.

Sect. 54. It is enacted by 18 *El.* 5. Par. 1. *That every Informer, upon any penal Statute, shall exhibit his Suit in proper Person, and pursue the same only by himself, or by his Attorney in Court; and that he shall not use any Deputy or Deputies at all.*

Sect. 55. It is recited by 29 *El.* 5. Par. 21. *That divers of her Majesty's Subjects, dwelling in the remote Parts of the Realm, had been many Times maliciously troubled upon Informations and Suits, exhibited in the Courts of the King's Bench, Common Pleas, and Exchequer, upon penal Statutes, and had been drawn up upon Process out of the Countries where they dwell, and driven to attend and put in Bail, to their great Trouble, and Undoing; and for Reformation thereof, it is enacted, That if any Person or Persons shall be sued or informed against, upon any penal Law, in any the said Courts, where such Person or Persons are bailable by Law, or where, by the Leave or Favour of the Court, such Person or Persons may appear by Attorney; in every such Case, the Person or Persons so to be impleaded or sued, shall and may, at the Day and Time contained in the first Process served for his Appearance, appear by Attorney of the same Court where the Process is returnable, to answer and defend the same, and not be urged to personal Appearance, or to put in Bail for the answering such Suits.*

[a] Bro. Attorn. 53, 54, 63, 101. 9 Ed. 4. 2. pl. 8. 9 Ed. 4. 4. pl. 44. 22 Ass. pl. 73.
[b] Bro. Attor. 63.
[c] Dy. 346. 9. 1 Lev. 145. Vide 21 Ed. 4. 77. pl. 12. 7 H. 6. 21. a.
[d] Fitz. Attor. 48, 53, 104. 3 Inst. 125. 39 Ed. 3. 7. 15 H. 7. 9. pl. 12. F. N. B. 66. Lett. H. & M. Vide Bro. Attorn. 69, 81, 82. 37 H. 6. 27. b. 3 H. 7. 6. pl. 4. Cro. Jac. 462, 616. 22 Ed. 4. 33, 34.
[e] See Cases cited to Lett. d.
[f] 15 H. 7. 9. pl. 12. 39 E. 3. 7.
[g] 1 Rol. Rep. 190. Vide 2 Bulst. 299.

Sect. 56. And it is enacted by 31 *El.* 10. Par. 20. *That this shall extend only to the natural Subjects born, or to be born, within the Dominions of the Queen's Majesty, her Heirs or Successors, and to Persons made free Denizens, and to no others.*

As to the ninth Particular, *viz.* In what Cases there shall be Costs on such an Action or Information, I shall endeavour to shew,

1. Whether an Informer shall in any Case have his Costs.
2. In what Cases the Defendant shall have them.

Sect. 57. As to the first of these Particulars, I take it to be in a great Measure settled, [h] That an Informer upon a Popular Statute, shall in no Case whatsoever have his Costs, unless they be expresly given him by such Statute; for it is certain that he cannot recover them by the Common Law, for that doth not [i] give Costs in any Case: Neither can he recover them by the Statute of *Glocester*, 1. which gives the Demandant his Costs in all Cases wherein he shall recover his Damages; for this seems to suppose some Damage to have been done to the Demandant in particular, which cannot be said in any Popular Action; and therefore such Actions have always been construed to be out of the Be-

[h] 2 Keb. 781. pl. 12. 1 Rol. A. 574. pl. 4. 1 Lutw. 200, 201. 1 Vent. 133. Salk. 206. pl. 4. Contra Moor 65. pl. 175. 3 Lev. 374.
[i] 2 Inst. 288.

 nefit

[a] 2 Keb. 781. pl. 12. 1 Rol. Abr. 574. Pl. 1, 2, 3, 4. 1 Jon. 447. Cro. Ca. 559, 560. 1 Lutw. 200, 201. 2 Inſt. 289. See Carth. 230, 231. Skin. 363, 367, 368. [b] 1 Rol. Ab. 574. pl. 1. 1 Lutw. 200, 201. 10 Co. 116. Cro. Ca. 560. Salk. 206. pl. 4.

nefit of this Statute. But it ſeems agreed, [a] That an Action on a Statute, by the Party grieved, for a certain Penalty given by ſuch Statute, is within the Statute of *Glouceſter*, becauſe ſuch Penalty is intended him by way of Recompence for his particular Damage by the Offence prohibited; and if he could recover that only, and no more, by way of Coſts, it would be in moſt Caſes in vain for him to ſue for it, ſince the Coſts of Suit would exceed it. But it is ſaid, That no Coſts ſhall be recovered in an Action on a Statute, which gives no certain Penalty to the Party grieved, but only his Damages in general, *&c.* if ſuch a Statute be introductive of a new Law, and give a Remedy in a [b] Point not remediable at the Common Law. But there is not that Inconvenience in this Caſe as in the former; becauſe no certain Sum being ſpecified, the Jury may give the Plaintiff a full Satisfaction by way of Damages.

Sect. 58. As to the ſecond Particular, *viz.* In what Caſes the Defendant ſhall have Coſts: It is enacted by 18 *El.* 5. which is made perpetual by 27 *El.* 10. *That if any Informer or Plaintiff, on a penal Statute, ſhall willingly delay his Suit, or ſhall diſcontinue, or be nonſuit in the ſame, or ſhall have the Trial or Matter paſs'd againſt him therein, by Verdict or Judgment of Law, that then, in every ſuch Caſe, the ſame Informer or Plaintiff ſhall yield, ſatisfy, and pay unto the Party Defendant, his Coſts, Charges, and Damages, to be aſſigned by the Court in which the ſame Suit ſhall be attempted,* &c.

In the Conſtruction hereof, I ſhall take Notice of the following Particulars;

[c] 1 Salk. 30. 1 And. 116. Cro. El. 177. pl. 4. Noy 71. 2 Leon. 116. [d] Vide Cro. El. 177. pl. 4. [e] Hutt. 22. [f] Vide 2 Danv. Abr. 224. pl. 1, 2, 3. [g] Vide 2 Danv. 225. pl. 9.

Sect. 59. *Firſt*, That it ſeems to be agreed, That no Action on any Statute, by the Party [c] grieved, is within the Purview of this Statute, the whole Purport whereof ſeems clearly to relate only to Common Informers: Yet, if ſuch Action, by the Party grieved, be *for any Offence or Wrong* [d] *perſonal, immediately ſuppoſed to be done to the Plaintiff or Plaintiffs*; or whatſoever the Nature of the Action may be, *if the Plaintiff* [e] *might have Coſts, in Caſe Judgment ſhould be given for him*, he ſhall pay them on a Nonſuit or Verdict againſt him, *&c.* by Virtue of [f] 23 *H.* 8. 15. and [g] 4 *Jac.* 1. 3.

[h] 2 Keb. 581. pl. 42. 1 Sid. 311. [i] 2 Keb. 106. 42. Quære Hutt. 35, 36.

Sect. 60. *Secondly*, That it hath been holden, That where Judgment is given againſt an Informer, becauſe the Court in which he [h] ſues has no Juriſdiction of the Cauſe, or [i] becauſe the Statute on which he grounds his Information is diſcontinued, yet he ſhall pay Coſts within the Intent of the ſaid Statute of 18 *Eliz.* which ſhall have a liberal Conſtruction, and was intended to prevent all vexations Informations; and ſurely ſuch ill grounded Proſecutions cannot but be thought ſuch.

[k] 10 H. 7. 18. pl. 18. Br. Ley gage. 63, 106. Co. Lit. 295. [l] Vide 21 H. 7. 15.

Sect. 61. As to the tenth Particular, *viz.* Whether the Defendant, in ſuch an Action or Information, may wage his Law, or take Advantage of a Protection? It is ſaid [k] to have been ruled, That the Defendant onght not to be admitted to wage his Law in any ſuch Action or Information, becauſe they are founded on a Statute; nor do I find any Authority to the contrary. But perhaps it may be queſtioned, How far the Reaſon given for the Opinion above-mentioned may be concluſive, ſince ſuch an Action or Information doth not ſeem ſo [l] properly to be grounded on a Statute, as on the Contempt of it. But as to the Queſtion, Whether the Defendant can take Advantage of a Protection? There ſeems to be near the ſame Number of Authorities on each [m] Side. But there is no great

[m] In the Affirmative, Fitz. Protect. 98, 122. Keil. 135. b. In the Negative, Fitz. Protection, 61, 105. 21 Ed. 3. 13. pl. 12. Co. Lit. 131. Vide 2 Rolle's Abr. 323. Letter G.

Need nicely to examine these Matters, since generally it is expresly provided by penal Statutes, That neither Wager of Law, nor Protection, shall be admitted in any Suit brought upon them.

Sect. 62. As to the eleventh Particular, *viz.* In what Manner the Defendant is to plead to such an Information, or Action, I shall take it for granted, That he must answer to the whole [a] Time laid in such Information or Action; and that if he have any [b] special Matter for his Excuse or Justification, he must set it forth with all convenient Certainty; and that if he plead the General Issue to the Whole, he must depend upon it, and not [c] together with it plead also a special Plea either to the Whole or Part of the Charge; but for these Matters I shall refer the Reader to the Books which treat of Pleading in general; and in this Place shall only consider,

[a] Bridg. 115. [b] Vide Bridg. 114, 115. [c] 1 Rol. Rep. 49, 50, 134.

1. Where a prior Suit depending may be pleaded to such an Information or Action.
2. Where a Pardon, or Release, or a Recovery in a former Suit.
3. What is a good General Issue; and where it may be pleaded.

Sect. 63. As to the first Point, *viz.* Where a prior Suit depending may be pleaded to such an Information or Action: It seems agreed, [d] That where-ever any Suit on a penal Statute may be said to be actually depending, it may be pleaded in Abatement of a subsequent Prosecution, being expresly averred to be for the same Offence. [e] Neither will it be any Exception to such a Plea, That the Offence in the subsequent Prosecution is laid on a Day different from that in the former. [f] Neither doth a Mistake in such a Plea of the very Day whereon the Suit pleaded as prior was commenced, seem to be material on the Issue of *Nul tiel Record*, if it appear in Truth to have been commenced before the other, and for the same Matter. And if two Informations be exhibited on the very same Day, it seems [g] that they may mutually abate one another, because there is no Priority to attach the Right of the Suit in one Informer more than in the other. Also it seems, That an [h] Information or Bill [i] the same Day that they are filed, may be so far said to be depending, before any Process sued upon them, that they may be pleaded in Abatement of any other Suit on the same Statute. And from the same Reason it seems also, That a Writ of Debt may be so pleaded after it is returned; because then it seems to be agreed, That it may properly be said to be depending; and whether it may not also be so pleaded before it be returned, seems questionable; Because, according to some [k] Opinions, a Writ may be said to be depending as soon as purchased.

[d] Cro.El. 261. 1 Ro. Re. 49, 50, 134. [e] Cro.El. 261. Vide 1 Ro. Re. 49, 50. [f] Hob. 209. [g] Hob. 138. [h] Cro.El. 261. [i] 10 Ed. 4. 13. pl. 2. [k] Cro.El. 677. pl. 7.

Sect. 64. As to the second Point, *viz.* Where a Pardon, or Release, or a Recovery in a former Suit, may be pleaded to such an Information, or Action? It seems agreed, That notwithstanding the King have such an Interest in every penal Statute, That he may [l] proceed in a Suit brought upon it by a common Informer, after the Death, Release, or Nonsuit of such Informer, hanging the Prosecution; and may also totally prevent any such Suit, by first [m] suing for the whole Penalty himself; or may totally bar it by a Pardon or Release [n] precedent to its Commencement; yet if it be actually commenced before any Suit by the King, the Informer hath such an Interest in the Part of the Penalty assigned him

Cro. Jac. 11. 5 Co. 48. a. b. 1 Rol. Rep. 379. pl. 37. Cont. Salk. 89. pl. 11. Far. 5. 2 Ed. 4. 11. pl. 3. 7 Co. 30. a. [l] 11 Co. 65. b. 66. a. 5 Co. 48. b. Noy 100.

3 Inst. 194. 2 Bulst. 261, 262. Cro. El. 583. Moore 541. Cont. Cro. El. 138. pl. 13. 37 H. 6. 5. a. 20 H. 7. 5. b. 6. a. Bro. Attaint, 130. Vide 2 Rol. Re. 33. Hutt. 82. [m] Crompton, Jurisdiction, 38. a. 3 Inst. 194. 11 Co. 65. b. 66. a. [n] Fitz. Decies tantum, 5. Charter, 21. Bro. Action Popular, 3, 4. 1 H. 7. 3. pl. 2. 37 H. 6. 4. 3 Inst. 194. 5 Ed. 4. 2, 3.

by

by the Statute, that the King can no [a] way diſcharge, or ſuſpend the Suit, as to [b] ſuch Part. Alſo it ſeems that the King can in [c] no Caſe bar the Suit of a Party grieved, nor proceed in it after the Death of the Plaintiff, *&c.* Alſo it ſeems agreed, [d] That a Conviction or Acquittal *bona fide* in any Action or Information on a penal Statute, whether by the Party grieved, or a Common Informer, or a Releaſe *bona fide*, from the Party grieved, or Common Informer, [e] after ſuch a Conviction, hath always been a good Bar of any ſubſequent Proſecution for the ſame Offence. But for the better ſettling of theſe Matters, the Statute of 4 *H.* 7. 20. was made, by which is recited, *That it had been uſual for Offenders againſt penal Statutes, to cauſe Popular Actions to be commenced againſt them by Covin of the Plaintiffs, or elſe when ſuch Actions had been commenced againſt them, to delay the ſame either by Non-appearance, or by Traverſe; and hanging the ſame, to cauſe the like Action Popular to be brought againſt them by Covin for the ſame Cauſe and Offence, and therein by Covin of the Plaintiff to be condemned, either by Confeſſion, feigned Trial, or Releaſe, which Condemnation or Releaſe, ſo had by Colluſion and Covin, did uſe to bar the Plaintiff in the Action ſued in good Faith*; and thereupon it is enacted, *That if any Perſon ſue with good Faith any Action Popular, and the Defendant plead any Manner of Recovery of Action Popular in Bar of the ſaid Action; or elſe, that he before that Time barr'd the Plaintiff in any ſuch Action Popular, that then ſuch Plaintiff, with good Faith, may aver, That ſuch Recovery or Bar were by Covin; and if ſuch Colluſion or Covin ſo aver'd, be lawfully found, ſuch Plaintiff ſhall recover,* &c. *and the Defendant condemned of Covin or Colluſion, as aforeſaid, ſhall have two Years Impriſonment,* &c. *and that no Releaſe of any Common Perſon to any ſuch Party, whether before or after any Action Popular, or Indictment of the ſame, had, or commenced or made, hanging the ſaid Action, ſhall be any wiſe available or effectual to let or ſurceaſe the ſaid Action, Indictment, Proceſs, or Execution. Provided always, That no Plaintiff or Plaintiffs be receiv'd to aver any Covin in any Action Popular, where the Point of the ſame Action, or elſe the Covin or Colluſion, have been once tried, or lawfully found with the Plaintiff or Plaintiffs, or againſt them, by Trial of twelve Men, and not otherwiſe.*

[a] Cro. El. 138. pl. 13. 1 Leon. 119. 1 H. 7. 3. pl. 2. 37 H. 6. 4. Hutt. 82. Bro. Action Popular, 3, 4. 3 Inſt. 194. [b] Sav. 23. [c] Noy 100. Moor 58. [d] Fitz. Decies tantum, 4, 5. Bro. Action Popular, 4, 7. Cro. Jac. 480, 481, 482. 1 H. 7. 3. pl. 2. 11 Co. 65. b. 66. a. 9 Ed. 4. 4. pl. 15. [e] 2 Rol. Re. 33. Bro. Action Popular, 7. 5 Ed. 4. 2, 3.

Sect. 65. It is [f] ſaid, That if a Recovery in a former Suit be pleaded in Bar of any Popular Action, the Plaintiff may, by Reaſon of the expreſs Words of the Statute, aver, That ſuch Recovery was by Covin, without ſhewing wherein the Covin conſiſted; but otherwiſe ſuch a general Pleading would be vicious.

[f] Pl. Com. 49. b. 50.

As to the third Point, *viz.* What is a good General Iſſue, and where it may be pleaded? I ſhall obſerve the following Particulars?

Sect. 66. *Firſt*, That if the Defendant plead *Nil debet* to an Action or Information *qui tam*, it is ſafeſt to ſay, That he owes [g] nothing to the Informer, nor to the King; becauſe if he only plead, that he owes nothing to the Informer, it may be objected, [h] That the whole Declaration is not anſwered, which makes a Demand for the King as well as the Informer: Yet perhaps it may be a good Anſwer [i] to ſuch Objection, That in the Plea, that he owes nothing to the Informer, it is neceſſarily implied that he owes nothing to the King, and therefore needs not be expreſſed.

Sect. 67. *Secondly*, That if there be more than one Defendant, they ought [k] not to plead jointly that they are Not guilty, but ſeverally That neither they, nor any of them, are guilty, *&c.*

[g] Vide Co. Ent. 165. b. 167. b. [h] Hob. 327, 328. 1 Vent. 122. [i] 3 Lev. 375. Vide Cro. Ca. 10, 11. [k] 21 H. 6. 20. pl. 37. Fitz. Decies tantum, 6. 2 Rol. Abr. 707 pl. 48.

Sect. 68. *Thirdly*, That where-ever the Breach of the Statute, whereon ſuch Suit is grounded, is alledged only from a Matter *in Pais*, and not from Matter of Record, the Defendant [a] may plead, that he owes nothing, or that he is not guilty, *&c.* but if it be alledged from a Matter of Record, ſuch a Plea is not good; becauſe a Record is not triable by the Country, but only by itſelf.

[a] 21 H. 7. 14. pl. 20. Bro. Iſſues joins, 23. Vide 21 Jac. 14. par. 4.

Sect. 69. *Fourthly*, That if the Defendant be within the Benefit of any *Proviſo* of a penal Statute, he might, according to ſome, always give it in [b] Evidence on the General Iſſue, in a Suit on ſuch Statute: But if he have Matter in his Diſcharge depending on a ſubſequent Statute, it hath been holden [c] (even ſince the Statute of 21 *Jac.* 1. 4.) That he muſt plead it ſpecially, and cannot give it in Evidence. But this ſeems contrary to the expreſs Purview of the ſaid Statute; by which it is enacted, *That if any Suit ſhall be brought againſt any Perſon for any Offence againſt any penal Law, either by, or on the Behalf of the King, or by any other, or on the Behalf of the King and any other, it ſhall be lawful for ſuch Defendant, to plead the General Iſſue, that he is Not guilty, or that he owes nothing, and to give ſuch ſpecial Matter in Evidence to the Jury that ſhall try the ſame, which Matter being pleaded, had been ſufficient in Law to have diſcharged the ſaid Defendant againſt the ſaid Suit, and the ſaid Matter ſhall be then as available, to all Intents and Purpoſes, as if it had been ſufficiently pleaded in Bar.*

[b] 2 Rol. Abr. 683, pl. 10, 12. Cont. pl. 11.

[c] 2 Rol. Abr. 683. pl. 13.

Sect. 70. Alſo it is enacted by the ſame Statute, *Par.* 2. *That if the Defendant to any Suit, commenced by, or on the Behalf of the King, or any other, for any Offence againſt any penal Statute, plead, That he oweth nothing, or, that he is Not guilty, and the Plaintiff or Informer, upon Evidence to the Jury, ſhall not prove the Offence laid in the ſaid Suit, and that the ſame Offence was committed in the ſame County in which it is laid, the Defendant ſhall be found Not guilty.*

Sect. 71. It is provided by the laſt Paragraph of the ſaid Statute, *That no Clauſe thereof ſhall extend to any Suit on any Law againſt Popiſh Recuſants,* &c. *or againſt Champerty,* &c. *or concerning defrauding the King of his Cuſtom,* &c. *or the tranſporting of Gold, or Silver, or Munition,* &c. *or Wool, or Leather, but that ſuch Offence may be laid in any County, at the Pleaſure of the Informer.* But *Quære*, if the laſt Words of this *Proviſo*, *viz. but that ſuch Offence may be laid in any County*, do not reſtrain the Exception intended by it to that Part of the Statute only which relates to the Laying the Offence in the proper County? For if ſo, the Defendant in a Suit on the Laws, mentioned in it, may give the ſpecial Matter in Evidence on the General Iſſue, as well as in a Suit on any other penal Statute.

Vide ſupra Sect. 50.

Sect. 72. As to the twelfth Particular, *viz.* By whom the Replication is to be made in ſuch an Information or Action: It ſeems agreed, [d] That regularly a Replication to a ſpecial Plea to an Information in the Courts of *Weſtminſter-Hall*, ſhall be made by the Attorney General only, who, in Reſpect of the King's Intereſt in the Suit, is preſumed to be moſt proper to be conſulted concerning it; and by the ſame Reaſon it [e] ſeems that ſuch Replication in a Suit before Juſtices of Aſſize, ſhall be made by the Clerk of the Aſſizes only. Alſo it is ſaid, [f] That the Replication to a General Iſſue in an Information *qui tam* in the Courts of King's Bench or Exchequer, may be made in the Name of the Attorney General only, by the Uſage of thoſe Courts. But in moſt of the [g] Precedents I can find of Actions *qui tam*, the Replication is made by the Plaintiff only. Alſo I find a Demurrer by the Informer only to a Plea in Bar to an [h] Information *qui tam*, without any Mention of the Attorney General. And if the Attorney General, *&c.* ſhall abſolutely refuſe to make a Replication to

[d] 6 Co. 20. a. Vide Cro. Jac. 538. Cro. El. 138. pl. 13. 2 Rol. Re. 33. Bro. Attaint, 127. Co. Ent. 365. a. 366. a. 367. a. 368. a. 395. a. Ra. Ent. 410 a.

[e] Vide Cro. Jac. 502.

[f] 1 And. 49.

[g] Co. Ent. 159. b. 163. a. b. 165. b. 166. a. 167. b.

[h] Co. Ent. 371 a.

[a] Vide ſupra Sect. 64. 5 Co. 48. b.

any Plea to an Information, ſurely the Informer may be [a] admitted to make it himſelf; for otherwiſe it would be in the Power of the Attorney General, *&c.* by refuſing to make a Replication, wholly to defeat the Suit.

Sect. 73. As to the thirteenth Particular, *viz.* In what Manner the Iſſue is to be joined in ſuch an Information or Action, and where it ſhall be tried: It hath been laid down [b] as a ſettled Rule, That where the King is to have no Part of the Thing demanded in an Action on a penal Statute, but only a Fine or Amercement, there is no Neceſſity either in the Joining of the Iſſue or *Venire facias*, to uſe the Words *qui tam pro Domino Rege, &c.* but that it is ſufficient ſimply to name the Party, as in Actions at Common Law; for the King ſeems to have little more Intereſt in ſuch Suits than in Actions at Law. Yet where-ever the Plaintiff may declare *tam pro Domino Rege quam pro ſeipſo*, it ſeems, [c] That it can be no Fault to uſe thoſe Words as well in the Joining of the Iſſue, *&c.* as in the Beginning of the Suit. And if the King be to have Part of the Penalty demanded, it hath been [d] adjudged to be a fatal Fault, and not amendable after Verdict, not to mention that the Plaintiff ſues *tam pro Domino Rege quam pro ſeipſo*, in the Joining of the Iſſue. But *Quære*; for there are many [e] Precedents where the Iſſues in ſuch Actions have not mentioned the Plaintiff, as ſuing for the King; but have ſimply named him by his proper Name, as in other Actions. And where he is expreſly named in the Declaration, as ſuing for the King as well as for himſelf, Why ſhould it be intended that he ſues otherwiſe in the Progreſs of the Action?

[b] Cro. Ca. 336, 337. Vide Coke's Ent. 160. b. 161. b. 164. a. 348. b. 350. b.

[c] Ra. Ent. 406. b. 407. a. Co. Ent. 349. b.

[d] 1 Vent. 122. 2 Keb. 788. Vide ſupra Sect. 17, 20.

[e] Co. Entr. 159. b. 163. a. b. 165. b. 166. a. 167. b. Vide ſupra Sect. 17, 20.

Sect. 74. As to the Place where ſuch Iſſues ſhall be tried, it is enacted by 18 *El.* 5. *That no Jury ſhall be compelled to appear in any of the Queen's Courts at* Weſtminſter, *for the Trial of any Iſſue in any Suit* (by a Common [f] Informer) *upon any penal Law, for any Offence committed above thirty Miles from the City of* Weſtminſter; *except in Caſe where the Attorney General for the Time being, for ſome reaſonable Cauſe in that Behalf to be ſhewed, ſhall require the ſame to be tried at the Bar, in any of the Courts of the Queen's Majeſty, her Heirs or Succeſſors, at* Weſtminſter *aforeſaid: Which Requeſt ſhall be noted on the Backſide of the Writ of* Diſtringas *thereupon awarded, to the End the Sheriff, or his Bailiff, may, and ſhall ſignify the ſame to the Jury that are in ſuch Caſe impanelled.*

[f] See the three laſt Sections of the Statute, and the 22d, 47th and 49th Sections of this Chapter.

Sect. 75. As to the fourteenth Particular, *viz.* Where a Verdict may be found as to Part againſt the Informer, and as to Part for him: It ſeems, [g] That regularly, if an Offence againſt a Statute be of ſuch a Nature that it may be committed by a ſingle Perſon, without the Concurrence of any other, and ſeveral Perſons be jointly charged in one Information, for one Act done by them all againſt ſuch Statute, one of them only may be found guilty, and the reſt acquitted; becauſe, tho' the Words of the Information ſeem to import a joint Charge againſt all the Defendants, yet in Judgment of Law each of them is charged ſeverally for his own Offence, which cannot but be ſeveral, whether the Act, in the doing whereof it conſiſted, were done by one or more; and accordingly the Iſſue muſt be, that [h] neither they, nor any of them, are guilty. And for the like Reaſons, if one be informed againſt for having offended againſt a Statute for more Times, or in a higher Degree than can be proved; as for not coming to Church during the Space of ten Months, where he can be proved to have been abſent but eight Months, *&c.* or for [i] ingroſſing 1000 Quarters of Wheat, where the Evidence amounts but to 700, he may be found guilty ſo far as the Evidence goes, and Not guilty for the

[g] 2 Rol. Abr. 707. pl. 45, 48. 708. pl. 50. Lane 19, 59, 60.

[h] Supra Sect. 67.

[i] 2 Rol. Abr. 707. pl. 48. Lane 59, 60.

the Reſidue; for ſuch Offences are not in the Nature of entire Contracts, which regularly muſt be fully proved in the ſame Manner as they are alledged, but are in the Nature of Treſpaſſes, which it is ſufficient to prove for any Part. But if the Offence againſt a Statute conſiſt in making a Contract contrary to the Purview of it; as in the Caſe of Uſury, it is [a] ſaid, That if it be alledged as having been made by two, it muſt be ſo proved likewiſe, becauſe it is a Rule of Law, That if Contracts be not proved as they are laid, they ſhall not be taken to be the ſame.

Sect. 76. As to the fifteenth Particular, *viz.* What Judgment on ſuch an Information or Action is good? It hath been adjudged, That where a Statute (as that of Recuſancy, for Inſtance) ordains that the Offender ſhall forfeit ſuch a Sum, and that the Sum ſo forfeited ſhall be divided into three Parts whereof one Third ſhall go to the King, and one to the Informer, and the other to the Poor, *&c.* and that if the Offender do not pay, *&c.* within ſuch a Time, that he ſhall be committed, *&c.* the Judgment on an Information *qui tam* on ſuch Statute may be general, that the [b] King and Informer ſhall recover the whole [c] Sum, without making any Mention how it ſhall be diſtributed, or that the Party ſhall be committed [d] for Non-payment, *&c.* But on ſuch an Information, if the Judgment for the Recovery of the Forfeiture be given wholly for the Informer, without any Mention of the King, it hath been holden, [e] That it is totally erroneous. Yet it hath been adjudged, That if on an Information *qui tam*, wherein, as it is laid, the Informer hath no Right to any Part, but the King ought to have the Whole, Judgment be given that the Defendant ſhall forfeit the Sum mentioned by the Statute, and that the King ſhall have one Moiety, and the Informer the other, ſuch Judgment is erroneous [f] only as to the later Part, wherein it awards to whom the Penalty ſhall go; but ſhall ſtand for the Clauſe concerning the Forfeiture, which ſufficiently entitles the King to the Whole. And it hath been adjudged, [g] That if there be no Clauſe at all concerning the Forfeiture in a Conviction on a penal Statute, but only a Judgment *Quod Convictus eſt*, it is ſufficient, for the Forfeiture is implied.

Sect. 77. As to the ſixteenth Particular, *viz.* Whether the Penalty of a penal Statute, may be compounded or granted over? It is enacted by 18 *El.* 5. *That no Informer, or Plaintiff, ſhall, or may compound or agree with any Perſon or Perſons, that ſhall offend, or that ſhall be ſurmiſed to offend againſt any Penal Statute, for an Offence committed or pretended to be committed; but after Anſwer made in Court unto the Information or Suit in that Behalf exhibited, or proſecuted: Nor after Anſwer, but by the Order or Conſent of the Court in which the ſame Information or Suit ſhall be depending; on Pain that whoſoever ſhall offend, in making of Compoſition, or other Miſdemeanor, contrary to the true Intent and Meaning of this Statute, or ſhall by Colour or Pretence of Proceſs, or without Proceſs, upon Colour or Pretence of any Matter of Offence againſt any penal Law, make any Compoſition, or take any Money, Reward, or Promiſe of Reward, for himſelf, or to the Uſe of any other, without Order or Conſent of ſome of her Majeſty's Courts at* Weſtminſter, *and ſhall be thereof convict, ſhall ſtand on the Pillory,* &c. *and for ever be diſabled to purſue, or be Plaintiff or Informer in any Suit or Information upon any Statute Popular or Penal; and ſhall alſo forfeit ten Pounds,* &c.

Sect. 78. It ſeems [h] clear, both from the Preamble and the whole Tenor of the Statute, that it extends only to Suits by Common Informers, and not to thoſe by a Party grieved.

[a] Lane 19, 59, 60.

[b] 1 And. 139, 140. Vide Style Rep. 329, 330.

[c] 2 Rol. Abr. 102. Lett. K. Vide 2 Keb. 820. pl. 30.

[d] 1 And. 139, 140.

[e] Style's Rep. 329, 330.

[f] 2 And. 128, 129, 130.

[g] Dominus Rex verſus Hawkins, Mich. 3 Geo. 1.

[h] See the three laſt Sections of the Statute, and the 22d, 47th, and 49th Sections of this Chapter.

Sect. 79.

[a] Hutt. 35. *Sect.* 79. But it hath been [a] holden, That it extends as well to ſubſequent penal Statutes, as to thoſe which were in Being when it was made. [b] 1 Keb. 106. pl. 42. 1 Sid. 311. [b] And alſo that it extends to the compounding of Suits commenced in Courts which have no Juriſdiction, as much as if they had a Juriſdiction.

Sect. 80. It is enacted and declared by 21 *Jac.* 1. 3. (which, as to theſe Matters, appears both by the Preamble, and Body of the Statute, and many [c] 7 Co. 36, 37. Moore 763. Hob. 183. 3 Inſt. 186, 187. 2 Rol. Abr. 187. pl. 12. ſeems contrary. former [c] Reſolutions, to be made in Affirmance of the Common Law) *That all Commiſſions, Grants, Licences, Charters, and Letters Patents, made or to be made to any Perſon or Perſons, Bodies politick or corporate whatſoever, of Power, Liberty, or Faculty, to diſpenſe with any others, or to give Licence, or Toleration, to do, uſe, or exerciſe any Thing againſt the Tenour or Purport of any Law or Statute, or to give or make any Warrant for any ſuch Diſpenſation, Licence, or Toleration to be had or made, or to agree, or compound with any others for any Penalty or Forfeitures limited by any Statute, or of any Grant or Promiſe of the Benefit, Profit, or Commodity of any Forfeiture, Penalty, or Sum of Money, that is or ſhall be due by any Statute, before Judgment thereupon had, and all Proclamations,* &c. *any way tending to the furthering of the ſame, are altogether contrary to the Laws of this Realm, and ſhall be utterly void,* &c. And it is farther enacted, *That all ſuch Commiſſions,* &c. *ſhall be examined, heard, tried and determined by, and according to the Common Laws of this Realm, and not otherwiſe.*

Sect. 81. But it is provided, *That this Act ſhall not extend to any Warrant or Privy Seal, made or directed by the King to the Juſtices of either Bench, or the Exchequer, or of Aſſiſe, or of* Oyer *and* Terminer *and Gaol-Delivery, or Peace, or other Juſtices for the Time being, having Power to hear and determine Offences done againſt any penal Statute, to compound for the Forfeitures of any penal Statutes, depending in Suit and Queſtion before them, or any of them reſpectively, after Plea pleaded by the Defendant.*

[d] 3 Inſt. 178. *Sect.* 82. It is ſaid by Sir [d] *Edward Coke*, That ſuch Juſtices, by ſuch Warrant, *&c.* can make ſuch Compoſition for the Uſe of the King only; However it ſeems, That by 18 *El.* they may give Leave to an Informer [e] Vide ſupra Sect. 64, 65, 66. to [e] compound with a Defendant after Plea pleaded.

Sect. 83. Alſo it is provided, *That the ſaid Act ſhall not extend to any Grants, Letters Patents, or Commiſſion heretofore granted, of, for, or concerning the licenſing of the keeping of any Tavern or Taverns, or ſelling, uttering or retailing of Wines to be drunk, or ſpent in the Manſion-Houſe or Houſes, or other Place, in the Tenure or Occupation of the Party or Parties, ſo ſelling or uttering the ſame; or for or concerning the making of any Compoſitions for ſuch Licences, ſo as the Benefit of ſuch Compoſitions be reſerved and applied, to and for the Uſe of his Majeſty, his Heirs or Succeſſors, and not to the private Uſe of any other Perſon or Perſons.*

CHAP. XXVII.

Of Process.

AND Now I am come to ſuch Proceſs as is to be awarded upon an Appeal, Indictment, or Information; for the better Underſtanding the Nature whereof, (having premiſed that it ſeems plain, from the Nature of the Thing, that there can be [a] no Need of it where the Defendant is preſent in Court, but only where he is abſent,) I ſhall conſider it,

[a] Lamb. B. 4. Ch. 8. Dalt. Ch. 132. Cromp. 150. a.

1. In General; without any particular Regard to Proceſs of Outlawry.
2. In Particular; with Regard to ſuch Proceſs only.

And *Firſt*, I ſhall examine the Nature of ſuch Proceſs in general, without any particular Regard to Proceſs of Outlawry, under the following Particulars;

1. Where it is well awarded into a County different from that wherein the Court ſits from which it is awarded.
2. What Kind of Proceſs ſhall iſſue on an Indictment, Appeal, and Information.
3. In what Manner it is to be executed.
4. What is required by Statute, in Relation to Proceſs on Informations.
5. What is the Proper Proceſs on a Default.
6. What after a Removal by *Certiorari.*
7. Where it ſhall be ſaid to be diſcontinued, or miſcontinued, or put without Day.
8. How far an Error in Proceſs is fatal.

Sect. 1. As to the firſt Particular, *viz.* Where ſuch Proceſs is well awarded into a County different from that wherein the Court ſits from which it is awarded: It ſeems [b] to be a good general Rule, That no Proceſs without Writ can be well awarded on any Indictment, or Appeal, *&c.* from any Court, out of the County wherein it ſits: But it ſeems agreed, [c] That ſuch Proceſs by Writ may, by the Common Law, be well awarded into any County of *England*, either by the Court of King's Bench, or by Juſtices of *Eyre*, upon an Indictment, *&c.* before them. Alſo it is clear, That Juſtices of *Oyer* and *Terminer* have the ſame Power, in Relation to Perſons indicted or appealed before them of Felony, by Force of 5 *Ed.* 3. 11. whereby it is recited, *That in Times paſt ſome Perſons appealed or indicted of divers Felonies in one County, or outlawed in the ſame County, had been dwelling, or received in another County, whereby ſuch felonious Perſons indicted and outlawed, had been encouraged in their Miſchief, becauſe they might* not

[b] 19 Aſſ. pl. 6. Fitz. Barr. 279. Bro. Juriſ. 105. Vide Fitz. Aſſiſe, 446.

[c] S.P.C. 146. a. H. P. C. 196. 2 H. H. P. C. 198, 199. Vide ſupra Ch. 24. Sect. 22.

not be attached in another County; and thereupon it is enacted, *That Justices assigned to hear and determine such Felonies, shall direct their Writs to all the Counties of* England, *where need shall be to take such Persons indicted.*

Sect. 2. It is observable, That the Mischief complained of in the Preamble of this Statute relates as well to Persons appealed, as to those who are indicted; and therefore it seems reasonable to construe them also to be within the Meaning of the Purview, though they be not within the Letter of it, which extends only to Persons indicted.

a Vide Crom. Justice 149. b. Lamb. B. 4. Ch. 8. b Vide supra Ch. 8. Sect. 33.

Sect. 3. It seems questionable, [a] Whether Justices of Peace, being assigned [b] by their Commission to hear and determine Felonies, are as well within the Meaning as Letter of this Statute? For, as on the other Side it may be argued, That this being a remedial Law, ought to receive as favourable and large an Interpretation as the Words will admit; so on the other Side it may be said, That the Preamble of the Statute making Mention as well of Persons appealed, as of those who are indicted, cannot be thought to have any manner of Regard to Justices of the Peace, before whom no Appeal lies; and nothing can be more reasonable than to construe one Part of a Statute by another.

Sect. 4. But by 22 *H.* 8. 5. Par. 5. *Justices of Peace of the Shire,* &c. *wherein any decayed Bridge shall be,* &c. *shall make Process into every Shire within this Realm, against any Persons who ought to amend such Bridge, being presented before them to be decayed,* &c. Also they have the like Power by other Statutes in many other Cases, for which, not being so proper for this Treatise, I shall refer the Reader to the [c] Authors which more particularly treat of the *Office of a Justice of Peace.*

c Crompton's Justice 151, 152. Lamb. B. 4. Ch. 8.

As to the second Particular, *viz.* What Kind of Process shall issue on an Appeal, Indictment, and Information; I shall endeavour to shew,

First, Where such Process ought to have the Clause of *Non omittas.*
Secondly, In whose Name, and under what *Teste*, it is to be made.
Thirdly, What is the proper Process on Indictments for Crimes of an Inferior Nature.
Fourthly, What is the proper Process on Informations.
Fifthly, What is the proper Process on Appeals, and on Indictments of Treason, Felony and Mayhem.
Sixthly, How many Days there ought to be between the *Teste* and Return of such Process.

Sect. 5. As to the first Point, *viz.* Where such Process ought to have the Clause of *Non omittas:* It is laid [d] down in some Books as a general Rule, That in every Suit, to which the King is a Party, the Process ought to have the Clause *Non omittas propter aliquam libertatem, &c.*

d Crompton's Just. 149. b. Lamb. B. 4. Ch. 8. Dalt. Ch. 132. 41 Ass. 17. Bro. Franc. 18. Process, 102. Fitz. Prerog. 21. 1 H. H. P. C. 577. 2 H. H. P. C. 202. Vide infra Sect. 17.

Sect. 6. But I do not find this Rule observed as to all Kinds of Suits by the King, in the best Precedents; for though the said Clause is mentioned in every Award of Process on [e] Indictments (except only [f] one) and even on [g] Informations *qui tam*, in *Coke's Entries*; yet it is omitted in all the Awards of Process I can find on Informations of [h] Intrusion on the King's Lands, or of [i] Trover and Conversion of his Goods; and yet these are at least as much, if not more properly, the Suits of the King, than the former.

e Coke's Ent. from 352 to 363. f Co. Ent. 358. b. g Co. Ent. 365. a. 366. a. 367. a. 368. a. h Co. Entr. 372. a. 376. a. 379. a. 381. a. 387. b. 1 Co. 16, 17. i Coke's Entr. 390. b.

Sect. 7. As to the second Point, *viz.* In whose Name, and under what *Teste* such Process is to be made. It is expresly [a] enacted by 27 *H.* 8. 24. *Par.* 3. *That all Manner of Process upon Indictments of Treason, Felony, or Trespass to be made in every County-Palatine, and other Liberty, shall be made only in the Name of the King; and that every Person having such County-Palatine, or any other such Liberty, to make Process,* &c. *shall make the* Teste *in the Name of the Person that hath such County-Palatine,* &c.

Sect. 8. And as to Process on Indictments in any other Courts, there can be no [b] Doubt but that it ought also to be in the Name of the King: And if it issue from the Court of King's Bench, it [c] seems clear, That it ought to be under the *Teste* of the Chief Justice, or of the Senior Judge of the Court, if there be no Chief Justice; and if it issue from any other Court, there seems to be the same Reason that it ought to be under the *Teste* of the first in the Commission; and that such a *Teste* will be sufficient. It is holden indeed by [d] *Lambard,* That every Process on an Indictment before Justices of Peace, ought to be under the *Teste* of some two Justices: But there are Precedents to the contrary in [e] *Crompton;* and even in [f] *Lambard.* Neither do the [g] Authorities cited by *Lambard* seem to come up fully to his Point; for they seem to amount to no more than this, That one Justice of the Peace cannot award Process on an Indictment, but that two of them at the least must do it, and that sitting the Court in the Sessions: And indeed it seems plainly to appear, from the [h] Commission it self, That one Justice has no Authority either to take an Indictment, or to proceed upon it: But I do not see the Consequence, That because an Indictment cannot be taken, nor proceeded upon, by less than two, therefore the Process cannot be tested by less than two.

Sect. 9. As to the third Point, *viz.* What is the proper Process on Indictment for Crimes of an inferior Nature: It seems clear, both from the [i] Books which speak of this Matter, and the constant Course of [k] Precedents, That a *Venire facias* (which is but in Nature of a Summons to cause the Party to appear) is a proper Process to be first awarded on an Indictment for any Crime (whether against the Common Law, or Statute,) under the Degree of Treason, Felony, or [l] Maihem, except in such Cases wherein other [m] Process is directed by some Statute. Also such a *Venire* seems to be the first proper Process on an [n] Information in the Crown-Office, for a Debt claimed by the King, as having been forfeited by a *Felo de se.*

Sect. 10. If it appear by the [o] Return to such *Venire,* that the Party has Lands in the County whereby he may be distrained, the [p] Distress infinite shall be awarded from Time to Time, till he do appear, and by Force hereof he shall [q] forfeit on every Default so much as the Sheriff shall return upon him in Issues. But if a *Nihil* be returned on such a *Venire,* a [r] *Capias, Alias* and *Pluries,* shall issue, *&c.*

Sect. 11. It is said in *Fitzherbert*'s [s] *Abridgment, That in* Oyer *and* Terminer, *if the Party at the first Day make Default, a Man may have a* Venire Facias, *or a* Pone per vadios, &c. *at his Election;* the Meaning whereof perhaps may be this, That if the Defendant, being summoned on the *Venire,* do not appear, the Prosecutor may either take out a second *Venire,* or a [t] *Pone per vadios, &c.* But I cannot [u] find any express Authority, or Precedent, to justify the making either a *Pone per vadios, &c.* or a *Capias,*

[a] Vide 4 Inst. 205.

[b] Vide Lamb. B. 4. Ch. 8. Dalt. Just. Ch. 132.

[c] Finch of Law 436. Cro. Ca. 393. 2 H. H. P. C. 199.

[d] Lamb. B. 4. Ch. 8. See Dalt. Just. Ch. 132.

[e] Crompton, 232, 233.

[f] See the printed Precedents in the End of his Eirenarcha.

[g] Bro. Peace, 6, 7. Vide 14 H. 7. 8. b. Crompt. 151. b.

[h] Vide supra Ch. 8. Sect. 24, 25. Dalt. Ch. 132.

[i] Crompt. 150. b. 151. Dalt. ch. 132. Lamb. B. 4. Ch. 8. Fitz. Assise, 17. 32 H. 6. 10. b.

[k] Co. Entr. 358. pl. 10. 362. pl. 17, 18. 363. a.

[l] Finch of Law 356.

[m] Vide supra Ch. 23. Sect. 156. Ra. Ent. 263. pl. 11.

[n] 1 Saund. 271.

[o] Crompt. 150, 151. Lambard B. 4. Ch. 8. Dalt. Just. Ch. 132. Dalt. Sheriff, Ch. 34, 78.

[p] Register Judicial 1. Finch 352, 353. Dalton's Sheriff, Ch. 34, 78. Dalt. Just. Ch. 132.

[q] Vide 2 Danv. Abr. 296. f. 5. 2 Inst. 453, 454.

[r] Lamb. B. 4. Ch. 8. Crompt. 150, 151. Fitz. Trespass, 232. Dalt. Just. Ch. 132. 11 H. 6. 4. a. Finch of Law 352.

[s] Fitz. Process, 188.

[t] Vide Finch of Law 352.

[u] Vide supra Sect. 9, 10. Fitz. Pro. 213. Tres. 232. 29 Ed. 4. 18. a. b.

pias, the first Process on any Indictment under the Degree of Maihem, or Felony, *&c.* except only where such Process is expresly given by some Statute.

Sect. 12. As to the fourth Point, *viz.* What is the proper Process on Informations: It seems, that a *Capias* against a [a] Commoner, and a [b] *Distringas* against a Peer, are the first proper Processes on an Information for an Intrusion on the King's Lands, or for a [c] Trover and Conversion of his Goods: And either an [d] Attachment or [e] *Subpœna*, at the Election of the Informer, were by the Common Law proper Processes on all Informations *qui tam* on Popular Statutes. And so was a [f] Summons in all Originals in Debt on such Statutes, in the same Manner as in an Action of Debt at [g] Common Law; and an [h] Attachment or *Pone per vadios, &c.* in other Actions on such Statutes, in the same Manner as in Actions upon the Case, and in Actions of Trespass at [i] Common Law.

Sect. 13. And it is enacted by 21 *Jac.* 1. 4. By which all Popular Suits on penal Statutes are restrained to their proper Counties, as is shewn at Large in the precedent [k] Chapter of Informations, *That the like Process in every Popular Action, Bill, Plaint, Information, or Suit, to be commenced, sued or prosecuted, by Force of, or according to the Purport of the said Act, be had and awarded, to all Intents and Purposes, as in an Action of Trespass* Vi & Armis *at the Common Law.* And [l] consequently the Process in all such Suits must now be by Attachment or *Pone per vadios, &c.* and after by Distress infinite, where by the Return the Party appears to be sufficient, [m] otherwise by *Capias*.

Sect. 14. It is, as I take it, the usual Practice of the Crown-Office, on a Criminal Information, first, to award a *Subpœna*; and after the Return thereof if no Appearance be entered in four Days, and an Affidavit be made of the Service of the *Subpœna*, to make out a *Capias* of Course, where the Defendants are informed against in their private Capacity, and a [n] *Distringas*, where they are sued as a Corporation aggregate.

Sect. 15. As to the fifth Point, *viz.* What is the proper Process on Appeals, and on Indictments of Treason, Felony and Maihem: It seems certain, That a *Capias* is the first Process in all Indictments of [o] Treason or Felony, and in [p] all Appeals whether of Maihem or Felony; from whence it seems reasonable to conclude, That it ought also to be the first Process in an Indictment of Mayhem, as well as of Felony or Treason.

Sect. 16. As to the sixth Point, *viz.* How many Days there must be between the *Teste* and Return of all such Process: It seems agreed, That there ought to be at least fifteen Days between the *Teste* and Return of every Process awarded from the King's Bench into any [q] Foreign County: But that this is not required in Process awarded into the same County wherein the Court sits.

Sect. 17. As to the third Particular, *viz.* In what Manner such Process is to be executed: It is laid down as a [r] general Rule, That where-ever the King is a Party to the Suit, (as he certainly is to all Informations and Indictments) the Process ought to be executed by the Sheriff himself, and not by the Bailiff of any Franchise, [s] whether it have the Clause *Non omittas, &c.* or not, and whether the Defendant be within a Franchise, or in the County at large; for the King's Prerogative shall be preferred to any Franchise: But it is said, [t] That this is to be intended only where in the Grant of the Franchise no Mention is made of Causes to which the King is a Party.

[a] Coke's Ent. 372.a. 367.a. 379.a. 381.a. 1 Co. 16. b.
[b] Co. Ent. 387. b.
[c] Co. Ent. 390. b.
[d] Coke's Ent. 365.a. 366. a. 367. a. 368.
[e] Co. Ent. 370. b. 371. b. 395. a. 1 And. 48.
[f] Co. Entr. 158.a. 164. b. 166. a. Ra. Entr. 599. pl. 2, 3.
[g] Finch of Law 352.
[h] Co. Ent. 43.b. 44. pl. 3. 46. a. 348. a. 349.a. 350.a. 351. a. Ra Ent. 406. a. b.
[i] Finch of Law 355.
[k] Vide Ch. 26. Sect. 32. to Sect. 39.
[l] See Finch of Law 345, 352, 355.
[m] 1 Rol. Abr. 463. pl. 11. 780. pl. 6. 793. pl. 4. the same Case. Palm. 449. 1 Keb. 159. pl. 109. 2 Rol. Abr. 277. D.
[n] Vide Salk. 374. pl. 15.
[o] 3 Mod. 265. 2 H. H. P. C. 194, 195.
[p] Co. Ent. 50. pl. 1. Fitz. Exigent, 28. Finch of Law 346, 351. Ra. Ent. 45. pl. 1. there is a Precedent seemingly contrary.
[q] Co. Lit. 134. b. Salk. 374. pl. 15. 1 Lev. 61.
[r] Co. 118. b. [r] Dalt. Ch. 132. Bro. Franchise, 18. 1 H. H. P. C. 577. 2 H. H. P. C. 202.
[s] 41 Aff. 17. Bro. Process, 102. Fitz. Prerog. 21. [t] Bro. Prerog. 109. Franch. 31.

Sect. 18. As to the fourth Particular, *viz.* What is required by Statute in Relation to Process on Informations: It is enacted by 4 & 5 *Will. & M.* 18. That no Process shall issue on any Information to be exhibited by the Master of the Crown Office, till the Prosecutor have given such a [a] Recognizance as by the said Act, is directed. Also it is enacted by 18 *El.* 5. That [b] no Process shall issue on any Information on a penal Statute, till a special Note be made of the Time when such Information was exhibited, &c. But these Matters having been already handled in the Chapter of *Informations*, in the Places cited in the Margin, I shall refer the Reader thither, for the fuller Consideration of them.

Sect. 19. As to the fifth Particular, *viz.* What is the proper Process upon a Default: It seems, That if a Defendant appear to an [c] Indictment or [d] Appeal of Felony, and afterwards, before Issue joined, make an Escape, whether from his [e] Bail, or from an actual [f] Prison, the Common *Capias*, *Alias* and *Pluries*, &c. shall be awarded against him, unless there had been an Exigent before, in which Case a new [g] Exigent shall be immediately awarded. And if a Defendant, against whom no Exigent had been before awarded, make such Default after Issue joined, and an Inquest awarded to try it, it seems [h] that a *Capias*, &c. shall be awarded against him *ad audiendum juratam*, &c. and, as I take it, the same Day on which the *Capias* is returnable, shall be given to the Inquest, (for it seems [i] agreed, That the Inquest shall never be taken by Default in the Case of Felony, as it may for an inferior Crime.) But in such Case, if the Exigent had before been awarded, it [k] seems, That a new Exigent in the Common Form shall be awarded; and that thereby both the Issue and Inquest are without Day. And it is said in some [l] Books, That such Exigent shall be *Ad audiendum judicium*: But this seems questionable; since it seems to be [m] agreed, That the Defendant may save himself from Judgment by a Render at any Time before the Return of the Exigent.

Sect. 20. It is said [n] by Sir *Matthew Hale*, That the Defendant in such Case appearing on the Exigent, shall plead *de novo*, because the Issue and Inquest are *sine die* by the Award of the Exigent; but this seems to be made a *Quære* by [o] *Staundforde*, and the [p] Authorities whereon it seems to be chiefly founded, are very obscure; and as it seems may well be understood in this [q] Sense, That the Court may cause the same Inquest to come to try the same Issue, which (according to [r] *Brook*) tho' it be put without Day by the Exigent, is not waived by it, unless the Defendant fail to render himself before the Return of it.

Sect. 21. Before I proceed to the sixth Particular, *viz.* What is the proper Process to be awarded after a Removal by *Certiorari*, it may not be improper to premise some Things concerning the Nature of a *Certiorari*; [s] as,

1. To what Courts it lies.
2. Where the Court of King's Bench uses a Discretionary Power in granting, denying, and filing it.
3. What Restraints are put upon it by Statute.
4. How the *Fiat* for it is to be signed.
5. To whom it ought to be directed.

[a] Vide supra ch. 26. sect. 5, 6, 10.
[b] Vide supra ch. 26. sect. 40, 41, 42, 44, 45, 46, 47.
[c] H. P. C. 211. 2 H. H. P. C. 201, 202.
[d] 16 Ass. pl. 13. 26 Ass. pl. 51.
[e] 16 Ass. pl. 13. Fitz. Exigent 10. But this is made a Quære Crompt. 150. b.
[f] 26 Ass. pl. 51.
[g] 19 H. 8. 1. pl. 1. Bro. Process, 1. seems to be contrary.
[h] S. P. C. 70. Letter E. F. 2 H. H. P. C. 224. Bro. Waiver de Choses, 39. Fitz. Exigent, 10. Process, 113, 127.
[i] S. P. C. 70. Letter E. Fitz. Exigent, 10. Coro. 173. Bro. Waiver de choses, 39. 16 Ass. pl. 13. Bro. Appeal, 54.
[k] 26 Ass. pl. 51. S. P. C. 70. Letters E, F. H. P. C. 211. Bro. Waiver de choses, 39. Fitz. Exigent, 10. Coro. 196.
[l] 26 Ass. 51. Crompt. 150. b. Fitz. Coro. 196.
[m] Fitz. Exigent, 10. Bro. Waiver de choses, 39. Coro. 192. H. P. C. 211.
[n] H. P. C. 211. 2 H. H. P. C. 225.
[o] S. P. C. 70. Letters E, F.
[p] Fitz. Exigent, 10. 16 Ass. pl. 13.
[q] Vide Fitz. Coro. 173.
[r] Bro. Waiver de choses, 39. Process, 148. Exigent, 67.
[s] 2 H. H. P. C. 210 to 216.

6. Where a Record may be removed into the Court of King's Bench without it.
7. What is to be done by a Defendant before the Allowance of it.
8. How far it is a *Superſedeas* to the Court below.
9. In what Manner it is to be returned.
10. Where a Record is removed by it.
11. What is to be done by the Court above, where the Record is not removed.

As to the firſt Point, *viz.* To what Courts a *Certiorari* lies: I ſhall endeavour to ſhew,

1. Whether it lie to all inferior Courts in general.
2. Whether to thoſe of the *Cinque-Ports.*
3. Whether to thoſe of *Wales.*
4. Whether to thoſe of *London.*

Sect. 22. As to the firſt Point, *viz.* Whether regularly it lie to all inferior Courts in general: It ſeems agreed at this Day, That regularly the Court of King's Bench having a general [a] Superintendency over all other Courts of Criminal Juriſdiction, whether they be of an antient or [b] newly created Juriſdiction, may award a *Certiorari* as well as the Court of Chancery, to remove the Proceedings before any ſuch Courts, unleſs the Statute or [c] Charter which erects them, expreſly give them an abſolute Judicature, exempt from ſuch Superintendency; as the [d] Statutes concerning the Commiſſioners of the *Cambridgſhire Fens,* &c. are ſaid by ſome to have done.

Sect. 23. And accordingly it ſeems to be agreed, That ſuch a *Certiorari* lies to [e] Juſtices in *Eyre,* and alſo to thoſe of [f] Gaol-Delivery, or of a [g] County-Palatine, and to the [h] College of Phyſicians, having a ſpecial Power by Statute to fine and impriſon for certain Offences; and to Juſtices of Peace, *&c.* even in ſuch [i] Caſes which they are impowered by Statute finally to hear and determine, and alſo to [k] Commiſſioners of Sewers, notwithſtanding the Clauſe in 13 *El.* 9. *Par.* 5. *That the ſaid Commiſſioners ſhall not be compelled to make any Certificate or Return of their Commiſſions, or of their Ordinances, Laws, or Doings,* &c. For it hath been adjudged, [l] That this is intended to exempt them from returning their Orders into Chancery, as by the Statute of *H.* 8. they were obliged to do, and ſhall not be conſtrued to take away the Superintendency of the Court of King's Bench, without expreſs Words.

Sect. 24. As to the ſecond Point, *viz.* Whether a *Certiorari* lie to the Courts of the *Cinque-Ports*? It hath been adjudged, That ſuch a *Certiorari* lies to ſuch Courts to remove an [m] Indictment of Sodomy there found, or an [n] Order made by the Juſtices of Peace at a Seſſions there holden. It is ſaid indeed, by [o] *Rolle,* That the Reaſon why ſuch an Indictment may be removed is, becauſe the Offence is made Felony by a late Statute, and therefore the Courts of the *Cinque-Ports* cannot hold Plea of it without a new Charter; by which it ſeems to be implied, That in his Opinion Indictments in ſuch Courts of Crimes whereof they have Juriſdiction, are not removeable. But the other Books above cited, ſeem to ſpeak generally of all Indictments, and to lay it down as a Rule, That the Privilege

[a] Carth. 494. S. P. C. 70. 1 Salk. 144. pl. 3. 146. pl. 7. 148. 2 Lev. 86. 1 Lev. 312. Contr. 41 Aſſ. pl. 22. Br. Coro. 193. Certiorari, 8.

[b] 1 Salk. 144. pl. 3. 148.

[c] Cro. Ca. 265. 3 Mod. 93, 94.

[d] 1 Sid. 296. Contra 1 Keb. 43. pl. 87. 2 Keb. 722. pl. 124.

[e] 1 Sid. 226. 2 Keb. 81, 82. 4 Inſt. 294, 295.

[f] 1 Salk. 144. pl. 2. Far. 118.

[g] 3 Mod. 229, 230. 2 Lev. 223. 1 Salk. 146. pl. 7. 148. 1 Rol. Abr. 395. pl. 4, 5. Aleyn 49. Far. 138. 1 H. H. P. C. 158. 5 and 6 Gul. and Mar. 11. Par. 5.

[h] Carth. 194. 1 Salk. 144. pl. 3.

[i] 3 Mod. 93, 94.

[k] 1 Salk. 145. pl. 6. 1 Keb. 129. pl. 85. March 196, 197, 199. Raym. 186.

[l] 1 Mod. 44, 45. 1 Lev. 288. 1 Ventr. 66, 67, 68.

[m] Cro. Ca. 252, 253, 264, 291. 1 Rol. Abr. 395. pl. 6. Style 14. 2 H. H. P. C. 212.

[n] 2 Lev. 86. 1 Sid. 356. 3 Keb. 154.

[o] 1 Rol. Abr. 395. pl. 6.

vilege of the Courts of the *Cinque-Ports*, used Time out of Mind, that the King's Writ doth not run there, is to be intended only of Civil [a] Causes between Party and Party.

Sect. 25. As to the third Point, *viz.* Whether a *Certiorari* lie to the Courts of *Wales*? It seems to be settled, That such a *Certiorari* lies to remove any Indictment taken in *Wales* for a Crime not capital, either at the [b] Grand Sessions or at a [c] Sessions of the Peace: But it is [d] said, That it hath never been granted to remove an Appeal from *Wales*; [e] neither doth it seem to be clearly settled, That it lies to remove an Indictment of Felony from thence, for such Indictments are never [f] quashed, as Indictments for inferior Crimes are. Neither do I find it agreed, [g] in what Manner the King's Bench shall proceed on any Indictment removed from *Wales*. [74] But it is said, That an Indictment of Felony so removed, may be tried in the next [h] *English* County, by force of [i] 26 *H.* 8. But it seems [k] agreed, That this Statute extends not to Appeals.

Sect. 26. As to the fourth Point, *viz.* Whether a *Certiorari* lie to the Courts of *London*? It seems to be admitted in the late [l] Reports, That a *Certiorari* may be granted to remove any Indictment from *London* or *Middlesex*; but it is [m] said, That he who prays it ought to give three Days Notice to the other Side: Also it is said, [n] That by a *Certiorari* to *London*, the Tenor of the Indictment only shall be removed by the City-Charters. And it seems, [o] That anciently that City insisted on a Privilege, That all Indictments and Proceedings for any Cause, except Felony, should be tried and determined there, and not elsewhere.

Sect. 27. As to the second Particular, *viz.* Where the Court of King's Bench uses a Discretionary Power, in granting, denying and filing a *Certiorari*; It hath been [p] adjudged, That where-ever a *Certiorari* is by Law grantable for an Indictment, the Court is bound of Right to award it at the Instance of the King, because every Indictment is the Suit of the King, and he has a Prerogative of suing in what Court he pleases. But it seems to be agreed, That it is left to the Discretion of the Court either to grant or deny it at the Prayer of the Defendant: And agreeably hereto, it is laid [q] down as a general Rule, That the Court will never grant it for the Removal of an Indictment before Justices of Gaol-Delivery, without some special Cause; [r] as where there is just Reason to apprehend that the Court below may be unreasonably prejudiced against the Defendant; [s] or where there is so much Difficulty in the Case, that the Judge below desires that it may be determined in the King's Bench, [t] or where the King himself gives a special Direction that the Cause shall be removed; or where the [u] Prosecution appears to be for a Matter not properly criminal.

Sect. 28. It seems, [x] That the Court will not ordinarily, at the Prayer of the Defendant, grant a *Certiorari* for the Removal of an Indictment of Perjury, or Forgery, or other heinous Misdemeanor; for such Crimes deserve all possible Discountenance, and the *Certiorari* might delay, if not wholly discourage their Prosecution,

Sect. 29. Also it is said, [y] That the Court of King's Bench will never grant a *Certiorari* for a Conviction of Recusancy upon a Default at Sessions; be-

[a] Vide Cro. El. 910, 911. Palm. 54, 55, 56, 96. Cro. Jac. 531. 1 Sid. 432. pl. 21. Hardr. 475, 476.
[b] 1 Rol. Abr. 394. pl. 1, 2. 2 Ro. Re. 28, 29. Cro. Jac. 484. Poph. 144. 2 Keb. 471. pl. 63. Cro. Car. 248. 1 H. H. P. C. 157, 158.
[c] 1 Salk. 146. pl. 7.
[d] Cro. Car. 248. 2 Keb. 797, 798.
[e] 1 Mod. 64, 68. 2 Keb. 685. pl. 8. 724. Cro. Ca. 331, 332. 1 Rol. Abr. 394. pl. 3. 1 Ventr. 93, 146. 1 H. H. P.C. 158.
[f] Vide ch. 25. sect. 146.
[g] Vide 1 Rol. Abr. 394. B. 1, 2, 3. 2 Keb. 685. pl. 8. 724.
[h] 2 Keb. 798, 799. 1 Vent. 146. Quære 1 Rol. Abr. 394, 395.
[i] Supra ch. 25. sect. 41. 42.
[k] Cro. Ca. 248. 2 Keb. 797. 798. 1 Vent. 146. 1 H. H. P. C. 157. See B. 1. ch. 31. Sect. 41.
[l] Raym. 74. 1 Keb. 352. pl. 20. 3 Mod. 230, &c. Hardr. 409, 410. 6 Mod. 246. Vide 5 & 6 W. & M. 11.
[m] Raym. 74.
[n] 1 Keb. 252. pl. 20. 1 Sid. 155, 230. Vide supra ch. 25. sect. 99.
[o] Cro. Ca. 128, 265.
[p] Term. Pasch. 5 Georg. 1. Vide 1 Vent. 63. 1 Mod. 41.
[q] Salk. 144. pl. 2. 1 Keb. 4. Far. 118.
[r] 1 Salk. 150. pl. 18.
[s] 1 Salk. 149. pl. 15.
[t] 1 Vent. 63. 1 Mod. 41.
[u] 1 Salk. 151. pl. 20.
[x] 1 Sid. 54. pl. 19.
[y] 1 Salk. 145. pl. 5.

cause

[a] 3 Jac. 1. 4. Par. 9. Vide B. 1. Ch. 10. Sect. 23.

cause by the [a] Statute such Convictions are to be removed into the Exchequer, and from thence Process is to be awarded upon them. But the Court of King's Bench cannot proceed upon them, and therefore will not suffer them to come thither, lest the Statute should be evaded. [75]

[b] 16 Ed. 4. 5. pl. 3. Bro. Coro. 162.

Sect. 30. It seems from the *Year-Book* of 16 *E.* 4. That it is a good Objection against the granting a *Certiorari*, that Issue is joined in the Court below, and a *Venire* awarded for the Trial of it; for it appears by that [b] Book, where a *Certiorari* had been granted in such a Case, that the Court being afterwards apprised of the Matter, remanded the Cause.

[c] 1 Salk. 149. pl. 15. 6 Mod. 17.

Sect. 31. It seems [c] agreed, That a *Certiorari* shall never be granted to remove an Indictment or Appeal after a Conviction, [76] unless for some special Cause; as where the Judge below is doubtful what Judgment is proper to be given; for unless there be some such Reason, the Judge who tried the Cause, shall not be prevented from giving Judgment in it; for it cannot be intended but that he is best acquainted with the Circumstances of it, and consequently best able to Judge what Fine, or other Punishment is proper for it.

[d] 1 Sid. 296. 2 Keb. 81, 82.

Sect. 32. But it hath been adjudged, That a *Certiorari* for the Removal of a Presentment before Justices in *Eyre*, of a Matter which is inquirable and punishable by the Forest Law only, shall not be granted before, but only after Conviction; for if it should be granted before, the Offence would be dispunished; but if it may be granted after Conviction, in order to give the Party, the Right of whose Freehold is concerned in it, an Opportunity so far to [e] traverse it.

[e] Vide Fitz. Ass. 442. 4 Inst. 294. 295. 21 Ed. 3. 48. pl. 70. Bro. Forest, 3. 1 Sid. 296. 2 Keb. 81, 82.

Sect. 33. The Court has [f] refused to grant a *Certiorari* to remove a Recognizance of Appearance before Justices of *Oyer* and *Terminer*, *&c.* because the Court below is most proper to judge, upon the whole Circumstances of the Case, which are equitably to be considered, whether it ought to be estreated or not.

[f] Dominus Rex versus Combs, Hill. 1 Georgii 1.

[g] Vide 1 Salk. 145. pl. 5. 2 Keb. 137. pl. 1. seems contrary.

Sect. 34. There is a Rule in the Court of King's Bench, That no Order of Commissioners of Sewers ought to be filed without Notice given to the Parties concerned. Also it is every [g] Day's Practice of that Court, before it will suffer the Return of a *Certiorari* for the Removal of the Orders of such Commissioners to be filed, to hear Affidavits concerning the Facts whereon they are grounded; and if the Matter shall still appear doubtful, to direct the Trial of feigned Issues, and either to file the Return, or supersede the *Certiorari*, and grant a *Procedendo*, as shall appear to be most reasonable for the Trial of such Issues, and to give [h] Costs against the Prosecutor of the *Certiorari*, if it appear to have been groundless.

[h] Vide 2 Keb. 500. pl. 63.

Sect. 35. As to the third Particular, *viz.* What Restraints have been put by Statute upon the granting a *Certiorari*; It is enacted by 1 & 2 *Ph.* & *M.* 13. pl. 7. *That no Writs of* Habeas Corpus, *or* Certiorari, *shall be granted to remove any Prisoner out of any Gaol, or to remove any Recognizance, except the same Writs be* [i] *signed with the proper Hands of the Chief Justice, or in his Absence, of one of the Justices of the Court out of which the same Writ shall be awarded or made, upon Pain that he that writeth any such Writs, not being signed, as is aforesaid, to forfeit for every such Writ five Pounds.*

[i] Vide Salk. 150. pl. 19.

Sect. 36. Also it is enacted by 5 & 6 *Will.* & *Ma.* 11. *That in Term-Time, no Writ of* Certiorari *whatsoever, at the Prosecution of any Party indicted, be granted out of the King's Bench, to remove any Indictment or Presentment from any General or Quarter-Sessions, before Trial, but upon Motion of Counsel, and by Rule of Court made in open Court.* But it is provided, *That in Vacation ſuch Writ may be granted by any Juſtices of the ſaid Court, whoſe Names ſhall be endorſed thereon, and alſo the Name of the Perſon at whoſe Inſtance it is granted.*

Sect. 37. It is enacted by 22 *Ca.* 2. 12. Par. 4. *That all Defects of Repairs of Cauſeys, Pavements, Highways, or Bridges, ſhall be preſented in the County only where ſuch Cauſeys,* &c. *lie, and not elſewhere; and that no Indictment or Preſentment ſhall be removed by* Certiorari, *or otherwiſe out of the ſaid County, till ſuch Indictment or Preſentment ſhall be traverſed, and Judgment thereupon given.* And it is farther enacted by 3 & 4 *W.* & *M.* 11. *That all Matters concerning Highways,* &c. *ſhall be determined in the County where they lie, and not elſewhere; and that no Preſentment, Indictment, or Order made by Virtue of that Act ſhall be removed by* Certiorari, &c. But it is enacted by 5 & 6 *W.* & *M.* 11. *That if the Right or Title to repair ſuch Cauſeys,* &c. *may come in Queſtion, upon Suggeſtion and Affidavit of the Truth thereof, a* Certiorari *may be granted to remove ſuch Indictment or Preſentment into the King's Bench,* &c. upon the like Recognizance as is required by the ſaid Statute as to other[a] *Certiorari's*, for the Removal of Indictments from Seſſions, for which I ſhall refer the Reader to the forty-ſixth and following Sections. Alſo it hath been adjudged, That if the Seſſions manifeſtly exceed their Authority, in making Orders concerning Highways, ſuch [b] Orders may be removed by *Certiorari* into the King's Bench, and quaſhed.

[a] See the Statute of 13 & 14 Car. 2. 6. Par. 16.

[b] See B. 1. Ch. 67. Sect. 10.

Sect. 38. It is enacted by 7 & 8 *Will.* & *Ma.* 6. made for the Recovery of ſmall Tithes before Juſtices of Peace, *That no Proceedings or Judgment by Virtute thereof ſhall be removed or ſuperſeded by any Writ of* Certiorari *out of any Court whatſoever, unleſs the Title of the Tithes,* &c. *ſhall come in Queſtion.* And in the Conſtruction hereof, it hath been adjudged, [c] That if the Party inſiſt on any Matter of Law before the Juſtice of Peace, which is any way doubtful, as on a Cuſtom in a Pariſh to be diſcharged of a certain Kind of Tithe, *&c.* the Order may be removed within the Intent of the Statute.

[c] Dominus Rex ver. Furnace. Term. Hill. ſexto Geo. 1.

Sect. 39. And it is enacted by 12 *Car.* 2. 23. Concerning the Exciſe, *Par.* 35. *That no Writ of* Certiorari *ſhall ſuperſede Execution or other Proceedings, upon any Order by Juſtices of Peace in purſuance of that Statute, but that Execution, and other Proceedings, ſhall and may be had thereupon, any ſuch Writ, or Allowance thereof notwithſtanding.* And the like is generally enacted by other Statutes concerning the Revenue; for which I ſhall refer the Reader to the ſeveral Statutes.

Vide 1 Keb. 818. pl. 10.

Sect. 40. As to the fourth Point, *viz.* How the *Fiat* for a *Certiorari* is to be ſigned: It is ſaid, [d] That if a *Certiorari* be taken out in Vacation, and teſted of the precedent Term, the *Fiat* for it muſt be ſigned by ſome Judge of the Court, ſome Time before the Eſſoin-Day of the ſubſequent Term, otherwiſe it is irregular, and the Court upon Motion will order a *Procedendo.* But it is ſaid, That there is no Need for any Judge to ſign the Writ of *Certiorari* it ſelf, but only in ſuch Caſes wherein it is required by Statute.

[d] 1 Sal 150. pl. 19.

Sect. 41. As to the fifth Point, *viz.* To whom the Writ of *Certiorari* is to be directed; It ſeems, That notwithſtanding [e] regularly it ought to be directed to the Judge of the inferior Court, yet in ſome Caſes it may be directed to the proper [f] Officer known to have the Cuſtody of the Record to be removed, and in ſome other Caſes to [g] others, as ſhall be moſt agreeable to the uſual Courſe of approved Precedents, which [h] ſeems to be the beſt Guide whereby to judge of this Matter. And accordingly

[e] 3 Keb. 13. pl. 17. 4 H. 6. 15.b. 16. a. S.P. C. 64. Letter B. Hob. 135.

[f] Dalt. Ch. 134. Style 371. 2 Lev. 223. Raſt. Entr. 110. pl. 4.

[g] See the Caſes cited to the other Parts of this Section.

[h] Dyer 163. pl. 56.

cordingly it seems, That for an Indictment or Confession of an Approver before a Coroner, it shall be directed to the Coroner alone [a], and for an Appeal, both [b] to the Sheriff and Coroner; and for an Indictment in the *Cinque-Ports*, to the [c] Mayor and Jurats; and for an Indictment at an Assise in a County Palatine, to the Chancellor of such [d] County, who shall send for it to the Justices of Assise.

Sect. 42. If the Person who ought to certify a Record, as a Justice of [e] Peace, *&c.* who hath taken a Recognizance, *&c.* or a [f] Judge of *Nisi Prius*, who hath taken a Verdict, or a [g] Coroner, who hath taken an Inquest, *&c.* happen to die, having such a Record in his Custody, it seems, That a *Certiorari* may be directed to his Executor or Administrator to certify it. [h] Also it hath been adjudged, That it may be directed to a Justice of Assise to certify a Record of Assise taken before his Companion in his Absence.

Sect. 43. All the Precedents, I am able to find, of *Certiorari's* for the Removal either of [i] Indictments, or [k] Recognizances from Sessions, are directed either to the Justices of Peace for the County generally, or to some of them in particular by Name, and not to the *Custos Rotulorum*; and according to [l] *Lambard*, they are never directed to him: Yet it is taken for granted in the [m] *Year-Book* of *H.* 7. That after a Recognizance for the Peace is brought in to the *Custos Rotulorum*, it shall be certified by him. But surely, if the *Certiorari* be directed generally to the Justices of the County, or any one of them, it may be as well returned by any of them, as by the *Custos Rotulorum*. And I question whether it can be well [n] returned by him, unless he do it as Justice of Peace, naming himself such? But if there are sufficient Precedents to warrant the directing the *Certiorari* to him as *Custos Rotulorum*, there can be no Doubt but that a Return by him as such will be good.

Sect. 44. As to the sixth Point, *viz.* Where a Record may be removed into the Court of King's Bench without any Writ of *Certiorari*: It seems agreed, That if [o] a Justice of Peace, or other Judge of Record, having taken Recognizance, or Inquisition, or recorded a Riot, or done any other executory Matter, within his Jurisdiction, have still continued in the same Commission, *&c.* without any Interruption, the Court of King's Bench shall receive such Record from his Hands, without any Writ of *Certiorari*. Also it seems to be [p] agreed, That upon the Death of both the Justices of Assise, the Clerk of the Assise may, without any *Certiorari*, bring in the Records of the Verdicts of *Nisi Prius*: But that the [q] Executors or Administrators of a Judge, can in no Case bring in a Record without a Writ to authorise them to do it. Also it seems to be [r] agreed, That no Record which is executed as by Acquittal, *&c.* can be brought into a higher Court without a Writ. And it seems to be the stronger [s] Opinion that neither a Justice who is out of Commission at the Time, nor one who has been out of Commission, but is afterwards restored, can certify any Record without a Writ of *Certiorari*.

Sect. 45. As to the seventh Point, *viz.* What is to be done by a Defendant before the Allowance of a *Certiorari*; It is enacted by 21 *Jac.* 8. *Par.* 7, 8. *That all Writs of* Certiorari *for the Removal of any Indictment of Riot, Forcible Entry, or of Assault and Battery, at any Quarter-Sessions of the Peace, or otherwise, shall be delivered at some Quarter-Sessions of the Peace in*

[a] Register Judic. 74. b. 78. a. Rast. Ent. 55. a. 263. b.
[b] Register Judic. 76. Supra ch. 9. sect. 42.
[c] 2 H. H P. C. 211. Cro. Ca. 252, 253, 264.
[d] 2 Lev. 223. 3 Keb. 279.
[e] 2 Keb. 750. pl. 4. 8 H. 4. 3. a. 5. b. Cro. Jac. 669. 21 H. 7. 21. pl. 4.
[f] Dyer 163. pl. 54, 55. 56. Rast. Entr. 439. pl. 14. 2 Inst. 424. 2 Rol. Abr. 629. Lett. S.
[g] Bro. Certiorari, 9. Indictment, 23. 43 Ass. pl. 40.
[h] Bro. Rec. 81. 11 H. 7. 5. pl. 21.
[i] Register Judic. 76. b. 77. a. Rast. Ent. 263. b.
[k] Register Orign. 90. F. N. B. 81. c.
[l] Lamb. B. 4. ch. 7.
[m] 2 H. 7. 1. pl. 2.
[n] Vide Hob. 135.
[o] Dalt. Ch. 134. Lamb. B. 4. ch. 7. 8 Ed. 4. 18. pl. 28. Bro. Record, 17, 64. 8 H. 4. 4. a. 5. b. Crompt. 132, 133. b.
[p] Dyer 163. pl. 54, 55, 56. 2 Inst. 424. See March 112, 113.
[q] 1 Dyer 163. pl. 54, 55, 56. Rastal's Entr. 439. pl. 14. 8 H. 4. 4. a.
[r] 8 Ed. 4. 18. pl. 28. Lamb. B. 4. ch. 7. f. 517. Crompt. 133. b.
[s] Dalt. ch. 134. 8 H. 4. 4. a. 5. b. Bro. Garrantie d' Attorney, 9. Bro. Record, 17, 64. Bro. Certiorari, 9. Dyer 163. pl. 54. Rast. Ent. 438. a. b.

open Court; and that the Party indicted shall before the Allowance thereof, become bound to the Prosecutor in 10 l. *with such sufficient Sureties as the Justices of Peace, at their Quarter-Sessions, shall think fit, with Condition to pay unto such Prosecutor within one Month after Conviction, such reasonable Costs and Damages as the said Justices of Peace of such Counties where such Indictments shall be found in the said Sessions of the Peace, shall assess or allow; and in Default thereof, it shall be lawful for the said Justices to proceed to Trial of such Indictments, any such Writs of* Certiorari *notwithstanding.*

Sect. 46. And the like Recognizance in the Sum of 40 *l.* is required by 13 & 14 *Car.* 2. 6. *Par.* 16. concerning the Highways, on the Removal of every Indictment, *&c.* on that Statute.

Sect. 47. It is observable, That these Statutes do not [a] extend to all Indictments at Sessions in general, but only to those particular Ones therein mentioned: But this Defect was in a great Measure [b] supplied by the Rules of the Court of King's Bench, which upon the Removal of an Indictment from *London* or *Middlesex*, required a Recognizance from the Defendant to carry down the Record to Trial the same Term, on which the *Certiorari* was returnable, or the Sittings after; and on the Removal of an Indictment from other Counties [c] required such Recognizance for a Trial at the next Assises. [77]

[a] 1 Keb. 225. pl. 38. 727. pl. 69.
[b] Vide 1 Keb. 33. pl. 88. 6 Mod. 246. 2 Salk. 564. pl. 3. Far. 10.
[c] Show. Rep. 336.

Sect. 48. And agreeably hereto, it is enacted by 5 & 6 *W.* & *M.* 11. and 8 & 9 *Guil.* 3. 33. *That all the Parties indicted at a General or Quarter-Sessions of the Peace, prosecuting a* Certiorari, *before the Allowance thereof, shall find two sufficient Manucaptors, who shall enter into a Recognizance in the Sum of* 20 l. *before one or more Justices of the Peace of the County or Place, (or* [d] *else before one of the Judges of the King's Bench, in which Case such Judge shall make Mention of it under his Hand, on the Back of the Writ) and the Recognizance shall be with Condition, at the Return of such Writ, to appear and plead to the Indictment or Presentment in the Court of King's Bench, and at his own Costs to procure the Issue that shall be joined upon the said Indictment or Presentment, or any Plea relating thereto, to be tried at the next Assises for the County wherein the Indictment was found after such* Certiorari *shall be returnable, if not in* London, Westminster *or* Middlesex; *and if there, then to cause it to be tried the next Term after wherein such* Certiorari *shall be granted or at the Sitting after the said Term, if the Court of King's Bench shall not appoint any other Time for the Trial thereof: And if any other Time shall be appointed by the Court, then at such other Time, and to give due Notice of such Trial to the Prosecutor, or his Clerk, in Court, and* [e] *also, That the Party or Parties, prosecuting such* Certiorari, *shall appear from Day to Day in the said Court of King's Bench, and not depart until he or they shall be discharged by the said Court: And such Recognizances,* Certiorari's, *and Indictments, shall be filed in the King's Bench, and the Name of the Prosecutor (if he be the Party grieved or injured) or some Publick Officer, endorsed on the Back of the Indictment; and if the Person prosecuting such* Certiorari, *being the Defendant, shall not, before Allowance thereof, procure such Manucaptors to be found as aforesaid, the Justices of Peace shall, and may proceed to Trial of the Indictment notwithstanding such* Certiorari.

[d] Viz. By Force of 8 & 9 Guil. 3. 33.
[e] Viz. by 8 & 9 Guil. 3. 33.

Sect. 49. And it is farther enacted by the said Statute of 5 & 6 *W.* & *M.* 11. *That if the Defendant prosecuting such* Certiorari, *be convicted, the King's Bench shall give reasonable Costs to the Prosecutor, if he be the Party grieved or injured, or be a Civil Officer who shall prosecute on Account of any Fact that concerned him as Officer to prosecute or present; which Costs shall be taxed according to the Course of the said Court; and the Prosecutor for the Recovery of*

such

ſuch Coſts, ſhall within ten Days after Demand made of the Defendant, and Refuſal of Payment on Oath, have an Attachment granted againſt the Defendant by the ſaid Court for ſuch his Contempt; and the ſaid Recognizance ſhall not be diſcharged till the Coſts ſo taxed ſhall be paid.

[a] See the fifth Parag.

Sect. 50. And the like in Effect is [a] enacted by the ſaid Statute of 5 & 6 *W.* & *M.* 11. concerning the Removal of Indictments by *Certiorari* within the Counties Palatine of *Cheſter*, *Lancaſter*, and *Durham*.

In the Conſtruction of theſe Statutes, the following Points ſeem moſt remarkable.

Sect. 51. *Firſt*, That notwithſtanding by the expreſs Words, Juſtices of Peace may proceed to Trial of the Indictments, notwithſtanding the *Certiorari*, if a proper Recognizance be not given; yet they will be in Contempt to the Court that awarded the *Certiorari*, if they make no [b] Return to it; for all Writs muſt be obeyed unleſs good Cauſe be ſhewn to the contrary; and the proper way of ſhewing it is to return it.

[b] 1 Keb. 225. pl. 38. 231. pl. 51. 598. pl. 68. 903. pl. 1. 1 Sid. 70.

Sect. 52. *Secondly*, That it appears from the manifeſt Purport of theſe Statutes, That they extend only to *Certiorari's* procured by Perſons indicted; from whence it follows, That thoſe, which are procured by the Proſecutor of an Indictment, remain as they were at [c] Common Law.

[c] 6 Mod. 246.

Sect. 53. *Thirdly*, That [d] theſe Statutes, being in the Affirmative, as to the Taking of Recognizances, do not take away the Power which the Juſtices of the King's Bench have by the Common Law of taking Recognizances upon their granting *Certiorari's*; from whence it follows, That if any ſuch Juſtice, granting a *Certiorari*, ſhall take a Recognizance variant from that preſcribed by the Act, either as to the Sum or Condition, &c. Such Recognizance will have the ſame Force as it would have had, if theſe Statutes had not been made; but it is ſaid, That the *Certiorari*, if procured by the Defendant, will not in ſuch Caſe be a *Superſedeas* to the Proceedings below, as it would have been at the Common Law; for the Statutes ſeem to be expreſs, That the Seſſions may proceed notwithſtanding any *Certiorari* procured by a Defendant whereon ſuch Recognizance is not given, as is expreſly preſcribed.

[d] 2 Salk. 564. pl. 3. Far. 10.

Sect. 54. *Fourthly*, That if the Perſons offering to be Sureties, appear to be worth 20 *l.* the Juſtices [e] cannot refuſe them.

[e] March 27.

Sect. 55. *Fifthly*, That if divers be indicted [f] in the ſame Indictment, and ſome of them find Sureties, and others not, the Indictment ought to be removed as to thoſe who find Sureties, (becauſe they ſhall not be prejudiced by the Default of the others.) And, as [g] ſome ſay, It ſhall be removed as to the others alſo.

[f] March 27.

[g] 1 Keb. 231. pl. 51. Vide 6 Ed. 4. 5. a. March 111.

Sect. 56. *Sixthly*, [h] That the Maſter of the Crown-Office, in taxing the Coſts, ought only to conſider thoſe which are ſubſequent to the *Certiorari*.

[h] 1 Salk. 55. pl. 5.

Sect. 57. *Seventhly*, That the Proſecutor, by accepting the Coſts ſo taxed, is not reſtrained from aggravating the Fine to be ſet on the Defendant, becauſe he has a Right to ſuch Coſts by the expreſs Words of the Statutes; and therefore the Defendant can claim no Indulgence from having paid them: But in other Caſes, after a Proſecutor has excepted Coſts from a Defendant, he cannot by the Rules of the Court, aggravate his Fine; becauſe in ſuch Caſes, having no Right to demand Coſts, if he take them at all, he muſt take them by way of Satisfaction of the Wrong, after which it is unreaſonable in him to harraſs the Defendant. And this I take to be a common Practice; tho' in [i] *Salkeld's Reports* there ſeems to be a Note to the contrary.

[i] 1 Salk. 55. pl. 5.

Sect. 58. *Eighthly*, [a] That notwithstanding the Condition of the Recognizance seem to be express, That the Defendant shall procure a Trial at the next Assises, *&c.* yet it shall not be forfeited, unless the Prosecutor of the Indictment give Rules according to the Course of the Court.

Sect. 59. *Ninthly*, That after such [b] Recognizance is forfeited by the Defendant's not procuring a Trial according to the Purport of the Condition, the Court will not hear any Motion to quash the Indictment, or *Certiorari.*

Sect. 60. It is enacted by 3 & 4 *W.* & *M.* 10. Par. 6. against Deer-stealers, *That no* Certiorari *shall be allowed to remove any Proceedings on that Act, unless the Party convict shall become bound, with good Sureties, in fifty Pounds to pay full Costs and Damages within one Month after the Conviction shall be confirmed, or a* Procedendo *granted.* [78]

Sect. 61. And the like in Effect is enacted by 4 & 5 *W.* & *M.* 23. and 5 *Annæ*, *Sess.* 2. *Ch.* 14. in Relation to Convictions, on those Acts of Offences concerning the Game.

Sect. 62. As to the eighth Point, *viz.* How far a *Certiorari* is a *Supersedeas* to the Court below: It is [c] agreed by all the Books, That after it is allowed by such Court, it makes all its subsequent Proceedings on the Record, that is removed by it, erroneous. Also it seems to be generally [d] agreed, That a *Certiorari*, for the Removal of an Indictment of Forcible Entry found at the Sessions of the Peace, being delivered to any one Justice of Peace of the same Place, before the Statute of 21 *Jac.* 1. set forth more at Large *Sect.* 45. which requires, That every such *Certiorari* shall be delivered at some Quarter-Sessions in open Court, did (by such Delivery without more) so far supersede the Power of the Sessions, that all its subsequent Proceedings thereon, and even an Execution of a prior Award on the same Indictment, would have been erroneous. And it seems to be generally [e] agreed that any one such Justice to whom such *Certiorari* should be delivered, might and ought thereupon immediately to have awarded a *Supersedeas* to the Sheriff in order to have stopped the Execution of any prior Award of such Court upon such Indictment.

Sect. 63. It seems to be the better [f] Opinion, That a *Supersedeas* on such a *Certiorari*, being delivered to the Sheriff before he hath begun to put a Process in Execution, will make his subsequent Execution of it wholly void; because it is a ministerial Act, and not a judicial one. But if such *Supersedeas* be not delivered to the Sheriff till after he have in Part executed such Award, it [g] seems, That he may afterwards be authorised to go thro' with it by a Writ of *Venditioni exponas*, in the same Manner as he may in the like Case after a Writ of Error; but I [h] question, Whether he can lawfully proceed after such *Supersedeas* actually delivered to him, without the Writ of *Venditioni exponas*?

Sect. 64. It seems to be the stronger Opinion, That a *Certiorari*, being once delivered, makes all subsequent Proceedings on the Record that ought to be removed by it, [i] erroneous, by Force of these Words, *Coram nobis terminari volumus, & non alibi*, whether such Proceedings are before or after its Return; and notwithstanding the Party who prosecuted it, never make any other Suit to have the Record certified, but only by causing the *Certiorari* to be delivered. And in this Respect a *Certiorari* hath a stronger Force than a Writ of Error; for that becomes [k] of no Effect,

[a] 1 Salk. 370. pl. 4.

[b] 1 Salk. 380. pl. 26. Dominus Rex versus Somers, Mich. 6 Geo. 1.

[c] Cro. Car. 261, 262. 1 Salk. 148, 149.

[d] Cro. El. 915, 916. 2 Keb. 306. pl. 5. Moor 677. pl. 921. 1 Salk. 151. pl. 22.

[e] Cro. El. 915. 916. Moor 677. pl. 921. This seems to be a Quære. F. N. B. 237. Letter E. Dalt. Ch. 134.

[f] Cro. El. 915, 916. Moor 677. pl. 921. 2 H. H. P. C. 215.

[g] Dy. 98. pl. 57. Yelv. 6. Cro. Eliz. 597. pl. 2. 1 Rol. Abr. 894. pl. 4. 2 Rol. Abr. 491. D. 5, 6. 3 Keb. 169. pl. 4. 174. pl. 9. 309. pl. 51.

[h] See the Books next above cited, and Moor 542. pl. 718. 1 Salk. 147. pl. 12.

[i] Yel. 32. Dy. 245. pl. 63. 6 H. 7. 15. b. 16. a. Bro. Recordare, 8. Dalt. Ch. 134. Lamb. B. 4. Ch. 7. fol. 516. Cont. Crompt. 132. b. 133. a. 2 H. H. P. C. 215.

[k] Dyer 245. pl. 63. 1 Keb. 14. pl. 35, 54. pl. 12. 107. pl. 123. 118. pl. 25. 1 Sid. 268. pl. 20. 2 Rol. Abr. 491. pl. 7.

if the Party who proſecuted it, neglect to get the Record certified in a reaſonable Time. Alſo it ſeems to be holden in ſome [a] Books, That the very Iſſuing of a *Certiorari* is of itſelf a *Superſedeas* to the inferior Court, whether the *Certiorari* be ever delivered or not: In the ſame Manner as an Appearance in the Court above, and a *Superſedeas* purchaſed there, will avoid [b] an Outlawry pronounced after, though ſuch *Superſedeas* were not delivered to the Sheriff before the *quinto exactus*; but the Contrary hereto, in Relation to a *Certiorari*, ſeems more agreeable to the general Tenor of the [c] Books, and the Reaſon of the Thing. And it hath been [d] adjudged, That if a *Certiorari* for the Removal of an Indictment before Juſtices of Peace be not delivered, before the Jury be ſworn for the Trial of it, the Juſtices may proceed. Alſo it hath been [e] holden, That a *Certiorari* is of no Effect, unleſs it be delivered before its Return is expired. And it is certain that by Force of the Statute it cannot at this Time be any [f] *Superſedeas* to the Proceedings on an Indictment at Seſſions, without a proper Recognizance, *&c.*

Sect. 65. It hath been [g] holden, That a *Certiorari* for the Removal of a Recognizance for the Good Behaviour, or for an Appearance at Seſſions, will ſuperſede its Obligation. But this would be highly inconvenient; and the contrary Opinion ſeems to be ſupported by the better [h] Authority.

Sect. 66. It [i] ſeems, That if an Indictment be removed by *Certiorari* after Iſſue joined, and afterwards remanded, the Inferior Court ſhall proceed to Trial, in the ſame Manner as it would have done, if no *Certiorari* had been granted.

Sect. 67. I ſhall take it for [k] granted, That inferior Courts proceeding after a *Certiorari* delivered, where by Law they ought not, are puniſhable for a Contempt; as hath been more fully ſhewn, *Chap.* 22. *Sect.* 28.

Sect. 68. Alſo it ſeems, That by the Common Law if a *Certiorari* be once filed, the Proceeding below can [l] never be revived by any *Procedendo.*

Sect. 69. As to the ninth Point, *viz.* In what Manner a *Certiorari* is to be returned: [79] I ſhall refer the Reader to the Form in which it is to be done, to [m] *Lambard* and [n] *Dalton*, and ſhall farther take Notice only of theſe following Particulars;

Sect. 70. *Firſt*, That every ſuch Return ought to be under the Seal [o] of the Inferior Court, or of the Juſtice, or Juſtices to whom it is directed; and if ſuch Court have no proper Seal, it ſeems, [p] That the Return may be well made under any other.

Sect. 71. *Secondly*, That every ſuch Return muſt be made by the very ſame Perſon to whom the *Certiorari* is directed; for if it be directed to the Juſtices of Peace of ſuch a Place, and the [q] Clerk of the Peace only return it or to the Conſtable, or to the Recorder of *B.* and the [r] Deputy Conſtable, or Deputy Recorder, return it, (without ſhewing in the Return that the Principal had Power to make a Deputy); or to the Steward of St. *Paul's*, and the Steward of the Church of St. [s] *Peter* and St. *Paul* return it, nothing is removed. Yet it is [t] certain, That if it be directed to the Juſtice of *Cheſter*, it may be returned by *A. B.* Chief Juſtice; for the ſame Officer is known to be meant, in the Writ and Return, and his Deſcription in both is in Subſtance the ſame. Alſo it is [u] ſaid, That if a Writ of Error be

[a] Moor 73. pl. 199. 1 Keb. 93. pl. 79.
[b] Dy. 222, 223. Mo. 73. pl. 199. 1 Inſt. 128. b.
[c] Cro. Jac. 282. pl. 2. Vide ſupra Ch. 5. S. 8, 9, 10, 11. Cro. El. 152. pl. 29. 915, 916. Cro. Jac. 43. pl. 10. Yelv. 52, 57, 121. Cro. Ca. 79. 2 Jon. 209.
[d] 1 Salk. 144. pl. 1. 150. pl. 17.
[e] 1 Keb. 944. pl. 3.
[f] Vide ſupra Sect. 45 to 62.
[g] 2 R. A. 492. Lett. F. pl. 12. Dalt. Ch. 75.
[h] Cro. Jac. 282. Yelv. 207. 2 Bulſt. 155, 156.
[i] 16 Ed. 4. 5. pl. 3. Vide Bro. Diſcontinuance de Proceſs, 52.
[k] Raym. 186. Far. 38. 1 Vent. 66. 1 Salk. 144, 145.
[l] Agreed by the Court of King's Bench, in the Caſe of the King againſt Whitlow, Hil. 6 Geo. 1.
[m] Lamb. B. 2. Ch. 2. 107, 108.
[n] Dalt. Ch. 73. and 134.
[o] Cro. El. 821. pl. 17.
[p] 1 Lev. 311.
[q] 2 Salk. 479.
[r] 1 Rol. Ab. 752. pl. 27. 754. pl. 14. 2 Keb. 385. pl. 56.
[s] Cited 2 Keb. 385. pl. 56.
[t] 1 Sid. 64. 1 Lev. 50. 2 Salk. 452. 1 Keb. 165. pl. 120. 187. pl. 168.
[u] Yel. 212. Cro. Jac. 254, 255. 1 Sid. 349. 1 Keb. 941. pl. 62. 2 Keb. 385. pl. 56. 1 Rol. Abr. 753, 754.

directed to ſeveral Juſtices, and returned by Part of them only; yet if it [a] truly recite the Record, it ſo far removes it, that a new Writ of Error lies, *de recordo quod coram nobis reſidet, &c.* And [b] *Quære* how the Court ſhall proceed upon the like Miſ-return of a *Certiorari?*

Sect. 72. *Thirdly*, That [c] regularly a Recognizance taken by a Juſtice of Peace, whether it ſtill actually continue in the Hands of ſuch Juſtice, or [d] have been ſent by him to the Clerk of the Peace, ought to be certified on a *Certiorari* for the Removal of it by ſuch Juſtice only, until it be made a Record of the Seſſions, [e] after which it ſhall be certified in the ſame Manner as the other Records thereof ſhall be.

Sect. 73. *Fourthly*, That it is [f] adviſeable, That a Return to a *Certiorari* directed to Juſtices of Peace, for the Removal of an Indictment taken before them, have the Clauſe *Necnon ad diverſas Felonias, &c.* as well in the [g] Deſcription of the Juſtices who make the Certificate, as of thoſe before whom the Indictment is ſaid to be taken in the Caption; which Matter hath been already conſidered, *Ch.* 8. *Sect.* 33. and *Ch.* 25. *Sect.* 121, 122, 123.

Sect. 74. *Fifthly*, [h] That the Perſon to whom a *Certiorari* is directed, may make what Return to it he pleaſes; and the Court will not ſtop the Filing of it on Affidavits of its Falſity, except only where the Publick Good requires it, (as in the Caſe of the [i] Commiſſioners of Sewers) or for ſome other ſpecial Reaſon: But regularly the [k] only Remedy againſt ſuch a Falſe Return, is an Action on the Caſe at the Suit of the Party injured by it, and an Information, *&c.* at the Suit of the King.

Sect. 75. *Sixthly*, [l] That whatſoever Matters are put into the Return of a *Certiorari*, by way of Explanation or otherwiſe, beſides thoſe which are expreſly ordered to be certified, are put in without any Warrant or Authority, and conſequently ſhall be no more regarded by the Court above, than if they had been wholly omitted.

Sect. 76. *Seventhly*, That [m] generally the Return to a *Certiorari* ought to certify the Record itſelf, or the Tenor of it, or the [n] Tenor of the Tenor, [o] according as the Writ requires: And agreeably hereto it hath been [p] adjudged, That if on a *Certiorari* to return an Order of Juſtices of Peace, the Tenor of ſuch Order be certified, the Return is naught; yet a Return of the Tenor of an Indictment from *London* on a *Certiorari* to remove the Indictment it ſelf, is good by the City-Charter, as hath been already ſhewn, *Sect.* 26. Alſo, it [q] ſeems to have been generally holden, That where-ever the Purport of a *Certiorari* is not to proceed upon the Record to be removed, but only to try an Iſſue of *Nul tiel Record*, it is ſufficient to certify the Tenor of the Record, whether the *Certiorari* require a Certificate of the Record itſelf, or of the Tenor of it only. However, I take it to be clear, That if the Court which awards ſuch a *Certiorari*, have no Juriſdiction to proceed on the Record thereby ordered to be removed; as where the Court of [r] Common Pleas award a *Certiorari* for the Removal of an Indictment on the Iſſue of *Nul tiel Record*, concerning ſuch Indictment, the Court below ought only to certify the Tenor of it, leſt there ſhould be a Failure of Juſtice.

Sect. 77. As to the tenth Point, *viz.* Where a Record is removed by a *Certiorari*: Having premiſed that nothing can be removed by it where it is improperly [s] directed, or [t] returned, for which I ſhall refer the Reader to the foregoing Parts of this Chapter; I ſhall in this Place obſerve only the following Particulars;

[a] Vide Yelv. 6, 7. 28 H. 6. 12, pl. 24. 1 Rol. Abr. 753. Let. Q. 754.
[b] Vide F.N.B. 71. Letter. D.
[c] 21 H. 7. 21. pl. 4. Cro. Jac. 669. 2 H. 7. 1. pl. 2. Supra Sect. 43.
[d] Domina Regina verſus Randal, Paſch. 13 Annæ.
[e] Vide ſupra Sect. 43. Regiſter Origin. 90, 151, b. 283. b. 284, &c. F.N.B. 81. Letter C. 2 H. 7. pl. 2. Bro. Peace, 11. Dalt. Ch. 70.
[f] Crompton, 131. b. 132. a. Lamb. B. 4. Ch. 7. fol. 516, 517. Dalt. Ch. 134.
[g] 22 Ed. 4. 12. b. 13. a. 12 H. 7. 25. pl. 3. 2 R. 3. 9. pl. 20. Bro. Indictment, 32, 50. Cauſe a Remover Plea, 27. Vide 1 Keb. 263. pl. 48.
[h] 6 Mod. 90. Domina Regina verſus Norton, Paſ. 11 Annæ.
[i] Supra Sect. 34.
[k] 6 Mod. 90.
[l] 2 Salk. 492, 493.
[m] Regiſter Origin. 151. a. 169. a. b. F. N. B. 245. Letter B.
[n] F. N. B. 245. Lett. B. 3 Keb. 13. pl. 17.
[o] F. N. B. 245. Lett. B. Crompt. 131. b. Dalt. Ch. 134. Lamb. B. 4. Ch. 7. f. 515.
[p] 1 Salk. 147. pl. 10. 2 Salk. 492, 493.
[q] 3 Keb. 13. pl. 17. Dyer 187. pl. 4. 1 Keb. 107. pl. 127.
[r] 1 Rol. Abr. 394. pl. 2. 395. pl. 1, 2. Hob. 135.
[s] Vide ſupra Sect. 41, 42, 43.
[t] Vide ſupra Sect. 69, &c.

Sect. 78. *Firſt*, That it ſeems to be ſettled at this Day, That as a Writ of [a] Error may remove a Judgment given; and a [b] *Recordare* may remove a Plaint entered, after its *Teſte* and before its Return: So likewiſe a [c] *Certiorari* may remove a Record that ſhall come within its Deſcription before the Time of its Return, tho' there where no ſuch Record *in eſſe* at the Time of its *Teſte*, [d] nor at the Time when it was firſt delivered to the Court below.

Sect. 79. *Secondly*, That as a *Recordare* will remove a Plaint that was [e] diſcontinued below, becauſe the Court above will proceed only on the Plaint, and all the other Proceedings thereon below are to no Purpoſe; there ſeems to be the like Reaſon that a *Certiorari* alſo may remove an Indictment which was diſcontinued below.

Sect. 80. *Thirdly*, That as a Writ of Error can remove no Record which materially varies from the Deſcription ſet forth in ſuch Writ, ſo neither can a *Certiorari*; as in the following Inſtances.

Sect. 81. *Firſt*, Where the Writ deſcribes an Indictment or other Record, taken before *A. B.* and eight others, and that certified appears to have been taken before [f] *A. B.* and ſeven others only, or [g] before him and the other eight mentioned, and others alſo beſides them; or where the Writ deſcribes a Record [h] *coram A. & B. & ſociis ſuis*; and the Record certified appears to have been taken *coram C. D. & ſociis ſuis*; or [i] where the Writ calls the Juſtices, before whom the Record is taken, *Juſticiarios noſtros*, and in the Record certified they appear to have taken it as Juſtices of a former King.

Sect. 82. *Secondly*, Where the Writ deſcribes an Indictment for ſtealing [k] two Horſes, and that certified is for ſtealing one Horſe only.

Sect. 83. *Thirdly*, [l] Where the Writ deſcribes an Order concerning Foreign Salt, and that certified is concerning Salt in general.

Sect. 84. *Fourthly*, [m] Where the Writ deſcribes an Order concerning the Town of *Needham-Market*, or concerning the Manor of *Anſly*, and an Order concerning the Town of *Needham*, or the Manor of *Aneſley*, is returned, without ſhewing in the Return that they are both the ſame Town.

Sect. 85. *Fifthly*, Where the Writ mentions only [o] Orders againſt *A. B. & C.* or Indictments wherein *A. B. & C.* are indicted, and thoſe certified are againſt *A.* only, or againſt *A. & B.* only. Yet [p] it is taken for granted in many Books, neither do I find it any where denied, That a *Certiorari* for the Removal of all Indictments againſt *A.* may remove one wherein the ſaid *A.* is indicted, together with twenty others, ſo far as it concerns him; becauſe in Judgment of Law it is a ſeveral Indictment as to every one of the Perſons indicted. But I do not find it [q] agreed, Whether in ſuch a Caſe the Indictment ſhall be removed ſo far as it concerns the other twenty?

Sect. 86. *Sixthly*, Where there is a [r] material Variance between the Writ and the Record certified, in the Names or Additions of the Parties; as where the Writ gives the Defendant the Surname of [s] *Giggure*, and the Record certified that of *Giggeer*; or where the Writ commands the Removal of all Convictions againſt [t] *Henry*, Coachman, *quocunque no-*

[a] 1 R. 3. 4. pl. 8. Bro. Recordare, 9. 1 Mod. 112. 3 Keb. 308. pl. 51. Cont. Noy 54. 1 Rol. Abr. 749. M. 1.
[b] 1 R. 3. 4. pl. 8. Bro. Recordare, 9.
[c] 1 R. 3. 4. pl. 8. Dyer 222. pl. 23. 1 Vent. 63. Bro. Recor. 9. 1 Mod. 41. 1 Salk. 149. pl. 13. Far. 138. Lamb. B. 4. Ch. 7. fol. 517. Crompt. 132. b. Dalt. Ch. 134. 1 Mod. 112. Yelv. 32. Cont. 1 Sid. 317. 2 Keb. 141. pl. 13. 142. pl. 15. Noy 54. 1 Rol. Abr. 749. M. 1.
[d] 1 Rol. Abr. 395. B. 1.
[e] 3 H. 6. 30. pl. 17. F. N. B. 71. Lett. A. Fitz. Recordare, 2.
[f] Cro. Jac. 254, 255. Yelv. 42. Plow. Com. 392.
[g] Vide Bro. Error, 13. 28 H. 6. 11. pl. 24. 1 Keb. 129. pl. 51. 282. pl. 86. 102. pl. 106.
[h] 1 Sid. 448. Parallel Caſe, 1 Rol. Abr. 753. pl. 14. 1 Rol. Abr. 753. pl. 3.

[i] 1 Rol. Abr. 754. pl. 7. 13. Dyer 105. pl. 6. Yelv. 212. [k] 2 Aſſ. pl. 3. S. P. C. 70. Letter C. Bro. Variance, 62. Lamb. B. 4. Ch. 7. fol. 518. Bro. Coro. 69. Crompt. 132. b. 1 Bulſt. 155. [l] 1 Salk. 145. pl. 4. Far. 97. [m] 2 Salk. 452. See Cro. El. 882. pl. 14. [n] 12 Aſſ. pl. 2. Bro. Variance, 66. [o] 1 Salk. 146. pl. 9. 151. pl. 21. Domina Regina verſus Hotſpurt, Hill. 12 Ann. Cont. 1 Rol. Ab. 395. B. 2. [p] 6 Ed. 4. 5. pl. 13. Bro. Record 57. Lamb. B. 4. Ch. 7. f. 517. Crompt. 132. a. Dalt. Ch. 134. March 112. [q] Affirmed 6 Ed. 4. 5. pl. 13. Bro. Record, 57. Lamb. B. 4. Ch. 7. f. 517. Crompt. 132. a. Dalt. Ch. 134. Denied, March 112. 2 Keb. 231. pl. 51. [r] Vide 1 Rol. Abr. 754. pl. 5, 6. [s] Salk. 264. pl. 8. [t] Adjudged Mich. tertio Geo. 1.

mine cenſeatur, and thoſe certified are againſt *Henry Munton*, Coachman;[a] or where the Writ calls the Defendant *John* [a] *of Stiles*, and the Record *John Stiles*; or where the one calls him [b] Knight and Baronet, and the other Baronet only; or the one [c] *Garret Malines*, and the other *Gerrard Malines*; or the one *J. S.* [d] *nuper de B.* and the other *J. S. nuper de C.* or the one *J. S.* of *B.* [e] *Sadler*, and the other *J. S.* of *B. Salter*. Yet if the Variance be only in the Spelling, and the Words have the very ſame Sound either Way, as [f] *Bird* and *Burd*, [g] *Shelbury* and *Shelbery*, it ſeems that it will not be material; becauſe it appears not by any Record of the Court, but that the Name in the *Certiorari* may be the true Name, and the Record certified deſcribing one by a Name of the ſame Sound, ſhall be intended to mean the ſame Perſon. Alſo, if a *Certiorari* name the Party without any Addition, and the Record certified, name him with an Addition; yet it ſeems that it may be probably argued, that the Record may be well removed by ſuch Writ, in the ſame Manner as it may be by a Writ of [h] Error, which has the like Variance. But if a Writ of Error deſcribe a Perſon with an Addition, which is omitted in the Record certified, it hath been [i] lately adjudged contrary to the Opinion in Sir *Edward Coke*'s [k] Third Report to the contrary (which ſeems to be rather contradicted than ſupported by the [l] Authorities cited to maintain it) that it cannot remove the Record; and the Reaſon ſeems to be the ſame in Reſpect of a *Certiorari*.

Sect. 87. As to the eleventh Point, *viz.* What is to be done by the Court above, where the Record mentioned in a *Certiorari* is not removed by it: It is [m] ſaid, That ſuch Court cannot in ſuch Caſe proceed upon the Record; becauſe in Judgment of Law it ſtill remains in the Court below, but will either [n] quaſh the Writ, and [o] award a new one, or ſuffer the Court below to proceed in the Cauſe, and take ſuch [p] Order in Relation to the Defendant's Appearance either in the one Court, or the other, to anſwer the farther Proſecution of the Cauſe againſt him, as ſhall in Diſcretion appear to be moſt proper.

Sect. 88. And now I ſhall conſider the ſixth Particular, *viz.* What Proceſs is to be awarded after the Removal of a Record by *Certiorari* into a ſuperior Court: As to which I take it to be agreed, That, after ſuch Removal, if the Defendant do not appear in the Court of King's Bench, the ſame [q] Kind of Proceſs lies againſt him as if the Cauſe had been originally commenced there. Alſo I take it to be [r] agreed, That ſeeing by ſuch Removal the Cauſe below is wholly put without Day, there is no Way to nonſuit the Plaintiff, before he hath appeared in the Court of King's Bench, but by taking out a *Scire facias* to warn him to proſecute his Appeal in that Court; whereupon if the Sheriff return a *Scire feci*, he ſhall be nonſuit. And if the Sheriff return a *Nihil*, a *Scire facias ſicut alias* ſhall be awarded; whereon, if the Sheriff return a ſecond *Nihil*, I do not find it [s] agreed what ought farther to be done.

Sect. 89. As to the ſeventh Particular, *viz.* Where the Proceſs on an Appeal, Indictment, or Information ſhall be ſaid to be diſcontinued, or miſcontinued, or put without Day; having premiſed, that it ſeems

[a] 26 Aſſ. pl. 31.
[b] Cro. Ja. 633.
[c] Vide Cro. Ja. 477. 2 Rol. Abr. 329. pl. 17. Such a Variance between a Protection and the Writ adjudged fatal.
[d] Adjudged in a Writ of Error between Ainſworth and Wilſon, Hil. 5 Geo. 1. Par. Caſe, 1. Sid. 193. pl. 23.
[e] Dy. 173. pl. 16. 1 Rol. Abr. 753. pl. 4.
[f] Cro. El. 172. pl. 14. Cont. 25 Ed. 3. 43. pl. 3.
[g] Vide Cro. El. 172. pl. 14. 1 Rol. Abr. 797. Lett. H. 2 Rol. Ab. 329. pl. 14.
[h] 1 Sid. 193. pl. 23. 9 H. 6. 1. pl. 3. Dyer 25. pl. 161.
[i] Shute and Car, adjudged Hill. tertio Georgii 1. 9 H. 6. 1. pl. 13. Bro. Variance, 6. Vide Dy. 25. pl. 161. Cont. 1 Sid. 104. 2 Rol. Abr. 328, 329.
[k] 3 Co. 2. a. 1 Rol. Abr. 752. a.
[l] 9 H. 6. 1. 7 Aſſ. pl. 5. 26 Aſſ. pl. 31.
[m] 12 H. 7. 25. pl. 3. 2 R. 3. 9. pl. 20. 3 Aſſ. pl. 3. Vide 1 Sid. 193. pl. 23. 2 Keb. 142. pl. 15.
[n] 1 Keb. 102. pl. 106. 1 Salk. 147. pl. 10.
[o] Vide 3 Aſſ. pl. 3.
[p] Vide 12 H. 7. 25. pl. 3. 3 Aſſ. pl. 3. 2 R. 3. 9. pl. 20. Bro. Indictment, 50. Bro. Coro. 69. 2 Keb. 142. pl. 15. Lam. B. 4. Ch. 7. f. 518. Supra Ch. 25. Sect. 11. 2 H. H. P. C. 198.
[q] S. P. C. 70. Lett. D. E. H. P. C. 211. Carth. 223.
[r] S. P. C. 70. Lett. D. H. P. C. 211. 48 Ed. 3. 22. pl. 2. 48 Aſſ. pl. 3. 1 Salk. 61, 62. 6 Mod. 246. Bro. Appeal, 15, 140. Fitz. Coro. 105.
[s] Vide S. P. C. 70. Lett. D. E. 72. Lett. A. 48 Ed. 3. 22. pl. 2. 48 Aſſ. pl. 3. Bro. Appeal, 15, 140. Fitz. Coro. 105.

to be agreed, That every Suit, whether Civil or Criminal, and also every Process in such Suit against Jurors, ought to be properly continued from Day to Day, from its Commencement to its Conclusion, without any the least Gap or Chasm; and that the Suffering any such Gap or Chasm, is properly [a] called a Discontinuance; and the continuing of the Suit by [b] improper Process, (as by a *Capias* instead of a *Distringas*) or by giving the Parties an [c] illegal Day, is properly called a Miscontinuance: I shall for the more distinct Understanding of the Learning of this Kind, endeavour more particularly to shew;

[a] Fitz. Judgment, 12. Finch of Law 431. Co. Lit. 325, a. Bro. Amend. 17. Fitz. Process, 124, 127. 1 H. 7. 2. b. 22 E. 3. 2. pl. 12. 22 E. 4. 3. pl. 12. 12 H. 4. 3. pl. 5.

First, In what particular Instances Process is generally said to be discontinued.

Secondly, Where to be miscontinued.

Thirdly, Where to be put without Day.

[b] 21 H. 7. 16. pl. 27. 8 H. 6. 29. pl. 24. 12 H. 4. 3. pl. 5. 10 H. 7. 21. pl. 15. Keilw. 36. Finch of Law 431, 432. Co. Lit. 325. Bro. Discontinuance de Process, 11, 23, 50, 57, 61. 12 H. 4. 18. pl. 15. Cont. 40 E. 3. 16. pl. 5. Fitz. Amend. 12.

And first, Process is generally said to be discontinued in the following Instances.

Sect. 90. *First*, Where the second is not tested on the very same [d] Day on which the first is returnable; as where a *Venire facias* is returnable on the 23d of *January*, and the *Distringas* is tested on the 24th or any other subsequent Day.

Sect. 91. *Secondly*, Where there is a Term intervening between the *Teste* and Return of a [e] *Capias*; for the Law will not suffer any such *Capias*, lest thereby the Defendant should be imprisoned an unreasonable Time; but an Original may be continued by any [f] other Process, except a *Capias*, tho' it have a Term or more intervening between its *Teste* and Return. [g] Neither is it any Objection to an Exigent, That it is not made returnable on the next Term after its *Teste*, because it must allow Time enough for five Counties to be holden between its *Teste* and Return.

[c] Bro. Discontinuance de Process, 23. 21 H. 7. 16. pl. 27.

Sect. 92. *Thirdly*, [h] Where, after Issue or Demurrer, the Court give the Parties a Day to a distant Term, without making any Continuance to that immediately following.

[d] 1 Bulst. 141, 142, 143. Yelv. 204, 205. Cro. Jac. 283. 284. 6 Mod. 281, 282, 283. 1 Salk. 51.

Sect. 93. *Fourthly*, Where the Term to which the Suit is continued is adjourned, and the Suit is [i] not adjourned accordingly.

Sect. 94. *Fifthly*, Where any of the Parties are described in any Continuance of the Suit, whether on the [k] Roll, or by [l] Process, by a Name or Addition variant from those in the Original, &c. tho' [m] only in one Letter.

[e] 8 Ed. 4. 13. pl. 10. Dy. 175. pl. 23. Cro. El. 467. the first. Fitz. Continuance, 3.

Sect. 95. *Sixthly*, Where after Issue joined the Process is [n] not continued from Time to Time against the Jurors, returnable on the same Days to which the Suit is continued on the Roll against the Parties.

Sect. 96. *Seventhly*, where [o] a joint *Venire* is first awarded for the Trial of all the Defendants together, and afterwards several *Venires* for the Trial of each of them.

Sect. 97. *Eighthly*, Where [p] a *Venire* omits Part of the Issue, or Issues to be tried.

[f] 8 Ed. 4. 13. pl. 10. Dalis. 108. Dyer 175. pl. 23. Quære Bro. Discontinuance de Process, 23. 21 H. 7. 16. pl. 27. [g] Dalis. 108. 1 Rol. Abr. 484. pl. 1. 3. [h] Cro. Jac. 236. Yelv. 169. 21 H. 7. 16. pl. 27. 1 Rol. Abr. 484. pl. 8, 9, 10. Cont. 1 Bulst. 144. 3 Bulst. 233. [i] Vide 1 Danv. Abr. 243. 4 E. 4. 40. Fitz. Discontinuance, 27. [k] Fitz. Discontinuance, 1. Bro. Amendm. 22. 4 H. 6. 6. pl. 17. 40 E. 3. 18. pl. 10. [l] Fitz. Amendm. 13, 17, 21, 27, 69, 77. Discontinuance, 7, 12, 17, 40, 42. Error, 15. Bro. Discontinuance de Process, 46. Amendm. 50. 38 Ed. 3. 22. b. 39 Ed. 3. 21. a. 40 Ed. 3. 31. pl. 9. 34. pl. 18. 8 H. 5. 2. pl. 9. 7 H. 6. 27. pl. 20. 9 H. 6. 39. a. [m] Quære 4 H. 6. 6. b. Bro. Amendm. 45. Fitz. Amendm. 21. [n] 21 Ed. 4. 20. pl. 27. Bro. Discontinuance de Process, 53. Continuance, 82. [o] Quære 22 H. 6. 3. b. 4. a. Fitz. Discontinuance, 11. Vide 7 H. 6. 27. pl. 19. [p] Fitz. Discontinuance, 14, 35. 2 H. 5. 3. pl. 16. Vide Bro. Discontinuance de Process, 63. Quære Cro. El 622. pl. 14.

Sect. 98. *Ninthly*, [a] Where a *Venire* omits any of the Parties.

Sect. 99. *Tenthly*, Where a Juror is named in the *Habeas Corpora*, by a Name [b] different from that in the Panel returned on the *Venire*; or where a Juror returned on ſuch a Panel is wholly omitted in the *Habeas Corpora*; but in theſe Caſes, if the Juror ſo miſnamed, or [c] omitted, be not ſworn at the Trial of the Cauſe, it is [d] queſtionable, Whether there be any Diſcontinuance at all?

Sect. 100. *Eleventhly*, Where a *Venire* or *Diſtringas* are iſſued without any [e] Award on the Roll to warrant them.

Sect. 101. It [f] ſeems, That before the Making of the Statutes of 11 *H.* 6. 6. and 1 *E.* 6. 7. all Pleas and Proceſſes before Juſtices of Aſſiſe, Gaol-Delivery, *Oyer* and *Terminer*, or *Peace*, or other the King's Commiſſioners, were diſcontinued by the Making a new Commiſſion, or Aſſociation, or by altering the Names of the Juſtices or Commiſſioners; but this Miſchief is fully remedied by thoſe Statutes.

Sect. 102. If an [g] Indictment be removed by *Certiorari*, after Iſſue joined, and Proceſs awarded for the Trial; *Quære*, If it ſhall be diſcontinued, if not remanded before the Return of ſuch Proceſs?

Sect. 103. As to the ſecond Point, *viz.* Where Proceſs is generally ſaid to be miſcontinued: It ſeems, that where-ever an Error in Proceſs doth not amount to a Diſcontinuance, it is generally called a Miſcontinuance; and this ſeems agreeable to the proper Notion of the Word; for as a Cauſe may then properly be ſaid to be diſcontinued, when there is either nothing at all done to continue it, or nothing but what is as to this Purpoſe merely void in Law; ſo it ſeems to be properly ſaid to be miſcontinued, where it is continued amiſs, or by an [h] erroneous and not void Continuance. And agreeably hereto, the Books which ſpeak of Errors in Proceſs, ſeem generally to include them all, without [i] Exception, under the general Heads of Miſcontinuance and Diſcontinuance. And this, as I apprehend, was alſo the Opinion of the greater Part of the Court of King's Bench, in the late Caſe of [k] *Widdrington* and *Charlton.*

Sect. 104. As to the third Particular, *viz.* Where Proceſs ſhall be ſaid to be put without Day: It ſeems [l] agreed, That by the Common Law all Proceedings upon any Indictment, Information, or Popular Action, whereon no Judgment had been given, were wholly determined by the Demiſe of the King, and that nothing remained but the Indictment or Information, Original Writ, or Bill, which were put without Day till re-continued by Re-attachment to bring in the Defendants to plead *de novo.* But this is fully [m] provided for by 4 & 5 *W.* 3. 18. and 1 *Annæ*, 8. By which it is enacted, That ſuch Proceſs, *&c.* ſhall continue in the ſame Force after the King's Demiſe, as it would have had if he had lived.

Sect. 105. As for Appeals, [n] I do not find it any where ſaid, That the Pleas, and other Proceedings therein, being put without Day by the Demiſe of the King might not be revived by a ſpecial Re-attachment, in the ſame Manner as in any other Action: However it is certain at this Day, That by Force of 1 *Ed.* 6. 7. and 1 *Annæ*, 8. neither the Writ nor Bill, nor any Plea, nor Proceedings therein, ſhall be any way diſcontinued or put without Day by ſuch Demiſe.

[a] Fitz. Diſcontinuance, 10, 35. 1 Rol. Re. 22. pl. 30. 3 Bulſt. 311. Winch 73. Br. Amendm. 50. 39 E. 3. 21. a. [b] Fitz. Repleader, 4. Amendm. 26. 4 H. 6. 7, 8. pl. 20. 19 H. 6. 39. a. 9 Ed. 4. 13. pl. 7. 27 H. 6. 5. pl. 33. Bro. Diſcontinuance, 47. Vide 1 Danv. Abr. 330, 331. 5 Co. 42. a. b. [c] Fitz. Amendm. 57. 37 H. 6. 12. a. b. Br. Amendm. 51. [d] 1 Sid. 66. 1 Keb. 182, 191, 198, 215. 6 Mod. 285. Fitz. Diſcontinuance, 4. ſeem to make it no Diſcontinuance. But 19 H. 6. 39. a. 34 H. 6. 20. pl. 39. 27 H. 6. 5. pl. 33. Fitz. Enqueſt, 18. 5 Co. 36. b. 37. a. Fitz. Diſc. 37, 38. Br. Amendm. 10, 37, 92. are to the contrary. Vide Cro. E. 586. pl. 17. [e] Fitz. Error, 16. 7 H. 6. 28. [f] Vide ſupra Ch. 5. Sect. 5, 6, 7, 8, 9, 10, 11, 12. Ra. Ent. 77. pl. 2, 3. [g] Vide Bro. Diſcontinuance de Proceſs, 52. 15 Ed. 4. 5. pl. 3. Supra Sect. 66. [h] Vide Finch of Law 431. Supra Sect. 89. 21 H. 7. 16 pl. 27. 39 E. 3. 20. b. [i] 21 H. 7. 16. pl. 27. Bro. Diſcontinuance de Proceſs, 11, 47, 50, 57. Amendment, 17. Cro. Jac. 283, 284. 1 Bulſt. 142, 143. [k] Trin. 11 Annæ. [l] 7 Co. 30, 31. Cro. Jac. 14. Moore 748. 2 H. H. P. C. 189, 209. [m] Vide Supra Ch. 1. Sect. 12, 13. [n] Vide 7 Co. 30.

Sect. 106. It ſeems to be holden by [a] ſome, That all Cauſes, whether Civil or Criminal, are diſcontinued; and by [b] others, who ſeem to ſpeak more accurately, That they are put without Day, by the Juſtices before whom they were depending, not coming on the Day to which they are continued, whether ſuch Abſence were occaſioned by [c] Death, or any other Cauſe. But it ſeems to be agreed by all, That a Cauſe ſo diſcontinued, or put without Day, cannot be revived without a Re-ſummons, or Re-attachment; which if they are [d] Special, may revive the whole Proceedings; but if general, the original Record only. Nor do I find that any Statute hath remedied this Miſchief, except in the Caſe of Aſſiſes, and *Juris utrum*, which are provided for by 1 *E.* 6. 7.

Sect. 107. As to the eighth Particular, *viz.* How far Errors in Proceſs are fatal: It ſeems to be generally taken [e] as an undoubted Principle, That a Diſcontinuance, by ſuffering a total Chaſm in the Proceedings, whether on the Roll or in the Proceſs, by not giving a freſh Continuance *inſtanter* upon the Determination of the Precedent, ſhall never be aided by an Appearance and pleading over: And the Book [f] of 9 *H.* 5. 2. *pl.* 7. ſeems to have an Opinion, That the Miſreturn of a Sheriff, as where he returns a *Cepi* on the Award of an Exigent, is not ſaved by the Defendant's Pleading over; but this is [g] queſtioned by *Staundforde*, and ſeems contrary to the general Tenor of the other [h] Books, and contradicted both by [i] *Brook* and [k] *Fitzherbert*, in their Abridgment of this very Caſe. And in all Probability the Book is miſ-printed; for, as it ſtands at preſent, it is hardly Senſe, or reconcileable with [l] itſelf. But if a Defendant appearing on erroneous Proceſs, expreſly except to it before he have pleaded over, there have been many [m] Authorities, that he ought to be diſcharged, and that [n] new Proceſs ſhall iſſue where the Defect firſt happened. But there is a greater [o] Number of Authorities to the contrary; by which it appears, That if the Original be good, and the Defendant preſent in Court, he ſhall be compelled to anſwer it, let the Proceſs whereon he came in, or the Execution of it, be never ſo erroneous, or defective, ſo that it never were diſcontinued; for the End of Proceſs is to compel an Appearance; and that End being ſerved, and a legal Charge appearing againſt the Defendant no way diſcontinued, the Law will not ſo far regard a Slip in the Proceſs, as to let the Defendant out of Court in order only to have him brought in again in better Form. And therefore where a Defendant hath excepted to the Proceſs whereon he hath appeared, that he was [p] never ſerved with it, or that [q] no ſuch Proceſs lies in the Caſe, or that it bore [r] *Teſte* before the Original, or that

[a] Dy. 226. pl. 38. Keil. 2. pl. 3. Cro. E. 12. pl. 1. Bro. Diſcontinuance de Proceſs, 29. 25 Aſſ. pl. 5. Vide 1 Co. 38.
[b] Co. Litt. 135. b. Finch of Law 432, 433. Ra. Ent. 77. pl. 1. Fitz. Diſcontinuance, 19. Re-attachment, 1, 17, 23, 24. 9 H. 6. 40. a. 24 E. 3. 23. pl. 17. 28 Aſſ. pl. 42. 30 Aſſ. pl. 39. Bro. Diſcontinuance de Proceſs, 2.
[c] Vide Bro. Re-attachment, 18. 4 H. 7. 7. pl. 6. F. N. B. 111. D. 287. B. 188. A.
[d] 7 Co. 29. b. Fitz. Re-attachment, 1.
[e] 1 Bulſt. 143. Yelv. 204. Cro. Ja. 283, 284. 8 H. 6. 29. pl. 24. 21 H. 6. 16. pl. 27. 12 H. 4. 17. pl. 15. 34 H. 6. 20. pl. 39. 18 H. 6. 15. a. b. Co. Lit. 325. a. Bro. Diſcontinuance de Proceſs, 4, 11, 47. Amendment, 17. Fitz. Proceſs, 127. Diſcontinuance, 40. Amendment, 27. 38 E. 3. 22. b. 19 H. 6. 39. a. See Bro. Error, 3. Repleader, 2. and Diſc. 1. Where the contrary Opinion is ſaid to have been holden; but this ſeems not to be warranted by the Caſe at Large in the Year-Book. [f] Vide ſupra Ch. 23. Sect. 143. [g] S. P. C. 169. b. [h] 5 Co. 45. a. Fitz Coro. 444. Co. Lit. 325. a. Salk. 59. pl. 2. 1 Sid. 260. pl. 7. 1 Rol. Abr. 779. Lett. L. 780. Yelv. 158. Cro. El. 582. pl. 6. Cro. Jac. 311. pl. 10. See the Books cited to the other Parts of this Section. In 1 Rol. Abr. 380. pl. 6. Notice is taken of three Reſolutions that a Capias where it lies not, is not aided by an Appearance and pleading over, and of a ſubſequent one contradicting them. [i] Bro. Reſtitution, 8. [k] Fitz. Coro. 68. But in another Part of his Book he abridges this Caſe, without taking any Exception to it. Fitz. Damage, 50. [l] Alſo it is cited in Yelv. 204. Cro. Jac. 284. 1 Bulſt. 142. for the Proof of the contrary Opinion. [m] 40 E. 3. 31. pl. 10. 47 Ed. 3. 14. pl. 16. 18 H. 6. 15. a. b. 3 H. 6. 9. a. Fitz. Repleader, 1. Amendm. 14. Proceſs, 154. Error, 82. Bro. Diſcontinuance de Proceſs, 50, 57. Default and Appearance, 11. 1 Rol. Abr. 779. L. 3. 3 Mod. 265. But the Year-Book of 8 H. 6. 29. b. from which the above-cited Authority in Brook, Diſcontinuance, 50. is taken, ſeems rather to contradict than warrant it. [n] 8 H. 6. 29. pl. 24. 12 H. 6. 18. pl. 15. 18 H. 6. 15. b. 47 E. 3. 14. pl. 16. Bro. Diſcontinuance de Proceſs, 11, 50, 57. Fitz. Proceſs, 127. Diſcontinuance, 17. [o] 21 H. 7. 16. pl. 27. Fitz. Error, 47. 46 E. 3. 30. pl. 28. Bro. Error, 28. Reſponder, 12. Faux Judgment, 4. 10 H. 7. 21. pl. 15. Yelv. 158. 1 Sid. 100. pl. 10. 260. pl. 7. and ſee the other Books under cited. [p] Fitz. Diſcontinuance, 36. 9 H. 5. 3. pl. 8. 1 Rol. Abr. 779. L. 1, 2. 46 Ed. 3. 30. pl. 28. Bro. Faux Judgment, 4. [q] 10 H. 7. 21. pl. 15. 12 H. 4. 18. pl. 15. Bro. Error, 109. Proceſs, 173. Jour. 36, 54. 21 H. 7. 16. pl. 27. 8 H. 6. 29. pl. 24. Fitz. Proceſs, 127. [r] 1 Sid. 406. pl. 16.

it was not awarded into the [a] proper County, or that it was [b] not returnable at a proper Day, or that it was [c] directed to one who was no Officer, or that it had not ſo many Days as it ought [d] between its *Teſte* and Return, or for any [e] other ſuch like Defect; yet he hath been compelled to anſwer the Original. And agreeably hereto it was lately [f] reſolved, upon great Deliberation by the Court of King's Bench, againſt the Opinion of Mr. Juſtice *Powell*, That the Defendant in an Appeal of Death, coming in upon an Exigent, which was erroneous for want of the Words *de morte viri*, *&c.* had ſalved the Error by his Appearance, notwithſtanding he had done all he could to take Advantage of it, by craving *Oyer* of the Proceſs, and then demurring. And [g] *Note*, That in all the *Year-Books* above cited to this Point, except [h] one, it is ſaid generally, That ſuch Errors are ſalved by an Appearance, without any Mention of any Amendment: But in that one it is ſaid, That they ſhall be amended. Alſo it ſeems, that where-ever Proceſs is awarded [i] *inſtanter* from Time to Time, without any the leaſt Break or Chaſm, and the Parties [k] have always a Day upon the Roll, all other Kinds of Errors whatſoever that come under the Name of Diſcontinuances, are [l] ſalved by an Appearance, for there are [m] Caſes by which it appears, That Defendants appearing, and taking Exceptions to ſuch Errors, have been compelled to anſwer to the Original, which they would not have been, if ſuch Original had been taken to have been diſcontinued by ſuch Errors, as they certainly are by an Error, in ſuffering a total Chaſm in the Continuance. And if the Original be not diſcontinued by ſuch Errors, Why ſhould they not be as much ſalved by an Appearance, as any of the other Errors above mentioned? For would it not be altogether as trifling in this, as in any other Caſe, to diſmiſs a Perſon only in order to ſend for him again? And in Criminal Caſes this could not but be of the utmoſt ill Conſequence, by giving the Defendant, who is actually in the Power of the Court, an Opportunity of eſcaping.

Sect. 108. But it ſeems agreed by all the [n] Books, That any other Diſcontinuance in the Proceſs againſt Jurors, ſhall have the ſame Effect as a Diſcontinuance in ſuffering a Chaſm in the Proceſs; but it ſeems, That no ſuch [o] Diſcontinuance, whether in the Proceſs or in the Roll, ſhall in any Caſe diſcontinue or abate the Original Suit; but if it appear before Trial, ſhall cauſe [p] new Proceſs to be awarded where the firſt Fault happened; and if after Trial, a new [q] *Venire* to have the whole [r] Iſſue tried over again; becauſe the firſt *Venire* was executed, and the whole Trial unwarranted. But [s] if Judgment be given on a Verdict by Jurors appearing on a Proceſs any way erroneous, It will be totally erroneous; becauſe the Trial was wholly unwarranted, and conſequently the Iſſue miſ-tried.

Sect. 109. Alſo, as I apprehend, any other Error in the Proceſs againſt the Jurors, who actually try a Cauſe, will make a [t] Miſ-trial, as much as thoſe which are called Diſcontinuances; as where ſuch Proceſs of this Kind is awarded which is not [u] proper in the Caſe, or where it is directed to a [x] wrong Officer, or has a [y] wrong Viſne, or [z] miſrecites the

[a] 38 E. 3. 20. b. 29 E. 3. 31. Fitz. Diſcontinuance, 39

[b] 21 H. 7. 16. pl. 27. Cont. 40 E. 3. 31. pl. 10. Fitz. Amendment, 14.

[c] Cro. El. 582. pl. 6.

[d] Bro. Jour. 36, 54. Diſcontinuance, 23. Error, 169. Amendment, 60. Fitz. Jour. 37, 38. 12 E. 4. 11. pl. 1. 9 E. 4. 18. pl. 20. 2 H. 7. 11. pl. 11.

[e] Fitz. Diſcontinuance, 51. 3 H. 4. 10. pl. 10.

[f] Widdrington v. Charlton, Trin. 11 Annæ. Vide 1 Salk. 59, 60.

[g] Vide 40 E. 3. 31. pl. 10. Fitz. Amendment, 14, 59.

[h] 2 H. 7. 11. pl. 11.

[i] Vide 1 Bulſt. 141, 142, 143. Yelv. 204, 205. 6 Mod. 281, 282, 283, 285, 286. 1 Salk. 51. Cro. Jac. 284.

[k] 1 Rol. Abr. 779. L. 3. 12 H. 4. 18. pl. 15. 21 H. 7. 16. pl. 27. 38 E. 3. 20. b. 12 H. 4. 3. pl. 5. Bro. Diſcontinuance de Proceſs, 11. Fitz. Diſcontinuance, 39.

[l] Cro. Jac. 311. pl. 10.

[m] 38 E. 3. 22. b. Fitz. Diſcont. 40. 19 H. 6. 39. a. Amendment, 27. Bro. Repleader, 2. Diſcontinuance de Proceſs, 1. Error, 3. 3 H. 6. 9. a.

[n] Fitz. Amendment, 26. Bro. Amendment, 10, 92. Diſcontinuance de Proceſs, 4. 19 H. 6. 39. a. 27 H. 6. 5. pl. 33. 3 H. 6. 20. pl. 39.

[o] 30 Aſſ. pl. 36. Cont. Bro. Diſcontinuance, 47. But his Note is not warranted by the Books at Large, which are 27 H. 6. 5. pl. 33, and 34 H. 6. 20. pl. 39.

[p] 19 H. 6. 39. a. 34 H. 6. 20. pl. 39. Fitz. Amendment, 26, 57. Enqueſt, 18. 29 E. 3. 31. Bro. Amendment, 10. Diſcontinuance, 30. 30 Aſſ. pl. 36.

[q] 6 Mod. 286, 287. Fitz. Diſcontinuance, 24, 38. 22 H. 6. 3. b. 4. a.

[r] 2 H. 5. 3. pl. 16. Fitz. Diſc. 35. Vide 9 H. 4. 7. b. Bro. Enqueſt, 98.

[s] Faux Judgment, 12. Error, 16. 22 E. 3. 2. pl. 12. 7 H. 6. 28. 29 E. 3. 31. a.

[t] Vide 1 Danv. Abr. 334, 335, 352, 357, 455, 456.

[u] 7 H. 6. 28. Fitz. Error, 16.

[x] 1 Brow. 134. Cro. El. 574. pl. 15. 586. pl. 16. Moore 356. pl. 482. Yelv. 15. 5 Co. 36. b.

[y] Cro. El. 468. the firſt. Vide ſupra ch. 23. ſect. 92. 2 D. Abr. 455, 456. 21 Jac. ch. 13, 16 and 17 Car. 2. 8.

[z] Cro. Jac. 89. pl. 15.

former Process, or is [a] misreturned, or [b] not returned at all, *&c.* For if Error of this Kind have such Effect even in Civil Actions, where they are not within some of the Statutes of *Amendments* or *Jeofails*, as it seems to be admitted that they have, it plainly follows, That they must always have it in Criminal Proceedings, since [c] no such Proceedings are within the Benefit of any of those Statutes. But if an Error of this Kind, owing wholly to the Misprision of the Clerk, be discovered before Trial, and the Amendment of it will set the whole Matter right, perhaps it may be [d] amended by the Common Law. And it hath been [e] holden clearly, That even a Discontinuance of Process may be amended by Consent of the Parties.

Sect. 110. Howsoever an Error may be so far salved by the Party's Appearance, that he shall be as much compellable to answer the Original, as if there had been no such Error: Yet if he were subject to any Disadvantage in Respect of having such Process awarded against him; as to the Loss of his Goods upon an Exigent, or to the Forfeiture of the Privilege of Appearance by Attorney upon a *Pluries*, he [f] shall wholly avoid such Disadvantage when such Award, which should have caused it, appears to be any way erroneous, whether in Respect of a Discontinuance, or Miscontinuance, or otherwise.

Sect. 111. Also, for the like Reason, it seems to be [g] agreed, That if a Man be outlawed, or condemned by Default, for not appearing to Process, which is any way erroneous, he may take Advantage of the Error in Avoidance of such Outlawry, or other Condemnation; for no one shall be condemned barely for not appearing, where that which should have compelled him to have appeared is defective. But it [h] seems, That a Defect in Process in an Outlawry, may be salved by the Defendant's Purchasing a Pardon, and shewing it to the Court; for that supposes that there was such an Outlawry against him, as needed a Pardon, which, if it were erroneous, it would not do.

Sect. 112. How far a Discontinuance of one Appeal will be a Bar to another, hath been already considered, *Chap.* 23. *Sect.* 132.

And now I am in the second Place particularly to consider the Nature of Process on a Criminal Accusation, with a particular Regard to Process of Outlawry only; and for the better Understanding thereof, shall consider the following Points;

1. Whether Process of Outlawry lie in all Criminal Cases?
2. In what Manner it is to be awarded in general.
3. What is particularly required in the Award of it against the Principal and Accessary.

Sect. 113. As to the first Point, *viz.* Whether Process of Outlawry lie in all Criminal Cases: I take it to be certain, That it lies in all Appeals, [i] whether of Felony or Maihem, and in all Indictments of Treason or Felony, and on all [k] Returns of a Rescous; and also in all Indictments of [l] Trespass *Vi & Armis*. Also it seems probable, That it lies on an Indictment of [m] Conspiracy, or [n] Deceit, or any other Crime of a higher Nature than a Trespass with Force and Arms, but [o] not on any Indictment for a Crime of an inferior Nature.

[a] Cro. Jac. 467. pl. 14. 1 Danv. Abr. 354, 355, 357.
[b] Vide 21 Jac. 13. 1 Danv. Ab. 340. pl. 2, 3. 341. pl. 4, 5. 8 Co. 163. a.
[c] 6 Mod. 283, 284, 285. 1 Salk. 51.
[d] Long quint. E. 4. 140. Bro. Amend. 10, 17, 66, 92. Discontinuance de Process, 4, 47. Vide Fitz. Amendment, 59, 75. 29 E. 3. 32.
[e] 21 H. 7. 40. pl. 65. Fitz. Amendment, 78.
[f] 10 H. 7. 21. pl. 15. 12 H. 4. 18. pl. 15. 19 H. 6. 29. a. 3 H. 4. 10. pl. 10. S. P. C. 184. Letter D. Vide Bro. Att. 82, 84. Exigent, 20. H. P. C. 271. Fitz. Amendment, 27. Discontinuance, 40, 51. Error, 82. But 8 H. 5. 2. pl. 9. 43 E. 3. 17. b. 18. a. 34. pl. 47. Fitz. Amendment, 77. Bro. Appeal, 7. seem contrary.
[g] 3 H. 7. 8. b. 9. a. Fitz. Replead. 1. Error, 47. Discontinuance de Process, 17. 1 Sid. 100. pl. 3. 260. pl. 7. Bro. Restitution, 8. Amendment, 60. 9 E. 4. 18. pl. 20.

[h] 3 H. 7. 10. pl. 10. Fitz. Charter, 25. Discontinuance, 51. [i] Finch of Law 346. Theloal Digest of Writs, B. 1. ch. 15. pl. 1. 35 H. 6. 6. pl. 9. [k] 13 H. 7. 21. pl. 5. 2 Inst. 665. Cont. Fitz. Process, 56, 213. 29 E. 3. 18. a. b. [l] 22 E. 4. 11. pl. 31. Finch of Law 355. Bro. Exigent, 51. 35 H. 6. 6. pl. 9. 2 H. H. P. C. 194. [m] 8 H. 6. 9. pl. 21. Fitz. Pro. 89. Bro. Exigent, 25, 28, 46. S. P. C. 172. 22 H. 6. 7. pl. 11. [n] 35 H. 6. 6. pl. 9. [o] Vide 22 E. 4. 11. pl. 31. 35 H. 6. 6. pl. 9. Cont. 8 H. 6. 9. pl. 21. Theloal B. 1. ch. 15.

Sect. 114. It ſeems [a] agreed, That it lies not on any Action on a Statute, unleſs it be given by ſuch Statute, either expreſly, as in the Caſe of a [b] *Præmunire*, and many other Caſes; or impliedly, as where a Recovery is given by an Action wherein ſuch Proceſs lay before. And agreeably hereto it hath been adjudged, That it lies not in an Action on the Statutes of [c] Liveries, or of [d] Maintenance, nor in a [e] *decies tantum*, and that it lay not in a Writ of [f] Entry on 5 *Ric.* 2. 7. till it was given by 23 *H.* 8. 14. But that it lies on a Writ of Treſpaſs for a [g] Forcible Entry on 8 *H.* 6. 9. becauſe the Statute expreſly gives a Recovery by ſuch Writ, and ſuch Proceſs lies in it by the Common Law. It ſeems to be holden in the [h] *Year-Book* 8 *H.* 6. That it lies on all Indictments on Statutes; but the contrary is adjudged in [i] 22 *E.* 4. as to the Statutes againſt *Foreſtalling*; and it is there laid down as a general Rule, That it lies not on an Indictment any more than in an Action on a Statute, unleſs it be expreſly or impliedly given by ſuch Statute.

As to the ſecond Point, *viz.* In what Manner Proceſs of Outlawry is to be awarded in general: I ſhall obſerve the following Particulars;

Sect. 115. *Firſt*, That it ſeems to be agreed [k] That in every Indictment or Appeal, for any Crime under the Degree of Capital, there muſt be three *Capias's* to the Sheriff of the ſame County wherein the Proſecution is commenced, before the Exigent ſhall be awarded, unleſs it be after [l] Judgment; in which Caſe one *Capias* is ſufficient. And [m] *Quære*, If three *Capias's* be not ſtill neceſſary in an Appeal of Rape, as they were at the Common Law, notwithſtanding it be made [n] Felony by Statute?

Sect. 116. *Secondly*, That it ſeems to be [o] agreed, That one *Capias*, before the Award of the Exigent, hath always been ſufficient in an Indictment or Appeal of Death, or High Treaſon; but that it ſeems [p] doubtful whether two *Capias's* were not required by the Common Law, in all Indictments and Appeals of any other Felony. However it is certain, That they are required in all Indictments of any other Felony, by 25 *E.* 3. 14. by which it is recorded, *That if after any Man be indicted of Felony, before the Juſtices in their Seſſions, to hear and determine, it ſhall be commanded to the Sheriff, to attach his Body by Writ or Precept, which is called a* Capias; *and if the Sheriff return that the Body is not found, another ſhall be incontinently made, returnable at three Weeks after, wherein it ſhall be compriſed, that the Sheriff ſhall cauſe to be ſeiſed his Chattels, and ſafely to keep them till the Day of the Writ or Precept returned. And if the Sheriff return, That the Body is not found, and the Indictee cometh not, the Exigent ſhall be awarded, and the Chattels ſhall be forfeit, as the Law of the Crown ordaineth. But if he come and yield himſelf, or be taken by the Sheriff, or by other Miniſter, before the Return of the ſecond* Capias, *then the Goods and Chattels ſhall be ſaved.* It ſeems to have been the general [q] Opinion, That this Statute extends to Appeals as well as Indictments, tho' it mention only the latter; but that it extends not to any Indictment or Appeal of Death, tho' it ſpeak of Felony in general.

Sect. 117. *Thirdly*, [r] That after the Sheriff hath returned a *Cepi*, if he have not the Body at the Day, the Court will not award an Exigent on the Suggeſtion of an Eſcape, unleſs the Sheriff will return one.

[a] 22 E. 4. 11. b. 8 H. 6. 9. pl. 21. Fitz. Proceſ. 81. Bro. Proceſs, 57. Exigent, 25. [b] Fitz. Proceſs, 106. 9 E. 4. 2. pl. 8. See the Statute againſt Proviſors, 27 E. 3. [c] 8 H. 6. 9. pl. 21. [d] 22 E. 4. 11. b. Cont. Fitz. Proceſs, 89. 22 H. 6. 7. pl. 11. Quære Bro. Exigent, 28. [e] 8 H. 6. 9. pl. 21. 35 H. 6. 6. pl. 9. Bro. Proceſs, 145. [f] 35 H. 6. 6. pl. 9. Fitz. Proceſs, 101. Bro. Proceſs, 16. [g] Bro. Exigent, 35. 37 H. 6. 23. pl. 11. [h] 8 H. 6. 9. pl. 21. Fitz. Proceſs, 81. [i] 22 E. 4. 11. b. Bro. Exigent, 51. Vide 35 H. 6. 6. pl. 9. 37 H. 6. 23. pl. 11. [k] Finch of Law, 351, 355. Raſt. Entr. 188. pl. 18. 302. pl. 1, 2, 3. 26 E. 3. 72. pl. 13. Fitz. Exigent, 30. Utlagary, 17. Error, 82. Vide 3 H. 6. 9. a. 3 H. 4. 11. pl. 10. [l] 40 E. 3. 25. pl. 28. Fitz. Exigent, 7, 27. Finch 476. [m] 1 Vide 16 Aſſ. pl. 13. Fitz. Exigent, 10. Coro. 173. Bro. Proceſs, 148. Exigent, 67. [n] Vide ſupra ch. 23. ſect. 59 to 70. [o] S. P. C. 67. a. H. P. C. 209. 2 H. H. P. C. 194. Fitz. Coro. 234. 1 H. 5. 5. pl. 8. Finch 351. [p] Fitz. Coro. 184, 234. 22 Aſſ. pl. 97. Cont. 8 H. 5. 6. pl. 25. Fitz. Exigent, 3. [q] S. P. C. 67. H. P. C. 209. Vide Fitz. Exigent, 3, 28, 30. Proceſs, 226. 8 H. 5. 6. pl. 25. 1 H. 5. 6. pl. 8. S. P. C. 70. Letter G. Fitz. Exigent, 25. 30 Aſſ. pl. 23.

Sect. 118. *Fourthly*, That if there be feveral Appellees, fome of which appear, and others make Default, and thofe who appear plead a Plea in Abatement of the Writ, or any fuch Plea in Bar as goes to the Whole, the Suit [a] fhall be continued againft thofe who made Default by *Capias* only, and no Exigent fhall iffue till fuch Plea or Pleas fhall be determined.

Sect. 119. *Fifthly*, That an Exigent fhall [b] never be awarded to the Sheriff of any other County than that wherein the Offence is laid ; and that by the [c] Common Law there was no [d] Neceffity of a *Capias* to the Sheriff of any other County. But the Law relating to this Matter, having been altered by feveral Statutes, I fhall fet forth thofe Statutes in particular, and endeavour to fhew how they are to be underftood.

Sect. 120. And firft it is enacted by 6 *H.* 6. 1. *That before any Exigent be awarded againft Perfons indicted in the King's Bench, of Treafon or Felony, Writs of* Capias *fhall be directed as well to the Sheriff or Sheriffs of the County wherein they be indicted, as to the Sheriff or Sheriffs of the County whereof they be named in the Indictments, the fame* Capias *having the Space of fix Weeks at the leaft, or longer Time, by the Difcretion of the faid Juftices, if the Cafe require it, before the Return of the fame ; which Writs fo returned, the Juftices fhall proceed in the Manner as they had done before the Statute : And if any Exigent be awarded or any Outlawry pronounced againft fuch Perfons before the Return of the faid Writs, the fame Exigent, fo awarded, with the Outlawry thereof pronounced, fhall be void, and holden for none.*

Sect. 121. And it is farther enacted by 8 *H.* 6. 10. *That upon every Indictment or Appeal, by the which any Subject dwelling in other Counties than where fuch Indictments or Appeal fhall be taken, of Treafon, Felony, and Trefpafs, before the Juftices of Peace, or before any other, having Power to take fuch Indictments or Appeals, or other Commiffioners or Juftices, in any County, Franchife, or Liberty of* England, *before any Exigent awarded, prefently after the firft Writ of* Capias *returned, another Writ of* Capias *fhall be awarded, directed to the Sheriff of the County whereof he, who is fo indicted, is or was fuppofed to be converfant by the fame Indictment, returnable before the fame Juftices, before whom he is indicted, or appealed, at a certain Day, containing the Space of three Months, from the Date of the faid laft Writ, where the Counties be holden from Month to Month ; and where the Counties be holden from fix Weeks to fix Weeks, the Space of four Months, until the Day of the Return of the faid Writ ; by which Writ of fecond* Capias, *the Sheriff fhall be commanded to take him which is fo indicted or appealed, by his Body, if he can be found within his Bailiwick : And if he cannot be found within his Bailiwick to make Proclamation in two Counties before the Return of the fame Writ, that he which is fo indicted or appealed, fhall appear before the faid Juftices,* &c. *at the Day contained in the faid Writ, to anfwer,* &c. *After which Writ fo ferved and returned, if he which is fo indicted or appealed, come not at the Day of fuch Writ returned, the Exigent fhall be awarded. And that every Exigent and Outlawry otherwife awarded, or pronounced, fhall be holden for none, and void.*

Sect. 122. But it is exprefly provided, *That the above-recited Statute, concerning Procefs to be made before the King in his Bench, ftand in force. And that this prefent Statute fhall not extend to Indictments or Appeals taken within the County of* Chefter. *And that if any Perfon fhall be indicted or appealed of Felony or Treafon, and at the Time of the fame Felony or Treafon fuppofed, was converfant within the County, whereof the Indictment or Appeal makes mention, the like Procefs be made againft him as was ufed before.*

[a] H. P. C. 210. S. P. C. 70. Letter B.
[b] Fitz. Exigent, 26. Default 10, 97. 22 E. 3. 11. pl. 4. 30 H. 6. 2. pl. 7. 11 H. 4. 72. pl. 6.
[c] Fitz. Procefs, 4, 34. See the Preamble of 6 H. 6. 1. and 8 H. 6. 10.
[d] Vide Fitz. Procefs, 1, 3, 34, 155, 164. 22 E. 3. 11. pl. 4. 47 Ed. 3. 4. pl. 7. Dyer 295. pl. 18. 30 H. 6. 2. pl. 7. 11 H. 4. 72. pl. 6.

Sect. 123. And it is farther enacted by 10 *H.* 6. 6. *That such second* Capias, *as is required by* 8 H. 6. 10. *shall be awarded upon Indictments or Appeals, removed into the King's Bench, or elsewhere, by* Certiorari *or otherwise.*

Sect. 124. It is observable that it seems to be holden generally in many [a] Books, That every Outlawry whatever, on an Indictment or Appeal against a Person living in a County different from that wherein the Court sits, is erroneous, if no such *Capias*, with a Command to the Sheriff to make Proclamation, as is given by 8 *H.* 6. were awarded to the Sheriff of the County wherein the Party is supposed to be conversant, before the Award of the Exigent: And there are [b] Precedents wherein Outlawries in Appeals, originally commenced in the King's Bench, have been reversed for want of such a *Capias.* Yet it seems, That on the other Side it may be probably argued, That Indictments of Treason or Felony, originally commenced in the King's Bench, are expresly provided for by the [c] Statute of 6 *H.* 6. which requires, That a *Capias*, having the Space of six Weeks or more, shall be awarded to the Sheriff of the County whereof the Indictee shall be named; and this Statute is taken Notice of by that of 8 *H.* 6. which expresly enacts, That it shall stand in its full Force, and therefore cannot well be imagined to intend either to supersede or repeal it. Especially, considering that it begins with Justices of Peace, and makes no express Mention of the King's Bench: And it is a [d] general Rule, in the Construction of Statutes, That where Things of an inferior Degree are first mentioned, those of a higher Dignity shall not be included under subsequent general Words. Also it appears from the Preamble of 10 *H.* 6. 6. That neither Indictments nor Appeals, removed into the King's Bench by *Certiorari*, were within the Benefit of 8 *H.* 6. 10. before the Making of that Statute, which expresly provides for Indictments and Appeals so removed; and there seems at least as good Reason, that Indictments and Appeals, originally commenced in the King's Bench, shall not be taken to be within the Benefit of it. To which may be added, That it seems to have been admitted in the *Year-Book* of [e] 31 *H.* 6. that an Appeal, originally commenced in the King's Bench, is within the Equity of 6 *H.* 6. 1. and that an Outlawry thereon is erroneous, if there were no *Capias* containing the Space of six Weeks, directed to the Sheriff of the County whereof the Appellee is named, as that Statute requires; by which it seems to be implied, That such an Appeal is not within the 8 but 6 *H.* 6. and that the same is still in Force.

[a] 1 E. 4. 1. pl. 3. 19 H. 6. 2. pl. 2. S. P. C. 67, 68, 69. H. P. C. 209. Fitz. Process, 103. 39 H. 6. 1. pl. 2.
[b] Ra. Entr. 304. pl. 2, 3. Vide 19 H. 6. 2. pl. 2. Fitz. Error, 26. Ra. Ent. 52. pl. 1, 2.
[c] Vide supra Sect. 120. 2 H. H. P. C. 195.
[d] 2 Co. 46. b.
[e] 31 H. 6. 11. pl. 8.

Sect. 125. It seems to have been [f] agreed, That by Force of these Statutes, a *Capias* shall be awarded into a County Palatine, where the Defendant is named of any Place in such County, in any Indictment or Appeal; and it seems, That such *Capias* shall be directed to, and returned by the [g] Chancellor of such County; and it hath been [h] said, That if he will not return it, the Exigent may be awarded as well as if he had returned it; because the Court cannot compel him to return it, and the Prosecution might be unreasonably delayed, if the Proceedings were to be stayed till he should return it. But [i] *Staundeforde* makes a *Quære*, Whether the Court of King's Bench may not enforce a Return of the Writ?

Sect. 126. If a Defendant be expresly named of the same County wherein he is indicted or appealed, and be also named under an *Alias dictus* of another, it hath been [k] adjudged, That there is no Need of any *Capias*,

[f] S. P. C. 68. Letter D. H. P. C. 209, 210. 2 H. H. P. C. 196, 197. 19 H. 6. 2. 31 H. 6. 11. pl. 11. Fitz. Cor. 19. Bro. Cinque Ports, 22. Sed vide 1 H. 6. 10.
[g] Ra. Entr. 52 pl. 1, 2. 19 H. 6. 2. 31 H. 6. 11. Cont. S. P. C. 68. Lett. D. Fitz. Process, 197. Bro. Cinque Port, 22.
[h] 31 H. 6. 11. pl. 8.
[i] S. P. C. 69. a. Vide Cro. Car. 252, 253.
[k] 1 E. 4. 1. pl. 3. Fitz. Process, 103. Dyer 214. pl. 44. Bro. Proclamation, 5. S. P. C. 68. b.

[a] Supra Ch. 25. Sect. 70. [b] S. P. C. 68. Lett. B. Fitz. Procefs, 192. Crompton 152.

with a Command for Proclamation, according to 8 *H.* 6. becaufe that which comes under the *alias dictus* is [a] no way traverfable nor material. Alfo if a Defendant be named of *B.* and late of *C.* there is [b] no Need of any *Capias* to the Sheriff of the County wherein *C.* lies, becaufe it appears that the Defendant is at prefent converfant at *B.* But if a Defendant be named of no certain Place at prefent, but only late of *B.* and late of *C.* and late of *D. &c.* being all of them in Counties different from that wherein the Profecution is commenced, a *Capias* fhall go to the Sheriff of [c] every one of thofe Counties.

[c] H.P.C.210. 2 H. H. P. C. 196. [d] 39 H. 6. 1. pl. 2. Bro. Utlagary, 34. Error, 16. 19 H. 6. 2. pl. 2. Fitz. Error, 26. Cro. El. 179. pl. 10. 3 Co. 59. b. Plow. Com. 137. b.

Sect. 127. Notwithftadning the Words are exprefs, That any Outlawry pronounced contrary to the Directions of the Statutes, fhall be void: Yet it feems to be agreed, [d] That it is not to be taken to be utterly void, but only voidable by Writ of Error.

Sect. 128. As to the third Point, *viz.* What is particularly required in the Award of Procefs of Outlawry againft the Principal and Acceffary, it is recited by the Statute of *Weftminfter*, 1. 14. *That it had been ufed in fome Counties to outlaw Perfons being appealed of Commandment, Force, Aid or Receipt, within the fame Time that he which is appealed for the Deed is outlawed: And thereupon it is provided, That none be outlawed upon Appeal of Commandment, Force, Aid or Receipt, unlefs he that is appealed of the Deed be attainted: So that one like Law be ufed therein thro' the Realm; neverthelefs, he that will fo appeal, fhall not, by Reafon of this, intermit or leave off to commence his Appeal at the next County againft them, no more than againft their Principals, which be appealed of the Deed, but their Exigent fhall remain, until fuch as be appealed of the Deed be attainted by Outlawry or otherwife.*

In the Conftruction of this Statute, the following Particulars feem moft remarkable;

[e] H. P. C. 210. 2 H. H. P. C. 200. 2 Inft. 183. S. P. C. 46. 69. Lett. A. [f] 9 Co. 119. a. [g] S. P. C. 44. Lett. G. 46. Lett. A. 69. Lett. B. [h] Bract. f. 127. b. 128. a. See Britt. f. 5. 2 Inft. 183. [i] 43 E. 3. 17. b. 18. a. 34. pl. 47. 44 Aff. pl. 16. Ra. Entr. 48. b. [k] Vide H.P.C. 210. 2 H. H. P.C. 200. 2 Inft. 183. S. P. C. 46. Lett. B. 70. Lett. A. 148. Lett. A.

Sect. 129. *Firft*, That it feems to be [e] agreed, That it extends as well to Indictments as to Appeals, not only becaufe the Word [f] Appeal in the Statute may, in a large Senfe, be taken for any Accufation in general; but becaufe Indictments are certainly as much within the Reafon of the Statute, as Appeals; and the Common Law, for the [g] Settling whereof this Statute was made, did [h] not make any Diftinction in this Refpect between Appeals and Indictments.

Sect. 130. *Secondly*, That it feems alfo to be [i] agreed, That whereever fome of the Defendants are exprefly charged as Principals, and others as Acceffaries, before the Award of this Exigent, the Outlawry thereon of thofe charged as Acceffaries, cannot but be reverfible; becaufe it appears upon the Record, That the Exigent iffued contrary to the Directions of the Statute. But if feveral be outlawed on a Writ of Appeal, which [k] chargeth them all alike, without any Diftinction, I [l] fee not how any Advantage can be taken of the Appellant's not having purfued the Statute, fince it appears not but that he might have charged them all as Principals.

Sect. 131. *Thirdly*, That it is holden both by [m] *Staundeforde*, [n] *Coke*, and [o] *Hale*, That if an Appellant take out the Exigent at the fame Time againft all the Defendants, he muft, when they appear, count againft them all as Principals, and fhall be concluded to count againft fome as

[l] Vide 43 E. 3. 17. b. 18. a. 34. pl. 47. 44 Aff. pl. 16. Bro. Appeal, 7. 79. Bro. Exigent, 44. Fitz. Forfeiture, 14. [m] S. P. C. 46. Lett. B. 70. Lett. A. [n] 2 Inft. 183. [o] H. P. C. 210. 2 H. H. P. C. 200. The Principal Authorities in the Old Books for the Maintenance of this Opinion feem to be 7 H. 4. 27. Fitz. Coro. 80. 20 E. 3. 7. b.

Principals, and others as Acceſſaries, becauſe he has taken out ſuch Proceſs againſt them which is erroneous, where all are not Principals. But granting that an Exigent taken out at the ſame Time againſt all the Defendants, appear to have been erroneous, when by the Declaration it appears that ſome of the Defendants are accuſed only as Acceſſaries, and therefore ought not to have had an Exigent awarded againſt them, till the Principal had been attainted: Yet ſeeing this is only an Error in the Proceſs to bring in the Defendant, and all ſuch Errors are ſalved by an Appearence, as the Law ſeems to be now ſettled, and hath been more fully ſhewn, *Sections* 107, *&c.* It ſeems [a] queſtionable at this Day, Whether an Appellant may not be at Liberty to declare as he pleaſes againſt Defendants appearing on ſuch an Exigent? However, it is certainly ſafeſt, [b] and moſt adviſable for an Appellant when he comes to the Exigent to ſhew which of the Defendants he intends to charge as Principals, and which of them as Acceſſaries, and to take out the Exigent againſt the Former only, and a *Capias* againſt the others.

[a] See 40 Aſſ. pl. 25. where it appears that Perſons appealed as Acceſſaries, and brought in by Exigent were ſtill proceeded againſt as Acceſſaries. See alſo 43 E. 3. 17. b. 18. a. 35. pl. 47. 44 Aſſ. pl. 16.

Sect. 132. *Fourthly*, That it ſeems the better [c] Opinion, That where there are more than one Principal, the Exigent ought not to iſſue till all of them are attainted.

Bro. Appeal, 7. Exigent, 44. Fitz. Forfeiture, 14. [b] Bro. Appeal, 107. 20 E. 3. 7. b. [c] 2 Inſt. 183. 1 H. H. P. C. 624. 2 H. H. P. C. 200, 201. Plowd. Com. 29. a. *dubitatur* 7 H. 4. 36. pl. 5. Bro. Appeal, 22. Contr. Fitz. Exigent, 4.

CHAP. XXVIII.

☞ *Of Arraignment in general.* [80]

HAving ſhewn in what Manner a Perſon under a Criminal Accuſation is to be brought into Court; I ſhall in the next Place endeavour to ſhew in what Manner he is to be arraigned or put upon his Trial; and this I conſider, 2 H. H. P. C. 216 to 225

Firſt, As it relates to all Criminals in general.
Secondly, As it relates to Principal and Acceſſaries in particular.

And firſt, As to the Arraignment of all Criminals in general: Having already ſhewn in the Twenty-fifth [d] Chapter, That regularly the Court will not arraign a Man upon an Indictment while an Appeal for the ſame Crime is depending againſt him; I ſhall here conſider only the following Particulars:

[d] Sect. 15.

Firſt, In what Manner a Criminal is to be arraigned.
Secondly, Whether the Omiſſion of it will be Error.
Thirdly, Where a Perſon ſhall be arraigned upon ſeveral Appeals or Indictments.

As

As to the firſt Particular, *viz.* In what Manner a Criminal is to be arraigned, I ſhall obſerve,

Sect. 1. *Firſt*, That every Perſon at the Time of his Arraignment, ought to be uſed with all the [a] Humanity and Gentleneſs which is conſiſtent with the Nature of the Thing, and under no other Terror or Uneaſineſs than what proceeds from a Senſe of his Guilt, and the Misfortune of his preſent Circumſtances; and therefore ought not to be brought to the Bar in a contumelious Manner; as with his [b] Hands tied together, or any other Mark of Ignominy and Reproach: Nor even with Fetters on [c] his Feet, unleſs there be ſome Danger of a Reſcous or Eſcape. [81] It ſeems indeed to have been holden by [d] ſome, That this is a particular Privilege of Perſons in Holy Orders. But it ſeems the [e] better Opinion, That the Law makes no Diſtinction in this Reſpect, between them and Laymen.

Sect. 2. *Secondly*, That there is no Neceſſity that a Priſoner at the Time of his Arraignment hold up his Hand at the Bar, or be commanded ſo to do; for this is [f] only a Ceremony for making known the Perſon of the Offender to the Court; and if he anſwer that he is the ſame Perſon, it is all one.

Sect. 3. *Thirdly*, That on every Indictment the Arraignment muſt be in *Engliſh*, by Virtue of 37 *E.* 3. 15. by which it is enacted, *That all Pleas which ſhall be pleaded in any Courts whatſoever, before any of the King's Juſtices whatſoever, or in his other Places, or before any of his other Miniſters whatſoever, or in the Courts and Places of any other Lords whatſoever within the Realm, ſhall be pleaded, ſhewed, defended, anſwered, debated, and judged in the* Engliſh *Tongue, and entered and inrolled in* Latin. But it ſeems to have been always taken, That Appeals are not within this Statute, but that they are to be arraigned, and the Plea of the Defendant to be read, in [g] *French*, in the ſame Manner as anciently; and thus I have often known it done in my own [h] Experience; but upon what Reaſon this Difference between Appeals and all other Proſecutions is grounded, I have never heard. [82]

Sect. 4. *Fourthly*, [i] That an Appeal in the King's Bench ought to be arraigned on the Plea-ſide, unleſs it come in by *Certiorari*, in which Caſe it is ſaid, That it ought to be arraigned on the Crown-ſide.

Sect. 5. *Fifthly*, That where a Writ of Appeal is abated, the Priſoner ſhall not [k] be arraigned on the Count, at the Suit of the Party, becauſe the Count depends upon the Writ, and that being determined, all [l] falls to the Ground. Yet it ſeems certain, That if the Writ were good, the Appellee may in many Caſes be arraigned at the Suit of the King upon the Count, as hath been more fully ſhewn, *Ch.* 23. *Sect.* 7, 8, 9, 10, 11, 12, 13.

Sect. 6. As to the ſecond Particular, *viz.* Whether the Omiſſion of an Arraignment will be Error: It is ſaid in the Third [m] *Modern Report*, That an Attainder of High Treaſon was reverſed for this and other Errors. Neither do I find any Precedent of an Attainder in *Coke's Entries*, on an

[a] 3 Inſt. 34, 35. 2 Inſt. 315, 316.
[b] Bracton 137. p. 3. Briton 14, 17. Fleta, Lib. 1. cap. 31.
[c] Bracton 137. pl. 3. 3 Inſt. 34, 35. H. P. C. 212. 2 H. H. P. C. 219. Kely. 10.
[d] Fitz. Coro. 432. S. P. C. 133. Lett. H.
[e] 3 Inſt. 34, 35. H. P. C. 212. 2 Inſt. 315. Briton 14, 17. Bracton 137. pl. 3. S. P. C. 133. Letters F, G. Kely. 10.
[f] Agreed by all the Judges in the Lord Stafford's Caſe, Raym. 408.
[g] 1 Sid. 324. pl. 4. 2 Jon. 210. Cro. El. 69. pl. 22. 1 Salk. 61.
[h] As in the Caſe of Smith and Bowen, Mich. 7. Ann. And that of Widdrington and Carlton, Trin. 11 Annæ. And that of Reeve and Trundal, Paſch. 3 Geo. 1.
[i] 2 Jon. 210. 1 Sid. 324. pl. 4. 1 Salk. 62. Raym. 408.
[k] Style's Rep. 7.
[l] Bro. App. 44. 4 H. 6. 16. Vide ſupra Ch. 23. Sect. 10.
[m] 3 Mod. 265. Vide 2 H. H. P. C. 217, 218.

Indictment of [a] Treason or [b] Felony, in which it is not expressed either in these Words, *Ad barram hic ductus in propria persona sua committitur mareschallo, &c. & statim de præmissis* (in Case of Felony, or *de altis proditionibus*, in Case of High Treason) *ei superius impositis allocutus qualiter se velit inde acquietare dicit, &c.* or in Words [c] tantamount. And therefore it is certainly safest to express it in every Record of such Attainder, where the Party appears and is condemned, whether upon Confession or Verdict, or standing Mute, *&c.* Yet I find it wholly omitted in every Attainder upon an [d] Appeal in *Coke's Entries*, and much oftner [e] omitted than expressed [f] in such Attainders in *Rastal*.

Sect. 7. As to the third Particular, *viz.* Where a Person shall be arraigned upon several Appeals or Indictments: It seems, that by the Common Law, if a Man be appealed of divers Robberies at the Suit of divers Persons, he may be severally [g] arraigned on each Appeal, and then severally tried on each, that each Appellant may be equally intitled to the Restitution of his Goods, upon the Conviction of the Appellee. And in like Manner at this Day a Person charged with several [h] Indictments of Robbery at the Prosecution of several Persons, may be severally arraigned and tried on each Indictment; because the Prosecutor since the Statute of 21 *H.* 8. 11. is intitled to a Restitution of his Goods upon a Conviction on such an Indictment, in the same Manner as the Plaintiff is upon a Conviction in an Appeal. And it is holden both by [i] *Staundforde* and [k] *Hale*, that even a Person attainted of Robbery at the Suit of one Person, may be arraigned and tried at the Suit of another, if such Suit were commenced before the Attainder: But *Quære:* For of the Authorities cited for the Maintenance of this Opinion two [l] seem to be directly against it; and the [m] other, which seems most to the Point, does not come up to it.

Sect. 8. It is made a *Quære* by [n] *Staundforde*, Whether a Prisoner before his Attainder shall answer to divers Appeals of Death or Rape, in the same Manner as in Case of Robbery?

[a] Coke's Ent. 360. pl. 14. 361. pl. 15, 16.

[b] Coke's Ent. 352. pl. 2, 3. 354. b. 355. pl. 7, 8. 356. pl. 9. 358. pl 11. 360. pl 13.

[c] See Rast. Ent. 42. pl. 2.

[d] See Coke's Ent. from f. 53 to 60.

[e] See Ra. Ent. 47. a. b. 48. a. b. 49. a. b. 50. a. b. 52. a. 54. a. 55. b.

[f] See Rast. Ent. 42. pl. 2. 53. pl. 6.

[g] 4 E. 4. 11. pl. 18. H. P. C. 212. S. P. C. 66. Letters A, B. 107. Letter B. 160. b. Fitz. Coro. 26, 27.

[h] S. P. C. 66. Letter E. H. P. C. 212.

[i] S. P. C. 66. a. b.

[k] H. P. C. 212, 258. [l] Fitz. Coro. 379. 7 H. 4. 31. pl. 16. Abridged Fitz. Coro. 81. [m] 4 Ed. 4. 11. pl. 18. Abridged Fitz. Coro. 26, 27. See 44 E. 4. 44. pl. 57. Abridged Fitz. Coro. 95. See also Chap. 23. Sect. 53. and the Chapter concerning the Plea of Autrefoits convict and attaint. [n] S. P. C. 66. Lett. C.

CHAP. XXIX.

Of the Arraignment of the Principal and Acceſſary.

AND now I am in the ſecond Place to conſider the Nature of Arraignment, ſo far as it particularly relates to Principals and Acceſſaries; for the better Underſtanding whereof, it may not be improper to conſider,

1. In what Caſes, in Judgment of Law, a Man ſhall be ſaid to be a Principal, and in what Caſes he ſhall be ſaid to be an Acceſſary.
2. Where he ſhall be adjudged an Acceſſary before.
3. Where an Acceſſary after.

1 H. H. P. C. 612 to 618.
1 H. H. P. C. 618 to 622.

Sect. 1. And 1ſt, For the better Underſtanding in what Caſes a Man ſhall be ſaid to be a Principal, and in what an Acceſſary; having premiſed, that where a Felony is committed by divers Perſons, the [a] ſame Man may be a Principal and Acceſſary in it, and ſo charged in the [b] ſame Indictment or Appeal; as where *A.* commands *B.* to kill *C.* and afterwards actually joins with him in the Fact. And having alſo farther premiſed, that it is agreed by all the Books, that a Man may be an Acceſſary after the Fact, by [c] receiving one who was an Acceſſary before, as well as by receiving a Principal; and that there ſeems to be the ſame [d] Reaſon, that a Man may be an Acceſſary before the Fact, by procuring another to be in ſuch Manner an Acceſſary to the Principal, I ſhall endeavour to ſhew,

1. In what Offences there can be no Acceſſaries, but all muſt be Principals, if any way guilty:
2. Where thoſe who only abet a Fact, ſhall be eſteemed as much Principals in it as thoſe who actually do it.
3. Where thoſe who are actually abſent when a Fact is committed may be eſteemed Principals in it.
4. Where one ſhall be adjudged a Principal in an Offence againſt a Statute.
5. Whether the Offence of an Acceſſary can ever riſe higher than that of the Principal.

[a] H. P. C. 219. 3 Inſt. 139. Keilw. 107. Fitz. Coro. 80.
[b] 7 H. 4. 27. pl. 4. Fitz. Coro. 80. Vide Fitz. Coro. 176, 285.
[c] Lamb. B. 2. Ch. 7. f. 291. 26Aſſ. pl. 52. Bro. Coro. 104. Fitz. Coro. 196. Crompt. Juſt. 42. pl. 24. S. P. C. 43. Letter D.
[d] See the Books above cited, and H. P. C. 219.

Sect. 2. As to the firſt Particular, *viz.* In what Offences there can be no Acceſſaries, but all muſt be Principals, if any way guilty: It ſeems to have been always an uncontroverted Maxim, that there can be no Acceſſaries in [e] High Treaſon, or [f] Treſpaſs. Alſo it ſeems to have been always agreed, That whatſoever will make a Man an Acceſſary before in

[e] 3 Inſt. 20, 21, 138. Dalif. 16. pl. 11. H. P. C. 215. 1 H. H. P. C. 613. 12 Co. 81, 82. 2 Inſt. 183. Bro. Treaſon, 19. 3 H. 7. 10. pl. 2. Fitz. Coro. 55. 19 H. 6. 47. pl. 103. S. P. C. 3. Lett. A. 40. Lett. C. Bro. Coro. 135. Dalt. Ch. 108. Crompt. 42. pl. 19. Co. Litt. 57. [f] 12 Co. 81, 82. 2 Inſt. 183. Bro. Rape, 3. Co. Litt. 57. 2 H. H. P. C. 613.

Felony, will make him a Principal in [a] High Treason and Trespass; as [b] Battery, [c] Riot, Rout, [d] Forcible Entry, and even in [e] Forgery and [f] Petit Larceny. And therefore, where-ever a Man commands another to commit a Trespass, who afterwards commits it in Pursuance of such Command, he [g] seems by necessary Consequence to be as guilty of it, as if he had done it himself; from whence it follows, that being in Judgment of Law a Principal Offender, he may be tried and found [h] Guilty, before any Trial of the Person who actually did the Fact.

Sect. 3. It was formerly a [i] Question, Whether the same Receipt of an Offender, which will make the Receiver an Accessary after the Fact in the Case of Felony, will make him a Principal in High Treason, as it seems to be [k] settled at this Day that it will? For if it should be adjudged a Misprision only, as [l] some have contended, a Man would be subject to a less Punishment for receiving a Traitor than for receiving a Felon; for he who receives a Felon is certainly liable to Judgment of Death, as being an Accessary to the Felony, but he who receives a Traitor would be liable only to Fine and Imprisonment, as being guilty of a Misprision only.

Sect. 4. It seems [m] agreed, That whosoever agrees to a Trespass on Lands or Goods done to his Use, thereby becomes a Principal in it. But that no one can become a Principal in a Trespass on the Person of a Man by any such Agreement. Also it seems [n] agreed, that no one shall be adjudged a Principal in any common Trespass, or inferior Crime of the like Nature, for barely receiving, comforting and concealing the Offender, though he know him to have been guilty, and that there is a Warrant out against him, which by Reason of such Concealment, cannot be executed. And if he cannot be punished as a Principal, it is certain that he cannot be punished as an Accessary; because in such Offences, all who are punished as Partakers of the Guilt of him who did the Fact, must be punished as Principals in it, or not at all. Yet if a Man knowing that there is a Warrant against such Offender, advise and perswade him to absent himself, [o] perhaps he may be indictable for a Contempt of the Law in hindring the due Course of Justice.

Sect. 5. It is certain, That in [p] Petit Treason, and also such Felony as shall have [q] Judgment of Death, there may be Accessaries both before and after the Fact, who must be proceeded against as such, and not as Principals, as shall be more fully shewn in the following Part of this Chapter. Also it seems, [r] that there may be Accessaries before the Fact in Mayhem, but that the Appellant hath his [s] Election to proceed against them either as Principals, or as Accessaries. [t] But I find it no where holden, that there can be Accessaries in Mayhem after the Fact.

Sect. 6. I do not find it agreed, [u] Whether there can be any Accessaries in *Præmunire*?

Sect. 7. As to the second Particular *viz.* Where those who only abet a Fact, shall be esteemed as much Principals in it as those who actually do it: It seems to have been [x] anciently the more prevailing Opinion, that

[a] 19 H. 6. 47. pl. 103. Bro. Treason, 9. Fitz. Coro. 8. 3 Inst. 138. [b] 38 Aff. pl. 9. Keilw. 55. pl. 4. [c] Co. Litt. 57. [d] B. 1. Ch. 64. S. 22. Co. Litt. 57. Fitz. Gard. 99. [e] Moor 666. pl. 913. Vide 1 Sid. 312. pl. 25. [f] Cro. E. 750. pl. 4. 2 Inst. 183. 12 Co. 81. Cont. H. P. C. 223. 1 H. H. P. C. 616. [g] Moor 787. H. P. C. 217. Pl. Com. 475. Vide infra, Sect. 7. Fitz. Coro. 314, 433. S. P. C. 41. Lett. D. Quære Moor 53. pl. 155. [h] Bro. Tres. 256. 1 Lev. 124. 29 Aff. pl. 59. Fitz. Aff. 291. Cont. 27 Aff. pl. 4. Quære Vaugh. 115, 116. [i] Dyer 296. pl. 21. 12 Co. 81, 82. 3 Inst. 138. Dalt. Ch. 89, 108. Crompt 42. pl. 19. Vide 3 H. 7. 10. pl. 2. S. P. C. 3. Lett. A. [k] H. P. C. 215. 3 Inst. 138. Dalt. Ch. 108. Crompt. 42. pl. 19. Vide supra Sect. 2. and B. 1. Ch. 20. Sect. 3, 4. S. P: C. 3. Lett. A. Bro. Treason, 19. Bro. Coro. 135. [l] Dyer 296. pl. 21. [m] Cro. El. 824. 38 Aff. pl. 9. Bro. Disseisor, 98. Bro. Ejectione Custodiæ, 8. Bro. Trespass, 256. 38 E. 3. 18. a. b. Co. Litt. 180. b. Fitz. Gard. 89. [n] Popham 134. 2 Rol. Abr. 75. Lett. A. pl. 3. [o] 2 Roll. Ab. 75. Lett. A. pl. 4. [p] Dalis. 16. pl. 11. 3 Inst. 20, 21. Crompton 42. pl. 19. S. P. C. 40. Lett. C. B. 1. Ch. 32. Sect. 5, 6. [q] 12 Co. 81, 82. Cro. El. 750. pl. 4. 2 Inst. 183. [r] See the Citations to the next Letter. Cont. Bro. Appeal, 154. [s] Vide supra Ch. 23. Sect. 19. 22 Aff. pl. 82. Fitz. Coro. 11, 182, 215, 221. Cont. 40. Aff. pl. 1. Bro. Appeal, 71, 154. [t] Vide supra Sect. 4. 1 H. H. P. C. 613. [u] Vide S. P. C. 44. Lett. F. Dalt. Ch. 108. Bro. Præmunire, 4, 6. Pl. Com. 97. b. 1 H. H. P. C. 613. [x] Pl. Com. 99. b. Fitz. Coro. 90, 216. 40 Aff. pl. 8. & 25. Bro. Coro. 11. 40 E. 3. 42. pl. 22. S. P. C. 48. Lett. G, H. 41. Lett. A, B. 44 E. 3. 38. pl. 35. See Bract. B. 3. Ch. 12. Sect. 10, 11, 13. Ch. 19. S. 11. Ch. 21. Sect. 8, 10, 11. Lamb. B. 2. ch. 7. fol. 282. Stat. of West. 1. ch. 14. Cont. Fitz. Coro. 433.

those

thoſe only were to be adjudged Principals in Felony who actually did the Fact; as in Murder, thoſe only who gave the Mortal Blow; in Rape, thoſe only who actually raviſhed the Party, *&c.* and that thoſe in the Company who were only preſent and abetted and encouraged the Doing it, were to be eſteemed Acceſſaries; or at moſt Principals in the [a] ſecond Degree only. But I take it to be ſettled at this Day, that all thoſe who [b] aſſemble themſelves together with a felonious Intent, the Execution whereof cauſes either the Felony intended, or any other to be committed, or with an Intent to commit a [c] Treſpaſs, the Execution whereof cauſes a Felony to be committed, and continuing together abetting one another till they have actually put their Deſign in Execution; and alſo all thoſe who are [d] preſent when a Felony is committed, and abet the Doing of it as by holding the [e] Party while another ſtrikes him; or by [f] delivering a Weapon to him that ſtrikes, or by moving [g] him to ſtrike, are Principals in the higheſt [h] Degree, in Reſpect of ſuch Abetment, as much as the Perſon who does the Fact, which in Judgment of Law is as [i] much the Act of them all, as if they had all actually done it; [k] and if there were Malice in the Abettor, and none in the Perſon who ſtruck the Party, it will be Murder as to the Abettor, and Manſlaughter only as to the other.

Sect. 8. It doth not ſeem neceſſary to the Making an Abettor a Principal, that the Perſon on whom the Felony is committed ſhould be under any [l] Terror from the Abetment, and by Reaſon thereof diſcouraged from making that Defence which otherwiſe he might have made; but it ſeems to be ſufficient for this Purpoſe, that the Perſon who does the Fact is encouraged and emboldened in it from the Hopes of preſent and immediate Aſſiſtance from the Abettor, whether he be within View of the Fact, or [m] not. And upon this Ground it hath been adjudged, [n] That where Perſons combine together, to ſtand by one another in a Breach of the Peace, with a general Reſolution to reſiſt all Oppoſers, and in the Execution of their Deſign a Murder is committed, all of the Company are equally Principals, tho' at the Time of the Fact ſome of them were at ſuch a Diſtance as to be out of View. Alſo upon the ſame Reaſon it hath been adjudged, [o] That where a Company of Rogues aſſault a Man in the Highway, who eſcapes from them, and then one of them rides from the reſt, in the ſame Highway, and robs another out of the View of his Companions, and then returns to them, they are all of them equally Principals. And the like hath been [p] adjudged in Relation to all thoſe who accompany one another with an Intent to commit a Burglary, in the Execution whereof ſome ſtand to watch only in the adjacent Places, and the reſt actually break, and enter the Houſe.

Sect. 9. But [q] where divers Perſons accompany one another in the doing of a lawful Act, and one of them happens to kill a Man, he that gives the Wound is only guilty of the Homicide, and the reſt of the Company ſhall neither be eſteemed Principals nor Acceſſaries. [r] Alſo if

[a] Pl. Com. 97.

[b] 11 H. 4. 13. pl. 30. Fitz. Coro. 86, 228. Bro. Appeal, 32. Moor 53. pl. 155. 9 Co. 67. b. Kely. 47. Pl. Com. 97, 98. 4 Co. 42. See the Caſes cited to the other Parts of this and the next Section, and B. 1. ch. 31. ſect. 31. ch. 32. ſect. 5. and ch. 41. ſect. 6.

[c] B. 1. ch. 31. ſect. 46. H. P. C. 216, 217. Fitz. Coro. 60, 314, 350, 433. Bro. Coro. 172. Keil. 161. Kely. 47. Salk. 334, 335. S. P. C. 40. Lett. D, E.

[d] See B. 1. ch. 32. ſect. 6. Moor 53. pl. 155. 2 Inſt. 182. 3 Inſt. 138. 59. Bro. Appeal, 19, 132. Bro. Coro. 19, 167, 188. S. P. C. 40. Lett. D. 44. Lett. B, C. 41 Lett. B. 10 E. 4. 14. pl. 8. H. P. C. 215, 216. Fitz. Coro. 99, 309, 433. Dalt. ch. 108. Lamb. B. 2. ch. 7. fol. 283. 7 H. 4. 27. pl. 4. Preſence holden not to be neceſſary for this Purpoſe. Fitz. Coro. 60. 4 H. 7. 18. pl. 10.

[e] H. P. C. 216. Fitz. Coro. 135. S. P. C. 40. Lett. F. 13 H. 7. 10. pl. 7.

[f] H. P. C. 216. 2 Inſt. 41, 82.

[g] Fitz. Coro. 60. S. P. C. 40. Lett. D. H. P. C. 216. 4 H. 7. 18. pl. 10. Bro. Coro. 141. Bro. Appeal, 85.

[h] H. P. C. 215, 216. Pl. Com. 98. Supra ch. 23. ſect. 76. ch. 25. ſect. 64.

[i] Pl. Com. 98, 100. Fitz. Coro. 60. Bro. Coro. 141. Bro. Appeal, 85. 4 H. 7. 18. pl. 10. 9 Co. 67. b.

[k] B. 1. ch. 31. ſect. 49 to ſect. 54.

[l] But this ſeems required in Pl. Com. 98.

[m] Fitz. Coro. 60. H. P. C. 216, 217. 4 H. 7. 18. pl. 10. Salk. 334, 335. B. 1. ch. 35. ſect. 7. ch. 38. ſect. 8.

[n] See B. 1. ch. 31. ſect. 46. H. P. C. 216, 217. Bro. Coro. 172. Salk. 334, 335. Keilw. 161. a. Fitz. Coro. 60, 314, 350, 433. S. P. C. 40. Lett. D, E. Vide Kely. 47.

[o] B. 1. ch. 34. ſect. 7. Vide Moor 53. pl. 155. S. P. C. 40. Lett. D, E.

[p] B. 1. ch. 38. ſect. 8, 9. 11 H. 4. 13, 30. Vide Moor, 53. pl. 155.

[q] Keilw. 161. a.

[r] Kely. 47.

the Act intended tho' unlawful, were a bare Treſpaſs, and one of the Company be guilty of Larceny, it is a Felony in ſuch Offender only, becauſe it is a Crime of a Nature entirely different from that intended, and not cauſed by the Execution of it.

Sect. 10. Alſo thoſe who by Accident are barely preſent when a Felony is committed, and are merely paſſive, and neither any Way encourage it, nor endeavour to hinder it, nor to apprehend the Offenders, ſhall [a] neither be adjudged Principals nor Acceſſaries; [b] yet if they be of full Age, they are highly puniſhable by Fine and Impriſonment for their Negligence, both in not endeavouring to [c] prevent the Felony, and in not endeavouring [d] to apprehend the Offender. And [e] if they any way ſhewed an Aſſent to the Felony, it ſeems, That they may be puniſhed as Principals in it; becauſe the Shewing ſuch an Aſſent could not but give Encouragement to it.

Sect. 11. As to the third Particular, *viz.* Where thoſe who are actually abſent when a Felony is committed may be eſteemed Principals in it: I take it to be a ſettled Rule, That where-ever a Man procures a Felony to be committed, and is abſent at the Time when it is committed, and no other Perſon but himſelf can be adjudged a Principal in it, he ſhall be eſteemed as much a Principal as if he had been preſent; for no one can be [f] puniſhed as a Felon, but either as a Principal or as an Acceſſary; and therefore where the Procurer of a Felony cannot be puniſhed as an Acceſſary, becauſe there is no other to whom he can be an Acceſſary, he muſt be puniſhed as a Principal, or not at all. And upon this Ground, it ſeems to be clear, That if a Man [g] perſuade another to drink a Poiſonous Liquor, under the Notion of a Medicine, who afterwards drinks it in his Abſence; [h] or if *A.* intending to poiſon *B.* put Poiſon into a Thing and deliver it to *C.* who knows nothing of the Matter, to be by him delivered to *B.* and *C.* innocently deliver it accordingly in the Abſence of *A.* or if one [i] incite a Madman to kill another, who afterwards kills him in the Abſence of the Perſon that incited him; in all theſe and the like Caſes, the Procurer of the Felony is as much a Principal as if he had been preſent when it was done. And ſo [k] likewiſe all thoſe ſeem to be, who were preſent when the Poiſon was infuſed, and privy to, and conſenting to the Deſign. But [l] thoſe who only abetted their Crime by their Command, Counſel or Advice, but were Abſent when the Poiſon was infuſed, are Acceſſaries, and not Principals. Alſo if *A.* intending to poiſon *B.* deliver a poiſonous Thing to *C.* to be by him delivered to *B.* and *C.* knowing it to be poiſoned deliver it to *B.* in the Abſence of *A.* In this Caſe *C.* [m] only is a Principal in the Felony, and *A.* an Acceſſary.

Sect. 12. By force of 3 *H.* 7. 2. All thoſe who are Acceſſaries before to the forcible taking away of a Woman, made Felony by that Statute, whether they were preſent or abſent at the Time of the Taking, or Acceſſaries after, by wittingly receiving the Woman ſo taken away, ſhall be puniſhed as [n] Principals; but this depends on the expreſs Words of the Statute, and not on any Conſtruction from the Reaſon of the Common Law.

[a] S. P. C. 40. Letters D, E. H. P. C. 216. Fitz. Coro. 92, 197, 395. Bro. Indict. 5. 14 H. 7. 31. pl. 7. Cont. Fitz. Coro. 314, 197. Lamb. B. 2. ch. 7. f. 289. Vide ſupra ch. 23. ſect. 66.
[b] S. P. C. 40. Letter E. Fitz Coro. 395.
[c] Noy 50. Dalt. ch. 108.
[d] Supra ch. 12. ſect. 1, 2, 3, 4.
[e] Vide infra ſect. 15. S. P. C. 40. Letters D, E. H. P. C. 217. Fitz Coro. 150. Dalt. ch. 108. Lamb. B. 2. ch. 7. f. 282. My Pleas of the Crown, B. 1. ch. 20. ſect. 3. But Fitz. Coro. 92. and Crompt. 41. pl. 7, 8. ſeems contrary.
[f] 4 Co. 44. b. Pult. 122 a.
[g] 4 Co. 44. b. 2 Inſt. 183. Crompt. 44. pl. 43. H.P.C 216. 1 H. H. P. C. 435, 615, 616 Pult. 122. a. Dalt. ch. 108. 9 Co. 81. 3 Inſt. 138.
[h] H.P.C. 218. 9 Co. 81. Kely. 52, 53.

[i] See B. 1. ch. 1 ſect. 7. 1 H. H. P. C. 617. [k] H. P. C. 216. [l] 4 Co. 44. b. Cromp. 44. pl. 43.
[m] Kely. 52, 53. [n] See B. 1. ch. 42. ſect. 8, 9. and H. P. C. 217. 1 H. H. P. C. 614.

Sect. 13. As to the fourth Particular, *viz.* Where a Man ſhall be adjudged a Principal in an Offence againſt a Statute: It ſeems to have been always [a] generally agreed, That notwithſtanding all penal Statutes are to be conſtrued ſtrictly; yet where-ever a Statute ordains, That thoſe who are guilty of the Thing prohibited by it, ſhall be adjudged Traitors or Felons, it by a neceſſary Implication makes all the Procurers and Abettors of it Principals or Acceſſaries before, upon the ſame Circumſtances which will make them ſuch in a Treaſon or Felony at Common Law; becauſe ſuch Perſons may properly be ſaid to have done the Thing in ſuch a Manner cauſed by them, and conſequently to come within the very Words of the Statute. And therefore it ſeems to have been generally unqueſtionable, That thoſe who procure the [b] Clipping of the King's Coin, or other Offence, made High Treaſon by Statute, in ſuch a Manner as will make them principal Traitors in a Treaſon at Common Law, ſhall be adjudged principal Traitors by the Statute. And that thoſe who abet a [c] Petit Treaſon, or a Felony by Statute; as a [d] Rape, or [e] Buggery, &c. ſhall be adjudged Principals if preſent when it was committed, and Acceſſaries if abſent, in the ſame Manner as in Felonies at Common Law, unleſs the Statute expreſly provide otherwiſe; as that of 3 *H.* 7. 2. does, as hath been ſhewn in the foregoing Section.

Sect. 14. But there [f] ſeems to have been formerly ſome Opinions, That the Receivers of a Felon by Statute, ſhall not be adjudged Acceſſaries to the Felony after the Fact, in the ſame Manner as the Receivers of a Felon at Common Law; becauſe ſuch Perſons can in no Propriety of Speech be ſaid to have done the Thing prohibited, as the Procurers of it may be ſaid to have done: But this [g] ſeems to have been more ſtrongly holden in Reſpect of thoſe Statutes, which expreſly provide that Acceſſaries before to the Offence prohibited, ſhall be puniſhed as Felons, &c. but ſay nothing of Acceſſaries after; from which Words it may be argued, That they muſt be either intended to exclude Acceſſaries after the Fact, or have no manner of Effect. Yet I take it to be ſettled at this Day, That in theſe and all other Caſes, where a Statute makes any Offence [h] Treaſon or [i] Felony, it involves the Receiver of the Offender in the ſame Guilt with himſelf, in the ſame Manner as in Treaſon or Felony at Common Law, unleſs there be an expreſs Proviſion to the contrary. For ſince it is agreed, That ſuch new Treaſon or Felony ſhall have the ſame Conſtruction with a Treaſon or Felony at Common Law to all other [k] Intents and Purpoſes, Why ſhould it not alſo have the ſame in Relation to thoſe who are to be eſteemed Principals and Acceſſaries in it? And as to the Objection, That the Receivers of the Offender cannot thereby be ſo properly ſaid to have done the Offence, as the Acceſſaries before, it may be anſwered, That they may properly enough be ſaid to be Partakers in the Guilt of the Offender; and what Crime ſuch a Partaking ſhall be adjudged to amount to, is moſt reaſonably determined by the Rules of Law in other Caſes of like Nature. And as to the Objection, That a Statute by expreſſing Acceſſaries before, muſt be intended to exclude Acceſſaries after, or to have no manner of Effect, it may be anſwered, That nothing is more common than for Statutes to expreſs thoſe Things which the Law would have implied, in which Caſes it ſeems a very reaſonable Conſtruction, That *Expreſſio eorum quæ tacite inſunt nihil operatur.*

[a] S. P. C. 44. Lett. A, B, C. 19 H. 6. 47. pl. 103. 3 Inſt. 45, 59, 72. B. 1. ch. 40. ſect. 4. Crompt. 42. pl. 13. Dalt. ch. 108. Lamb. B. 2. ch. 7. f. 286, 287. Daliſ. 11. pl. 12. 22. pl. 3. H. P. C. 215. 1 H. H. P. C. 613, 614. Quære Dy. 88. pl. 105. Daliſ. 11. pl. 12. H. P. C. 223. in the Additions printed in the ſecond Edition.

[b] Vide ſupra ſect. 2. B. 1. ch. 17. ſect. 55. 19 H. 7. 47. pl. 103. S. P. C. 3. Letter A. H. P. C. 18.

[c] See B. 1. ch. 32. Sect. 5, 6.

[d] H. P. C. 187, 215. See B. 1. ch. 41. Sect. 6. S. P. C. 44. Letter B. 11 H. 4. 13. Daliſ. 22. pl. 3. Fitz. Coro. 86, 228. Bro. Rape, 2, 3.

[e] 3 Inſt. 59. H. P. C. 215. See B. 1. ch. 38. Sect. 18.

[f] Vide S. P. C. 44. Letter C. and ſupra ſect. 3.

[g] Vide S. P. C. 44. Lett. C. Lamb. B. 2. ch. 7. fol. 284, 285. 1 H. H. P. C. 614.

[h] Vide ſupra ſect. 3. Bro. Treaſon, 19. S. P. C. 3. Lteter A. 3 H. 7. 10. pl. 2.

[i] H. P. C. 215. Daliſ. 22. pl. 3. Lamb. B. 2. ch. 7. f. 284, 285. 3 Inſt. 45, 61, 72, 73.

[k] See B. 1. ch. 40, ſect. 4. Supra ch. 18. ſect. 13. S. P. C. 168. Letter D. H. P. C. 230, 231.

Sect. 15. As to the fifth Particular, *viz.* Whether the Offence of the Accessary can ever rise higher than that of the Principal: I take it to be an uncontroverted [a] Rule, That it never shall; it seeming incongruous and absurd that he who is punished only as a Partaker of the Guilt of another, should be adjudged guilty of a higher Crime than the other. And therefore it seems clear, [b] That if a Wife or Servant cause a Stranger to murder the Husband or Master, and are absent when the Murder is committed, they cannot be said to be Accessaries to Petit Treason, but to Murder only, because the Offence of the Principal is but Murder. But if such Wife or Servant had been [c] present when the Murder was committed, they would have been guilty of Petit Treason, and the Stranger of Murder; because in Respect of such [d] Presence they would have been Principals in killing, as hath been more fully shewn *B.* 1. in the Chapter of *Petit Treason, Sect.* 6.

Sect. 16. As to the second Point, *viz.* In what Cases a Man shall be adjudged an Accessary before: It seems to be [e] agreed, That those who by Hire, Command, Counsel or Conspiracy; and it seems to be generally [f] holden, That those who by shewing an express Liking, Approbation or Assent to another's felonious Design of committing a Felony, abet and encourage him to commit it, but are so far [g] absent when he actually commits it, that he could not be encouraged by the Hopes of any immediate Help or Assistance from them, are all of them Accessaries before the Fact, both to the Felony intended, and to all other Felonies which shall happen in and by the Execution of it, if they do not [h] expresly retract and countermand their Encouragement, before it is actually committed.

Sect. 17. But it doth not seem necessary in any Indictment or Appeal against a Man as Accessary before the Fact, to set forth the special Manner by which he abetted it, but only to charge him [i] generally, *Quod Felonice, &c. abettavit, incitavit & procuravit, &c.* Also the like general Way of setting forth the Aid given to a Felon, seems to be sufficient both as to those who are [k] Principals, by being present when the Felony is committed, and also as to those who are [l] Accessaries after.

Sect. 18. It cannot be doubted, But that if a Man advise a Woman to kill her Child as soon as it shall be born, and she kill it in Pursuance of such Advice, he is an [m] Accessary to the Murder, tho' at the Time of the Advice, the [n] Child not being born, no Murder could be committed of it; for the Influence of the felonious Advice continuing till the Child was born, makes the Adviser as much a Felon as if he had given his Advice after the Birth. Also it seems [o] agreed, That if I command another to beat a Man, and he beat him in such a Manner that he dies thereof, I am an Accessary before to the Felony; [p] because it happened in the Execution of a Command, which naturally tended to endanger the Life of the other. And [q] *a fortiori* therefore it follows, That if a Man Commands another to rob a Man, and he in robbing him kill him; or to burn the House of *J. S.* and he by burning it, burn also the House of *J. N.* the Commander is as much an Accessary to the subsequent Felony, as to that which was directly commanded. Also it is said, [r] That if I command

[a] 3 Inst. 20, 139. H. P. C. 215. Bro. Coro. 119. Vide Keilw. 34. pl. 9 and inf. sect. 21, 22.
[b] 3 Inst. 20. Dalis. 16. pl. 11. Dyer 254. pl. 103. 332. pl. 25. 128. pl. 57. H. P. C. 24, 25, 215. Crompt. 19. pl. 8. Bro. Coro. 119. But 40 Ass. 25. whereof this Note in Brook is an Abridgment, seems contrary. See also Fitz. Coro. 216. which is an Abridgment of the same Case.
[c] 3 Inst. 20. H. P. C. 24, 25. 1 H. H. P. C. 615. Dy. 128. pl. 57, 254. pl. 103. 332. pl. 25. Crompt. 19. pl. 8. Moore 91. pl. 227. Dalis. 16. pl. 11.
[d] Vide supra Sect. 7.
[e] 2 Inst. 182. Dalt. ch. 108. Lamb. B. 2. ch. 7. S. P. C. 40. Letter D. Crompt. 41. pl. 1, 7, 8. H. P. C. 217.
[f] 2 Inst. 182. Dalt. ch. 108 Lamb. B. 2. ch. 7. f. 286. H. P. C. 217. Pl. Com. 475. b. Cont. Cromp. 41. pl. 7, 8.

[g] Vide supra sect. 7, 8. S. P. C. 40. Letter D, E. &c. Bro. Appeal, 19. Bro. Coro. 183. [h] 3 Inst. 51. Crompt. 42. pl. 16. H. P. C. 217, 218. Lamb. B. 2. ch. 7. f. 289. Dalt. ch. 108. Pl. Com. 475. a. 476. b. [i] Coke's Ent. 56. pl. 5. 57. pl. 6. Rast. Ent. 51. pl. 6. Fitz. Coro. 433. seems somewhat contrary. [k] 4 Co. 41. Co. Ent. 57. pl. 6. [l] Co. Ent. 56. pl. 5. Ra. Ent. 48. pl. 4. 52. pl. 15. [m] Dyer 186. 3 Inst. 51. Dalt. ch. 108. Lamb. B. 2. ch. 7. f. 286. Crompt. 41. pl. 2. 1 H. H. P. C. 617. [n] See B. 1. ch. 31. sect. 16, 17. [o] H. P. C. 217. Pl. Com. 475. b. Lamb. B. 2. ch. 7. f. 386. Pl. Com. 475. 1 H. H. P. C. 617. [p] S. P. C. 41. Letter D. Fitz. Coro. 314. Vide Pl. Com. 475. b. Dalt. ch. 108. Crompt. 43. pl. 35. [q] Pl. Com. 475. b. [r] Pl. Com. 475. a. b. Dalt. ch. 108. Lamb. B. 2. ch. 7. f. 286. Crompt. 42. pl. 34, 35.

a Man to rob another, and he kill him in the Attempt, but do not rob him, I am guilty of the Murder, becauſe it was the direct and immediate Effect of an Act done in Execution of my Command to commit a Felony. But if I perſuade *A.* to poiſon *B.* and *A.* accordingly give Poiſon to *B.* who eats Part of it, and gives the reſt to *C.* who is killed by it, I am guilty of a great Miſdemeanor only in Reſpect of *C.* but not [a] an Acceſſary to his Murder, becauſe it was not the direct and immediate Effect of the Act done in Purſuance of my Command, but happened accidentally thro' the Act of *B.* to which I being no way Privy, cannot be made Acceſſary by Reaſon of it. Yet in this Caſe *A.* is certainly guilty of the Murder of *C.* as hath been more fully ſhewn, *Book* 1. *Chap.* 31. *Sect.* 42, 43.

Sect. 19. It ſeems to be holden generally in ſome [b] Books, That whereever a Felony enſues, and follows upon any unlawful Act commanded by another, and executed in the ſame Manner as it was commanded, the Commander is an Acceſſary to the Felony. But this [c] ſeems to be too large a Rule, and liable to great Difficulties, unleſs limited by ſome Diſtinctions; but finding little in the Books concerning this Matter, I ſhall leave it to be farther conſidered by others.

Sect. 20. It ſeems to be [d] agreed, That if the Felony committed be the ſame in Subſtance with that which was intended, and variant only in ſome Circumſtance, as in Reſpect of the Time or Place, at which, or the Mean whereby it was effected, the Abettor of the Intent is altogether as much an Acceſſary as if there had been no Variance at all between it and the Execution of it; as where a Man adviſes another to kill ſuch an one in the Night, and he kills him in the Day, or to kill him in the Fields, and he kills him in the Town, or to poiſon him, and he ſtabs or ſhoots him.

Sect. 21. But if a Man command another to commit a Felony on a particular Perſon or Thing, and he do it on [e] another; as to kill *A.* and he kill *B.* or to burn the Houſe of *A.* and he burn the Houſe of *B.* or to ſteal an Ox, and he ſteal an Horſe; or to ſteal ſuch an Horſe, and he ſteal another; or to commit a Felony of one Kind, and he commit another [f] of a quite different Nature; as to rob *J. S.* of his Plate as he is going to Market, and he break open his Houſe in the Night, and there ſteal the Plate; it is ſaid, That the Commander is not an Acceſſary, becauſe the Act done varies in Subſtance from that which was commanded.

Sect. 22. But it is obſervable, That [g] *Plowden*, in his Report of *Saunder*'s Caſe, which ſeems to be the chief Foundation of what is ſaid by others concerning theſe Points, in putting the Caſe of a Command to burn the Houſe of *A.* which ſhall not make the Commander an Acceſſary to the Burning the Houſe of *B.* unleſs it were cauſed by burning that of *A.* ſtates it in this [h] Manner, *If I command a Man to burn the Houſe of ſuch an one, which he well knows, and he burn the Houſe of another, there I ſhall not be Acceſſary, becauſe it is another diſtinct Thing, to which I did not give Aſſent*, &c. By which it ſeems to be implied, That it is a neceſſary Ingredient in ſuch a Caſe to make *B.* no Acceſſary, that he knew the Houſe which he was commanded to burn; for if he did not know it, but miſtook another for it, and intending only to burn the Houſe which he was commanded to burn, happen by ſuch Miſtake to burn the other, it may probably be argued, That the Commander ought to be eſteemed an Acceſſary to ſuch Burning, becauſe it was the direct and immediate

[a] Pl. Com. 474, 475. Dalton, ch. 108. Lambard, B. 2. ch. 7. f. 288. Crompt. 42. pl. 10.

[b] Plow. Com. 475. a. Moore 487. Dalt. ch. 108. 3 Inſt. 51.

[c] S. P. C. 41. Letter D. Fitz. Coro. 314. Dalt. ch. 108. Moore 53. pl. 155.

[d] Pl. Com. 475. b. H. P. C. 217. 1 H. H. P. C. 617. Lamb. B. 2. ch. 7. f. 287. 3 Inſt. 51. Crompt. 42. pl. 14. Dalt. ch. 108.

[e] H. P. C. 217. 1 H. H. P. C. 617. Pl. Com. 475. Dalt. ch. 108. Lamb. B. 2. ch. 7. f. 287. Crompt. 42. pl. 11.

[f] Pl. Com. 475. 3 Inſt. 51. Dalt. ch. 108. Lambard, B. 2. ch. 7. fol. 287, 288. Crompt. 42. pl. 11.

[g] Pl. Com. 475. b.

[h] But this Caſe is not ſtated in this Manner, either by Lambard, Dalton or Crompton. See Lamb. 2. ch. 7. fol. 287. Dalt. ch. 108. Crompt. 42. pl. 36.

Effect of an Act wholly influenced by his Command, and intended to have purſued it.

Sect. 23. It ſeems to be generally agreed, [a] That he who barely conceals a Felony, which he knows to be intended, is guilty only of a Miſpriſion [b] of Felony, and ſhall not be adjudged an Acceſſary.

Sect. 24. It ſeems to be certain, That no one can be any [c] way puniſhed as an Acceſſary to Homicide *per infortunium*, or *ſe defendendo*, becauſe they are not Felonies; from whence it follows, That if he who is indicted or appealed, as a Principal in Murder, be found guilty of ſuch Homicide only, thoſe who are only charged as his Acceſſaries before or after, ſhall be diſcharged. [d] And ſo alſo ſhall thoſe who are charged only as Acceſſaries before, where the Principal is found guilty of Manſlaughter; becauſe that neceſſarily ſuppoſes the Fact to have happened on a ſudden; for if it had been done upon Premeditation, it would have been Murder. And *Quære*, If they who are charged as Acceſſaries [e] after, ſhould not alſo be diſcharged at Common Law, where the Principal was found guilty of Manſlaughter, and admitted to the Benefit of his Clergy, becauſe in ſuch Caſe it could not appear by any Judgment that there was a Principal; but the Law in this Reſpect ſeems to be altered by 1 *Annæ*, 9. ſet forth more at large in the following Part of this Chapter, which makes a Conviction equivalent as to this Purpoſe to an Attainder.

Sect. 25. Before the Statute of 11 & 12 *W.* 3. Acceſſaries to Piracy were not within the Purview of 28 *H.* 8. by which Piracy is triable according to the Courſe of the Common Law; but for this I ſhall refer the Reader to *B.* 1. Ch. 37.

As to the third Point, *viz.* In what Caſes a Man ſhall be adjudged an Acceſſary after: I ſhall endeavour to ſhew,

1. What Kind of Receipt of a Felon will make the Receiver ſuch an Acceſſary.
2. Whether it be neceſſary that ſuch Receiver know of the Felony.
3. Where the Receivers of a Felon ſhall be excuſed in Reſpect of the Relation they bear to him.
4. How far the Felony muſt be complete at the Time of the Receipt, to make the Receiver an Acceſſary.

Sect. 26. As to the firſt Particular, *viz.* What kind of Receipt of a Felon will make the Receiver an Acceſſary after the Fact: It ſeems agreed, [f] That generally any Aſſiſtance whatſoever given to one known to be a Felon, in order to hinder his being apprehended or tried, or ſuffering the Puniſhment to which he is condemned, is a ſufficient Receipt for this Purpoſe; as where one aſſiſts him with a [g] Horſe to ride away with, or with Money or Victuals to ſupport him in his Eſcape; or where one harbours and [h] conceals in his Houſe a Felon under Purſuit, by Reaſon whereof the Purſuers cannot find him; and much more, where one harbours in his Houſe, and openly [i] protects ſuch a Felon, by Reaſon whereof the Purſuers dare not take him.

[a] Lamb. B. 2. ch. 8. f. 289. Moore 8. pl. 29. S. P. C. 37. Letter C. H. P. C. 219. 3 Inſt. 139, 140. 2 Inſt. 183. But this is made a Quære by Dalton, ch. 108.

[b] See B. 1. ch. 59.

[c] Fitz. Coro. 116, 172. Bro. Coro. 33, 80. 15 Aſſ. pl. 7. 11 H. 4. 93. pl. 53. Crompt. 43. pl. 38. Bro. Forfeiture, 13. 1 H. H. P. C. 615, 616.

[d] 4 Co. 43, 44. H. P. C. 217. 1 H. H. P. C. 615, 616. Moore 461. pl. 645. Cro. El. 540. pl. 4. Crompt. 43. pl. 40. Dalt. ch 108. See B. 1. ch. 30.

[e] Vide Crom. Juſt. 44. pl. 41. 3 Inſt. 55. Moore 461. pl. 645. Cro. El. 540. pl. 4.

[f] 2 Inſt. 183. S. P. C. 41. Letter E. Dalt. ch. 108. Lamb. B. 2. ch. 7. f. 289, &c. H. P. C. 218. 1 H. H. P. C. 618. Dalt. ch. 108. Crompt. 43. pl. 39.

[g] H.P.C, 218. Dalt. ch. 108. Crompt. 43. pl. 39. Crompt. 42. pl. 20.

[h] Dalt. ch. 108. Fitz. Coro. 427. Lamb. B. 2. ch. 7. f. 291. S. P. C. 43. Letter C.

[i] 26 Aſſ. pl. 47. Adjudged Bro. Coro. 130. Fitz. Coro. 195.

Sect. 27. Alſo I take it to be ſettled at this Day, That whoever [a] reſcues a Felon from an Arreſt for the Felony, or voluntarily [b] ſuffers him to eſcape, is an Acceſſary to the Felony: [c] Alſo ſome have ſaid, That all thoſe are in like Manner guilty who oppoſe the Apprehending of a Felon; but for theſe Matters I ſhall refer the Reader to the former Part of this Book, wherein they are more fully handled.

Sect. 28. It ſeems to be holden both by [d] *Brook* and [e] *Staundforde*, That the bare Receiving into one's Houſe a Perſon known to be a Felon, is ſufficient without any farther Circumſtances to make a Man an Acceſſary to the Felony: And this ſeems to be favoured by the *Year-Books* of [f] 25 *E.* 3. and [g] 7 *H.* 6. Alſo it ſeems to be holden both by [h] *Standforde* and [i] *Dalton*, That not only ſuch a Receipt of ſuch a Felon into one's Houſe, but any other Favour or Aid voluntarily afforded him, as by relieving him with Money, Meat or Drink, is ſufficient for this Purpoſe. But it is obſervable, That the Caſe in the Book of [l] *Aſſiſes*, whereon *Dalton* ſeems chiefly to ground his Opinion, and which is more accurate than any other *Year-Book* I met with on this Subject, is of one who was indicted *for having received a Felon, and for that no one by Reaſon of him dared to take him:* Whereupon it is ſaid by *Shard*, *If one receive a Felon in Favour and Aid of the Felony, I hold ſuch a one an Acceſſary to the Felony.* Alſo it is farther obſervable, That the *Year-Book* of 9 [m] *H.* 4. on which the above-mentioned Opinion of *Brook* ſeems to be grounded, ſeems to prove only that every Receiver of a Felon, knowing him to be ſuch, is indictable, but not that he is indictable for Felony; and the chief Purport of the Caſe is to ſhew, That one who having a Felon in his Houſe, voluntarily ſuffers him to go at large, is not guilty of a felonious Eſcape, unleſs he had arreſted him. To which may be added, That [n] *Lambard* doth not ſay generally, That all thoſe who receive a Felon, knowing him to be ſuch, are Acceſſaries after; but all thoſe who feloniouſly, and with an evil Mind, receive a Felon, *&c.* And Sir *Edward Coke*, in his [o] *Second Inſtitute*, deſcribes ſuch Acceſſaries as thoſe who knowing a Felony receive the Felon, and not only conceal his Offence, but favour and aid him, that he be not known. And in his [p] *Third Inſtitute* he ſaith, If one receive a Thief, and aid and maintain him in his Felony, he is an Acceſſary; by which Expreſſions it ſeems to be implied, That there ought to be ſome other Circumſtance beſides that of the bare Suffering of a Perſon known to be a Felon to be in one's Houſe, to make a Man an Acceſſary. [83]

☞ *Sect.* 29. However, it ſeems to be [q] agreed, That no one ſhall be adjudged an Acceſſary to a Felony for receiving into his Houſe a Perſon under Bail for ſuch Crime, or for relieving with Money or Victuals a Perſon ſo bailed, or in Priſon; and the Reaſon given by [r] *Dalton* is, becauſe the Felony cannot be concealed, nor the Trial hindred by it. And if this be a ſufficient Reaſon, Why may not any other Receipt or Relief of a Felon, whereby the Felony is not concealed, nor the Trial, *&c.* hindred, come under the like Rule? As it ſeems [s] agreed, That the ſending a Letter to procure the Deliverance of a Felon, or the inſtructing him to [t] read, in order to entitle him to the Benefit of Clergy, ſhall do; and even the [u] adviſing his Friends to perſuade Witneſſes not to come againſt him at

[a] Supra ch. 21 Sect. 7, 8. Fitz. Coro. 158, 433. H. P. C. 116. Cont. Fitz. Coro. 48. S. P. C. 43. Lett. D. Dalt. ch. 108. 1 H. 7. 6. pl. 2. Bro. Coro. 130.

[b] Supra ch. 19 ſect. 10, 22, 26.

[c] Supra ſect. 10. and ch. 17. ſect. 1.

[d] Bro. Eſcape, 43.

[e] S. P. C. 41. Letter E.

[f] 25 E. 3. 39. pl. 2. Abridg. Fitz. Coro. 126.

[g] 7 H. 6. 42. pl. 18. Abridg. Bro. Indictm. 4. Fitz. Indict. 11.

[h] S. P. C. 41. Lett. E.

[i] Dalt. ch. 108. See alſo Crom. 42. pl. 25.

[l] 26. Aſſ. pl. 47. Abridg. Bro. Coro. 103. Fitz. Coro. 195.

[m] 9 H. 4. 1. pl. 3. Abridg. Fitz. Coro. 76. Bro. Coro. 26. Bro. Eſcape, 43.

[n] Lamb. B. 2. ch. 7. f. 289.

[o] Page 183.

[p] Page 134.

[q] H. P. C. 218. 1 H. H. P. C. 620, 621. Dalton, ch. 108. Crompt. 42. pl. 25.

[r] Dalt. ch. 108. Crompt. 42. pl. 25. and Lamb. B. 2. fol. 209. are to the ſame Purpoſe.

[s] 26 Aſſ. pl. 47. Bro. Coro. 103. Fitz. Coro. 195. S. P. C. 41. Lett. E. H. P. C. 219, 1 H. H. P. C. 621. 3 Inſt. 139. Lamb. b. 2. ch. 7. fol. 289, 290.

[t] 3 Inſt. 139. H. P. C. 219. 1 H. H. P. C. 621.

[u] 3 Inſt. 139. H. P. C. 219.

his Trial; and also the [a] Labouring of Witnesses in Pursuance of such Advice. And yet the two last of these Practices are certainly very highly criminal; and tho' they do not tend totally to prevent the Trial, yet are the most likely Means to make it fruitless and ineffectual. Also it seems to be agreed, That the suffering a Felon to escape [b] without arresting him, [c] or the bare Concealment of a Felony, tho' they are Crimes of a very high Nature, do not make a Man an Accessary.

Sect. 30. Also I take it to have been generally agreed, before the Statute of 3 & 4 *W. & M.* 9. That neither the Receiving of [d] other Men's Goods, known to have been stolen, nor the taking of one's [e] own Goods again, from one that had stolen them, on an Agreement not to prosecute him, nor the taking of any other [f] Reward on such an Agreement, did make a Man an Accessary to the Felony, unless he also had received the Thief. But now it is enacted by that Statute, *That if any Person or Persons shall buy or receive any Goods or Chattels that shall be feloniously taken or stolen from any other Person, knowing the same to be stolen, he or they shall be taken and deemed an Accessary or Accessaries to such Felony after the Fact, and shall incur the same Punishment as an Accessary or Accessaries to the Felony, after the Felony committed.* [84.] And it is farther enacted by 1 *Anne*, 9. That such Persons may be prosecuted for a Misdemeanor, before the Principal shall be convicted, as shall be shewn more at large in the following Part of this Chapter, *Sect.* 44.

Sect. 31. It doth not seem to be settled, [g] Whether the Receipt of a Felon who is pardoned by the King, but still liable to an Appeal, may not make the Receiver an Accessary.

Sect. 32. As to the second Particular, *viz.* Whether it be necessary that a Man know of the Felony, in order to make him an Accessary by receiving the Felon; There can be no Doubt but that it is necessary that such Receiver have [h] Notice of the Felony either express or implied; and therefore it is the settled Form of all [i] Indictments and Appeals [k] against Accessaries after the Fact, expresly to charge them with having known that the Person received by them, had committed the Principal Felony.

Sect. 33. But it is not clearly settled, Whether in some Cases an implied Notice of the Felony be not sufficient for this Purpose? As where a Man receives a Person attainted of Felony, in the same County wherein he is attainted, in which Case it hath been [l] holden, That he is an Accessary to the Felony, whether he had actually Notice of the Attainder or not; because it appears by Matter of Record in the same County, whereof every Man is said to be conusant. But to this it may be answered, That Felony implies in it something of Wilfulness and Baseness; something [m] *fellco animo perpetratum*; and that it would be extremely hard, by such a forced way of Reasoning, to presume a Man guilty of it, who probably may be entirely innocent: And to this Opinion the greater Number of [n] Authorities seem to incline.

[a] 3 Inst. 139.

[b] H.P.C. 219. 1 H. H. P.C. 618. Supra Sect. 10 and 27. Moore 8. pl. 29.

[c] Supra Sect. 10. and 27. B. 1. ch. 59.

[d] Aleyn 57. Style 91. Cro. El. 888. pl. 1. Yelv. 4, 5. Lamb. B. 2. ch. 7. f. 290, 291. 1 Rol. Abr. 68. pl. 29. H.P.C. 218. 1 H. H. P. C. 619, 620. 25 E. 3. 39. pl. 2. Abridg. Fitz. Coro. 126. 27 Ass. 69. Abridg. Fitz. Coro. 208. Bro. Coro. 114. Cont. Cromp. 42. pl. 3. 43. pl. 37, 39. It is made a Quære Crom. 42. pl. 17. and S. P. C. 43. Lett. C.

[e] H.P.C. 130. 1 H. H. P. C. 619. Dalt. ch. 108. Moore 8. pl. 29. Crompt. 41. pl. 5. 42. pl. 23. Lamb. B. 2 ch. 7. fol. 290. 1 Rol. Ab. 67. pl. 27. Cro. El. 486. pl. 3. Vide Noy 90.

[f] H.P.C. 130. 3 Inst. 134, 138. B. 1. ch. 59. Quære Moore

Sect. 5, 6, 7. Cont. Crompt. 41. pl. 4. 5. Lamb. B. 2. ch. 7. f. 290. 2 And. pl. 35. It is made a Quære Moore 8. pl. 29. and Dalt. ch. 108. [g] Vide Pl. Com. 476. Dalt. ch. 108. [h] S. P. C. 41. Lett. E. H. P. C. 218. 1 H. H. P. C. 622. [i] 7 H. 6. 42. pl. 18. Abridged Bro. Indict. 4. 3 H. 7. 10. pl. 2. Bro. Coro. 150. Fitz. Cor. 55, 285, 429. 22 Ass. pl. 55. H. P.C. 218. [k] Ra. Ent. 43. b. 54. pl. 3, 4. 51. pl. 15. Coke's Ent. 56. pl. 5. 57. pl. 6. [l] S. P. C. 41. Lett. E. 96. Lett. G. Crompt. 43. pl. 28, 31, 32. H. P. C. 218. Dyer, 355. pl. 36. Fitz. Coro. 377. Dalt. ch. 108. Quære 7 H. 6. 42. b. 43. a. [m] Co. Litt. 391. a. [n] S. P. C. 41. Letter E. Dalt. ch. 108. Lamb. B. 2. ch. 7. f. 293. H. P. C. 218.

Sect. 34.

Sect. 34. As to the third Particular, *viz.* Where the Receivers of a Felon shall be excused in Respect of the Relation they bear to him: It seems agreed, [a] That the Law hath such a Regard to that Duty, Love and Tenderness, which a Wife owes to her Husband, as not to make her an Accessary to Felony by any Receipt whatsoever given to her Husband; yet if she be any way guilty of [b] procuring her Husband to commit it, it seems to make her an Accessary before the Fact in the same Manner as if she had been Sole. Also it seems agreed, That no other Relation besides that of a Wife to her Husband, will exempt the Receiver of a Felon from being an [c] Accessary to the Felony; from whence it follows, That if a Master receive a Servant, or a Servant a Master, or a Brother a Brother, or even a Husband a Wife, they are Accessaries in the same Manner as if they had been mere Strangers to one another.

[a] Lamb. B. 2. ch. 9. Bract. B. 3. ch. 32. S. 9. Dalt. ch. 108. 1 H. H. P. C. 621. H. P. C. 219. Crompt. 42. Sect. 22. S. P. C. 26. See B. 1. ch. 1. Sect. 9, 10.
[b] Bract. Lib. 3. ca. 32. Sect. 9, 10. Dalt. ch. 108. See B. 1. ch. 1. Sect. 11, 12. Fitz. Coro. 383.
[c] Dalt. ch. 108. Crompt. 42. Sect. 22. H. P. C. 219. S. P. C. 26. Lett. C.

Sect. 35. As to the fourth Particular, *viz.* How far the Felony must be complete at the Time of the Receipt, to make the Receiver an Accessary: It seems to be clearly agreed, [d] That a Man shall never be construed an Accessary to a Felony, in Respect of the Receipt of an Offender, who at the Time of the Receipt was not a Felon, but afterwards becomes such by Matter subsequent; as where one receives another who has wounded a Person dangerously, that happens to die after such Receipt; for tho' the Offender be for special Reasons adjudged to some Purposes guilty of Homicide *ab initio*, yet he shall not be so esteemed in Respect of any others but himself; for Fictions of Law shall never be carried farther than the Reasons which introduce them necessarily require.

[d] 21 H. 7. 34. pl. 34. See Bro. Coro. 62. 1 H. H. P. C. 622. H. P. C. 219. Crompt. 42. pl. 15. Dalt. ch. 108. Lamb. B. 2. ch. 7.

Having thus shewn who are to be esteemed Principals, and who Accessaries; I am now to shew in what Manner they are to be arraigned, and shall endeavour to shew,

1. How far it is necessary that the Principal be actually attainted or convicted before the Accessary shall be proceeded against.
2. Whether the Accessary shall in any Case be arraigned or tried before any Principal hath appeared.
3. Whether a Person charged as Accessary to more than one, may be tried before all the Principals have appeared.
4. Whether the Principal and Accessary may be both tried by the same Inquest, and in what Manner they are to be tried.
5. In what Manner the Accessary shall be tried, where his Offence arises in a different County from that of the Principal.

[e] Supra ch. 18. Sect. 13. ch. 19. S. 25.

Sect. 36. As to the first Point, *viz.* How far it is necessary that the Principal be actually attainted [f] or convicted before the Accessary shall be proceeded against: It seems clear, That whatsoever the Nature of the Felony be, if the Principal be in such Manner [g] acquitted of it, [h] whether at the Suit of the King, or of the Party, that he may plead such Acquittal in [i] Bar of any subsequent Prosecution for the same Felony, the Accessary shall not be arraigned, but shall be discharged, according to the Rule, *Ubi factum* [k] *nullum, ibi fortia nulla.*

[f] Vide 9 Ass. pl. 5. Bract. 128. pl. 13, 14. and the Notes to the fourth of these Points.
[g] Fitz. Ass. 291. Conspira. 4. H. P. C. 221. 1 H. H. P. C. 623. 624. S. P. C. 47. Lett. F. 48. Lett. A. Supra ch. 23. Sect. 140. Fitz. Coro. 222. 33 H. 6. 1 pl. 6. 29 Ass. pl. 60. Ra. Ent. 57. pl. 6. Raym. 477. Fitz. Office de Court, 23.
[h] Fitz. Coro. 277.
[i] Vide supra ch. 23. Sect. 142.
[k] 4 Co. 43. b. S. P. C. 47. Lett. F.

Sect. 37. How far the Acceſſary ſhall be diſcharged upon the Principal's being found guilty of Manſlaughter, *&c.* hath been already ſhewn *Section* 24.

Sect. 38. It is certain that the Exigent ſhall not be awarded againſt the Acceſſary before the Principal is attainted, as hath been more fully ſhewn, *Ch.* 27. *Sect.* 128, *&c.*

Sect. 39. It ſeems alſo to be clear, That where the Law requires the Attainder or Conviction of the Principal before the Acceſſary ſhall be convicted, it requires that ſuch Attainder and Conviction of the Principal be on the [a] ſame Suit, and for the ſame Crime, of which the Acceſſary is to be convicted; for it is agreed, That an Attainder of the Principal at the Suit of the [b] King no way helps the Proceedings againſt the Acceſſary at the Suit of the Party, and *ſic e converſo:* Alſo it ſeems to be agreed, That the Attainder of the Principal of one Felony is no way [c] material as to the Proceedings againſt the Acceſſary for another.

Sect. 40. But where the Principal is actually attainted, tho' erroneouſly, of the ſame Felony with which the Acceſſary is charged, it ſeems [d] agreed, That ſuch Attainder, while it ſtands unreverſed, is as ſufficient for this Purpoſe as it would have been if there had been no Error in it. Yet it ſeems [e] certain, That if the Principal be attainted, and then the Acceſſary, the Reverſal of the Attainder of the Principal, *ipſo facto* reverſes the Attainder of the Acceſſary; and that the Heir may have an Aſſiſe of *Mordanceſtor* againſt the Lord of the Fee, having entred into the Lands of ſuch an Acceſſary, as having eſcheated to him by Reaſon of the Attainder.

Sect. 41. It ſeems to have been in a great Meaſure ſettled [f] before the Statute of 1 *Annæ*, 9. notwithſtanding the great Variety of Opinions in the *Old Books* concerning this Matter, That where-ever the Attainder of the Principal was prevented by his [g] Death, or [h] ſtanding Mute, or challenging [i] peremptorily above the Number allowed him by Law, or being admitted [k] to the Benefit of Clergy, or [l] pardoned, whether before or after his Conviction, the Acceſſary ſhould not be arraigned.

Sect. 42. But it ſeems to have been generally agreed, [m] That after the Principal is actually attainted, whether after a Conviction by Verdict, or by [n] Outlawry, *&c.* his Death or Pardon, *&c.* ſubſequent, will no way avail the Acceſſary.

[a] Bro.Appeal, 19.
[b] 2 Inſt. 184. Plowd. 98. b. 99. a. H. P. C. 221. S. P. C. 47. Letter A. Bro.Coro. 19. 7 H. 4. 27. Vide Dyer 133. pl. 4.
[c] 40 Aſſ. pl. 25. H. P. C. 221. 1 H. H. P. C. 625. 22 Aſſ. pl. 40.
[d] Fitz. Coro. 58. 2 R. 3. 21. b. 22. a. H. P C. 222, 223. 2 Inſt. 184. Crompt. 43. pl. 29. Bro. Coro. 164 or 5. 174 or 5. S. P. C. 47. Letter D. 7 H. 4. 16. pl. 5. 9 Co. 68. b. 119.
[e] H.P.C. 164. 270. Bro.Coro. 156. 18 E. 4. 9. pl. 16. Crompton's Juſtice 41. pl. 9. 1 Rol. Ab. 777. pl. 10. 9 Co. 119. b. Fitz. Mortdanceſter, 46.
[f] See the Preamble of 1 Annæ, 9. [g] Bro. Appeal, 19. Coro. 86. 7 H. 4. 27. pl. 4. Fitz. Coro. 378. Conſpiracy, 4. Reſponder, 35. F. N. B. 115. Letter F. H. P. C. 221. 44 E. 3. 7. pl. 6. 33 H. 6. 1. 2. pl. 6. 21 H. 7. 31. pl. 15. 22 Aſſ. pl. 40. [h] H. P. C. 221. 2 Inſt. 184. Cont. Fitz. Coro. 58. this is made a Quære S. P. C 47. Letter C. [i] See the Statute of 1 Annæ, 9. But this is made a Quære S. P. C. 47. Letter C. Fitz. Coro. 51. 3 H. 7. 12. pl. 5, 8. [k] Cro. El. 541. 4 Co. 43. b. 44. a. H. P. C. 221. 3 Inſt. 114, 139. 3 H. 7. 1. pl. 3. Cro. Ca. 566, 567. Crompton's Juſtice 43. pl. 26. 44. pl. 42. Raym. 477. Fitz. Coro. 145, 176, 193, 252, 376, 450. Bro. Coro. 18, 70, 71, 83, 84, 101, 131 or 132, 137 or 138. 18 Aſſ. pl. 13. 26 Aſſ. pl. 27. 5 Aſſiſe, pl. 5. 7 H. 4. 16. pl. 5. Bro. Clergy, 15. Cont. Fitz. Coro. 58, 53, 270, 406. Crompton's Juſtice 42. pl. 26. 10 H. 4. 15. pl. 17. Bro. Coro. 157 or 158. Quære 3 H. 7. 12. pl. 10. S. P. C. 47. H. 48. A. [l] H. P. C. 221. F. N. B. 115. Letter F. Cro. El. 541. Fitz. Coro. 53. Fitz. Conſpiracy, 4. 33 H. 6. 1. pl. 6. Bro. Coro. 18. 4 Co. 43. b. 44. a. 3 Inſt. 139. Crompt. Juſtice, 44. pl. 42. 3 H. 7. 12. pl. 10. 7 H. 4. 16. pl. 5. Raym. 477. This is made a Quære, Crompton's Juſtice, 42. pl. 26, and S. P. C. 47. G. Cont. Fitz. Coro. 151, 260. Bro. Coro. 70. 3 Aſſiſe, pl. 14. Vide Dyer 88. pl. 105. [m] Cro. Eliz. 541. 4 Co. 43. b. 44. a. H. P. C. 221. Raym. 477. Cont. Fitz. Cor. 450. [n] 4 Co. 43. b. Dyer 120. pl. 10. Fitz. Coro 58, 93. 40 Aſſiſe, pl. 8. 43 E. 3. 17. pl. 21. 3 H. 7. 1. pl. 3. 9 H. 4. 8. b. 9. a. Bro. Coro. 164 or 5. 174 or 5. Bro. Mainpriſe, 58. Cont. as to Abjuration, 7 H. 4. 16. pl. 5. Bro. Coro. 18.

Sect. 43. And it is enacted by the ſaid Statute of 1 *Annæ*, Seſſ. 2. c. 9. Par. 1. *That if any principal Offender ſhall be convicted of any Felony, or ſhall ſtand Mute, or ſhall peremptorily challenge above the Number of twenty Perſons, returned to ſerve on the Jury, it ſhall and may be lawful to proceed againſt any Acceſſary, either before or after the Fact, in the ſame Manner as if ſuch principal Felon had been attainted thereof, notwithſtanding any ſuch principal Felon ſhall be admitted to the Benefit of his Clergy, pardoned, or otherwiſe delivered before his Attainder; and ſuch Acceſſary ſhall ſuffer the ſame Puniſhment, if he or ſhe ſhall be convicted, or ſhall ſtand Mute, or peremptorily challenge above the Number of twenty Perſons returned to ſerve on the Jury, as he or ſhe ſhould have ſuffered if the Principal had been attainted.*

Sect. 44. And it is recited by the ſame Statute, *Par.* 2. *That the Buyers and Receivers of ſtolen Goods had oftentimes conveyed away and concealed the Principal Felons, ſo that they could not be convicted of ſuch principal Felony, and thereby ſuch Buyers and Receivers had eſcaped all Manner of Puniſhment, which had greatly encouraged the Buying and Receiving of ſuch ſtolen Goods*; and thereupon it is enacted, *That it ſhall and may be lawful to proſecute and puniſh every ſuch Perſon or Perſons buying or receiving any ſtolen Goods, knowing the ſame to be ſtolen, as for a Miſdemeanor, to be puniſhed by Fine and Impriſonment, altho' the principal Felon be not convicted before of the ſaid Felony, which ſhall exempt the Offender from being puniſhed as Acceſſary, if the Principal ſhall be afterwards convicted.* [85]

Sect. 45. As to the ſecond Point, *viz.* Whether the Acceſſary ſhall in any Caſe be arraigned or tried before any Principal hath appeared: Notwithſtanding the numerous [a] Authorities in the Old Books, that an Acceſſary ſhall not be compelled to anſwer before the Principal have appeared and anſwered, I take the contrary Opinion to be in a great Meaſure [b] ſettled at this Day. And yet it ſeems to have been always agreed, [c] That his Plea cannot be tried before ſuch Appearance or Attainder, [d] unleſs he deſires it himſelf; in which Caſe it is agreed, That he may be tried without the Principal, according to the Rule that *Quilibet poteſt renunciare juri pro ſe introducto.*

Sect. 46. As to the third Point, *viz.* Whether a Perſon charged as Acceſſary to more than one Principal, may be tried before all of them have appeared: It ſeems to be holden by Sir [e] *Matthew Hale*, agreeably to what ſeems to be the ſtronger [f] Opinion in *Plowden*, That if a Man be indicted as Acceſſary to more than one, and one of the Principals appear and be convict, the Court may, if they pleaſe, try the Acceſſary, as being Acceſſary to ſuch Principal, and alſo condemn him, if the Iſſue be found againſt him; and if it be found for him, may afterwards arraign and try him as Acceſſary to the other when they ſhall appear. But the contrary Opinion is certainly ſupported by great [g] Authorities; neither do I find any Inſtance in the Books wherein the Court hath actually proceeded to the Trial of an Acceſſary in ſuch a Caſe before all the Principals have either appeared, or been attainted: And [h] unleſs there be ſome very particular Circumſtances in the Caſe, it cannot be doubted but that it will be a weighty Motive to induce the Court in Diſcretion to reſpite the Trial of an Acceſſary, to ſhew that ſome of thoſe to whom he is charged as an Acceſſary, are neither attainted, nor have appeared; for

[a] Bro. Coro. 11, 20, 118. 9 H. 7. 19. pl. 14. Bract. 128. pl. 11. 139. pl. 11. 142. pl. 8. 148. pl. 4. Fitz. Reſponder, 35, 36. Coro. 33, 82, 90, 135, 136, 216, 350. Treſpaſs, 199. 44 E. 3. 38, pl. 35. 9 E. 4. 48. pl. 1. 40 E. 3. 42. pl. 22. 44 E. 3. 7. pl. 6. 25 E. 3. 44. pl. 14. 40 Aſſ. pl. 8. 25. Bro. Appeal, 9, 189. 2 R. 3. 21. pl. 50. Bro. Mainpriſe, 58. S.P.C. 46. D. 'Tis ſaid that the Law was ſo anciently, but that it is now changed. Yet Dalton ch. 108. ſeems to be for the old Opinion. [b] H. P. C. 222. 9 H. 4. 3. a. Fitz. Coro. 77. Bro. Appeal, 28. S. P. C. 46. Lett. D. [c] H. P. C. 222. 1 H. H. P. C. 623. 2 H. H. P. C. 223, 224. Bro. Appeal, 28. 9 H. 4. 3. a. Fitz Coro. 77. S. P. C. 46. Letter D. 1 And. 109. [d] Fitz. Coro. 12, 124, 463. H. P. C. 222. S. P. C. 46. Letter D. [e] H. P. C. 222. 1 H. H. P. C. 624. [f] Plowd. Com. 98. b. 99. [g] S. P. C. 46. G. See the Books cited to Section 47. 7 H. 4. 36. pl. 5. Quære Bro. Appeal, 22. 7 H. 4. 36. pl. 5. Keil. 107. [h] Plow. Com. 99. b. 7 H. 4. 36. pl. 5.

it muſt be owned, That it is a ſtrong Objection againſt the Trying him immediately, as Acceſſary to thoſe who do appear, that thereby the Country may be ſubject to the Trouble of attending two Trials where one might do as well; and the Perſon tried may be ſubject to the Hardſhip and Hazard of two Trials for his Life, which is contrary to the general Courſe of the Law, (as ſhall be more fully ſhewn under the Chapter concerning the Plea of *Auterfoits acquit*,) whereas if the Trial ſhould be deferred till all the Principals be attainted or appear, he would be tried but once. [a] But if there be ſeveral Principals, and a Perſon be charged as Acceſſary to one of them only, it ſeems clear, That it is no Objection againſt his being tried as Acceſſary to ſuch a Principal, that the others have not yet appeared, nor are attainted, *&c.*

Sect. 47. As to the fourth Point, *viz.* Whether the Principal and Acceſſary may be both tried by the ſame Inqueſt, and in what Manner they are to be ſo tried: It ſeems [b] to be ſettled at this Day, That if the Principal and Acceſſary appear together, and the Principal plead the general Iſſue, the Acceſſary ſhall be put to plead alſo; and that if he likewiſe plead the general Iſſue, both may be tried by [c] one Inqueſt; but that the Principal muſt be [d] firſt convicted; and that the Jury ſhall be charged, that if they find the Principal not guilty, they ſhall find the Acceſſary not guilty. But it ſeems agreed, That if the Principal plead a Plea in Bar, or to the Writ, the Acceſſary ſhall not [e] be driven to anſwer till ſuch Plea be determined.

Sect. 48. As to the fifth Point, *viz.* In what Manner the Acceſſary ſhall be tried, where his Offence ariſes in a different County from that of the Principal: It ſeems to have been [f] agreed antiently, That by the Common Law, if a Town extended into more than one County, and a Felony were committed in that Part of it which lay in one County, and there were Acceſſaries in that Part of it which lay in another County, an Appeal might be brought againſt the Acceſſaries as well as the Principals, in that County in which the principal Felony was committed; and where the Counties were at a Diſtance, it ſeems that it may be probably argued, [g] That an Appeal might be brought in like Manner againſt all in the County wherein the principal Felony was committed; becauſe in an Appeal the Trial may be by a Jury returned from each County. But where one of the Counties can not join with any other in taking an Inqueſt; as that of *London*, &c. it [h] hath been adjudged, That an Appeal againſt the Acceſſary could not be brought in either. Alſo, becauſe there can be no [i] Joinder of Counties for the finding of an Indictment, it ſeems to have been very [k] doubtful at the Common Law, where the Offence of the Acceſſary aroſe in a different County from that of the Principal, whether it could be indicted at all; becauſe the County in which it aroſe could

[a] S. P. C. 46. Lett. G.

[b] H.P.C. 222. 1 H. H. P.C. 624. 2 H. H. P. C. 222, 223. Dy. 120. pl. 10 2 Inſt. 184. 28 E. 3. 94. pl. 3. Fitz. Coro. 10, 17. S. P. C. 46. Lett. F. Raſt. Ent. 50. pl. 18. 52. a. pl. 15. 54. pl. 5. Fitz. Exigent, 4. Mainpriſe, 3. Cont. Bract. 128. pl. 13. 139. pl. 11. 142. pl. 8. 148. pl. 4. 44 E. 3. 7. pl. 6. Fitz. Coro. 82, 90, 135, 216, 350. Treſpaſs, 199. 40 E. 3. 42. pl. 22. 25 E. 3. 44. pl. 14. 40 Aſſ. pl. 8. 25. 44 E. 3. 8. pl. 35. Bro. Appeal, 9. Coro. 11, 118. Mainpriſe, 58. 2 R. 3. 21. pl. 50. In all which Books it ſeems to be holden, That the Acceſſary is not compellable to anſwer till all the Principals be convict.

[c] See the Books cited to Letter b. Cont. Fitz. Coro. 10, 77, 82. 9 H. 4. 3. a. 7 H. 4. 36. pl. 5. Dyer 120. pl. 10, 11. S. P. C. 46. Letters D, E, F, G.

[d] H. P. C. 222. Fitz. Coro. 10. Raſt. Entr. 50. b. 51. a. 52. pl. 15. 54. b. 9 Co. 117.

[e] Bro. Peremptory, 43. 2 Inſt. 184. S. P. C. 46. Letter F.

[f] 44 Aſſ. pl. 16. 43 E. 3. 17. pl. 21, and f. 34. b. Fitz. Coro. 93. Bro. Coro. 125. 45 Aſſ. pl. 9. Bro. Appeal, 80. But S. P. C. 63. Letter H. this Caſe ſeems to be cited with ſome Doubt.

[g] 3 H. 7. 12. pl. 4. See B. 1. Ch. 31. Sect. 18, and Dyer 38, 39, 40. 7 Co. 2. b. But Fitz. Coro. 93, and Bro. Coro. 125 or 6. and Bro. Appeal, 7, and 45 Aſſ. pl. 9. S. P. C. 63. Letter H. ſeem to be contrary. And in S. P. C. 65. Letter D. there is an Opinion, That in this Caſe there ſhall be ſeveral Appeals in the ſeveral Counties. But now one Appeal is ſufficient, in the Caſe of Murder, by Force of 2 & 3 Ed. 6. 24. ſet forth more at large in the next Section. See H. P. C. 188. Quære 44 Aſſ. pl. 16. 43 E. 17. pl. 21, and f. 34. b.

[h] Dyer 38, 39, 40. 7 Co. 2. b.

[i] Finch of Law 411. B. 1. Ch. 31. Sect. 13.

[k] Keilw. 67. the Acceſſary in ſuch Caſe is ſaid to be indictable in the County in which the principal Felony was committed. But in the Year-Book of 9 E. 4. 48. pl. 1. Abridged Fitz. Coro. 33. and Brook, Indictment, 52. the Acceſſary was indicted in the County in which he was Acceſſary, and the Court wrote to the Juſtices of the County wherein the principal Felony was committed, to certify whether the Principal were indicted before them. And in S. P. C. 90. Letter C. this Caſe is holden to be Law. See alſo 3 Inſt. 49, 135. but in S. P. C. 63. Letter H. It is ſaid, That there was no Remedy at Common Law againſt the Acceſſary where his Offence was in a different County from that of the Principal, and 1 H. H. P. C. 623.

not take Conusance of the principal Felony arising in another County, without which they could not find that of the Accessary.

Sect. 49. But these Matters are fully cleared by the Statute of 2 & 3 E. 6. 24. by which it is enacted, *Par.* 3. *That an Appeal of Murder may be sued in the same County where the Party feloniously striken or poisoned shall die, as well against the Principals as Accessaries, in whatsoever County or Place the Accessaries shall be guilty; and the Justices before whom any such Appeal shall be commenced, sued and taken, within the Year and Day after such Murder and Manslaughter committed and done, shall proceed against such Accessaries in the same County where such Appeal shall be so taken, in like Manner and Form, as if the same Offence of Accessaries had been committed in the same County where such Appeal shall be so taken, as well concerning the Trial by the Jurors, or twelve Men of such County where such Appeal shall be taken upon the Plea of not guilty, as otherwise.*

Sect. 50. And it is farther enacted, *Par.* 4. *That where any Murder or Felony shall be hereafter committed and done in one County, and another Person, or more, shall be Accessary or Accessaries in any Manner of wise, to any such Murder or Felony in any other County, that then an Indictment found or taken against such Accessary or Accessaries upon the Circumstances of such Matter before the Justices of the Peace, or other Justices or Commissioners, to enquire of Felonies in the County where such Offences of Accessary or Accessaries in any manner of wise shall be committed or done, shall be as good and effectual in the Law, as if the said principal Offence had been committed or done in the same County where the same Indictment against such Accessary shall be found: And that the Justices of Gaol-Delivery, of* Oyer *and* Terminer, *or two of them, of or in such County where the Offence of any such Accessary shall be hereafter committed and done, upon Suit to them made, shall write to the* Custos Rotulorum, *or Keepers of the Records, where such Principal shall be attainted or convict, to certify them whether such Principal be attainted, convicted or otherwise discharged of such principal Felony; who upon such writing to them, or any of them, directed, shall make sufficient Certificate in Writing under their Seal or Seals, to the said Justices, whether such Principal be attainted, convicted or otherwise discharged, or not: And after they that so shall have the Custody of such Records, do certify that such Principal is attainted, convicted, or otherwise discharged of such Offence by the Law; that then the Justices of Gaol-Delivery, or of* Oyer *and* Terminer, *or other thereto authorised, shall proceed upon every such Accessary, in the County where such Accessary or Accessaries became Accessary, in such Manner and Form, as if both the said principal Offence and Accessary had been committed and done in the same County where the Offence of Accessary was, or shall be committed or done: And that every such Accessary shall answer upon his Arraignment, and receive such Trial, Judgment, Order and Execution, and suffer such Forfeitures, Pains and Penalties, as is used in other Cases of Felony; any Law or Custom to the contrary before used in any wise notwithstanding.*

In the Construction of this Statute, the following Points seem most remarkable, *viz.*

8 Co. 118. a. Vide supra Ch. 25. Sect. 60.

Sect. 51. *First*, An Indictment against an Accessary, in Pursuance of this Statute, in the County wherein he was Accessary, ought expresly to recite that the Principal did the Felony in the other County, and not barely that he was indicted for it; for that is only an Argument, and no direct Affirmation that he did it.

Sect. 52. *Secondly*, The Court of [a] King's Bench, in Relation to a Perſon, there indicted as an Acceſſary in the County wherein the ſaid Court happens to ſit, to a Felony in another County; and the Lord [b] High Steward, in Relation to a Peer to be tried before the Lords on an Indictment againſt him as Acceſſary in one County to a Felony in another, are within the Purview of the ſaid Statute; not only becauſe it is a remedial Law, and made to ſupply a very miſchievous Defect of the Common Law, which oftentimes neceſſarily occaſioned a Failure of Juſtice, and therefore ought to have a beneficial Conſtruction; but alſo becauſe the Court of King's Bench being the [c] ſupreme Court of *Oyer* and *Terminer*, and Gaol-Delivery, may naturally be included in the very Words of a Statute which gives ſuch Juſtices any new Power; or if it be not thought to be ſtrictly within the Words, it is at leaſt within the Meaning of them, which otherwiſe would give a higher Privilege to an inferior Court than to a ſuperior: And the like in Effect may be ſaid in the Caſe of the Lord [d] Steward, who by the Words of his Commiſſion, as well as the Nature of the Thing, ſeems to be a Juſtice of *Oyer* and *Terminer*, and within the very Words of the Statute, or at leaſt within the Meaning. To which may be added, that theſe Words in the latter Part of the Statute, *That then the Juſtices of Gaol-Delivery, or of* Oyer *and* Terminer, *or other there authorized, ſhall proceed againſt ſuch Acceſſaries*, &c. ſeem plainly to imply, That ſuch other ſo authorized may alſo ſend for a Certificate of the Record relating to the Principal; for nothing can be more Natural than to expound one Part of the Statute by another. As to the Objection, That the Words of the Statute are, that the ſaid Juſtices, *or two of them*, ſhall write to the *Cuſtos Rotulorum*, *&c.* And therefore that the Lord Steward cannot do it, becauſe he is but one, it may be [e] anſwered, That thoſe Words are to be thus conſtrued, That where there are two or more ſuch Juſtices, they muſt write, *&c.* but not where there is but one.

[a] 3 Inſt. 49, 135. 9 Co. 118. H. P. C. 223. See the Notes to Sect. 48. under Lett. k

[b] 3 Inſt. 49. 135. H. P. C. 223.

[c] Vide ſupra ch. 3. ſect. 11.

[d] 3 Inſt. 136.

[e] 3 Inſt. 136.

Sect. 53. *Thirdly*, Not only the Juſtices of the King's Bench, the Pleas before whom are properly ſtyled [f] *Placita coram Rege*, and not *coram Juſticiariis*, but any other Juſtices, writing for a Certificate in Purſuance of the Statute, ought to do it by Writ in the King's Name, and not by a Precept in their own Names, and under their own Seals; and the Reaſon given by *Dyer* is becauſe it is a Writing from Juſtices to Juſtices.

[f] Dyer 253. pl. 103. 254. a. 12 Co. 32. H. P. C. 223. But Sir Edw. Coke in 3 Inſt. 49, 135. ſeems to make it neceſſary for the Juſtices of the King's Bench only to write in the King's Name.

Sect. 54. *Fourthly*, Where ſome of thoſe ſuppoſed to have been Acceſſaries to a Felony in a different County, are proceeded againſt in the King's Bench, in Purſuance of the Statute, if there be a Likelihood that others will be in the ſame Manner proceeded againſt in another Court, it ſeems moſt adviſeable [g] to ſend for the Record relating to the Principal by a ſpecial Writ formed upon the Matter according to the Words of the Statute, and not by *Certiorari*, becauſe that would wholly [h] remove the Record from the Court below into the Court of King's Bench, which might cauſe a Doubt, whether either the Court below, or that of King's Bench could certify it upon a ſubſequent Writ; for as to the Court below, it might be objected, That being no longer a Record of that Court, it cannot be certified by it; and as to the King's Bench, it might be objected, That the Principal was neither attainted nor convicted there: Whereas the Words of the Statute are, *That the Juſtices ſhall write to the Keepers of the Records where ſuch Principal ſhall be attainted or convicted.* But theſe Doubts are avoided by [i] directing a ſpecial Writ to the Court below,

[g] 3 Inſt. 49, 136.

[h] Vide ſupra ch. 27. ſect. 62 to 69. and ſect. 77 to 87.

[i] 3 Inſt. 49, 136. Vide H. P. C. 223.

below, on which a ſpecial Certificate ſhall be made in Purſuance of the Statute, and the Record ſhall ſtill remain below, and conſequently may be certified from thence on a ſubſequent Writ.

CHAP. XXX.

Of ſtanding Mute.

HAVING ſhewn in what Manner a Priſoner is to be arraigned, I am in the next Place to examine in what Manner he is to be dealt with afterwards; and to that End ſhall endeavour to ſhew what is to be done with him,

1. Upon his ſtanding Mute.
2. Upon his Confeſſion.
3. Upon his Pleading.

And firſt, as to the Priſoner's ſtanding Mute, I ſhall conſider,

1. Where he ſhall be ſaid to ſtand Mute.
2. How it ſhall be tried whether he do ſo of Malice, or by the Act of God.
3. What ſhall be done where one is found to ſtand Mute by the Act of God.
4. Where he who ſtands Mute ſhall be awarded to the ſame Execution as if he had not ſtood Mute, and where he ſhall be adjudged to his Penance.
5. What is the Nature of ſuch Penance.
6. What he ſhall forfeit, and to whom.
7. Whether the Proſecutor of an Indictment or Appeal of Larceny be entitled to a Reſtitution of the Goods ſtolen, upon the Defendant's ſtanding Mute.
8. Where one that ſtands Mute ſhall have the Benefit of Clergy.

Sect. 1. As to the firſt Point, *viz.* In what Caſes a Man ſhall be ſaid to ſtand Mute: I take it to be agreed, That he who anſwers impertinently, or ineffectually, or refuſes to put himſelf upon his Trial in ſuch Manner as the Law directs, may as properly be ſaid to ſtand Mute as he who makes no Anſwer at all; as where a Man [a] refuſes to plead a Plea in Chief, or the General Iſſue, but inſiſts on ſome frivolous Defence, or even to plead a good [b] dilatory Plea, and refuſes to plead over to the Felony, in which Caſe, after ſuch a Plea is found againſt him, he ſhall not [c] be admitted to plead in Chief, but ſhall be adjudged to his Penance in the ſame Manner as if he had made no Plea at all. And ſo ſhall he be who

[a] Dyer 49, 241. 2 H. H. P.C. 316, 317. H. P. C. 226. S. P. C. 150. Letter E.
[b] Keilw. 70. a. Vide Bro. Coro. 22.
[c] Keilw. 70. a.

who pleads a good Plea in Chief, or the General Iſſue, but [a] refuſeth to put himſelf upon the Inqueſt (that is, to be tried by God and his Country if a Commoner, or by God and his [b] Peers, if a Lord) or to wage Battle where ſuch Trial is [c] allowed.

Sect. 2. It ſeems to be holden in the [d] ſecond *Inſtitute*, and alſo in the latter Part of Sir *Matthew Hale's Pleas of the* [e] *Crown*, That if a Priſoner on his Trial peremptorily challenge above the Number allowed him by Law, he ſhall not be dealt with as one that ſtands Mute, but ſhall be hanged: But this very Point is made a *Quære* in another [f] Part of *Hale's Pleas of the Crown*; and alſo in [g] *Kelynge*, and the Contrary is holden in the third [h] *Inſtitute*: Neither does it ſeem eaſy to aſſign a Reaſon why he who challenges more Jurors than he ought, ſhall, in Reſpect of an implied Refuſal of a legal Trial, be thought worthy of a greater Puniſhment than he who obſtinately, directly, and expreſly refuſes it. To which may be added, That there ſeems to be but one [i] full Authority in the Old Books for the Maintenance of this Opinion, whereas there is a great [k] Number of the other Side. [86]

Sect. 3. But it is clear, [l] That he who demurs in Law to an Indictment or Appeal, ſhall not be eſteemed to ſtand Mute, nor be dealt with as ſuch, as having refuſed a Trial by his Country, for he puts himſelf upon a Trial by the Court, which is the proper Trial of a Matter in Law.

Sect. 4. Alſo it ſeems clear, That after a Man hath [m] confeſſed himſelf guilty, or pleaded, and put himſelf upon his [n] Country, he ſhall not afterwards be demeaſned as one that ſtands Mute, in Reſpect of his ſubſequent Silence: But the Jury ſhall be charged, and the Trial ſhall proceed, and the like Judgment ſhall be given as in Common Caſes.

Sect. 5. As to the ſecond Point, *viz.* In what Caſes, and in what Manner it ſhall be tried, whether one who ſtands Mute do ſo of Malice, or of the Act of God: It ſeems agreed, [o] That where a Priſoner wholly ſtands Mute without making any Anſwer at all, the Court ſhall take an Inqueſt of Office by the Oath of any [p] twelve Perſons that [q] happen to be preſent, whether he do ſo of Malice, or by the Act of God. But [r] after an Iſſue hath been joined, if the Priſoner ſtand Mute when the Jury are in Court, if there be any Need for ſuch Inquiry, it ſhall be made by them, and not by an Inqueſt of Office.

Sect. 6. Where [s] a Man anſwers, but not effectually, it ſeems needleſs to make any Inquiry whether his Refuſal be owing to his Malice or not, becauſe it is apparent.

Sect. 7. As to the third Point, *viz.* What ſhall be done where one is found to ſtand Mute by the Act of God: It is agreed, [t] That in ſuch a Caſe, the Judges of the Court, (who are always to be of Counſel with the Priſoner, to ſee that he have Law and Juſtice) ſhall not only cauſe the Felony to be enquired of, but alſo whether the Priſoner be the ſame Perſon, and all other Matters which he might have pleaded in his Defence. And ſuch Inquiry ſhall be made, as I ſuppoſe, not by an Inqueſt of Office,

[a] Bro. Pain 2, 14, 15. S. P. C. 150. Lett. E. Bro. App. 93. 2 Inſt. 178. H. P. C. 226. Fitz. Coro. 27, 30, 359. 4 E. 4. 11. pl. 18. 7 E. 4. 29. pl. 13. 14 E. 4. 7. pl. 10. 3 Inſt. 227. Vide Bro. Coro. 149. 8 E. 4. 3. pl. 6.
[b] Kely. 57.
[c] For this ſee Chapter of the Trial by Battle, and S. P. C. 81. Letter E.
[d] 2 Inſt. 178.
[e] H. P. C. 259.
[f] H. P. C. 226.
[g] Kely. 36.
[h] 3 Inſt. 227.
[i] 3 H. 7. 12. pl. 5. Abridged Fitz. Coro. 56. And Bro. Cor. 135 or 6. And Bro. Pain 5. And note, there is no other Authority cited for this Opinion by Coke, Hale, or Kelynge. 2 Inſt. 178. H. P. C. 259. Kely. 36.
[k] Fitz. Coro. 359. 3 H. 7. 12. pl. 8. Abridged Fitz. Coro. 51. and Bro. Clergy, 27. And note that this Caſe is the more remarkable, becauſe of the very ſame Year with the former, and ſubſequent to it. Vide Kely. 36. 3 H. 7. 2. pl. 5. the like is ſaid to be adjudged by all the Juſtices but Keble; and this Caſe is abridged Bro. Appeal, 82. Pain, 4. 2 H. H. P. C. 316.
[l] See the next Chapter ſect. 5.
[m] S. P. C. 150. Lett. C. Same Point admitted, 8 H. 4. 3. pl. 5. which is abridged Bro. Pain 2. but in theſe Books it is incidentally holden, That where a Man does not confeſs, but pleads Not guilty, and after ſtands Mute, he ſhall be put to his Penance.
[n] Kely. 36, 37. H. P. C. 225, 226. 2 H. H. P. C. 316. 15 E. 4. 33. pl. 19. Abridged Bro. Penance, 9. and Bro. Coro. 51. Cont. 8 H. 4. 3. pl. 5. for which ſee the Note next above.
[o] H. P. C. 225. S. P. C. 150. Lett. C. 2 Inſt. 177, 178. 8 H. 4. 1. pl. 2. Fitz. Coro. 71, 225. 43 Aſſ. pl. 30. Bro. Appeal, 24.
[p] Ra. Ent. 385. pl. 3.
[q] 8 H. 4. 1. pl. 2. Fitz. Coro. 71. Bro. Appeal, 24.
[r] S. P. C. 150. Lett. D. from the Authority of 8 H. 4. 3. for which ſee the Notes to the precedent Section.
[s] Vide H. P. C. 225, 226. S. P. C. 150. Lett. D 2 Inſt. 177, 178.
[t] S. P. C. 150. Lett. D. 2 Inſt. 177, 178. H. P. C. 225. 2 H. H. P. C. 317.

but by a Jury returned by the Sheriff in the ſame Manner as if the Defendant had actually pleaded; for ſince it is no way his Fault that he did not ſo plead, there is no Reaſon why his Trial ſhould be in a more looſe and ſummary Manner, or any way leſs regular, or ſolemn, than if he had. To which may be added, That Sir *Matthew Hale* ſaith, [a] *That the Felony ſhall be enquired of*, &c. *in the ſame Manner as if the Priſoner had pleaded Not guilty*; from which Words it ſeems plain, That in his Opinion the Inquiry ought to be an Inqueſt returned by the Sheriff as in other Trials at the Miſe of the Parties, becauſe if the Defendant had pleaded, it muſt certainly have been ſo. And therefore it ſeems reaſonable, That where Sir *William Staundeforde* [b] having ſpoken of ſuch Inquiry, adds immediately, That it is but an Inqueſt of Office, ought to be underſtood, not of the Inquiry of the Felony, whereof he had laſt ſpoken, but of the Inquiry whether the Priſoner ſtood Mute of Malice, or by the Act of God, whereof he had ſpoken in the Sentence next before. And I the rather incline to think that this is his Meaning, becauſe the [c] Books cited by him, to this Point, relate to this Inquiry only.

[a] H. P. C. 225.

[b] S. P. C. 150. Lett. D.

[c] Fitz. Coro. 225. 43 Aſſ. pl. 30. 8 H. 4. 1. pl. 2.

2 H. H. P. C. 316, 317. accords.

As to the fourth Point, *viz.* in what Caſes he that ſtands Mute ſhall be awarded to the ſame Execution as if he had not ſtood Mute, and where he ſhall be adjudged to his Penance, I ſhall conſider,

1. What ſhall be done to him who ſtands Mute after an Attainder.
2. What to a Perſon arraigned for High Treaſon.
3. What to one arraigned for Petit Larceny.
4. What to one arraigned for a Felony by Statute.
5. What to one arraigned upon an Appeal.
6. What to one indicted of a Capital Felony, or Petit Treaſon.

Sect. 8. As to the firſt Particular, *viz.* What is to be done to him who ſtands Mute after an Attainder: It ſeems to be ſettled [d] at this Day, That where-ever one who is attainted, either by Judgment on a Verdict, or Confeſſion, or by Outlawry, or Abjuration, ſtands Mute to the Demand why Execution ſhould not go againſt him, he ſhall not be awarded to his Penance, but to the ſame kind of Execution, if any, that would have been awarded, if he had not ſtood Mute. Yet there ſeems to be this Difference, That where one who hath always continued in Priſon, after an Attainder by Verdict or Confeſſion, ſtands Mute to the Demand why Execution ſhould not go, it ſhall be awarded [e] againſt him, without any Inquiry whether he ſtand Mute by Malice, or otherwiſe, or whether he be the ſame Perſon who is ſo attainted or not; becauſe it ſufficiently appears that he is the ſame Perſon, and that is ſufficient to juſtify an Award of Execution againſt him, where nothing appears to the contrary. But if a Perſon ſo attainted, be re-taken after an Eſcape; or if one be taken after an Outlawry or Abjuration, and ſtand Mute to the Demand, Why Execution ſhould not go againſt him? It ſhall be inquired, whether he ſtand Mute of Malice, or of the Act of God; and if it be found of Malice, it ſeems that Execution ſhall be awarded without any farther Inquiry: [f] But if it be found to be of the Act of God, it ſeems That it ought to be alſo inquired, whether he be the ſame Perſon or not, in the ſame Manner as where one ſtands Mute by the Act of God, when firſt brought upon his Trial.

[d] H P.C. 226. 2 H. H. P.C. 315, 316. Kely. 36. S. P. C. 150. Lett. C, D. So adjudged 8 H. 4. 3. pl. 5. Abridged Bro. Pain, 2. Coro. 22. as to the Caſe of Abjuration or any other Attainder after a Confeſſion; but the contrary is inſinuated as to other Attainders. But in 26. Aſſ. pl. 19. Abridged Fitz. Coro. 191. Bro. Pain, 12. Coro. 99. one who had abjured ſtanding Mute, was put to his Penance, and not hanged.

[e] S. P. C. 150. Lett. C. D. 10 E. 4. 19. pl. 26. Fitz. Coro. 36. Bro. Coro. 155.

[f] S. P. C 150. Lett. C. D. 10 E. 4. 19. pl. 26. Fitz. Coro. 36. Bro. Coro. 155.

Sect. 9. As to the ſecond Point, *viz.* What is to be done to one who ſtands Mute to an Arraignment for High Treaſon: It is clearly ſettled [a] at this Day, That ſtanding Mute upon an Arraignment for High Treaſon is equivalent to a Conviction by Verdict, or Confeſſion, and conſequently ſubjects the Criminal to the ſame Kind of Judgment and Execution as ſuch a Conviction would do. But I take it for granted, That ſuch ſtanding Mute muſt in [b] like manner appear to be obſtinate; and that if it be found to be the Act of God, the whole Matter ſhall in like Manner [c] be inquired of, as hath been more fully ſhewn in the former Part of this Chapter. But where ſuch Perſon appears to ſtand obſtinately Mute, I do not find it any where holden, that there is any Neceſſity that he probably appear to be Guilty, or that any Evidence be examined to prove him ſo, before he ſhall be condemned or executed. But this is adviſeable, where one ſtands obſtinately Mute on an Arraignment for Felony by Statute, as ſhall be more fully ſhewn in the fourteenth and fifteenth *Sections*.

Sect. 10. As to the third Particular, *viz.* What is to be done to one who ſtands Mute to an Arraignment for Petit Larceny: I take it to be agreed, [d] That if a Man appear to ſtand obſtinately Mute on an Arraignment for Petit Larceny, he ſhall have the like Judgment, *&c.* as if he had confeſſed the Indictment.

Sect. 11. As to the fourth Particular, *viz.* What is to be done to thoſe who ſtand Mute to an Arraignment for Felony by Statute: It is expreſly enacted by 33 *H.* 8. 12. *Par.* 12. *That if a Perſon indicted, and arraigned of Treaſon, Miſpriſion of Treaſon, Murder, Manſlaughter, or Bloodſhed,* &c. *againſt that Act, within the Verge of the Court, ſhall obſtinately refuſe to anſwer directly, or ſhall ſtand Mute, he ſhall have the like Judgment,* &c. *as if he were found Guilty,* &c. But [e] where a Statute, as that of *Piracy, &c.* ordains a Trial by the Common Courſe of the Law, it hath been adjudged, That the Criminal ſhall have Judgment of his Penance, *&c.* as in other Felonies.

Sect. 12. As to the fifth Particular, *viz.* What is to be done to one who ſtands Mute to an Arraignment on an Appeal: It is holden by Sir *Matthew Hale*, [f] That an Appellee of Felony ſtanding Mute ſhall not have ☞ Judgment of Penance, but to be hanged; [87] but this is made a *Quære* in [g] *Staundforde*, and [h] *Brook*; and the contrary Opinion ſeems to be favoured by Sir [i] *Edward Coke*, and is expreſly holden by [k] *Kelynge*, and ſupported by ſeveral [l] Reſolutions in the Old Books. Whereas the *Year-Book* of 21 [m] *E.* 3. ſeems to be the only Reſolution in favour of the other Side; to which it may be anſwered, Not only that three of the above-cited Reſolutions to the contrary, are much later, but alſo that the Appellee in this Caſe appears to have been taken with the Manner, [n] which probably might be a Circumſtance of conſiderable Weight in the Judgment.

Sect. 13. As to the ſixth Particular, *viz.* What is to be done to one who ſtands Mute to an Indictment of a Capital Felony, or a Petit Treaſon: It is enacted by the [o] above-mentioned Statute of *Weſtminſter*, 1. 12. *That notorious Felons which openly be of evil Fame, and will not put themſelves*

[a] H. P. C. 226. 2 H. H. P. C. 317. Skin. 145. Savil 56. pl. 121. Kely. 57. Dyer 205. pl. 4. 1 Inſt. 177, 178. Bro. Pain, 19. Co. Litt. 391. 3 Inſt. 14. S. P. C. 150. Letter C. Cont. Fitz. Coro. 283.

[b] Vide ſupra Sect. 5, 6. 18 E. 3. pl. 26. 8. S. C. 150. Letter D.

[c] Vide ſupra Sect. 7. S. P. C. 150. Letter D.

[d] 2 Inſt. 177.

[e] Dyer 241. pl. 49. 3 Inſt. 114. 2 H. H. P. C. 320. St. Tr. v. 1. p. 367. B. 1. ch. 37. ſect. 9. S. P. C. 150. Letter C. H. P. C. 226. 2 H. H. P. C. 318, 319.

[f] H. P. C. 226.

[g] S. P. C. 150. Letter B.

[h] Bro. Pain, 8, 19.

[i] 2 Inſt. 178, 179.

[k] Kely. 37.

[l] 8 H. 4. 1. pl. 2. Abrid. Bro. Pain, 1. Forfeiture, 11. Appeal, 24. Fitz. Coro. 71. 4 E. 4. 11. pl. 18. Abridg. Fitz. Coro. 71. Bro. Appeal, 93. Pain, 14. 43 Aſſ. pl. 30. Abridged Bro. Pain, 13. Appeal, 78. Coro. 123 or 124. Fitz. Coro. 225. 14 E. 4. 7. pl. 10. This Point is made a Quære; but in the very next Folio, pl. 17. Abridged Bro. Coro. 160 or 161 it is adjudged by all the Juſtices, That the Appellee in ſuch Caſe ſhould have his Penance.

[m] 21 E. 3. 18 pl. 26. Abridged Bro. Pain, 8. Appeal, 40. Coro. 43. But neither Fitz. Coro. 56. nor 3 H. 7. 2 pl. 5. nor 3 H. 7. 12. pl. 5. cited by Staundforde, ſeem to come up to this Point, but rather to be Authorities of the other Side. See Bro. Coro. 82.

[n] Vide ſupra Ch. 15. Sect. 41.

[o] Vide 2 Inſt. 177, 178.

in Enqueſts of Felonies, that Men ſhall charge them with before the Juſtices at the King's Suit, ſhall have ſtrong and hard Impriſonment, as they which refuſe to ſtand to the Common Law of the Land. But this is not to be underſtood of ſuch Priſoners as be taken on light Suſpicion.

[a] 2 Inſt. 177.

Sect. 14. Sir [a] *Edward Coke*, in the Conſtruction of this Statute, ſaith, That no Perſon ſhall be put to this Puniſhment, unleſs the Matter be evident, or probable, which it is the Duty of the Judge to look into; and Sir *William* [b] *Staundforde*, ſaith, That there ought to be evident or probable Matter to convince the Party of the Crime whereof he is arraigned, or otherwiſe that he be a notorious Felon, or openly of bad Fame; and therefore he adviſes the Judge, for the Satisfaction of this Statute, and Diſcharge of his Duty, to examine the Evidence which proves the Priſoner Guilty of the Fact, before he proceed to the Judgment of *Pain fort & dure.* Yet I cannot find any Book which takes Notice of any Examination of this Kind, or of any Entry that the Defendant appeared to be a notorious Felon, before ſuch Judgment given againſt him, upon his ſtanding Mute, whether upon an [c] Indictment or [d] Appeal: But all the Books cited in the Margin ſeem to intimate, That the ſtanding Mute is of itſelf a ſufficient Ground for ſuch Judgment. Yet all that can be inferred from thence ſeems to be this, That it is not neceſſary to make any thing of this Kind Part of the Record, it being a Matter left to the Diſcretion and Conſcience of the Judge, and to be preſumed where it is not expreſſed. But as to all Capital Appeals whatſoever, and all Indictments and Appeals of Petit Treaſon, perhaps it may be ſaid, That [e] not being within this Statute, but remaining as they were at the Common Law, the Obſtinacy of a Criminal in ſtanding Mute to them, may be of it ſelf, without more, a ſufficient Inducement to a Judge to award him to his Penance. But conſidering that ſuch Appeals and Indictments are within the ſame Reaſon with thoſe mentioned in the Statute; and it is uncertain how the Common Law ſtood in Relation to theſe Matters, as appears by the beſt Authors, [f] differing among themſelves concerning them; and ſeeing the Method preſcribed by the Statute is very juſt and equitable, it ſeems prudent at leaſt in a Judge to obſerve the ſame Rules in all Caſes of this Kind.

[b] S. P. C. 150. Letter A. Vide H. P. C. 226. 2 H. H. P. C. 320, 321, 322.

[c] Ra. Ent. 385. pl. 2, 3. Keilw. 70. a. 7 E. 4. 29. pl. 13. 3 H. 7. 12. pl. 5, 8.

[d] 8 H. 4. 1. pl. 2. 4 E. 4. 11. pl. 18. 14 E. 4. 7. pl. 10. 43 Aſſ. pl. 30. 21 E. 3. 18. pl. 26. 3 H. 7. 2. pl. 5.

[e] S. P. C. 150. Letters B, C. 2 Inſt. 177, 178, 179. And the Books cited, Sect. 12. under Lett. [l].

[f] S. P. C. 149. Letter F. 2 Inſt. 178, 179.

Sect. 15. I do not find it ſaid in any Book, what ſhall be done to a Priſoner who obſtinately ſtanding Mute to an Arraignment, ſhall appear to be charged upon very light Suſpicion; but I take it for granted, That he may be ſeverely fined and impriſoned for the Contempt.

Sect. 16. As to the fifth Point, *viz.* What is the Nature of the Penance to which a Priſoner is to be adjudged upon his obſtinately ſtanding Mute: It is obſervable, That the above-cited Statute of *Weſtminſter* 1. ſays only in general, That Felons ſtanding Mute ſhall be put *in Priſon fort & dure*, without ſaying any Thing of the Manner of it, which it ſeems to leave as a known Thing to the uſual Practice in ſuch Caſes; which we ſhall beſt find from the Books of Entries, and other Law Books, all of which generally agree, That the Priſoner ſhall be remanded [g] to the Place from whence he came, and put [h] in ſome low dark Room, [i] and

[g] H. P. C. 227. 2 H. H. P. C. 319, 399, 400. S. P. C. 150. Letter E. Keilw. 70. a. 4 E. 4. 11. pl. 18. 14. E. 4. 8. pl. 17. Abridged Bro. Coro. 160. 2 Inſt. 178. Ra. Ent. 385. pl. 17. 8 H. 4. 1. pl. 2.

[h] This Clauſe is omitted in Keilw. 70. a. 4 E. 4. 11. pl. 18. but it is mentioned in all the other Books above cited, but with this Difference, That 14 E. 4. 11. pl. 17. ſays only that he ſhall be put in a Chamber, without adding that it ſhall be low or dark.

[i] In this all the Books above cited ſeem to agree. And 14 E. 4. 8. pl. 17. and S. P. C. 150. Letter E. and 2 Inſt. 178. add, That he ſhall lie without any Litter or other Thing under him, and that one Arm ſhall be drawn to one Quarter of the Room with a Cord, and the other to another, and that his Feet ſhall be uſed in the ſame Manner. But theſe Clauſes are wholly omitted in all the other Books above cited, except H. P. C. which takes Notice of the latter of them only. And Ra. Ent. 385. pl. 2. adds, That an Hole ſhall be made for the Head, and Keil. 70. a. ſays, That the Head ſhall not touch the Earth; but none of the other mention either of theſe Clauſes.

there laid on his Back, without any manner of Covering, except for the Privy Parts, and [a] that as many Weights shall be laid upon him as he can bear, and more, and that he shall have no Manner of Sustenance but of the worst [b] Bread and [c] Water, and that he shall [d] not eat the same Day in which he drinks, nor drink the same Day on which he eats; and that he shall so continue till he [e] die. But it is said, [f] That anciently the Judgment was not, That he should so continue till he should die, but till he should answer, and that he might save himself from the Penance by putting himself on his Trial, which he cannot do at this Day after the Judgment of Penance is once given.

Sect. 17. It seems clear, [g] That Women upon standing Mute, are liable to such Penance as well as Men.

Sect. 18. It is said [h] to be the constant Practice of *Newgate* Sessions, where a Prisoner refuses to plead, to endeavour to compel him to do it by tying his Thumbs together with Whipcord, and not to proceed to the Judgment and Penance, before all Methods of persuading him to plead, are found ineffectual.

Sect. 19. As to the fifth Point, *viz.* What he who obstinately stands Mute shall forfeit, and to whom: There is no Doubt but that in Case of [i] High Treason he shall forfeit both Lands and Goods, in the same Manner as if he had been attainted any other way. Also I take it for granted that in the Case of Felony and Petit Treason, where a Person by standing Mute shall not avoid being attainted for such Crimes, he shall forfeit his Lands and Goods in the same Manner as on other Attainders. But where ever a Person standing Mute is adjudged to his Penance, and thereby prevents that Attainder which otherwise he might have incurred, it seems agreed, [k] That he forfeits his Chattels only, and not his Lands.

Sect. 20. It is agreed in the *Year-Book* of 8 [l] *H.* 4. That the Goods so forfeited ought not to be delivered to any Person claiming them under a Grant from the Crown, till he have shewed a good Title to them in the King's Court, by some Grant sufficient to pass them.

Sect. 21. And it seems [m] That such Goods will not pass by Grant of all Felons Goods, having no Words specially extending to the Goods of those who stand Mute, *&c.* because a Person adjudged to his Penance for standing Mute, does not seem to suffer as a Felon, being neither attainted nor convicted of any Felony, but as a Person refusing to stand to the Law of the Land. And it seems rather the stronger Opinion, [n] That they pass not by the Grant of *all Goods of Felons and Fugitives of all Persons within such a District; so that if such Persons for any Trespass or other Fault ought to lose Life or Member; or shall fly and refuse to stand to Judgment, or do any other Trespass for which they ought to lose their Chattels.*

Sect. 22. As to the sixth Point, *viz.* Whether the Prosecutor of an Indictment or Appeal of Larceny be intitled to a Restitution of the Goods stolen, upon the Defendant's standing Mute: It seems agreed, [o] That by the Common Law, where a Person stands Mute to an Appeal of Larceny, it is proper to charge the same Inquest which is to enquire whether the standing Mute be of Malice or not, to enquire also whether the Goods mentioned in the Appeal are the Goods of the Appellant, and whether the Defendant were taken upon a fresh Suit [p] made by such Appellant,

[a] In this all the Books above-cited agree.

[b] But 14 E. 4. 8. pl. 17. S. P. C. 150. Lett. E. and 2 Inst. 178. are, That he shall only have three Morsels of Barley Bread a Day. Keilw. 70. a. that he shall have only Rye Bread; and Ra. Ent. 385. pl. 2. and 2 H. 4. 1. pl. 2. generally that he shall have of the worst Bread.

[c] 14 E. 4. 8. pl. 17. S. P. C. 150. Letter E. 2 Inst. 178. and 8 H. 4. 1. pl. 2. and Keilw. 70. a. are, That he shall have the Water next the Prison, so that it be not current; but Ra. Ent. 385. pl. 5. is general, That he shall have the worst Water.

[d] This is omitted in Keilw. 70. a. and in 8 H. 4. 1. pl. 2.

[e] This is omitted in none of the Books above-cited, except 14 E. 4. 11. and H P. C. 227. but neither of these Books give the whole Judgment at Large.

[f] S. P. C. 150. Lett. F. 151. Letter E. Briton 11.

[g] 2 Inst. 177. 2 H. H. P. C. 319. [h] Kely. 27, 28. [i] See the Books cited to Sect. 9. [k] 14 E. 4. 7. pl. 10. H. P. C. 226, 227. 2 H. H. P. C. 319. Co. Litt. 391. Fitz. Esc. 10. Coro. 51. Ass. 421. S. P. C. 151. a. Bro. Forfeiture, 11, 64. Appeal, 24. 8 H. 4. 1. b. 2. a. b. 3 H. 7. 12. pl. 8. [l] 8 H. 4. 2. a. Bro. Appeal, 24. [m] Dy. 268. pl. 18. 8 H. 4. 2. a. b. Bro. Forfeitnre, 11. [n] Dy. 268. pl. 18. 8 H. 4. 2. a. b. Bro. Forfeit. 11. [o] Vide supra ch. 23. sect. 53. Letter F. 8 H. 4. 1. pl. 2. 2. Abridged Bro. Appeal, 24. S. P. C. 166. [p] Vide ch. 23. sect. 50, 51, 52.

which Points being found [a] for him, he ſhall have an Award of Reſtitution to ſuch Goods, and to ſuch only, [b] in whoſe Hands ſoever [c] they are found. And it is ſaid in general in ſome Books, [d] That in an Appeal of Larceny there ſhall be a Reſtitution of the Goods, upon the Appellee's ſtanding Mute, without ſaying any thing of any Inquiry concerning the Property, or freſh Suit: But I take it for granted, That where it is ſo omitted, it is taken as a Thing known, and done of Courſe, and therefore needleſs to be expreſly mentioned.

Sect. 23. But it ſeems queſtionable, Whether the Proſecutor of an Indictment of Larceny, be in like manner intitled to a Reſtitution, upon the Defendant's ſtanding Mute? Becauſe it ſeems agreed, [e] That by the Common Law there could be no ſuch Reſtitution upon any other Proſecution but an Appeal; and it is certain, That the Proſecutor of an Indictment is not intitled to a Reſtitution by the expreſs Words of 21 [f] *H.* 8. 11. which require, *That the Felon be found guilty, or otherwiſe attainted,* &c. And I do not know that he is intitled to it by any other Statute, or any equitable Conſtruction of this.

Sect. 24. As to the ſeventh Point, *viz.* Where one who ſtands Mute ſhall have the Benefit of his Clergy: It ſeems clear, [g] That unleſs it happen to be otherwiſe ſpecially provided by ſome Statute, where-ever he ſhall be allowed it upon a Conviction, by Verdict or Confeſſion, he ſhall have it upon his ſtanding Mute. Alſo I take it to be agreed, [h] That a Statute taking away the Benefit of Clergy from thoſe who ſhall be convicted of a Crime, doth not thereby take it away from thoſe who ſtand Mute on an Indictment or Appeal for ſuch Crime. But it is enacted by 3 & 4 *W.* & *M.* 9. ſet forth more at large in the Chapter of Clergy, *That if any Perſon ſhall be indicted of any Offence, for which by Virtue of any former Statute, he is excluded from the Benefit of his Clergy, if he had been thereof convicted by Verdict or Confeſſion, if he ſtand Mute he ſhall not be admitted to it.* But Appeals and Offences excluded from the Benefit of Clergy by ſubſequent Statutes, ſeem not to be within the Purview of this Statute; for the fuller Conſideration whereof I ſhall refer the Reader to the Chapter of *Clergy.*

[a] Supra ch. 23. ſect. 53.
[b] Supra ch. 23. ſect. 57.
[c] Supra ch. 23. ſect. 54.
[d] 21 E. 3. 18. pl. 26. Abrid. Bro. Appeal, 40. 43 Aſſ. pl. 30. Abrid. Bro. Appeal, 78. Coro. 123 or 124. Fitz. Coro. 225. Vide 40 Aſſ. pl. 39. Abrid. Fitz. Coro. 217.
[e] Supra ch. 23. ſect. 55, 56.
[f] Set forth more at large, ch. 23. ſect. 55.
[g] Fitz. Coro. 233, 283. Aſſ. 421. 8 H. 4. 3. pl. 5. H. P. C. 231. 2 H. H. P. C. 320, 380. Moore 550. pl. 738. 3 H. 7. 12. pl. 8. Abrid. Bro. Clergy, 27. Fitz. Coro. 51. 3 H. 7. 12. pl. 10. Abrid. Fitz. Coro. 53. Fitz. Cor. 58. ſeems contrary, but I cannot find any thing in 3 H. 7. 1. which is the Year-Book cited to this Note to warrant this Opinion.
[h] See H. P. C. 232 to 238. 2 H. H. P. C. 345.

CHAP. XXXI.

Of Confeſſion and Demurrer.

AND now I am to conſider what is to be done to a Priſoner upon his Confeſſion, which may be either,

1. Expreſs, or,
2. Implied.

Sect. 1. An expreſs Confeſſion is where a Perſon directly confeſſes [a] the Crime with which he is charged, which is the higheſt Conviction that can be, and may be received [b] after the Plea of Not guilty recorded notwithſtanding the Repugnancy; for the Entry is, That the Defendant *poſtea* or *relicta verificatione, cognovit indictamentum.*

Sect. 2. Such a Confeſſion carries with it ſo ſtrong a Preſumption of Guilt, that an Entry [c] on Record *quod cognovit indictamentum, &c.* in an Indictment of Treſpaſs, eſtops the Defendant to plead Not guilty to an Action brought afterwards againſt him for the ſame Matter. But it ſeems queſtionable, Whether ſuch Entry of a Confeſſion of an Indictment of a Capital Crime, will in the like Manner eſtop a Defendant to plead Not guilty to an Appeal, becauſe in Caſe of Life, the Court will be very tender in going upon Preſumptions. And where a Perſon upon his Arraignment actually confeſſes [d] himſelf Guilty, or unadviſedly diſcloſes the Special [e] Manner of the Fact, ſuppoſing that it doth not amount to Felony, where it doth, yet the Judges, upon probable Circumſtances, that ſuch Confeſſion may proceed from Fear, Menace, or Dureſs, or from Weakneſs or Ignorance, may refuſe to record ſuch Confeſſion, and ſuffer the Party to plead Not guilty.

Sect. 3. An implied Confeſſion is where a Defendant in a Caſe not Capital, doth not directly own himſelf Guilty, but in a Manner admits it by yielding to the King's Mercy, and deſiring to ſubmit to a ſmall Fine; in which Caſe, if the Court think fit to accept of ſuch Submiſſion, and make an Entry that the Defendant *poſuit ſe in gratiam Regis*, without putting him to a direct Confeſſion, or Plea, (which in ſuch Caſes ſeems to be left to Diſcretion) the Defendant ſhall [f] not be eſtopped to plead Not guilty to an Action for the ſame Fact, as he ſhall [g] be where the Entry is *quod cognovit indictamentum.*

Sect. 4. I take it for granted, That no Confeſſion whatever ſhall, before final [h] Judgment, deprive the Defendant of the Privilege of taking Exceptions in Arreſt of Judgment to Faults apparent in the Record; [i] for the Judges muſt *ex officio* take Notice of all ſuch Faults, and any one, as *amicus Curiæ*, may inform them of them.

[a] Vide S.P.C. 142. Lett. C. Lamb. B. 4. ch. 9. Finch of Law 38.

[b] Kely. 11. Quære if the Law be the ſame in Civil Actions. Affirmed Cro. E. 144. pl. 3. Denied 2 Jon. 156.

[c] 9 H. 6. 60. a. Fitz. Eſtopp. 24. 102. 11 H. 6. 65. pl. 21. Lamb. B. 4. ch. 9. Trial per Pais 25.

[d] S.P.C. 141. Letter C. 2 H. H. P. C. 225.

[e] 22 Aſſ. pl. 71. Abridged Fitz. Coro. 180. 27 Aſſ. pl. 40.

[f] 9 H. 6. 60. a. Abridged Fitz. Eſtoppel, 24. 11 H. 4. 65. pl. 21. Lamb. B. 4. ch. 9. Far. 40.

[g] Supra § 2.

[h] 1 Salk. 77, 78. Far. 100.

[i] Finch of Law 226. 2 Danv. Abr. 252. 2 Lev. 223.

Sect. 5. It seems to be taken for granted, both by [a] *Brook* and [b] *Staundforde*, [c] *Coke* and [d] *Hale*, speaking as I suppose, of a general Demurrer, That it amounts so far to a Confession of the Indictment as laid, that if the Indictment be good, Judgment and Execution shall go against the Prisoner. [88] But it is observable, That no adjudged Case is cited for the Maintenance of this Opinion, nor any Authority from the old Books except the *Year-Book* of 14 *Ed.* 4. 7. *a. pl.* 10. in which it is reported to have been said by *Choke*, That if a Defendant demur to a Plea, he shall be hanged, *quod fuit concessum.* But to this it may be said, That it was only spoken incidentally, and not a Point adjudged; and besides that it is so short and obscure that it is scarce intelligible, which appears by *Brook*'s abridging it in different Senses; for in one Place [e] he seems to understand it of a Demurrer by a Defendant to a Plea in Bar, which seems impossible; and in another [f] Place he seems to understand it in a different Sense. And therefore perhaps the Meaning of it may be only this, That after a Defendant hath pleaded such a Bar, as confesses the Fact, and concludes him to plead the General Issue afterwards, as some Pleas are said [g] to do; if he afterwards demur to a Replication to such Plea, he shall be condemned if the Demurrer be adjudged against him, and the Indictment or Appeal be good.

Sect. 6. But howsoever the Law may stand in Relation to a [h] General Demurrer concluding in Bar of an Appeal, or Indictment, as in Common Demurrers in Civil Actions, or a Demurrer to a Plea in Bar, [i] which admits the Fact, or to a [k] Replication to such a Plea: It hath been adjudged, That if an Appellee demur in Law to an Appeal by Reason of the [l] Insufficiency of the Declaration or generally demur to the Declaration, with a [m] Conclusion *& petit judicium de narratione illa & quod narratio illa cassetur*; or having prayed [n] *Oyer* of the Writ and Process, demand Judgment of the Appeal, *quia dicit quod breve de appello prædict. & process. inde minus sufficient' in lege existunt ad ipsum W. C. ad dictum breve de Appello respondere compellend'; & hoc parat. est verificare prout Cur', &c. unde petit judicium de brevi de Appello prædict. & petit inde allocationem, & quod breve illud de Appello cassetur*; such Demurrer shall not conclude him from pleading over to the Felony, either at the same Time [o] with the Demurrer, or [p] after it shall be adjudged against him.

Sect. 7. But it seems, That in Criminal Cases not Capital, if the Defendant demur to an Indictment, *&c.* whether in Abatement or otherwise, the Court will not give Judgment against him to answer over, but final [q] Judgment; for it seems, That in such Cases there can be no Demurrer properly in Abatement, except [r] it be to a Plea in Abatement, or to a [s] Replication to such a Plea.

Sect. 8. A Demurrer to an Appeal hath been [t] received after Issue joined: But it hath been adjudged, [u] That a Demurrer to an Indictment ought not to be received after Verdict.

[a] Bro. Peremptory, 86.
[b] S. P. C. 150. Letter C.
[c] 2 Inst. 178.
[d] H. P. C. 243. 2 H. H. P. C. 315.
[e] Bro. Demurrer, 17.
[f] Bro. Peremptory, 86.
[g] Vide supra ch. 23. sect. 137.
[h] See the precedent Sect.
[i] Vide Bro. Peremptory, 86. Fitz. Coro. 12.
[k] Vide Bro. Perempt. 86.
[l] Dyer 38. pl. 51. 39. pl. 65. Cro. Eliz. 196. pl. 13.
[m] As it was done in the Case of Smith and Bowen, Mich. 7. Ann. Vid. Salk. 59. pl. 2.
[n] As it was done in the Case of Widdrington and Charlton, Hill. 10 Ann.
[o] Smith and Bowen, Mic. 7 Annæ; In which Case the Demurrer was continued on the Record with a Cesset triatio exitus, &c. and after the Demurrer was determined against the Defendant, a Venire was awarded.
[p] Dyer 38. pl. 51. Salk. 59, 60. Cro. E. 196. pl. 13.
[q] Vide Salk. 220.
[r] Salk. 218.
[s] Ra. Ent. 160. pl. 1, 2, 3. 611.
[t] Cro. E. 196. pl. 13.
[u] 1 Sid. 208. wherein the Precedent in Co. Ent. 363. b. to the contrary is denied to be Law.

CHAP. XXXII.

Of Sanctuary.

BEFORE I consider in the third Place, how a Prisoner is to be demesned upon his Pleading; I shall examine the Nature of the several Kinds of Pleas in Criminal Cases, which are either,

1. Dilatory, or,
2. In Chief.

Dilatory Pleas are either,

1. Declinatory, or,
2. In Abatement.

Declinatory Pleas are either,

1. Of the Privilege of Sanctuary, or,
2. Of the Benefit of Clergy.

Sect. 1. As to the Plea of the Privilege of Sanctuary, the Learning relating to it being made in a great Measure useless by the Statute of 21 *Jac.* 1. 28. *Par.* 7. by which it is enacted, *That no Sanctuary or Privilege of Sanctuary shall after that Time be admitted or allowed in any Case.* I shall but briefly consider it under the following Heads,

1. What was the Nature of the Privilege of Sanctuary.
2. What Authority was necessary for the creating it.
3. To what Matters it extended.
4. At what Time, and in what Manner it was to be pleaded.

Sect. 2. As to the first Point, *viz.* What was the Nature of the Privilege of Sanctuary: It seems to be agreed, [a] That so far as a Place was allowed to have it, it gave all those that fled to it for Safeguard, and continued within its [b] Precincts, a [c] Freedom from being apprehended, or compelled to answer in any Court of Justice, and a Right to be remanded, if taken out against their Will.

[a] Finch of Law 374. S. P. C. 108. Letter B. 2 H. H. P. C. 323, 324.

[b] What those Precincts were, Keilw. 189. a. b. 191. 9 H. 7. 20. pl. 15. S. P. C. 113. a. Bro. Sanctuary, 10.

[c] Keilw. 188, 189, 190, 191. 8 H. 6. 4. b. Abridged Fitz. Coro. 5. 1 H. 7. 23. b. Abridged Fitz. Coro. 49. 9 E. 4. 28. b. Abridged Fitz. Coro. 32. Keilw. 107, 188.

Sect. 3.

Sect. 3. As to the second Point, *viz.* What Authority was necessary for the creating it: It seems, that it belonged of Common [a] Right to every Church and Churchyard, for the Space of forty Days, but could not be claimed for a longer Time, either by Force of any Bull from the [b] Pope, nor even by [c] Prescription, ([d] especially in the Case of High Treason) but only by a Grant [e] from the King, made, or at least confirmed [f] or allowed [g] in *Eyre*, since the Time of Memory. But it is said, That it did not gain [h] the Name of a Sanctuary till it had the Pope's Bull, tho' it had the [i] full Privilege of one, as to all Exemption from Temporal Courts, by the King's Grant only.

Sect. 4. As to the third Point, *viz.* To what Matters it extended: It seems agreed, That it never was any farther a Protection against any Action merely Civil, [k] than to save the Defendant from Execution of his Body. Also it seems to be generally agreed, That if it were granted by general Words, it extended not to [l] High Treason. But it seems agreed, [m] That in such Case it extended to all Felonies except [n] Sacrilege, and to all inferior Crimes, except such as were committed by a Sanctuary Man [o] within the Sanctuary, or even [p] out of it, *sub spe redeundi.*

Sect. 5. As to the fourth Point, *viz.* At what Time, and in what Manner it was to be pleaded: It seems agreed, That the Defendant lost the Benefit of it, unless he pleaded it before any [q] other Plea, and properly made out his Case; but for this Matter I shall wholly refer the Reader to the Old [r] Books.

Sect. 6. For the Learning of Abjuration, [s] depending much upon that of Sanctuaries, and seeming to be of very little Use at this Day, I shall refer to *Staundforde's Pleas of the Crown, Book* 2. *Chap.* 40. and to what hath been said already concerning that Matter, in the Chapter concerning *Coroners*, *Sect.* 44.

[a] 32 H. 8. ch. 12. Finch of Law 383. 3 H. 7. 12. pl. 6. Abridg. Fitz. Coro. 54. 21 E. 3. 17. pl. 21. Abridg. Bro. Sanctuary, 2. Supra ch. 9. sect. 44. Keilw. 189. a. Bro. Sanctu. 11, 14, 16. Rast. Ent. 583. pl. 1, 2.

[b] Keilw. 189, 190, 191. S. P. C. 110. b. 111. Lett. A. Bro. Sanctu. 6, 15. 5 Co. de jure Regis Eccles. 26.

[c] 1 Inst. 114. Keilw. 188, &c. But Quære if such Prescription were confirmed by King, or allowed in Eyre since Time of Memory. Keilwey, 188, 189, 190, 191.

[d] S. P. C. 112. a. 1 H. 7. 23, 25, 26. Abridged Fitz. Coro. 49. Prescription, 20. Vide Ra. Ent. 584. pl. 3, 4, 5.

[e] S. P. C. 108. Letter B. 110, 111. 1 H. 7. 25. b. 26. Bro. Sanctuary, 7. Keilw. 189, 190, 191.

[f] Keilw. 189, 190. 1 H. 7. 23. 2 Rol. Abr. 268, 269.

[g] Keilw. 189, 190. 2 Rol. Abr. 268, 269. 1 H. 7. 23. Bro. Sanctuary, 7. 15. this is made a Quære. S. P. C. 112.

[h] Finch of Law 375.

[i] Finch of Law 374, 375.

[k] Bro. Sanctuary, 3, 11. 7 H. 6. 8. pl. 34. Abridged Fitz. Jurisdiction, 2. Dyer 295. pl. 11, 12.

[l] 21 E. 3. 17. pl. 21. Denied 29 Ass. pl. 24. Abridged Fitz. Grant, 77. Bro. Sanctuary, 6. 1 H. 7. 23, 25, 26. Abridged Fitz. Coro. 49. Prescription, 20. Cont. Keilw. 190, 191. Quære Finch 374.

[m] See the Books cited to the other Parts of this Section. Quære if in such Case it extended to Petit Treason. Bro. Sanctuary, 2.

[n] 3 Inst. 115. Fitz. 420.

[o] Agreed by all the Canonists. Keilw. 191. b.

[p] Denied by many of the Canonists, Keilw. 191. b.

[q] S. P. C. 113. Letter B. Fitz. Coro. 438. Bro. Sanctuary, 5. 21 E. 3. 17. pl. 21. Abridged Bro. Sanctuary, 2. Fitz. Coro. 447. 9 E. 4. 28. b. Abridged Fitz. Coro. 32.

[r] Keilw. 90, 107, 188, 189. S. P. C. 113. a. 1 H. 7. 23, 24, 25, 26 9 H. 7. 20. pl. 15. Ra. Ent. 584. pl. 3, 4, 5. 683. pl. 3.

[s] 3 Inst. 115. Fitz. Aiel, 5.

CHAP. XXXIII.

Of Clergy.

FOR the better Underſtanding the Nature of the Benefit of Clergy, (or rather of the [a] Statute at this Day, I ſhall endeavour to ſhew,

[a] See the latter Part of this Chapter.

1. By what kind of Perſons it is demandable.
2. For what Crimes.
3. At what Times.
4. Whether it ſhall be allowed where it is not demanded.
5. Who is to judge whether the Perſon who demands it have a Right to it or not.
6. How far the Ordinary was puniſhable at Law for demanding or refuſing a Clerk againſt Law.
7. In what Manner at the Common Law a Clerk was to be delivered to the Ordinary, and what is to be done to him afterwards.
8. What is to be done to him at this Day, and how far it ſhall be to his Benefit.

Sect. 1. As to the firſt Point, *viz.* By what kind of Perſons the Benefit of Clergy, (or rather of the Statute at this Day) is demandable: It may not be improper to look a little back into the Original of it, whereby we ſhall find, That anciently the Clergy [b] ſtrongly inſiſted, that by the Law of God their Perſons were ſo ſacred, that they could not, without a Violation of that Law, be convened before, and much leſs be puniſhed with the Loſs of Life, or Member by any ſecular Judge, for any Crime whatſoever. But there ſeems to be ſo little [c] Colour for any Pretence of this Kind from Scripture, that I almoſt wonder how it was poſſible that any Perſons could be ſo far prejudiced, as ſeriouſly to be perſuaded that it is deducible from thence.

[b] Keilw. 181, 182, 183, 184, 185. See 2 H. H. P. C. 323, 324, &c.

[c] Keilw. 181, &c.

Sect. 2. But it ſeems agreed, [d] That all Perſons in Holy Orders have this Privilege by the Canon Law; but this Law being no farther in [e] Force here than as it hath been received, and is conſiſtent with the Common or Statute Law; it will be proper to ſhew how far it hath

[d] See Lyndw. Book 2. in the Chapter De foro Competente, Kely. 99, 100, 101. Keilw. 180. &c. S. P. C. 123, 124. Finch of Law 462, 463.

[e] Keilw. 181, &c. Kely. 99, &c. 5 Co. de jure Regis eccleſ. 13, &c 2 H. H. P. C. 325.

been received, and is consistent with those Laws; which I shall at present consider under this Head, so far as it relates to the Persons intitled to this Privilege; and shall farther consider it as to other Matters, in the following Part of this Chapter.

Sect. 3. It seems agreed, That before the Statute of *Articuli cleri*, *Ch.* 15. made in the ninth Year of *Ed.* 2. it was [a] generally denied to those who had abjured, or who had any other way confessed themselves guilty: But by a favourable Interpretation of that Statute, which expresly extends only to those who fly to the Church for Safeguard, it hath been allowed [b] to all those who have confessed themselves guilty, upon their Arraignment or otherwise, in the same Manner as if they had not confessed.

Sect. 4. Also it seems, That notwithstanding the Clergy [c] contended, That the Word *Clericus* (which is the Word generally used by the [d] Canon Law as well as ours, [e] to express those who are intitled to this Privilege) did include those of the inferior Orders, [f] as well as Bishops, Priests and Deacons: Yet it seems, [g] That the Temporal Judges sometimes denied it to those in inferior Orders, as well as to mere [h] Laymen, before the Statute of 25 *E.* 3. *ch.* 4. which reciting, *That the Prelates had grievously complained, That secular Clerks, as well Chaplains, as other Monks, and other People of Religion, had been drawn and hanged by Award of the secular Justices, in Prejudice of the Franchise of Holy Church,* &c. *doth enact, That all Manner of Clerks, as well Secular as Religious,* &c. *shall freely enjoy the Privilege of Holy Church,* &c.

Sect. 5. It seems that by a favourable Interpretation of this Statute, which universally prevailed soon [i] after it was made, not only those actually admitted into some inferior Order of the Clergy, [k] but also those who were never qualified to be admitted into Orders, (which was tried [l] by putting them to read a Verse) have been taken to have a [m] Right to this Privilege, as much as Persons in Holy Orders, whether they were Persons lawfully born, or [n] Bastards, [o] Aliens or Denizens, in the Communion of the Church or [p] Excommunicate, within the Common Benefit of the Law, or [q] Outlaws, *&c.* so that they were not [r] Hereticks convict, nor [s] Jews, Mahometans, nor Pagans; nor under [t] perpetual Disability of going into Orders, admitting of no Dispensation, as [u] blind and maimed Persons formerly were, and Women [x] still are; nor liable to the Objection of Bigamy, *viz.* (of having [y] married two different Women successively, or a Widow) which by a Constitution of the Council of *Lyons*, [z] received in this Kingdom, was a Bar to the Demand of the Privilege of the Clergy; and by Force of 18 *E.* 3. 2. was triable by the Certificate [aa] of the Bishop.

Sect. 6. But it is expresly enacted by 1 *E.* 6. 12. *Par.* 16. *That any Person who by the Law of this Realm ought to have the Benefit of his Clergy, shall be admitted to it, altho' he have been divers Times married to any single Woman,*

[a] Fitz. Coro. 155. 11 Co. 29. b. S. P. C. 124. Lett. G. Vide Keilw. 186. b. Selden's Janus Anglor', ch. 10.

[b] Bro. Clergy, 3, 7, 8. 9 E. 4. 28. pl. 40. 8 H. 4. 3. pl. 5. 1 Ass. pl. 4. 27 H. 6. 7. b. Fitz. Coro. 191.

[c] Kely. 99, 100.

[d] Lyndw. B. 2. in the Chapter De foro competente.

[e] See the Statute of Marlb. ch. 28. and Westm. 1. ch. 2. and Articuli cleri, ch. 15. and the Old Books cited, 2 Inst. 633, 634, &c.

[f] Keilw. 181. Kely. 99, 100.

[g] Kely. 99, 100

[h] Fitz. Coro. 233. But they sometimes allowed it to mere Laymen, being able to read, Fitz. Coro. 117.

[i] Yet it was holden the next Year after the Statute quod literatura non facit clericum nisi habeat sacram tonsuram. 26. Ass. pl. 19. Abridged Fitz. Coro. 191. S. P. C. 124. Lett. B. 2 H. H. P. C. 372, 373. [k] Kely. 100, 101, 102. Bro. Clergy, 7, 20. [l] Kely. 100, 101. Finch 462, 463. S. P. C. 133. Letters A, B, C, D. 34 H. 6. 49. pl. 16. Fitz. Coro. 44. See the Cases cited to the fourth general Point of this Chapter. [m] 9 E. 4. 28. pl. 40. Abridged Bro. Clergy, 7. [n] Bro. Clergy, 22. 2 H. H. P. C. 373. [o] Bro Clergy, 20. [p] Bro. Clergy, 20. H. P. C. 229. 11 Co. 29. b. [q] See 3 & 4. W. & M. 9. 11 Co. 29. b. [r] S. P. C. 133. Lett. B. Bro. Clergy, 20. 11 Co. 29. b. [s] Bro. Clergy, 20. 11 Co. 29. b. H. P. C. 229. 2 H. H. P. C. 373. [t] 11 Co. 29. b. [u] 11 Co. 29. b. H. P. C. 229. Cont. Bro. Clergy, 21. [x] Finch 463. 11 Co. 29. b. See the Preambles of 21 Ja. 1. ch. 6. and of 3 & 4 W. M. 9. Par. 7. Yet 'tis admitted Fitz. Coro. 461. That a Woman might claim the Benefit of Clergy. [y] S. P. C. 134, 135. Ra. Ent. 106. a. b. 2 H. H. P. C. 372. [z] See the Statute of Bigamy, 4 E. 1. ch. 5. 5 Co. de jure Regis ecclesiastico, 13. S. P. C. 125. Lett. F. [aa] Ra. Ent. 160. a. b. S. P. C. 134. Lett. C. 135. a. 11 H. 4. 11. pl. 24. Abridged Fitz. Coro. 85. 40 E. 3. 42. pl. 23. Abridged Fitz. Attorney, 39.

or single Women, or to any Widow or Widows, or to two Wives or more. But it bore some [a] Question whether this Statute were not impliedly repealed by 1 & 2 *Ph. & Ma.* 8. while it stood in Force, *Which repealed all Clauses,* &c. *against the See of* Rome.

[a] Vide S. P. C. 134. Dalis. 21. pl. 1. Dyer 201. pl. 67.

Sect. 7. As to Women it is enacted by 21 *Jac.* 1. 6. *That on a Conviction of Grand Larceny under the Value of* 10 *s. being no Burglary, nor Robbery in or near the Highway, nor a felonious private Taking from the Person,* &c. *but only such an Offence for which a Man might have his Clergy, they shall be burnt in the Hand, and imprisoned,* &c.

Bro. Clergy, 20. H. P. C. 229. 2 H. H. P. C. 372.

Sect. 8. But it is enacted by 3 & 4 *W. & M.* 9. Par. 7. *That where a Man being convicted of any Felony may demand the Benefit of his Clergy; if a Woman be convicted for the same or the like Offence, upon her Prayer to have the Benefit of this Statute, Judgment of Death shall not be given against her upon such Conviction, or Execution awarded upon any Outlawry for such Offence, but she shall suffer the same Punishment as a Man should suffer, that has the Benefit of his Clergy allowed him in the like Case; that is to say, shall be burnt in the Hand by the Gaoler in open Court, and further be kept in Prison for such a Time as the Justices in their Discretion shall think fit, so as the same do not exceed one Year's Imprisonment.*

Sect. 9. It seems, [b] That one who had been guilty of Sacrilege, or of breaking the Prison of the Ordinary, had no Right to the Benefit of Clergy, but at the [c] Discretion of the Ordinary.

Sect. 10. It seems clear, [d] That before the Statute of 4 *H.* 7. 13. He who had been admitted to the Benefit of Clergy, might have it a second Time as well as the first, unless he had broken the Prison of the Ordinary, to which he was committed when Clergy was first allowed him; in which Case it seems, [e] That he could not save himself from a second Prosecution, tho' for the very same Felony for which he was before convicted, unless he could shew a Purgation.

Sect. 11. But it is enacted by 4 *H.* 7. 13. *That every Person, not being within Orders, who hath once been admitted to the Benefit of his Clergy, eftsoons arraigned of any such Offence, be not admitted to have the Benefit or Privilege of the Clergy,* &c. *And it is provided, that if any Person at the second Time of asking his Clergy, because he is within Orders, hath not there ready his Letters of his Orders, or a Certificate of his Ordinary, witnessing the same: That then the Justices afore whom he is so arraigned, shall give him a Day by their Discretion to bring in his said Letter or Certificate; and if he fail, and bring not at such a Day his said Letters or Certificate, then the Person to lose the Benefit of his Clergy as he shall do that is without Orders.*

[b] S. P. C. 31. Lett. F 32. Lett. A. 123. Lett. D. 124. Lett. B. 133. Lett. A. Fitz. Coro. 112, 117, 120, 250, 257. 4 Inst. 314. 12 Ass. 39. Abridg. Bro. Clergy, 10. 17 Ass. pl. 4. 17 E. 3. 13. pl. 47. Abridg. Fitz. Coro. 112. 9 E. 4. 28. pl. 40. Abridg. Bro. Clergy, 7. 27 Ass. 42. Abridged Fitz. Coro. 205. Bro. Clergy, 13. 11 Co. 29. b.

[c] Yet it seems to be holden, 26 Ass. pl. 19. and 27. Abridged Bro. Clergy, 11, 12. Fitz. Coro. 191, 193. That one who had been guilty of Sacrilege might demand it as well as any other. 2 H. H. P. C. 333, 366. And it seems to be holden, Fitz. Co. 232, 250, 257, 419. 2 H. H. P. C. 372. That one who had broken the Prison of the Ordinary had no Manner of Right to it. Vide 12 Ass. 39. Abridged Bro. Clergy, 10. This Point is made a Quære, 9 E. 4. 28. pl. 40. Abridged Bro. Clergy 7. [d] H. P. C. 230. S. P C. 31. Lett. F. 32. Letter A. 107. Letter B. 124. Letter C. 135. Letters B. D. See the Preamble of 4 H. 7. 13. But 17 Ass. pl. 4. 17 E. 3. 13. pl. 47. Abridged Fitz. Coro. 112. It seems to have been doubted where the Clerk was attainted before he first had the Benefit of Clergy. [e] Fitz. Coro. 232. and to the Books cited to Letter C. and to the former Section.

Sect. 12. But it is enacted by 28 *H.* 8. *Par.* 7. *That Persons within Holy Orders, shall be under the same Pains and Dangers for the Offences referred to by that Statute, and be used and ordered to all Intents and Purposes, as other Persons, not being within Holy Orders. And it is farther enacted by* 32 H. 8. 3. Par. 8. *That Persons within Holy Orders who shall be admitted to their Clergy, shall be burnt in the Hand in like Manner as lay Clerks, and shall suffer and incur all such Pains, Dangers, and Forfeitures, and be ordered and used for their Offences of Felony, to all Intents, Purposes and Constructions, as lay Persons admitted to their Clergy be, or ought to be*, &c.

Sect. 13. But it is enacted by 1 *E.* 6. 12. *par.* 10. That in all Cases of Felony, other than those in that Act mentioned, every Person who shall be found Guilty, or confess, or stand Mute, or not answer directly, shall have the Benefit of his Clergy, in like Manner and Form as before the first Year of King *Henry* VIII. And therefore it seems plain, That where lay Persons are not excluded from the Benefit of Clergy the first Time; Persons in Holy Orders may have it as often as they want it, in the same Manner as they might upon the Foot of the said Statute of 4 *H.* 7. 13. [a] except they shall be outlawed, or challenge above the Number of twenty, [89] in which Case they are not within the Purview of 1 *E.* 6. which extends only to those who shall be found Guilty, or confess, or stand Mute, *&c.* But [b] where the Crime itself charged against a Person in Holy Orders, is by any Statute generally excluded from Clergy, such Person shall no more have the Benefit of it than if he were a mere Layman.

[a] H. P. C. 238, 239. S. P. C. 135. Lett. B.

[b] S.P.C. 135. Lett. D. 136. H. P. C. 235, 236. 2 H. H. P. C. 374.

Sect. 14. It is recited by 34 & 35 *H.* 8. 14. *That divers Persons had been indicted and attainted, and some of them Clerks convict, and some of them Clerks attainted*, &c. *before Justices of Peace, Gaol-Delivery*, &c. *within divers Cities, Counties and Franchises*, &c. *the Records of which Attainders and Convictions often, by Negligence of the Clerks*, &c. *having the Rule and Keeping thereof, had been embezled, and not ready to be objected against such Persons, being newly arraigned before other Justices*, &c. *And for that it had not been known certainly whether to resort for the same Records, because they were not certified into any Place certain, such Offenders had often had the Benefit of the Clergy where they ought not*, &c. And thereupon it is enacted, *That the Clerk of the Crown, Clerks of the Peace, and Clerks of Assize, where any such Attainder, or Conviction shall be so had, shall certify a Transcript, briefly containing the Effect of every such Indictment*, &c. *and Clerk attainted*, &c. *that is to say, the Name, Surname, and Addition of every such Person, &c. and the Certainty of the Offence*, &c. *and the Day and Place of his Attainder or Conviction*, &c. *and the Day and Place of his Offence*, &c. *before the King in his Bench at* Westminster, *there to remain of Record for ever, within forty Days after such Attainder*, &c. *if the Term be then, and if not, then within twenty Days after the next Term*, &c. *on Pain of* 40 s. &c. *And that the Clerk of the Crown in the King's Bench, shall receive the same without Fee, under the like Pain.*

Sect. 15. *Provided, That if there be more Persons contained in any such Indictment, other than such Person so attainted or convicted, that then such Clerk shall certify such Transcript only* [c] *concerning the Person or Persons so attainted or convicted, which shall be as effectual against such Person and Persons against whom it shall be so objected, alledged or pleaded, as if the very Record were present.*

[c] Note, That this is omitted in Keble's Statutes.

2 *Sect.* 16.

Sect. 16. And it is farther enacted, *That the ſaid Clerk of the Crown in the King's Bench, ſhall at all ſuch Times as the Juſtices of the Gaol-Delivery, or Juſtices of the Peace, in every County within this Realm of* England, *do write unto him for the Names of ſuch Perſons, which be ſo attainted or convict, and certified in the ſaid Bench, ſhall incontinently certify the ſaid Names and Surnames of the ſaid Perſons, with the Cauſes why and wherefore they were convicted or attainted, unto the Juſtices of Gaol-Delivery, or Juſtices of the Peace,* &c. *on Pain of* 40 s.

Sect. 17. But it is provided, *That this Act ſhall not extend to the Clerks of the Crown,* &c. *in* Wales *or* Cheſter, *or Counties Palatine of* Lancaſter *and* Durham, *to make any Tranſcript of any ſuch Attainder or Conviction, before the King's Juſtices of his Counties in* Wales, &c.

Sect. 18. It ſeems, [a] That the Juſtices may, by force of this Act, write in their own Names to the Clerk of the Crown in the King's Bench, for a Certificate of the Tranſcript of an Attainder or Conviction, and need not do it by Writ in the King's Name under their *Teſte, &c.* which is required [b] by the Conſtruction of 2 & 3 *E.* 6. 24. where the Juſtices of one County write to thoſe of another for the Certificate of the Attainder, or Acquittal of the Principal, in order to proceed againſt the Acceſſary. And the Reaſon of the Difference is, becauſe in this laſt Caſe Juſtices write to Juſtices, but in the former to an Officer only.

[a] Dy. 253. pl. 103.

[b] Vide ſupra ch. 29. ſect. 53.

Sect. 19. It is farther provided by 3 & 4 *W. & M.* 9. *Par.* 7. as followeth, *Foraſmuch as ſuch Men and Women who have once had their Clergy,* &c. *may happen to be indicted for an Offence committed afterwards in ſome other County, Be it therefore enacted, That the Clerk of the Crown, Clerk of the Peace, Clerk of the Aſſiſes where ſuch Man or Woman ſhall be convicted, ſhall, at the Requeſt of the Proſecutor, or any other in his Majeſty's Behalf, certify a Tranſcript briefly, and in few Words, containing the Effect and Tenor of every Indictment and Conviction of ſuch Man or Woman, of his or her having the Benefit of the Clergy,* &c. *and Addition of every ſuch Perſon or Perſons, and the Certainty of the Felony and Conviction, to the Judges and Juſtices in ſuch other County where ſuch Man or Woman ſhall be indicted, which Certificate being produced in Court, ſhall be ſufficient Proof that ſuch Man or Woman have before had the Benefit of Clergy,* &c.

As to the ſecond Point, *viz.* For what Crimes the Benefit of Clergy, or rather of the Statute may be demanded, I ſhall premiſe,

Sect. 20. *Firſt*, That it ſeems to be generally agreed, That by the Common Law it is demandable as well upon an [c] Appeal as Indictment, for any Crime whatſoever, which ſubjects the Offender to the [d] Loſs of Life or Member, except [e] High Treaſon, (whether againſt the King's Perſon or [f] not,) and Sacrilege; for the firſt of which the Common Law ſeems to give the Offender no manner of Right to the Benefit of his Clergy, and for the latter to have left it to the Diſcretion of the Ordinary, as hath been more fully ſhewn, *Sect.* 9.

[c] 11 Co. 29. b.

[d] S. P. C. 124. Lett. E. Bro. Clergy, 19. Finch of Law 462, 463.

[e] S.P.C. 124. Letter E. Fitz. Coro. 283. 19 H. 6. 47. pl. 103. Abridged Fitz. Coro. 8. Bro. Clergy, 6 Vide 2 Inſt. 634.

[f] So it appears from the Books cited to Letter E. Yet in H. P. C. 330. and 11 Co. 29. b. and Bro. Clergy, 25, 31. it ſeems to be holden, That by the Common Law Clergy was excluded from ſuch High Treaſon only as was againſt the Perſon of the King. But Quære upon what Ground this is holden. [90] And ſee 25 E. 3. De Clero, ch. 5.

Sect. 21. *Secondly*, That it ſeems to be doubtful, [b] whether it were demandable at the Common Law for Petit Treaſon; but this was ſettled by 25 *E.* 3. *de clero*, *Ch.* 4. which expreſly allows it for *any Treaſons or Felonies, touching other Perſons than the King himſelf, or his Royal Majeſty.*

Sect. 22. *Thirdly*, That after this a Conſtruction [b] prevailed, That Clergy might be denied to Felons charged as *inſidiatores viarum, & depopulatores agrorum*; but this is remedied by 4 *H.* 4. 2.

From theſe Premiſſes it ſeems to be generally agreed, [c] That the following Concluſions neceſſarily follow.

Sect. 23. *Firſt*, So far as a Perſon, who in Reſpect of his Orders or Learning, or otherwiſe, is qualified to be admitted to the Benefit of Clergy, is denied it in Reſpect of his [d] Crime, not amounting to High Treaſon or Sacrilege; ſuch Denial muſt be grounded on ſome Act of [e] Parliament, made ſince 25 *E.* 3.

Sect. 24. *Secondly*, Where-ever an Offence is made Felony by Statute, it [f] ſhall have the Benefit of Clergy, unleſs it be expreſly excluded from it.

Sect. 25. *Thirdly*, Where-ever a Perſon is denied the Benefit of Clergy, in Reſpect of a Statute, excluding it from the Crime charged againſt him, the [g] Indictment or Appeal, and the [h] Evidence thereon, muſt expreſly bring his Caſe within the Words of ſuch Statute: And therefore, if a [i] Murder be not expreſly laid, and proved to have been done of Malice prepenſe; and the Offence of an Acceſſary [k] before, to have been done maliciouſly; and that of a [l] Cut-purſe *clam & ſecrete a perſona, &c.* the Offender ſhall have his Clergy. And agreeably hereto it hath been adjudged, [m] That an Indictment of Robbery *in quadam via Regia pedeſtri ducent' de* London *ad* Iſlington, ſhall not ouſt the Offender of the Benefit of his Clergy; becauſe the Words of the Statute [n] to this Purpoſe are *In, or about, or near the Highway.* Yet it hath been adjudged, [o] That an Indictment againſt a Man as Acceſſary to Murder before the Fact, by the Words *malitioſe excitavit, movit & procuravit, &c.* is ſufficient to ouſt the Offender of the Benefit of Clergy, by Force of 4 & 5 *Ph. & M.* the Words whereof are, *That all Perſons who ſhall maliciouſly command, hire, or counſel any Perſon*, &c. which are not expreſly purſued in ſuch Indictment. But the Counſelling another being neceſſarily included in the Moving, Procuring, and Exciting him, which therefore are tantamount in Senſe, and different only in the Manner of Expreſſion, ſuch an Indictment is as [p] much within the Statute as if it followed the very Words. Alſo it hath been [q] adjudged, That in order to ouſt a Man of the Benefit of Clergy by Force of a Statute, which takes it away from a Capital Offence at Common Law, there is no Need that the Indictment or Appeal conclude *contra formam Statuti*, becauſe the Statute doth no way alter the Nature of the Offence, but only leaves it to its proper Judgment, and takes away a perſonal Privilege of Exemption from ſuch Judgment.

Sect. 26. *Fourthly*, A Statute excluding the Principals from the Benefit of Clergy, doth [r] not thereby exclude the Acceſſaries before or after; Neither [s] doth a Statute, excluding the Acceſſaries, thereby exclude

[a] Vide S. P. C. 124. Letter E. H. P. C. 230. Finch of Law 463. 11 Co. 29. b.
[b] Supra ch. 25. ſect. 59. S. P. C. 124. Letter D. 2 H. H. P. C. 328, 333.
[c] H. P. C. 230, 231.
[d] S. P. C. 124, 125, &c. H. P. C. 232, 233, &c.
[e] 2 H. H. P. C. 332. H. P. C. 230.
[f] H. P. C. 230. 2 H. H. P. C. 330, 334, 335.
[g] H. P. C. 231. 2 H. H. P. C. 336, 344. 11 Co. 37. S. P. C. 114. Lett. A. 130. Letter B.
[h] S. P. C, 130. Letter B. Dy. 261. pl. 26. 224. pl. 30.
[i] H. P. C. 231. S. P. C. 130. Letter B. Dyer 261. pl. 26. Vid. 23 H. 8. ch. 1. 1 E. 6. 12. par. 10.
[k] H. P. C. 231. 1 And. 195. 11 Co. 37. Dyer 183. pl. 59. Vid. 4 & 5. Ph. & M. 4.
[l] H. P. C. 231. 8 El. ch. 4.
[m] Moore 5. pl. 16. 2 H. H. P. C. 349.
[n] 23 H. 8. ch. 1. par. 3. 1 E. 6. ch. 12 Par. 10. 4 & 5 Ph. & M. 4.
[o] 1 And. 195.
[p] See B. 1. ch. 32. ſect. 3.
[q] See B. 1. ch. 30. ſect. 9. 1 Vent. 13.
[r] See B. 1. ch. 3. ſect. 4. ch. 30. ſect. 7. H. P. C. 7, 58, 231. 2 H. H. P. C. 335, 336. 11 Co. from 29 to 36. 1 And. 195. Dyer 99. pl. 59. 183. pl. 59. See 4 & 5 Ph. & Ma. 4.
[s] 11 Co. from 29 to 36. Sav. 46. pl. 98.

the Principals. And it ſeems agreed, [a] That where a Statute excludes thoſe from the Clergy who ſhall be found guilty of Petit Treaſon, Murder, Burglary, Robbery, or any other Kind of Crimes, it ſhall be conſtrued to intend only to exclude the Principals, and not Acceſſaries before or after, notwithſtanding they are certainly in a high Degree Partakers in the Guilt of the Principal Offender, as hath been more fully ſhewn *Chap.* 29. *Sect.* 13, 14. Yet inaſmuch as ſuch Statutes taking away a Privilege of ſo high a Conſequence to the Subject, ought to receive the ſtricteſt Interpretation; and the Words of them may, without any manner of Strain, or Repugnance to the general Rules of Law, be taken in ſuch a Senſe as will include the Principals only; I do not know that they have ever been carried farther.

[a] H. P. C. 7, 58. 1 And. 195. Dy. 99. pl. 59. 183. pl. 59.

Sect. 27. *Fifthly*, Where Clergy is allowable, it ſhall be as much allowed to one who ſtands [b] Mute, or Challenges peremptorily [c] above the Number of twenty, or is [d] outlawed, *&c.* as to one who is convicted by Verdict, or Confeſſion, *&c.*

Sect. 28. *Sixthly*, A Statute Taking the Benefit of Clergy from thoſe who ſhall be found guilty, doth not [e] thereby take it from thoſe who ſtand Mute, or challenge peremptorily above the Number of twenty, or are outlawed, *&c.* But it ſeems [f] clear, That a Statute taking it away from thoſe who ſhall be found Guilty, extends as well to thoſe who ſhall confeſs themſelves guilty upon Record, as to thoſe who ſhall be found guilty by Verdict; for as the latter are found guilty by a Jury, ſo are the former by the Court, and their Conviction being from their own Mouths, is of the higheſt Nature poſſible.

[b] H. P. C 231. 25 H. 8. 3. par. 2. Supra ch. 30. ſect. 24. Moore 550. pl. 738. Cont. Fitz. Coro. 283.

[c] 3 H. 7. 12. pl. 8. Abrid. Bro. Clergy, 27. Fitz. Coro. 51. H. P. C. 231. 25 H. 8. 3. Par. 2. 3 & 4 W. & M. 9.

[d] 11 Co. 29. b. See 3 & 4 W. & M. 9.

[e] See 25 H. 8. 3 Par. 2. 3 & 4 W. & M. 9. 11 Co. Poulter's Caſe. 2 H. H. P. C. 335.

[f] 11 Co. 29. a.

Sect. 29. And now I ſhall endeavonr to ſhew for what Crimes Perſons are excluded from the Benefit of Clergy by Statutes made ſince 25 *E.* 3. which being ſomewhat perplexed and intricate, I ſhall, for the better clearing of this Matter, firſt take a general View of thoſe Statutes ſo far as they are in Force at this Day, and then ſhall more diſtinctly conſider them, as they particularly concern the ſeveral Kinds of Capital Crimes.

Sect. 30. The firſt of thoſe Statutes I ſhall take Notice, is 23 *H.* 8. *Ch.* 1. by which it is enacted, *Par.* 3. *That no Perſon who ſhall be found guilty after the Laws of this Land, for any Manner of Petit Treaſon, or for any wilful Murder of Malice prepenſed, or for robbing any Churches, Chapels, or other Holy Places, or for robbing of any Perſon or Perſons, in their Dwelling Houſes, or Dwelling Place, the Owner or Dweller in the ſame Houſe, his Wife, his Children, or Servants, then being within, and put in Fear and Dread by the ſame, or for robbing of any Perſon or Perſons in or near about* [g] *the Highways, or for wilful burning of any Dwelling-Houſes or Barns, wherein any Grain of Corn ſhall happen to be; nor any Perſon or Perſons being found guilty of any Abetment, Procurement, Helping, Maintaining, or Counſelling of, or to any ſuch Petit Treaſons, Murders or Felonies, ſhall be admitted to his Clergy; ſuch as be within Holy Orders only excepted.*

[g] So Raſtal's Statutes; but Poulton omits the Word *about*, and Keble the Word *near*.

Sect. 31. *Note*, That this Statute extends [h] as well to Appeals as to Indictments, and to thoſe who ſhall confeſs [i], as much as thoſe who ſhall plead and be found Guilty; for the Words are general, *That no Perſon who ſhall be found guilty, after the Laws of this Realm,* &c. *ſhall be admitted to his Clergy,* &c. But it extends not [k] to Perſons outlawed, and was eaſily evaded [l] by Perſons brought to their Trials, by ſtanding Mute, or challenging peremptorily above the Number of twenty, whereby they prevented their being found guilty.

[h] 11 Co. 30. b.

[i] 2 H. H. P. C. 338. Supra ſect. 28.

[k] 11 Co. 30. b.

[l] See the Preamble of 25 H. 8. 3. And 11 Co. 30. b.

Sect. 32.

Sect. 32. But these two last Defects are provided for by 25 *H.* 8. *Ch.* 3. by which it is enacted, Par. 2. *That every Person who shall from thenceforth be indicted of Petit Treason, wilful burning of Houses, Murder, Robbery or Burglary, or other Felony, according to the Tenor and Meaning of* 23 H. 8. *and thereupon arraigned, do stand Mute of Malice or froward Mind, or challenge peremptorily above the Number of twenty, or else will not, or do not answer directly to the same Indictment and Felony, whereupon he is so arraigned, shall from thenceforth lose the Benefit and Privilege of his Clergy, in like Manner and Form as if he had directly pleaded to the said Petit Treason, Murder, Robbery, Burglary, or other Felony, whereupon he is so arraigned, and thereupon had been found guilty, after the Laws of the Land.* [91]

[a] 11 Co. 31. 32. 1 H. H. P. C. 573. 2 H. H. P. C. 339.

Sect. 33. But this Statute extends not [a] to those who are outlawed, any more than 23 *H.* 8. neither doth it extend to Appeals, nor to Accessaries before, both of which are included in 23 *H.* 8.

Sect. 34. After came the Statute of 1 *E.* 6. 12. Par. 10. *That no Person who shall be in due Form of the Laws attainted or convicted of Murder of Malice prepensed, or of Poisoning of Malice prepensed, or of breaking of any House by Day or by Night, any Person being then in the same House where the same Breaking shall be committed, and thereby put in Dread; or of robbing any Person in the Highway, or near the Highway; or for felonious stealing of Horses, Geldings, or Mares; or of felonious Taking of any Goods out of any Parish Church, or other Church or Chappel; or being indicted or appealed of any of the same Offences, and thereupon found guilty by Verdict of twelve Men, or shall confess the same upon his Arraignment; or will not answer directly according to the Laws of this Realm, or shall stand wilfully, or of Malice, Mute, shall not be admitted to the Benefit of his Clergy; And that in all other Cases of Felony, all Persons that shall be arraigned, or found guilty upon their Arraignment, or shall confess, or stand Mute, in Form aforesaid, or will not answer directly in Form aforesaid, shall have their Clergy in the same Manner as before the first Year of King* Henry VIII.

[b] 11 Co. 32. b. 2 H. H. P. C. 343. [c] 11 Co. 31, 32. [d] Supra sect. 30. [e] Supra sect. 32.

Sect. 35. *Note*, That this Statute extends as well to [b] Appeals as to Indictments, in which Respect it is more fully penned than 25 *H.* 8. And that it extends to Persons in Holy [c] Orders, as much as to Lay-men, and to all Persons attainted in general, and consequently to those who are outlawed, in which Respects it is more fully penned than either, [d] 23 or [e] 25 *H.* 8. Yet it hath several considerable Defects; as,

[f] 11 Co. 32. a. Sup. sect. 27, 28. But S. P. C. 126. Lett. A. it is made a Quære whether those who challenge more than twenty, are not included under the Word Convict.

Sect. 36. *First*, In that it doth not exclude those from the Benefit of the Clergy, who challenge above the Number of twenty; so that it is easily made ineffectual [f] by taking such Challenges, as to Crimes excluded from the Benefit of Clergy, by this Statute, and no other. But as to the Crimes within 25 *H.* 8. it [g] seems plain, That a Person that takes such Challenges might be excluded from his Clergy by Force of that Statute even before it was revived by 5 & 6 *E.* 6. set forth more at Large *Sect.* 42, &c. because 1 *E.* 6. restores the Benefit of Clergy, as it was before the Reign of *Henry* 8. to such only as shall be found guilty, or confess, or stand Mute, or not answer directly, and consequently [h] those who challenge above the Number of twenty, seem clearly to be excluded in the same Manner as if 1 *E.* 6. had never been made.

[g] But in 11 Co. 32. a it seems to be otherwise holden. [h] Vide H. P. C. 239. and Additions N° [89] [91] [102]

Sect. 37. *Secondly*, In that it omits Acceſſaries in the Clauſe which takes away Clergy, but includes them in that which reſtores it, which is general as to all Caſes of Felony, not mentioned in the Act, whereof any Perſon ſhall be found guilty, and conſequently as to Acceſſaries wholly takes off the Force of 23 *H.* 8. which extends [a] only to thoſe who ſhall be found guilty, and is the only Statute in this Reign which excludes Acceſſaries from the Clergy. And accordingly we find, [b] That after this Statute Acceſſaries were admitted to their Clergy, in the ſame Manner as before the Reign of *Henry* 8. till the making of 4 & 5 *Ph.* & *Mar.* ſet forth more at large *Sect.* 45.

[a] Vide ſupra ſect. 30, 33.
[b] 11 Co. 31. b. Dy. 133. pl. 4.

Sect. 38. *Thirdly*, In that it alſo omits Arſon in the Clauſe which takes away Clergy, but includes it in the general Words of that which reſtores it, and conſequently re-intitled thoſe [c] Convict of it to Clergy, in all Caſes but that of challenging more than twenty, till the making of 5 & 6 *E.* 6. as ſhall be more fully ſhewn hereafter.

[c] 11 Co. 31, 32, &c. Vide ſupra ſect. 36.

Sect. 39. *Fourthly*, In that the Clauſe which ouſts Horſe-ſtealers of their Clergy is worded in ſuch a Manner as makes it doubtful whether it extend to thoſe who ſteal but one, which occaſioned the Making of 2 [d] & 3. *E.* 6. 33, which declares, *That a Perſon feloniouſly ſtealing one Horſe, Gelding or Mare, ſhall be put from his Clergy in the ſame Manner as if he had been indicted, or appealed for ſtealing of two*, &c.

[d] Vide infra ſect. 61.

Sect. 40. *Fifthly*, In that the Clauſe which ouſts Houſe-breakers of their Clergy, is not worded in ſuch a Manner as fully brings their Offence under the Notion of Felony; for it is thus expreſſed, *Any Perſon who ſhall be attainted*, &c. *of breaking any Houſe by Day or Night, any Perſon being therein and put in Fear, or Dread*, &c. But ſuch a Breaking, even in the Night is no Felony unleſs it be done with an Intent to commit a Felony, which makes it Burglary; neither can it be Felony, if done in the Day with any Intent whatſoever; for tho' a Felony follow, which may make the Houſe-breaking, done with an Intent to commit it, properly enough to be called felonious: Yet it ſeems, That it cannot make it become [e] a Felony, becauſe it is not reducible to any Species of Felony. And therefore the Statute muſt be ſupplied by a reaſonable Intendment, and [f] conſtrued to mean ſuch Houſe-breaking only as amounts to, or is attended with Felony.

[e] Yet quære, for this Matter is doubtfully expreſs'd, S. P. C. 126. Lett. A. and 11 Co. 31. b. 32. a.
[f] S.P.C. 125. Lett. D. 126. Lett. A. 11 Co. 31. b. 32. a.

Sect. 41. It is [g] holden by Sir *Edward Coke*, That Piracy was reſtored to the Benefit of Clergy by this Statute; but as to Piracy on the High Sea, the contrary hath been ſolemnly [h] adjudged and confirmed by conſtant Experience, and is certainly agreeable to the [i] legal Notion of Piracy in other Caſes; which being a Capital Offence by the Civil Law only, (even after the Statute of 28 *H.* 8. 15. which altered not the Nature of the Offence, but only the Manner of the Trial) ſhall not be included in a Statute ſpeaking generally of Felonies, which ſhall be conſtrued only of thoſe Felonies which are ſuch by our Law; as thoſe Piracies are [k] which are committed in a Creek or Port within the Body of a County, but no other.

[g] 11 Co. 31. b.
[h] Moor 756. pl. 1044. Vide 3 Inſt. 111.
[i] B. 1. ch. 37. ſect. 6, 7. 2 H. H. P. C. 370.
[k] B. 1. ch. 37. ſect. 11. 2 H. H. P. C. 369.

Sect. 42. The next general Statute relating to theſe Matters, is 5 & 6 *E.* 6. 10. which firſt recites the above-mentioned [l] Clauſe of 23 *H.* 8. concerning Clergy, and takes Notice that it was defective in omitting thoſe who rob, &c. in one County, and remove the Thing taken into another, and there are tried, &c. and that this Omiſſion was ſupplied by 25 *H.* 8. and that the ſaid Statute of 25 *H.* 8. was in this Reſpect made ineffectual by 1 *E.* 6. 12. which reſtored Clergy as it ſtood before the Reign of *H.* 8. to all the Felonies not therein mentioned; and that by Rea-

[l] Vide ſupra ſect. 30.

2 H. H. P. C. 341. ſon of the ſaid Statute of 1 *E.* 6. divers Perſons had committed Robberies, *&c.* in one County, and after had been taken, *&c.* and tried in another, and there had their Clergy, which they would not have had, if the ſaid Statute of 25 *H.* 8. had ſtood in force; and then goes on in theſe Words, *For Redreſs whereof from henceforth to be had, be it enacted, &c. That the ſaid Act made in the ſaid 25th Year, touching the putting of ſuch Offenders from their Clergy; and every Article Clauſe and Sentence, contained in the ſame, touching Clergy, ſhall from henceforth, touching ſuch Offence from henceforth to be committed and done, ſtand, remain and be in full Strength and Virtue, in ſuch Manner and Form, as it did before the making of the ſaid Act in the firſt Year of the Reign of our Sovereign Lord the King that now is: Any Clauſe, Article, or Sentence compriſed therein to the contrary notwithſtanding.*

Sect. 43. It was for ſome Time a great Queſtion, Whether this Statute revived 25 *H.* 8. for the whole, or only for ſuch Part of it which relates to Felons removing the Thing feloniouſly taken into a different County from that wherein they took it, and there tried, *&c.* And Sir
[a] S.P.C. 128. Letter A. [a] *William Staundforde* inclines to the latter Opinion; becauſe the Words are, *That the ſaid Act made in the ſaid 25th Year, touching the putting ſuch Offenders from their Clergy, ſhall be revived,* &c. where the Word *ſuch* ſhall have Relation only to the Offenders mentioned before; which are thoſe who ſteal in one County, and remove the Thing ſtolen into another;
[b] Vide 11 Co. 33. a. and this Objection is ſtrengthened [b] by the Title of the Act, which is only this, *That ſuch as rob in one Shire, and fly into another, ſhall not have their Clergy.* To which it may be added, That all Statutes which take away Clergy, are to be conſtrued ſtrictly *in favorem vitæ.* Yet it hath
[c] 11 Co. 33, 34, 35. [d] H. P. C. 232 to 237. 2 H. H. P. C. 341. See Raſtal's Statutes, Title Clergy, Par. 16. been adjudged, [c], and is, as I take it, fully [d] ſettled, That this Statute revived 25 *H.* 8. as to every other Part of it, as well as that concerning Felons carrying the Thing ſtolen from one County into another; for granting that the Makers of the Statute of 5 & 6 *E.* 6. had the Caſe of ſuch Felons principally in their View; which appears pretty plainly, not only from the Title of the Statute, but alſo from the Preamble and Purview, for the Preamble expreſly takes Notice of no other Miſchief from the Repeal of 25 *H.* 8. but only this, That thereby many of ſuch Felons had their Clergy; and then follows the enacting Clauſe, which begins in theſe Words, *For Redreſs whereof,* and then goes on *be it enacted,* &c. *That* 25 *H.* 8. *touching ſuch Offenders, and ſuch Offences, remain in full Force.* Yet conſidering that the Statute of 5 & 6 *E.* 6. begins with a Recital of the whole Clauſe of 23 *H.* 8. wherein there are ſeveral other Offences contained, and that the Words, *ſuch Offenders and ſuch Offences* in the enacting Clauſe of 5 & 6 *E.* 6. may properly enough refer to them, as well as to the Offence of the Felons mentioned next immediately before: And farther conſidering that the Words, *ſuch Offenders and ſuch Offences,* may properly enough be taken to include *all ſuch in Miſchief, and ſuch in In-*
[e] 11 Co. 33. b. *convenience,* according to the received [e] Conſtruction of the Word *ſuch,* in ſome other Statutes, and *a fortiori* thoſe in greater Miſchief and greater Inconvenience, as almoſt all the other Offences ſpecified in 25 *H.* 8. are; as for Inſtance, Petit Treaſon, Murder, Arſon, *&c.* and it is a received
[f] 11 Co. 33, 34. Vide ſupra ſect. 25. and *B.* 1. ch. 32. ſect. 3. [f] Conſtruction of penal Statutes, to extend them to all Caſes that come within the Meaning of the Words. And it would be abſurd to imagine that the Makers of the Statute intended to put thoſe, who carried Goods ſtolen into a different County, in a worſe Caſe in ſuch County than in that wherein they ſtole them, as they muſt be, if 25 *H.* 8. were only revived againſt them where they carried the Thing ſtolen into a different County;

County; for by ſuch a Conſtruction they would have been excluded from Clergy, in the County wherein they committed the Robbery, by 1 *E.* 6. 12. only, which not extending to thoſe who challenge above the Number of twenty, might eaſily be evaded; whereas in a different County they would be excluded from it in ſuch Caſe by 25 *H.* 8. To which may be added, [a] That the firſt Sentence of the Purview of 5 & 6 *E.* 6. *viz. That the ſaid Act of* 25 *H.* 8. *touching the putting ſuch Offenders from their Clergy*, had been ſufficient, if no more had been intended but the Excluding thoſe who rob in one County and fly into another; and therefore it is moſt natural to intend that it was the Meaning of the Makers of the Statute, by adding thoſe farther Words, *That every Article, Clauſe, and Sentence in the ſame, touching Clergy, ſhall, touching ſuch Offences, remain,* &c. to revive the whole Statute ſo far as it related to Clergy. [a] 11 Co. 34.

Sect. 44. And ſince the whole Statute of 25 *H.* 8. is revived, it follows by a neceſſary Conſequence, That ſo much of 23 *H.* 8. alſo as is expreſly affirmed by it, is revived alſo. And therefore ſince 25 *H.* 8. having recited the Clauſe of 23 *H.* 8. concerning Clergy, and the Miſchief that it extended only to thoſe who are found Guilty, expreſly enacts, *That whoever ſhall be indicted of Petit Treaſon, wilful burning of Houſes, Murder, Robbery or Burglary, or other Felony, according to the Tenor and Meaning of the ſaid Statute, and ſtand Mute, or challenge peremptorily above twenty,* &c. *ſhall loſe the Benefit of the Clergy, in like Manner as if he had pleaded, and been found guilty*; whereby it affirms and inforces the 23 *H.* 8. as to thoſe found guilty of ſuch Crimes; it follows by a neceſſary Conſequence, That Perſons not in Holy Orders found guilty of Petit Treaſon, or [b] Arſon, which were omitted by 1 *E.* 6. are excluded from Clergy by 23 *H.* 8. thus affirmed and enforced by 25 *H.* 8. and conſequently revived by 5 & 6 *E.* 6. [b] 11 Co. 34. b. 35. a. H. P. C. 232, 233.

Sect. 45. But it is obſervable, That the ſaid Statute of 25 *H.* 8. wholly omits [c] Acceſſaries, as well as 1 *E.* 6. But to remedy this Defect, it is enacted by 4 & 5. *P.* & *M.* 4. *That every Perſon that ſhall maliciouſly command, hire, or counſel any Perſon or Perſons, to commit or do any Petit Treaſon, wilful Murder, or to do any Robbery in any Dwelling-Houſe or Houſes, or to commit or do any Robbery in or near the Highway in the Realm of* England, *or in any other the Queen's Dominions, or to commit or do any Robbery in any Place within the Marches of* England *againſt* Scotland, *or wilfully to burn any Dwelling Houſe, or any Part thereof, or any Barn then having Corn or Grain in the ſame, that then every ſuch Offender, being outlawed thereof, or being thereof arraigned and found guilty by the Order of the Law, or being otherwiſe lawfully attainted or convicted of the ſame Offence, or being arraigned thereof, do ſtand Mute of Malice or froward Mind, or do challenge peremptorily above the Number of twenty Perſons, or will not anſwer directly to ſuch Offence, ſhall not have the Benefit of his Clergy.* 1 H. H. P. C. 570, 571, &c. 2 H. H. P. C. 345, 346. Cont. Savil 46. pl. 98. S. P. C. 125. [c] Vide ſupra ſect. 33.

Sect. 46. It is obſervable, 1. That this Statute is general as to all Robberies in any Dwelling-Houſe; Yet it ſeems to have been always taken as a [d] reaſonable Conſtruction, That it ſhall be reſtrained to ſuch Robberies of this Kind as were excluded from the Benefit of Clergy, by ſome former Statute; for it cannot be well imagined that the Makers of this, or any other Statute, intended in any Caſe to take away Clergy from the Acceſſary, where the Principal is left to the full Benefit of it. [d] 11 Co. 35, 36, 37. Vide H. P. C. 235, 236, 237. 2 H. H. P. C. 342. Cont. Savil 46. pl. 98.

Sect. 47. 2dly, That an Indictment or Appeal, in order to ouſt an Acceſſary of his Clergy by force of this Statute, muſt expreſly purſue it, in Subſtance [a] at leaſt, as hath been already ſhewn, *Sect.* 25.

[a] Vide Dy. 186. pl. 2, 3.

That the Words Wilful Murder, in an Indictment on the Statute, are ſufficiently purſued by laying the Murder done ex malitia præcogitata.

Sect. 48. It is farther enacted by 3 & 4 *W.* & *M.* 9 Par. 3. *That if any Perſon or Perſons whatſoever be indicted of any Offence, for which by Virtue of any former Statute, he or they are excluded from having the Benefit of his or their Clergy, if he or they had been thereof convicted by Verdict or Confeſſion, if he or they ſtand Mute, or will not anſwer directly to the Felony, or ſhall challenge peremptorily above the Number of twenty Perſons returned to be on the Jury, or ſhall be outlawed thereupon, ſhall not be admitted to the Benefit of his or their Clergy.*

Sect. 49. But *Note*, That this Statute extends not to Appeals, nor to Offences made Felonies by ſubſequent Statutes.

And now I am in the ſecond Place more diſtinctly to conſider the ſeveral Statutes which take away the Benefit of Clergy, ſo far as they particularly relate to the ſeveral Kinds of Crimes; for the better Illuſtration whereof having referred the Reader, as to the Felonies made ſuch by Statute, to the ſeveral Chapters in the firſt Book wherein ſuch Felonies are handled, I ſhall here conſider the Statutes which take away Clergy from Capital Offences at the Common Law, under the following Heads, as they relate,

1. To Petit Treaſon.
2. To Homicide.
3. To Larceny.
4. To Sacrilege.
5. To Robbery.
6. To Burglary.
7. To Arſon.

Sect. 50. And firſt as to Petit Treaſon; It is certain, that by Force of 23 & 25 *H.* 8. revived [b] by 5 & 6 *E.* 6. the Principal not being a [c] Clerk in Holy Orders, is excluded from the Benefit of Clergy, upon a [d] Conviction, [e] ſtanding Mute, or challenge of more than twenty, upon an [f] Indictment.

Sect. 51. And Sir [g] *Matthew Hale* ſeems to be of Opinion, That the Principal is likewiſe ouſted of his Clergy, by 23 *H.* 8. in Appeal of Petit Treaſon, if he be convict by Verdict or Confeſſion, but not in other Caſes: But *Quære*, How this can be? For ſince ſo much [h] only of 23 *H.* 8. ſeems to be revived, as is affirmed and enforced by 25 *H.* 8. and that no way extends to Appeals but only to Indictments, it ſeems difficult to make out that any Part of 23 *H.* 8. ſo far as it relates to Appeals, is revived by 25 *H.* 8.

Sect. 52. But I would rather incline to think that the Principal in an Appeal of Petit Treaſon may be excluded from his Clergy by 1 [i] *E.* 6. 12. in all Caſes except that of challenging above the Number of twenty, under the Words *Murder of Malice prepenſed* in that Statute; becauſe all Petit Treaſon, in the very Notion of it, neceſſarily [k] includes ſuch Murder and more.

[b] Vide ſupra ſect. 43, 44. H. P. C. 232. 2 H. H. P. C. 341.
[c] Vide ſupra ſect. 13.
[d] Vide ſupra ſect. 30, 31.
[e] Vide ſupra 32, 33.
[f] Vide ſupra ſect. 33.
[g] 2 H. H. P. C. 338, 339, 341. H. P. C. 232.
[h] Vide ſupra ſect. 43, 44.
[i] Vide ſupra ſect. 34, 35.
[k] B. 1. ch. 32. ſect. 6. 2 H. H. P. C. 340.

Sect. 53. However the Makers of 4 [a] & 5 *Ph.* & *M.* 4. ſeem plainly to have been of Opinion, That the Principals in Petit Treaſon are excluded from Clergy in all Caſes, as well upon an Appeal as Indictment; becauſe they have in all Caſes expreſly excluded the Acceſſaries maliciouſly before, as well upon an Appeal as Indictment; and [b] it cannot be well imagined that they intended to make the Law more ſevere againſt them than againſt the Principals.

[a] Vide ſupra ſect. 45.

[b] Vide 11 Co. 35. a. 2 H. H. P. C. 342, 346. And ſupra ſect. 46.

Sect. 54. *Secondly*, As to Homicide: It is certain that wilful Murder of Malice prepenſed is excluded from the Benefit of Clergy upon Indictments in all Caſes by [c] 23 & [d] 25 *H.* 8. and by 1 [e] *E.* 6. 12.

[c] Vide ſupra S. 25, 30, 31.

[d] Vide ſupra ſect. 32, 33.

[e] Vide ſupra ſect. 34, &c.

Sect. 55. Alſo it ſeems [f] to be the Opinion of Sir *Matthew Hale*, That it likewiſe is excluded from Clergy in all Caſes as well upon Appeals as Indictments; but this ſeems queſtionable; for Appeals are certainly not [g] within 25 *H.* 8. and therefore ſince ſo much only of 23 *H.* 8. is revived by 5 & 6 *E.* 6. as is affirmed and enforced by 25 *H.* 8. I do not ſee how it can be revived as to any Appeal. From whence it ſeems to follow, That the only Statute which expreſly excludes them is 1 *E.* 6. 12. which [h] omits the Caſe of challenging more than twenty. Neither is this Defect ſupplied by 3 & 4 *W.* & *M.* 9. for this extends [i] only to Indictments.

[f] H.P.C. 232. 2 H. H. P. C. 343.

[g] Vide ſupra ſect. 42, 43, 51.

[h] Vide ſupra ſect. 34, 36.

[i] Supra ſect. 48, 49.

Sect. 56. But Acceſſaries maliciouſly before to ſuch Murder are expreſly excluded from Clergy in all Caſes, as well upon Appeals as Indictments by 4 & 5 *P.* & *M.* 4. and how far the Paincipal may [k] hereby in like Manner be implicitly excluded alſo in all Caſes, I ſhall leave to be conſidered. [92]

[k] Vide 11 Co. 35. a. and ſupra ſect. 46, 53.

☞ *Sect.* 57. By 1 *Jac.* 1. 8. He that ſhall be convicted by Verdict of twelve Men, or Confeſſion, or otherwiſe according to the Laws of this Realm, of Homicide, by ſtabbing, (but not thoſe who abet them, &c. for which I ſhall refer to *Book* 1. *Chap.* 30. *Sect.* 4, 5, &c.) ſhall be excluded from the Benefit of his Clergy, &c.

Sect. 58. And this Statute ſeems plainly to extend as well to Appeals as Indictments, but not to the Caſe of ſtanding Mute, or challenging above twenty, &c. But thoſe who are indicted of ſuch Manſlaughter are excluded from Clergy in all ſuch Caſes, as well as on a Conviction, by 3 & 4 *W.* & *M.* 9. Supra ſect. 48. 49.

Thirdly, Larceny is excluded from the Benefit of Clergy in the following Caſes:

1. In that of a felonious ſecret Taking from the Perſon.
2. In that of Horſe-ſtealing.
3. In that of ſtealing from a Shop or Dwelling-Houſe, &c.
4. In that of ſtealing Woollen Manufactures from the Tenters.
5. In that of ſtealing the King's Naval Stores.

Sect. 59. And firſt, As to a felonious ſecret Taking from the Perſon: It is enacted by 8 *Eliz.* 4. *That no Perſon who ſhall be indicted or appealed for felonious Taking of any Money, Goods, or Chattels, from the Perſon of any other, privily without his Knowledge, in any Place whatſoever, and thereupon found guilty by Verdict of twelve Men, or ſhall confeſs the ſame upon his or their Arraignment, or will not anſwer directly to the ſame according to the Laws of the Realm, or ſhall ſtand wilfully or of Malice, or obſtinately Mute, or challenge peremptorily above the Number of twenty, or ſhall be upon ſuch Indictment or Appeal outlawed, ſhall be admitted to his Clergy*, &c.

Vide ſect. 26, 45, 46. *Sect.* 60. But *Note*, That this Statute extends not to any Acceſſaries before or after.

[a] Vide ſupra ſect. 34, 39. 2 H. H. P. C. 364, 365. *Sect.* 61. *Secondly*, As to Horſe-ſtealers: It ſeems that they are [a] ouſted of their Clergy in all Caſes, as well upon Appeals, as Indictments, by 1 *E.* 6. 12. and 2 & 3 *E.* 6. 33. by the latter of which Statutes it is enacted, *That all Perſons feloniouſly Taking or ſtealing any Horſe Gelding, or Mare, ſhall not be admitted to the Privilege of the Clergy, but ſhall be put from the ſame, in like Manner and Form as though they had been indicted or appealed for felonious Stealing of two Horſes, two Geldings, or two Mares, of any other, and thereupon found guilty by Verdict of twelve Men, or confeſſed the ſame upon their Arraignment, or ſtand wilfully or of Malice Mute.*

[b] S. P. C. 125. Letters B, C. H. P. C. 238. 2 H. H. P. C. 365. *Sect.* 62. It ſeems a reaſonable [b] Conſtruction of this Statute to extend it as well to thoſe who are outlawed, or challenge more than twenty, as to thoſe who are found guilty by Verdict, &c. becauſe it is general, That all ſuch Perſons *ſhall be put from their Clergy*, &c. *in ſuch Manner as if they had been found guilty*, &c. and if they had been found guilty, it is certain that they would have been ouſted of their Clergy by the expreſs Words of 1 *E.* 6. 12. *Par.* 10. (Supra 34, &c.)

[c] H. P. C. 238. *Sect.* 63. But I do not find that any [c] Statute excludes any Acceſſaries to this Offence from their Clergy. [93]

Vide ſupra ſect. 26, 45, 46. *Sect.* 64. *Thirdly*, As to Larceny from a Dwelling-Houſe, Shop, &c. it is enacted by 10 & 11 *W.* 3. 23. *That all Perſons who by Night or Day, ſhall in any Shop, Ware-houſe, Coach-houſe, or Stable, privately and feloniouſly ſteal any Goods, Wares, or Merchandizes, of the Value of* 5 s. *or more, though ſuch Shop*, &c. *be not broke open, and tho' the Owner, or any other Perſon be not in ſuch Shop*, &c. *or that ſhall aſſiſt, hire or command any Perſon to commit ſuch Offence, being thereof convict, or attainted by Verdict or Confeſſion, or being indicted thereof ſhall ſtand Mute, or challenge above twenty of the Jury, ſhall be excluded from the Benefit of the Clergy.*

Sect. 65. But this Statute ſeems defective in neither mentioning Perſons [d] outlawed, nor [e] Acceſſaries; neither is it help'd by 3 & 4 *W.* & *M.* 9. becauſe [f] it is ſubſequent to it.

[d] Vide ſect. 26, 27, 28.
[e] Vide ſupra ſect. 26, 45, 46.
[f] Vide ſupra ſect. 48, 49.

Sect. 66. It is enacted by 12 *Annæ*, 7. *That every Perſon who ſhall feloniouſly ſteal any Money, Goods or Chattels, Wares or Merchandizes of the Value of* 40 s. *or more, being in a Dwelling-houſe, or Out-houſe thereunto belonging, although ſuch Houſe or Out-houſe be not actually broken by ſuch Offender, and altho' the Owner of ſuch Goods, or any other Perſon or Perſons be or be not in ſuch Houſe or Out-houſe, or ſhall aſſiſt, or aid any Perſon or Perſons, to commit any ſuch Offence, being thereof convicted or attainted by Verdict or Confeſſion, or being indicted thereof ſhall ſtand Mute, or will not directly anſwer to the Indictment, or ſhall peremptorily challenge above the Number of twenty returned to be of the Jury, ſhall be abſolutely debarred of and from the Benefit of Clergy*, &c.

Sect. 67. But it is provided, *That nothing in this Act ſhall extend to Apprentices under the Age of fifteen Years, who ſhall rob their Maſters as aforeſaid.*

Vide ſect. 26, 27, 28, 64, 65. *Sect.* 68. This Statute ſeems alſo defective like the former, as to Perſons outlawed, and Acceſſaries.

Sect. 69. *Fourthly*, As to thoſe who ſhall feloniouſly ſteal Woollen Manufactures from the Tenters: It is enacted by 22 *Car.* 2. 5. *That no Perſon who ſhall be indicted for feloniouſly cutting and taking, ſtealing or carrying away of any Cloth or Woollen Manufactures from the Rack or Tenter in the Night-Time, and thereupon found guilty by Verdict of twelve Men, or ſhall confeſs the ſame on Arraignment, or will not anſwer directly to the ſame, according to the Laws of the Realm, or shall stand wilfully of Malice Mute; or challenge peremptorily above the Number of twenty, or shall be upon such Indictment outlawed, shall be admitted to the Benefit of Clergy*, &c. [94]

☞ *Sect.* 70. *Fifthly*, As to those who steal Naval Stores: It is observable, That those who *shall steal or embezzle any of his Majesty's Sail, Cordage, or any other his Majesty's Naval Stores*, are in the like Manner excluded from Clergy by 22 *Car.* 2. 5. as those who steal Woollen Manufactures from the Tenters, *&c.* See the precedent Section.

Sect. 71. But *Note*, That this Statute extends neither to Appeals, nor to [a] Accessaries.

Sect. 72. As to Sacrilege: It is observable, That all Persons not in Holy Orders, who shall be indicted, whether in the same County wherein the Fact was committed, or in a [b] different County, of *robbing any Church, Chapel, or other holy Place*, are excluded from their Clergy by [c] 23 *H.* 8. 1. and 25 [d] *H* 8. 3. revived [e] by 5 & 6 *E.* 6. 10. upon a Conviction, standing Mute, or peremptorily challenge of more than twenty; and by 3 & [f] 4 *W.* & *M.* 9. upon an Outlawry.

Sect. 73. But the Word *Robbing* [g] being always taken to carry with it some Force, as shall be more fully shewn, *Sections* 88, 92; 96; it seems that no Sacrilege is within any of these Statutes, which is not accompanied with the actual Breaking of a Church, *&c.*

Sect. 74. But by 1 *E.* 6. 12. [h] *Par.* 10. all Persons in general are ousted of their Clergy for the *felonious Taking of any Goods out of any Parish Church, or other Church or Chapel*, in all Cases, except that of challenging more than twenty; and by 3 & [i] 4 *W.* & *M.* 9. upon such a Challenge as well as upon a Conviction, *&c.* upon an Indictment [k] whether in the same County wherein the Sacrilege was committed, or in a different one.

Sect. 75. But it seems, That Accessaries to such a Robbery, or felonious Taking are excluded from their Clergy by no Statute; for tho' they are expresly mentioned by 23 *H.* 8. 1, yet since they are omitted by 25 *H.* 8. 3. and so much only [l] of 23 *H.* 8. 1. is revived as is affirmed and enforced by 25 *H.* 8. 3. they seem to remain in the same Case as if they had been wholly omitted by 23 *H.* 8. 1. which is the only Statute I know of which extends to them, except the Offence amount to Burglary; in which Case Accessaries before are ousted of their Clergy by 3 & 4 *W.* & *M.* 9.

Sect. 76. But *Quære* if there be Need of any Statute to exclude them, since the Common Law seems to have given no Person whatsoever any Right to demand the Privilege of the Clergy for Sacrilege, but only at the Discretion of the Ordinary, as hath been more fully shewn, *Section* the ninth. 2 H. H. P. C. 333.

[a] Vide sect. 26, & 45, 46.
[b] Infra 80, 81, 82.
[c] Vide supra sect. 30, 31. 2 H. H. P. C. 365.
[d] Vide supra sect. 32, 33.
[e] Vide supra sect. 42, 43, 44.
[f] Vide supra sect. 48, 49.
[g] Kely. 58, 69, 70. Dyer 224. pl. 30.
[h] Vide supra sect. 34, 35, 36, 37.
[i] Vide supra sect. 48, 49.
[k] Infra 80, 81, 82. 2 H. H. P. C. 365, 366.
[l] Vide supra sect. 43, 44, 52, 55.

Fifthly, As to Robbery, I shall particularly consider the Statutes excluding it from Clergy, as they relate,

1. To Robbery in or near the Highway.
2. To Robbery in a Dwelling-House, Booth or Tent.
3. To Robbery in general.

Sect. 77. And first, as to Robbery in or near the Highway: It is observable, That all Persons, not in Holy Orders, who shall be indicted [m] of *Robbing any Person or Persons in or near the Highways*, are ex-

[m] Vide supra sect. 30.

[a] Vide supra sect. 30, 31. [b] Vide supra sect. 32, 33. [c] Vide supra S. 42, 43, 44. [d] Vide supra sect. 48, 49. [e] Vide supra sect. 34, 35, 36, 37.

excluded from the Clergy by 23 [a] *H.* 8. 1. and 25 [b] *H.* 8. 3. revived [c] by 5 & 6 *E.* 6. 10. upon a Conviction, standing Mute, or peremptorily Challenge of more than twenty; and by 3 & 4 [d] *W.* & *M.* 9. upon an Outlawry.

Sect. 78. And *Note*, That all Persons in general, *who shall be guilty of robbing any Person or Persons in the Highway, or near to the Highway*, are excluded from the Clergy both upon an Appeal and Indictment by [e] 1 *E.* 6. 12. *Par.* 10. in all Cases except that of challenging more than twenty; and by 3 & 4 *W.* & *M.* 9. upon such a Challenge upon an Indictment.

[f] Vide supra sect. 25. [g] Supra sect. 73. And Dy. 224. pl. 30. And B. 1. ch. 35. sect. 13. [h] Vide supra sect. 43, 44. [i] Vide B. 1. ch. 33. S. 9.

Sect. 79. *Note*, That no Robbery is within these Statutes, but such as is laid in the Indictment to have been committed in or near the [f] Highway, and to have [g] put the Person robbed in Fear.

Sect. 80. It is recited by 25 *H.* 8. 3. revived [h] by 5 & 6 *E.* 6. 10. *That divers Felons and Robbers that had committed many heinous Robberies and Burglaries in one Shire, and conveyed the Spoil and Robbery into another Shire, and had been there* [i] *taken, indicted and arraigned upon Felony, and felonious taking of the same Goods, and not upon the same Robbery nor Burglary; for that it was not committed nor done in the same Shire where they had been so indicted and arraigned, and by Reason thereof the same Felons, Robbers, and Burglars had enjoyed the Privilege of their Clergy.* And thereupon it is enacted, *That if any Person or Persons be indicted of Felony for stealing of any Goods or Chattels, in any County within this Realm of* England, *and thereupon arraigned and be found guilty, or stand Mute of Malice, or challenge peremptorily above the Number of twenty Persons, or will not directly answer to the Law, shall lose and be put from the Benefit of the Clergy, in like Manner and Form as they should have been if they had been indicted and arraigned, and found guilty in the same County where the same Robbery or Burglary was done or committed; if it shall appear to the Justices before whom any such Felons or Robbers be arraigned, by Evidence given before them, or by Examination that the same Felonies, whereupon they were so arraigned, had been such Robberies or Burglaries, in the same Shire wherein such Robberies or Burglaries were committed or done, by Reason whereof they should have lost the Benefit of their Clergy by Force of* 23 *H.* 8. *in Case they had been found guilty thereof in the same Shire where such Robberies or Burglaries were so committed and done.*

[k] 11 Co. 31. a. 1 H. H. P. C. 518. 2 H. H. P. C. 349.

Sect. 81. But *Note*, That this Statute extends [k] not to those who are outlawed; nor to those who are indicted out of the Realm of *England*; nor to those who are indicted of such Stealing as is excluded from Clergy by subsequent Statutes; nor to Appellees; but the three first of these Defects are supplied by 3 & 4 *W.* & *M.* 9. by which it is enacted, *That if any Person or Persons be indicted of Felony for stealing of any Goods or Chattels in any County within this Realm of* England, *Dominion of Wales, or Town of* Berwick *upon* Tweed, *and thereof be convicted or attainted, or upon his or their Arraignment shall stand Mute, or will not directly answer to the Indictment, or shall challenge peremptorily above the Number of twenty Persons returned to be of the Jury, he or they shall be totally excluded from having the Benefit of his or their Clergy, if it appear upon Evidence or Examination before the Justices, that the said Goods or Chattels were taken by Robbery or Burglary, or in any other Manner, in any other County, whereof if such Person or Persons had been convicted by a Jury of the said other County, he or they are excluded by Virtue of this or any other Act from having the Benefit of his or their Clergy.*

Sect. 82. *Note*, That [a] the Words *If it shall appear upon Evidence before the Justices*, &c. are to be intended where the Party pleads Not guilty, and is found guilty by the Jury, and the Words *If it shall appear upon Examination*, &c. are to be intended where he stands Mute, or challenges peremptorily above the Number of twenty, or is outlawed, or confesses [b], *&c.* And it hath been [c] adjudged, That there is no Need to make any Entry on the Record, that it appears by such Evidence, or Examination, that the Felony was originally commenced in a different County, and was of such a Nature that the Offender could not have his Clergy. But it is said, [d] That it is usual to write in the Margent of the Indictment, that it is for Robbery, *&c.* in another County.

Sect. 83. It is said to [e] have been holden by all the Justices, That if the Felony, whereof a Man is found guilty in the County wherein he is indicted, be such as doth not need the Benefit of Clergy, as amounting only to Petit Larceny, *&c.* the Offender shall have only the proper Judgment for such Offence, and no other, in Respect of the Robbery, *&c.* proved upon the Evidence, *&c.* in the first County, for being convicted of no Offence which will warrant a Judgment of Death, and consequently having no Need to demand his Clergy, he cannot be hurt by being excluded from it.

[a] 11 Co. 31.
[b] Vide supra sect. 28, 31. 11 Co. 31. Cont. 1 And. 114.
[c] 1 And. 114. 2 H. H. P. C. 518.
[d] H. P. C. in the old Edition printed in the Year, 1678.
[e] Mo. 550. pl. 739 H. P. C. 241. 1 H. H. P. C. 536. 2 H. H. P. C. 349.

Sect. 84. It is enacted by 3 & 4 [f] *Ph. & M.* 4. *That those who shall maliciously command, hire or counsel any Person or Persons to commit or do any Robbery in or near any Highway in this Realm of* England, *or in any other the Queen's Dominion, shall be ousted of their Clergy, on a Conviction, standing Mute, peremptory Challenge of more than twenty, or Outlawry.*

[f] Vide supra sect. 45, 46. How such Offence must be laid in the Indictment. Vide supra sect. 25.

Secondly, As to Robbery in a Dwelling-house, Booth or Tent, I shall consider the Statutes concerning it as they relate.

1. To such Robbery putting some Persons in Fear.
2. To such Robbery putting no Person in Fear.

Sect. 85. *First*, As to such Robbery putting some Person in Fear: It is observable, That all Persons not in Holy Orders, *who shall rob any Person or Persons in their Dwelling-houses, or Dwelling-place, the Owner or Dweller in the same House, his Wife, his Children or Servants then being within, and put in Fear and Dread by the same*, and indicted, [g] are excluded from their Clergy by 23 *H.* 8. 1. and 25 *H.* 8. 3. revived by 5 & 6 *E.* 6. 10. upon a Conviction, standing Mute, or peremptory Challenge of more than twenty, and by 3 & 4 *W. & M.* 9. upon an Outlawry.

Sect. 86. And *Note*, [h] That by 25 *H.* 8. 3. and 3 & 4 *W. & M.* 9. they are excluded from their Clergy on an Indictment in a Foreign County. And their Accessaries before are excluded in all Cases by 3 & 4 [i] *Ph. & Ma.* 4.

Sect. 87. And by 1 [k] *Ed.* 6. 12. *Par.* 10. all Persons in general who shall *break any House by Day or by Night*, (*viz.* [l] who shall break a House burglarily, if in the Night, or shall break a House or commit a Felony therein, if in the Day) [m] *any Person being then in the same House where the same Breaking shall be, and thereby put in Fear or Dread*, are excluded from their Clergy, as well upon an Appeal as an Indictment, in all Cases, [n] except that of challenging more than twenty; and by 3 [o] & 4 *W. & M.* 9. upon such a Challenge, as well as upon a Conviction, *&c.* upon an Indictment, whether in the same County wherein the Breaking and Felony was

2 H. H. P. C. 351, 352, &c.
[g] Vide supra sect. 30, 31, 32, 33, 42, 43, 44, 48, 49, 72, 77.
[h] Vide supra sect. 80, 81, 82, 83.
[i] Vide supra sect. 45, 46.
[k] Vide supra sect. 34, &c.
[l] Vide supra sect. 40. 11 Co. 36. a. b.
[m] Vide infra sect. 93.
[n] Vide supra sect. 36.
[o] Vide supra sect. 48, 49.

 was

[a] Vide ſupra ſect. 80, 81, 82, 83. [b] H. P. C. 236. Supra ſect. 45, 46. [c] Vide ſupra ſect. 73. And infra ſect. 82, 92, 96. [d] Supra ſect. 48, 49.

was committed, or in a [a] different County; and the Acceſſaries before to ſuch a Breaking, if accompanied with ſtealing in a Dwelling-houſe, are ouſted of their Clergy in all [b] Caſes by 4 & 5 *Ph. & M.* 4. becauſe the felonious Taking being accompanied with a Breaking, ſeems properly [c] enough to come under the Notion of Robbery in a Dwelling-houſe, all Acceſſaries to which before the Fact are expreſly excluded from their Clergy by that Statute, as Acceſſaries before to Robbery in general are by 3 & [d] 4 *W. & M.* 9.

[e] Kely. 58, 59, 70. Supra ſect. 73, 87. infra Sect. 92, 96. H. P. C. 237, 238.

Sect. 88. But [e] no Breaking is within the Statute of 1 *E.* 6. which doth not amount to an actual Breaking of an Houſe, or of ſome Part of it; as of a Cupboard or Door, *&c.* fixed to the Freehold; and therefore the Breaking of a Trunk or Box, *&c.* ſeem plainly not to be within the Statute. But by 3 & 4 *W. & M.* 9. *Every Perſon or Perſons that ſhall feloniouſly Take away any Goods or Chattels, being in any Dwelling-houſe, the Owner, or any other Perſon being therein, and put in Fear, or ſhall comfort, aid, abet, aſſiſt, counſel, hire, or command any Perſon to commit ſuch Offence, being thereof convicted or attainted, or indicted, and ſtanding Mute, or peremptorily challenging above twenty, ſhall be ouſted of the Benefit of their Clergy.*

2 H. H. P. C. 354, 355, &c.

Secondly, As to ſuch Robbery, putting no Perſon in Fear: I ſhall conſider the Statutes concerning it as they relate,

1. To ſuch Robbery in a Houſe, which ſome Perſon is in at the Time.
2. To ſuch Robbery in a Houſe, which no Perſon is in at the Time.

Sect. 89. As to the firſt of theſe, it is enacted by 5 & 6 *E.* 6. 9. *That if it happen any Perſon or Perſons to be found guilty according to the Laws of this Realm, for robbing of any Perſon or Perſons in any Part or Parcel of their Dwelling-houſes, or Dwelling-places, the Owner or Dweller in the ſame Houſe, or his Wife, his Children or Servants being then within the ſame Houſe or Place where it ſhall happen the ſame Robbery and Felony to be committed and done, or in any other Place within the Precinct of the ſame Houſe or Dwelling-place, that ſuch Offenders ſhall in no wiſe be admitted to their Clergy, whether the Owner or Dweller in the ſame Houſe, his Wife or Children then and there being, ſhall be waking or ſleeping.*

Sect. 90. *And that no Perſon or Perſons which ſhall happen to be found guilty after the Laws of this Realm, of and for robbing any Perſon or Perſons, in any Booth or Tent, in any Fair or Market, the Owner, his Wife, his Children, or Servants or Servant then being within the Booth or Tent, ſhall not be admitted to the Benefit of his or their Clergy, but utterly be excluded thereof,* &c. *without having any Reſpect or Conſideration whether the Owner or Dweller in ſuch Booths and Tents, his Wife, Children or Servants being in the ſame Booths or Tents at the Time of ſuch Robberies and Felonies committed, ſhall be ſleeping or waking.*

[f] H. P. C. 236, 237. 2 H. H. P. C. 355. [g] Vide ſupra ſect. 48, 49.

Sect. 91. This Statute [f] ſeems plainly to extend to all who ſhall be convicted by Verdict or Confeſſion, whether upon an Appeal or Indictment; but not to thoſe who ſhall be outlawed, or ſtand Mute, or challenge peremptorily above twenty Jurors; but theſe Defects are ſupplied as to Indictments by 3 [g] & 4 *W. & M.* 9.

Sect. 92. It seems to be generally agreed, That no Robbery is within this Statute which is not accompanied with an actual [a] Breaking of an House, or of some Part of it.

[a] For this Vide supra sect. 73, 87, 88, 96.

Sect. 93. Also it seems to be agreed, [b] That a Sojourner's Being in an House at the Time of the Robbery doth not bring it within this Statute; for the Words are *The Owner or Dweller in the same House, or his Wife, his Children, or Servants, being then within the same House*, &c. Yet it is said in [c] *Hale's Pleas of the Crown* to have been ruled by Advice of the Justices, That where one entered into the Lodging of Sir *H. Hungate*, being Parcel of *Whitehall*, and broke open a Chamber and took away his Goods, his Case was within this Statute, and that the Indictment ought to be for breaking the King's House, called *Whitehall*, and for stealing the Goods of Sir *H. H.* divers Persons being in the House: But *Note*, That this Case is wholly omitted in the first Edition of *Hale's Pleas of the Crown*, ☞ and I cannot but think that it is misprinted in the Second; [95] because such a Robbery seems by no Means within the Purview of this Statute, which extends only to such Robberies as are done to a Man in such a Place as may be called *his Dwelling-house or Dwelling-place, his Wife, Children, or Servants being at the same Time within the same.* But in the State of this Case it seems to be admitted, That *Whitehall*, wherein the Felony was committed, could not properly be called, nor ought to be laid in the Indictment as the Dwelling-house or Dwelling-place of the said Sir *H. H.* who was the Person robbed, but of the King: Also it seems to be admitted, That it is sufficient to set forth generally in the Indictment that divers Persons were in the House, without shewing that they were under any Relation to the Person robbed, as his Children or Servants, *&c.* which [d] seems to be necessarily required by 5 & 6 *E.* 6. 9. And therefore I take it, that the Statute here intended is not 5 & 6 *E.* 6. 9. but rather 1 *E.* 6. [e] 12. *Par.* 10. or 39 [f] *El.* 15. Yet *Quære*, for neither of these Statutes seem to extend to this Case as it is here put. However 3 & 4 *W.* & *M.* 9. seems fully to extend to it. By which it is enacted, *That all those who shall rob any Dwelling-house in the Day-time, any Person being therein, or shall comfort, aid, abet, assist, counsel, hire, or command any Person to commit such Offence, being thereof convicted or attainted, or indicted, and standing Mute, or challenging peremptorily above twenty, shall be ousted of their Clergy.* But I do not [g] find that any Statute excludes those from their Clergy who are Accessaries to a Robbery in a Booth or Tent, except it be from the Person of a Man, in which Case the Accessaries before the Fact seem to be excluded from their Clergy by 3 & 4 *W.* & *M.* 9. as shall be more fully shewn hereafter.

H. P. C. 237, 238. 2 H. H. P. C. 354. Yet in Pop. 84. there is a Case seemingly contrary.
[b] Hetley 64. S. P. C. 129. H. P. C. 236, 237. 11 Co. 36. b.
[c] Folio 237. 238.
[d] Vide Hetl. 64. H. P. C. 235, 236. 11 Co. 36. b. S. P. C. 129. b. Popham 84.
[e] Vide supra sect. 87.
[f] Vide infra S. 95, 96, 97.
[g] See the Statute of 3 & 4 Ph. & M. supra sect. 45, 46.

Sect. 94. It seems plain, That those who are guilty of a Felony within these Statutes, are excluded from their Clergy by 3 & 4 *W.* & *M.* 9. on an Indictment in a Foreign County, in the same Manner as if they had been convicted in the first County, as hath been more fully shewn, *Sect.* 80, 81, 82, 83.

Sect. 95. *Secondly*, As to such Robbery in a House which no Person is in at the Time: It is recited by 39 *El.* 15. *That then of late divers lewd and felonious Persons, understanding that the Robbing of Houses in the Day-time, no Person being therein at the Time, is not so penal as where some Person is therein, had been emboldened to take their Opportunity to commit many heinous Robberies, in breaking and entring divers Houses*, &c. and thereupon it is enacted, *That if any Person shall be found guilty, and convicted by Verdict, Confession, or otherwise, according to the Laws of this Realm, for the felonious taking*

2 H. H. P. C. 356.

away in the Day-time, of any Money, Goods or Chattel, being of the Value of 5 s. *or upwards, in any Dwelling-house or Houses, or any Part thereof, or any Out-house or Out-houses, belonging and used to and with any Dwelling-house or Houses, altho' no Person shall be in the said House or Out-houses at the Time of such Felony committed, then such Person shall not be admitted to the Benefit of his Clergy.*

Sect. 96. Notwithstanding the Words of the Purview of this Statute seem plainly to include all felonious Takings to the Value of 5 *s.* out of an House, *&c.* whether with or without Force; yet since the Mischief complained of in the Preamble, and intended to be redressed is the frequent Committing of many *heinous Robberies in breaking and entring*, &c. and since all other [a] Statutes excluding the Benefit of Clergy from Robberies in Houses, have been construed to extend to such Larcenies only as are accompanied with a Breaking of a House, or of some Part of it; it seems agreed, [b] That this Statute also shall extend only to such a felonious Taking as is accompanied with the like Breaking.

[a] Supra sect. 73, 87, 88, 92, 96.
[b] Kely. 30, 58, 69, 70. H. P. C. 237. 238. 2 H. H. P. C. 356.

Sect. 97. It seems agreed, [c] That a Chamber in one of the Inns of Court, wherein a Person usually lodges, is properly a Dwelling-house within this Statute, and may be so called in an Indictment, because every Owner of such a Chamber hath a separate Interest in it. But that a Lodging in *Whitehall* or *Somerset-house* is not [d] a Dwelling-house within this Statute; from whence it seems to follow, That a Robbery in such a Lodging is not excluded from the Clergy by this Statute, if any Person were at the Time in any other Part of the Palace, because the Whole is but one Dwelling-house.

11 Co. 36. b. Cro. Ca. 473, 474.
[c] Cro. Ca. 473, 474. 1 Jon. 394. H. P. C. 83, 237. 2 H. H. P. C. 358. Kely. 27, 52. See B. 1. ch. 38. Sect. 13.
[d] Kely. 27, 52. Vide supra sect. 93.

Sect. 98. It seems agreed, [e] That no Accessary is ousted of his Clergy by this Statute. Also it hath been adjudged, [f] That he who stands by and abets another while he breaks and enters the House, and afterwards divides the Money with him, but doth not actually enter the House himself, is not within the Statute, the Reason whereof seems to be this, That the Words, *If any Person shall be convicted*, &c. *of a felonious taking*, &c. *in a Dwelling-house*, &c. shall in so penal a Law be intended only of an actual Taking, and not of a constructive one. [96] But this seems an extremely nice Case, and if it were a new Point, and not confirmed by Experience, the Authority of it might perhaps be justly questioned; for if the Person, who only stood by and entred not the House, had actually entred it, and the other only had taken the Money, and had not given him any Part of it till both had gone out of the House; in this Case, as well as in the other, it might be said, That he, who actually received not any Part of the Money till he was gone out of the House was guilty only of a constructive Taking in the House, and consequently not within this Statute. But I cannot easily persuade my self but that in such a Case both must be adjudged equally within the Statute; and why not as well in the other, it seeming an uncontroverted [g] Rule, That where divers are present and abet one another in committing any Felony, the Act of one shall be looked on as the Act of all. And upon this Ground, as I take it, it hath been always agreed, That those who are present, and abetting, when a Murder or Robbery is committed, are all of them equally excluded from their Clergy, whether they actually gave the Stroke or took the Money or not; and yet the Statutes to this Purpose mention only those who shall be found guilty of Murder or Robbing, *&c.* Nor do I find any Resolution to the contrary on any other Statute concerning Clergy, except only the [h] Statute of *Stabbing*, whereon it hath been adjudged, [i] That the Person only who gives the Stab is within the

[e] H. P. C. 237. 2 H. H. P. C. 357. Supra sect. 45, 46.
[f] Cro. Ca. 473, 474. 2 H. H. P. C. 358. Note, That the same Case is in 1 Jon. 394. but this Point is not taken Notice of.
[g] Vide supra ch. 29. sect. 7, 8, 13.
[h] 1 Jac. 1. 8.
[i] Aleyn 44. H. P. C. 58. B. 1. ch. 30. sect. 71.

the Purview of it: But this ſeems plainly to depend on the particular Circumſtances of this Offence, which is excluded from Clergy in Reſpect of the Cruelty and Bloody Mind of him who gives the Stab, which certainly is peculiar to himſelf.

Sect. 99. However it is certain at this Day, *That whoever ſhall comfort, aid, abet, aſſiſt, counſel, hire or command any Perſon or Perſons to break any Dwelling-houſe, Shop, or Ware-houſe thereunto belonging, or therewith uſed, in the Day-time, and feloniouſly take away any Money, Goods, or Chattel of the Value of* 5 s. *or upwards therein being, altho' no Perſon ſhall be within ſuch Dwelling-houſe, Shop or Ware-houſe, being convicted or attainted, or being indicted and ſtanding Mute, or challenging peremptorily above twenty, ſhall be excluded from their Clergy, by the expreſs Words of* 3 & 4 W. & M. 9.

Sect. 100. But *Note*, That this Clauſe mentioning only a felonious Taking in a Dwelling-houſe, Shop, or Ware-houſe thereunto belonging, and not mentioning Out-houſes in general, as 39 *El.* doth, ſeems to have done it with a View to leave Out-houſes to the ſame Conſtruction which prevailed before; and therefore I take it that an Aſſiſtant to ſuch a Felony in an Out-houſe, not being ſuch a Shop or Ware-houſe, without entring into it, is clearly intitled to the Benefit of his Clergy ſince this Statute, however it might be diſputed before. Vide ſupra ſect. 98.

Sect. 101. *Note* alſo, That the Acceſſaries before to ſuch a Felony in any Out-houſe, not being ſuch a Shop or Ware-houſe, are ſtill intitled to the Benefit of their Clergy, becauſe the only [a] Law which excludes them is the [b] above-cited Clauſe of 3 & 4 *W. & M.* 9. which extends only to ſuch Felonies in a Dwelling-houſe, Shop or Ware-houſe thereunto belonging.

[a] H. P. C. 227.
[b] Supra ſect. 99.

Sect. 102. But all Principals in any Felony within the ſaid Statute of 39 *El.* are excluded from their Clergy by the ſame Statute upon any Conviction, whether upon an Indictment or Appeal; and by the ſaid Statute of 3 [c] & 4 *W. & M.* upon an Outlawry, ſtanding Mute, or peremptory Challenge of more than twenty, upon an Indictment, whether in the ſame County in which the Felony was firſt committed, or in a different [d] County.

[c] Supra ſect. 48, 49.
[d] Supra ſect. 81, 82, 83.

Sect. 103. *Thirdly*, As to Robbery in general, it is enacted by 3 & 4 *W. & M.* 9. *That all and every Perſon or Perſons that ſhall rob any other Perſon, or ſhall comfort, aid, abet, aſſiſt, counſel, hire or command any Perſon or Perſons to commit ſuch Offence, being thereof convicted or attainted, or being indicted and ſtanding Mute, or challenging peremptorily above twenty, ſhall not have the Benefit of his Clergy.*

Sect. 104. *Sixthly*, As to Burglary: [e] If any Perſon be in the Houſe at the Time of the Breaking, and thereby put in Fear, the Principal is excluded from his Clergy by 1 *E.* 6. 12 *Par.* 10. in all Caſes, except that of challenging more than twenty, and by 25 *H.* 8. revived [f] by 5 & 6 *E.* 6. or at leaſt by 3 & 4 *W. & M.* 9. upon ſuch a Challenge, upon an Indictment.

[e] Vide 11. Co. 35. b. 36. 2 H. H. P. C. 360, 361. Supra ſect. 34, 36, 40.
[f] Vide ſupra ſect. 42, 43, 44.

Sect. 105. Alſo the Principal in every Burglary, whether [g] any Perſon were in the Houſe at the Time or not, is excluded from his Clergy by 18 *El.* 7. upon a [h] Conviction by Verdict, Outlawry, or Confeſſion; and by 3 & 4 *W. & M.* upon ſtanding Mute, or challenging peremptorily more than twenty upon an Indictment.

[g] Poph. 42, 52. 1 And. 302. Moore 660. 4 Co. 40. a. B. 1. ch. 38. ſect. 11.
[h] 11 Co. 35. b. H. P. C. 233.

Sect. 106. Alſo by [a] the ſame Statute of 3 & 4 *W. & M.* 9. *Every Perſon who ſhall counſel, hire or command any Perſon to commit any Burglary, being thereof convicted, or attainted, or being indicted, and ſtanding Mute, or challenging peremptorily above twenty, ſhall not have his Clergy.*

Sect. 107. *Seventhly*, As to Arſon: It hath been clearly [b] ſettled, ſince *Poulter*'s Caſe, that the Principal [c] not being in Holy Orders, is excluded from Clergy upon an Indictment in all Caſes, except Outlawry, by 23 *H.* 8. and 25 *H.* 8. as [d] revived by 5 & 6 *E.* 6. 10. And it is certain that he is excluded upon an Outlawry on an Indictment by 3 & 4 *W. & M.* 9.

Sect. 108. Alſo Acceſſaries to the Fact before, maliciouſly, are excluded in all Caſes by 4 & [e] 5 *Ph. & M.* 4.

Sect. 109. *Note*, That by 1 *E.* 6. 12. *Par.* 14. [f] Every Lord of Parliament is allowed his Clergy in all Caſes, wherein others are excluded by that Act, except wilful Murder, and conſequently cannot be denied his Clergy for any other Felony wherein it was grantable at Common Law, unleſs it be ouſted by ſome Statute made ſince the firſt Year of *Edward* VI. or [g] revived by 5 & 6 *E.* 6. 10.

Sect. 110. As to the third general Point of this Chapter, *viz.* At what Time the Benefit of Clergy is demandable: It ſeems, [h] That it might be demanded by the ancient Common Law as ſoon as the Priſoner was brought to the Bar, before any Indictment or other Proceeding againſt him; for it is plain, That anciently the Clergy claimed, and were in a great Meaſure indulged a Privilege of being wholly [i] free from ſecular Juriſdiction for Crimes puniſhable with Loſs of Life or Member. But after the Stat. of *Weſtminſter* 1. *Ch.* 2. which ſtrictly enjoined the Ordinaries not to ſuffer Clerks who have been indicted by ſolemn Inqueſts to be delivered without due Purgation, the Judges ſoon made a ſettled Rule [k] not to deliver any Clerk to the Ordinary, before he had been firſt indicted and arraigned, and his Offence had been inquired of and found by an Inqueſt of Office, which was done both to the End that if the Priſoner were found guilty, he [l] might abſolutely forfeit his Goods, (which anciently were ſaved by a Purgation) and alſo that the Court might be appriſed, whether it were proper from the Circumſtances of the Caſe, diſcloſed upon ſuch an Inquiry, to deliver the Clerk to the Ordinary generally, in which Caſe he was allowed to make his Purgation [m], or ſpecially, [n] *abſque purgatione facienda.* But this Practice being found inconvenient to Priſoners, becauſe they loſt their Goods, if found guilty by ſuch Inquiry, and yet could take no Challenge to any of the Jury, it being but an Inqueſt of Office; it hath been the general Practice [o] ever ſince the Reign of *H.* 6. to oblige thoſe who demand the Benefit of Clergy to plead and put themſelves upon their Trial, under [p] Pain of being dealt with as thoſe that ſtand Mute, whereby they forfeit their Goods [q] without any Inquiry concerning their Crime; but yet [r] cannot be denied their Clergy, where they ſhould be intitled to it in caſe they were convicted, unleſs they be ſpecially excluded by ſome Statute. But after a Clerk hath put himſelf upon his Trial, and the Inqueſt are charged with him, it is ſaid that he [s] may, if he deſire it, be admitted to his Clergy, before the Jury come back; but ſhall not forfeit his Goods unleſs they find him guilty.

[a] Vide 11 Co. 36. a. H. P. C. 233, 234.
[b] H. P. C. 233. 2 H. H. P. C. 345, 346. 11 Co. 29, &c.
[c] Vide ſupra ſect. 10, 11, 12, 13, 30, 32.
[d] Vide ſupra ſect. 43, 44.
[e] Supra ſect. 25, 45.
[f] S. P. C. 130. 2 H. H. P. C. 376.
[g] Supra ſect. 42, 43, 44.
[h] See the Statute of Marl. ch. 28. Weſtmin. 1. ch. 2. Articuli Cler. ch. 15. 2 Inſt. 150, 163, 164, 633. S. P. C. 123. Lett. C. 130. b. 131. a. 185. 2 H. H. P. C. 377, 378, &c. Bract. lib. 3. ch. 9. Supra ch. 15. ſect. 84. Hob. 288, 289. Yet in Kely. 100. the contrary ſeems to be holden.
[i] Vide Bract. lib. 3. cap. 9. Articuli Cleri, ch. 15. S. P. C. 138. Lett. E. 139. Lett. A. 140. Supra ſect. 1, 2. Fitz. Coro. 118.
[k] S P. C. 131, 185. 2 Inſt. 164, 633, 634. H. P. C. 239. Finch of Law 463. Fitz. Coro. 232, 376, 382, 386, 417. But this ſeems to be doubtful, Fitz. Coro. 233.
[l] S. P. C. 131, 185. 5 Co. 110. Regiſt. 68. Pl. Com. 262. b. Cont. 40 Aſſ. 42. pl. 23. Abridged Fitz. Coro. 91. Bro. Forfeiture, 5. Hob. 289. 'tis holden, That the Goods are not forfeit without a Conviction.
[m] H. P. C. 240. Hob. 288, 289. S. P. C. 139. Letter D. 5 Co. 109.
[n] Vide Fitz. Coro. 109, 417. H. P. C. 240. Raſt. Ent. 121. pl. 1. Hob. 288, 289. Kely. 100.
[o] H. P. C. 239. 2 H. H. P. C. 378. 2 Inſt. 164. Fitz. Coro. 53, 58. S. P. C. 131. Salk. 61. Finch of Law 463. Hob. 288.
[p] Fitz. Coro. 58. ſo ſaid in a Note of a Caſe in 3 H. 7. 1. But I do not find it made out by the Books at large. But this is clearly holden 3 H. 7. 12. pl. 10. Abridged Fitz. Coro. 53.
[q] Supra ch. 30. ſect. 19.
[r] 8 H. 4. 3. pl. 5. Abridged Fitz. Coro. 72. Supra ch. 30. ſect. 24.
[s] S. P. C. 131. a. b. Finch of Law 463.

Sect. 111. Also I take it to be generally agreed in the later [a] Books, That a Person may demand his Clergy after a *Non legit* recorded; and also after Judgment given against him, whether of [b] Death, or of [c] *Pain fort & dure*, or of [d] Outlawry, *&c.* as well as before Judgment, and even [e] under the Gallows, if there be a Judge there who has Power to allow it; as a Justice of the King's Bench, if the Party were condemned there; or a Justice of Gaol-Delivery, if he were condemned before him, and the Commission of Gaol-Delivery be not [f] yet adjourned, and according to some [g] Opinions, even tho' the Commission were adjourned.

Sect. 112. As to the fourth general Point of this Chapter, *viz.* Whether the Benefit of Clergy shall be allowed where it is not demanded: I take it to be generally agreed, That notwithstanding it was anciently the [h] usual Method for the Ordinary to demand the Criminal as his Clerk, before the Court allowed him the Benefit of his Clergy: Yet there was no [i] Necessity that any such Demand should be made by the Ordinary: But the Court might without it admit a Person to the Benefit of his Clergy, upon sufficient Evidence of his being a Clerk, as upon his producing Letters of Orders, or reading as a Clerk, *&c.* except he appears to have been guilty of Sacrilege, or of breaking the Prison of the Ordinary, in which Cases it is said to have been in a great Measure left to the [k] Discretion of the Ordinary, whether he should have his Clergy or not. And as there is no Necessity that the Ordinary should demand the Benefit of Clergy for a Clerk; so [l] neither doth there seem to be any that the Prisoner himself should demand it, where it sufficiently appeared to the Court that he has a Right to it in Respect of his being in Orders, *&c.* in which Case, if the Prisoner does not demand it, it seems to be left to the Discretion of the Judge, whether he will allow it him or not.

Sect. 113. As to the fifth general Point of this Chapter, *viz.* Who is to judge whether a Person who demands the Benefit of Clergy, have a Right to it or not: I take it, That in all Cases the Temporal Judge is to determine both, whether the Crime be within the Benefit of Clergy, and also whether the Person who demands it to be qualified to demand it or not; for notwithstanding it had its [m] original Commencement from the Canon Law; yet it being no [n] otherwise to be allowed here than as it hath been received by, and is agreeable to the Common or Statute Law, whereof the Temporal Courts are the Judges, it seems very reasonable that all Questions [o] of this Kind be determined by those Courts. And therefore even in those Cases, wherein by the old Books the Ordinary seems to have been allowed a discretionary Power of demanding or refusing a Clerk, as where he hath been guilty of [p] Sacrilege, and also in Cases wherein it is said generally, That a Prisoner hath no Right to his Clergy, as where he is convict of [q] Heresy, *&c.* it seems to be taken as a Ground by *Staundforde*, That the temporal Judge, where the Ordinary refuses a Prisoner, has a Power to determine whether still he may be allowed his Clergy or not. And this seems to be ground-

[a] H. P. C. 239, 240. 2 H. H. P. C. 378, 379, 380. S. P. C. 132. Letter B. Finch of Law 363, 364. Fitz. Coro. 99, 109. Dy. 205. pl. 6. This seems doubtful, 12. Aff. pl. 15. Abrid. Fitz. Coro. 117. Cont. Fitz. Coro. 233
[b] 40 Aff. 42. pl. 23. Abrid. Fitz. Coro. 91. Dy. 183. pl. 89. 34 H. 6. 49. pl. 16. Abrid. Fitz. Coro. 20. Bro. Cler. 1.
[c] H. P. C. 239. 1 H. H. P. C. 380. Supra ch. 30. Sect. 24.
[d] 9 E. 4. 28. 8 H. 4. 3. pl. 5. Abrid. Fitz. Coro. 72.
[e] 34 H. 6. 49. pl. 16. Abrid. Fitz. Coro. 20. Bro. Cler. 1. H. P. C. 239. 240. Dy. 205. pl. 5, 6. S. P. C. 132. Letter B. Crompt. Jurisd. 126. a.
[f] S. P. C. 132. Letter B. H. P. C. 240. Cro. Jurisd. 126. a.
[g] As it seems from Dy. 205. pl. 5, 6. 2 H. H. P. C. 379.
[h] Bra. B. 3. c. 9. West. 1. ch. 2. 2 Inst. 163, 164. S. P. C. 130. b. 9 E. 4. 28. 12 Aff. pl. 15. 34 H. 6. 49. pl. 16. Kely. 99.
[i] S. P. C. 131. b. 132, 133. Hob. 289, 290. Fitz. Coro. 117. Bro. Clergy, 1, 9. See the following Section. But this Matter seems to be left doubtful, 12 Aff. pl. 15. Abridged Bro. Clergy, 9. 34 H. 6. 49. pl. 16. Kely. 99. Fitz. Coro. 44, 120, 191. 9 E. 4. 28. F. N. B. 66. Letter B.
[k] Vide supra sect. 9. Fitz. Coro. 112, 120. S. P. C. 133. b. 27 Aff. pl. 42. Abridged Fitz. Coro. 205.
[l] S. P. C. 131. b. Fitz. Coro. 191, 254. 26 Aff. pl. 19. H. P. C. 239. 2 H. H. P. C. 321, 378, 379. Bro. Clergy, 1, 9. Coro. 73. Hob. 288, 289.
[m] Vide supra sect. 2. Hob. 288.
[n] Vide supra sect. 2. 110. Hob. 288.
[o] Vide 1 E. 3. 13. pl. 8. 1 Aff. pl. 4. Abridged Fitz. Coro. 155. Bro. Cler. 8. Where the Court refused to deliver to the Ordinary a Clerk who had abjured, till he should get the King's Pardon of his Return into the Land without Licence. See Kely. 28.
[p] S. P. C. 133. Letter B. Supra sect. 9.
[q] S. P. C. 133. Letter B. But 21 E. 4. 21. pl. 1. Abridged Bro. Clergy, 18. 9 E. 4. 28. pl. 41. Abridged Bro. Clergy, 7. seem to be contrary, where the Ordinary assigns no particular Cause of Refusal.

ed on good Reason; for otherwise in such Cases the Ordinary by such Pretences might have an absolute Power of controlling the Temporal Courts in a Matter properly determinable by such Courts. And therefore whatever Point it may turn upon, whether a Prisoner ought to have his Clergy or not, as the Validity of his Letters of Orders, or his being a Heretick convict, *&c.* howsoever the Temporal Courts may pay the highest Regard to the Certificate of the Ordinary; yet I take it to be generally [a] holden, That they only are finally to determine whether upon the Whole the Prisoner be well intitled to his Clergy, or not, because the Ordinary is not in this Respect esteemed as a Judge, but [b] only as a Minister to the Court. However it was certainly the [c] settled Practice (while the Method of trying the Prisoner's Capacity of receiving Orders was by putting him to read a Verse,) for the Judges of the Common Law to over-rule the Ordinary as to the Point, Whether the Prisoner read as a Clerk or not; and to record a *Legit* or *Non legit*, according to their own Judgment.

Sect. 114. But the Necessity of such an Ability to read in the Case of a Peer, was taken away by 1 *E.* 6. [d] 12. *Par.* 15. by which it is enacted, *That in every Case where any of the King's Subjects shall upon his Prayer have the Privilege of his Clergy,* &c. *every Lord having Place and Voice in Parliament, shall by Virtue of that Act of Common Grace, upon his Request or Prayer, alledging that he is a Lord or Peer of this Realm, and claiming the Benefit of this Act tho' he cannot read, without any Burning in the Hand, Loss of Inheritance, or Corruption of Blood, be adjudged, deemed, taken and used for the first Time only, to all Intents, Constructions and Purposes, as a Clerk convict, and shall be in Case of a Clerk convict, which may make Purgation, without any further or other Benefit or Privilege of Clergy, to any such Lord or Peer from thenceforth, at any Time after, for any Cause to be allowed,* &c.

Sect. 115. The Necessity of such reading is also taken away, as to every common Person, by 5 *Annæ*, 6. by which it is enacted, *That if any Person convict of such Felony, for which he ought to have the Benefit of Clergy, pray the Benefit of that Act, he shall not be required to read, but shall be punished as a Clerk convict.*

Sect. 116. As to the sixth general Point of this Chapter, *viz.* How far the Ordinary was punishable at Law for demanding or refusing a Clerk against Law: It seems agreed, [e] That anciently this was such a Contempt for which his Temporalities might be seised: But since the Statute of 25 *E.* 3. 6. which provides, *That Prelates shall be admitted to pay a reasonable Fine for Contempts to Writs of* Quare non admisit, *and such like,* it seems to have been generally [f] agreed, That the Ordinary is liable only to be fined, but to no such Seizure for a Contempt of this Kind, as in obstinately [g] persisting to return that a Prisoner reads as a Clerk, or the contrary, *&c.* against the declared Sense of the Court.

[a] Hob. 290. See the Notes to the other Parts of this and the foregoing Section; yet 9 E. 4. 28. Abrid. Bro. Clergy, 7. This Matter seems to be left doubtful. Vide Fitz. Coro. 44. F. N. B. 66. Letter B. [b] 7 E. 4. 29. pl. 12. Abrid. Fitz. Fines, 24. Bro. Clergy, 17. Ordinary, 16. 34 H. 6. 49. pl. 16. Abrid. Fitz. Fines, 19. Bro. Clergy, 1. 7 H. 4. 41. pl. 6. Abrid. Bro. Clergy, 2. Ordinary, 20. 15 H. 7. 9. pl. 8. Abrid. Fitz. Imprisonm. 28. Bro. Ordinary, 11. Kely. 51, 89. Fin. of Law 463, 464. S. P. C. 131. Lett. C. 132. Letters A, B, C, D. 133. Letters A, B, C, D. 141. Letter B. H. P. C. 240. 2 H. H. P. C. 378, 381. 21 E. 4. 21. pl. 1. Abridged Bro. Clergy, 18. [c] Kely. 28, 51. 9 E. 4. 28. pl. 41. Abridged Fitz. Coro. 32. Bro. Ordin. 12. See the Cases cited to the precedent Letter. [d] Vide supra sect. 109. S. P. C. 129. b. 130. [e] Fitz. Coro. 32, 191, 233. 9 E. 4. 28. pl. 41. Vide 21 E. 3. 3. pl. 7. Bro. Contempt, 19 S. P. C. 132. Letter D. Hob. 290. 2 Inst. 164. See the Notes under the next Letter. [f] 9 E. 4. 28. a. Abridged Fitz. Coro. 32. Bro. Clergy, 7. 7 E. 4. 29. pl. 12. Abridged Fitz. Fines, 24. Bro. Clergy, 17. Ordinary, 16. 34 H. 6. 49. pl. 16. Abridged Fitz. Fines, 19. Bro Clergy, 1. 15 H. 7. 9. pl. 8. Abridged Fitz. Imprisonm. 28. Bro. Ordinary, 11. Kely. 28, 51. Finch of Law 463. 2 Inst. 164. Yet see the contrary holden the very next Year, 26 Aff. pl. 19. Abridged Fitz. Coro. 191. And also 7 H. 4. 41. pl. 6. Abridged Bro. Clergy, 2. Ordinary, 20. And S. P. C. 132. Letter D. [g] See the Books cited to the other Parts of this Section.

Sect. 117. As to the ſeventh general Point of this Chapter, *viz.* In what Manner a Clerk was to be delivered to the Ordinary, and afterwards demeſned by the Common Law: It ſeems [a] plain, That anciently whereever a Clerk was delivered to the Ordinary by a temporal Judge, his Perſon ought to be kept in the Ordinary's Priſon, till [b] he had been tried before him by a Jury of twelve Clerks; for the Clergy never pretended to an abſolute Exemption from all kind of Puniſhment for their Crimes, but only to a Privilege of being tried only by Eccleſiaſtical Judges; and this was anciently ſo far indulged them, that after they had been once delivered to the Ordinary, they could not afterwards be remanded to any temporal Court, before the Statute of 8 *Eliz.* 4. ſet forth more at large *Section* 122, *&c.* either for the ſame Crime wherewith they had been charged in ſuch Court, or for any other [c] committed before the Time when the Benefit of Clergy was allowed them, whether ſuch other Crimes were within the Benefit of Clergy, or not. And if they could acquit themſelves on their Trial before the Ordinary of the Crimes for which they had been arraigned in the Temporal Courts, which Acquittal was called a Purgation, [d] they anciently claim'd a Right not only to be delivered out of Priſon, but alſo to be reſtored [e] to their Goods, *&c.* But to render ſuch Purgation the more difficult, and alſo to delay the Delivery of Great Offenders as much as poſſible, the Judges anciently often refuſed [f] to deliver them to the Ordinary till they had been arraigned of all the Crimes whereof they ſtood indicted. But after the Statute of [g] 25 *E.* 3. the Judges could not refuſe the Delivery of Clerks Convict in Reſpect of any Crime whereof they had not been actually arraigned; and therefore they uſed to arraign them at once for all the Crimes whereof they ſtood indicted.

Sect. 118. And if ſuch Clerks could not purge themſelves upon ſuch a Trial, I do not [h] find that they were anciently liable to any greater Puniſhment than Degradation, and the [i] Loſs of their Goods, and the Profits of their Lands, unleſs they had been guilty of Apoſtacy, *&c.* But afterwards, [k] by a Provincial Conſtitution, if they were notoriouſly ſcandalous, they were to be kept in a perpetual Priſon, on ſlender Diet, *&c.*

Sect. 119. If the Ordinary had refuſed to admit a Clerk delivered to him to make his Purgation, he might be compelled [l] by a ſpecial Writ for that Purpoſe.

Sect. 120. But this Privilege was often very much abuſed; and therefore after the Statute of *Weſtminſter*, 1. *Ch.* 2. which requires that no Clerk ſhall be delivered without due Purgation, the Courts of Common Law would never deliver over a Clerk to the Ordinary, without a [m] previous Inquiry into, or Trial of his Crime; whereupon if the Clerk were found Guilty, he abſolutely forfeited his Goods, and the Judges would [n] often in their Diſcretion make a Special Delivery, *abſque purga-*

2 H. H. P. C. 382, 383, &c.

[a] Bract. lib. 3. c. 9. S. P. C. 137. C.

[b] See the Statute of Weſt. 1. ch. 2. 2 Inſt. 163, 164. S. P. C. 137. Lett. C. 138. Lett. A, B. if the Ordinary ſuffered a Clerk to go at large without making ſuch Purgation, he might be fined by the Temporal Courts. 15 H. 7. 9. pl. 8. 9 E. 4. 28. a.

[c] And this Privilege was expreſly confirmed, 25 E. 3. ch. 5. and appears from the Recital of 8 El. c. 4. Vide Dyer 214. pl. 48. 215. pl. 49. H. P. C. 213, 249. And. 114. S. P. C. 108. Lett. A. Finch of Law 464. Poph. 107.

[d] Finch of Law 464, 465.

[e] H. P. C. 241. 5 Co. 110. b. S. P. C. 185. In the Regiſter 68. b. there are three Writs to this Purpoſe. S. P. C. 52. Lett. C. 185, 192. Lett. B. 193. Reg. 68. b. Vide 1 Rich. 3. ch. 3.

[f] Fitz. Coro. 394, 461. Bro Clergy, 24, 30. S. P. C. 66. Lett. D. 108. Lett. A. H. P. C. 213. Bro. Coro. 11.

[g] S. P. C. 108. Lett. A. 142. Lett. B. Dy. 214, 215.

[h] Bract. lib. 3. c. 9. ſect. 2. S. P. C. 138. Lett. B.

[i] H. P. C. 241. 5 Co. 110. b. Bracton and Staundforde in the Places cited to the precedent Letter ſeem to hold generally, That Degradation was the only Puniſhment; but I ſuppoſe that they mean the only Puniſhment to the Perſon.

[k] S. P. C. 140, 141. See Cro. Ja. 431.

[l] Bract. lib. 3. cap. 9 ſect. 3. S. P. C. 137. Lett. C. 138. Lett. A. 15 H. 7. 9. pl. 8. Cro. Jac. 431. Bro. Coro. 223.

[m] Vide ſupra ſect. 117.

[n] H. P. C. 240. 2 Inſt. 195. Hob. 289.

tione facienda; as where it appeared that a Priſoner was a common [a] Thief, *&c.* or where in an Appeal of Robbery a Reſtitution of the Goods ſtolen had been awarded [b] to the Appellant, which Judgment they would not ſuffer to be contradicted by a Purgation. And both in ſuch a Caſe, and alſo *a fortiori* where a Clerk is admitted to his Clergy after an Attainder, whether by an expreſs Judgment or by Outlawry, *&c.* or even after a Confeſſion [c] though he were not ſpecially delivered *abſque purgatione facienda*, the Ordinary ſeems by the ſtronger [d] Opinions to have been liable to an Eſcape, if he had admitted him to his Purgations, becauſe it could not but contradict a Judgment, or the Party's own Confeſſion, which is the higheſt Conviction. Neither was any Purgation thought lawful without a previous Notice to the [e] King of the Time when it was intended to be made.

Sect. 121. As to the Eighth general Point of this Chapter, *viz.* What ſhall be done to one who is allowed the Privilege of Clergy at this Day, and how far it ſhall be for his Benefit: It is enacted by 4 *H.* 7. 13. *That if any Perſon, not in Orders, ſhall be convict of Murder, he ſhall be marked with an* M. *and if of any other Felony, with a* T. *on the Brawn of the Left Thumb, in open Court, before he ſhall be delivered to the Ordinary.* And it is ſaid by [f] *Hale*, That by 3 *H.* 7. 1. A Clerk convicted of Manſlaughter ſhall be committed, or bailed at Diſcretion till the Year be paſſed. But the contrary hath been [g] adjudged; for the ſaid Statute mentions only thoſe who are acquitted of Murder at the King's Suit, within the Year and Day, in which Caſe it directs that they ſhall be committed or bailed, till the Year and Day be paſſed, that they may be forthcoming, in order to anſwer to an Appeal, if brought within that Time. But it admits the Clergy once had to be a good Bar to an Appeal, even after an Attainder, and therefore cannot be thought to have intended to make Proviſion in any Caſe for the Parties being forthcoming to anſwer an Appeal after Clergy hath been allowed him, which makes it ineffectual. But it is certain, that any Perſon who hath his Clergy may be committed for any Time within a Year by 18 *Eliz.* 7. *Par.* 3. ſet forth more at large, *Sect.* 125.

Sect. 122. It is recited by 8 *Eliz.* 4. *Par.* 3. *That divers Perſons had oft times committed ſundry deteſtable Felonies, for the which Clergy is not allowable, and afterwards had fled to Places remote where they were not known, and committed ſome other Felony within the Benefit of Clergy, and being arraigned for the ſame had had their Clergy allowed them, and thereupon been committed to the Cuſtody of the Ordinary, the former Offence being then not known, and ſo by that Means could not after be impeached for the ſame, to the great encouraging of Offenders, uſing ſuch Practices of Fore-knowledge and ſet Purpoſe for their Diſcharge of the ſame.*

Sect. 123. *For Reformation whereof it is enacted, That every Perſon or Perſons, who ſhall hereafter upon his or their Arraignment for any Felony, be admitted to the Benefit of his Clergy, and delivered to the Ordinary for the ſame, and ſhall make his due Purgation for the ſame Offence or Offences, whereupon he was ſo admitted to his Clergy, and ſhall, before the ſame Admiſſion to his Clergy, have committed any other ſuch Offence, whereupon Clergy is not allowable, and not being thereof indicted and acquitted, convicted or attainted, or pardoned, ſhall and may be indicted or appealed for the ſame, and thereupon put to anſwer, and ordered and uſed in all Things according to the Laws and Statutes of this Realm, in ſuch like Manner and Form, as though no ſuch Admiſſion of Clergy had been; any Law, Cuſtom, or Uſage to the contrary notwithſtanding.*

[a] S.P.C. 139. Lett. D. Hob. 289. Fitz. Coro. 247.
[b] Finch of Law 464. S. P. C. 139. Lett. B. Fitz. Coro. 109, 247.
[c] But this is left a Quære, S. P. C. 138. Lett. E. 139. Lett. A. but it ſeems agreed, That a Clerk might be admitted to his Purgation after a Conviction by Verdict. Fitz. Coro. 393. 5 Aſſ. pl. 5. Abridg. Fitz. 145. Cont. Fitz. Coro. 417.
[d] S. P. C. 48. 138. Lett. C. 27 H. 6. 7. b. Abridg. Fitz. Coro. 16. 13 E. 4. 3. pl. 6. Abridg. Bro. Coro. 158. Fitz. Cor. 38. 3 H. 7. 12. pl. 5. Abridg. Fitz. Coro. 56, 136. 9 E. 4. 28. a. Abridg. Bro. Coro. 55. Bro. Coro. 4. Finch 464, 465. Cont. Hob. 289. Fitz. Coro. 109, 128, 247, 450. 18 Aſſ. pl. 13. Abridg. Fitz. Coro. 176. Utlagary 2. Theloal, B. 1. ch. 15. ſect. 26.
[e] Finch 464. S.P.C. 138. Lett. B. Fitz. Coro. 152.
[f] H. P. C. 240.
[g] Kely. 25.

Sect. 124. *And for the avoiding of ſundry Perjuries and other Abuſes, in and about the Purgation of Clerks Convict, delivered to the Ordinaries,* it is enacted by 18 *Eliz.* 7. *That every Perſon who ſhall be admitted to his Clergy, ſhall not thereupon be delivered to the Ordinary, but after ſuch Clergy allowed, and burning in the Hand, according to the* [a] *Statute in that Behalf provided, ſhall forthwith be enlarged and delivered out of Priſon by the Juſtices before whom ſuch Clergy ſhall be granted, that Cauſe notwithſtanding.* [a] 4 H. 7. 13. for which ſee ſect. 121.

Sect. 125. But it is provided, Par. 3. *That the Juſtices before whom any ſuch Allowance of Clergy ſhall be had, ſhall and may, for the further Correction of ſuch Perſons to whom Clergy ſhall be allowed, detain and keep them in Priſon for ſuch convenient* [b] *Time, as the ſame Juſtices in their Diſcretions ſhall think convenient, ſo as the ſame do not exceed one Year's Impriſonment.* [b] 2 Bulſt. 137.

Sect. 126. And it is farther provided, Par. 5. *That all Perſons admitted to their Clergy, ſhall notwithſtanding ſuch Admiſſion, be put to anſwer to all other Felonies whereof they ſhall be indicted or appealed, and not being thereof before acquitted, convicted, attainted or pardoned, and ſhall in ſuch Manner and Form be arraigned, tried, adjudged, and ſuffer ſuch Execution for the ſame, as they ſhould have done, if, as Clerks Convicts, they had been delivered to the Ordinary, and there had made their Purgations; any thing in this Act contained to the contrary notwithſtanding.*

Upon theſe Statutes the following Points ſeem moſt remarkable.

Sect. 127. *Firſt,* Inaſmuch as it plainly appears, not only from the Preamble, but alſo from the expreſs Words of the above recited Clauſe of 8 *Eliz.* 4. That it had nothing elſe in View but only to prevent the Inconvenience that Offenders ſhould be diſcharged of Crimes not within the Benefit of Clergy, by being admitted to their Clergy for Crimes within the Benefit of it, as they were [c] before this Statute; and inaſmuch as the above-recited *Proviſo* of 18 *Eliz.* 7. though it be more largely worded than 8 *Eliz.* 4. hath a plain Relation to it, and therefore may reaſonably receive the ſame Conſtruction; it ſeems to have been agreed, [d] ever ſince theſe Statutes, That a Conviction for a Felony within the Benefit of Clergy, and an Allowance of Clergy thereon, is as much a Diſcharge of all precedent Felonies within the Benefit of Clergy (though not of any others) as it was before theſe Statutes. [c] Vide ſupra ſect. 117. [d] H. P. C. 213, 249. 2 H. H. P. C. 388. 1 And. 114. Poph. 107.

Sect. 128. *Secondly,* Inaſmuch as the Statute of 18 *Eliz.* 7. is expreſs, *That every Perſon admitted to his Clergy, ſhall not be delivered to the Ordinary, but after ſuch Clergy allowed, and burning in the Hand, ſhall forthwith be enlarged and delivered out of Priſon,* &c. *with a* Proviſo *neverthe leſs, that for further Correction he may be kept in Priſon,* &c. *and alſo with a farther* Proviſo, *that he ſhall anſwer to all former Felonies, in the ſame Manner as if he had made his Purgation.* It ſeems to be the more prevailing Opinion, [e] That a Clerk Convict being admitted to his Clergy, may either be taken to have a Kind of a Statute-pardon, or elſe to be in the ſame Caſe as if he had made his Purgation at the Common Law. And both theſe Conſtructions ſeem reaſonable. For as to the firſt it may be ſaid, That the Statute by ordaining that the Party ſhall be forthwith enlarged and delivered out of Priſon, under certain *Proviſoes,* ſeems plainly to imply that he ſhall be liable to no other Puniſhment, and conſequently in Effect pardons him. And as to the ſecond it may be ſaid, That the Statute ſeems only to intend to take away the Practice of making Purgation, which had been ſo much abuſed, but not the Benefit accruing to the Subject by it, [e] Vide Kely. 37, 102.

it, but rather to make it more univerſal, by giving the ſame Advantage to all by a direct and expreſs Law, attended with no Inconvenience, which before ſome only gained by an uſurped Practice, very frequently abuſed, and highly derogatory from the Honour of the Common Law. But [a] Sir *Edward Coke* is of Opinion, That it ſhall enure by way of Purgation in Reſpect of ſuch Perſons only who might be admitted to make their Purgation before the Statute, and in Reſpect of others by way of Pardon. And [b] *Hobart* argues, That becauſe many Offenders before the Statute might have their Clergy, who yet could not be diſcharged by making their Purgation; and the Statute intends that all in general who are admitted to their Clergy, ſhall be diſcharged, *&c.* And alſo becauſe all Purgations diſcredited a Trial at Law, therefore is it not reaſonable to intend that the Statute meant that ſuch a Diſcharge ſhould enure by way of a Purgation, but only by way of a Statute-pardon. But to this it ſeems a reaſonable Anſwer, That it doth by no Means follow, that becauſe the Statute intended that ſuch Diſcharge ſhould extend to Perſons who could not have the Benefit of a Purgation, therefore it did not intend that it ſhould have the Effect of a Purgation; neither doth it ſeem to follow, That becauſe a Purgation diſcredited the Acts of a Jury, therefore ſuch a Diſcharge, if it have to ſome Purpoſes the ſame Effect as a Purgation, muſt diſcredit them likewiſe.

Sect. 129. *Thirdly*, Taking the Statute to enure either by way of a Statute-pardon, or Purgation, it ſeems that it reſtores [c] the Party to his Credit, and conſequently enables [d] him to be a good Witneſs; which it hath been queſtioned whether a Pardon by the King can do, as ſhall be ſet forth more at large in the Chapter of *Pardon*. Alſo it ſeems agreed, That it gives him a Capacity to purchaſe [e] Goods, and to retain the [f] Profits of his Land, but gives him no Right to be reſtored to thoſe which he had at the Time of the Conviction, which being veſted in the King by the Forfeiture upon the Conviction, [g] ſhall not be deveſted either by a [h] Pardon or [i] Purgation. For it is certain that a Pardon never avoids [k] any precedent legal Act, as ſhall be more fully ſhewn in the Chapter of *Pardon*. Neither would the Common Law endure that Purgation, which was introduced by a Connivance, or rather tolerated than allowed, ſhould ſo far control its Proceedings.

Sect. 130. *Fourthly*, Whether the Statute enure as a Pardon or Purgation, it [l] ſeems to take from the Spiritual Court the Power of depriving the Party for the Crime for which he has had his Clergy. For if it enure as a Pardon, ſurely it cannot be doubted but that it frees the Party from all ſubſequent Puniſhment, and conſequently from a Deprivation. And if it enure as a Purgation, which is admitted [m] to have been a good Bar to a Deprivation before the Statute, why ſhould it not have the ſame Effect as a Purgation had formerly, in this as well as in other Reſpects. Yet [n] *Watſon*, in his *Clergyman's Law*, holds an Opinion on the Authority of [o] *Croke's Second Report*, that a Clergyman may be deprived for Manſlaughter after he has had his Clergy, not obſerving, as I ſuppoſe, that what is

[a] 5 Co. 110. a. b.

[b] Hob. 292, 293.

[c] H. P. C. 241.

[d] Kely. 37. Raym. 369, 370, 380. Vide 1 Sid. 222. State Trials, Vol. 2. 523. Vol. 4. 379 to 386. 5 Mod 15.

[e] H. P. C. 241. 5 Co. 110. Hob. 293.

[f] 5 Co. 110. Fitz. Coro. 393. Forfeit. 34.

[g] 12 Co. 121. 5 Co. 110. b. H. P. C. 241. Co. Lit. 391. a. 3 H. 7. 12. pl. 10. Fitz. Coro. 53, 356, 365, 393. Fitz. Forfeit. 23, 34. Bro. Forf. 11. 8 H. 4. 2. b. Plow. Com. 262. b. S. P. C. 185. 20 E. 4. 5. pl. 3. Bro. Coro. 166. But it is holden 40 E. 3. 42. pl. 23. Abridged Fitz. Coro. 91. and Bro. Forfeit. 5. That nothing is forfeited unleſs there be an Attainder. Alſo 'tis ſaid, that the Profits of Lands are not forfeited. 20 E. 4. 5. pl. 3. Bro. Coro. 166.

[h] 1 Saund. 362. 1 Lev. 8. 120.

[i] Vide ſupra ſect. 110. Fitz. Coro. 356. Finch 464. Cont. Fitz. Coro. 365. Bro. Forfeit. 113. F. N. B. 66. Lett. A. Bro. Clergy, 28.

[k] 1 Saund. 362. 1 Lev. 8. 120.

[l] Hob. 292, 293. 2 Roll. Ab. 305. pl. 3.

[m] Cro. Jac. 431.

[n] Ch. 6. fol. 35, 36. in the Folio Edition.

[o] Cro. Jac. 430, 431.

said in this Book was only on the sudden on a Motion for a Prohibition in the King's Bench; and that in the same Case a Prohibition was afterwards actually brought and declared on in the [a] Common Place, and Judgment thereupon solemnly given for the Plaintiff upon open Argument by all the Judges.

Sect. 131. *Fifthly*, It seems agreed, that where a Person exempt from burning in the Hand, (either in Respect of his [b] Peerage or [c] Orders, or a [d] Special Pardon,) is admitted to the Benefit of his Clergy, he shall have the same Advantage of the Statute without being burnt in the Hand, as others shall have upon such Burning; for the Words of the Statute, that the Party *after such Clergy allowed, and Burning in the Hand, shall be enlarged*, &c. shall have this Construction, that he shall be enlarged, *&c.* upon burning where Burning ought to be.

Sect. 132. It is holden, That after a Man is admitted to his Clergy, it is [e] actionable to call him Felon, *&c.* because his Offence being pardoned by the Statute, all the Infamy and other Consequences of it are discharged.

Sect. 133. How far a Person convicted of a Crime within the Clergy, and praying or being ready to pray it, but not actually admitted to it, shall be within these Statutes, shall be considered, *Ch.* 37.

[a] Hobart 288. 2 H. H. P. C. 389. 2 Roll. Abr. 305. pl. 3. Also a Prohibition was granted in the like Case, 27 & 28 Eliz. Rotulo 2574. cited, Hob. 294. a.
[b] 1 Lev. 180.
[c] Hob. 294.
[d] 5 Co. 110. b.
[e] Hob. 294. Vide Hob 67. 81. 1 Danv. 163. pl. 6. and the Chapter of Pardon.

Sect. 134. It is enacted by 5 *Annæ*, 6. *That where any Person shall be convict of Larceny, the Judges shall at their Discretion award him to the Work-house, or House of Correction, there to be kept without Bail, not less than six Months, nor more than two Years from the Conviction; an Entry whereof is to be made of Record*, &c. *And if such Offender escape, he shall be committed to some such House, there to remain not less than twelve Months, nor more than four Years*, &c.

Sect. 135. It is enacted by 4 *Geo.* 1. c. 11. and 6 *Geo.* 1. c. 23. *That where any Person or Persons shall be convicted of Grand or Petit Larceny, or any felonious stealing or taking of Money, Goods, or Chattels, either from the Person, or the House of any other, or in any other Manner, and who by the Law shall be intitled to the Benefit of Clergy, and liable only to the Penalties of burning in the Hand or whipping, (except Persons convicted for receiving or buying stolen Goods, knowing them to be stolen) it shall and may be lawful for the Court before whom they were convicted, or any Court held at the same, or any* [f] *other Place with the like Authority, if they think fit, instead of ordering any such Offenders to be burnt in the hand, or whipt, to order and direct that such Offenders shall be sent, as soon as conveniently may be, to some of his Majesty's Colonies, and Plantations in* America, *for the Space of seven Years: And that Court before whom they were convicted, or any subsequent Court, with like Authority as the former, shall have Power to convey, transfer, and make over such Offenders, by Order of Court, to the Use of any Person or Persons who shall contract for the Performance of such Transportation, to him, or them, and his and their Assigns, for such Term of seven Years. And where any Persons shall be convicted of any Crimes for which they are excluded their Clergy, and the King shall extend his Mercy to them upon Condition of Transportation to any Part of* America, *and such Intention of Mercy be signified by a Principal Secretary of State, it shall be lawful for any Court, having proper Authority to allow such Offenders the Benefit of a Pardon, to order and direct the like Transportation, to any Person (who will contract for the Performance thereof) of any such Offenders, as also of any Person convict of receiving or buying stolen Goods, knowing them to be stolen, for the Term of fourteen Years, in Case such Condition of Transportation be general, or else for such other Term as shall be made Part of such Condition; and such Person so con-*

[f] Viz. by 6. Geo. 1. ch. 23.

tracting, and his Assigns, shall have an Interest in the Service of the said Offenders for such Term of Years; And if any such Offender return into Great Britain *or* Ireland *before the End of his Term, he shall be liable to be punished as any Person attainted of Felony, without the Benefit of Clergy,* &c. *Provided, that the King may pardon and dispense with any such Transportation, and allow of the Return of such Offender, paying his Owner at the Time, such Sum as shall be adjudged reasonable by any two Justices of the Peace where such Owner dwells; and where any such Offenders shall be transported, and shall have served their Terms, such Services shall have the Effect of a Pardon, as for the Crimes for which they were transported,* &c.

Sect. 136. And it is farther enacted, That *every such Person to whom any such Court shall order any such Offenders to be transferred or conveyed, shall before such Offenders shall be delivered to them, contract with such Person as shall be appointed by such Court, and shall give sufficient Security to the Satisfaction of such Court, for the transporting such Offenders to some Plantation in* America, *to be ordered by such Court, and the Procuring an authentick Certificate from the Governor or Chief Custom-House Officer of the Place, of the Landing of such Offenders,* &c. *and their not returning by the wilful Default of such Contractor.*

Sect. 137. And it is farther enacted by 6 *Geo.* 1. c. 23. *That the Court may nominate two or more Justices of the Peace for the Place where such Offenders shall be convicted, who shall have Power to contract with any Person or Persons for the Performance of the Transportation of such Offenders; and to order such and the like Security as the said former Act directs to be taken by Order of Court, and to cause such Felons to be delivered to such Contractors; which said Contracts and Security shall be certified by the said Justices to the next Court held with the like Authority, to be filed,* &c.

Sect. 138. And it is farther enacted, *That all Charges in or about such Contracts,* &c. *shall be born by each County,* &c. *for which the Court was held; and that the respective Treasurers shall pay the same. And that all Securities for Transportation shall be by Bond in the Name of the Clerks of the Peace,* &c. *and the Money recovered shall be to the Use of the respective Counties,* &c.

Sect. 139. And it is farther enacted, *That the Persons so contracting,* &c. *may carry such Offenders towards the Sea Port,* &c. *and that if any Person shall rescue such Offenders, or aid them in making their Escape,* &c. *they shall be deemed guilty of Felony, without Clergy. And that if any Felon ordered for Transportation shall be afterwards at large within any Part of* Great Britain, *without some lawful Cause before the Expiration of his Term, and be lawfully convict thereof, he shall suffer Death without Clergy. And may be tried before Justices of Assise,* Oyer *and* Terminer, *or Gaol-Delivery, for the County where he shall be apprehended,* &c. *or from whence he was ordered to be transported,* &c. *and that the Clerk of Assise, and Clerk of the Peace, where such Orders of Transportation shall be made, shall on Request of the Prosecutor,* &c. *certify briefly a Transcript containing the Tenor of every Indictment, Conviction and Order of Transportation to the Justices of Assise,* &c. *which shall be a sufficient Proof of such Conviction and Order of Transportation.*

CHAP. XXXIV.

Of Pleas in Abatement.

AND now I come to *Pleas in Abatement*, which having already considered so far as they particularly relate to Appeals, Indictments, and Informations, in the several Chapters concerning them, and shewn in *Chap.* 23. from *Section* 102. to *Section* 128. what Pleas are good in Abatement of an Appeal; and in *Sections* 128, and 137. That an Appellee may plead as many of them as he pleases, unless they be repugnant to one another, and afterwards take the General Issue; and in *Chap.* 25. *Sect.* 12. That the same Matters may be pleaded to an Appeal on an Arraignment thereon at the Suit of the King, as on an Arraignment at the Suit of the Party, and in the same Chapter, *Sections* 68, 69, 70, 71. what Misnosmers, *&c.* may be pleaded in Abatement of an Indictment; and in *Chap.* 26. *Sections*, 63, 64, 65. What Pleas are good in Abatement of an Information; and having considered Demurrers in Abatement, *Chap.* 31. *Sect.* 5, 6, 7. I shall in this Place take Notice only of the following Particulars;

Sect. 1. *First*, That it hath been holden [a] that it is no good Plea in Abatement of an Indictment, as it is of an Appeal [b], or Information, [c] that there is another Indictment against the Defendant for the same Offence. But in such [d] a Case the Court in Discretion will quash the first Indictment if any Fault can be found in it.

[a] 1 Jon. 199. Cro. Ca. 147.
[b] Ch. 23. sect. 126.
[c] Ch. 26. sect. 63.
[d] Cro. Car. 147. 1 Jo. 199.

Sect. 2. *Secondly*, That where an Indictment of a Capital Crime is abated for a Misnosmer of the Defendant's [e] Christian Name, the Court will not dismiss him, but cause him to be Indicted *de novo* [f] by his true Name, and arraign him again on such new Indictment. For I take it to be settled [g] at this Day, That regularly a Defendant shall not be dismissed for an Insufficiency in an Indictment or Appeal for a capital Crime.

[e] Vide ch. 25. sect. 70, 71.
[f] H.P.C. 243. 2 H. H. P. C. 176, 238. Cro. Ca. 371, 372.
[g] Vide ch. 23. sect. 4. 133. ch. 25. sect. 9, 10, 11.

Sect. 3. *Thirdly*, That a Defendant appearing *Gratis*, and by Attorney to an Information, may [h] plead a Misnosmer in Abatement, as well as if he had appeared in proper Person; for if he be not the Person intended, the Attorney General may reject the Plea, and sign Judgment on a *Nihil dicit*; but if he accept the Plea, he thereby admits him that pleads it to be the Person concerned to make a Defence, and therefore shall not afterwards say that it doth not appear but that the Plea might be put in by a Stranger.

cont. 11 H. 4. 41. pl. 7. Fitz. Misnosmer, 18. Coro. 88. Bro. Misnos. 23.

See the Books cited ch. 23. sect. 11. Lett. a.

[h] Adjudged Trin. 4 Geo. 1. between the King and Westby.

CHAP.

CHAP. XXXV.

Of the Plea of Autrefoits acquit.

PLeas in Chief are either,

1. In Bar, or
2. The General Iſſue.

As to the Pleas in Bar, having ſhewn already, *Chap.* 23. *Sect.* 130. what Pleas of this Kind to an Appeal are good, which ſhew that the Plaintiff had never any Right to bring it; and in *Sections* 131, 132, 133. where a *Retraxit*, Nonſuit, Diſcontinuance, or Abatement, of one Appeal may be pleaded in Bar of another; and in *Section* 134. where the Bringing of an Appeal againſt one Perſon will be a Bar to a ſubſequent one againſt another Perſon not named in the Firſt; and in *Section* 135. where a Releaſe will bar an Appeal; and in *Section* 136. where an Appellant may be barred as to one Apellee, and continue his Suit againſt the Reſt; and in *Section* 137. what Pleas of this Kind are conſiſtent with the General Iſſue, and in *Ch.* 26. *Sect.* 64, 65. what is a good Plea in Bar to an Information, I ſhall in this Place only conſider,

1. The Plea of *Autrefoits acquit.*
2. The Plea of *Autrefoits attaint* or *convict.*
3. The Plea of a Pardon.

Sect. 1. And firſt of the Plea of *Autrefoits acquit*, which is grounded on this *Maxim*, [a] That a Man ſhall not be brought into Danger of his Life for one and the ſame Offence, more than once. From whence it is generally taken, by all the Books, [b] as an undoubted Conſequence, that where a Man is once found Not guilty on an Indictment or Appeal free [c] from Error, and [d] well commenced before any [e] Court which hath Juriſdiction of the Cauſe, he may by the Common Law in all [f] Caſes whatſoever plead ſuch Acquittal in Bar of any ſubſequent Indictment or Appeal for the ſame Crime. But for the more diſtinct Underſtanding hereof I ſhall particularly conſider,

1. How far he who pleads this Plea muſt be ready to produce the Record of his former Acquittal.
2. Where a Variance between the Record of the former Acquittal and the Indictment or Appeal to which it is pleaded, may be helped.
3. How far other Diſcharges of a former Proſecution have the ſame Effect as an Acquittal by Verdict.

[a] S. P. C. 105. Lett. A. 4 Co. 40. a 45. a. 47. a. 9 H. 7. 19. pl. 14. Fitz. Pard. 3. Bro. Appeal, 9, 12, 89. Coro. 11. Cromp. Juſt. 111. pl. 1.
[b] See the Authorities cited to all the other Parts of this Chapter, and 5 E. 3. 25. pl. 36.
[c] Vide infra ſect. 8.
[d] Vide infra ſect. 9.
[e] Vide infra ſect. 10.
[f] 25 E. 3. 44. pl. 16. Abridged Fitz. Coro. 136. 41 Aſſ. 9. Abridged Fitz. Coro. 220. Bro. Coro. 120 or 121. 2 Leon. 161. Vide infra ſect. 14, 15. 47 E. 3. 16. pl. 27. Abridged Fitz. Coro. 104. Bro. Appeal, 14.

4. How far it is neceſſary that the Indictment or Appeal in the Record of Acquittal be free from Error, and well commenced.

5. Whether an Acquittal in any Court which has a Juriſdiction be ſufficient for this Purpoſe.

6. How far an Acquittal of a Perſon as Principal will bar a ſubſequent Proſecution againſt him as Acceſſary, & *e converſo*, how far an Acquittal of a Man as Acceſſary will bar a Proſecution againſt him as Principal.

7. How far the Law is altered in theſe Reſpects as to an Indictment of Death, by 3 *H.* 7. 1.

Sect. 2. As to the firſt Particular, *viz.* How far he who pleads this Plea muſt be ready to produce the Record of his formal Acquittal, I take it to be [a] agreed, that ſuch Plea being a Plea in [b] Bar, and the Record not in the Cuſtody of, nor the Property of him that pleads it, there is no need to plead with a *profert ſub pede ſigilli*; but the Defendant ſhall have a [c] Day given him to bring it in. And there is in *Brook* a Note of a [d] Caſe in the Time of *Edw.* 3. wherein a Plea of *Autrefoits acquit* was diſallowed, becauſe the Defendant ſhewed forth the Record when he pleaded it; and the Book gives this Reaſon, That *the Record ought to come before the Court by Writ.*

Sect. 3. As to the ſecond Particular, *viz.* Where a [e] Variance between the Record of the former Acquittal, and the Indictment or Appeal to which it is pleaded, may be helped: I take it to be clear, That if the Nature of the Crime be in [f] Subſtance the ſame, a Variance may generally be helped by proper [g] Averments. And therefore if a Man be named in the firſt Record *Yeoman*, and in the ſecond *Gentleman*, yet it ſeems [h] clear, That he may make good the Variance, with an Averment that he only was meant under each Addition. Alſo if a Man be acquitted of an Indictment of Murder or Robbery *cujuſdam* [i] *ignoti*, and afterwards arraigned on an Indictment for the ſame Fact, deſcribing the Perſon killed or robbed by his proper Name; yet it hath been holden, [k] That he may plead the Acquittal in Bar, averring that both the Indictments are for the very ſame Felony. Alſo if the Perſon kill'd be deſcribed by his proper Name and Surname in the firſt Indictment, and by the ſame Chriſtian but by a different Surname in the ſecond, yet it hath been [l] adjudged, That he may plead an Acquittal on the firſt in Bar of the ſecond Indictment, averring that the Perſon ſo differently named was one and the ſame Perſon. But it ſeems [m] adviſeable in ſuch Caſe to add a farther Averment, That the Perſon killed was known as well by the Name in the firſt, as by that in the ſecond Indictment; for if he were never known by the Name in the firſt Indictment, I much queſtion whether the Defendant could be found guilty upon it; and if he could not, it ſeems plain that his Life having never been in Danger by it, the Acquittal upon it [n] cannot be any Bar to a ſubſequent Indictment. But if there be no other Variance between the firſt and ſecond Indictment but only as to the [o] Times when the Crime is alledged to have been committed, or as to the [p] Places being both in the ſame County, there is no Doubt but

[a] S. P. C. 105. Letter A. H. P. C. 245. 2 H. H. P. C. 241, 242, 243. Fitz. Coro. 33. Fitz. Monſtrans de faits, 33. Vide Raſt. Entr. 385. pl. 4. ſeems contrary.

[b] Co. Litt. 128. See the Chapter of Pardon.

[c] Co. Litt. 128. b. Fitz. Coro. 232.

[d] Bro. Coro. 218. But 26 Aſſ. pl. 15. Abridged Fitz. Coro. 189. 11 H. 4. 41. pl. 6. Abridged Fitz. Monſtrans de faits, 128. Bro. Coro. 29. 9 H. 7. 19. pl. 14. Abridged Bro. Appeal, 89. ſeems contrary.

[e] Vide 2 Keb. 705. pl. 71.

[f] 14 H. 7. 2. pl. 8. S. P. C. 168. Letter B.

[g] S. P. C 105. H. P. C. 246.

[h] Vide Keil. 58. a.

[i] Vide ſupra ch 25. ſect. 73.

[k] Keil. 25. b. Dy. 285. pl. 38. Vide Fitz. Coro. 159.

[l] 26 Aſſ. pl. 15. Abridged Bro. Coro. 98. Fitz. Coro. 189. Crompt. Juſt. 112. pl. 12. S. P. C. 105. Letter C. 2 H. H. P. C. 244. Vide 11 H. 4. 41. pl. 6. Abridged Fitz. Monſtrans de faits, 128. Bro. Variance, 31. Coro. 29. 1 Rol. Rep. 368. pl. 22.

[m] Vide H. P. C. 246. S. P. C. 105. Letter C. Crompt. Juſt. 112. pl. 12.

[n] Vide ſupra ſect. 1. & infra ſect. 8, 9, 10.

[o] Dy. 285. pl. 31. H. P. C. 246. 2 H. H. P. C. 244. Vide 22 Aſſ. pl. 55. Abridged Fitz. Coro. 179. S. P. C. 105. Letter C. 11 H. 4. 41. pl. 6. Abridged Bro. Coro. 29. Variance, 31. Fitz. Monſtrans de faits, 128. 25 Ed. 3. 44. pl. 16. Abridged Fitz. Coro. 136. 3 Aſſ. pl. 15. Abridged Fitz. Coro. 166. Crompt. Juſt. 112. pl. 13.

[p] H. P. C. 246. 2 H. H. P. C. 245. S. P. C. 105. Letter C. 106. Letter A.

that regularly it may be helped by an Averment, that the Felony in both is one and the ſame, becauſe neither the Time nor Place laid in an Indictment, *&c.* are material upon Evidence, ſo that the Defendant be proved guilty at any other [a] Time before the Indictment, or at any other Place [b] within the County. And it is holden by [c] *Staundforde*, That an Acquittal of Murder in one County may be pleaded in Bar of a ſubſequent Indictment in another County for the ſame Murder. But this ſeems queſtionable, becauſe all Indictments are local; and therefore if the firſt were laid in an improper County, the Defendant could not be found guilty upon it, and conſequently was in no Danger of his Life, and therefore [d] cannot plead an Acquittal upon it in Bar of a ſubſequent Indictment in the proper County: But if the firſt Indictment were in the proper County, the ſecond cannot but be in an improper one, and conſequently the Defendant not being liable to be found guilty upon it, cannot be ſaid to be reduced by it to the Inconvenience of being twice brought into Danger of his Life for one and the ſame Offence, the Avoiding of which Inconvenience [e] ſeems the chief Inducement for which the Law allows the Plea of *Autrefoits acquit.*

[a] H.P.C. 264. Salk. 288.
[b] See the Chapter of Evidence; and H. P. C. 264.
[c] S.P.C. 105. Letter C. See Crompt. Juſt. 12. pl. 9.
[d] Vide ſect. 1, 8, 9, 10.
[e] Supra ſect. 1, 8, 9, 10.

Sect. 4. But if a Man ſteal Goods in one County, and then carry them into another, in which Caſe it is certain [f] that he may be indicted and found guilty in either, it ſeems very reaſonable, that an Acquital in the one County for ſuch Stealing may [g] be pleaded in Bar of a ſubſequent Proſecution for the ſame Stealing in another County, becauſe the Defendant may be altogether as well convicted in the one County, as in the other; and therefore if he could not bar the ſecond Proſecution by the Acquittal on the firſt, his Life would be twice in Danger from that which is in Truth but one and the ſame Offence, and only conſidered as a new one by a mere Fiction or Conſtruction of Law, which ſhall hardly [h] take Place againſt a Maxim made in Favour of Life. And as to the [i] Objection, That the Jurors of the one County can take no Manner of Conuſance of what is done in the other, and conſequently cannot try whether the Felony whereof the Party is indicted in the ſecond County be the very ſame with that of which he is acquitted in the firſt, it may be anſwered, That it appears from the old Books, that anciently the Judges often ſatisfied themſelves of the Truth of an Averment that the Offences in both Indictments were the ſame, by [k] Witneſſes, or by an [l] Inqueſt of Office, without putting it to a Trial by Jury, upon an Iſſue joined, on the Denial thereof by the Proſecutor, which ſeems [m] to have been of later Years the uſual Method. But granting, that it is to be tried by ſuch Jury, I do not ſee how it follows, That becauſe they cannot convict a Defendant upon Evidence of a Fact done out of their own County, therefore they cannot collaterally inquire whether an Offence laid in their own County be in Subſtance the ſame with that done in another, ſince it cannot be denied but that in Abundance of Caſes a Jury of one County may receive Evidence of Facts done in another. To which may be added, That in the *Year-Book* of 4 *H.* 7. 5. *pl.* which is the [n] Chief Authority for the contrary Opinion, it is admitted that an Acquittal of an Appeal of Larceny in the one County, may be pleaded in Bar of a ſubſequent Appeal in the other; becauſe ſuch an Appeal intitles the Plaintiff to a Reſtitution of the Goods, whereof being once

[f] Supra ch. 23. ſect. 47. ch. 25. ſect. 38. and B. 1. ch. 33. ſect. 9.
[g] 41 Aſſ. pl. 9. Fitz. Coro. 220. But this is left doubtful, S. P. C. 105. Lett. C. 106. Lett. A. H. P. C. 246. Crompt. Juſt. 112. pl. 9. Bro. Coro. 139 or 140. 4 H. 7. 5. pl. 1. Fitz. Coro. 62.
[h] Vide ſupra ch. 18. ſect. 13. and ch. 19. ſect. 25. and ch. 29. ſect. 35.
[i] 4 H. 7. 5. pl. 1. Fitz. Cor. 62.
[k] 26 Aſſ. pl. 15. Abridged Fitz. Coro. 189. Bro. Coro. 98. 41 Aſſ. pl. 9. Abridged Fitz. Coro. 220.
[l] 3 Aſſ. pl. 15. Abridged Fitz. Coro. 166. See the ſixth Section.
[m] 9 H. 7. 19. pl. 14. Abridged Bro. Appeal, 89. H. P. C. 245.
[n] Vide Bro. Coro. 139 or 140. Fitz. Coro. 62. S. P. C. 106. H. P. C. 246. 2 H. H. P. C. 245.

barred he is barred for ever. But granting this to be a good Reaſon, which yet it ſeems difficult to make out, the very ſame may be ſaid at this Day as to an Indictment, which ſince [a] 21 *H.* 8. 11. intitles the Proſecutor to a Reſtitution alſo. Beſides, taking the Law as it ſtood formerly, why may not a Jury of one County try whether a Felony therein indicted, be the ſame whereon the Party was before acquitted in another County, in the Caſe of a ſecond Indictment, as well as of a ſecond Appeal?

Sect. 5. It ſeems [b] that it is no Plea to an Appeal of Larceny, That the Defendant hath been found Not guilty in an Action of Treſpaſs brought againſt him by the ſame Plaintiff for the ſame Goods; for Larceny and Treſpaſs are entirely different: Alſo it ſeems a general [c] Rule, That a Bar in an Action of an inferior Nature, will not bar another of a ſuperior. Yet it ſeems, [d] That an Acquittal in an Indictment of Murder, will be a good Bar of an Indictment of Petit Treaſon, becauſe both Offences are in Subſtance the ſame. But it is clear, That an Acquittal of one Felony is [e] no Manner of Bar to a Proſecution for another in Subſtance different, whether committed before or at the ſame Time with that of which he is acquitted; and therefore if a Man commit a Burglary, and ſteal the Goods of *A.* and *B.* and be indicted for the Burglary, and ſtealing the Goods of *A.* and acquitted; it hath been adjudged, [f] that he cannot plead ſuch Acquittal to an Indictment for ſtealing the Goods of *B.* But it ſeems agreed, That he may plead it to a ſecond Indictment for the Burglary.

Sect. 6. As to the third Particular, *viz.* How far other Diſcharges of a legal Proſecution have the ſame Effect as an Acquittal by Verdict: Having ſhewn already in the [g] Chapter of *Appeals*, how far the Diſcharge of one Appeal will bar another, I ſhall only add in this Place, That notwithſtanding the [h] Allowance of a Pardon, or any other Bar of one Indictment, ſeems to be pleadable in Bar of another; and by the like Reaſon whatever hath been allowed a good Bar of one Appeal may be pleaded in Bar of another: Yet it ſeems that no other Diſcharge of an Indictment will bar an Appeal, and no other Diſcharge of an Appeal will bar an Indictment, but only an [i] Acquittal by Battel, or an Acquittal by Verdict on the General Iſſue, finding the Defendant's [k] Innocence; as where it finds him Not guilty on ſuch an Iſſue, on an Indictment or Appeal of any Felony whatſoever; or where it finds [l] him guilty of Homicide *ſe defendendo*, or *per infortunium*, on an Indictment of Murder. But it hath been adjudged, [m] That where a Demurrer by an Appellant to a Tender of Battel, or to a Plea, hath been adjudged againſt him, yet the Appellee may be afterwards arraigned at the Suit of the King.

Sect. 7. It is ſaid by Sir *Matthew Hale* in the [n] Chapter of *Autrefoits acquit*, That an Acquittal by Battel in an Appeal is no Bar of an Indictment. But I find no other Authority to this Point but a Note in *Fitzherbert* [o] of a Caſe to this Purpoſe in the Time of King *Edward* the Second. To which it may be anſwered, That this Matter is only ſpoken of incidentally, and not adjudged. And that *Staundforde* in the ſame Place [p] where he cites it, makes a *Quære*, whether it be Law or not. And it is expreſly holden by *Bracton*, [q] That an Appellee who vanquiſhes the Appellant in Battel, ſhall go quit not only from all other Appeals, *but alſo from the Suit of the King; becauſe by this he clears his Innocence againſt all, in the ſame Manner, as if he had put himſelf upon his Country, and his Country had acquitted him.* Alſo it is admitted by Sir *Matthew Hale* in the

Chapter

[a] Vide ſupra ch. 23. ſect. 55, 56.

[b] 2 Ric. 3. 14. a. Bro. Appeal, 121. Vide infra ch. 36. ſect. 7.

[c] Co. Litt. 146. a. 2 Ri. 3. 14. 15.

[d] 3 Inſt. 213. H. P. C. 246. 2 H. H. P. C. 246.

[e] S. P. C. 105. Letter A. H. P. C. 244. Bro. Coro. 11.

[f] Kely. 30, 52.

[g] Ch. 23. ſect. 129, 130, 131.

[h] 11 H. 4. 41. pl. 6. Abridged Fitz. Monſtrans de faits, 128. Bro. Coro. 29. Appeal, 33. Variance, 31. Vide S. P. C. 106. Lett. B.

[i] 2 H. H. P. C. 246. See the next Section.

[k] S. P. C. 169. a.

[l] 3 Inſt. 213. Crompt. Juſt. 111. pl. 6. 4 Co. 46. b.

[m] Dy. 120. pl. 13. Crompt. Juſt. 112. pl. 18.

[n] H. P. C. 245. 2 H. H. P. C. 249.

[o] Fitz. Coro. 375.

[p] S. P. C. 106. Letter D.

[q] Lib. 3. ch. 19 ſect. 8.

[a] Chapter of *Indictments*, That if an Approver be vanquiſhed in Battel joined on his Appeal, he ſhall be hanged, and the Appellee diſcharged, without being arraigned at the Suit of the King. Alſo it hath been [b] adjudged, That upon ſuch a Vanquiſhment the Appellee is intitled to his Damages againſt the Appellant, as being *legitimo modo acquietatus*, which ſeems [c] neceſſarily to imply that he is finally acquitted as well againſt the King as againſt the Party.

Sect. 8. As to the fourth Particular, *viz.* How far it is neceſſary that the Indictment or Appeal in the Record of Acquittal be free from Error, and well commenced: I take it to be ſettled [d] at this Day, [e] That where-ever the Indictment, or Appeal, whereon a Man is acquitted, is ſo far erroneous (either for want of Subſtance in ſetting out the Crime, or of Authority in the [f] Judge before whom it was taken,) that no good Judgment could have been given upon it againſt the Defendant, the Acquittal can be no Bar of a ſubſequent Indictment or Appeal, becauſe in Judgment of Law the Defendant was never in Danger of his Life from the firſt; for the Law will preſume *prima facie* that the Judges would not have given a Judgment, which would have been liable to have been reverſed. But if there be no Error in the Indictment or Appeal, but [g] only in the Proceſs, it ſeems agreed, That the Acquittal will be a good Bar of a ſubſequent Proſecution, notwithſtanding ſuch Error; the beſt Reaſon whereof ſeems to be this, That ſuch Error is [h] ſalved by the Appearance.

Sect. 9. It ſeems agreed, [i] That an Acquittal on an Appeal brought by one who had no Right to bring it, as by any other Woman [k] except the Wife of the deceaſed, or by any other Man [l] except the next Heir, is no more a Bar to an Appeal by another Appellant, or to an Indictment, than an Acquittal on an inſufficient Appeal or Indictment would have been.

Sect. 10. As to the fifth Particular, *viz.* Whether an Acquittal in any Court which has a Juriſdiction, be ſufficient for this Purpoſe: Notwithſtanding the [m] Opinion in the Book of *Aſſizes*, That no Acquittal in any other Court can be any Bar to a Proſecution in the Court of King's Bench, becauſe that is the Higheſt Court, I take it to be ſettled [n] at this Day, That an Acquittal in any Court whatſoever, which has a Juriſdiction of the Cauſe, is as good a Bar of any ſubſequent Proſecution for the ſame Crime, as an Acquittal in the Higheſt Court. And therefore it hath been adjudged, [o] That an Acquittal of Murder at a Grand Seſſions in *Wales*, may be plead to an Indictment for the ſame Murder in *England*. For the [p] Rule is, That a Man's Life ſhall not be brought into Danger for the ſame Offence more than once.

[a] H.P.C.200. 2 H.H.P.C. 233, 234. Vide ſupra ch. 25. ſect. 10. Letter t. 21 H. 6. 34. pl. 1. S.P.C. 168. Letter B. [b] Fitz. Coro. 98. S.P.C. 168. Letter E. Supra ch. 23. ſect. 140. [c] S.P.C.169. Supra ch. 23. ſect. 140. [d] 4 Co. 45. a. 47. a. H.P.C.244, 245. 2 H.H.P.C. 248, 251. 3 Inſt. 214. Fitz. Coro. 444. Supra ch. 23. ſect. 140. Crompt. Juſt. 112. pl. 14, 15, 16, 19. 20 H. 7. 11. b. 12 a. 9 H.5.2.pl.7. Abridged Bro. Appeal, 39. Coro. 35. Fitz. Cor. 68. [e] But Staundforde ſeems to be of Opinion, That an Acquittal on an erroneous Appeal, is a good Bar to an Indictment till it be reverſed by Error. S.P.C. 106. Lett. B. cited in Crompt. Juſt. 112. pl.15. But this ſeems repugnant to all other Books, and to what is ſaid by Staundforde himſelf, in the very ſame Page. Indeed in the ſecond Edition of Hale's Pleas of the Crown, there is a Note to the ſame Effect with what is ſaid in Staundforde; but this is manifeſtly miſprinted, and the Word Acquit put for Attaint. [f] Crompt. Juſt. 111. pl. 4, 5. Supra ch. 9. ſect. 15, 16. 4 Co. 46. [g] Fitz. Coro. 444. 9 H. 5. 2. pl. 7. Abridged Bro. Appeal, 39. Coro. 35. Fitz. Coro. 68. S. P. C. 106. Letter B. 169. Letter A. Crompt. Juſt. 112. pl. 15. 2 H. H. P. C. 248. [h] Supra ch. 27. ſect. 107. [i] 20 H. 7. 11. b. 12. a. 21 H. 6. 28. b. 29. a. Abridged Bro. Appeal, 41. Crompt. Juſt. 112. pl. 14. S. P. C. 106. Letter B. H. P. C. 245. 2 H. H. P. C. 249. [k] Supra ch. 23. ſect. 36, 37, 38. [l] Supra ch. 23. ſect. 39, 40, 41, 42. [m] 9 Aſſ. pl. 15. [n] 4 Co. 45. b. Raſt. Ent. 385. pl. 4. 11 H. 4. 41. pl. 6. Abridged Fitz. Monſtrans de faits, 128. 25 E. 3. 44. pl. 16. Abridged Fitz. Coro. 136. 41 Aſſ. pl. 9. Abridged Bro. Coro. 120 or 121. Crompt. Juſt. 112. pl. 8. Fitz. Coro. 220. [o] 1 Lev. 118. 1 Sid. 179. Supra ch. 25. ſect. 41, 42. [p] Supra ſect. 1, 8, 9.

Sect. 11. As to the sixth Particular, *viz.* How far an Acquittal of a Person as Principal will bar a subsequent Prosecution against him as Accessary; *& è converso*, how far an Acquittal of a Man as Accessary will bar a Prosecution against him as Principal: It seems to be [a] settled at this [b] Day, That an Acquittal of a Man as Principal is no Bar of a subsequent Prosecution against him as Accessary after the Fact, because such Acquittal clears him only of the Charge of having committed the Fact, which being a Crime entirely different from that of receiving him that hath committed it, there seems no more Reason that the Acquittal of it should Bar a Prosecution for the Receipt, than if they were Offences that bore no Manner of Relation to one another. But it is [c] holden in many Books of good Authority, (contrary to what is admitted [d] to have been the ancient Law,) that the Acquittal of a Man as Principal is a good Bar of a subsequent Prosecution against him as Accessary before; for it is said, That such an Accessary is in some Measure [e] guilty of the Fact, and therefore that an Acquittal which clears a Man from being guilty of the Fact, doth by Consequence clear him from being such an Accessary. And this seems reasonable upon the Supposition that a Man may be found guilty of an Indictment against him as Principal, upon Evidence which only proves him to have been an Accessary before. But if a Man cannot be found guilty of such an Indictment upon such Evidence, as it is strongly [f] holden that he cannot, it may with great Reason be said, that the Acquittal of him as Principal no way acquits him as Accessary before; for if so, he might save himself by a mere Slip in the Indictment, and bar all other Prosecutions by an Acquital on a Trial, which in Truth never brought him into [g] Danger of his Life. And it is upon this Supposition, as I suppose, that it is holden in some [h] Books, contrary to those abovecited, that one who has been acquitted as Principal may be tried Aagain as cceffary before, as well as after.

Sect. 12. But it seems [i] agreed, that an Acquittal of a Man as Accessary before, or after, is no Bar to a subsequent Prosecution against him as Principal.

Sect. 13. Also it hath been holden, that an Acquittal of a Man as Accessary to one Principal, will not save him from being arraigned afterwards as Accessary to another in the same Fact; but for this I shall refer to *Chap.* 29. *Sect.* 46.

Sect. 14. As to the seventh Particular, *viz.* How far the Law is altered in these Respects as to an Indictment by 3 *H.* 7. 1. It seems agreed, [k] That by the Common Law an Acquittal on an Indictment might be pleaded in Bar of an Appeal of Death, in the same Manner as an Acquittal of any other Felony might be pleaded in Bar of a subsequent Prosecution, and therefore in Favour of Appeals a general Practice was introduced, [l] not to try any Person on an Indictment of Death, till after

[a] Kely. 25, 26. H. P. C. 244. 2 H. H. P. C. 244. S. P. C. 105. Lett. A. Cromp. Just. 42. pl. 18. 112. pl. 7. 27 Ass. pl. 10. Abridged Fitz. Coro. 200. Bro. Coro. 105. Lamb. B. 2. ch. 7.

[b] Cont. Fitz. Coro. 282.

[c] S. P. C. 44. Lett. C. 105. Lett. A. B. Kely. 25, 26. Lamb. B. 2. ch. 7. H. P. C. 224. 244. 2 H. H. P. C. 244. Crompt. Just. 42. pl. 18. 112. pl. 7. But the Principal Authority in the old Book is 2 E. 3. 20. pl. 14. Abridged Fitz. Coro. 150. which seems inconsistent with it self; for the Words are for an Example, that a Man may in such Case be twice put to answer, We award that you go quit. And Fitz. Coro. 282. is contradicted by all other Books; for it says, That a Man acquitted as Principal, cannot be so much as arraigned as an Accessary after. And 27 Ass. pl. 10. Abridged Bro. Coro. 105. and Fitz. Coro. 200. extend only to the Case of an Accessary after. And 8 H. 5. 6. pl. 26. Abridged Fitz. Coro. 463. expresly goes upon the Supposition, that a Man may be found guilty as Principal, upon Evidence which only proves him Accessary. [d] S. P. C. 105. Lett. B. Fitz. Coro. 424. 2 H. H. P. C. 244. [e] Vide supra ch. 29. sect. 13, 14. [f] H. P. C. 266. Keilw. 107. Dalis. 14. [g] Vide supra sections 1, 8, 9, 10. [h] Keilw. 107. Dalis. 14. Lamb. B. 2 ch. 7. [i] Crompton's Justice 43. pl. 30. Bro. Coro. 186. [k] Vide supra ch. 25. sect. 15. 21 H. 6. 28, 29. Abridged Bro. Appeal 41. 44 E. 3. 25. pl. 36. Abridged Bro. App. 12. H. P. C. 244, 245. 47 E. 3. 16. pl. 27. Abridged Fitz. Coro. 104. Bro. Appeal, 33, 35, 102. 2 Leon. 161. But this is made a Quære, 17 Ass. pl. 1. [l] Vide supra ch. 25. sect. 15. Crompt. Justice 111. pl. 2, 3. Kely. 95, 96, 97, 98. 2 Leon. 161. H. P. C. 244, 245. S. P. C. 107. Lett. A. Bro. Appeal, 9. 32 Ass. pl. 8. Abridged Bro. Appeal 119. 45 E. 3. 25. pl. 36. Abridged Bro. Appeal, 12. 11 H. 4. 94. pl. 56. Abridged Bro. Appeal, 36, 41 Ass. pl. 14. Abridged Bro. Appeal, 75.

the Year and Day had been paſſed, by which Time it often happened that all was forgotten; and *for Reformation thereof it is enacted, That if any Man be ſlain or Murdered, and thereof the Slayers, Murderers, Abettors, Maintainers and Comforters of the ſame, be indicted, that the ſame Slayers and Murderers, and all other Acceſſaries of the ſame, be arraigned and determined of the ſame Felony and Murder at any Time at the King's Suit, within the Year after the ſame Felony and Murder done, and not tarry the Year and Day for any Appeal to be taken for the ſame Felony or Murder. And if it happen any Perſon named as Principal or Acceſſary to be acquitted of any ſuch Murder at the King's Suit, within the Year and Day, that then the ſame Juſtices afore whom he is acquitted, ſhall not ſuffer him to go at large, but* [a] *either to remit him again to the Priſon, or elſe to let him to Bail after their Diſcretion till that Year and Day be paſſed. And if it fortune the ſame Felons or Murderers, and Acceſſaries ſo arraigned or any of them to be acquit, or the Principal of the ſaid Felony, or any of them to be attainted, the Wife or next Heir to him ſo ſlain, as ſhall require, may take and have their Appeal of the ſame Death and Murder, within the Year and Day after the ſame Felony and Murder done, againſt the ſaid Perſons ſo arraigned and acquit, and all other their Acceſſaries, or againſt the Acceſſaries of the ſaid Principal, or any of them, ſo attainted, or againſt the ſaid Principals ſo attainted, if they be on live, and the Benefit of his Clergy thereof before not had; and that the Apellant ſhall have ſuch and like Advantage, as if the ſaid Acquittal or Attainder had not been, the ſaid Acquittal or Attainder notwithſtanding* [b].

[a] Vide ſupra ch. 33. S. 121. F. N. B. 251. Lett. G. Crompt. Juſt. 111. pl. 2. 3.

[b] Vide S. P. C. 107. and Raſt. Statutes, Title Murder, 2.

Sect. 15. It ſeems [c] agreed, That this Statute ſhall not be conſtrued to extend to any other Appeal but of Death, nor to any other Acquittal but upon an Indictment; from whence it follows, That an Acquittal on an Indictment, or Appeal, for any other [d] Felony except Death, may ſtill be pleaded in Bar of an Appeal for the ſame Crime, and that an Acquital on an Appeal of Death [e] may ſtill be pleaded in Bar of an Indictment, in the ſame Manner as by the Common Law.

Sect. 16. How far a Perſon found guilty of Manſlaughter, or of Homicide *ſe defendendo*, on an Indictment of Murder, is liable to be tried again upon an Appeal by Force of this Statute, ſhall be conſidered in the next Chapter.

[c] H. P. C. 244, 245. 2 H. H. P. C. 250. S. P. C. 107. Lett. A.

[d] H. P. C. 244, 245. S. P. C. 107. Lett. A.

[e] H. P. C. 244, 245. S. P. C. 107. Lett. A. Crompton's Juſtice, 111. pl. 2, 3.

CHAP. XXXVI.

Of the Plea of Autrefoits attaint *or* convict.

Sect. 1. IT ſeems to be generally agreed, [a] That where-ever a Man is attained of Felony, either by Judgment upon a Verdict, or by [b] Outawry, or Abjuration, whether upon an Indictment or Appeal, he may plead ſuch Attainder to any ſubſequent Indictment or Appeal, for the ſame or any other Felony. And two Reaſons are given for ſuch Plea to a ſecond Proſecution for the ſame Felony; Firſt, [c] Becauſe the Life of the Defendant was in Danger by the firſt; and it is againſt a Maxim of Law to bring a Man into ſuch Danger more than once for one and the ſame Offence: 2dly, [d] Becauſe generally the proceeding in ſuch ſecond Proſecution cannot be to any Purpoſe, becauſe the Party is dead in Law by the firſt Attainder, and hath forfeited all that he can forfeit, and therefore it is ſaid, That it is equally abſurd to attaint him a [e] ſecond Time, as to attempt to kill one who is already dead. And this is the only [f] Reaſon I find any where given for the Plea of *Autrefoits attaint* of one Felony to a Proſecution for another. But where both of theſe Reaſons fail in the firſt Caſe, and the latter of them in the ſecond; and alſo in ſome other Caſes, for ſpecial Reaſons, the Plea of *Autrefoits attaint* ſeems to be of little Effect, as in the following Inſtances.

Sect. 2. Firſt, where the firſt Attainder is reverſed for Error, after which it can neither be pleaded to a Proſecution for the ſame or any other Felony; becauſe by ſuch Reverſal the Attainder is of no [g] more Force than if it had never been: And if an Acquittal on an erroneous Indictment or Appeal will not bar a ſubſequent Proſecution, ſurely *a fortiori* an Attainder reverſed will not do it. But it is agreed to be a good Bar while it ſtands unreverſed, becauſe it is not void but voidable only.

Sect. 3. *Secondly*, Where the Attainder was at the Suit of the King and [h] pardoned, and after the Party is proſecuted upon an Appeal; for it is an allowed Maxim, that the King cannot bar the Suit of the Subject, and if he cannot bar an Appeal by pardoning the Offender before it appear whether he be guilty or innocent, there cannot but be much leſs Reaſon that he ſhould bar it after the Guilt appears by a Judgment upon Record.

[a] H.P.C.247. 2 H. H. P. C. 251, 252. S. P. C. 107. Lett. B. 12 Co. 100. 6 Co. 13. b. 3 Inſt. 213, 214. Supra ch. 23. ſect. 38.
[b] Yet this is made a Quære 28 E. 3. 90. pl. 3. but no Notice is taken of the Quære in the Abridgment of the Caſe in Fitz. Coro. 136. Vide 18 H.8. 2 pl. 12. 12 Co. 100.
[c] 9 H. 7. 19. pl. 14. Abridged Bro. Appeal, 89. Coro. 11.
[d] S. P. C. 107. Lett. B. H. P. C. 247. 12 Co. 100. Cro. El. 516. Cromp. 113. pl. 1.
[e] Bro. App.9. 44 E. 3. 44. pl. 57. Abridged Fitz.Coro.95. 6H.4.6.pl.29. Abridged Fitz. Coro. 227. Bro. Appeal, 10. Popham 107. 7. H. 4. 31. pl. 16. Fitz. Eſcheat, 14. Bro. Coro. 11. Fitz. Coro. 81, 95. Cont. 4 E. 4. 11. pl. 18. Fitz. Coro. 27. See the Chapter of Judgment.
[f] See the Books cited to the precedent Lett.
[g] S. P. C. 106. Lett. B. 12 Co. 100. H. P. C. 247. 4 Co. 45. a.
[h] Bro. Coro. 11. 28 E. 3. 90. pl. 3. Abridged Fitz. Coro. 139. S. P. C. 107. Lett. B. 3 Inſt. 213. Crompton's Juſtice 113. pl. 3. 6 H. 4. 6. pl. 29. Abridged Fitz. Coro. 227. Bro. Appeal, 10. cont. 12 Co. 100.

Sect. 4. *Thirdly*, Where a Perſon attainted of Felony, is afterwards indicted of High Treaſon, whether before or after his [a] Attainder; for the Judgment of Death in High Treaſon is not only different from that in Felony, but the Forfeiture is alſo more general, (extending to Land in Tail as well as to Land in Fee-ſimple, ſince [b] the Statutes of 26 *H.* 8. 13. and 33 *H.* 8. 20.) But if the Felony were firſt committed, it ſeems [c] agreed, That the Title of Eſcheat to the Felons Lands in Fee-ſimple, veſted in the Lords of whom they are holden from the Time of the Felony, ſhall not be deveſted by the ſubſequent Attainder for the Treaſon, as it would be if the Treaſon had been firſt committed.

Sect. 5. *Fourthly*, Where an Appellee of Larceny hath a ſecond Appeal brought againſt him hanging the firſt, and afterwards is attainted in the firſt, in which Caſe, according to ſome [d] Opinions the Court may, in order to entitle the ſecond Apellant to a Reſtitution, inquire by an Inqueſt of Office, and according to others [e] by an Inqueſt taken at the Miſe of the Parties, whether ſuch Apellee be guilty of the Larceny or not. And the Law ſeems to be the ſame in Relation to an Indictment of [f] Larceny ſince the Statute of 21 *H.* 8. 11. which entitles the Proſecutor to a Reſtitution of his Goods, upon the Offender's being found guilty, &c. in the ſame Manner as upon an Appeal. Alſo it hath been [g] adjudged, that a Perſon attainted is as liable to anſwer a Perſonal Action, as if he had not been attainted. For otherwiſe his Attainder would give him a Privilege and Protection, which the Law is far from intending in allowing the Plea of *Autrefoits attaint* to a ſecond Proſecution for a new Crime, which is chiefly grounded on this Reaſon, that the Law will not ſuffer an abſurd and vain Thing in attainting one who is attainted already.

Sect. 6. *Fifthly*, Where a Perſon attainted of one Felony, is afterwards proſecuted as a Principal in another, and others are alſo proſecuted together with him as his Acceſſaries, in which Caſe it is ſaid, [h] That for the Benefit of Publick Juſtice he is compellable to plead, &c. to the ſecond Proſecution in the ſame Manner as if he had not been attainted, becauſe otherwiſe the Acceſſaries to ſuch ſecond Felonies could not [i] be brought to their Trials for want of a Conviction of their Principal.

Sect. 7. It ſeems [k] clear, That a Judgment againſt a Man on an Indictment or Action of Treſpaſs, is no Bar to an Indictment or Appeal of Larceny, for the ſame taking, becauſe Treſpaſs and Larceny are Offences of a different Nature, and the Judgment for the one entirely differs from that for the other. Alſo I take it to be in a great Meaſure [l] agreed, That the Judgment of *Pain fort & dure* in one Felony is no Bar to a Proſecution for another; becauſe ſuch Judgment neither corrupts the Blood, nor forfeits the Lands, as an Attainder doth. But it ſeems queſtionable, whether it may not bar a ſecond Proſecution for the ſame Felony, becauſe the Life of the Party was brought into Danger by the firſt.

Sect. 8. It is [m] ſaid, That *Autrefoits attaint* or *convict* was no Plea for one who had broken the Priſon of the Ordinary; but for this I ſhall refer to the Books cited, *Ch.* 33. *Sect.* 9, 10.

[a] 1 H. 6. 5. 22. Abridged Bro. Treaſon, 11. Fitz. Coro. 2. 3 Inſt. 213. Poph. 107. H. P. C. 213. 214. 2 H. H. P. C. 252. And the Obſervation to the contrary in 2 Inſt. 590. and S. P. C. 107. Lett. B. Crompt. Juſt. 113. pl. 2. on the above cited Year-Book of H. 6. 5. to the plain Purport of it ſeems repugnant.

[b] Co. Lit. 372, 392. See the chapter of Forfeiture.

[c] 3 Inſt. 213. S. P. C. 137. Lett. B.

[d] Vide ſupra ch. 23. ſect. 53. and ch. 28. ſect. 7. 2 H. H. P. C. 252. Fitz. Coro. 379. 7 H. 4. 31. pl. 16. Abridged Fitz. Coro. 81. Bro. Appeal, 21. Vide 44 E. 3. 44. pl. 57. Abridged Bro. Appeal, 11. Fitz. Coro. 95.

[e] 4 E. 4. 11. pl. 18. S. P. C. 66. Lett. E. H. P. C. 212. 248. Bro. Appeal, 93. Fitz. Coro. 26. Vide 6 Ed. 4. 4. Abridged Bro. Coro. 147.

[f] Vide ſupra ch. 23. ſect. 55, 56. H. P. C. 212, 248. [g] 3. Inſt. 213, 215. Cro. El. 516. cont. Cro. El. 213. [h] Poph. 107. [i] Vide ſupra ch. 29. from ſect. 36. to ſect. 45. [k] Vide ſupra ch. 35. ſect. 5. 7 H. 4. 35. pl. 4. Fitz. Coro. 82. [l] 3 Inſt. 213. Crompt. Juſt. 113. pl. 4. Dy. 308. pl. 73. [m] S. P. C. 31, 32.

Sect. 9. It is certain that an Attainder on an Indictment of Death is no Bar to an Appeal, by Reason of 3 *H.* 7. 1. set forth more at large in the precedent Chapter, which gives an Appeal against Persons attainted of Death, the Benefit of Clergy thereof being not had, as it is certain that it cannot at this Day. But it seems [a] agreed, That in all other Cases the Plea of *Autrefoits attaint* is still of the same Force as it was by the Common Law.

Sect. 10. The Plea of *Autrefoits convict* seems chiefly to depend on this Reason, [b] That the Party ought [c] not to be brought twice into Danger of his Life for the same Crime. Upon which Ground it seems [d] agreed, That a Conviction on an Appeal or Indictment of Burglary, or other Felony, may be pleaded to an Indictment or Appeal for the same Felony: And that a Conviction of Manslaughter in an Appeal of Death may be pleaded in Bar of a subsequent Indictment or Appeal of the same Death; and that the Reason why such a Conviction on an Indictment of Death cannot be pleaded to an Appeal as well as to an Indictment (unless the Person so convicted be admitted to his Clergy, or at least have prayed it,) [e] depends entirely on 3 *H.* 7. 1. which expressly giving an Appeal against a Person attainted on an Indictment of Death, who hath not had his Clergy, cannot but be thought to give it as well against a Person convicted, since every Attainder includes a Conviction and more; and it is wholly owing to the Default of the Court which shall not prejudice any one, that a Person convicted is not attainted [f]. But I do not find any Authority that a Conviction of one Felony may be pleaded in Bar of another; but on the contrary it is plain, That it was anciently the usual [g] Practice, where a Clerk was indicted of several Felonies, and tried and convicted of one of them, and demanded by the Ordinary, not to deliver him upon such Demand, but to detain him in Prison till he had been arraigned of all the Felonies whereof he stood indicted. Also it seems [h] agreed, That even after the Statute of 25 *E.* 3. 5. *de clero*, a Clerk convict of one Felony, might immediately, while he stood at the Bar, be arraigned of any other.

Sect. 11. But it seems to be admitted [i] as a general Rule, That after a Clerk convict was once delivered to the Ordinary, he could not afterwards be impeached either for the same, or any other Felony committed before such Delivery to the Ordinary, whether it were within the Benefit of Clergy or not: And tho' this be so far remedied [k] by 8 *El.* 4. and 18 *El.* 7. That a Person admitted to his Clergy, for any Felony, shall not in Respect thereof bar a subsequent Prosecution for another Felony not within the Benefit of Clergy; yet, as I take it, the Law generally still continues as it was, as to the Felony whereof the Party who is admitted to his Clergy is convicted, and also as to other Felonies within the Benefit of Clergy committed before such Admittance, whereof it seems agreed, That regularly one admitted to his Clergy shall not be afterwards arraigned.

Sect. 12. It seems to have been long settled, That not only he who hath been admitted [l] to his Clergy on a Conviction of Manslaughter, upon an Indictment of Murder, but also that he who being called to Judgment on such a Conviction, hath [m] prayed his Clergy, but hath not

[a] H.P.C. 247. 2 H. H. P.C. 250, 251.
[b] Vide supra sect. 1.
[c] Vide 4 Co. 39. b. 40. a. 47. a. 2 Leon. 83.
[d] 4 Co. 39. b. 40. a. 2 Leon. 83. Crompt. Just. 113. pl. 5. Kely. 94, 98. 4 Co. 46. 1 Salk. 62, 63. Cro. Ca. 147.
[e] Vide 1 And. 68. 4 Co. 46. 3 Mod. 156, 157. Infra sect. 17.
[f] Vide S. P. C. 108. Lett. A. H.P. C. 247. 248. Crompt. Just. 113.
[g] Fitz. Coro. 394, 461. S. P. C. 108. Letter A. Supra ch. 33. sect. 117. See the Preamble of 25 E. 3. 5.
[h] S.P.C. 108. Letter A. Dyer 215. pl. 49.
[i] Dyer 214, 215. H. P. C. 248, 249. Supra ch. 33. sect. 117 to 121. 18 H. 8. 2. pl. 12. 3 Inst. 131. Kely. 93, 103. Crompt. Just. 113. pl. 8, 9, 10. Fitz. Coro. 232.
[k] Vide supra ch. 33 from sect. 121 to 130.
[l] 4 Co. 40. Wetherel's Case, 45. b. 46. Crompt. Just. 102. pl. 10. Vide Cro. Ja. 282. Yelv. 204, 205. 1 Bulst. 241. See the Cases cited to the next Letter.
[m] 2 Leon. 160, 161. 1 And. 68. 4 Co. 45. b. 46. a. Kely. 93, &c. 3 Inst. 161. Co. Ent. 55. b. Salk. 63. 2 H. H. P. C. 250, 390. This is left doubtful, 2 Rol. Rep. 478.

been actually admitted to it, may bar any subsequent Appeal for the same Death, as he might by the Common Law. And so to the Objection from the seeming Absurdity, that if the Law be so, he that hath his Clergy on a Conviction of Manslaughter will be in a better Case than if he had been wholly acquitted, it may be answered, That this doth not depend on any Reasoning from the Nature of the Thing, but from the Statute of 3 *H.* 7. 1. which expresly takes away the Plea of *Autrefoits acquit* in this Case, but by suffering even Persons attainted on an Indictment of Death, who have been admitted to their Clergy to plead such Admission in Bar of an Appeal, plainly seems to have intended to leave the Benefit of Clergy, as it stood before.

Sect. 13. Also it hath been adjudged, [a] That it is not material whether the Appeal, in Bar whereof such Conviction and Clergy are pleaded, were depending at the Time of such Conviction or not; since the Judges [b] may, if they think fit in their Discretion, proceed on an Indictment of Death, notwithstanding an Appeal thereof be depending; and therefore as on the one Side the Party is liable to be hanged, if found guilty of Murder on a Verdict against him on such Indictment, pending an Appeal, it cannot but be equitable, that on the other Side he should have the full Benefit of the Verdict, if found in his Favour.

[a] Salk. 63. Kely. 91, 92, 94, 104, 107, 108. But the contrary seems to be holden in 3 Inst. 131.
[b] Supra ch. 25. sect. 15. and the Notes to ch. 35. sect. 14. Kely. 94, 95, 96, 97, 98.

Sect. 14. But there have been many [c] Opinions, That unless the Court call a Man to Judgment on a Conviction of Manslaughter on an Indictment of Murder, he cannot demand the Privilege of his Clergy, and consequently cannot plead such Conviction and Clergy thereon had or prayed, in Bar of an Appeal. And accordingly it was solemnly resolved [d] by all the Judges, except one, in the latter End of the Reign of King *James* the second, That the Court might delay the Calling a Convict to Judgment, to hinder him from praying his Clergy, (especially if an Appeal be depending,) in Order to make him liable to an Appeal. But the contrary seems [e] to be fully settled in the Case of *Armstrong* and *Lisle*, wherein it was adjudged upon great Deliberation, That a Conviction of Manslaughter on an Indictment of Murder, and the [f] Prayer of Clergy thereupon, may be pleaded in Bar of an Appeal of the same Death, whether such Prayer were made upon the Party's being called to Judgment or not. For it seems to be [g] admitted, even by those of the contrary Opinion, That the Delay of the Court in not admitting a Man to his Clergy who prays it when called to Judgment, shall no Way prejudice him, but that he may bar an Appeal by pleading a Conviction and Prayer of Clergy as much as if he had been actually admitted to it. And why should it be more reasonable that the Delay of the Court in not calling a Man to Judgment, shall put it in the Power of the Court to make so high a Privilege in Favour of Life, wholly precarious and discretionary? To which may be added, That a Demand of Clergy by a Convict before he is called to Judgment, seems in Strictness to be as legal as a Demand after a Call to Judgment; since whenever a Person appears to have a Right to his Clergy, as he seems plainly to do, when his Crime is found to be such as is within the Benefit of it, it seems a necessary Consequence that he has a Right to pray it. And it seems [h] agreed, That by the ancient Common Law, Clergy might be demanded upon the Prisoner's first Arraignment. And tho' afterwards for special Reasons, the Judges made it a Rule not to admit any one to it till after he had pleaded; yet I find it no where holden in the old

[c] 1 Sid. 316. Carth. 17, 18. Kely. 106. Vide Dyer 214. pl. 48. 215. pl. 49. 296. pl. 60.
[d] 3 Mod. 156, 157, 158. Kely. 106.
[e] Skin. 670, 671. Carth. 394, 395. Kely. 93. 103, 104, 105, 107. Salk. 62, 63.
[f] But Note, That in this Case the Party was actually admitted to his Clergy in the King's Bench.
[g] Vide supra sect. 12. 1 And. 68. 4 Co. 45, 46. Kely. 105. Salk. 63.
[h] Supra ch. 33. sect. 110. 111.

Books, That a Man could not legally demand it till called to Judgment. Neither doth the [a] Opinion to the contrary, in the Report of the Case of *Armstrong* and *Lisle*, grounded upon the Authority of [b] *Searl*'s Case, seem to be at all made out by that Case.

[a] 1 Salk. 63. Kely. 105.
[b] Hob. 289.

Sect. 15. But it seems clearly settled, That whenever the Record on which a Man is convicted of Manslaughter, and admitted to his Clergy, on an Indictment or Appeal of Murder, is erroneous, either in Respect of Insufficiency [c] in the Indictment or Appeal, or for a [d] Mis-trial, *&c.* so that his Life was not in Danger at the Trial, *&c.* he cannot plead such Conviction and Clergy thereon had, in Bar of a second Indictment or Appeal.

[c] 4 Co. 39. b. 40. a. 47. a. Crompt. Just. 111. pl. 4, 5.
[d] 6 Co. 14. b.

Sect. 16. It hath been adjudged, [e] That the Conclusion of a Plea of *Autrefoits convict* of Manslaughter, and Clergy thereon, *&c.* may be either *petit judicium si prædict' A. B. iterum de eadem morte, de qua semel convictus est, respondere compelli debeat*; or thus, [f] *petit judicium si prædict' A. B. appellum suum prædict' versus eum de morte prædict' habere seu manutenere debeat.*

[e] 3 Inst. 131.
[f] Coke's Entr. 55. b. 3 Inst. 131.

Sect. 17. It is said [g] to have been adjudged in *Holcroft*'s Case, That a Verdict finding a Man guilty of Homicide *se defendendo* on an Indictment of Murder may be pleaded to an Appeal of the same Death; but this was certainly not the very Point [h] in Question in that Case; neither do I find it expresly taken Notice of in any Report of it. However, since it seems clear, That such a Conviction would be a good Bar of an Appeal at the Common [i] Law; and since it is not within the Letter of 3 *H.* 7. 1. which mentions only Persons acquitted or attainted, it shall not easily be construed to be within the Meaning of it, [k] being in this Respect a penal Statute, and derogatory from a Maxim of the Common Law in Favour of Life. And tho' it be in a great Measure [l] agreed, That the Statute in giving an Appeal against a Person attainted of Murder doth by necessary Consequence give it as well against one convict of Murder, because every Person attainted is convict and more; and if an Appeal should not lie against a Person convicted, until he were attainted, it would be wholly in the Power of the Court, by delaying to give Judgment on a Person convicted, to bar an Appeal. Yet since these Reasons hold not in the Case of one convict of *Homicide se defendendo* only, it may well be argued, That a Conviction thereof may still be a good Bar of an Appeal.

[g] Crompt. Just. 111. pl. 6.
[h] Coke's Ent. 55. 4 Co. 45. b. 46. 3 Leon. 160, 161. 3 Inst. 131.
[i] 1 And. 68.
[i] Vide supra sect. 10.
[k] Vide 3 Inst. 131. Kely. 104.
[l] 1 And. 68. 4 Co. 46. Supra sect. 10.

CHAP.

CHAP. XXXVII.

Of Pardon.

BEFORE I proceed to consider in what Manner a Pardon is to be taken Advantage of, it may not be improper to premise some Things concerning the Nature of Pardon in general, as,

1. By whom it is grantable.
2. Where it is grantable of Right.
3. What is the Nature of a Pardon of Grace.

Sect. 1. As to the first Point, *viz.* By whom a Pardon is grantable: It seems that anciently the Right of pardoning Offences within certain Districts was claimed by the Lords Marchers and others, who had *Jura regalia*, by ancient Grants [a] from the Crown, or by prescription; but it is enacted by 27 *H.* 8. 24. *Par.* 1. *That no Person or Persons, of what Estate or Degree soever they be, shall have Power to pardon or remit any Treasons or Felonies whatsoever, nor any Accessaries to the same, nor any Outlawries for such Offences, whether committed in* England *or* Wales, *or the Marches of the same; but that the King shall have the whole and sole Power and Authority thereof united and knit to the Imperial Crown of this Realm, as of good Right and Equity it appertaineth.*

[a] See the Statute of 27 H. 8. ch. 24. Co. Litt. 114. b. Crompt. Just. 116. pl. 19. S. P. C. 104. Letter C. 3 Inst. 233.

As to the second Point, *viz.* Where a Pardon is grantable of Right, I shall endeavour to shew where it is to be so granted.

1. To Persons found guilty of excusable Homicide.
2. To an Approver who hath convicted an Appellee.
3. To Robbers, Clippers, Burglars, &c. who shall discover two or more guilty of Robbery, &c.

Sect. 2. And first, As to Persons found guilty of excusable Homicide, it is enacted by the Statute of *Gloucester* 9. *That in Case it be found by the Country, that a Person tried for the Death of a Man, did it in his Defence or by Misfortune, then by the Report* [b] *of the Justices to the King, the King shall take him to his Grace, if it please him.* By which at first Sight it seems to be implied, That it is left to the Discretion of the King, whether he will grant a Pardon in such Case or not. And agreeably hereto it is said in four several Notes [c] in *Fitzherbert*'s *Abridgment* of Cases in the Time of *Edward* 3. That a Person found guilty of Homicide *se defendendo* is to be remitted to Prison in Order to attend the King's Grace: And yet in two other Notes of [d] Cases in the very same Year, it is said,

[b] For the Form of a Certiorari in such Case, and a Pardon thereon, See Register 190.

[c] Fitz. Coro. 284, 286. 287, 354. Also Fitz. Coro. 305. and 44 Ed. 3. 44. pl. 55. Abr. Fitz. Coro. 94. and 2 H. 4. 18. pl. 5. Abr. Bro. Forfeiture, 9. are to the same Purpose.

[d] Fitz. Coro. 297, 361.

That in such a Case, if the Prisoner cause the Record to come into the Chancery, the Chancellor will make him a Charter of Pardon, without speaking to the King; and this seems to be [a] settled at this Day, and agreeable to the ancient [b] Common Law, which shall not without express Words be restrained by a Statute which seems to be made in Affirmance of it. And therefore these Words in the Statute, *If it shall please the King*, shall be taken as spoken only out of Reverence to him, and not as intended to make the Right of the Subject to such a Pardon precarious. And the Cases above-cited, which seem to be contrary, may be reconciled with the others, by intending them to mean only the Grant of the King's Pardon to a Person represented to him as guilty of Homicide *se defendendo* only, without any Certificate of the Verdict upon Record; for none of those Cases make any Mention of such Certificate, as the others do; and if there be no such Certificate, it seems plain that the Grant of a Pardon is a mere Matter of Favour. However it seems to have been always [c] agreed, That the Forfeiture of Goods by such Homicide may be saved by a Pardon, (which in this particular Case seems to purge the Offence *ab initio.*) And it hath been [d] adjudged, That such a Pardon is as necessary for one who is indicted only of Homicide *se defendendo* and confesses it, as for one who is found guilty of Homicide *se defendendo* on an Indictment of Murder. And if he were found guilty of having fled [e], &c. I question whether the Pardon will save the Forfeiture of the Goods by Reason of the Flight; for that is grounded not on the Homicide, but on the Contempt of the Law in not standing to it's Judgment.

Sect. 3. Secondly, In what Manner an Approver who convicts the Appellee is intitled to a Pardon, hath been already shewn, *Chap.* 24. *Sect.* 27.

Sect. 4. Thirdly, As to Robbers, Clippers and Coiners, and Burglars, &c. who shall discover two or more guilty of Robbery, &c. it is enacted by 4 & 5 *W. & M.* 8. *That if any Person or Persons, being out of Prison, shall after the 25th Day of* March, 1691. *commit any Robbery, and afterwards discover two or more, who then had, or afterwards shall commit any Robbery, so as two or more of the Persons discovered shall be convicted of such Robbery, any such Discoverer shall himself have, and is hereby entitled to the gracious Pardon of their Majesties, their Heirs and Successors for all Robberies which he or they shall have committed at any Time or Times before such Discovery made, which Pardon shall be likewise a good Bar to any Appeal brought for any such Robbery.*

Sect. 5. Also it is enacted by 6 & 7 *W.* 3. 17. *That if any Person or Persons, being out of Prison, shall after the first Day of* May, 1695. *be guilty of clipping, coining, counterfeiting, washing, filing, or otherwise diminishing the Coin of this Realm, and afterwards discover two or more who then had, or afterwards shall commit any of the said Crimes, so as two or more of the Persons discovered shall be convicted of the same, any such Discoverer shall himself have, and is hereby intitled to the gracious Pardon of his Majesty, his Heirs and Successors, for all such his Crimes, which he or they have committed at any Time or Times before such Discovery made.*

Sect. 6. Also it it is enacted by 10 & 11 *W.* 3. 23. (which excludes [f] all Persons from their Clergy who shall by Night or Day, in any Shop, Ware-house, Coach-house or Stable, privately and feloniously steal any Goods, Wares or Merchandizes, being of the Value of 5 *s.* or more, altho' such Shop, &c. be not actually broken open, and altho' no Person be therein, or shall

[a] S. P. C. 15. Lett. C. 16. Letter D. 2 Inst. 316, 317. H. P. C. 250. Book 1. ch. 29. sect. 24. Bro. Chart. de Pardon, 65. Keilw. 108. pl. 27.

[b] Vide Kelw. 122, 123. Bract. Lib. 3. cap. 17. Book 1. ch. 29. from sect. 19 to the end of the Chapter.

[c] See the Books cited to the other Parts of this Section, and 4 H. 7. 2. pl. 3. Abridged Fitz. Coro. 61. Bro. Coro. 138 or 139. Forfeit. 51. 2 H. 4. 18. pl. 6. Abridged Fitz. Coro. 69. Bro. Forfeit. 9.

[d] Keilw. 53. pl. 8. 4 H. 7. 2. pl. 3. Abridged Fitz. Coro. 61.

[e] Vide Fitz. Coro. 286, 287. and infra, in the Chapter of Falsifying Attainders.

[f] Vide supra ch. 33. sect. 64, 65.

assist, hire or command any Person to commit such Offence,) *That if any Person or Persons after the twentieth Day of* May, 1699. *shall commit any Burglary, House-breaking, or Felony in stealing of any Horse or Horses, or any Money, Wares or Goods, from whom the Benefit of Clergy is by the said Act taken away, and being out of Prison, shall discover two or more, who then had or after shall commit any such Burglary, Horse-stealing or Felony, as aforesaid, and shall be convicted thereof, or cause to be discovered and apprehended two or more, who shall be convicted, as aforesaid, every such Discoverer shall have, and is hereby intitled to his Majesty's most gracious Pardon for the Burglaries, House-breakings, Horse-stealings or Felonies as aforesaid, which he or she or they shall have committed at any Time or Times before such Discovery made; which Pardon shall be likewise a good Bar to an Appeal for any such Burglary,* &c.

Sect. 7. And it is farther enacted by 5 *Annæ*, 31. *Sect.* 4. *That every Person who shall be guilty of Burglary, or of the* [a] *felonious breaking and entering any House in the Day-time, and after shall discover two who shall have committed such Burglary or Felony, so as they be convict,* &c. *shall have* 40 l. &c. *and be entitled to a Pardon of all Burglaries and Felonies, except Murder and Treason; which Pardon shall be a Bar to an Appeal,* &c. [97] [98] ☞

[a] Vide ch. 33. from sect. 85 to sect. 106.

As to the third Point, *viz.* What is the Nature of a Pardon of Grace, I shall consider the following Particulars;

1. Where such Pardon is good in Law.
2. What is the Effect of it.
3. Whether it may be waived.

As to the first Point, *viz.* Where such a Pardon is good in Law, I shall consider.

1. What is required to make a good Pardon of Felony in general.
2. What is particularly required in a Pardon of Treason, Murder, or Rape.
3. How far the Pardon of one Man may discharge another.
4. How far it is necessary that the Pardon of several Persons for Felony, be several.
5. Whether the King's Grant of a Protection, or of a Place of Trust to a Traitor or Felon, carry with it an implied Pardon of his Crime.
6. What is required to make a good Pardon of Offences not capital.
7. Whether any Offence can be pardoned before it is committed.
8. Whether there be any Offence which cannot be pardoned after it is committed.
9. How far a Pardon may be of Force against the private Interest of the Subject.
10. Whether it may be conditional.
11. Where a Pardon is void in Respect of a wrong Recital.

Sect. 8. As to the first Particular, *viz.* What is required to make a good Pardon of Felony in general: It seems to be laid down as a general Rule in many Books, that where-ever it may be reasonably intended-ed that the King, when he granted such Pardon, was not fully [a] apprised both of the Heinousness of the Crime, and also how far the Party stands convicted thereof upon Record, the Pardon is void, as being gained by Imposition upon the King. And this is very agreeable to the Reason of the Law, which seems to have intrusted the King with this high Prerogative, upon a special Confidence that he will spare those only whose Case, could it have been foreseen, the Law it self may be presumed willing to have excepted out of its general Rules, which the Wit of Man cannot possibly make so perfect as to suit every particular Case. And upon this Ground it hath been holden, [b] that if one be indicted by these Words, that he had slain a Man for having sued him in the King's Court, and the King make him a Charter of all Manner of Felonies; this Charter shall not be allowed, because it shall be intended that the King was not acquainted with the Heinousness of the Crime, but deceived in his Grant. Also where one outlawed in an Appeal of Felony prayed his Clergy, which was counterpleaded on the Account of Bigamy, *&c.* and afterwards purchased a Pardon, and sued a *Scire facias* against the Appellant, *&c.* it is [c] said, That the Pardon was not allowed, because it made no mention of the Bigamy. Also it seems agreed by all the [d] Books That if a Man be attainted of any Felony, whether by Abjuration, or Outlawry, or otherwise, and afterwards get a Pardon which doth not expresly mention the Attainder, the Pardon will not avail him; [e] because it shall be intended that the King had not Conusance of the Attainder, but was deceived in his Grant, which shall not grieve him when he has true Notice of the Matter. And upon the like Ground it hath been holden [f] that the Pardon of one who is convicted by Verdict of a Felony is not good, unless it recite the Indictment and Conviction. Also it hath been [g] questioned, whether the Pardon of one who is barely indicted of Felony be good, if it do not mention the Indictment. But this hath been [h] adjudged to be helped by the Words *sive indictatus sive non.*

Sect. 9. It hath been holden, That anciently [i] a Pardon of all Felonies, included all Treasons, as well as Felonies whatsoever, and might be pleaded to an Indictment for them: And it seems to be taken for granted, in many [k] Books, that a Pardon of all Felonies in general, without describing any one particular Felony, may even at this Day, if the Party be neither [l] attainted nor indicted, be pleaded in Bar of any Felony whatsoever, coming within the general Limitations of the Pardon, except Murder or Rape, and that the only [m] Reason why it cannot be also pleaded to Murder or Rape, is because the Statute of 13 *R.* 2. set forth more at large under the next Point, requires an express Mention of them. But I find this Point no [n] where solemnly debated; neither doth it seem easy to reconcile it with the general Rules concerning Pardons, agreed to be good in other Cases; for if a Felony cannot be

[a] 8 H. 6. 20. a. Abridged Bro. Charter of Pardon 19. 8 H. 6. 21. Abridged Bro. Patents, 15. 6 Co. 13. 3 Inst. 238.
[b] 8 H. 6. 20. a. But Note, that Brook in abridging this Case in the Title of Charter of Pardon, 19. omits the Words, because he sued him in the King's Court.
[c] Fitz. Charter, 16. S. P. C. 102. Letter C. Crompt. Just. 115. pl. 4. from the Authority of the Year-Book of 11 H. 4. 11. pl 24. and 48. pl. 23. where on the Debate of this Case it seems admitted that the Pardon was not good because it made no Mention of the Bigamy, and yet it is said that upon the Non-appearance of any one to maintain the Appeal, the Pardon was afterwards allowed. Ergo Quære.
[d] 8 H. 6. 21. Abridged Bro. Patents, 15. 9 Ed. 4. 28. pl. 41. Abridged Fitz. Charter, 23. Bro. Charter, 23. 6 Ed. 4. 4. 1 Ed. 3. 13. pl. 8. 1 Ass. pl. 4. Abridged Fitz. Coro. 155. Same Point admitted, 36 H. 6. 25. a. b. 26. a. Abridged Bro. Charter, 25. 6 Co. 13. b. Fitz. Coro. 124. Crompt. Just. 115. pl. 1. 2. 3 Inst. 238. H. P. C 251. S. P. C. 102. Lett. C. 123. Lett. A. Dalt. ch. 94. Kely. 28.
[e] These are the very Words of 8 H. 6. 21. Abridged Bro. Patent, 15.
[f] 1 Sid. 366. pl. 2. 430. pl. 18. 2 Keb. 363. pl. 11. 3 Keb. 694. pl. 24.
[g] 2 Jon. 56. 3 Keb. 30. pl. 55.
[h] 2 Jon. 56. 3 Keb. 30. pl. 55. 694. pl. 24. Crompt. Just. 115. pl. 11.
[i] 10. Ed. 4. 10. pl. 14. Co. Litt. 391. a. 3 Inst. 236. Vide 22 Ass. pl. 49. S. P. C. 2. Lett. E. 102. Lett. F. Fitz. Charter, 13. Dy. 124. pl. 39. March 214, &c.
[k] Keilw. 91. b. Bro. Coro. 147. Co. Lit. 391. a. S. P. C. 2. Lett. E. 102. Lett. F. 3 Inst. 236. 22 E. 4. 7. pl. 22. See the Books cited to the other Parts of this Section.
[l] 8 H. 6. 21. Abridged Bro. Patents, 15. Fitz. Coro. 24. 2 Keb. 574. pl. 92. 10 Ed. 4. 10. pl. 14. 36 H. 6. 25. a. b. 26. a. H. P. C. 251. 2 Jon. 56. 6 Ed. 4. 4. Bro. Chart. Pardon, 10.
[m] Keilw. 91. b. 9 Ed. 4. 26. b. Crompton's Justice 115. pl. 12.
[n] Vide 2 Keb. 363. pl. 11. 415. pl. 45. 574 pl. 92.

well

well [a] pardoned where it may be reaſonably intended that the King, when he granted the Pardon was not fully appriſed of the State of the Caſe, much leſs doth it ſeem reaſonable that it ſhould be pardoned where it may be well intended that he was not appriſed of it at all. And if a Felony whereof a Perſon be attainted cannot be well pardoned, even tho' it appear that the King was informed of all the Circumſtances of the Fact, unleſs it alſo appear that he was informed of the Attainder, much leſs doth it ſeem reaſonable that a Felony ſhould be well pardoned where it doth not appear that he knew any Thing of it: For by this Means, where the King in Truth intends only to pardon one Felony, which may be very proper for his Mercy, he may by Conſequence pardon the greateſt Number of the moſt heinous Crimes, the leaſt of which, had he been appriſed of it, he would not have pardoned. And for theſe Reaſons, as I ſuppoſe, general Pardons are commonly made by Act of Parliament; and have been of late Years [b] very rarely granted by the Crown, without a particular Deſcription of the Offence intended to be pardoned. As to the [c] Precedents of ſuch general Pardons in *Raſtal's Entries*, it may be anſwered, That their Authority ſeems to be of leſs weight when compared with thoſe many Precedents of Pardons in the Regiſter, every [d] one of which particularly deſcribes the Offence which is pardoned, and even thoſe which relate to [e] Homicide by Lunaticks, or Infants, or in Self-Defence, &c. except only one which pardons Eſcapes, but expreſly excepts all voluntary ones. And therefore where the Books ſpeak of Pardons of all Felonies in general as good, perhaps it may be reaſonable for the moſt part to intend that they either ſpeak of a Pardon by Parliament, or that they ſuppoſe [f] that the particular Crime is mentioned in the Pardon, tho' they do not expreſs it.

Sect. 10. It is enacted by 27 *E.* 3. 2. *That in every Charter of Pardon of Felony, which ſhall be granted at any Man's Suggeſtion, the ſaid Suggeſtion and the Name of him that makes it ſhall be compriſed; and if after the ſame Suggeſtion be found untrue, the Charter ſhall be diſallowed. And the Juſtices before whom ſuch Charters ſhall be alledged, ſhall enquire of the ſame* [g] *Suggeſtion, and if they find it untrue, ſhall diſallow the Charters ſo alledged.* And it is enacted by 5 *H.* 4. 2. That if an Approver become a Felon again after a Pardon, he who procured the Pardon ſhall forfeit 100 *l.*

Sect. 11. It is certain that a general Pardon of Felonies extends not to Piracy, as hath been more fully ſhewn, *Book* 1. *Ch.* 37. *Sect.* 6.

Sect. 12. It ſeems a ſettled Rule, That no Pardon of Felony ſhall be carried farther than the expreſs Purport of it; and therefore where a Man was attainted on an Appeal of Robbery, and the King reciting the Attainder pardoned the Execution, it is ſaid, [h] That becauſe the Pardon did not expreſly mention the Felony, it was diſallowed. But it does not appear how it was pleaded, nor to what Purpoſe it was attempted to be made Uſe of, nor how far, or in what Reſpect it was diſallowed; and therefore tho' [i] ſome Books ſeem to hold generally on the Authority of this Caſe, that ſuch a Pardon is no way good, yet I do not well ſee how any more can be proved from it than this, That it ſhall neither amount to a Pardon of the Felony it ſelf, nor of any other Conſequence of the Attainder beſides the Execution. But it ſeems difficult to give a Reaſon why it ſhould not well pardon the Execution, ſince the King doth not appear to have been any way deceived; and [k] it hath been clearly adjudged, that the King may, if he think fit, pardon the Execution, and no more.

[a] See the precedent Section.
[b] Vide 2 Keb. 575. pl. 92.
[c] Raſt. Ent. 455. pl. 1, 2, 3. 459. pl. 21.
[d] Regiſter of Original Writs from fol. 308 to 313.
[e] Regiſter of Original Writs 309.
[f] See Dyer 124. pl. 39. Vide 22 Aſſ. 47. Abridged Fitz. Chart. 14.
[g] Vide Raym. 13. 1 Sid. 41.
[h] 8 H. 4. 21. pl. 7. Abridged Fitz. Chart. 26. Bro. App. 27. Charter de Pardon, 13. Coro. 24. 6 Co. 13. b. S. P. C. 102. Letter C.
[i] Crompt. Juſt. 115. pl. 3. H. P. C. 251.
[k] 6 H. 4. 6. pl. 29. Abridged Fitz. Coro 227. See the Chapter of Execution and Reprieve. State Trials, Vol. 1. f. 261.

4

Sect. 13. It ſeems [a] agreed, That where a general Act of Pardon excepts ſome particular Kinds of Felony, ſuch Exception extends as well to thoſe whereof any Perſons are attainted as to others; for if thoſe whoſe Guilt appears not on Record are excepted, much greater Reaſon is there that thoſe whoſe Guilt appears in ſo high a Manner ſhould be excepted; and therefore being within the Letter of the Exception, they cannot but be intended to be within the Meaning of it alſo. Neither doth it follow, That becauſe the Pardon of a Felony whereof a Perſon is attainted is not [b] good without mentioning the Attainder, therefore ſuch a general Exception of all Felonies ſhall not extend to thoſe whereon there hath been an Attainder; for the Caſe of ſuch a Pardon depends on this ſpecial Reaſon, That the King ought to be fully appriſed of the Proceedings againſt the Party before he pardons him, as hath been more fully ſhewn, *Sect.* 8.

[a] 6 Co. 13. H.P.C. 251. 3 Inſt. 238.

[b] Vide ſupra ſect. 8, 9.

Sect. 14. As to the ſecond Particular, *viz.* What is particularly required in a Pardon of Treaſon, Murder or Rape: I do not [c] find that the Common Law required any Thing particular in the Form of Pardons of ſuch Crimes, which was not equally requiſite in the Pardon of any Felony whatever. But it being enacted by the Statute of 2 *Ed.* 3. 2. which is confirmed by ſeveral [d] ſubſequent Statutes, *That Charters of Pardon of Manſlaughters ſhall not be granted, but only where the King may do it by his Oath, that is to ſay, where a Man ſlayeth another in his own Defence, or by Miſfortune.* And there being no Precedent in the Regiſter [e] of a Pardon of any other Homicide, but ſuch as is done either in Self-defence or by Miſadventure, or by Infants or Madmen; [f] ſome have gone ſo far as to hold that the King's Pardon of any other Homicide is not good unleſs it be confirmed by Parliament, or at leaſt have a *Non obſtante* of theſe Statutes. But this ſeems contrary not only to the general Tenour of the Books, which clearly [g] admit the King's Power to pardon any Homicide in general, but alſo to the expreſs Purport of 13 *R.* 1. which by ſhewing in what Form the King ſhall make a Pardon of Murder, plainly allows that he has a Power to make it. Beſides, the ſame Reaſons hold as ſtrongly againſt the King's Power to pardon Manſlaughter as Murder, which yet I never knew diſputed. However it ſeems reaſonable that thus much at leaſt be allowed to follow from the Arguments above-mentioned, that too great Caution cannot well be [h] taken in the Grant of Pardons of any Homicide, that there be ſome ſuch favourable Circumſtances in Extenuation of it, as may bring it ſome Way within the Equity of the Caſes in the Regiſter, and thoſe old Statutes.

[c] Vide ſupra ſect 9. Moor 752. pl. 1033. 3Mod. 37, 38. Fitz. Charter, 13. Coro. 25. Keilw. 91.

[d] 4 Ed. 3. ch. 13. 10 Ed. 3. 2. 14 E. 3. 14.

[e] Regiſt. 309.

[f] S.P.C. 101. Letter A. 3 Inſt. 236. Style 375. 377. March 217. Bract. 133. a. Show. Rep. 283, 284. 1 Keb. 67. 1 Lev. 8.

[g] 11 H. 4. 11. pl. 24. Abr. Fitz. Chart. 16. 4 Ed. 4. 10. pl. 14. Abr. Fitz. Coro. 25. 9 H. 7. 5. pl. 1. Abr. Fitz. Scire fac. 56. 9 H. 4. 1. pl. 2. Abrid. Fitz. Scire fac. 63. 13 H. 4. 6. pl. 14. Abr. Fitz. Coro. 266. Dy. 34. pl. 20.

Sect. 15. It is recited by the Statute of 13 *Ric.* 2. 1. *That the Commons had grievouſly complained of the outragious Miſchiefs which had happened to the Realm, for that Treaſons, Murders and Rapes had been commonly done, and the more becauſe Charters of Pardon had been eaſily granted in ſuch Caſes, and that hereupon the Commons had requeſted the King that ſuch Charters might not be granted, to which the King had anſwered, That he would ſave his Liberty and Regality, as his Progenitors had done*; and thereupon it is enacted, *That no Charter of Pardon ſhall from henceforth be allowed before any Juſtice for Murder, or for the*

in all which Books it is clearly admitted, That an Outlawry in an Appeal of Death may be pardoned by the King ſo far as the Publick Juſtice is concerned in it. See alſo Show. Rep. 283, 284. 2 Jon. 56. Kely. 24, 25. 1 Sid. 366. pl. 2. Moor 752. pl. 1033. Raym. 13. 2 Keb. 363. pl. 11. 415. pl. 45. 574. pl. 92. 3 Keb. 30. pl. 55. 694. pl. 24. 3 Mod. 37. [h] See Bracton 133. a.

Death of a Man slain by Await, Assault or Malice prepensed, Treason, or Rape of a Woman, unless the same Murder, Death of a Man slain by Await, Assault or Malice prepensed, Treason, or Rape of a Woman, be specified in the same Charter. And if the Charter of the Death of a Man be alledged before any Justices, in which Charter it is not specified, That he of whose Death any such is arraigned, was murdered or slain by Await, Assault or Malice prepensed, the same Justices shall enquire by a good Inquest, of the Visne *where the dead was slain, if he were murdered or slain by Await, Assault or Malice prepensed; and if they find that he was murdered, or slain by Await, Assault or Malice prepensed, the Charter shall be disallowed, and further it shall be done as the Law alloweth.*

Sect. 16. Also the said Statute required, That the Name of him who sued for such a Charter should be endorsed upon the Bill under a great Penalty, *&c.* But to this, and all other Matters, except only what is contained in the precedent Section, it is repealed by 16 *Rich.* 2. 6.

Sect. 17. It so fully appears from the express Words of 13 *Rich.* 2. That the King's Pardon of Murder, Rape or Treason cannot be good, without a Clause of *Non obstante*, unless the Crime be specified in the Pardon, that I do not [a] know that it hath ever been disputed. But it hath been often formerly [b] adjudged, That a Murder might be well pardoned under the general Description of a felonious Killing, if the Charter had the Clause of *Non obstante* of this Statute. Which Construction seems in a great Measure to evacuate so excellent a Law, by barely changing the Form of the Charter. But it seems difficult to give a good Reason why this Statute should so easily be evaded, which was made for the Prevention of such great Mischiefs, and no Way tends to abolish the King's Prerogative, but only to put such a Restraint upon the Abuse of it, which every one must own to be reasonable. But if such Opinions were founded on the King's Power of dispensing with Statutes, they seem to have been of [c] little Force since the Statute of 1 *Will. & Mar. Sess.* 2. *ch.* 2. by which it is declared and enacted, *That from and after that Session, no Dispensation by* Non obstante *of or to any Statute, or any Part thereof, shall be allowed,* &c.

Sect. 18. But it seems plain, That Pardons of Manslaughter, or any other Felony, except Murder or Rape, remain as they were at Common Law, for which I shall refer to *Section* 8, 9, 10, 11, 12, 13. from whence it follows, that the Pardon of the [d] felonious Killing of *J. S.* may be well pleaded to an Indictment of Manslaughter for Killing him. But where such a Pardon hath been pleaded to an Indictment of Manslaughter by the Coroner's Inquest, the Court in Prudence hath refused [e] to allow it till the Fact hath been found Manslaughter only, by a Jury directed by a higher Court.

Sect. 19. It hath been [f] adjudged, That where a general Act of Pardon expresly pardons all Petit Treasons, but excepts Murder it cannot be avoided by indicting one for Murder only, without the Word *Proditorie*, *&c.* who has been guilty of Petit Treason; for the less Offence being included, and consequently drowned in the greater, cannot but be pardoned by a Pardon of it; and therefore the Exception of Murder in such a Pardon must be construed of such Murder only as is specially so called, and doth not amount to Petit Treason.

[a] Vide Bro. Charter of Pardon, 10. Crompt Just. 115. pl. 12. Keilw. 91. b. Cro. Ja. 495. March 213, 214, &c. 1 H. H. P. C. 466, 467. Yet in Rast. Ent. 455. there are Precedents of Pardons of all Murders in general, without any Non obstante, and in Dyer 124. pl. 39. there is Mention of a Pardon of all Treasons, &c. but I suppose that the particular Treason was also expresly pardoned; for it appears that the Attainder for it was expresly mentioned.

[b] 2 Keb. 363. pl. 11. 574. pl. 92. Show. Rep. 283, 284. Skin. 157. 1 Sid. 366. pl. 2. 3 Mod. 37, 38. Kely. 24, 25. Moor 752. pl. 1033. 12 Co. 18. 2 Jon. 56. Rast. Ent. 455. pl. 3. the same Point is admitted and complained of, S. P. C. 132. Letter A. H. P. C. 250. Vide 3 Inst. 136. 2 H. 7. 6. b. March 214. Sty. Rep. Rickabee's Case.

[c] Show. Rep. 283, 284. [d] 2 Keb. 363. pl. 11. 574. pl. 92. Kely. 24, 25. 2 Jon. 56.

[e] 2 Keb. 415. pl. 45. [f] Dy. 50. pl. 4, 5. 235. pl. 19. 6 Co. 13. b. Crompt. 115. pl. 5, 6, 8.

Sect. 20. Alſo it hath been [a] adjudged, That a general Act of Pardon of all Felonies, *&c.* except Murder, ſhall extend to a *felo de ſe*; for notwithſtanding his Offence may in Strictneſs be called Murder, and conſequently may ſeem naturally enough to come within the Exception, yet ſince the general Words of an Act of Parliament are to be expounded according to the Common Uſe of them, and the Offence of *felo de ſe* and Murder are generally underſtood as diſtinct Offences, and as ſuch are diſtinctly treated by all Authors, who when they uſe the Word Murder as ſignifying a certain Species of Offences, always mean by it the Murder of another; and farther, ſince there is greater Reaſon to except the Murder of another out of a Pardon, than that of a Man's ſelf, becauſe both the Law of God and Nature ſeem generally to require Blood for Blood, which can be applied only to the Murder of another, the Word Murder ſhall in ſuch an Exception be taken only to ſignify the Murder of another.

Sect. 21. Alſo it hath been [b] adjudged, That if a general Act of Pardon extend to all Felonies, Offences, Injuries, Miſdemeanors, and other Things done before ſuch a Day, it pardons a Homicide from a Wound given before the Day, whereof the Party died not till after the Day, becauſe the Stroke which is the Cauſe of the Death being pardoned, all the Effects of it are conſequently pardoned.

Sect. 22. As to the third Particular, *viz.* How far the Pardon of one Man may diſcharge another: It ſeems to be generally [c] agreed, That notwithſtanding all Felonies are [d] ſeveral, and conſequently a Pardon of one Man cannot be a direct Diſcharge of another, yet in ſome Caſes the Felony of one Man may be ſo far dependent upon that of another, that the Pardon of the one will by a neceſſary Conſequence enure to the Benefit of the other. As where the Principal pleaded his [e] Pardon, and was allowed it at the Common Law, [f] before his Attainder, or where he pleads and is allowed it at this Day before his [g] Conviction, in which Caſe it ſeems that the Acceſſary may by a neceſſary Conſequence take Benefit of it, becauſe he cannot be arraigned till after the Principal is convicted.

Sect. 23. It is [h] agreed, That if a Man be bound to the King as Surety for another, for the Payment of a certain Fine or other Debt due to the Crown, the Pardon of the Principal is a Diſcharge of the Surety alſo. But it ſeems to have been [i] holden as a general Rule, That where a Man is bound as Surety for another for the Performance of a future Act, the Diſcharge of the Principal before the Time of the Performance will not diſcharge the Surety, becauſe nothing was due to the King at the Time of ſuch Diſcharge: But this ſeems extremely nice; neither do the Caſes [k] brought for the Proof of it ſeem any Way to come up to it. For as to the firſt of them, *viz.* That of the King's Releaſe of a Recognizance for the Peace to the Principal, before it is forfeited, which ſhall not diſcharge the Sureties; it may be anſwered, that it will [l] not ſo much as diſcharge the Principal. And as to the other Caſe [m] cited for this Purpoſe, *viz.* That of the King's Pardoning *J. N.* the Building of ſuch a Houſe, for his Building whereof *J. S.* is bound to the King, which ſhall be no Diſcharge to *J. S.* it may be anſwered, that as this Caſe is put, *J. N.* doth not ſeem to be bound

[a] 1 Lev. 8. 120. 1 Sid. 150. 1 Keb. 66, 548.

[b] Pl. Com. 401. 1 H. H. P.C. 426. Crompt. Juſt. 116. pl. 20. This is left a Quære Dyer 99. pl. 65.

[c] Vide ſupra ch. 29. ſect. 41 Letter [l], 34 H. 6. 9. pl. 19. 42 Aſſ. pl. 16. Bro. Charter of Pardon, 33. Coro. 122 or 123. Fitz. Charter, 15.

[d] Cro. Eliz. 30, 31. 22 Ed. 4. 7. pl. 22. See the next Section, Dy. 34. pl. 21, 22.

[e] F.N.B. 115. Letter [e]. 7 H. 4. 16. pl. 5. Supra ch. 29. ſect. 41. Let. [l].

[f] Supra ch. 29. ſect. 41, 42.

[g] Supra ch. 29. ſect. 43.

[h] 1 H. 7. 10. pl. 12. Fitz. Pardon, 4. Bro. Charter of Pardon, 36.

[i] See the Books next above-cited.

[k] See the Books next above cited.

[l] See B. 1. ch. 60. ſect. 17.

[m] 1 H. 7. 10. pl. 12, &c.

at

at all, but only *J. S.* who therefore doth not ſeem to come under the Notion of a Surety, but of a Principal.

Sect. 24. As to the fourth Particular, *viz.* How far it is neceſſary that the Pardon of ſeveral Perſons for Felony be ſeveral: It ſeems [a] agreed, That the Pardon of *A. B.* and *C.* of all Felonies by them done, without adding, or any of them, is void; becauſe it ſuppoſes them jointly guilty, and extends to no other but joint Felonies, whereas all Felony is ſeveral [b] in each Offender, and cannot be joint. And the *Year-Book* of [c] 22 *E.* 4. goes ſo far as to hold, That the Addition of the Words, *or any of them*, will not help a Pardon beginning with ſuch joint Words. But this is [d] ſaid to be miſreported, and contrary to the Roll, and ſeems to be agreed [e] not to be Law at this Day.

Sect. 25. As to the fifth Particular, *viz.* Whether the King's Grant of a Protection, or of a Place of Truſt to a Traitor or Felon, carry with it an implied Pardon of his Crime: It is generally [f] agreed, That a Protection granted to a Felon ſhall be ſo far from enuring as a Pardon, that it ſhall not ſo much as privilege him from anſwering immediately to an Indictment, in the ſame Manner as if he had no Protection at all. But there is a ſhort [g] Note of a Caſe in *Fitzherbert*'s *Abridgment*, where one being indicted and found guilty of Felony, produced a Charter whereby it appeared that the King had hired him to go into *Gaſcoign*, to the Army, whereupon the Court allowed the Charter. And Sir *Edward Coke* [h] ſuppoſes that the Offence was ſpecially recited in the Charter, and that ſuch Recital varies this Caſe from that of a Protection, which muſt be a formed Writ, and therefore can have no ſuch Recital. But however ſuch a Charter may enure as a [i] Suſpenſion of the Proceedings againſt a Felon for a Time, I do not ſee how it can be collected from this Caſe, that it ſhall enure as a Pardon of the Felony by Implication, which ſeems contrary to the Rule [k] of Law in other Caſes, which will not ſuffer a Pardon of Felony to be carried beyond the expreſs Purport of it. However it was ſolemnly adjudged [l] in Sir *Walter Raleigh*'s Caſe, That the King's Grant of a military Command to a Perſon attainted of High Treaſon, wherein he called him his true and loyal Subject, and gave him judicial Power over the Lives of others, did not pardon the High Treaſon, becauſe every Pardon of High Treaſon requires an expreſs Mention of it, if not by the Common Law, yet at leaſt by the Statute of 13 [m] *R.* 2. Beſides if the Offence had been but Felony, yet after an Attainder it could not have been pardoned without an expreſs Mention both of the [n] Felony, and alſo of the [o] Attainder.

Sect. 26. As to the ſixth Particular, *viz.* What is required to make a good Pardon of Offences not Capital: It hath been adjudged, That a Pardon of all Miſpriſions, Treſpaſſes, Offences and Contempts, will pardon a Contempt in making a [p] falſe Return, *&c.* and a [q] Striking in *Weſtminſter-Hall*, and [r] Barratry, and even a [s] *Præmunire*: And it hath been laid down as a [t] general Rule, That it will pardon any Crime which is not Capital. But it is ſaid [u] to have been holden, That ſuch a Par-

[a] 22 Ed. 4. 7. pl. 22. Bro. Charter of Pardon, 51. Dyer 34. pl. 21, 22. S. P. C. 102. Letter D.
[b] See the precedent Section.
[c] 22 E. 4. 7. pl. 22.
[d] Bro. Charter of Pardon, 51. Dyer 34. pl. 21, 22. S. P C. 102. Letter D.
[e] Dyer 34. pl. 21, 22. H. P. C. 252.
[f] S. P. C. 104. Letter D. Co. Lit. 130. b. 7 Ed. 4. 29. pl. 13. Abr. Fitz. Coro. 30. 3 Inſt. 239, 240. 2 Rol. Abr. 323. Lett. G. Fitz. Cor. 61. But Fitz. Coro. 122. ſeems contrary.
[g] Fitz. Coro. 239. cited. 3 Inſt. 239. 240. S. P. C. 140. Letter D. 2 Rol. Rep. 50.
[h] 3 Inſt. 240.
[i] Vide S. P. C. 104. Lett. D. 3 Inſt. 239, 240. 2 Rol. Rep. 50.
[k] Vide ſupra ſect. 12, &c.
[l] Cro. Ja. 494. 2 Rol. Rep. 50. State Trials, Vol. 1. f. 187, 188, 877.
[m] Supra ſect. 15.
[n] Vide ſupra ſect. 8, 9.
[o] Vide ſupra ſect. 8, 9.
[p] 36 H. 6. 24. pl. 21. 37 H. 6. 21, 22. Abr. Fitz. Charter, 22. Bro. Charter of Pardon, 25.
[q] 1 Lev. 106. 1 Sid. 211. 1 Keb. 852. pl. 56.
[r] 1 Mod. 102.
[s] Cro. Jac. 336. 2 Bulſt. 299.
[t] 1 Mod. 102. Vide Keilw. 159, 198. pl. 2. Fitz. Coro. 122.
[u] Watſon's Clergy-Man's Law, ch. 5. 1 Sid. 170, 222. the ſame Caſe is in Keble 780. but this Point is not taken Notice of. And the contrary ſeems to be admitted, Cro. El. 685. pl. 21. Moor 916. pl. 1292. And is agreed 2 Mod. 52.

don will not extend to Simony, becauſe it is *malum in ſe*; but this ſeems to be no good Reaſon? for Barratry, and the injurious Striking of another, and generally all Offences at Common Law are alſo *mala in ſe*; and yet it ſeems clear, that unleſs they be Capital, they may be pardoned by ſuch a Pardon.

Sect. 27. It hath been queſtioned [a] whether a general Pardon of all Treſpaſſes extends to Champerty or Confederacy.

Sect. 28. As to the ſeventh Particular, *viz.* Whether any Offence can be pardoned before it is committed: It ſeems agreed [b], That the King can by no previous Licence, Pardon, or Diſpenſation whatſoever, make an Offence diſpuniſhable which is [c] *malum in ſe, i. e.* unlawful in itſelf, as being againſt the Law of Nature, or ſo far againſt the Publick Good, as to be indictable at Common Law. For a Grant of this Kind tending to encourage the Doing of Evil, which it is the Chief End of Government to prevent, is plainly againſt Reaſon, and the Common Good, and therefore void. Yet it ſeems to have been adjudged [d], That the King's Grant to the Biſhop of *Saliſbury*, and his Succeſſors, having the Cuſtody of a Priſon, that they ſhall be quit from all Eſcapes, &c. having been allowed in *Eyre*, ſhall be a good Diſcharge from any Fine for a negligent Eſcape out of ſuch Priſon. And yet it is admitted that ſuch a Grant is no Diſcharge of a voluntary Eſcape; but it is ſaid, that it ſhall diſcharge a negligent one, becauſe it is puniſhable only by a pecuniary Penalty; and it is a general Rule, That the King may diſcharge a [e] Poſſibility of an Intereſt before it happens; as where the Tenants of his Manor are to be amerced for a Default in Reſpect of their Tenures, which the King may pardon beforehand. But if it be a good Rule that the King cannot pardon an Offence which is *malum in ſe* before it happens, and the negligent keeping of a Priſon be ſuch an Offence, which I think cannot be denied; and farther if it be alſo a good Rule, That where the King's Grant is plainly againſt the Common Good, as a Grant of this Kind ſeems to be, as tending to make a Gaoler leſs diligent in his Duty, by taking off the legal Puniſhment of his Negligence, I do not well ſee how this Caſe can be maintained. For it ſeems by no Means to follow, that becauſe the King can diſcharge his Right to an Amercement before it happens, for a Default of his Tenants in a Matter relating barely to the Revenue of the Crown, which it is admitted that in the like Caſe any other Lord may do as well; therefore he can diſcharge a pecuniary Penalty for an Offence of a publick Nature before it happens. Neither doth it ſeem that a negligent Eſcape is only puniſhable by a pecuniary Penalty; for in ſome [f] Books it is ſaid to be fineable, by which it is implied, that the Offender may be impriſoned. Beſides it ſeems [g] agreed, That many negligent Eſcapes will forfeit the Office of keeping a Gaol, and therefore it is plain that a pecuniary Penalty cannot be ſaid to be their only Puniſhment. However this is the only Caſe I [h] meet with which looks like an Exception out of the General Rule that the King cannot pardon an Offence that is *malum in ſe* before it happens.

Sect. 29. But where [i] a Thing, which is lawful in its own Nature, is made unlawful by the Prohibition of an Act of Parliament only, as the Carrying [k] Bell-metal or [l] Beer, &c. out of the Realm, Importing [m] certain Merchandiſes in Foreign Ships, &c. Selling [n] Wines beyond a cer-

[a] 7 H. 4. 9. pl. 11.

[b] Finch of Law 234, 235. 19 H. 6. 62. b. 37 H. 6. 4. b. 5. a. 11 H. 7. 11, 12. pl. 35. Bro. Charter de Pardon, 76. Davis's Rep. 75. 5 Co. 35. b. 12 Co. 29, 30.

[c] But Chief Juſtice Vaughan in Sorrel's Caſe, fol. 332, &c. ſeems to find fault with the Diſtinction between malum in ſe & Prohibitum, as not fully anſwering all the Caſes concerning Diſpenſations.

[d] 3 H. 7. 15. pl. 30. Abridged Fitz. Grant, 37. Bro. Patents, 51. Cited S. P. C. 102 Lett. E.

[e] Dy. 52. pl. 2. 19 H. 6. 62, 63, 64. Abridged Bro. Patents, 16.

[f] Vide ſupra 19 ſect. 31.

[g] Supra ch. 19 ſect. 29, 30.

[h] But Chief Juſtice Vaughan in Sorrel's Caſe, 335, 336. ſeems to argue to the contrary.

[i] Dav. Rep. 75, 76. Finch 234, 235.

[k] Dyer 52. pl. 1, 2.

[l] Dyer 92. pl. 18.

[m] Dyer 54. pl. 17, 18.

[n] Dyer 270. pl. 22.

certain Price, [a] Exporting Wool to any other Place than *Calais*, Selling [b] Wines without a Licence, Multiplying [c] Gold or Silver, [d] Coining Money of a baſe Alloy, and [e] other Matters of the like Nature, it ſeems to have been formerly taken [f] for granted, that generally the King might diſpenſe with it as to a [g] particular Time, or Place, or Perſon or even a [h] Corporation aggregate, &c. ſo far as the Publick was concerned in it. Yet where ſuch Diſpenſation could not but be atttended with a great Inconvenience, as the Introducing a Monopoly, or Fruſtrating the End for which the Law was made, as the Licenſing [i] a particular Perſon to import Foreign Cards or Wines prohibited by Parliament, and [k] *a fortiori* if it tended to ſuſpend the whole Statute in general, it was commonly agreed to be void. Alſo where ever an Act of Parliament gives a particular Intereſt, or Right of Action, to the Party [l] grieved by the Breach of it, as the Statutes of [m] *Mortmain*, which give an Entry to the next immediate Lord for an Alienation to a Corporation, the [n] Statutes againſt Maintenance, Forcible Entries, Carrying Diſtreſſes out of the Hundred, [o] Suffering one in Execution to eſcape, &c. which give an Action to the Party grieved by the Offence prohibited; it ſeems to have been always agreed, That no Charter by the King can be of any Force to bar the Right of the Party grounded upon ſuch Statute, becauſe it is a ſettled Rule, that the King cannot Prejudice the Intereſt of the Party. Alſo where a Statute is expreſs, that the King's Charter againſt the Purport of it, whether with or without a Clauſe of *Non obſtante*, ſhall be void; it is ſaid by Sir [p] *Edward Coke*, that no Clauſe of *Non obſtante* can diſpenſe with it, unleſs it tend to reſtrain ſome Prerogative, ſolely and inſeparably incident to the Perſon of the King, as the Right of pardoning, or of commanding the Service of the Subject, for the publick Weal, which being, [q] as he ſeems to argue, founded on the Law of Nature, are ſo far inſeparable from the King, that by a Clauſe of *Non obſtante* he may diſpenſe with any Statute whatſoever, which tends to deprive him of them. And on this Ground the Reſolution of the Judges in the [r] *Year-Book* of *H.* 7. is ſaid to be maintainable, whereby it was adjudged, without any Difficulty, That where the Statute of 23 *H.* 6. *ch.* 8. expreſly enacts, That Patents to Sheriffs to continue longer than a Year ſhall be void, and the Party diſabled to bear the Office of Sheriff notwithſtanding any Clauſe of *Non obſtante*, yet the King by the Clauſe of *Non obſtante* might make a good Patent of ſuch Office for Life. Which is in Effect to ſay that let there be never ſo good Reaſons for the making a new Law for the Reſtraint of the Prerogative in any Particular relating to the Service of the Subject, yet it is not in the Power of the Legiſlature to make ſuch a Law; and yet no one will deny that where-ever the Law of Nature leaves a Matter indifferent, there the Law of Man ought to prevail. Neither is there any Pretence to ſay, that the King has a Right by the Law of Nature to appoint Sheriffs, ſince it is plain that before the [s] Statute of 9 *Ed.* 2. the Freeholders choſe them, unleſs they had a Fee in their Office. And what Reaſon can there be, that the Statute-Law, which gives the Crown the Power of making Sheriffs, may not alſo qualify that Power, as ſhall be thought convenient? But it is obſervable, that the Reſolution above-mentioned does not go upon any particular Reaſon which may di-

[a] 2 Rich. 2. 11, 12. pl. 26. 11 H. 7. 11, 12. pl. 35. 37 H. 6. 4. 2 H. 7. 6. b. Bro. Charter de Pardon, 24, 76. Parliament, 98. 13 H. 7. 8. b. Fitz. Charter, 21. Grant, 33.

[b] Vaughan 330. 1 Lev. 217. 1 Sid. 6, 7.

[c] Vaughan, 344.

[d] 11 H. 7. 11. pl. 26. Vaugh. 344.

[e] 2 Rich. 3. 12. a. 2 H. 7. 6. b. 12 H. 3. a. by Martyn. Dyer 224. pl. 31. 225. pl. 35. 303. pl. 49.

[f] See the Books above cited to the other Parts of this Section, and State Trials, Vol. 3. f. 799 to 810. f. 845.

[g] 11 Co. 88. a. 7 Co. 36. b. 1 Lev. 218. Co. Litt. 99. a. Vide 3 Lev. 389.

[h] Vaugh. 352. 1 Lev. 217.

[i] Vaugh. 344. 11 Co. 88. See the Books above-cited.

[k] State Trials, Vol. 3. fol. 793, 796, 808, 809.

[l] Supra ch. 26. ſect. 64. 37 H. 6. 4. a. b. 2 Rich. 3. 12. a. Vaugh. 342, 343. Infra ſect. 34.

[m] 11 Co. 98, 99. Vide Keilw. 134. pl. 15. But now by 7 & 8 W. 3. 37. ſuch Licence may be granted by the King alone.

[n] Vaugh. 342, 343. [o] Dyer 162. pl. 50. 297. pl. 24. [p] 12 Co. 18, 19. [q] 7 Co. Calvin's Caſe, 14. a. [r] 2 H. 7. 6. b. Abridged Fitz. Grant, 33. Bro. Patents, 102. Vide Finch of Law 234, 235. 13 H. 7. 8. b. Plow. Com. 502. b. [s] 2 Inſt. 558, 559.

ſtinguiſh the Caſe of a Sheriff, from any other Caſe, but only on the King's Power by *Non obſtante* to diſpenſe with the Statutes concerning the Tranſporting Wool, the Pardoning of Murder, and the Expreſſing the Quantities of the Land granted by the King's Patents, and ſuch like, which becauſe they may be diſpenſed with by Clauſes of *Non obſtante*, it is taken for granted, that the Statute of 23 *H.* 6. might as well be diſpenſed with by them; as if it were a plain Conſequence that becauſe Statutes which ſay nothing concerning the Clauſe of *Non obſtante*, may be diſpenſed with by it; therefore a Statute which expreſly provides againſt it, may alſo as well be diſpenſed with by it.

Sect. 30. It is [a] ſaid, That the King may diſpenſe with the Statutes of *Mortmain*, without any Clauſe of *Non obſtante*; and this ſeems very reaſonable, becauſe thereby he only gives up that Right of Entry which thoſe Statutes give him for the Forfeiture, which every meſne Lord might alſo do as well ſo far as he had a Right by thoſe Statutes. Alſo it ſeems to be holden [b] by ſome Books, That the Clauſe of *Non obſtante* was only requiſite in Reſpect of ſuch Statutes which expreſly ſaid it ſhould be void. But the far greater Number of [c] Authorities ſeem to be to the contrary.

Sect. 31. But the diſpenſing Power was carried ſo very high in a late Reign, and found to be of ſuch dangerous Conſequence as to make the Execution of the moſt neceſſary Laws in Effect precarious, and merely dependent on the Pleaſure of the Prince. And it ſeeming highly incongruous that the King ſhould have a Kind of abſolute unlimited Power in diſpenſing with Laws wherein the Church and State have the higheſt Intereſt, when at the ſame Time he has no Power at all to diſpenſe with any Law which veſts the leaſt Right or Intereſt in a Private Subject, it was found by Experience neceſſary to *declare and enact by* 1 Will. & Mar. Seſſ. 2. ch. 2. *That no Diſpenſation by* Non obſtante *of or to any Statute, or any Part thereof, be allowed, but that the ſame ſhall be held void and of none Effect, except a Diſpenſation be allowed in ſuch Statute. But it is provided that no Charter, Grant, or Pardon, granted before* 23 October, 1689. *ſhall be any way impeached or invalidated by that Act, but that the ſame ſhall be and remain of the ſame Force and Effect in Law, and no other, as if the ſaid Act had never been made.*

Sect. 32. It hath been always [d] agreed, That the King never could diſpenſe with a Statute before it was made.

Sect. 33. As to the eighth Particular, Whether there be any Offence which cannot be pardoned after it is committed: I take it to be a ſettled Rule [e], That the King may Pardon any Offence whatever, whether againſt the Common or Statute Law, ſo far as the Publick is concerned in it, after it is over, and conſequently [f] may prevent any popular Action on a penal Statute by a Pardon of the Offence before any Suit commenced by an Informer. But while a Publick Nuſance continues unreformed, it ſeems [g] agreed, That the King cannot wholly pardon it, becauſe ſuch Pardon would take away the only Means of compelling a Redreſs of it. But it hath been [h] holden by ſome, That a Pardon of ſuch Offence will ſave the Party from any Fine for the Time Precedent to the Pardon.

[a] Co. Lit. 99. Plowd. Com. 502. b. Dyer 269. pl. 19. where the Grant is made ex certa Scientia. Cont. by Dy. in Plow. Com. 502. Vide Raſt. Ent. 302. a. Fitz. Grant, 36. Entry congeable, 28. Plow. Com. 334. b.

[b] Finch 234, 235. Plow. Com. 502.

[c] 2 H. 7. 6. b. Abridged Bro. Patents, 109. Fitz. Charter, 33. 2 Rich. 3. 12. a. 43 Aſſ. pl. 19. Vide Dyer 52. pl. 1. 54. pl. 17. 29. pl. 17. 18. 270. pl. 22. 303. pl. 49. 352. pl. 25.

[d] Finch 235. 1 Sid. 6. Dy. 52. pl. 2.

[e] See the Books cited to the other Parts of this and the next Section.

[f] Vide ſupra ch. 26. ſect. 64. See the following Section.

[g] 3 Inſt. 237. Vaugh. 333. 37 H. 6. 4. b. Plow. Com. 487. Vide Fitz Aſſiſe, 445. Keilw. 134. pl. 15. 12 Co. 29, 30. State Trials, Vol. 1. fol. 578.

[h] 12 Co. 30.

Sect. 34. As to the ninth Particular, *viz.* How far a Pardon may be of Force againſt the private Intereſt of the Subject: I take it to be a [a] ſettled Rule, That the King cannot by any Diſpenſation, Releaſe, Pardon or Grant whatſoever, bar any Right, whether of Entry, or Action, or any legal Intereſt, Benefit or Advantage whatſoever before veſted in the Subject; and upon this Ground it ſeems clear, That the King can no way bar any Action on a Statute by the Party [b] grieved; nor even a popular [c] Action by a Common Informer, if commenced before his Pardon or Releaſe; and that he cannot diſcharge a Recognizance [d] for the Peace, before it is forfeited.

Sect. 35. And upon the ſame Ground, it ſeems to be clearly agreed, That as the Releaſe of a Perſon robbed, or of the Wife or Heir of a Perſon killed, will not [e] bar an Indictment, or a Demand of Execution at the Suit of the King; ſo neither will a Pardon [f] by the King be any Bar to an Appeal, except only where it is carried on at the Suit of the King, after a Nonſuit of the Party, in which Caſe it may be barred by a [g] Pardon in the ſame Manner as an Indictment. But if one who appears to be attainted of Felony, whether by Outlawry, or otherwiſe, on an Appeal carried on at the Suit of the Party, get a Pardon from the King, he [h] muſt ſue a [i] *Scire facias* againſt the Appellant before the Pardon ſhall be allowed, unleſs the Appellant appear [k] *gratis*, and confeſs that he will ſue no farther, *&c.*

Sect. 36. If the Appellant appear on the *Scire facias*, it is [l] certain that he may pray Execution notwithſtanding the Pardon: But if the Sheriff have returned a [m] *Scire facias*, or two [n] *Nihils*, and the Appellant appear not [o] upon Demand, the Appellee ſhall be diſcharged. Yet if the Appeal be of Death, and the Sheriff return the Appellant dead, there are ſome [p] Authorities that a *Scire facias* ought to go againſt the next Heir to the deceaſed, but the greater Number of [q] Authorities ſeem to be to the contrary.

Sect. 37. There is ſaid [r] to be no Need of any *Scire facias* on ſuch a Pardon againſt the Lords mediate or immediate, becauſe the Pardon no way tends to reverſe the Attainder, and conſequently can do no Hurt to their Title of Eſcheat, *&c.* grounded on the Attainder, but rather affirms it.

[a] Supra S. 29. 8 H. 6. 19. Abridged Fitz. Grant, 4. 37 H. 6. 4. b. Abridged Bro. Charter de Pardon, 24. 2 Rich. 3. 12. a. Pl. Com. 487. a. b. Fitz. Aſſiſe, 445. Cro. Ca. 199. 2 Roll. Abr. 178. Lett. S. 304. Lett. S. Cro. Ja. 159. [b] Supra ch. 26. ſect. 64. 2 Rich. 3. 12. a. Vide Keilw. 134. pl. 15. Fitz. Chart. 21. [c] Supra ch. 26. ſect. 64. 37 H. 6. 4. a. b. Abridged Fitz. Grant, 21. Bro. Charter, de Pardon, 24. 2 Rich. 3. 12. a. 5 Ed. 4. 3. pl. 25. [d] 37 H. 6. 4. b. Fitz. Charter, 21. Pardon, 4, 5. Bro. Charter de Pard. 24. Recogniſ. 22. 11 H. 7. 12. pl. 35. 12 Co. 29, 30. Book 1. ch. 60. ſect. 17. [e] 8 H. 4. 22. pl. 17. Abridged Fitz. Charter, 26. Bro. Charter de Pardon, 13. Appeal, 27, 33, 41, 128. 11 H. 4. 16. pl. 36. [f] See the Authorities cited to the other Parts of this Section, and Bro. Appeal, 150. 3 Inſt. 237. [g] Supra ch. 25. ſect. 13. Bro. Appeal, 33. [h] Dy. 34. pl. 20. S. P. C. 104. Lett. B. H. P. C. 251. 11 H. 4. 11. pl. 24. 11 H. 4. 48. pl. 23. 9 H. 7. 5. pl. 1. 2 Rich. 3. 8. pl. 17. 9 H. 4. 1. pl. 2. 13 H. 4. 6. pl. 14. 38 H. 6. 13. pl. 26. and the Authorities cited to the other Parts of this Section. [i] That the Apellee may have ſuch a Scire facias of Courſe on ſuch a Pardon, without producing a Releaſe or other Deed from the Appellant. 9 H. 7. 5. pl. 1. Abridged Fitz. Scire facias, 56. Bro. Scire Facias, 166. 2 Rich. 3. 8. pl. 17. S. P. C. 104. Lett. B. cont. 11 H. 4. 16. pl. 36. Abridged Bro. Scire fa' 73. That there was no Need of any Scire facias where an Appeal was abated by the King's Death, and the Year and Day were paſſed. 2 H. 7. 10. pl. 5. Bro. Charter of Pardon, 69. [k] 11 H. 4. 16. pl. 36. Fitz. Coro. 87. Same Caſe Bro. Confeſſion, 12. and Jour in Court, 21. But 'tis made a Wonder that a Scire facias was not awarded. [l] S. P. C. 104. Lett. B. H. P. C. 251. 11 H. 4. 1. pl. 2. [m] S. P. C. 104. Lett. B. H. P. C. 251. [n] Finch 477. Vide Dy. 168. pl. 17. 172. pl. 10, 11. [o] 2 Rich. 3. 8. pl. 17. 9 H. 4. 1. pl. 2. Abridged Fitz. Scire facias, 63. Bro. Charter de Pardon, 14. [p] 11 H. 4. 11. pl. 24. 11 H. 4. 48. pl. 23. 19 H. 4. 6. pl. 14. Abridged Fitz. Coro. 266. Vide Fitz. Coro. 85. Supra ch. 23. ſect. 38 & 41. [q] 9 H. 7. 5. pl. 1. Abridged Fitz. Scire fac' 56. Bro. Scire Facias, 166. Appeal, 88, 144. 38 H. 6. 13. pl. 26. Bro. Appeal, 141. Charter de Pardon, 28. Supra ch. 23. ſect. 38, 41. [r] Dyer 34. pl. 20.

Sect. 38. If ſeveral Perſons be outlawed in an Appeal, and one of them be pardoned, and get his Pardon allowed on the Non-appearance of the Appellant on a *Scire facias*, *&c.* and afterwards another of them get his Pardon; it ſeems, That he ſhall take no [a] Advantage of the Appellant's Default on the firſt *Scire facias*, but muſt ſue out his *Scire facias*, *&c.* in the ſame Manner as if there had been no ſuch Default.

Sect. 39. It is holden by great [b] Authorities, That if a Perſon be convicted of Manſlaughter upon an Appeal of Death, the King may pardon the Burning in the Hand; for which this Reaſon is given by Sir *Edward Coke*, That it is no Part of the Judgment at the Suit of the Party, but a collateral and exemplary [c] Puniſhment inflicted by the Statute of 4 *H.* 7. 13. But this made a *Quære* by [d] others, and the principal Caſe wherein it is ſaid to have been reſolved, is very differently [e] reported, and was never [f] adjudged: And the Ground laid down that the King may pardon it becauſe it is no Part of the Judgment at the Suit of the Party, by which it ſeems admitted, That if it were Part of the Judgment, the Law would be otherwiſe, ſeems rather to make againſt it than for it; for there are [g] Precedents of expreſs Judgments, *quod cautariſetur in manu ſua læva.* Alſo it is [h] admitted, That where a Defendant is to have a certain Impriſonment, *&c.* at the Suit of the Party upon a Statute, the King cannot diſpenſe with it, except in ſome ſpecial [i] Caſes, wherein it may be reaſonably intended that ſuch Impriſonment was given by the Statute, by Way of Satisfaction to the Publick Juſtice only, in which Caſe it ſeems agreed, [k] That the King may diſpenſe with it, as it is ſaid that he may, with finding of Sureties by one convict on the Statute againſt Treſpaſſes in Parks. But it ſeems doubtful, whether the Statute of 4 *H.* 7. 13. which appoints the Burning of the Hand can well admit of ſuch a Conſtruction; for the Words are, *whereas upon Truſt of the Privilege of the Church, diverſe have been more bold to commit Murder*, &c. *becauſe they have been admitted to their Clergy as oft as they have offended; for avoiding of ſuch preſumptuous Boldneſs*, It is enacted, *That every Perſon not being in Orders, who hath once been admitted to his Clergy, be not again admitted thereto, and that every ſuch Perſon convict*, &c. *ſhall be marked*, &c. from whence it ſeems plain, That the Statute expreſly intends ſuch Marking as a Diſcouragement of the Offence; and it ſeems difficult to give a Reaſon why it ſhould be conſtrued to mean it only as a collateral and not as a direct Puniſhment. Neither doth it ſeem a plain Reaſon, That becauſe the Statute intended it an exemplary Puniſhment, the King may diſpenſe with it; for ſurely the Execution of an Appellee attainted of Murder, and the perpetual Impriſonment of a Clerk delivered to the Ordinary upon a Conviction on an Appeal, who could not make his Purgation, were alſo exemplary Puniſhments; and yet it is generally [l] agreed, That the King never could diſpenſe with them. And therefore upon the Whole this ſeems to be a Point that deſerves to be farther conſidered.

Sect. 40. But granting that the King may pardon the Burning the Hand in an Appeal, it ſeems a very reaſonable [m] Conſequence that the Party ſhall immediately be delivered by Force of the Statute of 18 *Eliz.* 7. which ſays, That after Burning he ſhall be delivered, which ought to have this Conſtruction, That he ſhall be delivered after Burning, where he is to be burned.

[a] 1 H. 4. 1. pl. 2. Fitz. Scire facias, 63. But Bro. Charter de Pardon, 14. in the Abridgment of the ſame Caſe holds the contrary.

[b] H.P.C. 252. 3 Inſt. 237. Hob. 294. cited, State Trials, Vol. 4. f. 382.

[c] But my Lord Hobart f. 294 ſays, That it is no Part of the Judgment, nor ſo much as in the Nature of the Puniſhment, but only a Mark to notify that the Party may have his Clergy but once.

[d] Raym. 369, 370. Dyer 202. pl. 68. 261. pl. 26. Cro. El. 464. the firſt, pl. 13.

[e] Biggins's Caſe, 5 Co. 50. Cro. Eliz. 632. pl. 27. 682. pl. 14. Moor 571. pl. 782.

[f] Raym. 371.

[g] Raſt. Ent. 1. b. pl. 2. 56. a. pl. 1. Yet it is omitted, 55. b. pl. 6.

[h] 5 Co. 50. b. Dy. 261. pl. 26. 323. pl. 28.

[i] 3 Inſt. 171, 237. 2 Inſt. 200. 439.

[k] Dy. 238. pl. 34, 35. 3 Inſt. 171. 2 Inſt 200.

[l] Vide ſupra ſect. 35. 5 Co. 50. b. Dy. 261. pl. 26. Yet 'tis made a Quære, Dy. 200. pl. 68. whether the King could not pardon ſuch Impriſonment.

[m] 5 Co. 50. b. Vide ch. 33. ſect. 131. Cro. Ca. 596, 597. Hob. 294.

Sect. 41. It ſeems to have been always agreed, [a] That the King's Pardon will diſcharge any Suit in the Spiritual Court *ex officio*: Alſo it ſeems to be [b] ſettled at this Day, That it will diſcharge any Suit in ſuch Court *ad inſtantiam partis pro reformatione morum*, or *ſalute animæ*, as for Defamation, or laying violent Hands on a Clerk, and ſuch like; for ſuch Suits, like thoſe in the Star-Chamber, are in Truth the Suits of the King, tho' proſecuted by the Party. Alſo it ſeems to be [c] agreed, That if the Time to which ſuch Pardon hath Relation, be prior to the Award of Coſts to the Party, it ſhall diſcharge them: And it ſeems to be the general [d] Tenour of the Books, That tho' it be ſubſequent to the Award of the Coſts, yet if it be prior to the Taxation of them, it ſhall diſcharge them; becauſe nothing appears in certain to be due for Coſts before they are taxed. [e] Alſo if a Perſon be impriſoned on a Writ of *Excommunicato capiendo* for his Contumacy in not paying Coſts, and afterwards the King pardon all Contempts, it ſeems, That he ſhall be diſcharged of ſuch Impriſonment without any *Scire facias* againſt the Party, becauſe it is grounded on the Contempt which is wholly pardoned; and the Party muſt begin anew to compel a Payment of the Coſts.

Sect. 42. But it ſeems agreed, [f] That a Pardon ſhall not diſcharge a Suit in the Spiritual Court, any more than in a Temporal, for a Matter of Intereſt or Property in the Plaintiff, as for Tithes, Legacies, Matrimonial Contracts and ſuch like. Alſo it is [g] agreed, That after Coſts are taxed in a Suit in ſuch Court at the Proſecution of the Party, whether for a Matter of private Intereſt, or *pro reformatione morum*, or *pro ſalute animæ* as for Defamation, *&c.* they ſhall not be diſcharged by a ſubſequent Pardon.

Sect. 43. If the Offence be pardoned after Coſts are taxed, and then the Defendant appeal to a Superior Court, which gives new Coſts, whether upon the Affirmance or Reverſal of the firſt Sentence, they ſhall [h] not be avoided by Reaſon of the Pardon, becauſe they are not given in Reſpect of the Offence, but of the Award of the former Coſts, which being taxed before the Pardon, are not avoided by it, and therefore the Appeal was proper for determining whether they were well given or not. But if the Offence for which the Suit was in the Spiritual Court be pardoned, hanging an Appeal, and ſuch Pardon relate to a Time precedent to the Award of the Coſts, and after ſuch Pardon the Appellant deſert his Appeal, and the Spiritual Court award Coſts againſt him in Reſpect of ſuch Deſertion, it ſeems, [i] That he may have a Prohibition, becauſe the Pardon having diſcharged the Coſts of the firſt Suit as well as the Offence, made the Appeal to be to no Purpoſe. It is [k] ſaid, That Coſts taxed to the Party grieved for a Contempt in a Court of Equity are not diſcharged by a general Pardon of all Contempts, becauſe it is the Common Courſe of a Court of Equity to award ſuch Coſts at the Pleaſure of the Judge. But it hath been queſtioned whether Coſts taxed by the Prothonotary upon an Attachment to the Party grieved be not diſcharged by a general Pardon of all Contempts.

Sect. 44. It was inſiſted [l] by the Houſe of Commons in the Earl of *Danby*'s Caſe, and it is enacted by 12 & 13 *W.* 3. *ch.* 2. *That no Pardon under the Great Seal be pleaded to an Impeachment by the Commons in Parliament.*

Sect. 45. As to the tenth Particular, *viz.* Whether a Pardon may be conditional: It ſeems agreed, [m] That the King may extend his Mercy on what Terms he pleaſes, and conſequently may annex to his Pardon any Condition that he thinks fit, whether precedent or ſubſequent, on the Performance whereof the Validity of the Pardon will depend.

[a] 5 Co. 51. Cro. Eliz. 684. pl. 18. Cro. Ca. 113, 114.
[b] 5 Co. 51. Winch 125. Cro. Ja. 335. Hob. 81. Cont. Cro. El. 684. pl. 18.
[c] Cro. Ja. 335. Cro. Ca. 9. Vide Cro. Ca. 667, 668.
[d] 2 Roll. Abr. 304. pl. 1. 299. pl. 8. 5 Co. 51. Latch 190. Noy 85, 91. Cro. Ca. 46, 47. Vide Cro. Ca. 9. wherein it is holden that an Award of Coſts tho' they have not been taxed, ſhall not be avoided by a Pardon, but the other Books ſeem contrary.
[e] 1 Jon. 227. 2 Rol. 178. Letter S. Cont. adjudged. Cro. Jac. 159. And 'tis made a Quære Cro. Ja. 212. whether an Excommunication can be diſcharged by the King's Pardon. 8 Co. 68, 69.
[f] 5 Co. 51.
[g] Latch 190. 5 Co. 51. Cr. Ca. 46, 47. and the Authorities cited to the precedent Sect.
[h] Cro. Ca. 46, 47. Winch 125.
[i] 2 Rol. Abr. 304. pl. 2. Noy 85. Latch 155.
[k] 2 Vent. 194.
[l] State Trials, Vol. 2. f. 199, 723.
[m] Moor 466. pl. 662. Co. Li. 274. b.

Sect. 46. As to the eleventh Particular, *viz.* Where a Pardon is void in Respect of a wrong Recital: It being a general Rule, [a] That where-ever the King appears to have been deceived, his Grant is void, I take it to be agreed, That if it appears from the Recital of a Pardon, that the King was misinformed either as to the [b] Nature of the Case, or the Proceedings thereupon, the Pardon is void; as where the [c] King pardons a Man for Felony whereof he stands indicted, or indicted and attainted, and in Truth he never was indicted, &c.

Sect. 47. How a Pardon of Felony shall be avoided by Statute in Respect of a wrong Suggestion, hath been already shewn, *Sect.* 10.

Sect. 48. As to the second general Point, *viz.* What is the Effect of a Pardon: I take it to be settled at this Day, That the Pardon of a Treason or Felony even after a Conviction or Attainder, does so far clear the Party from the Infamy and all other [d] Consequences of his Crime, that he may not only have an Action [e] for a Scandal in calling him Traitor or Felon after the Time of the Pardon, but may also be a good Witness notwithstanding the [f] Attainder or Conviction; because the Pardon makes [g] him as it were a new Man, and gives him a new Capacity and Credit.

Sect. 49. And it hath been [h] admitted, That the King's Pardon of the Burning of the Hand on a Conviction of Manslaughter hath the same Effect as to this Purpose, as the Burning would have had, which is [i] agreed to restore the Party to his Credit.

Sect. 50. But it hath been adjudged, [k] That a Pardon is of no Manner of Force, as to this Purpose, till it have passed the Great Seal.

Sect. 51. Also it is said, [l] That the Pardon of a Felony will not make an Arrest for it, by one who did not know of the Pardon, unlawful, because such Arrests being for the Publick Good are to be favoured; and therefore shall not be actionable by Reason of such a Pardon, as scandalous Words shall be, because they deserve no Favour.

Sect. 52. I do not [m] find it clearly settled, Whether the Pardon of a Conviction of Perjury make the Party a good Witness.

Sect. 53. If a Man be convicted, or deprived, or otherwise punished for an Offence during a Session of Parliament, and at the same Session an Act passeth which pardons the Offence: It seems agreed, "That the Conviction or Deprivation, &c. are *ipso facto* avoided, because the Act taking Effect from the first Day of the Session, it now appears that the Offence was pardoned at the Time of the Conviction, &c. Also it hath been adjudged, That where an Act of Parliament expresly pardons such and such Crimes from a certain Day before the Session, it thereby avoids all [o] Convictions and [p] Deprivations, and [q] Awards of Costs and Amerciaments, [r] &c. for such Crimes, whether such Convictions, &c. were before or after the Sessions, because it appears to be the Intent of the Parliament that such Crimes shall no Way be punished, which cannot take Effect if such Convictions, &c. continue in Force.

[a] Yelv. 43. 47, 48. Cro. Jac. 18, 34. 2 Rol. Abr. 188. Letters N. O. Dy. 352. pl. 26. Cro. Ja. 548.
[b] Raym. 13. 1 Sid. 41.
[c] 3 Inst. 238. H. P. C. 251.
[d] Vide 1 Keb. 940. pl. 59. Fitz. Coro. 154, 281. 1 Aff. 3. Cro. Ca. 55. 1 Sid. 222. 5 Co. 49.
[e] Hob. 67, 81, 82. Moor 863. pl. 1187. 872. pl. 1213. 1 Rol. Abr. 87. pl. 6. Owen 150. 1 Brownl. 10. Raym. 23. Cont. Cro. Ja. 622. pl. 14.
[f] State Trials, Vol. 2. f. 269. Vol. 3. f 552, 553, 585, 596, 610. Vol. 4. 119. 5 Mod. 15, 16. Raym. 369. 370. 2 H. H. P. C. 278. But the contrary is held Bulst. 154. and State Trials, Vol. 2. 520 to 524. Raym. 379, 380.
[g] Skin. 578, 579. State Trials, Vol. 4. 119.
[h] State Trials, Vol. 4. 379. to 386.

[i] Supra ch. 33. sect. 129. [k] By the Lords in the Earl of Warwick's Trial, State Trials, Vol. 4. 379 to 386. [l] Hob. 67, 82. [m] Vide State Trials, Vol. 2. 520 to 524. 1 Keb. 780. pl. 24. 5 Mod. 15, 16. Ray. 369, 370, 379. 380. Kely. 37, 38. 1 Sid. 52, 221, 222. 3 Lev. 426. [n] Cro. Eliz 41. pl. 4. Vide Latch 22. [o] 6 Co. 14. a. Cro. Ca. 67, 68, 114, 115. Vide Latch 22, 141. 8 H. 5. 2. pl. 6 35 H. 6. 1. 2. Fitz. Fines, 21. Pardon, 6. [p] Burton's Case, 6 Co. 13. b. 14. a. But this Case hath often been denied to be Law, 1 Keb. 780. pl. 24. 1 Sid. 164, 222. [q] Latch 190. Noy 91. Cro. Ca. 47. [r] 36 H. 6. 24, 25. 37 H. 6. 21. Fitz. Charter 22. 5 Co. 49. Co. Litt. 126. b. Cro. Ja. 64. Moor 394. pl. 511. Cro. Eliz. 768, 778. Whether an Excommunication be pardoned by a general Pardon of all Contempts, &c. Supra sect. 41.

Sect. 54.

Sect. 54. But it seems to be a settled [a] Rule, That no Pardon by the King, without express Words of Restitution, shall devest, either from the King or [b] Subject, an Interest either in Lands or Goods, vested in them, by an Attainder or Conviction precedent. Yet it seems [c] agreed, That a Pardon prior to a Conviction, shall prevent any Forfeiture either of Lands or Goods.

Sect. 55. It hath been adjudged, [d] That a Clause of Release of all Judgments and Executions in a general Pardon, extends as well to Debts due to the King by Assignment or Forfeiture, as to those originally due to him, and that it doth not restore them to the Person who assigned or forfeited them, but extinguishes them in the Hands of the Debtor.

Sect. 56. It seems agreed, That notwithstanding the King's Pardon to a Simonist coming into Church contrary to the Purport of 31 *El.* 6. or to an Officer coming into his Office by a corrupt Bargain, contrary to the Purport of 5 & 6 *Ed.* 6. 16. may save [e] such Clerk or Officer from any Criminal Prosecution in Respect of the corrupt Bargain; yet shall it not [f] enable the Clerk to hold the Church, nor the [g] Officer to retain the Office, because they are absolutely disabled by Statute.

Sect. 57. Also it seems [h] agreed, That the King's Pardon cannot salve the Corruption of Blood by Attainder of Treason or Felony.

Sect. 58. As to the third general Point, *viz.* Whether a Pardon may be waived: I take it to be [i] agreed, That a general Pardon by Parliament cannot be waived, because no one by his Admittance can give a Court a Power to proceed against him, when it appears there is no Law to punish him.

Sect. 59. But it is [k] certain, That a Man may waive the Benefit of a Pardon under the Great Seal, as where one who has such a Pardon doth not plead it, but takes the General Issue, after which he shall not resort to the Pardon.

And now I am to shew in what Manner a Pardon is to be taken Advantage of, which I shall consider,

1. In Relation to a general Pardon by Parliament.
2. In Relation to a particular Pardon under the Great Seal.

Sect. 60. And first, As to the Pleading of a general Pardon by Parliament: It seems [l] agreed, That if any Persons are excepted out of it, the Court is not bound, and some [m] have holden that it hath no Power in Discretion to give any Person the Benefit of it, unless it be pleaded. Also it seems generally agreed, That if the Body of such a Pardon either excepts divers particular Persons by Name, or excepts all those who come under a general Description, as all those who adhered to *J. S.* &c. no one can demand the Benefit of it, without expresly shewing in the [n] first Case that he is not one of the Persons excepted; and in the latter [o] Case, that he is not included in such Description. And if he

[a] 1 Lev. 8. 120. 2 Mod. 53. 1 Keb. 695, 757, 817, 921, 922. 3 Mod. 101, 241, 242. 1 Saund. 362, 363. 1 Sid. 167, 168, 264. Theloal, lib. 1. ch. 85. sect. 8.

[b] Dy. 34. pl. 20. Finch of Law 467. Theloal, lib. 1. ch. 15. sect. 3.

[c] 5 Co. 110. b. Owen 87. State Trials, Vol. 4. 119. 2 Mod. 53.

[d] 1 Lev. 120, 121. 1 Keb. 695, 757, 817, 921, 922. 1 Saund. 362, 363. 1 Sid. 167, 168, 264.

[e] Supra sect. 26, 33. Owen 87, 88.

[f] Hetl. 104. Co. Lit. 120. a. Watson's Clergy-man's Law, ch. 5.

[g] 3 Inst. 154. 3 Bulst. 90, 91. See B. 1. ch. 67. sect. 5. 1 Keb. 781. pl. 24.

[h] Co. Litt. 8, a. 391. b. 3 Inst. 233, 240, 241. 1 H. H. P. C. 358.

[i] See B. 1. ch. 64. sect. 63. S. P. C. 173. Lett. A. 169, 103. Lett. A. Bro. Notice, 1. 26 H. 8. 7. pl. 34. 11 H. 4. 41. pl. 8. Bro. Coro. 30, 200. Indictment, 2. Fitz. Coro. 89. Crompt. Just. 115. pl. 13.

[k] S. P. C. 173. Letter A. 169. N. Bro. Coro. 200. Kely. 24, 25.

[l] H. P. C. 252. 8 E. 4. 7. pl. 1. Cro. Ca. 32. Crompt. Just. 115. pl. 13, 14. Cro. El. 768. pl. 9. 778. pl. 11. 6 Co. 79. b. Moor 770. pl. 664. Raym. 23. 2 Inst. 234. 2 Rol. Rep. 307. Cro. El. 4. pl. 2. Moor 619. pl. 845.

[m] 1 Leon. 300. Cro. El. 125. pl. 4. Cont. Lane 71. Moor 394. Vide 5 Co. 49. Cro. Ca. 32. Yel. 126.

[n] 8 E. 4. 7. pl. 1. S. P. C. 103. Letter A. Fitz. Pardon, 3. Bro. Pleadings, 124. Contra 2 Leon. 26.

[o] 8 E. 4. 7. pl. 1. S. P. C. 103. Letter A. Fitz. Pardon, 3. Plowd. Com. 103. a. 484. b. Bro. Chart. 66. 4 H. 7. 8. pl. 9. Dy. 27. pl. 180. State Trials, Vol. 2. f. 5.

happen to be of the same Name with one of the Persons excepted by Name, it is said that it will not [a] be sufficient for him to aver that he was none of the Persons excepted, without adding that he is a different Person from such other of the same Name. Which, how it can be tried, unless it appear by some Additions to the Name in the Statute, may deserve to be considered. But if the Body of a Statute be general as to all Persons whatsoever, and afterwards some are excepted in the Provisoes, [b] perhaps it may be sufficient to plead such a Pardon, without any Averment, That he who pleads it is none of the Persons so excepted; it being a [c] general Rule, that where a Man is within the general Words of the Body of a Record or Deed, which is qualified by subsequent Provisoes, it is sufficient for him to bring his Case within such general Words and that the Exceptions in such Provisoes ought to be shewn of the other Side. [99.]

Sect. 61. But it seems agreed, [d] That the Court is so far bound to take Notice *ex Officio* of a general Pardon by Parliament, which extends to all Persons in general without Exception, That it cannot proceed against any Person whatsoever as to any of the Offences pardoned, tho' he be so far from pleading it, or praying the Benefit of it, that he does all he can to [e] waive it.

Sect. 62. Also where a general Act of Pardon excepts certain Kinds of Crimes, there is [f] no Need to aver that the Crime whereof a Person is indicted is not one of such excepted Crimes; but the Court ought judicially to take Notice whether it be excepted or not.

Sect. 63. Also where such a Statute excepts only one Particular Person, it hath been [g] said, that there is no Need of an Averment that a Person indicted is not such Person; but that the Court is to take Notice whether he be or not.

Secondly, As to the Taking Advantage of a particular Pardon under the [h] Great Seal, I shall observe only the following Particulars.

Sect. 64. First, That it will be [i] Error to allow a Man the Benefit of such a Pardon, unless it be pleaded.

Sect. 65. Secondly, That he who pleads such a Pardon, ought to [k] produce it *sub pede sigilli*, tho' it be a Plea in Bar, because it is presumed to be in his Custody, and the [l] Property of it belongs to him. Yet if a Man plead such Pardon without producing it, it seems [m] that the Court may in Discretion indulge him a farther Day to put in a better Plea; and that at such Day he may perfect his Plea by producing the Charter. Also it seems [n] agreed, that there is no Need in a Plea of *Autrefoits acquit, &c.* to produce the Record immediately, because it is pleaded in Bar, and he that pleads it hath neither the Custody nor Property of it.

[a] 8 E. 4. 7. pl. 1. S. P. C. 103. Letter A. Fitz. Pardon. 3.
[b] Vide 1 Lev. 26. 4 H. 7. 8. pl. 9. Raym. 23.
[c] 1 Lev. 26, 88. Raym. 65. Cro. Ca. 515.
[d] H. P. C. 252. Plow. Com. 83. b. 26 H. 8. 7. pl. 34. Bro. Notice 1. Dy. 28. pl. 188. 5 Co. 49. 3 Inst. 234. 11 H. 4. 41. pl. 8. Bro. Coro. 30. Indictment, 2. 2 Rol. Rep. 307.
[e] Vide supra Sect. 58.
[f] Noy 100. Black versus Allen. Cro. Ca. 449. Moore 620. pl. 845. Vide 2 Leon. 26. Carth. 132. Crompt. Just. 116. pl. 17. 8 Co. 68. 3 Inst. 234.
[g] Cro. Eliz. 125. pl. 4. Vide 2 Leon. 26.
[h] That no such Pardon is good unless under the Great Seal, and consequently that Articles of Surrender cannot be pleaded as amounting to a Pardon, State Trials, Vol. 1. fol. 578, &c.
[i] Cro. Eliz. 153. pl. 33.
[k] H. P. C. 252. S. P. C. 103. Letter B. 11 H. 4. 41. pl. 6.
[l] See the Books above cited, and Cro. Ja. 70, 317. Cro. Ca. 441, 442. 1 Jon. 377. 1 Sid. 311. Cro. El. 217. pl. 2. 547. pl. 21. 716. pl. 42.
[m] 11 H. 4. 41. pl. 6. S. P. C. 103. Letter B.
[n] Vide supra ch. 35. sect. 2.

Sect. 66. Thirdly, That if there be a Variance [a] between the Record on which a Man is convicted or attainted, and his Charter of Pardon; yet if there be no Repugnancy to intend that the ſame Perſon or Thing are meant in both, it may be ſupplied by proper Averments: And therefore if one be indicted by the Name of *J. S.* [b] Yeoman, and pardoned by the Name of *J. S.* Gentleman, or indicted by the Name of *B.* the Tasker, and pardoned by the Name of *B.* the Son of *W.* he may make good the Variance by averring, that he is the ſame Perſon intended in ſuch Indictment and Pardon: Or if in an Indictment [c] of the Death of *J. S.* the Stroke be ſuppoſed to have been given on the firſt of *Auguſt*, and in the Pardon on the third, the Party may aver that the Death of one and the ſame *J. S.* are intended in both. And if ſuch a variant Pardon be pleaded without any ſuch Averment, it ſeems that the Court may in Diſcretion give the Party a farther Day either to [d] perfect his Plea, or to [e] purchaſe a better Pardon. And there are ſome [f] Inſtances in the old Books, where upon ſuch Variance the Court took an Inquiry of Office, whether the ſame Perſon were meant in both Records.

Sect. 67. Fourthly, That no ſuch Pardon can be pleaded together with, or after the General Iſſue, unleſs it be of a Date ſubſequent to the Time of the Pleading ſuch Iſſue, becauſe otherwiſe it is waived by it; as hath been more fully ſhewn, *Sect.* 59.

Sect. 68. Fifthly, [g] That the Party ſhall not be obliged to lay the Streſs of his Caſe on any particular Words or Clauſe in ſuch Pardon, but may take Advantage of the Whole.

Sect. 69. Sixthly, That after an [h] Amerciament in the King's Bench hath been eſtreated into the Exchequer, and the Party being taken upon Proceſs from thence hath inſiſted upon a Pardon, and been denied any Benefit from it, yet he may be brought by a *Habeas Corpus cum cauſa* to the King's Bench, becauſe the Record remains there, and the Tranſcript is only ſent into the Exchequer, and may plead the ſame Pardon in the King's Bench; and if it be adjudged ſufficient, may have a *Superſedeas* to the Barons, *&c.*

Sect. 70. Seventhly, That while the Statute of 10 *Ed.* 3. 2. ſtood in Force, (which required all Perſons pardoned for Felony to find Sureties for their Good Behaviour before the Sheriff and Coroners within three Months, *&c.*) no Pardon of [i] Felony could be allowed, without a Writ out of Chancery, commonly called a Writ of Allowance, teſtifying that the Party had found [k] Sureties, *&c.* according to that Statute, unleſs it were diſpenſed with by a Special Clauſe of *Non obſtante, &c.* But the Neceſſity hereof is taken away by 5 & 6 *W. & M.* 13. which hath repealed the ſaid Statute of 10 *Ed.* 3. *but hath provided, that the Juſtices before whom any Pardon for Felony ſhould be pleaded, may at their Diſcretion, remand, or commit the Perſon that pleads it to Priſon, till he or they ſhall enter into a Recognizance with two ſufficient Sureties for the Good Behaviour for any Time, not exceeding ſeven Years. Provided that if ſuch Perſon be an Infant or Feme covert, he or ſhe may find two ſufficient Sureties, who ſhall enter into a Recognizance for his or her Being of the Good Behaviour, as is aforeſaid.*

[a] H.P.C. 253. Supra ch. 35. ſect. 3, 4. 5. 3 Inſt. 240. S.P.C. 104. Letter a. Crompt. Juſt. 116. pl. 18. [b] Keilw. 58. a. Dy. 34. pl. 20. 1 Rol. Rep. 368. Fitz. Coro. 294. but 18. E. 3. 33. pl. 11. Abridged Fitz. Brief, ſeems contrary. 364. [c] 11 H. 4. 41. pl. 6. Abridged Fitz. Monſtrans de faits, 128. Bro. Variance, 38. Coro. 29. Charter de Pardon, 15. But Note, that none of theſe Books make mention of any Averment but ſeem to imply that the Pardon was allowed without it, notwithſtanding the Variance. [d] 11 H. 4. 41. pl. 6. Fitz. Monſt. de faits, 128. [e] 3 Inſt. 240. 1 Sid. 41. 26 Aſſ. pl. 46. Raym. 13. Fitz. Office de Court, 34. Bro. Charter de Pard. 32. Office de Court, 25. [f] Fitz. Coro. 294. 3 Aſſ. pl. 15. Abridged Fitz. Coro. 166. Bro. Cor. 190 or 191. Variance, 63. But Bro. in abridging this Caſe under the Title of Charter of Pardon, 29 makes this Remark, quod mirum mihi. [g] 37 H. 6. 4. a. Fitz. Chart. 21. [h] 36 H. 6. 24, 25. Fitz. Chart. 22. Bro. Charter, 25. [i] S. P. C. 103. Letter C. Crompt. Juſt. 115. pl. 15. 3 H. 7. pl. 5. Plow. Com. 502. b. 1 Keb. 9. pl. 11. 1 Sid. 41. Raym. 13. 3 Inſt. 234, 235. Carth. 121. But there never was any Neceſſity for ſuch Writ upon a Pardon of Treaſon, Cro. Eliz. 814. pl. 2. Noy 31. [k] That a Breach of the Recognizance avoided the Pardon, 3 H. 7. 7. pl. 5. S. P. C. 103. Letter C. Crompt Juſtice, 115. pl. 16.

Sect. 71. Eighthly, That the Judges may insist on the usual Fee of Gloves [a] to themselves and Officers, before they allow a Pardon.

[a] Fitz. Coro. 294. 4 E. 4. 10. b. 2 Jon. 56. 1 Sid. 452. pl. 18. Kely. 25. Pulton de pace, 88. a.

CHAP. XXXVIII.

Of the General Issue.

Sect. 1. HAVING shewn already, *Ch.* 23. *Sect.* 128 and 137. that the General Issue is pleadable in capital Cases, together with any other Plea in Bar or Abatement, which is not repugnant to it; and that it may also be pleaded even after such Plea found against a Defendant; and having also shewn, *Ch.* 37. *Sect.* 59. That the Plea of the General Issue amounts to a Waiver of a Pardon; and *Ch.* 26. *Sect.* 66, &c. what is a good General Issue to an Information on a penal Statute; and in the same Chapter, *Sect.* 73, 74. In what Manner the Issue is to be joined on such an Information, and where it is to be tried, I shall in this Place take Notice only of the following Particulars;

Sect. 2. First, That in a criminal Information or Indictment in the [b] King's Bench, for a Misdemeanour, and also in an Indictment before [c] Justices of the Peace, the Issue is well joined for the King by the Words *A. B. qui pro Rege sequitur similiter*, &c. without any Addition, shewing that *A. B.* is the proper Officer for this Purpose; for it shall be intended that he was sufficiently known to be such by the Court. But in all [d] Precedents I meet with of Informations of Intrusion, the Issue for the King is joined by the Attorney General, naming himself such.

Sect. 3. Secondly, That in Indictments of [e] capital Crimes, after the Defendant hath pleaded *quod ipse in nullo est inde culpabilis, & inde de bono & malo ponit se super patriam*, (which is the general Form of pleading the General Issue in capital Cases, both in [f] Indictments and [g] Appeals,) the Usage seems to have been immediately to award Process against the Jury, without any express Joining of Issue on the Part of the King. But in the Precedents of Appeals of Felony, whether by an [h] Appellant or [i] Approver, generally the Issue is expresly joined by the Appellant and Approver as well as the Appellee.

Sect. 4. Thirdly, That it seems [k] the better Opinion, that if an Issue be joined in Process on a Recognizance for the Peace, whether the Defendant killed *J. S.* and such Issue be found for the King, yet shall it not estop the Defendant to plead Not guilty to an Indictment or Appeal for the Death of the same *J. S.*

[b] 1 Sid. 230, 231. Coke's Entr. 363. a.

[c] Cro. Ca. 315.

[d] 1 Co. 17. a. 27. a. Coke's Entr. 372. a. 379. a. 381 a. 385. a. 387. b. 390. b. Raft. Ent. 412. a.

[e] Coke's Entr. 352. a. 353. b. 354. b. 355. b. 356. b. 358. a. 360. a. 361. a. Raft. Ent. 385. pl. 5. 9.

[f] See the Precedents above cited.

[g] Coke's Ent. 57. b. Raft. Ent. 47. a. b. 48. a. 49. a. b. 50. a. b. 51. a. 52. a. 53. a. 54. a. 55. b.

[h] See the Precedents cited to the Precedent Letter. But in Raft. Ent. 43. b. after the General Issue with an &c. the Process is immediately awarded against the Jury.

[i] Raft. Ent. 42. b.

[k] 7 H. 4. 35. b. Bro. Appeal, 19.

CHAP.

CHAP. XXXIX.

Where a Prisoner shall be allowed Counsel, and a Copy of the Indictment, &c.

A Person having pleaded Not guilty is to be tried either,

1. By his Country, or
2. By his Peers, or
3. By Battle.

But before I consider what is proper to each of these in their Order, I shall endeavour to shew,

1. In what Cases a Prisoner may have Counsel to assist him in his Defence.
2. Where he may have a Copy of the Indictment.

Sect. 1. As to the first of these Particulars, I take it to be a settled [a] Rule at Common Law, that no Counsel shall be allowed a Prisoner, whether he be a [b] Peer or Commoner, upon the General Issue, on an Indictment of Treason or Felony, unless some Point of Law arise, proper to be debated.

Sect. 2. This indeed many have complained of as very unreasonable, yet if it be considered, that generally every one of Common Understanding may as properly speak to a Matter of Fact, as if he were the best Lawyer; and that it requires no manner of Skill to make a plain and honest Defence, which in Cases of this Kind is always the best, the Simplicity and Innocence, artless and ingenuous Behaviour of one whose Conscience acquits him, having something in it more moving and convincing than the highest Eloquence of Persons speaking in a Cause not their own. And if it be farther considered that it is the [c] Duty of the Court to be indifferent between the King and Prisoner, and to see that the Indictment be good in Law, and the Proceedings regular, and the Evidence legal, and such as fully proves the Point in Issue, there seems no great Reason to fear but that, generally speaking, the Innocent, for whose Safety alone the Law is concerned, have rather an Advantage than Prejudice in having the Court their only Counsel. Whereas on the other Side, the very Speech, Gesture and Countenance, and Manner of Defence of those who are guilty, when they speak for themselves, may often help to disclose the Truth, which probably would not so well be discovered from the artificial Defence of others speaking for them.

[a] 3 Inst. 29. 137. 7 H. 4. 35. b. Finch 386. 2 Bulst. 147. Bro. Coro. 54. Fitz. Coro. 31. Cro. Ca. 147. S. P. C. 151. B. 9 E. 4. 2. pl. 4. 1 Lev. 86. Dr. and Stud. B. 2. ch. 48. State Trials, Vol. 1. fol. 70. V. 2. f. 1002. See the Books cited to the other Parts of this Chapter.

[b] State Trials, Vol. 1. f. 70, 265, 614. Vol. 4. f. 355. 3 Inst. 29. Rushw. Col. Part 2. Vol. 1. f. 94.

[c] 2 Bulst. 147. 3 Inst. 29.

Sect. 3. But the Law allows a Defendant the ſame Benefit of Counſel in an [a] Appeal, whether Capital or not Capital, as in any other Action. Perhaps for this Reaſon among [b] others, becauſe Appeals are preſumed to be generally carried on with greater Heat and Spleen than Indictments, and yet are not ſo much to be favoured as being for the moſt part rather grounded on a Deſire of private Revenge than of Publick Juſtice; and therefore the Defendant ſhall have at leaſt the ſame Advantage in them as in Common Actions.

Sect. 4. Alſo upon Indictments, the Court will never refuſe to aſſign a Priſoner Counſel to argue a doubtful Point of Law, happening to ariſe at or after his Trial; as where it ſhall appear queſtionable whether the Facts proved, if true, fully [c] amount to the Crime charged againſt him; or whether the Perſons offered to be Evidence againſt him be [d] legal Witneſſes in Reſpect of ſuch or ſuch Exceptions againſt them; or whether certain Perſons returned [e] of his Jury can be lawful Jurors, in Reſpect of certain Objections againſt them; or whether the [f] Indictment or [g] Proceſs, *&c.* be ſtrictly legal: In all which Caſes the Priſoner muſt [h] propoſe the Point, and [i] if the Court think it will bear a Debate, they will aſſign him Counſel to argue it.

Sect. 5. Alſo where-ever a Priſoner hath a [k] Pardon or other [l] Special Matter to plead to an Indictment, or an [m] Error to aſſign in Order to reverſe an Outlawry, the Court will of Courſe aſſign him Counſel. And it is [n] ſaid, That for ſuch collateral Matters any one may be of Counſel for a Priſoner without any Aſſignment.

Sect. 6. But if a Queſtion ariſe on the Trial of a Peer concerning the Courſe of Parliamentary Proceedings, the Lords will not [o] ſuffer it to be argued by Counſel, but will debate it among themſelves.

Sect. 7. There is a Caſe in the *Year-Book* of [p] *H.* 4. Where a Serjeant at Law, as *amicus Curiæ*, offered his Opinion to the Court, concerning the Trial of an Indictment of Death, That it was not proper to proceed in it till the Year and Day were paſſed, nor doth he appear to have been any Way reprehended for it. [q] But it is not ſafe for any one to be either Counſel or Solicitor to one in Priſon for a Capital Crime, in Order to Prepare him for his Trial, without an Aſſignment from the Court. But by Leave of the Court Priſoners have ſometimes been indulged the Aſſiſtance of Counſel, not only to [r] adviſe them in Priſon, but [s] alſo to ſtand by them at the Bar: But it is ſaid, [t] That in Strictneſs they ought not to be prompted by them as to Matters of Fact, [u] nor to have the Aſſiſtance of any Papers drawn up by Counſel to prepare them for their Trial.

Sect. 8. After a Priſoner hath had Counſel aſſigned him, the Court will not [x] diſcharge them without his Conſent, tho' they deſire it, but will ſometimes add others to them.

Sect. 9. It is [y] ſaid, That the Court cannot aſſign an Appellee any of the King's Counſel; but that if they will they may be either for or againſt him.

[a] S.P.C. 151. B. Dr. & Stud. B. 2. ch. 48. Dy. 296. pl. 20. Keilw. 176. b. Finch of Law 386. 1 Bulſt. 85. 9 E. 4. 2. pl. 4. Bro. Coro. 54. Fitz. Coro. 31.

[b] Dr. & Stud. B. 2. ch. 48.

[c] 3 Inſt. 137. State Trials, Vol. 1. f. 569. Ruſhworth's Stafford 671.

[d] State Trials, Vol. 2. 520.

[e] State Trials, Vol. 3. f. 135.

[f] 3 Inſt. 29. 1 Lev. 68. Cro. Ca. 147. 2 H. H. P. C. 236.

[g] 3 Inſt. 29. 137. 6 Co. 14.

[h] 3 Inſt. 137. State Trials, Vol. 2. f. 762.

[i] State Trials, Vol. 2. f. 694, 701, 709, 763, 764. Vol. 3. 867.

[k] 3 Inſt. 29 137. Vide 26 Aſſ. pl. 46. Fitz. Office de Court, 34. 11 H. 7. 23. a. Bro. Coro. 128, 129. Finch of Law, 386.

[m] 2 Jo. 180. Cro. Ca. 365. Yet in the Year-Book of 1 H. 7. 13. the Court refuſed it, becauſe the Party was of very bad Fame.

[n] 2 Jo. 180.

[o] State Trials, Vol. 2. 694. 699. [p] 7 H. 4. 36. a. S. P. C. 151. B. 3 Inſt. 29, 137. [q] State Trials, Vol. 2. f. 272, 273, 712, 743, 763, 768. [r] State Trials, Vol. 3. f. 133. [s] State Trials, Vol. 2. f. 614. [t] State Trials, Vol. 2. f. 614. [u] State Trials, Vol. 1. f. 732. Vol. 2. f. 743, 762, 763, 770. [x] State Trials, Vol. 2 f. 711, 712. [y] 1 Bulſt. 85.

Sect. 10. It having been found by Experience that Prisoners have been often under great Disadvantages from the Want of Counsel, in Prosecutions of High Treason against the King's Person, which are generally managed for the Crown with greater Skill and Zeal than ordinary Prosecutions, it is enacted by 7 *W.* 3. 3. *That all and every Person and Persons whatsoever, that shall be accused and indicted for High Treason, whereby any Corruption of Blood may or shall be made to any such Offender or Offenders, or to any the Heir or Heirs of any such Offender or Offenders, or for Misprision of such Treason, shall be received and admitted to make his and their full Defence by Counsel learned in the Law: And in Case any Person or Persons so accused or indicted shall desire Counsel, the Court, before whom such Person or Persons shall be tried, or some Judge of that Court is authorised and required, immediately upon his or their Request, to assign to such Person and Persons, such and so many Counsel, not exceeding two, as the Person or Persons shall desire, to whom such Counsel shall have free Access at all seasonable Hours; any Law or Usage to the contrary notwithstanding.*

Sect. 11. But it is provided, *S.* 3. *That any Person being indicted of such Treason may be outlawed,* &c. *and where by the Law, after such Outlawry, he may come in and be tried, he shall upon such Trial have the Benefit of the said Act.*

Sect. 12. And it is farther provided, *S.* 12, 13. *That nothing in the said Act shall extend, or be construed to extend to any Impeachment or other Proceedings in Parliament whatsoever. And also that it shall not any Ways extend to any Indictment of High Treason, nor to ony Proceedings thereupon, for counterfeiting his Majesty's Coin, his Great or Privy Seal, his Sign Manual, or Privy Signet.*

[a] 1 Lev. 68. Moor, 666. State Trials, Vol. 1. f. 644. Vol. 2. f. 711, 763. Vol. 3. f. 861, 862, 863, 864. Show. 131. 1 Sid. 85. 2 H. H. P. C. 236.
[b] Lev. 68. 1 Sid. 85.
[c] State Trials, Vol. 2. f. 711.

Sect. 13. As to the second Particular, *viz.* Where a Prisoner may have a Copy of the Indictment against him: It is said, [a] That by the Common Law it is always denied in Cases of Treason or Felony. Yet if a Prisoner take a legal Exception to an Indictment, it is said, [b] That the Court will grant him a Copy of so much as concerns his Exception. Also if he have such Matter to plead which cannot well be put into Form without Knowledge of the Charge against him as laid in the Indictment, as *Autrefoits acquit, &c.* it is [c] said, That the Court will give him the Heads of the Indictment, to enable him to have his Plea so drawn as to suit the Charge against him.

Sect. 14. But it is enacted by 7 *W.* 3. *That every Person and Persons indicted for High Treason, except for counterfeiting the Coin, or the Great or Privy Seal, or Sign Manual or Privy Signet, shall have a true Copy of the whole Indictment, but not the Names of the Witnesses, five Days at the least before Trial, to advise with Counsel thereupon, to plead and make their Defence, his or their Attorney, or Agent, requiring the same, and paying the Officer his reasonable Fees for writing thereof not exceeding five Shillings for the Copy of every such Indictment.* [100]

Sect. 15. What Exceptions may be taken to such Indictment, and when, hath been shewn, *Ch.* 25. *Sect.* 146, 147, 148, 149.

CHAP. XL.

From what County the Jury is to be returned, &c.

FOR the better Underſtanding what more particularly relates to a Trial by the Country in Capital Caſes, having ſhewn, *Ch.* 5. *Sect.* 18. That by Virtue of a ſpecial Commiſſion, Juſtices of *Oyer* and *Terminer* may ſit in one County, for the Trial of a Fact in another by the proper Jurors. And having alſo ſhewn, *Ch.* 23. *Sect.* 92, 93. what is a proper Place from whence a *Viſne* may come, I ſhall in this Place only conſider,

1. From what County the Jury is to be returned.
2. By Virtue of what Proceſs.
3. Before what Court.
4. How they may be challenged.

As to the firſt of theſe Particulars, *viz.* From what County the Jury is to be returned: I ſhall endeavour to ſhew,

1. From what County they are to be returned for the Trial of the General Iſſue.
2. From what County for the Trial of a Foreign Plea.

Sect. 1. As to the firſt Point, *viz.* From what County a Jury is to be returned for the Trial of the General Iſſue: I take it to be [a] agreed, That [b] regularly by the Common Law they muſt be returned in all Caſes, for the Trial of the General iſſue from the ſame County wherein the Fact was committed. And it is ſaid, That in an Appeal of Death, where the Wound was given in one County, and the Party died in another, the Jury [c] ought to be returned from each County before the Statute of 2 & 3 *Ed.* 6. 24. ſince which the whole may be tried either upon an [d] Indictment or Appeal, in the County wherein the Death happens.

Sect. 2. But it is enacted by 33 *H.* 8. 23. *That if any Perſon being examined by the King's Council, or three of them, upon any Manner of Treaſons, Miſpriſions of Treaſons, or Murders, do confeſs any ſuch Offences, or that the ſaid Council, or three of them, upon ſuch Examination, ſhall think any Perſon ſo examined, to be vehemently ſuſpected of any Treaſon, Miſpriſions of Treaſons or Murder, that then in every ſuch Caſe by the King's Commandment his Majeſty's Commiſſion of* Oyer *and* Terminer *under the Great Seal, ſhall be made by the Chancellor of* England *to ſuch Perſons and into ſuch Vills and Places as ſhall be nam'd and appointed by the King, for the ſpeedy Trial, Conviction or Delivery of ſuch Offenders; which Commiſſioners ſhall have Power to enquire, hear and determine all ſuch Treaſons, Miſpriſions of Treaſons and Murders, within the Places limited by their Commiſſion, by ſuch good and lawful Perſons as ſhall be returned before them by the Sheriff, or his Miniſter, or any other having Power to return Writs and Proceſs for that*

[a] S.P.C. 154. Dy. 132. pl. 75. 286. pl. 5. Fitz. Coro. 194. 3 Inſt. 27. 26 Aſſ. pl. 32. Vide ſupra ch. 5. ſect. 19.

[b] Vide infra ſect. 5.

[c] Book 1. ch. 31. ſect. 13. Supra ch. 23. ſect. 35. Fitz. Coro. 59, 60.

[d] Vide ſupra ch. 25. ſect. 35. 2 H. H. P. C. 262.

that Purpoſe, in whatſoever other Shire or Place within the King's Dominions, or without, ſuch Offences were done or committed, and that in ſuch Caſes, no Challenge for the Shire or Hundred ſhall be allowed.

Sect. 3. It hath been [a] adjudged, That this Statute as far as it relates to Treaſon done within the Realm, is repealed by 1 & 2 *P. & M.* 10. which enacts, That all Trials for Treaſon ſhall be according to the Common Law. But as to [b] Murder and [c] Miſpriſion of Treaſon, it ſtill ſeems to continue in Force. And as to High [d] Treaſon done without the Realm, it doth not ſeem material whether it be in Force or not, becauſe that is fully provided for by 35 *H.* 8. 2. as hath been more fully ſhewn *Ch.* 25. *Sect.* 49, 50, 51, 52, 53.

Sect. 4. It hath been [e] adjudged, That the Word *Murder* in this Statute ſhall have the ſame ſtrict Conſtruction as in the [f] Statutes which take away the Benefit of Clergy from Murder, and conſequently ſhall not extend to one examined before the Council as Acceſſary only, and not as Principal; for Murder is one Offence, and the being Acceſſary to it is another.

Sect. 5. Having ſhewn already that he, who ſteals [g] Goods in one County, and carries them into another, or does a Fact in one County which proves a [h] Nuſance to another, may be indicted or appealed in either, from whence it follows, That he may be alſo tried in either: Having alſo [i] ſhewn, That he who marries two Wives, the firſt in a Foreign Country, and the ſecond in *England*, may be Indicted and tried in *England*; and that he who takes a Woman by Force out of one County, and carries her into another and there marries her, [k] may be indicted and tried in the ſecond County: And that Felonies in [l] *Wales* may by Force of 26 *H.* 8. 6. be indicted and tried in the next adjoining *Engliſh* County: And that Treaſons upon the Seas, [m] or in any Foreign [n] Country, and Felonies [o] and Piracies upon the Sea, may be indicted and tried in any County in *England*; and that an [p] Acceſſary in one County to Murder in another, may be appealed and tried in the County wherein the Stroke was given; and that an Acceſſary to Murder, or any other Felony in one County, may be indicted [q] and tried in the County wherein he was Acceſſary; I ſhall refer to the Places cited in the Margin for the farther Conſideration of theſe Matters.

Sect. 6. As to the ſecond Point, *viz.* From what County the Jury is to be returned for the Trial of a Foreign Plea, That is, the Plea of iſſuable Matter alledged in a different County from that wherein the Party is indicted or appealed; as where a Man indicted in the County of *A.* [r] pleads, That he was taken out of a Sanctuary in the County of *B.* Or where one appealed by a Woman for the Death of her Husband in one County, [s] pleads, That ſince the Death of her Husband ſhe hath married *J. S.* in another County; it is [t] agreed, That by the Common Law ſuch Pleas can only be tried by Juries returned from the Counties wherein they are alledged: And therefore if Iſſue be joined on ſuch Matters before a Court which has no Juriſdiction out of the County wherein it ſits, there ſeems to be [u] no Remedy by the Common Law, but to remove the Proceedings by *Certiorari* into the King's Bench, which having a Juriſdiction throughout the whole Kingdom, will award proper Proceſs for the Trial.

[a] 1 And 104, 105.
[b] 1 And 194, 195.
[c] Vide ſupra ch. 25. ſect. 143. Bro. Coro. 220. 3 Inſt. 24.
[d] Vide Dyer 286. pl. 45.
[e] 1 And. 194, 195.
[f] Supra ch. 33. ſect. 26. B. 1. ch. 31. ſect. 11.
[g] B. 1. ch. 33. ſect. 9. Supra ch. 23. ſect. 47. ch. 25. ſect. 38.
[h] Supra ch. 25. ſect. 37.
[i] B. 1. ch. 43. ſect. 7. Supra ch. 25. ſect. 39.
[k] B. 1. ch. 42. ſect. 10. Supra ch. 25. ſect. 40.
[l] B. 1. ch. 31. ſect. 14. Supra ch. 25. ſect. 41, 42.
[m] Supra ch. 25. ſect. 43, 44, 45.
[n] Supra ch. 25. ſect. 48 to 54.
[o] B. 1. ch. 37. ſect. 12, 13, 14, 15. Supra ch. 25. ſect. 43 to 48.
[p] Supra ch. 29. ſect. 49.
[q] Supra ch. 25. ſect. 54. and ch. 29. ſect. 50, 51. &c.
[r] Keilw. 175. pl. 10.
[s] Dy. 296. pl. 20.
[t] 3 Inſt. 27. S. P. C. 154. Keilw. 175. pl. 10. Dy. 296. pl. 20. H. P. C. 255. Vide 23 H. 8. 14. ſect. 5.
[u] Keilw. 175. pl. 10. Dy. 296. pl. 20. Vide Dy. 286. pl. 5.

Sect. 7. But *for the more speedy Trials of Murders and Felonies, it is enacted by* 23 H. 8. 14. Par. 5. *That all Manner of Foreign Pleas triable by the Country, upon any Indictment for any Petit Treason, Murder or Felony, shall be forthwith tried before the same Justices afore whom the Party shall be arraigned, and by the Jurors of the same County that shall try the Petit Treason, Murder or Felony, whereof he shall be so arraigned, without any further Respite or Delay, in whatsoever County or Counties, Place or Places of this Realm, the Matter of the same Pleas be supposed or alledged.*

Sect. 8. But this Statute extending neither to Indictments of High Treason, nor to Appeals, it [a] is said, That a Foreign Issue therein must still be tried by the Jury of the County wherein it is alledged.

[a] 3 Inst. 27. S. P. C. 154. H. P. C. 255. Vide Dyer 296 pl. 20.

CHAP. XLI.

Of Process against Jurors.

FOR the better Understanding the Nature of Process against Jurors in Criminal Cases, I shall endeavour to shew,

1. Where a Panel may be returned without any Precept by a bare Award.
2. In what Manner the Process is to be returnable.
3. Where a *Venire* may be joint or several.
4. What Process may be awarded by *Proviso.*
5. In what Cases, and in what Manner a *Tales* is grantable.
6. Where it is necessary to return a Panel into Court, before an Inquest can be taken upon it, and where the Prisoner may have a Copy of it.

Sect. 1. As to the first Point, *viz.* Where a Panel may be returned without any Precept by a bare Award, it is [b] agreed, That Justices of [c] Gaol-Delivery, may have a Panel so returned by the Sheriff, without any Precept or Writ; and the [d] Reason given for it is, That before their Coming, they always make a general [e] Precept to the Sheriff in Parchment under their Seals, *to bring before them at the Day of their Sessions twenty-four out of every Hundred,* &c. *to do those Things which shall be enjoined them on the Part of the King,* &c. And therefore it is said that they need not make any other Precept for the Return of a Jury, for the Trial of any Issue joined before them. But that their bare [f] Award that the Jury shall come is sufficient, because there are enow for that Purpose supposed to be present in Court, whom the Sheriff may return immediately whenever the Court shall require their Service. Also it is said, [g] that a Jury may be so returned before Justices of Peace at their Sessions, because the [h] Precept

[b] Fitz. Inquest, 55. 4 Inst. 168. 2 Inst. 568. H. P. C. 158, 256. 2 H. H. P. C. 261, 264. Crompt. Jur. 128. S. P. C. 155. Lett. E.

[c] Yet 'tis said that the Law is otherwise, if they have a Special Commission. Fitz. Inq. 55. 4 Inst. 168. Crompt. Jurisf. 128.

[d] Fitz. Inq. 55. Crompt. Jur. 128. 4 Inst. 168. 2 Inst. 568. 2 H. H. P. C. 34, 261.

[e] Vide Rast. Ent. 384. b. 385. a. pl. 1. Cro. Ca. 448.

[f] For the Form of such an Award, see Rast. Ent. 385. pl. 5. 6. State Trials, Vol. 4. fol. 182.

[g] 2 Inst. 568. Adjudged 1 Sid. 364. pl. 11.

[h] See Lambard's Just. B. 4. Ch. 2. and Crompt. Justice 232.

 for

for the Summons of the Seſſions hath a Clauſe to the ſame Effect for the Summons of twenty-four out of every Hundred, *&c.* Yet I much queſtion whether this Matter do not rather depend on [a] Practice, and the conſtant Courſe of Precedents, than any Argument from the Reaſon of the Thing. For the [b] Precept to the Sheriff from Juſtices of *Oyer* and *Terminer*, in order for the holding of their Seſſions, hath in Effect the very ſame Clauſe for the Bringing of twenty-four before them, out of each Hundred, at the Day of their Seſſions, *&c.* And yet it ſeems [c] agreed, that they cannot have a Jury returned for the Trial of an Iſſue joined before them, by Force of a bare Award, but ought to make a particular Precept to the Sheriff for that Purpoſe under their Seals.

Sect. 2. It ſeems [d] agreed, that by the Courſe of the King's Bench no Jury can be returned into it from a Foreign County, without proper Proceſs, under the [e] Seal of the Chief Juſtice, *&c.* But [f] *Quære* if it may not be returned for the Trial of an Indictment, *&c.* in the ſame County wherein it ſits, by a bare *præceptum eſt*, *&c.*

Sect. 3. As to the ſecond Point, *viz.* In what Manner the Proceſs againſt Jurors is to be returnable, it ſeems agreed, that it may be returnable immediately into the Court of King's Bench for the Trial of an Indictment in the ſame County wherein it ſits, whether for a Crime committed in ſuch County, or for a [g] Treaſon, *&c.* beyond the Sea. But that for the Trial of Indictments removed thither by *Certiorari* from other Counties, there [h] ought to be fifteen Days between the *Teſte* and Return of every Proceſs.

Sect. 4. Alſo it is [i] agreed, that Juſtices in *Eyre*, or of Gaol-Delivery, may Order a Jury to be returned immediately for the Trial of a Priſoner arraigned before them. Alſo it is clearly [k] holden by Sir *Edward Coke*, and hath been often [l] adjudged, That Juſtices of *Oyer* and *Terminer*, for the Trial of any Iſſue joined before them, might award a *Venire* returnable the ſame Day on which the Party is arraigned. Alſo it is holden by Sir [m] *Edward Coke*, and hath been [n] adjudged, That Juſtices of the Peace may do the like; but there are very [o] ſtrong Authorities to the contrary, unleſs the Crime amount [p] to Felony, or the Party [q] conſent to be tried immediately.

Sect. 5. *Quære* how far the Law is altered as to theſe Points by 4 & 5 *W. & M.* 24. and 7 & 8 *W.* 3. 32. which by requiring that Jurors ſhall be ſummoned ſix Days before they are to appear, ſeem to make it neceſſary whenever a [r] *Venire* or Particular Precept is required for the Return of a Jury, [s] that there be ſix Days between its *Teſte* and Return.

Sect. 6. It hath been [t] adjudged, That a *Venire* before Juſtices of *Oyer* and *Terminer* returnable at a Day certain is erroneous, unleſs the Seſſions appear to have been [u] adjourned to the ſame Day; becauſe otherwiſe it ſhall not be intended that their Commiſſion continued till ſuch Day; and if it did not, their Authority to try the Iſſue was determined. But it is admitted [x] that ſuch *Venire* may be made returnable at the next Aſſiſes, and then tried by Virtue of [y] 1 *E.* 6. 7.

[a] Vide 4 Inſt. 164. 2 H. H. P. C. 261. 1 Sid. 364. pl. 11. [b] Raſt Ent. 443. b. pl. 1. 2. [c] H. P. C. 162, 256. 4 Inſt. 164. 2 Inſt. 568. [d] S. P. C. 154. Lett. B. Vide 27 H. 6. 10. pl. 4. Supra ch. 27. ſect. 16. [e] Supra ch. 27. ſect. 8. [f] Vide Dyer 118. pl. 78. [g] Vide ch. 25, ſect. 49 to 70. [h] 2 Roll. A. 626. pl. 4. 5. 2 H. H. P. C. 260. Supra ch. 3. ſect. 12. and ch. 27. ſect. 16. 2 Inſt. 568. State Trials, Vol. 4. fol. 214. [i] Keilw. 159. b. H. P. C. 256. Crompt. Juſt. 152. a. Cro. Ca. 315. 1 Sid. 335. pl. 20. Fitz. Inq. 55. Vide Kely. 7. [k] 2 Inſt. 568. 4 Inſt. 164. [l] Cro. Ca. 340, 583. 2 Roll. Ab. 96. pl. 1. H. P. C. 161. 2 H. H. P. C. 261. Admitted 2. Keb. 212. pl. 49. 292. pl. 75. 718. pl. 109. 2 Keb. 433. pl. 13. 1 Sid. 334. pl. 20. 1 Roll. Abr. 96. pl. 1. Cro. Ca. 340, 583. Cont. Keilw. 159. b. Trial per pais 26. 2 Rol. Ab. 625. pl. 2. H. P. C. 266. [m] 2 Inſt. 563. 4 Inſt. 164. [n] Cro. Ja. 404. pl. 2. And in this Book it is ſaid that Common Experience is ſo. [o] Fitz. Coro. 44. Keilw. 159. b. 1 Jon. 379. pl. 10. S. P. C. 156. a. 1 Keb. 433. pl. 3. Trial per pais 25, 26. 2 Keb. 212. pl. 49. Crompt. Juſtice 152. a. 1 Sid. 99. pl. 2. 335. pl. 20. Cro. Ca. 438, 448. 2 Roll. Abr. 625. L. 1. 3. H. P. C. 256. [p] 1 Sid. 335. pl. 20. In Crompt. Juſtice 150. b. 'tis ſaid that the Seſſions for the Peace may award Proceſs for the Trial of an Indictment of Felony, the next Day after it is traverſed. Quære if the Party's Being in Gaol make no Difference? Cro. Ca. 340. 2 Roll. Abr. 96. pl. 1. 1 Sid. 335. pl. 20. [q] 1 Keb. 433. pl. 3. 1 Sid. 99. pl. 2. 334. pl. 20. [r] Vide ſupra ſect. 1. [s] State Trials, Vol. 4. fol. 99, 100. [t] 1 Sid. 348. pl. 15. 2 Keb. 284. pl. 53. 292. pl. 75. 718. pl. 109. 854. pl. 6. And in theſe Books ſuch Error is ſaid not to be helped by the next Aſſiſes happening to fall on the ſame Day. [u] Vide ſupra ch. 5. ſect. 7. 15. [x] 1 Sid. 348. pl. 15. 2 Keb. 284. pl. 53, 718. pl. 109, 854. pl. 6. Cro. Ca. 340. [y] Vide ch. 5. ſect. 12.

Sect. 7. It hath been [a] adjudged, That the Award of a *Venire* returnable at a certain Day before Justices of *Oyer*, &c. needs not expresly mention before what Justices it shall be returnable; for it cannot but be intended that it ought to be before the same Court which awards it.

Sect. 8. As to the third Point, *viz.* Where a *Venire* may be joint or several: It seems agreed, that where several Persons are arraigned upon the same [b] Indictment or [c] Appeal, and severally plead not guilty, it is in the [d] Election of the Prosecutor, &c. either to take out [e] joint *Venires* against them all, or [f] several against each of them. But in an Appeal, if one plead Not guilty, and the other plead a Release made at *A.* it seems [g] that there must be several *Venires.*

Sect. 9. It seems generally [h] agreed, that where the same Jury is returned on such a Joint Process against several Defendants, if a Juror be challenged by any one Defendant, and the Challenge allowed, and the Juror thereupon [i] drawn, he is by necessary Consequence drawn as to all the other Defendants also, because there being but one Panel, the same Person cannot at the same Time be taken from it, and yet continue in it. But where one Jury is jointly returned for the Trial of several Defendants before Justices of Gaol-Delivery, it is [k] certain that they may afterwards sever the Panel, if they find it expedient, for the Prevention of this Inconvenience. But I do not find [l] that this can be done in any other Case. And it seems agreed, That after an Apellant hath taken out a joint *Venire* against all the Apellees, he cannot [m] afterwards take out several ones, tho' the first be never returned; and the Reason seems to be because it would amount to a [n] Discontinuance.

Sect. 10. As to the fourth Point, *viz.* Where Process may be taken out by the Defendant in Criminal Cases by *Proviso*, (*i. e.* with a [o] Clause that if two Writs come to the Sheriff he shall execute one of them only.) I take it to be agreed [p] That it may be so awarded in any Appeal, whether Capital or not Capital, in the same Manner as in other Actions, after the Apellant hath made Default in [q] Relation to the very same Kind of Process. And therefore if the Appellant, after Issue joined, either neglects to take out any [r] *Venire* the same Term, &c. or takes one out but doth not [s] get it returned, it seems that the Defendant may take one out by *Proviso*, &c. And in like Manner if the Appellant make the like Default in suing out an *Habeas Corpora*, or other subsequent Process, the Defendant may sue out the like Process by *Proviso*. But where the Defendant hath sued out any Process by *Proviso*, there are [t] Authorities that

[a] 29 Ed. 3. 30. b. 31. a. In Dy. 315. pl. 99. The same Case is taken Notice of, and it is there said, that the Venire it self needs not shew before what Justice it is returnable; but this seems not to be warranted by the Book at large. Vide 2 Keb. 855. pl. 6.

[b] H. P. C. 256. 2 H. H. P. C. 263.

[c] State Trials, Vol. 4. fol. 100. H. P. C. 256. S.P.C. 155. a. 1 Jo. 425. But Cro. Eliz. 541. pl. 4. it is said to be the Course to try the Defendants in Appeal by several Venires. S.P.C. 155. a. It is said, that where there are three Defendants the Plaintiff may join two of them in one Venire, and take out another against the third.

[d] See the Books above cited, and 1 Jon. 425. and Fitz. Quare Impedit, 199. 21 H. 6. 22. pl. 46. [e] See the Books above cited. Also the same is adjudged 1 Jon. 425. Where one Appellee was charged with doing the Fact proditorie, the others Felonice. See Fitz. Quare impedit, 199. Visne, 11, 14. Keilw. 106. b. [f] Dy. 120. pl. 10. 131. pl. 72. Cro. Eliz. 541. pl. 4. [g] 50 E. 3. 1. pl. 1. Bro. Visne, 27. Vide 11 H. 7. 5. pl. 9. Bro. Disc. de Process, 62. Fitz. Execut. 114. Nisi prius, 7, 8. [h] S. P. C. 155. a. H. P. C. 256. 2 H. H. P. C. 263. 9 Ed. 4. 27. pl. 40. Moor 13. pl. 48. Co. Litt. 156. b. Dyer 246. pl. 70. Plowd. Com. 100. Bro. Challenge, 84. Parallel Case. Co. Litt. 130. b. 4 H. 4. 4. a. Dyer 246. pl. 70. 50 Ed. 3. 1. pl. 1. Fitz. Protection, 21, 126. 3 H. 4. 5. pl. 24. Crompt. Just. 113. b. pl. 1. But this is made a Quære Dyer 152. pl. 8. And denied in the same Case in Dalis. 25. pl. 11. [i] But if no Judgment be given that the Juror who is challenged by one shall be drawn, but only that he shall stand aside for a Time, it is said that he may try those who do not actually challenge him. Dyer 120. pl. 8. Cont. Bendloe 58. pl. 95. [k] Kely. 7. H. P. C. 256. 2 H. H. P. C. 264. Plow. Com. 100. 9 Ed. 4. 27. pl. 40. Crompt. Just. 113. b. pl. 2. [l] Plow. Com. 100. 2 H. H. P. C. 263, 264. [m] 8 Co. 66. a. S. P. C. 155. Lett. A. 27 H. 6. 4. pl. 28. Fitz. Process, 94. S. P. C. 155. Lett. A. Bro. Venire facias, 32. 9 Ed. 4. 27. pl. 40. Fitz. Challenge, 56. Vide Fitz. Inquest, 59. Executors, 114. [n] Supra ch. 27. sect. 96. [o] 8 H. 6. 6. pl. 14. Fitz. Process, 79. Vide 2 Rol. Ab. 666. B. 1. 2. Rast. Ent. 625. pl. 7. [p] H. P. C. 257. S. P. C. 155. Lett. B. Fitz. Process, 211. 15 H. 7. 9. pl. 10. Keil. 176. pl. 10. [q] See the Books cited to the other Parts of this Section. 33 H. 6. 14 a. [r] Dyer 215. pl. 51, 52. Cro. Ca. 484. Vide Dyer 284. pl. 34, 319. pl. 13. 2 Roll. Ab. 666. B. 1. 2. 2 Jon. 34. Keilw. 176. pl. 11. [s] 8 H. 6. 6. pl. 14. Fitz. Process, 79. Bro Nisi prius, 13. [t] 15 H. 7. 9. pl. 10. 14 H. 7. 7. pl. 16. Fitz. Process, 211. Dyer 318. pl. 10. H. P. C. 257. Cro. Ca. 484. 2 Roll. Ab. 666. pl. 1, 2, 3, 4. Bro. Octo Tales, 8. S. P. C. 71. Lett. A. 155. Lett. G. Dyer 284. pl 34. 193. pl. 28. Cont. Fitz. Process 68. Dyer 215. pl. 51, 52, 217. pl. 51.

the

the Plaintiff is to sue out the proper subsequent Process upon it in the same Manner as if he had sued out the first; and that it is irregular for a Defendant to take out any such subsequent Process till the Plaintiff has made a [a] Default in Respect of the same Kind of Process, except only in such Actions wherein the Defendant is an Actor as well as the Plaintiff, as in [b] Replevin, or [c] Error, or [d] *Quare impedit* against the Patron only, or [e] Prohibition, *&c.* in which Actions the Defendant may either take out Process by *Proviso*, without any Default in the Plaintiff, or [f] may, if he think fit, take it out in the same Manner as the Plaintiff, without any Clause of *Proviso*. But it seems agreed, That neither in Actions wherein the King is sole [g] Party, nor in [h] Indictments, there can be any Process taken out by *Proviso*, because no Laches is imputable to the King. Also it hath been [i] questioned, whether there can be any such Process in Informations *qui tam*, because the King is in some Sort a Party.

As to the fifth Point, *viz.* In what Cases, and in what Manner a *Tales* is grantable, I shall observe the following Particulars.

Sect. 11. I. That if a full Jury appear not in an Appeal whether by Reason of the [k] Death of some of the Persons returned, or for any other Cause, or if so many be [l] challenged and drawn that there do not remain enow to make a Jury; or if after the Jury is charged, one [m] or more of them die, the Appellant [n] may pray a *Tales*, in the same Manner as a Plaintiff in other Actions. And so also may the Appellee, if the Appellant neglect to pray one the same [o] Term, *&c.* But it seems that a Defendant cannot regularly pray it till there has been a Default in the Plaintiff.

Sect. 12. II. That in Capital Cases, a *Tales* may be granted for a larger Number than the first Process, as for [p] sixty or forty, or any other even [q] Number that the Court thinks proper, in order to prevent the Delay, which may be occasioned by the Defendant's peremptory Challenges. And in this Respect the Law in Respect of a *Tales* in Capital Cases is different from what it is in any other Case; it being an allowed Rule, that in all [r] other Cases the *Tales* must be for a less Number than the first Process.

Sect. 13. III. That every subsequent *Tales*, in Capital as well as in all [s] other Cases, must be for a [t] less Number than the former, except the former were quashed, in which [u] Case the next may be for the same Number.

[a] Dyer 215. pl. 51, 52. Bro. Nisi prius, 40. 6 Mod. 246. [b] Dy. 193. pl. 28. 21 H. 6. 22. pl. 2. 16 H. 7. 14. pl. 10. Fitz. Nisi prius, 9. Bro. Nisi prius, 40. [c] 2 Lev. 5. 6. 2 Saund. 336. [d] 6 Mod. 246. Fitz. Nisi prius, 6. [e] Par. Case, 2 Roll. Abr. 666. Lett. R. Fitz. Nisi prius, 3. [f] 2 Lev. 5, 6. 16 H. 7. 14. pl. 10. Bro. Nisi prius, 40. 21 H. 6. 22. pl. 2. Bro. Octo Tales, 17. 2 Saund. 336. [g] 2 Leon. 110. [h] 6 Mod. 246, 247. 1 Keb. 195. pl. 184. Cont. 1 Sid. 316. [i] 2 Leon. 110. [k] S. P. C. 155. Lett. F. 10 Co. 104. b. H. P. C. 257. 20 Ed. 3. 11. pl. 13. [l] State Trials, Vol. 1. f. 502. and the Books next above cited. [m] S. P. C. 155. Lett. F. 12 H. 4. 10. a. S. 10 Co. 104. b. Quære 2 Roll. Abr. 671. pl. 2. [n] H. P. C. 257. S. P. C. 155. Lett. C. 14 H. 7. 7. pl. 16. [o] Cro. Ca. 484. 14 H. 7. 7. pl. 16. 10 Co. 104. b. See the Books cited to the precedent Section, under the Letter r. Yet 'tis said in Dyer 359. pl. 2. That if a full Jury do not appear, and the Plaintiff pray a Distringas without praying any Tales, the Court ought to grant it at the Prayer of the Defendant. Vide 2 Roll. Abr. 671. N. [p] 14 H. 7. 7. pl. 16. H. P. C. 257. 2 H. H. P. C. 266. S. P. C. 155. Lett. C. Finch 415. Bro. Octo Tales, 6, 8, 19. Keilw. 176. pl. 10. Dyer 213. pl. 43. 1 Bulst. 121. 15 Ed. 4. 33. pl. 19. 16 Ed. 4. 5. pl. 3. 10 Co. 104. b. 105. a. [q] 10 Co. 105. a. Finch of Law, 414. But a Tales de circumstantibus may be of any uncertain Number, 10 Co. 105. a. [r] 14 H. 7. 7. pl. 16. Finch of Law 414. 10 Co. 104. b. 105. a. 2 Roll. Abr. 672. Lett. Q. 37 H. 6. 12. pl. 1. Bro. Octo Tales, 11, 16. Fitz. Inquest, 20, 40. 18 Ed. 4. 6. pl. 31. [s] Finch of Law 414. 2 Roll. Abr. 672. Letters Q. S. Bro. Octo Tales, 15, 16. Bro. Attaint, 7. 10 Co. 105. 47 Ass. pl. 10. 14 H. 7. 2. pl. 6. [t] S. P. C. 155. Lett. C. H. P. C. 257. 2 H. H. P. C. 266. Keilw. 176. pl. 10. 10 Co. 105. a. Fitz. Inquest, 40. It is said that there may be 12 Tales; but this is contrary to all the other Books. [u] S. P. C. 155. Lett. C. H. P. C 257. Fitz. Challenge 36. 20 H. 6. 38. pl. 2.

Sect. 14. IV. That the Quaſhing the Array of the principal Panel doth [a] not quaſh that of the *Tales*, but the Inqueſt ſhall be taken of thoſe returned on the *Tales* if there be enow, and if not, others ſhall be added to them by a new *Tales*. Yet it ſeems [b] agreed, That if all the Perſons returned on a *Habeas Corpora*, be challenged and drawn, there ſhall not be a *Tales awarded*, but a new *Venire facias*; for the Word *Tales* plainly refers to ſome others, to whom the Perſons returned are to be like. Alſo it ſeems agreed, [c] That if the firſt *Habeas Corpora* be quaſhed, the *Habeas Corpora* with a *Tales* cannot but be quaſhed with it, and the Party muſt go on in the ſame Manner, as if the *Venire* had been only returned, and nothing done upon it; for where a Proceſs is quaſhed, all that follows it and depends upon it, ſeems of Courſe to fall with it.

Sect. 15. V. That it ſeems the ſtronger Opinion, That a *Tales* is not grantable upon the Return of a *Venire*, but only [d] upon the Return of a *Habeas Corpora* or *Diſtringas*, becauſe it appears not before ſuch Return, but that a full Jury may appear.

Sect. 16. VI. That the [e] *Diſtringas* or [f] *Habeas Corpora*, with a Command to add ſo many more to thoſe ſummoned on the *Venire*, is the firſt Proceſs againſt the *Tales*; but it is [g] ſaid not to be grantable with a *Niſi Prius*, without having been firſt returned into the Court.

Sect. 17. VII. That [h] if a Juror be withdrawn after a Trial is commenced whereon a *Tales de Circumſtantibus* was awarded, and afterwards a new *Habeas Corpora* be taken out with a *Tales*, it ſhall appoint ſuch *Tales* to be added to the Jurors returned on the firſt *Venire*, and alſo to thoſe returned on the *Tales de Circumſtantibus*; becauſe the Court above will take judicial Notice of what is done at *Niſi Prius* being entred on Record.

Sect. 18. VIII. That the [i] Statutes which authoriſe Juſtices of *Niſi Prius* to award a *Tales de Circumſtantibus*, extend [k] as well to all Capital Caſes, whether of Treaſon or Felony, as to others. But it ſeems, That ſuch a *Tales* cannot be prayed for the King upon an Indictment, or Criminal Information, without a [l] Warrant from the Attorney General, or an expreſs [m] Aſſignment from the Court before which the Inqueſt is taken. But for the fuller Underſtanding of theſe Matters, not being ſo proper for this Treatiſe, I ſhall refer to the Statutes in the Margin.

Sect. 19. IX. That it hath been [n] queſtioned whether any *Tales* be grantable by Juſtices of *Oyer* and *Terminer*; and it hath been [o] holden, That it is not grantable by Juſtices of Gaol-Delivery: [101] And therefore if a Trial before ſuch Juſtices be put off for Want of a ſufficient Number of Jurors, it ſeems the uſual Practiſe for the Court not to order a *Tales*, but a [p] larger Panel, whereon the former Jurors ſhall be returned in the ſame Order as before, and called to be ſworn as they ſtand, without any more Regard to thoſe who were ſworn before than to the others. Which is the Method likewiſe to be obſerved in the like Caſe, [q] as to the Swearing of a Jury returned with a *Tales*.

[a] Fitz. Inqueſt, 30. S. P. C. 155. Lett. G. Dy. 245. pl. 64. 10 Co. 104. b. 105. a.
[b] S. P. C. 155. Lett. E. Finch 414.
[c] 34 H. 6. 20. pl. 39. Fitz. Inqueſt, 20.
[d] Cro. Eliz. 502, 503. 27 H. 6. 10. pl. 4. Bro. Niſi prius, 1. and Octo Tales, 1. 34 H. 6. 21. pl. 39. 2 Roll. Abr. 671. O. pl. 2. Cont. Bro. Octo Tales, 10. 15 H. 7. 9. pl. 10.
[e] 1 Roll. Abr. 798. pl. 9.
[f] 27 H. 6. 10. pl. 4. Bro. Niſi prius, 1. and Octo Tales, 1.
[g] 27 H. 6. 10. pl. 4. Bro. Niſi prius, 1. and Octo Tales, 1. 1 H. 5. 11. pl. 22. S.P.C. 157. a.
[h] Cro. Ja. 677.
[i] 35 H. 8. 6. Par. 6, 7, 8. made perpetual by 2 & 3 Ed. 6. 32. 4 & 5 Ph. & Ma. 7. 14 El. 9.
[k] Raym. 367. 1 Lev. 223. 1 Keb. 490. pl. 30.
[l] 1 Lev. 223.
[m] See the Statute of 14 El. 9. [n] State Trials, Vol. 4. f. 179 to 182. [o] State Trials, Vol. 4. f. 179 to 182. Yet there is an Inſtance in Keilw. 176. pl. 10. of the Tales awarded in an Appeal before ſuch Juſtices. And the like was done Plow. Com. 100. upon an Indictment of Murder. [p] State Trials, Vol. 4. f. 179 to 182. [q] Yelv. 23.

Sect. 20. As to the sixth Point, *viz.* Where it is necessary to return a Panel into Court, before an Inquest can be taken upon it, and where the Prisoner may be demand a Copy of it. It is recited by 42 *Ed.* 3. 11. *That divers Mischiefs had happened, because that the Panels of Inquests which had been taken before Justices by Writ of* Scire facias, *and other Writs, had not been returned before the Sessions of the Justices at the* Nisi prius, *and otherwise, so that the Parties could not have Knowledge of the Names of the Persons which should pass in the Inquest, whereby divers of the People had been disherited and oppressed, and thereupon it is ordained that no Inquest* [a] *but Assises and Deliverances of Gaols, be taken by Writ of* Nisi Prius, *nor in any other Manner, at the Suit of the Great or Small, before the Names of all them that shall pass in the Inquest, be returned in the Court.*

[a] Note, That 6 H. 6. ch. 2. provides also for Assises, 3 Inst. 175.

Sect. 21. It seems [b] agreed, That this Statute extends as well to Writs of *Nisi Prius* in Criminal Cases as in Civil, and to Jurors returned upon a *Tales* as well as to those returned upon a Principal Panel.

[b] S. P. C. 156. 157. H. P. C. 258. Quære, If the Statute extends to Justices of Oyer and Terminer, for it is said to be the Practice for Trials before them for Treason to be on the Venire and not to award any Habeas Corpora. State Trials, Vol. 4. f. 102.

Sect. 22. But it seems, [c] That in Trials before the Justices of Gaol-Delivery the Prisoner has no Right to a Copy of the Panel before the Time of his Trial, except only in Cases within the Purview of 7 & 8 *W.* 3. 3. which enacts, *That every Person indicted and tried for High Treason, or Misprision thereof (except it be for counterfeiting the Coin,* &c.) *shall have a Copy of the Panel of the Jurors, who are to try him, duly returned by the Sheriff, and delivered unto him two Days at least before he shall be tried.*

Sect. 23. It hath been [d] adjudged to be sufficient within the Intent of this Act to deliver to a Prisoner a Copy of a Panel arrayed by the Sheriff before it is returned into Court, if the very same Panel be afterwards returned.

[c] State Trials, Vol. 2. f. 762. Vol. 3. f. 4. 866, 867. Vol. 4. f. 6. [d] State Trials, Vol. 4. f. 101 to 104.

CHAP.

CHAP. XLII.

Before what Court the Jury is to be returned.

Sect. 1. AND now I am to consider before what Court the Process against Jurors in Criminal Cases is returnable: As to which there can be no [a] Doubt but that by the Common Law it is returnable only into the Court wherein the Prosecution was depending.

Sect. 2. But the Statute of [b] *Westm.* 2. *Ch.* 30. having ordained that all Pleas in either Bench, which require only an easy Examination, shall be determined in the Country before the Justices of Assise, by Virtue of the Writ prescribed by that Statute, commonly called the Writ of *Nisi Prius*: It seems to have been universally agreed, [c] That an Issue join'd in the King's Bench upon an [d] Indictment or [e] Appeal, whether for Treason or [f] Felony, or a Crime of an inferior [g] Nature, committed in a different County from that wherein the Court sits, may be tried in the proper County by Writ of *Nisi Prius* by Virtue of the said Statute.

Sect. 3. Yet inasmuch as the King is not expresly named in this Statute, and it is a general Rule, That he shall not be bound by a Statute which doth not expresly name him; it seems to have been generally holden, That where-ever the King is a Party it is irregular to grant a Trial by *Nisi Prius* without his [h] special Warrant, or the [i] Assent of his Attorney. But I do not find it denied, [k] but that regularly the Court may grant it in an [l] Appeal in the same Manner as in any other Action.

Sect. 4. Having shewn already, *Ch.* 7. *Sect.* 17, 18. and *Ch.* 23. *Sect.* 146. that Justices of *Nisi Prius* have Power by 14 *H.* 6. 1. to give Judgment in Felony and Treason, and how far they have Power to give Damages in an Appeal, and having also shewn *Ch.* 25. from *Sect.* 7 *to* 14. in what Cases they may arraign an Appellee at the Suit of the King, after a Nonsuit of the Party, I shall refer to what is there said concerning these Matters.

[a] Vide 4 Inst. 159.
[b] 2 Inst. 421. 423, 424. Cro. Ca. 349.
[c] 2 Inst. 424. 4 Inst. 160. See the Books cited to the other Parts of this Section.
[d] Bro. Coro. 231.
[e] 4 Co. 43. pl. 9. 4 Inst. 160. Dy. 46. pl. 8. 261. pl. 26. 21 H. 7. 34. pl. 35. Rast. Ent. 47. a. 55. a. Vide supra ch. 7. sect. 18. ch. 23. sect. 146.
[f] Bro. Coro. 231. 4 Inst. 160. Raym. 367.
[g] Cro. Ca. 348, 349. 6 Mod. 246, 247.
[h] Fitz. Nisi prius, 16. 2 Leon. 110. 2 Inst. 424. F. N. B. 241. Lett. A. Bro. Nisi prius, 16.
[i] 2 Inst. 424. F. N. B. 241. Lett. A. Crompt. Jurisdict. 211. b. 6 Mod. 246, 247. S. P. C. 156. Lett. A. H. P. C. 258. In Cro. Ca. 348, 349. In an Indictment of Barratry, which seemed to require great Examination, the Court refused to grant a Trial by Nisi prius at the Motion of the Attorney General, till the King by his Letters, had signified his Pleasure, that it should be so tried. Vide 6 Mod. 123.
[k] But not where the Jury is to be from two Counties, Dy. 46. pl. 6.
[l] See the Books cited to the precedent Section under Letter [e].

CHAP.

CHAP. XLIII.

Of Challenges.

AND now I am to ſhew in what Manner the Jurors returned for the Trial of a Criminal may be challenged, which I ſhall conſider,

1. So far as it relates to all Perſons in general.
2. With Regard to Aliens only.

Sect. 1. As to the Learning of this Kind, ſo far as it relates to all Perſons in general, having premiſed, That no Challenge [a] can be taken, either to the Array or to the Polls, till a full Jury have appeared; and that no Juror can be [b] challenged either by the King or Priſoner, without [c] Conſent, after he hath been ſworn, whether on the ſame Day, or (according to the greater Number of [d] Authorities,) on a former, on the ſame Trial, unleſs it be for ſome Cauſe which happened [e] ſince he was ſworn, I ſhall endeavour to ſhew,

[a] Hob. 235. [b] Yelv. 23. Cro. Ca. 291. Co. Litt. 158. a. 22 Ed. 3. 8. pl. 20. 2 Roll. Abr. 658. pl. 5. 6. 7, 8, 9. 659. pl. 4, 5. 661. Lett. Q. 12 H. 4. 10. a. Fitz. Challenge, 64. 14 H. 7. 6. pl. 13. Bro. Challenge, 73. 9 H. 5. 7. pl. 21. Abridged Fitz. Challenge, 72. Bro. Challenge, 50. 14 H. 7. 19. pl. 8. Abridged Bro. Challenge, 75. State Trials, Vol. 3. f. 379.

1. How Jurors may be challenged on the Part of the King.
2. How on the Part of the Priſoner.

Sect. 2. And firſt, As to ſuch Challenges on the Part of the King: It ſeems [f] agreed, That by the Common Law the King might challenge peremptorily as many as he thought fit, of any Jury returned to try any Cauſe in which he was a Party. But this is remedied by 33 *Ed.* 1. commonly called an Ordinance for Inqueſts, which is enacted as followeth. *Of Inqueſts to be taken before any of the Juſtices, and wherein our Lord the King, is Party, howſoever it be: It is agreed and ordained by the King and all his Counſel, that from henceforth, notwithſtanding it be alledged by them that ſue for the King, that the Jurors of thoſe Inqueſts, or ſome of them be not indifferent for the King, yet ſuch Inqueſts ſhall not remain untaken for that Cauſe; but if they that ſue for the King will challenge any of thoſe Jurors, they ſhall aſſign of their Challenge a Cauſe certain, and the Truth of the ſame Challenge ſhall be inquired of according to the Cuſtom of the Court.*

Neither can a Challenge be taken to the Array after any of the Jurors are ſworn. Hob. 235. [c] Cro. Ca. 291. State Trials, Vol. 3. f. 379. [d] 22. Ed. 3. 8. pl. 20. 2 Rol. Abr. 658. pl. 5, 6, 7, 8. 659. pl. 4. 5. 661. Lett. Q. 12 H. 4. 10. a. 14 H. 7. 6. pl. 14. Bro. Challenge, 50, 73, 130. Fitz. Challenge, 143. 28 Aſſ. pl. 44. Yelv. 23. Yet adjudged, That a Juror after he is ſworn may be peremptorily challenged another Day, tho' not on the ſame wherein he is ſworn, 32 H. 6. 26. pl. 14. Abridged Bro. Challenge, 193. 14 H. 7. 19. pl. 8. Abr. Bro. Challenge, 75. S. P. C. 158. 2 Rich. 3. 19. pl. 34. Abr. Bro. Challenge, 194. [e] 22 Ed. 3. 8. pl. 20. Yelv. 23. 2 Roll. Abr. 658. pl. 5, 6, 7, 8, 9. Bro. Challenge, 130. 28 Aſſ. pl. 44. Co. Litt. 158. a. 14 H. 7. 6. pl. 14. Bro. Challenge, 50, 73, 75. Fitz. Challenge, 64, 72, 143. 2 H. H. P. C. 270. [f] Co. Lit. 156. b H. P. C. 259. S. P. C. 162. Lett. A. 1 Roll. Ab. 645. X. pl. 2. 3.

Sect. 3. It seems to be clearly settled [a] at this Day, that this Statute being general, extends as well to all Criminal as Civil Causes: However if the King challenge a Juror before the Panel is perused, it is [b] agreed that he needs not shew any Cause of his Challenge till the whole Panel be gone thro', and it appear that there will not be a full Jury without the Person so challenged. And if the Defendant, in order to oblige the King to shew Cause, presently challenge *touts paravaile* [c], yet it hath been adjudged that the Defendant shall be first put to shew all his Causes of Challenge, before the King need to shew any.

Sect. 4. As to the second Point, *viz.* How Jurors may be challenged on the Part of the Prisoner: Having premised that a [d] Peer can take no Challenge to any of his Peers; and that where several are tried on a joint [e] *Venire*, a Juror challenged and drawn as to one, cannot but be drawn as to all, I shall farther endeavour to shew,

1. How Jurors may be challenged peremptorily.
2. How they may be challenged for Cause.

As to the first Particular, *viz.* How Jurors may be challenged peremptorily, having premised that the Prisoner must take all such Challenges himself, [f] even in such Cases wherein he may have Counsel, I shall endeavour to shew,

1. In what Cases a peremptory Challenge is allowable.
2. How many Jurors may be so challenged.

Sect. 5. As to the first Particular, I take it to be agreed, that a peremptory Challenge was allowable by the Common Law, in all [g] capital Cases both upon Indictments and [h] Appeals, and also in [i] Misprision of High Treason; but it was enacted by 33 *H.* 8. 23. *Par.* 3. *That it should not be allowed in any Cases of High Treason, nor Misprision of High Treason.* Nor do I know that any Statute hath revived it as to the latter of these; for it is said that the Statute of 1 *Ph. & M.* 10. which by restoring the old Course of the Common Law as to Trials of Treason, has revived [k] such Challenge as to Treason, doth not [l] extend to Misprision of High Treason.

Sect. 6. It hath been anciently [m] adjudged, and is holden both by [n] *Staundforde* and [o] *Coke*, That a Man shall have the same peremptory Challenges on an Issue joined upon collateral Matter alledged in Avoidance of an Outlawry for a capital Crime, as he may on the general Issue: But the contrary is holden by [p] *Hale*, and is said to have been [q] adjudged in the Case of *Okey* and *Berkstead.*

Sect. 7. As to the second Particular, *viz.* How many Jurors may be challenged peremptorily: It seems to have been the settled [r] Rule of the Common Law, where-ever such Challenge was allowed, to suffer the

[a] Moor 595. pl. 809. S. P. C. 162. Lett. A. H. P. C. 259. Co. Litt. 159. b. and the Books cited to other Parts of this Section. Yet peremptory Challenges were taken for the Queen in Throckmorton's Trial. 1 Mar. State Trials Vol. 1. fol. 48.

[b] 1 Ventr. 309, 310. S. P. C. 162. Lett. A. State Trials, Vol. 2. 744. Vol. 3. fol. 52. 869. Skin. 82. H. P. C. 259. 2 H. H. P. C. 271.

[c] State Trials, Vol. 3. fol. 52. Raym. 473, 474. Skin. 82. See State Trials, Vol. 3. f. 4. Vol. 4. f. 177, 407.

[d] Rushw. Collections, 2. V. 1. f. 94. Moor 621, 622. Co. Lit 156. b. State Trials, Vol. 1. fol. 164, 265. Trial per pais ch. 9. 2 H. H. P. C. 275.

[e] Supra ch. 41. sect. 9.

[f] State Trials, Vol. 4. f. 105. Vol. 1. fol. 601. V. 2. fol. 743, 744.

[g] Co. Litt. 156. b. Moor 12. pl. 46. [h] Moor 12. pl. 46. Bendl. 42. pl. 77. 9 H. 5. 7. pl. 21. Abridged Fitz. Challenge, 72. Bro. Challenge, 50. 14 H. 7. 7. pl. 16. Bro. Challenge, 74, 75, 211. 3 H. 7. 2. pl. 5. [i] 3 Inst. 27. But in no other Case that is not Capital. State Trials, Vol. 2. fol. 254. [k] 3 Inst. 227. S. P. C. 157. Lett. B. 158. 1 And. 107, 108. Co. Litt. 156. b. State Trials, Vol. 2. fol. 764, &c. But this is made a Quære Savil 57. [l] Supra, ch. 25. sect. 145. Yet 3 Inst. 27. a. it is said that for Misprision of Treason one may peremptorily challenge 35. [m] Fitz. Challenge, 153, 165. [n] S. P. C. 163. Lett. A. Yet the same Point is made a Quære, S. P. C. 158. [o] Co. Litt. 157. b. [p] H. P. C. 259. 2 H. H. P. C. 267. [q] 1 Lev. 61. But the other Books which report the same Case take no Notice of this Point. 1 Sid. 72. Kely. 13. [r] Co. Litt. 156. b. Crompt. Just. 114. pl. 4. 9 H. 5. 7. pl. 21. 14 H. 7. 7 pl. 16. Bro. Challenge, 70, 74, 75, 217. 19 Ed. 4. 33. b. 3 H. 7. 2 pl. 5. Abridged Bro. Challenge, 211. 17 Ass. pl. 6. 17 Ed. 3. 23. pl. 8. Abridged Bro. Challenge, 105. Trial per pais, ch. 9. S. P. C. 157. b. 158. See the Books cited, ch. 30. sect. 2 Lamb. B. 4. ch. 14, says that it was doubtful at Common Law how many might be challenged.

Prisoner to challenge as many as he thought fit under the Number of three full Juries, *i. e.* not amounting to more than thirty-five. But if a Criminal challenge more than that Number, [a] it seems the more prevailing Opinion that he is to be dealt with as one that stands Mute.

Sect. 8. It is enacted by 22 *H.* 8. 14. *Par.* 7. made perpetual by 32 *H.* 8. 3. *That no Person arraigned for any Petit Treason, Murder or Felony, be admitted to any peremptory Challenge above the Number of twenty.* But it seems [b] agreed, That 1 & 2 *Ph.* & *Ma.* 10. which restores the Course of the Common Law as to Trials of Treason, has revived the old Challenge of 35 in Trials of Petit Treason.

Sect. 9. It seems to have been holden by Sir [c] *Edward Coke*, that he who challenges more than twenty upon an Arraignment of Felony, since the above-mentioned Statute of 22 *H.* 8. shall [d] neither forfeit his Goods, nor have Judgment of Death, nor of *Pain fort & dure*, but shall only be over-ruled as to his Challenges so far as they exceed twenty, and put upon his Trial. But this seems to have been doubted by Sir *Matthew* [e] *Hale*, [102] and the contrary is holden by [f] *Crompton*, and seems more agreeable to the most natural Construction of 22 *H.* 8. which seems to have intended no Alteration as to the Nature or Effect of peremptory Challenges, but only as to their Number. To which may be added, That nothing is more Common than for [g] subsequent Statutes which take from Felons the Benefit of Clergy, [h] expresly to exclude those who challenge more than twenty, which would be needless if their Challenge were only to be over-ruled, and did not subject them to Judgment of [i] Death, &c.

Sect. 10. As to the second Particular, *viz.* How Jurors may be challenged for Cause, having premised that it is a [k] general Rule, That whereever [l] the King is a Party, as he is in every [m] Indictment, and in some Sort also in [n] Appeals of Felony, he who takes a Challenge for Cause must shew it presently, and shall not have Time till the Panel is perused, as the King shall where he takes a Challenge, as hath been more fully shewn, *Sect.* 3. and having also farther premised that after a Prisoner hath challenged a Juror for Cause, and his Cause hath been disallowed, or found against him, he may [o] challenge the same Juror peremptorily, before he is [p] sworn, I shall endeavour to shew,

1. What shall be a good Challenge of a Juror, in Respect of his Honour or Insufficiency.
2. What in Respect of his Unindifferency.

And first as to the Challenge of a Juror for his Honour or Insufficiency; having premised that it is agreed to be a good Challenge of this Kind that a Juror is an [q] Alien, [r] Minor, or [s] Villein, I shall more fully endeavour to shew,

[a] Supra ch. 30. sect. 2.

[b] Bro. Challenge, 217. H. P. C. 260. 2 H. H. P. C. 269. 3 Inst. 227. Vide supra sect. 5. and ch. 25. sect. 132, 144. S. P. C. 158. a. Co. Lit. 156. b.

[c] 3 Inst. 227. 228.

[d] Vide ch. 30. sect. 19. Staund. Prer. 46. a.

[e] H. P. C. 260.

[f] Crompton's Just. 114. pl. 4.

[g] Supra ch. 33. sect. 32, 45, 48, 59. 64, 66, 69, &c.

[h] Vide supra ch. 33. sect. 27, 36. 11 Co. 31. a. 32. a. 35. b. S. P. C. 126. Lett. A.

[i] Vide ch. 33. sect. 20.

[k] Co. Litt. 158. a. Fitz. Challenge, 128. State Trials, Vol. 3. f. 235. S. P. C. 162. Lett. C. 2 Roll. Abr. 659. pl. 6, 7, 8. 38 Aff. pl. 22. 1 Sid. 244. Cont. 19 Aff. pl. 6. Abridged Bro. Chal. 107.

[l] Except in Inquests, Fitz. Challenge, 105, 107. 2 Roll. Abr. 659. pl. 9. 660. N. 2.

[m] That Cause must be shewn presently on Indictments. Co. Litt. 158. a. 1 Sid. 244. 1 H. 5. pl. 1. Abridged Fitz. Challenge, 70. Skin. 82.

[n] That Cause must be shewn presently in Appeals. Co. Lit. 158. a. This is left a Quære S. P. C. 162. Lett. D.

[o] Co. Litt. 158 a. 37 H. 6. 8. pl. 17. Abridged, Fitz. Challenge, 48. Bro. Challenge, 86. Cont. 10 H. 4. 9. pl. 7. Abridged Fitz. Challenge, 180.

[p] Vide supra sect. 1.

[q] Co. Litt. 156. b. Theloal, B. 1. ch. 6. sect. 14. 14 H. 4. 19. pl. 23. Bro. Challenge, 48. Fitz. Challenge, 91. 2 Roll. Abr. 656. pl. 2. Calvin's Case, 18. b.

[r] Co. Litt. 157. b. 172. b. Litt. sect. 259.

[s] 2 Roll. Abr. 657. pl. 1. Co. Litt. 156. b. 9 Ed. 4. 16. pl. 16. 26 Aff. pl. 28. F. Challenge, 135. Bro. Challenge, 64, 118. But the contrary is holden in the Year-Book of 10 H. 7. 20. Abridged Bro. Challenge, 220. and a Quære by the Reporter and Brook.

1. Where Peerage is a good Cause of Challenge.
2. Where the Want of Freehold.
3. Where Infamy.
4. Whether old Age, Sicknefs, or Non-Refidence in the County be in any Cafe a good Caufe of Challenge.

Sect. 11. As to the firft Particular, *viz.* Where Peerage is a good Caufe of Challenge, it is [a] agreed, That if a Peer be returned on a Jury and bring a Writ of Privilege, he fhall be difcharged. Alfo it feems to have been [b] holden, that even without fuch a Writ he may either challenge himfelf, or be challenged by the Party. *Quære.*

Sect. 12. As to the fecond Particular, *viz.* Where the Want of Freehold is a good Caufe of Challenge: It feems to be admitted by the Statute of 21 E. 1. *de his qui ponendi funt in Affifis*, and alfo by the Regifter, That at the Common Law there was no [c] Neceffity that Jurors fhould have any Freehold, as to Inquefts before Juftices in *Eyre*, or in Cities or Burghs, as hath been more fully fhewn, *Chap.* 25. *Sect.* 21. Alfo it feems [d] agreed, That the Common Law doth not require that a Juror fhould in any Cafe have a Freehold of any certain Value; and upon this Ground it hath been adjudged, That a Freehold worth but [e] 20 *s.* or [f] 5 *s.* or even a [g] Penny, is ftill a fufficient Qualification for a Juror in fuch Cafes as are not within the Statutes which require a Freehold of a greater Value. Alfo it hath been [h] adjudged, that the Common Law did not require that a Juror fhould in any Cafe have any Freehold: But this is not only contrary to what feems implied by all the Authorities above-cited, which in faying that the Common Law did not require a Freehold of any certain Value, plainly feem to fuppofe that it required fome Freehold, but hath been alfo contradicted by many exprefs [i] Authorities; agreeably to which it feems to be [k] fettled at this Day, that the Want of Freehold is a good Challenge of a Juror in all Cafes not otherwife provided for by [l] Statute, and confequently in a Trial for High Treafon in *London* as well as in any other County.

Sect. 13. But it feems agreed, that where-ever the Letter of the Common or Statute Law require that a Juror fhould have a Freehold, the Meaning is fully fatisfied, by his having the [m] Ufe of a Freehold; and that it is not material whether he have it in his own or his [n] Wife's Right, or whether it be [o] Abfolute or upon Condition, or an Eftate of Inheritance, or only [p] for Term of one's own or another's Life, fo that it be in the fame [q] County, wherein the Suit is brought, and actually continue in the Juror [r] till the Time when he is fworn.

[a] 48 Aff. pl. 6.
[b] 48 Ed. 3. 30. pl. 18. Bro. Challenge, 18, 37. 209. Dy. 314. pl. 98. 35 H. 6. 46. pl. 8. Moor 767.
Regift. 179. F. N. B. 165. E. 166.
[b] 22 E. 3. 18. pl. 75. Fitz. Challenge, 119. 2 Roll. Abr. 646. Y. 1. 2. but his Notes are not warranted by the Books at large.
Co. Litt. 157. b. 9 Co. 49. 27 H. 8. 22. pl. 18. cont. 35 H. 6. 46. pl. 8. Bro. Challenge, 8. Finch of Law 506. 6 Co. 53. a. Fitz. Challenge, 44. 1 Jon. 153. F. N. B. 166. [r] Vide Raym. 485, 486. 1 Vent. 366. Infra fect. 21.

[d] Keilw. 46. pl. 2. 54. pl. 19. 92. pl. 5. Cro. El. 413. See the Citations to the next three Letters, and Litt. fect. 464. and 2 Roll. Abr. 647, 648. [e] 10 H. 6. 7. pl. 24. Abridged Fitz. Challenge, 29. Bro. Challenge, 189. 19 H. 6. 9. pl. 21. Abridged Fitz. Challenge, 32. Bro. Challenge, 60. 2 H. 7. 13. pl. 17. Bro. Challenge, 152. 10 H. 6. 18. pl. 59. Bro. Challenge, 192. [f] 3 H. 4. 4. pl. 14. Abridged, Fitz. Challenge, 78. Bro. Challenge, 32. [g] Keilw. 46. pl. 2. [h] 28 Aff. pl. 15. Abridged Bro. Challenge, 106. 10 H. 7. 13. pl. 7. State Trials, Vol. 3. f. 135 to 140. Vide 16 H. 7. 14. pl. 10. 7 H. 6. 44. pl. 23. Abridged Fitz. Challenge, 24. Bro. Challenge, 57. It feems to be holden that by the Common Law it is a Challenge only to the Favour. [i] Cro. Eliz. 413. pl. 4. Trial per pais, ch. 9. 3 H. 4. 4. pl. 14. Abridged Fitz. Challenge, 78. Bro. Challenge, 32. 4 H. 4. 1. pl. 2. Vide Keilw. 54. pl. 14. Co. Litt. 156. b. 157. a. 2 Roll. Abr. 647. pl. 9, 10. 7 H. 4. 1. pl. 4. Abridged Bro. Challenge, 34. Fitz. Challenge, 58. 21 H. 7. 29. pl. 10. Abridged Bro. Challenge, 90. 10 H. 7. 11. pl. 30. It feems taken for granted that Iffues in all Cafes are to be returned upon Jurors, by which it feems to be implied that they ought to have Land, &c. [k] State Trials, Vol. 3. 869. Vol. 4. fol. 874. [l] Vide infra fect. 19, &c. [m] Keilw. 46. pl. 2. 92. pl. 5. Dyer 9. pl. 26. Fitz. Challenge, 27. 13 H. 7. 7. b. 5 Ed. 4. 7. pl. 15. Bro. Challenge, 165. Co. Litt. 272. Plow. Com. 58. a. 15 H. 7. 13. b. S. P. C. 160 Lett. b. Bro. Jurors, 14. [n] Fitz. Challenge, 27. 9 H. 7. 1. pl. 2. Bro. Challenge, 157. 12 H. 7. 4. pl. 2. Bro. Challenge, 160. Co. Lit. 156. b. [o] Co. Litt. 156. b. Keilw. 167, 168. 2 Rol. Abr. 648. pl. 20. cont. 7 H. 4. 1. pl. 4. Fitz. Challenge, 158. But Bro. in abridging this Cafe in Title Challenge, 53. fays quod mirum. [p] 9 H. 7. 1. pl. 2. 12 H. 7. 4. pl. 2. Bro. Challenge, 160. Co. Litt. 156. b. Bro. Challenge, 157. See F. N. B. 14. Lett. e. 166. Lett. f. [q] 9 H. 7. 1. pl. 2. Bro. Challenge, 157. Co. Litt. 157. a. Raft. Ent. 118. b 19 H. 6. 9. pl. 21. [r] 12 H. 7. 4. pl. 2. Bro. Challenge, 160. Co. Lit. 157. a. 7 H. 4. 1. pl. 4. Abridged Fitz. Challenge, 158.

Sect. 14.

Sect. 14. It is enacted by the [a] Statutes of *Westminster*, 2. 38. and 21 *Ed.* 1. *de his qui ponendi sunt in Assisis*, that none shall be put in Assises or Juries, except in Cities, Burghs or trading Towns, who have not Tenements to the yearly Value of 40 *s.* *&c.* But it seems to have been [b] generally agreed that a Juror can neither be challenged by the Parties for being returned contrary to these Acts, nor alledge such Matter himself for his Discharge, but must take his Remedy by Action against the Sheriff, or by Writ of Privilege for his Discharge.

Sect. 15. It is farther enacted by 2 *H.* 5. 3. *That no Person shall be admitted to pass in any Inquest upon Trial of the Death of a Man, nor in any Inquest betwixt Party or Party in Plea Real, nor in Plea Personal, whereof the Debt or the Damage declared amount to forty Marks, if the same Person have not Lands or Tenements of the yearly Value of forty Shillings, above all Charges of the same; so that it be challenged by the Party, that any such Person so impanelled in the same Cases, hath not Lands or Tenements of the yearly Value of forty Shillings above the Charges as afore is said.*

Sect. 16. It hath been [c] adjudged, that this Statute extends as well to a Collateral Issue, as to the General one, but not to an Indictment or Information for a Crime not [d] Capital, for the Words are, *Upon Trial of the Death of a Man, nor in any Inquest between Party and Party in Plea Real or Personal*, &c.

Sect. 17. It seems [e] agreed, That a *Cestuy que use* of any Freehold in the same County, of the yearly Value of 40 *s.* is a good Juror within this Statute. And some have [f] holden, That the Law is the same as to a Feoffee of such Land in Trust for another, or a [g] Remainder Man of a State of Freehold expectant on a Lease for Years. But this seems not to be maintainable, because the Statute in requiring that a Juror shall have Lands of the yearly Value of 40 *s.* above all Charges, plainly seems to intend that he ought to have Lands of the clear [h] Income whereof at the Time he can expend so much. But a Man cannot expend any Thing out of Lands whereof he is enfeoffed to the Use of another, or wherein he has only a dry Remainder.

Sect. 18. It hath been [i] adjudged, that this Statute is repealed as to Treasons by 1 [k] & 2 *Ph.* & *Ma.* 10. which enacts that all Trials for Treason shall be according to the Common Law.

Sect. 19. It is recited by 23 *H.* 8. 13. *That Trials in Murders and Felonies in Cities, Buroughs, and Towns corporate within this Realm having Authority to proceed in the Deliverance of such Offenders, had been oftentimes deferred and delayed, by Reason of Challenge of such Offenders, for lack of Sufficiency of Freehold, to the great Hindrance of Justice.* And thereupon it is enacted, *That every Person and Persons being the King's natural Subject born, which either by the Name of a Citizen, or of a Freeman, or any other Name, doth enjoy and use the Liberties and Privileges of any City, Borough or Town corporate where he dwelleth or maketh his Abode, being worth in moveable Goods and Substance to the clear Value of forty Pounds, be admitted in Trial of Murders and Felonies in every Sessions and Gaol-Delivery, to be kept and holden in and for the Liberty of such Cities, Boroughs, and Towns Corporate, albeit they have no Freehold; any Act, Statute, Use, Custom or Ordinance to the contrary hereof notwithstanding.*

Sect. 20. *Provided that this Act no way extend to any Knight or Esquire, dwelling, abiding, or resorting in or to any such City*, &c.

[a] Vide supra ch. 25. sect. 21, 22, 30.

[b] 2 Inst. 448. 28 Ass. pl. 15. Abridged Bro. Challenge, 106. 3 H. 4. 4. pl. 14. Abridged Bro. Challenge, 32. Fitz. Challenge, 78. F. N. B. 166. State Trials, Vol. 2. fol. 744. But 38 Ass. pl. 19. is contrary.

[c] Keilw. 92. pl. 5. 16 H. 7. 14. pl. 10. 2 Rol. Abr. 647, 648.

[d] Cro. Eliz. 413. pl. 4. Raym. 485, 486.

[e] Vide supra sect. 13.

[f] Keilw. 92. pl. 5. and Bro. Challenge, 202. Jurors, 14. in an Abridgment of the Year-Book of 15 H. 7. 13. pl. 1. But I do not find this Point in the Book at large.

[g] Keilw. 168. pl. 2.

[h] Vide Keil. 92. a. 18 Ed. 4. 13. pl. 8. 19 H. 6. 9. pl. 21. Fitz. Challenge, 32. 36 H. 6. 23. pl. 16. 2 Rol. Abr. 647. pl. 11, 648. pl. 28. 649. pl. 29.

[i] State Trials, Vol. 3. f. 135 to 140.

[k] Vide ch. 25. sect. 132, 142, 143, 144.

Sect. 21. Alſo ſpecial Proviſion is made by 11 *H.* 7. 21. and 4 *H.* 8. 3. for Jurors in *London* in real and Perſonal Actions above the Value of forty Marks, for which I ſhall refer to the Statutes at large.

Sect. 22. It is enacted by 4 & 5 *W.* & *M.* 24. *That all Jurors* (*other than Strangers upon Trials* per medietatem linguæ) *who are to be returned for Trials of Iſſues joined, in any of the Courts of King's Bench, Common Pleas or Exchequer, or before Juſtices of Aſſiſe or* Niſi Prius, Oyer *and* Terminer, *Gaol-Delivery, or General Quarter-Seſſions of the Peace in any County of this Realm of* England, *ſhall every of them have in their own Name, or in Truſt for them within the ſame County, ten Pounds by the Year at leaſt above Repriſes, of Freehold or Copyhold Lands or Tenements, or of Lands or Tenements of Ancient* [a] *Demeſne, or in Rents, or in all or any of the ſaid Lands, Tenements or Rents, in Fee-ſimple, Fee-tail, or for the Life of themſelves or ſome other Perſon; and that in every County in* Wales *every ſuch Juror ſhall have in the ſame County ſix Pounds by the Year at leaſt, in Manner aforeſaid above Repriſes.*

Sect. 23. But it is provided, *That it ſhall be lawful to return any Perſon on a* Tales *in* England, *who ſhall have five Pounds by the Year, or in* Wales, *who ſhall have three Pounds by the Year, in Manner aforeſaid.*

[a] But by the Common Law a Freehold in Ancient Demeſne was not ſufficient. 9 H. 7. 1. pl. 2. Bro. Challenge, 157. Co. Litt. 156. b.

Sect. 24. Alſo there is a Saving to all [b] Cities, Boroughs and Towns Corporate, of their ancient Uſage of returning Jurors of ſuch Eſtate, and in ſuch Manner as before had been uſed and accuſtomed. But there is no expreſs Saving of any Trial contrary to the Purview of this Statute and made good by ſome other; and therefore it may be argued that the Trial of Felonies in Towns by Jurors worth 40 *l.* in Goods by Virtue of the above-cited Statute of 23 *H.* 8. is no longer lawful, it not being a Trial by Uſage, but by Statute. Yet ſeeing 4 & 5 *Gul.* & *Mar.* ſeems plainly to have a View to Trials in Counties only, and the Statute of 16 & 17 *Ca.* 2. 3. which is penned almoſt in the very ſame Words, was taken [c] no Way to alter the former Method of Trials in Towns, leſt it ſhould cauſe a Failure of Juſtice; and it being generally impracticable to get a ſufficient Number of ſuch Freeholders as the Statute requires in Towns, it ſeems a reaſonable Conſtruction of 4 & 5 *W.* & *M.* That the Trial by 23 *H.* 8. ſtill continues lawful as before. But it hath been [d] agreed, That for Trials in *London* for High Treaſon, every Juror ought to have ſuch Freehold or Copyhold as is required by 4 & 5 *W.* & *M.* [103].

[b] Vide ſupra ſect. 12. and there is the like Exception in 27 El. 6. Par. 7 and in 16 & 17 Ca. 2. 3. Par. 4.

[c] 1 Vent. 366.

[d] State Trials, Vol. 4. f. 186. and in Francia's Trial.

Sect. 25. As to the third Particular, *viz.* Where Infamy is a good Cauſe of Challenge, it ſeems that it is a good Challenge of a Juror that he is [e] outlawed, or that he hath been [f] adjudged to any Corporal Puniſhment whereby he becomes infamous, or that he hath been convicted of Treaſon, or [g] Felony, or [h] Perjury, or [i] Conſpiracy or of [k] Forgery on 5 *Eliz.* 14. or attainted in an [l] Attaint for giving a falſe Verdict. And it hath been [m] holden, That ſuch Exceptions are not ſalved by a Par-

[e] Co. Litt. 158. a. 21 H. 6. 30. pl. 17. 11 H. 4. 41. pl. 8. Bro. Indict. 2. 2 Rol. Abr. 657. pl. 3. Bro. Challenge, 64. Fitz. Proceſs, 208. Cro. Ca. 134. Trials per pais, ch. 9. [f] Co. Litt. 6. b. 156. a. Trials per pais, ch. 9. [g] Co. Litt. 6. b. 158. a. 2 Bulſt. 154. State Trials, Vol. 2. f. 521 to 524. Trials per pais, ch. 9. Cont. 1 Lev. 263. [h] Bract. Lib. 4. c. 19. ſect. 2. Fleta, Lib. 4. c. 8. ſect. 2. Trials per pais, ch. 9. [i] See B. 1. ch. 72. ſect. 9. Co. Litt. 6. b. 158. a. It ſeems to be holden, That the Conviction for Conſpiracy ought to be at the King's Suit. But 33 H. 6. 55. pl. 45. Bro. Challenge, 15. Fitz. Challenge, 41. make no ſuch Diſtinction. [k] Co. Litt. 6. b. and the Reaſon ſeems to be becauſe the Statute is expreſs that the Offender ſhall be ſet on the Pillory, &c. but it was adjudged, 33 H. 6. 55. pl. 45. Abridged Fitz. Challenge, 41. Bro. Challenge, 15. 2 Rol. Abr. 649. pl. 5. That a Conviction on 1 H. 5. 3. was not a good Challenge to a Juror, becauſe it was not a Conviction on an Action at the Common Law. Vide 44 Ed. 3. 39. pl. 39. Fitz. Decies tantum, 11, 12. [l] See the Authorities under the precedent Letter. [m] State Trials, Vol. 2. f. 521 to 524. 2 Bulſt. 154. 2 H. H. P. C. 278 Vide ſupra ch. 37. ſect. 48 to 53.

don. And it was anciently [a] holden that Excommunication was alſo a good Challenge. Yet it [b] ſeems that none of the above-cited Challenges are principal ones, but only to the Favour, unleſs the Record of the Outlawry, Judgment or Conviction be produced, if it be a Record of another Court, or the Term, *&c.* be ſhewn, if it be a Record of the ſame Court.

Sect. 26. As to the fourth Particular, *viz.* Whether old Age, or Sickneſs, or Non-reſidence in the County be in any Caſe a good Cauſe of Challenge of a Juror, I take it to be agreed, That notwithſtanding the [c] Statute of *Weſtm.* 2. 38. be expreſs that neither old Men above the Age of Seventy Years, nor Perſons perpetually ſick, nor thoſe who are infirm at the Time of their Summons, nor thoſe who do not reſide in the County ſhall be put in Juries, or in the leſſer Aſſiſes; and therefore ſuch Perſons may ſue out a Writ of [d] Privilege for their Diſcharge, grounded on this Statute; yet if they be [e] actually returned and appear, they can neither be challenged by the Party, nor excuſe themſelves from not ſerving if there be not enow without them.

Sect. 27. As to the ſecond Point, *viz.* What ſhall be a good Challenge of a Juror in Reſpect of his Indifferency: It is expreſly enacted by 25 *Ed.* 3. *ch.* 3. which ſeems to have been made in [f] Affirmance of the Common Law, *That no Indictor ſhall be put in Inqueſts upon Deliverance of the Indictees of Felonies or* [g] *Treſpaſs, if he be challenged for that ſame Cauſe by him which is ſo indicted.* And this Exception againſt a Juror that he hath found an Indictment againſt the Party for the ſame Cauſe, hath been adjudged good, not only upon the Trial of [h] ſuch Indictment, but alſo upon the Trial of another Indictment or Action, [i] whereein the ſame Matter is either in Queſtion, or happens to be material, tho' not directly in Iſſue.

Sect. 28. It hath been allowed a good Cauſe of Challenge on the Part of the Priſoner, That the Juror [k] hath a Claim to the Forfeiture, which ſhall be cauſed by the Party's Attainder or Conviction; or that he hath declared his [l] Opinion before-hand that the Party is guilty, or will be hanged, or the like. Yet it hath been [m] adjudged, That if it ſhall appear that the Juror made ſuch Declaration from his Knowledge of the Cauſe, and not out of any Ill-will to the Party, it is no Cauſe of Challenge.

Sect. 29. But it hath been [n] adjudged to be no good Cauſe of Challenge, that the Juror hath found others guilty on the ſame Indictment; for the Indictment is in Judgment of Law ſeveral againſt each Defendant, for every one muſt be convicted by particular Evidence againſt himſelf.

Sect. 30. It hath been [o] ruled to be a good Challenge of a Juror, on the Part of the King, that he hath given his Dogs the Names of the King's Witneſſes.

[a] Co. Litt. 158.
[b] Co. Litt. 157. b. 33 H. 6. 55. pl. 45. 43 Aſſ. pl. 46. 8 H. 5. 11. a. 21 Ed. 4. 74. b. pl. 5. 2 Rol. Abr. 649. pl. 13. 650. pl. 11. 658. Lett. K. 33 H. 6. 1. pl. 1. Bro. Challenge, 15, 147.
[c] 2 Inſt. 446. 447, 448.
[d] F. N. B. 165. b. 166. D. Regiſter 179, 180.
[e] State Trials, Vol. 2. f. 744 2 Inſt. 448.
[f] 12 Aſſ. pl. 36. 19 Aſſ. pl. 6. Bro. Challenge, 101, 107. S. P. C. 158. Lett. B.
[g] Yet in 7 Ed. 4. 4. pl. 11. Abridged Bro. Challenge, 166. Fitz. Challenge, 53. It is holden to be no principal Challenge in Treſpaſs.
[h] State Trials, Vol. 2. f. 379. Vol. 4. f. 186. In the Year-Book of 40 Aſſ. pl. 10. Abridged, Bro. Challenge, 142. An Indictor being returned on the Petit Jury and giving a Verdict, was fined becauſe he did not challenge himſelf. Yet 27 Aſſ. pl. 13. Abridged Bro. Challenge, 120. and Fitz. Challenge, 137. 'tis not allowed to be a principal Challenge, even upon the Trial of the ſame Indictment. [i] 8 H. 4. 2. pl. 4. Abridged Bro. Challenge, 42. Fitz. Challenge, 79. Co. Lit. 157. b. 1 Syd. 244. 2 Rol. Abr. 649. pl. 9. [k] State Trials, Vol. 1. f. 502. [l] 21 H. 7. 29. pl. 10. Bro. Challenge, 90. State Trials, Vol. 4. f. 184, 185. and ruled, That the Priſoner ſhall not examine a Juror concerning ſuch Matter on a Voir dire, becauſe it ſounds in Reproach. Vide 49 Ed. 3. 1. pl. 2. Abridged Bro. Challenge, 25. Fitz. Challenge, 100. [m] 7 H. 7. 25. pl. 8. Abridged Bro. Challenge, 55. Fitz. Challenge, 22. 20 H. 6. 40. 2 Rol. Abr. 657. Lett. I. Vide 49 Ed. 3. 1. pl. 2. Abridged Bro. Challenge, 25. Fitz. Challenge, 100. [n] Kely. 9. State Trials, Vol. 4. f. 141, 175. [o] State Trials, Vol. 2. f. 738.

Sect. 31. It seems to be [a] settled, That where the King is a Party he may take either a principal Challenge, or to the Favour.

Sect. 32. It is [b] said, That the Subject cannot take a Challenge for the Favour against the King, because every one is bound by his Allegiance to favour the King. But if [c] no more be meant by these Books, than that such a Challenge is not good without shewing some actual Partiality in such Sheriff or Juror, or some particular Cause in Respect whereof the King may influence them, it seems not clearly settled how the King in this Respect hath a greater [d] Privilege than the Subject, which yet it seems agreed [e] that he hath.

Sect. 33. It hath been [f] said to be no principal Challenge where the King is a Party, that a Juror is of the King's Livery, or his immediate Tenant; but it is said, That a Challenge for such Cause ought to conclude to the [g] Favour. But these Matters seeming to be unsettled, I shall leave them to be farther considered by others.

For other Matters relating to Challenges, being not so proper for this Treatise, I shall refer to the [h] Books which more particularly treat of them.

Sect. 34. And now I am in the second Place to consider the Learning of Challenges, so far as it particularly relates to Aliens; as to whom it is enacted by 28 *Ed.* 3. 13. *Par.* 2. *That in all Manner of Inquests and Proofs, which be to be taken or made amongst Aliens and Denizens, be they Merchants or* [i] *other, as well before the Mayor of the Staple as before any other Justices or Ministers, altho' the King be Party, the one Half of the Inquest or Proof shall be Denizens, and the other Half of Aliens, if so many Aliens and Foreigners be in the Town or Place where such Inquest or Proof is to be taken, that be not Parties, nor with the Parties in Contracts, Pleas or other Quarrels, whereof such Inquests or Proofs, ought to be taken: And if there be not so many Aliens, then shall be put in such Inquests or Proofs, as many Aliens as shall be found in the same Towns or Places which be not thereto Parties, nor with the Parties, as aforesaid, and the Remnant of Denizens, which be good Men, and not suspicious to the one Party nor to the other.*

Sect. 35. It is declared by 9 *H.* 6. 29. that the above recited Statute of 2 *H.* 5. which requires that the Jurors in certain Cases shall have Tenements to the yearly Value of 40 *s. shall be no wise prejudicial to this Statute of* 28 Ed. 3. *nor extend it self but only to the Inquests to be taken between Denizen and Denizen.* Also it seems agreed, [k] That the subsequent Statutes which require that Jurors shall have Tenements to a greater Value no way repeal the said Statute of 28 *E.* 3. Yet it seems, [l] That the *English* Half of the Jury ought to have Tenements to the same Value as in other Cases. And it hath been [m] adjudged, That the Words *quorum quilibet habeat quatuor libratas terræ, &c.* shall be applied to the *English* only.

Sect. 36. It seems [n] agreed, that there is no need that any of those who find an Indictment against an Alien should be Aliens.

[a] Co. Lit. 156. a. 4 H. 7. 8. pl. 7. Fitz. Challenge, 63. 44 Ed. 3. 38. pl. 32. Bro. Challenge, 22. 2 Rol. Abr. 645. pl. 5.
[b] Fitz. Challenge, 63, 65. Co. Lit. 156. a. 2 Rol. Abr. 646. pl. 8. 4 H. 7. 8. pl. 3. Trials per pais, ch. 9. State Trials, Vol. 3. f. 235, 236. Vol. 4. f. 70, 661. Cro. Eliz. 663. pl. 12.
[c] Vide 2 Rol. Abr. 646. pl. 8. 640. pl. 6. 1 Vent. 309.
[d] For in the Year-Book of 20 H. 6. 40. a. Abridged 2. Rol. Abr. 641. pl. 5, 6. It is holden in the Case of the Subject to be no Cause of Challenge, that the Sheriff hath Malice against the Party without shewing some particular Instance of Partiality.
[e] See the Books cited to the other Parts of this and the next Section.
[f] Fitz. Challenge 17. S. P. C. 162. Lett. C. 2 Rol. Abr. 646. pl. 10. It is said generally in some Books that it is a good Challenge of a Juror that he is the King's menial Servant, or a Valet of the Crown. Co. Lit. 156. a. Fitz. Cor. 63. Trials per pais, ch. 9. 2 Rol. Abr. 646 pl. 11. But State Trials, Vol. 3. f. 235, 236. Vol. 4. f. 70. And in other Books the contrary is ruled. Bro. Challenge, 154. 4 H. 7. 3. pl. 5. Cro. Eliz. 663. pl. 12.
[g] Vide supra sect. 33.
[h] Co. Lit. 157, 158. Trials per pais, ch. 9. 2 Rol. Abr. 635 to 666.
[i] Fitz. Inquest, 22. 3 Ed. 4. 11. pl. 3.
[k] Cro. El. 272. Vide H. P. C. 260, 261.
[l] Cro. El. 272.
[m] Cro. El. 272, 841. pl. 18.
[n] H. P. C. 260. S. P. C. 159.

Sect. 37. Alſo it hath been adjudged, [a] That the ſaid Statute of 28 *E.* 3. is repealed as to Trials for Treaſon, by [b] 1 & 2 *Ph.* & *Ma.* 10. which enacts that all Trials for Treaſon ſhall be according to the Courſe of the Common Law. Yet it ſeems that the [c] King may, if he thinks fit, make a ſpecial Grant to an Alien to be tried for Treaſon by a Jury whereof the one Half ſhall be Aliens.

Sect. 38. [d] Alſo it hath been adjudged that the ſaid Statute of 28 *Ed.* 3. doth not extend to an Appeal, or other Action by an Alien againſt an Alien, for the Words are *all Inqueſts*, &c. *between Aliens and Denizens.*

Sect. 39. It is [e] holden, That by Denizens in this Statute are meant not only thoſe who are born within the King's Ligeance, but alſo thoſe who are made Denizens by the King's Letters Patents.

Sect. 40. It ſeems to be [f] ſettled, That no Alien whether he be Plaintiff or Defendant, can take any Advantage of the Statute, unleſs he [g] pray it in Time; and that if he have neglected to pray it before the Return of a Common *Venire*, he can neither except to ſuch *Venire*, nor pray a *Tales* or other Proceſs *de medietate linguæ.*

Sect. 41. It was [h] holden, even before the Union of the two Kingdoms under King *James* the firſt, That no *Scot* was an Alien within the Meaning of this Statute, not only becauſe the *Scotch* Language is the ſame with the *Engliſh*, but alſo [i] becauſe the *Scots* were never reckoned Aliens, but rather Subjects.

Sect. 42. *Note*, That [k] ſome of the Precedents for the Award of a *Venire* of a Jury of half Denizens and half Aliens, in Purſuance of 28 *E.* 3. mention, that the Aliens ſhall be of the ſame Country whereof the Party alledges himſelf; and others direct [l] generally that one Half of the Jury ſhall be Aliens, without ſpecifying any Country in particular. And this Form ſeems moſt agreeable to the Statute which ſpeaks of Aliens in general, and ſeems to be confirmed both by late [m] Practice, and the greater Number of [n] Authorities.

Sect. 43. If on a *Venire* of half Denizens and half Aliens, the Sheriff return 12 as Aliens, and among them ſome who in Truth are not ſuch, it ſeems [o] that the Party ſhall not be concluded by ſuch Return, but may notwithſtanding challenge the Array for Want of a ſufficient Number of Aliens.

Sect. 44. It ſeems [p] agreed, That the Return of a *Venire* of half Denizens, and half Aliens, ought to ſpecify which of the Jurors are Denizens and which Aliens, and that a full Number of each muſt appear to be ſworn.

Sect. 45. If one or more be wanting to make up the full Number of ſix Denizens or Aliens, the Juſtices of *Niſi prius*, by a reaſonable [q] Conſtruction of the Statutes which give a *Tales de Circumſtantibus* may award ſuch a *Tales* for ſo many Denizens or Aliens as ſhall be wanting.

Sect. 46. It is expreſly enacted by 2 & 3 *P.* & *M.* and 4 & 5 *El.* 20. ſet forth more at large *B.* 1 *Ch.* 54. that thoſe adjudged Felons, as *Egyptians* by Virtue of thoſe Statutes, ſhall be tried by the Inhabitants of the County or Place where they ſhall be taken, and not *per medietatem linguæ.*

[a] Daliſ. 22. Dy. 144, 145. pl. 61. 3 Inſt. 27. H. P. C. 260. [b] Vide ſupra ch. 25. ſect. 132, 142, 144. [c] S. P. C. 158. Fitz. Trial, 71. 22 Ed. 3. 14. pl. 38. [d] 21 H. 6. 4. pl. 10. Fitz. Trial, 32. Bro. Trial, 42. S. P. C. 260. Lett. C. H. P. C. 261. But by 27 Ed. 3. 8. it is enacted, That in Pleas between Aliens concerning the Staple there ſhall be a Jury of none but Aliens. S. P. C. 159. Lett. C. [e] Bro. Den. 4. [f] Dy. 28. pl. 180. 145. pl. 60, 61. 304. pl. 51. 357. pl. 45. 3 Ed. 4. 11. pl. 3. 22 Ed. 3. 14. pl. 38. 2 Rol. Abr. 643. P. 1. Fitz. Inq. 22. Trial, 71. H. P. C. 261. Bro Panel, 3. Cont. 21 H. 7. 32. pl. 23. Bro. Deniz. 4. S. P. C. 259. 'Tis holden Cro. Eliz. 869. pl. 3. by two Judges againſt one, that tho' the Defendant appear by the Declaration to be Alien, yet the Common Venire is well awarded, unleſs a Venire de medietate be prayed. [g] For the Form of ſuch a Prayer, Raſt. Ent. 7. a. pl. 2. 158. b. 159. a. 264. b. pl. 1, 2. 265. a. Dy. 144. pl. 60. S. P. C. 259. Pl. Com. 2. b. [h] Dy. 304. pl. 51. H. P. C. 261. [i] But Quære of this Reaſon, for it ſeems contrary to what is admitted in the whole Argument of Calvin's Caſe, 7 Co. See State Trials, Vol. 1. f. 572, 573. Vol. 4. f. 652, &c. [k] Dy. 144. pl. 60. Raſt. Ent. 7. b. pl. 2. 159. a. 264. b. pl. 1, 2. [l] Raſt. Ent. 265. a. 10 Co. 104. a. [m] State Trials, Vol. 3. f. 3. [n] H. P. C. 261. S. P. C. 158. Lett. C. Bro. Denizen, 4. Bro. Panel, 3. Cont. Fitz. Trial, 30. By five Judges againſt one. [o] 2 Rol. Abr. 643. pl. 2. Vide S. P. C. 158. Lett. C. [p] Cro. El. 818. pl. 10. 84. 1. pl. 18. But this being only a Miſ-return is helped by Verdict in Caſes within the Statute of Jeoſails. [q] 10 Co. 104. a. Cro. Eliz. 305. pl. 3. 818. pl. 10. 841. pl. 18.

CHAP. XLIV.

Of a Trial by Peers.

AS to a Trial by Peers, having ſhewn already, *Ch.* 39. *Sect.* 1. That a Peer has no more Privilege than a Commoner as to having the Benefit of Counſel. And *Ch.* 43. *Sect.* 4. That a Peer cannot challenge any of his Peers, I ſhall now endeavour to ſhew,

1. The particular Form and Solemnity to be obſerved in ſuch a Trial.
2. Who are to be Triers.
3. Who are to be ſo tried.
4. As to what Crimes.
5. Upon what Suits and Pleas.
6. Whether a Peer can waive a Trial by his Peers.
7. In what Manner the Peers may require the Opinion of the Lord Steward or of the Judges.
8. Whether the Court may be adjourned.

And firſt of the particular Form and Solemnity to be obſerved in ſuch a Trial.

Sect. 1. When an Indictment is found againſt a Peer for a Crime for which he ought to be tried by his Peers, the King by his Commiſſion under the Great Seal reciting the Indictment, conſtitutes ſome [a] Peer, High [b] Steward of the Kingdom *pro hac vice*, and by the ſame Commiſſion gives him Power to receive and proceed on ſuch Indictment, and requires the Peers to be attendant on him, and the Lieutenant of the Tower to bring the Priſoner before him.

[a] Supra ch. 2.
[b] 1 H. 4. 1. 3 Inſt. 28. 13 H. 8. 11. pl. 1. S. P. C. 152. the Neceſſity of making a High Steward for the Trial of an Impeachment for High Treaſon was denied by the Houſe of Commons in the Earl of Danby's Caſe. State Trials, Vol. 2. fol. 198, 199.

Sect. 2. Alſo [c] a *Certiorari*, (which may either have the ſame Date with the Steward's Commiſſion, or a ſubſequent one) goes out of Chancery to certify the Indictment before the Steward *indilate*; and the Steward by his Precept under his Seal, directed to thoſe before whom the Indictment was found, appoints a certain Day and Place, at which it ſhall be certified. And another Writ goes out of Chancery to the Lieutenant of the Tower, &c. to bring the Priſoner before the Steward at ſuch Day and Place as he ſhall appoint, and thereupon the Steward by his Precept under his Seal directed to the Lieutenant, &c. appoints the Day and Place.

[c] 3 Inſt. 28.

Sect. 3. Alſo the Steward makes [d] another Precept under his Seal to the Serjeant at Arms, appointed to ſerve him during the Time of his Commiſſion, to ſummon the [e] Peers before him at ſuch a Place, Day and Hour, &c.

[d] This is to be intended when the Parliament is not ſitting, but is either diſſolved or prorogued, State Trials, Vol. 3. fol. 659 to 663. 3 Inſt. 28. S. P. C. 152. a. 13 H. 8. 11. pl. 1.
[e] 'Tis ſaid 13 H. 8. 11. pl. 1. S. P. C. 157. a. That the Steward ſhall make ſuch Precept to cauſe 20 or 18 Peers to come before him, but Sir Edward Coke, 3 Inſt. 28. ſays that the Precept doth not mention any certain Number; and now by 7 W. 3. all the Peers are to be ſummoned.

Sect. 4. At the Time appointed the Steward, attended [a] with six or [b] seven Serjeants at Arms carrying Maces before him, and by the King at Arms, and the Usher of the Black Rod, enters the Place of Trial uncovered, and ascends a Chair of State which always is [c] provided for that Purpose, and then the [d] Clerk of the Crown, or a [e] Master in Chancery delivers to him his Commission, and he delivers it again to the Clerk [f] of the Crown, and then a Serjeant at Arms makes three [g] Oyes, and a Proclamation for Silence in the Name of the Steward, and then the Lord Steward and all the other Lords [h] standing up uncovered, the Commission is read, and then the [i] Usher on his Knees delivers to the Steward a White Rod, who redelivers it to him or to a Serjeant at Arms, who holds it by him during the Trial: Then an [m] Oyes is made, and a Command given in the Name of the Steward to all Justices and Commissioners to certify all Indictments, *&c.* which being delivered into Court, the Clerk of the Crown reads the Return. Another Oyes is made that the Lieutenant of the Tower, *&c.* return his Writ and Precept, and bring the Prisoner to the Bar, and then the Prisoner is brought to the Bar, the [n] Gentleman-Gaoler of the Tower carrying the Ax before him, which being [o] done the Clerk reads the Return.

Sect. 5. All things being thus prepared, the High Steward [p] acquaints the Prisoner with the Nature of the Crime, and such like Matters proper for such an Occasion, and then the Clerk of the Crown arraigns him, [q] but is not to insist on his holding up his Hand.

Sect. 6. After the Prisoner hath pleaded and put himself upon God and his Peers, the King's Counsel go thro' with their Evidence; and after the Prisoner hath made his Defence, and the King's Counsel have been fully heard, the Prisoner is withdrawn from the Bar, and the Lords go together to consider of their Evidence; and when a Majority of them are agreed, they return to the Place of Trial, and the Lord Steward demands of them one by one, beginning with the Puisne, whether the Person arraigned be Guilty or Not guilty, and they [r] all answer one by one, not upon their Oaths but on their [s] Honours and Ligeances. And the Lord Steward gives Judgment according to the Determination of the [t] Majority being more than twelve, but gives no Vote himself on a Trial by [u] Commission, but only on a Trial by the House of Peers, while the Parliament is sitting.

Sect. 7. As to the second Point, *viz.* Who are to be Triers: It is agreed, [x] That none but Lords, who have a Vote in Parliament can pass on such a Trial; and before 7 *W.* 3. 3. when the Trial was by Commission, it seems to have been the Practice for the Lord Steward to cause as many Temporal Lords to be summoned as he thought fit; and for the Lords so summoned alone to pass on the Trial. But this is remedied by that Statute set forth more at large in the next Section.

[a] 3 Inst 28.
[b] Rushw. Col. Part 2. Vol. 1. f. 96. Vide 2. Jon. 54.
[c] 3 Inst. 28. S.P.C. 152. 1 H. 4. 1. 13 H. 8. 11. pl. 1.
[d] 3 Inst. 21.
[e] Rushw. Col. Part 2. Vol. 1. fol. 96.
[f] 3 Inst. 28. Rushw. Col. Part 2. Vol. 1. fol. 96.
[g] 1 H. 4. 1. 3 Inst. 28.
[h] State Trials, Vol. 3. f. 955. Vol. 4. fol. 350.
[i] 3 Inst. 28. Rushw. Col. Part 2. Vol. 1. fol. 96.
[m] 3 Inst. 28.
[n] State Trials, Vol. 3. f. 955. Vol. 4. fol. 355.
[o] By 3 Inst. 28. All this is to precede the Call of the Peers and their Seating themselves; but 1 H. 4. 1. and 13 H. 8. 11. b. and S. P. C. 152. a. and State Trials, Vol. 1. f. 266. Vol. 3. f. 955, 956. and Vol. 4. f. 353 to 355. and 2 Jon. 55. are contrary.
[p] 3 Inst. 29. S.P.C. 152. a. 2 Jon. 55. and the other Books cited to the precedent Section.
[q] Raym. 408. State Trials, Vol. 3. fol. 658, 957. Vol. 2. 702, 703.
[r] 3 Inst. 30. 2 Inst. 49. Fitz. Coro. 34. 1 H. 4. 1. a. S. P. C. 152. 13 H. 8. 12. 2 Jon. 55, 56. 10 Ed. 4. 61. pl. 17.
[s] See the Books above-cited, and 1 Co. 30. b. 2 Inst. 49.
[t] 1 H. 4. 1. 13 H. 8. 12. S.P.C. 153. E. 3 Inst. 30. Moor 622.
[u] State Trials, Vol. 2. fol. 702. Vol. 3. fol. 657, 679.
[x] 2 Inst. 48. Co. Litt. 156.

Sect. 8. It is agreed, That at a Trial before the House of Peers, every Temporal Lord who has a Right to vote in that House, has a Right to pass on such Trial. But it is said in the *Year-Book* of 10 *Ed.* 4. 6. [a] *pl.* 17. That upon the Trial of a Peer in Parliament, the Bishops shall make a Procurator, because they cannot consent to the Death of a Man; but this is [b] said to be wholly grounded on a Canon not in Force at this Day; neither do I find any Precedent wherein they have been excluded against their Consent, or have withdrawn themselves without a Protestation of their Right, or making a Proxy; and the Judgment against the *Spencers*, was expresly reversed for this Reason among others, because the Bishops were not present; and in the Precedents chiefly insisted on of the other Side, it is not expresly said that they were not present, and it doth not clearly appear, but that they might be included under the Word Peers. However it hath been always [c] admitted that they have a Right to vote in a Bill of Attainder: Also in the Earl of *Danby*'s Case, they were adjudged [d] by the House of Lords to have a Right to vote in Questions previous to the Trial of a Peer, tho' this was strongly opposed by the House of Commons. And their Right to vote at the Trial itself, if they think fit, seems fully implied in 7 *W.* 3. 3. which enacts, *That upon the Trial of any Peer or Peeress for Treason or Misprision, all the Peers who have a Right to sit and vote in Parliament shall be summoned twenty Days at least before every such Trial, to appear at every such Trial, and that every Peer so summoned and appearing, shall vote at the Trial, every such Peer first taking the Oaths of Allegiance and Supremacy, and subscribing and repeating the* [e] *Declaration against Popery.*

Sect. 9. As to the third Point, *viz.* What Persons are to be thus tried: It is [f] agreed, That no Lord of any [g] other Country, or even of [h] *Scotland*, before the Union under Queen *Anne*, or of [h] *Ireland*, nor the Son and Heir [i] apparent of any Peer, or any other Man whatsoever, who is not at the Time a Lord of Parliament, hath any Right to such a Trial in this Kingdom. But that every Lord of Parliament hath a Right to such a Trial [k] by Virtue of that Clause in *Magna Charta*, *ch.* 29. *Nec super eum ibimus, nec super eum mittemus, nisi per legale judicium parium suorum vel per legem terræ.*

Sect. 10. It is recited by 20 *H.* 6. 9. *to have been a Doubt in the Law of* England *how Ladies of great Estate in Respect of their Husbands, Peers of the Land, married or sole, that is to say, Dutchesses, Countesses or Baronesses, shall be put to answer, and judged upon Indictments of Treasons and Felonies, because they are not mentioned in the said Statute of* Magna Charta, ch. 29. *and thereupon to put out such Doubts,* [l] *it is declared, That such Ladies so indicted of any Treason or Felony, whether they be married or sole, shall thereof be brought to answer, and judged before such Judges and Peers of the Realm, as Peers of the Realm should be, if they were indicted or impeached of such Treasons or Felonies.*

Sect. 11. It seems [m] agreed, that a Queen, the King's Consort, and also a Queen Dowager, whether she continue sole after the King's Death, or take a second Husband, be he a Peer or Commoner; and also all Peeresses by Birth, whether they be sole or [n] married to Peers or Commoners; and also all Marchionesses and Viscountesses, are intitled to a Trial by the Peers, tho' none of them be expresly mentioned in this Act, or in *Magna Charta*. But it is [o] agreed, that a Peeress by Marriage loses her Dignity by marrying a Commoner.

[a] Abridged Fitz. Coro. 34. cited S. P. C. 153. Lett. B. Brook in a Note of the same Case, Coro. 153. says that they shall make Proxies. Sir Edward Coke, 3 Inst. 31. says that they must withdraw and make their Proxies.

[b] See Bishop Stillingfleet, of the Bishops Jurisdiction in Criminal Cases, ch. 2, 3. and Hunt's Argument ch. 9, 10, 11.

[c] See Hunt's Argument for the Right of Bishops, &c. ch. 12. and Stillingfleet of the Bishops Jurisdiction in Capital Cases, ch. 1. sect. 3. and ch. 2.

[d] State Trials, Vol. 2. f. 179 to 202.

[e] B. 1. ch. 14. sect. 1.

[f] 2 Inst. 48. 3 Inst. 30. Co. Lit. 156. b

[g] Vide Fitz. Brief, 473. 20 Ed. 4. 6. pl. 6. Bro. Nosme de Dignity, 49.

[h] 9 Co. 117. Vide 39 Ed. 3. 35. b. Bro. Nosme de Dignity, 29. Vide supra ch. 25. sect. 50.

[i] Bro. Treason, 2.

[k] Such Trial is said to be very ancient, 2 Inst. 50.

[l] 2 Inst. 45, 50.

[m] 2 Inst. 50. Crompt. Jurisd. 33. b.

[n] See the Citations to the next Letter.

[o] 2 Inst. 50. Co. Litt. 16. b. 6 Co. 53. b. Dy. 79. pl. 51.

Sect. 12. It is said by [a] *Staundforde* and [b] *Coke*, that those who are Lords of Parliament, not in Respect of their Nobility, but of their Baronies which they hold of the Crown, as Bishops now do, and some Abbots and Priors [c] did formerly, are not within the Intent of *Magna Charta*, to be tried by the Peers. And [d] *Selden* seems clear, that this is the only Privilege which Bishops have not in Common with other Peers. And those who seem [e] most for the contrary Opinion admit that the Law hath been generally so taken. Neither do they produce any Precedent where a Bishop or Abbot has been tried by the Peers upon a Commission; but on the contrary admit that there are [f] two Precedents of their being tried by the Country. And it is said by [g] others, that there are divers Precedents of this Kind; yet *Selden*, with his utmost Diligence, seems able to produce but two, which clearly and fully come up to his Point, *viz.* those of Archbishop *Cranmer* and Bishop *Fisher*. However it seems to be [h] agreed, that while the Parliament is sitting a Bishop shall be tried by the Peers.

Sect. 13. As to the fourth Point, *viz.* As to what Crimes a Peer is to be tried by his Peers: I take it to be [i] agreed, That he has a Right to be so tried upon an Indictment of Treason or Felony, [k] whether such Treason or Felony be made such by the Common Law, or by Statute; and also upon an Indictment for a Misprision of Treason or Felony; but it [l] seems that regularly he is to be tried by the Country for all other Crimes, out of Parliament, as [m] *Præmunire*, [n] Riot, [o] Seducing a young Lady from her Parents in order to debauch her, *&c.*

Sect. 14. As to the fifth Point, *viz.* Upon what Suits and Pleas a Peer is to be tried by his Peers, it hath been [p] adjudged, That he shall not be so tried upon an Appeal of Felony, but only upon an Indictment; and the Reason given for it is, that those Words in *Magna Charta*, *ch.* 29. *nec super eum ibimus*, *&c.* are to be intended only of the Suit of the King, and not of the Suit of the Subject.

Sect. 15. Also it hath been [q] adjudged, and appears from constant [r] Experience, that neither the said Clause of *Magna Charta*, nor any other Law privileges a Peer from being indicted by a Grand Jury of Commoners, either in the King's Bench, or before Commissioners of *Oyer*, or the Coroner, *&c.*

Sect. 16. Also it seems [s] to be clear, That if a Peer absent himself, and cannot be found, he may be outlawed *per judicium coronatorum*, *&c.*

Sect. 17. Also it is said that the Court of King's Bench may allow a [t] Pardon pleaded by a Peer to an Indictment in that Court: But that it cannot receive either his Plea of Not guilty, or Confession, but only the Lord Steward on an Arraignment before the Lords.

Sect. 18. It seems clear, that if a Peer be [u] attainted of Treason or Felony, he may be brought before the King's Bench and demanded, What he has to say why Execution should not be awarded against him? And if he plead any Matter to such Demand, his Plea shall be discussed and Execution awarded by the said Court, upon its being adjudged against him.

[a] S. P. C. 152. A.

[b] 3 Inst. 30. But in Fitz. Coro. 161. seems admitted that a Bishop shall be tried by the Peers in Cases proper for such Trial, and Brook tit. Trial, 142. cites a Note from Fitz. Challenge, 115. wherein he says it was holden, that Bishops shall be tried by the Peers, but this is mistaken, for there is no such Opinion there holden,

[c] Co. Lit. 97. Fuller's Ch. History B. 6. fol. 292.

[d] Selden of Baronage, p. 152. Titles of Honour, 1st. Edit. pa. 347.

[e] Hunt's Argument for the Bishops Right in Capital Cases, ch. 18. Gibson's Codex, 154. Stillingfleet of the Bishops Jurisdiction in Capital Cases, ch. 4.

[f] Bro. Trial, 142. See Hunt's Argument ch. 18. and Stillingfleet of the Bishops Juridiction in Capital Cases.

[g] S. P. C. 153. Lett. A. Seld. Baron. 142 to 155. Vide 3 Inst. 30.

[h] See Hunt's Argument, ch. 18. Trials per pais, ch. 2. par. 8. State Trials, Vol. 1. f. 374. Stillingfleet of the Bishops Jurisdiction in Capital Cases.

[i] 3 Inst. 30. 2 Inst. 49. S. P. C. 153. Lett. D. 1 Bulst. 198.

[k] S. P. C. 158. Lett. D. E. F. 1 Bulst. 198.

[l] See the Books above-cited, State Trials, Vol. 2. fol. 3. Fitz. Coro. 161.

[m] 1 Bulst. 198, 199. 3 Inst. 30. 12 Co 93.

[n] State Trials, Vol. 3. fol. 79.

[o] State Trials, Vol. 3. fol. 52. 12 Co. 93.

[p] 10 Ed. 4. 6. pl. 17. Fitz. Coro. 34. Bro. Coro. 153. S. P. C. 152. Lett. A. 2 Inst. 49. 3 Inst. 30. Rast. Ent. 50. pl. 7.

[q] 3 Inst. 26, 28. 2 Inst. 49.

[r] 1 H. 4. 1. State Trials, Vol. 3. fol. 52, 79, 657, 951. Vol. 4. fol. 351, &c. Skin. 683.

[s] 3 Inst. 31. 2 Inst. 49.

[t] 2 Inst. 49.

[u] 1 H. 7. 22, 23. pl. 15. Bro. Coro. 129. Treason 18. Fitz. Coro. 49.

Sect. 19.

Sect. 19. As to the ſixth Point, *viz.* Whether a Peer can waive a Trial by his Peers, it hath been [a] adjudged, That if a Peer on an Arraignment before the Lords refuſe to put himſelf upon his Peers, he ſhall be dealt with as one that ſtands Mute; for it is as much the Law of the Land that a Peer be tried by his Peers, as a Commoner by Commoners. Yet if one who has a Title to Peerage, be indicted and arraigned as a Commoner, and plead Not guilty, and put himſelf upon his Country, it hath been [b] adjudged that he cannot afterwards ſuggeſt that he is a Peer, and pray a Trial by his Peers.

Sect. 20. As to the ſeventh Point, *viz.* In what Manner the Peers may require the Opinion of the Lord Steward, or of the Judges: It was [c] reſolved by all the Judges in the Lord *Dacre's* Caſe, who was tried by Commiſſion, that no Queſtion ought to be asked of the Lord Steward or of the Judges in the Abſence of the Priſoner. And it was [d] adjudged by the Lord Steward, in the Earl of *Warwick*'s Caſe, who was tried by the Houſe of Peers in Parliament, that no Queſtion ought to be asked of the Judges in the Abſence of the Priſoner. But in the Lord *Audley*'s Caſe, who was tried by Commiſſion, the Lords Triers, [e] after they were withdrawn, conſulted with the Lord Chief Juſtice four ſeveral Times, and alſo ſent to conſult with the Lord Steward. Yet, notwithſtanding this Precedent, the Judges [f] reſolved in the Lord *Morley*'s Caſe, who was likewiſe tried by Commiſſion, that if after the Lords were withdrawn they ſhould ſend for any of the Judges to deſire their Opinions on a Point in Law, and the Lord Steward ſhould permit them to go, they would tell the Lords, if they ſhould ask them any Queſtion, that they were not to give any private Opinion, without Conference with the reſt of the Judges, and that openly in Court. But they reſolved that if the Lord Steward ſhould ask them any Queſtion in open Court, tho' in the Abſence of the Priſoner, they would anſwer it, becauſe they are call'd to aſſiſt the Court, and the Demand of any Queſtion in ſuch Caſe is to be referred to the Diſcretion of the Lord Steward.

Sect. 21. When a Peer is tried before the Houſe of Peers in Parliament, the Lord Steward [g] withdraws with the reſt of the Lords, and conſults with them.

Sect. 22. As to the eighth Point, *viz.* Whether the Court may be adjourned: It is agreed, [h] That where a Peer is tried by the Houſe of Lords in full Parliament, the Houſe may be adjourned as often as there is Occaſion, and the Evidence taken by Parcels: Alſo it hath been [i] adjudged, That where the Trial is by Commiſſion, the Lord Steward, after a Verdict is given, may take Time to adviſe upon it, and that his Office continues 'till he has given Judgment. Alſo it was [k] ſaid to have been agreed by the Judges in the Lord *Dacre*'s Caſe, That on ſuch a Trial the Court might be adjourned, and that if the Lords Triers did not agree, it was holden by ſome they ought to be kept together all Night, and by others that they might go to their ſeveral Houſes. But it is ſaid, [l] That there is no Precedent of the Lords Triers ever having ſeparated upon a Trial by Commiſſion, after the Evidence has been given for the King; and it is ſaid to have been [m] reſolved by all the Judges in the Caſe of the Duke of *Norfolk*, That the Peers in ſuch Caſe muſt continue together 'till they agree to give Verdict, and the like was [n] adjudged by the Lord Steward in the Lord *Delamere*'s Caſe.

[a] Ruſhw. Collections, Part. 2. Vol. 1. f. 94. 3 Inſt. 30. Kely. 57. Yet there is ſaid to be a Record in 4 Edw. 3. That T. Lord Berkley, put himſelf on his Country, and was tried by a Jury of Knights.

[b] Dalis. 16.

[c] 3 Inſt. 29, 30. 2 Inſt. 49. Kely. 57. State Trials, Vol. 3. f. 679.

[d] State Trials, Vol. 4. f. 381.

[e] Ruſhw. Collections, Part 2. Vol. 1. f. 101. State Trials, Vol. 1. f. 271.

[f] Kely. 54.

[g] State Trials, Vol. 3. f. 679.

[h] State Trials, Vol. 2. f. 654. Vol. 3. f. 677 to 680.

[i] Ruſhw. Collections, Part 2. Vol. 1. f. 95. State Trials, Vol. 1. f. 265. But Moor 622. ſeems contrary.

[k] Kely. 57. But Moor 622. in a Report of the very ſame Caſe it is ſaid that the contrary was holden.

[l] State Trials, Vol. 3. f. 678. But ſee Moor 622.

[m] 3 Inſt. 30. in the Margin.

[n] State Trials, Vol. 3 f. 677 to 680.

CHAP. XLV.

Of Trial by Battel.

Sect. 1. A Trial by Battel, at the [a] Defendant's Choice, is allowable in Appeals [b] of Treaſon before the Conſtable and Marſhal, and in Appeals [c] of Felony, whether by Appellants or [d] Approvers.

Sect. 2. For the Manner of waging Battel in an Appeal of Treaſon being according to the Civil Law, I ſhall refer to *Ruſhworth*'s Collections, *Part.* 2. *Vol.* 1. *fol.* 112. *to* 128.

Sect. 3. When an Appellee of Felony wages Battel, he pleads [e] that he is Not guilty, and that he is ready to defend the ſame by his Body and then [f] flings down his Glove, and if the Appellant will join Battel, he replies, That he is ready to make good his Appeal by his Body upon the Body of the Appellee, and takes up the Glove: And then the Appellee lays his [g] right Hand on the Book, and with his left Hand takes the Appellant by the Right, and [h] ſwears to this Effect, *Hear this thou who calleſt thy ſelf* John *by the Name of Baptiſm, that I, who call my ſelf* Thomas *by the Name of Baptiſm, did not feloniouſly murder thy Father* W. *by Name,* (*on the Day of in the Year of at* B.) *as you ſurmiſe, nor am any way guilty of the ſaid Felony*; *ſo help me God,* (and then he ſhall kiſs the Book and ſay) *and this I will defend againſt thee by my Body as this Court ſhall award.* And then the Appellant lays his right Hand on the Book, and with his left Hand takes the Appellee by the Right, and ſwears to this Effect, *Hear this thou who calleſt thy ſelf* Thomas *by the Name of Baptiſm, that thou feloniouſly* (*on the Day of in the Year of at* B.) *didſt murder my Father* W. *by Name, ſo help me God,* (and then he ſhall kiſs the Book and ſay) *and this I will prove againſt thee by my Body, as this Court ſhall award.* And then the Court ſhall [i] appoint a Day and Place for the Battel, and in the mean while the Appellee ſhall be kept in the [k] Cuſtody of the Marſhal, and the Appellant ſhall find [l] Sureties to be ready to fight at the Time and Place, unleſs he be an Approver, in which Caſe [m] he ſhall alſo be kept by the Marſhal. And the [n] Night before the Day of Battel, both Parties ſhall be arraigned by the Marſhal, and ſhall be brought into the Field before the [o] Juſtices of the Court where the Appeal is depending, at the Riſing of the Sun, [p] bare headed, and bare legged from the Knee downwards, and bare in the Arms to the Elbows, and armed only with Baſtons an Ell long, and four cornered Targets, and before they engage they ſhall both take this [q] Oath, *Hear this ye Juſtices, that I,* A. B. *have neither eat nor drunk, nor done any thing elſe, nor any other for me, by which the Law of God may be depreſſed, and the Law of the Devil exalted.* And then after [r] Proclamation for Silence under Pain of Impriſonment for a Year and a Day,

[a] Finch of Law 421. S. P. C. 176. Letter F. Fleta, lib. 1. ch. 34. ſect. 27. Trials per pais, ch. 2. ſect. 19.

[b] Vide ſupra ch. 23. ſect. 29. Crompt. Jur. 82. b. 88. a. Bro. Battel, 15.

[c] Raſt. Ent. 50. pl. 10. Cro. Eliz. 69. pl. 22. Dyer 120. pl. 10. S. P. C. 176. ch. 13, 14. and the Books cited to the other Parts of this Chapter.

[d] Raſt. Ent. 42. pl. 3. S.P.C 178. b. 9 Co. 31. b.

[e] Cro. Eliz. 69. pl. 22. Raſt. Ent. 42. pl. 3. 50. pl 10. Dyer 120. pl. 10. 9 H. 4. 3. pl 16.

[f] S. P. C. 178. Letter K. Fitz. Coro. 385. Vide 1 H. 6. 6. b.

[g] Bro. Battel, 1. 6. 9 H. 4. 3. pl. 16. 17 Aſſ. pl. 1. 17 Ed. 3. 2. pl. 6. Britton, 41. S.P.C. 178. A.

[h] Fleta B. 1. ch. 34. ſect. 28, 29. 9 H. 4. 3. pl. 16. 17 Aſſ. pl. 1. Bro. Battel, 1, 6. 17 Ed. 3. 2. pl. 6. Britton, 41. Bract. B. 3. ch. 21. ſect. 2. [i] Raſt. Ent. 42. b. pl. 2. S. P. C. 178. B. [k] Fleta, B. 1. ch. 33. ſect. 28. Raſt. Ent. 42. b. pl. 2. 9 H. 4. 3. pl. 16. S. P. C. 178. Bro. Battel, 1. Fitz. Coro. 78, 111. [l] Fleta B. 1. ch. 34. ſect. 28. 9 H. 4. 3. pl. 16. 17 Aſſ. pl. 1. S. P. C. 178. Letter B. Fitz. Cor. 78, 111. Bro. Battel, 1, 6. 17 Ed. 3. 2. pl. 6. Bract. B. 3. ch. 21. ſect. 3. ſays that both Parties ſhall be kept in Cuſtody. [m] Raſt. Ent. 42. b. pl. 2. [n] 9 H. 4. 3. pl. 16. Bro. Battel, 1. [o] Fleta B. 1. ch. 34. ſect. 30, 31. Dyer 301. Bro. Battel, 15. S. P. C. 177, 178. Bract. B. 3. ch. 21. ſect. 4, 5. Britt. 40. Cont. 37 H. 6. 20. [p] Britt. 41. By ſome the Appellant's Head ſhall be covered. 9 H. 4. 3. pl. 16. Bro. Battel, 1. Vide 1 H. 6. 6. 7. Dy. 301. [q] Fleta, B. 1. ch. 34. ſect. 30. Bract. B. 3. ch. 21. ſect. 4. Britt. f. 40. [r] Fleta, B. 1. ch. 34. ſect. 31.

&c. they ſhall begin the Combat, wherein if the Appellee be ſo far vanquiſhed that he cannot or will not fight any longer, he may be adjudged to be [a] hanged immediately; but if he can maintain the Fight 'till the Stars appear, he ſhall have [b] Judgment to go quit of the Appeal. And if the Appellant become Recreant, that is, a Crying Coward or Craven, the Appellee ſhall not only recover his Damages, but may alſo, as it [c] ſeems, plead his Acquittal in Bar of a ſubſequent Indictment or Appeal, and the Appellant [d] ſhall for his Perjury loſe his *liberam Legem.* Yet if there be other Appellees in the ſame Appeal, it hath been adjudged, [e] that it ſhall ſtill ſtand in Force againſt them. But for theſe Matters I ſhall refer to *Ch.* 24. *Sect.* 24.

Sect. 4. In Appeals each Party muſt fight in proper [f] Perſon, and not by Champions. And therefore if the Appellant be under an apparent Diſability of fighting, as being a [g] Woman, or in [h] Holy Orders, or under [i] Age, or of the Age of [k] ſixty, [l] or maimed, or [m] blind, he may counterplead the Wager of Battel, and compel the Appellee to put himſelf upon his Country. [n] Alſo if an Appellant become blind by the Act of God after he has waged Battel, the Court will diſcharge him of the Battel; and in ſuch Caſe it is [o] ſaid that the Appellee ſhall go free.

Sect. 5. Alſo if a [p] Peer of the Realm, and much more if the King bring an Appeal, the Defendant ſhall not be admitted to wage Battel, by Reaſon of the Dignity of their Perſons.

Sect. 6. Alſo the Citizens of *London* have a ſpecial [q] Privilege by Charter, that in Appeals brought by any of them, there ſhall be no Wager of Battel.

Sect. 7. Alſo any Plaintiff may counterplead a Wager of Battel, by alledging ſuch Matters againſt the Defendant as induce a violent Preſumption of Guilt; as in an Appeal of Robbery, by ſhewing [r] that the Defendant was taken with the Manner, *&c.* And in an Appeal of Death, that he was found lying upon the deceaſed [s] with a bloody Knife in his Hand; and in any Appeal by ſhewing that the Defendant being under an Arreſt for the Crime charged againſt him, [t] brake the Priſon, or [u] eſcaped, unleſs ſuch Breaking or Eſcape be [x] pardoned. For the Law will [y] not oblige a Plaintiff to make good his Accuſation in ſo extraordinary a Manner, when in all Appearance he may prove it in the ordinary Way. It is alſo a good Counterplea of Battel that the Defendant hath been [z] indicted for the ſame Fact, unleſs the Indictment were inſufficient.

Sect. 8. It is enacted by 6 *Ric.* 2. That the Defendant ſhall not be received to wage Battel in an Appeal of Rape.

[a] S. P. C. 178. b. See where this is done accordingly. 19 H. 6. 35. pl. 75. Fitz. Coro. 6. Bro. Coro. 46. Bract. B. 1. ch. 21. ſect. 6.

[b] Trials per pais, ch. 2. ſect. 19. 3 Inſt. 221. Fleta, B. 1. ch. 34. ſect. 32. Bract. B. 3. ch. 21. ſect. 5.

[c] Supra ch. 23. ſect. 140. and ch. 35. ſect. 6. Fitz. Cor. 98. Fleta, B. 1. ch. 34. ſect 32.

[d] 3 Inſt. 221. Co. Lit. 6. b.

[e] Fitz. Coro. 98.

[f] Finch of Law 421, 422. 9 Co. 31. b. 3 Inſt. 221. Plow. Com. 335. b. Trials per pais, ch. 2. ſect. 19.

[g] Keilw. 120. pl. 66. Fleta, B. 1. ch. 34. ſect. 25. S. P. C. 180. Letter A.

[h] Britton 40.

[i] Keilw. 120. pl. 66. Finch of Law 423. Fitz. Droit, 3. S. P. C. 60. Letter D. 180. Letter A. 22 Ed. 4. 20. a. Fleta, B. 1. ch. 34 ſect. 25.

[k] S. P. C. 60. Lett. D. 180. Lett. A. Fitz. Coro. 385. 22 Ed. 4. 20. a. Trials per pais, ch. 2. ſect. 19. Fleta, B. 1. ch. 34. ſect. 25.

[l] Finch of Law 423. Fitz. Coro. 230, 268. S. P. C. 180. Letter A. 22 Ed. 4. 20. a. Trials per pais, ch. 2. ſect. 19. Fleta, B. 1. ch. 34. ſect. 25.

[m] Fitz. Droit, 57. 3 Inſt. 158, 159.

[n] Fitz. Droit, 57. 3 Inſt. 158, 159.

[o] 3 Inſt. 158, 159.

[p] Finch of Law 423. S. P. C. 152. Letter A. Plow. Com. 335. b. Fleta B. 1. ch. 34 ſect. 25.

[q] S. P. C. 180. Letter C. Fitz. Coro. 125, 187.

[r] Finch of Law 422, 423. S. P. C. 179. Fitz. Coro. 100, 125, 144, 157, 230, 268, 375. 4 Aſſ. pl. 1. 22 Ed. 4. 19. b. Bro. Battel, 5, 7. Appeal, 114. 20 H. 7. 8. pl. 18. Vide ſupra ch. 15. ſect. 41.

[s] Finch of Law 422. S. P. C. 179. Fitz. Coro. 411.

[t] Finch of Law 422. S. P. C. 180. 1 Aſſ. pl. 3, 6. Hob. 82. Fitz. Coro. 154, 157, 164, 251, 281.

[u] Finch of Law 422. Hob. 82. S. P. C. 80. Bro. Battel, 3. Aſſ. pl. 6. Fitz. Coro. 164, 251.

[x] S. P. C. 100. Hob. 82. Fitz. Coro 154, 281. Bro. Battel, 3. 1 Aſſ. pl. 3.

[y] Trials per pais, ch. 2. ſect. 19.

[z] Finch of Law 422. 22 Ed. 4. 19. b. Bro. Battel, 7, 11. Appeal, 114. 20 Ed. 4. 6. pl. 5. Raſt. Ent. 50. pl. 10.

CHAP.

CHAP. XLVI.

Of Evidence.

Sect. 1. AS to the Nature of Evidence, ſo far as it more particularly concerns Criminal Caſes, having premiſed that it is a ſettled Rule, That in Caſes of Life no [a] Evidence is to be given againſt a Priſoner but in his Preſence; and that it hath been [b] adjudged, That no Bill of Exceptions is grantable on an Indictment of Treaſon or Felony, the Statute of *Weſtm.* 2. 3. *cum aliquis implacitatus, &c. proponat exceptionem, &c.* having been never thought to extend to any ſuch Caſe, it being plain that it could not but cauſe an infinite Delay of Juſtice, if it ſhould; I ſhall more fully conſider the following Points.

1. How many Witneſſes are required in Criminal Caſes.
2. What is to be allowed as Evidence.
3. Who may be Witneſſes.
4. In what Manner the Witneſſes for the Defendant are to give their Evidence.
5. Whether a Defendant have Right to Proceſs to bring in his Witneſſes.
6. What Evidence maintains an Indictment, &c.
7. What may be given in Evidence on the Part of the Defendant.

Sect. 2. As to the firſt Point, *viz.* How many Witneſſes are required in Criminal Caſes: Having already endeavoured to ſhew that the Common Law did [c] not require any certain Number of Witneſſes for the Trial of any Crime whatſoever, I ſhall only add in this Place, That it ſeems to have been the more [d] prevailing Opinion, That 1 [e] *E.* 6. 12. and 5 & 6 *E.* 6. 11. which required two Witneſſes in Treaſon, were not repealed by 1 & 2 *P.* & *M.* 10. which ordered that all Trials of Treaſon ſhould be according to the Courſe of the Common Law; [104] and therefore that it was ſtill neceſſary in all Trials of High Treaſon, not concerning the Coin, to have either two Witneſſes to the [f] ſame Overt-Act, or one Witneſs to one, and another [g] Witneſs to another Overt-Act, of the ſame Kind of Treaſon, or at leaſt one Witneſs to an Overt-Act, and [h] another to a material Circumſtance to prove it. In Relation to which Matters the Law ſeeming to be ſettled by 7 [i] *W.* 3. which is expreſs, *That no Perſon ſhall be indicted, tried or attainted for High Treaſon, but upon the Oaths of two lawful Witneſſes, either both of them to the ſame Overt-Act, or one of them to one, and the other of them to another Overt-Act of the ſame Treaſon*; it will be needleſs

[a] State Trials, Vol. 4. f. 277, 310.

[b] Sir Henry Vane's Caſe, State Trials, Vol. 1. f. 938. wherein it is ſaid that ſuch Bill never was nor ought to be allowed in any Capital Caſe, and as this Caſe is reported in 1 Sid. 85. 1 Keb. 384. it ſeems to have been holden that it is not grantable on any Indictment; and as it is reported in 1 Lev. 68. and Kely. 15. That it is not grantable in any Criminal Caſe whatſoever. Vide 2 Inſt. 427.

[c] Ch. 25. ſect. 129.

[d] H.P.C. 262. and the Authorities cited to the other Parts of this Section. Cont. State Trials Vol. 1. f. 180, 181, 636. Vol 2. f. 408. and ſupra ch. 25. ſect. 129.

[e] For theſe Statutes, and their Expoſition, See ch. 25. ſect. 130 to 146. [f] Raym. 407, 408. State Trials, Vol. 2. f. 533. Vol. 3. fol. 688, 689. [g] State Trials, Vol. 1. f. 697, 723, 724. Vol. 2. f. 317, 695, 785, 829, 830. Vol. 3. f. 149, 156, 228. Vol. 4. f. 86, 87, 88, 117. Raym. 407, 408. Kely. 9. [h] State Trials, Vol. 2. f. 408. Vol. 3. f. 228, 229, 688, 689, 894 to 901, 928, 929, 930. Vide State Trials, Vol. 1. fol. 636. But State Trials, Vol. 1. f. 180, 181. 'tis holden that Circumſtantial Evidence alone is ſufficient. [i] Vide ch. 25. ſect. 134 to 146.

lefs at this Day to examine how far thefe Opinions were reconcileable with 1 *Ph. & Ma.*

As to the fecond Point, *viz.* What is to be allowed as Evidence in Criminal Cafes, I fhall confider.

1. Where the Confeffion of the Defendant or the Depofitions of others out of Court may be allowed as Evidence.
2. How far Hearfay is Evidence.
3. Whether Similitude of Hands be any Evidence in Criminal Cafes.

Sect. 3. As to the firft Particular, *viz.* Where the Confeffion of the Defendant, or the Depofitions of others, out of Court, may be allowed as Evidence: It feems that the Confeffion of the Defendant himfelf, whether taken upon an [a] Examination before Juftices of Peace, in Purfuance of 1 & 2 *Ph. & M.* 13. or of 2 & 3 *Ph. & Ma.* 10. upon [b] a Bailment or [c] Commitment for Felony, or taken by the Common Law upon an Examination before a Secretary of State, or other Magiftrates for [d] Treafon, or [e] other Crimes, not within thofe Statutes, or in [f] Difcourfe with private Perfons, hath always been allowed to be given in Evidence againft the Party confeffing, but [g] not againft others.

Sect. 4. Alfo it was [h] holden, That two Witneffes of a Confeffion of High Treafon, upon an Examination before a Juftice of Peace, were fufficient to convict the Perfon fo confeffing, within the Meaning of 1 *E.* 6. 12. and 5 & 6 *E.* 6. 11. which required two Witneffes in High Treafon, *unlefs the Offender fhould willingly without Violence confefs the fame*: But this is remedied by 7 *W.* 3. 3. which requires two Witneffes, *unlefs the Party fhall willingly, without Violence, in open Court confefs, &c.*

Sect. 5. It [i] feems an eftablifhed Rule, that where-ever a Man's Confeffion is made Ufe of againft him, it muft all be taken together, and not by Parcels.

Sect. 6. It feems [k] fettled, that the Examination of an Informer taken upon [l] Oath, and [m] fubfcribed by him either before a [n] Coroner upon an Inquifition of Death in Purfuance of 1 & 2 *Ph. & M.* 13. or before [o] Juftices of Peace in Purfuance of 1 & 2 *Ph. & M.* 13. and 2 & 3 *P. & M.* 10. upon a [p] Bailment or [q] Commitment for any Felony, may be given in Evidence at the Trial of fuch Inquifition, or of an Indictment for the fame Felony, if it be made out by Oath to the Satisfaction of the Court, that fuch Informer is [r] dead, or unable to [s] Travel, or kept [t] away by the Means or Procurement of the Prifoner, and that the Examination offered in Evidence is the very fame [u] that was fworn before the Coroner or Juftice, without any Alteration whatfoever.

[a] H. P. C. 102, 262, 263, 264. 1 H. H. P. C. 304. State Trials, Vol. 1. fol. 265. Vol. 3. fol. 8, 9.
[b] Supra ch. 15. Sect. 58, 59, 60, 61.
[c] Supra ch. 15. fect. 11, 12.
[d] State Trials, Vol. 1. f. 87, 181, 963. Francia's Trial. Kely. 18.
[e] 5 Mod. 164, 165. State Trials, Vol. 2. fol. 426. Vol. 3. fol. 131, 132.
[f] Dyer 215. pl. 50. H. P. C. 102, 193. 1 H. H. P. C. 306.
[g] Kely. 18, 19. State Trials, Vol. 3. fol. 8, 9. Vol. 4. f. 33. See the contrary practifed State Trials, Vol. 1. in Sir Jerv. Ellis's Trial, and in Throgmorton's Trial, fol. 49 to 56. Duke of Norfolk's Trial, fol. 73 to 85. and 97, 98. Other Trials from fol. 118 to 122. Earl of Effex's Trial, 167, 168. Sir Walter Raleigh's Trial, fol. 177, 178, 181.
[h] Kely. 18. Supra ch. 25. fect. 140.
[i] 5 Mod. 165. Cont. State Trials, Vol. 1. fol. 53. Throgmorton's Trial.
[k] Kely. 55. H. P. C. 262, 263. 1 Lev. 180. Salk. 281. pl. 8. 2 Keb. 19. Vide Cro. El. 901. Dalt. ch. 111, 112, 113.
[l] State Trials, Vol. 1. fol. 265. H. P. C. 262, 263.
[m] H. P. C. 262, 263.
[n] Supra ch. 9. fect. 31. 2 Jon. 53.
[o] See the Books above-cited; but 2 Jon. 53. 'tis adjudged that Depofitions before a Coroner may be read, but faid that thofe taken before a Juftice of Peace can in no Cafe be read.
[p] Supra ch. 15. fect. 59, 60, 61.
[q] Supra ch. 16. fect. 11.
[r] Kely. 55. 1 Lev. 180. 2 Keb. 19. pl. 39. H. P. C. 263.
[s] Kely. 55.
[t] Kely. 55. in Harrifon's Cafe, State Trials, Vol. 3. fol. 941. fuch an Examination was read in Evidence, upon Proof that the Witnefs had been enticed away, tho' it did not directly appear to have been done by the Procurement of the Prifoner.
[u] Kely. 55. 2 Keb. 19. pl. 39. H. P. C. 263. 2 H. H. P. C. 284, 285.

Sect. 7. But it hath been [a] adjudged, that it is not ſufficient to authorize the Reading ſuch an Examination, to make Oath that the Proſecutors have uſed all their Endeavours to find the Witneſs, but cannot find him.

Sect. 8. Alſo it hath been [b] adjudged, that Depoſitions taken before a Coroner upon an Inquiſition of Death *ſuper viſum corporis*, cannot be given in Evidence upon an Appeal for the ſame Death, becauſe it is a different Proſecution from that wherein they were taken.

Sect. 9. There are many [c] Inſtances in the Reigns of Queen *Elizabeth* and King *James* I. wherein the Depoſitions of abſent Witneſſes were allowed as Evidence in Treaſon and Felony, even where it did not appear but that the Witneſſes might have been produced *viva voce*. And it was adjudged in [d] the Earl of *Strafford*'s Trial, that where Witneſſes could not be produced *viva voce*, by Reaſon of Sickneſs, &c. their Depoſitions might be read for or againſt the Priſoner on a Trial of High Treaſon, but not where they might have been produced in Perſon. And it was admitted [e] in the Lord *Stafford*'s Trial, that the Depoſitions taken by a Witneſs before a Juſtice of the Peace might at the Priſoner's Deſire be read at the Trial, in order to take off the Credit of the Witneſs by ſhewing a Variance between ſuch Depoſitions and the Evidence given in Court *viva voce*. And for the ſame Reaſon it ſeems [f] agreed, That where a Witneſs at one Trial varies from his own Evidence at another, in Relation to the ſame Matter, ſuch Variance may alſo be given in Evidence to invalidate his Teſtimony at the ſecond Trial.

Sect. 10. But it is [g] ſaid to have been adjudged in the ſeventh Year of *Will.* 3. by the Court of King's Bench upon Advice with the Juſtices of the Common Pleas, upon an Indictment for a Libel, that Depoſitions taken before a Juſtice of Peace relating to the Fact, could not be given in Evidence, tho' the Deponent were dead; and that the Reaſon why ſuch Depoſitions may be given in Evidence in Felony depends upon the Statutes of *Ph. & Ma.* And that this cannot be extended farther than the particular Caſe of Felony. But in the Report of this Caſe in 5 [h] *Mod.* it is ſaid that the Reaſon why ſuch Depoſitions could not be read, was becauſe the Defendant was not preſent, when they were taken, and therefore had not the Benefit of a Croſs Examination.

Sect. 11. However it was [i] agreed in Sir *John Fenwick*'s Caſe, that the Information of a Witneſs taken upon Oath before a Juſtice of Peace, being joined with the Evidence of one other Witneſs only *viva voce*, could not in the ordinary Courſe of Juſtice, amount to ſufficient Evidence within the 7th of *W.* 3. which requires two Witneſſes in High Treaſon; and therefore it was thought neceſſary to proceed in that Caſe by Bill of Attainder in Parliament, whoſe Power can be reſtrained by no Rules but thoſe of natural Juſtice.

Sect. 12. And in the ſame Caſe it was [k] agreed, that the Evidence given by a Witneſs at one Trial, could not in the ordinary Courſe of Juſtice be made Uſe of againſt a Defendant on the Death of ſuch Witneſs, at another Trial.

[a] Kely. 55.

[b] 2 Rol. Rep. 460, 461. Vide 1 Sid. 325. 2 Keb. 384. pl. 54.

[c] State Trials, Vol. 1. Duke of Norfolk's Trial, f. 84. Abington's Trial, f. 118, 119. Udal's Trial, fol. 148, 149. Earl of Eſſex's Trial, fol. 166. Sir Walter Raleigh's Trial, fol. 181. 182. and the like was admitted in the Lord Audley's Caſe on an Indictment for a Rape on his own Lady. State Trials, Vol. 1. fol. 268, 269.

[d] Ruſhw. Strafford, fol. 231, 526 to 531.

[e] State Trials, Vol. 2. fol. 622 to 627, 644, 647, 651. See Vol. 1. f. 911.

[f] State Trials, Vol. 2. f. 343, 344, 528, 529. See ſect. 12.

[g] Salk. 281. Vide ſupra ſect. 3.

[h] 5 Mod. 165. Vide Ruſhw. Strafford, 524 to 531. and State Trials, Vol. 2. fol. 420. and Vol. 4. fol. 261. and 2 Rol. Rep. 460, 461.

[i] State Trials, Vol. 4. f. 237, &c.

[k] State Trials, Vol. 4. fol. 265 to 272. Vide ſupra ſect. 9. 1 Sid. 325. 2 Keb. 384. pl. 54.

Sect. 13. Also it seems clear that Depositions taken in the Spiritual Court in a Cause of Divorce for a Forcible Marriage cannot [a] be given in Evidence upon an Indictment for such Marriage on the [b] Statute of 3 *H.* 7. 2.

[a] H.P.C. 263. 2 H.H.P.C. 285.
[b] Vide B. 1. ch. 42.

Sect. 14. As to the second Particular, *viz.* How far Hearsay is Evidence: It seems [c] agreed, That what a [d] Stranger has been heard to say is in Strictness no Manner of Evidence either for or against a Prisoner, not only because it is not upon Oath, but also because the other Side hath no Opportunity of a cross Examination; and therefore it seems a settled Rule, that it shall never be made use of but only by way of Inducement [e] or Illustration of what is properly Evidence; yet it seems [f] that what the Prisoner hath been heard to say at another Time, may be given in Evidence for him, as well as against [g] him, and also what a [h] Witness hath been heard to say at another Time, may be given in Evidence in order either to invalidate or confirm the Testimony which he gives in Court.

[c] State Trials, Vol. 2. f. 332, 414, 415, 761, 802, 803. Vol. 3. fol. 145, 210, 252. Vol. 4. f. 33.
[d] Vide supra sect. 3.
[e] State Trials, Vol. 2. f. 325, 328, 332, 333, 414, 415. Vol. 3. fol. 144, 145, 209, 210. Vol. 4. f. 33.
[f] State Trials, Vol. 3. f. 254, 255.
[g] Vide supra sect. 3.
[h] State Trials, Vol. 2. fol. 529, 802, 803. Vol. 3. fol. 218 to 222, 428, 429. Vol. 4. fol. 51, 52, 53. Vide supra sect. 9. & 12.

Sect. 15. As to the third Particular, *viz.* Whether Similitude of Hands be any Evidence in Criminal Cases: It is observable that this with other Circumstances in [i] *Algernoon Sidney*'s Case was ruled to be good Evidence of his having written a Paper charged against him as an Overt-act of High Treason: Yet in the Trial of the seven [k] Bishops, the Court was divided in Opinion, whether Similitude of Hands were Evidence of the Defendants having signed the Paper charged against them as a Libel; and the Parliament having declared an Opinion in the Reversal of *Algernoon Sidney*'s Attainder, that Comparison of Hands is no Evidence of a Man's Hand-Writing in Criminal Cases: It seems to have been generally holden [l] since that Time, that it is not Evidence in any Criminal Case, whether capital or not capital. [105]

[i] State Trials, Vol. 3. f. 213, 216, 217, 226, 230.
[k] State Trials, Vol. 3. fol. 762 to 767.
[l] Vide State Trials, Vol. 3. fol. 892, 893. Vol. 4. fol. 271, 272. and Ftancia's Trial.

As to the third Point, *viz.* Who may be Witnesses in Criminal Cases, I shall endeavour to shew,

1. Whether a Husband or Wife may be Witnesses for or against one another.
2. Whether a Judge or Juror may be a Witness.
3. Where an Accomplice in the Crime charged against a Prisoner may be a Witness against him or for him.
4. Where a Person shall be disabled to be a Witness in Respect of his having been attainted or convicted of a Crime.
5. Where it is a good Exception against a Witness that his Interest is concerned.
6. What other Exceptions are good against a Witness.

Sect. 16. As to the first of these Particulars, *viz.* Whether a Husband or Wife may be Witnesses for or against one another: It seems [m] agreed, That the Husband and Wife being as one and the same Person in Affection and Interest, can no more give Evidence for one another in any Case whatsoever than for themselves; and that regularly the one shall not be admitted to give Evidence against the other, nor the Examination of the one be made Use of against the other, by Reason of the implacable Dissension which might be caused by it, and the great Danger of Perjury from taking the Oaths of Persons under so great a Biass, and the extreme Hard-

[m] Co. Litt. 6. b. 2 Rol. Abr. 686. pl. 4. H.P.C. 263. 1 H.H.P.C. 301. 2 H.H.P.C. 279. 1 Brownl. 47. Hutton 116. Raym. 1. 2 Keb. 403. pl. 12. State Trials, Vol. 4. fol. 608.

Hardſhip of the Caſe: And therefore it hath been [a] adjudged, That the Husband cannot be a Witneſs againſt the Wife, nor the Wife againſt the Husband, to prove the firſt Marriage on an Indictment on the Statute of 1 [b] *Jac.* 1. 11. for a ſecond Marriage. Yet [c] ſome Exceptions have been allowed to this general Rule in Caſes of evident Neceſſity, as in the Lord [d] *Audley*'s Caſe who held his Wife's Hands and Legs while his Servant, by his Command, raviſhed her; or where a Man is indicted for a [e] forcible Marriage againſt the [f] Purport of 3 *H.* 7. or where either a Husband or Wife have Cauſe to demand [g] Sureties of the Peace againſt the other, *&c.*

Sect. 17. As to the ſecond Particular, *viz.* Whether a Judge or Juror may be a Witneſs: It ſeems [h] agreed, that it is no Exception againſt a Perſon's giving Evidence either for or againſt a Priſoner, that he is one of the Judges or Jurors who are to try him. And in the Caſe of [i] *Hacker*, two of the Perſons in the Commiſſion for the Trial came off from the Bench, and were ſworn and gave Evidence, and did not go up to the Bench again during his Trial.

Sect. 18. As to the third Particular, *viz.* Where an Accomplice in the Crime charged againſt a Priſoner may be a Witneſs againſt him or for him: It has been long ſettled [k], That it is no Exception againſt a Witneſs that he hath confeſſed himſelf guilty of the ſame Crime, if he have not been [l] indicted for it; for if no Accomplices were to be admitted as Witneſſes, it would be generally impoſſible to find Evidence to convict the greateſt Offenders. Alſo it hath been often [m] ruled, That Accomplices who are indicted, are good Witneſſes for the King, until they be convicted. Alſo it hath been [n] adjudged, That ſuch of the Defendants in an Information againſt whom no Evidence is given, may be Witneſſes for the others. It hath been alſo [o] adjudged that where *A. B.* and *C.* are ſued in three ſeveral Actions on the Statute for a ſuppoſed Perjury in their Evidence concerning the ſame Thing, they may be good Witneſſes in ſuch Actions for one another.

Sect. 19. As to the fourth Particular, *viz.* Where a Perſon ſhall be diſabled to be a Witneſs in Reſpect of his having been attainted, or convicted of a Crime: It ſeems agreed, That a Conviction, and therefore *a fortiori* an Attainder, or Judgment of [p] Treaſon, [q] Felony, [r] Piracy, [s] *Præmunire* or [t] Perjury, or of Forgery [u] on 5 *Eliz.* and alſo a [x] Judgment in Attaint for giving a falſe Verdict, or in Conſpiracy at the Suit of [y] the King, and alſo [z] Judgment for any [aa] Crime whatſoever to ſtand in the Pillory, or to be whipt or branded, being in a Court which had a [bb] Juriſdiction, are good Cauſes of Exception againſt a Witneſs, while they continue in Force.

[a] Raym. 1. and the ſame Point was admitted in Fielding's Trial. State Trials, Vol. 4. f. 754. [b] Vide B. 1. ch. 43. [c] In Raym. 1. There is an Opinion that a Husband and Wife may be Witneſſes againſt one another in Treaſon, but the contrary is adjudged, 1 Brownl. 47. See 2 Keb. 403. 1 H. H. P. C. 301. [d] State Trials, Vol. 1. f. 265, 269. Hutt. 116. Ruſhw. Collections, Part 2. Vol. 1. f. 94, 99. But this Caſe is denied to be Law, Raym. 1. [e] Cro. Ca. 488. State Trials, Vol. 4. fol. 588. 3 Keb. 193. pl. 43. [f] See B. 1. ch. 42. [g] See B. 1. ch. 60. ſect. 4. Hutt. 116. [h] State Trials, Vol. 2. fol. 257, 632, 674. Kely. 12. 1 Sid. 133. pl. 6. [i] Kely. 12. [k] State Trials, Vol. 1. f. 96, 696, 697, 723. Vol. 2. fol. 334, 501. Vol. 3. fol. 161, 217, &c. 595, 668, 669. Vol. 4. fol. 12, 33. 1 H. H. P. C. 303, 304. See Hale's Opinion to the contrary arguendo. State Trials, Vol. 1. fol. 724. and Bracton 118. b. [l] State Trials, Vol. 1. fol. 96. Vol. 2. fol. 501. [m] State Trials, Vol. 1. fol. 966. Vol. 4. fol. 12. Kely. 17, 18. 3 Keb. 136. pl. 70. Vide Vol. 1. fol. 697. [n] 1 Sid. 237. pl. 4. Vide Trials per pais 148. Style 401. 12 Aſſ. 12. Savil 34. [o] 2 Rol. Abr. 685. pl. 3. [p] 5 Mod. 16. Kely. 33. [q] Raym. 369. Co. Litt. 6. b. 2 Bulſt. 154. [r] 2 Rol. Abr. 686. H. 2. 3. [s] Co. Litt. 6. b. [t] Raym. 32. infra Sect. 22, 23. Supra ch. 37. ſect. 52. Co. Litt. 6. b. H. P. C. 263. [u] Co. Litt. 6. b. Vide ſupra ch. 43. Sect. 25. 33 H. 6. 55. pl. 45. 2 H. H P. C. 277. But H. P. C. 263. 'tis ſaid in general that one attaint of Forgery cannot be a Witneſs. [x] Co. Litt. 6. b. 2 Roll. 684. pl. 4. [y] 33 H. 6. 55. pl. 45. 24 E. 3. 34. pl. 34 Vide ſupra ch. 43. ſect. 25. B. 1. ch. 72. ſect. 9. Co. Litt. 6. b. 2 H. H. P. C. 277. But H. P. C. 263. 'tis ſaid in general that one attaint of Conſpiracy cannot be a Witneſs. [z] That it is not material whether ſuch Judgment were actually executed. 2 Salk. 689. 3 Inſt. 219. 3 Lev 426. But Co. Litt. 6. b. Kely. 37. 38. H. P. C. 263. 2 H. H. P. C. 277. 5 Mod. 75, 76. ſeem to make the Execution of the Judgment material. [aa] 2 Salk 689. 3 Lev. 426. This Point is made a Quære, 5 Mod. 15, 16, 75, 76. Skin. 578, 579. And it is ſaid that by the Civil and Canon Law no ſuch Judgment diſables a Witneſs, unleſs the Nature of the Crime be infamous. 3 Lev. 426, 427. [bb] 1 Sid. 51. pl. 16. Raym. 32.

Sect. 20. But it is [a] agreed, That no such Conviction or Judgment can be made Use of to this Purpose, unless the Record be actually produced in Court. Also it is a general Rule, That a [b] Witness shall not be asked any Question the Answering to which might oblige him to accuse himself of a Crime; and that his Credit is to [c] be impeached only by general Accounts of his Character and Reputation, and not by Proofs of particular Crimes, whereof he never was convicted.

Sect. 21. It seems clear [d] at this Day, That Outlawry in a personal Action is not a good Exception against a Witness, as it is against a Juror. And that a Person convicted of Felony, who is admitted to his Clergy and [e] burnt in the Hand, is thereby re-enabled to be a Witness.

Sect. 22. It seems [f] agreed, That the King's Pardon of Treason or Felony after a Conviction or Attainder, restores the Party to his Credit: Also it was holden by the late Chief Justice [g] *Holt*, That the King's Pardon will remove a Man's Disability to be a Witness in all Cases whatsoever, wherein it is only the Consequence of the Conviction or Judgment against him, and not an express Part of the Judgment, as it is in in Conspiracy [h] at the Suit of the King, and in Perjury on the Statute. But this Matter ☞ [i] seems not to be fully settled. [106]

Sect. 23. It hath been [k] ruled, That a Conviction of Perjury doth not disable a Man from making an Affidavit in Relation to the Irregularity of a Judgment.

Sect. 24. As to the fifth Particular, *viz.* Where it is a good Exception against a Witness that his Interest is concerned: It seems an uncontested [l] Rule, in all Cases whatsoever, That it is a good Exception against a Witness, that he is either to be a Gainer or Loser by the Event of the Cause; whether such Advantage be direct and immediate, or consequential only. And this seems to be the Reason why he who is Bail for the Defendant, [m] cannot be an Evidence for him without Consent. Also upon the same Ground it is [n] agreed, That he who borrows Money upon an usurious Contract, cannot be a Witness upon an Information for the Usury (unless he [o] hath paid the Money) whether such Information be brought by himself or any other; for if in such Case a Man might be a Witness, he would in Effect swear for himself, by proving a Matter which may avoid his own Contract. And upon the like Reason it hath been [p] ruled, That he who by a Slight has been imposed upon to set his Hand to a Note for more Money than he intended, is no good Witness on an Information for the Cheat; because a Conviction may be a Means to avoid the Note, by being made Use of by the Party when sued upon it, as a Motive to influence the Jury, which cannot well be prevented, tho' in Law it be no [q] Evidence. And for the like Reason I take it to be generally [r] agreed, That he whose Property may be prejudiced by a Forgery, is no Evidence to prove it on an Indictment or Information. And if it be a Forgery within 5 *Eliz.* a farther Reason may be offered why such a Person cannot be an Evidence because he may have an Action on the Statute; and upon this Reason alone it hath been [s] adjudged, That he against whom a Verdict is given, cannot be a Witness to prove Perjury in the Evidence. And yet it appears from daily Experience, That [t] a Person beaten, and generally any other Person to whose [u] Damage a criminal Information concludes, is a

[a] State Trials, Vol. 1. f. 268. Vol. 2. f. 307, 436, 445. Vol. 3. f. 425. Vol. 4. f. 130.
[b] State Trials, Vol. 2. f. 268, 472. Vol. 3. f. 387, 1010. Vol. 4. f. 44. Cont. Rushw. Strafford, 605. & ibid. 558. one was not admitted to speak to clear himself.
[c] State Trials, Vol. 3. f. 256. 257, 680. Vol. 4. f. 129, 130. Vide Vol. 2. f. 151, 267, 297.
[d] Co. Lit. 6. b. 1 H. H. P. C. 303. But 33 H. 6. 32. pl. 2. taken Notice of 2 Rol. Abr. 675. pl. 4. seems contrary.
[e] Supra ch. 33. sect. 129. ch. 37. sect. 49.
[f] Supra ch. 37. sect. 48, 49, 50.
[g] 2 Salk. 514, 689. But see 2 Brow. 47.
[h] B. 1. ch. 72. sect. 9.
[i] Vide supra ch. 37. sect. 52.
[k] 2 Salk. 461. pl. 3.
[l] Co. Lit. 6. 1 Sid. 237. pl. 5. 1 Keb. 836. pl. 17. 1 H. H. P. C. 302, 303. 2 H. H. P. C. 279.
[m] State Trials, Vol. 3. f. 253.
[n] Co. Lit. 6. b. 2 Rol. Abr. 685. pl. 2. 1 H. H. P. C. 302.
[o] Raym. 191. Vide 2 Keb. 384. pl. 54.

[p] 1 Salk. 283. Yet between the King and Paris, 1 Sid. 431. 2 Keb. 572. pl. 84. 1 Vent. 49. the contrary was ruled in a stronger Case, by three Judges against the Opinion of Twisden. [q] Salk. 283. pl. 12. 1 Sid. 325. [r] Salk. 283. pl. 12. [s] 2 Rol. Ab. 685. pl. 4. and the same Point is taken for granted. 1 Sid. 237. pl. 5. 1 Keb. 836. pl. 17. Vide 1 Salk. 283. pl. 12. [t] 2 Rol. Abr. 685. pl. 5. 2 Keb. 572. pl. 84. [u] 1 Sid. 237. pl. 5. 2 Keb. 384. pl. 54. 572. pl. 84. 1 Keb. 836. pl. 17. 1 Salk. 286. pl. 20. 1 Sid. 211. pl. 8.

good Evidence to prove ſuch Battery or other Miſdemeanor, notwithſtanding the Objection that he may have an Action. And therefore, upon the Whole, the Rules of Evidence concerning this Matter ſeem not to be clearly ſettled.

Sect. 25. It ſeems [a] agreed, That it is no good Exception againſt a Witneſs, That he has a Maintenance from the King; for every one may maintain his own Witneſſes. Alſo it hath been [b] adjudged to be no good Exception againſt a Witneſs, That he has received a Reward for having made a Diſcovery of the Crime to be proved againſt the Priſoner. Alſo it hath been [c] Ruled to be no good Exception, That a Witneſs hath the Promiſe of a Pardon or other Reward on Condition of giving his Evidence, unleſs ſuch Reward be promiſed by Way of Contract for giving ſuch and ſuch particular Evidence, or full Evidence, or any Way in the leaſt to biaſs him to go beyond the Truth; which not being eaſily avoided in Promiſes or Threats of this Kind, it is certain that too great Caution cannot be uſed in making them.

Sect. 26. As to the ſixth Particular, *viz.* What other Exceptions are good againſt a Witneſs: It ſeems [d] agreed to be a good Exception, That a Witneſs is an Infidel; That is, as I [e] take it, That he believes neither the Old nor New Teſtament to be the Word of God; on one of which our Laws require the Oath ſhould be adminiſtred.

Sect. 27. Alſo it is [f] certain, That want of Diſcretion is a good Exception againſt a Witneſs; on which Account alone [g] it ſeems, That an Infant may be excepted againſt; for in ſome Caſes an Infant of nine Years of Age has been allowed to give Evidence.

Sect. 28. But it ſeems agreed, That it is no good [h] Exception againſt a Witneſs that he is an Alien, or Villein, or Bondman, &c.

Sect. 29. As to the fourth Point, *viz.* In what Manner the Witneſſes for the Defendant are to give their Evidence: It hath always been [i] agreed, That the Evidence for the King muſt in all Caſes be upon Oath, and alſo that the Evidence for the Defendant in an [k] Appeal, whether capital or not capital, or in an Indictment or Information for a [l] Miſdemeanor, muſt alſo be upon Oath. And it is ſaid by Sir *Edward* [m] *Coke*, *That we never read in any Statute, ancient Author, Book-Caſe or Record, that in Criminal Caſes the Party accuſed ſhould not have Witneſſes ſworn for him, and therefore that there is not ſo much as* ſcintilla juris *againſt it.* And it is ſaid by Sir [n] *Matthew Hale*, That there is no known Law, againſt it. However there having been a conſtant immemorial [o] Practice not to ſuffer Witneſſes to be ſworn againſt the King upon Indictments of capital Crimes [p] except in ſome Caſes ſpecially provided for by Statute; and the Judges being always tender of departing from the ſettled Practice of their Predeceſſors, and generally chooſing rather to preſume it originally founded on ſome Statute or other good Foundation, than to ſuffer the Reaſonableneſs of it to be nicely inquired into, which might be an Inlet to endleſs Uncertainties, it was thought neceſſary to enact by 1 *Annæ*, 9. *Par.* 3. *That after the twelfth of* February 1702, *every Perſon who ſhall be produced or appear as a Witneſs on the Behalf of the Priſoner, before he or ſhe be admitted to depoſe, or give any Manner of Evidence, ſhall firſt take an Oath to depoſe the Truth, the whole Truth, and nothing but the Truth, in ſuch Manner as the Witneſſes for the Queen are by Law obliged to do; and if convicted of any wilful Perjury in ſuch Evidence, ſhall ſuffer all the Puniſhments, Penalties, Forfeitures and Diſabilities, which by any of the Laws and Statutes of this Realm, are or may be inflicted upon Perſons convicted of wilful Perjury.*

[a] State Trials, Vol. 2. f. 334, 335, 691, 693.

[b] State Trials, Vol. 1. f. 723, 724. Vol. 2. f. 334, 335. Vol. 4. f. 121. Kely. 18.

[c] Kely. 18. State Trials, Vol. 2. f. 334, 335, 693. Vol. 3. f. 221, 222. But Sir Matthew Hale is of a different Opinion, 1 H. H. P. C. 304. 2 H. H. P. C. 280. Kely. 18. Vide State Trials, Vol. 4. f. 121.

[d] Co. Lit. 6. 2 H. H. P. C. 279. State Trials, Vol. 4. f. 131.

[e] Vide Trials per pais 165. 2 Keb. 314. pl. 23.

[f] Co. Lit. 6.

[g] H. P. C. 263. 2 H. H. P. C. 278. 1 Brownl. 47.

[h] State Trials, Vol. 1. f. 253.

[i] H. P. C. 264. 2 H. H. P. C. 283. 2 Bulst. 147.

[k] State Trials, Vol. 2. f. 737. 1 Sid. 325.

[l] 1 Sid. 211.

[m] 3 Inst. 79.

[n] H. P. C. 264. 2 H. H. P. C. 283.

[o] Cro. Ca. 292. 2 Bulst. 147. State Trials, Vol. 1. f. 55, 148. Vol. 2. f. 296, 737. H. P. C. 264.

[p] Vide 31 El. ch. 4. 4 Jac. ch. 1.

Sect. 30. As to the fifth Point, *viz.* Whether a Defendant in criminal Cases have Right to Process to bring in his Witnesses: I take it that in Prosecutions for [a] Misdemeanors the Defendant may take out *Subpœnas* of Course, but that in Capital Cases he hath no [b] Right by the Common Law to any Process against his Witnesses without a [c] special Order of the Court. But it is enacted by 7 *W.* 3. 3. *Par.* 7. *That all Persons accused and indicted for any High Treason, whereby any Corruption of Blood may ensue, shall have the like Process of the Court where they shall be tried, to compel their Witnesses to appear for them at any such Trial or Trials, as is usually granted to compel Witnesses to appear against them.* And it seems that since the Statute of 1 *Annæ*, 9. set forth more at large in the precedent Section, which ordains, That the Witnesses for the Prisoner shall be sworn, Process may be taken out against them of Course in any Case whatsoever.

Sect. 31. As to the sixth Point, *viz.* What Evidence maintains an Indictment, &c. Having already shewn, *Ch.* 25. *Sect.* 115. and *Book* 1. *Ch.* 30. *Sect.* 9. That according to the later Opinions, where one is indicted upon a Statute, and the Evidence doth not bring the Case within the Statute, but yet proves the Offence in the Indictment as it is an Offence at the Common Law, the Defendant may be found guilty at the Common Law, and the Words *contra formam Statuti* rejected as Surplus: Having also shewn, *Ch.* 35. *Sect.* 11. That it is strongly holden that a Man cannot be found guilty of an Indictment against him as Principal, upon Evidence which only proves him to have been Accessary before, but shall be discharged of the Indictment; I shall in this Place take Notice only of the following Particulars.

Sect. 32. *First*, That it is a settled Rule [d] in all Cases, whether capital or not capital, That the Day laid in the Indictment or [e] Appeal is not material upon Evidence, but that the Defendant may be convicted upon Proof of a Fact at any other Time, whether before or after the Day laid; so [f] that it were before the Time when the Indictment or Appeal were preferred. And agreeably hereto Sir [g] *Henry Vane* was found guilty of an Indictment of High Treason laid on the 30th of *May*, 11 *Car.* 2. upon Evidence of a Fact done the 30th of *January*, 1 *Car.* 2.

Sect. 33. *Secondly*, That where the Time proved varies from that laid in the Indictment or Appeal, the Jury may either find the Defendant guilty generally, in which Case the Forfeiture shall relate to the Time laid, till the Verdict be falsifyed by the Party interested, (as it may be in this [h] Respect, tho' not as to the Point of the Offence,) or they may [i] specially find him Guilty on the Day on which the Fact is proved, whether before or after the Day laid in the Indictment or Appeal, in which Case the Forfeiture shall relate to the Day so specially found. But where a Verdict expresly finds a Defendant guilty before the Time laid in the Indictment or Appeal, whether it may be falsifyed, as to the Time, by the Party interested, as it may be where it finds him guilty generally of the Offence in the Indictment or Appeal, upon Evidence of a Fact after the Time laid, may deserve to be considered.

Sect. 34. *Thirdly*, That where a certain [k] Place is made Part of the Description of the Fact which is charged against the Defendant, the least Variance as to such Place between the Evidence and Indictment is fatal; as where a Trespass in Taking away Goods, or any other Offence is alledged in such a Parish in the House of *J. S.* or in such a Parish in a Play-House in *Lincoln*'s-*Inn-Fields*, and upon Evidence it appear to have been done at the House of a different Person, or that there is no Play-House in *Lincoln*'s-*Inn-Fields*. But it is a settled [l] Rule, That a Place

laid

[a] State Trials, Vol. 1. f. 969. Vol. 3. f. 238, 252, 420.

[b] Vide State Trials, Vol. 1. f. 969. Vol. 3. f. 1002, 1003.

[c] But in Turner's Case, State Trials, Vol. 1. f. 995. 'Tis said that the Court can't grant the Prisoner any Precept to bring in his Witnesses, &c.

[d] H. P. C. 264. 1 H. H. P. C. 361. 2 H. H. P. C. 291. 3 Inst. 230. 1 Salk. 288. Kely. 16. 2 Inst. 318, 319. State Trials, Vol. 4. f. 9.

[e] H. P. C. 187.

[f] 1 Salk. 288. State Trials, Vol. 4. f. 9. 3 Kely. 16.

[g] H. P. C. 264. 2 Inst. 318. 3 Inst. 230.

[h] H. P. C. 264, 270. 3 Inst. 230. and infra in Chapter 51.

[i] Kely. 16. H. P. C. 264. 1 H. H. P. C. 361. 2 Inst. 318. 3 Inst. 230.

[k] Salk. 385, 661.

[l] H. P. C. 264, 265. Salk. 288. State Trials, Vol. 4. f. 9. Kely. 15, 33.

laid only for a Venue in an Indictment or Appeal is no Way material upon Evidence; but that a Proof of the ſame Crime at any other Place in the [a] ſame County, maintains the Indictment or Appeal as well as if it had been proved in the very ſame Place. Alſo it hath been [b] adjudged, That after a Crime hath been proved in the County in which it is laid, Evidence may be given of other Inſtances of the ſame Crime in another County, in Order to ſatisfy the Jury. Alſo it was [c] adjudged, in Sir *Henry Vane*'s Caſe, That where one is indicted for High Treaſon in compaſſing the King's Death in the County of *M.* and the Levying of War in the ſame County is laid as an Overt-Act of ſuch Treaſon, and [d] proved in the ſame County by one Witneſs, the Levying of War in another County may alſo be proved by another Witneſs. But it ſeems to have been [e] agreed at the ſame Time, That where the Levying of War is the Treaſon for which the Party is indicted, it muſt be fully proved in the County in which it is laid. Alſo it ſeems, That at this Day the Levying of War can in no Caſe be given in Evidence as an Overt-Act in any County in which it is not laid, unleſs it tend to prove ſome Overt-Act that is expreſly laid; for it is enacted by 7 *Wil.* 3. 3. *Par.* 8. *That no* [f] *Evidence ſhall be admitted or given of any Overt-Act that is not expreſly laid in the Indictment againſt any Perſon or Perſons whatſoever.* In the Conſtruction whereof it hath been [g] adjudged, That where one is indicted for High Treaſon in adhering to the King's Enemies, and certain Acts of Hoſtility done by him in a certain Ship called the *Clencarty*, are laid as the Overt-Acts of ſuch Adherence, no Evidence can be given of any other diſtinct Act of Adherence, having no Relation to, nor any Way tending to prove, what was done in the *Clencarty*, tho' it conduce to prove the ſame Species of Treaſon; and therefore that on ſuch an Indictment no Evidence can be given of the Priſoner's having run away to the Enemy in a Cuſtom-Houſe-Boat, *&c.* But it hath been [h] adjudged, That where one is indicted for High Treaſon in compaſſing the King's Death, and a Conſult and Agreement to aſſaſſinate the King is laid as one of the Overt-Acts of ſuch Treaſon, the Defendant's giving about among the Conſpirators a Liſt of the Perſons Names who where intended to be employed in the Aſſaſſination, may be given in Evidence againſt him upon ſuch Indictment, becauſe it naturally tends to prove his Agreement to the intended Aſſaſſination, which Agreement is one of the Overt-Acts laid in the Indictment. Alſo it hath been [i] adjudged, That where the Writing of ſeveral treaſonable Letters is laid as an Overt-Act of High Treaſon in Compaſſing the King's Death, and the Purport of ſuch Letters is only ſet forth in the Indictment without a particular Recital or Deſcription of any of them, the particular Letters making good ſuch Charge may be read at the Trial.

Sect. 35. *Fourthly*, That where ſeveral Overt-Acts, are laid in an Indictment of High Treaſon, the Proof of any [k] of them maintains the Indictment as much as if every one of them were proved.

Sect. 36. *Fifthly*, That where one is indicted for writing a [l] Libel *ſecundum tenorem ſequentem*, or for forging a Deed ſo and ſo deſcribed, any the leaſt Variance between the Libel recited, or Deed deſcribed, and thoſe given in Evidence, is fatal; but that where the Subſtance only of a Libel is ſet forth in *Latin*, it is ſufficient if the Libel be proved to have the ſame Senſe as is ſet forth. Yet it ſeems [m] agreed, That it is no Evidence in any criminal Caſe, that the Defendant ſaid ſo and ſo, or Words to the like Effect; becauſe the Court muſt know the very Words to judge of their Force and Effect.

[a] 2 H.H.P.C. 291. See the Books above-cited and ſupra ch. 25. ſect. 35 to 54. and Cro. El. 911.
[b] Kely. 33.
[c] Kely. 14, 15. State Trials, Vol. 1. f. 932. Vol. 2. f. 317, 776, 785. Vide Vol. 1. f. 843. Vol. 4. f. 78.
[d] For it is neceſſary that ſome Overt-Act be proved in the ſame County; for otherwiſe the compaſſing could no Way be ſaid to be proved in the County wherein it is laid. See the Books above cited.
[e] Kely. 15.
[f] Vide State Trials, Vol. 1. f. 843.
[g] State Trials, Vol. 4. f. 331, 332, 333.
[h] State Trials, Vol. 4. f. 124, 125, 132, 133, 134.
[i] Francia's Trial, Vide Vol. 1. f. 617, 950. Vol. 2. f. 98, 99, 112. &c. 322, 323. Vol. 3. f. 857, 1009. Yet in ſome Indictments the very Words charged to have been treaſonable have been ſet forth. State Trials, Vol. 2. f. 746. Vol. 3. f. 204, 219.
[k] State Trials, Vol. 1. f. 843, 851. Vol. 2. f. 430. Vol. 4. f. 159.
[l] Salk. 660, 661. Hob. 272.
[m] Hob. 294.

Sect. 37. *Sixthly*, That a Variance between an Indictment or Appeal of Death, and the Evidence, as to the Inſtrumental Cauſe mentioned in ſuch Indictment or Appeal, is no [a] way material, ſo that the Party be proved to have died by the ſame Kind of Death as is alledged in the Indictment or Appeal. And therefore it is [b] agreed, That if one be indicted or appealed for killing another with a Sword, and upon Evidence it appear that he killed him with a Staff, Hatchet, Bill or Hook, or any other Weapon with which a Wound may be given, he ought to be found guilty; for the Subſtance of the Matter is, whether he gave the Party a Wound of which he died, and it is not material with what Weapon he gave it, tho' for Form's ſake it be [c] neceſſary to ſet forth a particular Weapon. And on the ſame Ground it hath been alſo [d] adjudged That an Indictment, or Appeal for poiſoning a Man with one Kind of Poiſon, may be maintained by Evidence of a different Kind of Poiſon; for the Subſtance of the Matter is whether the Defendant did poiſon the Deceaſed or not. [e] Yet it ſeems clear, That Evidence of poiſoning, burning, or famiſhing, or any other Kind of killing wherein no Weapon is uſed, will not maintain an Indictment or Appeal of Death by killing with a Weapon; and that Evidence of killing with a Weapon will not maintain an Indictment or Appeal of Poiſoning, *&c.* becauſe they are different Kinds of Deaths; and in like Manner that an Indictment of Treaſon could [f] never be maintained by Evidence of Treaſon of a different Species.

Sect. 38. *Seventhly*, That it ſeems a [g] general Rule, That where-ever a Variance between an Indictment or Appeal, and the Evidence brought to ſupport them, is material or immaterial in Reſpect of the Principal; in the ſame Caſes alſo it will be material or immaterial in Reſpect of the Acceſſary.

Sect. 39. *Eighthly*, That it is [h] ſettled at this [i] Day, That if an Indictment or Appeal againſt *A. B.* and *C.* for the Death of *D.* charge *A.* as having given the mortal Blow, and *B.* and *C.* as having been preſent, procuring and abetting, and the Evidence prove that *B.* and *C.* gave the Blow, and that *A.* was only preſent procuring and abetting; yet it maintains the Indictment, becauſe in ſuch a Caſe in the [k] Judgment of Law, the Act of any of them is the Act of all.

Sect. 40. *Ninthly*, That it hath been [l] reſolved, That if one be indicted as Acceſſary to two, and upon Evidence appear to have been Acceſſary to one of them only, yet he ſhall be found guilty. But it is [m] holden by Sir *Edward Coke*, That if an Appeal be brought againſt two as Principals and againſt another as Acceſſary to them, and one of thoſe charged as Principals be found not guilty, the Acceſſary is diſcharged, for which he gives this Reaſon, That becauſe the Plaintiff made him Acceſſary to two, he cannot be found Acceſſary to one. But no Authority is cited for the Maintenance of this Opinion; neither doth it ſeem eaſy to reconcile it with the Reſolution above-mentioned, unleſs the Rules of Evidence on an Appeal differ from thoſe on an Indictment, which I do not [n] find that they do as to other Variances.

[a] 9 Co. 67. 2 Inſt. 319. 3 Inſt. 135. H. P. C. 265.
[b] See the Books above-cited, and ſupra ch. 23. ſect. 84.
[c] Vide ſupra ch. 23. ſ. 84.
[d] 3 Inſt. 135. H. P. C. 265. 3 Inſt. 319.
[e] H. P. C. 265. 2 H. H. P. C. 291. 2 Inſt. 319.
[f] State Trials, Vol. 4. f. 9.
[g] 2 H. H. P. C. 291. [g] H. P. C. 265. 2 H. H. P. C. 292. 3 Inſt. 165.
[h] But there were anciently ſome Opinions to the contrary Supra ch. 29. ſect. 7. Lett. x. S. P. C. 41. Lett. A. B.
[i] Plow. Com. 98, 100. a. 1 Salk. 334, 335. 3 Mod. 121. 9 Co. 67. b. 4 H. 7. 18. pl. 10. Abridged. Fitz. Coro. 60. Bro. Appeal 85. Coro. 140 or 141. S. P. C. 41. Letters A. B. 1 H. H. P. C. 437, 438. 2 H. H. P. C. 292. Supra ch. 23. ſect. 76. ch. 25. ſect. 64.
[k] See the Books above cited, and B. 1. ch. 32. ſect. 6. ch. 31. ſect. 31. and 50. ch. 34. ſect. 7. ch. 38. ſect. 8, 9. ch. 41. ſect. 6.
[l] 9 Co. 119. a. H. P. C. 222, 265. 2 H. H. P. C. 292. Vide Keilw. 107. and ſupra ch. 29. ſect. 46, 47.
[m] 2 Inſt. 183.
[n] Vide ſupra ſect. 32, 34, 37, 38, 39.

[a] 9 Co. 67. b. Cro. Jac. 280. H. P. C. 266.
[b] See B. 1. ch. 31. ſect. 18, 19. and ſ. 40 to 43.
[c] 9 Co. 67.
[d] 9 Co. 62, 63, 67.

Sect. 41. *Tenthly*, That it hath been [a] agreed, That if a Perſon be generally indicted for the Murder of another *ex malitia præcogitata*, and no expreſs Malice appear upon the Evidence but only [b] Malice implied by Law, yet he ſhall be found guilty. Alſo it hath been [c] adjudged, That where an Indictment ſets forth all the ſpecial Matter in Reſpect whereof the Law implies Malice, a Variance between the Indictment and Evidence as to the Circumſtances doth no Hurt, ſo that the Subſtance of the Matter be found. As [d] where an Indictment for the Murder of a Serjeant at Mace in *London* upon an Arreſt, ſuppoſes that the Sheriff made a Precept to ſuch Serjeant for the Arreſt, and upon the Evidence it appears that there was not any ſuch Precept, but that the Serjeant made the Arreſt *ex Officio* at the Plaintiff's Requeſt upon the Entry of the Plaint, according to the Cuſtom of the City; for the Subſtance of the Matter is whether the Defendant killed an Officer in the lawful Execution of legal Proceſs.

[e] Co. Litt. 6. b. S.P.C. 179. Letter A. Vide ſupra ch. 45. ſect. 10. and State Trials, Vol. 1. fol. 181, 636. Vol. 2. fol. 408, Vol. 3. f. 228, 229, 688, 689, 894 to 901, 928, 929, 930.
[f] Co. Litt. 6. b.

Sect. 42. *Eleventhly*, That violent [e] Preſumption from plain Circumſtances is in ſome Caſes taken for full Proof; as where a Man is ſtabbed in a Houſe, and another runs out with a bloody Knife in his Hand, and no one elſe is in the Houſe at the Time; alſo it is [f] ſaid, That a probable Preſumption is of ſome Weight, but that a light one is not to be regarded at all.

[g] Kely. 32. 2 H. H. P. C. 288, 289.
[h] Kely. 32, 33.
[i] Kely. 32.
[k] Kely. 33.

Sect. 43. *Twelfthly*, That it is enacted by 21 *Jac.* 27. *That if any Woman be delivered of any Iſſue of her Body, Male or Female, which being born alive ſhould by the Laws of this Realm be a Baſtard, and that ſhe endeavour privately, either by drowning, or ſecret burying thereof, or any other way, either by herſelf or the procuring of others, ſo to conceal the Death thereof, as it may not come to light, whether it were born alive or not, but be concealed; in every ſuch Caſe, the ſaid Mother ſo offending ſhall ſuffer Death as in Caſe of Murder, except ſuch Mother can make Proof by one Witneſs at the leaſt, that the Child whoſe Death was by her ſo intended to be concealed was born dead.* In the Conſtruction whereof it hath been [g] adjudged, That in order to convict a Woman by Force of this Statute, there is no need that the Indictment be drawn ſpecially, or conclude *contra formam Statuti*; but that it is the better Way to ſet forth only that the Defendant *infantem maſculum vivum parturiit, qui quidem infans maſculus adtunc & ibidem vivus exiſtens natus per legem hujus regni Angliæ Spurius fuit, Anglice* a Baſtard, and then to go on in the ordinary Way to ſhew that ſhe murdered him, *&c. contra pacem, &c.* for the Statute doth not make a new Offence, but only make ſuch Concealment an undeniable Evidence of Murder. Alſo it hath been [h] agreed, That where a Woman appears to have endeavoured to conceal the Death of ſuch Child within the Statute, there is no Need of any Proof that the Child was born alive, or that there were any Signs of Hurt upon the Body, but it ſhall be undeniably taken that the Child was born alive, and murdered by the Mother. But it hath been [i] adjudged, That where a Woman lay in a Chamber by herſelf, and went to Bed without Pain, and waked in the Night, and knocked for Help but could get none, and was delivered of a Child and put it in a Trunk, and did not diſcover it till the following Night, yet ſhe was not within the Statute, becauſe ſhe knocked for Help. Alſo it hath been [k] agreed, that if a Woman confeſs herſelf with Child before-hand, and afterwards be ſurpriſed and delivered, no Body being with her, ſhe is not within the Statute, becauſe there was no Intent of Concealment. And therefore in ſuch Caſes it muſt appear by Signs of Hurt upon the Body, or ſome other way, that the Child was born alive.

Sect. 44. As to the seventh Point, *viz.* What may be given in Evidence on the Part of the Defendant: It seems [a] agreed, that *son assault Demesne* may be given in Evidence on the General Issue in an Indictment, but not in an Acti on of Battery. Also it seems to have been always [b] agreed, that the Defendant in an Information on a Penal Statute may give in Evidence any Exception in his Favour in the Body of the Act. And it hath also been [c] holden that he may give in Evidence any such Exception in a *Proviso* of the Act, (because any such Exception shews that he did not act against the Form of the Statute;) but that he cannot [d] give in Evidence any Clause of Exemption in a latter Statute, but ought to plead it.

[a] B. 1. ch. 62. sect. 3. [b] Savil 32. pl. 75. 1 Jon. 157. 2 Rol. Abr. 683. pl. 11. [c] 2 Roll. Ab. 683. pl. 10, 12. But this is left a Quære Savil 32. pl. 75. Bro. General Issue, 3. Vide supra ch. 25. sect. 113. [d] 2 Koll. Abr. 683. pl. 13.

CHAP. XLVII.

Of Verdict.

FOR the general Learning of Verdicts I shall refer to other Books, and in this Place take Notice only of the following Particulars;

Sect. 1. 1st, That it seems to have been [a] anciently an uncontroverted Rule, and hath been allowed, even by those [b] of the contrary Opinion, to have been the general Tradition of the Law, that a Jury sworn and charged in a capital [c] Case, cannot be discharged (without the [d] Prisoner's Consent) till they have given a Verdict. And notwithstanding some [e] Authorities to the contrary in the Reign of King *Charles* II. this hath been holden for clear Law both in the Reign of King [f] *James* II. and [g] since the Revolution.

Sect. 2. 2dly, That it seems to have been [h] always agreed, that in all [i] capital Cases the Jury must give their Verdict openly in Court, and cannot give a privy Verdict.

Sect. 3. 3dly, That it is settled, [k] that the Jury may give a special Verdict in any criminal Case, whether Capital or not Capital, as well as in a Civil.

Sect. 4. 4thly, That it hath been [l] adjudged, that where the Jury find a Man not guilty of an Indictment or Appeal of Murder, they are not bound to make any Inquiry, whether he be guilty of Manslaughter, &c. But that if they will they may, according to the Nature of the Evidence, find him guilty of [m] Manslaughter or [n] Homicide *se defendendo*, or *per infortunium*; for the Killing is the Substance, and the Malice but a Circum-

[a] Co. Lit. 227. b. 3 Inst. 110. 1 And. 103, 104. H.P.C. 267. 2 H. H. P.C. 294, 295. [b] Raym. 84. [c] And the same is holden by Coke as to Larceny, and any Case of Member. 3 Inst. 110. Co.Litt. 227. b. but as to Cases of an Inferior Nature, the contrary hath been adjudged, Raym.84. [d] 1 And. 103, 104. [e] Kely. 47, 52. State Trials, Vol. 1. fol. 978. Vol. 2. fol. 155, 277, 389. Raym. 84. [f] State Trials, Vol. 3. f. 678. Vide supra ch. 44. sect. 22. [g] State Trials, Vol. 4. fol. 110, 178, 179. [h] Co. Litt. 227. b. 3 Inst. 110. Raym. 193. 2 H. H. P. C. 300. [i] The same is holden by Sir Edward Coke, as to Larceny, and any Case of Member, 3 Inst. 110. Co. Litt. 227. b. And it is said in Raym. 193. That no privy Verdict can be given in any Case where the Jury are to look upon the Prisoner when they give it. [k] S. P. C. 165. Letter C. H. P. C. 267. 2 H. H. P. C. 301, 302. 9 Co. 12. b. 63. 1 Bulst. 87. Vide infra sect. 6. But it is said, Kely. 29, 30. That it is dishonourable for the Court to suffer a special Verdict in a plain Case. [l] Cro. Eliz. 276. pl. 5. 296. pl. 2. 464. pl. 13. [m] Dyer 261. pl. 26. 4 Co. 43. b. 9 Co. 81. Dalis. 14. H. P. C. 267. Latch 126. Pl. Com. 101. Cro. Eliz. 276. pl. 5. 296. pl. 2. 464. pl. 13. Moor 407. pl. 546. Bro. Coro. 121 or 122. But 2 Roll. Re. 461. this was questioned as to an Appeal of Death. [n] Bro. Coro. 1 H. P. C. 267. 2 H. H. P. C. 302. Dalis. 14. S. P. C. 165. Letter A. See the Books cited to the following Section.

stance

ſtance, a [a] Variance as to which hurts not the Verdict. Yet the Books ſeem to make this Difference, that where the Jury find the Defendant guilty of Manſlaughter on an Indictment of Murder, they may give their Verdict [b] generally, without ſetting out any of the Circumſtances of the Fact: But that they ſhall not [c] be received to find him guilty generally of Homicide *ſe defendendo*, or *per infortunium*, but muſt ſet out the whole Circumſtances of the Fact, and in the [d] Concluſion ſhew of what Crime they find the Defendant guilty, wherein if they be miſtaken, it is [e] ſaid, that the Court may notwithſtanding give ſuch Judgment as ſhall appear to be proper from the Circumſtances of the Fact ſpecially ſet forth.

Sect. 5. 5thly, That it hath been [f] adjudged, That if the Jury on an Indictment or Appeal of Murder find the Defendant guilty of Manſlaughter, without ſaying any thing expreſly as to the Murder, it is inſufficient and void, as being only a Verdict for Part. And *Quære* if the Law be not the ſame where the Jury upon ſuch an Indictment find that the Defendant killed the Deceaſed *ſe defendendo* or *per infortunium*, and do not expreſly find that he did not murder him, according to the Generality of the ancient [g] Authorities.

Sect. 6. 6thly, That it is agreed, that on an Indictment for ſtealing Goods of a certain Value above 12 *d.* the [h] Jury may find the Defendant guilty, but that the Goods are but of the Value of 10*d.* &c. But it ſeems that if a Man be indicted for Felony generally, and upon the Evidence it [i] plainly appear that the Fact amounts to no more than a bare Treſpaſs, he cannot be found guilty of the Treſpaſs, but ought to be indicted anew. Yet if the ſpecial Circumſtances of the Caſe be ſet forth in an Indictment for an Offence laid as Felony, and the Defendant be found guilty generally, and afterwards the Court be of Opinion that the Fact doth not amount to Felony, but only to an enormous Treſpaſs, it ſeems [k] agreed, That Judgment may be given as for a Treſpaſs only. Alſo if the Jury find a ſpecial Verdict on a general Indictment for Felony; and the Crime be adjudged upon ſuch Verdict to be but a Treſpaſs, [l] Judgment may be given upon it as for a Treſpaſs only. Alſo if on an Indictment of Treſpaſs the Fact appear to have been felonious, it hath been [m] adjudged, That the Defendant may be found guilty of the Indictment as it is laid, becauſe the King may proceed againſt the Offender as he thinks fit, either as a Treſpaſſer or Felon. But the contrary is [n] ſaid to have been holden by the late Chief Juſtice *Holt*; and it hath been [o] adjudged, that if it appear in an Action of Treſpaſs that the Taking was felonious, no Verdict ought to be taken unleſs the Defendant have been before tried for the Felony, becauſe the Suffering ſuch Actions might be a Means to prevent Proſecutions for Felonies.

[a] 1 Bulſt. 87. 'Tis holden by two Judges againſt one That where the Appeal mentioned three Wounds, and the Verdict found but one, yet the Variance was immaterial. Vide ch. 46. ſect. 37.
[b] See the Books cited ſect. 4. under Lett. [m].
[c] H. P. C. 267. 2 H. H. P. C. 302. S. P. C. 15. Lett. B. 165. Lett. A. 3 Inſt. 56. 26 H. 8. 5. a. Aleyn 12.
[d] Fitz. Coro. 264, 286, 287, 305. Vide Benl. 47. 1 And. 41.
[e] 43 Aſſ. pl. 31. Fitz. Coro. 226. Crompt. Juſt. 114. pl. 1. S. P. C. 165. Letter A. Vide Benl. 47. 1 And. 41.
[f] 1 And. 103, 104. and Note, That in all the Books cited under the fourth Section to Letter p, where the Defendant is found guilty of Manſlaughter on an Indictment of Murder, he is expreſly acquitted of the Murder, but other Books, which ſpeak of this Matter, ſay in general that the Defendant may be found guilty of Manſlaughter on an Indictment of Murder, without ſaying any thing as to the Neceſſity of giving an expreſs Verdict upon the Murder. 9 Co. 67. b. Crompt. Juſt. 114. pl. 5. H. P. C. 267. 2 H. H. P. C 302. See 4 Co. 40. a. 46. b.
[g] Fitz. Coro. 284, 286, 287. Sed Vide 44 E. 3. 44. pl. 55. Fitz. Coro. 94. Benl. 47. 1 And. 41.
[h] Fitz. Coro. 115, 177, 451. 18 Aſſ. pl. 14. H. P. C. 267. 2 H. H. P. C. 302. S. P. C 165. Letter B. Crompt. Juſt. 114. pl. 2. B. 1. ch. 35. ſect. 4.
[i] Kely. 29, 30. Cro. Ca. 332. 'Tis made a Quære, 2 H. 7. pl. 22. and 10. pl. 6. whether where an Indictment of Larceny is inſufficient as to the Felony, the Party may be found guilty of the ſame taking as for a Treſpaſs.
[k] Kely. 29, 30. Cro. Ca. 376, 377. 1 Jon. 351.
[l] Cro. Ja. 497, 498.
[m] 18 Ed. 4. 10. pl. 28. 2 Lev. 208. Vide ſupra ch. 35. ſect. 5. and ch. 36. ſect. 6. That an Acquittal or Judgment againſt a Man in an Action or Indictment of Treſpaſs is no Bar on an Indictment or Appeal of Larceny. Kely. 30.
[n] 6 Mod. 77.
[o] 2 Roll. Abr. 556. pl. 19. 557. pl. 20, 21, 22, 33, 24. Noy 18. Vide 1 Jon. 147. Noy 82. Latch 145. 1 Mod. 283. Cont. Bract. cited S. P. C. 28. a. 83. b.

Sect. 7. 7thly, That it hath been holden, That a Verdict acquitting a Defendant of the Death of a Man found againſt him by the Coroner's Inqueſt, ought not to be received unleſs it ſhew what other Perſon did the ☞Fact; but for this I ſhall refer to *Ch.* 9. *Sect.* 33. [107]

2 H. H. P.C. 301, 305.

Sect. 8. 8thly, That on an Indictment for a Riot againſt three or more, if a Verdict acquit all but two, and find them guilty; or on an Indictment for a Conſpiracy, if the Verdict acquit all but one, and find him guilty, it is repugnant and [a] void as to the two found guilty in the firſt Caſe, and as to the one found guilty in the ſecond, unleſs the Indictment charge them with having made ſuch Riot or Conſpiracy, *ſimul cum aliis juratoribus ignotis*; for otherwiſe it appears that the Defendants are found guilty of an Offence whereof it is impoſſible that they ſhould be guilty; for there can be no Riot where there are no more Perſons than two, nor can there be a Conſpiracy where there is no Partner. Yet it ſeems [b] agreed, That if twenty Perſons are indicted for a Riot or Conſpiracy, and any three found guilty of the Riot, or any two of the Conſpiracy, the Verdict is good: And that [c] where ſeveral are indicted for Treaſon or Felony, or other Crime, which may be as well done by one only, as by more, a Verdict [d] may find one of the Defendants only guilty, and acquit all the reſt. And in like Manner it ſeems [e] agreed, That a Verdict on an Information on a penal Statute againſt ſeveral Perſons jointly charged with the Offence againſt the Statute, may acquit ſome and find others guilty; becauſe tho' the Words of the Information be joint, yet in Judgment of Law, each Defendant is ſeverally charged for his own Offence. And in like Manner [f] it ſeems, That the Defendant in ſuch Information may be found guilty for a leſs Time or Degree than is laid, unleſs the Offence conſiſt in the Doing ſome entire Thing, which muſt be preciſely proved in the ſame Manner as it is laid.

[a] Poph. 202. 1 Salk. 385. State Trials, Vol. 2. f. 60, 61. Vol. 4. f. 160, 161. In the Year-Book of 11 H. 4. 2. pl. 3. Abridged Fitz. Verdict, 18. It is agreed, That ſuch a Verdict is repugnant, and therefore the Court would not receive it, but ſent the Jury back again, whereupon they found both the Defendants guilty.

[b] State Trials, Vol. 4. f. 160, 161.

[c] State Trials, Vol. 4. f. 160, 161.

[d] Yet it hath been holden, That on an Indictment of Burglary and other Felony againſt A. and B. the Jury cannot, upon the very ſame Evidence againſt both, find A. guilty of the Burglary, and B. of the Felony only, 1 Sid. 171. pl. 4.

[e] Vide ſupra ch. 26. ſect. 75.

[f] Vide ſupra ch. 26. ſect. 75 and State Trials, Vol 4. f. 160, 161.

Sect. 9. 9thly, That the Court in judging upon a ſpecial Verdict is confined to the Facts expreſly found, and cannot ſupply the Want thereof, as to any material Part by any Argument or Implication from what is ☞expreſly found; [108] and therefore where an Indictment ſet forth that the Defendant diſcharged a Gun againſt *J. S.* and thereby gave him a mortal Wound, *&c.* and the Special Verdict found that he diſcharged a Gun and thereby killed *J. S.* but did not expreſly ſay, that he diſcharged it againſt *J. S.* it was [g] adjudged, That the Court could not take it from the other Circumſtances of the Fact, which were expreſly found, tho' they were as full to the Purpoſe as poſſibly they could well be, that the Defendant diſcharged the Gun againſt *J. S.*

Sect. 10. 10thly, That it hath been [h] adjudged, That where an Indictment found at the Aſſiſes is removed into the King's Bench by *Certiorari*, and there the Defendant pleads Not guilty, *& de hoc ponit ſe ſuper patriam*, *&* T. F. *Miles Coronator & attornatus Dom' Regis, &c. ſimiliter*, and thereupon the Defendant is found guilty of the Offence *in Indictamento prædict' interius ei impoſit' prout prædict'* T. F. *interius verſus eum queritur*, the Verdict is good; for theſe Words *prout prædict'* T. F. *interius verſus eum queritur* ſhall be rejected as Surplus, [i] repugnant and void, and the Verdict is compleat without them.

[g] Kely. 111. [h] 2 Saund. 308. [i] See B. 1. ch. 30. ſect. 9. What is a good Verdict on an Indictment of Forgery, B. 1. ch. 70. ſect. 27.

[a] 1 And. 104. Crompt. Just. 114. pl. 6. Aleyn 12. Vide State Trials Vol. 2. f. 60. 61.
[b] Crompt. Just. 114. pl. 6. Fitz. Coro. 108. 2 H. H. P. C. 299, 300, 310.
[c] Cro. Ca. 292. against the Opinion of Cro. and Berkely, and Cro. Jac. 507. Vide State Trials, Vol. 2. fol. 60, 61. where the Court upon the Acquittal of the Defendants of the Indictment against them for a Riot, committed them for their Contempt to the Court, during the Trial.

Sect. 11. 11thly, That it hath been [a] adjudged, That if the Jury acquit a Prisoner of an Indictment of Felony against manifest Evidence, the Court may, before the Verdict is recorded, but [b] not after, order them to go out again and reconsider the Matter; but this is by many thought hard, and seems not of late Years to have been so frequently practised as formerly. Also there are [c] Instances where Defendants acquitted against plain Evidence, of Felonies and other enormous Crimes, have been bound to their Good Behaviour. However it is settled, That the Court cannot set aside a Verdict which [d] acquits a Defendant of a Prosecution properly criminal, as it seems that they may a Verdict that [e] convicts him for having been given contrary to Evidence, and the Directions of the Judge, or any Verdict whatever for a [f] Mistrial.

[d] Agreed in the Case of the King and Bennet, Hill. 4 Georg. 1. wherein it was holden by six of the Judges against six, That a new Trial was not grantable upon an Acquittal on an Information in the Nature of a Quo Warranto, because it sounds in the Criminalty. 1 Keb. 124. pl. 33. 2 Keb. 403. pl. 14. 404. pl. 18. Whether it be grantable for a corrupt Practice in obtaining a Verdict. 1 Lev. 9, 10, 124. 1 Sid. 153, 154. 1 Keb. 546. pl. 47. 568. pl. 16. 590. pl. 54. 3 Keb. 179. pl. 2. 409. pl. 31. Shower 336. That it is not grantable where the Acquittal was occasioned by a Slip in an Indictment of Perjury in varying from the Original Record. 2 Keb. 409. pl. 31.
[e] Adjudged 2 Jon. 163. 3 Keb. 525. 1 Lev. 9. But it is doubted, 1 Keb. 124. pl. 33. 127. pl. 43. 5 Mod. 350. 1 Sid. 49. pl. 12. and the contrary is ruled. 2 Keb. 396. pl. 81. 403. pl. 14. [f] See Co. 14. b. 1 Keb. 546. Supra ch. 23. sect. 92. and ch. 36. sect. 15.

CHAP. XLVIII.

Of Judgment.

[a] Algernoon Sidney's Case State Trials, Vol. 3. fol. 207, 231. Rosewell's Case, State Trials, Vol. 3. Knightley's Case, State Trials, Vol. 4. fol. 215.

Sect. 1. HAVING shewn already what Judgment is good on an Information, or Action *qui tam*, and *Ch.* 33. *Sect.* 135, *&c.* where it may be saved by an Award of Transportation, and *Ch.* 25. *Sect.* 147. That Judgment in High Treason, not being for counterfeiting the Coin or Seal, *&c.* shall not be arrested for Miswriting or Misspelling, or false or improper *Latin*: Having also premised, That by the Course of the Court of King's Bench, upon every Conviction in that Court, of a Crime [a] capital or not [b] capital, whether by [c] Verdict or Confession, the Party is to have four Days to move in [d] Arrest of Judgment, if there be so many Days remaining of the Term; and if not, [e] then the longest Time that can be had in the Term: Having also premised, That on a Conviction of Homicide *se defendendo* or *per infortunium*, no [f] Judgment at all is to be given, but the Party let to Mainprise in Order to purchase his Pardon, I shall farther endeavour to shew the Nature,

[b] State Trials, Vol. 3. fol. 77. [c] State Trials, Vol. 4. fol. 210. [d] But in Saund. 301, 302. Chief Justice Hale refused to hear any Motion in Arrest of Judgment of a scandalous Conspiracy; but in my own Experience I never knew such a Motion refused to be heard. [e] State Trials, Vol. 4. fol. 217. Yet in the Lord Gray's Case, State Trials, Vol. 3. fol. 77. the Court would not give Judgment on a Conviction for a Misdemeanor, because there were not four Days left of the Term. [f] H. P. C. 269. 2 H. H. P. C. 395. B. 1. ch. 29. sect. 24. Supra ch. 37. sect. 2.

1. Of Judgment by exprefs Sentence to the Punifhment proper for the Crime.
2. Of Judgments without any fuch Sentence.

Of Judgments by fuch exprefs Sentence in Criminal Cafes there are two Kinds.

1. Such as are fixt and ftated, and always the fame for the fame Species of Crimes.
2. Such as are difcretionary and variable according to the different Circumftances of each Cafe.

Sect. 2. And firft of fixed and ftated Judgments; as to which it feems [a] agreed, That the Law makes no Diftinction between a Peer and a Commoner, or between a common and ordinary Cafe, and one attended with extraordinary Circumftances; for which Reafon it was [b] adjudged in *Felton*'s Cafe, who was convicted by Confeffion of the Murder of the Duke of *Buckingham*, that the Court could not order his Hand to be [c] cut off, nor make it Part of the Sentence that his Body fhould be hanged in Chains, but that the Body after Execution being at the King's Difpofal might be hanged in Chains, or otherwife ordered as the King fhould think fit.

[a] State Trials, Vol. 2. fol. 704. 3 Inft. 31.
[b] Hetl. 126. Litt. Rep. 237. Rufhworth's Collections, Part 1. fol. 640, 641.
[c] Agreed 3 Inft. 140. 12. Co. 71. That the Court cannot order the Hand to be cut off in any Cafe wherein it is not the ftated Judgment. See B. 1. ch. 21. fect. 1. to 7.

Of fuch fixt and ftated Judgments, the moft remarkable are thofe for Treafon and Felony, *Præmunire* and Mifprifions.

Sect. 3. The fettled [d] Judgment at [e] this Day againft a Man for High Treafon, not relating to the Coin, feems to be, That he fhall be [f] carried back to the Place from whence he came, and from thence be [g] drawn to the Place of Execution, and be there hanged by the [h] Neck, and cut [i] down alive, and that his [k] Entrails be taken out, and [l] burnt before his Face, and his Head cut off, and his Body divided into four Quarters, and his Head and Quarters difpofed of at the King's Pleafure. And I find little or no Variation in Subftance from this Judgment, but only in fome Circumftances, for which I fhall refer to the Notes in the Margin and the *State Trials*.

[d] 3 Inft. 210, 211. H.P.C. 268. 1 H. H. P.C. 350, 351. 2 H. H. P.C. 397. S. P. C. 182. Letter E. Plow. Com. 387. b. Co. Entr. 361. b.

[e] In the Time of Will. Rufus Judgment was given againft two convicted of High Treafon, that one fhould have his Eyes put out, and the other in crucem tollatur. Madox's Hiftory of the Exchequer, fol. 6. [f] S. P. C. 182. Letter E. But this Claufe is wholly omitted in H. P. C. 268. and 3 Inft. 210. and in Pl. Com. 387. b. it is thus expreffed, quod præd' R. D. duceretur per præfat' conftabular' ufque dictam turrim London, & deinde, &c. And in Co. Ent. 361. b. it is thus, Quod præd' T. B. ducatur per præfat' Marefc. ufque prifonam Mar' Marefc' Domini Regis, &c. [g] S. P. C. 182. Letter E. It is expreffed, That he fhall be drawn upon an Hurdle. And Plow. Com. 387. b. it is, That he fhall be drawn through the Middle of the City of London, to the Gallows at Tyburn, Alfo in Co. Entr. 361. b. and 3 Inft. 310. a particular Place of Execution is mentioned [h] S.P. C. 182. b. and 3 Inft. 110. But Plow. Com. 387. b. Co. Ent. 361. b. and H. P. C. 268. it is only faid Quod fufpendatur, without adding per Collum. [i] 3 Inft 110. S.P.C. 182. Letter E Plow. Com. 387. b. Co. Entr. 361. b. But this is omitted H. P. C. 268. [k] This Claufe is thus expreffed, 3 Inft. 210, 211. Plow. 387. b. Co. Entr. 361. b. Quod interiora fua extra ventrem fuum capiantur, without mentioning the Cutting off of the privy Members; and fo is H. P. C. 268. 2 H. H. P. C. 397. and the later Precedents. [109] But S. P. C. 182. Letter E. is exprefs that they fhall be cut off. [l] S. P. C. 102. Letter E But in Plow. Com. 387. b. Co. Ent. 361. b. 3 Inft. 211. it is thus expreffed, ipfoque vivente comburantur.

Sect. 4.

Sect. 4. It hath been always agreed to be the proper Judgment againſt a Man for High Treaſon at Common Law, in counterfeiting the King's [a] Coin or [b] Seal, That he ſhall be drawn to the Place of Execution, and there hanged by the Neck 'till he be dead. But there have been [c] great Opinions, That the Judgment againſt a Man for Clipping, and other Offences againſt the Coin, made Treaſon by Statute, ſhall be to be drawn, hanged and quartered, as for other High Treaſons; becauſe it is a general [d] Rule, That where a Statute makes an Offence Treaſon or Felony, it gives it the like Incidents that belong to a Treaſon or Felony by the Common Law; yet inaſmuch as High Treaſon at Common Law in counterfeiting the Coin had Judgment only of drawing and hanging; and it is a reaſonable Conſtruction, That the Makers of the Statutes, which made other Offences concerning the Coin High Treaſon, intended to give ſuch Offences the like [e] Incidents with High Treaſons againſt the Coin at the Common Law, and not to make inferior Offences of this Kind ſubject to a heavier Puniſhment than the greater; it ſeems to be [f] ſettled at this Day, That the Judgment for ſuch Offences ſhall be the ſame as for counterfeiting the Coin, *&c.* at the Common Law, *i. e.* of drawing and hanging, without quartering. [110]

Sect. 5. It hath been [g] long [h] agreed, That the Judgment againſt a Man for Petit Treaſon is the ſame with that for counterfeiting the Coin, *viz.* That he ſhall be [i] drawn to the Place of Execution and there hanged by the Neck 'till he be dead.

Sect. 6. The Judgment againſt a [k] Woman, in all Caſes of Treaſon, whether High or Petit Treaſon, is, That ſhe ſhall be drawn to the Place of Execution, and there burnt.

Sect. 7. The Judgment againſt a Man or [l] Woman for Felony of Death, hath always been the ſame [m] ſince the Reign of *H.* 1. *viz.* That he or ſhe be [n] hanged by the [o] Neck 'till [p] dead, which in the [q] Roll is ſhortly enter'd thus, *Suſ. per coll.*

Sect. 8. For the Judgment of *Pain fort & dure* upon all Offenders Standing Mute, I ſhall refer to *Ch.* 30. *ſect.* 16.

Sect. 9. Judgment in *Præmunire* at the Suit of the [r] King, againſt the Defendant, being in [s] Priſon, is, That he ſhall be out of the King's Protection, and that his Lands and Tenements, Goods and Chattels ſhall be forfeited to the King, and that his Body ſhall remain in Priſon at the King's Pleaſure; but if the Defendant be condemned upon his [t] Default in not appearing, whether at the Suit of the King or [u] Party, the ſame Judgment ſhall be given as to the Being out of

[a] S. P. C. 182. Lett. E. 3 Inſt. 17. H.P.C. 268. 1 H. H. P.C. 351. 2 H. H.P. C. 397. Cro. Ca. 383. 19 H. 6. 47. b. pl. 103. Abridged Fitz. Coro. 8. Bro. Treaſ. 9. [b] Fleta, B. 1. ch. 22. ſect. 1. [c] S.P.C. 182. Letter E. 3 Inſt. 17. H. P. C. 19. [d] See B. 1. ch. 40. ſect. 4. [e] See 2 Jon. 233. Supra ch. 25. ſect. 145. [f] Dyer 230. pl. 55. 2 Lev. 98. 2 Jon. 233. 3 Keb. 278. pl. 27. Raym. 234. 1 Vent. 254. [g] But Bract. 104. b. it is ſaid, That they are burnt, qui ſaluti dominorum ſuorum inſidiaverint. [h] 3 Inſt. 211. H. P. C. 268. 1 H. H. P. C. 382. 2 H. H. P.C. 399. S. P. C. 182. Letter F. 19 H. 6. 47. pl. 102. Abridged Fitz. Coro. 7. Bro. Treaſon, 8. 33 Aſſ. pl. 7. Abridged Bro. Treaſon, 15. Fitz. Coro. 210. [i] See 21 E. 3. 17. pl. 21. Abridged Fitz. Coro. 447. Bro. Coro. 38. where an Approver becoming Nonſuit, had Judgment to be hanged only, and not drawn, tho' he ſtood indicted of Petit Treaſon. But the Caſe is obſcure both in the Reports and Abridgments. [k] Preface to the 6th Report. H. P. C. 268. 3 Inſt. 211. S. P. C. 182. Letter F. Fitz. Coro. 383. 23 Aſſ. pl. 2. Abridged Bro. Treaſon, 26. 12 Aſſ 30. Abridged Bro. Coro. 73 or 74. Treaſon, 12. Fitz. Coro. 170. 1 Ric. 3. 4. pl. 5. Abridged Fitz. Coro. 46. [l] 1 Ric. 3. 4. pl. 5. Abridged Fitz. Coro. 46. [m] 3 Inſt. 53. [n] S. P. C. 182. Letter G. H. P. C. 268. 2 H. H. P. C. 399. 3 Inſt. 211. Fitz. Coro. 227. See the Citations to the next Letter. [o] The Words per collum are omitted. Co. Entr. 60. b. 352. b. pl. 2. 353. b. pl. 3. 355. b. pl. 7. 360. pl. 13. and Raſt. Entr. 42. b. pl. 2. 53. b. pl. 6. 55. b. pl. 6. [p] 3 Inſt. 53, 211. H. P. C. 268. 6 E. 4. 4. But this is omitted, 6 H. 4. 6. b. S. P. C. 182. Letter G. and in Raſt. Ent. 42. b. pl. 2. 53. b. pl. 6. 55. b. pl. 6. the Precedents in Coke's Entr. cited to Letter [o] comes only under an &c. [q] S. P. C. 182. Letter G. [r] Co. Lit. 129. b. 'tis agreed, 30 E. 3. 11. Abridged Fitz. Judgment, 145. And in 8 H. 4. 6. b. 7. a. Abridged Fitz. Forſeiture, 13. Bro. Forfeiture, 12. Præmunire, 6. and 20. That ſuch Judgment ſhall not be given at the Suit of the Party, on 27 Ed. 3. but in the two laſt Citations 'tis holden, That the ſame Judgment ſhall be given at the Suit of the Party on 16 Ric. 2. [s] 3 Inſt. 218. Supra B. 1. ch. 19. ſect. 14, 45. Co. Lit. 129. b. 130. a. [t] Vide B. 1. ch. 19. ſect. 14. Raſt. Entr. 466. b. 467. b. 3 Inſt. 125, 218. Dalt. ch. 90. [u] 8 H. 4. 6. b. 7. a. Abridged Fitz. Forfeiture, 13. Bro. Forfeiture, 12. Præmunire, 6, 20. 30 E. 3. 11. b. Abridged Fitz. Judgment, 145. 44 E. 3. 7. pl. 6. Abridged Fitz. Reſponder, 35. 39 E. 3. 37. Abridged Fitz. Retorn de Vicount, 61. Attorney, 36. 8 H. 6. 3. pl. 8. Abridged Bro. Præmunire, 8, 20.

the King's Protection, and the Forfeiture; but inſtead of the Clauſe, that the Body ſhall remain in Priſon, there ſhall be an Award of a *Capiatur*.

Sect. 10. The Judgment againſt a Man for Miſpriſion of High Treaſon [a] is, That he ſhall be impriſoned during his Life, and forfeit all his Goods, and the Profits of his Lands during his Life.

Sect. 11. The Judgment againſt a Man for drawing a Sword on a Judge, or ſtriking any Perſon in the [b] Preſence of the King's Higher Courts, is, that he ſhall be impriſoned during Life, and forfeit his Goods, and the Profits of [c] his Lands during Life, and that his [d] Right Hand ſhall be cut off at a certain Place.

Sect. 12. For the Judgments for [e] ſtriking in the King's Palace, for [f] reſcuing a Priſoner from the Superior Courts, [g] for Perjury, or [h] Forgery on the Statute, and for the Villainous [i] Judgment in Conſpiracy at the Suit of the King, I ſhall refer to the Citations in the Margin.

Sect. 13. The Entry of the Judgment for a Defendant upon an Acquittal by Verdict, or upon the Plea of a Pardon is, *ideo conſid' eſt quod præd'* A. B. *de* [k] *præmiſſis eat inde ſine die*, or *eat ſine die*, omitting [l] *de præmiſſis*; or *de proditionibus prædictis eat inde* [m] *quietus*; or [n] thus, *Quod ſit inde quietus, &c. & quod ipſe eat inde ſine die*; and upon the Plea of a Releaſe to an Appeal, and in other Caſes of like Nature, it is, *ideo conſid' eſt quod* [o] *præd'* A. *quoad ſectam præd'* B. *in præmiſſis eat inde ſine die.* And [p] *Staundforde* ſays, that upon the Acquittal of one arraigned of Treaſon or Felony, the Judgment is no other, but that the Court diſcharges the Defendant paying his Fees.

Sect. 14. *Secondly*, As to Judgments by expreſs Sentence, which are diſcretionary and variable according to different Circumſtances, I ſhall obſerve in general, that for Crimes of an infamous Nature, ſuch as Petit [q] Larceny, [r] Perjury, or [s] Forgery at Common Law, groſs [t] Cheats, Conſpiracy not requiring a villainous Judgment, keeping a Bawdy-houſe, bribing [u] Witneſſes to ſtifle their Evidence, and other Offences of the like Nature, againſt the firſt Principles of natural Juſtice, and common Honeſty, it ſeems to be in great Meaſure left to the Prudence of the Court to inflict ſuch corporal Puniſhment, and alſo ſuch Fine and Lien to the Good Behaviour for a [x] certain Time [y], *&c.* as ſhall ſeem moſt proper and adequate to the Offence, from the Conſideration of the Baſeneſs, Enormity, and dangerous Tendency of it, the Malice, Deliberation and Wilfulneſs, or the Inconſideration, Suddenneſs and Surprize with which it was committed, the Age, Quality and Degree of the Offender, and all other Circumſtances which may any way aggravate or extenuate the Guilt.

[a] H. P. C. 128, 269. 1 H. H. P. C. 374. 2 H. H. P. C. 400. 3 Inſt. 36, 218. Bro. Treaſon, 19, 25.

[b] See B. 1. ch. 21. ſect. 3. to ſect. 6.

[c] So is H. P. C. 131. And in 41. Aſſ. pl. 25. Abridged Bro. Fines, 11. Forfeiture, 41. Reſtitut. 32. Scire facias, 160. 2 Roll. Abr. 76. pl. 3. Judgment was given, that the Lands ſhould be ſeiſed into the King's Hands, and the King anſwered of the Profits; after which the King granted over the Lands as forfeited, and then pardoned the Offence; and the Heir was reſtored upon a Scire facias. By which it appears that the Inheritance of the Lands was not forfeited. (Vide ſupra ch. 37. ſect. 54). But in 1 Keb. 751 the Judgment is, that the Lands ſhall be forfeited during Life; and Daliſon 23. a Quære is made by what Law the Lands ſhall be forfeited any farther than during Life: Yet 3 Inſt. 140, 218. and 39 Aſſ. pl. 1. Abridged Bro. Contempts, 9. Fitz. Aſſiſe, 333. Dyer 188. pl. 10. Fitz. Judgment, 174. Coro. 280. S. P. C. 38. Lett. B. Owen 120. Cro. Eliz. 405. Daliſon 23. ſay, in general, that the Land ſhall be forfeited without adding for Life; and 22 Ed. 3. 12. pl. 26. Abridged Fitz. Forfeiture, 21. That the Offender ſhall be diſinherited. [d] In this Part of the Judgment the Books above cited generally agree. [e] B. 1. ch. 21. ſect. 1, 2. [f] B. 1. ch. 21. ſect. 5. [g] B. 1. ch. 69. ſect. 11, 13. [h] B. 1. ch. 70. ſect. 12. [i] B. 1. ch. 72. ſect. 9. [k] Co. Entr. 356. b. Raſt. Entr. 47. b. pl. 3. 48. a. pl. 4. [l] Co. Entr. 358. a. pl. 9, 10, 359. b. Raſt. Entr. 51. b. pl. 12. 56. a. pl. 5. 57. pl. 7. [m] Co. Entr. 360. b. Raſt. Entr. 51. pl. 11. [n] Raſt. Ent. 49. b. pl. 6. 57. pl. 7. [o] Raſt. Entr. 43. pl. 8. 50. pl. 10. [p] S. P. C. 182. Lett. I. [q] 3 Inſt. 218. B. 1. ch. 33. ſect. 36. [r] State Trials, Vol. 3. fol. 487, 488. Hob. 62. [s] Raym. 81. 1 Sid. 142, 278. 3 Leon. 170. [t] Cro. Ja. 498. 2 Rol. Abr. 78. H. 1. 1 Keb. 849. Noy 99, 103. [u] State Trials, Vol. 2. fol. 272. Raym. 376. [x] 1 Sid. 214. pl. 14. [y] See Cro. Ca. 55. a Decree of the Star-Chamber againſt a Judge for Bribery, that he ſhould be incapable of any Office of Judicature.

Sect. 15. And at this Day by Force of 5 *Annæ*, 6. and 4 *Georg*. 1. 11. and 6 *Georg*. 1. 23. set forth more at large, *Ch*. 33. *Sect*. 134 *to* 139. the Judges upon a Conviction for Larceny, may in their Discretion award the Offender to the House of Correction, and for that and other Felonies within the Benefit of Clergy, instead of giving the usual Sentence, *&c.* may direct that the Offender be transported.

[a] Dalison 20. [b] 2 Inst. 47, 201. Co. Lit. 135.

Sect. 16. But it [a] seems that the Court cannot be authorised by any Letters Patents, but only by Act of Parliament, to inflict a Punishment unknown to our Laws, as of [b] Banishment, *&c.*

[c] Salk. 56, 400. Skin. 684.

Sect. 17. [c] *Note*, That the Court may assess a Fine, but cannot award any corporal Punishment against a Defendant, unless he be actually present in the Court.

[d] 11 Co. 43. 44. 1 Roll. Rep. 74, &c. Supra ch. 9. sect. 16. 1 Lev. 126.

Sect. 18. *Note also*, That where there are several Defendants, a joint Award of one Fine against them all is [d] erroneous, for it ought to be several against each Defendant; for otherwise one who hath paid his proportionable Part might be continued in Prison till all the others have also paid theirs, which would be in Effect to punish him for the Offence of another.

[e] Dy. 232. pl. 6. [f] Co. Litt. 127. a.

Sect. 19. It hath been [e] adjudged, that where a Man is to make Fine and Ransom, the Ransom must be treble the Fine at least; but Sir [f] *Edward Coke* strongly argues, That Fine and Ransom are in legal Understanding the same Thing under different Names, called a *Fine*, because it makes an End of the Business, and a *Ransom*, because it redeems from Imprisonment; for if they were different Things, it would follow that where the Books say, That a Man shall make a Fine and Ransom, they must be taken to intend that he ought to pay two different Sums, of which there is no Precedent.

[g] Co. Litt. 260. a. Adjudged Raym. 376, 377. and there said that Cro. Ca. 251. is to be thus understood.

Sect. 20. A Fine is under the Power of the Court, during the Term in which it is set, and [g] may be mitigated as shall be thought proper; but after the Term it admits of no Alteration.

2dly, Of Judgments without an express Sentence to the Punishment proper to the Crime, there are two Kinds,

1. Outlawry.
2. Abjuration.

[h] Finch of Law 356. Dy. 223. pl. 24. Bro. Coro. 166. 3 Inst. 212. [i] If the Judgment appear not by the Return of the Exigent to have been given by the Coroner it is erroneous, except in London, where the Mayor by Custom is Coroner, and the Judgment is given by the Recorder. Co. Litt. 288. Bro. Utlagary, 31. Dy. 317. pl. 6. 8 Co. 126. a. 21 H. 7. 33. Cro. Eliz. 648. pl. 3.

Sect. 21. Judgment of Outlawry is [h] given by the [i] Coroner at the fifth County-Court upon the Party's not appearing to the Exigent, (which is a [k] Writ commanding the Sheriff to cause the Defendant to be demanded from County-Court to County-Court until he be outlawed, *&c.*) and such Judgment is [l] entred thus, *Ideo, &c. per judicium coronatoris Domini Regis comitatus prædict' utlagatus est.*

Sect. 22. It seems [m] agreed, that when a Judgment of Outlawry for Treason or Felony appears of Record by the Sheriff's Return of the Exigent, and it hath been [n] holden, That if it appears not by such Return, but only by the Coroners Return of a [o] *Certiorari* to them directed to certify whether the Party were outlawed or not, the Party is as much [p] at-

[k] Reg. Jud. 2. a. [l] 3 Inst. 212. [m] Co. Litt. 128. b. 288. b. 28 Ass. pl. 49. Abridged Bro. Nonability, 25. 3 Inst. 212. Theloal, B. 1. ch. 15. S. 20. [n] Co. Litt. 288. a. But the contrary seems to be holden, Dy. 223. pl. 23, 25. and it is made a Quære, 38 E. 3. 14. a. b. [o] Vide Rast. Ent. 332. a. b. 2 H. H. P. C. 399. [p] Finch of Law 467. 3 Inst. 52, 212, State Trials, Vol. 3. fol. 324. Bro. Coro. 166.

tainted,

tainted, and ſhall forfeit and loſe as much as if Sentence had been given againſt him upon Verdict or Confeſſion.

Sect. 23. If ſuch [a] Outlawry appear to the Court to be erroneous, whereof any one as *amicus Curiæ* may inform them, the Party ſhall have Counſel aſſigned him to take Advantage of the Error; but if he will neither bring a Writ of Error, nor plead in convenient Time, and the Outlawry be voidable only and not void, the proper Execution ſhall be [b] awarded againſt him, but no Sentence pronounced, becauſe the Outlawry is a Judgment, and no Man ſhall have [c] two Judgments for one Offence.

Sect. 24. For the Nature of Abjuration, (which was alſo an [d] Attainder of it ſelf) being wholly obſolete at this Day, I ſhall refer to the Citations [e] in the Margin.

Sect. 25. It ſeems to be generally [f] agreed, that a Man can no other way be attainted of Treaſon or Felony at this Day but only by Judgment by expreſs Sentence, or by Outlawry or Abjuration; and therefore where an Appellee was ſlain in the Field upon a Wager of Battle, [g] Judgment was given, *Quod ſuſpendatur per collum* in order to entitle the Lord to his Eſcheat. But I know of no other Caſe wherein it is clear at this Day, that a Man may be attainted after his Death: It is ſaid indeed in a Note in *Fitzherbert*'s [h] *Abridgment* of a Caſe in the Time of *Edward* III. that in *Eyre* it hath been ſeen that a Man hath been attainted by Preſentment after his Death; alſo it was holden by [i] *Markham* in the Time of *Henry* IV. that if he who levies War againſt the King be ſlain in Battle, his Lands may be ſeiſed by the King. And it is ſaid in the [k] *Fourth Report*, That if one aiding the King's Enemies be ſlain in open Rebellion, and the Chief Juſtice of the King's Bench, who is the Sovereign Coroner of *England*, make a Record of it upon the View of the Body, and return it into the King's Bench, he ſhall forfeit his Lands. [111] And this ſeems agreeable ☞ to 34 *E.* 3. 12. whereby the King expreſly reſerves his Prerogative as to Forfeiture of Wars, but grants that he will in no other Caſe ſeize Lands for Treaſon whereof the Party is not attainted in his Life. Yet the contrary Opinion ſeems to be holden in the *Firſt* and *Third* [l] *Inſtitutes*, and alſo by [m] *Hale*; and to this [n] *Staundforde* ſeems alſo to incline.

[a] 3 Inſt. 212, 213. 2 H. H. P. C. 408.
[b] State Trials, Vol. 3. f. 323, 324, 334, 335.
[c] Finch of Law 389, 467. S. P. C. 34. Lett. C. 217. Lett. C. Fitz. Coro. 313, 335. 11 H. 7. 4. pl. 10. Abridged Bro. Coro. 226 or 227. 27 Aff. pl. 54. Abridged Bro. Coro. 110. 9 Ed. 4. 28. b. pl. 41. Abridged Bro. Coro. 55. 12 Co. 100. Fitz. Eſcheat, 14. Supra ch. 23. ſect. 53. ch. 36. ſect. 1. Yet Sentence was given upon one Outlawed of Felony, 3 H. 7. 7. pl. 5. Abridged Bro. Coro. 134 or 135.
[d] Finch of Law 389. 467. S. P. C. 34. Lett. C. 117. Lett. C. 122. Lett. C. Fitz. Coro. 313, 335. 3 Inſt. 216, 217.
[e] Supra ch. 9. ſect. 44. and ch. 32. ſect. 6. 3 Inſt. 216, 217.
[f] Bro. Coro. 166. and the other Books under-cited.
[g] Fitz. Judgment, 225. Co. Lit. 390. a. 3 Inſt. 212. 2 Inſt. 283. Plowd. Com. 261. b. 262. a. Bro. Eſcheat, 24.
[h] Fitz. Petition, 2 Co. Lit. 390. a. Vide Fitz. Coro. 290, 312. 1 H. H. P. C. 342. and the next Chapter, ſect. 16. where a Felon killed in the Purſuit forfeited his Chattels, and the Year, Day and Waſte, and the Meſne Profits of his Lands from the Time of the Felony.
[i] 7 H. 4. 46. b. but denied by Gaſcoign; and 'tis ſaid by Brown, in Plowd. Com. 263. a. that the ancient Law was ſo. See alſo Plowd. Com. 262. a, and Dalt. ch. 89.
[k] 4 Co. 57. b.
[l] 3 Inſt. 27. Co. Lit. 13.
[m] H. P. C. 17. 1. H. H. P. C. 342, 343.
[n] S. P. C. 188, 189.

CHAP.

CHAP. XLIX.

Of Forfeiture of Lands and Goods, Loſs of Dower, and Corruption of Blood.

AND now I am to ſhew the Conſequences of an Attainder or Conviction of Treaſon and Felony, which I ſhall conſider under the following Particulars.

1. What ſhall be forfeited by the Offender.
2. Where his Wife loſes her Dower.
3. How far his Blood is corrupted.

As to the firſt Point, I ſhall endeavour to ſhew,

1 What is forfeited by the Common Law,
2. What by Statute,
3. To what Time the Forfeiture ſhall relate,
4. What ſhall be done with the Goods of an Offender before they are actually forfeited.

As to the firſt Particular, *viz.* What is forfeited by the Offender, by the Common Law, I ſhall endeavour to ſhew,

1. Where his Lands are forfeited by the Common Law.
2. Where his Goods.

Sect. 1. And firſt as to the Forfeiture of Lands, it ſeems agreed, that by the Common Law all Lands of Inheritance whereof the Offender was [a] ſeiſed in his own Right, and alſo all Rights of [b] Entry to Lands in the Hands of a Wrong-doer, are forfeited to the [c] King by an Attainder of High Treaſon, and to the Lord of whom they are immediately holden, by an Attainder of Petit Treaſon or Felony: And that the Lands whereof a Perſon attainted of High Treaſon dies [d] ſeiſed of an Eſtate in Fee are actually veſted in the King without any Office, becauſe they cannot deſcend, the Blood being corrupted, and the Freehold ſhall not be in Abeyance.

Sect. 2. But it ſeems [e] agreed, that by the Common Law ſuch Lands were not veſted in the actual Poſſeſſion of the King during the Life of the Offender without an Office.

Sect. 3. Alſo it [f] ſeems clear, That the Lord cannot enter into the Lands holden of him upon an Eſcheat for Petit Treaſon or Felony, without a ſpecial Grant, till it appear by due Proceſs that the King hath had his Prerogative of the Year, Day and Waſte.

[a] 3 Inſt. 19. 3 Co. 2, 3. 1 H. H. P. C. 240, 241, &c.
[b] 3 Inſt. 19. 3 Co. 2, 3.
[c] See the Statute of 25 Ed. 3, 2.
[d] Co. Lit. 2. 4 Co. 58. a. 1 Leon. 21. and infra S. 23. 1 H. H. P. C. 242.
[e] 3 Co. 10. Co. Lit. 2. S. P. C. 191. D. Bro. Coro. 208, 210. 1 Leon. 21. Infra S. 23.
[f] S. P. C. 191. D. Fitz. Trav. 48. Aſſiſe 166.

Sect. 4. It is [a] said, That the Inheritance of Things not lying in Tenure, as of Rents-Charge, Rents-Seck, Commons, *&c.* shall be forfeited to the King by an Attainder of High Treason, and that the Profits of them shall be also forfeited to the King by an Attainder of Felony during the Life of an Offender, and that the Inheritance shall be extinguished by his Death; for it cannot escheat, because there is no Tenure, nor descent because the Blood is corrupted.

Sect. 5. But it is [b] said, That no Right of Action whatsoever to Lands of an Estate of Inheritance are forfeited, either by the Common Law, or by the Statute; and it seems agreed, That no [c] Right of Entry into such Lands whereof there is a Tenant by Feoffment, or other Title, nor [d] Use, (except only Lands conveyed [e] fraudulently with an Intent to avoid a Forfeiture,) nor [f] Condition, were liable to be forfeited before the Statute of 33 *H.* 8. and that [g] Land in Tail could not be forfeited after the Statute of *Westm.* 2. but only for the Life of the Tenant in Tail, 'till the Statute of 26 *H.* 8. 13.

Sect. 6. It [h] seems, That the Profits of such Lands whereof a Person attainted of Felony is seised of an Estate of Inheritance in the Right of his Wife, or of an Estate for Life only in his own Right, are forfeited to the King, and that nothing thereof is forfeited to the Lord.

Sect. 7. It seems [i] agreed, That by Force of a special Custom a Copyhold of Inheritance may be forfeited by an Attainder or Conviction of Treason or Felony: Also it hath been [k] holden, That by Custom it may be forfeited for Treason or Felony, even without a Conviction; also it seems the stronger Opinion, That it shall be forfeited by an Attainder of Treason or Felony of Common Right, without any special Custom, but [m] not by a Conviction only.

Sect. 8. It seems [n] agreed, That by the Common Law upon an Attainder of Felony, the King had a Right utterly to waste the Lands holden of any but himself, whereof the Person attainted was seised of an Estate of Inheritance, either in his own or in his [o] Wife's Right. [p] And it is said by some, That the King hath both this Right, and also a Right to hold such Lands for a Year and a Day; but it is holden by others, That the Right to hold over the Lands for a Year and a Day was given to the King in Lieu of the Waste; and this seems [q] implied in *Magna Charta*, *Ch.* 22. which saying, That the King shall not hold over the Lands of those convicted of Felony, but for one Year and a Day, and making no Mention of the Waste, seems plainly to intimate that at the Time of the Making of that Statute the King was thought to have no other Right but only to the Year and Day. Yet the Statute of *Prærogativa Regis* made in the 17th of *Ed.* 2. having declared the King's Right to the Year and Day, and also to the Waste; it seems to have been the more general [r] Opinion since that Time, that he hath a Right to both. Indeed if this Statute had been against the express Purview of *Magna Charta*, it would have been clearly repealed by those many subsequent Statutes which repeal all Statutes contrary to *Magna Charta*; but

[a] 3 Inst. 19, 21.
[b] 3 Co. 2, 3. 7 Co. 13. 1 H. H. P. C. 242, 243. Vide infra S. 23, 24, 25.
[c] Fitz. Entry congeable 28. 3 Co. 2, 3. 3 Inst. 19.
[d] 3 Inst. 19. 1 H. H. P. C. 247.
[e] 2 Rol. Abr. 34. pl. 1, 2.
[f] 3 Inst. 19. 1 H. H. P. C. 244.
[g] 3 Inst. 19. S. P. C. 187. Plow. Com. 554, 555.
[l] Dyer 289. pl. 55. Co. Lit. 130, 372, 391. 1 H. H. P. C. 240.
[h] 3 Inst. 19. Fitz. Assise, 166. Forfeiture, 23. 4 Ass. pl. 4.
[i] 2 Jon. 151. 1 Lev. 263. 1 Leon. 1.
[k] 1 Bulst. 13. 2 Brownl. 217, 218, 219. 220. See Godbolt 267. 2 Vent. 38, 39.
[l] 2 Jon. 189. 2 Vent. 38, 39. 5 Co. 117. b. 2 Keb. 451. pl. 23. Coke's Copyholder, sect. 58.
[m] 1 Lev. 263. 2 Keb. 451. pl. 23.
[n] 4 Co. 124. b. S. P. C. 190, 191. Staundf. Prerog. 48, 49, 50. [o] Fitz. Coro. 327. Vide Fitz. Coro. 332. [p] Vide 2 Inst. 36, 37. S. P. C. 190, 191. Staundf. Prerog. 48, 49, 50. [q] See the Books above-cited; yet it seems admitted 8 Ed. 3. Fitz. Traverse, 489. Prescription, 50. That the King was intitled to the Waste as to the Year and Day since this Statute. [r] Bro. Coro. 206, 208, 209, 210. Fitz. Coro. 290, 308, 310, 312, 327, 358. Register 165. Fitz. Traverse, 19. S. P. C. 190, 191. Staundf. Prerog. 48, 49, 50. 49 Ed. 3. 11. pl. 3. 4 Co. 124. b. But 49 Ass. pl. 21. the contrary seems to be holden. 2 Inst. 36, 37. Fitz. Utlagary, 2. See also Fitz. Coro. 285, 390, 332, 344. And it seems agreed, That the King's Prerogative of the Waste is not grantable over, except only as to such Interests which by Virtue of it are actually vested in him. Fitz. Coro. 310. S. P. C. 191. Lett. E. Staundf. Prerog. 50.

being not contrary to the express Words of it, but only to what is argumentatively drawn from it, it may be well argued that it is still in Force.

As to the second Point, *viz.* Where the Goods of the Offender shall be forfeited for Treason or Felony, I shall endeavour to shew,

First, What Goods are liable to such Forfeiture.
Secondly, In what Cases.

[a] Staundf. Prerog. 45, 46. S. P. C. 187. D. Cro. Ca. 566. 12 Co. 121.

Sect. 9. As to the first of these Particulars, it seems [a] agreed, That all Things whatsoever which are comprehended under the Notion of a personal Estate, whether they be in Action or Possession, which the Party hath, or is intitled to in his own Right, and not as Executor or Administrator to another, are liable to such Forfeiture.

It is holden, Staundf. Prerog. 45. b. and S. P. C. 188. ch. 28. That a Felon shall forfeit the Goods of others stolen by him, but the Authorities cited to this Point, viz. 44 Ed. 3. 44. Fitz. Coro. 317, 318, 319, 323, 334, 379, 380. do not seem fully to come up to it except where such Goods are waived, or of such a Nature as not to be distinguishable from others of the like Kind, as Corn out of a Bag, &c. Vide 2 Leon. 5, 6. 1 And. 19. Moor 100. Dy. 309, 310. That a Term limited to Executors, and not vested in the Party himself is not forfeitable.

Sect. 10. Also it [b] seems to be settled, That a Bond taken in another's Name, or a Lease made to another in Trust for a Person who is afterwards convicted of Treason or Felony, are as much liable to be forfeited, as a Bond made to him in his own Name, or a Lease in Possession.

Sect. 11. Also it [c] seems to be in a great Measure settled, That the Trust of a Term granted by a Man for the Use of himself, his Wife and Children, *&c.* is liable in like Manner to be forfeited, if fraudulently made with an Intent to avoid a subsequent Forfeiture; but that it shall be forfeited so far only as it is reserved to the Benefit of the Party himself if made *bona fide*, whether before or after Marriage, for good Consideration without Fraud, which is to be left to a Jury on the whole Circumstances of the Case, and shall never be presumed by the Court where it is not expresly found.

Sect. 12. It hath been [d] adjudged, That a Power of Revocation of the Trust of a Settlement reserved to the Grantor is not liable to be forfeited, if it depend on something Personal to be done by the Grantor himself, as the Making the Deed of Revocation under his own Hand and Seal.

2. Personal Things liable to Forfeiture shall be forfeited in the following Cases.

Sect. 13. *1st*, Upon a [e] Conviction of Treason or Felony.

Sect. 14. *2dly*, Upon a *fugam fecit* found before a Coroner, upon an Inquisition of Death taken upon View of a dead Body; as to which it is [f] agreed, That where-ever a Person found Guilty by such Inquest either as a Principal or as an Accessary [g] before the Fact, is found also to have fled for the same, he forfeits his Goods absolutely, and the Issues of his Lands till he be acquitted or pardoned. Also it is [h] agreed, That where one indicted of any Capital Felony, either as Principal or Accessary before or after, before Justices of *Oyer*, *&c.* is acquitted at his Trial but found to have fled, he shall incur the like Forfeiture of his Goods, but not of the Issues of his Lands, because by the Acquittal the Land is discharged, and consequently the Issues. And it hath been [i] hol-

[b] Cro. Ja. 312, 313. Hob. 214. and the Books cited to the following Section. [c] 2 Keb. 564, 608, 644, 763, 772. 1 Lev. 279. Lane 54, 113. 1 Mod. 16, 38. Hardr. 466. 1 Ander. 294. Raym. 120. 2 Rol. Abr. 34. pl. 1, 2. 1 Rol. Abr. 343. F. 5, 6, 7. March 45, 88. 1 Sid. 260, 403. 1 Keb. 909. [d] 2 Keb. 564, 644, 763, 772. 1 Lev. 279. 1 Mod. 16, 38. Vide infra sect. 26. [e] 5 Co. 109. Supra ch. 33. sect. 129. and the Books cited to the three foregoing Sections. [f] S. P. C. 183, 184, 191. c. 192. a. H. P. C. 271. Staundf. Prerog. 46. Keilw. 68. b. Dy. 239. pl. 36. 5 Co. 110. [g] Secus if he be found Accessary after, for the Indictment is so far void. S. P. C. 184. A. B. Supra ch. 9. sect. 26. [h] S. P. C. 184. A. B. 191. G. H. P. C. 271. Keilw. 68. b. 5 Co. 110 Fitz. Forfeiture, 35. [i] H. P. C. 271. S. P. C. 184. B Fitz. Coro. 206.

den, That the Law is the same as to the Finding of a *fugam fecit* upon an Acquittal of an Indictment of Petit Larceny. But it is [a] certain, That the Party may in all Cases, except that of the Coroner's Inquest, traverse the finding of a *fugam fecit*. Also it seems [b] agreed, That whenever the Indictment against a Man is sufficient, the Finding a *fugam fecit* will not hurt him; and that in all Cases the Particulars of the Goods found to be forfeited may be traversed.

Sect. 15. 3*dly*, Upon a Default till the Award of an Exigent; as to which it is [c] agreed, That if one make such a Default either upon an Appeal or Indictment of a capital Felony, he forfeits his Goods unless he was pardoned before the Exigent was awarded; and it hath been [d] holden, That the Law is the same as to such a Default upon an Indictment of Petit Larceny: However it is clear, That where-ever Goods are so forfeited, they are not saved by an Acquittal at the Trial. But it seems [e] agreed, That they are saved by a Reversal of the Award of the Exigent, for an Error either in Fact or in Law; as for the Imprisonment of the Defendant at the Time when the Exigent was awarded, or for a Defect in the Indictment, Appeal or Process.

Sect. 16. 4*thly*, Upon a [f] Presentment by the Oaths of twelve Men, That a Person arrested for Treason or Felony, fled from, or resisted those who had him in Custody, and was killed by them in the Pursuit or Scuffle.

Sect. 17. 5*thly*, By being [g] waived or left by a Felon in his Flight, from those who either actually do pursue him, or are apprehended by him so to do, whereby he forfeits the Goods so waived, whether they be his own [h] proper Goods, or the Goods of others stolen by him, which shall not be restored to the right Owners but upon a proper Prosecution, as hath been more fully shewn, *Chap.* 23. from *Sect.* 49 *to* 58.

Sect. 18. As to the second Particular, *viz.* What is forfeited by Statute: It is enacted by 26 *H.* 8. 13. *That every Offender and Offenders being hereafter lawfully convicted of any Manner of High Treasons by Presentment, Confession, Verdict or Process of Outlawry, according to the due Course and Custom of the Common Laws of this Realm, shall lose and forfeit to the King, his Heirs and Successors, all such Lands, Tenements and Hereditaments, which any such Offender or Offenders shall have of any Estate of Inheritance, in Use or Possession, by any Right, Title or Means, within the Realm of* England, *or elsewhere within any the King's Dominions, at the Time of any such Treason committed, or any Time after. Saving to every Person and Persons, their Heirs and Successors, other than the Offenders in any Treasons, their Heirs and Successors, and such Person and Persons, as claim to any their Uses, all such Rights, Titles, Interests, Possessions, Leases, Rents, Offices and other Profits, which they shall have at the Day of committing such Treasons, or at any Time before, in as large and ample Manner as if this Act had never been had nor made.* And the same is enacted in near the same Words by 5 & 6 *Ed.* 6. 11.

Sect. 19. And it is farther enacted by 33 *Hen.* 8. *That if any Person or Persons shall be attainted of High Treason by the Course of the Common Laws, or Statutes of this Realm, in every such Case every such Attainder by the Common Law shall be of as good Strength, Value, Force and Effect, as if it had been done by Authority of Parliament; And that the King, his Heirs and Successors, shall have as much Benefit and Advantage by such Attainder, as well of Uses, Rights Entries, Conditions, as Possessions, Reversions, Remainders and all other Things,*

[a] H. P. C. 271. 36 H. 6. 26 a. Vide supra ch. 9. sect. 51, 52. Fitz. Coro. 22.
[b] H. P. C. 271. S. P. C. 184. 47 Ed. 3. 26. pl. 72. Abridged Fitz. Traverse, 18. Bro. Coro. 17.
[c] Fitz. Coro. 181. Forfeiture, 28. S. P. C. 183. 184. D. Staundf. Prerog. 47.
[d] Bro. Coro. 8. Finch 352. 1 Rol. Abr. 793. 41 Ass. pl. 13. 22 Ass. pl. 81. Cro. El. 472. 5 Co. 110. b. 111.
[e] H. P. C. 271. [e] 5 Co. 110. b. 111. 43 Ed. 3. 17, 18. H. P. C. 271. 1 Rol. Abr. 743. D. S. P C. 184. D. Co. Lit. 259. Staund. Prerog. 47. Cro. Ja. 464.
[f] 5 Co. 109. b. Fitz. Coro. 289, 290, 291. 312. S. P. C. 184. Lett. C. 189. 191. Lett. B. 192. A. 3 Inst. 56, 227. Plowd. Com. 260. b. But Staundf. makes a Quære whether the Law in this Point be not altered by 34 E. 3. 12. taken Notice of above, ch. 48. sect. 25. Staundf. Prerog. 46. a.
[g] S. P. C. 186. ch. 25. 5 Co. 109. Cro. Eliz. 611. pl. 18. 693. pl. 3.
[h] S. P. C. 186. ch. 25. and 29 E. 3. 29, b. Abridged Fitz. Avowry, 255. seems express to this Purpose. But 3 Inst. 227. and 5. Co. 109. b. it is said, That the Felon's proper Goods are not forfeited as Waifs, but as the Goods of a Fugitive.

as if it had been done and declared by Authority of Parliament, and ſhall be deemed and adjudged in actual and real Poſſeſſion of the Lands, Tenements, Hereditaments, Uſes, Goods, Chattels, and all other Things of the Offenders ſo attainted, which his Highneſs ought lawfully to have, and which they being ſo attainted ought or might lawfully loſe or forfeit, if the Attainder had been done by Authority of Parliament, without any Office, or Inquiſition to be found of the ſame; any Law, Statute or Uſe of the Realm to the contrary thereof in any wiſe notwithſtanding.

Sect. 20. *Saving to all and every Perſon and Perſons, and Bodies Politick, and their Heirs, Aſſigns and Succeſſors, and every of them (other than ſuch Perſon and Perſons which hereafter ſhall be attainted of High Treaſon, and their Heirs and Aſſigns, and every of them, and all and every other Perſon and Perſons, claiming by them or any of them, or to their Uſes, or to the Uſes of any of them after the ſaid Treaſons committed,) all ſuch Right, Title, Uſe, Poſſeſſion, Entry, Reverſions, Remainders, Intereſts, Conditions, Fees, Offices, Rents, Annuities, Commons, Leaſes, and all other Commodities, Profits and Hereditaments, whatſoever they or any of them ſhould, might or ought to have had, if this Act had never been had or made.*

In the Conſtruction of theſe Statutes the following Points ſeem moſt conſiderable.

Sect. 21. 1*ſt*, It is [a] ſettled, That they are not repealed by 1 *Ma. Seſſ.* 1. *ch.* 1. which enacts, *That no Pains of Death, Penalty or Forfeiture in any wiſe enſue or be to any Offender or Offenders, for the Doing or Committing any Treaſon, Petit Treaſon or Miſpriſion of Treaſon other than ſuch as be in the Statute* 25 Ed. 3. *ordained and provided*; for the Words, *other than ſuch as be within the Statute of* 25 *Ed.* 3, *&c.* ſhall not be taken to refer to the Pains, Penalties and Forfeitures which are mentioned in the Beginning of the Sentence, but to Treaſons, Petit Treaſons and Miſpriſion of Treaſon, which are laſt mentioned.

Sect. 22. 2*dly*, It is [b] agreed, That Eſtates in Tail are forfeited by Force of thoſe Words in 26 *H.* 8. *of any Eſtate of Inheritance*, which muſt be void, if they do not include Eſtates in Tail, for Eſtates in Fee-ſimple were forfeited before. Alſo it hath been [c] adjudged, That where Lands are given to a Man and his Wife, and the Heirs of their two Bodies, the Intail is forfeited by his Attainder, and the Heir as much diſabled as if the Gift had been made to the Heirs of his Body in general.

Sect. 23. 3*dly*, It was [d] ſettled in the Marqueſs of *Wincheſter*'s Caſe, That the Right to a Writ of Error to reverſe an erroneous Common Recovery is not forfeited by theſe Statutes; alſo it is [e] agreed, That a meer Right of Action to Lands in the Hands of a Stranger, as of a Diſcontinuee, or of the Heir of a Diſſeiſor, is not forfeited: [f] But, That a Right of Entry into Lands to which a Perſon attainted of High Treaſon is intitled, is as much forfeited as Lands in Poſſeſſion; but yet that the King ſhall [g] not be adjudged in Poſſeſſion of ſuch Lands without an Office, and *Scire facias*, or Seizure on ſuch Office; for the Words, *That the King ſhall be deemed in Poſſeſſion without Office*, ſhall have this Conſtruction, That he ſhall be in Poſſeſſion without Office in the ſame Manner as he ſhould have been upon an Office found at Common Law: But at the Common Law, if a Diſſeiſee had been attainted of High Treaſon, and the Seiſin found by Office, the King ſhould not have been in Poſſeſſion, without a *Scire facias*, or a Seiſure at leaſt.

[a] S.P.C. 187. 3 Inſt. 19. Dyer 28. 1 H. H. P. C. 241, 356.

[b] S.P.C. 187. Co. Lit. 372. 391. and the Books cited to the following Sections.

[c] Dy. 322. pl. 27.

[d] 3 Co. 2, 3. 1 Leon. 270, 271. Moor 125. Hob. 340, 341. Cro. El. 389. cited and agreed, Cro. Ca. 428. 7 Co. 13. Moor 323. Lit. Rep. 100. 1 H. H. P. C. 242.

[e] 3 Co. 2, 3. Hob. 340, 341. 7 Co. 13. 4 Co. 58. a.

[f] 3 Co. 2, 3, 10. 1 H. H. P. C. 242.

[g] 3 Co. 11. a. 4 Co. 58. a. 1 Leon. 21. 9 Co. 95. a. Supra ſect. 1, 2.

Sect. 24. 4thly, After two contradictory Judgments upon the ſame Point, it was at laſt [a] ſettled by a Majority of the Judges in *Stone* and *Newman*'s Caſe, That where a Tenant in Tail of the Gift of the Crown makes a Feoffment in Fee, the Reverſion being ſtill in the Crown, and afterwards is attainted of High Treaſon, the Right of the Intail is forfeited to the Crown; becauſe the Reverſion continuing always in the Crown, the Intail could not be diſcontinued, but the Heir might have entered after the Death of the Feoffor, without bringing any Action; and tho' the Intail by ſuch a Feoffment be put in Abeyance as to any Benefit which the Feoffor himſelf may claim from it; yet ſince it is not turned to a Right of Action, and would have continued ſtill in him for the Benefit of the Heir, if he had not been attainted, (as appears from the Form of a Writ of *Formedon*, which ſuppoſes that the Right deſcended to the Heir from the Feoffor, and conſequently that it was in him at his Death,) it ſhall likewiſe continue in him for the Benefit of the King.

[a] Cro. Ca. 427. Vide Plowd. Com. 552. 1 H. H. P. C. 243.

Sect. 25. 5thly, It was ſolemnly adjudged in the Exchequer Chamber in [b] *Sheffield*'s Caſe, and a Judgment to the contrary in the Exchequer reverſed, That where one attainted of High Treaſon is ſeiſed of a defeaſible Eſtate in Tail, and hath at the ſame Time a Right to an ancient Intail which is diſcontinued, he forfeits both the Intail in Poſſeſſion, and the Right to the old Intail; for the firſt is within the expreſs Words of 26 *H.* 8. and the latter within thoſe of 33. And it by no Means follows, that becauſe naked Rights of Action to Lands in the Hands of the Heir of a Diſſeiſor, or of a Diſcontinuee, are not within the Meaning of the Statute, as it is [c] ſettled that they are not; therefore alſo a Right to Lands in the Hands of the Perſon attainted himſelf is not within the Meaning of it; for the Forfeiture of ſuch naked Rights, might not only be of dangerous Conſequence in unſettling Poſſeſſions, but might alſo be highly prejudicial to Strangers whom the Statute by an expreſs Saving plainly intends to favour; but the Forfeiture of the Offender's Right to his own Lands can be of no Prejudice to any but himſelf and his Heirs, to whom the Statute is ſo far from intending any Favour, that it expreſly excludes them from all the Benefit of the ſaving Clauſe.

[b] Hob. 334. &c. Palmer 351, &c. 2 Rol. Rep. 305, &c.

[c] Supra Sect. 23.

Sect. 26. 6thly, It ſeems [d] agreed, That a Power of revoking the Uſes of a Settlement may be forfeited by Force of 33 *H.* 8. if the Execution of it require nothing but what may be as well performed by any other Perſon, as by the Party himſelf, by whom it was reſerved, as the Tender of a Ring, *&c.* Alſo it was adjudged in [e] *Englefield*'s Caſe, That the Mention of ſuch Conſiderations and Inducements for the reſerving of ſuch a Power of Revocation in the Preamble of it, as are inſeparable from the Perſon, do not alter the Caſe if nothing of this Kind be inſerted in the Proviſo it ſelf, by which it is reſerved. But it is agreed, That if the Proviſo by which ſuch a Power is reſerved require ſomething inſeparably annexed to the Perſon, it keeps it out of the Statute; and therefore in the [f] Duke of *Norfolk*'s Caſe, where there was this Proviſo, That if the Duke ſhould be minded to alter and revoke the Uſes, and ſignify his Mind in Writing under his Hand and Seal, that then, *&c.* it was clearly adjudged, That the Power of Revocation was not forfeitable, becauſe it depended on the Duke's Signifying his Mind in Writing under his proper Hand and Seal, which none but himſelf could do. Alſo it was adjudged in [g] *Main*'s Caſe, That the Law is the ſame where ſuch Proviſo doth not expreſly require the Party's Signifying a Change of Mind, but only that the Deed of Revocation be under his proper Hand

[d] 7 Co. 12, 13. 1 H. H. P. C. 245. Poph. 18. 1 And. 293. Moor 303. 4 Leon. 135. Palmer 433, &c. 1 Ro. Rep. 142.

[e] 7 Co. 12. and the other Books above cited. Cited and agreed 2 Keb. 566, 763, 773. 1 Lev. 279. Lane 44. 1 Rol. Rep. 142.

[f] 7 Co. 13. 1 H. H. P. C. 245. Cited and agreed 1 Lev. 279. 2 Keb. 566, 763, 773. 3 Inſt. 19.

[g] Supra Sect. 12. 1 H. H. P C 246.

Hand and Seal. [a] But if ſuch Proviſo require only the Tender of a Ring by the Feoffor, *ipſo adtunc declarante* that the Tender is to the Intent to avoid the Feoffment, it ſeems unſettled, whether it come within the ſame Conſtruction.

Sect. 27. 7thly, It [b] ſeems, That an Annuity granted to a Man *pro conſilio impendendo*, is not forfeitable by theſe Statutes: Alſo it ſeems [c] doubtful whether an Office granted to a Man for Life, and requiring Skill and Confidence, be forfeitable; but if it be [d] granted in Fee, it ſeems clear that it may be forfeited even by the Common Law; becauſe the Grantor in giving ſuch an Eſtate, which ſhall deſcend to all the Heirs of the Grantee however unqualified, ſeems plainly not to have been induced to make his Grant from any Conſideration of the peculiar Merit of the Perſons who are to execute the Office.

Sect. 28. It hath been [e] adjudged, but not without great Difficulty, That an Act of Parliament that certain Perſons ſhall forfeit all their Lands, Poſſeſſions, Rights, Intereſts and Hereditaments, and other Things of what Nature ſoever, extends to Eſtates in Tail, by force of the Words *all Intereſts of what Nature ſoever.* Yet it is [f] agreed, That the Statutes of *Præmunire*, which give a general Forfeiture of all the Lands and Tenements of the Offender, extend not to Land in Tail.

Sect. 29. It is [g] holden, That a Saving againſt the Corruption of Blood in a Statute concerning Felony, doth by a neceſſary Conſequence ſave the Land to the Heir; becauſe the Eſcheat to the Lord for Felony is only *pro defectu tenentis*, occaſioned by the Corruption of Blood. Alſo it is holden, That a Saving of the Land to the Heir prevents the Corruption of Blood, and alſo the Loſs of Dower. But it hath been [h] adjudged, That a Saving againſt the Corruption of Blood in a Statute concerning Treaſon, doth not ſave the Land to the Heir, becauſe in Treaſon the Land goes to the King by way of immediate Forfeiture, and not by Eſcheat.

Sect. 30. As to the third Particular, *viz.* To what Time the Forfeiture ſhall relate: It ſeems [i] agreed, That the Forfeiture upon an Attainder either of Treaſon or Felony, ſhall have Relation to the Time of the Offence, for the avoiding of all ſubſequent Alienations of the Lands, but to the Time of the [k] Conviction, or *fugam fecit* found, *&c.* only as to Chattels; unleſs the Party were [l] killed in flying from or reſiſting thoſe who had arreſted him; in which Caſe it is ſaid, That the Forfeiture ſhall relate to the Time of the Offence.

Sect. 31. But it ſeems [m] unſettled, Whether in *Præmunire* it ſhall relate to the Time of the Offence, or only to that of the Judgment.

Sect. 32. It ſeems the better [n] Opinion, That no Attainder whatſoever ſhall have any Relation as to the mean Profits of the Lands of the Perſon attainted, but only from the Time of the Attainder.

Sect. 33. As to the fourth Particular, *viz.* What ſhall be done with the Goods of an Offender both before and after they are actually forfeited: It ſeems to have been always [o] agreed, That one indicted or appealed of Treaſon or Felony may *bona fide* ſell any of his Chattels real or

[a] Palmer 429. Latch 25, 26, &c. 70, 102. 1 Jon. 135. 1 Ventr. 129. 1 Mod. 40.
[b] Plow. Com. 381, 382.
[c] Plow. Com. 379, &c.
[d] Plow. Com. 379.
[e] 2 Lev. 169. 3 Keb. 459, 651, 712. 2 Mod. 130, 131. 2 Jon. 57. 1 Ventr. 299.
[f] Co. Litt. 130. and the Books above-cited.
[g] H. P. C. 8. 1 H. H. P.C. 704. 3 Inſt. 47, 90. Salk. 85.
[h] Salk. 85.
[i] Fitz. Forf. 3, 30. 30 H. 6. 5. a. S. P. C. 192. ch. 31. Fitz. Counterplea de voucher, 30. Co. Litt. 2. b. 8 Co. 170. 38 Ed. 3. 32. a. Plow. Com. 488. b. 1 H. H. P.C. 360, 361.
[k] Fitz. Forfeiture 30. Staundf. Prerog. 48. S. P. C. 192. ch. 31. Bro. Relation, 31. Expoſition, 26. Forfeit. 119. Fitz. Coro. 296. 1 H. H. P. C. 362.
[l] Vide ſupra ſect. 16. S. P. C. 192. a. Fitz. Coro. 290. 1 H. H. P. C. 362.
[m] Cro. Car. 172, 173. 1 Jon. 217.
[n] 8 Co. 170. Plowd. Com. 488. b. 38 Ed. 3. 32. a. But this is made a Quære, S. P. C. 191. Lett. D. and the contrary ſeems holden, Fitz. Coro. 290, 344. See alſo Fitz. Forfeiture, 16. Coro. 374. Finch 326, 327.
[o] Bract. B. 3. ch. 8. ſect. 5. and ch. 18. ſect. 1, 2. Fleta, B. 1. ch. 26. ſect. 1, 2. 8 Co. 171. b. 7 H. 4. in the laſt Caſe. S. P. C. 193. a. State Trials, Vol. 1. fol. 994, 995. Vol. 4. fol. 65, 66, 454. 1 H. H. P. C. 362, 367.

personal for the Suſtenance of himſelf and Family until they be actually forfeited. [112]

Sect. 34. Alſo it ſeems [a] agreed, that the Goods of ſuch Perſon can in no Caſe be lawfully removed out of his Houſe until they be forfeited.

Sect. 35. Yet according to the general Tenor of the old [b] Books, the Goods of one [c] arreſted for Treaſon or Felony, may by the Purview of an ancient Statute, which [d] ſeems to continue ſtill in Force, be immediately inventoried and appraiſed, after which, and on Surety found that they ſhall be forth-coming, they ſhall be kept by the Bailiffs of the Party arreſted, and for want of ſuch Surety, by his Neighbours, till he be convicted, or found to have fled, *&c.* whereby they are actually forfeited.

Sect. 36. Alſo it was enacted by the Statute *de Officio Coronatoris*, (ſet forth more at large, *Ch.* 9. *Sect.* 19, 20.) That where one is found guilty of Murder by a Coroner's Inqueſt upon View of a dead Body, the Coroner ſhall inquire what Goods he hath, and cauſe them to be valued and delivered to the Townſhip, *&c.* But ſo much of this Statute as enables the Coroner to ſeiſe the Goods, [e] ſeems to be repealed by 1 *Rich.* 3. (ſet forth more at large *Sect.* 38.) unleſs the Party indicted be found alſo to have fled.

Sect. 37. Alſo it was enacted by 25 *Ed.* 3. 14. (ſet forth more at large *Ch.* 27. *Sect.* 116.) That in the ſecond *Capias* given by that Statute on the Return of a *Non inventus*, it ſhall be compriſed, that the Sheriff ſhall cauſe the Party's Chattels to be ſeiſed, and ſafely kept till the Day of the Writ or Precept returned, *&c.* and this is ſtill in [f] Force notwithſtanding the Statute of 1 *R.* 3. 3. for this prohibits only the Seiſing of the Goods of thoſe who are arreſted; and ſo far as it relates to this Purpoſe, is enacted as followeth.

Sect. 38. *And that no Sheriff, under-Sheriff, nor Eſcheator, Bailiff of Franchiſe, nor any other Perſon, take or ſeiſe the Goods of any Perſon arreſted or impriſoned for Suſpicion of Felony, before that the ſame Perſon ſo arreſted and impriſoned be convicted or attainted of ſuch Felony according to the Law, or elſe the ſame Goods otherwiſe lawfully forfeited, upon Pain to forfeit the double Value of the Goods ſo taken, to him that is ſo hurt in that Behalf, by* [g] *Action of Debt*, &c.

Sect. 39. This Statute is ſaid to be in [h] Affirmance of the Common Law, and hath been [i] adjudged to extend as well to the Seizure of Money as of any other Chattel. [113]

Sect. 40. It ſeems plain from this Statute, That Goods may be ſeiſed as [k] ſoon as they are forfeited; and it ſeems the whole Townſhip is anſwerable [l] for them to the King, and may ſeiſe them [m] where-ever they can be found.

[a] See the Citations to the foregoing and following Section.

[b] Fleta, B. 1. ch. 26. ſect. 2. Bract. B. 3. ch. 18. ſect. 2. Britton, f. 4. S. P. C. 52. Letter C. 192. Letter B. Staundf. Prerog. 47. b. 48. a. 1 H. H. P. C. 363, 364. It is ſaid 26. Aſſ. pl. 32. Abridged Bro. Coro. 102. That Juſtices of Oyer, &c. ſhall put the Chattels of Felons in Eſtreat preſently, &c. and deliver them to the Towns, &c. to anſwer to the King in Eyre. But this ſeems intended of the Chattels of one convict of Felony. And in 44 Aſſ. pl. 13. and 43 E. 3. 24. pl. 1. Abridged Bro. Coro. 9. Forfeiture, 7. Reſeiſer, 3. Office and Officer, 3. Fitz. Treſp. 7. Bar, 196. the 2d. it is ſaid That no Miniſter of the King ought to take the Chattels of an Appellee of Felony away with him, but to ſeiſe them, and cauſe the Party to find Surety that they ſhall not be eloigned, &c. And if the Party cannot find Surety, he ought to deliver them to the Neighbours, &c. And in the laſt Caſe of 7 H. 4. Abridged Fitz. Coro. 83. and Bro. Forfeit. 10. It is ſaid, That where one is indicted of Felony until he be attainted, his Goods ſhall not be removed out of his Houſe, but ſhall be kept by his Neighbours until, &c. and in the mean Time the Felon ought to live upon his Goods, Vide 41 Aſſ. pl. 13. Abridged Fitz. Proceſs, 183. Bro. Forfeit. 40. 13 H. 3. 13 pl. 6. in which Books it is ſaid, That Goods ſhall not be ſeiſed till they be forfeited.

[c] The old Writ recited, Bract. B. 3. ch. 18. ſect. 2. and Fleta, B. 1. ch. 26. ſect. 2. is expreſs to this Purpoſe: Yet in 3 Inſt. 228. it is ſaid, That the Goods of any Delinquent cannot be inventoried, and the Town charged therewith before the Owner is indicted of Record; and a Note in H. P. C. 269. ſeems to be to the ſame Effect, and 1 H. H. P. C. 367.

[d] State Trials, Vol. 1. fol. 994, 995. Vol. 4. fol. 65, 66. S. P. C. 139.

[e] S. P. C. 52. Letter C.

[f] S. P. C. 193. 1 H. H. P. C. 366. Staundf. Prerog. 48.

[g] For Precedents of ſuch Actions, See 1 Lutw. 132. Cro. Eliz. 749.

[h] Vide ſupra ſect. 33, 34, 35. S. P. C. 193.

[i] Raym. 414.

[k] Co. Litt. 391.

[l] Fitz. Coro. 300, 347, 366. 13 H. 4. 13. pl. 6. Abridged Fitz. Forfeit. 32. 22 Aſſ. pl. 81. Abridged Fitz. Coro. 181. Bro. Charge, 45. Forfeiture, 32. S. P. C. 193. B. 194. A. B. Staundf. Prerog. 47. b. 47 E. 3. 26. a. b.

[m] 22 Aſſ. pl. 81. Abridged Fitz. Coro. 181. Bro. Charge, 45. Forfeiture, 32. Staundf. Prerog. 47. b.

Sect. 41. And at the Common Law it was no [a] Plea for ſuch Townſhip, That the Goods were delivered to the Cuſtody of *J. S.* who imbezilled them, *&c.* But it is enacted by 31 *E.* 3. 3. *That if any Man or Town be charged in the Exchequer by Eſtreats of the Juſtices of the Chattels of Fugitives and Felons, and will alledge in Diſcharge of him another which is chargeable, he ſhall be heard, and Right done to the other.*

Sect. 42. As to the ſecond Point, *viz.* Where the Wife loſes her Dower: It is agreed, that before the Statute of 1 *Ed.* 6. *ch.* 12. the Wife not only loſt her Dower at Common [b] Law, but alſo her Dower [c] *ad oſtium eccleſiæ*, or *ex aſſenſu patris*, or by Special [d] Cuſtom (except that of [e] Gavelkind) by an Attainder of any Treaſon or [f] capital Felony, whether [g] committed before or after the Marriage, and whether the Lands were in the Hands of a [h] Feoffee, or forfeited to the King, or eſcheated to the Lord of the Fee: And tho' the [i] Attainder were pardoned, *&c.*

Sect. 43. But it [k] ſeems that the Wife never forfeited Lands given jointly to her Huſband and her, whether by way of Frank-marriage or otherwiſe, but only [l] for the Year and Day and Waſte.

Sect. 44. Alſo it hath been [m] adjudged, That if a Huſband having levied a Fine with Proclamations, is afterwards erroneouſly attainted of High Treaſon, and the five Years paſs after his Death, and then the Outlawry is reverſed, the Wife may purſue her Title of Dower within five Years after ſuch Reverſal; becauſe being barred of her Dower by the Attainder while it ſtood in Force, which Attainder ſhe could no way reverſe, ſhe had no Remedy to purſue her Title of Dower within the five Years, and therefore ſhall not be barred by her Non-claim.

Sect. 45. It is enacted by 1 *Ed.* 6. 12. *Par.* 17. *That albeit any Perſon ſhall be attainted of any Treaſon or Felony whatſoever, yet that notwithſtanding every Woman that ſhall fortune to be Wife of the Perſon ſo attainted, ſhall be endowable and enabled to demand, have, and enjoy her Dower in like Manner and Form as tho' her Husband had not been attainted*, &c.

Sect. 46. But this is repealed as to Treaſon by 5 & 6 *Ed.* 6. 11. *Par.* 9. by which it is enacted, *That the Wife whoſe Husband ſhall be attainted of any Treaſon whatſoever, ſhall in no wiſe be received to ask, challenge, demand, or have Dowry of any the Lands, Tenements, or Hereditaments of the Perſon ſo attainted during the ſaid Attainder in Force.* And this hath been conſtrued [n] to extend as well to an Attainder of Petit Treaſon, as of High Treaſon.

As to the third Point, *viz.* How far the Blood is corrupted by an Attainder of Treaſon or Felony, the following Particulars ſeem moſt remarkable.

Sect. 47. 1ſt, It is [o] agreed, That by [p] ſuch an Attainder, the Blood is ſo far ſtained or corrupted that the Party loſes all the Nobility or Gentility he might have had before, and becomes ignoble.

Sect. 48. 2dly, It is alſo [q] agreed, That he can neither inherit as Heir to an Anceſtor, nor have an Heir.

Sect. 49. 3dly, It is alſo farther [r] agreed, That where-ever it is neceſſary for any one who would make a Title to another, to derive the De-

[a] Fitz. Coro. 300, 347. S. P. C. 194. Lett. B.
[b] S. P. C. 194. D. Co. Litt. 31. a. 37. a. 41. a. 392. b. Litt. §. 747. 3 Inſt. 47, 211. 1 H. H. P. C. 359.
[c] Co. Litt. 37. a. 41. a. S. P. C. 195. A. Bract. 311. pl. 13.
[d] Co. Litt. 41. a. Bract. 311. pl. 13. Winch 27.
[e] Bract. 311. pl. 13.
[f] Co. Litt. 41. a. 1 H. H. P. C. 359.
[g] Co. Litt. 31. a.
[h] 3 Inſt. 216. Savil 54, 55. Co. Litt. 41. a. Benl. 55, 56, 57. Dy. 140. pl. 42. Moor 639. pl. 879. Cont. by Vavaſor. Litt. ſect. 55.
[i] 1 Leon. 3.
[k] Co. Lit. 37. 3 Inſt. 216. Bract. 129. pl. 14. 130. pl. 23.
[l] Bract. 129. pl. 14. Supra ſect. 8. Cont. Bract. 130. pl. 23.
[m] 3 Inſt. 216. Moor 639. 879.
[n] S. P. C. 195. Dyer 140. pl. 42. Co. Litt. 37. a. 392. b. 1 H. H. P. C. 359.
[o] 3 Inſt. 211. S. P. C. 195. B.
[p] But an Attainder of Piracy, [114] (B. 1. ch. 37. ſect. 6, 8. Co. Litt. 391.) or Petit Larceny corrupts not the Blood. B. 1. ch. 33. ſect. 26. 3 Inſt. 112. Co. Litt. 41. a. Noy 170.
[q] Co. Litt. 8. a. 391. b. 392. S. P. C. 195. b. Bro. Nonability, 21. Coro. 60.
[r] Cro. Ca. 543. Litt. Rep. 28. 1 Vent. 413, 417. Noy, 159, 166, &c. 1 Lev. 60. 1 Sid. 200, 201.

ſcent thro' him, the Attainder is a Bar to ſuch Title, [a] unleſs the Land were intailed. And therefore if there be Grandfather, Father and Son, and the Father be attainted, it is clear, That the Son [b] cannot claim as Heir to the Grandfather of the Lands in Fee-ſimple, becauſe he muſt of Neceſſity derive the Deſcent thro' the Father, which by Reaſon of the Attainder he cannot do. And for the ſame Reaſon, if there be two Brothers, and one of them having Iſſue a Son, be attainted, and either the Son or Uncle purchaſe Land and die without Iſſue, the other [c] cannot be his Heir, becauſe the Blood of the Father thro' whom the Deſcent muſt be convey'd, is corrupted. But it ſeems a [d] general Rule, That the Attainder of a Perſon who needs not be mentioned in the Conveyance of the Deſcent, does no Hurt, let the Anceſtor be never ſo remote; and *a fortiori* therefore it ſeems clearly to follow, that where one may claim as immeditate Heir to another, without deriving the Deſcent thro' any other, he ſhall not be barred by the Attainder of any other. And therefore it ſeems [e] agreed, That if the Son of one attainted purchaſe Land, and have a Son and die, ſuch Son ſhall inherit him, becauſe he derives his Deſcent immediately from him. And for the like Reaſon it hath been [f] ſettled, That if a Man hath two Sons, and then be attainted, and one of the Sons Purchaſe Lands and die without Iſſue, the other ſhall be his Heir, becauſe he may make his Title without mentioning the Father.

But Sir *Edward Coke* [g] ſays, That the Reaſon of this Caſe is, *becauſe the Attainder of the Father corrupts only the lineal Blood, and not the collateral Blood between the Brethren which was veſted in them before the Attainder*; but he ſaith, *That ſome have holden that if a Man after he be attainted have Iſſue two Sons, the one cannot be Heir to the other, becauſe they could not be Heir to their Father, for that they never had any inheritable Blood in them.* But the Ground of this Opinion ſeems to be overthrown by the Reſolution in the Caſe of *Collingwood* and *Pace*, wherein it was adjudged [h] in the Exchequer-Chamber by ſeven Judges againſt three, that the Sons of an Alien might be Heirs to one another if born in *England* or naturalized; and yet it is certain that they could not be Heirs to their Father. Alſo it ſeems to [i] be the better Opinion, that where a Perſon attainted hath Iſſue by a Woman ſeiſed of Lands of Inheritance, ſuch Iſſue may inherit the Mother, tho' he never had any inheritable Blood from the Father.

Sect. 50. *4thly*, It ſeems clear, That notwithſtanding a Perſon attainted be to many Purpoſes looked upon as dead in Law, yet he hath a Capacity to [k] purchaſe Land, which the King ſhall have upon Office found. Alſo if the Father of a Perſon attainted die ſeiſed of an Eſtate of Inheritance during his Life, no [l] younger Brother can be Heir, but the Land ſhall rather eſcheat; for the elder Brother, tho' attainted, is ſtill a Brother, and no other can be Heir to the Father while he is alive: But it ſeems [m] agreed at this Day, That if he die before the Father, the younger Brother ſhall be Heir.

[a] 3 Co. 10. b. Lit. S. 746, 747. 1 H. H. P. C. 356. 8 Co. 166. a.
[b] 1 Vent. 416, 418. Dalif. 14. pl. 3. 1 H. H. P. C. 356. Co. Lit. 392.
[c] Cro. Ca. 543. Dy. 274. pl. 40. 1 Vent. 413, 416, 425. 1 H. H. P. C. 357.
[d] Cro. Ca. 543. 1 Vent. 413, 417, &c. Lit. Rep. 28. Noy 159, 166, &c. 1 Lev. 60. 1 Sid. 200, 201. Vide Bract. B. 3. ch. 14. Sect. 17.
[e] 1 Vent. 416.
[f] Co. Lit. 8. a. 1 H. H. P. C. 357. 4 Leon. 5. Cro. Ja. 539. 1 Rol. Abr. 625. pl. 5. Cro. Ca. 543. 1 Vent. 425. Palm. 19. 1 Lev. 59. 2 Rol. Rep. 93. 2 Sid. 25, 27. This is left doubtful Moor 569. pl. 775. Noy 158, &c. Cont. Lit. Rep. 28.
[g] Co. Lit. 8. a. 1 Rol. Abr. 625. pl. 5.
[h] 1 Sid. 193. Hard. 224. 1 Vent. 413. 1 Lev. 59.
[i] 1 Sid. 201. 1 Vent. 422, 426. Noy 159, 167, 168, 169. 2 Sid. 248. This alſo appears from 13 H. 7. 17. cited S. P. C. 196. Abridged Bro. Tenant by Curteſy, 15. and wherein it is holden, That if the Husband of an Inheritrix have Iſſue, and be attainted of Felony and pardoned, he ſhall not be Tenant by Curteſy by Reaſon of the Iſſue born before the Pardon, but by Reaſon of Iſſue born after he ſhall; from whence it neceſſarily follows, that ſuch Iſſue muſt be inheritable to the Wife. Alſo it is admitted, Co. Lit. 84. b. That the Iſſue of an Inheritrix by an Alien or a Perſon attainted may be in Ward, which could not be unleſs he could inherit the Mother. Vide Cro. Ja. 539. Lit. Rep. 28. 1 Lev. 59, 60. But the contrary was anciently holden. 3 Co. 41. Bract. B. 3. ch. 13. ſect. 19, 20.
[k] Co. Lit. 2. b.
[l] Fleta, B. 1. Ch. 28. ſect. 9. Co. Lit. 8. a. 13. a. Bro. Mortdanceſter, 36. S. P. C. 195. B. Bract. B. 5. ch. 6. ſect. 7. Fitz Petition, 20. Mortdanceſter, 28. Diſcent, 7. 1 Vent. 413, 417. 1 Lev. 60. Deſcent, 17. 29 Aſſ. pl. 11. Noy 166, 170. 1 Sid. 195. 26 Aſſ. pl. 2.
[m] See the Books next above cited, and Bro. Diſcent, 64 Cont. Bract. B. 3. ch. 14. ſect. 17.

Sect. 51. *5thly*, It is clear, That the Corruption of Blood from an Attainder is so High that it cannot be absolutely salved but by Act of Parliament; for it seems [a] agreed, That the King's Pardon cannot restore the Blood so as to make the Person attainted capable either of inheriting others, or of being inherited himself by any one born before the Pardon. [b] Yet if such Person have a Son born after the Pardon, and purchase Lands and die, such Son may be his Heir, unless he have an elder Brother alive born before the Pardon; for a Pardon doth as it were make a Man a new Creature, and give him a new Capacity, in Respect whereof his Issue born after the Pardon may be his Heir, as to Lands Purchased after the Pardon in the same Manner as if he had never been attainted. [115]

[a] Co. Lit. 8. a. 391. b. 392. a. S. P. C. 195. B. 3 Inst. 233. Dalis. 14. pl. 3. 1 H. H. P. C. 358. Cont. 9 H. 5. 9. a.

[b] See the Books next above cited.

CHAP. L.

Of avoiding Judgments in Criminal Cases.

FOR the better Understanding the Learning concerning the avoiding of Judgments in criminal Cases, I shall endeavour to shew,

1. How such Judgments may be avoided.
2. The Effect of such Avoidance.

And first, such Judgments may be avoided either,

1. Without Writ of Error.
2. By Writ of Error.

They may be avoided without Writ of Error two Ways.

1. For Faults apparent in the Record.
2. For other Matters *dehors* the Record.

Sect. 1. And first I shall endeavour to shew where such Judgments may be avoided by Plea without any Writ of Error for Faults apparent in the Record; as to which it is observable, That notwithstanding it be the allowed Practice of the Court of Common Pleas to suffer a Defendant coming in by [c] *Capias Utlagatum* the same [d] Term in which an Exigent is returnable, to avoid the Outlawry without Writ of Error, by shewing that he purchased a [e] *Supersedeas* out of the [f] same Court, and

[c] Co. Lit. 259. b. 1 And. 36. pl. 92. Vide infra sect. 9. Secus if he comes in gratis. Dyer 192. pl. 25. Cont. 39 H. 6. 27. b. Abridged Fitz. Responder, 52. Bro. Utlagary, 35. Vide 14 H. 4. 27. a. b. Fitz. Idempnitate nominis, 3. Bro. Utlagary, 28. 30 H. 6. 3. a. [d] 8 H. 6. 37. pl. 8. Abridged Fitz. Error, 19. 19 H. 6. 2. a. Abridged Fitz. Error, 26 But some have holden, That an Outlawry cannot be avoided for this or any other Cause in another Term. Co. Lit. 259. b. 37 H. 6. 17. a. b. Abridged Fitz. Utlagary, 28. Bro. Error, 97. 37 H. 6. 17. a. b. Abridged Fitz. Utlagary, 28. Bro. Error, 97. 8 H. 6. 37. a. b. Con. adjudged 1 And. 36. pl. 93. [e] 19 H. 6. 44. a. b. Abridged Fitz. Utlagary, 20. Bro. Utlagary, 21. 33 H. 6. 1. b. Abridged Fitz. Utlagary, 27. Bro. 2. 30 H. 6. 3. a. Abridged Fitz. Protection, 11. Bro. Utlagary, 74. 12 H. 4. 18. a. Abridged Bro. Utlagary, 14. 7 H. 4. 1. a. Abridged Bro. Utlagary, 5. 8 H. 6. 7. a. b. Fitz. Error, 42. 11 H. 4. 34. 33 H. 6. 1. b. 45. a Abridged Fitz. Utlagary, 27. 1 And. 36. pl. 93. But 1 Rol. Abr. 743. pl. 2. The contrary is said to have been holden 39. Eliz. [f] 30 H. 6. 3. a. Abridged Fitz. Protection, 11. Secus if the Supersedeas were from the Chancery, 7 H. 4. 5. b. Abridged Fitz. Supersedeas, 10. Bro. Utlagary, 65. Supersedeas, 8. Vide 18 H. 6. 18. a. b. Abridged Fitz. Error, 24. 7 Ed. 4. 9. b. Abridged Fitz. Exigent, 1. Bro. Supersedeas, 31. F. N. B. 236. A.

[a] delivered it to the Sheriff before the *Quinto exactus*, *&c.* or by fhewing any [b] other Matter apparent on Record which makes the Outlawry erroneous, as the Want of an [c] Original, or the [d] Omiffion of Procefs, or Want [e] of Form in a Writ of Proclamation, *&c.* or a [f] Return by a Perfon appearing not to be Sheriff, or a [g] Variance between the Original and Exigent or other Procefs, or the Want of fuch Addition as [h] required by 1 *H.* 5. Yet it is faid in many [i] Books, to be the conftant Courfe of the Court of King's Bench, never to reverfe an Outlawry on the Crown-fide either in the fame or a different Term, for [k] thefe or other Errors of the like Nature (as the [l] Want of a *Capias* to the Sheriff of the County whereof the Party is named, or a [m] Fault in the Indictment) without a Writ of Error; yet fince Sir *Edward* [n] *Coke* feems to be of another Opinion, and fince alfo it is clearly holden, That one may plead even a Matter of Fact in the King's Bench in Avoidance of an Outlawry of Felony, which cannot be pleaded in Avoidance of any other Outlawry, as fhall be more fully fhewn, *Sect.* 6. I fhall leave this Point to be farther confidered. However it is [o] agreed, That Conviction of Felony whereon the Party hath had his Clergy may be difcharged by Exception to the Indictment, becaufe no Writ of Error lies of fuch a Conviction, not being a Judgment.

Sect. 2. As to the fecond Particular, *viz.* Where a Judgment may be avoided without Writ of Error for Matters *dehors* the Record, it is holden, That he who purchafes Land of a Perfon who afterwards is [p] outlawed of Felony, or condemned upon his own [q] Confeffion, may falfify the Record not only as to the Time wherein the Felony is fuppofed to have been committed, but alfo as to the Point of the Offence. But it is [r] agreed, That where a Man is found guilty by Verdict, a Purchafer cannot falfify as to the Point of the Offence, but that he may falfify for the Time where the Party is found Guilty generally of the Offence in the Appeal or Indictment; becaufe the Time is not material upon Evidence.

Sect. 3. Alfo it feems [s] agreed, That any Judgment whatfoever given by Perfons who had no good Commiffion to proceed againft the Perfon condemned, may be falfify'd by fhewing the Special Matter without Writ of Error, becaufe it is void; as where a Commiffion authorifes to proceed on an Indictment taken before *A. B. C.* and twelve others, and by Colour thereof the Commiffioners proceed on an Indictment taken before eight Perfons only.

Sect. 4. Alfo it feems [t] agreed, That if the Treafon or Felony of which a Man is attainted, be afterwards pardoned by Parliament, the Attainder may be falfify'd by himfelf or his Heir without Plea.

[a] 14 H. 4. 27. a. b. Abridged Bro. Utlagary, 15. Long quinto Ed. 4. 5. Abridged Bro. Error, 155. Dyer 222. pl. 23. 223. pl. 26. and it is faid not to be material whether it were delivered to the Sheriff or not. Co. Lit. 128. b. Bro. Utlag. 8. 4 E. 4. 42. a. Cont. Fitz. Error, 77. Vide Fitz. Error, 42. [b] Co. Lit. 259. b. 33 H. 6. 1. b. 45. a. Abridged Fitz. Utlagary, 27. [c] 11 H. 7. 4. b. Abridged Bro. Utl. 78. 16 E. 4. 9. b. Abridged Bro. Error, 172. Fitz. Utl. 41. Vide 19 Ed. 4. 8. b. But it is agreed, That an Outlawry without any Original is not void, but voidable only. Fitz. Color, 45. Utlagary, 18. V. 7 H. 7. 5. b. Abridged Fitz. Error, 52. Keilw. 19. b. Bro. Utlagary, 45. Long quinto Ed. 4. 116. b. [d] 33 H. 6. 1. b. 45. a. Abridged Fitz. Utl. 27. 8 H. 6. 37 pl. 8. Abridged Fitz. Error, 19. Bro. Utlagary, 19. 19 H. 6. 2. a. Abridged Fitz. Error, 26. Long quinto Ed. 4. 116. b. Bro. Utlagary, 45. [e] Dy. 206. pl. 10. 11 H. 4. 34. a. [f] Dy. 41. pl. 7. [g] Fitz. Utlagary, 41. 38 H. 6. 31. a. Abridged Fitz. Utlagary, 31. 21 Ed. 3. 56. b. Abridged Fitz. Difcontinuance, 3. 16 Ed. 4. 9. b. Bro. Error, 172. Fitz. Difcontinuance, 17. 20 H. 6. 18. Abridged Fitz. Difcontinuace, 22. 2 Rich. 3. 13. b. Bro. Mifnofmer, 80. Variance, 90. [h] 8 H. 6. 37. a. Abridged Fitz. Error, 19. 1 And. 36. pl. 92. 1 Rol. Abr. 743. pl. 6, 7. 2 Inft. 670. Cont. Bro. Utlagary, 34. 39 H. 6. 1. b. [i] 1 Rol. Abr. 743. Let. C. 37 H. 6. 17. b. Abridged Fitz. Utlagary, 28. 4 E. 4. 42. a. b. 43. Abridged Bro. Error, 158. Utlagary, 67. 19 H. 6. 2. a. Abridged Fitz. Error, 26. Vide Palmer 43. Contra, 11 H. 7. 4. b. Abridged Bro. Utlagary, 78. [k] Not for the Want of an Addition, 19 H. 6. 2. a. Abr. Fitz. Error, 26. 11 H. 6. 15. b. 54. [l] Supra ch. 27. fect. 127. 9 H. 6. 15. b. Bro. Utlagary, 20, 34. 39 H. 6. 1. b. [m] 1 Bulft. 109. 1 Sid. 144. [n] Co. Lit. 259. b. Vide 11 H. 7. 4. b. Bro. Utlagary, 78. 33 H. 6. 1. b.. Abridged Fitz. Utlagary, 27. 8 H. 6. 37. a. b. Abridged Bro. Utlagary, 19. [o] Cro. Eliz. 489, 490. [p] H. P. C. 270. 1 H. H. P. C. 361. 3 Inft. 230. Yet the contrary feems holden, 49 Ed. 3. 11. 49 Aff. pl. 2. Bro. Coro. 205 or 6. 207 or 8. Fitz. Traverfe, 19. [q] H. P. C. 270. 1 H. H. P. C. 361. 3 Inft. 231. Bro. Traverfe de Office, 35. 7 Ed. 4. 1. 2. Fitz. Eftoppel, 91. [r] See the Books above cited. [s] H. P. C. 270. 3 Inft. 231. Plow. Com. 392, &c. [t] 3 Inft. 232. H. P. C. 271. 8 Co. 79. b. Vide fupra ch. 37. S. 53. Cro. El. 72. Cro. Eliz. 4. 'Tis faid that a Writ of Error lies on fuch a Pardon. But this is contrary to 3 Inft. 231. and 6. Co. 14. a. For the avoiding of an Outlawry by the King's Pardon, vide fupra ch. 49. S. 15. Fitz. Chart. 27. Bro. Error, 56. 18 Ed. 3. 38. Bro. App. 7. 92. 9 H. 5. 14. b. 15. a.

Sect. 5. But it hath been [a] adjudged, that the King's Letters Patents reversing an Attainder are void, unless they be afterwards made good by Act of Parliament.

Sect. 6. It seems generally agreed, that by the Common Law, in [b] *favorem vitæ*, an Outlawry of Treason or Felony might be avoided by Plea that the Defendant was in [c] Prison, or in the King's Service beyond the [d] Sea, *&c.* at the Time of the Outlawry [e] pronounced against him. But I take it to be generally [f] agreed, that no Outlawry for any other Crime, (against a Party [g] rightly described) can be avoided by the Plea of any Matter [h] of Fact whatsoever.

Sect. 7. And it is enacted by 26 *H.* 8. 13. *and* 5 *&* 6 *Ed.* 6. 11. *That all Process of Outlawry to be had or made within this Realm, against any Offenders in Treason, being resiant or inhabited out of the Limits of this Realm, or in any of the Parts beyond the Seas at the Time of the Outlawry pronounced against them, shall be as good and effectual in Law to all Intents and Purposes, as if such Offenders had been resident and dwelling within this Realm at the Time of such Process awarded, and Outlawry pronounced;* [i] *Provided, that the Party so to be outlawed, shall, within one Year next after the said Outlawry pronounced,* [k] *yield himself to the Chief Justice of* England *for the Time being, and offer to traverse the Indictment or Appeal whereon the said Outlawry shall be pronounced as is aforesaid, that then he shall be received to the same Traverse, and being thereupon found not guilty by the Verdict of twelve Men, he shall be clearly acquitted and discharged of the said Outlawry, &c.*

Sect. 8. And it hath been [l] resolved, that these Statutes extend as well to Treasons by subsequent Statutes as to those within 25 *Ed.* 3.

Sect. 9. It seems generally agreed, That any Outlawry whatsoever may be avoided by a Defendant's Coming in upon the [m] *Capias Utlagatum*, and pleading a [n] Misnosmer either of the Name or Addition in the Writ, *&c.* as by shewing that whereas he is called by such a Name of [o] Baptism, or [p] Surname, he hath been always known by a different one, and not by that in the Writ, *&c.* or whereas he is named of such Estate, Degree, or Mystery, that he hath some other [q] Addition, and not that in the Writ, *&c.* Also it is said in many [r] Books, that he may plead, that there is no such Town as that whereof he is named. And it seems clearly agreed, That he may plead that at the Time of the Writ purchased, and ever since, he hath made his Abode at some [s] other Town, and not at that in the Writ, *&c.*

[a] 29 Ed. 3. 25. a. 1 Rol. A. 489. Letter Y.
[b] Co. L. 269. b. V. 10. H. 4. 7. a. Abridged Fitz. Respon. 101.
[c] Fitz. Utl. 2, 11, 18, 27. 33 H. 6. 1. b. 7 H. 6. 25. a. Br. Utl. 18, 40. 38 Ass. pl. 17. 27 Ass. pl. 47. Vide Fitz. Coro. 123. 8 H. 4. 13. b. 3 Inst. 32. Cont. 21 Ed. 4. 73. b. Bro. Utl. 57. 1 H. 7. 13. Bro. Utlaga. 68. Coro. 128. That he who pleads this Plea must shew in whose Custody he was, and in what County, and must also aver his Plea; and by 5 Ed. 3. 13. an Averment is given against the Testimony of a Sheriff or others, having no Record testifying such Imprisonment.

[d] Fitz. Utl. 11. 2 E. 4. 1. a. b. Abridged Fitz. Respond. 54. 9 H. 4. 3. a. Fitz. Scire Facias, 64. 11 H. 7. 5. a. Bro. Utl. 79. 4 Ed. 4. 10. b. Cont. Fitz. Coro. 123. Vide 10 H. 4. 7. a. Abridged Fitz. Ref. 201. Co. 31. b. Co. Lit. 74. a. [e] Skin. 16. Fitz. Utlagary, 2, 48. Forfeiture, 19. Respond. 54, 101. 7 H. 6. 25. a. Abridged Bro. Utlagary, 18. 16 Ed. 4. 6. a. [f] Co. Lit. 259. b. [g] Vide infra sect. 9. [h] Not by the Plea of Imprisonment. Fitz. Utl. 27, 47. 33 H. 6. 1. b. 45. a. Nor by the Plea of being beyond Sea. Fitz. Utl. 27. 33 H. 6. 1. 45. a. [i] 5 & 6. E. 6. 4. [k] Vide State Trials. V. 3. f. 335. 3 Mod. 47. and Skin. 195. Sir Tho. Armstrong's Case. [l] 3 Inst. 32, 216. But see Dyer, 287. pl. 48. See also 2 Jon. 180. Error assigned for the Reversal of an Outlawry of High Treason, that the Defendant was beyond Sea at the Time. [m] 33 H. 6. 1. b. 38. 45 a. Fitz. Utlagary, 22, 23, 26, 27, 29, 32, 35, 37, 44. Nonsuit, 6. Estoppel, 47, 54, 67. Dyer 192. pl. 25. Bro. Utlagary, 1, 22, 23, 24, 25, 26. Misnosmer, 52. 1 Ed. 4. 2. b. 21 H. 6. 50. b. 5 H. 7. 16. a. 7 Ed. 4. 1. 27 H. 8. 11, 12. 22 H. 6. 23. a. 19 H. 6. 80. a. b. 5 H. 5. 7. b. 28 H. 6. 2. b. Vide Fitz. Variance, 74. 19 H. 6. 58. a. 22 Ed. 4. 37, 38. [n] 33 H. 6. 1. b. 45. a. But in the Abridgment of this Case, Bro. Utlagary, 2. The contrary seems to be holden Fitz. Utlagary, 27. [o] Fitz. Utlagary, 44. Bro. Utlagary, 1. 27 H. 8. 11, 12. [p] 14 Ed. 4. 6. b. Bro. Utlagary, 53. 19 Ed. 4. 24, 25. Bro. Scire Facias, 132. Misnosmer, 1. 27 H. 8. 11, 12. 12 H. 6. 7. b. So if one be called in the Writ the Son of J. S. he may plead that he is the Son of W. S. 10 Ed. 4. 12. b. Bro. Idempnitate nominis, 9. [q] Fitz. Nonsuit, 6. Estoppel, 47, 67. 1 Ed. 4. 2. b. 21 H. 6. 50. b. 28 H. 6. 2. b. Fitz. Utlagary, 32, 35, 37. Bro. Utlagary, 15, 24, 78. Misnos. 52. 5 H. 7. 16. a. 7 Ed. 4. 1. 5 H. 5. 7. b. Abridged Bro. Utl. 15. Fitz. Utl. 37. But 'tis there said, that some were of Opinion, That the Party should be put to his Writ of Error, because he is the same Person. See 38 H. 6. 1. Bro. Utl. 32, 51. 10 Ed. 4. 16. a. Bro. Scire Facias, 132. 9 Ed. 4. 24, 25. [r] Fitz. Utl. 23, 26. 22 Ed. 4. 37. b. 22 H. 6. 23 a. 33 H. 6. 51. a. Bro. Utl. 26. the 2d. Vide Rast. Entr. 300. pl. 24. 301. pl. 25, 26. But the contrary is holden 33 H. 6. 1. b. Because such Plea would avoid the Outlawry against all Persons. Bro. Utl. 29. There is an Opinion to the contrary, but it seems not warranted by the Year-Book. [s] Fitz. Utl. 22, 23, 25, 29, 30, 33. Estoppel, 54. Error, 23. 38 H. 6. 1. a. b. 28 H. 6. 2. a b. 33 H. 6. 38. 22 H. 6. 7. a. 16. a. 23. a. b. 19 H. 6. 80. a. b. Dyer 192. pl. 25. 2 E. 4. 1. b. Bro. Utl. 22, 25, 32, 33, 58. 21 Ed. 4. 79. Keil. 101. Such Matter is pleaded without any Traverse of the Place in the Indictment. Vide 22 E. 4. 37, 38. 20 H. 6. 19. b. It is adjudged 28 H. 6. Abridged Fitz. Utl. 25. That it is no Plea for one named of the Parish of C. that there are 3 Vills in the same Parish, viz. D. E. F. and that he was commorant at D. and therefore ought to have been named of it.

and it is [a] ſaid, That by ſuch Plea, the Outlawry ſhall only be avoided as to the Perſon who pleads it, (who ſhall [b] not be intended to be the Perſon meant) and ſhall ſtand in Force againſt the Perſon of the Name and Addition in the Record. But it is ſaid, That a Perſon of the ſame Name and Addition as are mentioned in a Record of Outlawry, [c] cannot avoid it by averring that there are two Perſons of ſuch Name and Addition, and that the Perſon intended is the Elder, and he himſelf is the Younger, but ſhall be put to his Writ of *idempnitate nominis*, which is ſaid by ſome to be the [d] only Remedy in ſuch Caſe after an Outlawry returned. And it ſeems, That notwithſtanding in Civil Cauſes [e] before an Outlawry is returned, one of the ſame Name may come into Court, and ſhew [f] that he is not the Perſon intended; whereupon if the Plaintiff confeſs it, the Diverſity of the Names ſhall be entered on the Roll, and a new Exigent ſhall iſſue with a fuller Deſcription of the Perſon intended: Yet this [g] cannot be done upon an Indictment, without a Writ of *idempnitate nominis*, becauſe it would make the Proceſs variant from the Indictment, which cannot be altered without the Conſent of the Jurors.

And now I am to ſhew how Judgments in Criminal Caſes may be avoided by Writs of Error; as to which having ſhewn already, *Ch.* 29. *Sect.* 40. That the Reverſal of the Attainder of the Principal *ipſo facto* reverſes that of the Acceſſary, I ſhall in this Place only obſerve the following Particulars.

Sect. 10. *1ſt*, That it ſeems to be in a great Meaſure [h] ſettled, That a Writ of Error to reverſe an Attainder of Treaſon or Felony, may be brought as well by the Executor as by the Heir of the Party, but [i] no other Perſon whatſoever.

Sect. 11. *2dly*, That a Perſon attainted of Treaſon or Felony, before he can have a writ of Error to reverſe his attainder, muſt [k] aſſign his Errors, and thereupon have Leave from the Court to proſecute his Writ of Error.

Sect. 12. *3dly*, That no Writ of Error for the Reverſal of an Attainder of Treaſon or Felony is to be [l] allowed without an expreſs Warrant from the King, or the Conſent of the Attorney General.

Sect. 13. *4thly*, That an Attainder of Felony of a Perſon who had any Lands, ſhall never be reverſed by Writ of Error [m] without a *Scire facias* againſt all the Ter-tenants and Lords mediate and immediate; but it is [n] ſettled, That ſuch *Scire facias* is not neceſſary in the Caſe of High Treaſon. Alſo it is [o] ſaid, That it is not neceſſary in the Caſe of Felony when it is ſuggeſted on the Roll that the Party had no Lands, and the Attorney General confeſſes it.

Sect. 14. *5thly*, That it hath been [p] ſettled, That the Statute of 33 *H.* 8. 29. which enacts, *That if any Perſon ſhall be attainted of High Treaſon by the Courſe of the Common Laws or Statutes of this Realm, that in every ſuch Caſe, every ſuch Attainder by the Common Law ſhall be of as good Strength, Value, Force and Effect, as if it had been done by Authority of Parliament*, is to be intended of lawful Attainders by due Courſe of the Common Law, and not of erroneous and void Attainders, which therefore may be avoided in the ſame Manner as before.

[a] 39 H.6.1.b. Bro. Utl. 34. 73. 10 H. 6. 4. b. 30H.6.2.pl 9. Fitz. Er. 23. 21 H. 7. 13. pl. 16. But it is ſaid, 21 H. 6. 21. b. Abridged Fitz' Scire facias, 55. Bro. Utl. 23. That a Cap. ad ſatisfac. the Judgment is affirmed or diſaffirmed by the Affirmance or Avoidance of the Outlawry. Vide 22 H.6. 16. a. Bro. Utl. 25. 19 H. 6. 58. a. b. Fitz. Utl. 21.
[b] And for this Cauſe this is a good Plea in Avoidance of the Plea of Outlawry in Diſability. Fitz. Nonability, 14. 21 H. 7. 13. pl. 16. 7 E. 4. 1. Br. Nona. 50.
[c] 21 H. 7. 13. pl. 16. 14H.4.27.a.b. Fitz. Idempn. nominis, 2. 3. Vide Bro.Utl. 29, 55, 56. 21 Ed. 4. 15. a. 54. a. 13 H. 6. 7. b. Fitz. Utl. 1, 24, 43. Variance, 74.
[d] Fitz. Utl. 6. 16. Reſp. 21. Nona. 17
[e] 21 E.4.15.a. 13 H. 7.12.a. Bro. Idempn. nominis, 3. 5, 7, 8. Fitz. Idempn. nomi. 3, 6, 7. Cont. F. N. B. 268. Lett. B.

[f] F. N. B. 268. Lett A. Bro. Idemp nominis, 3, 4, 11. 14 H. 4. 27. Fitz. Idemp. nominis, 5. 21 Ed. 3. 36. b. Cont. Fitz. Idemp. nominis, 4. Bro. Idemp. nominis, 6. Long quinto Ed. 4. 51. [g] Fitz. Idemp. nominis, 3. F. N. B. 268. Lett. B. Bro. Idemp. nominis, 2, 11. 9 H. 4. 3. [h] Cro. El. 225, 273, 558. 5 Co. 111. a. Owen 147, 148. 1 Leon. 325, 326. Salk. 295. Shower 13. [i] Vide Salk. 60, 61. [k] 1 H. 7. 13. b. Bro. Err. 135. [l] 1 Sid. 69. 1 Bulſt. 71. 3 Mod. 42. 1 Ro. Rep. 175. [m] Dy. 34. pl. 20. 1 Keb. 141. pl. 11. 1 Sid. 316. 22 E. 4. 37. b. 3 Keb. 29. 4 E. 4. 10. pl. 14. Fitz. Err. 52. 7 H. 7. 5. b. 4 Ed. 4. 10. pl. 14. [n] The Queen and Strafford, Mich. 12 Annæ, upon Examination of all the Precedents. [o] 2 Salk. 495. pl. 5. Vide 3 Keb. 29. [p] 3 Inſt. 214, 215. 1 H. H. P. C. 353.

[a] Which is called the 29th in the printed Statutes by a Mistake. 3. Lev. 333. [b] 3 Inst. 31. 213. 1 H. H. P. C. 353. [c] 1 Sid. 208.

Sect. 15. *6thly*, That it is also clear, That the Statute of [a] 28 *Eliz.* 2. which enacts, *That no Record of Attainder that then was of High Treason, where the Party is or hath been executed, shall be reversed, avoided or impeached by any Plea or Writ of Error*, extends not [b] to Attainders since that Time.

Sect. 16. *7thly*, [c] That it hath been holden, That a Writ of Error lies in the King's Bench of an Attainder before the Lord High Steward.

And now I am in the second Place to shew the Effect of the Avoidance of a Judgment, as to which I shall take Notice only of the following Particulars.

[d] Bro. Coro. 27, 143 or 144. 164, or 165. 7 H. 7. 5. pl. 7. 18 Ed. 4. 9. pl. 16. 3 Mod. 42. Cro. Ja. 464. Fitz. Error, 52. Cro. Ca. 365. [e] That the Law is the same in civil Causes. Fitz. Err. 41.

Sect. 17. *1st*, That it is [d] agreed, That after an Outlawry of Treason or Felony is reversed, the Party shall be put to [e] plead to the Indictment, for that still remains good.

Sect. 18. *2dly*, That it is said by Sir *Edward Coke*, If the Judgment be erroneous, both that, and the Execution thereupon, and all former Proceedings shall be [f] reversed by Writ of Error; but if the Execution be erroneous that only shall be reversed.

Sect. 19. *3dly* That it hath been [g] adjudged, That if the King grant over the Lands of a Person outlawed for Treason or Felony, and afterwards the Outlawry be reversed, the Party may enter on the Patentee, and needs neither to sue a Petition to the King, nor a *Scire facias* against the Patentee.

37 H. 6. 17. Bro. Utlagary, 28. 20 H. 6. 3. a. Abridged Fitz. Protection, 11. Bro. Utlagary, 74. Contra 21 H. 6. 50. pl. 3. Abridged Fitz. Nonsuit, 6. Bro. Utlagary, 24. Vide Bro. Utlagary, 35. [f] 3 Inst. 2, 10. [g] 1 And. 188.

CHAP. LI.

Of Execution and Reprieve.

AND now nothing remains but to shew in what Manner a Person condemned is to be executed or reprieved; as to which, having shewn already, *Ch.* 30. *Sect.* 8. That a Person attainted, standing mute to a Demand why Execution shall not go against him, shall not be awarded to his Penance, but to the ordinary Execution proper for the Crime, I shall farther observe only the following Particulars,

[a] 1 Sid. 72. 1 Lev. 61. 1 Keb. 244. Supra ch. 44. sect. 18.

Sect. 1. *First*, That the Court of King's Bench hath not only Power to award Execution against Persons attainted there, but also against Persons attainted in [a] Parliament, or any other [b] Court, the Record of their Attainder, or a Transcript thereof, being first [c] removed into the Court of King's Bench, and themselves brought thither by [d] *Habeas Corpus*.

[b] 2 H. H. P. C. 4. Poph. 131. Cro. Ca. 176. Cro. Ja. 495. [c] Cro. Ca. 176. Cro. Ja. 495. 1 Sid. 72. 1 Lev. 61. 1 Keb. 244. [d] Cro. Ca. 176. Cro. Ja. 495. 1 Sid. 72, 73.

Sect. 2. 2*dly*, That Execution ought [a] not to be awarded into a different County from that wherein the Party was tried and convicted, except only where a Record of Attainder is removed into the Court of King's Bench, which [b] may award the Execution in the same County wherein it sits.

Sect. 3. 3*dly*, That where a Person attainted hath been at large after his Attainder, and afterwards is brought into Court and demanded why Execution should not be awarded against him, [c] if he deny that he is the same Person, it shall be [d] immediately tried by a Jury returned for that Purpose.

Sect. 4. 4*thly*, That the Court [e] may command Execution to be done without any Writ.

Sect. 5. 5*thly*, That it is [f] holden by *Coke* and *Hale*, That no Execution can be warranted unless it be pursuant to the Judgment, and therefore that it cannot be altered by the King, as from hanging to beheading. Yet since there is a great Number of Precedents, where [g] Men condemned to be hanged for Felony, and Women condemned to be burnt [h] for Treason, have been beheaded by Force of a special Warrant from the King to that Purpose; and since [i] *Bracton* and [k] *Staundforde* and the [l] *Year-Book* of 35 *H.* 6. speaking of this Matter, are not so express as *Coke* and *Hale*, but say only in general, That the Sheriff cannot lawfully behead a Man who is only condemned to be hanged; by which they may perhaps intend no more than that he cannot lawfully do it of his own Authority; I shall leave this Matter to be farther considered. However it is agreed, That where Beheading is Part of the Judgment, as in Case of High Treason, the King may [m] pardon all the rest, and consequently in such Case the Judgment will be well executed by Beheading only.

Sect. 6. 6*thly*, That it seems [n] agreed at this Day, That an Execution cannot be lawfully executed by any but the proper Officer.

Sect. 7. 7*thly*, That it is [o] clear, That if a Man condemned to be hanged, come to Life after he be hanged, he ought to be hanged again; for the Judgment was not Executed 'till he was dead.

Sect. 8. 8*thly*, That it seems agreed, That every Court which has Power to award an Execution, has also of Common Right a discretionary Power of granting a Reprieve; as [p] where a Person pleads a Pardon defective in Point of Form, but sufficiently shewing the King's Intention of Mercy; or where it is [q] doubtful whether the Offence be not included in a general Statute-Pardon; or [r] whether as it is laid in the Indictment, it amounts to so high a Crime, as that with which the Prisoner was charged. And it seems [s] agreed at this Day, that Judges continue to have this Power after their Commission is determined.

[a] Cro. Ca. 176. 3 Mod. 124, 125.

[b] Co. Ca. 176. Cro. Ja. 495.

[c] Poph. 131. Cro. Ca. 176. Cro. Ja. 495. Crompt. Just. 183. b. 2 H. H. P. C. 407.

[d] 1 Sid. 72. 1 Lev. 61.

Whether the Party may have peremptory Challenges on such a Trial. Supra ch. 43. sect. 6.

[e] Finch of Law 478. 3 Mod. 42. 2 H. H. P. C. 409.

But sometimes Execution is commanded by Writ, as in Sir Walter Raleigh's Case. Cro. Ja. 496. and in Lord Stafford's Case, State Trials, Vol. 2. f. 704, 705. being both in the Custody of the Lieutenant of the Tower, and beheaded only.

[f] 3 Inst. 52. 211, 212, 217. 12 Co. 130. H. P. C. 272. 2 H. H. P. C. 411. and accordingly Lord Dacres, Lord Stourton, and Sanchar, a Scotch Lord, were hanged for Murder. 3 Inst. 211, 212. 9 Co. 121. b. [g] Lord Hungerford in 32 H. 8. 3 Inst. 211. Duke of Somerset in 5 Ed. 6. 3 Inst. 211. Lord Audley in 6 Car. 1. State Trials, Vol. 1. f. 271. [h] Queen Catherine Howard, Lady Jane Grey, Countess of Salisbury, Lady Alice Lisle. [i] Bracton 104. b. Vide 3 Inst. 217. [k] S. P. C. 13. a, [l] 35 H. 6. 38. [m] H. P. C. 273. 3 Inst. 31, 52, 212. 12 Co. 130. Supra ch. 37. sect. 12. 3 Inst. 31. It is said, That such a Pardon must be under the Great Seal; but it seems admitted, that it may be by Writ. State Trials, Vol. 2. f. 704, 705. [n] See B. 1. ch. 28. sect. 8, 9. 2 H. H. P. C. 411. [o] 6 Ed. 4. 4. Fitz. Coro. 335. Finch of Law 389, 467. 2 H. H. P. C. 412. Vide supra ch. 48. sect. 7. [p] 26 Ass. pl. 46. Abridged Fitz. Office de Court, 34. [q] Dy. 235. pl. 19. [r] Dy. 295. pl. 2[illegible]. [s] Dy. 205. pl 5. Supra ch. 6. sect. 7.

[a] H. P. C. 272. 2 H. H. P. C. 413. 3 Inst. 17. [b] Quære if before Justices of Peace, Keilw. 51. a. [c] S.P.C. 198. Letter C. 22 Ass. pl. 71. Abridged Fitz. Coro. 180. Bro. Coro. 88. [d] 3 Inst. 17. Finch of Law 478.

Sect. 9. 9*thly*, That it is clear, That if a Woman quick with Child be condemned either for [a] Treason or [b] Felony, she may alledge her being with Child in Order to get the Execution respited, and thereupon the Sheriff [c] or Marshal shall be commanded to take her into a private Room, and to impanel a Jury of [d] Matrons to try and examine whether she be quick with Child or not; and if they find her quick with Child, the Execution shall be respited [e] 'till her Delivery. But it is agreed, That a Woman [f] cannot demand such Respite of Execution by Reason of her being quick with Child more than once; and that she can neither save herself by this Means from [g] pleading upon her Arraignment, nor from having [h] Judgment pronounced against her upon her Conviction. Also it is said both by [i] *Staundford* and *Coke*, That a Woman can have no Advantage from being found with Child, unless she be also found quick with Child.

S. P. C. 198. Letter. C. [e] State Trials Vol. 4. f. 612. S. P. C. 198. Letter C. 3 Inst. 17. State Trials, Vol. 4. f. 612. Fitz. Coro. 253, 410. 23 Ass. pl. 2. Abridged Bro. Coro. 97. Fitz. Coro. 188. 25 Ed. 3. 42. b. Abridged Fitz. Coro. 130. 12 Ass. pl. 11. Abridged Fitz. Coro. 168. Bro. Coro. 72. Bro. Pain, 11. [f] Finch of Law 478. S. P. C. 198. Letter C. Fitz. Coro. 168, 253. 3 Inst. 17. H. P. C. 272. 23 Ass. pl. 2. Abridged Bro. Coro. 97. Fitz. Coro. 188. 25 Ed. 3. 42. b. Abridged Fitz. Coro. 130. 12 Ass. 11. Bro. Coro. 72. Pain, 11. [g] Finch of Law 478. 3 Inst. 17. 22 Ass. pl. 71. Abridged Fitz. Coro. 180. Bro. Coro. 88. [h] State Trials, Vol. 4. f. 611. S. P. C. 198. Letter C. 3 Inst. 17. 2 H. H. P. C. 413. [i] 3 Inst. 17. S. P. C. 198. Letter C. and in 22 Ass. pl. 71. Abridged Fitz. Coro. 180. Bro. Coro. 88. it is expresly said, That the Inquiry was whether the Woman were enseint with a live Child or not. See also H. P. C. 272. and Finch of Law 478. Yet Fitz. Coro. 120, 168, 388, 240, 410. 22 Ass. pl. 2. 25 Ed. 3. 42. b. 12 Ass. pl. 11. Bro. Coro. 72. Bro. Pain, 11. 'tis said only, That the Woman was found enseint or pregnant.

F I N I S.

Notes and Additions to the Second Book.

THE Court of Honour is no Court of Record, and therefore cannot enforce the Payment of a Fine by Impriſonment, *Far.* 128. where (*Page* 125 *to* 129.) ſee the Caſe of a Prohibition upon a Suit by Libel in this Court, for ſcandalous Words, and the ſame Caſe in *Salk.* 553. Page 14. N° [1]

2 *H. H. P. C.* 35. ſays, only that Juſtices of *Gaol-Delivery* may receive Appeals by Bill againſt any Perſon being in Gaol. In the Beginning of the ſame Page indeed it is ſaid, that the Juſtices of *Gaol-Delivery* may take an Indictment againſt one let to Bail, as well as if he were actually in Gaol. But the Books there cited do not ſupport this Opinion; for 39 *H.* 6. 27. *b.* and 9 *Ed.* 4. 2. *a.* ſeem only to prove that one mainpriſed is not ſuppoſed in Cuſtody; and 21 *H.* 7. 33. *a.* proves no more, than that if one *in cuſtodia Mareſchalli* be let to Bail, yet he ſhall anſwer a Bill; and this is ſaid to be *per curſum curiæ.* Page 25. N° [2]

The Opinion, that Juſtices of Aſſiſe may deliver Gaols without any ſpecial Commiſſion, is taken Notice of in 2 *H. H. P. C.* 403. but it is farther obſerved, that this has not been uſed, and that it is not ſafe without a Commiſſion of *Gaol-Delivery.* Page 29. N° [3]

By Stat. 9 Geo. 1. c. 7. ſect. 3. For the greater Eaſe of Juſtices of Peace for Counties, it is enacted, *That if any Juſtice of Peace ſhall happen to dwell in any City, or other Precinct, that is a County of itſelf, ſituate within the County at large, for which he ſhall be appointed Juſtice of Peace, although not within the ſame County, it ſhall be lawful for any ſuch Juſtice to grant Warrants, or Orders, at his own Dwelling-Houſe, tho' out of the County where he is authorized to act as a Juſtice of Peace, and in ſome City or Precinct adjoining, that is a County of itſelf; and that all ſuch Warrants or Orders, and the Acts of any Conſtable, Overſeer of the Poor, Surveyor of the Highways,* &c. *in Obedience to ſuch Warrant or Order, ſhall be good and effectual in Law. Provided that nothing in this Act ſhall extend to give Power to the Juſtices of Peace for the Counties at large, to hold their General Quarter-Seſſions of the Peace, in Cities or Towns, which are Counties of themſelves, nor to impower Juſtices of Peace, Sheriffs, Conſtables, or other Peace Officers, to act in any Matters ariſing within ſuch Cities or Towns, but that all ſuch Actings ſhall be of the ſame Effect, and no other, as if this Act had never been made.* Page 37. N° [4]

The Chief Juſtice of the King's Bench is, by Virtue of his Office, the Chief Coroner of *England,* 2 *H. H. P. C.* 53. and *ibid. p.* 5. the like is affirmed of the Court of King's Bench, which therefore may take Appeals of Death, *&c.* by Bill. 4 *Inſt.* 73. Page 42. N° [5]

By chooſing another Coroner, the Power and Authority of the firſt *ipſo facto* ceaſes. *Godb.* 105. Page 44. N° [6]

The Coroner of the Verge was antiently appointed by the King's Letters Patent. 2 *H. H. P. C.* 54. Page 46. N° [7]

It is a Matter indictable, to bury a Man that dies a violent Death, before the Coroner's Inqueſt have ſat upon him. *Far.* 10. *per Holt.* Page 48. N° [8]

In 2 *H. H. P C.* 65, 66. It is expreſly ſaid, that the Coroner hath no Power to take an Inquiſition of any other Felony, than the Death of a Man; only by the Cuſtom of *Northumberland,* the Coroner has Power to inquire of other Felonies. 35 *H.* 6. 27. *b.* Page 50. N° [9]

Though by *Magna Charta, c.* 17. the Coroner cannot determine the Appeal; yet he may outlaw the Defendant. 2 *H. H. P. C.* 67. Page 51. N° [10]

Sir *Matthew Hale* ſays, That the Coroner being the principal Judge, a *Certiorari* to remove a Bill of Appeal may be directed to him alone. 2 *H. H. P. C.* 67. Page 51. N° [11]

If there be two Coroners in a County, one may execute the Writ, as in Caſe of an *Exigent,* but the Return muſt be in the Name of both. 2 *H. H. P. C.* 56. Page 52. N° [12]

Page 53. N° [13] The Reason given in 1 *H. H. P. C.* 363. why the Finding of the Jury at the Trial (as to the Flight) shall not avoid the Coroner's Inquisition, is, because the latter is best for the King; and *Fitz. Forfeiture*, 35. seems agreeable to this.

Page 54. N° [14] If the Inquisition *super visum Corporis* had been quashed a long Time (as a Year) after the Death, a *Melius inquirendum* might have been granted, but not another Inquisition *super visum, &c.* yet where the Coroner had actually taken such other Inquisition, a *Melius inquirendum* was denied; for *factum valet quod fieri non debet.* Carth. 72.

If the Coroner's Inquest find the Death of the Party to be *per Infortunium*, and it be suggested on the Part of the King, or Almoner, that he was *felo de se*; yet a *Melius inquirendum* ought not to be granted; and if granted, and an Inquisition taken, it has been held void. 2 *And.* 204. by the Stat. 28 *Ed.* 3. *c.* 9. 1 *H. H. P. C.* 415. 2 *H. H. P. C.* 59, 69.

Page 62. N° [15] 2 *H. H. P. C.* 88. says generally, That by Law a Constable may make a Deputy, and he is within the 7 *Jac.* 5. to plead the general Issue. *Moor* 845. *pl.* 1141. Yet in 1 *H. H. P. C.* 581. it is said, That if a Warrant be directed to a Constable, he must execute it himself, and may not substitute another.

Page 75. N° [16] By the Stat. 8 Geo. 2. c. 16. (for the Amendment of the Law relating to Actions on the Statute of Hue and Cry) it is enacted, sect. 1. *That no Person shall maintain any Action against any Hundred, by Virtue of the Statutes* 13 Ed. 1. *and* 27 Eliz. c. 13. *unless he shall, over and besides the Notice already required, with as much convenient Speed as may be, after any Robbery on him committed, give Notice thereof to one of the Constables of the Hundred, or to some Constable, Bosholder, Headborough, or Tithingman of some Town, Parish or Tithing, near the Place wherein such Robbery shall happen, or shall leave Notice in Writing at the Dwelling-House of such Constable,* &c. *describing in such Notice, so far as the Circumstances of the Case will admit, the Felons, and the Time and Place of the Robbery; and also shall, within twenty Days, cause Notice to be given in the* London Gazette, *therein likewise describing the Felons, and the Time and Place, together with the Goods whereof he was robbed; and shall also, before Action be commenced, go before the chief Clerk or Secondary, or the Filazer of the County wherein such Robbery shall happen, or the Clerk of the Pleas of that Court, wherein such Action is intended to be brought, or before the Sheriff of the County, and enter into a Bond to the High Constable of the Hundred, in the penal Sum of* 100 l. *with two sufficient Sureties to be approved of by such chief Clerk,* &c. *with Condition for securing to such High Constable (who is required to enter an Appearance, and defend such Action) the Payment of Costs, in Case Judgment shall be against such Plaintiff.*

And it is farther enacted by the said Statute, sect. 11. *That every Constable, Bosholder, Headborough, or Tithingman, to whom Notice shall be given, and every Constable,* &c. *of any Town, Parish, Hamlet or Tithing, within the Hundred, or the Franchises within the Precinct thereof, wherein such Robbery shall happen, as soon as the same shall come to his Knowledge, shall with the utmost Expedition make fresh Suit, and Hue and Cry after the Felons; and if any Constable,* &c. *shall offend in the Premisses, every such Offender shall forfeit* 5 l.

Sect. 12. *Every Forfeiture hereby incurred shall be recovered with Costs, and shall be one Moiety to the King's Majesty, and the other Moiety to such Person who shall sue for the same within six Months after such Forfeiture incurred.*

Page 77. N° [17] But an Assault, with an Intent to rob, is now made Felony, by 7 *Geo.* 2. *c.* 21. *See the Additions to Book* 1. N° [37]

Page 77. N° [18] It seems, that to make an Arrest of a Night-Walker justifiable, there ought to be probable Causes of Suspicion; and so it was ruled in the Case of the *Queen* and *Tooley*, *Mich.* 1709. for the Murder of *Dent*, who was killed in aiding the Constable, who had taken up a Woman walking the Street, upon Suspicion of her being of ill Fame. C. J. *Holt* delivered the Opinion of the Court, that it was not Murder, and that it was not lawful, even for a legal Constable, to take up a Woman upon a bare Suspicion only, having been guilty of no Breach of the Peace nor any unlawful Act. 2 *H. H. P. C.* 89. *in Notis.*

Page 79. N° [19] By Stat. 9 Geo. 1. c. 22. sect. 12. it is enacted, *That if any Person shall apprehend or, cause to be convicted, any of the Offenders against this Act*, (commonly called the Black Act; See the Additions to Book 1. N° [66]) *and shall be killed,, or wounded so as to lose an Eye, or the Use of any Limb, in apprehending, or endeavouring to apprehend, any such Offenders, upon Proof thereof made at the General Quarter-Sessions of the Coun-*

ty, &c. *The Justices shall give a Certificate thereof to such Person so wounded, or to the Executors or Administrators of the Person killed, by which he or they shall be intitled to receive of the Sheriff of the said County* fifty Pounds, *which Sum the Sheriff is required to pay within thirty Days, from the Day on which the said Certificate shall be shewn to him, under the Penalty of forfeiting* 10 l. *to the Persons to whom such Certificate is given, for which* 10 l. *as well as for the* 50 l. *such Person is authorized to bring an Action on the Case*, &c. *against the Sheriff.*

By the Stat. 8 Geo. 2. c. 16. (*for the Amendment of the Law relating to Actions on the Statute of Hue and Cry*) Any Person who shall apprehend a Felon within the Time limited by that Act, whereby the Hundred shall be discharged, shall be intitled to a Reward of *ten Pounds* which shall be raised on the Hundred by a Taxation. Page 79. N° [20]

It having been enacted by Stat. 9 Geo. 2. c. 35. (*for preventing the Clandestine running of Goods*) sect. 10. set forth more at large in the Additions to B. 1. N° [76] that any Persons, to the Number of three or more, armed with Fire Arms, *&c.* assisting in the clandestine running of Goods, should be guilty of Felony, It is farther enacted,

Sect. 11. *That every Person who shall apprehend any Person guilty of the Offences last mentioned, shall have, for every Offender convicted,* 50 l. *and if any Person shall be maimed, or dangerously wounded, in endeavouring to apprehend such Offenders, every Person so maimed or wounded, shall, upon such Conviction, have* 50 l. *over and above any other Reward; and in Case any Person shall be killed in Pursuit after such Offenders, the Executors or Administrators of such Person killed (upon Certificate of the Justices of Assize, or the two next Justices of Peace, of such Person's being so killed) shall have* 50 l. *over and above any other Reward.*

Sect. 15. *If any Officer of the Customs or Excise shall be maimed, or dangerously wounded, by any Offenders herein last mentioned (in* sect. 13. See the Additions to B. 1. N° [76]) *in the Execution of his Office, or in apprehending such Offenders, all such Officers and Persons so maimed and wounded, shall, upon the Conviction of such Offenders, have* 50 l. *over and above any other Reward; and in Case any Person be killed in the apprehending such Offenders, the Executors or Administrators of such Person killed, (upon Certificate of the Justices of Assize, or the two next Justices of Peace) shall have* 50 l. *over and above any other Reward.*

And it is to be observed, that not only the Apprehending, but also the Discovering and Convicting Runners of Foreign Goods, is rewarded; for which Purpose it is enacted by Stat. 8 Geo. 1. c. 18. sect. 8. *That any Person discovering and convicting a Runner of Foreign Goods* (within that Act) *shall have* 40 l. *over and above any other Reward he may be intitled to, on Account of Goods conveyed away, which shall be recovered by Means of such Discovery, or on Account of the Penalties recovered for the Running the said Goods, so as the Value of such Goods recovered for the Use of his Majesty shall exceed* 50 l.

And by Stat. 9 Geo. 2. c. 35. sect. 16. it is enacted, *That if any Person shall, within three Months after any of the Offences last mentioned (in* sect. 13. See the Additions in B. 1. N° [76]) *have been committed, discover to the Commissioners of the Customs or Excise, any Person guilty of such Offence, so as such Offender be convicted, such Discoverer shall have* 50 l. *for every Offender so convicted, over and above any other Reward.*

The Opinion of Sir *Edward Coke* 4 *Inst.* 177. taken Notice of in this Section, seems to be adopted by Sir *Matthew Hale* in his *Summary of the Pleas of the Crown*; but his *Historia Placitorum Coronæ, Vol.* 1. *p.* 579, 580, 583. and *Vol.* 2. *p.* 79, 80, 107 *to* 110. is very full to the contrary, and *Vol.* 2. *p.* 119. he says, If a Justice of Peace have Jurisdiction in the Case, (as in Felonies and Breaches of the Peace, and even in High Treason, so far as it is a Breach of the Peace) tho' he err in granting his Warrant, yet the Officer that executes it is excusable. Page 83. N° [21]

An Arrest by a Constable, or other Person, by the Command, and in the Presence of a Justice of Peace, without any Warrant, or any Cause alledged, was held justifiable. *Moor* 408. *pl.* 551. 1 *H. H. P. C.* 585. Page 83. N° [22]

As to Warrants to search for stolen Goods, Sir *Matthew Hale* lays down these Rules. 1st, That they are not to be granted without Oath, made before a Justice, of a Felony committed, and that the Party complaining has probable Cause to suspect they are in such a House or Place, and do shew his Reasons for his Suspicion; and therefore Page 84. N° [23]

therefore a general Warrant to ſearch all ſuſpected Places is not good; nor are general Warrants dormant, which are many Times made before any Felony committed, juſtifiable, nor do they give any more power to the Officer or Party, than what he had without them. 2dly, It is fit to expreſs, that Search be made in the Day-time. 3dly, They ſhould be directed to Conſtables, *&c.* and not to private Perſons, tho' the Party complaining ſhould be preſent, becauſe he knows his Goods. 4thly, It ought to command, that the Goods found, together with the Party in whoſe Cuſtody they are found, be brought before ſome Juſtice of Peace. 2 *H. H. P. C.* 150.

As to the Execution of ſuch Warrant, it is there (*p.* 151.) farther laid down, 1ſt, Whether the ſtolen Goods be in the ſuſpected Place, or not, the Officer in the Day-time may enter *per Oſtia aperta.* 2dly, If the Door be ſhut, and upon Demand it be refuſed to be opened, the Officer or Party may juſtify breaking open the Door. 3dly, If the Goods be not in the Houſe, yet it ſeems the Officer is excuſed; but it ſeems the Party that made the Suggeſtion is puniſhable in ſuch a Caſe; for as to him, the Breaking of the Door is *in eventu* lawful, if the Goods be there; unlawful, if not there. See alſo 2 *H. H. P. C.* 113, 114.

Page 85. N° [24] But Sir *Matthew Hale*, in his *Hiſtoria Placitorum Coronæ*, *V.* 2. *p.* 108, 109, 110. aſſerts, not only that a Juſtice of Peace has Power to iſſue a Warrant to apprehend a Perſon accuſed of Felony, though not indicted; but alſo, that he may iſſue a Warrant to apprehend a Perſon ſuſpected of Felony, tho' the original Suſpicion be not in himſelf, but in the Party that prays the Warrant, and he ſays the Reaſon is, becauſe the Juſtice is a competent Judge of the Probabilities offered to him of ſuch Suſpicion. See alſo 1 *H. H. P. C.* 579, 580. where after Mention made of Lord *Coke*'s Opinion, that the Party may arreſt one on his own Suſpicion, but not by Warrant of a Juſtice; it is ſaid, that the Law is not ſo, and that the conſtant Practice is againſt it, and that it would be pernicious to the Kingdom, if it were as Lord *Coke* delivers it.

Page 87. N° [25] But in 1 *H. H. P. C.* 579, 580. it is ſaid, that upon a Warrant for probable Cauſe of Suſpicion of Felony, the Perſon to whom ſuch Warrant is directed may break open Doors to take the Perſon ſuſpected, if upon Demand he will not ſurrender himſelf, as well as if there had been an expreſs and poſitive Charge of Felony ſworn againſt him.

Page 94. N° [26] According to Sir *Matthew Hale*, Lord *Coke*, 2 *Inſt.* 190. in ſaying generally, that *the Writ of Mainprize is taken away*, is certainly miſtaken; for this Writ hath ſtill it's Uſe in Caſes of Perſons committed by Juſtices of Peace, and in ſome other Caſes. See 2 *H. H. P. C.* 142, 143.

Page 96. N° [27] *Mandatum Domini Regis* in the Stat. of *Weſtm.* 1. according to *Hale*, is not intended of the perſonal Command of the King; for regularly, as the King cannot in Perſon arreſt or impriſon, ſo he cannot command another to impriſon; but it muſt be done by ſome Order, Writ, or Proceſs of ſome of his Courts. And though ſuch a Mandate be by Commiſſion under the great Seal, it is void. 2 *H. H. P. C.* 131.

Page 98. N° [28] *Manner*, or *Mainer*, is by Sir *Matthew Hale* called *Mainouvre*, or *Mainovre*, *cum manu opere*, 1 H. H. P. C. 187, 348, 349. 2 H. H. P. C. 133, 156. And Lord *Coke* ſays, it was antiently called *Hand-habbend* and *Backberend*, which *Bracton* and *Britton* uſe for *furtum manifeſtum*. *Quære* if it may not be derived from the *French*, *Main-avoir*, which anſwers to the *Saxon*, *Hand-habbend.*

Page 106. N° [29] It was reſolved by all the Judges in *England*, 7 *Car.* 1. that a Man is not bailable for Manſlaughter; and Chief Juſtice *Hyde* ſet a Fine of 20 *l.* on a Juſtice of Peace, for bailing a Man in ſuch a Caſe, 2 *H. H. P. C.* 138, 139. where it is farther ſaid, that two Juſtices of Peace, whereof one of the *Quorum*, cannot bail, even in the Caſe of *ſe defendendo*, if the Fact be apparent; or if the Party be indicted of Manſlaughter, though but *ſe defendendo*. But that the Statute of *Weſtminſter* 1. which takes away Bail, in Caſes of the Death of a Man, muſt be intended, when the Offender is certainly known; for it generally provides that Perſons taken upon light Suſpicion ſhall be bailed.

Page 111. N° [30] The Caſe here cited from *Shower* 100. is more fully reported in *Carth.* 131, 132, 133. It was the Caſe of the Earl of *Salisbury*, who was impeached for High Treaſon, in the Convention Parliament, 1 *W. & M.* for being reconciled to the Church of *Rome*, and committed to the Tower, where he continued till the next Parliament. And it appears from this Report, that the Parliament was adjourned at the Time of the Motion for bailing the Earl, and that the Court refuſed to bail him, be-

 cauſe

cauſe of the ſhort Adjournment, the Parliament being the proper Place for an Application to that Purpoſe; and as to Lord *Danby*'s Caſe, who was bailed, though committed by the Peers in Parliament, and which was here cited by the Counſel for the Earl, it was ſaid, the chief Reaſon for bailing him was, becauſe the then Parliament was prorogued, and the Time uncertain for it's Meeting again, and ſo no Proſpect of applying himſelf that way; beſides, he was denied to be bailed by ſeveral Judges of *B. R.* until Chief Juſtice *Jefferies* came in. The Court alſo cited the Caſe of Lord *Stafford*, who was committed by the Houſe of Peers, and notwithſtanding the Diſſolution of that Parliament, yet he continued a Priſoner, and was tried upon the ſame Impeachment, convicted and executed; which fully proves, that Commitments by the Peers are not made void by the Prorogation or Diſſolution of the Parliament. This is alſo confirmed by the Caſe of Lord *Danby*, who was bailed to appear at the next Seſſions of Parliament, which was an Affirmance of the Commitment, and a plain Proof of the Opinion of the Court, that the Commitment was not avoided or diſcharged by the Prorogation of the Parliament. As to the Plea of Pardon in this Caſe of the Earl of *Salisbury*, *vide infra* N° [99].

In *Skin.* 56. Lord *Danby*'s Caſe, it is ſaid by *Pemberton*, Ch. Juſt. that if one be detained after a Prorogation, an Action of falſe Impriſonment lies. But ſee the foregoing Caſe of the Earl of *Salisbury*, and *Skin.* 163.

Sir *Matthew Hale* is of Opinion, that the Gaoler may juſtify in falſe Impriſonment, by Virtue of a general Warrant for Felony, and that (contrary to the Opinion of Lord *Coke*) if an Eſcape be ſuffered willingly by the Gaoler, on ſuch Warrant, it will be Felony in him. 2 *H. H. P. C.* 123. This is alſo aſſerted in 1 *H. H. P. C.* 595, 596. which ſays farther, that if the *Mittimus* be general, and contain no certain Cauſe, tho' the Gaoler is not bound to receive the Priſoner upon ſuch *Mittimus*; yet if he be acquainted what the Crime is for which he is committed, and ſuffer him voluntarily to eſcape, it is Felony. For if a private Perſon or Conſtable arreſt a Man for Felony, and carry him to the common Gaol (as he may do, by 13 *Ed.* 4. 9. and the Gaoler is bound to receive him, by 4 *Ed.* 3. *c.* 10.) if the Conſtable, or Perſon that delivers him, acquaints the Gaoler it is for Felony, it is at the Peril of the Gaoler if he lets him eſcape; and yet there is no *Mittimus* in that Caſe, but only Notice *ore tenus*. Page 119. N° [31]

The Omiſſion of the Words, *until he be delivered by due Courſe of Law*, makes no Nullity in a Juſtice of the Peace's *Mittimus*. 3 *Keb.* 531. *New Abr. Vol.* 1. *p.* 381. And according to *Hale*, though a *Mittimus* for Felony want the regular Concluſion (*till he be delivered by due Courſe of Law*) yet this will not excuſe the Breach of Priſon from Felony. 1 *H. H. P. C.* 609. So if the Cauſe be expreſſed, and the Concluſion irregular, *as till farther Order given by the Juſtices*; yet a Breach of Priſon, or voluntary Eſcape, under ſuch Warrant, will be Felony. And ſuch Warrants will be good Juſtifications in falſe Impriſonment. 1 *H. H. P. C.* 584, 595. Page 120. N° [32]

It is alſo to be obſerved, that a Commitment, grounded on an Act of Parliament, ought to be conformable to the Method preſcribed by it. As where the *Mayor of Northampton* committed the Church-wardens for refuſing to account before him, and the Warrant concluded in the common Form, *until they be duly diſcharged according to Law*; upon the Return of an *Habeas Corpus*, the Court held the Commitment void, becauſe the Warrant ought to have concluded, *there to remain until he ſhall account*, as the 43 *Eliz.* 2. appoints. And a Difference is, where a Man is committed as a Criminal, and where only for Contumacy: In the firſt Caſe, the Commitment muſt be until diſcharged according to Law, but in the latter until he comply. *Carth.* 152, 153. So alſo where one *Bracey* was committed by Commiſſioners of the Statute of Bankrupts for refuſing to anſwer, and they concluded their Warrant, *Until he conform himſelf to our Authority, and be thence delivered by due Courſe of Law*; upon the Return of an *Habeas Corpus* he was diſcharged, for the Statute only impowers them to commit *until he ſubmit himſelf to be by them examined.* Carth. 153. Salk. 348. 5 Mod. 308. S. C. Page 120. N° [33]

So in *Yaxley*'s Caſe, who was committed by the *Earl of Nottingham*, *Secretary of State*, by Virtue of 35 *Eliz. c.* 2. for refuſing to anſwer whether he was a *Jeſuit*, *Seminary*, *or Maſſing Prieſt*; the Concluſion of the Commitment being, *there to remain until he ſhall be from thence diſcharged by due Courſe of Law*, when the Words of the Statute are, *until he ſhall anſwer unto the Queſtions.* The Court held the Commitment ill; And they aſking the ſame Queſtions of the Defendant, and he anſwering openly and directly in the Negative, he was discharged. *Carth.* 291. See also the Case of *Baxter*, *Mich.* 20 *Car.* 2. *in C. B. New Abrid. Vol.* 1. *p.* 382.

Page 125. N° [34] A lawful Commitment may be for Suspicion of Felony. 2 *H. H. P. C.* 109, 110. and *supra* N° [24] and is within the Statute *de frangentibus Prisonæ.* 1 H. H. P. C. 610. Notwithstanding the Warrant should want some Formalities. 1 *H. H. P. C.* 609. & *supra* N° [32].

Page 128. N° [35] If a Man be indicted of Felony, and committed, and then breaks Prison, and be arraigned of the principal Felony, and found Not guilty, he shall not be indicted for the Breach of Prison, or if indicted for it, he may plead the Acquittal in Bar to the Felony for Breach of Prison. 1 *H. H. P. C.* 611, 612. 2 *H. H. P. C.* 224, 254, 255.

Page 130. N° [36] If the Prisoner be rescued by Rebels, though this excuse not the Gaoler or Sheriff in civil Actions, because they have their Remedy over; yet it excuses the Gaoler from Felony, and also from a Fine, if it be *vis major, quam cui resisti potest.* 1 H. H. P. C. 596.

Page 131. N° [37] But in 1 *H. H. P. C.* 596, 597. a Justice of Peace or Officer letting one, not bailable, to Bail, is said to be only guilty of a negligent Escape, unless done by Design to deliver the Prisoner for ever.

Page 131. N° [38] According to *Hale*, If a Gaoler licence a Felon to wander out of the Prison on Promise of returning, if the Prisoner return before the Gaoler be indicted, yet he is punishable as for a Misdemeanor; and if the Prisoner had never returned, it would be Felony in the Gaoler. 1 *H. H. P. C.* 597.

Page 132. N° [39] Sir *Matthew Hale* is of Opinion, That if a Felon escape by Negligence, the Gaoler may retake him any Time after; but this shall not discharge the Gaoler's Fine, and that this is the Sense of 13 *Ed.* 4. 9. *a.* 1 *H. H. P. C.* 602.

Page 132. N° [40] 1 *H. H. P. C.* 602. shews that which is here called the better Opinion, to be agreeable to *Hale*'s, altho' *H. P. C.* 114. seems contrary: For in 1 *H. H. P. C.* 602. it is said, That if the Gaoler once lost View of his Prisoner it is an Escape, but if he retake him upon a fresh Pursuit, and hath still the View of him, it is no Escape.

Page 133. N° [41] If the Gaoler being called, cannot give an Account where a Prisoner is, this is a Conviction of an Escape, but seems not a Conviction of a voluntary Escape, unless the Gaoler confesses it. 1 *H. H. P. C.* 603. And the Gaoler may be fined in such a Case, but not convicted of Felony, without Indictment or Presentment. 1 *H. H. P. C.* 599, 600.

Page 134. N° [42] If a Prisoner acquitted on an Indictment, be continued in Gaol till the Year and Day be passed, to give the Widow or Heir an Opportunity of an Appeal, and the Gaoler suffer the Prisoner to escape within the Year, it is *prima facie* Felony in the Gaoler; but if the Appeal be not brought, or the Prisoner acquitted on such Appeal, the Gaoler ought also to be acquitted. 1 *H. H. P. C.* 593.

If a Prisoner convicted of Felony prays his Clergy, and he be continued in Gaol till the Court advise upon it, if in the mean Time the Gaoler voluntarily suffer him to escape, this is Felony; but if the Felon be retaken and has his Clergy, the Felony in the Escape is purged, and the Gaoler is not indictable after, or if indicted before Clergy allowed, he is to be acquitted. *Hale Ibid.*

So if one be indicted for Felony, and has his Clergy, but is continued six Months in Prison, according to 18 *Eliz. c.* 7. the Gaoler suffering him to escape voluntarily, is guilty of a Misdemeanor, punishable by Fine and Imprisonment, but no Felony. *Hale Ibid.*

Page 134. N° [43] Sir *Matthew Hale*'s Opinion is not different from what is here laid down, though *H. P. C.* be quoted as contrary; for in 1 *H. H. P. C.* 595. it is expresly asserted, that though the Warrant be not formal, yet if the Gaoler let the Prisoner voluntarily escape, it is Felony. *Vide supra* N° [32].

Page 135. N° [44] But according to *Hale*, he that rescues a Person imprisoned for Treason, or suffers him voluntarily to escape, shall not be arraigned for that Offence, till the principal Offender be convicted; for if such principal Offender be acquitted, the Gaoler that suffered the Escape, and he that made the Rescue, shall be discharged. 1 *H. H. P. C.* 237, 238.

Page 144. N° [45] Persons undertaking to act as Attornies, without being admitted and sworn, are now liable to a Forfeiture, by 2 *Geo.* 2. *c.* 23. *sect.* 24. by which it is enacted, *That in Case any Person shall in his own Name, or in the Name of any other Person, sue out any Writ or Process, or prosecute or defend any Action or Suit, or any Proceedings in* any

any Court of Law or Equity, as an Attorney or Solicitor, for any Fee or Reward, without being admitted and inrolled, as by this Act is directed, every such Person for every such Offence shall forfeit fifty Pounds, *to the Use of such Person who shall prosecute him for such Offence, and is hereby made incapable to prosecute any Action or Suit, in any Court of Law or Equity, for any Fee, Reward or Disbursement, on Account of prosecuting, carrying on or defending, any such Action, Suit or Proceeding.*

It is also enacted by the said Statute, sect. 17. *That if any Sworn Attorney of any of the Courts of Law, shall knowingly permit any other Person to sue out any Writ or Process,* &c. *in his name, not being a Sworn Attorney of some other Court of Law, or a Sworn Solicitor of the Court of Chancery, or other Court of Equity, and shall be thereof lawfully convicted, every Person so convicted shall, from the Time of such Conviction, be disabled, and made incapable to act in any of the Courts of Law aforesaid; and the Admittance of such Person to be an Attorney of any of the said Courts of Law shall from thenceforth cease and be void.*

But *Vide Skin.* 634. where the Court ordered a Roll to be made, and a Copy of Page 155. N° [46]
it to be delivered to the Appellee, and gave him a Day to plead.

Where an Appeal is commenced in the Court below, and removed into the Page 156. N° [47]
King's Bench, the Appellee is to be arraigned *de novo*, on the same Bill of Appeal, and it is not necessary to exhibit a new Bill against him *in Custodia Mareschalli*; and if the Appellant will not appear to prosecute his Appeal, the Appellee may sue out a *Scire Facias* reciting the whole Matter, warning him to appear at a certain Day; and if he make Default, the Court on Demand will nonsuit him; but the Appellant may appear *gratis*, and prosecute without any *Scire Facias*. Carth. 394, 395. Skin. 670. New Abr. Vol. 1. p. 126.

But the Law is now altered by Stat. 2 *Geo.* 2. *ch.* 21. See *the Additions to Book* 1. Page 157. N° [48]
N° [30]

In 1 *H. H. P. C.* 349. it is said, That Proceedings by way of Appeal in the Page 161. N° [49]
King's ordinary Courts in Cases of Treason have been long disused, and seem to be wholly taken away by the Statutes of the 5 *Ed.* 3. *c.* 9. and 25 *Ed.* 3. *c.* 4. by which none shall be put to answer, but by Indictment or Presentment.

It seems that the Appellant must appear once in proper Person, before he can Page 176. N° [50]
make an Attorney. *Skin.* 48, 670. *Carth.* 394, 395.

The Writ in an Appeal is an Original issuing out of Chancery, returnable into Page 184. N° [51]
the King's Bench only; before the Return thereof, the Court of Chancery only can set it aside, where it appears to have issued *erronicè* or *improvidè*, by some Error extrinsick to the Writ itself; but for any Error or Defect on the Face of it, it may be quashed after it is returned into the King's Bench. *New Abr. Vol.* 1. *p.* 126. and see *Cases in Equity abridged, p.* 416.

It seems from *Carth.* 56. that if the Appellee plead in Abatement, and doth not Page 191. N° [52]
plead over to the Felony, that the Appellant ought to move the Court for Judgment against the Defendant; but in that particular Case, the Plea being accepted by the Plaintiff, it was held good without pleading over.

But 2 *H. H. P. C.* 233. agrees with *Staundford*, that the Approver's being above Page 205. N° [53]
seventy Years of Age, or maimed, whereby the Appellee loses his Trial by Battle, is a good Exception.

Sir *Matthew Hale* seems to think the Court may in Discretion admit one to be an Page 206. N° [54]
Approver at any Time before Verdict given, and for this Purpose cites 12 *Ed.* 4. 10 *b.* and 11 *H.* 7. 5. *b.* which he says is of greater Weight than the other Books. 2 *H. H. P. C.* 228, 229.

But 2 *H. H. P. C.* 229. is express, that a Man cannot become an Approver, be- Page 207. N° [55]
fore Justices of *Oyer and Terminer*, because they cannot assign a Coroner.

Quære whether *H. P. C.* 194. where it is said, that the *High Steward* may take the Page 207. N° [56]
Appeal of an Approver, must not be understood of the Lord Steward, or Lord Great Master of the King's House, who by the Stat. 33 *H.* 8. *c.* 12. *sect.* 3. (referred to in 2 *H. H. P. C.* 54. & *supra, ch.* 9. *sect.* 8.) may from Time to Time assign a Coroner to take Inquisitions, upon a View of Persons slain within the King's Palace? If this be Sir *Matthew Hale*'s Meaning, the Contradiction between him and Sir *Edward Coke*, 3 *Inst.* 130, who speaks of the *Lord High Steward of England* is avoided.

According to *Britton*, the Approver shall have three half Pence *per diem*, till he Page 207. N° [57]
has convicted the Appellee. 2 *H. H. P. C.* 230.

Page 208. N° [58] Juſtices of *Gaol-Delivery* may award Proceſs of Outlawry againſt the Appellee of an Approver, though he be neither in Gaol nor in the ſame County. 2 *H. H. P. C.* 37.

Page 211. N° [59] Sir *Matthew Hale* makes a Diſtinction in this Caſe; his Words are, "If a Statute "prohibit any Act to be done, and by a ſubſtantive Clauſe gives a Recovery by "Action of Debt, Bill, Plaint or Information, but mentions not Indictment, the "Party may be indicted upon the prohibitory clauſe, and thereupon fined, but not "to recover the Penalty, as upon the Stat. 3 *Jac.* 1. *c.* 5. prohibiting Recuſants to "baptize their Children by a Popiſh Prieſt, *Hill.* 7 *Car.* 1. B. R. *per Cur'*; but then "it ſeems the Fine ought not to exceed the Penalty, *Paſch.* 22 *Car.* 1. College of "Phyſicians, *Vide tamen Cro. Jac.* 644. to be contrary. But if the Act be not prohi- "bitory, but only that if any Perſon ſhall do ſuch a Thing, he ſhall forfeit 5 *l.* to be "recovered by Action of Debt, Bill, Plaint or Information, he cannot be indicted "for it; but the Proceeding muſt be by Action, Bill, Plaint or Information, *Paſch.* "6 *Car.* 1. B. R. *Day's Caſe*, 2 *H. H. P. C.* 171." But *Quære* this Diſtinction, for it is ſaid by *Holt* in *Carth.* 252. that a Penalty implies a Prohibition, though there are no Prohibitory Words in the Statute.

Page 211. N° [60] In 1 *H. H. P. C.* 187. Notice is taken of an Arraignment of Treaſon without Indictment, upon the Perſon's being found with the *Mainouvre* or *Manner*, and *P.* 21 *Ed.* 3. *B. R. Rot.* 46. *Midd' Rex* is there refered to. See alſo 1 *H. H. P. C.* 349. 2 *H. H. P. C.* 156, 149 *. in which laſt cited Page it is ſaid, that Proceedings upon the *Mainouvre* are wholly taken away by 25 *Ed.* 3. 4. 28 *Ed.* 3. 3. and 42 *Ed.* 3. 3.

Page 216. N° [61] Sir *Matthew Hale* is of Opinion that Grand Jurors ought to be Freeholders. 2 *H. H. P. C.* 155 *.

Page 222. N° [62] All Perſons declared Acceſſaries by the 11 & 12 *W.* 3. *c.* 7. are by the 8 *Geo.* 1. *c.* 24. *ſect.* 3. declared principal Offenders, See *Addit. B.* 1. N° [41]

Page 223. N° [63] But in the Caſe of Lord *Macguire*, State Trials Vol. 1. p. 928. and in 1 *H. H. P. C.* 155, 284. it was ruled, that an *Iriſh* Peer, for Treaſon committed in *Ireland*, might be indicted and tried in *England* by a common Jury, and the Opinion in *Dyer* 360. was ruled to be no Law.

Page 230. N° [64] *Hale* makes it a *Quære* whether a Miſtake in an Indictment, of the Surname of the Offender, be not a good Plea in Abatement. 2 *H. H. P. C.* 175, 176. and as to a Miſnomer of the Chriſtian Name, tho' ſome Books hold it a good Plea, yet he thinks other Books of greater and later Authority, are to the contrary. 2 *H. H. P. C.* 238. See alſo *Layer*'s Trial, *St. Tr. Vol.* 6. *p.* 237.

Page 231. N° [65] According to 2 *H. H. P. C.* 177. If ſeveral Perſons be indicted of one Offence, Miſnomer or want of Addition of one, quaſhes the Indictment only againſt him, and the reſt ſhall be put to anſwer; for they are in Law ſeveral Indictments, and ſo in Treſpaſs. 7 *Ed.* 4. 10. *b.*

Page 236. N° [66] So it is in an Information, as where it ſet forth that a Ferry-man, *between* 7 Sept. 2 W. & M. *and the Day of exhibiting the Information, did extort diverſe Sums of diverſe Subjects, exceeding the ancient Rate*, &c. The Defendant was found guilty; but upon Motion in arreſt of Judgment, the whole Court was of Opinion, that in every ſuch Information, a ſingle Offence ought to be laid and aſcertained, becauſe every Extortion from every particular Perſon is a ſeparate and diſtinct Offence; and therefore ſuch Extortions ought not to be accumulated under a general Charge; becauſe each Offence requires a diſtinct Puniſhment; and 'tis not poſſible for the Court to proportion the Puniſhment to an Offence not ſingly and certainly laid: It is true, all Informations in the Exchequer are general, as this is, but the Reaſon is, becauſe they are for certain Penalties: and Judgment was arreſted. *Carth.* 226, 227.

Page 240. N° [67] But theſe Niceties about Abbreviations and the Latin of Indictments are taken away by 4 *Geo.* 2. *c.* 26. by which it is enacted, *That all Writs, Proceſs and Returns thereof and Proceedings thereon, and all Pleadings, Rules, Orders, Indictments, Informations, Inquiſitions, Preſentments, Verdicts, Prohibitions, Certificates, and all Patents, Charters, Pardons, Commiſſions, Records, Judgments, Statutes, Recognizances, Bonds, Rolls, Entries, Fines and Recoveries, and all Proceedings whatſoever, in any Courts of Juſtice, ſhall be in the* Engliſh *Language, and ſhall be written in ſuch common legible Hand and Character as the Acts of Parliament are uſually ingroſſed in, and in Words at length and not abreviated: And every Perſon Offending againſt this Act, ſhall for every ſuch Of-*

fence forfeit 50 l. *to any Person who shall sue for the same, by Action of Debt, Plaint, Bill, or Information in any of the Courts of* Westminster Hall.

Sir *Matthew Hale* is also of Opinion, that an Indictment need not conclude *contra Coronam & Dignitatem, &c.* though it be usual in many Cases; and for this he cites *M.* 23 *Car.* 1. *B. R.* 2 *H. H. P. C.* 188. Page 243. N° [68]

Most of the Indictments in *Tremaine's* Entries, which lay the Offence *contra pacem*, lay it also *contra Coronam & Dignitatem.*

But in this Case, if the Indictment conclude generally *contra formam Statuti in hujusmodi casu edit' & provis.* it is good, for the Court takes Notice of the true Statute, and will reject the Misrecital as Surplusage. 2 *H. H. P. C.* 172, 173. Page 246. N° [69]

Sir *Matthew Hale* lays it down as a Rule, " That if an Offence were Felony at " Common Law, but a special Act of Parliament ousts the Offender of some other " Benefit (that the Common Law allowed him,) when certain Circumstances are in " the Fact, though the Body of the Indictment must express those Circumstances ac" cording as they are prescribed in the Statute; yet the Indictment need not con" clude *contra formam Statuti.*" Thus on the Stat. 21 *Jac.* 1. concerning the Murder of Bastard Children, the Indictment must shew it was a Bastard Child, but need not conclude *contra formam Statuti:* So where *Clergy* is taken away, as by 8 *Eliz.* 4. in Cases of Pick-pockets; 18 *El.* 7. and 39 *El.* 15. in Cases of Burglary; 23 *H.* 8. in Cases of Petit Treason, Murder or Robery, *&c.* The Body of the Indictment must bring the Offenders within the express Purview of the Statutes, otherwise they shall have their Clergy, but need not conclude *contra formam Statuti.* Tho' if it should so conclude, it will not vitiate the Indictment; this being now the usual Course, and ruled good in the Case of *Bradley* and *Banks. Cro. Car.* 283. 2 *H. H. P. C.* 190, 191. Page 251. N° [70] Vide ch. 46. sect. 43.

Sir *Matthew Hale* in his *Summary, p.* 208. agrees with 3 *Inst.* 25, 26. that the Necessity of two Witnesses on an Indictment of High Treason (other than for counterfeiting the Coin) is not taken away by the Stat. 1 & 2 *Ph. & Ma.* But in 1 *H. H. P. C.* 299, 300. many strong Reasons and Authorities are brought against Lord *Coke's* Opinion, which *Hale* thinks not so well supported as the contrary Opinion. Page 256. N° [71]

But a Hearsay from the Offender himself confessing the Fact, makes a good Witness within the Statute. 1 *H. H. P. C.* 306. Page 258. N° [72]

An Information was granted against an Attorney for speaking scandalous and reproachful Words against Sir *J. K.* Knight of the Shire for the County of *York*, and a Justice of the Peace, concerning his said Office of Justice of the Peace, and the exercising thereof: Because the Words related to him as a publick Magistrate, and one who is subordinate to the Government; and therefore such Words are a Reproach to the supreme Governor by whom Magistrates are intrusted; and it cannot be denied that Words reflecting on the publick Government are punishable at the Suit of the King by Information. *Carth.* 14, 15. Page 260. N° [73]

According to Sir *Matthew Hale*, a *Certiorari* (upon an Indictment of Felony in *Wales*) may issue for a special Purpose, as to quash the Indictment for Insufficiency, or to plead a Pardon, but not as to the Trial of the Fact; but it shall be sent down by *Mittimus*, according to the Stat. 6 *H.* 8. *c.* 6. because it is in a Manner essential for Felony or Treason to be tried in the proper County, unless otherwise provided by Statute, as 26 *H.* 8. But see 1 *Vent.* 93, 146. Page 287. N° [74]

James Duke of *York* being presented at the Quarter-Sessions, upon 3 *Jac.* 1. *c.* 4. for not coming to Church, it was removed into the King's Bench by *Certiorari.* But *per Holt* this was the only Case wherein it was ever done. *Salk.* 145. *pl.* 5. Page 288. N° [75]

In the Case of the *King* and *Baker*, the Defendant was indicted and convicted at *Kingston upon Hull*, for speaking seditious Words, and the Proceedings being removed into the King's Bench by *Certiorari*, the Court was moved to give Judgment. But this was opposed because irregular; for this Court never gives Judgment upon a Conviction in another Court; but after Issue joined below, and the Indictment removed, the Party is always admitted to wave such Issue below, and to plead *de novo*, and to go on to Trial upon Issue joined in this Court; they directed a new Trial, and the Defendant was found guilty a second Time. *Carth.* 6. Page 288. N° [76]

By Stat. 5 Geo. 2. c. 19. sect. 2. it is enacted, *That no* Certiorari *shall be allowed to remove any Judgment or Order of the Justices of the Peace at their General or Quarter-Sessions, unless the Party prosecuting such* Certiorari, *before the Allowance thereof, shall enter into a Recognizance with sufficient Sureties, before one or more Justices of the Peace of the County or Place, or before the Justices at their Quarter or General Sessions, where such Judgment or Order shall have been given, or before any of the Justices of the King's Bench, in the Sum of* fifty Pounds, *with Condition to prosecute the same at his* Page 291. N° [77]

 own

own Charges with Effect, without any wilful Delay, and to pay to the Party, in whose Favour such Judgment or Order was given, within one Month after the said Judgment or Order shall be confirmed, their full Costs to be taxed according to the Course of the Court where such Judgment or Order shall be confirmed; and in Case the Party prosecuting shall not enter into such Recognizance, or shall not perform the Conditions, it shall be lawful for the said Justices to proceed as if no Certiorari *had been granted.*

Sect. 3. it is farther enacted, *That the Recognizance taken as aforesaid, shall be certified into the Court of King's Bench, and there filed with the* Certiorari, *and the Order or Judgment removed thereby; and if the said Order or Judgment shall be confirmed, the Person entitled to Costs, within ten Days, after Demand made of the Person who ought to pay the said Costs, upon Oath made of the making such Demand, and Refusal of Payment, shall have an Attachment granted against him for such Contempt, and the said Recognizance shall not be discharged until the Costs shall be paid, and the Order so confirmed complied with.*

Page 293. N° [78] This Clause of 3 & 4 W. & M. 10. is enforced and enlarged by 5 Geo. 1. c. 15. sect. 1. which enacts, *That no* Certiorari *shall be allowed to remove any Proceedings on the said Statute, unless the Party convicted shall, at the same Time that Security is given for the Payment of Costs and Damages, become also bound to the Justice or Justices of Peace before whom such Conviction was made, with sufficient Sureties in the Penalty of* sixty Pounds *for each Offence, with Condition to prosecute such* Certiorari *with Effect, and to pay the Forfeitures due by such Conviction, or to render the Persons convicted to such Justice or Justices, within one Month after such Conviction shall be confirmed, or a* Procedendo *granted.*

Page 294. N° [79] Upon a *Certiorari* to remove an Indictment upon 5 *Eliz.* into *B. R.* for exercising a Trade in a Borough, not being bound Apprentice to it; the Mayor's Return was *Humillime certifico quod ad sessionem pacis, &c. per juratores præsentatum existit quod billa sequens est vera, (viz.) Quod prædict'* B. did exercise, &c. omitting the Clause *juratores pro Domino Rege præsentant quod, &c.* And the Court held this to be no Return to the *Certiorari*, for the Writ commands to return an Indictment; but this is none; therefore they could not quash it, neither would they suffer this Return to be filed, because insufficient, and the Mayor was ordered to amend it: And a Return *quod humillime certifico* was held not good. *Carth.* 223.

Page 307. N° [80] Arraignment is the Calling of the Offender to the Bar of the Court, to answer the Matter charged upon him by Indictment or Appeal. The Latin *arrenare* signifies *ad rationem ponere*, and in French *ad reson*, or abreviated *a resn.* This is the Etymology given in 2 *H. H. P. C.* 216, 218.

Page 308. N° [81] But in *Layer*'s Case, a Difference was taken between the Time of Arraignment and the Time of Trial, and accordingly the Prisoner stood in Irons at the Bar during his Arraignment. See *St. Tr. Vol.* 6. *p.* 230, 231.

Page 308. N° [82] Not only Arraignments, but also Indictments and all other proceedings in Courts of Justice must now be in *English*, by 4 Geo. 2. c. 26. *supra* N° [67]

Page 318. N° [83] If *B.* commit a Felony, and come to the House of *A.* before he be arrested, and *A.* suffer him to escape without Arrest, knowing him to have committed a Felony, this doth not make *A.* Accessary; but if he take Money of *B.* to suffer him to escape, this makes him accessary, 9 *H.* 4. 1. and so it is if *A.* shut the fore Door of his House, whereby the Pursuers are deceived, and the Felon hath Opportunity to escape, this makes *A.* Accessary; for here is not a bare Omission, but an Act done by *A.* to accommodate *B.*'s Escape. 8 *Ed.* 2. *Fitz. Cor.* 427. 1 *H. H. P. C.* 619.

Page 319. N° [84] By Stat. 5 An. c. 31. sect. 5. it is enacted, *That if any Person shall receive or buy any Goods or Chattels, that shall be feloniously taken or stoln from any other Person, knowing the same to be stoln, or shall receive, harbour or conceal any Burglars, Felons or Thieves, knowing them to be so; such Person shall be taken as Accessary to the said Felonies, and being convicted shall suffer as a Felon.*

And by Stat. 4 Geo. 1. c. 11. sect. 1. *Persons convicted of receiving or buying stoln Goods, knowing them to be stoln, may be transported for the Term of fourteen Years.* See also the same *Stat. sect.* 4. in what Cases taking a Reward to help Persons to their stoln Goods, is made Felony. *Additions to Book* 1. N° [62.]

Page 322. N° [85] This is also enacted by 5 Ann. c. 31. sect. 6. which says, *That such Offender (by buying or receiving stolen Goods, knowing,* &c.) *shall be punished by Fine and Imprisonment, or other such corporal Punishment as the Court shall think fit to inflict.*

Page 327. N° [86] Notwithstanding the Authority of 3 *H.* 7. 12. *pl.* 5. the better Opinion according to *Hale* is, that at Common Law in Case of a Peremptory Challenge of above thirty-five, (the Number allowed before 22 *H.* 8.) in Case of Felony, the Judgment was not an Attainder, but only Penance. 2 *H. H. P. C.* 268, 399. but *Pag.* 269, 316. in the same Book seem contrary.

But in 2 *H. H. P. C.* 317, 322. the Law is held the same in Case of an Appeal Page 329. N° [87] and of an Indictment.

Sir *Matthew Hale* has given his Opinion at large on this Subject, *Hist. Plac. Cor.* Page 334. N° [88] *Vol.* 2. *p.* 257. and says, that regularly in all Cases of Felony or Treason, where a Man pleads a special Matter, whether or not he conclude his Plea with *Not guilty* to the Felony, yet if his Plea be found against him, he shall be tried for the Felony; for though a Man in some Cases shall lose his Land, yet he shall not lose his Life for mis-pleading. Therefore 14 *Ed.* 4. 7. *a.* must be understood *cum grano salis:* And the true Difference seems to be this, if a Person indicted for Felony demur to the Indictment, and it be judged against him, he shall have Judgment to be hanged; for it is a wilful Confession, since he may have all the Advantages of the Insufficiency of the Indictment, by way of Exception, either before his Plea of *Not guilty*, or after Conviction and before Judgment, as he might have by Demurrer; and in Case of Demurrer, Judgment of *Peine forte & dure* cannot be given, because it is a Plea; and thus are 14 *Ed.* 4. 7. *a.* 7 *Ed.* 4. 29. *a.* and 2 *Inst.* 178. to be understood. But if the Prisoner pleads in Bar, and concludes to the Felony, or pleads a Pardon, and concludes not to the Felony, and the Attorney General demurs, and he joins in the Demurrer, and it be adjudged against him, yet he shall be put to answer the Felony; for this Demurrer is no Confession of the Indictment. As to the Plea of Pardon, it seems according to the same Author, *ibid. p.* 256. a Kind of Confession of the Fact, but *in favorem vitæ* the Party is put to answer the Felony, in Case the Pardon be adjudged against him.

But according to *Hale* it is a Mistake to say, that a Person in Orders challenging Page 340. N° [89] above twenty shall not have his Clergy a second Time, because in 1 *Ed.* 6. this Case is not mentioned; for upon challenging above twenty, there follows neither Penance nor Judgment of Death, but only the Challenge shall be over-ruled. 2 *H. H. P. C.* 376. *vide infra*, N° [102]. But Outlawry is *casus omissus.* ibid. & p. 341, 342.

Before the Stat. 25 *Ed.* 3. *de Clero*, there were two Sorts of Treasons that con- Page 341. N° [90] cerned the King, one of greater Note, *as Conspiring the King's Death*, *Levying War against the King*, *Adhering to his Enemies*, and two others since abrogated by 25 *Ed.* 3. which came under the obscure Names of *Sedition*, *and Accroaching Royal Power*; and in these Cases the Party convict had not his Clergy by the Common Law, as appears by a Judgment cited 2 *H. H. P. C.* 327. But in other Treasons of inferior Note, as *Counterfeiting the Seal*, *and Counterfeiting the Coin*, the Judgment was as in *Petit Treason* to be drawn and hanged. And it seems before 25 *Ed.* 3. *de proditionibus* Clergy was allowed in both these Cases, as appears by the Book of *Ed.* 3. *B. R.* Title *Clergy*, *placito ultimo*, and the Judgment in Parliament of 18 *Ed.* 1. in *Berton*'s Case, who being convict for counterfeiting the King's Seal had his Clergy, but *tradatur ordinario sine Purgatione.* But at this Day in all Cases of High Treason, Clergy is taken away. 2 *H. H. P. C.* 331, 332.

According to *Hale*, as the Law was taken (in the Time of *H.* 8.) challenging a- Page 344. N° [91] bove twenty had been a Conviction, or at least had put the Party to his Penance, but now the Clause of challenging above twenty, mentioned in the Stat. 25 *H.* 8. and other Statutes imports nothing as to the Point of Clergy, for the Challenge is over-ruled. 2 *H. H. P. C.* 339, 345. *Vide infra* N° [102].

Accessaries after the Fact in Petit Treason and Murder are in no Case ousted of Page 349. N° [92] Clergy. 2 *H. H. P. C.* 342, 344.

Accessaries before and after in Horse stealing are excluded from their Clergy in Page 350. N° [93] like Manner as the Principals are by 31 *El. c.* 12. *sect.* 5.

Stealing Linen, *&c.* to the Value of ten Shillings, from any bleaching Field, or Page 351. N° [94] Buying the same knowing it to be stolen, is Felony without Benefit of Clergy, by 4 *Geo.* 2. *c.* 16. See *the Additions to Book* 1. N° [71].

This Case of a Robbery in Sir *H. Hungate*'s Lodgings at *Whitehall*, is also re- Page 355. N° [95] ported in 1 *H. H. P. C.* 522, 523. where it is said, that *Croke* and *Crawley* were advised with to pen the Indictment, who agreed, that upon the Statute of 5 & 6 *Ed.* 6. the Indictment need only be, that he broke the King's House called *Whitehall*, and stole the Goods of Sir *H. Hungate*, diverse of the King's Servants then being in the House. And accordingly at the *Gaol-Delivery* at the *Old Baily*, the 29th of *August*, 14 *Car.* 1. those two Justices being present, the Prisoners were indicted, one fled, the other two were found guilty; one was reprieved before Judgment, and the other was executed; *ex libro Twisden.*

The Case taken Notice of in this Section from *Cro. Car.* 473, 474. is that of Page 356. N° [96] *Evans* and *Finch*, mentioned in 1 *H. H. P. C.* 527. and 2 *H. H. P. C.* 358. And

Hale makes a *Quære* whether possibly the same Law might not be upon the Statute of 5 & 6 *Ed.* 6. *c.* 9. "That he only, that enters the House in the Day-time "without putting in Fear, and actually takes the Goods, shall be excluded from "Clergy, and those that stand without the House and are present and abetting, tho' "all principals, yet shall have their Clergy;" and he says, "He can see no Dif-"ference in the Cases. 2 *H. H. P. C.* 359." But in 1 *H. H. P. C.* 521. he delivers it as his own Opinion, that they ought all to be excluded of their Clergy upon this Statute of 5 & 6 *Ed.* 6. because the Stat. 4 & 5 *Ph.* & *Ma. c.* 4. excluding those from Clergy *who shall maliciously command, hire or counsel any Person to commit any Robbery in any Dwelling-House*, cannot be intended to take away Clergy from those who at most are but Accessaries, and yet leave it to those who are present and abetting, which is certainly more; yet he says the contrary has been held by the Opinion of divers Judges at a Meeting in *Serjeants-Inn*, *Nov.* 30. 1664. who grounded themselves principally upon the said Case in *Cro. Car.* 473.

Page 382. N° [97] By the Stat. 8 Geo. 1. c. 18. sect. 7. it is enacted, *That if any Runner of Foreign goods as aforesaid* (sect. 6. see the Additions to Book 1. N° [65]) *shall within two Months after his Offence, and before his Conviction, discover two or more of his Accomplices, so as they or two of them at least be convicted of such Offence, the Offender discovering shall receive* 40 l. *for every Offender so convicted, so as the Value of the Goods recovered for the Use of his Majesty shall exceed the Sum of fifty Pounds, and such Person so discovering shall be discharged of his Offence.*

Page 382. N° [98] Stat. 9 Geo. 2. c. 35. sect. 12. *If any Offender shall, within three Months after such Offence* (mentioned in sect. 10. see Additions to Book 1. N° [76]) *and before Conviction, discover two Accomplices to the Commissioners of the Customs or Excise, so as they be convicted, the Offender discovering shall have* 50 l. *for every Offender so convicted, and shall be discharged of such Offence.*

Page 397. N° [99] In the Case of the Earl of *Salisbury* (*supra* N° [30]) The Counsel for the Earl moved, that he might be discharged upon the Act of Oblivion, wherein neither his Crime nor his Person were excepted. But the Court held, that Notice could not be taken of this Act of Pardon, unless it were pleaded with the Averments, because of several Exceptions in it both as to Crimes and Persons; and therefore the Party, who would have the Benefit thereof, should aver himself by Plea capable of such Benefit; (for which *Plowd.* 401, 484. *b.* 8 *Co.* 68. 4 *H.* 7. 8. *Rast. Ent.* 665. *a.* were cited) and that here the Lord at the Bar cannot plead this Pardon, because there was nothing before the Court whereupon to ground such Plea. Whereupon the Reporter makes this *Quære*, whether he might not plead it in Discharge of the Matter returned by the *Habeas Corpus*, and enter it as the same Roll. *Carth.* 132.

Page 402. N° [100] By Stat. 7 An. c. 21. sect. 11. it is enacted, *That from and after the Decease of the Pretender, when any Person is indicted of High Treason, or Misprision of Treason, a List of the Witnesses that shall be produced on the Trial for proving the said Indictment, and of the Jury, mentioning the Names, Profession, and Place of Abode of the said Witnesses and Jurors, be also given at the same Time that the Copy of the Indictment is delivered to the Party indicted; and that the Copies of all Indictments for the Offences aforesaid, with such Lists, shall be delivered to the Party indicted, ten Days before the Trial, and in the Presence of two or more credible Witnesses.*

Page 409. N° [101] If an Indictment be before Justices of *Oyer* and *Terminer*, the *Tales* as well as the principal Panel ought to be by Precept in the Name of three of the Justices, and may be made returnable *de die in diem*, or *de hora in horam* of the same Day. 2 *H. H. P. C.* 266. where it is farther said, that as to the Number, Manner, and Times of granting a *Tales*, the Proceedings before these Justices resemble those in the King's Bench. But as to Justices of *Gaol-Delivery*, the Learning of *Tales* is not of much Use in Proceedings before them; because there is no particular Precept to the Sheriff to return either Jury or *Tales*, but the general Precept before the Sessions, and the Award or Command of the Court upon the Plea of the Prisoner; for which 4 *H.* 5. *Fitz. Enquest*, 55. *S. P. C. B.* 3. *c.* 6. *f.* 155 *b.* are cited. Yet *Vide Plowd. Com.* 100. *a. Salisbury*'s Case, where before Justices of Peace and *Gaol-Delivery* a *Tales* was granted returnable the next Day.

Page 414. N° [102] But Sir *Matthew Hale* in his *Historia Placitorum Coronæ*, *Vol.* 2. *p.* 270, 345. is of Opinion with Sir *Edward Coke*, that he that challenges above twenty, as the Law stands at this Day, shall not have Judgment of Death, nor of *Peine forte & dure* (ibid. p. 399.) but only his Challenge shall be over-ruled, and the Jurors sworn. *Vide supra*, N° [89] [91]

By the Stat. 3 Geo. 2. c. 25. ſect. 18. it is enacted, *That Perſons having an Eſtate in Poſſeſſion in Land, in their own Right, of the yearly Value of twenty Pounds or upwards, over and above the reſerved Rent payable thereout, ſuch Lands being held by Leaſe, for the abſolute Term of five hundred Years or more, or for ninety-nine Years, or any other Term determinable on one or more Life or Lives; ſuch Leaſeholders may be ſummoned and impanelled to ſerve on Juries, in like manner as Freeholders may be.* Page 417. N° [103]

Sect. 19. It is farther enacted, *That the Sheriffs of* London *ſhall not impanel or return any Perſon, to try any Iſſue joined in any of his Majeſty's Courts of* King's Bench, Common Pleas, *and* Exchequer, *or to ſerve on any Jury at the Seſſions of* Oyer *and* Terminer, Gaol-Delivery, *or* Seſſions of the Peace, *to be held for the ſaid City, who ſhall not be a Houſholder, and have Lands, Tenements, or Perſonal Eſtate, to the Value of one hundred Pounds; and the ſame Matter and Cauſe alledged by way of Challenge, and ſo found, ſhall be taken and admitted as a principal Challenge, and the Perſon ſo challenged may be examined on Oath, as to the Truth of the ſaid Matter.*

Sect. 20. It is farther enacted, *That the Sheriffs, or other returning Officer, ſhall not impanel or return any Perſon to ſerve on any Jury for the Trial of any capital Offence, who at the Time of ſuch Return would not be qualified to ſerve as Jurors in civil Cauſes; and the ſame Matter and Cauſe alledged by way of Challenge, and ſo found, ſhall be taken as a principal Challenge; and the Perſon ſo challenged may be examined on Oath as to the Truth of the ſaid Matter.*

Alſo by the Stat. 4 Geo. 2. c. 7. ſect. 3. it is enacted, *That all Leaſeholders upon Leaſes, where the improved Rents or Value ſhall amount to* fifty Pounds *or upwards* per Annum, *over and above all Ground Rents, or other Reſervations, payable by Virtue of the ſaid Leaſes, ſhall be obliged to ſerve upon Juries.*

Both theſe Acts are made perpetual by 6 *Geo.* 2. *c.* 37. *Sect.* 1.

But Sir *Matthew Hale* in his *Hiſtoria Placitorum Coronæ, Vol.* 1. *p.* 298. contradicts his own *Summary of the Pleas of the Crown, p.* 262. and ſays, that it is on all Hands agreed, That the Stat. of 1 *&* 2 *Ph. & Ma.* takes away the Neceſſity of two Witneſſes on the Trial for Treaſon; though it has been doubted, whether it take away the Neceſſity of two Witneſſes on the Indictment, or not; and as to this laſt Queſtion, he admits the Reaſons for the Affirmative to be the ſtrongeſt. *Vide ſupra*, N° [71] Page 428. N° [104]

Skin. 579. Compariſon of Hands was held not to be good Evidence, except the Papers are found in the Cuſtody of the Perſon, but where in the Cuſtody of another, it is not Evidence. Page 431. N° [105]

Hale thinks one convict of Conſpiracy, Perjury or Forgery, may be a good Witneſs, if pardoned. 1 *H. H. P. C.* 306. Page 433. N° [106]

But this, according to *Hale*, is now only a Buſineſs of Form, for if the Jury know not who did the Murder or Manſlaughter, they uſually ſay *John a Nokes* did it; for this 37 *H.* 8. *Bro. Coron.* 32. 21 *Ed.* 3. 17. *b. Bro. Cor.* 39. *Dy.* 238. *b.* are cited, 2 *H. H. P. C.* 301. Page 441. N° [107]

If the Verdict do not aſcertain the Fact ſufficiently, for this Imperfection a *Venire facias de novo* ought to iſſue, and a new Trial and Verdict ought to be had, for there cannot be an Amendment of a ſpecial Verdict found of a Felony; *per Holt* Ch. Juſt. *Skin.* 667. Page 441. N° [108]

In the Caſe of the *King* and *Tucker*, *Skin.* 442. The Judgment was held good notwithſtanding the Omiſſion of *ſecreta ſua amputentur*; and *per Holt*, though this be always pronounced, it is never entred as Part of the Judgment; and to reverſe a Judgment for this Reaſon, would be to overthrow the greateſt Part of all the Judgments which have been given in High Treaſon. It was objected to the ſame Judgment, that the Clauſe *quod interiora, &c. in ignem ponantur*, was wholly omitted; but upon View of Precedents this Objection was alſo over-ruled. *Carth.* 318. But ſee in the ſame Book, *p.* 349. the Reverſal of an Attainder for High Treaſon, for omitting the Words *ipſoque vivente comburentur*, which were held a material Part of the Judgment; and upon a Writ of Error in the Houſe of Lords, this Judgment of Reverſal was affirmed by the Majority of one Vote. And it is obſerved, that before the Time of *Henry* VII. the Judgment in Treaſon was very uncertain, and that there are ſcarce two Records which agree in the ſame Form. Page 443. N° [109]

Sir *Matthew Hale* in his *Summary* is of Opinion with *Staundford* and *Coke*, that the Judgment for Clipping, *&c.* ought to be, to be Drawn, Hanged and Quartered; but in his *Hiſtoria Placitorum Coronæ, Vol.* 1. 352, 353, and *Vol.* 2. 398. he is of the contrary Opinion, that it ought only to be Drawing and Hanging; and he gives his Reaſons at large, which ſee. Page 444. N° [110]

Page 447. N° [111] 2 *H. H. P. C.* 53. takes Notice of this Opinion in 4 *Co.* 57. *b.* and ſays it may be true as to Goods, but not as to Lands; becauſe none can be attainted after his Death but by Act of Parliament. See this Point largely treated of in 1 *H. H. P. C.* 342 to 349.

Page 455. N° [112] One *Jones* being in Newgate made a Bill of Sale of his Goods to his Son, and upon *Trover* brought by the Son againſt the Sheriffs of *London*, the Bill was ruled fraudulent by *Holt*; for though a Sale *bona fide*, and for a valuable Conſideration, had been good, becauſe the Party had a Property in the Goods till Conviction, yet ſuch a Conveyance as this, cannot be intended to any other Purpoſe than to prevent a Forfeiture, and defraud the King; and this he ſaid was a Fraud at Common Law. *Skin.* 357, 358.

Page 455. N° [113] *Staundford* thinks the Stat. 1 *Ric.* 3. 3. but an Affirmance of the Common Law, but *Hale* ſays, it ſeems to be ſomewhat more, for this Statute prohibits the Seizure of the Goods of the Party impriſoned, though he were alſo indicted, but not yet convicted; but unqueſtionably the Common Law allowed ſuch a Seizure, if the Party or his Friends did not ſecure the forth-coming of the Goods where the Party was indicted. 1 *H. H. P. C.* 365.

This Statute ſeems to extend to Treaſon according to *Hale*, tho' he ſays he knew it otherwiſe held in the Caſe of Sir *Henry Vane*, whoſe Rents were ſtopped in the Tenants Hands, and no Precept granted for their Delivery, tho' before Conviction, and even before Indictment, tho' after Impriſonment, in 1661. 1 *H. H. P. C.* 366.

According to the ſame Author, Lord *Coke* has truly ſtated the Law as it ſtands on the Stat. 1 *Ric.* 3. 1ſt, That before Indictment, the goods of any Perſon cannot be ſearched, inventoried, nor in any Sort ſeized. 2dly, That after Indictment, they cannot be ſeized and removed before Conviction or Attainder. And *Hale* thinks the Perſon indicted is not bound to find Sureties, neither has the Officer at this Day any Power to remove the Goods, in Default of Sureties, and commit them to the Vill, but only to inventory them and leave them where he found them (unleſs in the Caſe of a ſecond *Capias*, by 25 *Ed.* 3. *c.* 14.) and there is this Advantage by the viewing and appraiſing, that thereby the King is aſcertained what the Goods are, and may purſue thoſe that take or imbezzle them, by Information, (if the Party happen to be convict) and try whether they were really ſold for a valuable Conſideration, or only fraudulently to prevent the Forfeiture, and ſo forfeited by the Stat. of 13 *El.* *c.* 5. notwithſtanding ſuch fraudulent Sale. 1 *H. H. P. C.* 367.

Page 456. N° [114] As to the Effect of an Attainder of Piracy, it is aſſerted in 3 *Inſt.* 112. that it corrupts not the Blood; but the contrary ſeems aſſerted in *Co. Lit.* 391. Sir *Matthew Hale* endeavours to reconcile this ſeeming Contradiction; he obſerves, that if a Man be attainted before the Admiral, of Treaſon or Felony committed upon the Sea, according to the Courſe of the Civil Law, this works no Corruption of Blood: But if there be an Attainder of Treaſon or Felony done upon the Sea, upon the Statute of 28 *H.* 8. by Jury, according to the Courſe of the Common Law, he thinks the Judgment thereon works a Corruption of Blood; becauſe the Commiſſion it ſelf is under the Great Seal warranted by Act of Parliament, and the Trial according to the Common Law; and therefore the Proceeding and Judgment thereon is of the ſame Effect as an Attainder of foreign Treaſon, by Commiſſion upon the Statute of 35 *H.* 8. *c.* 2. or any other Attainder by Courſe of the Common Law; and he ſays, *Co. Lit.* 391. agrees with this; he thinks farther, that if the Indictment of Piracy before ſuch Commiſſioners upon the Statute of 28 *H.* 8. be formed as an Indictment of Robbery at Common Law, *viz. vi & armis & felonicè, &c.* the Offender might be thereon attainted, and the Blood corrupted; for it is out of Queſtion that Piracy upon the Statute is Robbery, and Offenders have been indicted, convicted and executed for it in the King's Bench, as for a Robbery, as he ſays he has elſewhere made evident. (*Quære.*) But indeed if the Indictment before theſe Commiſſioners run only according to the Stile of the Civil Law, *viz. piraticè deprædavit*, then the Attainder upon 28 *H.* 8. corrupts not the Blood. And thus he thinks 3 *Inſt.* 112. and *Co. Lit.* 391. may be reconciled. 1 *H. H. P. C.* 355.

Page 458. N° [115] By the Stat. 7 Ann. c. 21. Sect. 10. it is enacted, *That after the Deceaſe of the Pretender, no Attainder for Treaſons ſhall extend to the Diſheriting of any Heirs, nor to the Prejudice of the Right or Title of any Perſon or Perſons, other than the Offender, during his natural Life only; and that it ſhall and may be lawful to every Perſon, to whom the Right or Intereſt of any Lands, Tenements, or Hereditaments, after the Death of any ſuch Offender, ſhould or might have appertained, if no ſuch Attainder had been, to enter into the ſame.*

An

An Alphabetical Index of the Principal Matters contained in this Book.

No

The

Aſſiſe.

Index to the Second Book.

Autrefoits.

Autrefoits acquit.

Award.

Bail.

B.

Index to the Second Book.

It

Challenge.

A.

B.

C.

D.

E.

E.

F.

G.

H.

Clerk.

Whether

Eves-droppers.

Evidence.

A.

B.

C.

D.

E.

F.

Examination.

Where

Whether

When

Whether

Whether

How

Larceny.

Malum

In

Where

Whether

Whether

Whether

Where

Trial.

FINIS.

www.ingramcontent.com/pod-product-compliance
Lightning Source LLC
LaVergne TN
LVHW081947200926
848484LV00009B/2522
* 9 7 8 1 5 8 4 7 7 9 3 6 0 *